C++ Master Reference

C++ Master Reference

Clayton Walnum

IDG Books Worldwide, Inc.

An International Data Group Company

Foster City, CA ■ Chicago, IL ■ Indianapolis, IN ■ New York, NY

C++ Master Reference

Published by
IDG Books Worldwide, Inc.
An International Data Group Company
919 E. Hillsdale Blvd., Suite 400
Foster City, CA 94404
www.idgbooks.com (IDG Books Worldwide Web site)

Library of Congress Catalog Card No.: 99-65414

ISBN: 0-7645-7524-4

Printed in the United States of America

10 9 8 7 6 5 4 3 2 1

1P/QZ/QZ/ZZ/FC

Distributed in the United States by IDG Books Worldwide, Inc.

Distributed by CDG Books Canada Inc. for Canada; by Transworld Publishers Limited in the United Kingdom; by IDG Norge Books for Norway; by IDG Sweden Books for Sweden; by IDG Books Australia Publishing Corporation Pty. Ltd. for Australia and New Zealand; by TransQuest Publishers Pte Ltd. for Singapore, Malaysia, Thailand, Indonesia, and Hong Kong; by Gotop Information Inc. for Taiwan; by ICG Muse, Inc. for Japan; by Norma Comunicaciones S.A. for Colombia; by Intersoft for South Africa; by Eyrolles for France; by International Thomson Publishing for Germany, Austria and Switzerland; by Distribuidora Cuspide for Argentina; by LR International for Brazil; by Galileo Libros for Chile; by Ediciones ZETA S.C.R. Ltda. for Peru; by WS Computer Publishing Corporation, Inc., for the Philippines; by Contemporanea de Ediciones for Venezuela; by Express Computer Distributors for the Caribbean and West Indies; by Micronesia Media Distributor, Inc. for Micronesia; by Grupo Editorial Norma S.A. for Guatemala; by Chips Computadoras S.A. de C.V. for Mexico; by Editorial Norma de Panama S.A. for Panama; by American Bookshops for Finland. Authorized Sales Agent: Anthony Rudkin Associates for the Middle East and North Africa.

For general information on IDG Books Worldwide's books in the U.S., please call our Consumer Customer Service department at 800-762-2974. For reseller information, including discounts and premium sales, please call our Reseller Customer Service department at 800-434-3422.

For information on where to purchase IDG Books Worldwide's books outside the U.S., please contact our International Sales department at 317-596-5530 or fax 317-596-5692.

For consumer information on foreign language translations, please contact our Customer Service department at 800-434-3422, fax 317-596-5692, or e-mail rights@idgbooks.com.

For information on licensing foreign or domestic rights, please phone +1-650-655-3109.

For sales inquiries and special prices for bulk quantities, please contact our Sales department at 650-655-3200 or write to the address above.

For information on using IDG Books Worldwide's books in the classroom or for ordering examination copies, please contact our Educational Sales department at 800-434-2086 or fax 317-596-5499.

For press review copies, author interviews, or other publicity information, please contact our Public Relations department at 650-655-3000 or fax 650-655-3299.

For authorization to photocopy items for corporate, personal, or educational use, please contact Copyright Clearance Center, 222 Rosewood Drive, Danvers, MA 01923, or fax 978-750-4470.

ABOUT IDG BOOKS WORLDWIDE

Welcome to the world of IDG Books Worldwide.

IDG Books Worldwide, Inc., is a subsidiary of International Data Group, the world's largest publisher of computer-related information and the leading global provider of information services on information technology. IDG was founded more than 30 years ago by Patrick J. McGovern and now employs more than 9,000 people worldwide. IDG publishes more than 290 computer publications in over 75 countries. More than 90 million people read one or more IDG publications each month.

Launched in 1990, IDG Books Worldwide is today the #1 publisher of best-selling computer books in the United States. We are proud to have received eight awards from the Computer Press Association in recognition of editorial excellence and three from Computer Currents' First Annual Readers' Choice Awards. Our best-selling *...For Dummies®* series has more than 50 million copies in print with translations in 31 languages. IDG Books Worldwide, through a joint venture with IDG's Hi-Tech Beijing, became the first U.S. publisher to publish a computer book in the People's Republic of China. In record time, IDG Books Worldwide has become the first choice for millions of readers around the world who want to learn how to better manage their businesses.

Our mission is simple: Every one of our books is designed to bring extra value and skill-building instructions to the reader. Our books are written by experts who understand and care about our readers. The knowledge base of our editorial staff comes from years of experience in publishing, education, and journalism — experience we use to produce books to carry us into the new millennium. In short, we care about books, so we attract the best people. We devote special attention to details such as audience, interior design, use of icons, and illustrations. And because we use an efficient process of authoring, editing, and desktop publishing our books electronically, we can spend more time ensuring superior content and less time on the technicalities of making books.

You can count on our commitment to deliver high-quality books at competitive prices on topics you want to read about. At IDG Books Worldwide, we continue in the IDG tradition of delivering quality for more than 30 years. You'll find no better book on a subject than one from IDG Books Worldwide.

 John Kilcullen
Chairman and CEO
IDG Books Worldwide, Inc.

Steven Berkowitz
President and Publisher
IDG Books Worldwide, Inc.

*Eighth Annual
Computer Press
Awards 1992*

WINNER

*Ninth Annual
Computer Press
Awards 1993*

WINNER

*Tenth Annual
Computer Press
Awards 1994*

*Eleventh Annual
Computer Press
Awards 1995*

IDG is the world's leading IT media, research and exposition company. Founded in 1964, IDG had 1997 revenues of $2.05 billion and has more than 9,000 employees worldwide. IDG offers the widest range of media options that reach IT buyers in 75 countries representing 95% of worldwide IT spending. IDG's diverse product and services portfolio spans six key areas including print publishing, online publishing, expositions and conferences, market research, education and training, and global marketing services. More than 90 million people read one or more of IDG's 290 magazines and newspapers, including IDG's leading global brands — Computerworld, PC World, Network World, Macworld and the Channel World family of publications. IDG Books Worldwide is one of the fastest-growing computer book publishers in the world, with more than 700 titles in 36 languages. The "...For Dummies®" series alone has more than 50 million copies in print. IDG offers online users the largest network of technology-specific Web sites around the world through IDG.net (http://www.idg.net), which comprises more than 225 targeted Web sites in 55 countries worldwide. International Data Corporation (IDC) is the world's largest provider of information technology data, analysis and consulting, with research centers in over 41 countries and more than 400 research analysts worldwide. IDG World Expo is a leading producer of more than 168 globally branded conferences and expositions in 35 countries including E3 (Electronic Entertainment Expo), Macworld Expo, ComNet, Windows World Expo, ICE (Internet Commerce Expo), Agenda, DEMO, and Spotlight. IDG's training subsidiary, ExecuTrain, is the world's largest computer training company, with more than 230 locations worldwide and 785 training courses. IDG Marketing Services helps industry-leading IT companies build international brand recognition by developing global integrated marketing programs via IDG's print, online and exposition products worldwide. Further information about the company can be found at www.idg.com. 1/24/99

Credits

Acquisitions Editor
Greg Croy

Development Editor
Terri Varveris

Technical Editor
Greg Guntle

Copy Editors
Rich Adin
Amy Eoff
Eric Hahn

Book Designer
Kurt Krames

Production
IDG Books Worldwide Production

Proofreading
York Production Services

About the Author

Clayton Walnum started programming computers in 1982 when he traded in an IBM Selectric typewriter to buy an Atari 400 computer (16K of RAM!). Clay soon learned to combine his interest in writing with his newly acquired programming skills and started selling programs and articles to computer magazines. In 1985, *ANALOG Computing*, a nationally distributed computer magazine, hired him as a technical editor, and, before leaving the magazine business in 1989 to become a freelance writer, Clay had worked his way up to Executive Editor. He has since acquired a degree in Computer Science, as well as written over 40 books (translated into many languages) covering everything from computer gaming to 3D graphics programming. He's also written hundreds of magazine articles and software reviews, as well as countless programs. His most recent IDG books include *Visual Basic 6 Master Reference* (IDG Books Worldwide) and *Windows 98 Programming Secrets* (IDG Books Worldwide). His other books include *AFC Black Book, Special Edition Using MFC and ATL, Java By Example*, and the award-winning *Building Windows 95 Applications with Visual Basic*. Clay's biggest disappointment in life is that he wasn't one of the Beatles. To compensate, he writes and records rock music in his home studio. You can reach Clay at his homepage, which is located at www.claytonwalnum.com.

To Lynn

Preface

C++ is one of the most-used programming languages in the world. The reason for its success is obvious: C++ is a high-level language that almost gives a programmer the power of assembly language. Of course, this power comes with a price. Although the basic C++ language is actually quite small, mastering its intricacies can take years. Moreover, C++ defines, outside of the basic language, a huge set of functions and class libraries that themselves require a lot of practice to master.

In any case, no programmer, no matter how experienced, can possibly keep in his head all the information needed to program C++ applications. That would be like trying to fit the Atlantic ocean into a drinking glass. That's where *C++ Master Reference* comes in. Using this book, you can quickly find the answers to most questions without having to dig through multiple volumes filled with information you'll probably never use. *C++ Master Reference* provides an alphabetized list of keywords, functions, operators, classes, concepts, techniques, and other entry types, all formatted in an easy-to-read, quick-reference style.

Who Should Use This Book

This book is not a C++ tutorial (although some C++ topics are presented as mini-tutorials). In order to understand the information presented here, you must already have at least a basic understanding of C++. If you're new to C++, you should pick up a good general C++ programming book such as *Teach Yourself... C++, 5th Edition*, by Al Stevens (IDG Books Worldwide). Once you've worked through that book (or some similar book), *C++ Master Reference* can be your main reference guide.

What This Book Covers

When we first set out to outline the contents of this book, we expected to be able to cover everything there is to know about C++. (Okay, you can stop laughing now.) However, as you may have guessed, we soon discovered that such an undertaking would require a book twice this size, not to mention bury the reader under hundreds of pages of esoteric information that he'll probably never need.

So we started with the core language and worked our way up, adding material until we got the maximum size book we thought would be reasonable, yet would still cover the most important elements of the C++ language. As it turned out, we managed to cram in enough information to cover the basic C++ language, as well as the most commonly used libraries and classes. The types of entries you'll find in this book include the following:

- *Class* — Each Class entry includes a brief description of the class, the class's declaration, and a table that describes the class members. Example entries include `exception`, `fstream`, and `stdiostream`.

- *Concept* — Each Concept entry describes a C++ programming concept, such as abstract classes, header files, and virtual functions.

- *Directive* — Each Directive entry describes a compiler directive and shows an example of usage. Entries of this type include `#include`, `#define`, and `#if`.

- *Function* — Each Function entry includes a description and a declaration. Function entries include `_wcsinc()`, `printf()`, or `sin()`. These entries also include short example programs that show the function being used.

- *Keyword* — Each Keyword entry describes a C or C++ keyword and includes an example of usage.

- *Manipulator* — Each Manipulator entry includes a description of a stream manipulator (such as `dec`, `endl`, and `hex`), along with an example of usage.

- *Operator* — Each Operator entry (such as `&`, `->`, and `sizeof`) includes a description of the operator, as well as an example of usage.

- *Standard C Library Header File* — Each Standard C Library Header File entry includes a brief description of the file, as well as a list of the symbols (such as functions, constants, structures, etc.) defined in the file. Examples include `float.h`, `stdlib.h`, and `string.h`.

- *Standard C++ Library Header File* — Each Standard C++ Library Header File entry includes a brief description of the file, as well as a list of the symbols (such as functions, constants, structures, etc.) defined in the file. Examples include `cfloat`, `cstdlib`, and `cstring`.

- *Stream* — Each Stream Object entry (such as `stdout`, `stdin`, and `stderr`) includes a description of the stream and an example of usage.

- *Stream Object* — Each Stream Object entry (such as `cerr`, `cin`, and `cout`) includes a description of the object and an example of usage.

- *Technique* — Each Technique entry is a "mini-tutorial" that describes an important C++ programming technique, such as creating classes, using polymorphism, and handling exceptions.

- *Template Class* — Each Template Class entry includes a brief description of the template class, the class' declaration, and a table that describes the class' members. Examples include `bitset`, `list`, and `map`.

In addition, to the above entry types, this book contains punctuator, structure, and macro entry types. Each contains a description and a usage example.

How This Book Is Organized

The entire contents of this book, regardless of the topic, are arranged in alphabetical order. This means that no matter what you're looking for — a class description, the use of a function, or a programming technique — you need look in only one book, rather than having to search through several manuals. For example, if you want to know about the stdlib.h header file, look it up in the S's. If you want to know what the `cprintf()` function does, look in the C's.

Please note that the book begins with a symbols chapter, which includes entries for nonalphabetic characters, such as &, !, and /*. The remaining chapters are organized alphabetically, except that entries that begin with one or more underscore characters (e.g., `_close()`, `_exit()`, and `__int16`) or with a pound sign (e.g., `#define`, `#if`, and `#include`) are at the beginning of the appropriate chapter. That is, `#define` is located near the beginning of Chapter D, and `_close()` is located near the beginning of Chapter C.

Understanding the Program Listings

Most of the entries in this book feature a short program that demonstrates how to use that particular element of the language. The program listings shown in the book were developed using Microsoft Visual C++. However, all the program source code that appears in the book is included on the accompanying CD-ROM. These programs include both Visual C++ and Borland C++ Builder versions.

To put it more specifically, everywhere you see a program listing in the book, you can find the complete program on the book's CD-ROM. If you're looking over this book as you sit in your favorite comfy chair (you know the one), you can just look over the printed program listing to see what's going on. If, however, you're perched in front of your computer, you can load the program from the CD-ROM and run it.

The programs are ordered alphabetically just as the entries are ordered in the book. For example, if you want to find the demo program for the `printf()` function, you look in the P folder for the printf folder. To run the program from the CD-ROM, find the project file (the file with the .dsw file-name extension for Visual C++ or the .bpr file-name extension for Borland C++ Builder) and double-click it. This action will load the program into the appropriate compiler, assuming you have that compiler installed on your system.

Note that all of the projects for both the Microsoft Visual C++ and Borland C++ Builder were started using the development environment's code-generator. Please see the "What's on the CD-ROM" appendix at the end of this book for more information.

System Requirements

The system and software requirements for the programs in this book are the same as the requirements for whatever system you're running and whatever compiler you're using.

In Closing

A huge amount of effort went into making this book as accurate as possible. However, the rules of this universe forbid such an immense task to be free of all errors. For this reason, please forgive any errors and oversights and notify me of any such discoveries. Your help will be greatly appreciated. You can reach me at my home page located at `www.claytonwalnum.com`.

Acknowledgments

I would like to thank the many people who had a hand in getting this book from the author's head to the bookshelf. Special thanks go to Greg Croy for trusting me with this project, to Terri Varveris for keeping things rolling and ensuring that the text made sense; to Eric Hahn, Amy Eoff, and Rich Adin for polishing things up; to Susan Parini and Linda Marousek for working on the production aspects of the book; and to Greg Guntle for verifying the technical accuracy of this book. As always, thanks go to my family: Lynn, Christopher, Justin, Stephen, and Caitlynn.

Contents

' (character literal indicator)

Operator

The single quote is used to indicate a character literal.

Syntax

```
'char'
```

- *char* — A value that represents a single character.

Example

The following program displays the message "C++" followed by newlines. The program's output looks like the following:

```
C++

Press any key to continue
```

Although the newlines are represented in the program by a backslash and an "n", it is still considered to be a single character. The backslash simply acts as an escape sequence. Here is the program source code that produced the output:

```
#include "stdafx.h"

int main(int argc, char* argv[])
{
    putchar('C');
    putchar('+');
    putchar(43);
    putchar('\n');
    putchar('\n');

    return 0;
}
```

CROSS-REFERENCE
See also " (string literal indicator).

- (subtraction)

Operator

The subtraction operator subtracts the value on the right of the operator from the value on the left.

Syntax

```
result = value1 - value2;
```

- *result*— The result of the operation.
- *value1*— The value from which value2 should be subtracted.
- *value2*— The value to subtract from value1.

Example

The following program demonstrates the use of the subtraction operator. The program's output looks like the following:

```
result: 13
result: 15
Press any key to continue
```

Here is the program source code that produced the output:

```
#include "stdafx.h"
#include <iostream>

using namespace std;

int main(int argc, char* argv[])
{
    int val1 = 20;
    int val2 = 7;

    int result = val1 - val2;
    cout << "result: " << result << endl;
    result = val1 - 5;
    cout << "result: " << result << endl;
```

```
      return 0;
  }
```

 CROSS-REFERENCE
See also — (decrement), -= (subtraction assignment), + (addition), += (addition assignment), * (multiplication), *= (multiplication assignment), / (division), and /= (division assignment).

— (decrement)

Operator

The decrement operator subtracts one from the value of its operand. If placed in front of its operand, the operator performs its subtraction before the value is accessed by the program statement. In this case, — is called a prefix decrement operator. If placed after its operand, the operator performs its subtraction after the value is accessed by the program statement. In this case, — is called a postfix decrement operator.

Syntax

```
–value
```

or

```
value–
```

■ *value*—The value to be decremented.

Example

The following program uses both prefix and postfix decrement operators and displays the results of the subtractions. The program's output looks like the following:

```
9
9
20
19
Press any key to continue
```

In the case of val1, the program first subtracts 1 from val1 before the first call to cout displays its value, which is now 9. The second cout displays val1 after the decrement, showing that it is still 9. In the case of val2, the third cout displays the value before performing the subtraction, and so displays the value 20. The fourth cout displays val2 again, which is now 19, proving that val2 was decremented after it was first displayed. Here is the program source code that produced the output:

```
#include "stdafx.h"
#include <iostream>

using namespace std;

int main(int argc, char* argv[])
{
    int val1 = 10;
    int val2 = 20;

    cout << -val1 << endl;
    cout << val1 << endl;
    cout << val2- << endl;
    cout << val2 << endl;

    return 0;
}
```

CROSS-REFERENCE
See also ++ (increment).

-= (subtraction assignment)

Operator

The subtraction-assignment operator subtracts the value on the right of the operator from the value on the left of the operator and then assigns the result to the left-hand value. For example, the line val1 -= 3 is equivalent to val1 = val1 - 3.

Syntax

var1 -= *exp1*;

- *exp1* — A valid expression.
- *var1* — Before the operation, var1 is the variable that contains the value from which exp1 is to be subtracted. After the operation, var1 will contain the result of the operation.

Example

The following program displays the value of the val1 variable both before and after a subtraction-assignment operation. The output looks like the following:

```
val1 = 12
val1 = 9
Press any key to continue
```

Before the operation, val1 is 12. After the operation, val1 is 9. Here is the program source code that produced the output:

```cpp
#include "stdafx.h"
#include <iostream>

using namespace std;

int main(int argc, char* argv[])
{
    int val1 = 12;
    cout << "val1 = " << val1 << endl;
    val1 -= 3;
    cout << "val1 = " << val1 << endl;

    return 0;
}
```

CROSS-REFERENCE

See also %= (remainder assignment), &= (bitwise AND assignment), *= (multiplication assignment), /= (division assignment), ^= (bitwise exclusive OR assignment), |= (bitwise OR assignment), += (addition assignment), <<= (left shift assignment), = (simple assignment), and >>= (right shift assignment).

-> (object pointer dereference)

Operator

The object pointer dereference operator dereferences a pointer to an instantiation of a class.

Syntax

objectPtr->member

- *objectPtr*—A pointer to an instantiation of a class.
- *member*—A member of the instantiated class.

Example

The following program demonstrates how to use the object pointer dereference operator. The program's output looks like the following:

```
Class value: 10
Press any key to continue
```

Here is the program source code that produced the output:

```cpp
#include "stdafx.h"
#include <iostream>
#include "MyClass.h"

using namespace std;

int main(int argc, char* argv[])
{
    MyClass* pMyClass = new MyClass(10);
    int value = pMyClass->GetValue();
    cout << "Class value: " << value << endl;
    delete pMyClass;

    return 0;
}

// Class header file.
class MyClass
{
protected:
    int value;

public:
    MyClass(int val);
    ~MyClass();
    int GetValue();
};

// Class implementation file.
#include "stdafx.h"
#include "MyClass.h"
```

```
MyClass::MyClass(int val)
{
    value = val;
}

MyClass::~MyClass()
{
}

int MyClass::GetValue()
{
    return value;
}
```

CROSS-REFERENCE
See also & (address of), & (reference), and * (pointer).

! (logical NOT)

Operator

The logical NOT operator reverses the value of a Boolean expression. That is, a true expression becomes false and vice versa.

Syntax

!*exp*

- *exp* — The Boolean expression whose value is to be reversed.

Example

The following program demonstrates the use of the logical NOT operator. The program's output looks like the following:

```
result: 1
!result: 0
Press any key to continue
```

Here is the program source code that produced the output:

```
#include "stdafx.h"
#include <iostream>
```

```
using namespace std;

int main(int argc, char* argv[])
{
    int x = 10;
    bool result = (x == 10);
    cout << "result: " << result << endl;
    cout << "!result: " << !result << endl;

    return 0;
}
```

CROSS-REFERENCE
See also bool (Keyword).

!= (not equal)

Operator

The not-equal operator compares two values and returns 1 (true) if the values are not equal or returns 0 (false) if the values are equal.

Syntax

```
result = exp1 != exp2;
```

- *exp1* — A valid expression.
- *exp2* — A valid expression.
- *result* — The value 1 or 0.

Example

The following program uses the not-equal operator to compare two values. The program's output looks like the following:

```
The values are not equal
Press any key to continue
```

Here is the program source code that produced the output:

```
#include "stdafx.h"
#include <iostream>
```

```
using namespace std;

int main(int argc, char* argv[])
{
    int val1 = 10;
    int val2 = 15;

    if (val1 != val2)
        cout << "The values are not equal" << endl;
    else
        cout << "The values are equal" << endl;

    return 0;
}
```

CROSS-REFERENCE
See also < (less than), <= (less than or equals), == (equals), > (greater than), and >= (greater than or equals).

" (string literal indicator)

Operator

The double quote is used to indicate a string literal.

Syntax

```
"str"
```

- *str*—A string.

Example

The following program displays a string, followed by newlines. The output looks like the following:

```
C++
```

```
Press any key to continue
```

Here is the program code that produced the output:

```
#include "stdafx.h"
#include <stdio.h>
```

```
int main(int argc, char* argv[])
{
    printf("C++\n\n");
    return 0;
}
```

CROSS-REFERENCE
See also ' (character literal indicator).

% (modulus)

Operator

The modulus operator divides the value on the left of the operator by the value on the right and returns the remainder of the division.

Syntax

```
result = exp1 % exp2;
```

- *exp1* — A valid expression.
- *exp2* — A valid expression.
- *result* — The result of the modulus operation.

Example

The following program displays the value of the `result` variable both before and after modulus operations. The output looks like the following:

```
result = 6
result = 0
Press any key to continue
```

Before the operation, `val1` is 20. After the modulus operation with `val2`, `result` is 6 (which is the remainder of 20/7). After the second operation, result is 0 (which is the remainder of 20/5). Here is the program source code that produced the output:

```
#include "stdafx.h"
#include <iostream>

using namespace std;
```

```
int main(int argc, char* argv[])
{
    int val1 = 20;
    int val2 = 7;

    int result = val1 % val2;
    cout << "result: " << result << endl;
    result = val1 % 5;
    cout << "result: " << result << endl;

    return 0;
}
```

CROSS-REFERENCE

See also %= (remainder assignment), / (division), and /= (division assignment).

%= (remainder assignment)

Operator

The remainder-assignment operator divides the value on the left of the operator by the value on the right of the operator, and then assigns the remainder of the division to the left-hand value. For example, the line `val1 %= 4` is equivalent to `val1 = val1 % 4`.

Syntax

```
var1 %= exp2;
```

- *exp2* — A valid expression.
- *var1* — A variable that contains the dividend before the operation and will contain the result after the operation.

Example

The following program displays the value of the `val1` variable both before and after the remainder-assignment operation. The output looks like the following:

```
val1 = 25
val1 = 1
Press any key to continue
```

Before the operation, val1 is 25. After the operation, val1 is 1 (which is the remainder of 25/4). Here is the program source code that produced the output:

```
#include "stdafx.h"
#include <iostream>

using namespace std;

int main(int argc, char* argv[])
{
    int val1 = 25;
    cout << "val1 = " << val1 << endl;
    val1 %= 4;
    cout << "val1 = " << val1 << endl;

    return 0;
}
```

CROSS-REFERENCE

See also -= (subtraction assignment), &= (bitwise AND assignment), *= (multiplication assignment), /= (division assignment), ^= (bitwise exclusive OR assignment), |= (bitwise OR assignment), += (addition assignment), <<= (left shift assignment), = (simple assignment), and >>= (right shift assignment).

& (address of)

Operator

The address-of operator returns the address in memory of an object, including variables, functions, and structures.

Syntax

&obj

- *obj*—The object for which to get the address in memory.

Example

The following program displays the address of a variable and uses the address to change the variable's value. The program's output looks something like the following:

```
val1 = 25
&val1 = 006AFDF4
val1 = 50
&val1 = 006AFDF4
Press any key to continue
```

Before any operations, val1 is 25. The first two couts display val1's current value and its address. The program then loads var1's address into a pointer and dereferences the pointer in order to change the value stored in val1. The third and fourth couts display the variable's new value and its address, which hasn't changed. Here is the program source code that produced the output:

```cpp
#include "stdafx.h"
#include <iostream>

using namespace std;

int main(int argc, char* argv[])
{
    int val1 = 25;
    cout << "val1 = " << val1 << endl;
    cout << "&val1 = " << &val1 << endl;
    int* adr = &val1;
    *adr = 50;
    cout << "val1 = " << val1 << endl;
    cout << "&val1 = " << adr << endl;

    return 0;
}
```

CROSS-REFERENCE

See also -> (object pointer dereference), & (reference), and * (pointer).

& (bitwise AND)

Operator

The bitwise-AND operator ANDs the value on the left of the operator with the value on the right of the operator and returns the result.

Syntax

```
result = exp1 & exp2;
```

- *exp1* — A valid expression.
- *exp2* — A valid expression.
- *result* — The result of the bitwise-AND operation.

Example

The following program performs bitwise-AND operations on a variable. The output looks like the following:

```
result: 0
result: 4
Press any key to continue
```

Here is the program source code that produced the output:

```cpp
#include "stdafx.h"
#include <iostream>

using namespace std;

int main(int argc, char* argv[])
{
    int val1 = 20;
    int val2 = 2;

    int result = val1 & val2;
    cout << "result: " << result << endl;
    result = val1 & 5;
    cout << "result: " << result << endl;

    return 0;
}
```

CROSS-REFERENCE

See also &= (bitwise AND assignment), ^ (bitwise exclusive OR), ^= (bitwise exclusive OR assignment), | (bitwise OR), and |= (bitwise OR assignment).

& (reference)

Operator

The reference operator enables a function to accept arguments by reference rather than by value. The reference to the argument can then be used just as if the argument were "global" between the calling and called functions. That is, changes to the argument's value also change the value of the original data item. This is similar to passing the address of a variable (a pointer to a variable) to a function, except you don't need to use the dereference operator (*) on a reference (which you must do to access the contents of a variable passed as a pointer).

Syntax

```
&val1
```

- *val1* — The argument to be received by reference.

Example

The following program demonstrates passing a variable by reference. The output looks like the following:

```
var1 in main: 25
arg1 in MyFunc: 25
arg1 in MyFunc: 50
var1 in main: 50
Press any key to continue
```

The program first displays the value of `var1` before passing it to the `MyFunc()` function. `MyFunc()` receives a reference to `var1`, naming the reference `arg1`. That is, now both `var1` and `arg1` represent the same storage location in memory. `MyFunc()` displays the value of `arg1`, showing that it is indeed the same value as `var1`. The function then changes the value of `arg1` to 50, displaying the changed value before returning to `main()`. Finally, `main()` displays the value of `var1`, which has also changed to 50. Here is the program source code that produced the output:

```
#include "stdafx.h"
#include <iostream>
```

```
using namespace std;

void MyFunc(int &arg1)
{
    cout << "arg1 in MyFunc: " << arg1 << endl;
    arg1 = 50;
    cout << "arg1 in MyFunc: " << arg1 << endl;
}

int main(int argc, char* argv[])
{
    int var1 = 25;
    cout << "var1 in main: " << var1 << endl;
    MyFunc(var1);
    cout << "var1 in main: " << var1 << endl;

    return 0;
}
```

Here is the equivalent code using a pointer to var1 instead of a reference:

```
#include "stdafx.h"
#include <iostream>

using namespace std;

void MyFunc(int* arg1)
{
    cout << "arg1 in MyFunc: " << *arg1 << endl;
    *arg1 = 50;
    cout << "arg1 in MyFunc: " << *arg1 << endl;
}

int main(int argc, char* argv[])
{
    int var1 = 25;
    cout << "var1 in main: " << var1 << endl;
    MyFunc(&var1);
    cout << "var1 in main: " << var1 << endl;

    return 0;
}
```

CROSS-REFERENCE
See also -> (object pointer dereference), & (address of), and * (pointer).

&& (logical AND)

Operator

The logical AND operator returns the Boolean value true if the expressions on the left and the right of the operator are both true. Otherwise, the operator returns false.

Syntax

```
result = expr1 && expr2;
```

- *expr1* — Any valid expression.
- *expr2* — Any valid expression.
- *result* — The Boolean value true (nonzero) or false (0).

Example

The following program demonstrates using the logical AND operator. The output looks like the following:

```
TRUE
FALSE
TRUE
```

Here is the program source code that produced the output:

```
#include "stdafx.h"
#include <iostream>

using namespace std;

int main(int argc, char* argv[])
{
    int var1 = 25;
    int var2 = 35;

    if ((var1 == 25) && (var2 == 35))
        cout << "TRUE" << endl;
    else
        cout << "FALSE" << endl;

    if ((var1 == 20) && (var2 == 35))
        cout << "TRUE" << endl;
    else
```

```
            cout << "FALSE" << endl;

        if ((var1) && (var2))
            cout << "TRUE" << endl;
        else
            cout << "FALSE" << endl;

        return 0;
    }
```

CROSS-REFERENCE
See also || (logical OR).

&= (bitwise AND assignment)

Operator

The bitwise-AND-assignment operator ANDs the value on the left of the operator with the value on the right of the operator and then assigns the result to the left-hand value. For example, the line `val1 &= 3` is equivalent to `val1 = val1 & 3`.

Syntax

```
var1 &= exp2;
```

- *exp2* — A valid expression.
- *var1* — Before the operation, a variable that contains the value with which to AND `exp2`. After the operation, `var1` will contain the result of the operation.

Example

The following program displays the value of the `val1` variable both before and after the bitwise-AND-assignment operation. The output looks like the following:

```
val1 = 27
val1 = 3
Press any key to continue
```

Before the operation, `val1` is 27. After the operation, `val1` is 3. Here is the program source code that produced the output:

```
#include "stdafx.h"
#include <iostream>

using namespace std;

int main(int argc, char* argv[])
{
    int val1 = 27;
    cout << "val1 = " << val1 << endl;
    val1 &= 3;
    cout << "val1 = " << val1 << endl;

    return 0;
}
```

CROSS-REFERENCE
See also -= (subtraction assignment), %= (remainder assignment), *= (multiplication assignment), /= (division assignment), ^= (bitwise exclusive OR assignment), |= (bitwise OR assignment), += (addition assignment), <<= (left shift assignment), = (simple assignment), and >>= (right shift assignment).

* (multiplication)

Operator

The multiplication operator multiplies the value on the right of the operator by the value on the left.

Syntax

```
result = value1 * value2;
```

- *result* — The result of the operation.
- *value1* — The value by which value2 should be multiplied.
- *value2* — The value by which value1 should be multiplied.

Example

The following program demonstrates the use of the multiplication operator. The program's output looks like the following:

```
result: 140
```

```
result: 100
Press any key to continue
```

Here is the program source code that produced the output:

```cpp
#include "stdafx.h"
#include <iostream>

using namespace std;

int main(int argc, char* argv[])
{
    int val1 = 20;
    int val2 = 7;

    int result = val1 * val2;
    cout << "result: " << result << endl;
    result = val1 * 5;
    cout << "result: " << result << endl;

    return 0;
}
```

CROSS-REFERENCE

See also - (subtraction), — (decrement), -= (subtraction assignment), + (addition), += (addition assignment), *= (multiplication assignment), / (division), and /= (division assignment).

* (pointer)

Operator

The pointer operator is used to declare or dereference a pointer.

Syntax

type *varl*

or

varl

- *type* — The data type to which the pointer will point.
- *varl* — The symbol that represents the pointer.

Example

The following program demonstrates declaring and dereferencing pointers. The output looks something like the following:

```
var1 in main: 25
address of var1: 006AFDF4
arg1 in MyFunc: 25
address of arg1: 006AFDF4
arg1 in MyFunc: 50
var1 in main: 50
Press any key to continue
```

The program first defines an integer (var1) and a pointer to that integer (pVar1). The program then displays the value and address of var1 before passing the pVar1 pointer to the MyFunc() function. MyFunc() receives the pointer to var1, naming the pointer arg1. MyFunc() then displays the value pointed to by arg1, as well as the address contained in arg1, showing that it is indeed the same value as var1. The function then changes the value pointed to by arg1 to 50, displaying the changed value before returning to main(). Finally, main() displays the value of var1, which has also changed to 50. Here is the program source code that produced the output:

```cpp
#include "stdafx.h"
#include <iostream>

using namespace std;

void MyFunc(int* arg1)
{
    cout << "arg1 in MyFunc: " << *arg1 << endl;
    cout << "address of arg1: " << arg1 << endl;
    *arg1 = 50;
    cout << "arg1 in MyFunc: " << *arg1 << endl;
}

int main(int argc, char* argv[])
{
    int var1 = 25;
    int* pVar1 = &var1;
    cout << "var1 in main: " << var1 << endl;
    cout << "address of var1: " << pVar1 << endl;
    MyFunc(pVar1);
    cout << "var1 in main: " << var1 << endl;

    return 0;
}
```

CROSS-REFERENCE
See also -> (object pointer dereference), & (address of), and & (reference).

*/ (end comment)

Punctuator

The end-comment punctuator marks the end of a C-style comment.

Syntax

```
/* comment */
```

- *comment*— Any text that should be ignored by the compiler.

Example

The following program demonstrates the use of C-style comments in source code. The program displays no output except the default message displayed by Visual C++, which looks like the following:

```
Press any key to continue
```

Here is the program source code:

```
#include "stdafx.h"

int main(int argc, char* argv[])
{
    /* This text will be completely ignored */

    /* A comment can even take up more
       than a single line because the compiler
       ignores all characters up to the
       end-comment punctuation */

    return 0;
}
```

CROSS-REFERENCE
See also /* (start comment) and // (C++ comment).

*= (multiplication assignment)

Operator

The multiplication-assignment operator multiplies the value on the left of the operator with the value on the right of the operator, and then assigns the result to the left-hand value. For example, the line `val1 *= 3` is equivalent to `val1 = val1 * 3`.

Syntax

```
var1 *= exp2;
```

- *exp2* — A valid expression.
- *var1* — Before the operation, a variable that contains the value with which to multiply `exp2`. After the operation, `var1` will contain the result of the operation.

Example

The following program displays the value of the `val1` variable both before and after the multiplication-assignment operation. The program output looks like the following:

```
val1 = 15
val1 = 45
Press any key to continue
```

Before the operation, `val1` is **15**. After the operation, `val1` is **45**. Here is the program source code that produced the output:

```
#include "stdafx.h"
#include <iostream>

using namespace std;

int main(int argc, char* argv[])
{
    int val1 = 15;
    cout << "val1 = " << val1 << endl;
    val1 *= 3;
    cout << "val1 = " << val1 << endl;

    return 0;
}
```

CROSS-REFERENCE
See also -= (subtraction assignment), %= (remainder assignment), &= (bitwise AND assignment), /= (division assignment), ^= (bitwise exclusive OR assignment), |= (bitwise OR assignment), += (addition assignment), <<= (left shift assignment), = (simple assignment), and >>= (right shift assignment).

/ (division)

Operator

The division operator divides the value on the left of the operator by the value on the right.

Syntax

```
result = value1 / value2;
```

- *result*—The result of the operation.
- *value1*—The value to be divided by `value2`.
- *value2*—The value by which `value1` should be divided.

Example

The following program demonstrates the use of the division operator. The program's output looks like the following:

```
result1: 2
result2: 2
result3: 2.85714
result4: 2
Press any key to continue
```

The first division operation divides an integer by an integer and yields an integer result. The floating-point portion of the result is truncated. In the second operation, an integer is again divided by another integer, but the variable that receives the result is declared as `float`. Still, the floating-point portion of the result is truncated. In the third operation, the dividend and divisor are cast to floating-point values, which yields a floating-point result. Finally, in the fourth division operation, the result is an integer, even though both the dividend and divisor were cast to floating-point values. Here is the source code that produced the output:

```
#include "stdafx.h"
#include <iostream>
```

```
using namespace std;

int main(int argc, char* argv[])
{
    int val1 = 20;
    int val2 = 7;
    int result1 = val1 / val2;
    float result2 = val1 / val2;
    float result3 = (float)val1 / (float)val2;
    int result4 = (float)val1 / (float)val2;

    cout << "result1: " << result1 << endl;
    cout << "result2: " << result2 << endl;
    cout << "result3: " << result3 << endl;
    cout << "result4: " << result4 << endl;

    return 0;
}
```

CROSS-REFERENCE
See also - (subtraction), — (decrement), -= (subtraction assignment), + (addition), += (addition assignment), * (multiplication), *= (multiplication assignment), and /= (division assignment).

/* (start comment)

Punctuator

The start-comment punctuator marks the start of a C-style comment.

Syntax

```
/* comment */
```

- *comment* — Any text that should be ignored by the compiler.

Example

The following program demonstrates the use of C-style comments in source code. The program displays no output except the default message displayed by Visual C++, which looks like the following:

```
Press any key to continue
```

Here is the program source code:

```
#include "stdafx.h"

int main(int argc, char* argv[])
{
    /* This text will be completely ignored */

    /* A comment can even take up more
        than a single line because the compiler
        ignores all characters up to the
        end-comment punctuation */

    return 0;
}
```

CROSS-REFERENCE
See also */ (end comment) and // (C++ comment).

// (C++ comment)

Punctuator

The C++-comment punctuator marks the start of a C++-style comment. Unlike a C-style comment, a C++-style comment has no ending punctuation and thus can be only a single line.

Syntax

```
// comment
```

- *comment*—Any text that should be ignored by the compiler.

Example

The following program demonstrates the use of C++-style comments in source code. The program displays no output except the default message displayed by Visual C++, which looks like the following:

```
Press any key to continue
```

Here is the program source code:

```
#include "stdafx.h"

int main(int argc, char* argv[])
{
    // This text will be completely ignored

    // Each line of a multiline C++ comment must
    // begin with the comment punctuator. That is,
    // unlike C style comments, which can be
    // multiple lines, C++ comments can only
    // be a single line.


    return 0;
}
```

CROSS-REFERENCE
See also */ (end comment) and /* (start comment).

/= (division assignment)

Operator

The division-assignment operator divides the value on the left of the operator by the value on the right of the operator, and then assigns the result to the left-hand value. For example, the line `val1 /= 3` is equivalent to `val1 = val1 / 3`.

Syntax

```
var1 /= exp2;
```

- *exp2*—A valid expression.
- *var1* — Before the operation, a variable that contains the divisor. After the operation, `var1` will contain the result of the operation.

Example

The following program displays the value of the `val1` variable both before and after the division-assignment operation. The program's output looks like the following:

```
val1 = 15
val1 = 5
```

```
Press any key to continue
```

Before the operation, val1 is 15. After the operation, val1 is 5. Here is the program source code that produced the output:

```cpp
#include "stdafx.h"
#include <iostream>

using namespace std;

int main(int argc, char* argv[])
{
    int val1 = 15;
    cout << "val1 = " << val1 << endl;
    val1 /= 3;
    cout << "val1 = " << val1 << endl;

    return 0;
}
```

CROSS-REFERENCE

See also -= (subtraction assignment), %= (remainder assignment), &= (bitwise AND assignment), *= (multiplication assignment), ^= (bitwise exclusive OR assignment), l= (bitwise OR assignment), += (addition assignment), <<= (left shift assignment), = (simple assignment), and >>= (right shift assignment).

[] (array elements)

Operator

The array-elements operator is used to declare arrays and access elements of an array.

Syntax

type array1[num];

or

array1[index]

- *array1* — The symbol that represents the array.
- *index* — The value that specifies the number of the array element to access.

- *num* — The number of elements to define in the array.
- *type* — The array's data type.

Example

The following program demonstrates how to declare, define, and access an array. The program's output looks like the following:

```
array1[0] = 10
array1[1] = 20
array1[2] = 30
Press any key to continue
```

Note that, although this program demonstrates only a one-dimensional array, you can declare multidimensional arrays by using more than one set of [] operators. For example, to declare a two-dimensional array, you might write something like int array1[10][10], which represents a 10 10 grid of array elements. Here is the source code that produced the output:

```
#include "stdafx.h"
#include <iostream>

using namespace std;

int main(int argc, char* argv[])
{
    int array1[3];
    array1[0] = 10;
    array1[1] = 20;
    array1[2] = 30;
    for (int x=0; x<3; ++x)
        cout << "array1[" << x << "] = " << array1[x] << endl;

    return 0;
}
```

^ (bitwise exclusive OR)

Operator

The bitwise-exclusive-OR operator exclusive ORs the value on the left of the operator with the value on the right of the operator.

Syntax

```
result = exp1 ^ exp2;
```

- *exp1* — The expression to be exclusive ORed with `exp2`.
- *exp2* — The expression to be exclusive ORed with `exp1`.
- *result* — The result of the operation.

Example

The following program performs bitwise-exclusive-OR operations on a variable. The output looks like the following:

```
result: 22
result: 17
Press any key to continue
```

Here is the program source code that produced the output:

```cpp
#include "stdafx.h"
#include <iostream>

using namespace std;

int main(int argc, char* argv[])
{
    int val1 = 20;
    int val2 = 2;

    int result = val1 ^ val2;
    cout << "result: " << result << endl;
    result = val1 ^ 5;
    cout << "result: " << result << endl;

    return 0;
}
```

CROSS-REFERENCE
See also & (bitwise AND), &= (bitwise AND assignment), ^= (bitwise exclusive OR assignment), | (bitwise OR), and |= (bitwise OR assignment).

^= (bitwise exclusive OR assignment)

Operator

The bitwise-exclusive-OR-assignment operator exclusive ORs the value on the left of the operator with the value on the right of the operator and then assigns the result to the left-hand value. For example, the line `val1 ^= 3` is equivalent to `val1 = val1 ^ 3`.

Syntax

```
var1 ^= exp2;
```

- *exp2* — A valid expression.
- *var1* — Before the operation, a variable that contains the value to be exclusive ORed with `exp2`. After the operation, `var1` will contain the result of the operation.

Example

The following program displays the value of the `val1` variable both before and after a bitwise-exclusive-OR-assignment operation. The program's output looks like the following:

```
val1 = 15
val1 = 12
Press any key to continue
```

Before the operation, `val1` is 15. After the operation, `val1` is 12. Here is the source code that produced the output:

```
#include "stdafx.h"
#include <iostream>

using namespace std;

int main(int argc, char* argv[])
{
    int val1 = 15;
    cout << "val1 = " << val1 << endl;
    val1 ^= 3;
    cout << "val1 = " << val1 << endl;

    return 0;
}
```

CROSS-REFERENCE

See also -= (subtraction assignment), %= (remainder assignment), &= (bitwise AND assignment), *= (multiplication assignment), /= (division assignment), |= (bitwise OR assignment), += (addition assignment), <<= (left shift assignment), = (simple assignment), and >>= (right shift assignment).

| (bitwise OR)

Operator

The bitwise-OR operator ORs the value on the left of the operator with the value on the right of the operator.

Syntax

```
result = exp1 | exp2;
```

- *exp1* — The expression to be ORed with exp2.
- *exp2* — The expression to be ORed with exp1.
- *result* — The result of the operation.

Example

The following program performs bitwise-OR operations on a variable. The program's output looks like the following:

```
result: 22
result: 21
Press any key to continue
```

Here is the program source code that produced the output:

```
#include "stdafx.h"
#include <iostream>

using namespace std;

int main(int argc, char* argv[])
{
    int val1 = 20;
    int val2 = 2;

    int result = val1 | val2;
```

```
    cout << "result: " << result << endl;
    result = val1 | 5;
    cout << "result: " << result << endl;

    return 0;
}
```

CROSS-REFERENCE

See also & (bitwise AND), &= (bitwise AND assignment), ^ (bitwise exclusive OR), ^= (bitwise exclusive OR assignment), and |= (bitwise OR assignment).

|| (logical OR)

Operator

The logical OR operator returns the Boolean value true if either (or both) of the expressions on the left and the right of the operator is true. Otherwise, the operator returns false.

Syntax

```
result = expr1 || expr2;
```

- *expr1* — Any valid expression.
- *expr2* — Any valid expression.
- *result* — The Boolean value true (nonzero) or false (0).

Example

The following program demonstrates using the logical OR operator. The program's output looks like the following:

```
TRUE
TRUE
FALSE
TRUE
Press any key to continue
```

Here is the program source code that produced the output:

```
#include "stdafx.h"
#include <iostream>
```

```
using namespace std;

int main(int argc, char* argv[])
{
    int var1 = 25;
    int var2 = 35;

    if ((var1 == 25) || (var2 == 10))
        cout << "TRUE" << endl;
    else
        cout << "FALSE" << endl;

    if ((var1 == 25) || (var2 == 35))
        cout << "TRUE" << endl;
    else
        cout << "FALSE" << endl;

    if ((var1 == 20) || (var2 == 10))
        cout << "TRUE" << endl;
    else
        cout << "FALSE" << endl;

    if ((var1) || (var2))
        cout << "TRUE" << endl;
    else
        cout << "FALSE" << endl;

    return 0;
}
```

CROSS-REFERENCE
See also && (logical AND).

|= (bitwise OR assignment)

Operator

The bitwise-OR-assignment operator ORs the value on the left of the operator with the value on the right of the operator, and then assigns the result to the left-hand value. For example, the line val1 |= 3 is equivalent to val1 = val1 | 3.

Syntax

```
var1 |= exp1;
```

- *exp1* — A valid expression.
- *var1* — Before the operation, a variable that contains the value to be ORed with exp2. After the operation, var1 will contain the result of the operation.

Example

The following program displays the value of the val1 variable both before and after a bitwise-OR-assignment operation. The program's output looks like the following:

```
val1 = 12
val1 = 15
Press any key to continue
```

Before the operation, val1 is 12. After the operation, val1 is 15. Here is the source code that produced the output:

```cpp
#include "stdafx.h"
#include <iostream>

using namespace std;

int main(int argc, char* argv[])
{
    int val1 = 12;
    cout << "val1 = " << val1 << endl;
    val1 |= 3;
    cout << "val1 = " << val1 << endl;

    return 0;
}
```

CROSS-REFERENCE

See also -= (subtraction assignment), %= (remainder assignment), &= (bitwise AND assignment), *= (multiplication assignment), /= (division assignment), ^= (bitwise exclusive OR assignment), += (addition assignment), <<= (left shift assignment), = (simple assignment), and >>= (right shift assignment).

~ (ones complement)

Operator

The ones-complement operator returns the ones complement of its operand.

Syntax

```
~value
```

- *value* — The value for which to calculate the ones complement.

Example

The following program demonstrates the use of the ones-complement operator. The program's output looks like the following:

```
var1: 0
ones complement: -1
Press any key to continue
```

Here is the program source code that produced the output:

```
#include "stdafx.h"
#include <iostream>

using namespace std;

int main(int argc, char* argv[])
{
    int var1 = 0;

    cout << "var1: " << var1 << endl;
    cout << "ones complement: " << ~var1 << endl;

    return 0;
}
```

CROSS-REFERENCE
See also & (bitwise AND), ^ (bitwise exclusive OR), and | (bitwise OR).

+ (addition)

Operator

The addition operator sums two values.

Syntax

```
result = value1 + value2;
```

- *result* — The result of the operation.
- *value1* — The first value to sum.
- *value2* — The second value to sum.

Example

The following program demonstrates the use of the addition operator. The program's output looks like the following:

```
result: 27
result: 25
Press any key to continue
```

Here is the program source code that produced the output:

```cpp
#include "stdafx.h"
#include <iostream>

using namespace std;

int main(int argc, char* argv[])
{
    int val1 = 20;
    int val2 = 7;

    int result = val1 + val2;
    cout << "result: " << result << endl;
    result = val1 + 5;
    cout << "result: " << result << endl;

    return 0;
}
```

CROSS-REFERENCE
See also - (subtraction), — (decrement), -= (subtraction assignment), * (multiplication), *= (multiplication assignment), / (division), /= (division assignment), and += (addition assignment).

++ (increment)

Operator

The increment operator adds one to the value of its operand. If placed in front of its operand, the operator performs its addition before the value is accessed by the program statement. In this case, ++ is called a prefix increment operator. If placed after its operand, the operator performs its addition after the value is accessed by the program statement. In this case, ++ is called a postfix increment operator.

Syntax

```
++value
```

or

```
value++
```

- *value* — The value to be incremented.

Example

The following program uses both prefix and postfix increment operators and displays the results of the additions. The program's output looks like the following:

```
11
11
20
21
Press any key to continue
```

In the case of val1, the program first adds 1 to val1 before the first call to cout displays its value, which is now 11. The second cout displays val1 after the increment, showing that it is still 11. In the case of val2, the third cout displays the value before performing the addition, and thus displays the value 20. The fourth cout displays val2 again, which is now 21, proving that val2 was incremented after it was first displayed. Here is the source code that produced the output:

```
#include "stdafx.h"
#include <iostream>

using namespace std;

int main(int argc, char* argv[])
{
    int val1 = 10;
    int val2 = 20;

    cout << ++val1 << endl;
    cout << val1 << endl;
    cout << val2++ << endl;
    cout << val2 << endl;

    return 0;
}
```

CROSS-REFERENCE
See also — (decrement).

+= (addition assignment)

Operator

The addition-assignment operator sums the value on the left of the operator with the value on the right of the operator and then assigns the result to the left-hand value. For example, the line val1 += 3 is equivalent to val1 = val1 + 3.

Syntax

var1 += exp2;

- *exp2*—A valid expression.
- *var1* — Before the operation, a variable that contains the value to be summed with exp2. After the operation, var1 will contain the result of the operation.

Example

The following program displays the value of the val1 variable both before and after an addition-assignment operation. The output looks like the following:

```
val1 = 12
val1 = 15
Press any key to continue
```

Before the operation, val1 is 12. After the operation, val1 is 15. Here is the source code that produced the output:

```cpp
#include "stdafx.h"
#include <iostream>

using namespace std;

int main(int argc, char* argv[])
{
    int val1 = 12;
    cout << "val1 = " << val1 << endl;
    val1 += 3;
    cout << "val1 = " << val1 << endl;

    return 0;
}
```

CROSS-REFERENCE
See also -= (subtraction assignment), %= (remainder assignment), &= (bitwise AND assignment), *= (multiplication assignment), /= (division assignment), ^= (bitwise exclusive OR assignment), |= (bitwise OR assignment), <<= (left shift assignment), = (simple assignment), and >>= (right shift assignment).

< (less than)

Operator

The less-than operator compares two values and results in 1 (true) if the left-hand value is less than the right-hand value, or 0 (false) if the left-hand value is greater than or equal to the right-hand value.

Syntax

result = exp1 < exp2;

- *exp1* — A valid expression.
- *exp2* — A valid expression.
- *result* — The value 1 or 0.

symbols & numbers

Example

The following program compares two values and displays the results. The program's output looks like the following:

```
Val1 is less than val2.
Press any key to continue
```

Here is the program source code that produced the output:

```
#include "stdafx.h"
#include <iostream>

using namespace std;

int main(int argc, char* argv[])
{
    int val1 = 10;
    int val2 = 15;

    if (val1 < val2)
        cout << "Val1 is less than val2." << endl;
    else
        cout << "Val1 is not less than val2." << endl;

    return 0;
}
```

CROSS-REFERENCE

See also != (not equal), <= (less than or equal), == (equals), > (greater than), and >= (greater than or equal).

<< (left shift)

Operator

The left-shift operator left shifts the bits of the value on the left of the operator by the number of bits specified by the value on the right of the operator.

Syntax

```
result = var1 << exp2;
```

- *exp2* — The number of bits to shift.

- *result*—The result of the operation.
- *var1*—The value to be shifted.

Example

The following program displays the value of the results of a left-shift operation. The program's output looks like the following:

```
val1 = 256
result = 2048
Press any key to continue
```

Before the operation, val1 is 256. After the operation, the result is 2,048. Here is the source code that produced the output:

```cpp
#include "stdafx.h"
#include <iostream>

using namespace std;

int main(int argc, char* argv[])
{
    int val1 = 256;
    int result;

    cout << "val1 = " << val1 << endl;
    result = val1 << 3;
    cout << "result = " << result << endl;

    return 0;
}
```

CROSS-REFERENCE
See also <<= (left shift assignment), >> (right shift), and >>= (right shift assignment).

<<= (left shift assignment)

Operator

The left-shift-assignment operator left shifts the bits of the left-hand value by the number of places in the right-hand value, and then assigns the result

symbols &
numbers

to the left-hand value. For example, the line `val1 <<= 3` is equivalent to `val1 = val1 << 3`.

Syntax

```
var1 <<= exp2;
```

- *exp2* — A valid expression.
- *var1* — Before the operation, a variable that contains the value to be shifted. After the operation, `var1` will contain the result of the shift.

Example

The following program displays the value of the `val1` variable both before and after a left-shift-assignment operation. The output looks like the following:

```
val1 = 12
val1 = 96
Press any key to continue
```

Before the operation, `val1` is 12. After the operation, `val1` is 96. Here is the source code that produced the output:

```
#include "stdafx.h"
#include <iostream>

using namespace std;

int main(int argc, char* argv[])
{
    int val1 = 12;
    cout << "val1 = " << val1 << endl;
    val1 <<= 3;
    cout << "val1 = " << val1 << endl;

    return 0;
}
```

CROSS-REFERENCE

See also -= (subtraction assignment), %= (remainder assignment), &= (bitwise AND assignment), *= (multiplication assignment), /= (division assignment), ^= (bitwise exclusive OR assignment), |= (bitwise OR assignment), += (addition assignment), = (simple assignment), and >>= (right shift assignment).

<= (less than or equal)

Operator

The less-than-or-equal operator compares two values and results in 1 (true) if the left-hand value is less than or equal to the right-hand value, or 0 (false) if the left-hand value is greater than the right-hand value.

Syntax

```
result = exp1 <= exp2;
```

- *exp1* — A valid expression.
- *exp2* — A valid expression.
- *result* — The value 1 or 0.

Example

The following program compares two values and displays the results. The program's output looks like the following:

```
Val1 is less than or equal to val2.
Press any key to continue
```

Here is the program source code that produced the output:

```cpp
#include "stdafx.h"
#include <iostream>

using namespace std;

int main(int argc, char* argv[])
{
    int val1 = 10;
    int val2 = 15;

    if (val1 < val2)
        cout << "Val1 is less than or equal to val2." << endl;
    else
    {
        cout << "Val1 is not less than or equal to val2.";
        cout << endl;
    }

    return 0;
}
```

CROSS-REFERENCE
See also != (not equal), < (less than), == (equals), > (greater than), and >= (greater than or equal).

= (simple assignment)

Operator

The simple assignment operator assigns the value on the right of the operator to the data item on the left.

Syntax

```
var1 = exp1;
```

- *exp1*—A valid expression.
- *var1*—The data item that is assigned the value of exp1.

Example

The following program displays the value of the val1 variable both before and after a simple assignment operation. The program's output looks like the following:

```
val1 = 12
val1 = 3
Press any key to continue
```

Here is the program source code that produced the output:

```cpp
#include "stdafx.h"
#include <iostream>

using namespace std;

int main(int argc, char* argv[])
{
    int val1 = 12;
    cout << "val1 = " << val1 << endl;
    val1 = 3;
    cout << "val1 = " << val1 << endl;

    return 0;
}
```

CROSS-REFERENCE
See also -= (subtraction assignment), %= (remainder assignment), &= (bitwise AND assignment), *= (multiplication assignment), /= (division assignment), ^= (bitwise exclusive OR assignment), |= (bitwise OR assignment), += (addition assignment), <<= (left shift assignment), and >>= (right shift assignment).

== (equals)

Operator

The equals operator compares two values and results in 1 (true) if the left-hand value is equal to the right-hand value or results in 0 (false) otherwise.

Syntax

```
result = exp1 == exp2;
```

- *exp1* — A valid expression.
- *exp2* — A valid expression.
- *result* — The value 1 or 0.

Example

The following program compares two values and displays the results. The program's output looks like the following:

```
Val1 equals val2.
Press any key to continue
```

Here is the program source code that produced the output:

```
#include "stdafx.h"
#include <iostream>

using namespace std;

int main(int argc, char* argv[])
{
    int val1 = 20;
    int val2 = 20;

    if (val1 == val2)
        cout << "Val1 equals val2." << endl;
```

```
        else
            cout << "Val1 does not equal val2." << endl;

        return 0;
    }
```

CROSS-REFERENCE

See also != (not equal), < (less than), <= (less than or equal), > (greater than), and >= (greater than or equal).

> (greater than)

Operator

The greater-than operator compares two values and results in 1 (true) if the left-hand value is greater than the right-hand value, or 0 (false) if the left-hand value is less than or equal to the right-hand value.

Syntax

```
result = exp1 > exp2;
```

- *exp1* — A valid expression.
- *exp2* — A valid expression.
- *result* — The value 1 or 0.

Example

The following program compares two values and displays the results. The program's output looks like the following:

```
Val1 is greater than val2.
Press any key to continue
```

Here is the program source code that produced the output:

```
#include "stdafx.h"
#include <iostream>

using namespace std;

int main(int argc, char* argv[])
{
```

```
int val1 = 20;
int val2 = 15;

if (val1 > val2)
    cout << "Val1 is greater than val2." << endl;
else
    cout << "Val1 is not greater than val2." << endl;

return 0;
}
```

CROSS-REFERENCE
See also != (not equal), < (less than), <= (less than or equal), == (equals), and >=
(greater than or equal).

>= (greater than or equal)

Operator

The greater-than-or-equal operator compares two values and results in 1
(true) if the left-hand value is greater than or equal to the right-hand value, or
0 (false) if the left-hand value is less than the right-hand value.

Syntax

```
result = exp1 >= exp2;
```

- *exp1* — A valid expression.
- *exp2* — A valid expression.
- *result* — The value 1 or 0.

Example

The following program compares two values and displays the results. The program's output looks like the following:

```
Val1 is greater than or equal to val2.
Press any key to continue
```

Here is the program source code that produced the output:

```
#include "stdafx.h"
#include <iostream>
```

```
using namespace std;

int main(int argc, char* argv[])
{
    int val1 = 20;
    int val2 = 15;

    if (val1 >= val2)
        cout << "Val1 is greater than or equal to val2." <<
endl;
    else
        cout << "Val1 is less than val2." << endl;

    return 0;
}
```

CROSS-REFERENCE
See also != (not equal), < (less than), <= (less than or equal), == (equals), and >
(greater than).

>> (right shift)

Operator

The right-shift operator right shifts the bits of the value on the left of the operator by the number of bits specified by the value on the right of the operator.

Syntax

```
result = var1 >> exp2;
```

- *exp2* — The number of bits to shift.
- *result* — The result of the operation.
- *var1* — The value to be shifted.

Example

The following program displays the value of the results of a right-shift operation. The program's output looks like the following:

```
val1 = 256
```

```
result = 32
Press any key to continue
```

Before the operation, val1 is 256. After the operation, the result is 32. Here is the source code that produced the output:

```
#include "stdafx.h"
#include <iostream>

using namespace std;

int main(int argc, char* argv[])
{
    int val1 = 256;
    int result;

    cout << "val1 = " << val1 << endl;
    result = val1 >> 3;
    cout << "result = " << result << endl;

    return 0;
}
```

 CROSS-REFERENCE
See also << (left shift), <<= (left shift assignment), and >>= (right shift assignment).

>>= (right shift assignment)

Operator

The right-shift-assignment operator right shifts the bits of the left-hand value by the number of places in the right-hand value, and then assigns the result to the left-hand value. For example, the line val1 >>= 3 is equivalent to val1 = val1 >>3.

Syntax

```
var1 >>= exp2;
```

- *exp2* — A valid expression.
- *var1* — Before the operation, a variable that contains the value to be shifted. After the operation, var1 will contain the result of the shift.

symbols & numbers

Example

The following program displays the value of the `val1` variable both before and after a right-shift-assignment operation. The program's output looks like the following:

```
val1 = 100
val1 = 12
Press any key to continue
```

Before the operation, `val1` is 100. After the operation, `val1` is 12. Here is the source code that produced the output:

```cpp
#include "stdafx.h"
#include <iostream>

using namespace std;

int main(int argc, char* argv[])
{
    int val1 = 100;
    cout << "val1 = " << val1 << endl;
    val1 >>= 3;
    cout << "val1 = " << val1 << endl;

    return 0;
}
```

CROSS-REFERENCE

See also -= (subtraction assignment), %= (remainder assignment), &= (bitwise AND assignment), *= (multiplication assignment), /= (division assignment), ^= (bitwise exclusive OR assignment), |= (bitwise OR assignment), += (addition assignment), <<= (left shift assignment), and = (simple assignment).

A

__asm

Keyword

The __asm keyword enables a program to contain assembly language instructions. For example, the following program includes a single line of assembly language in the main() function:

```
int main(int argc, char* argv[])
{
    __asm xor bx,bx

    return 0;
}
```

Multiple lines of assembly language can be included by enclosing the lines in braces, as follows:

```
int main(int argc, char* argv[])
{
    __asm
    {
        mov ax,0e07h
        xor bx,bx
    }

    return 0;
}
```

_access()

Function

The _access() function returns information about the accessibility of a file. The function returns 0 if the access verified is valid, or returns -1 if it is not valid.

NOTE
Borland users should refer to the access() function later in this chapter.

Header File

```
#include <io.h>
```

Declaration

```
int _access(const char* fileName, int access);
```

- *access* — The type of access for which to check. Can be 0 (existence), 2 (write), 4 (read), 6 (read and write).
- *fileName* — The path to the file to check.

Example

The following program demonstrates how to use the _access() function. The program's output looks like the following:

```
The file exists.
The file can be written to.
Press any key to continue
```

Here is the program source code that produced the output:

```cpp
#include "stdafx.h"
#include <io.h>
#include <iostream>

using namespace std;

int main(int argc, char* argv[])
{
    int result = _access("access.cpp", 0);
    if (result != -1)
    {
        cout << "The file exists." << endl;
        result = _access("_access.cpp", 2);
        if (result != -1)
            cout << "The file can be written to." << endl;
        else
            cout << "The file cannot be written to." << endl;
    }
    else
```

```
        else
            cout << "The file does not exist." << endl;

        return 0;
    }
```

CROSS-REFERENCE
See also _chmod(), _waccess(), _wchmod(), and access().

_atoi64()

Function

The _atoi64() function converts a string containing digits to a 64-bit integer value. The function returns 0 if the conversion cannot be performed successfully.

Header File

```
#include <stdlib.h>
```

Declaration

```
__int64 _atoi64(const char* str);
```

- *str* — The string to convert to a 64-bit integer.

Example

The following program demonstrates how to use the _atoi64() function. The program's output looks like the following:

```
The string is: 12345
The converted value is: 12345
Press any key to continue
```

Here is the program source code that produced the output:

```
#include "stdafx.h"
#include <stdlib.h>
#include <iostream>

using namespace std;
```

```
        char str[81];
        strcpy(str, "12345");
        __int64 result = _atoi64(str);
        cout << "The string is: " << str << endl;
        cout << "The converted value is: " << (int)result << endl;

        return 0;
}
```

 CROSS-REFERENCE
See also atof(), atoi(), and atol().

abort()

Function

The abort() function terminates a process, returning an exit code of 3.

Header File

```
#include <stdlib.h>
```

Declaration

```
void abort(void);
```

Example

The following program demonstrates how to use the abort() function. The program attempts to open a file and calls abort() if the file doesn't open successfully. The program's output looks like the following:

```
File open error.

abnormal program termination
Press any key to continue
```

Here is the program source code that produced the output:

```
#include "stdafx.h"
#include <stdlib.h>
#include <fcntl.h>
#include <io.h>
```

a

b

c

```
#include <iostream>

using namespace std;

int main(int argc, char* argv[])
{
    int fileHandle = _open("MyFile.dat", O_RDONLY);

    if (fileHandle != -1)
    {
        cout << "File opened successfully." << endl;
        _close(fileHandle);
    }
    else
    {
        cout << "File open error." << endl;
        abort();
    }

    return 0;
}
```

CROSS-REFERENCE
See also _exit() and exit().

abs()

Function

The abs() function returns the absolute value of its argument.

Header File

```
#include <stdlib.h>
```

Declaration

```
int abs(int num);
```

- *num* — The number for which to return the absolute value.

Example

The following program demonstrates how to use the abs() function. The program's output looks like the following:

```
The absolute value of -25 is 25
Press any key to continue
```

Here is the program source code that produced the output:

```
#include "stdafx.h"
#include <stdlib.h>
#include <iostream>

using namespace std;

int main(int argc, char* argv[])
{
    int var1 = -25;
    int result = abs(var1);
    cout << "The absolute value of " << var1;
    cout << " is " << result << endl;

    return 0;
}
```

CROSS-REFERENCE
See also _cabs(), fabs(), and labs().

Abstract Class

Concept

An *abstract class* is a class that contains one or more pure virtual functions. Such a class cannot be instantiated, but can be used to derive a more specific class that implements all pure virtual functions declared in the base class. For example, the following class is an abstract class:

```
// Class header file.
class MyClass
{
protected:
    int value;

public:
```

```
     MyClass();
     ~MyClass();
     int GetValue();

     // This is the pure virtual function.
     virtual int MultValue() = 0;
};


// Class implementation file.
#include "stdafx.h"
#include "MyClass.h"

MyClass::MyClass()
{
}

MyClass::~MyClass()
{
}

int MyClass::GetValue()
{
     return value;
}
```

Notice that, in the class's header file, a function called `MultValue()` is declared as a pure virtual function by using the `=0` pure virtual function specifier. Also, the class's implementation file has no definition for the `MultValue()` function.

The following class, `MyNewClass`, is derived from the abstract class, but implements the `MultValue()` function so that `MyNewClass` is not an abstract class, but still inherits the functionality of the base class, `MyClass`.

```
// Class header file.
#include "MyClass.h"

class MyNewClass : public MyClass
{
public:
     MyNewClass(int val);
     ~MyNewClass();

     virtual int MultValue();
};
```

```
// Class implementation file.
#include "stdafx.h"
#include "MyNewClass.h"

MyNewClass::MyNewClass(int val)
{
    value = val;
}

MyNewClass::~MyNewClass()
{
}

int MyNewClass::MultValue()
{
    return value * value;
}
```

Finally, the following program tests the `MyClass` and `MyNewClass` classes. The program's output looks like the following:

```
Return from GetValue: 10
Return from MultValue: 100
Press any key to continue
```

Here is the program source code that, along with the source code for the previously discussed classes, produced the output:

```
#include "stdafx.h"
#include <iostream>
#include "MyNewClass.h"

using namespace std;

int main(int argc, char* argv[])
{
    MyNewClass obj(10);

    int value = obj.GetValue();
    int result = obj.MultValue();
    cout << "Return from GetValue: " << value << endl;
    cout << "Return from MultValue: " << result << endl;

    return 0;
}
```

access()

Function

The `access()` function returns information about the accessibility of a file. The function returns 0 if the access verified is valid, or returns -1 if it is not valid.

Header File

```
#include <io.h>
```

Declaration

```
int access(const char* fileName, int access);
```

- *access* — The type of access for which to check. Can be 0 (existence), 2 (write), 4 (read), 6 (read and write).
- *fileName* — The path to the file to check.

Example

The following program demonstrates how to use the `access()` function. The program's output looks like the following:

```
The file exists.
The file can be written to.
Press any key to continue
```

Here is the program source code that produced the output:

```cpp
#include "stdafx.h"
#include <io.h>
#include <iostream>

using namespace std;

int main(int argc, char* argv[])
{
    int result = access("access.cpp", 0);
    if (result != -1)
    {
        cout << "The file exists." << endl;
        result = access("access.cpp", 2);
```

```
            if (result != -1)
                cout << "The file can be written to." << endl;
            else
                cout << "The file cannot be written to." << endl;
        }
        else
            cout << "The file does not exist." << endl;

        return 0;
    }
```

CROSS-REFERENCE
See also _access(), _chmod(), _waccess(), and _wchmod().

acos()

Function

The acos() function returns the arccosine of its argument.

Header File

```
#include <math.h>
```

Declaration

```
double acos(double num);
```

- *num* — The number (from –1 to 1) for which to return the arccosine.

Example

The following program demonstrates how to use the acos() function. The program's output looks like the following:

```
The arccosine of 0.345 is 1.21856
Press any key to continue
```

Here is the program source code that produced the output:

```
#include "stdafx.h"
#include <math.h>
```

```
#include <iostream>

using namespace std;

int main(int argc, char* argv[])
{
    double var1 = 0.345;
    double result = acos(var1);
    cout << "The arccosine of " << var1;
    cout << " is " << result << endl;

    return 0;
}
```

CROSS-REFERENCE
See also acosf(), acosl(), asin(), atan(), atan2(), cos(), cosh(), sin(), sinh(), tan(), and tanh().

acosf()

Function

The `acosf()` function returns, as a `float` value, the arccosine of its argument.

NOTE
Borland does not support this function.

Header File

```
#include <math.h>
```

Declaration

```
float acosf(float num);
```

- *num* — The number (from -1 to 1) for which to return the arccosine.

Example

The following program demonstrates how to use the `acosf()` function. The program's output looks like the following:

```
The arccosine of 0.345 is 1.21856
Press any key to continue
```

Here is the program source code that produced the output:

```
#include "stdafx.h"
#include <math.h>
#include <iostream>

using namespace std;

int main(int argc, char* argv[])
{
    float var1 = (float)0.345;
    float result = acosl(var1);
    cout << "The arccosine of " << var1;
    cout << " is " << result << endl;

    return 0;
}
```

CROSS-REFERENCE

See also acos(), acosl(), asin(), atan(), atan2(), cos(), cosh(), sin(), sinh(), tan(), and tanh().

acosl()

Function

The `acosl()` function returns, as a `long double` value, the arccosine of its argument.

Header File

```
#include <math.h>
```

Declaration

```
long double acosl(long double num);
```

- *num* — The number (from –1 to 1) for which to return the arccosine.

Example

The following program demonstrates how to use the `acosl()` function. The program's output looks like the following:

```
The arccosine of 0.345 is 1.21856
Press any key to continue
```

Here is the program source code that produced the output:

```cpp
#include "stdafx.h"
#include <math.h>
#include <iostream>

using namespace std;

int main(int argc, char* argv[])
{
    long double var1 = 0.345;
    long double result = acosl(var1);
    cout << "The arccosine of " << var1;
    cout << " is " << result << endl;

    return 0;
}
```

CROSS-REFERENCE

See also acos(), acosl(), asin(), atan(), atan2(), cos(), cosh(), sin(), sinh(), tan(), and tanh().

alloca()

Function

The `alloca()` function allocates memory on the program stack, returning a pointer to the allocated memory. You should not call `free()` for memory allocated in this way, because it is freed automatically.

Header File

```cpp
#include <malloc.h>
```

Declaration

```
void* alloca(size_t size);
```

- *size* — The number of bytes to allocate on the stack.

Example

The following program demonstrates how to use the `alloca()` function. The program allocates a block of memory on the stack, and then displays the address of the allocated memory. The program's output looks something like the following:

```
Memory located at: 006AFCA4
Press any key to continue
```

Here is the program source code that produced the output:

```
#include "stdafx.h"
#include <malloc.h>
#include <iostream>

using namespace std;

int main(int argc, char* argv[])
{
    void* pStackMem = alloca(256);

    if (pStackMem)
        cout << "Memory located at: " << pStackMem << endl;
    else
        cout << "Memory allocation unsuccessful." << endl;


    return 0;
}
```

CROSS-REFERENCE
See also calloc(), malloc(), and realloc().

asctime()

Function

The asctime() function converts the contents of a tm structure (which holds time and date information) to a string, returning a pointer to the string.

Header File

```
#include <time.h>
```

Declaration

```
char* asctime(const strict tm* pTm);
```

- *pTm*—A pointer to the tm structure that contains the time data to be converted to a string.

Example

The following program demonstrates how to use the asctime() function. The program initializes a tm structure, converts the structure to a string, and then displays the result. The program's output looks like the following:

```
Thu Jan 21 05:17:00 1999
Press any key to continue
```

Here is the program source code that produced the output:

```
#include "stdafx.h"
#include <iostream>
#include <time.h>

using namespace std;

int main(int argc, char* argv[])
{
    struct tm tmTime;

    tmTime.tm_mday  = 21;
    tmTime.tm_mon   = 0;
    tmTime.tm_year  = 99;
    tmTime.tm_wday  = 4;
    tmTime.tm_yday  = 0;
    tmTime.tm_isdst = 0;
```

```
            tmTime.tm_sec    = 0;
            tmTime.tm_min    = 17;
            tmTime.tm_hour   = 5;

            char* str = asctime(&tmTime);
            cout << str << endl;

            return 0;
        }
```

CROSS-REFERENCE

See also _tasctime() and _wasctime().

asin()

Function

The asin() function returns the arcsine of its argument.

Header File

```
#include <math.h>
```

Declaration

```
double asin(double num)
```

- *num* — The number (from –1 to 1) for which to return the arcsine.

Example

The following program demonstrates how to use the asin() function. The program's output looks like the following:

```
The arcsine of 0.345 is 0.352239
Press any key to continue
```

Here is the program source code that produced the output:

```
#include "stdafx.h"
#include <math.h>
#include <iostream>
```

```
using namespace std;

int main(int argc, char* argv[])
{
    double var1 = 0.345;
    double result = asin(var1);
    cout << "The arcsine of " << var1;
    cout << " is " << result << endl;

    return 0;
}
```

CROSS-REFERENCE
See also acos(), atan(), atan2(), cos(), cosh(), sin(), sinh(), tan(), and tanh().

asinf()

Function

The asinf() function returns, as a float value, the arcsine of its argument.

NOTE
Borland does not support this function.

Header File

```
#include <math.h>
```

Declaration

```
float asinf(float num)
```

- *num*—The number (from -1 to 1) for which to return the arcsine.

Example

The following program demonstrates how to use the asinf() function. The program's output looks like the following:

```
The arcsine of 0.345 is 0.352239
Press any key to continue
```

Here is the program source code that produced the output:

```
#include "stdafx.h"
#include <math.h>
#include <iostream>

using namespace std;

int main(int argc, char* argv[])
{
    float var1 = (float)0.345;
    float result = asinf(var1);
    cout << "The arcsine of " << var1;
    cout << " is " << result << endl;

    return 0;
}
```

CROSS-REFERENCE

See also acos(), asin(), asinl(), atan(), atan2(), cos(), cosh(), sin(), sinh(), tan(), and tanh().

asinl()

Function

The asinl() function returns, as a long double value, the arcsine of its argument.

Header File

```
#include <math.h>
```

Declaration

```
long double asinl(long double num)
```

- *num* — The number (from –1 to 1) for which to return the arcsine.

Example

The following program demonstrates how to use the asinl() function. The program's output looks like the following:

```
The arcsine of 0.345 is 0.352239
Press any key to continue
```

Here is the program source code that produced the output:

```cpp
#include "stdafx.h"
#include <math.h>
#include <iostream>

using namespace std;

int main(int argc, char* argv[])
{
    long double var1 = 0.345;
    long double result = asinl(var1);
    cout << "The arcsine of " << var1;
    cout << " is " << result << endl;

    return 0;
}
```

CROSS-REFERENCE

See also acos(), asin(), asinf(), atan(), atan2(), cos(), cosh(), sin(), sinh(), tan(), and tanh().

assert()

Function

The assert() function checks the validity of an expression and aborts the program if the statement is false.

Header File

```cpp
#include <assert.h>
```

Declaration

```cpp
void assert(int exp);
```

- *exp* — The expression to evaluate for validity.

Example

The following program demonstrates how to use the assert() function. Because the expression evaluated by assert() is true, program execution ends normally. The program's output looks like the following:

```
Press any key to continue
```

Here is the program source code that produced the output:

```
#include "stdafx.h"
#include <assert.h>

int main(int argc, char* argv[])
{
    int var1 = 25;
    assert(var1 > 10);

    return 0;
}
```

 CROSS-REFERENCE
See also abort() and exit().

atan()

Function

The atan() function returns the arctangent of its argument.

Header File

```
#include <math.h>
```

Declaration

```
double atan(double num);
```

■ *num* — The number for which to return the arctangent.

Example

The following program demonstrates how to use the atan() function. The program's output looks like the following:

```
The arctangent of 98.5 is 1.56064
Press any key to continue
```

Here is the program source code that produced the output:

```cpp
#include "stdafx.h"
#include <math.h>
#include <iostream>

using namespace std;

int main(int argc, char* argv[])
{
    double var1 = 98.5;
    double result = atan(var1);
    cout << "The arctangent of " << var1;
    cout << " is " << result << endl;

    return 0;
}
```

CROSS-REFERENCE
See also acos(), asin(), atan2(), cos(), cosh(), sin(), sinh(), tan(), and tanh().

atan2()

Function

The atan2() function returns the arctangent of arg1/arg2.

Header File

```cpp
#include <math.h>
```

Declaration

```cpp
double atan2(double arg1, double arg2);
```

- *arg1* — The first double-precision floating-point value.
- *arg2* — The second double-precision floating-point value.

Example

The following program demonstrates how to use the `atan2()` function. The program's output looks like the following:

```
The arctangent of 98.5/35.87 is 1.22156
Press any key to continue
```

Here is the program source code that produced the output:

```cpp
#include "stdafx.h"
#include <math.h>
#include <iostream>

using namespace std;

int main(int argc, char* argv[])
{
    double var1 = 98.5;
    double var2 = 35.87;
    double result = atan2(var1, var2);
    cout << "The arctangent of " << var1 << "/" << var2;
    cout << " is " << result << endl;

    return 0;
}
```

CROSS-REFERENCE

See also acos(), asin(), atan(), atan2f(), atan2l(), atanf(), atanl(), cos(), cosh(), sin(), sinh(), tan(), and tanh().

atan2f()

Function

The `atan2f()` function returns, as a `float` value, the arctangent of arg1/arg2.

NOTE

Borland does not support this function.

Header File

```cpp
#include <math.h>
```

Declaration

```
float atan2f(float arg1, float arg2);
```

- *arg1* — The first double-precision floating-point value.
- *arg2* — The second double-precision floating-point value.

Example

The following program demonstrates how to use the `atan2f()` function. The program's output looks like the following:

```
The arctangent of 98.5/35.87 is 1.22156
Press any key to continue
```

Here is the program source code that produced the output:

```cpp
#include "stdafx.h"
#include <math.h>
#include <iostream>

using namespace std;

int main(int argc, char* argv[])
{
    float var1 = (float)98.5;
    float var2 = (float)35.87;
    float result = atan2f(var1, var2);
    cout << "The arctangent of " << var1 << "/" << var2;
    cout << " is " << result << endl;

    return 0;
}
```

CROSS-REFERENCE
See also acos(), asin(), atan(), atan2(), atan2l(), atanf(), atanl(), cos(), cosh(), sin(), sinh(), tan(), and tanh().

atan2l()

Function

The `atan2l()` function returns, as a `long double` value, the arctangent of arg1/arg2.

Header File

```
#include <math.h>
```

Declaration

```
long double atan2l(long double arg1, long double arg2);
```

- *arg1* — The first double-precision floating-point value.
- *arg2* — The second double-precision floating-point value.

Example

The following program demonstrates how to use the `atan2l()` function. The program's output looks like the following:

```
The arctangent of 98.5/35.87 is 1.22156
Press any key to continue
```

Here is the program source code that produced the output:

```
#include "stdafx.h"
#include <math.h>
#include <iostream>

using namespace std;

int main(int argc, char* argv[])
{
    long double var1 = 98.5;
    long double var2 = 35.87;
    long double result = atan2l(var1, var2);
    cout << "The arctangent of " << var1 << "/" << var2;
    cout << " is " << result << endl;

    return 0;
}
```

CROSS-REFERENCE

See also acos(), asin(), atan(), atan2(), atan2f(), atanf(), atanl(), cos(), cosh(), sin(), sinh(), tan(), and tanh().

atanf()

Function

The `atanf()` function returns, as a `float` value, the arctangent of its argument.

NOTE
Borland does not support this function.

Header File

```
#include <math.h>
```

Declaration

```
float atanf(float num);
```

- *num* — The number for which to return the arctangent.

Example

The following program demonstrates how to use the `atanf()` function. The program's output looks like the following:

```
The arctangent of 98.5 is 1.56064
Press any key to continue
```

Here is the program source code that produced the output:

```cpp
#include "stdafx.h"
#include <math.h>
#include <iostream>

using namespace std;

int main(int argc, char* argv[])
{
    float var1 = (float)98.5;
    float result = atanf(var1);
    cout << "The arctangent of " << var1;
    cout << " is " << result << endl;

    return 0;
}
```

CROSS-REFERENCE
See also acos(), asin(), atan(), atan2(), atan2f(), atan(), atanl(), cos(), cosh(), sin(), sinh(), tan(), and tanh().

atanl()

Function

The atanl() function returns, as a long double value, the arctangent of its argument.

Header File

```
#include <math.h>
```

Declaration

```
long double atanl(long double num);
```

- *num* — The number for which to return the arctangent.

Example

The following program demonstrates how to use the atanl() function. The program's output looks like the following:

```
The arctangent of 98.5 is 1.56064
Press any key to continue
```

Here is the program source code that produced the output:

```
#include "stdafx.h"
#include <math.h>
#include <iostream>

using namespace std;

int main(int argc, char* argv[])
{
    long double var1 = 98.5;
    long double result = atanl(var1);
    cout << "The arctangent of " << var1;
    cout << " is " << result << endl;

    return 0;
}
```

CROSS-REFERENCE
See also acos(), asin(), atan(), atan2(), atan2f(), atan(), atanf(), cos(), cosh(), sin(),
sinh(), tan(), and tanh().

atexit()

Function

The atexit() function registers one or more functions that should run when
the program exits normally. The function returns 0 if successful or returns a
nonzero value if unsuccessful.

Header File

```
#include <stdlib.h>
```

Declaration

```
int atexit(void(__cdecl *func)(void));
```

- *func* — A pointer to the function that should execute.

Example

The following program demonstrates how to use the atexit() function. The
program displays the following output:

```
Hello from MyExitFunc2.
Press Enter to continue

Hello from MyExitFunc1.
Press Enter to continue
Press any key to continue
```

Here is the program source code that produced the output:

```
#include "stdafx.h"
#include <stdlib.h>
#include <iostream>

using namespace std;

void MyExitFunc1()
{
```

```
        cout << endl << "Hello from MyExitFunc1.";
        cout << endl << "Press Enter to continue";
        getchar();
    }

    void MyExitFunc2()
    {
        cout << endl << "Hello from MyExitFunc2.";
        cout << endl << "Press Enter to continue";
        getchar();
    }

    int main(int argc, char* argv[])
    {
        atexit(MyExitFunc1);
        atexit(MyExitFunc2);

        return 0;
    }
```

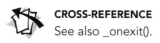

CROSS-REFERENCE
See also _onexit().

atof()

Function

The atof() function converts a string containing digits to a floating-point value. The function returns 0 if the conversion cannot be performed successfully.

Header File

```
#include <stdlib.h>
```

Declaration

```
double atof(const char* str);
```

- *str* — The string to convert to a floating-point value.

a
b
c

Example

The following program demonstrates how to use the atof() function. The program's output looks like the following:

```
The string is: 1234.56
The converted value is: 1234.56
Press any key to continue
```

Here is the program source code that produced the output:

```cpp
#include "stdafx.h"
#include <stdlib.h>
#include <iostream>

using namespace std;

int main(int argc, char* argv[])
{
    char str[81];
    strcpy(str, "1234.56");
    double result = atof(str);
    cout << "The string is: " << str << endl;
    cout << "The converted value is: " << result << endl;

    return 0;
}
```

CROSS-REFERENCE
See also _atoi64(), atoi(), and atol().

atoi()

Function

The atoi() function converts a string containing digits to an integer value. The function returns 0 if the conversion cannot be performed successfully.

Header File

```cpp
#include <stdlib.h>
```

Declaration

```
int atoi(const char* str);
```

- *str*—The string to convert to an integer.

Example

The following program demonstrates how to use the atoi() function. The program's output looks like the following:

```
The string is: 12345
The converted value is: 12345
Press any key to continue
```

Here is the program source code that produced the output:

```cpp
#include "stdafx.h"
#include <stdlib.h>
#include <iostream>

using namespace std;

int main(int argc, char* argv[])
{
    char str[81];
    strcpy(str, "12345");
    int result = atoi(str);
    cout << "The string is: " << str << endl;
    cout << "The converted value is: " << result << endl;

    return 0;
}
```

CROSS-REFERENCE
See also _atoi64(), atof(), and atol().

atol()

Function

The atol() function converts a string containing digits to a long integer value. The function returns 0 if the conversion cannot be performed successfully.

Header File

```
#include <stdlib.h>
```

Declaration

```
long atol(const char* str);
```

- *str*—The string to convert to a long integer.

Example

The following program demonstrates how to use the `atol()` function. The program's output looks like the following:

```
The string is: 12345
The converted value is: 12345
Press any key to continue
```

Here is the program source code that produced the output:

```
#include "stdafx.h"
#include <stdlib.h>
#include <iostream>

using namespace std;

int main(int argc, char* argv[])
{
    char str[81];
    strcpy(str, "12345");
    long result = atol(str);
    cout << "The string is: " << str << endl;
    cout << "The converted value is: " << result << endl;

    return 0;
}
```

CROSS-REFERENCE
See also _atoi64(), atof(), and atoi().

auto

Keyword

The `auto` keyword is used in declarations to specify a storage type of *automatic*. Because `auto` is the default storage class for declarations within program blocks, the actual specifier is usually not included in the declaration. For example, the declaration

```
auto int var1;
```

is equivalent to

```
int var1;
```

CROSS-REFERENCE
See also extern, register, and static.

B

basic_filebuf

Template Class

The `basic_filebuf` template class represents a stream buffer that controls the flow of data to and from a file.

Class Declaration

```
template <class E, class T = char_traits<E> >
    class basic_filebuf : public basic_streambuf<E, T> {
public:
    basic_filebuf();
    bool is_open() const;
    basic_filebuf *open(const char *s,
        ios_base::openmode mode);
    basic_filebuf *close();
protected:
    virtual pos_type seekoff(off_type off,
        ios_base::seekdir way,
        ios_base::openmode which = ios_base::in |
        ios_base::out);
    virtual pos_type seekpos(pos_type pos,
        ios_base::openmode which = ios_base::in |
        ios_base::out);
    virtual int_type underflow();
    virtual int_type pbackfail(int_type c = T::eof());
    virtual int_type overflow(int_type c = T::eof());
    virtual int sync();
    virtual basic_streambuf<E, T> *setbuf(E *s, streamsize n);
    };
```

Class Members

Table B-1 lists and describes the class members of the `basic_filebuf` template class.

Table B-1 Class Members of the basic_filebuf Template Class

Member	Description
close()	Closes the stream, returning a null pointer if unsuccessful
is_open()	Returns true if the stream is open
open()	Opens the file in the specified mode, returning a null pointer if unsuccessful
overflow()	Inserts a data element into an output stream, returning not_eof() for the element type if successful or returning eof() for the element type if unsuccessful
pbackfail()	Places a data element back into the input stream, returning not_eof() for the element type if successful or returning eof() for the element type if unsuccessful
seekoff()	Repositions the stream pointer in the stream, returning an invalid stream position if unsuccessful
seekpos()	Repositions the stream pointer in the stream, returning an invalid stream position if unsuccessful
setbuf()	Sets the buffer size, returning a null pointer if unsuccessful
sync()	Flushes all output to the stream, returning 0 if unsuccessful
underflow()	Reads a data element from an input stream, returning the value converted to int_type if successful or returning eof() for the element type if unsuccessful

CROSS-REFERENCE
See also basic_fstream, basic_ifstream, basic_ios, basic_iostream, basic_istream, basic_istringstream, basic_ofstream, basic_ostream, basic_ostringstream, basic_streambuf, basic_string, basic_stringbuf, and basic_stringstream.

basic_fstream

Template Class

The basic_fstream template class controls the flow of data to and from a stream buffer of the basic_filebuf type.

Class Declaration

```
template <class E, class T = char_traits<E> >
    class basic_fstream : public basic_iostream<E, T> {
public:
    explicit basic_fstream();
    explicit basic_fstream(const char *s,
```

```
        ios_base::openmode mode = ios_base::in |
        ios_base::out);
    basic_filebuf<E, T> *rdbuf() const;
    bool is_open() const;
    void open(const char *s,
        ios_base::openmode mode = ios_base::in |
        ios_base::out);
    void close();
    };
```

Class Members

Table B-2 lists and describes the class members of the `basic_fstream` template class.

Table B-2 Class Members of the basic_fstream Template Class

Member	Description
close()	Closes the stream
is_open()	Returns true if the stream is open
open()	Opens the stream in the specified mode
rdbuf()	Returns a pointer to the `basic_filebuf` object that represents the stream's buffer

CROSS-REFERENCE
See also basic_filebuf, basic_ifstream, basic_ios, basic_iostream, basic_istream, basic_istringstream, basic_ofstream, basic_ostream, basic_ostringstream, basic_streambuf, basic_string, basic_stringbuf, and basic_stringstream.

basic_ifstream

Template Class

The `basic_ifstream` template class controls the input of data from a stream buffer of the `basic_filebuf` type.

Class Declaration

```
template <class E, class T = char_traits<E> >
    class basic_ifstream : public basic_istream<E, T> {
```

```
public:
    explicit basic_ifstream();
    explicit basic_ifstream(const char *s,
        ios_base::openmode mode = ios_base::in);
    basic_filebuf<E, T> *rdbuf() const;
    bool is_open() const;
    void open(const char *s,
        ios_base::openmode mode = ios_base::in);
    void close();
    };
```

Class Members

Table B-3 lists and describes the class members of the `basic_ifstream` template class.

Table B-3 Class Members of the basic_ifstream Template Class

Member	Description
is_open()	Returns true if the stream is open
open()	Opens the stream in the specified mode
close()	Closes the stream
rdbuf()	Returns a pointer to the basic_filebuf object that represents the stream's buffer

CROSS-REFERENCE
See also basic_filebuf, basic_fstream, basic_ios, basic_iostream, basic_istream, basic_istringstream, basic_ofstream, basic_ostream, basic_ostringstream, basic_streambuf, basic_string, basic_stringbuf, and basic_stringstream.

basic_ios

Template Class

The `basic_ios` template class represents the functions required to manage both input and output streams, which are represented by objects of the `basic_istream` and `basic_ostream` template classes, respectively.

Class Declaration

```
template <class E, class T = char_traits<E> >
    class basic_ios : public ios_base {
public:
    typedef E char_type;
    typedef T::int_type int_type;
    typedef T::pos_type pos_type;
    typedef T::off_type off_type;
    explicit basic_ios(basic_streambuf<E, T>* sb);
    virtual ~basic_ios();
    operator void *() const;
    bool operator!() const;
    iostate rdstate() const;
    void clear(iostate state = goodbit);
    void setstate(iostate state);
    bool good() const;
    bool eof() const;
    bool fail() const;
    bool bad() const;
    iostate exceptions() const;
    iostate exceptions(iostate except);
    basic_ios& copyfmt(const basic_ios& rhs);
    E fill() const;
    E fill(E ch);
    basic_ostream<E, T> *tie() const;
    basic_ostream<E, T> *tie(basic_ostream<E, T> *str);
    basic_streambuf<E, T> *rdbuf() const;
    basic_streambuf<E, T> *rdbuf(basic_streambuf<E, T> *sb);
    locale imbue(const locale& loc);
    E widen(char ch);
    char narrow(E ch, char dflt);
protected:
    basic_ios();
    void init(basic_streambuf<E, T>* sb);
    };
```

Class Members

Table B-4 lists and describes the class members of the basic_ios template class.

Table B-4 Class Members of the basic_ios Template Class

Member	Description
bad()	Returns true if the stream is in a bad state (rdstate() & badbit)
char_type	A synonym for the template's E parameter
clear()	Resets the stream's state
copyfmt()	Copies the stream's given fill character, tie pointer, and formatting information into the stream object
eof()	Returns true if the stream position is at the end of the stream (rdstate() & eofbit)
exceptions()	Returns the stream's exception mask
fail()	Returns true if the stream is in a failed state (rdstate() & failbit)
fill()	Returns the stream object's fill character
good()	Returns true if the stream's state is good (rdstate() & goodbit)
imbue()	Calls the stream buffer's pubimbue() member
init()	Initializes all class member objects
int_type	A synonym for T converted to int_type
narrow()	Returns use_facet<ctype<E>(getloc()).narrow(ch, dflt)
off_type	A synonym for T converted to off_type
pos_type	A synonym for T converted to pos_type
rdbuf()	Returns the address of the stream object's buffer
rdstate()	Returns state information about the stream
setstate()	Sets the stream's state
tie()	Returns the stream object's tie pointer
widen()	Returns use_facet<ctype<E>(getloc()).widen(ch)

CROSS-REFERENCE

See also basic_filebuf, basic_fstream, basic_ifstream, basic_iostream, basic_istream, basic_istringstream, basic_ofstream, basic_ostream, basic_ostringstream, basic_streambuf, basic_string, basic_stringbuf, and basic_stringstream.

basic_iostream

Template Class

The basic_iostream template class controls the flow of data to and from the associated basic_ostream and basic_istream objects.

Class Declaration

```
template <class E, class T = char_traits<E> >
    class basic_iostream : public basic_istream<E, T>,
        public  basic_ostream<E, T> {
public:
    explicit basic_iostream(basic_streambuf<E, T> *sb);
    virtual ~basic_iostream();
    };
```

Class Members

The `basic_iostream` template class does not have any class members.

CROSS-REFERENCE
See also basic_filebuf, basic_fstream, basic_ifstream, basic_ios, basic_istream, basic_istringstream, basic_ofstream, basic_ostream, basic_ostringstream, basic_streambuf, basic_string, basic_stringbuf, and basic_stringstream.

basic_istream

Template Class

The `basic_istream` template class controls the input of data from a stream buffer.

Class Declaration

```
template <class E, class T = char_traits<E> >
    class basic_istream : virtual public basic_ios<E, T> {
public:
    class sentry;
    explicit basic_istream(basic_streambuf<E, T> *sb);
    virtual ~istream();
    bool ipfx(bool noskip = false);
    void isfx();
    basic_istream& operator>(basic_istream&
        (*pf)(basic_istream&));
    basic_istream& operator>(basic_ios<E, T>&
        (*pf)(basic_ios<E, T>&));
    basic_istream& operator>(ios_base<E, T>&
```

```
    (*pf)(ios_base<E, T>&));
basic_istream& operator>(basic_streambuf<E, T> *sb);
basic_istream& operator>(bool& n);
basic_istream& operator>(short& n);
basic_istream& operator>(unsigned short& n);
basic_istream& operator>(int& n);
basic_istream& operator>(unsigned int& n);
basic_istream& operator>(long& n);
basic_istream& operator>(unsigned long& n);
basic_istream& operator>(void *& n);
basic_istream& operator>(float& n);
basic_istream& operator>(double& n);
basic_istream& operator>(long double& n);
streamsize gcount() const;
int_type get();
basic_istream& get(E& c);
basic_istream& get(E *s, streamsize n);
basic_istream& get(E *s, streamsize n, E delim);
basic_istream& get(basic_streambuf<E, T> *sb);
basic_istream& get(baiic_streambuf<E, T> *sb, E delim);
basic_istream& getline(E *s, streamsize n)E
basic_istream& getline(E *s, streamsize n, E delim);
basic_istream& ignore(streamsize n = 1,
    int_type delim = T::eof());
int_type peek();
basic_istream& read(E *s, streamsize n);
streamsize readsome(E *s, streamsize n);
basic_istream& putback(E c);
basic_istream& unget();
pos_type tellg();
basic_istream& seekg(pos_type pos);
basic_istream& seekg(off_type off,
    ios_base::seek_dir way);
int sync();
};
```

Class Members

Table B-5 lists and describes the class members of the basic_istream template class.

Table B-5 Class Members of the basic_istream Template Class

Member	Description
gcount()	Returns the extraction count
get()	Retrieves data from the stream
getline()	Retrieves a line of data from the stream
ignore()	Retrieves and ignores data from the stream
ipfx()	Prepares the stream for input
isfx()	Performs cleanup after data transfer
peek()	Retrieves the next data element from the stream buffer
putback()	Places a data element back in the stream
read()	Reads a given number of data elements from the stream
readsome()	Reads a given number of data elements from the stream
seekg()	Changes the position in the stream, returning a pointer to the stream
sync()	Synchronizes the stream with any external streams, returning 0 if successful or –1 if unsuccessful
tellg()	Changes the position in the stream, returning the new position
unget()	Places a data element back in the stream

CROSS-REFERENCE
See also basic_filebuf, basic_fstream, basic_ifstream, basic_ios, basic_iostream, basic_istringstream, basic_ofstream, basic_ostream, basic_ostringstream, basic_streambuf, basic_string, basic_stringbuf, and basic_stringstream.

basic_istringstream

Template Class

The basic_istringstream **template class controls the input of data from a** basic_stringbuf **stream buffer.**

Class Declaration

```
template <class E,
    class T = char_traits<E>,
    class A = allocator<E> >
    class basic_istringstream : public basic_istream<E, T> {
public:
    explicit basic_istringstream(ios_base::openmode
        mode = ios_base::in);
```

```
explicit basic_istringstream(const
    basic_string<E, T, A>& x,
    ios_base::openmode mode = ios_base::in);
basic_stringbuf<E, T, A> *rdbuf() const;
basic_string<E, T, A>& str();
void str(const basic_string<E, T, A>& x);
};
```

Class Members

Table B-6 lists and describes the class members of the basic_istringstream template class.

Table B-6 Class Members of the basic_istringstream Template Class

Member	Description
rdbuf()	Returns the address of the stream's buffer object
str()	Returns a basic_string object from the stream

CROSS-REFERENCE
See also basic_filebuf, basic_fstream, basic_ifstream, basic_ios, basic_iostream, basic_istream, basic_ofstream, basic_ostream, basic_ostringstream, basic_streambuf, basic_string, basic_stringbuf, and basic_stringstream.

basic_ofstream

Template Class

The basic_ofstream template class controls the flow of data into a stream buffer of the basic_filebuf type.

Class Declaration

```
template <class E, class T = char_traits<E> >
    class basic_ofstream : public basic_ostream<E, T> {
public:
    explicit basic_ofstream();
    explicit basic_ofstream(const char *s,
        ios_base::openmode mode = ios_base::out |
        ios_base::trunc);
```

```
basic_filebuf<E, T> *rdbuf() const;
bool is_open() const;
void open(const char *s,
    ios_base::openmode mode = ios_base::out |
    ios_base::trunc);
void close();
};
```

Class Members

Table B-7 lists and describes the class members of the basic_ofstream template class.

Table B-7 Table Members of the basic_ofstream Template Class

Member	Description
is_open()	Returns true if the stream is open
open()	Opens the stream
close()	Closes the stream
rdbuf()	Returns a pointer to the basic_filebuf object that represents the stream's buffer

CROSS-REFERENCE
See also basic_filebuf, basic_fstream, basic_ifstream, basic_ios, basic_iostream, basic_istream, basic_istringstream, basic_ostream, basic_ostringstream, basic_streambuf, basic_string, basic_stringbuf, and basic_stringstream.

basic_ostream

Template Class

The basic_ostream template class controls the flow of data into a stream buffer.

Class Declaration

```
template <class E, class T = char_traits<E> >
    class basic_ostream {
public:
    class sentry;
```

```
explicit basic_ostream(basic_streambuf<E, T> *sb);
virtual ~ostream();
bool opfx();
void osfx();
basic_ostream& operator<<(basic_ostream&
    (*pf)(basic_ostream&));
basic_ostream& operator<<(basic_ios<E, T>&
    (*pf)(basic_ios<E, T>&));
basic_ostream& operator<<(ios_base<E, T>&
    (*pf)(ios_base<E, T>&));
basic_ostream& operator<<(basic_streambuf<E, T> *sb);
basic_ostream& operator<<(const char *s);
basic_ostream& operator<<(char c);
basic_ostream& operator<<(bool n);
basic_ostream& operator<<(short n);
basic_ostream& operator<<(unsigned short n);
basic_ostream& operator<<(int n);
basic_ostream& operator<<(unsigned int n);
basic_ostream& operator<<(long n);
basic_ostream& operator<<(unsigned long n);
basic_ostream& operator<<(float n);
basic_ostream& operator<<(double n);
basic_ostream& operator<<(long double n);
basic_ostream& operator<<(void * n);
basic_ostream& put(E c);
basic_ostream& write(E *s, streamsize n);
basic_ostream& flush();
pos_type tellp();
basic_ostream& seekp(pos_type pos);
basic_ostream& seekp(off_type off,
    ios_base::seek_dir way);
};
```

Class Members

Table B-8 lists and describes the class members of the `basic_ostream` template class.

Table B-8 Class Members of the basic_ostream Template Class

Member	Description
flush()	Synchronizes the stream
opfx()	Flushes the stream

Member	Description
osfx()	Flushes the stream
put()	Sends data to the stream
seekp()	Changes the position in the stream, returning a pointer to the stream
tellp()	Changes the position in the stream
write()	Sends a given number of data elements to the stream

CROSS-REFERENCE

See also basic_filebuf, basic_fstream, basic_ifstream, basic_ios, basic_iostream, basic_istream, basic_istringstream, basic_ofstream, basic_ostringstream, basic_streambuf, basic_string, basic_stringbuf, and basic_stringstream.

basic_ostringstream

Template Class

The `basic_ostringstream` template class controls the flow of data to a `basic_stringbuf` stream buffer.

Class Declaration

```
template <class E,
    class T = char_traits<E>,
    class A = allocator<E> >
    class basic_ostringstream : public basic_ostream<E, T> {
public:
    explicit basic_ostringstream(ios_base::openmode
        mode = ios_base::out);
    explicit basic_ostringstream(const
        basic_string<E, T, A>& x,
        ios_base::openmode mode = ios_base::out);
    basic_stringbuf<E, T, A> *rdbuf() const;
    basic_string<E, T, A>& str();
    void str(const basic_string<E, T, A>& x);
    };
```

Class Members

Table B-9 lists and describes the class members of the `basic_ostringstream` template class.

Table B-9 Class Members of the basic_ostringstream Template Class

Member	Description
rdbuf()	Returns the address of the stream's buffer object
str()	Returns a basic_string object from the stream

CROSS-REFERENCE
See also basic_filebuf, basic_fstream, basic_ifstream, basic_ios, basic_iostream, basic_istream, basic_istringstream, basic_ofstream, basic_ostream, basic_streambuf, basic_string, basic_stringbuf, and basic_stringstream.

basic_streambuf

Template Class

The basic_streambuf **template class represents a stream buffer.**

Class Declaration

```
template <class E, class T = char_traits<E> >
    class basic_streambuf {
public:
    typedef E char_type;
    typedef T traits_type;
    typedef T::int_type int_type;
    typedef T::pos_type pos_type;
    typedef T::off_type off_type;
    virtual ~streambuf();
    locale pubimbue(const locale& loc);
    locale getloc() const;
    basic_streambuf *pubsetbuf(E *s, streamsize n);
    pos_type pubseekoff(off_type off, ios_base::seekdir way,
        ios_base::openmode which = ios_base::in |
        ios_base::out);
    pos_type pubseekpos(pos_type sp,
        ios_base::openmode which = ios_base::in |
        ios_base::out);
    int pubsync();
    streamsize in_avail();
    int_type snextc();
    int_type sbumpc();
```

```
        int_type sgetc();
        streamsize sgetn(E *s, streamsize n);
        int_type sputbackc(E c);
        int_type sungetc();
        int_type sputc(E c);
        streamsize sputn(const E *s, streamsize n);
protected:
    basic_streambuf();
    E *eback() const;
    E *gptr() const;
    E *egptr() const;
    void gbump(int n);
    void setg(E *gbeg, E *gnext, E *gend);
    E *pbase() const;
    E *pptr() const;
    E *epptr() const;
    void pbump(int n);
    void setp(E *pbeg, E *pend);
    virtual void imbue(const locale &loc);
    virtual basic_streambuf *setbuf(E *s, streamsize n);
    virtual pos_type seekoff(off_type off,
        ios_base::seekdir way,
        ios_base::openmode which = ios_base::in |
        ios_base::out);
    virtual pos_type seekpos(pos_type sp,
        ios_base::openmode which = ios_base::in |
        ios_base::out);
    virtual int sync();
    virtual int showmanyc();
    virtual streamsize xsgetn(E *s, streamsize n);
    virtual int_type underflow();
    virtual int_type uflow();
    virtual int_type pbackfail(int_type c = T::eof());
    virtual streamsize xsputn(const E *s, streamsize n);
    virtual int_type overflow(int_type c = T::eof());
    };
```

Class Members

Table B-10 lists and describes the class members of the basic_streambuf template class.

Table B-10 Class Members of the basic_streambuf Template Class

Member	Description
char_type	A synonym for the template's E parameter
eback()	Returns the address of the stream's input buffer
egptr()	Returns a pointer past the end of the stream's input buffer
epptr()	Returns a pointer past the end of the output buffer
gbump()	Adds the given value to the input buffer's next pointer
getloc()	Returns the locale object
gptr()	Returns the address of the next data element in the stream's input buffer
imbue()	Does nothing in this class
in_avail()	Returns the remaining number of data elements in the stream
int_type	A synonym for T converted to int_type
off_type	A synonym for T converted to off_type
overflow()	Places the given data element into the output stream
pbackfail()	Places a data element back into the input stream and sets the stream's next pointer to the data element
pbase()	Returns the address of the start of the output buffer
pbump()	Adds the given value to the output buffer's next pointer
pos_type	A synonym for T converted to pos_type
pptr()	Returns the address of the next data element in the output buffer
pubimbue()	Stores the given locale object and then calls imbue()
pubseekoff()	Calls seekoff() and returns the result
pubseekpos()	Calls seekpos() and returns the result
pubsetbuf()	Calls setbuf() and returns the result
pubsync()	Calls sync() and returns the result
sbumpc()	Returns the next data element in the stream and advances the next input buffer pointer
seekoff()	Sets the stream's positions
seekpos()	Sets the stream's position to the specified position
setbuf()	Sets the buffer's size
setg()	Sets the input buffer's start, next, and end pointers
setp()	Sets the output buffer's start, next, and end pointers
sgetc()	Returns the next data element in the stream or calls underflow() and returns the result
sgetn()	Returns a given number of data elements from the stream
showmanyc()	Returns the number of characters that can be read from the input stream without the program's having to wait
snextc()	Returns the next data element in the stream
sputbackc()	Decrements the input buffer's next pointer, returning the given character

Member	Description
sputc()	Places a data element in the current stream position and increments the input buffer's next pointer
sputn()	Places a specified number of data elements in the stream
sungetc()	Decrements the input buffer's next pointer and returns the next character
sync()	Synchronizes the streams with any external streams
traits_type	A synonym for the template's T parameter
uflow()	Retrieves a data element from the input stream and increments the buffer's next pointer
underflow()	Retrieves a data element from the input stream without incrementing the buffer's next pointer
xsgetn()	Retrieves the specified number of data elements from the input stream
xsputn()	Places the specified number of data elements into the output stream

CROSS-REFERENCE

See also basic_filebuf, basic_fstream, basic_ifstream, basic_ios, basic_iostream, basic_istream, basic_istringstream, basic_ofstream, basic_ostream, basic_ostringstream, basic_string, basic_stringbuf, and basic_stringstream.

basic_string

Template Class

The basic_string template class controls a set of elements of varying length and is the template class used to represent strings.

Class Declaration

```
template<class E,
    class T = char_traits<E>,
        class A = allocator<T> >
    class basic_string {
public:
    typedef T traits_type;
    typedef A allocator_type;
    typedef T::char_type char_type;
    typedef A::size_type size_type;
    typedef A::difference_type difference_type;
    typedef A::pointer pointer;
```

```
typedef A::const_pointer const_pointer;
typedef A::reference reference;
typedef A::const_reference const_reference;
typedef A::value_type value_type;    typedef T0 iterator;
typedef T1 const_iterator;
typedef reverse_iterator<iterator, value_type,
    reference, pointer, difference_type>
    reverse_iterator;
typedef reverse_iterator<const_iterator, value_type,
    const_reference, const_pointer, difference_type>
        const_reverse_iterator;
static const size_type npos = -1;
explicit basic_string(const A& al = A());
basic_string(const basic_string& rhs);
basic_string(const basic_string& rhs,
    size_type pos, size_type n,
    const A& al = A());
basic_string(const E *s, size_type n, const A& al = A());
basic_string(const E *s, const A& al = A());
basic_string(size_type n, E c, const A& al = A());
basic_string(const_iterator first, const_iterator last,
    const A& al = A());    basic_string&
    operator=(const basic_string& rhs);
basic_string& operator=(const E *s);
basic_string& operator=(E c);
iterator begin();
const_iterator begin() const;
iterator end();
const_iterator end() const;
reverse_iterator rbegin();
const_reverse_iterator rbegin() const;
reverse_iterator rend();
const_reverse_iterator rend() const;
const_reference at(size_type pos) const;
reference at(size_type pos);
const_reference operator[](size_type pos) const;
reference operator[](size_type pos);
const E *c_str() const;
const E *data() const;
size_type length() const;
size_type size() const;
size_type max_size() const;
void resize(size_type n, E c = E());
size_type capacity() const;
```

```
void reserve(size_type n = 0);
bool empty() const;
basic_string& operator+=(const basic_string& rhs);
basic_string& operator+=(const E *s);
basic_string& operator+=(E c);
basic_string& append(const basic_string& str);
basic_string& append(const basic_string& str,
    size_type pos, size_type n);
basic_string& append(const E *s, size_type n);
basic_string& append(const E *s);
basic_string& append(size_type n, E c);
basic_string& append(const_iterator first,
    const_iterator last);
basic_string& assign(const basic_string& str);
basic_string& assign(const basic_string& str,
    size_type pos, size_type n);
basic_string& assign(const E *s, size_type n);
basic_string& assign(const E *s);
basic_string& assign(size_type n, E c);
basic_string& assign(const_iterator first,
    const_iterator last);
basic_string& insert(size_type p0,
    const basic_string& str);
basic_string& insert(size_type p0,
    const basic_string& str, size_type pos, size_type n);
basic_string& insert(size_type p0,
    const E *s, size_type n);
basic_string& insert(size_type p0, const E *s);
basic_string& insert(size_type p0, size_type n, E c);
iterator insert(iterator it, E c);
void insert(iterator it, size_type n, E c);
void insert(iterator it,
    const_iterator first, const_iterator last);
basic_string& erase(size_type p0 = 0, size_type n = npos);
iterator erase(iterator it);
iterator erase(iterator first, iterator last);
basic_string& replace(size_type p0, size_type n0,
    const basic_string& str);
basic_string& replace(size_type p0, size_type n0,
    const basic_string& str, size_type pos, size_type n);
basic_string& replace(size_type p0, size_type n0,
    const E *s, size_type n);
basic_string& replace(size_type p0, size_type n0,
    const E *s);
```

a
b
c

```
basic_string& replace(size_type p0, size_type n0,
    size_type n, E c);
basic_string& replace(iterator first0, iterator last0,
    const basic_string& str);
basic_string& replace(iterator first0, iterator last0,
    const E *s, size_type n);
basic_string& replace(iterator first0, iterator last0,
    const E *s);
basic_string& replace(iterator first0, iterator last0,
    size_type n, E c);
basic_string& replace(iterator first0, iterator last0,
    const_iterator first, const_iterator last);
size_type copy(E *s, size_type n,
    size_type pos = 0) const;
void swap(basic_string& str);
size_type find(const basic_string& str,
    size_type pos = 0) const;
size_type find(const E *s, size_type pos,
    size_type n) const;
size_type find(const E *s, size_type pos = 0) const;
size_type find(E c, size_type pos = 0) const;
size_type rfind(const basic_string& str,
    size_type pos = npos) const;
size_type rfind(const E *s, size_type pos,
    size_type n = npos) const;
size_type rfind(const E *s, size_type pos = npos) const;
size_type rfind(E c, size_type pos = npos) const;
size_type find_first_of(const basic_string& str,
    size_type pos = 0) const;
size_type find_first_of(const E *s, size_type pos,
    size_type n) const;
size_type find_first_of(const E *s,
    size_type pos = 0) const;
size_type find_first_of(E c, size_type pos = 0) const;
size_type find_last_of(const basic_string& str,
    size_type pos = npos) const;
size_type find_last_of(const E *s, size_type pos,
    size_type n = npos) con/t;
size_type find_last_of(const E *s,
    size_type pos = npos) const;
size_type find_last_of(E c, size_type pos = npos) const;
size_type find_first_not_of(const basic_string& str,
    size_type pos = 0) const;
size_type find_first_not_of(const E *s, size_type pos,
```

```
        size_type n) const;
size_type find_first_not_of(const E *s,
    size_type pos = 0) const;
size_type find_first_not_of(E c, size_type pos = 0) const;
size_type find_last_not_of(const basic_string& str,
    size_type pos = npos) const;
size_type find_last_not_of(const E *s, size_type pos,
     size_type n) const;
size_type find_last_not_of(const E *s,
    size_type pos = npos) const;
size_type find_last_not_of(E c,
    size_type pos = npos) const;
basic_string substr(size_type pos = 0,
    size_type n = npos) const;
int compare(const basic_string& str) const;
int compare(size_type p0, size_type n0,
    const basic_string& str);
int compare(size_type p0, size_type n0,
    const basic_string& str, size_type pos, size_type n);
int compare(const E *s) const;
int compare(size_type p0, size_type n0,
    const E *s) const;
int compare(size_type p0, size_type n0,
    const E *s, size_type pos) const;
A get_allocator() const;protected:
A allocator;
};
```

Class Members

Table B-11 lists and describes the class members of the `basic_string` template class.

Table B-11 Class Members of the basic_string Template Class

Member	Description
allocator_type	A synonym for the template's A parameter
append()	Appends a given sequence to the current sequence
assign()	Replaces the current sequence with the given sequence
at()	Returns a reference to the specified element

Continued

Table B-11 *Continued*

Member	Description
begin()	Returns a random-access iterator that points to the sequence's first element
c_str()	Returns the address of the C-style string represented by the sequence
capacity()	Returns the amount of allocated storage for a sequence
char_type	A synonym for the template's E parameter
compare()	Compares the sequence with another sequence
const_iterator	Object type for a constant random-access iterator
const_pointer	A synonym for A converted to const_pointer
const_reference	A synonym for A converted to const_reference
const_reverse_iterator	Object type for a constant reverse iterator
copy()	Copies a portion of the sequence
data()	Returns the address of the first element in the sequence
difference_type	A synonym for A converted to difference_type
empty()	Returns true if the sequence is empty
end()	Returns a random-access iterator that points to the next element beyond the end of the sequence
erase()	Erases a portion of the sequence
find()	Finds a subsequence
find_first_not_of()	Finds the first occurrence of an element that does not match the given element
find_first_of()	Finds the first occurrence of an element in the sequence
find_last_not_of()	Finds the last occurrence of an element that does not match the given element
find_last_of()	Finds the last occurrence of an element in a sequence
get_allocator()	Returns the allocator
insert()	Inserts a given sequence into the current sequence
Iterator	Object type for a random-access iterator
length()	Returns the length of the sequence
max_size()	Returns the maximum possible size of a sequence
npos	Largest possible value of size_type
pointer	A synonym for A converted to pointer
rbegin()	Returns a reverse iterator that points to the next element beyond the end of the sequence
reference	A synonym for A converted to reference
rend()	Returns a reverse iterator that points to the sequence's first element
replace()	Replaces a portion of a sequence
reserve()	Sets the amount of allocated storage for a sequence
resize()	Resizes the sequence

Member	Description
reverse_iterator	Object type for a reverse iterator
rfind()	Finds a subsequence using a reverse search
size()	Returns the length of the sequence
size_type	A synonym for A converted to size_type
substr()	Returns a subsequence from the specified position in the sequence
swap()	Swaps one sequence with another
traits_type	A synonym for the template's T parameter
value_type	A synonym for the template's E parameter

CROSS-REFERENCE

See also basic_filebuf, basic_fstream, basic_ifstream, basic_ios, basic_iostream, basic_istream, basic_istringstream, basic_ofstream, basic_ostream, basic_ostringstream, basic_streambuf, basic_stringbuf, and basic_stringstream.

basic_stringbuf

Template Class

The basic_stringbuf template class represents a stream buffer for string-type objects.

Class Declaration

```
template <class E,
    class T = char_traits<E>,
    class A = allocator<E> >
    class basic_stringbuf {
public:
    basic_stringbuf(ios_base::openmode mode =
        ios_base::in | ios_base::out);
    basic_stringbuf(basic_string<E, T, A>& x,
        ios_base::openmode mode = ios_base::in |
        ios_base::out);
    basic_string<E, T, A> str() const;
    void str(basic_string<E, T, A>& x);
protected:
    virtual pos_type seekoff(off_type off,
        ios_base::seekdir way,
        ios_base::openmode mode = ios_base::in |
```

```
        ios_base::out);
virtual pos_type seekpos(pos_type sp,
    ios_base::openmode mode = ios_base::in |
    ios_base::out);
virtual int_type underflow();
virtual int_type pbackfail(int_type c = T::eof());
virtual int_type overflow(int_type c = T::eof());
};
```

Class Members

Table B-12 lists and describes the class members of the basic_stringbuf template class.

Table B-12 Class Members of the basic_stringbuf Template Class

Member	Description
overflow()	Places an element into the output buffer
pbackfail()	Places an element back in the input buffer and sets the buffer's next pointer to the element
seekoff()	Changes the stream's current position
seekpos()	Changes the stream's current position to the given position
str()	Returns a basic_string object
underflow()	Returns an element from the input stream and advances the buffer's next pointer

CROSS-REFERENCE
See also basic_filebuf, basic_fstream, basic_ifstream, basic_ios, basic_iostream, basic_istream, basic_istringstream, basic_ofstream, basic_ostream, basic_ostringstream, basic_streambuf, basic_string, and basic_stringstream.

basic_stringstream

Template Class

The basic_stringstream template class controls the flow of data to and from a basic_stringbuf stream buffer.

Class Declaration

```
template <class E,
    class T = char_traits<E>,
    class A = allocator<E> >
    class basic_stringstream : public basic_iostream<E, T> {
public:
    explicit basic_stringstream(ios_base::openmode mode =
        ios_base::in | ios_base::out);
    explicit basic_stringstream(const
        basic_string<E, T, A>& x,
        ios_base::openmode mode = ios_base::in |
        ios_base::out);
    basic_stringbuf<E, T, A> *rdbuf() const;
    basic_string<E, T, A>& str();
    void str(const basic_string<E, T, A>& x);
    };
```

Class Members

Table B-13 lists and describes the class members of the `basic_stringstream` template class.

Table B-13 Class Members of the basic_stringstream Template Class

Member	Description
rdbuf()	Returns the address of the stream's buffer object
str()	Returns a `basic_string` object from the stream

CROSS-REFERENCE
See also basic_filebuf, basic_fstream, basic_ifstream, basic_ios, basic_iostream, basic_istream, basic_istringstream, basic_ofstream, basic_ostream, basic_ostringstream, basic_streambuf, basic_string, and basic_stringbuf.

binary

Manipulator

The `binary` manipulator, which is defined in the `ios` base I/O class, sets a stream's mode to binary.

CROSS-REFERENCE
See also boolalpha, dec, hex, oct, and text.

bitset

Template Class

The bitset template class allows the manipulation of a sequence of bits.

Class Declaration

```
template<size_t N>
    class bitset {
public:
    typedef bool element_type;
    class reference;
    bitset();
    bitset(unsigned long val);
    template<class E, class T, class A>
        explicit bitset(const string<E, T, A>& str,
            string<E, T, A>size_type pos = 0,
            string<E, T, A>size_type n =
            string<E, T, A>::npos);
    bitset<N>& operator&=(const bitset<N>& rhs);
    bitset<N>& operator|=(const bitset<N>& rhs);
    bitset<N>& operator^=(const bitset<N>& rhs);
    bitset<N>& operator<<=(const bitset<N>& pos);
    bitset<N>& operator>=(const bitset<N>& pos);
    bitset<N>& set();
    bitset<N>& set(size_t pos, bool val = true);
    bitset<N>& reset();
    bitset<N>& reset(size_t pos);
    bitset<N>& flip();
    bitset<N>& flip(size_t pos);
    reference operator[](size_t pos);
    bool operator[](size_t pos) const;
    reference at(size_t pos);
    bool at(size_t pos) const;
    unsigned long to_ulong() const;
    template<class E, class T, class A>
```

```
    string to_string() const;
size_t count() const;
size_t size() const;
bool operator==(const bitset<N>& rhs) const;
bool operator!=(const bitset<N>& rhs) const;
bool test(size_t pos) const;
bool any() const;
bool none() const;
bitset<N> operator<<(size_t pos) const;
bitset<N> operator>(size_t pos) const;
bitset<N> operator~();
static const size_t bitset_size = N;
};
```

Class Members

Table B-14 lists and describes the class members of the `bitset` template class.

Table B-14 Class Members of the bitset Template Class

Member	Description
any()	Returns true if any bit in the bitset is set
at()	Returns the value of the requested bit
bitset_size	Stores the size of the bitset
count()	Returns the number of set bits in the bitset
flip()	Flips the value of bits in a bitset
none()	Returns true if none of the bits in the bitset are set
reset()	Resets bits in the bitset
set()	Sets bits in the bitset
size()	Returns the size of the bitset
test()	Returns true if the requested bit is set
to_string()	Returns the bitset as a string
to_ulong()	Returns (as an unsigned long) the sum of all the bits in the bitset

CROSS-REFERENCE

See also deque, list, map, queue, set, stack, valarray, and vector.

bool

Keyword

The `bool` keyword is used to declare Boolean values, which are values that represent true and false outcomes. For example, the following line declares a variable of the `bool` type:

```
bool result;
```

CROSS-REFERENCE
See also int.

boolalpha

Manipulator

The `boolalpha` manipulator, which is defined in the `ios` base I/O class, sets a stream's mode so that Boolean values are represented by the words true and false, rather than by numeric values.

CROSS-REFERENCE
See also binary, dec, hex, oct, and text.

break

Keyword

The `break` keyword can be used to terminate `switch`, `do`, `for`, and `while` statements. For example, the following `switch` statement displays a message based on the value of the variable `var1`. In this case, the `case 3` portion of the statement executes, displaying the message "Three". The `break` keywords in each `case` clause assure that program execution breaks out of the `switch` statement before executing more than one `case` clause. Without the `break` keywords, every `case` clause after the `case 3` would also execute. The final `case` clause doesn't need a `break` because there are no other `case` clauses following it.

```
int var1 = 3;

switch (var1)
{
```

```
        case 1:
            cout << "One" << endl;
            break;
        case 2:
            cout << "Two" << endl;
            break;
        case 3:
            cout << "Three" << endl;
            break;
        case 4:
            cout << "Four" << endl;
            break;
        case 5:
            cout << "Five" << endl;
    }
```

CROSS-REFERENCE
See also continue, do, for, switch, and while.

bsearch()

Function

The bsearch() function performs a binary search of a previously sorted array. The function returns a pointer to the requested object if the object is found, or returns NULL if the object is not found.

Header File

```
#include <stdlib.h>
```

Declaration

```
void *bsearch(const void *key, const void *base,
    size_t num, size_t width,
    int (__cdecl *compare)(const void *elem1,
    const void *elem2));
```

- *base* — The address of the data to search.
- *compare* — The function that compares two elements.
- *elem1* — The address of the search key.

- *elem2* — The address of the element to compare with the key.
- *key* — The object for which to search.
- *num* — The number of elements in the data.
- *width* — The width of an element.

Example

The following program demonstrates how to use the bsearch() function, searching a string array (or, more precisely, an array of char pointers) for the word "eggs". The program's output looks like the following:

```
eggs found!
Press any key to continue
```

The program source code that produced the output follows:

```
#include "stdafx.h"
#include <iostream>
#include <stdlib.h>

using namespace std;

int compare(char **str1, char **str2)
{
    int result = strcmpi(*str1, *str2);
    return result;
}

int main(int argc, char* argv[])
{
    char* data[] = {"apple", "boat", "cattle", "diamond",
                    "eggs", "flag", "goat", "hat", "insect",
                    "junk"};
    char *key = "eggs";

    char** item = (char **)bsearch(&key, data, 5,
        sizeof(char *),
        (int(*)(const void*, const void*))compare);

    if (item != NULL)
        cout << *item << " found!" << endl;
    else
        cout << "No eggs here." << endl;

    return 0;
}
```

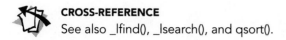

CROSS-REFERENCE
See also _lfind(), _lsearch(), and qsort().

_c_exit()

Function

The _c_exit() function performs the fast cleanup tasks associated with a process and then returns to the process. That is, unlike the _cexit() function, _c_exit() does not flush and close buffers and streams, or call the functions registered on behalf of the process by the atexit() and _onexit() functions.

Header File

```
#include <process.h>
```

Declaration

```
void _c_exit(void);
```

Example

The following program demonstrates how to use the _c_exit() function. When run, the program calls _c_exit() and displays a message when the exit processing is complete. The program's output looks like the following:

```
_c_exit() processing complete.
Press any key to continue
```

Here is the program source code that produced the output:

```
#include "stdafx.h"
#include <iostream>
#include <process.h>

using namespace std;

int main(int argc, char* argv[])
{
    _c_exit();
```

```
        cout << "_c_exit() processing complete." << endl;

        return 0;
}
```

CROSS-REFERENCE
See also cexit(), exit(), _onexit(), atexit(), and exit().

_cabs()

Function

The _cabs() function returns the absolute value of a complex number. If an overflow occurs during the calculation, the function returns HUGE_VAL. The errno global error variable will then be set to ERANGE.

Header File

```
#include <math.h>
```

Declaration

```
double _cabs(struct _complex z);
```

- z — The complex number for which to calculate the absolute value. This value must be stored in a _complex structure.

Example

The following program demonstrates how to use the _cabs() function. When run, the program calculates the absolute value of a complex number and displays the results. The program's output looks like the following:

```
result = 4.47214
Press any key to continue
```

Here is the program source code that produced the output:

```
#include "stdafx.h"
#include <math.h>
#include <iostream>

using namespace std;
```

```
int main(int argc, char* argv[])
{

    struct _complex val = {4.0, 2.0};

    double result = _cabs(val);
    cout << "result = " << result << endl;

    return 0;
}
```

CROSS-REFERENCE

See also _cabsl(), _finite(), _hypot(), _logb(), _scalb(), abs(), acos(), asin(), atan(), atan2(), atof(), cabs(), ceil(), cos(), cosh(), exp(), fabs(), floor(), fmod(), frexp(), labs(), ldexp(), log(), log10(), modf(), pow(), sin(), sinh(), sqrt(), tan(), and tanh().

_cabsl()

Function

The _cabsl() function returns, as a long double, the absolute value of a complex number. If an overflow occurs during the calculation, the function returns HUGE_VAL. The errno global error variable will then be set to ERANGE.

Header File

```
#include <math.h>
```

Declaration

```
long double _cabsl(struct _complex z);
```

- *z*—The complex number for which to calculate the absolute value. This value must be stored in a _complex structure.

Example

The following program demonstrates how to use the _cabsl() function. When run, the program calculates the absolute value of a complex number and displays the results. The program's output looks like the following:

```
result = 4.47214
Press any key to continue
```

Here is the program source code that produced the output:

```cpp
#include "stdafx.h"
#include <math.h>
#include <iostream>

using namespace std;

int main(int argc, char* argv[])
{

    struct _complex val = {4.0, 2.0};

    long double result = _cabsl(val);
    cout << "result = " << result << endl;

    return 0;
}
```

CROSS-REFERENCE
See also _cabs(), _finite(), _hypot(), _logb(), _scalb(), abs(), acos(), asin(), atan(), atan2(), atof(), cabs(), ceil(), cos(), cosh(), exp(), fabs(), floor(), fmod(), frexp(), labs(), ldexp(), log(), log10(), modf(), pow(), sin(), sinh(), sqrt(), tan(), and tanh().

_cexit()

Function

The _cexit() function performs the cleanup tasks associated with a process, including flushing and closing all buffers and streams and calling the functions registered on behalf of the process by the atexit() and _onexit() functions. However, _cexit() does not actually terminate the process.

Header File

```
#include <process.h>
```

Declaration

```
void _cexit(void);
```

Example

The following program demonstrates how to use the _cexit() function. When run, the program calls _cexit() and displays a message when the exit processing is complete. The program's output looks like the following:

```
_cexit processing complete
Press any key to continue
```

Here is the program source code that produced the output:

```cpp
#include "stdafx.h"
#include <iostream>
#include <process.h>

using namespace std;

int main(int argc, char* argv[])
{
    _cexit();
    printf("_cexit processing complete\n");

    return 0;
}
```

CROSS-REFERENCE
See also _c_exit(), _exit(), _onexit(), atexit(), and exit().

_cgets()

Function

The _cgets() function reads a string from the console and stores the string in the specified buffer. Before calling _cgets(), the first byte of the buffer must contain the maximum number of characters that can be read (including a null at the end of the string). The function will not allow the user to enter more than the maximum number of characters. After the function call, the second byte of the buffer will contain the number of characters read. In order to accommodate the maximum length and the returned length, the buffer must be two bytes larger than needed for the string and its terminating null character. The _cgets() function returns a pointer to the characters that were read. This line of text begins at the third byte in the buffer.

NOTE
Borland users should refer to the cgets() function later in this chapter.

Header File

```
#include <conio.h>
```

Declaration

```
char* _cgets(char* buf);
```

- *buf* — The buffer that will receive the string.

Example

The following program demonstrates how to use the _cgets() function. The program output looks something like the following:

```
Enter a line of text below:
This is a test!
The line you entered is:
This is a test!
The length of the entry is 15
Press any key to continue
```

Here is the program source code that produced the output:

```cpp
#include "stdafx.h"
#include <iostream>
#include <conio.h>

using namespace std;

int main(int argc, char* argv[])
{
    char buf[83];
    char* input;

    buf[0] = 80;
    cout << "Enter a line of text below: " << endl;
    input = _cgets(buf);
    cout << "The line you entered is:" << endl;
    cout << input << endl;
    cout << "The length of the entry is ";
    cout << (int)buf[1] << endl;
```

```
        return 0;
    }
```

CROSS-REFERENCE
See also cgets(), cputs(), and getch().

_chdir()

Function

The _chdir() function changes the current directory. If the function is successful, it returns 0. Otherwise, it returns –1.

NOTE
Borland users should refer to the chdir() function later in this chapter.

Header File

```
#include <direct.h>
```

Declaration

```
int _chdir(const char* dir)
```

- *dir*— The path of the new current directory.

Example

By changing the current directory to C:\Windows, the following program demonstrates how to use the _chdir() function. The program's output looks like the following:

```
Current directory is now c:\Windows
Press any key to continue
```

Here is the program source code that produced the output:

```
#include "stdafx.h"
#include <direct.h>
#include <iostream>

using namespace std;
```

```
int main(int argc, char* argv[])
{
    int result = _chdir("c:\\Windows");
    if (result != -1)
    {
        cout << "Current directory is now c:\\Windows";
        cout << endl;
    }
    else
        cout << "Directory doesn't exist" << endl;

    return 0;
}
```

CROSS-REFERENCE

See also chdir(), mkdir(), and rmdir().

_chdrive()

Function

The _chdrive() function changes the currently active working directory. The function returns 0 if the function call is successful and returns −1 if unsuccessful.

Header File

```
#include <direct.h>
```

Declaration

```
int _chdrive(int drive_num);
```

- *drive_num* — The number of the drive to which to change, where 1 is drive A, 2 is drive B, 3 is drive C, and so forth.

Example

The following program demonstrates how to use the _chdrive() function. When run, the program changes the current drive to drive C and displays a message. The program's output looks like the following:

```
Current drive successfully changed.
Press any key to continue
```

Here is the program source code that produced the output:

```cpp
#include "stdafx.h"
#include <iostream>
#include <direct.h>

using namespace std;

int main(int argc, char* argv[])
{
    int result = _chdrive(3);
    if (result == 0)
        cout << "Current drive successfully changed." << endl;
    else
        cout << "Current drive not changed." << endl;

    return 0;
}
```

CROSS-REFERENCE

See also chdir(), _getcwd(), _getdcwd(), _getdrive(), _mkdir(), _rmdir(), _searchenv(), _wchdir(), _wgetcwd(), _wgetdcwd(), _wmkdir(), _wrmdir(), and _wsearchenv().

_chmod()

Function

The _chmod() function changes the access permission of a specified file. The function returns 0 if the function call is successful and returns −1 if unsuccessful.

Header File

```cpp
#include <io.h>
#include <sys\stat.h>
```

Declaration

```cpp
int _chmod(const char* fileName, int pMode);
```

- *fileName* — The name of the file whose access permission is to be changed.
- *pMode* — The access to which to set the file. This can be S_IREAD and/or S_IWRITE, both of which are defined in the stat.h header.

Example

The following program demonstrates how to use the _chmod() function. When run, the program changes the access permission on the chmod.cpp file to allow both reading and writing. The program's output looks like the following:

```
File permission changed.
Press any key to continue
```

Here is the program source code that produced the output:

```cpp
#include "stdafx.h"
#include <iostream>
#include <io.h>
#include <sys\stat.h>

using namespace std;

int main(int argc, char* argv[])
{
    int result = _chmod("chmod.cpp", S_IWRITE);
    if (result == 0)
        cout << "File permission changed." << endl;
    else
        cout << "File not found." << endl;

    return 0;
}
```

CROSS-REFERENCE
See also _access(), _fullpath(), _get_osfhandle(), _makepath(), _mktemp(), _open_osfhandle(), _splitpath(), _stat(), _stati64(), _umask(), _unlink(), _waccess(), _wchmod(), _wfullpath(), _wmakepath(), _wmktemp(), _wremove(), _wrename(), _wsplitpath(), _wstat(), _wstati64(), _wunlink(), remove(), and rename().

_chsize()

Function

The _chsize() function changes the size of the given file. If the file is made smaller, the truncated portion is lost. If the file is made larger, the file is padded with null characters. The function returns 0 if successful or returns –1 if unsuccessful.

NOTE
Borland users should refer to the chsize() function later in this chapter.

Header File

```
#include <io.h>
```

Declaration

```
int _chsize(int handle, long size)
```

- *handle* — The handle of the file whose size is to be changed.
- *size* — The file's new size.

Example

By changing the size of the file MyFile.txt to 10 bytes, the following program demonstrates how to use the _chsize() function. The program's output looks like the following:

```
File size changed
Press any key to continue
```

Here is the program source code that produced the output:

```
#include "stdafx.h"
#include <iostream>
#include <sys/stat.h>
#include <io.h>
#include <fcntl.h>
```

```
using namespace std;

int main(int argc, char* argv[])
{
    int fileHandle =
        open( "MyFile.txt", O_RDWR, S_IREAD | S_IWRITE);

    if (fileHandle != -1)
    {
        int result = _chsize(fileHandle, 10);
        if (result != -1)
            cout << "File size changed" << endl;
        else
            cout << "File size not changed" << endl;
        close(fileHandle);
    }
    else
        cout << "Could not open file" << endl;

    return 0;
}
```

CROSS-REFERENCE
See also _open(), chsize(), and close().

_clear87()

Function

The _clear87() function obtains the value of the floating-point status word, and then clears the floating-point status word. Unlike the _clearfp() function, _clear87() is compatible only with Windows systems.

Header File

```
#include <float.h>
```

Declaration

```
unsigned int _clear87(void);
```

Example

The following program demonstrates how to use the `_clear87()` function. When run, the program displays the value of the floating-point status word and then performs an operation that causes an underflow error. After the underflow, the program displays the new value of the floating-point status word. The program's output looks like the following:

```
Floating-point status: 0
Floating-point status: 3
Press any key to continue
```

Here is the program source code that produced the output:

```cpp
#include "stdafx.h"
#include <iostream>
#include <float.h>

using namespace std;

int main(int argc, char* argv[])
{
    double arg1 = 1e-50;
    float arg2;

    unsigned int result = _clear87();
    cout << "Floating-point status: " << result << endl;
    arg2 = arg1;
    result = _clear87();
    cout << "Floating-point status: " << result << endl;

    return 0;
}
```

CROSS-REFERENCE
See also _clearfp().

_clearfp()

Function

The `_clearfp()` function obtains the value of the floating-point status word, and then clears the floating-point status word. Unlike the `_clear87()` function, `_clearfp()` is platform-independent.

Header File

```
#include <float.h>
```

Declaration

```
unsigned int _clearfp(void);
```

Example

The following program demonstrates how to use the _clearfp() function. When run, the program displays the value of the floating-point status word and then performs an operation that causes an underflow error. After the underflow, the program displays the new value of the floating-point status word. The program's output looks like the following:

```
Floating-point status: 0
Floating-point status: 3
Press any key to continue
```

Here is the program source code that produced the output:

```cpp
#include "stdafx.h"
#include <iostream>
#include <float.h>

using namespace std;

int main(int argc, char* argv[])
{
    double arg1 = 1e-50;
    float arg2;

    unsigned int result = _clearfp();
    cout << "Floating-point status: " << result << endl;
    arg2 = arg1;
    result = _clear87();
    cout << "Floating-point status: " << result << endl;\

    return 0;
}
```

CROSS-REFERENCE
See also _clear87().

_close()

Function

The _close() function closes a file, using the supplied file's handle. The function returns 0 if successful or returns –1 if unsuccessful.

Header File

```
#include <io.h>
```

Declaration

```
int _close(int fileHandle);
```

- *fileHandle* — The handle of the file to close.

Example

The following program demonstrates how to use the _close() function. When run, the program opens and closes a file, displaying appropriate messages as it goes. The program's output looks like the following:

```
File opened successfully.
File closed successfully.
Press any key to continue
```

Here is the program source code that produced the output:

```cpp
#include "stdafx.h"
#include <fcntl.h>
#include <io.h>
#include <iostream>

using namespace std;

int main(int argc, char* argv[])
{
    int fileHandle = _open("close.cpp", O_RDONLY);

    if (fileHandle != -1)
    {
        cout << "File opened successfully." << endl;
        int result = _close(fileHandle);
        if (result == 0)
```

```
                    cout << "File closed successfully." << endl;
                else
                    cout << "File close error." << endl;
            }
            else
                cout << "File open error." << endl;

            return 0;
        }
```

 CROSS-REFERENCE
See also _creat(), _dup(), _dup2(), _eof(), _lseek(), _lseeki64(), _open(), _open(),
_read(), _sopen(), _tell(), _telli64(), _umask(), _unlink(), _wcreat(), _wopen(),
_write(), and _wsopen().

_control87()

Function

The _control87() function retrieves or sets the floating-point control word on
Windows machines. The function returns the current value of the control word.

Header File

```
#include <float.h>
```

Declaration

```
unsigned int _control87(unsigned int newValue,
    unsigned int mask);
```

- *newValue* — The value to which to set the floating-point control
  word, which can be a value from Table C-1.
- *mask* — The control-word mask, which can be a value from Table C-2.

Table C-1 Values for the Floating-Point Control Word

Value	Description
DN_FLUSH	Use with the MCW_DN mask
DN_SAVE	Use with the MCW_DN mask

Value	Description
EM_DENORMAL	Use with the MCW_EM mask
EM_INEXACT	Use with the MCW_EM mask
EM_INVALID	Use with the MCW_EM mask
EM_OVERFLOW	Use with the MCW_EM mask
EM_UNDERFLOW	Use with the MCW_EM mask
EM_ZERODIVIDE	Use with the MCW_EM mask
IC_AFFINE	Use with the MCW_IC mask
IC_PROJECTIVE	Use with the MCW_IC mask
PC_24	Use with the MCW_PC mask
PC_53	Use with the MCW_PC mask
PC_64	Use with the MCW_PC mask
RC_CHOP	Use with the MCW_RC mask
RC_DOWN	Use with the MCW_RC mask
RC_NEAR	Use with the MCW_RC mask
RC_UP	Use with the MCW_RC mask

Table C-2 Masks for the Floating-Point Control Word

Value	Description
MCW_DN	Denormal control
MCW_EM	Interrupt exception
MCW_IC	Infinity control
MCW_PC	Precision control
MCW_RC	Rounding control

Example

The following program demonstrates how to call the _control87() function. When run, the program retrieves and displays the current floating-point control word value, and then resets the control word to 24 bits of precision. The program's output looks like the following:

```
Control word value: 589855
Press any key to continue
```

Here is the program source code that produced the output:

```
#include "stdafx.h"
#include <iostream>
```

```
#include <float.h>

using namespace std;

int main(int argc, char* argv[])
{
    unsigned int result = _control87(0,0);
    cout << "Control word value: " << result << endl;
    result = _control87(MCW_PC, PC_24);

    return 0;
}
```

CROSS-REFERENCE
See also _controlfp().

_controlfp()

Function

The _controlfp() function retrieves or sets the floating-point control word. The function returns the current value of the control word. Unlike the _control87() function, _controlfp() is platform-independent.

NOTE
There is no Borland version of this function.

Header File

```
#include <float.h>
```

Declaration

```
unsigned int _controlfp(unsigned int newValue,
    unsigned int mask);
```

- *newValue* — The value to which to set the floating-point control word, which can be a value from Table C-3.
- *mask* — The control-word mask, which can be a value from Table C-4.

Table C-3 Values for the Floating-Point Control Word

Value	Description
DN_FLUSH	Use with the MCW_DN mask
DN_SAVE	Use with the MCW_DN mask
EM_DENORMAL	Use with the MCW_EM mask
EM_INEXACT	Use with the MCW_EM mask
EM_INVALID	Use with the MCW_EM mask
EM_OVERFLOW	Use with the MCW_EM mask
EM_UNDERFLOW	Use with the MCW_EM mask
EM_ZERODIVIDE	Use with the MCW_EM mask
IC_AFFINE	Use with the MCW_IC mask
IC_PROJECTIVE	Use with the MCW_IC mask
PC_24	Use with the MCW_PC mask
PC_53	Use with the MCW_PC mask
PC_64	Use with the MCW_PC mask
RC_CHOP	Use with the MCW_RC mask
RC_DOWN	Use with the MCW_RC mask
RC_NEAR	Use with the MCW_RC mask
RC_UP	Use with the MCW_RC mask

Table C-4 Masks for the Floating-Point Control Word

Value	Description
MCW_DN	Denormal control
MCW_EM	Interrupt exception
MCW_IC	Infinity control
MCW_PC	Precision control
MCW_RC	Rounding control

Example

The following program demonstrates how to call the _controlfp() function. When run, the program retrieves and displays the current floating-point control word value, and then resets the control word to 24 bits of precision. The program's output looks like the following:

```
Control word value: 589855
Press any key to continue
```

Here is the program source code that produced the output:

```
#include "stdafx.h"
#include <iostream>
#include <float.h>

using namespace std;

int main(int argc, char* argv[])
{
    unsigned int result = _controlfp(0,0);
    cout << "Control word value: " << result << endl;
    result = _controlfp(MCW_PC, PC_24);

    return 0;
}
```

CROSS-REFERENCE
See also _control87().

_cprintf()

Function

The _cprintf() function displays formatted data output on the console. The function returns the number of displayed characters.

NOTE
Borland users should refer to the cprintf() function later in this chapter.

Header File

```
#include <conio.h>
```

Declaration

```
int _cprintf(const char *format [, argument] ... );
```

- *format*—The format string that specifies how the data should be converted. The format string takes the same form as the format string used with the printf() function. Table C-5 lists the available format specifiers.

- *argument*—Pointers to variables that match the type specifiers in *format*. The function will read data directly into the given variables.

Table C-5 Format Specifiers for _cprintf()

Specifier	Description
%c	Specifies a character
%C	Specifies a wide character (printf()) or single-byte character (wprintf())
%d	Specifies a signed decimal integer
%e	Specifies a signed double-precision floating-point value using scientific notation with a lowercase "e"
%E	Specifies a signed double-precision floating-point value using scientific notation with an uppercase "E"
%f	Specifies a signed double-precision floating-point value
%g	Specifies a signed double-precision floating-point value using either normal notation or scientific notation with a lowercase "e"
%G	Specifies a signed double-precision floating-point value using either normal notation or scientific notation with an uppercase "E"
%I	Specifies a signed decimal integer
%n	Specifies an integer pointer
%o	Specifies an unsigned octal integer
%p	Specifies a void pointer
%s	Specifies a string
%S	Specifies a wide-character string (printf()) or single-byte-character string (wprintf())
%u	Specifies an unsigned decimal integer
%x	Specifies an unsigned hexadecimal integer with lowercase letters
%X	Specifies an unsigned hexadecimal integer with uppercase letters

Example

The following program demonstrates how to use the _cprintf() function. When run, the program requests that the user type a string and an integer. The program then displays the given input. The program's output looks something like the following:

```
Enter a text string and an integer:
abcdefghij 25

The items are as follows:
     abcdefghij 25
```

```
Press any key to continue
```

Here is the program source code that produced the output:

```
int main(int argc, char* argv[])
{
    int val1;
    char str[81];

    cout << "Enter a text string and an integer:" << endl;
    _cscanf( "%s %i", str, &val1);
    cout << endl << endl;
    cout << "The items are as follows:" << endl;
    _cprintf("     %s %d\r\n\r\n", str, val1);

    return 0;
}
```

CROSS-REFERENCE
See also cprintf(), cscanf(), fprintf(), fscanf(), fwprintf(), fwscanf(), printf(), scanf(), sscanf(), swprintf(), swscanf(), vfprintf(), vfwprintf(), vprintf(), vsprintf(), vswprintf(), vwprintf(), wprintf(), and wscanf().

_cputs()

Function

The _cputs() function displays a string on the console. If the function is successful, it returns a 0; otherwise, it returns a nonzero value.

NOTE
Borland users should refer to the cputs() function later in this chapter.

Header File

```
#include <conio.h>
```

Declaration

```
int _cputs(const char* str);
```

■ *str*—The string to display.

Example

The following program demonstrates how to use the _cputs() function by displaying the following output:

```
This is a test.
Press any key to continue
```

Here is the program source code that produced the output:

```cpp
#include "stdafx.h"
#include <iostream>
#include <conio.h>

using namespace std;

int main(int argc, char* argv[])
{
    _cputs("This is a test.\r\n");

    return 0;
}
```

CROSS-REFERENCE
See also cgets(), cputs(), and getch().

_creat()

Function

The _creat() function creates a file, returning the file's handle if successful or returning –1 if unsuccessful.

Header File

```cpp
#include <io.h>
#include <sys\stat.h>
```

Declaration

```cpp
int _creat(const char* fileName, int mode);
```

- *fileName* — The name of the file to create.

■ *mode* — A value that specifies the file-creation mode. This value can be S_IREAD and/or S_IWRITE, which are defined in the stat.h header file.

Example

The following program demonstrates how to use the _creat() function. When run, the program creates a file in read-and-write mode and then closes a file, displaying appropriate messages as it goes. The program's output looks like the following:

```
File created successfully.
File closed successfully.
Press any key to continue
```

Here is the program source code that produced the output:

```cpp
#include "stdafx.h"
#include <fcntl.h>
#include <sys\stat.h>
#include <io.h>
#include <iostream>

using namespace std;

int main(int argc, char* argv[])
{
    int fileHandle = _creat("test.dat", S_IREAD | S_IWRITE);

    if (fileHandle != -1)
    {
        cout << "File created successfully." << endl;
        int result = _close(fileHandle);
        if (result == 0)
            cout << "File closed successfully." << endl;
        else
            cout << "File close error." << endl;
    }
    else
        cout << "File create error." << endl;

    return 0;
}
```

CROSS-REFERENCE
See also _close(), _dup(), _dup2(), _eof(), _lseek(), _lseeki64(), _open(), _open(), _read(), _sopen(), _tell(), _telli64(), _umask(), _unlink(), _wcreat(), _wopen(), _write(), and _wsopen().

_cscanf()

Function

The _cscanf() function reads input from the console. The function returns the number of data items that were accepted from the input.

NOTE
Borland users should refer to the cscanf() function later in this chapter.

Header File

```
#include <conio.h>
```

Declaration

```
int _cscanf(const char *format [, argument] ... );
```

- *format* — The format string that specifies how the input should be converted. The format string takes the same form as the format string used with the printf() function. Table C-6 lists the available format specifiers.

- *argument* — Pointers to variables that match the type specifiers in *format*. The function will read data directly into the given variables.

Table C-6 Format Specifiers for _cscanf()

Specifier	Description
%c	Specifies a character
%C	Specifies a wide character (printf()) or single-byte character (wprintf())
%d	Specifies a signed decimal integer
%e	Specifies a signed double-precision floating-point value using scientific notation with a lowercase "e"

Continued

Table C-6 *Continued*

Specifier	Description
%E	Specifies a signed double-precision floating-point value using scientific notation with an uppercase "E"
%f	Specifies a signed double-precision floating-point value
%g	Specifies a signed double-precision floating-point value using either normal notation or scientific notation with a lowercase "e"
%G	Specifies a signed double-precision floating-point value using either normal notation or scientific notation with an uppercase "E"
%I	Specifies a signed decimal integer
%n	Specifies an integer pointer
%o	Specifies an unsigned octal integer
%p	Specifies a void pointer
%s	Specifies a string
%S	Specifies a wide-character string (printf()) or single-byte-character string (wprintf())
%u	Specifies an unsigned decimal integer
%x	Specifies an unsigned hexadecimal integer with lowercase letters
%X	Specifies an unsigned hexadecimal integer with uppercase letters

Example

The following program demonstrates how to use the _cscanf() function. When run, the program requests that the user type a string and an integer. The program then displays the given input. The program's output looks something like the following:

```
Enter a text string and an integer:
abcdefghij 25

You entered 2 items.
The items are as follows:
    abcdefghij
    25

Press any key to continue
```

Here's the program source code that produced the output:

```
#include "stdafx.h"
#include <conio.h>
#include <iostream>
```

```
using namespace std;

int main(int argc, char* argv[])
{
    int val1;
    char str[81];

    cout << "Enter a text string and an integer:" << endl;
    int numItems = _cscanf( "%s %i", str, &val1);
    cout << endl << endl;
    cout << "You entered " << numItems << " items." << endl;
    cout << "The items are as follows:" << endl;
    cout << "     " << str << endl;
    cout << "     " << val1 << endl << endl;

    return 0;
}
```

CROSS-REFERENCE

See also cprintf(), cscanf(), fprintf(), fscanf(), fwprintf(), fwscanf(), printf(), scanf(), sscanf(), swprintf(), swscanf(), vfprintf(), vfwprintf(), vprintf(), vsprintf(), vswprintf(), vwprintf(), wprintf(), and wscanf().

cabs()

Function

The cabs() function returns the absolute value of a complex number. If an overflow occurs during the calculation, the function returns HUGE_VAL. The errno global error variable will then be set to ERANGE.

Header File

```
#include <math.h>
```

Declaration

```
double cabs(struct _complex z);
```

- z — The complex number for which to calculate the absolute value. This value must be stored in a _complex structure.

Example

The following program demonstrates how to use the cabs() function. When run, the program calculates the absolute value of a complex number and displays the results. The program's output looks like the following:

```
result = 4.47214
Press any key to continue
```

Here is the program source code that produced the output:

```
#include "stdafx.h"
#include <math.h>
#include <iostream>

using namespace std;

int main(int argc, char* argv[])
{

    struct _complex val = {4.0, 2.0};

    double result = cabs(val);
    cout << "result = " << result << endl;

    return 0;
}
```

CROSS-REFERENCE
See also _cabs(), _finite(), _hypot(), _logb(), _scalb(), abs(), acos(), asin(), atan(), atan2(), atof(), ceil(), cos(), cosh(), exp(), fabs(), floor(), fmod(), frexp(), labs(), ldexp(), log(), log10(), modf(), pow(), sin(), sinh(), sqrt(), tan(), and tanh().

calloc()

Function

The calloc() function allocates a block of memory and initializes the block to all zeroes. The function returns a pointer to the block of memory, or, in the case of failure, returns NULL.

Header File

```
#include <stdlib.h>
```

Declaration

```
void* calloc(size_t num, size_t size);
```

- *num* — The number of data elements to allocate.
- *size* — The size of each data element.

Example

The following program demonstrates how to use the `calloc()` function. When run, the program attempts to allocate enough memory to hold 256 integer values (1,024 bytes), displaying a message that indicates whether the memory allocation was successful. The program's output looks like the following:

```
Memory allocated successfully
Press any key to continue
```

Here is the program source code that produced the output:

```cpp
#include "stdafx.h"
#include <iostream>
#include <stdlib.h>

using namespace std;

int main(int argc, char* argv[])
{
    int* pMem = (int*)calloc(256, sizeof(int));

    if (pMem)
    {
        cout << "Memory allocated successfully" << endl;
        free(pMem);
    }
    else
        cout << "Memory allocation failed" << endl;

    return 0;
}
```

CROSS-REFERENCE

See also _alloca(), _expand(), _heapadd(), _heapchk(), _heapmin(), _heapset(), _heapwalk(), _msize(), free(), malloc(), and realloc().

case

Keyword

The case keyword is part of the switch statement, which enables program branching based on the value of an expression. For example, the following switch statement displays a message based on the value of the variable var1. In this case, the case 3 portion of the statement executes, displaying the message "Three".

```
int var1 = 3;

switch (var1)
{
    case 1:
        cout << "One" << endl;
        break;
    case 2:
        cout << "Two" << endl;
        break;
    case 3:
        cout << "Three" << endl;
        break;
    case 4:
        cout << "Four" << endl;
        break;
    case 5:
        cout << "Five" << endl;
}
```

CROSS-REFERENCE
See also break, for, and switch.

cassert

Standard C++ Library Header File

The cassert header file includes the C library header file assert.h into the source code. The assert.h header file defines the assert macro that's used for debugging source code.

CROSS-REFERENCE
See also assert().

Casting

Concept

Type *casting* enables a program to convert explicitly one type of data to another. For example, most memory allocation functions return a void pointer. If you want to use the allocated memory to store integers, you can cast the void pointer to an integer pointer, as follows:

```
int* buf = (int*)calloc(256, sizeof(int));
```

In the preceding case, the void pointer returned by the calloc() function is cast to an integer pointer. Notice the syntax used to perform the type cast. The required type is enclosed in parentheses and placed immediately in front of the function's name.

You can also use type casts in many other programming situations. Another example would be when you want to control the type of result you obtain from a mathematical operation. Here's an example:

```
int val1 = 20;
int val2 = 7;
int result1 = val1 / val2;
float result2 = val1 / val2;
float result3 = (float)val1 / (float)val2;
```

Here, the first division operation divides an integer by an integer and yields an integer result. The floating-point portion of the result is truncated. In the second operation, an integer is again divided by another integer, but the variable that receives the result is declared as float. Still, the floating-point portion of the result is truncated. In the third operation, the dividend and divisor are cast to floating-point values, which yield a floating-point result.

CROSS-REFERENCE
See also char, double, float, int, and long.

catch

Keyword

The catch keyword is used as part of a try statement, and enables the program to respond to exceptions that may be generated by the code in a try program block. The general syntax for a try statement follows.

```
try
{
    // Code that may cause an exception
    // goes here.
}
catch( ... )
{
    // Code that responds to the exception
    // goes here.
}
```

CROSS-REFERENCE
See also Exception Handling.

cctype

Standard C++ Library Header File

The cctype header file includes the C library header file ctype.h into the source code. The ctype.h header file declares constants, functions, data types, and macros for manipulating character data, as listed in the following:

Defined Constants

_ALPHA	_LEADBYTE
_BLANK	_LOWER
_CONTROL	_PUNCT
_DIGIT	_SPACE
_HEX	_UPPER

Defined Functions

isalnum()	iswctype()
isalpha()	iswdigit()
iscntrl()	iswgraph()
isdigit()	iswlower()
isgraph()	iswprint()
isleadbyte()	iswpunct()
islower()	iswspace()
isprint()	iswupper()
ispunct()	iswxdigit()
isspace()	isxdigit()
isupper()	tolower()
iswalnum()	toupper()
iswalpha()	towlower()
iswascii()	towupper()
iswcntrl()	

Defined Data Types

_ctype[]	wchar_t
_pctype	wctype_t
_pwctype	wint_t

Defined Macros

WEOF

CROSS-REFERENCE
See also ctype.h.

ceil()

Function

The ceil() function returns the smallest integer (returned as a double) that is greater than or equal to a given value.

Header File

```
#include <math.h>
```

Declaration

```
double ceil(double num);
```

- *num* — The value for which to return the ceiling.

Example

The following program demonstrates how to use the ceil() function, displaying the ceiling of two values. The program output looks like the following:

```
The ceiling of 34.7 is 35
The ceiling of -23.56 is -23
Press any key to continue
```

Here is the program source code that produced the output:

```
#include "stdafx.h"
#include <iostream>
#include <math.h>

using namespace std;

int main(int argc, char* argv[])
{
    double val1 = 34.7;
    double val2 = -23.56;
    double result = ceil(val1);
    cout << "The ceiling of " << val1;
    cout << " is " << result << endl;
    result = ceil(val2);
    cout << "The ceiling of " << val2;
    cout << " is " << result << endl;

    return 0;
}
```

CROSS-REFERENCE
See also ceilf(), ceill(), and floor().

ceilf()

Function

The `ceilf()` function returns the smallest integer (returned as a `float`) that is greater than or equal to a given value.

 NOTE
Borland does not support this function.

Header File

```
#include <math.h>
```

Declaration

```
float ceilf(float num);
```

- *num* — The value for which to return the ceiling.

Example

The following program demonstrates how to use the `ceilf()` function, displaying the ceiling of two values. The program output looks like the following:

```
The ceiling of 34.7 is 35
The ceiling of -23.56 is -23
Press any key to continue
```

Here is the program source code that produced the output:

```
#include "stdafx.h"
#include <iostream>
#include <math.h>

using namespace std;

int main(int argc, char* argv[])
{
    float val1 = (float)34.7;
    float val2 = (float)-23.56;
    float result = ceilf(val1);
    cout << "The ceiling of " << val1;
```

```
        cout << " is " << result << endl;
        result = ceilf(val2);
        cout << "The ceiling of " << val2;
        cout << " is " << result << endl;

        return 0;
}
```

CROSS-REFERENCE
See also ceil(), ceill(), and floor().

ceill()

Function

The ceill() function returns the smallest integer (returned as a long double) that is greater than or equal to a given value.

Header File

```
#include <math.h>
```

Declaration

```
long double ceill(long double num);
```

- *num* — The value for which to return the ceiling.

Example

The following program demonstrates how to use the ceill() function, displaying the ceiling of two values. The program output looks like the following:

```
The ceiling of 34.7 is 35
The ceiling of -23.56 is -23
Press any key to continue
```

Here is the program source code that produced the output:

```
#include "stdafx.h"
#include <iostream>
#include <math.h>
```

```
using namespace std;

int main(int argc, char* argv[])
{
    long double val1 = 34.7;
    long double val2 = -23.56;
    long double result = ceill(val1);
    cout << "The ceiling of " << val1;
    cout << " is " << result << endl;
    result = ceill(val2);
    cout << "The ceiling of " << val2;
    cout << " is " << result << endl;

    return 0;
}
```

CROSS-REFERENCE
See also ceil(), ceilf(), and floor().

cerr

Stream Object

cerr is a predefined stream object of the ostream class that places output into the standard error output stream.

Header File

```
#include <iostream.h>
```

Example

By displaying an error message if a value doesn't fit a required range, the following program demonstrates how to use the cerr stream object. The program's output looks something like the following:

```
Enter a value from 1 to 5:
7
ERROR: Value out of range!

Press any key to continue
```

Note that endl is a stream manipulator that places a carriage return and line feed onto the stream. Other manipulators include hex for obtaining hexadecimal output (cout << hex << 2000 << endl), oct for obtaining octal output (cout << oct << 2000 << endl), and dec for obtaining decimal output (cout << dec << 2000 << endl). Here is the program source code that produced the output:

```
#include "stdafx.h"
#include <iostream>

using namespace std;

int main(int argc, char* argv[])
{
    char s[81];

    cout << "Enter a value from 1 to 5:" << endl;
    cin > s;
    int val = atoi(s);
    if ((val < 1) || (val > 5))
        cerr << "ERROR: Value out of range!" << endl << endl;
    else
        cout << "Value OK" << endl << endl;

    return 0;
}
```

CROSS-REFERENCE

See also cin, clog, cout, istream, and ostream.

cerrno

Standard C++ Library Header File

The cerrno header file includes the C library header file errno.h into the source code. The errno.h file defines the many error codes needed to report system errors, and also defines the global variables. The error codes and variables defined in errno.h are listed as follows:

Defined Error Codes

E2BIG	ENAMETOOLONG
EACCES	ENFILE
EAGAIN	ENMFILE
EBADF	ENODEV
EBUSY	ENOENT
ECHILD	ENOEXEC
ECONTR	ENOFILE
ECURDIR	ENOMEM
EDEADLOCK	ENOPATH
EDOM	ENOSPC
EEXIST	ENOTBLK
EFAULT	ENOTDIR
EFBIG	ENOTSAM
EINTR	ENOTTY
EINVACC	ENXIO
EINVAL	EPERM
EINVDAT	EPIPE
EINVDRV	ERANGE
EINVENV	EROFS
EINVFMT	ESPIPE
EINVFNC	ESRCH
EINVMEM	ETXTBSY
EIO	EUCLEAN
EISDIR	EXDEV
EMFILE	EZERO
EMLINK	

b
c
d

Defined Global Variables

errno

CROSS-REFERENCE

See also errno.h.

cfloat

Standard C++ Library Header File

The cfloat header file includes the C library header file float.h into the source code. The float.h file defines constants and functions that are used with floating-point operations. The symbols defined in float.h include the following:

Defined Constants

_DBL_RADIX

_DBL_ROUNDS

_DN_FLUSH

_DN_FLUSH_OPERANDS_SAVE_RESULTS

_DN_SAVE

_DN_SAVE_OPERANDS_FLUSH_RESULTS

_EM_DENORMAL

_EM_INEXACT

_EM_INVALID

_EM_OVERFLOW

_EM_UNDERFLOW

_EM_ZERODIVIDE

_FPCLASS_ND

_FPCLASS_NINF

_FPCLASS_NN

_FPCLASS_NZ

_FPCLASS_PD

_FPCLASS_PINF

_FPCLASS_PN

_FPCLASS_PZ

_FPCLASS_QNAN

_FPCLASS_SNAN

_FPE_DENORMAL

_FPE_EXPLICITGEN

_FPE_INEXACT

_FPE_INVALID

_FPE_OVERFLOW

_FPE_SQRTNEG

_FPE_STACKOVERFLOW

_FPE_STACKUNDERFLOW

_FPE_UNDERFLOW

_FPE_UNEMULATED

_FPE_ZERODIVIDE

_IC_AFFINE

_IC_PROJECTIVE

_LDBL_RADIX

_LDBL_ROUNDS

_MCW_DN

_MCW_IC

_MCW_PC

_MCW_RC

_PC_24

_PC_53

_PC_64

_RC_CHOP

_RC_DOWN

_RC_NEAR

_RC_UP

_SW_DENORMAL

_SW_INEXACT

_SW_INVALID

_SW_OVERFLOW

_SW_SQRTNEG

_SW_STACKOVERFLOW

_SW_STACKUNDERFLOW

_SW_UNDERFLOW

_SW_UNEMULATED

_SW_ZERODIVIDE

CW_DEFAULT

DBL_DIG

DBL_EPSILON

DBL_MANT_DIG

DBL_MAX

DBL_MAX_10_EXP

DBL_MAX_EXP

DBL_MIN

DBL_MIN_10_EXP

DBL_MIN_EXP

DBL_RADIX

DBL_ROUNDS

EM_DENORMAL

EM_INEXACT

EM_INVALID

EM_OVERFLOW

EM_UNDERFLOW

EM_ZERODIVIDE

FLT_DIG

FLT_EPSILON

FLT_GUARD

FLT_MANT_DIG

FLT_MAX

FLT_MAX_10_EXP

FLT_MAX_EXP

FLT_MIN

FLT_MIN_10_EXP

FLT_MIN_EXP

FLT_NORMALIZE

FLT_RADIX

FLT_ROUNDS

FPE_DENORMAL

FPE_EXPLICITGEN

FPE_INEXACT

FPE_INVALID

FPE_OVERFLOW

FPE_SQRTNEG

FPE_STACKOVERFLOW

FPE_STACKUNDERFLOW

FPE_UNDERFLOW

FPE_UNEMULATED

FPE_ZERODIVIDE

IC_AFFINE

IC_PROJECTIVE

LDBL_DIG

LDBL_EPSILON

LDBL_MANT_DIG

LDBL_MAX

LDBL_MAX_10_EXP

LDBL_MAX_EXP

LDBL_MIN

LDBL_MIN_10_EXP

LDBL_MIN_EXP

LDBL_RADIX

LDBL_ROUNDS

MCW_EM

MCW_IC

MCW_PC

MCW_RC

PC_24

PC_53

PC_64

RC_CHOP

RC_DOWN

RC_NEAR

RC_UP

SW_DENORMAL

SW_INEXACT

b
c
d

SW_INVALID	SW_STACKUNDERFLOW
SW_OVERFLOW	SW_UNDERFLOW
SW_SQRTNEG	SW_UNEMULATED
SW_STACKOVERFLOW	SW_ZERODIVIDE

Defined Functions

_chgsign()	_fpreset()
_clearfp()	_isnan()
_control87()	_logb()
_controlfp()	_nextafter()
_copysign()	_scalb()
_finite()	fpreset()
_fpclass()	statusfp()

CROSS-REFERENCE
See also float.h.

cgets()

Function

The cgets() function reads a string from the console and stores the string in the specified buffer. Before calling cgets(), the first byte of the buffer must contain the maximum number of characters that can be read (including a null at the end of the string). The function will not allow the user to enter more than the maximum number of characters. After the function call, the second byte of the buffer will contain the number of characters read. In order to accommodate the maximum length and the returned length, the buffer must be two bytes larger than needed for the string and its terminating null character. The cgets() function returns a pointer to the characters that were read. This line of text begins at the third byte in the buffer.

Header File

```
#include <conio.h>
```

Declaration

```
char* cgets(char* buf);
```

- *buf*— The buffer that will receive the string.

Example

The following program demonstrates how to use the cgets() function. The program output looks something like the following:

```
Enter a line of text below:
This is a test!
The line you entered is:
This is a test!
The length of the entry is 15
Press any key to continue
```

Here is the program source code that produced the output:

```
#include "stdafx.h"
#include <iostream>
#include <conio.h>

using namespace std;

int main(int argc, char* argv[])
{
    char buf[83];
    char* input;

    buf[0] = 80;
    cout << "Enter a line of text below: " << endl;
    input = cgets(buf);
    cout << "The line you entered is:" << endl;
    cout << input << endl;
    cout << "The length of the entry is ";
    cout << (int)buf[1] << endl;

    return 0;
}
```

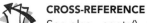

CROSS-REFERENCE
See also _cgets(), cputs(), and getch().

char

Keyword

The char keyword is used to declare character values, which are one-byte values typically used to represent alphanumeric characters and symbols. For example, the following line defines a variable of the char type:

```
char ch = 'a';
```

CROSS-REFERENCE
See also int.

char_traits

Template Class

The char_traits template class represents character traits for the specified type E.

Class Declaration

```
struct char_traits<E> {
    typedef E char_type;
    typedef T1 int_type;
    typedef T2 pos_type;
    typedef T3 off_type;
    typedef T4 state_type;
    static void assign(E& x, const E& y);
    static E *assign(E *x, size_t n, const E& y);
    static bool eq(const E& x, const E& y);
    static bool lt(const E& x, const E& y);
    static int compare(const E *x, const E *y, size_t n);
    static size_t length(const E *x);
    static E *copy(E *x, const E *y, size_t n);
    static E *move(E *x, const E *y, size_t n);
    static const E *find(const E *x, size_t n, const E& y);
    static E to_char_type(const int_type& ch);
    static int_type to_int_type(const E& c);
    static bool eq_int_type(const int_type& ch1,
        const int_type& ch2);
    static int_type eof();
    static int_type not_eof(const int_type& ch);
    };
```

Class Members

Table C-7 lists and describes the class members of the char_traits template class.

Table C-7 Class Members of the char_traits Template Class

Member	Description
assign()	Assigns a value to one or more elements in the sequence.
char_type	A synonym for the template's E parameter.
compare()	Compares the first sequence to the second for the length n, returning a negative value if a value in the first sequence is less than the same value in the second, 0 if the two sequences are equal, and a positive value if a value in the first sequence is larger than the same value in the second.
copy()	Copies elements starting at the element specified in the second argument to the array specified in the first argument. The third argument specifies the number of elements to copy. The function returns a pointer to the destination array.
eof()	Returns the end-of-file value.
eq()	Compares two elements for equality.
eq_int_type()	Compares the two given values and returns true if they are equal.
find()	Searches for the first occurrence of the element specified by the third argument in the sequence given in the first argument, returning a pointer to the matching element if found or else returning a null pointer. The second argument specifies the number of elements to search.
int_type	An integer type that can represent any value in the sequence controlled by the class.
length()	Returns the length of the sequence starting at the given element.
lt()	Determines if the first argument is less than the second.
move()	Copies elements starting at the element specified in the second argument to the array specified in the first argument. The third argument specifies the number of elements to copy. The function returns a pointer to the destination array. Note that move() allows the source and destination sequences to overlap.
not_eof()	Returns the given value, if that value equals eof(); otherwise, returns something other than eof().
off_type	A type that represents an offset in a stream.
pos_type	A type that represents a position in a stream.
state_type	A type that represents a conversion state.
to_char_type()	Converts the given value to the template's type E.
to_int_type()	Converts the given value to the template's int_type.

CROSS-REFERENCE
See also basic_ios and basic_string.

chdir()

Function

The `chdir()` function changes the current directory. If the function is successful, it returns 0. Otherwise, it returns −1.

Header File

```
#include <direct.h>
```

Declaration

```
int chdir(const char* dir)
```

- *dir*—The path of the new current directory.

Example

By changing the current directory to C:\Windows, the following program demonstrates how to use the `chdir()` function. The program's output looks like the following:

```
Current directory is now c:\Windows
Press any key to continue
```

Here is the program source code that produced the output:

```
#include "stdafx.h"
#include <direct.h>
#include <iostream>

using namespace std;

int main(int argc, char* argv[])
{
    int result = chdir("c:\\Windows");
    if (result != -1)
    {
        cout << "Current directory is now c:\\Windows";
        cout << endl;
```

```
    }
    else
        cout << "Directory doesn't exist" << endl;

    return 0;
}
```

CROSS-REFERENCE
See also mkdir() and rmdir().

chmod()

Function

The chmod() function changes the access permission of a specified file. The function returns 0 if the function call is successful and returns –1 if unsuccessful.

Header File

```
#include <io.h>
#include <sys\stat.h>
```

Declaration

```
int chmod(const char* fileName, int pMode);
```

- *fileName* — The name of the file whose access permission is to be changed.
- *pMode* — The access to which to set the file. This can be S_IREAD and/or S_IWRITE, both of which are defined in the stat.h header.

Example

The following program demonstrates how to use the chmod() function. When run, the program changes the access permission on the chmod.cpp file to allow both reading and writing. The program's output looks like the following:

```
File permission changed.
Press any key to continue
```

Here is the program source code that produced the output:

```
#include "stdafx.h"
#include <iostream>
#include <io.h>
#include <sys\stat.h>

using namespace std;

int main(int argc, char* argv[])
{
    int result = chmod("chmod.cpp", S_IWRITE);
    if (result == 0)
        cout << "File permission changed." << endl;
    else
        cout << "File not found." << endl;

    return 0;
}
```

CROSS-REFERENCE
See also _access(), _chmod(), _fullpath(), _get_osfhandle(), _makepath(), _mktemp(), _open_osfhandle(), _splitpath(), _stat(), _stati64(), _umask(), _unlink(), _waccess(), _wchmod(), _wfullpath(), _wmakepath(), _wmktemp(), _wremove(), _wrename(), _wsplitpath(), _wstat(), _wstati64(), _wunlink(), remove(), and rename().

chsize()

Function

The chsize() function changes the size of the given file. If the file is made smaller, the truncated portion is lost. If the file is made larger, the file is padded with null characters. The function returns 0 if successful or returns −1 if unsuccessful.

Header File

```
#include <io.h>
```

Declaration

```
int chsize(int handle, long size)
```

- *handle* — The handle of the file whose size is to be changed.
- *size* — The file's new size.

Example

By changing the size of the file MyFile.txt to 10 bytes, the following program demonstrates how to use the chsize() function. The program's output looks like the following:

```
File size changed
Press any key to continue
```

Here is the program source code that produced the output:

```cpp
#include "stdafx.h"
#include <iostream>
#include <sys/stat.h>
#include <io.h>
#include <fcntl.h>

using namespace std;

int main(int argc, char* argv[])
{
    int fileHandle =
        open( "MyFile.txt", O_RDWR, S_IREAD | S_IWRITE);

    if (fileHandle != -1)
    {
        int result = chsize(fileHandle, 10);
        if (result != -1)
            cout << "File size changed" << endl;
        else
            cout << "File size not changed" << endl;
        close(fileHandle);
    }
    else
        cout << "Could not open file" << endl;

    return 0;
}
```

CROSS-REFERENCE
See also _open() and close().

cin

Stream Object

cin is a predefined stream object of the istream class that can be used to obtain input from the standard input stream.

Header File

```
#include <iostream.h>
```

Example

By retrieving a string from the user and redisplaying the acquired string on the screen, the following program demonstrates how to use the cin stream object. The program's output looks something like the following:

```
Enter a string below:
abcdefghijklmnopqrstuvwxyz

You typed the following:
abcdefghijklmnopqrstuvwxyz

Press any key to continue
```

Note that endl is a stream manipulator that places a carriage return and line feed onto the stream. Other manipulators include hex for obtaining hexadecimal output (cout << hex << 2000 << endl), oct for obtaining octal output (cout << oct << 2000 << endl), and dec for obtaining decimal output (cout << dec << 2000 << endl). Here is the program source code that produced the output:

```
#include "stdafx.h"
#include <iostream>

using namespace std;

int main(int argc, char* argv[])
{
    char str[81];
```

```
cout << "Enter a string below:" << endl;
cin > str;
cout << endl << "You typed the following:" << endl;
cout << str << endl << endl;

    return 0;
}
```

CROSS-REFERENCE
See also cerr, cin, and cout.

ciso646

Standard C++ Library Header File

The ciso646 header file includes the C library header file iso646.h into the source code. The ios646.h header file defines alphabetic symbols for logical and bitwise operators. The symbols defined are listed as follows:

Defined Alphabetical Symbols

#define and	&&	#define not_eq	!=
#define and_eq	&=	#define or	||
#define bitand	&	#define or_eq	|=
#define bitor	|	#define xor	^
#define compl	~	#define xor_eq	^=
#define not	!		

class

Keyword

The class keyword is used to declare a class. For example, the following code example declares a simple class called MyClass, which provides member functions for setting and getting an internal value named, appropriately enough, value. The main() function in the main test program creates an object of the MyClass class and calls the object's two member functions, displaying the results on the screen. The program's output looks like the following:

```
Class value: 10
Class value: 20
Press any key to continue
```

Here is the program source code that produced the output:

```cpp
#include "stdafx.h"
#include <iostream>

using namespace std;

class MyClass
{
protected:
    int value;

public:
    MyClass() {};
    MyClass(int val) { value = val; };
    ~MyClass() {};

    void SetValue(int val) { value = val; };
    int GetValue() { return value; };
};

int main(int argc, char* argv[])
{
    MyClass myClass(10);

    int val = myClass.GetValue();
    cout << "Class value: " << val << endl;
    myClass.SetValue(20);
    val = myClass.GetValue();
    cout << "Class value: " << val << endl;

     return 0;
}
```

CROSS-REFERENCE
See also Creating a Class.

Class Hierarchies

Technique

A *class hierarchy* is a set of related classes that you can use in your programs to perform various types of programming tasks more easily. The hierarchy starts with very general classes from which more specific classes are derived. You can build your own class hierarchies using object-oriented programming techniques.

The Base Class

A simple class hierarchy starts with a base class that represents common attributes and functions in all the classes in the hierarchy. Suppose, for example, you want to build a class hierarchy to represent collectible items, such as books, videos, coins, or stamps. Your first task is to determine what these items have in common. For the sake of this example, let's say that you want each item to have an item number, a value, and a description. You can then define a class for the items; the header and implementation files for the class might look as follows:

Header File

```
class Item
{
protected:
    int itemNumber;
    int value;
    char* description;

public:
    Item();
    Item(int num, int val, char* desc);
    ~Item();

    int GetItemNum();
    void SetItemNum(int num);
    int GetValue();
    void SetValue(int num);
    char* GetDescription();
    void SetDescription(char* desc);
};
```

Implementation File

```
#include "stdafx.h"
#include "Item.h"
#include "string.h"
#include "malloc.h"

Item::Item()
{
    itemNumber = 0;
    value = 0;
    description = (char*)calloc(81, sizeof(char));
    strcpy(description, "");
}

Item::Item(int num, int val, char* desc)
{
    itemNumber = num;
    value = val;
    description = (char*)calloc(81, sizeof(char));
    strcpy(description, desc);
}

Item::~Item()
{
    free(description);
}

int Item::GetItemNum()
{
    return itemNumber;
}

void Item::SetItemNum(int num)
{
    itemNumber = num;
}

int Item::GetValue()
{
    return value;
}

void Item::SetValue(int val)
{
```

```
        value = val;
}

char* Item::GetDescription()
{
    return description;
}

void Item::SetDescription(char* desc)
{
    strcpy(description, desc);
}
```

As you can see, the Item class includes not only data members in which to store the item's number, value, and description, but also a complete set of member functions for getting and setting the data members. The following program shows how a program would create instances of an item using the two different constructors. The output for the program looks like the following:

```
Item Number: 1
Item Value: 10
Item Description: This is item #1

Item Number: 2
Item Value: 25
Item Description: This is item #2

Press any key to continue
```

Here is the program source code that produced the output:

```
#include "stdafx.h"
#include <iostream>
#include "Item.h"

using namespace std;

int main(int argc, char* argv[])
{
    Item item1(1, 10, "This is item #1");
    cout << "Item Number: " << item1.GetItemNum() << endl;
    cout << "Item Value: " << item1.GetValue() << endl;
    cout << "Item Description: " << item1.GetDescription();
    cout << endl << endl;

    Item item2;
```

```
    item2.SetItemNum(2);
    item2.SetValue(25);
    item2.SetDescription("This is item #2");
    cout << "Item Number: " << item2.GetItemNum() << endl;
    cout << "Item Value: " << item2.GetValue() << endl;
    cout << "Item Description: " << item2.GetDescription();
    cout << endl << endl;

    return 0;
}
```

A More Specific Class

Your next task is to derive new, more specific classes from your general Item class. For example, suppose you want to create classes for books, videos, coins, and stamps. What do these objects have in common, besides the fact that they are all some sort of item? Books and videos are similar in that they both have titles and lengths. Coins and stamps, however, are different from books and videos, sharing few attributes with those items. Coins and stamps share attributes, such as the year and the condition. This means that you can create a new class, derived from the Item class, for books and videos, but you'll also have to derive a second class from Item for items like coins and stamps.

You might call the new class for books and videos something like TitleItem, since both of these types of items have titles. The header and implementation files for the class then might look something like the following:

Header File
```
#include "Item.h"

class TitleItem: public Item
{
protected:
    char *title;
    int length;

public:
    TitleItem();
    TitleItem(int num, int val, char* desc,
        char* str, int len);
    ~TitleItem();

    char* GetTitle();
    void SetTitle(char* str);
    int GetLength();
```

```
    void SetLength(int len);
};
```

Implementation File

```
#include "stdafx.h"
#include "string.h"
#include "malloc.h"
#include "TitleItem.h"

TitleItem::TitleItem() : Item(0, 0, "")
{
    title = (char*)calloc(81, sizeof(char));
    strcpy(title, "");
    length = 0;
}

TitleItem::TitleItem(int num, int val, char* desc,
    char* str, int len) : Item(num, val, desc)
{
    title = (char*)calloc(81, sizeof(char));
    strcpy(title, str);
    length = len;
}

TitleItem::~TitleItem()
{
    free(title);
}

char* TitleItem::GetTitle()
{
    return title;
}

void TitleItem::SetTitle(char* str)
{
    strcpy(title, str);
}

int TitleItem::GetLength()
{
    return length;
}

void TitleItem::SetLength(int len)
```

```
{
    length = len;
}
```

This class is derived from the Item class, so it inherits Item's data members and member functions. In addition, the TitleItem class adds data members and member functions for managing an item's title and length. The following program puts the new TitleItem class to the test. The program's output looks like the following:

```
Item Number: 1
Item Value: 10
Item Description: This is item #1
Item Title: This is title 1
Item Length: 150

Item Number: 2
Item Value: 25
Item Description: This is item #2
Item Title: This is title 2
Item Length: 120


Press any key to continue
```

Here is the program source code that produced this output:

```
#include "stdafx.h"
#include <iostream>
#include "TitleItem.h"

using namespace std;

int main(int argc, char* argv[])
{
    TitleItem item1(1, 10, "This is item #1",
        "This is title 1", 150);
    cout << "Item Number: " << item1.GetItemNum() << endl;
    cout << "Item Value: " << item1.GetValue() << endl;
    cout << "Item Description: " << item1.GetDescription();
    cout << endl;
    cout << "Item Title: " << item1.GetTitle() << endl;
    cout << "Item Length: " << item1.GetLength();
    cout << endl << endl;

    TitleItem item2;
    item2.SetItemNum(2);
```

```
    item2.SetValue(25);
    item2.SetDescription("This is item #2");
    item2.SetTitle("This is title 2");
    item2.SetLength(120);
    cout << "Item Number: " << item2.GetItemNum() << endl;
    cout << "Item Value: " << item2.GetValue() << endl;
    cout << "Item Description: " << item2.GetDescription();
    cout << endl;
    cout << "Item Title: " << item2.GetTitle() << endl;
    cout << "Item Length: " << item2.GetLength();
    cout << endl << endl;

    return 0;
}
```

You would create your base class for stamp- and coin-type items similarly by deriving the class from Item. However, in this case, you would need to create year and condition data members, as well as create the member functions to manipulate them. You might call this new class YearItem, and its header and implementation files might look as follows:

Header File

```
#include "Item.h"

class YearItem: public Item
{
protected:
    int year;
    int condition;

public:
    YearItem();
    YearItem(int num, int val, char* desc, int yr, int cond);
    ~YearItem();

    int GetYear();
    void SetYear(int yr);
    int GetCondition();
    void SetCondition(int cond);
};
```

Implementation File

```
#include "stdafx.h"
#include "string.h"
#include "malloc.h"
```

```
#include "YearItem.h"

YearItem::YearItem() : Item(0, 0, "")
{
    year = 0;
    condition = 0;
}

YearItem::YearItem(int num, int val, char* desc,
    int yr, int cond) : Item(num, val, desc)
{
    year = yr;
    condition = cond;
}

YearItem::~YearItem()
{
}

int YearItem::GetYear()
{
    return year;
}

void YearItem::SetYear(int yr)
{
    year = yr;
}

int YearItem::GetCondition()
{
    return condition;
}

void YearItem::SetCondition(int cond)
{
    condition = cond;
}
```

This class, like TitleItem, is also derived from the Item class, so it inherits Item's data members and member functions. In addition, the YearItem class adds data members and member functions for managing an item's year and condition. The following program puts the new YearItem class to the test. The program's output looks like the following:

```
Item Number: 1
Item Value: 10
Item Description: This is item #1
Item Year: 1998
Item Condition: 2


Item Number: 2
Item Value: 25
Item Description: This is item #2
Item Year: 1951
Item Condition: 4


Press any key to continue
```

Here is the program source code that produced the output:

```cpp
#include "stdafx.h"
#include <iostream>
#include "YearItem.h"

using namespace std;

int main(int argc, char* argv[])
{
    YearItem item1(1, 10, "This is item #1", 1998, 2);
    cout << "Item Number: " << item1.GetItemNum() << endl;
    cout << "Item Value: " << item1.GetValue() << endl;
    cout << "Item Description: " << item1.GetDescription();
    cout << endl;
    cout << "Item Year: " << item1.GetYear() << endl;
    cout << "Item Condition: " << item1.GetCondition();
    cout << endl << endl;

    YearItem item2;
    item2.SetItemNum(2);
    item2.SetValue(25);
    item2.SetDescription("This is item #2");
    item2.SetYear(1951);
    item2.SetCondition(4);
    cout << "Item Number: " << item2.GetItemNum() << endl;
    cout << "Item Value: " << item2.GetValue() << endl;
    cout << "Item Description: " << item2.GetDescription();
    cout << endl;
    cout << "Item Year: " << item2.GetYear() << endl;
    cout << "Item Condition: " << item2.GetCondition();
```

```
        cout << endl << endl;

        return 0;
}
```

The Final Classes in the Hierarchy

Now, finally, you're ready to define the classes that will actually represent the book, video, coin, or stamp items. What additional information do you need to represent a book object that isn't already part of a TitleItem object? How about the book's author and publisher? So, you now derive a class from TitleItem that supplies these new data members and defines the functions needed to manage these data members. You would probably call this class Book, and its header and implementation files might look something like the following:

Header File

```
#include "TitleItem.h"

class Book: public TitleItem
{
protected:
    char* author;
    char* publisher;

public:
    Book();
    Book(int num, int val, char* desc,
        char* str, int len, char* auth,
        char* pub);
    ~Book();

    char* GetAuthor();
    void SetAuthor(char* auth);
    char* GetPublisher();
    void SetPublisher(char* pub);
};
```

Implementation File

```
#include "stdafx.h"
#include "string.h"
#include "malloc.h"
#include "Book.h"
```

```
Book::Book() : TitleItem(0, 0, "", "", 0)
{
    author = (char*)calloc(81, sizeof(char));
    publisher = (char*)calloc(81, sizeof(char));
    strcpy(author, "");
    strcpy(publisher, "");
}

Book::Book(int num, int val, char* desc,
    char* str, int len, char* auth, char* pub) :
    TitleItem(num, val, desc, str, len)
{
    author = (char*)calloc(81, sizeof(char));
    publisher = (char*)calloc(81, sizeof(char));
    strcpy(author, auth);
    strcpy(publisher, pub);
}

Book::~Book()
{
    free(author);
    free(publisher);
}

char* Book::GetAuthor()
{
    return author;
}

void Book::SetAuthor(char* auth)
{
    strcpy(author, auth);
}

char* Book::GetPublisher()
{
    return publisher;
}

void Book::SetPublisher(char* pub)
{
    strcpy(publisher, pub);
}
```

b
c
d

Now that you have your `Book` class, you can create book objects as demonstrated by the following program. The program's output looks like the following:

```
Book Number: 1
Book Value: $10
Book Description: This is a cool cookbook
Book Title: The Big Book of Pancakes
Book Length: 250 pages
Book Author: Gary Griddle
Book Publisher: Chef Press

Book Number: 2
Book Value: $25
Book Description: This is one creepy story
Book Title: The Worm That Ate Mama
Book Length: 194 pages
Book Author: Willy Long
Book Publisher: Shriek Books

Press any key to continue
```

Here is the program source code that produced the output:

```
#include "stdafx.h"
#include <iostream>
#include "Book.h"

using namespace std;

int main(int argc, char* argv[])
{
    Book book1(1, 10, "This is a cool cookbook",
        "The Big Book of Pancakes", 250,
        "Gary Griddle", "Chef Press");
    cout << "Book Number: " << book1.GetItemNum() << endl;
    cout << "Book Value: " << "$" << book1.GetValue() << endl;
    cout << "Book Description: " << book1.GetDescription();
    cout << endl;
    cout << "Book Title: " << book1.GetTitle() << endl;
    cout << "Book Length: " << book1.GetLength() << " pages";
    cout << endl;
    cout << "Book Author: " << book1.GetAuthor() << endl;
    cout << "Book Publisher: " << book1.GetPublisher();
    cout << endl << endl;

    Book book2;
```

```
book2.SetItemNum(2);
book2.SetValue(25);
book2.SetDescription("This is one creepy story");
book2.SetTitle("The Worm That Ate Mama");
book2.SetLength(194);
book2.SetAuthor("Willy Long");
book2.SetPublisher("Shriek Books");
cout << "Book Number: " << book2.GetItemNum() << endl;
cout << "Book Value: " << "$" << book2.GetValue() << endl;
cout << "Book Description: " << book2.GetDescription();
cout << endl;
cout << "Book Title: " << book2.GetTitle() << endl;
cout << "Book Length: " << book2.GetLength() << " pages";
cout << endl;
cout << "Book Author: " << book2.GetAuthor() << endl;
cout << "Book Publisher: " << book2.GetPublisher();
cout << endl << endl;

    return 0;
}
```

You should now have a good idea of how to build a class hierarchy. To get some practice, complete this hierarchy by creating the classes for videos (derived from `TitleItem` and adding `director` and `studio` data members), coins (derived from `YearItem` and adding a `mint` data member), and stamps (also derived from `YearItem`, but adding a `country` data member).

This process may seem like a lot of work, but keep in mind that the next time you want to create a new class for a collectible item, you can derive that class from one of the classes you've already created, and save a great deal of work. This is how object-oriented programming enhances the reusability of your code.

CROSS-REFERENCE
See also Creating a Class, Encapsulation, Header Files, Implementation File, Polymorphism, and Virtual Functions.

clear87()

Function

The `clear87()` function obtains the value of the floating-point status word, and then clears the floating-point status word. Unlike the `_clearfp()` function, `clear87()` is compatible only with Windows systems.

> **NOTE**
> Borland users should refer to the _clear87() function.

Header File

```
#include <float.h>
```

Declaration

```
unsigned int clear87(void);
```

Example

The following program demonstrates how to use the clear87() function. When run, the program displays the value of the floating-point status word and then performs an operation that causes an underflow error. After the underflow, the program displays the new value of the floating-point status word. The program's output looks like the following:

```
Floating-point status: 0
Floating-point status: 3
Press any key to continue
```

Here is the program source code that produced the output:

```
#include "stdafx.h"
#include <iostream>
#include <float.h>

using namespace std;

int main(int argc, char* argv[])
{
    double arg1 = 1e-50;
    float arg2;

    unsigned int result = clear87();
    cout << "Floating-point status: " << result << endl;
    arg2 = arg1;
    result = clear87();
    cout << "Floating-point status: " << result << endl;

    return 0;
}
```

CROSS-REFERENCE
See also _clear87() and _clearfp().

clearerr()

Function

The `clearerr()` function clears a stream's error indicator and resets the stream's file pointer.

Header File

```
#include <stdio.h>
```

Declaration

```
void clearerr(FILE* stream)
```

- *stream* — A pointer to the stream's `FILE` structure.

Example

The following program demonstrates how to call the `clearerr()` function to clear the indicator for the `stdout` stream. The program's output looks like the following:

```
Error indicator cleared.
Press any key to continue
```

Here is the program source code that produced the output:

```
#include "stdafx.h"
#include <iostream>
#include <stdio.h>

using namespace std;


int main(int argc, char* argv[])
{
    clearerr(stdout);
```

```
        cout << "Error indicator cleared." << endl;

        return 0;
    }
```

 **CROSS-REFERENCE**
See also ferror().

climits

Standard C++ Library Header File

The climits header file includes the C library header file limits.h into the source code. The limits.h header file defines constants for the limits of the various data types. The definition of some of the constants, which are listed below, is implementation-dependent.

Defined Constants

_I128_MAX	_POSIX_PIPE_BUF
_I128_MIN	_POSIX_SSIZE_MAX
_I16_MAX	_POSIX_STREAM_MAX
_I16_MIN	_UI128_MAX
_I32_MAX	_UI16_MAX
_I32_MIN	_UI32_MAX
_I64_MAX	_UI64_MAX
_I64_MIN	_UI8_MAX
_I8_MAX	ARG_MAX
_I8_MIN	CHAR_BIT
_POSIX_ARG_MAX	CHAR_MAX
_POSIX_CHILD_MAX	CHAR_MIN
_POSIX_LINK_MAX	INT_MAX
_POSIX_MAX_CANON	INT_MIN
_POSIX_MAX_INPUT	LINK_MAX
_POSIX_NAME_MAX	LONG_MAX
_POSIX_NGROUPS_MAX	LONG_MIN
_POSIX_OPEN_MAX	MAX_CANON
_POSIX_PATH_MAX	MAX_INPUT

MB_LEN_MAX	SHRT_MAX
NAME_MAX	SHRT_MIN
NGROUPS_MAX	SSIZE_MAX
OPEN_MAX	STREAM_MAX
PATH_MAX	TZNAME_MAX
PIPE_BUF	UCHAR_MAX
POSIX_TZNAME_MAX	UINT_MAX
SCHAR_MAX	ULONG_MAX
SCHAR_MIN	USHRT_MAX

CROSS-REFERENCE
See also limits.h.

clocale

Standard C++ Library Header File

The clocale header file includes the C library header file locale.h into the source code. The locale.h header file defines constants, function, and data structures needed by the localization routines. The symbols defined include those in the following list.

Defined Constants

LC_ALL	LC_MIN
LC_COLLATE	LC_MONETARY
LC_CTYPE	LC_NUMERIC
LC_MAX	LC_TIME

Defined Functions

_wsetlocale()	setlocale()
localeconv()	

Defined Structures

```
struct lconv {
        char *decimal_point;
        char *thousands_sep;
```

```
            char *grouping;
            char *int_curr_symbol;
            char *currency_symbol;
            char *mon_decimal_point;
            char *mon_thousands_sep;
            char *mon_grouping;
            char *positive_sign;
            char *negative_sign;
            char int_frac_digits;
            char frac_digits;
            char p_cs_precedes;
            char p_sep_by_space;
            char n_cs_precedes;
            char n_sep_by_space;
            char p_sign_posn;
            char n_sign_posn;
            };
```

CROSS-REFERENCE
See also locale.h.

clock()

Function

The clock() function returns the number of timer ticks that have elapsed. If the function cannot return the number of timer ticks, it returns –1.

Header File

```
#include <time.h>
```

Declaration

```
clock_t clock(void);
```

Example

The following program demonstrates how to call the clock() function to get the number of elapsed timer ticks. The program displays the number of ticks and seconds that it takes for a loop to complete. The output looks something like the following:

```
Starting a loop...
Loop finished.
Number of ticks: 1920
Time in seconds: 1.92
Press any key to continue
```

Here is the program source code that produced the output:

```cpp
#include "stdafx.h"
#include <iostream>
#include <time.h>

using namespace std;

int main(int argc, char* argv[])
{
    cout << "Starting a loop..." << endl;
    clock_t begin = clock();

    for (int x=0; x<99999999L; ++x)
        ;

    clock_t end = clock();
    cout << "Loop finished." << endl;

    double elapsed = double(end - begin);
    cout << "Number of ticks: " << elapsed << endl;
    double secs = elapsed / CLOCKS_PER_SEC;
    cout << "Time in seconds: " << secs << endl;

    return 0;
}
```

CROSS-REFERENCE
See also difftime() and time().

clog

Stream Object

clog is a predefined stream object of the ostream class that places buffered output into the standard error output stream.

Header File

```
#include <iostream.h>
```

Example

By displaying an error message if a value doesn't fit a required range, the following program demonstrates how to use the clog stream object. The program's output looks something like the following:

```
Enter a value from 1 to 5:
7
ERROR: Value out of range!

Press any key to continue
```

Note that endl is a stream manipulator that places a carriage return and line feed onto the stream. Other manipulators include hex for obtaining hexadecimal output (cout << hex << 2000 << endl), oct for obtaining octal output (cout << oct << 2000 << endl), and dec for obtaining decimal output (cout << dec << 2000 << endl). Here is the program source code that produced the output:

```
#include "stdafx.h"
#include <iostream>

using namespace std;

int main(int argc, char* argv[])
{
    char s[81];

    cout << "Enter a value from 1 to 5:" << endl;
    cin > s;
    int val = atoi(s);
    if ((val < 1) || (val > 5))
        cerr << "ERROR: Value out of range!" << endl << endl;
    else
        cout << "Value OK" << endl << endl;

    return 0;
}
```

CROSS-REFERENCE
See also cerr, cin, cout, istream, and ostream.

close()

Function

The close() function closes a file given the file's handle. The function returns 0 if successful or returns −1 if unsuccessful.

Header File

```
#include <io.h>
```

Declaration

```
int close(int fileHandle);
```

- *fileHandle* — The handle of the file to close.

Example

The following program demonstrates how to use the close() function. When run, the program opens and closes a file, displaying appropriate messages as it goes. The program's output looks like the following:

```
File opened successfully.
File closed successfully.
Press any key to continue
```

Here is the program source code that produced the output:

```cpp
#include "stdafx.h"
#include <fcntl.h>
#include <io.h>
#include <iostream>

using namespace std;

int main(int argc, char* argv[])
{
    int fileHandle = open("close.cpp", O_RDONLY);

    if (fileHandle != -1)
    {
        cout << "File opened successfully." << endl;
        int result = close(fileHandle);
        if (result == 0)
```

```
                    cout << "File closed successfully." << endl;
               else
                    cout << "File close error." << endl;
          }
          else
               cout << "File open error." << endl;

          return 0;
     }
```

CROSS-REFERENCE
See also _open() and creat().

cmath

Standard C++ Library Header File

The cmath header file includes the C library header file math.h into the source code. The math.h header file defines a set of constants and functions used in mathematical operations. The symbols defined in math.h include the following:

Defined Constants

_DOMAIN	_UNDERFLOW
_OVERFLOW	EDOM
_PLOSS	ERANGE
_SING	HUGE_VAL
_TLOSS	

Defined Functions

_hypot()	_yn()
_hypotf()	abs()
_j0()	acos()
_j1()	acosf()
_jn()	acosl()
_matherr()	asin()
_y0()	asinf()
_y1()	asinl()

atan()

atan2()

atan2f()

atan2l()

atanf()

atanl()

cabs()

ceil()

ceilf()

ceill()

cos()

cosf()

cosh()

coshf()

coshl()

cosl()

exp()

expf()

expl()

fabs()

fabsf()

fabsl()

floor()

floorf()

floorl()

fmod()

fmodf()

fmodl()

frexp()

frexpf()

frexpl()

hypot()

hypotf()

j0()

j1()

jn()

labs()

ldexp()

ldexpf()

ldexpl()

log()

log10()

log10f()

log10l()

logf()

logl()

matherr()

modf()

modff()

modfl()

pow()

powf()

powl()

sin()

sinf()

sinh()

sinhf()

sinhl()

sinl()

sqrt()

sqrtf()

sqrtl()

tan()

tanf()

tanh()

tanhf()

tanhl()

tanl()

y0()

y1()

yn()

b

c

d

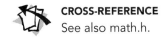
CROSS-REFERENCE
See also math.h.

complex

Template Class

The complex template class represents the real and imaginary parts of a complex number.

Class Declaration

```
template<class T>
    class complex {
public:
    typedef T value_type;
    T real() const;
    T imag() const;
    complex(const T& re = 0, const T& im = 0);
    complex(const complex& x);
    complex& operator=(const complex& rhs);
    complex& operator+=(const complex& rhs);
    complex& operator-=(const complex& rhs);
    complex& operator*=(const complex& rhs);
    complex& operator/=(const complex& rhs);
    complex& operator=(const T& rhs);
    complex& operator=(const T& rhs);
    complex& operator+=(const T& rhs);
    complex& operator-=(const T& rhs);
    complex& operator*=(const T& rhs);
    complex& operator/=(const T& rhs);
    friend complex<T>
        operator+(const complex<T>& lhs, const T& rhs);
    friend complex<T>
        operator+(const T& lhs, const complex<T>& rhs);
    friend complex<T>
        operator-(const complex<T>& lhs, const T& rhs);
    friend complex<T>
        operator-(const T& lhs, const complex<T>& rhs);
    friend complex<T>
        operator*(const complex<T>& lhs, const T& rhs);
    friend complex<T>
```

```
      operator*(const T& lhs, const complex<T>& rhs);
friend complex<T>
      operator/(const complex<T>& lhs, const T& rhs);
friend complex<T>
      operator/(const T& lhs, const complex<T>& rhs);
friend bool operator==(const complex<T>& lhs,
      const T& rhs);
friend bool operator==(const T& lhs,
      const complex<T>& rhs);
friend bool operator!=(const complex<T>& lhs,
      const T& rhs);
friend bool operator!=(const T& lhs,
      const complex<T>& rhs);
};
```

Class Members

Table C-8 lists and describes the class members of the `complex` template class.

Table C-8 Class Members of the complex Template Class

Member	Description
value_type	A synonym for the template's type T
real()	Returns the real portion of the complex number
imag()	Returns the imaginary portion of the complex number

const

Keyword

The `const` keyword specifies that a data object cannot be modified. For example, in the following lines, the program can assign the value of x to the variable y, but it cannot change the value of x because x has been declared as `const`.

```
const int x = 10;

int y = x; // This is OK.
x = 20; // This causes compiler error.
```

CROSS-REFERENCE
See also auto, extern, register, and static.

Constructor

Technique

A *constructor* is a special member function in a class that initializes a new instance (also called an object) of the class. The constructor is called automatically when a program tries to instantiate an object from the class. For example, take a look at the following class, as found in the MyClass.h header file and the MyClass.cpp implementation file:

Header File

```
class MyClass
{
protected:
    int value;

public:
    MyClass();
    MyClass(int val);
    ~MyClass();

    void SetValue(int val);
    int GetValue();
};

#include "stdafx.h"
#include "MyClass.h"

MyClass::MyClass()
{
    value = 0;
}
```

Implementation File

```
MyClass::MyClass(int val)
{
    value = val;
}

MyClass::~MyClass()
{
}

int MyClass::GetValue()
{
```

```
        return value;
}

void MyClass::SetValue(int val)
{
    value = val;
}
```

The class's constructor is easy to spot because it has the same name as the class. In fact, this class has two constructors, enabling a program to create an instance of the class in two ways. The first constructor requires no arguments, setting the `value` data member to 0 automatically. Using this constructor, you would create an object of the class as follows:

```
MyClass myClass1;
```

The second constructor enables the program to create an object of the class and, at the same time, initialize the object to any valid value. Using this constructor, you would create an instance of the class as follows:

```
MyClass myClass2(25);
```

The following program demonstrates how to construct objects of the `MyClass` class in a program, and also how to call the object's member functions to manipulate the `value` data member. The program's output looks like the following:

```
Value = 0
Value = 25
Value = 55
Value = 99


Press any key to continue
```

Here is the program source code that produced the output:

```
#include "stdafx.h"
#include <iostream>
#include "MyClass.h"

using namespace std;

int main(int argc, char* argv[])
{
    MyClass myClass1;
    MyClass myClass2(25);

    int val = myClass1.GetValue();
```

```
cout << "Value = " << val << endl;
val = myClass2.GetValue();
cout << "Value = " << val << endl;

myClass1.SetValue(55);
myClass2.SetValue(99);

val = myClass1.GetValue();
cout << "Value = " << val << endl;
val = myClass2.GetValue();
cout << "Value = " << val << endl;

return 0;
}
```

CROSS-REFERENCE
See also Creating a Class and Destructor.

continue

Keyword

The `continue` keyword causes a `for`, `do`, or `while` loop to jump back to the beginning of the loop without executing statements in the body of the loop that follow the `continue` keyword. For example, the following program uses a `for` loop to count from 1 to 10, displaying a message for each count except 6. When `count` equals 6, the `continue` statement causes the loop to skip the `count` statement in the body of the loop. The program's output looks like the following:

```
count = 1
count = 2
count = 3
count = 4
count = 5
count = 7
count = 8
count = 9
count = 10
Press any key to continue
```

Here is the program source code that produced the output:

```
#include "stdafx.h"
```

```
#include <iostream>

using namespace std;

int main(int argc, char* argv[])
{
    int count;

    for (count=1; count<11; ++count)
    {
        if (count == 6)
            continue;
        cout << "count = " << count << endl;
    }

    return 0;
}
```

CROSS-REFERENCE
See also break, do, for, and while.

control87()

Function

The control87() function retrieves or sets the floating-point control word on Windows machines. The function returns the current value of the control word.

NOTE
Borland users should refer to the _control87() function.

Header File

```
#include <float.h>
```

Declaration

```
unsigned int control87(unsigned int newValue,
    unsigned int mask);
```

- *newValue* — The value to which to set the floating-point control word, which can be a value from Table C-9.
- *mask* — The control-word mask, which can be a mask value from Table C-10.

Table C-9 Values for the Floating-Point Control Word

Value	Description
DN_FLUSH	Use with the MCW_DN mask
DN_SAVE	Use with the MCW_DN mask
EM_DENORMAL	Use with the MCW_EM mask
EM_INEXACT	Use with the MCW_EM mask
EM_INVALID	Use with the MCW_EM mask
EM_OVERFLOW	Use with the MCW_EM mask
EM_UNDERFLOW	Use with the MCW_EM mask
EM_ZERODIVIDE	Use with the MCW_EM mask
IC_AFFINE	Use with the MCW_IC mask
IC_PROJECTIVE	Use with the MCW_IC mask
PC_24	Use with the MCW_PC mask
PC_53	Use with the MCW_PC mask
PC_64	Use with the MCW_PC mask
RC_CHOP	Use with the MCW_RC mask
RC_DOWN	Use with the MCW_RC mask
RC_NEAR	Use with the MCW_RC mask
RC_UP	Use with the MCW_RC mask

Table C-10 Masks for the Floating-Point Control Word

Value	Description
MCW_DN	Denormal control
MCW_EM	Interrupt exception
MCW_IC	Infinity control
MCW_PC	Precision control
MCW_RC	Rounding control

Example

The following program demonstrates how to call the `control87()` function. When run, the program retrieves and displays the current floating-point control word value, and then resets the control word to 24 bits of precision. The program's output looks like the following:

```
Control word value: 589855
Press any key to continue
```

Here is the program source code that produced the output:

```cpp
#include "stdafx.h"
#include <iostream>
#include <float.h>

using namespace std;

int main(int argc, char* argv[])
{
    unsigned int result = control87(0,0);
    cout << "Control word value: " << result << endl;
    control87(MCW_PC, PC_24);

    return 0;
}
```

CROSS-REFERENCE
See also _control87() and _controlfp().

cos()

Function

The `cos()` function returns the cosine of its argument.

Header File

```cpp
#include <math.h>
```

Declaration

```
double cos(double num);
```

- *num* — The value for which to return the cosine.

Example

The following program demonstrates how to use the cos() function. The program's output looks like the following:

```
The cosine of 1.387 is 0.182763
Press any key to continue
```

Here is the program source code that produced the output:

```
#include "stdafx.h"
#include <math.h>
#include <iostream>

using namespace std;

int main(int argc, char* argv[])
{
    double var1 = 1.387;
    double result = cos(var1);
    cout << "The cosine of " << var1;
    cout << " is " << result << endl;

    return 0;
}
```

CROSS-REFERENCE

See also _cabs(), _finite(), _hypot(), _logb(), _scalb(), abs(), acos(), asin(), atan(), atan2(), atof(), ceil(), cosh(), cosl(), exp(), fabs(), floor(), fmod(), frexp(), labs(), ldexp(), log(), log10(), modf(), pow(), sin(), sinh(), sqrt(), tan(), and tanh().

cosf()

Function

The cosf() function returns, as a float, the cosine of its argument.

NOTE

Borland does not support this function.

Header File

```
#include <math.h>
```

Declaration

```
float cosf(float num);
```

- *num* — The value for which to return the cosine.

Example

The following program demonstrates how to use the cosf() function. The program displays the following output:

```
The cosine of 1.387 is 0.182763
Press any key to continue
```

Here is the program source code that produced the output:

```
#include "stdafx.h"
#include <math.h>
#include <iostream>

using namespace std;

int main(int argc, char* argv[])
{
    float var1 = (float)1.387;
    float result = cosf(var1);
    cout << "The cosine of " << var1;
    cout << " is " << result << endl;

    return 0;
}
```

CROSS-REFERENCE

See also _cabs(), _finite(), _hypot(), _logb(), _scalb(), abs(), acos(), asin(), atan(), atan2(), atof(), ceil(), cos(), cosh(), cosl(), exp(), fabs(), floor(), fmod(), frexp(), labs(), ldexp(), log(), log10(), modf(), pow(), sin(), sinh(), sqrt(), tan(), and tanh().

cosh()

Function

The cosh() function returns the hyperbolic cosine of its argument.

Header File

```
#include <math.h>
```

Declaration

```
double cosh(double num);
```

- *num* — The value for which to return the hyperbolic cosine.

Example

The following program demonstrates how to use the cosh() function. The program's output looks like the following:

```
The hyperbolic cosine of 1.387 is 2.12632
Press any key to continue
```

Here is the program source code that produced the output:

```
#include "stdafx.h"
#include <math.h>
#include <iostream>

using namespace std;

int main(int argc, char* argv[])
{
    double var1 = 1.387;
    double result = cosh(var1);
    cout << "The hyperbolic cosine of " << var1;
    cout << " is " << result << endl;

    return 0;
}
```

CROSS-REFERENCE
See also _cabs(), _finite(), _hypot(), _logb(), _scalb(), abs(), acos(), asin(), atan(), atan2(), atof(), ceil(), cos(), coshf(), coshl(), cosl(), exp(), fabs(), floor(), fmod(), frexp(), labs(), ldexp(), log(), log10(), modf(), pow(), sin(), sinh(), sqrt(), tan(), and tanh().

coshf()

Function

The `coshf()` function returns, as a `float`, the hyperbolic cosine of its argument.

NOTE
Borland does not support this function.

Header File

```
#include <math.h>
```

Declaration

```
float coshf(float num);
```

- *num* — The value for which to return the hyperbolic cosine.

Example

The following program demonstrates how to use the `coshf()` function. The program displays the following output:

```
The hyperbolic cosine of 1.387 is 2.12632
Press any key to continue
```

Here is the program source code that produced the output:

```
#include "stdafx.h"
#include <math.h>
#include <iostream>

using namespace std;
```

```
int main(int argc, char* argv[])
{
    float var1 = (float)1.387;
    float result = coshf(var1);
    cout << "The hyperbolic cosine of " << var1;
    cout << " is " << result << endl;

    return 0;
}
```

 CROSS-REFERENCE
See also _cabs(), _finite(), _hypot(), _logb(), _scalb(), abs(), acos(), asin(), atan(), atan2(), atof(), ceil(), cos(), cosh(), coshl(), cosl(), exp(), fabs(), floor(), fmod(), frexp(), labs(), ldexp(), log(), log10(), modf(), pow(), sin(), sinh(), sqrt(), tan(), and tanh().

coshl()

Function

The coshl() function returns, as a long double, the hyperbolic cosine of its argument.

Header File

```
#include <math.h>
```

Declaration

```
long double coshl(long double num);
```

- *num* — The value for which to return the hyperbolic cosine.

Example

The following program demonstrates how to use the coshl() function. The program displays the following output:

```
The hyperbolic cosine of 1.387 is 2.12632
Press any key to continue
```

Here is the program source code that produced the output:

```
#include "stdafx.h"
#include <math.h>
#include <iostream>

using namespace std;

int main(int argc, char* argv[])
{
    long double var1 = 1.387;
    long double result = coshl(var1);
    cout << "The hyperbolic cosine of " << var1;
    cout << " is " << result << endl;

    return 0;
}
```

CROSS-REFERENCE
See also _cabs(), _finite(), _hypot(), _logb(), _scalb(), abs(), acos(), asin(), atan(), atan2(), atof(), ceil(), cos(), cosh(), coshf(), cosl(), exp(), fabs(), floor(), fmod(), frexp(), labs(), ldexp(), log(), log10(), modf(), pow(), sin(), sinh(), sqrt(), tan(), and tanh().

cosl()

Function

The cosl() function returns, as a long double, the cosine of its argument.

Header File

```
#include <math.h>
```

Declaration

```
long double cosl(long double num);
```

- *num* — The value for which to return the cosine.

Example

The following program demonstrates how to use the cosl() function. The program's output looks like the following:

```
The cosine of 1.387 is 0.182763
Press any key to continue
```

Here is the program source code that produced the output:

```cpp
#include "stdafx.h"
#include <math.h>
#include <iostream>

using namespace std;

int main(int argc, char* argv[])
{
    long double var1 = 1.387;
    long double result = cosl(var1);
    cout << "The cosine of " << var1;
    cout << " is " << result << endl;

    return 0;
}
```

CROSS-REFERENCE

See also _cabs(), _finite(), _hypot(), _logb(), _scalb(), abs(), acos(), asin(), atan(), atan2(), atof(), ceil(), cos(), cosh(), cosf(), exp(), fabs(), floor(), fmod(), frexp(), labs(), ldexp(), log(), log10(), modf(), pow(), sin(), sinh(), sqrt(), tan(), and tanh().

cout

Stream Object

cout is a predefined stream object of the ostream class that can be used to send output to the standard output stream.

Header File

```cpp
#include <iostream.h>
```

Example

By retrieving a string from the user and redisplaying the acquired string on the screen, the following program demonstrates how to use the cout stream object. The program's output looks something like the following:

```
Enter a string below:
abcdefghijklmnopqrstuvwxyz

You typed the following:
abcdefghijklmnopqrstuvwxyz

Press any key to continue
```

Note that endl is a stream manipulator that places a carriage return and line feed onto the stream. Other manipulators include hex for obtaining hexadecimal output (cout << hex << 2000 << endl), oct for obtaining octal output (cout << oct << 2000 << endl), and dec for obtaining decimal output (cout << dec << 2000 << endl). Here is the program source code that produced the output:

```cpp
#include "stdafx.h"
#include <iostream>

using namespace std;

int main(int argc, char* argv[])
{
    char str[81];

    cout << "Enter a string below:" << endl;
    cin > str;
    cout << endl << "You typed the following:" << endl;
    cout << str << endl << endl;

    return 0;
}
```

CROSS-REFERENCE
See also cerr and cin.

cprintf()

Function

The cprintf() function displays formatted data output on the console. The function returns the number of displayed characters.

Header File

```
#include <conio.h>
```

Declaration

```
int cprintf(const char *format [, argument] ... );
```

- *format*—The format string that specifies how the data should be converted. The format string takes the same form as the format string used with the `printf()` function. Table C-11 lists the available format specifiers.

- *argument*—Pointers to variables that match the type specifiers in *format*. The function will read data directly into the given variables.

Table C-11 Format Specifiers for cprintf()

Specifier	Description
%c	Specifies a character
%C	Specifies a wide character (`printf()`) or single-byte character (`wprintf()`)
%d	Specifies a signed decimal integer
%e	Specifies a signed double-precision floating-point value using scientific notation with a lowercase "e"
%E	Specifies a signed double-precision floating-point value using scientific notation with an uppercase "E"
%f	Specifies a signed double-precision floating-point value
%g	Specifies a signed double-precision floating-point value using either normal notation or scientific notation with a lowercase "e"
%G	Specifies a signed double-precision floating-point value using either normal notation or scientific notation with an uppercase "E"
%I	Specifies a signed decimal integer
%n	Specifies an integer pointer
%o	Specifies an unsigned octal integer
%p	Specifies a void pointer
%s	Specifies a string
%S	Specifies a wide-character string (`printf()`) or single-byte-character string (`wprintf()`)
%u	Specifies an unsigned decimal integer
%x	Specifies an unsigned hexadecimal integer with lowercase letters
%X	Specifies an unsigned hexadecimal integer with uppercase letters

Example

The following program demonstrates how to use the `cprintf()` function. When run, the program requests that the user type a string and an integer. The program then displays the given input. The program's output looks something like the following:

```
Enter a text string and an integer:
abcdefghij 25

The items are as follows:
     abcdefghij 25

Press any key to continue
```

Here is the program source code that produced the output:

```cpp
#include "stdafx.h"
#include <conio.h>
#include <iostream>

using namespace std;

int main(int argc, char* argv[])
{
    int val1;
    char str[81];

    cout << "Enter a text string and an integer:" << endl;
    cscanf( "%s %i", str, &val1);
    cout << endl << endl;
    cout << "The items are as follows:" << endl;
    cprintf("     %s %d\r\n\r\n", str, val1);

    return 0;
}
```

CROSS-REFERENCE

See also _cprintf(), cscanf(), fprintf(), fscanf(), fwprintf(), fwscanf(), printf(), scanf(), sscanf(), swprintf(), swscanf(), vfprintf(), vfwprintf(), vprintf(), vsprintf(), vswprintf(), vwprintf(), wprintf(), and wscanf().

cputs()

Function

The cputs() function displays a string on the console. If the function is successful, it returns a 0; otherwise, it returns a nonzero value.

Header File

```
#include <conio.h>
```

Declaration

```
int cputs(const char* str);
```

- *str*—The string to display.

Example

The following program demonstrates how to use the cputs() function. The program's output looks like the following:

```
This is a test.
Press any key to continue
```

Here is the program source code that produced the output:

```
#include "stdafx.h"
#include <iostream>
#include <conio.h>

using namespace std;

int main(int argc, char* argv[])
{
    cputs("This is a test.\r\n");

    return 0;
}
```

CROSS-REFERENCE
See also _cputs(), cgets(), and getch().

creat()

Function

The creat() function creates a file, returning the file's handle if successful or returning –1 if unsuccessful.

Header File

```
#include <io.h>
#include <sys\stat.h>
```

Declaration

```
int creat(const char* fileName, int mode);
```

- *fileName* — The name of the file to create.
- *mode* — A value that specifies the file-creation mode. This value can be S_IREAD and/or S_IWRITE, which are defined in the stat.h header file.

Example

The following program demonstrates how to use the creat() function. When run, the program creates a file in read-and-write mode and then closes a file, displaying appropriate messages as it goes. The program's output looks like the following:

```
File created successfully.
File closed successfully.
Press any key to continue
```

Here is the program source code that produced the output:

```
#include "stdafx.h"
#include <fcntl.h>
#include <sys\stat.h>
#include <io.h>
#include <iostream>

using namespace std;

int main(int argc, char* argv[])
{
```

```
int fileHandle = creat("test.dat", S_IREAD | S_IWRITE);

if (fileHandle != -1)
{
    cout << "File created successfully." << endl;
    int result = close(fileHandle);
    if (result == 0)
        cout << "File closed successfully." << endl;
    else
        cout << "File close error." << endl;
}
else
    cout << "File create error." << endl;

return 0;
}
```

CROSS-REFERENCE
See also _open() and close().

Creating a Class

Technique

In the simplest terms, a *class* is little more than a special type of structure that can contain functions and data members. Much like a structure, a class is meant to represent a type of object. For example, you might have a structure that holds the coordinates of a point on the screen. The following sections show how a class is similar to a structure, as well as how to define and use classes.

Defining a Structure for a Point

The following source code demonstrates how you might define a structure for a point and use it in a program. The program's output looks like the following:

```
p.x data member = 100
p.y data member = 200
Press any key to continue
```

Here is the program source code that produced the output:

```
#include "stdafx.h"
#include <iostream>
```

```
using namespace std;

typedef struct point
{
    int x;
    int y;
} POINTXY;

int main(int argc, char* argv[])
{
    POINTXY p;

    p.x = 100;
    p.y = 200;

    cout << "p.x data member = " << p.x << endl;
    cout << "p.y data member = " << p.y << endl;

    return 0;
}
```

This program first defines a data type called POINTXY, which is a structure that can hold the X and Y coordinates of a point on the screen. The main() function creates an object of the POINTXY structure, assigns values to the two data members, and then displays the values on the screen.

Defining a Class for a Point

While a structure is a powerful object for managing various kinds of data, it has limitations — one of which is the inability to encapsulate into the structure not only the data members themselves, but also the functions needed to manipulate those data members. That's where a class comes in. By changing the POINTXY structure to a class called Point, you can not only represent the values of a point object, but also represent the actions that can be taken by a point object. The following program demonstrates how you might convert the structure POINTXY to a class called Point. This program's output looks like the following:

```
p.x data member = 100
p.y data member = 200
p.x data member = 150
p.y data member = 250
Press any key to continue
```

Here is the program source code that produced the output:

```
#include "stdafx.h"
#include <iostream>

using namespace std;

class Point
{
protected:
    int x;
    int y;

public:
    Point(int xPos, int yPos)
    {
        x = xPos;
        y = yPos;
    }

    ~Point() {};

    void SetX(int xPos)
    {
        x = xPos;
    }

    void SetY(int yPos)
    {
        y = yPos;
    }

    int GetX()
    {
        return x;
    }

    int GetY()
    {
        return y;
    }
};

int main(int argc, char* argv[])
{
    Point p(100, 200);
```

```
int x = p.GetX();
int y = p.GetY();
cout << "p.x data member = " << x << endl;
cout << "p.y data member = " << y << endl;

p.SetX(150);
p.SetY(250);

x = p.GetX();
y = p.GetY();
cout << "p.x data member = " << x << endl;
cout << "p.y data member = " << y << endl;

    return 0;
}
```

Exploring the Class Definition

The new version of the program defines a class for points that not only contains the coordinates of a point, but also contains functions for initializing, setting, and getting the coordinates. Take a closer look at the class definition. The first two lines tell the compiler that you're defining a class, provide the class's name, and supply the definition's opening brace:

```
class Point
{
```

The next three lines tell the compiler that no program should have direct access to the x and y data members, and declares the data members themselves:

```
protected:
    int x;
    int y;
```

In place of the `protected` keyword, you could have also used `public` or `private`. If you had used `public`, the data members would have been directly accessible from the program, just as with a conventional structure. If you had used `private`, not only would the data members be inaccessible to the program, but they would also be inaccessible to any class derived from the `Point` class. (For more information on deriving classes, please refer to the Deriving Classes entry.)

The next line of the class definition tells the compiler that the following members are to be accessible from outside the class:

```
public:
```

It's important that the class's member functions be declared as `public` so that the main program can call those functions. Often, you'll declare member functions as `protected` or `private`, which means those functions can be called only from within the class.

Next, the class defines a special function known as a *constructor*. A constructor initializes an object instantiated from the class. That is, when the program creates an object from the `Point` class, it must supply the two integers that represent the point's coordinates. When the point object is created, the constructor gets called first and transfers the values supplied by the program into the object's data members. Here's the class's constructor:

```
Point(int xPos, int yPos)
{
    x = xPos;
    y = yPos;
}
```

As you can see, the name of the constructor is the same as the name of the class.

The next line in the class defines another special function — a *destructor*. A destructor is the opposite of a constructor. Whereas the class's constructor is called first when a program creates an object of the class, the destructor is called last, just before the object is removed from memory. The destructor gives the object a chance to perform any cleanup chores that may need to be completed before the object disappears. For example, if a class allocates memory on the heap, the destructor can release the memory before the object is deleted. The `Point` class's destructor looks like the following:

```
~Point() {};
```

Notice that, like the constructor, the destructor's name is the same as the class's name. However, in the destructor's case, the name is prefaced by a tilde (~). Notice that the `Point` class's destructor does nothing. Technically, because the `Point` class needs to perform no cleanup, you could have declared the class without a destructor. In that case, the compiler would provide a default destructor automatically. However, it's always a good programming practice to provide both a constructor and a destructor, even if neither of these special functions do anything.

You may recall that the class's two data members `x` and `y` were declared as `protected`, which means that the program cannot access them directly. That is, if you tried to write, in the main program, a line like

```
p.x = 100;
```

or

```
int x1 = p.x;
```

the compiler would generate an error. This means that you must supply the class with `public` functions that a program can call to manipulate the class's data members. The `Point` class defines a member function for changing the value of the point's X coordinate as follows:

```
void SetX(int xPos)
{
    x = xPos;
}
```

This function is generally just like any other C++ function.

As you may have guessed, the class also defines a function for changing the value of the point's Y coordinate:

```
void SetY(int yPos)
{
    y = yPos;
}
```

Not surprisingly, the class also defines functions for retrieving the current values of the point's coordinates:

```
int GetX()
{
    return x;
}
```

```
int GetY()
{
    return y;
}
```

Finally, the class definition ends with a closing brace and a semicolon:

```
};
```

Exploring the Main Program

Now, turn your attention to the main program where the `Point` class gets put through its paces. First, the program creates an object of the `Point` class:

```
Point p(100, 200);
```

Creating an object from a class is called *instantiating the class* or *creating an instance of the class*. This process is little different from creating an instance of any data object. For example, the line

```
int x = 12;
```

creates an instance of an integer and initializes it to the value 12.

You can think of the object declaration as the calling of the class's constructor on behalf of the object. For example, in the case of

```
Point p(100, 200);
```

you're telling the program to create an instance (also called an object) of the `Point` class. To do this, the p object's constructor gets called with the values 100 and 200. The constructor plugs these values into the object's x and y data members, and you're ready to go.

The program gets the current values of the x and y data members by calling the object's `GetX()` and `GetY()` member functions, as follows:

```
int x = p.GetX();
int y = p.GetY();
```

The program then calls upon the `cout` stream object (which, by the way, is an instantiation of the `ostream` class) to display the values of the two data members:

```
cout << "p.x data member = " << x << endl;
cout << "p.y data member = " << y << endl;
```

Next, the program changes the values of the x and y data members by calling the p object's `SetX()` and `SetY()` data members:

```
p.SetX(150);
p.SetY(250);
```

Finally, the program retrieves the new values from the object and displays them, proving that the data members' values were actually changed:

```
x = p.GetX();
y = p.GetY();
cout << "p.x data member = " << x << endl;
cout << "p.y data member = " << y << endl;
```

Using Header and Implementation Files

In the previous program, the class is declared and defined in the same file as the main program. Although this practice is perfectly acceptable for a short program, when you develop a larger program using classes, you're going to want to place your classes in separate source-code files. The traditional way to do this is to place the class's declaration in a header file and the class's definition in an implementation file.

The header file does nothing more than describe the class to the compiler. The information in the class's header file is sometimes called the class's *inter-*

face, because it describes all the data members and member functions of the class. The header file for the `Point` class, called Point.h, looks like the following:

Header File
```
class Point
{
protected:
    int x;
    int y;

public:
    Point(int xPos, int yPos);
    ~Point();

    void SetX(int xPos);
    void SetY(int yPos);
    int GetX();
    int GetY();
};
```

Notice how the details of each member function's implementation are left out, with the header file providing only function prototypes.

The class's definition appears in the implementation file, called Point.cpp, which looks like the following:

Implementation File
```
#include "stdafx.h"
#include "Point.h"

Point::Point(int xPos, int yPos)
{
    x = xPos;
    y = yPos;
}

Point::~Point()
{
};

void Point::SetX(int xPos)
{
    x = xPos;
}

void Point::SetY(int yPos)
{
```

```
    y = yPos;
}

int Point::GetX()
{
    return x;
}

int Point::GetY()
{
    return y;
}
```

Examine the syntax used to define each function. First, notice that each function's name is prefaced by the class's name followed by a double set of colons. Also notice that the implementation file contains the complete functions, which match up with the function prototypes in the class's header file. Finally, notice that the implementation file includes the class's header file, as follows:

```
#include "Point.h"
```

To use the `Point` class in your project, you must include the Point.h header file in any file that references the class. In this way, the compiler obtains the information it needs to compile the program successfully. You must also add the class's implementation file to your project. This enables the linker to find the function definitions referred to in the class's header file. The main program from the preceding example now looks like the following:

```
#include "stdafx.h"
#include <iostream>
#include "Point.h"

using namespace std;

int main(int argc, char* argv[])
{
    Point p(100, 200);

    int x = p.GetX();
    int y = p.GetY();
    cout << "p.x data member = " << x << endl;
    cout << "p.y data member = " << y << endl;

    p.SetX(150);
```

```
    p.SetY(250);

    x = p.GetX();
    y = p.GetY();
    cout << "p.x data member = " << x << endl;
    cout << "p.y data member = " << y << endl;

    return 0;
}
```

Notice that, although the `Point` class has been divided into separate header and implementation files and removed from the main file, the main program has not changed — except for the line:

```
#include "Point.h"
```

CROSS-REFERENCE

See also Abstract Class, Deriving a Class, Encapsulation, Inheritance, inline, Polymorphism, and Virtual Functions.

cscanf()

Function

The `cscanf()` function reads input from the console. The function returns the number of data items that were accepted from the input.

Header File

```
#include <conio.h>
```

Declaration

```
int cscanf(const char *format [, argument] ... );
```

- *format* — The format string that specifies how the input should be converted. The format string takes the same form as the format string used with the `printf()` function. Table C-12 lists the available format specifiers.
- *argument* — Pointers to variables that match the type specifiers in *format*. The function will read data directly into the given variables.

Table C-12 Format Specifiers for cscanf()

Specifier	Description
%c	Specifies a character
%C	Specifies a wide character (printf()) or single-byte character (wprintf())
%d	Specifies a signed decimal integer
%e	Specifies a signed double-precision floating-point value using scientific notation with a lowercase "e"
%E	Specifies a signed double-precision floating-point value using scientific notation with an uppercase "E"
%f	Specifies a signed double-precision floating-point value
%g	Specifies a signed double-precision floating-point value using either normal notation or scientific notation with a lowercase "e"
%G	Specifies a signed double-precision floating-point value using either normal notation or scientific notation with an uppercase "E"
%I	Specifies a signed decimal integer
%n	Specifies an integer pointer
%o	Specifies an unsigned octal integer
%p	Specifies a void pointer
%s	Specifies a string
%S	Specifies a wide-character string (printf()) or single-byte-character string (wprintf())
%u	Specifies an unsigned decimal integer
%x	Specifies an unsigned hexadecimal integer with lowercase letters
%X	Specifies an unsigned hexadecimal integer with uppercase letters

Example

The following program demonstrates how to use the cscanf() function. When run, the program requests that the user type a string and an integer. The program then displays the given input. The program's output looks something like the following:

```
Enter a text string and an integer:
abcdefghij 25

You entered 2 items.
The items are as follows:
    abcdefghij
    25
```

```
Press any key to continue
```

Here's the program source code that produced the output:

```cpp
#include "stdafx.h"
#include <conio.h>
#include <iostream>

using namespace std;

int main(int argc, char* argv[])
{
    int val1;
    char str[81];

    cout << "Enter a text string and an integer:" << endl;
    int numItems = cscanf( "%s %i", str, &val1);
    cout << endl << endl;
    cout << "You entered " << numItems << " items." << endl;
    cout << "The items are as follows:" << endl;
    cout << "     " << str << endl;
    cout << "     " << val1 << endl << endl;

    return 0;
}
```

CROSS-REFERENCE
See also cprintf(), fprintf(), fscanf(), fwprintf(), fwscanf(), printf(), scanf(), sscanf(), swprintf(), swscanf(), vfprintf(), vfwprintf(), vprintf(), vsprintf(), vswprintf(), vwprintf(), wprintf(), and wscanf().

csignal

Standard C++ Library Header File

The csignal header file includes the C library header file signal.h into the source code. The signal.h header file defines signal constants and functions, including the following:

Defined Constants

SIG_ACK	SIGBREAK
SIG_DFL	SIGFPE
SIG_ERR	SIGILL
SIG_IGN	SIGINT
SIG_SGE	SIGSEGV
SIGABRT	SIGTERM

Defined Functions

raise()

signal()

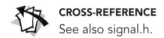

CROSS-REFERENCE
See also signal.h.

cstdarg

Standard C++ Library Header File

The cstdarg header file includes the C library header file stdarg.h into the source code. The stdarg.h header file defines macros needed to support variable-argument lists. The macros defined in stdarg.h include those in the following list.

Defined Macros

_INTSIZEOF(n)	va_end(ap)
va_arg(ap,t)	va_start(ap,v)

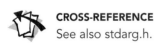

CROSS-REFERENCE
See also stdarg.h.

cstddef

Standard C++ Library Header File

The cstddef header file includes the C library header file stddef.h into the source code. The stddef.h header file defines useful general-purpose constants, type definitions, macros, and functions as listed in the following:

Defined Constants

NULL

Defined Functions

__threadhandle(void);

Defined Data Types

ptrdiff_t;   wchar_t;

size_t;

Defined Macros

offsetof()   _threadid

CROSS-REFERENCE

See also stddef.h.

cstdio

Standard C++ library header file

The cstdio header file includes the C library header file stdio.h into the source code. The stdio.h header file defines data types, constants, functions, data types definitions, structures, and macros that make up the standard I/O library. The symbols defined in stdio.h include the following:

Defined Constants

_IOAPPEND	_IORW
_IOB_ENTRIES	_IOSTRG
_IOEOF	_IOWRT
_IOERR	_NSTREAM_
_IOFBF	_SYS_OPEN
_IOLBF	BUFSIZ
_IOMYBUF	EOF
_IONBF	FILENAME_MAX
_IOREAD	FOPEN_MAX

NULL	SEEK_SET
SEEK_CUR	TMP_MAX
SEEK_END	

Defined Functions

_fcloseall()	_wperror()
_fdopen()	_wpopen()
_fgetchar()	_wremove()
_fgetwchar()	_wtempnam()
_filbuf()	_wtmpnam()
_fileno()	clearerr()
_flsbuf()	fclose()
_flushall()	fcloseall()
_fputchar()	fdopen()
_fputwchar()	feof()
_fsopen()	ferror()
_getmaxstdio()	fflush()
_getw()	fgetc()
_getws()	fgetchar()
_pclose()	fgetpos()
_popen()	fgets()
_putw()	fgetwc()
_putws()	fgetws()
_rmtmp()	fileno()
_setmaxstdio()	flushall()
_snprintf()	fopen()
_snwprintf()	fprintf()
_tempnam()	fputc()
_unlink()	fputchar()
_vsnprintf()	fputs()
_vsnwprintf()	fputwc()
_wfdopen()	fputws()
_wfopen()	fread()
_wfreopen()	freopen()
_wfsopen()	fscanf()

fseek()

fsetpos()

ftell()

fwprintf()

fwrite()

fwscanf()

getc()

getchar()

gets()

getw()

getwc()

getwchar()

perror()

printf()

putc()

putchar()

puts()

putw()

putwc()

putwchar()

remove()

rename()

rewind()

rmtmp()

scanf()

setbuf()

setvbuf()

sprintf()

sscanf()

swprintf()

swscanf()

tempnam()

tmpfile()

tmpnam()

ungetc()

ungetwc()

unlink()

vfprintf()

vfwprintf()

vprintf()

vsprintf()

vswprintf()

vwprintf()

wprintf()

wscanf()

b

c

d

Declared Data Types

fpos_t

size_t

wchar_t

wctype_t

wint_t

Defined Structures

```
struct _iobuf {
        char *_ptr;
        int   _cnt;
        char *_base;
        int   _flag;
        int   _file;
```

```
        int    _charbuf;
        int    _bufsiz;
        char *_tmpfname;
        };
typedef struct _iobuf FILE;
```

Defined Macros

_fileno()	L_cuserid
_FPOSOFF	L_tmpnam
_P_tmpdir	putc()
_wP_tmpdir	putchar()
feof()	putwc()
ferror()	putwchar()
getc()	stderr
getchar()	stdin
getwc()	stdout
getwchar()	WEOF
L_ctermid	

CROSS-REFERENCE
See also stdio.h.

cstdlib

Standard C++ Library Header File

The cstdlib header file includes the C library header file stdlib.h into the source code. The stdlib.h header file defines the constants, functions, general data types, variables, structures, and macros used in program development. The defined symbols include the following:

Defined Constants

_MAX_DIR	_OUT_TO_DEFAULT
_MAX_DRIVE	_OUT_TO_MSGBOX
_MAX_EXT	_OUT_TO_STDERR
_MAX_FNAME	_REPORT_ERRMODE
_MAX_PATH	EXIT_FAILURE

EXIT_SUCCESS   NULL
MB_CUR_MAX   RAND_MAX

b
c
d

Defined Functions

_atoi64()   _wgetenv()
_atold()   _wmakepath()
_ecvt()   _wperror()
_exit()   _wputenv()
_fcvt()   _wsearchenv()
_fullpath()   _wsplitpath()
_gcvt()   _wsystem()
_i64toa()   _wtoi()
_i64tow()   _wtoi64()
_itoa()   _wtol()
_itow()   abort()
_lrotl()   abs()
_lrotr()   atexit()
_ltoa()   atof()
_ltow()   atoi()
_makepath()   atol()
_mbstrlen()   bsearch()
_onexit()   calloc()
_putenv()   div()
_rotl()   ecvt()
_rotr()   exit()
_searchenv()   fcvt()
_set_error_mode()   free()
_splitpath()   gcvt()
_strtold()   getenv()
_swab()   itoa()
_ui64toa()   labs()
_ui64tow()   ldiv()
_ultoa()   ltoa()
_ultow()   malloc()
_wfullpath()   mblen()

mbstowcs()	strtol()
mbtowc()	strtoul()
onexit()	swab()
perror()	system()
putenv()	ultoa()
qsort()	wcstod()
rand()	wcstol()
realloc()	wcstombs()
srand()	wcstoul()
strtod()	wctomb()

Defined Data Types

size_t	wchar_t

Defined Variables

__argc	_sys_nerr
__argv	_wenviron
__wargv	_winmajor;
_environ	_winminor;
_fileinfo	_winver;
_fmode	_wpgmptr
_osver;	doserrno
_pgmptr	environ
_sys_errlist[]	errno

Defined Structures

```
typedef struct _div_t {
        int quot;
        int rem;
} div_t;

typedef struct _ldiv_t {
        long quot;
        long rem;
} ldiv_t;
```

Defined Macros

__argc	_pgmptr
__argv	_wenviron
__max()	_wpgmptr
__min()	max()
__wargv	min()
_environ	

CROSS-REFERENCE
See also stdlib.h.

cstring

Standard C++ Library Header File

The cstring header file includes the C library header file string.h into the source code. The string.h header file defines the constants, functions, and data types used for string manipulation. The defined symbols include those in the following:

Defined Constants

_NLSCMPERROR	NULL

Declared Functions

_memccpy()	_strrev()
_memicmp()	_strset()
_strcmpi()	_strupr()
_strdup()	_wcsdup()
_strerror()	_wcsicmp()
_stricmp()	_wcsicoll()
_stricoll()	_wcslwr()
_strlwr()	_wcsncoll()
_strncoll()	_wcsnicmp()
_strnicmp()	_wcsnicoll()
_strnicoll()	_wcsnset()
_strnset()	_wcsrev()
	_wcsset()

_wcsupr()	strstr()
memccpy()	strtok()
memchr()	strupr()
memcmp()	strxfrm()
memcpy()	wcscat()
memicmp()	wcschr()
memset()	wcscmp()
strcat()	wcscoll()
strchr()	wcscpy()
strcmp()	wcscspn()
strcmpi()	wcsdup()
strcoll()	wcsicmp()
strcpy()	wcsicoll()
strcspn()	wcslen()
strdup()	wcslwr()
strerror()	wcsncat()
stricmp()	wcsncmp()
strlen()	wcsncpy()
strlwr()	wcsnicmp()
strncat()	wcsnset()
strncmp()	wcspbrk()
strncpy()	wcsrchr()
strnicmp()	wcsrev()
strnset()	wcsset()
strpbrk()	wcsspn()
strrchr()	wcsstr()
strrev()	wcstok()
strset()	wcsupr()
strspn()	wcsxfrm()

Defined Data Types

size_t	wchar_t

CROSS-REFERENCE
See also string.h.

ctime()

Function

The ctime() function converts the contents of a time_t structure to a string.

Header File

```
#include <time.h>
```

Declaration

```
char* ctime(const time_t* time);
```

- *time* — The address of the time_t structure that should be converted to a string.

Example

The following program demonstrates how to use the ctime() function. When run, the program calls the time() function to get the current time in a time_t structure, and then converts the structure to a string for display. The program's output looks something like the following:

```
Mon Jan 11 15:29:21 1999

Press any key to continue
```

Here is the program source code that produced the output:

```
#include "stdafx.h"
#include <iostream>
#include <time.h>

using namespace std;

int main(int argc, char* argv[])
{
    time_t curTime;
    time(&curTime);
    char* timeStr = ctime(&curTime);
    cout << timeStr << endl;

    return 0;
}
```

CROSS-REFERENCE
See also _ftime(), asctime(), and time().

ctime

Standard C++ Library Header File

The ctime header file includes the C library header file time.h into the source code. The time.h header file defines the constants, functions, type definitions, global variables, and structures needed to manipulate time data in a program. The defined symbols include those in the following lists:

Defined Constants

CLK_TCK	NULL
CLOCKS_PER_SEC	

Defined Functions

_strdate()	difftime()
_strtime()	gmtime()
_wasctime()	localtime()
_wctime()	mktime()
_wstrdate()	strftime()
_wstrtime()	time()
asctime()	tzset()
clock()	wcsftime()
ctime()	

Defined Data Types

clock_t	time_t
size_t	wchar_t

Defined Variables

_daylight	_tzname[]
_dstbias	daylight
_timezone	timezone

Defined Structures

```
struct tm {
        int tm_sec;
        int tm_min;
        int tm_hour;
        int tm_mday;
        int tm_mon;
        int tm_year;
        int tm_wday;
        int tm_yday;
        int tm_isdst;
        };
```

CROSS-REFERENCE
See also time.h.

ctype.h

Standard C Library Header File

The ctype.h header file defines constants, functions, and data types for manip-ulating character data. The following lists shows the symbols defined in this header file.

Defined Constants

_ALPHA	_LOWER
_BLANK	_PUNCT
_CONTROL	_SPACE
_DIGIT	_UPPER
_HEX	MB_CUR_MAX
_LEADBYTE	WEOF

Defined Functions

__isascii()	_toupper()
__iscsym()	isalnum()
__iscsymf()	isalpha()
__toascii()	isascii()
_tolower()	iscntrl()

iscsym()	iswascii()
iscsymf()	iswcntrl()
isdigit()	iswdigit()
isgraph()	iswgraph()
isleadbyte()	iswlower()
islower()	iswprint()
isprint()	iswpunct()
ispunct()	iswspace()
isspace()	iswupper()
isupper()	iswxdigit()
iswalnum()	isxdigit()
iswalpha()	toascii()

Defined Data Types

wchar_t;	wint_t;
wctype_t;	

CROSS-REFERENCE
See also cctype.

cwchar

Standard C++ Library Header File

The cwchar header file includes the C library header file wchar.h into the source code. The wchar.h header file defines constants, functions, type definitions, structures, and macros for handling wide characters. The symbols defined include those in the following lists:

Defined Constants

_ALPHA	_HEX
_BLANK	_LEADBYTE
_CONTROL	_LOWER
_DIGIT	_PUNCT

_SPACE
_UPPER
NULL

WCHAR_MAX
WCHAR_MIN

Defined Functions

_fgetwchar()
_fputwchar()
_getws()
_i64tow()
_itow()
_ltow ()
_putws()
_snwprintf()
_ui64tow()
_ultow()
_vsnwprintf()
_waccess()
_wasctime()
_wchdir()
_wchmod()
_wcreat()
_wcsdup()
_wcsicmp()
_wcsicoll()
_wcslwr()
_wcsncoll()
_wcsnicmp()
_wcsnicoll()
_wcsnset()
_wcsrev()
_wcsset()
_wcsupr()
_wctime()
_wexecl()

_wexecle()
_wexeclp()
_wexeclpe()
_wexecv()
_wexecve()
_wexecvp()
_wexecvpe()
_wfdopen()
_wfindfirst()
_wfindfirsti64()
_wfindnext()
_wfindnexti64()
_wfopen()
_wfreopen()
_wfsopen()
_wfullpath()
_wgetcwd()
_wgetdcwd()
_wgetenv()
_wmakepath()
_wmkdir()
_wmktemp()
_wopen()
_wperror()
_wpopen()
_wputenv()
_wremove()
_wrename()
_wrmdir()

_wsearchenv()

_wsetlocale()

_wsopen()

_wspawnl()

_wspawnle()

_wspawnlp()

_wspawnlpe()

_wspawnv()

_wspawnve()

_wspawnvp()

_wspawnvpe()

_wsplitpath()

_wstat()

_wstati64()

_wstrdate()

_wstrtime()

_wsystem()

_wtempnam()

_wtmpnam()

_wtoi()

_wtoi64()

_wtol()

_wunlink()

btowc()

fgetwc()

fgetws()

fputwc()

fputws()

fwide()

fwprintf()

fwscanf()

getwc()

getwchar()

isleadbyte()

iswalnum()

iswalpha()

iswascii()

iswcntrl()

iswctype()

iswdigit()

iswgraph()

iswlower()

iswprint()

iswpunct()

iswspace()

iswupper()

iswxdigit()

mbrlen()

mbrtowc()

mbsinit()

mbsrtowcs()

putwc()

putwchar()

putwchar()

swprintf()

swscanf()

towlower()

towupper()

ungetwc()

vfwprintf()

vswprintf()

vwprintf()

wcrtomb()

wcscat()

wcschr()

wcscmp()

wcscoll()

wcscpy()

wcscspn()

wcsdup()

b
c
d

wcsftime()	wcsstr()
wcsicmp()	wcstod()
wcsicoll()	wcstok()
wcslen()	wcstol()
wcslwr()	wcstoul()
wcsncat()	wcsupr()
wcsncmp()	wcsxfrm()
wcsncpy()	wctob()
wcsnicmp()	wmemchr()
wcsnset()	wmemcmp()
wcspbrk()	wmemcpy()
wcsrchr()	wmemmove()
wcsrev()	wmemset()
wcsrtombs()	wprintf()
wcsset()	wscanf()
wcsspn()	

Defined Data Types

_dev_t	mbstate_t
_fsize_t	off_t
_ino_t	size_t
_iob[]	time_t
_off_t	va_list
_wint_t	wchar_t
dev_t	wctype_t
ino_t	wint_t

Defined Structures

```
struct _iobuf {
        char *_ptr;
        int   _cnt;
        char *_base;
        int   _flag;
        int   _file;
        int   _charbuf;
        int   _bufsiz;
        char *_tmpfname;
```

```
                };
typedef struct _iobuf FILE;

struct _wfinddata_t {
        unsigned attrib;
        time_t   time_create;
        time_t   time_access;
        time_t   time_write;
        _fsize_t size;
        wchar_t  name[260];
};

struct _wfinddatai64_t {
        unsigned attrib;
        time_t   time_create;
        time_t   time_access;
        time_t   time_write;
        __int64  size;
        wchar_t  name[260];
};

struct _stat {
        _dev_t st_dev;
        _ino_t st_ino;
        unsigned short st_mode;
        short st_nlink;
        short st_uid;
        short st_gid;
        _dev_t st_rdev;
        _off_t st_size;
        time_t st_atime;
        time_t st_mtime;
        time_t st_ctime;
        };

struct stat {
        _dev_t st_dev;
        _ino_t st_ino;
        unsigned short st_mode;
        short st_nlink;
        short st_uid;
        short st_gid;
```

```
        _dev_t st_rdev;
        _off_t st_size;
        time_t st_atime;
        time_t st_mtime;
        time_t st_ctime;
        };

struct _stati64 {
        _dev_t st_dev;
        _ino_t st_ino;
        unsigned short st_mode;
        short st_nlink;
        short st_uid;
        short st_gid;
        _dev_t st_rdev;
        __int64 st_size;
        time_t st_atime;
        time_t st_mtime;
        time_t st_ctime;
        };

struct tm {
        int tm_sec;
        int tm_min;
        int tm_hour;
        int tm_mday;
        int tm_mon;
        int tm_year;
        int tm_wday;
        int tm_yday;
        int tm_isdst;
        };
```

Defined Macros

getwc()	iswprint()
iswalnum()	iswpunct()
iswalpha()	iswspace()
iswascii()	iswupper()
iswcntrl()	iswxdigit()
iswdigit()	putwc()
iswgraph()	WEOF
iswlower()	

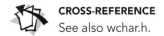

CROSS-REFERENCE
See also wchar.h.

cwctype

Standard C++ Library Header File

The cwctype header file includes the C library header file wctype.h into the source code. The wctype.h header file defines constants, functions, data types, definitions, variables, and macros for handling ctype wide characters. The symbols defined include those in the following lists. Please refer to the wctype.h entry elsewhere in this book for more information.

Defined Constants

_ALPHA	_LEADBYTE
_BLANK	_LOWER
_CONTROL	_PUNCT
_DIGIT	_SPACE
_HEX	_UPPER

Defined Functions

isleadbyte()	iswpunct()
iswalnum()	iswspace()
iswalpha()	iswupper()
iswascii()	iswxdigit()
iswcntrl()	towctrans()
iswctype()	towlower()
iswdigit()	towupper()
iswgraph()	wctrans()
iswlower()	wctype()
iswprint()	

Defined Data Types

wchar_t	wctype_t
wctrans_t	wint_t

Defined Variables

`_ctype[]`   `_pwctype`
`_pctype`

Defined Macros

`WEOF`

CROSS-REFERENCE
See also wctype.h.

#define

Directive

The #define directive defines a symbol to be used by the compiler in preprocessing. The following example of the #define directive, along with the #ifndef and #endif directives, protects this header file from being included more than once into a compilation:

```
#ifndef __MYCLASS
#define __MYCLASS

class MyClass
{
protected:
    int value;

public:
    MyClass();
    MyClass(int val);
    ~MyClass();

    virtual void SetValue(int val);
    virtual int GetValue();
};

#endif
```

CROSS-REFERENCE
See also defined, #elif, #else, #endif, #if, #ifdef, and #ifndef.

_dup()

Function

The _dup() function creates a duplicate handle for an open file. A return value of –1 indicates an error.

 NOTE
Borland users should refer to the dup() function later in this chapter.

Header File

```
#include <io.h>
```

Declaration

```
int _dup(int fileHandle);
```

- *fileHandle* — The file handle to duplicate.

Example

The following program demonstrates how to use the _dup() function. When run, the program creates a file in read-and-write mode, writes a string to the file, duplicates the file handle, writes another string using the new file handle, and then closes the file, displaying appropriate messages as it goes. The program's output looks like the following:

```
File created successfully.
File closed successfully.
Press any key to continue
```

Here is the program source code that produced the output:

```
#include "stdafx.h"
#include <sys\stat.h>
#include <io.h>
#include <iostream>

using namespace std;

int main(int argc, char* argv[])
{
    char* buf1 = "ABCDEFGHIJ";
    char* buf2 = "1234567980";
```

```
    int fileHandle = _creat("test.dat", S_IREAD | S_IWRITE);

    if (fileHandle != -1)
    {
        cout << "File created successfully." << endl;
        _write(fileHandle, buf1, 10);
        int newHandle = _dup(fileHandle);
        _write(newHandle, buf2, 10);
        int result = _close(newHandle);
        if (result == 0)
            cout << "File closed successfully." << endl;
        else
            cout << "File close error." << endl;
    }
    else
        cout << "File create error." << endl;

    return 0;
}
```

CROSS-REFERENCE
See also dup().

dec

Manipulator

The dec manipulator is used to generate decimal numerical data in an input or output stream. For example, the following program displays the hexadecimal value 0xa3d5 as the equivalent decimal value. The program's output looks like the following:

```
41941
Press any key to continue
```

Here is the program source code that produced the output:

```
#include "stdafx.h"
#include <iostream>

using namespace std;

int main(int argc, char* argv[])
```

```
{
    cout << dec << 0xa3d5 << endl;

    return 0;
}
```

 CROSS-REFERENCE
See also hex and oct.

default

Keyword

The default keyword is used as part of a switch statement, enabling the programmer to code for a default result. That is, if none of the case clauses match the switch value, the program executes the default clause. The program's output looks like the following:

```
var1 is not 1, 2, or 3
Press any key to continue
```

Here is the program source code that produced the output:

```
#include "stdafx.h"
#include<iostream>

using namespace std;

int main(int argc, char* argv[])
{
    int var1 = 5;

    switch(var1)
    {
    case 1:
        cout << "var1 is 1" << endl;
        break;
    case 2:
        cout << "var1 is 2" << endl;
        break;
    case 3:
        cout << "var1 is 2" << endl;
        break;
    default:
```

```
            cout << "var1 is not 1, 2, or 3" << endl;
        }


    return 0;
}
```

CROSS-REFERENCE
See also break, case, and switch.

Default Arguments

Concept

Default arguments enable a function to supply a value for a parameter when the function call does not supply that parameter. Using default arguments, a function call needs to supply a complete set of arguments only when the needed arguments differ from the norm. For example, the following program defines a function named Mult() that multiples the value supplied as the first argument by the value supplied in the second argument. If the programmer wants to multiply the given value by 2, he needs only call the function with the first parameter, because Mult() provides a default argument of 2 for the second argument. The program's output looks like the following:

```
Result = 20
Result = 30
Press any key to continue
```

Here is the program source code that produced the output:

```
#include "stdafx.h"
#include <iostream>

using namespace std;

int Mult(int val, int multiplier = 2)
{
    return val * multiplier;
}

int main(int argc, char* argv[])
{
    int var1 = 10;
    int result = Mult(var1);
```

```
        cout << "Result = " << result << endl;
        result = Mult(var1, 3);
        cout << "Result = " << result << endl;

        return 0;
}
```

As you can see in the Mult() function, to define a default argument, you simply follow the argument's name by an equals sign and the default value. If the function call supplies a value for the argument, the function ignores the default value; otherwise, the function uses the default value.

defined

Directive

The defined compiler directive is used with the #if and #elif directives to test whether a symbol has already been defined. For example, the following program displays the message "In debug mode". The program's output looks like the following:

```
In debug mode
Press any key to continue
```

Here is the program source code that produced the output:

```
#include "stdafx.h"
#include <iostream>

using namespace std;

#define DEBUG

int main(int argc, char* argv[])
{

#if defined(DEBUG)
    cout << "In debug mode" << endl;
#elif defined(NODEBUG)
    cout << "Not in debug mode" << endl;
#endif

    return 0;
}
```

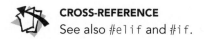

CROSS-REFERENCE
See also #elif and #if.

delete

Keyword

The delete keyword is used to remove an object from memory that was created using the new keyword. For example, the following program creates on the heap an instance of the MyClass class with the new keyword, calls the class's member functions, and then deletes the instance from memory using the delete keyword. The program's output looks like the following:

```
pMyClass->Value = 10
pMyClass->Value = 15
Press any key to continue
```

Here is the program source code that produced the output:

```
#include "stdafx.h"
#include <iostream>

using namespace std;

class MyClass
{
protected:
    int value;

public:
    MyClass(int val) { value = val; };
    ~MyClass() {};

    void SetValue(int val) { value = val; };
    int GetValue() { return value; };
};


int main(int argc, char* argv[])
{
    MyClass* pMyClass = new MyClass(10);

    cout << "pMyClass->Value = " << pMyClass->GetValue();
    cout << endl;
```

```
            pMyClass->SetValue(15);
            cout << "pMyClass->Value = " << pMyClass->GetValue();
            cout << endl;

            delete pMyClass;

        return 0;
    }
```

CROSS-REFERENCE
See also new.

deque

Template Class

The deque template class represents a list of data items of type E in which new
items can be added efficiently to the start or end of the list.

Class Declaration

```
template<class T, class A = allocator<T> >
    class deque {
public:
    typedef A allocator_type;
    typedef A::size_type size_type;
    typedef A::difference_type difference_type;
    typedef A::reference reference;
    typedef A::const_reference const_reference;
    typedef A::value_type value_type;
    typedef T0 iterator;
    typedef T1 const_iterator;
    typedef reverse_iterator<iterator, value_type,
        reference, A::pointer, difference_type>
            reverse_iterator;
    typedef reverse_iterator<const_iterator, value_type,
        const_reference, A::const_pointer, difference_type>
            const_reverse_iterator;
    explicit deque(const A& al = A());
    explicit deque(size_type n, const T& v = T(),
        const A& al = A());
    deque(const deque& x);
```

```
        deque(const_iterator first, const_iterator last,
            const A& al = A());
        iterator begin();
        const_iterator begin() const;
        iterator end();
        iterator end() const;
        reverse_iterator rbegin();
        const_reverse_iterator rbegin() const;
        reverse_iterator rend();
        const_reverse_iterator rend() const;
        void resize(size_type n, T x = T());
        size_type size() const;
        size_type max_size() const;
        bool empty() const;
        A get_allocator() const;
        reference at(size_type pos);
        const_reference at(size_type pos) const;
        reference operator[](size_type pos);
        const_reference operator[](size_type pos);
        reference front();
        const_reference front() const;
        reference back();
        const_reference back() const;
        void push_front(const T& x);
        void pop_front();
        void push_back(const T& x);
        void pop_back();
        void assign(const_iterator first, const_iterator last);
        void assign(size_type n, const T& x = T());
        iterator insert(iterator it, const T& x = T());
        void insert(iterator it, size_type n, const T& x);
        void insert(iterator it,
            const_iterator first, const_iterator last);
        iterator erase(iterator it);
        iterator erase(iterator first, iterator last);
        void clear();
        void swap(deque x);
    protected:
        A allocator;
        };
```

Class Members

Table D-1 lists and describes the members of the deque template class.

Table D-1 Members of the deque Template Class

Member	Description
allocator_type	A synonym for the template's A parameter
append()	Appends a given sequence to the current sequence
assign()	Replaces the current sequence with the given sequence
at()	Returns a reference to the specified element
back()	Returns a reference to the last element
begin()	Returns a random-access iterator that points to the sequence's first element
clear()	Removes all elements from the list
const_iterator	Object type for a constant random-access iterator
const_pointer	A synonym for A as a const_pointer
const_reference	Refers to an element reference
const_reverse_iterator	Object type for a constant reverse iterator
difference_type	A value that can represent the difference between two element addresses
empty()	Returns true if the sequence is empty
end()	Returns a random-access iterator that points to the next element beyond the end of the sequence
erase()	Erases an element
front()	Returns a reference to the first element
get_allocator()	Returns the allocator
iterator	Object type for a random-access iterator
max_size()	Returns the maximum possible size of a sequence
pop_back()	Removes an element from the end of the list
pop_front()	Removes an element from the front of the list
push_back()	Adds an element to the end of the list
push_front()	Adds an element to the front of the list
rbegin()	Returns a reverse iterator that points to the next element beyond the end of the sequence
reference	A synonym for A as an element reference
rend()	Returns a reverse iterator that points to the sequence's first element
resize()	Resizes the sequence
reverse_iterator	Object type for a reverse iterator
size()	Returns the length of the sequence
size_type	An unsigned integer used to represent the length of the list
swap()	Swaps one sequence with another
value_type	A synonym for the template's A parameter

CROSS-REFERENCE
See also list and vector.

Deriving a Class

Concept

Deriving a class is the process of using object-oriented programming (OOP) inheritance to create a customized class from a pre-existing base class. For example, consider the following class declaration and definition:

```
class MyClass
{
protected:
    int value;

public:
    MyClass(int val);
    ~MyClass();
    void SetValue(int val);
    int GetValue();
};

MyClass::MyClass(int val)
{
    value = val;
}

MyClass::~MyClass()
{
}

void MyClass::SetValue(int val)
{
    value = val;
}

int MyClass::GetValue()
{
    return value;
}
```

If you wanted to create a new version of the `MyClass` class that has an additional data member named `value2`, as well as the member functions required to set and get the value of `value2`, you could derive this new class directly from `MyClass`, as follows:

```
class MyCustomClass : public MyClass
{
protected:
    int value2;

public:
    MyCustomClass(int val1, int val2);
    ~MyCustomClass();
    void SetValue2(int val);
    int GetValue2();
};

MyCustomClass::MyCustomClass(int val1, int val2) :
    MyClass(val1)
{
    value2 = val2;
}

MyCustomClass::~MyCustomClass()
{
}

void MyCustomClass::SetValue2(int val)
{
    value2 = val;
}

int MyCustomClass::GetValue2()
{
    return value2;
}
```

CROSS-REFERENCE
See also Inheritance.

Destructor

Technique

A *destructor* is a special member function in a class that performs cleanup tasks for an instance (also called an object) of a class. The destructor is called automatically when a program deletes the object from memory. For example, take a look at the following class, as found in the MyClass.h header file and the MyClass.cpp implementation file:

Header File

```
class MyClass
{
protected:
    int value;

public:
    MyClass();
    MyClass(int val);
    ~MyClass();

    void SetValue(int val);
    int GetValue();
};
```

Implementation File

```
#include "stdafx.h"
#include "MyClass.h"
#include <iostream>

using namespace std;

MyClass::MyClass()
{
    value = 0;
}

MyClass::MyClass(int val)
{
    value = val;
}

MyClass::~MyClass()
{
    cout << "Destructor called" << endl;
```

```
    }

    int MyClass::GetValue()
    {
        return value;
    }

    void MyClass::SetValue(int val)
    {
        value = val;
    }
```

The class's destructor is easy to spot because it has the same name as the class, prefaced by a tilde (~). The following program demonstrates how to construct objects of the MyClass class in a program, and how to call the object's member functions to manipulate the value data member. When the MyClass objects are deleted from memory, their destructors display the message "Destructor called". The program's output looks like the following:

```
Value = 0
Value = 25
Value = 55
Value = 99
Destructor called
Destructor called
Press any key to continue
```

Here is the program source code that produced the output. In this case, the MyClass objects' destructors are called when they go out of scope in the main() function.

```
#include "stdafx.h"
#include <iostream>
#include "MyClass.h"

using namespace std;

int main(int argc, char* argv[])
{
    MyClass myClass1;
    MyClass myClass2(25);

    int val = myClass1.GetValue();
    cout << "Value = " << val << endl;
    val = myClass2.GetValue();
    cout << "Value = " << val << endl;
```

```
myClass1.SetValue(55);
myClass2.SetValue(99);

val = myClass1.GetValue();
cout << "Value = " << val << endl;
val = myClass2.GetValue();
cout << "Value = " << val << endl;

return 0;
}
```

CROSS-REFERENCE
See also Constructor and Creating a Class.

difftime()

Function

The `difftime()` function returns the difference in seconds between two times.

Header File

```
#include <time.h>
```

Declaration

```
double difftime(time_t timer1, time_t timer0);
```

- *timer0* — The time to subtract from `timer1`.
- *timer1* — The time from which to subtract `timer0`.

Example

The following program demonstrates how to use the `difftime()` function. When run, the program displays 20,000 numbers on the screen and then computes and displays how long in seconds it took to display the numbers. The program's output looks something like the following:

```
Starting a loop...
196461964719648196491965019651196521965319654196551965619657 19
```

```
19662196631966419665196661966719668196691967019671196721967319
19678196791968019681196821968319684196851968619687196881968919
19694196951969619697196981969919700197011970219703197041970519
19710197111971219713197141971519716197171971819719197201972119
19726197271972819729197301973119732197331973419735197361973719
19742197431974419745197461974719748197491975019751197521975319
19758197591976019761197621976319764197651976619767197681976919
19774197751977619777197781977919780197811978219783197841978519
19790197911979219793197941979519796197971979819799198001980119
19806198071980819809198101981119812198131981419815198161981719
19822198231982419825198261982719828198291983019831198321983319
19838198391984019841198421984319844198451984619847198481984919
19854198551985619857198581985919860198611986219863198641986519
19870198711987219873198741987519876198771987819879198801988119
19886198871988819889198901989119892198931989419895198961989199
9819999Loop finished...
Time in seconds: 6
Press any key to continue
```

Here is the program source code that produced the output:

```cpp
#include "stdafx.h"
#include <iostream>
#include <time.h>

using namespace std;

int main(int argc, char* argv[])
{
    cout << "Starting a loop..." << endl;
    time_t begin;
    time(&begin);

    for (int x=0; x<20000; ++x)
        cout << x;

    time_t end;
    time(&end);
    cout << "Loop finished." << endl;

    double elapsed = difftime(end, begin);
    cout << "Time in seconds: " << elapsed << endl;

    return 0;
}
```

CROSS-REFERENCE
See also clock() and time().

div()

Function

The div() performs a division and returns the quotient and remainder in a div_t structure.

Header File

```
#include <stdlib.h>
```

Declaration

```
div_t div(int numer, int denom);
```

- *denom* — The value by which numer should be divided.
- *numer* — The value to be divided by denom.

Example

The following program demonstrates how to use the div() function. When run, the program calls the div() function to perform a division and displays the results. The program's output looks like the following:

```
Quotient: 4
Remainder: 1
Press any key to continue
```

Here is the program source code that produced the output:

```cpp
#include "stdafx.h"
#include <iostream>
#include <stdlib.h>

using namespace std;

int main(int argc, char* argv[])
{
    int val1 = 21;
    int val2 = 5;
```

```
        div_t result = div(val1, val2);
        cout << "Quotient: " << result.quot << endl;
        cout << "Remainder: " << result.rem << endl;

        return 0;
}
```

CROSS-REFERENCE
See also _cabs(), _cabsl(), _hypot(), abs(), acos(), asin(), atan(), atan2(), ceil(), cos(), cosh(), exp(), fabs(), fabsl(), floor(), fmod(), frexp(), labs(), ldexp(), ldexpl(), ldiv(), log(), log10(), pow(), sin(), sinh(), sqrt(), tan(), and tanh().

do

Keyword

The do keyword is part of a do-while loop. A do-while loop loops a specified number of times, evaluating the loop-control expression at the end of each loop. Because the loop-control expression is evaluated at the end of the loop, a do-while loop is, unlike a while loop, guaranteed to execute at least once. The following program gives an example of a do loop. The program's output looks like the following:

```
x = 0
x = 1
x = 2
x = 3
x = 4
x = 5
x = 6
x = 7
x = 8
x = 9
Press any key to continue
```

Here is the program source code that produced the output:

```
#include "stdafx.h"
#include <iostream>

using namespace std;

int main(int argc, char* argv[])
```

```
    {
        int x = 0;

        do
        {
            cout << "x = " << x << endl;
            ++x;
        }
        while (x < 10);

        return 0;
    }
```

CROSS-REFERENCE
See also while.

double

Keyword

The `double` keyword is used to declare double-precision floating-point values. For example, the following line defines a variable of the `double` type:

```
double var1 = 2345.989465;
```

CROSS-REFERENCE
See also float.

dup()

Function

The `dup()` function creates a duplicate handle for an open file. A return value of −1 indicates an error.

Header File

```
#include <io.h>
```

Declaration

```
int dup(int fileHandle);
```

■ *fileHandle* — The file handle to duplicate.

Example

The following program demonstrates how to use the dup() function. When run, the program creates a file in read-and-write mode, writes a string to the file, duplicates the file handle, writes another string using the new file handle, and then closes the file, displaying appropriate messages as it goes. The program's output looks like the following:

```
File created successfully.
File closed successfully.
Press any key to continue
```

Here is the program source code that produced the output:

```cpp
#include "stdafx.h"
#include <sys\stat.h>
#include <io.h>
#include <iostream>

using namespace std;

int main(int argc, char* argv[])
{
    char* buf1 = "ABCDEFGHIJ";
    char* buf2 = "1234567980";

    int fileHandle = creat("test.dat", S_IREAD | S_IWRITE);

    if (fileHandle != -1)
    {
        cout << "File created successfully." << endl;
        write(fileHandle, buf1, 10);
        int newHandle = dup(fileHandle);
        write(newHandle, buf2, 10);
        int result = close(newHandle);
        if (result == 0)
            cout << "File closed successfully." << endl;
        else
            cout << "File close error." << endl;
    }
```

```
        else
            cout << "File create error." << endl;

        return 0;
    }
```

CROSS-REFERENCE
See also _dup().

dynamic_cast

Keyword

The `dynamic_cast` operator defined by RTTI enables a program to determine at runtime what type of object is represented by a pointer or reference, and perform any necessary conversions between pointers. For example, the following line downcasts a base class pointer to a pointer to a class derived from the base class.

```
MyDerivedClass* pObj =
    dynamic_cast<MyDerivedClass*>(myClass);
```

CROSS-REFERENCE
See also Dynamic Casting and Polymorphism.

Dynamic Casting

Technique

Run-Time Type Information (RTTI), which includes dynamic casting, enables programmers to get information about objects at runtime. In the case of dynamic casting, the `dynamic_cast` operator defined by RTTI enables a program to determine at runtime what type of object is represented by a pointer or reference. This determination can be a critical task when dealing with polymorphic objects.

Dynamic downcasting converts a base-class pointer to a pointer to a class derived from the base class. An example might be the following:

```
ObjType* pObj = dynamic_cast<ObjType*>(Pointer);
```

Here, `ObjType` is the type to which the object should be cast, and `Pointer` is a pointer to the object to be downcast. If the downcast fails, the `dynamic_cast` operator returns 0.

For example, say that you've written a base class called `MyClass` and a class derived from `MyClass` called `MyDerivedClass`. Using polymorphism, the program gets a pointer to `MyDerivedClass` as follows:

```
MyClass* myDerivedClass = new MyDerivedClass;
```

Although the program creates a `MyDerivedClass` object, the pointer is to a `MyClass` object, which is an object of the base class, `MyClass`. The program can safely downcast the `MyClass` pointer to a `MyDerivedClass` pointer as follows:

```
MyDerivedClass* pObj =
    dynamic_cast<MyDerivedClass*>(myDerivedClass);
```

A Working Example

Now, how about a more complex example that actually runs? The following source code listings define a class called `MyClass`, which contains two virtual functions, `GetValue()` and `SetValue()`:

The Header File

```
#ifndef __MYCLASS
#define __MYCLASS

class MyClass
{
protected:
    int value;

public:
    MyClass();
    MyClass(int val);
    ~MyClass();

    virtual void SetValue(int val);
    virtual int GetValue();
};

#endif
```

The Implementation File

```
#include "stdafx.h"
#include <iostream>
#include "MyClass.h"
```

```
using namespace std;

MyClass::MyClass()
{
    value = 0;
}

MyClass::MyClass(int val)
{
    value = val;
}

MyClass::~MyClass()
{
}

int MyClass::GetValue()
{
    cout << "In MyClass.GetValue()" << endl;
    return value;
}

void MyClass::SetValue(int val)
{
    cout << "In MyClass.SetValue()" << endl;
    value = val;
}
```

The following listings show the source code for a class called MyDerivedClass that is derived from MyClass and supplies its own versions of the virtual functions GetValue() and SetValue():

The Header File

```
#ifndef __MYDERIVEDCLASS
#define __MYDERIVEDCLASS

#include "MyClass.h"

class MyDerivedClass: public MyClass
{
public:
    MyDerivedClass();
    MyDerivedClass(int val);
    ~MyDerivedClass();
```

```
        void SetValue(int val);
        int GetValue();
};

#endif
```

The Implementation File

```
#include "stdafx.h"
#include <iostream>
#include "MyDerivedClass.h"

using namespace std;

MyDerivedClass::MyDerivedClass() : MyClass(0)
{
}


MyDerivedClass::MyDerivedClass(int val) : MyClass(val)
{
}


MyDerivedClass::~MyDerivedClass()
{
}


int MyDerivedClass::GetValue()
{
    cout << "In MyDerivedClass.GetValue()" << endl;
    return value;
}


void MyDerivedClass::SetValue(int val)
{
    cout << "In MyDerivedClass.SetValue()" << endl;
    value = val;
}
```

Finally, the next listing is a program that tests the two classes:

```
#include "stdafx.h"
#include "MyClass.h"
#include "MyDerivedClass.h"
#include <iostream>

using namespace std;
```

```
int main(int argc, char* argv[])
{
    MyClass* myClass = new MyClass(10);
    MyClass* myDerivedClass = new MyDerivedClass(20);

    int val = myClass->GetValue();
    cout << "value = " << val << endl;
    myClass->SetValue(30);
    val = myClass->GetValue();
    cout << "value = " << val << endl;

    cout << endl;

    val = myDerivedClass->GetValue();
    cout << "value = " << val << endl;
    myDerivedClass->SetValue(40);
    val = myDerivedClass->GetValue();
    cout << "value = " << val << endl;

    delete myClass;
    delete myDerivedClass;

    return 0;
}
```

This program creates an object from each class, with both pointers being of the MyClass type. Although both pointers are of the MyClass type, when each object calls its GetValue() and SetValue() functions, the appropriate versions of the functions are called for the object type. This situation is polymorphism working right before your eyes. The program's output looks like the following:

```
In MyClass.GetValue()
value = 10
In MyClass.SetValue()
In MyClass.GetValue()
value = 30

In MyDerivedClass.GetValue()
value = 20
In MyDerivedClass.SetValue()
In MyDerivedClass.GetValue()
value = 40
Press any key to continue
```

As you can see from the output, even though both myClass and myDerivedClass are pointers of the MyClass type, the program knows which version of the virtual functions GetValue() and SetValue() to call.

Overridden Instead of Virtual

Now, what if you change the declaration of GetValue() in the base class so that it is no longer a virtual function. The header file would then look like the following:

```
#ifndef __MYCLASS
#define __MYCLASS

class MyClass
{
protected:
    int value;

public:
    MyClass();
    MyClass(int val);
    ~MyClass();

    virtual void SetValue(int val);
    int GetValue();
};

#endif
```

When you run the test program now, you get the following output:

```
In MyClass.GetValue()
value = 10
In MyClass.SetValue()
In MyClass.GetValue()
value = 30

In MyClass.GetValue()
value = 20
In MyDerivedClass.SetValue()
In MyClass.GetValue()
value = 40
Press any key to continue
```

Notice that the MyDerivedClass version of GetValue() is never called. That's all well and good because that's the way you'd expect a call to GetValue() on a MyClass pointer to work. But what if you have overridden

GetValue() in the derived class (as you have) and want that overridden version to be called rather than the base class's version? Now, you have trouble.

The solution is to downcast the class pointers when you need to be sure that the derived class's version of the function is called rather than the base class's version. The following program demonstrates how this technique works:

```
#include "stdafx.h"
#include "MyClass.h"
#include "MyDerivedClass.h"
#include <iostream>

using namespace std;

int main(int argc, char* argv[])
{
    MyClass* myClass = new MyClass(10);
    MyClass* myDerivedClass = new MyDerivedClass(20);

    int val = myClass->GetValue();
    cout << "value = " << val << endl;
    myClass->SetValue(30);
    val = myClass->GetValue();
    cout << "value = " << val << endl;

    cout << endl;

    MyDerivedClass* ptr =
        dynamic_cast<MyDerivedClass*>(myDerivedClass);

    val = ptr->GetValue();
    cout << "value = " << val << endl;
    ptr->SetValue(40);
    val = ptr->GetValue();
    cout << "value = " << val << endl;

    delete myClass;
    delete myDerivedClass;

    return 0;
}
```

Notice how the myDerivedClass pointer is downcast before it is used. The program uses the new downcast version of the pointer, called ptr, to call the object's member functions. Now, the program always calls the correct version of the GetValue() member function, as shown in the following output:

```
In MyClass.GetValue()
value = 10
In MyClass.SetValue()
In MyClass.GetValue()
value = 30

In MyDerivedClass.GetValue()
value = 20
In MyDerivedClass.SetValue()
In MyDerivedClass.GetValue()
value = 40
Press any key to continue
```

What's the Point?

It may seem a little silly to define the myDerivedClass pointer as a pointer to MyClass in the first place. Why not define myDerivedClass as a pointer to MyDerivedClass and be done with it? The answer is that it isn't always that simple. Suppose, for example, your program was storing pointers to objects in an array. Because all of the elements of the array have to be the same type, you decide to make each element a pointer to MyClass. The following program demonstrates how dynamic downcasting can help you in this situation:

```
#include "stdafx.h"
#include "MyClass.h"
#include "MyDerivedClass.h"
#include <iostream>

using namespace std;

int main(int argc, char* argv[])
{
    int x;

    MyClass* objPtrs[3];
    objPtrs[0] = new MyClass(10);
    objPtrs[1] = new MyDerivedClass(20);
    objPtrs[2] = new MyClass(30);

    cout << "***** No Downcasting *****" << endl;
    for (x=0; x<3; ++x)
    {
```

```
        int val = objPtrs[x]->GetValue();
        cout << "value = " << val << endl;
    }

    cout << endl << "***** With Downcasting *****" << endl;
    for (x=0; x<3; ++x)
    {
        MyDerivedClass* ptr =
            dynamic_cast<MyDerivedClass*>(objPtrs[x]);

        if (ptr)
        {
            int val = ptr->GetValue();
            cout << "value = " << val << endl;
        }
        else
        {
            int val = objPtrs[x]->GetValue();
            cout << "value = " << val << endl;
        }

        delete objPtrs[x];
    }


    return 0;
}
```

This program first fills an array with pointers of the type `MyClass`. However, one of those pointers, the second, is actually a pointer to an object of the derived class, `MyDerivedClass`. In the first `for` loop, the program calls the non-virtual `GetValue()` function on behalf of each of the pointers in the array. Because all the array elements are defined as pointers to `MyClass`, the program calls only the `MyClass` version of `GetValue()`.

In the second `for` loop, the program uses dynamic downcasting to determine exactly what type of pointer with which it's currently working. If the downcast is successful, the program has a pointer to a `MyDerivedClass` object and uses the downcast pointer, `ptr`, to call `GetValue()`. If the downcast fails and returns 0, the program has a pointer to a `MyClass` object, and so uses the pointer in the array to call `GetValue()`. The program's output looks like the following:

```
***** No Downcasting *****
In MyClass.GetValue()
value = 10
```

```
In MyClass.GetValue()
value = 20
In MyClass.GetValue()
value = 30

***** With Downcasting *****
In MyClass.GetValue()
value = 10
In MyDerivedClass.GetValue()
value = 20
In MyClass.GetValue()
value = 30
Press any key to continue
```

With Visual C++, in order to use RTTI in your program, you must first turn it on. To do this, press Alt+F7 to bring up the Project Settings property sheet. Then, go to the C/C++ tab, select C++ Language in the Category box, and select the Enable Run-Time Type Information (RTTI) check box.

CROSS-REFERENCE
See also Creating a Class, Polymorphism, and Virtual Functions.

#elif

Directive

The #elif directive provides an "else if" type of branch for conditional compilation. The following example of the #elif directive, along with the #if and #endif directives, prints a message depending on whether the symbol DEBUG has been defined. The program's output looks like the following:

```
Debugging is off.
Press any key to continue
```

Here is the program source code that produced the output:

```cpp
#include "stdafx.h"
#include <iostream>

#define DEBUG 0

using namespace std;

int main(int argc, char* argv[])
{
#if DEBUG == 1
    cout << "Debugging is on." << endl;
#elif DEBUG == 0
    cout << "Debugging is off." << endl;
#endif

    return 0;
}
```

CROSS-REFERENCE

See also #else, #endif, #if, #ifdef, and #ifndef.

#else

Directive

The #else directive provides an "else" type of branch for conditional compilation. The following example of the #else directive, along with the #if and #endif directives, prints a message depending on whether the symbol DEBUG has been defined. The program's output looks like the following:

```
Debugging is off.
Press any key to continue
```

Here is the program source code that produced the output:

```
#include "stdafx.h"
#include <iostream>

#define DEBUG 0

using namespace std;

int main(int argc, char* argv[])
{
#if DEBUG
     cout << "Debugging is on." << endl;
#else
     cout << "Debugging is off." << endl;
#endif

     return 0;
}
```

CROSS-REFERENCE
See also #elif, #endif, #if, #ifdef, and #ifndef.

#endif

Directive

The #endif directive marks the end of an #if compiler directive. The following example of the #endif directive, along with the #if, #elif, and #else directives, prints a message depending on the value of the symbol COUNT. The program's output looks like the following:

```
COUNT = 10
Press any key to continue
```

Here is the program source code that produced the output:

```
#include "stdafx.h"
#include <iostream>

#define COUNT 10

using namespace std;

int main(int argc, char* argv[])
{
#if COUNT == 5
    cout << "COUNT = 5" << endl;
#elif COUNT == 10
    cout << "COUNT = 10" << endl;
#else
    cout << "COUNT = ?" << endl;
#endif

    return 0;
}
```

CROSS-REFERENCE
See also #elif, #else, #if, #ifdef, and #ifndef.

#error

Directive

The #error directive displays error messages during compilation. The following example of the #error directive, along with the #if and #endif directives, prints an error message if the symbol VALUE equals 10. The compiler produces the following error:

```
fatal error C1189: #error :   "Value cannot be 10"
```

Here is the program source code that produced the error:

```
#include "stdafx.h"
#include <iostream>

#define VALUE 10
```

```
using namespace std;

int main(int argc, char* argv[])
{
#if VALUE == 10
#error "Value cannot be 10"
#endif

    return 0;
}
```

CROSS-REFERENCE
See also #elif, #else, #endif, #if, #ifdef, and #ifndef.

_ecvt()

Function

The _ecvt() function converts a double floating-point value to a string of digits.

Header File

```
#include <stdlib.h>
```

Declaration

```
char* _ecvt(double value, int count,
    int* decPosition, int* sign);
```

- *count* — The number of digits to return.
- *decPosition* — A pointer to an integer that will receive the position of the decimal point.
- *sign* — A pointer to an integer that will receive the value's sign, where 0 specifies a positive value and any other value specifies negative.
- *value* — The value to convert.

Example

The following program demonstrates how to use the _ecvt() function. When run, the program converts a value to a string of digits, and then displays the converted value along with its decimal-position and sign values. The program's output looks like the following:

```
Buffer: 24358756
Decimal position: 4
Sign: 0
Press any key to continue
```

Here is the program source code that produced the error:

```cpp
#include "stdafx.h"
#include <iostream>
#include <stdlib.h>

using namespace std;

int main(int argc, char* argv[])
{
    int decPosition;
    int sign;

    char* buf = _ecvt(2435.87564, 8, &decPosition, &sign);
    cout << "Buffer: " << buf << endl;
    cout << "Decimal position: " << decPosition << endl;
    cout << "Sign: " << sign << endl;

    return 0;
}
```

CROSS-REFERENCE
See also _fcvt(), _gcvt(), atof(), and ecvt().

_exit()

Function

The _exit() function performs the fast cleanup tasks associated with a process and then terminates the process. That is, unlike the exit() function, _exit() does not flush and close buffers and streams, or call the functions registered on behalf of the process by the atexit() and _onexit() functions.

Header File

```
#include <process.h>
```

Declaration

```
void _exit(int status);
```

- *status* — A value that indicates the status of the terminating process.

Example

The following program demonstrates how to use the _exit() function. When run, the program displays a message, after which the _exit() function terminates the process. The program's output looks like the following:

```
About to exit process.
Press any key to continue

Press any key to continue
```

Here is the source code that produced the output:

```cpp
#include "stdafx.h"
#include <iostream>
#include <process.h>

using namespace std;

int main(int argc, char* argv[])
{
    cout << "About to exit process." << endl;
    cout << "Press any key to continue" << endl;
    getchar();
    _exit(0);

    return 0;
}
```

 CROSS-REFERENCE
See also _c_exit(), _cexit(), _onexit(), atexit(), and exit().

_expand()

Function

The _expand() function enlarges or reduces the size of a block of allocated memory, without moving the block in memory. The function returns a pointer to the allocated memory if successful, or returns NULL if an error occurs.

Header File

```
#include <malloc.h>
```

Declaration

```
void *_expand(void* memblock, size_t size);
```

- *memblock* — A pointer to the memory block that should be resized.
- *size* — The memory block's requested new size.

Example

The following program demonstrates how to use the _expand() function. When run, the program allocates a block of memory and then resizes the memory block, displaying messages as it goes. The program's output looks like the following:

```
1024 bytes allocated.
Memory allocation reduced.
Press any key to continue
```

Here is the program source code that produced the output:

```
#include "stdafx.h"
#include <iostream>
#include <malloc.h>

using namespace std;

int main(int argc, char* argv[])
{
    char* buf = (char *)calloc(1024, sizeof(char));

    if (buf != NULL )
    {
```

```
                cout << "1024 bytes allocated." << endl;
                buf = (char *) _expand(buf, 246);

                if (buf != NULL )
                    cout << "Memory allocation reduced." << endl;
                else
                    cout << "Expansion error." << endl;

                free(buf);
            }
        else
            cout << "Allocation error." << endl;

        return 0;
    }
```

CROSS-REFERENCE
See also _msize() and realloc().

ecvt()

Function

The ecvt() function converts a double floating-point value to a string of digits.

Header File

```
#include <stdlib.h>
```

Declaration

```
char* ecvt(double value, int count,
    int* decPosition, int* sign);
```

- *count* — The number of digits to return.
- *decPosition* — A pointer to an integer that will receive the position of the decimal point.

- *sign*—A pointer to an integer that will receive the value's sign, where 0 specifies a positive value and any other value specifies negative.
- *value*—The value to convert.

Example

The following program demonstrates how to use the `ecvt()` function. When run, the program converts a value to a string of digits, and then displays the converted value along with its decimal-position and sign values. The program's output looks like the following:

```
Buffer: 24358756
Decimal position: 4
Sign: 0
Press any key to continue
```

Here is the source code that produced the output:

```cpp
#include "stdafx.h"
#include <iostream>
#include <stdlib.h>

using namespace std;

int main(int argc, char* argv[])
{
    int decPosition;
    int sign;

    char* buf = _ecvt(2435.87564, 8, &decPosition, &sign);
    cout << "Buffer: " << buf << endl;
    cout << "Decimal position: " << decPosition << endl;
    cout << "Sign: " << sign << endl;

    return 0;
}
```

CROSS-REFERENCE
See also _ecvt(),_fcvt(), _gcvt(), and atof().

else

Keyword

The else keyword is part of an if statement, enabling program execution to branch based on the value of a specified expression if the if portion of the statement evaluates to false. For example, the following program prints the message "x = 10" because both the if and else if clauses evaluate to false, causing the default else clause to execute. The program's output looks like the following:

```
x = 10
Press any key to continue
```

Here is the program source code that produced the output:

```cpp
#include "stdafx.h"
#include <iostream>

using namespace std;

int main(int argc, char* argv[])
{
    int x = 10;

    if (x == 15)
        cout << "x = 15" << endl;
    else if (x == 20)
        cout << "x = 20" << endl;
    else
        cout << "x = " << x << endl;

    return 0;
}
```

CROSS-REFERENCE
See also else if and if.

else if

Keyword

The else if keyword is part of an if statement, enabling program execution to evaluate subsequent expressions if the if portion of the statement evaluates to false. For example, the following program prints the message "x = 10" because both the if and else if clauses evaluate to false, causing the default else clause to execute. The program's output looks like the following:

```
x = 30
Press any key to continue
```

Here is the source code that produced the output:

```
#include "stdafx.h"
#include <iostream>

using namespace std;

int main(int argc, char* argv[])
{
    int x = 30;

    if (x == 15)
        cout << "x = 15" << endl;
    else if (x == 20)
        cout << "x = 20" << endl;
    else if (x == 30)
        cout << "x = 30" << endl;
    else if (x == 40)
        cout << "x = 40" << endl;
    else
        cout << "x = " << x << endl;

    return 0;
}
```

CROSS-REFERENCE
See also else and if.

Encapsulation

Technique

Encapsulation is a feature of object-oriented programming (OOP) that enables a program to specify that data and functions are to be part of a class. That is, a class encapsulates (encloses) its data members and member functions, creating another layer of scope in which to define variables and functions. In the following sections, you learn to use encapsulation.

Data Hiding

One of the most useful results of encapsulation is the ability to hide variables and functions from the main program, providing an interface for accessing protected parts of the class indirectly. For example, consider the following class declaration:

```
class MyClass
{
protected:
    int value;

public:
    MyClass();
    MyClass(int val);
    ~MyClass();

    int GetValue();
    void SetValue(int val);
};
```

The data member `value` is declared as `protected`, which prevents any code outside the class from accessing the variable directly. Instead, a program can access `value` by calling one of the two public member functions, `GetValue()` or `SetValue()`. The class's implementation looks like the following:

Implementation File

```
#include "stdafx.h"
#include "MyClass.h"

MyClass::MyClass()
{
    value = 0;
}

MyClass::MyClass(int val)
{
    value = val;
}

MyClass::~MyClass()
{
}

int MyClass::GetValue()
{
```

```
    return value;
}

void MyClass::SetValue(int val)
{
    value = val;
}
```

Using encapsulation in this way, you can protect the inner workings of your class from unwanted intrusion, as well as make the class easier to maintain. For example, notice how the MyClass constructor and member functions manage any integer values coming into the class, assigning them directly to the integer data member, value. The following program puts the class to the test. The program's output looks like the following:

```
value = 20
Press any key to continue
```

Here is the program source code that produced the output:

```
#include "stdafx.h"
#include <iostream>
#include "MyClass.h"

using namespace std;

int main(int argc, char* argv[])
{
    MyClass myClass(20);
    int val = myClass.GetValue();
    cout << "value = " << val << endl;

    return 0;
}
```

Safe Modification of the Class

Suppose now you wanted to change the class so that the value data member was a string rather than an integer. If you had allowed programs to get direct access to value, you'd not only have to change the class, but also every program that uses the class—a bit of nasty business. However, because you cleverly declared value as protected and provided an interface for accessing value indirectly, all you need to change is the class. The header file for the class now looks like the following:

Header File
```
class MyClass
{
protected:
    char value[81];

public:
    MyClass();
    MyClass(int val);
    ~MyClass();

    int GetValue();
    void SetValue(int val);
};
```

Here, the only difference between this class declaration and the original is that value is now declared as an 81-character string rather than an integer. The public parts of the class (the class's interface) have not changed. The implementation file for the class now looks like the following:

Implementation File
```
#include "stdafx.h"
#include <stdlib.h>
#include <string.h>
#include "MyClass.h"

MyClass::MyClass()
{
    strcpy(value, "0");
}

MyClass::MyClass(int val)
{
    itoa(val, value, 10);
}

MyClass::~MyClass()
{
}

int MyClass::GetValue()
{
    int val = atoi(value);
    return val;
}
```

```
void MyClass::SetValue(int val)
{
    itoa(val, value, 10);
}
```

Even though the class's implementation has changed drastically, any program that used the original version of the class will still run properly with the new version, because none of the class's public members are accessed differently from the original. That is, the class's interface is exactly the same. Running the program with the modified class produces the following output:

```
value = 20
Press any key to continue
```

Notice that this output is exactly the same as the output from the original version of the program.

CROSS-REFERENCE

See also Creating a Class, private, protected, and public.

endl

Manipulator

The `endl` manipulator is used with the `cout` and `cin` I/O objects to append a carriage return/line feed (CR/LF) pair to the end of a line of data. For example, the following program prints three lines of text, each followed by a CR/LF. The program's output looks like the following:

```
This is line #1
This is line #2
This is line #3

Press any key to continue
```

Here is the program source code that produced the output:

```
#include "stdafx.h"
#include <iostream>

using namespace std;

int main(int argc, char* argv[])
{
    cout << "This is line #1" << endl;
```

```
        cout << "This is line #2" << endl;
        cout << "This is line #3" << endl << endl;

        return 0;
}
```

CROSS-REFERENCE
See also dec, hex, and oct.

enum

Keyword

The enum keyword is used to define an enumeration, which is a set of constants with ascending values. For example, the following program defines an enumeration for the values 0 through 5. C++ automatically assigns 0 to the first symbol in the enumeration (Zero), 1 to the second (One), and so forth. The program's output looks like the following:

```
Zero = 0
One = 1
Two = 2
Three = 3
Four = 4
Five = 5
result = 6
Press any key to continue
```

Here is the program source code that produced the output:

```
#include "stdafx.h"
#include <iostream>

using namespace std;

enum
{
    Zero,
    One,
    Two,
    Three,
    Four,
    Five
```

```
    };

    int main(int argc, char* argv[])
    {
        cout << "Zero = " << Zero << endl;
        cout << "One = " << One << endl;
        cout << "Two = " << Two << endl;
        cout << "Three = " << Three << endl;
        cout << "Four = " << Four << endl;
        cout << "Five = " << Five << endl;

        int result = One * Two * Three;
        cout << "result = " << result << endl;

        return 0;
    }
```

You can change the default assignments made to the symbols in an enumeration by assigning one or more values explicitly. For example, the following enumeration assigns the values 1 through 5 to the five symbols, One, Two, Three, Four, and Five, respectively:

```
    enum
    {
        One = 1,
        Two,
        Three,
        Four,
        Five
    };
```

You can even have the automatic assignments jump over values by assigning an explicit value in the middle of an enumeration. The following example defines five constants with the values 1, 2, 10, 11, and 12:

```
    enum
    {
        One = 1,
        Two,
        Ten = 10,
        Eleven,
        Twelve
    };
```

CROSS-REFERENCE
See also struct.

eof()

Function

The eof() function returns 1 if the associated file is at end-of-file. Otherwise, the function returns 0 if not at end-of-file or –1 for an error.

Header File

```
#include <io.h>
```

Declaration

```
int eof(int handle)
```

- *handle* — The file handle for the file to check for end-of-file.

Example

The following program demonstrates how to use the eof() function. When run, the program opens its own source code file and reads the contents. The while loop that reads the file ends when the eof() function returns 1. If the program reads the file successfully, it displays the message "File read successfully". The program's output looks like the following:

```
File read successfully
Press any key to continue
```

Here is the program source code that produced the output:

```cpp
#include "stdafx.h"
#include <iostream>
#include <io.h>
#include <fcntl.h>

using namespace std;

int main(int argc, char* argv[])
{
    char buf[20];

    int fileHandle = open( "eof.cpp", O_RDONLY );
    if (fileHandle == - 1)
        cout << "Couldn't open file." << endl;
    else
```

```
    {
        while(!eof(fileHandle))
        {
            int count = read(fileHandle, buf, 20);
            if (count == -1)
            {
                cout << "File read error." << endl;
                exit(1);
            }
        }
    }

    close(fileHandle);
    cout << "File read successfully" << endl;

    return 0;
}
```

CROSS-REFERENCE

See also close(), open(), and read().

errno.h

Standard C Library Header File

The error.h header file defines constants that represent the various errors that can be generated by library functions.

Defined Constants

E2BIG	ENFILE
EACCES	ENODEV
EAGAIN	ENOENT
EBADF	ENOEXEC
EBUSY	ENOLCK
ECHILD	ENOMEM
EDEADLK	ENOSPC
EDOM	ENOSYS
EEXIST	ENOTDIR
EFAULT	ENOTEMPTY

EFBIG	ENOTTY
EILSEQ	ENXIO
EINTR	EPERM
EINVAL	EPIPE
EIO	ERANGE
EISDIR	EROFS
EMFILE	ESPIPE
EMLINK	ESRCH
ENAMETOOLONG	EXDEV

exception

Class

The `exception` class is the base class for exceptions thrown in C++ programs. The class is declared as follows:

```
class exception {
public:
    exception() throw();
    exception(const exception& rhs) throw();
    exception& operator=(const exception& rhs) throw();
    virtual ~exception() throw();
    virtual const char *what() const throw();
    };
```

CROSS-REFERENCE
See also catch, Exception Handling, and try.

Exception Handling

Technique

Exceptions provide a structured way to handle runtime errors in a program. When such an error occurs, the program can *throw* an exception, which can be *caught* in another part of the program. The keywords you need in order to perform simple exception handling are `throw`, `try`, and `catch`.

Catching Exceptions

The try keyword marks the beginning of the program block that might cause an exception. If no error occurs, the entire try program block executes as if it weren't enclosed in a try block. If, however, the try program block generates an exception, the catch program block, in which all error handling takes place, captures the exception.

The following program demonstrates how to set up simple exception handling. The program's output looks like the following:

```
Press any key to continue
```

Here is the program source code that produced the output:

```
#include "stdafx.h"
#include <iostream>
#include <malloc.h>

using namespace std;

int main(int argc, char* argv[])
{
    char* buf;
    char* errorMsg[] =
    {
        "Exception generated."
    };

    try
    {
        buf = (char*)calloc(256, sizeof(char));
        if (buf == NULL)
            throw *errorMsg;
        else
            free(buf);
    }
    catch (char* exception)
    {
        cout << exception << endl;
    }

    return 0;
}
```

In this program, if the memory allocation in the try program block fails, the block throws an exception, which is caught by the catch program block. If the memory allocation goes okay, the program ignores the `catch` block and program execution proceeds normally.

Throwing Exceptions

Of course, the previous program is a very simple example. Typically, exceptions are thrown by one function and caught by another, as you can see in this new version of the previous program. The program's output looks like the following:

```
Press any key to continue
```

Here is the program source code that produced the output:

```
#include "stdafx.h"
#include <iostream>
#include <malloc.h>

using namespace std;

char* AllocBuf()
{
    char* buf;
    char* errorMsg[] =
    {
        "Exception generated."
    };

    buf = (char*)calloc(256, sizeof(char));
    if (buf == NULL)
        throw *errorMsg;

    return buf;
}

int main(int argc, char* argv[])
{
    char* buf;

    try
    {
        buf = AllocBuf();
        free(buf);
    }
    catch (char* exception)
    {
```

```
        cout << exception << endl;
    }

    return 0;
}
```

In this example, a function called `AllocBuf()` takes care of the memory allocation details, throwing an exception if the memory allocation fails. This exception finds its way back to the `catch` program block in the `main()` function, where the program displays the error message.

Exception Objects

In these examples, the exception object thrown is a string. However, the `throw` statement can send off almost any kind of object, including objects instantiated from a custom exception class. By creating a class for an exception, you can transfer any type of data you like along with the exception. For example, the following program defines an exception class named `MyException` and uses that class to generate exceptions for the main program. The program's output looks like the following:

```
Press any key to continue
```

Here is the program source code that produced the output:

```
#include "stdafx.h"
#include <iostream>
#include <malloc.h>

using namespace std;

class MyException
{
protected:
    char errorMsg[81];

public:
    MyException()
    {
        strcpy(errorMsg, "");
    }

    MyException(char* msg)
    {
        strcpy(errorMsg, msg);
    }
```

```cpp
    ~MyException() {}

    char* GetMsg()
    {
        return errorMsg;
    }

    void SetMsg(char* msg)
    {
        strcpy(errorMsg, msg);
    }
};

char* AllocBuf()
{
    char* buf;

    buf = (char*)calloc(256, sizeof(char));
    if (buf == NULL)
    {
        MyException* exp = new MyException;
        exp->SetMsg("Memory allocation error");
        throw exp;
    }

    return buf;
}

int main(int argc, char* argv[])
{
    char* buf;

    try
    {
        buf = AllocBuf();
        free(buf);
    }
    catch (MyException* exception)
    {
        cout << exception->GetMsg() << endl;
    }
```

```
        return 0;
    }
```

CROSS-REFERENCE
See also catch, throw, and try.

execl()

Function

The execl() function runs a child process given the process's path and name and additional arguments. This function does not return to the process that called it. If the called process does not run successfully, the function returns −1. In this case, the errno global variable will be set to one of the error values in Table E-1:

Table E-1 Error Values for execl()

Value	Description
E2BIG	The arguments and environment require more than 32K of space.
EACCES	There has been a sharing or locking violation.
EMFILE	Too many files are open.
ENOENT	The specified file cannot be found.
ENOEXEC	The specified file is not executable.
ENOMEM	Not enough memory to run the process.

Header File

```
#include <process.h>
```

Declaration

```
int execl(const char *cmdname,
    const char *arg0, ... const char *argn, NULL);
```

- *arg0* — A pointer to the first argument.
- *argn* — A pointer to the last argument.
- *cmdname* — The path and file name of the process to run.

Example

The following program demonstrates how to use the execl() function. When run, the program runs a process called TestProg.exe, displaying a message if an error occurs. The program's output looks like the following:

```
Running TestProg.exe
Press any key to continue
Child process running.
```

Here is the program source code that produced the output:

```cpp
#include "stdafx.h"
#include <iostream>
#include <process.h>
#include <errno.h>

using namespace std;

int main(int argc, char* argv[])
{
    cout << "Running TestProg.exe" << endl;

    int result = execl("TestProg.exe", "TestProg.exe",
        "arg2", "arg3", NULL);
    if (result == -1)
    {
        switch(errno)
        {
        case ENOEXEC:
            cout << "Not an executable file" << endl;
            break;
        case E2BIG:
            cout << "Space required exceeds 32K" << endl;
            break;
        case ENOMEM:
            cout << "Not enough memory" << endl;
            break;
        case EMFILE:
            cout << "Too many files open" << endl;
            break;
        case EACCES:
            cout << "Locking or sharing violation" << endl;
            break;
```

```
        case ENOENT:
            cout << "File not found" << endl;
        }
    }

    return 0;
}
```

CROSS-REFERENCE

See also _wexecl(), _wexecle(), _wexeclp(), _wexeclpe(), _wexecv(), _wexecve(), _wexecvp(), _wexecvpe(), _wspawnl(), _wspawnle(), _wspawnlp(), _wspawnlpe(), _wspawnv(), _wspawnve(), _wspawnvp(), _wspawnvpe(), execle(), execlp(), execlpe(), execv(), execve(), execvp(), execvpe(), spawnl(), spawnle(), spawnlp(), spawnlpe(), spawnv(), spawnve(), spawnvp(), and spawnvpe().

execle()

Function

The execle() function runs a child process given the process's path and name, additional arguments, and environment settings. This function does not return to the process that called it. If the called process does not run successfully, the function returns –1. In this case, the errno global variable will be set to one of error values in Table E-2:

Table E-2 Error Values for execle()

Value	Description
E2BIG	The arguments and environment require more than 32K of space.
EACCES	There has been a sharing or locking violation.
EMFILE	Too many files are open.
ENOENT	The specified file cannot be found.
ENOEXEC	The specified file is not executable.
ENOMEM	Not enough memory to run the process.

Header File

```
#include <process.h>
```

Declaration

```
int execle(const char *cmdname,
    const char *arg0, ... const char *argn,
    NULL, const char *const *envp)
```

- *arg0* — A pointer to the first argument.
- *argn* — A pointer to the last argument.
- *cmdname* — The path and file name of the process to run.
- *envp* — A pointer to the environment settings.

Example

The following program demonstrates how to use the execle() function. When run, the program runs a process called TestProg.exe, displaying a message if an error occurs. The program's output looks like the following:

```
Running TestProg.exe
Press any key to continue
Child process running.
```

Here is the program source code that produced the output:

```cpp
#include "stdafx.h"
#include <iostream>
#include <process.h>
#include <errno.h>

using namespace std;

char *envir[] =
{
   "ENVIR1=environment setting 1",
   "ENVIR2=environment setting 2",
   "ENVIR3=environment setting 3",
    NULL
};

int main(int argc, char* argv[])
{
    cout << "Running TestProg.exe" << endl;

    int result = execle("TestProg.exe", "TestProg.exe",
        "arg2", "arg3", NULL, envir);
```

```
if (result == -1)
{
    switch(errno)
    {
    case ENOEXEC:
        cout << "Not an executable file" << endl;
        break;
    case E2BIG:
        cout << "Space required exceeds 32K" << endl;
        break;
    case ENOMEM:
        cout << "Not enough memory" << endl;
        break;
    case EMFILE:
        cout << "Too many files open" << endl;
        break;
    case EACCES:
        cout << "Locking or sharing violation" << endl;
        break;
    case ENOENT:
        cout << "File not found" << endl;
    }
}

return 0;
}
```

CROSS-REFERENCE

See also _wexecl(), _wexecle(), _wexeclp(), _wexeclpe(), _wexecv(), _wexecve(), _wexecvp(), _wexecvpe(), _wspawnl(), _wspawnle(), _wspawnlp(), _wspawnlpe(), _wspawnv(), _wspawnve(), _wspawnvp(), _wspawnvpe(), execl(), execlp(), execlpe(), execv(), execve(), execvp(), execvpe(), spawnl(), spawnle(), spawnlp(), spawnlpe(), spawnv(), spawnve(), spawnvp(), and spawnvpe().

execlp()

Function

The execlp() function runs a child process given the process's path and name and additional arguments. This function does not return to the process that called it. If the called process does not run successfully, the function returns −1. In this case, the errno global variable will be set to one of the error values in Table E-3:

Table E-3 Error Values for execlp()

Value	Description
E2BIG	The arguments and environment require more than 32K of space.
EACCES	There has been a sharing or locking violation.
EMFILE	Too many files are open.
ENOENT	The specified file cannot be found.
ENOEXEC	The specified file is not executable.
ENOMEM	Not enough memory to run the process.

Header File

```
#include <process.h>
```

Declaration

```
int execlp(const char *cmdname,
    const char *arg0, ... const char *argn, NULL);
```

- *arg0*—A pointer to the first argument.
- *argn*—A pointer to the last argument.
- *cmdname*—The path and file name of the process to run.

Example

The following program demonstrates how to use the execlp() function. When run, the program runs a process called TestProg.exe, displaying a message if an error occurs. The program's output looks like the following:

```
Running TestProg.exe
Press any key to continue
Child process running.
```

Here is the program source code that produced the output:

```
#include "stdafx.h"
#include <iostream>
#include <process.h>
#include <errno.h>

using namespace std;
```

```cpp
int main(int argc, char* argv[])
{
    cout << "Running TestProg.exe" << endl;

    int result = execlp("TestProg.exe", "TestProg.exe",
        "arg2", "arg3", NULL);
    if (result == -1)
    {
        switch(errno)
        {
        case ENOEXEC:
            cout << "Not an executable file" << endl;
            break;
        case E2BIG:
            cout << "Space required exceeds 32K" << endl;
            break;
        case ENOMEM:
            cout << "Not enough memory" << endl;
            break;
        case EMFILE:
            cout << "Too many files open" << endl;
            break;
        case EACCES:
            cout << "Locking or sharing violation" << endl;
            break;
        case ENOENT:
            cout << "File not found" << endl;
        }
    }

    return 0;
}
```

CROSS-REFERENCE

See also _wexecl(), _wexecle(), _wexeclp(), _wexeclpe(), _wexecv(), _wexecve(), _wexecvp(), _wexecvpe(), _wspawnl(), _wspawnle(), _wspawnlp(), _wspawnlpe(), _wspawnv(), _wspawnve(), _wspawnvp(), _wspawnvpe(), execl(), execle(), execlpe(), execv(), execve(), execvp(), execvpe(), spawnl(), spawnle(), spawnlp(), spawnlpe(), spawnv(), spawnve(), spawnvp(), and spawnvpe().

execlpe()

Function

The `execlpe()` function runs a child process given the process's path and name, additional arguments, and environment settings. This function does not return to the process that called it. If the called process does not run successfully, the function returns −1. In this case, the `errno` global variable will be set to one of the error values in Table E-4:

Table E-4 Error Values for execlpe()

Value	Description
E2BIG	The arguments and environment require more than 32K of space.
EACCES	There has been a sharing or locking violation.
EMFILE	Too many files are open.
ENOENT	The specified file cannot be found.
ENOEXEC	The specified file is not executable.
ENOMEM	Not enough memory to run the process.

Header File

```
#include <process.h>
```

Declaration

```
int execlpe(const char *cmdname,
    const char *arg0, ... const char *argn,
    NULL, const char *const *envp)
```

- *arg0*—A pointer to the first argument.
- *argn*—A pointer to the last argument.
- *cmdname*—The path and file name of the process to run.
- *envp*—A pointer to the environment settings.

Example

The following program demonstrates how to use the `execlpe()` function. When run, the program runs a process called TestProg.exe, displaying a message if an error occurs. The program's output looks like the following:

```
Running TestProg.exe
Press any key to continue
Child process running.
```

Here is the program source code that produced the output:

```cpp
#include "stdafx.h"
#include <iostream>
#include <process.h>
#include <errno.h>

using namespace std;

char *envir[] =
{
   "ENVIR1=environment setting 1",
   "ENVIR2=environment setting 2",
   "ENVIR3=environment setting 3",
    NULL
};

int main(int argc, char* argv[])
{
    cout << "Running TestProg.exe" << endl;

    int result = execlpe("TestProg.exe", "TestProg.exe",
        "arg2", "arg3", NULL, envir);
    if (result == -1)
    {
        switch(errno)
        {
        case ENOEXEC:
            cout << "Not an executable file" << endl;
            break;
        case E2BIG:
            cout << "Space required exceeds 32K" << endl;
            break;
        case ENOMEM:
            cout << "Not enough memory" << endl;
            break;
        case EMFILE:
            cout << "Too many files open" << endl;
            break;
        case EACCES:
            cout << "Locking or sharing violation" << endl;
```

```
                            break;
                    case ENOENT:
                        cout << "File not found" << endl;
                    }
            }

            return 0;
    }
```

 CROSS-REFERENCE

See also _wexecl(), _wexecle(), _wexeclp(), _wexeclpe(), _wexecv(), _wexecve(), _wexecvp(), _wexecvpe(), _wspawnl(), _wspawnle(), _wspawnlp(), _wspawnlpe(), _wspawnv(), _wspawnve(), _wspawnvp(), _wspawnvpe(), execl(), execle(), execlp(), execv(), execve(), execvp(), execvpe(), spawnl(), spawnle(), spawnlp(), spawnlpe(), spawnv(), spawnve(), spawnvp(), and spawnvpe().

execv()

Function

The execv() function runs a child process given the process's path and name and additional arguments supplied as an array of char pointers. This function does not return to the process that called it. If the called process does not run successfully, the function returns –1. In this case, the errno global variable will be set to one of the error values in Table E-5:

Table E-5 Error Values for execv()

Value	Description
E2BIG	The arguments and environment require more than 32K of space.
EACCES	There has been a sharing or locking violation.
EMFILE	Too many files are open.
ENOENT	The specified file cannot be found.
ENOEXEC	The specified file is not executable.
ENOMEM	Not enough memory to run the process.

Header File

```
#include <process.h>
```

Declaration

```
int execv(const char *cmdname, const char *const *argv)
```

- *argv*—A pointer to an array of `char` pointers that point to the arguments.
- *cmdname*—The path and file name of the process to run.

Example

The following program demonstrates how to use the `execv()` function. When run, the program runs a process called TestProg.exe, displaying a message if an error occurs. The program's output looks like the following:

```
Running TestProg.exe
Press any key to continue
Child process running.
```

Here is the program source code that produced the output:

```cpp
#include "stdafx.h"
#include <iostream>
#include <process.h>
#include <errno.h>

using namespace std;

int main(int argc, char* argv[])
{
    char* args[] =
    {
        "TestProg.exe",
        "argument #1",
        "argument #2",
         NULL
    };

    cout << "Running TestProg.exe" << endl;

    int result = execv("TestProg.exe", args);
    if (result == -1)
    {
        switch(errno)
        {
```

```
                case ENOEXEC:
                    cout << "Not an executable file" << endl;
                    break;
                case E2BIG:
                    cout << "Space required exceeds 32K" << endl;
                    break;
                case ENOMEM:
                    cout << "Not enough memory" << endl;
                    break;
                case EMFILE:
                    cout << "Too many files open" << endl;
                    break;
                case EACCES:
                    cout << "Locking or sharing violation" << endl;
                    break;
                case ENOENT:
                    cout << "File not found" << endl;
                }
            }

        return 0;
    }
```

CROSS-REFERENCE

See also _wexecl(), _wexecle(), _wexeclp(), _wexeclpe(), _wexecv(), _wexecve(), _wexecvp(), _wexecvpe(), _wspawnl(), _wspawnle(), _wspawnlp(), _wspawnlpe(), _wspawnv(), _wspawnve(), _wspawnvp(), _wspawnvpe(), execl(), execle(), execlp(), execlpe(), execve(), execvp(), execvpe(), spawnl(), spawnle(), spawnlp(), spawnlpe(), spawnv(), spawnve(), spawnvp(), and spawnvpe().

execve()

Function

The execve() function runs a child process given the process's path and name, and additional arguments and environment settings supplied as an array of char pointers. This function does not return to the process that called it. If the called process does not run successfully, the function returns −1. In this case, the errno global variable will be set to one of the error values in Table E-6:

Table E-6 Error Values for execve()

Value	Description
E2BIG	The arguments and environment require more than 32K of space.
EACCES	There has been a sharing or locking violation.
EMFILE	Too many files are open.
ENOENT	The specified file cannot be found.
ENOEXEC	The specified file is not executable.
ENOMEM	Not enough memory to run the process.

Header File

```
#include <process.h>
```

Declaration

```
int execve(const char *cmdname, const char *const *argv,
    const char *const *envp);
```

- *argv* — A pointer to an array of `char` pointers that point to the arguments.
- *cmdname* — The path and file name of the process to run.
- *envp* — A pointer to an array of `char` pointers that point to the environment settings.

Example

The following program demonstrates how to use the `execve()` function. When run, the program runs a process called TestProg.exe, displaying a message if an error occurs. The program's output looks like the following:

```
Running TestProg.exe
Press any key to continue
Child process running.
```

Here is the program source code that produced the output:

```
#include "stdafx.h"
#include <iostream>
#include <process.h>
```

```cpp
#include <errno.h>

using namespace std;

char *envir[] =
{
   "ENVIR1=environment setting 1",
   "ENVIR2=environment setting 2",
   "ENVIR3=environment setting 3",
    NULL
};

char* args[] =
{
    "TestProg.exe",
    "argument #1",
    "argument #2",
     NULL
};

int main(int argc, char* argv[])
{
    cout << "Running TestProg.exe" << endl;

    int result = execve("TestProg.exe", args, envir);
    if (result == -1)
    {
        switch(errno)
        {
        case ENOEXEC:
            cout << "Not an executable file" << endl;
            break;
        case E2BIG:
            cout << "Space required exceeds 32K" << endl;
            break;
        case ENOMEM:
            cout << "Not enough memory" << endl;
            break;
        case EMFILE:
            cout << "Too many files open" << endl;
            break;
        case EACCES:
            cout << "Locking or sharing violation" << endl;
```

```
            break;
        case ENOENT:
            cout << "File not found" << endl;
        }
    }

    return 0;
}
```

CROSS-REFERENCE

See also _wexecl(), _wexecle(), _wexeclp(), _wexeclpe(), _wexecv(), _wexecve(), _wexecvp(), _wexecvpe(), _wspawnl(), _wspawnle(), _wspawnlp(), _wspawnlpe(), _wspawnv(), _wspawnve(), _wspawnvp(), _wspawnvpe(), execl(), execle(), execlp(), execlpe(), execv(), execvp(), execvpe(), spawnl(), spawnle(), spawnlp(), spawnlpe(), spawnv(), spawnve(), spawnvp(), and spawnvpe().

execvp()

Function

The `execvp()` function runs a child process given the process's path and name and additional arguments supplied as an array of `char` pointers. This function does not return to the process that called it. If the called process does not run successfully, the function returns −1. In this case, the `errno` global variable will be set to one of the error values in Table E-7:

Table E-7 Error Values for execvp()

Value	Description
E2BIG	The arguments and environment require more than 32K of space.
EACCES	There has been a sharing or locking violation.
EMFILE	Too many files are open.
ENOENT	The specified file cannot be found.
ENOEXEC	The specified file is not executable.
ENOMEM	Not enough memory to run the process.

Header File

```
#include <process.h>
```

Declaration

```
int execvp(const char *cmdname, const char *const *argv)
```

- *argv* — A pointer to an array of `char` pointers that point to the arguments.
- *cmdname* — The path and file name of the process to run.

Example

The following program demonstrates how to use the `execvp()` function. When run, the program runs a process called TestProg.exe, displaying a message if an error occurs. The program's output looks like the following:

```
Running TestProg.exe
Press any key to continue
Child process running.
```

Here is the program source code that produced the output:

```
#include "stdafx.h"
#include <iostream>
#include <process.h>
#include <errno.h>

using namespace std;

int main(int argc, char* argv[])
{
    char* args[] =
    {
        "TestProg.exe",
        "argument #1",
        "argument #2",
        NULL
    };

    cout << "Running TestProg.exe" << endl;

    int result = execvp("TestProg.exe", args);
    if (result == -1)
    {
        switch(errno)
        {
```

```
        case ENOEXEC:
            cout << "Not an executable file" << endl;
            break;
        case E2BIG:
            cout << "Space required exceeds 32K" << endl;
            break;
        case ENOMEM:
            cout << "Not enough memory" << endl;
            break;
        case EMFILE:
            cout << "Too many files open" << endl;
            break;
        case EACCES:
            cout << "Locking or sharing violation" << endl;
            break;
        case ENOENT:
            cout << "File not found" << endl;
        }
    }

    return 0;
}
```

 CROSS-REFERENCE
See also _wexecl(), _wexecle(), _wexeclp(), _wexeclpe(), _wexecv(), _wexecve(), _wexecvp(), _wexecvpe(), _wspawnl(), _wspawnle(), _wspawnlp(), _wspawnlpe(), _wspawnv(), _wspawnve(), _wspawnvp(), _wspawnvpe(), execl(), execle(), execlp(), execlpe(), execv(), execve(), execvpe(), spawnl(), spawnle(), spawnlp(), spawnlpe(), spawnv(), spawnve(), spawnvp(), and spawnvpe().

execvpe()

Function

The execvpe() function runs a child process given the process's path and name, and additional arguments and environment settings supplied as an array of char pointers. This function does not return to the process that called it. If the called process does not run successfully, the function returns –1. In this case, the errno global variable will be set to one of the error values in Table E-8:

Table E-8 Error Values for execvpe()

Value	Description
E2BIG	The arguments and environment require more than 32K of space.
EACCES	There has been a sharing or locking violation.
EMFILE	Too many files are open.
ENOENT	The specified file cannot be found.
ENOEXEC	The specified file is not executable.
ENOMEM	Not enough memory to run the process.

Header File

```
#include <process.h>
```

Declaration

```
int execvpe(const char *cmdname, const char *const *argv,
    const char *const *envp);
```

- *argv* — A pointer to an array of char pointers that point to the arguments.
- *cmdname* — The path and file name of the process to run.
- *envp* — A pointer to an array of char pointers that point to the environment settings.

Example

The following program demonstrates how to use the execvpe() function. When run, the program runs a process called TestProg.exe, displaying a message if an error occurs. The program's output looks like the following:

```
Running TestProg.exe
Press any key to continue
Child process running.
```

Here is the program source code that produced the output:

```
#include "stdafx.h"
#include <iostream>
#include <process.h>
#include <errno.h>

using namespace std;
```

```
char *envir[] =
{
    "ENVIR1=environment setting 1",
    "ENVIR2=environment setting 2",
    "ENVIR3=environment setting 3",
     NULL
};

char* args[] =
{
    "TestProg.exe",
    "argument #1",
    "argument #2",
     NULL
};

int main(int argc, char* argv[])
{
    cout << "Running TestProg.exe" << endl;

    int result = execvpe("TestProg.exe", args, envir);
    if (result == -1)
    {
        switch(errno)
        {
        case ENOEXEC:
            cout << "Not an executable file" << endl;
            break;
        case E2BIG:
            cout << "Space required exceeds 32K" << endl;
            break;
        case ENOMEM:
            cout << "Not enough memory" << endl;
            break;
        case EMFILE:
            cout << "Too many files open" << endl;
            break;
        case EACCES:
            cout << "Locking or sharing violation" << endl;
            break;
        case ENOENT:
            cout << "File not found" << endl;
        }
```

d
e
f

```
      }

      return 0;
}
```

CROSS-REFERENCE
See also _wexecl(), _wexecle(), _wexeclp(), _wexeclpe(), _wexecv(), _wexecve(),
_wexecvp(), _wexecvpe(), _wspawnl(), _wspawnle(), _wspawnlp(), _wspawnlpe(),
_wspawnv(), _wspawnve(), _wspawnvp(), _wspawnvpe(), execl(), execle(), exe-
clp(), execlpe(), execv(), execve(), execvp(), spawnl(), spawnle(), spawnlp(),
spawnlpe(), spawnv(), spawnve(), spawnvp(), and spawnvpe().

exit()

Function

The exit() function performs the cleanup tasks associated with a process and
then terminates the process. That is, unlike the _exit() function, exit()
flushes and closes buffers and streams, and calls the functions registered on
behalf of the process by the atexit() and _onexit() functions.

Header File

```
#include <process.h>
```

Declaration

```
void exit(int status);
```

- *status* — A value that indicates the status of the terminating process.

Example

The following program demonstrates how to use the exit() function. When
run, the program displays a message, after which the exit() function terminates the process. The program's output looks like the following:

```
About to exit process.
Press Enter to continue
```

```
Press any key to continue
```

Here is the program source code that produced the output:

```
#include "stdafx.h"
#include <iostream>
#include <process.h>

using namespace std;

int main(int argc, char* argv[])
{
    cout << "About to exit process." << endl;
    cout << "Press Enter to continue" << endl;
    getchar();
    exit(0);

    return 0;
}
```

CROSS-REFERENCE
See also _c_exit(), _cexit(), _exit(),_onexit(), and atexit().

exp()

Function

The exp() function returns the exponential of a given double value. If an overflow occurs, the function returns INF, or, in the case of an underflow, returns 0.

Header File

```
#include <math.h>
```

Declaration

```
double exp(double x);
```

- *x* — The value for which to calculate the exponential.

Example

The following program demonstrates how to use the exp() function. When run, the program calculates the exponential of a value and displays the result. The program's output looks like the following:

```
exp(4.98756) = 146.578
Press any key to continue
```

Here is the program source code that produced the output:

```
#include "stdafx.h"
#include <math.h>
#include <iostream>

using namespace std;

int main(int argc, char* argv[])
{
    double val = 4.98756;
    double result = exp(val);
    cout << "exp(4.98756) = " << result << endl;

    return 0;
}
```

CROSS-REFERENCE

See also abs(), acos(), asin(), atan(), cos(), cosh(), expf(), expl(), fabs(), log(), log10(), sin(), sinh(), tan(), and tanh().

expf()

Function

The expf() function returns the exponential of a given float value. If an overflow occurs, the function returns INF, or, in the case of an underflow, returns 0.

NOTE

Borland does not support this function.

Header File

```
#include <math.h>
```

Declaration

```
float expf(float x);
```

- *x* — The value for which to calculate the exponential.

Example

The following program demonstrates how to use the `expf()` function. When run, the program calculates the exponential of a value and displays the result. The program's output looks like the following:

```
exp(4.98756) = 146.578
Press any key to continue
```

Here is the program source code that produced the output:

```cpp
#include "stdafx.h"
#include <math.h>
#include <iostream>

using namespace std;

int main(int argc, char* argv[])
{
    float val = (float)4.98756;
    float result = expf(val);
    cout << "exp(4.98756) = " << result << endl;

    return 0;
}
```

CROSS-REFERENCE
See also abs(), acos(), asin(), atan(), cos(), cosh(), exp(), expl(), fabs(), log(), log10(), sin(), sinh(), tan(), and tanh().

expl()

Function

The `expl()` function returns the exponential of a given `long double` value. If an overflow occurs, the function returns INF, or, in the case of an underflow, returns 0.

Header File

```
#include <math.h>
```

Declaration

```
long double expl(long double x);
```

- *x*— The value for which to calculate the exponential.

Example

The following program demonstrates how to use the `expl()` function. When run, the program calculates the exponential of a value and displays the result. The program's output looks like the following:

```
exp(4.98756) = 146.578
Press any key to continue
```

Here is the program source code that produced the output:

```
#include "stdafx.h"
#include <math.h>
#include <iostream>

using namespace std;

int main(int argc, char* argv[])
{
    long double val = 4.98756;
    long double result = expl(val);
    cout << "exp(4.98756) = " << result << endl;

    return 0;
}
```

CROSS-REFERENCE

See also abs(), acos(), asin(), atan(), cos(), cosh(), exp(), fabs(), log(), log10(), sin(), sinh(), tan(), and tanh().

explicit

Keyword

The `explicit` keyword disallows the automatic conversion that occurs when the type of value accepted by the class's constructor is assigned directly to an object. For example, examine the following program. The program's output looks like the following:

```
value 1 = 10
value 2 = 20
Press any key to continue
```

Here is the program source code that produced the output:

```cpp
#include "stdafx.h"
#include <iostream>

using namespace std;

class MyClass
{
protected:
    int value;
public:
    MyClass(int val) { value = val; }
    int GetValue() { return value; }
};

int main(int argc, char* argv[])
{
    MyClass myClass1(10);
    MyClass myClass2 = 20;

    int val = myClass1.GetValue();
    cout << "value 1 = " << val << endl;
    val = myClass2.GetValue();
    cout << "value 2 = " << val << endl;

    return 0;
}
```

This source code defines a class named `MyClass`, as well as a `main()` function that tests the class. First, notice that the class's constructor takes a single parameter, an integer called `val`, which gets stored in the class's data member, `value`. Next, look at `main()` where the program creates the two `MyClass` objects, `myClass1` and `myClass2`. The program creates the first object in the conventional way:

```
MyClass myClass1(10);
```

However, the program can (and does) create the object more simply by assigning an integer to the object directly, like the following:

```
MyClass myClass2 = 20;
```

This works because the class's constructor takes an integer as its single parameter, and C++ is smart enough to pass the assigned integer on to the constructor just as it would with the more conventional construction syntax. If you run the previous program, you'll see the following output, proving that both methods of creating a `MyClass` object worked:

```
value 1 = 10
value 2 = 20
Press any key to continue
```

To disallow this type of object construction, you can add the `explicit` keyword to the class's constructor. The following program shows how this works:

```
#include "stdafx.h"
#include <iostream>

using namespace std;

class MyClass
{
protected:
    int value;
public:
    explicit MyClass(int val) { value = val; }
    int GetValue() { return value; }
};

int main(int argc, char* argv[])
{
    MyClass myClass1(10);
```

```
    // MyClass myClass2 = 20; Not legal now!

    int val = myClass1.GetValue();
    cout << "value 1 = " << val << endl;

    return 0;
}
```

In this version of the program, the commented line will cause a compiler error if it is uncommented. Because the class's constructor is declared as `explicit`, assigning an integer directly to an object of the `MyClass` class will no longer work.

CROSS-REFERENCE
See also Constructor.

extern

Keyword

The `extern` keyword specifies that a symbol can be seen in a file other than the one in which it's defined. For example, the following function is declared as having external linkage:

```
extern int MyFunc(int val)
{
    return val * 2;
}
```

The `extern` keyword can also be used to specify that another language's linkage conventions are being used. The following code, for example, tells the linker that the functions should be linked using C-language conventions:

```
extern "C"
{
    int MyFunc1(int);
    int MyFunc2(float);
}
```

CROSS-REFERENCE
See also auto, const, register, static, and volatile.

__fastcall

keyword

The __fastcall keyword specifies that all arguments in a function call should, if possible, be passed using the registers. For example, the following function is declared as using the fastcall calling convention:

```
void __fastcall MyFunction(int arg1, int arg2);
```

_fcloseall()

Function

The _fcloseall() function closes all streams, returning the number of streams closed if successful, or EOF if unsuccessful.

Header File

```
#include <stdio.h>
```

Declaration

```
int _fcloseall(void);
```

Example

The following program demonstrates how to use the _fcloseall() function. When run, the program attempts to open two streams, print status messages, and then close the streams if they opened successfully. The program's output looks like this:

```
First file opened successfully.
Second file opened successfully.
2 files closed successfully
Press any key to continue
```

Here is the program source code that produced the output:

```cpp
#include "stdafx.h"
#include <stdio.h>
#include <iostream>

using namespace std;

int main(int argc, char* argv[])
{
    FILE* file1 = fopen("_fcloseall.cpp", "r");
    if (file1 == NULL)
    {
        cout << "File open error." << endl;
        exit(1);
    }

    cout << "First file opened successfully." << endl;

    FILE* file2 = fopen("stdafx.cpp", "r");
    if (file2 == NULL)
    {
        cout << "File open error." << endl;
        exit(1);
    }

    cout << "Second file opened successfully." << endl;

    int numClosed = _fcloseall();
    cout << numClosed << " files closed successfully" << endl;

    return 0;
}
```

CROSS-REFERENCE

See also _close(), _creat(), _fdopen(), _fgetchar(), _fgetwchar(), _fileno(), _flushall(), _fputwchar(), _fsopen(), _getw(), _getws(), _lseeki64(), _open(), _putw(), _putws(), _read(), _rmtmp(), _tempnam(), _wcreat(), _wfdopen(), _wfopen(), _wfreopen(),_wfsopen(), _wopen(), _wtempnam(), _wtmpnam(), clearerr(), eof(), fclose(), feof(), ferror(), fflush(), fgetc(), fgetpos(), fgets(), fgetwc(), fgetws(), fopen(), fprintf(), fputc(), fputchar(), fputs(), fputwc(), fputws(), fread(), freopen(), fscanf(), fseek(), fsetpos(), ftell(), fwprintf(), fwrite(), fwscanf(), getc(), getchar(), gets(), getwc(), getwchar(), lseek(), putc(), putch(), putchar(), puts(), putwc(), putwchar(), rewind(), setbuf(), setvbuf(), tmpfile(), tmpnam(), ungetc(), ungetch(), ungetwc(), and write().

_fcvt()

Function

The _fcvt() function converts a floating-point value to a string of digits, returning a pointer to the resultant string.

Header File

```
#include <stdlib.h>
```

Declaration

```
char* _fcvt(double value, int count,
    int* decPosition, int* sign);
```

- *count* — The number of digits after the decimal point to return.
- *decPosition* — A pointer to an integer that will receive the position of the decimal point.
- *sign* — A pointer to an integer that will receive the value's sign, where 0 specifies a positive value and any other value specifies a negative value.
- *value* — The floating point value to convert.

Example

The following program demonstrates how to use the _fcvt() function. When run, the program converts a floating-point value to a string of digits, and then displays the converted value, along with its decimal-position and sign values. The program's output looks like this:

```
Buffer: 243587564000
Decimal position: 4
Sign: 0
Press any key to continue
```

Here is the program source code that produced the output:

```
#include "stdafx.h"
#include <iostream>
#include <stdlib.h>

using namespace std;
```

```
int main(int argc, char* argv[])
{
    int decPosition;
    int sign;

    char* buf = _fcvt(2435.87564, 8, &decPosition, &sign);
    cout << "Buffer: " << buf << endl;
    cout << "Decimal position: " << decPosition << endl;
    cout << "Sign: " << sign << endl;

    return 0;
}
```

CROSS-REFERENCE
See also _ecvt(), _gcvt(), atof(), and fcvt().

_fdopen()

Function

The _fdopen() function associates a stream with an open file, returning a pointer to the stream.

Header File

```
#include <stdio.h>
```

Declaration

```
FILE* _fdopen(int handle, const char *mode);
```

- *handle* — A handle to the open file.
- *mode* — The file access mode, which can be one of the mode values from Table F-1. The extension mode values shown in Table F-2 can be combined with the mode.

Table F-1 Mode Values for _fdopen()

Value	Description
"r"	Open for reading.
"w"	Open for writing, which erases the file if it already exists, or creates a new file if it doesn't exist.
"a"	Open for append, which writes to the end of an existing file, or creates the file if it doesn't already exist.
"r+"	Open for both reading and writing.
"w+"	Open for both reading and writing. If the file already exists, its contents are lost; if the file doesn't exist, it's created.
"a+"	Open for reading and appending. If the file doesn't exist, it's created.

Table F-2 Extension Mode Values for _fdopen()

Value	Description
T	Open for in text mode.
B	Open in binary mode.
C	Set the file's commit flag.
N	Turn off the file's commit flag.

Example

The following program demonstrates how to use the _fdopen() function. When run, the program opens a file for reading and then associates a stream with the open file. The program's output looks like this:

```
Stream created successfully.
Press any key to continue
```

Here is the program source code that produced the output:

```
#include "stdafx.h"
#include <fcntl.h>
#include <io.h>
#include <stdio.h>
#include <iostream>

using namespace std;

int main(int argc, char* argv[])
{
    int fileHandle = _open("_fdopen.cpp", O_RDONLY);
```

```
            if (fileHandle == -1)
                cout << "File open error." << endl;
            else
            {
                FILE* file = _fdopen(fileHandle, "r");

                if(file == NULL )
                    cout << "Stream creation error." << endl;
                else
                {
                    cout << "Stream created successfully." << endl;
                    fclose(file);
                }
            }

            return 0;
        }
```

CROSS-REFERENCE

See also _close(), _creat(), _fcloseall(), _fgetchar(), _fgetwchar(), _fileno(), _flushall(), _fputwchar(), _fsopen(), _getw(), _getws(), _lseeki64(), _open(), _putw(), _putws(), _read(), _rmtmp(), _tempnam(), _wcreat(), _wfdopen(), _wfopen(), _wfreopen(),_wfsopen(), _wopen(), _wtempnam(), _wtmpnam(), clearerr(), eof(), fclose(), feof(), ferror(), fflush(), fgetc(), fgetpos(), fgets(), fgetwc(), fgetws(), fopen(), fprintf(), fputc(), fputchar(), fputs(), fputwc(), fputws(), fread(), freopen(), fscanf(), fseek(), fsetpos(), ftell(), fwprintf(), fwrite(), fwscanf(), getc(), getchar(), gets(), getwc(), getwchar(), lseek(), putc(), putch(), putchar(), puts(), putwc(), putwchar(), rewind(), setbuf(), setvbuf(), tmpfile(), tmpnam(), ungetc(), ungetch(), ungetwc(), and write().

_fgetchar()

Function()

The _fgetchar() function reads a character from the standard input stream, returning the character read, or EOF in the case of an error.

Header File

```
#include <stdio.h>
```

Declaration

```
int _fgetchar(void);
```

Example

The following program demonstrates how to use the _fgetchar() function. When run, the program reads a line of text from the console. The program then displays the line of text. The program's output looks like this:

```
Enter a line of text:
This is a test

The text you entered:
This is a test

Press any key to continue
```

Here is the program source code that produced the output:

```
#include "stdafx.h"
#include <stdio.h>
#include <iostream>

using namespace std;

int main(int argc, char* argv[])
{
    char buf[81];

    cout << "Enter a line of text:" << endl;
    int i = 0;
    int ch = _fgetchar();
    while (ch != '\n')
    {
        buf[i] = (char)ch;
        ++i;
        ch = _fgetchar();
    }

    buf[i] = 0;
    cout << endl << "The text you entered:" << endl;
    cout << buf << endl << endl;

    return 0;
}
```

CROSS-REFERENCE
See also _close(), _creat(), _fcloseall(), _fdopen(), _fgetwchar(), _fileno(), _flushall(), _fputwchar(), _fsopen(), _getw(), _getws(), _lseeki64(), _open(), _putw(), _putws(), _read(), _rmtmp(), _tempnam(), _wcreat(), _wfdopen(), _wfopen(), _wfreopen(),_wfsopen(), _wopen(), _wtempnam(), _wtmpnam(), clearerr(), eof(), fclose(), feof(), ferror(), fflush(), fgetc(), fgetpos(), fgets(), fgetwc(), fgetws(), fopen(), fprintf(), fputc(), fputchar(), fputs(), fputwc(), fputws(), fread(), freopen(), fscanf(), fseek(), fsetpos(), ftell(), fwprintf(), fwrite(), fwscanf(), getc(), getchar(), gets(), getwc(), getwchar(), lseek(), putc(), putch(), putchar(), puts(), putwc(), putwchar(), rewind(), setbuf(), setvbuf(), tmpfile(), tmpnam(), ungetc(), ungetch(), ungetwc(), and write().

_fgetwchar()

Function()

The _fgetwchar() function reads a wide character from the standard input stream, returning the character read or returning WEOF in the case of an error.

Header File

```
#include <stdio.h>
```

Declaration

```
wint_t _fgetwchar(void);
```

Example

The following program demonstrates how to use the _fgetwchar() function. When run, the program reads a line of text from the console. The program then displays the line of text. The program's output looks like this:

```
Enter a line of text:
This is a test

The text you entered:
This is a test

Press any key to continue
```

Here is the program source code that produced the output:

```cpp
#include "stdafx.h"
#include <stdio.h>
#include <iostream>

using namespace std;

int main(int argc, char* argv[])
{
    wchar_t buf[81];

    cout << "Enter a line of text:" << endl;
    int i = 0;
    wint_t ch = _fgetwchar();
    while (ch != '\n')
    {
        buf[i] = (wchar_t)ch;
        ++i;
        ch = _fgetwchar();
    }

    buf[i] = 0;
    cout << endl << "The text you entered:" << endl;
    wcout << buf << endl << endl;

    return 0;
}
```

CROSS-REFERENCE

See also _close(), _creat(), _fcloseall(), _fdopen(), _fgetchar(), _fileno(), _flushall(), _fputwchar(), _fsopen(), _getw(), _getws(), _lseeki64(), _open(), _putw(), _putws(), _read(), _rmtmp(), _tempnam(), _wcreat(), _wfdopen(), _wfopen(), _wfreopen(),_wfsopen(), _wopen(), _wtempnam(), _wtmpnam(), clearerr(), eof(), fclose(), feof(), ferror(), fflush(), fgetc(), fgetpos(), fgets(), fgetwc(), fgetws(), fopen(), fprintf(), fputc(), fputchar(), fputs(), fputwc(), fputws(), fread(), freopen(), fscanf(), fseek(), fsetpos(), ftell(), fwprintf(), fwrite(), fwscanf(), getc(), getchar(), gets(), getwc(), getwchar(), lseek(), putc(), putch(), putchar(), puts(), putwc(), putwchar(), rewind(), setbuf(), setvbuf(), tmpfile(), tmpnam(), ungetc(), ungetch(), ungetwc(), and write().

_filelength()

Function()

The _filelength() function returns the number of bytes in a file or returns –1L in the case of an error.

 NOTE
Borland users should refer to filelength() later in this chapter.

Header File

```
#include <io.h>
```

Declaration

```
long _filelength(int handle);
```

- *handle* — The file's handle.

Example

The following program demonstrates how to use the _filelength() function. When run, the program opens a file and displays the file's byte size. The program's output looks like this:

```
Opening a file...
The file's length is 670 bytes.

Press any key to continue
```

Here is the program source code that produced the output:

```
#include "stdafx.h"
#include <io.h>
#include <fcntl.h>
#include <sys/types.h>
#include <sys/stat.h>
#include <iostream>

using namespace std;

int main(int argc, char* argv[])
{
    cout << "Opening a file..." << endl;
```

```
int fileHandle = open( "_filelength.cpp",
    O_RDONLY, S_IREAD);
if (fileHandle != -1)
{
    int fileSize = _filelength(fileHandle);
    cout << "The file's length is " << fileSize;
    cout << " bytes." << endl << endl;
    close(fileHandle);
}
else
    cout << "File open error." << endl;

return 0;
}
```

CROSS-REFERENCE
See also _filelengthi64() and filelength().

_filelengthi64()

Function()

The `_filelengthi64()` function returns, as a 64-bit integer, the number of bytes in a file, or –1L in the case of an error.

NOTE
Borland does not support this function.

Header File

```
#include <io.h>
```

Declaration

```
__int64 _filelengthi64(int handle);
```

- *handle* — The file's handle.

Example

The following program demonstrates how to use the _filelengthi64() function. When run, the program opens a file and displays the file's byte size. The program's output looks like this:

```
Opening a file...
The file's length is 697 bytes.


Press any key to continue
```

Here is the program source code that produced the output:

```cpp
#include "stdafx.h"
#include <io.h>
#include <fcntl.h>
#include <sys/types.h>
#include <sys/stat.h>
#include <iostream>

using namespace std;

int main(int argc, char* argv[])
{
    cout << "Opening a file..." << endl;
    int fileHandle = open( "_filelengthi64.cpp",
        O_RDONLY, S_IREAD);
    if (fileHandle != -1)
    {
        __int64 fileSize = _filelengthi64(fileHandle);
        cout << "The file's length is " << (int)fileSize;
        cout << " bytes." << endl << endl;
        close(fileHandle);
    }
    else
        cout << "File open error." << endl;

    return 0;
}
```

CROSS-REFERENCE
See also _filelength() and filelength().

_fileno()

Function()

The _fileno() function returns the file handle of the file attached to a stream.

Header File

```
#include <stdio.h>
```

Declaration

```
int _fileno(FILE *stream);
```

- *stream* — A pointer to the stream for which to get the file handle.

Example

The following program demonstrates how to use the _fileno() function. When run, the program opens a file and displays the file's handle. The program's output looks like this:

```
File opened successfully.
The file handle is 3
Press any key to continue
```

Here is the program source code that produced the output:

```
#include "stdafx.h"
#include <stdio.h>
#include <iostream>

using namespace std;

int main(int argc, char* argv[])
{
    FILE* file = fopen("_fileno.cpp", "r");

    if (file != NULL)
    {
        cout << "File opened successfully." << endl;
        int fileHandle = _fileno(file);
        cout << "The file handle is " << fileHandle << endl;
        fclose(file);
```

```
            }
        else
            cout << "File failed to open." << endl;

        return 0;
    }
```

CROSS-REFERENCE
See also _filelength(), _filelengthi64(), filelength(), and fileno().

_findclose()

Function

The _findclose() function closes a find handle created by the _findfirst() function, returning 0 if successful or returning –1 if unsuccessful.

NOTE
Borland users should refer to the findclose() function later in this chapter.

Header File

```
#include <io.h>
```

Declaration

```
int _findclose(long handle);
```

- *handle* — The find handle to close.

Example

The following program demonstrates how to use the _findclose() function. When run, the program looks for all files in the current directory, printing each file's name and size. The program's output looks like this.

```
FILE: . — 0 bytes
FILE: .. — 0 bytes
FILE: StdAfx.h — 667 bytes
FILE: StdAfx.cpp — 297 bytes
FILE: ReadMe.txt — 1232 bytes
FILE: _findclose.dsw — 545 bytes
```

```
FILE: _findclose.cpp — 847 bytes
FILE: Debug — 0 bytes
FILE: _findclose.dsp — 4584 bytes
FILE: _findclose.ncb — 0 bytes
FILE: _findclose.plg — 1646 bytes
Press any key to continue
```

Here is the program source code that produced the output:

```cpp
#include "stdafx.h"
#include <io.h>
#include <iostream>

using namespace std;

int main(int argc, char* argv[])
{
    struct _finddata_t fileData;

    long fileHandle = _findfirst("*.*", &fileData);

    if(fileHandle == -1L)
        cout << "No files found." << endl;
    else
    {
        cout << "FILE: " << fileData.name;
        cout << " — " << fileData.size << " bytes" << endl;

        int result = _findnext(fileHandle, &fileData);
        while(result == 0 )
        {
            cout << "FILE: " << fileData.name;
            cout << " — " << fileData.size << " bytes";
            cout << endl;
            result = _findnext(fileHandle, &fileData);
        }

        _findclose(fileHandle);
    }

    return 0;
}
```

CROSS-REFERENCE
See also _findfirst(), _findfirsti64(), _findnext(), _findnexti64(), _wfindclose(), _wfindfirst(), _wfindfirsti64(), _wfindnext(), findclose(), and findnext().

_findfirst()

Function

The _findfirst() function finds the first file that matches the given specification, returning a handle to the file. If the function fails, it returns –1, and the errno global variable is set to ENOENT (no matching files) or EINVAL (invalid file specification).

NOTE
Borland users should refer to the findfirst() function later in this chapter.

Header File

```
#include <io.h>
```

Declaration

```
long _findfirst(char *filespec, struct _finddata_t *fileinfo);
```

- *fileinfo* — A pointer to a _finddata_t structure in which the function will store information about the requested file.
- *filespec* — The file specification returned by _findfirst().

Example

The following program demonstrates how to use the _findfirst() function. When run, the program looks for all files in the current directory, printing each file's name and size. The program's output looks like this:

```
FILE: . - 0 bytes
FILE: .. - 0 bytes
FILE: StdAfx.h - 667 bytes
FILE: StdAfx.cpp - 297 bytes
FILE: ReadMe.txt - 1232 bytes
FILE: _findfirst.dsw - 545 bytes
FILE: _findfirst.cpp - 828 bytes
FILE: Debug - 0 bytes
```

```
FILE: _findfirst.dsp — 4584 bytes
FILE: _findfirst.ncb — 0 bytes
FILE: _findfirst.plg — 1275 bytes
Press any key to continue
```

Here is the program source code that produced the output:

```cpp
#include "stdafx.h"
#include <io.h>
#include <iostream>

using namespace std;

int main(int argc, char* argv[])
{
    struct _finddata_t fileData;

long fileHandle = _findfirst("*.*", &fileData);

    if(fileHandle == -1L)
        cout << "No files found." << endl;
    else
    {
        cout << "FILE: " << fileData.name;
        cout << " — " << fileData.size << " bytes" << endl;

        int result = _findnext(fileHandle, &fileData);
        while(result == 0 )
        {
            cout << "FILE: " << fileData.name;
            cout << " — " << fileData.size << " bytes";
            cout << endl;
            result = _findnext(fileHandle, &fileData);
        }

        _findclose(fileHandle);
    }

    return 0;
}
```

CROSS-REFERENCE

See also _findclose(), _findfirsti64(), _findnext(), _findnexti64(), _wfindclose(), _wfindfirst(), _wfindfirsti64(), _wfindnext(), _wfindnexti64, findclose(), findfirst(), and findnext().

_findfirsti64()

Function

The _findfirsti64() function finds the first file that matches the given specification, returning a handle to the file. If the function fails, it returns –1, and the errno global variable is set to ENOENT (no matching files) or EINVAL (invalid file specification).

 NOTE
Borland does not support this function.

Header File

```
#include <io.h>
```

Declaration

```
__int64 _findfirsti64(char *filespec,
    struct _finddatai64_t *fileinfo);
```

- *fileinfo* — A pointer to a _finddatai64_t structure in which the function will store information about the requested file.
- *filespec* — A pointer to the file specification.

Example

The following program demonstrates how to use the _findfirsti64() function. When run, the program looks for all files in the current directory, printing each file's name and size. The program's output looks like this:

```
FILE: . — 0 bytes
FILE: .. — 0 bytes
FILE: StdAfx.h — 667 bytes
FILE: StdAfx.cpp — 300 bytes
FILE: ReadMe.txt — 1250 bytes
FILE: _findfirsti64.dsw — 551 bytes
FILE: _findfirsti64.cpp — 878 bytes
FILE: Debug — 0 bytes
FILE: _findfirsti64.dsp — 4620 bytes
FILE: _findfirsti64.ncb — 0 bytes
FILE: _findfirsti64.plg — 1302 bytes
Press any key to continue
```

Here is the program source code that produced the output:

```cpp
#include "stdafx.h"
#include <io.h>
#include <iostream>

using namespace std;

int main(int argc, char* argv[])
{
    struct _finddatai64_t fileData;

    __int64 fileHandle = _findfirsti64("*.*", &fileData);

    if(fileHandle == -1)
        cout << "No files found." << endl;
    else
    {
        cout << "FILE: " << fileData.name;
        cout << " - " << (int)fileData.size;
        cout << " bytes" << endl;

        __int64 result = _findnexti64(fileHandle, &fileData);
        while(result == 0 )
        {
            cout << "FILE: " << fileData.name;
            cout << " - " << (int)fileData.size << " bytes";
            cout << endl;
            result = _findnexti64(fileHandle, &fileData);
        }

        _findclose(fileHandle);
    }

    return 0;
}
```

CROSS-REFERENCE

See also _findclose(), _findfirst(), _findnext(), _findnexti64(), _wfindclose(), _wfindfirst(), _wfindfirsti64(), _wfindnext(), _wfindnexti64, findclose(), and findnext().

_findnext()

Function

The _findnext() function finds the next file that matches the given specification, returning a handle to the file. If the function fails, it returns −1, and the errno global variable is set to ENOENT (no matching files).

> **NOTE**
> Borland users should refer to the findnext() function later in this chapter.

Header File

```
#include <io.h>
```

Declaration

```
int _findnext(long handle, struct _finddata_t *fileinfo);
```

- *fileinfo* — A pointer to a _finddata_t structure in which the function will store information about the requested file.
- *handle* — The file handle returned by _findfirst().

Example

The following program demonstrates how to use the _findnext() function. When run, the program looks for all files in the current directory, printing each file's name and size. The program's output looks like this:

```
FILE: . — 0 bytes
FILE: .. — 0 bytes
FILE: StdAfx.h — 667 bytes
FILE: StdAfx.cpp — 296 bytes
FILE: _findnext.dsw — 543 bytes
FILE: _findnext.cpp — 844 bytes
FILE: ReadMe.txt — 1226 bytes
FILE: _findnext.ncb — 0 bytes
FILE: _findnext.dsp — 4572 bytes
FILE: Debug — 0 bytes
FILE: _findnext.plg — 1266 bytes
Press any key to continue
```

Here is the program source code that produced the output:

```cpp
#include "stdafx.h"
#include <io.h>
#include <iostream>

using namespace std;

int main(int argc, char* argv[])
{
    struct _finddata_t fileData;

    long fileHandle = _findfirst("*.*", &fileData);

    if(fileHandle == -1L)
        cout << "No files found." << endl;
    else
    {
        cout << "FILE: " << fileData.name;
        cout << " - " << fileData.size << " bytes" << endl;

        int result = _findnext(fileHandle, &fileData);
        while(result == 0 )
        {
            cout << "FILE: " << fileData.name;
            cout << " - " << fileData.size << " bytes";
            cout << endl;
            result = _findnext(fileHandle, &fileData);
        }

        _findclose(fileHandle);
    }

    return 0;
}
```

CROSS-REFERENCE

See also _findclose(), _findfirst(), _findfirsti64(), _findnexti64(), _wfindclose(), _wfindfirst(), _wfindfirsti64(), _wfindnext(), _wfindnexti64, findclose(), and findnext().

_findnexti64()

Function

The _findnexti64() function finds the next file that matches the given specification, returning a handle to the file. If the function fails, it returns –1, and the errno global variable is set to ENOENT (no matching files).

 NOTE
Borland does not support this function.

Header File

```
#include <io.h>
```

Declaration

```
__int64 _findnexti64(long handle,
    struct _finddatai64_t *fileinfo);
```

- *fileinfo* — A pointer to a _finddatai64_t structure in which the function will store information about the requested file.
- *handle* — The file handle returned by _findfirsti64().

Example

The following program demonstrates how to use the _findnexti64() function. When run, the program looks for all files in the current directory, printing each file's name and size. The program's output looks like this:

```
FILE: . - 0 bytes
FILE: .. - 0 bytes
FILE: StdAfx.h - 667 bytes
FILE: StdAfx.cpp - 299 bytes
FILE: ReadMe.txt - 1244 bytes
FILE: _findnexti64.dsw - 549 bytes
FILE: _findnexti64.cpp - 892 bytes
FILE: Debug - 0 bytes
FILE: _findnexti64.dsp - 4608 bytes
FILE: _findnexti64.ncb - 0 bytes
FILE: _findnexti64.plg - 1668 bytes
Press any key to continue
```

Here is the program source code that produced the output:

```cpp
#include "stdafx.h"
#include <io.h>
#include <iostream>

using namespace std;

int main(int argc, char* argv[])
{
    struct _finddatai64_t fileData;

    __int64 fileHandle = _findfirsti64("*.*", &fileData);

    if(fileHandle == -1)
        cout << "No files found." << endl;
    else
    {
        cout << "FILE: " << fileData.name;
        cout << " - " << (int)fileData.size;
        cout << " bytes" << endl;

        int64 result = _findnexti64(fileHandle, &fileData);
        while(result == 0 )
        {
            cout << "FILE: " << fileData.name;
            cout << " - " << (int)fileData.size << " bytes";
            cout << endl;
            result = _findnexti64(fileHandle, &fileData);
        }

        _findclose(fileHandle);
    }

    return 0;
}
```

CROSS-REFERENCE

See also _findclose(), _findfirst(), _findfirsti64(), _findnext(), _wfindfirst(), _wfindfirsti64(), _wfindnext(), _wfindnexti64, findclose(), findfirst(), and findnext().

_finite()

Function

The _finite() function returns true if the given value is finite, and false if the value is infinite or NaN (not a number).

Header File

```
#include <float.h>
```

Declaration

```
int _finite(double value);
```

- *value* — The value to test.

Example

The following program demonstrates how to use the _finite() function. When run, the program calls _finite() to test a value and displays the result. The program's output looks like this:

```
Result = 1
Press any key to continue
```

Here is the program source code that produced the output:

```
#include "stdafx.h"
#include <iostream>
#include <float.h>

using namespace std;

int main(int argc, char* argv[])
{
    double value = 3456.09865;

    int result = _finite(value);
    cout << "Result = " << result << endl;

    return 0;
}
```

CROSS-REFERENCE

See also _fpclass() and _isnan().

_flushall()

Function

The _flushall() function flushes all open streams, returning the number of streams flushed.

Header File

```
#include <stdio.h>
```

Declaration

```
int _flushall(void);
```

Example

The following program demonstrates how to use the _flushall() function. When run, the program calls _flushall() to flush the standard I/O streams. The program's output looks like this:

```
Flushing all streams...
3 streams were flushed.
Press any key to continue
```

Here is the program source code that produced the output:

```
#include "stdafx.h"
#include <iostream>
#include <stdio.h>

using namespace std;

int main(int argc, char* argv[])
{
    cout << "Flushing all streams..." << endl;
    int num = _flushall();
    cout << num << " streams were flushed." << endl;

    return 0;
}
```

CROSS-REFERENCE
See also _close(), _creat(), _fcloseall(), _fdopen(), _fgetchar(), _fgetwchar(), _fileno(), _fputwchar(), _fsopen(), _getw(), _getws(), _lseeki64(), _open(), _putw(), _putws(), _read(), _rmtmp(), _tempnam(), _wcreat(), _wfdopen(), _wfopen(), _wfreopen(),_wfsopen(), _wopen(), _wtempnam(), _wtmpnam(), clearerr(), eof(), fclose(), feof(), ferror(), fflush(), fgetc(), fgetpos(), fgets(), fgetwc(), fgetws(), fopen(), fprintf(), fputc(), fputchar(), fputs(), fputwc(), fputws(), fread(), freopen(), fscanf(), fseek(), fsetpos(), ftell(), fwprintf(), fwrite(), fwscanf(), getc(), getchar(), gets(), getwc(), getwchar(), lseek(), putc(), putch(), putchar(), puts(), putwc(), putwchar(), rewind(), setbuf(), setvbuf(), tmpfile(), tmpnam(), ungetc(), ungetch(), ungetwc(), and write().

_fpclass()

Function

The _fpclass() function returns the floating-point status word, which contains information about the floating-point class of the function's argument. Table F-3 lists the possible return values.

NOTE
Borland does not support this function.

Table F-3 Return Values for _fpclass()

Value	Description
_FPCLASS_ND	Negative denormalized
_FPCLASS_NINF	Negative infinity
_FPCLASS_NN	Nonzero negative normalized
_FPCLASS_NZ	Negative zero
_FPCLASS_PD	Positive denormalized
_FPCLASS_PINF	Positive infinity
_FPCLASS_PN	Nonzero positive normalized
_FPCLASS_PZ	Positive zero
_FPCLASS_QNAN	Quiet NaN
_FPCLASS_SNAN	Signaling NaN

Header File

```
#include <float.h>
```

Declaration

```
int _fpclass(double value);
```

■ *value* — The value to test.

Example

The following program demonstrates how to use the _fpclass() function. When run, the program calls _fpclass() to test a value and displays the result. The program's output looks like this:

```
The value's class is: non-zero positive normalized
Press any key to continue
```

Here is the program source code that produced the output:

```
#include "stdafx.h"
#include <iostream>
#include <float.h>

using namespace std;

int main(int argc, char* argv[])
{
    double value = 3456.09865;

    int result = _fpclass(value);
    cout << "The value's class is: ";

    switch (result)
    {
    case _FPCLASS_ND:
        cout << "negative denormalized" << endl;
        break;
    case _FPCLASS_NINF:
        cout << "negative infinity" << endl;
        break;
    case _FPCLASS_NN:
        cout << "non-zero negative denormalized" << endl;
        break;
    case _FPCLASS_NZ:
```

```
                        cout << "negative zero" << endl;
                        break;
                case _FPCLASS_PD:
                        cout << "positive denormalized" << endl;
                        break;
                case _FPCLASS_PINF:
                        cout << "positive infinity" << endl;
                        break;
                case _FPCLASS_PN:
                        cout << "non-zero positive normalized" << endl;
                        break;
                case _FPCLASS_PZ:
                        cout << "positive zero" << endl;
                        break;
                case _FPCLASS_QNAN:
                        cout << "quiet NaN" << endl;
                        break;
                case _FPCLASS_SNAN:
                        cout << "signaling NaN" << endl;
                }

                return 0;
        }
```

CROSS-REFERENCE
See also _finite() and _isnan().

_fpreset()

Function

The _fpreset() function resets the floating-point package. The function returns no value.

Header File

```
#include <float.h>
```

Declaration

```
void _fpreset(void);
```

Example

The following program demonstrates how to use the _fpreset() function. When run, the program calls _fpreset() to reset the floating-point package. The program's output looks like this:

```
Floating-point package reset.
Press any key to continue
```

Here is the program source code that produced the output:

```cpp
#include "stdafx.h"
#include <iostream>
#include <float.h>

using namespace std;

int main(int argc, char* argv[])
{
    _fpreset();
    cout << "Floating-point package reset." << endl;

    return 0;
}
```

CROSS-REFERENCE
See also _clearfp(), _control87(), _controlfp(), and clear87().

_fputchar()

Function

The _fputchar() function writes a character into the standard output stream, returning the character written, or EOF in the case of an error.

Header File

```cpp
#include <stdio.h>
```

Declaration

```cpp
int _fputchar(int c);
```

- *c*—The character to write to the stream.

Example

The following program demonstrates how to use the _fputchar() function. When run, the program writes 25 Xs to the standard output stream. The program's output looks like this:

```
XXXXXXXXXXXXXXXXXXXXXXXXX

Press any key to continue
```

Here is the program source code that produced the output:

```cpp
#include "stdafx.h"
#include <stdio.h>
#include <iostream>

using namespace std;

int main(int argc, char* argv[])
{
    for (int x=0; x<25; ++x)
    {
        int result = _fputchar('X');
        if (result == EOF)
            cout << "_fputchar() error" << endl;
    }
    cout << endl << endl;

    return 0;
}
```

CROSS-REFERENCE

See also _close(), _creat(), _fcloseall(), _fdopen(), _fgetchar(), _fgetwchar(), _fileno(), _flushall(), _fputwchar(), _fsopen(), _getw(), _getws(), _lseeki64(), _open(), _putw(), _putws(), _read(), _rmtmp(), _tempnam(), _wcreat(), _wfdopen(), _wfopen(), _wfreopen(),_wfsopen(), _wopen(), _wtempnam(), _wtmpnam(), clearerr(), eof(), fclose(), feof(), ferror(), fflush(), fgetc(), fgetpos(), fgets(), fgetwc(), fgetws(), fopen(), fprintf(), fputc(), fputs(), fputwc(), fputws(), fread(), freopen(), fscanf(), fseek(), fsetpos(), ftell(), fwprintf(), fwrite(), fwscanf(), getc(), getchar(), gets(), getwc(), getwchar(), lseek(), putc(), putch(), putchar(), puts(), putwc(), putwchar(), rewind(), setbuf(), setvbuf(), tmpfile(), tmpnam(), ungetc(), ungetch(), ungetwc(), and write().

_fputwchar()

Function

The _fputwchar() function writes a wide character into the standard output stream, returning the character written, or WEOF in the case of an error.

Header File

```
#include <stdio.h>
```

Declaration

```
wint_t _fputwchar(wint_t c);
```

- *c*—The character to write to the stream.

Example

The following program demonstrates how to use the _fputwchar() function. When run, the program writes 25 Xs to the standard output stream. The program's output looks like this:

```
XXXXXXXXXXXXXXXXXXXXXXXXX

Press any key to continue
```

Here is the program source code that produced the output:

```
#include "stdafx.h"
#include <stdio.h>
#include <iostream>

using namespace std;

int main(int argc, char* argv[])
{
    for (int x=0; x<25; ++x)
    {
        wint_t result = _fputwchar(L'X');
        if (result == WEOF)
            cout << "_fputwchar() error" << endl;
    }
    cout << endl << endl;

    return 0;
}
```

CROSS-REFERENCE

See also _close(), _creat(), _fcloseall(), _fdopen(), _fgetchar(), _fgetwchar(), _fileno(), _flushall(), _fsopen(), _getw(), _getws(), _lseeki64(), _open(), _putw(), _putws(), _read(), _rmtmp(), _tempnam(), _wcreat(), _wfdopen(), _wfopen(), _wfreopen(),_wfsopen(), _wopen(), _wtempnam(), _wtmpnam(), clearerr(), eof(), fclose(), feof(), ferror(), fflush(), fgetc(), fgetpos(), fgets(), fgetwc(), fgetws(), fopen(), fprintf(), fputc(), fputchar(), fputs(), fputwc(), fputws(), fread(), freopen(), fscanf(), fseek(), fsetpos(), ftell(), fwprintf(), fwrite(), fwscanf(), getc(), getchar(), gets(), getwc(), getwchar(), lseek(), putc(), putch(), putchar(), puts(), putwc(), putwchar(), rewind(), setbuf(), setvbuf(), tmpfile(), tmpnam(), ungetc(), ungetch(), ungetwc(), and write().

_fsopen()

Function

The _fsopen() function opens a stream using file sharing.

Header File

```
#include <stdio.h>
```

Declaration

```
FILE* _fsopen(const char *filename,
    const char *mode, int shflag);
```

- *filename* — The name of the file to open.
- *mode* — The file access mode, which can be one of the mode values from Table F-4. The extension mode values shown in Table F-5 can be combined with the mode.
- *shflag* — The sharing flag for the stream, which can be a file sharing flag value (defined in share.h) from Table F-6.

Table F-4 Mode Values for _fsopen()

Value	Description
"r"	Open for reading.
"w"	Open for writing, which erases the file if it already exists or creates a new file if it doesn't exist.

Value	Description
"a"	Open for append, which writes to the end of an existing file or creates the file if it doesn't already exist.
"r+"	Open for both reading and writing.
"w+"	Open for both reading and writing. If the file already exists, its contents are lost; if the file doesn't exist, it's created.
"a+"	Open for reading and appending. If the file doesn't exist, it's created.

Table F-5 Extension Mode Values for _fsopen()

Value	Description
t	Open for in text mode.
b	Open in binary mode.
c	Set the file's commit flag.
n	Turn off the file's commit flag.

Table F-6 File Sharing Flag Values for _fsopen()

Value	Description
SH_COMPAT	Compatibility mode setting for 16-bit applications.
SH_DENYNO	Read and write access.
SH_DENYRD	No read access.
SH_DENYRW	No read or write access.
SH_DENYWR	No write access.

Example

The following program demonstrates how to use the _fsopen() function. When run, the program attempts to open a file that denies write access, prints a status message, and then closes the file if it opened successfully. The program's output looks like this:

```
File opened successfully.
Press any key to continue
```

Here is the program source code that produced the output:

```
#include "stdafx.h"
#include <stdio.h>
#include <iostream>
#include <share.h>

using namespace std;

int main(int argc, char* argv[])
{
    FILE* file = _fsopen("_fsopen.cpp", "r", _SH_DENYWR);

    if (file != NULL)
    {
        cout << "File opened successfully." << endl;
        fclose(file);
    }
    else
        cout << "File failed to open." << endl;

    return 0;
}
```

CROSS-REFERENCE

See also _close(), _creat(), _fcloseall(), _fdopen(), _fgetchar(), _fgetwchar(), _fileno(), _flushall(), _fputwchar(), _getw(), _getws(), _lseeki64(), _open(), _putw(), _putws(), _read(), _rmtmp(), _tempnam(), _wcreat(), _wfdopen(), _wfopen(), _wfreopen(),_wfsopen(), _wopen(), _wtempnam(), _wtmpnam(), clearerr(), eof(), fclose(), feof(), ferror(), fflush(), fgetc(), fgetpos(), fgets(), fgetwc(), fgetws(), fopen(), fprintf(), fputc(), fputchar(), fputs(), fputwc(), fputws(), fread(), freopen(), fscanf(), fseek(), fsetpos(), ftell(), fwprintf(), fwrite(), fwscanf(), getc(), getchar(), gets(), getwc(), getwchar(), lseek(), putc(), putch(), putchar(), puts(), putwc(), putwchar(), rewind(), setbuf(), setvbuf(), tmpfile(), tmpnam(), ungetc(), ungetch(), ungetwc(), and write().

_fstat()

Function

The _fstat() function retrieves status information about an open file, returning 0 if the information is obtained successfully, or –1 in the case of an error. The file information is returned into a _stat structure, which is defined as:

```
struct _stat
{
    _dev_t st_dev;    // Device handle or 0
    _ino_t st_ino;
    unsigned short st_mode; // File mode bit mask
    short st_nlink;   // Always 1 on non-NFTS
    short st_uid;
    short st_gid;
    _dev_t st_rdev;   // Device handle or 0
    _off_t st_size;   // File size
    time_t st_atime;  // Time of last access
    time_t st_mtime;  // Time of last modification
    time_t st_ctime;  // Creation time
};
```

NOTE

Borland users should refer to the fstat() function later in this chapter.

Header File

```
#include <sys/systypes.h>
#include <sys/stat.h>
```

Declaration

```
int _fstat(int handle, struct _stat *buffer);
```

- *buffer* — A pointer to the _stat structure that will hold the returned status information.
- *handle* — The handle of the file for which to acquire status information.

Example

The following program demonstrates how to use the _fstat() function. When run, the program acquires and displays size and time status information on a file. The program's output looks like this:

```
File Size: 772
Time: Wed Mar 10 00:00:00 1999
Press any key to continue
```

Here is the program source code that produced the output:

```cpp
#include "stdafx.h"
#include <fcntl.h>
#include <io.h>
#include <sys/types.h>
#include <sys/stat.h>
#include <time.h>
#include <iostream>

using namespace std;

int main(int argc, char* argv[])
{
    struct _stat statInfo;

    int fileHandle = _open( "_fstat.cpp", O_RDONLY);

    if(fileHandle ==  -1)
        cout << "File open error." << endl;
    else
    {
        int result = _fstat(fileHandle, &statInfo);
        if(result == 0)
        {
            cout << "File Size: " << statInfo.st_size << endl;
            cout << "Time: " << ctime(&statInfo.st_atime);
        }
        else
            cout << " _fstat() error" << endl;
    }
    close(fileHandle);

    return 0;
}
```

CROSS-REFERENCE

See also _fstati64(), _stat(), _stati64(), _wstat(), _wstati64, fstat(), and stat().

_fstati64()

Function

The _fstati64() retrieves, as a 64-bit integer, status information about an open file, returning 0 if the information is obtained successfully or returning -1 in the case of an error. The file information is returned into a _stati64 structure, which is defined as follows:

```
struct _stati64
{
    _dev_t st_dev;    // Device handle or 0
    _ino_t st_ino;
    unsigned short st_mode; // File mode bit mask
    short st_nlink;   // Always 1 on non-NFTS
    short st_uid;
    short st_gid;
    _dev_t st_rdev;   // Device handle or 0
    __int64 st_size;  // File size
    time_t st_atime;  // Time of last access
    time_t st_mtime;  // Time of last modification
    time_t st_ctime;  // Creation time
};
```

NOTE
Borland does not support this function.

Header File

```
#include <sys/systypes.h>
#include <sys/stat.h>
```

Declaration

```
__int64 _fstati64(int handle, struct _stati64 *buffer);
```

- *buffer*—A pointer to the _stati64 structure that will hold the returned status information.
- *handle*—The handle of the file for which to acquire status information.

Example

The following program demonstrates how to use the _fstati64() function. When run, the program acquires and displays size and time status information on a file. The program's output looks like this:

```
File Size: 772
Time: Wed Mar 10 00:00:00 1999
Press any key to continue
```

Here is the program source code that produced the output:

```cpp
#include "stdafx.h"
#include <fcntl.h>
#include <io.h>
#include <sys/types.h>
#include <sys/stat.h>
#include <time.h>
#include <iostream>

using namespace std;

int main(int argc, char* argv[])
{
    struct _stati64 statInfo;

    int fileHandle = open( "_fstati64.cpp", O_RDONLY);

    if(fileHandle ==  -1)
        cout << "File open error." << endl;
    else
    {
        __int64 result = _fstati64(fileHandle, &statInfo);
        if(result == 0)
        {
            cout << "File Size: " << (int)statInfo.st_size <<
endl;
            cout << "Time: " << ctime(&statInfo.st_atime);
        }
        else
            cout << "_fstati64() error" << endl;
    }
    close(fileHandle);

    return 0;
}
```

CROSS-REFERENCE
See also _fstat(), _stat(), _stati64(), _wstat(), _wstati64, fstat(), and stat().

_ftime()

Function

The _ftime() retrieves the current time. The function returns the time into a _timeb structure, which is defined as follows:

```
struct _timeb
{
    time_t time;    // Time in seconds since midnight 1/1/1970
    unsigned short millitm; // Milliseconds
    short timezone; // Difference from UTC in minutes
    short dstflag;  // Non-zero for DST
};
```

> **NOTE**
> Borland users should refer to the ftime() function later in this chapter.

Header File

```
#include <sys/types.h>
#include <sys/timeb.h>
```

Declaration

```
void _ftime(struct _timeb *timeptr);
```

- *timeptr* — A pointer to the _timeb structure that will hold the returned time information.

Example

The following program demonstrates how to use the _ftime() function. When run, the program acquires and displays time information. The program's output looks like this:

```
The current time is:
   Thu Mar 11 00:39:07 1999

Press any key to continue
```

Here is the program source code that produced the output:

```
#include "stdafx.h"
#include <sys/types.h>
```

```
#include <sys/timeb.h>
#include <time.h>
#include <iostream>

using namespace std;

int main(int argc, char* argv[])
{
    struct _timeb tb;

    cout << "The current time is:" << endl;
    _ftime(&tb);
    char* str = ctime(&tb.time);
    cout << "   " << str << endl;

    return 0;
}
```

CROSS-REFERENCE

See also asctime(), ctime(), ftime(), gmtime(), localtime(), and time().

_fullpath()

Function

The _fullpath() function creates a full path from a relative path name.

Header File

```
#include <stdlib.h>
```

Declaration

```
char* _fullpath(char *absPath,
    const char *relPath, size_t maxLength);
```

- *absPath*—A pointer to the character array that will hold the final path.
- *relPath*—The relative path for which the function should find the absolute path.

- *maxLength* — The maximum number of characters to return in the absolute path name.

Example

The following program demonstrates how to use the `_fullpath()` function. When run, the program creates and displays the full path for the program's source code file. The program's output looks like this:

```
Full Path:
C:\Microsoft\F\_fullpath\_fullpath.cpp
Press any key to continue
```

Here is the program source code that produced the output:

```cpp
#include "stdafx.h"
#include <stdlib.h>
#include <iostream>

using namespace std;

int main(int argc, char* argv[])
{
    char fullPath[_MAX_PATH];

    _fullpath(fullPath, "_fullpath.cpp", _MAX_PATH);
    if (fullPath == NULL)
        cout << "Error in path" << endl;
    else
    {
        cout << "Full Path: " << endl;
        cout << fullPath << endl;
    }

    return 0;
}
```

CROSS-REFERENCE

See also _getcwd(), _getdcwd(), _makepath(), _splitpath(), _wfullpath(), _wgetcwd(), _wgetdcwd(), _wmakepath(), and _wsplitpath().

_futime()

Function

The _futime() function sets the modification time on an open file, returning 0 if successful, or –1 in the case of an error.

NOTE
Borland does not support this function.

Header File

```
#include <sys/utime.h>
```

Declaration

```
int _futime(int handle, struct _utimbuf *filetime);
```

- *filetime* — A pointer to the _utimbuf structure that holds the new modification time. If this argument is NULL, then the function uses the current time.
- *handle* — The handle of the file for which to acquire time information.

Example

The following program demonstrates how to use the _futime() function. When run, the program displays a file's modification date both before and after a call to _futime(). The program's output looks like this:

```
Modification Time:
   Thu Mar 11 01:02:46 1999
Changing modification time...
New modification Time:
   Thu Mar 11 01:04:38 1999
Press any key to continue
```

Here is the program source code that produced the output:

```
#include "stdafx.h"
#include <fcntl.h>
#include <io.h>
#include <sys/types.h>
#include <sys/stat.h>
```

```cpp
#include <sys/utime.h>
#include <time.h>
#include <iostream>

using namespace std;

int main(int argc, char* argv[])
{
    struct _stat statInfo;

    int fileHandle = _open( "test.dat", O_RDWR);

    if (fileHandle ==  -1)
    {
        cout << "File open error." << endl;
        exit(1);
    }

    int result =_fstat(fileHandle, &statInfo);
    if(result != 0)
    {
        cout << " _fstat() error" << endl;
        close(fileHandle);
        exit(1);
    }

    cout << "Modification Time: " << endl;
    cout << "  " << ctime(&statInfo.st_mtime);
    cout << "Changing modification time..." << endl;
    result = _futime(fileHandle, NULL);
    if (result == 0)
    {
        _fstat(fileHandle, &statInfo);
        cout << "New modification Time: " << endl;
        cout << "  " << ctime(&statInfo.st_mtime);
    }
    else
        cout << "_futime() error" << endl;

    close(fileHandle);

    return 0;
}
```

e
f
g

CROSS-REFERENCE
See also _fstat(), _fstati64(), _stat(), _stati64(), _wstat(), _wstati64, fstat(), and stat().

fabs()

Function

The fabs() function gets the absolute value of floating-point value.

Header File

```
#include <math.h>
```

Declaration

```
double fabs(double x);
```

- *x*—The value for which to get the absolute value.

Example

The following program demonstrates how to use the fabs() function. When run, the program obtains and displays the absolute value of two floating-point values. The program's output looks like this:

```
var1 = 253.298
Absolute value of var1 = 253.298
var2 = -543.867
Absolute value of var2 = 543.867
Press any key to continue
```

Here is the program source code that produced the output:

```
#include "stdafx.h"
#include <math.h>
#include <iostream>

using namespace std;

int main(int argc, char* argv[])
{
    double var1 = 253.29834;
    double var2 = -543.86745;
```

```cpp
    cout << "var1 = " << var1 << endl;
        double result = fabs(var1);
        cout << "Absolute value of var1 = " << result << endl;
        cout << "var2 = " << var2 << endl;
        result = fabs(var2);
        cout << "Absolute value of var2 = " << result << endl;

        return 0;
    }
```

CROSS-REFERENCE

See also _cabs(), abs(), fabsf(), fabsl(), and labs().

fabsf()

Function

The `fabsf()` function gets the absolute value of floating-point value.

NOTE

Borland does not support this function.

Header File

```cpp
#include <math.h>
```

Declaration

```cpp
float fabsf(float x);
```

- *x* — The value for which to get the absolute value.

Example

The following program demonstrates how to use the `fabsf()` function. When run, the program obtains and displays the absolute value of two `float` values. The program's output looks like this:

```
var1 = 15.5
Absolute value of var1 = 15.5
var2 = 5.5
Absolute value of var2 = 5.5
Press any key to continue
```

Here is the program source code that produced the output:

```
#include "stdafx.h"
#include <math.h>
#include <iostream>

using namespace std;

int main(int argc, char* argv[])
{
    float var1 = 15.5;
    float var2 = 5.5;

    cout << "var1 = " << var1 << endl;
    float result = fabsf(var1);
    cout << "Absolute value of var1 = " << result << endl;
    cout << "var2 = " << var2 << endl;
    result = fabsf(var2);
    cout << "Absolute value of var2 = " << result << endl;

    return 0;
}
```

CROSS-REFERENCE
See also _cabs(), abs(), fabs(), fabsl(), and labs().

fabsl()

Function

The fabsl() function gets the absolute value of a long double value.

Header File

```
#include <math.h>
```

Declaration

```
long double fabsl(long double x);
```

- *x*—The value for which to get the absolute value.

Example

The following program demonstrates how to use the `fabsl()` function. When run, the program obtains and displays the absolute value of two `long double` values. The program's output looks like this:

```
var1 = 253.298
Absolute value of var1 = 253.298
var2 = -543.867
Absolute value of var2 = 543.867
Press any key to continue
```

Here is the program source code that produced the output:

```cpp
#include "stdafx.h"
#include <math.h>
#include <iostream>

using namespace std;

int main(int argc, char* argv[])
{
    long double var1 = 253.29834;
    long double var2 = -543.86745;

    cout << "var1 = " << var1 << endl;
    long double result = fabsl(var1);
    cout << "Absolute value of var1 = " << result << endl;
    cout << "var2 = " << var2 << endl;
    result = fabsl(var2);
    cout << "Absolute value of var2 = " << result << endl;

    return 0;
}
```

CROSS-REFERENCE
See also _cabs(), abs(), fabs(), fabsf(), and labs().

false

Keyword

The `false` keyword represents the false value of a Boolean data object. For example, the following program sets a Boolean variable to false and another

Boolean variable to true. The program then displays the variables' values on the screen. The program's output looks like this:

```
var1 = 0
var2 = 1
Press any key to continue
```

Here is the program source code that produced the output:

```
#include "stdafx.h"
#include <iostream>

using namespace std;

int main(int argc, char* argv[])
{
    bool var1 = false;
    bool var2 = true;

    cout << "var1 = " << var1 << endl;
    cout << "var2 = " << var2 << endl;

    return 0;
}
```

CROSS-REFERENCE
See also bool and true.

fclose()

Function

The fclose() function closes a stream, returning 0 if successful, or EOF if unsuccessful.

Header File

```
#include <stdio.h>
```

Declaration

```
int fclose(FILE *stream);
```

■ *stream* — A pointer to the stream to close.

Example

The following program demonstrates how to use the fclose() function. When run, the program attempts to open a file, print a status message, and then close the file if it opened successfully. The program's output looks like this:

```
File opened successfully.
Press any key to continue
```

Here is the program source code that produced the output:

```cpp
#include "stdafx.h"
#include <stdio.h>
#include <iostream>

using namespace std;

int main(int argc, char* argv[])
{
    FILE* file = fopen("fclose.cpp", "r");

    if (file != NULL)
    {
        cout << "File opened successfully." << endl;
        fclose(file);
    }
    else
        cout << "File failed to open." << endl;

    return 0;
}
```

CROSS-REFERENCE

See also _close(), _creat(), _fcloseall(), _fdopen(), _fgetchar(), _fgetwchar(), _fileno(), _flushall(), _fputwchar(), _fsopen(), _getw(), _getws(), _lseeki64(), _open(), _putw(), _putws(), _read(), _rmtmp(), _tempnam(), _wcreat(), _wfdopen(), _wfopen(), _wfreopen(),_wfsopen(), _wopen(), _wtempnam(), _wtmpnam(), clearerr(), eof(), feof(), ferror(), fflush(), fgetc(), fgetpos(), fgets(), fgetwc(), fgetws(), fopen(), fprintf(), fputc(), fputchar(), fputs(), fputwc(), fputws(), fread(), freopen(), fscanf(), fseek(), fsetpos(), ftell(), fwprintf(), fwrite(), fwscanf(), getc(), getchar(), gets(), getwc(), getwchar(), lseek(), putc(), putch(), putchar(), puts(), putwc(), putwchar(), rewind(), setbuf(), setvbuf(), tmpfile(), tmpnam(), ungetc(), ungetch(), ungetwc(), and write().

fcloseall()

Function

The fcloseall() function closes all streams, returning the number of streams closed if successful, or EOF if unsuccessful.

Header File

```
#include <stdio.h>
```

Declaration

```
int fcloseall(void);
```

Example

The following program demonstrates how to use the fcloseall() function. When run, the program attempts to open two files, print status messages, and then close the files if they opened successfully. The program's output looks like this:

```
First file opened successfully.
Second file opened successfully.
2 files closed successfully
Press any key to continue
```

Here is the program source code that produced the output:

```
#include "stdafx.h"
#include <stdio.h>
#include <iostream>

using namespace std;

int main(int argc, char* argv[])
{
    FILE* file1 = fopen("fcloseall.cpp", "r");
    if (file1 == NULL)
    {
        cout << "File open error." << endl;
        exit(1);
    }

    cout << "First file opened successfully." << endl;
```

```
FILE* file2 = fopen("stdafx.cpp", "r");
    if (file2 == NULL)
    {
        cout << "File open error." << endl;
        exit(1);
    }

    cout << "Second file opened successfully." << endl;

    int numClosed = fcloseall();
    cout << numClosed << " files closed successfully" << endl;

    return 0;
}
```

CROSS-REFERENCE

See also _close(), _creat(), _fcloseall(), _fdopen(), _fgetchar(), _fgetwchar(), _fileno(), _flushall(), _fputwchar(), _fsopen(), _getw(), _getws(), _lseeki64(), _open(), _putw(), _putws(), _read(), _rmtmp(), _tempnam(), _wcreat(), _wfdopen(), _wfopen(), _wfreopen(), _wfsopen(), _wopen(), _wtempnam(), _wtmpnam(), clearerr(), eof(), fclose(), feof(), ferror(), fflush(), fgetc(), fgetpos(), fgets(), fgetwc(), fgetws(), fopen(), fprintf(), fputc(), fputchar(), fputs(), fputwc(), fputws(), fread(), freopen(), fscanf(), fseek(), fsetpos(), ftell(), fwprintf(), fwrite(), fwscanf(), getc(), getchar(), gets(), getwc(), getwchar(), lseek(), putc(), putch(), putchar(), puts(), putwc(), putwchar(), rewind(), setbuf(), setvbuf(), tmpfile(), tmpnam(), ungetc(), ungetch(), ungetwc(), and write().

fcvt()

Function

The fcvt() function converts a floating-point value to a string of digits.

Header File

```
#include <stdlib.h>
```

Declaration

```
char* fcvt(double value, int count,
    int* decPosition, int* sign);
```

- *count* — The number of digits after the decimal point to return.
- *decPosition* — A pointer to an integer that will receive the position of the decimal point.
- *sign* — A pointer to an integer that will receive the value's sign, where 0 specifies a positive value and any other value specifies negative.
- *value* — The floating point value to convert.

Example

The following program demonstrates how to use the `fcvt()` function. When run, the program converts a floating-point value to a string of digits, and then displays the converted value, along with its decimal-position and sign values. The program's output looks like this:

```
Buffer: 243587564000
Decimal position: 4
Sign: 0
Press any key to continue
```

Here is the source code that produced the output:

```
#include "stdafx.h"
#include <iostream>

using namespace std;

int main(int argc, char* argv[])
{
    int decPosition;
    int sign;

    char* buf = fcvt(2435.87564, 8, &decPosition, &sign);
    cout << "Buffer: " << buf << endl;
    cout << "Decimal position: " << decPosition << endl;
    cout << "Sign: " << sign << endl;

    return 0;
}
```

 CROSS-REFERENCE
See also _ecvt(), _fcvt(), _gcvt(), and atof().

feof()

Function

The `feof()` function returns 0 if the given stream is not yet at the end of the file.

Header File

```
#include <stdio.h>
```

Declaration

```
int feof(FILE* stream);
```

- *stream* — A pointer to the stream.

Example

The following program demonstrates how to use the `feof()` function. When run, the program calls, reads, and displays its own source code file (as shown below), using the return value of the `feof()` function to control a `while` loop:

```
#include "stdafx.h"
#include <stdio.h>
#include <iostream>

using namespace std;

int main(int argc, char* argv[])
{
    char buf[2048];
    FILE *file;

    file = fopen("feof.cpp", "r");
    if (file == NULL)
        cout << "File open error" << endl;
    else
    {
        int i = 0;
        int ch = fgetc(file);
        while (!feof(file))
        {
            buf[i] = (char)ch;
```

```
                    ++i;
                    ch = fgetc(file);
                }

                buf[i] = 0;
                cout << buf << endl;
                fclose(file);
            }

        return 0;
    }
```

CROSS-REFERENCE

See also _close(), _creat(), _fcloseall(), _fdopen(), _fgetchar(), _fgetwchar(), _fileno(), _flushall(), _fputwchar(), _fsopen(), _getw(), _getws(), _lseeki64(), _open(), _putw(), _putws(), _read(), _rmtmp(), _tempnam(), _wcreat(), _wfdopen(), _wfopen(), _wfreopen(),_wfsopen(), _wopen(), _wtempnam(), _wtmpnam(), clearerr(), eof(), fclose(), ferror(), fflush(), fgetc(), fgetpos(), fgets(), fgetwc(), fgetws(), fopen(), fprintf(), fputc(), fputchar(), fputs(), fputwc(), fputws(), fread(), freopen(), fscanf(), fseek(), fsetpos(), ftell(), fwprintf(), fwrite(), fwscanf(), getc(), getchar(), gets(), getwc(), getwchar(), lseek(), putc(), putch(), putchar(), puts(), putwc(), putwchar(), rewind(), setbuf(), setvbuf(), tmpfile(), tmpnam(), ungetc(), ungetch(), ungetwc(), and write().

ferror()

Function

The ferror() function returns a nonzero value if an error occurs during stream manipulation, or 0 if no error occurs.

Header File

```
#include <stdio.h>
```

Declaration

```
int ferror(FILE* stream);
```

- *stream* — A pointer to the stream to test for an error.

Example

The following program demonstrates how to use the `ferror()` function. When run, the program calls, reads, and displays its own source code file, as shown below:

```cpp
#include "stdafx.h"
#include <stdio.h>
#include <iostream>

using namespace std;

int main(int argc, char* argv[])
{
    char buf[2048];
    FILE *file;

    file = fopen("ferror.cpp", "r");
    if (file == NULL)
        cout << "File open error" << endl;
    else
    {
        int i = 0;
        int ch = fgetc(file);
        while (!feof(file))
        {
            buf[i] = (char)ch;
            if (ferror(file))
                cout << "File error" << endl;
            ++i;
            ch = fgetc(file);
        }

        buf[i] = 0;
        cout << buf << endl;
        fclose(file);
    }

    return 0;
}
```

CROSS-REFERENCE

See also _close(), _creat(), _fcloseall(), _fdopen(), _fgetchar(), _fgetwchar(), _fileno(), _flushall(), _fputwchar(), _fsopen(), _getw(), _getws(), _lseeki64(), _open(), _putw(), _putws(), _read(), _rmtmp(), _tempnam(), _wcreat(), _wfdopen(), _wfopen(), _wfreopen(),_wfsopen(), _wopen(), _wtempnam(), _wtmpnam(), clearerr(), eof(), fclose(), feof(), fflush(), fgetc(), fgetpos(), fgets(), fgetwc(), fgetws(), fopen(), fprintf(), fputc(), fputchar(), fputs(), fputwc(), fputws(), fread(), freopen(), fscanf(), fseek(), fsetpos(), ftell(), fwprintf(), fwrite(), fwscanf(), getc(), getchar(), gets(), getwc(), getwchar(), lseek(), putc(), putch(), putchar(), puts(), putwc(), putwchar(), rewind(), setbuf(), setvbuf(), tmpfile(), tmpnam(), ungetc(), ungetch(), ungetwc(), and write().

fflush()

Function

The `fflush()` function flushes an open stream, returning 0 if successful, or `EOF` if unsuccessful.

Header File

```
#include <stdio.h>
```

Declaration

```
int fflush(FILE* stream);
```

- *stream* — A pointer to the stream to flush.

Example

The following program demonstrates how to use the `fflush()` function. When run, the program calls `fflush()` to flush the `stdout` standard output stream. The program's output looks like this:

```
Flushing the stdout stream...
Stream successfully flushed.
Press any key to continue
```

Here is the program source code that produced the output:

```
#include "stdafx.h"
#include <iostream>
#include <stdio.h>

using namespace std;

int main(int argc, char* argv[])
```

```
    {
        cout << "Flushing the stdout stream..." << endl;
        int result = fflush(stdout);
        if (result == 0)
            cout << "Stream successfully flushed." << endl;
        else
            cout << "fflush() error" << endl;

        return 0;
    }
```

CROSS-REFERENCE

See also _close(), _creat(), _fcloseall(), _fdopen(), _fgetchar(), _fgetwchar(), _fileno(), _flushall(), _fputwchar(), _fsopen(), _getw(), _getws(), _lseeki64(), _open(), _putw(), _putws(), _read(), _rmtmp(), _tempnam(), _wcreat(), _wfdopen(), _wfopen(), _wfreopen(),_wfsopen(), _wopen(), _wtempnam(), _wtmpnam(), clearerr(), eof(), fclose(), feof(), ferror(), fgetc(), fgetpos(), fgets(), fgetwc(), fgetws(), fopen(), fprintf(), fputc(), fputchar(), fputs(), fputwc(), fputws(), fread(), freopen(), fscanf(), fseek(), fsetpos(), ftell(), fwprintf(), fwrite(), fwscanf(), getc(), getchar(), gets(), getwc(), getwchar(), lseek(), putc(), putch(), putchar(), puts(), putwc(), putwchar(), rewind(), setbuf(), setvbuf(), tmpfile(), tmpnam(), ungetc(), ungetch(), ungetwc(), and write().

fgetc()

Function

The fgetc() function reads a character from a stream, returning the character read, or EOF in the case of an error or reaching the end of the file.

Header File

```
#include <stdio.h>
```

Declaration

```
int fgetc(FILE* stream);
```

- *stream* — A pointer to the stream from which to read a character.

Example

The following program demonstrates how to use the `fgetc()` function. When run, the program attempts to open a file and read the first line of text. The program then displays the line of text. The program's output looks like this:

```
// fgetc.cpp : Defines the entry point for the console
application.
Press any key to continue
```

Here is the program source code that produced the output:

```cpp
#include "stdafx.h"
#include <stdio.h>
#include <iostream>

using namespace std;

int main(int argc, char* argv[])
{
    char buf[81];
    FILE *file;

    file = fopen("fgetc.cpp", "r");
    if (file == NULL)
        cout << "File open error" << endl;
    else
    {
        int i = 0;
        int ch = fgetc(file);
        while (ch != '\n')
        {
            buf[i] = (char)ch;
            ++i;
            ch = fgetc(file);
        }

        buf[i] = 0;
        cout << buf << endl;
        fclose(file);
    }

    return 0;
}
```

CROSS-REFERENCE
See also _close(), _creat(), _fcloseall(), _fdopen(), _fgetchar(), _fgetwchar(), _fileno(), _flushall(), _fputwchar(), _fsopen(), _getw(), _getws(), _lseeki64(), _open(), _putw(), _putws(), _read(), _rmtmp(), _tempnam(), _wcreat(), _wfdopen(), _wfopen(), _wfreopen(),_wfsopen(), _wopen(), _wtempnam(), _wtmpnam(), clearerr(), eof(), fclose(), feof(), ferror(), fflush(), fgetpos(), fgets(), fgetwc(), fgetws(), fopen(), fprintf(), fputc(), fputchar(), fputs(), fputwc(), fputws(), fread(), freopen(), fscanf(), fseek(), fsetpos(), ftell(), fwprintf(), fwrite(), fwscanf(), getc(), getchar(), gets(), getwc(), getwchar(), lseek(), putc(), putch(), putchar(), puts(), putwc(), putwchar(), rewind(), setbuf(), setvbuf(), tmpfile(), tmpnam(), ungetc(), ungetch(), ungetwc(), and write().

fgetchar()

Function()

The `fgetchar()` function reads a character from the standard input stream, returning the character read, or `EOF` in the case of an error.

Header File

```
#include <stdio.h>
```

Declaration

```
int fgetchar(void);
```

Example

The following program demonstrates how to use the `fgetchar()` function. When run, the program reads a line of text from the console. The program then displays the line of text as shown in the following output:

```
Enter a line of text:
This is a test

The text you entered:
This is a test

Press any key to continue
```

Here is the program source code that produced the output:

```cpp
#include "stdafx.h"
#include <stdio.h>
#include <iostream>

using namespace std;

int main(int argc, char* argv[])
{
    char buf[81];

    cout << "Enter a line of text:" << endl;
    int i = 0;
    int ch = fgetchar();
    while (ch != '\n')
    {
        buf[i] = (char)ch;
        ++i;
        ch = fgetchar();
    }

    buf[i] = 0;
    cout << endl << "The text you entered:" << endl;
    cout << buf << endl << endl;

    return 0;
}
```

CROSS-REFERENCE

See also _close(), _creat(), _fcloseall(), _fdopen(), _fgetchar(), _fgetwchar(), _fileno(), _flushall(), _fputwchar(), _fsopen(), _getw(), _getws(), _lseeki64(), _open(), _putw(), _putws(), _read(), _rmtmp(), _tempnam(), _wcreat(), _wfdopen(), _wfopen(), _wfreopen(),_wfsopen(), _wopen(), _wtempnam(), _wtmpnam(), clearerr(), eof(), fclose(), feof(), ferror(), fflush(), fgetc(), fgetpos(), fgets(), fgetwc(), fgetws(), fopen(), fprintf(), fputc(), fputchar(), fputs(), fputwc(), fputws(), fread(), freopen(), fscanf(), fseek(), fsetpos(), ftell(), fwprintf(), fwrite(), fwscanf(), getc(), getchar(), gets(), getwc(), getwchar(), lseek(), putc(), putch(), putchar(), puts(), putwc(), putwchar(), rewind(), setbuf(), setvbuf(), tmpfile(), tmpnam(), ungetc(), ungetch(), ungetwc(), and write().

fgetpos()

Function

The fgetpos() function gets the position of the file pointer, returning 0 if successful, or a nonzero value if unsuccessful.

Header File

```
#include <stdio.h>
```

Declaration

```
int fgetpos(FILE* stream, fpos_t* pos);
```

- *pos* — A pointer to the variable that will hold the file position.
- *stream* — A pointer to the stream for which to get the file position.

Example

The following program demonstrates how to use the fgetpos() function. When run, the program attempts to open a file and read the first line of text, displaying the file pointer position as it goes. The program's output looks like this:

```
1 2 3 4 5 6 7 8 9 10 11 12 13 14 15 16 17 18 19 20 21 22 23 24
25 26 27 28 29 30 31 32 33 34 35 36 37 38 39 40 41 42 43 44 45
46 47 48 49 50 51 52 53 54 55 56 57 58 59 60 61 62 63 64 65 66
67 68 69
// fgetpos.cpp : Defines the entry point for the console
application.
Press any key to continue
```

Here is the program source code that produced the output:

```cpp
#include "stdafx.h"
#include <stdio.h>
#include <iostream>

using namespace std;

int main(int argc, char* argv[])
{
    char buf[81];
```

```
FILE *file;
fpos_t pos;

file = fopen("fgetpos.cpp", "r");
if (file == NULL)
    cout << "File open error" << endl;
else
{
    int i = 0;
    int ch = fgetc(file);
    while (ch != '\n')
    {
        int result = fgetpos(file, &pos);
        if (result != 0)
            cout << "fgetpos() error" << endl;
        else
            cout << (int)pos << " ";

        buf[i] = (char)ch;
        ++i;
        ch = fgetc(file);
    }

    cout << endl;
    buf[i] = 0;
    cout << buf << endl;
    fclose(file);
}

return 0;
}
```

CROSS-REFERENCE

See also _close(), _creat(), _fcloseall(), _fdopen(), _fgetchar(), _fgetwchar(), _fileno(), _flushall(), _fputwchar(), _fsopen(), _getw(), _getws(), _lseeki64(), _open(), _putw(), _putws(), _read(), _rmtmp(), _tempnam(), _wcreat(), _wfdopen(), _wfopen(), _wfreopen(),_wfsopen(), _wopen(), _wtempnam(), _wtmpnam(), clearerr(), eof(), fclose(), feof(), ferror(), fflush(), fgetc(), fgets(), fgetwc(), fgetws(), fopen(), fprintf(), fputc(), fputchar(), fputs(), fputwc(), fputws(), fread(), freopen(), fscanf(), fseek(), fsetpos(), ftell(), fwprintf(), fwrite(), fwscanf(), getc(), getchar(), gets(), getwc(), getwchar(), lseek(), putc(), putch(), putchar(), puts(), putwc(), putwchar(), rewind(), setbuf(), setvbuf(), tmpfile(), tmpnam(), ungetc(), ungetch(), ungetwc(), and write().

fgets()

Function

The `fgets()` function reads a string from a stream, returning a pointer to the string, or `NULL` in the case of an error or reaching the end of the file.

Header File

```
#include <stdio.h>
```

Declaration

```
char* fgets(char* string, int n, FILE* stream);
```

- *n* — The maximum number of characters to read.
- *stream* — A pointer to the stream from which to read a string.
- *string* — A pointer to the buffer into which to read the string.

Example

The following program demonstrates how to use the `fgets()` function. When run, the program attempts to open a file and read the first five lines of text. The program then displays the text. The program's output looks like this:

```
// fgets.cpp : Defines the entry point for the console
application.
//

#include "stdafx.h"
#include <stdio.h>

Press any key to continue
```

Here is the program source code that produced the output:

```
#include "stdafx.h"
#include <stdio.h>
#include <iostream>

using namespace std;

int main(int argc, char* argv[])
{
```

```
        char buf[81];
        FILE *file;

        file = fopen("fgets.cpp", "r");
        if (file == NULL)
            cout << "File open error" << endl;
        else
        {
            for (int x=0; x<5; ++x)
            {
                char* str = fgets(buf, 80, file);
                cout << str;
            }

            cout << endl;
            fclose(file);
        }

        return 0;
    }
```

CROSS-REFERENCE

See also _close(), _creat(), _fcloseall(), _fdopen(), _fgetchar(), _fgetwchar(), _fileno(), _flushall(), _fputwchar(), _fsopen(), _getw(), _getws(), _lseeki64(), _open(), _putw(), _putws(), _read(), _rmtmp(), _tempnam(), _wcreat(), _wfdopen(), _wfopen(), _wfreopen(),_wfsopen(), _wopen(), _wtempnam(), _wtmpnam(), clearerr(), eof(), fclose(), feof(), ferror(), fflush(), fgetc(), fgetpos(), fgetwc(), fgetws(), fopen(), fprintf(), fputc(), fputchar(), fputs(), fputwc(), fputws(), fread(), freopen(), fscanf(), fseek(), fsetpos(), ftell(), fwprintf(), fwrite(), fwscanf(), getc(), getchar(), gets(), getwc(), getwchar(), lseek(), putc(), putch(), putchar(), puts(), putwc(), putwchar(), rewind(), setbuf(), setvbuf(), tmpfile(), tmpnam(), ungetc(), ungetch(), ungetwc(), and write().

fgetwc()

Function

The fgetwc() function reads a wide character from a stream, returning the character read, or WEOF in the case of an error or reaching the end of the file.

NOTE

This function works only on systems, such as Windows NT, that support wide-character filenames.

Header File

```
#include <stdio.h>
```

Declaration

```
wint_t fgetwc(FILE* stream);
```

- *stream* — A pointer to the stream from which to read a character.

Example

The following program demonstrates how to use the `fgetwc()` function. When run, the program attempts to open a file and read 80 characters of text. The program's output looks like this:

```
// fgetwc.cpp : Defines the entry point for the application.
//

#include "stdaf
Press any key to continue
```

Here is the program source code that produced the output:

```
#include "stdafx.h"
#include <stdio.h>
#include <iostream>

using namespace std;

int main(int argc, char* argv[])
{
    wchar_t buf[81];
    FILE *file;

    file = _wfopen(L"fgetwc.cpp", L"r");
    if (file == NULL)
        cout << "File open error" << endl;
    else
    {
        int i = 0;
```

```
                   wint_t ch = fgetwc(file);
                   while (i < 80)
                   {
                       buf[i] = (wchar_t)ch;
                       ++i;
                       ch = fgetwc(file);
                   }

                   buf[i] = 0;
                   wcout << buf << endl;
                   fclose(file);
               }

               return 0;
           }
```

CROSS-REFERENCE

See also _close(), _creat(), _fcloseall(), _fdopen(), _fgetchar(), _fgetwchar(), _fileno(), _flushall(), _fputwchar(), _fsopen(), _getw(), _getws(), _lseeki64(), _open(), _putw(), _putws(), _read(), _rmtmp(), _tempnam(), _wcreat(), _wfdopen(), _wfopen(), _wfreopen(),_wfsopen(), _wopen(), _wtempnam(), _wtmpnam(), clearerr(), eof(), fclose(), feof(), ferror(), fflush(), fgetc(), fgetpos(), fgets(), fgetws(), fopen(), fprintf(), fputc(), fputchar(), fputs(), fputwc(), fputws(), fread(), freopen(), fscanf(), fseek(), fsetpos(), ftell(), fwprintf(), fwrite(), fwscanf(), getc(), getchar(), gets(), getwc(), getwchar(), lseek(), putc(), putch(), putchar(), puts(), putwc(), putwchar(), rewind(), setbuf(), setvbuf(), tmpfile(), tmpnam(), ungetc(), ungetch(), ungetwc(), and write().

fgetws()

Function

The fgetws() function reads a wide-character string from a stream, returning a pointer to the string, or NULL in the case of an error or when the end of the file is reached.

NOTE

This function works only on systems, such as Windows NT, that support wide-character filenames.

Header File

```
#include <stdio.h>
```

Declaration

```
wchar_t* fgetws(wchar_t* string, int n, FILE* stream);
```

- *n* — The maximum number of characters to read.
- *stream* — A pointer to the stream from which to read a string.
- *string* — A pointer to the buffer into which to read the string.

Example

The following program demonstrates how to use the `fgetws()` function. When run, the program attempts to open a file and read the first five lines of text. The program's output looks like this:

```
// fgetws.cpp : Defines the entry point for the application.
//

#include "stdafx.h"
#include <stdio.h>

Press any key to continue
```

Here is the program source code that produced the output:

```
#include "stdafx.h"
#include <stdio.h>
#include <iostream>

using namespace std;

int main(int argc, char* argv[])
{
    wchar_t buf[81];
    FILE *file;

    file = _wfopen(L"fgetws.cpp", L"r");
    if (file == NULL)
        cout << "File open error" << endl;
    else
    {
        for (int x=0; x<5; ++x)
```

```
      {
          wchar_t* str = fgetws(buf, 80, file);
          wcout << str;
      }

      cout << endl;
      fclose(file);
  }

  return 0;
}
```

CROSS-REFERENCE
See also _close(), _creat(), _fcloseall(), _fdopen(), _fgetchar(), _fgetwchar(), _fileno(), _flushall(), _fputwchar(), _fsopen(), _getw(), _getws(), _lseeki64(), _open(), _putw(), _putws(), _read(), _rmtmp(), _tempnam(), _wcreat(), _wfdopen(), _wfopen(), _wfreopen(),_wfsopen(), _wopen(), _wtempnam(), _wtmpnam(), clearerr(), eof(), fclose(), feof(), ferror(), fflush(), fgetc(), fgetpos(), fgets(), fgetwc(), fopen(), fprintf(), fputc(), fputchar(), fputs(), fputwc(), fputws(), fread(), freopen(), fscanf(), fseek(), fsetpos(), ftell(), fwprintf(), fwrite(), fwscanf(), getc(), getchar(), gets(), getwc(), getwchar(), lseek(), putc(), putch(), putchar(), puts(), putwc(), putwchar(), rewind(), setbuf(), setvbuf(), tmpfile(), tmpnam(), ungetc(), ungetch(), ungetwc(), and write().

filelength()

Function()

The `filelength()` function returns the number of bytes in a file, or −1L in the case of an error.

Header File

```
#include <io.h>
```

Declaration

```
long filelength(int handle);
```

- *handle* — The file's handle.

Example

The following program demonstrates how to use the `filelength()` function. When run, the program opens a file and displays the file's byte size. The program's output looks like this:

```
Opening a file...
The file's length is 676 bytes.


Press any key to continue
```

Here is the program source code that produced the output:

```cpp
#include "stdafx.h"
#include <io.h>
#include <fcntl.h>
#include <sys/types.h>
#include <sys/stat.h>
#include <iostream>

using namespace std;

int main(int argc, char* argv[])
{
    cout << "Opening a file..." << endl;
    int fileHandle = open( "filelength.cpp",
        O_RDONLY, S_IREAD);
    if (fileHandle != -1)
    {
        int fileSize = filelength(fileHandle);
        cout << "The file's length is " << fileSize;
        cout << " bytes." << endl << endl;
        close(fileHandle);
    }
    else
        cout << "File open error." << endl;

    return 0;
}
```

CROSS-REFERENCE

See also _chsize(), _filelength(), _filelengthi64(), and chsize().

fileno()

Function()

The `fileno()` function returns the file handle of the file attached to a stream.

Header File

```
#include <stdio.h>
```

Declaration

```
int fileno(FILE *stream);
```

- *stream* — A pointer to the stream for which to get the file handle.

Example

The following program demonstrates how to use the `fileno()` function. When run, the program opens a file and displays the file's handle. The program's output looks like this:

```
File opened successfully.
The file handle is 3
Press any key to continue
```

Here is the program source code that produced the output:

```cpp
#include "stdafx.h"
#include <stdio.h>
#include <iostream>

using namespace std;

int main(int argc, char* argv[])
{
    FILE* file = fopen("fileno.cpp", "r");

    if (file != NULL)
    {
        cout << "File opened successfully." << endl;
        int fileHandle = fileno(file);
        cout << "The file handle is " << fileHandle << endl;
        fclose(file);
    }
```

```
        else
            cout << "File failed to open." << endl;

        return 0;
    }
```

CROSS-REFERENCE
See also _filelength(), _filelengthi64(), _fileno(), and filelength().

findclose()

Function

The findclose() function closes a find handle created by the findfirst() function, returning 0 if successful, or −1 if unsuccessful.

NOTE
Microsoft users should refer to the _findclose() function earlier in this chapter.

Header File

```
#include <io.h>
```

Declaration

```
int findclose(long handle);
```

■ *handle* — The find handle to close.

Example

The following program demonstrates how to use the findclose() function. When run, the program looks for all files in the current directory, printing each file's name and size. The program's output looks like this.

```
FILE: findclose.obj — 111995 bytes
FILE: findclose.cpp — 928 bytes
FILE: findclose.bpr — 3990 bytes
FILE: findclose.~bp — 3990 bytes
FILE: findclose.tds — 524288 bytes
FILE: findclose.exe — 167936 bytes
Press any key to continue
```

Here is the program source code that produced the output:

```
#pragma hdrstop
#include <condefs.h>
#include <dir.h>
#include <stdio.h>
#include <iostream>

//————————————————————————
#pragma argsused
int main(int argc, char **argv)
{
    struct ffblk fileData;

    long fileHandle = findfirst("*.*", &fileData, 0);

    if(fileHandle == -1L)
        cout << "No files found." << endl;
    else
    {
        cout << "FILE: " << fileData.ff_name;
        cout << " — " << fileData.ff_fsize << " bytes" <<
endl;

        int result = findnext(&fileData);
        while(result == 0 )
        {
            cout << "FILE: " << fileData.ff_name;
            cout << " — " << fileData.ff_fsize << " bytes";
            cout << endl;
            result = findnext(&fileData);
        }

        findclose(&fileData);
    }

    cout << "Press Enter to continue" << endl;
    getchar();

    return 0;
}
```

CROSS-REFERENCE

See also _findclose(), _findfirst(), _findfirsti64(), _findnext(), _findnexti64(), _wfindfirst(), _wfindfirsti64(), _wfindnext(), _wfindnexti64, and findnext().

findfirst()

Function

The `findfirst()` function finds the first file that matches the given specification, returning a handle to the file. If the function fails, it returns –1, and the `errno` global variable is set to `ENOENT` (no matching files) or `EINVAL` (invalid file specification).

NOTE

Microsoft users should refer to the `_findfirst()` function earlier in this chapter.

Header File

```
#include <io.h>
```

Declaration

```
long findfirst(char *filespec, struct ffblk *fileinfo);
```

- *fileinfo* — A pointer to a `ffblk` structure in which the function will store information about the requested file.
- *filespec* — The file specification returned by findfirst().

Example

The following program demonstrates how to use the `findfirst()` function. When run, the program looks for all files in the current directory, printing each file's name and size. The program's output looks like this:

```
FILE: _findfirst.bpr – 3992 bytes
FILE: _findfirst.cpp – 928 bytes
FILE: _findfirst.obj – 111998 bytes
FILE: _findfirst.tds – 524288 bytes
FILE: _findfirst.exe – 167936 bytes
Press Enter to continue
```

Here is the program source code that produced the output:

```
#pragma hdrstop
#include <condefs.h>
#include <dir.h>
#include <stdio.h>
#include <io.h>
#include <iostream>

//————————————————————————————
#pragma argsused
int main(int argc, char **argv)
{
    struct ffblk fileData;

    long fileHandle = findfirst("*.*", &fileData, 0);

    if(fileHandle == -1L)
        cout << "No files found." << endl;
    else
    {
        cout << "FILE: " << fileData.ff_name;
        cout << " — " << fileData.ff_fsize << " bytes" <<
endl;

        int result = findnext(&fileData);
        while(result == 0 )
        {
            cout << "FILE: " << fileData.ff_name;
            cout << " — " << fileData.ff_fsize << " bytes";
            cout << endl;
            result = findnext(&fileData);
        }

        findclose(&fileData);
    }

    cout << "Press Enter to continue" << endl;
    getchar();

    return 0;
}
```

CROSS-REFERENCE

See also _findclose(), _findfirst(), _findfirsti64(), _findnext(), _findnexti64(), _wfindfirst(), _wfindfirsti64(), _wfindnext(), _wfindnexti64, findclose(), and findnext().

findnext()

Function

The findnext() function finds the next file that matches the given specification, returning a handle to the file. If the function fails, it returns –1, and the errno global variable is set to ENOENT (no matching files).

NOTE

Microsoft users should refer to the _findnext() function earlier in this chapter.

Header File

```
#include <io.h>
```

Declaration

```
int findnext(long handle, struct ffblk *fileinfo);
```

- *fileinfo* — A pointer to a ffblk structure in which the function will store information about the requested file.
- *handle* — The file handle returned by findfirst().

Example

The following program demonstrates how to use the findnext() function. When run, the program looks for all files in the current directory, printing each file's name and size. The program's output looks like this.

```
FILE: _findnext.bpr — 3990 bytes
FILE: _findnext.cpp — 928 bytes
FILE: _findnext.obj — 111992 bytes
FILE: _findnext.tds — 524288 bytes
FILE: _findnext.exe — 167936 bytes
Press Enter to continue
```

Here is the program source code that produced the output:

```cpp
#pragma hdrstop
#include <condefs.h>
#include <dir.h>
#include <stdio.h>
#include <io.h>
#include <iostream>

//─────────────────────────────────────
#pragma argsused
int main(int argc, char **argv)
{
    struct ffblk fileData;

    long fileHandle = findfirst("*.*", &fileData, 0);

    if(fileHandle == -1L)
        cout << "No files found." << endl;
    else
    {
        cout << "FILE: " << fileData.ff_name;
        cout << " - " << fileData.ff_fsize << " bytes" <<
endl;

        int result = findnext(&fileData);
        while(result == 0 )
        {
            cout << "FILE: " << fileData.ff_name;
            cout << " - " << fileData.ff_fsize << " bytes";
            cout << endl;
            result = findnext(&fileData);
        }

        findclose(&fileData);
    }

    cout << "Press Enter to continue" << endl;
    getchar();

    return 0;
}
```

CROSS-REFERENCE
See also _findclose(), _findfirst(), _findfirsti64(), _findnext(), _findnexti64(), _wfindfirst(), _wfindfirsti64(), _wfindnext(), _wfindnexti64, and findclose().

float

Keyword

The `float` keyword enables programs to declare single-precision floating-point values, which are 4-byte values that can range from 3.4E–38 to 3.4E+38. For example, the following line declares a floating-point variable and initializes its value to 36.894.

```
float var1 = 36.894;
```

CROSS-REFERENCE
See also char, double, int, long, short, signed, and unsigned.

float.h

Standard C Library Header File

The float.h header file defines constants and functions used to write programs that rely heavily on floating-point values.

Defined Constants

CW_DEFAULT	_EM_UNDERFLOW
_DBL_RADIX	_EM_ZERODIVIDE
_DBL_ROUNDS	_FPCLASS_ND
_DN_FLUSH	_FPCLASS_NINF
_DN_FLUSH_OPERANDS_SAVE_RESULTS	_FPCLASS_NN
	_FPCLASS_NZ
_DN_SAVE	_FPCLASS_PD
_DN_SAVE_OPERANDS_FLUSH_RESULTS	_FPCLASS_PINF
	_FPCLASS_PN
_EM_DENORMAL	_FPCLASS_PZ
_EM_INEXACT	_FPCLASS_QNAN
_EM_INVALID	_FPCLASS_SNAN
_EM_OVERFLOW	_FPE_DENORMAL

_FPE_EXPLICITGEN	_SW_STACKUNDERFLOW
_FPE_INEXACT	_SW_UNDERFLOW
_FPE_INVALID	_SW_UNEMULATED
_FPE_OVERFLOW	_SW_ZERODIVIDE
_FPE_SQRTNEG	CW_DEFAULT
_FPE_STACKOVERFLOW	DBL_DIG
_FPE_STACKUNDERFLOW	DBL_EPSILON
_FPE_UNDERFLOW	DBL_MANT_DIG
_FPE_UNEMULATED	DBL_MAX
_FPE_ZERODIVIDE	DBL_MAX_10_EXP
_IC_AFFINE	DBL_MAX_EXP
_IC_PROJECTIVE	DBL_MIN
_LDBL_RADIX	DBL_MIN_10_EXP
_LDBL_ROUNDS	DBL_MIN_EXP
_MCW_DN	DBL_RADIX
_MCW_EM	DBL_ROUNDS
_MCW_IC	EM_DENORMAL
_MCW_PC	EM_INEXACT
_MCW_RC	EM_INVALID
_PC_24	EM_OVERFLOW
_PC_24	EM_UNDERFLOW
_PC_53	EM_ZERODIVIDE
_PC_53	FLT_DIG
_PC_64	FLT_EPSILON
_PC_64	FLT_GUARD
_RC_CHOP	FLT_MANT_DIG
_RC_DOWN	FLT_MAX
_RC_NEAR	FLT_MAX_10_EXP
_RC_UP	FLT_MAX_EXP
_SW_DENORMAL	FLT_MIN
_SW_INEXACT	FLT_MIN_10_EXP
_SW_INVALID	FLT_MIN_EXP
_SW_OVERFLOW	FLT_NORMALIZE
_SW_SQRTNEG	FLT_RADIX
_SW_STACKOVERFLOW	FLT_ROUNDS

FPE_DENORMAL	LDBL_ROUNDS
FPE_EXPLICITGEN	MCW_EM
FPE_INEXACT	MCW_IC
FPE_INVALID	MCW_PC
FPE_OVERFLOW	MCW_RC
FPE_SQRTNEG	PC_24
FPE_STACKOVERFLOW	PC_53
FPE_STACKUNDERFLOW	PC_64
FPE_UNDERFLOW	RC_CHOP
FPE_UNEMULATED	RC_DOWN
FPE_ZERODIVIDE	RC_NEAR
IC_AFFINE	RC_UP
IC_PROJECTIVE	SW_DENORMAL
LDBL_DIG	SW_INEXACT
LDBL_EPSILON	SW_INVALID
LDBL_MANT_DIG	SW_OVERFLOW
LDBL_MAX	SW_SQRTNEG
LDBL_MAX_10_EXP	SW_STACKOVERFLOW
LDBL_MAX_EXP	SW_STACKUNDERFLOW
LDBL_MIN	SW_UNDERFLOW
LDBL_MIN_10_EXP	SW_UNEMULATED
LDBL_MIN_EXP	SW_ZERODIVIDE
LDBL_RADIX	

Defined Functions

__fpecode()	_isnan()
_chgsign()	_logb()
_clearfp()	_nextafter()
_control87()	_scalb()
_controlfp()	_statusfp()
_copysign()	clear87()
_finite()	control87()
_fpclass()	fpreset()
_fpecode()	status87()
_fpreset()	

floor()

Function

The floor() function returns the largest value that is less than or equal to the given double value.

Header File

```
#include <math.h>
```

Declaration

```
double floor(double value);
```

- *value* — The value for which to get the floor.

Example

The following program demonstrates how to use the floor() function. When run, the program calls floor() and displays the result. The program's output looks like this:

```
var1 = 32.789
Floor of var1 = 32
var2 = -15.895
Floor of var2 = -16
Press any key to continue
```

Here is the program source code that produced the output:

```
#include "stdafx.h"
#include <iostream>
#include <math.h>

using namespace std;

int main(int argc, char* argv[])
{
    double var1 = 32.789;
    double var2 = -15.895;

    cout << "var1 = " << var1 << endl;
    double result = floor(var1);
    cout << "Floor of var1 = " << result << endl;
```

```
        cout << "var2 = " << var2 << endl;
        result = floor(var2);
        cout << "Floor of var2 = " << result << endl;

        return 0;
    }
```

CROSS-REFERENCE
See also ceil(), ceill(), floorf(), and floorl().

floorf()

Function

The `floorf()` function returns the largest value that is less than or equal to the given floating-point value.

NOTE
Borland does not support this function.

Header File

```
#include <math.h>
```

Declaration

```
float floorf(float value);
```

- *value* — The value for which to get the floor.

Example

The following program demonstrates how to use the `floorf()` function. When run, the program calls `floorf()` and displays the result. The program's output looks like this:

```
var1 = 15.5
Floor of var1 = 15
var2 = -15.5
Floor of var2 = -16
Press any key to continue
```

Here is the program source code that produced the output:

```
#include "stdafx.h"
#include <iostream>
#include <math.h>

using namespace std;

int main(int argc, char* argv[])
{
    float var1 = 15.5;
    float var2 = -15.5;

    cout << "var1 = " << var1 << endl;
    float result = floorf(var1);
    cout << "Floor of var1 = " << result << endl;
    cout << "var2 = " << var2 << endl;
    result = floorf(var2);
    cout << "Floor of var2 = " << result << endl;

    return 0;
}
```

CROSS-REFERENCE
See also ceil(), ceill(), floor(), and floorl().

floorl()

Function

The floorl() function returns the largest value that is less than or equal to the given long double value.

Header File

```
#include <math.h>
```

Declaration

```
long double floorl(long double value);
```

- *value* — The value for which to get the floor.

Example

The following program demonstrates how to use the `floorl()` function. When run, the program calls `floorl()` and displays the result. The program's output looks like this:

```
var1 = 32.789
Floor of var1 = 32
var2 = -15.895
Floor of var2 = -16
Press any key to continue
```

Here is the program source code that produced the output:

```
#include "stdafx.h"
#include <iostream>
#include <math.h>

using namespace std;

int main(int argc, char* argv[])
{
    long double var1 = 32.789;
    long double var2 = -15.895;

    cout << "var1 = " << var1 << endl;
    long double result = floorl(var1);
    cout << "Floor of var1 = " << result << endl;
    cout << "var2 = " << var2 << endl;
    result = floorl(var2);
    cout << "Floor of var2 = " << result << endl;

    return 0;
}
```

CROSS-REFERENCE
See also ceil(), ceill(), floor(), and floorf().

flushall()

Function

The `flushall()` function flushes all open streams, returning the number of streams flushed.

Header File

```
#include <stdio.h>
```

Declaration

```
int flushall(void);
```

Example

The following program demonstrates how to use the flushall() function. When run, the program calls flushall() to flush the standard I/O streams. The program's output looks like this:

```
Flushing all streams...
3 streams were flushed.
Press any key to continue
```

Here is the program source code that generated the output:

```
#include "stdafx.h"
#include <iostream>
#include <stdio.h>

using namespace std;

int main(int argc, char* argv[])
{
    cout << "Flushing all streams..." << endl;
    int num = flushall();
    cout << num << " streams were flushed." << endl;

    return 0;
}
```

CROSS-REFERENCE

See also _close(), _creat(), _fcloseall(), _fdopen(), _fgetchar(), _fgetwchar(), _fileno(), _flushall(), _fputwchar(), _fsopen(), _getw(), _getws(), _lseeki64(), _open(), _putw(), _putws(), _read(), _rmtmp(), _tempnam(), _wcreat(), _wfdopen(), _wfopen(), _wfreopen(),_wfsopen(), _wopen(), _wtempnam(), _wtmpnam(), clearerr(), eof(), fclose(), feof(), ferror(), fflush(), fgetc(), fgetpos(), fgets(), fgetwc(), fgetws(), fopen(), fprintf(), fputc(), fputchar(), fputs(), fputwc(), fputws(), fread(), freopen(), fscanf(), fseek(), fsetpos(), ftell(), fwprintf(), fwrite(), fwscanf(), getc(), getchar(), gets(), getwc(), getwchar(), lseek(), putc(), putch(), putchar(), puts(), putwc(), putwchar(), rewind(), setbuf(), setvbuf(), tmpfile(), tmpnam(), ungetc(), ungetch(), ungetwc(), and write().

fmod()

Function

The `fmod()` function returns the floating-point remainder of a floating-point division operation.

Header File

```
#include <math.h>
```

Declaration

```
double fmod(double x, double y);
```

- x — The operation's dividend.
- y — The operation's divisor.

Example

The following program demonstrates how to use the `fmod()` function. When run, the program calls `fmod()` and displays the result. The program's output looks like this:

```
var1 = 32.789
var2 = -15.895
The fmod() result of var1/var2 = 0.999
Press any key to continue
```

Here is the program source code that produced the output:

```
#include "stdafx.h"
#include <iostream>
#include <math.h>

using namespace std;

int main(int argc, char* argv[])
{
    double var1 = 32.789;
```

```
                    double var2 = -15.895;

                    cout << "var1 = " << var1 << endl;
                    cout << "var2 = " << var2 << endl;
                    double result = fmod(var1, var2);
                    cout << "The fmod() result of var1/var2 = ";
                    cout << result << endl;

                    return 0;
                }
```

CROSS-REFERENCE
See also fmodf(), fmodl(), modf(), and modl().

fmodf()

Function

The `fmodf()` function returns the floating-point remainder of a floating-point division operation.

NOTE
Borland does not support this function.

Header File

```
#include <math.h>
```

Declaration

```
float fmodf(float x, float y);
```

- *x*—The operation's dividend.
- *y*—The operation's divisor.

Example

The following program demonstrates how to use the `fmodf()` function. When run, the program calls `fmodf()` and displays the result. The program's output looks like this:

```
var1 = 15.5
var2 = 5.5
The fmodf() result of var1/var2 = 4.5
Press any key to continue
```

Here is the program source code that produced the output:

```cpp
#include "stdafx.h"
#include <iostream>
#include <math.h>

using namespace std;

int main(int argc, char* argv[])
{
    float var1 = 15.5;
    float var2 = 5.5;

    cout << "var1 = " << var1 << endl;
    cout << "var2 = " << var2 << endl;
    float result = fmodf(var1, var2);
    cout << "The fmodf() result of var1/var2 = ";
    cout << result << endl;

    return 0;
}
```

CROSS-REFERENCE
See also fmod(), fmodl(), modf(), and modl().

fmodl()

Function

The `fmodl()` function returns the floating-point remainder of a floating-point division operation using long double values.

NOTE
Borland does not support this function.

Header File

```cpp
#include <math.h>
```

Declaration

```
long double fmodl(long double x, long double y);
```

- *x*—The operation's dividend.
- *y*—The operation's divisor.

Example

The following program demonstrates how to use the fmodl() function. When run, the program calls fmodl() and displays the result. The program's output looks like this:

```
var1 = 32.789
var2 = -15.895
The fmodl() result of var1/var2 = 0.999
Press any key to continue
```

Here is the program source code that produced the output:

```
#include "stdafx.h"
#include <iostream>
#include <math.h>

using namespace std;

int main(int argc, char* argv[])
{
    long double var1 = 32.789;
    long double var2 = -15.895;

    cout << "var1 = " << var1 << endl;
    cout << "var2 = " << var2 << endl;
    long double result = fmodl(var1, var2);
    cout << "The fmodl() result of var1/var2 = ";
    cout << result << endl;

    return 0;
}
```

CROSS-REFERENCE
See also fmod(), fmodf(), modf(), and modl().

fopen()

Function

The `fopen()` function opens a file as a stream, returning a pointer to the stream.

Header File

```
#include <stdio.h>
```

Declaration

```
FILE* fopen(const char *filename, const char *mode);
```

- *filename* — The name of the file to open as a stream.
- *mode* — The file access mode, which can be one of the mode values from Table F-7. The extension mode values shown in Table F-8 can be combined with the mode.

Table F-7 Mode Values for fopen()

Value	Description
`"r"`	Open for reading.
`"w"`	Open for writing, which erases the file if it already exists, or creates a new file if it doesn't exist.
`"a"`	Open for append, which writes to the end of an existing file, or creates the file if it doesn't already exist.
`"r+"`	Open for both reading and writing.
`"w+"`	Open for both reading and writing. If the file already exists, its contents are lost; if the file doesn't exist, it's created.
`"a+"`	Open for reading and appending. If the file doesn't exist, it's created.

Table F-8 Extension Mode Values for fopen()

Value	Description
t	Open for in text mode.
b	Open in binary mode.
c	Set the file's commit flag.
n	Turn off the file's commit flag.

Example

The following program demonstrates how to use the fopen() function. When run, the program attempts to open a file, prints a status message, and then closes the file if it opened successfully. The program's output looks like this:

```
File opened successfully.
Press any key to continue
```

Here is the program source code that produced the output:

```cpp
#include "stdafx.h"
#include <stdio.h>
#include <iostream>

using namespace std;

int main(int argc, char* argv[])
{
    FILE* file = fopen("fopen.cpp", "r");

    if (file != NULL)
    {
        cout << "File opened successfully." << endl;
        fclose(file);
    }
    else
        cout << "File failed to open." << endl;

    return 0;
}
```

CROSS-REFERENCE

See also _close(), _creat(), _fcloseall(), _fdopen(), _fgetchar(), _fgetwchar(), _fileno(), _flushall(), _fputwchar(), _fsopen(), _getw(), _getws(), _lseeki64(), _open(), _putw(), _putws(), _read(), _rmtmp(), _tempnam(), _wcreat(), _wfdopen(), _wfopen(), _wfreopen(),_wfsopen(), _wopen(), _wtempnam(), _wtmpnam(), clearerr(), eof(), fclose(), feof(), ferror(), fflush(), fgetc(), fgetpos(), fgets(), fgetwc(), fgetws(), fprintf(), fputc(), fputchar(), fputs(), fputwc(), fputws(), fread(), freopen(), fscanf(), fseek(), fsetpos(), ftell(), fwprintf(), fwrite(), fwscanf(), getc(), getchar(), gets(), getwc(), getwchar(), lseek(), putc(), putch(), putchar(), puts(), putwc(), putwchar(), rewind(), setbuf(), setvbuf(), tmpfile(), tmpnam(), ungetc(), ungetch(), ungetwc(), and write().

for

Keyword

The for keyword is used as part of the for loop construct, which enables a program to execute a block of code a given number of times. For example, the following program prints ten lines of text using a for loop. The program's output looks like this:

```
This is text line #0.
This is text line #1.
This is text line #2.
This is text line #3.
This is text line #4.
This is text line #5.
This is text line #6.
This is text line #7.
This is text line #8.
This is text line #9.

Press any key to continue
```

Here is the program source code that produced the output:

```cpp
#include "stdafx.h"
#include <iostream>

using namespace std;

int main(int argc, char* argv[])
{
    int x;
    char buf[81];

    for (x=0; x<10; ++x)
    {
        sprintf(buf, "This is text line #%d.", x);
        cout << buf << endl;
    }
    cout << endl;

    return 0;
}
```

Note the syntax of the for loop. The keyword for is followed by three expressions inside parentheses, with the expressions separated by a semicolon. The loop uses the expressions as follows:

- The first expression initializes the loop-control variable x to 0.
- The second expression specifies the condition under which the loop should continue. In this case, the loop iterates as long as x is less than 10.
- The third expression specifies how the program should increment the loop-control variable. In this case, the program increments x by 1 at the end of each loop iteration.

The code within the brackets that follow the for line is the program block that comprises the body of the loop. That is, the code in the parentheses is executed once for each iteration of the loop. If the loop's body contains only a single statement, the braces can be left off, as shown in the following example:

```
for (x=0; x<10; ++x)
    cout << "Text" << endl;
```

CROSS-REFERENCE
See also do and while.

fprintf()

Function

The fprintf() writes a formatted string to a stream, returning the number of bytes written or returning a negative value in the case of an error.

Header File

```
#include <stdio.h>
```

Declaration

```
int fprintf( FILE *stream, const char *format
    [, argument ]...);
```

- *argument*—A list of data items that match the format specifiers included in the format string *format*.
- *format*—The format string, which can include the format specifiers shown in Table F-9.
- *stream*—A pointer to the stream to which to write the string.

Table F-9 Format Specifiers for fprintf()

Specifier	Description
%c	Specifies a character.
%C	Specifies a wide character (printf()) or single-byte character (wprintf()).
%d	Specifies a signed decimal integer.
%e	Specifies a signed double-precision floating-point value using scientific notation with a lowercase e.
%E	Specifies a signed double-precision floating-point value using scientific notation with an uppercase E.
%f	Specifies a signed double-precision floating-point value.
%g	Specifies a signed double-precision floating-point value using either normal notation or scientific notation with a lowercase e.
%G	Specifies a signed double-precision floating-point value using either normal notation or scientific notation with an uppercase E.
%i	Specifies a signed decimal integer.
%n	Specifies an integer pointer.
%o	Specifies an unsigned octal integer.
%p	Specifies a void pointer.
%s	Specifies a string.
%S	Specifies a wide-character string (printf()) or single-byte-character string (wprintf()).
%u	Specifies an unsigned decimal integer.
%x	Specifies an unsigned hexadecimal integer with lowercase letters.
%X	Specifies an unsigned hexadecimal integer with uppercase letters.

Example

The following program demonstrates how to use the fprintf() function. When run, the program attempts to open a file for writing and then writes a formatted string to the file, displaying the string as it goes. The program's output looks like this:

```
Writing the following string:
var1 = 25 and var2 = 25.758
Press any key to continue
```

Here is the program source code that produced the output:

```
#include "stdafx.h"
#include <stdio.h>
#include <iostream>
```

```
using namespace std;

int main(int argc, char* argv[])
{
    FILE *file;
    int var1 = 25;
    double var2 = 25.758;

    file = fopen("test.txt", "w");
    if (file == NULL)
        cout << "File open error" << endl;
    else
    {
        cout << "Writing the following string:" << endl;
        cout << "var1 = " << var1;
        cout << " and var2 = " << var2 << endl;
        fprintf(file, "var1 = %d and var2 = %f\n",
            var1, var2);
        fclose(file);
    }

    return 0;
}
```

CROSS-REFERENCE

See also _close(), _creat(), _fcloseall(), _fdopen(), _fgetchar(), _fgetwchar(), _fileno(), _flushall(), _fputwchar(), _fsopen(), _getw(), _getws(), _lseeki64(), _open(), _putw(), _putws(), _read(), _rmtmp(), _tempnam(), _wcreat(), _wfdopen(), _wfopen(), _wfreopen(),_wfsopen(), _wopen(), _wtempnam(), _wtmpnam(), clearerr(), eof(), fclose(), feof(), ferror(), fflush(), fgetc(), fgetpos(), fgets(), fgetwc(), fgetws(), fopen(), fputc(), fputchar(), fputs(), fputwc(), fputws(), fread(), freopen(), fscanf(), fseek(), fsetpos(), ftell(), fwprintf(), fwrite(), fwscanf(), getc(), getchar(), gets(), getwc(), getwchar(), lseek(), putc(), putch(), putchar(), puts(), putwc(), putwchar(), rewind(), setbuf(), setvbuf(), tmpfile(), tmpnam(), ungetc(), ungetch(), ungetwc(), and write().

fputc()

Function

The fputc() function writes a character into a stream, returning the character written. or EOF in the case of an error.

Header File

```
#include <stdio.h>
```

Declaration

```
int fputc(int c, FILE* stream);
```

- *c* — The character to write to the stream.
- *stream* — A pointer to the stream to which to write a character.

Example

The following program demonstrates how to use the `fputc()` function. When run, the program attempts to open a file for writing and then writes 25 Xs to the file, displaying the characters as it goes. The program's output looks like this:

```
Data written to file:
XXXXXXXXXXXXXXXXXXXXXXXXX

Press any key to continue
```

Here is the program source code that produced the output:

```cpp
#include "stdafx.h"
#include <stdio.h>
#include <iostream>

using namespace std;

int main(int argc, char* argv[])
{
    FILE *file;

    file = fopen("test.dat", "w");
    if (file == NULL)
        cout << "File open error" << endl;
    else
    {
        cout << "Data written to file:" << endl;
        for (int x=0; x<25; ++x)
        {
            int result = fputc('X', file);
            if (result == EOF)
```

```
                              cout << "fputc() error" << endl;
                    else
                              cout << (char)result;
          }

          cout << endl << endl;
          fclose(file);
    }

    return 0;
}
```

 CROSS-REFERENCE
See also _close(), _creat(), _fcloseall(), _fdopen(), _fgetchar(), _fgetwchar(), _fileno(), _flushall(), _fputwchar(), _fsopen(), _getw(), _getws(), _lseeki64(), _open(), _putw(), _putws(), _read(), _rmtmp(), _tempnam(), _wcreat(), _wfdopen(), _wfopen(), _wfreopen(),_wfsopen(), _wopen(), _wtempnam(), _wtmpnam(), clearerr(), eof(), fclose(), feof(), ferror(), fflush(), fgetc(), fgetpos(), fgets(), fgetwc(), fgetws(), fopen(), fprintf(), fputc(), fputchar(), fputs(), fputws(), fread(), freopen(), fscanf(), fseek(), fsetpos(), ftell(), fwprintf(), fwrite(), fwscanf(), getc(), getchar(), gets(), getwc(), getwchar(), lseek(), putc(), putch(), putchar(), puts(), putwc(), putwchar(), rewind(), setbuf(), setvbuf(), tmpfile(), tmpnam(), ungetc(), ungetch(), ungetwc(), and write().

fputchar()

Function

The `fputchar()` function writes a character into the standard output stream, returning the character written, or `EOF` in the case of an error.

Header File

```
#include <stdio.h>
```

Declaration

```
int fputchar(int c);
```

- *c*—The character to write to the stream.

Example

The following program demonstrates how to use the `fputchar()` function. When run, the program writes 25 Xs to the standard output stream. The program's output looks like this:

```
XXXXXXXXXXXXXXXXXXXXXXXXX
```

```
Press any key to continue
```

Here is the program source code that produced the output:

```cpp
#include "stdafx.h"
#include <stdio.h>
#include <iostream>

using namespace std;

int main(int argc, char* argv[])
{
    for (int x=0; x<25; ++x)
    {
        int result = fputchar('X');
        if (result == EOF)
            cout << "fputchar() error" << endl;
    }
    cout << endl << endl;

    return 0;
}
```

CROSS-REFERENCE

See also _close(), _creat(), _fcloseall(), _fdopen(), _fgetchar(), _fgetwchar(), _fileno(), _flushall(), _fputwchar(), _fsopen(), _getw(), _getws(), _lseeki64(), _open(), _putw(), _putws(), _read(), _rmtmp(), _tempnam(), _wcreat(), _wfdopen(), _wfopen(), _wfreopen(),_wfsopen(), _wopen(), _wtempnam(), _wtmpnam(), clearerr(), eof(), fclose(), feof(), ferror(), fflush(), fgetc(), fgetpos(), fgets(), fgetwc(), fgetws(), fopen(), fprintf(), fputc(), fputs(), fputwc(), fputws(), fread(), freopen(), fscanf(), fseek(), fsetpos(), ftell(), fwprintf(), fwrite(), fwscanf(), getc(), getchar(), gets(), getwc(), getwchar(), lseek(), putc(), putch(), putchar(), puts(), putwc(), putwchar(), rewind(), setbuf(), setvbuf(), tmpfile(), tmpnam(), ungetc(), ungetch(), ungetwc(), and write().

fputs()

Function

The `fputs()` function writes a string into a stream, returning a positive value if successful, or `EOF` in the case of an error.

Header File

```
#include <stdio.h>
```

Declaration

```
int fputs(const char* string, FILE* stream);
```

- *stream* — A pointer to the stream to which to write the string.
- *string* — A pointer to the string to write to the stream.

Example

The following program demonstrates how to use the `fputs()` function. When run, the program attempts to open a file for writing and then writes ten strings to the file, displaying the strings as it goes. The program's output looks like this:

```
Data written to file:
String Output #0
String Output #1
String Output #2
String Output #3
String Output #4
String Output #5
String Output #6
String Output #7
String Output #8
String Output #9

Press any key to continue
```

Here is the program source code that produced the output:

```
#include "stdafx.h"
#include <stdio.h>
#include <iostream>
```

```cpp
using namespace std;

int main(int argc, char* argv[])
{
    FILE *file;
    char str[81];

    file = fopen("test.dat", "w");
    if (file == NULL)
        cout << "File open error" << endl;
    else
    {
        cout << "Data written to file:" << endl;
        for (int x=0; x<10; ++x)
        {
            sprintf(str, "String Output #%d", x);
            int result = fputs(str, file);
            if (result == EOF)
                cout << "fputs() error" << endl;
            else
                cout << str << endl;
        }

        cout << endl << endl;
        fclose(file);
    }

    return 0;
}
```

CROSS-REFERENCE

See also _close(), _creat(), _fcloseall(), _fdopen(), _fgetchar(), _fgetwchar(), _fileno(), _flushall(), _fputwchar(), _fsopen(), _getw(), _getws(), _lseeki64(), _open(), _putw(), _putws(), _read(), _rmtmp(), _tempnam(), _wcreat(), _wfdopen(), _wfopen(), _wfreopen(),_wfsopen(), _wopen(), _wtempnam(), _wtmpnam(), clearerr(), eof(), fclose(), feof(), ferror(), fflush(), fgetc(), fgetpos(), fgets(), fgetwc(), fgetws(), fopen(), fprintf(), fputc(), fputchar(), fputwc(), fputws(), fread(), freopen(), fscanf(), fseek(), fsetpos(), ftell(), fwprintf(), fwrite(), fwscanf(), getc(), getchar(), gets(), getwc(), getwchar(), lseek(), putc(), putch(), putchar(), puts(), putwc(), putwchar(), rewind(), setbuf(), setvbuf(), tmpfile(), tmpnam(), ungetc(), ungetch(), ungetwc(), and write().

fputwc()

Function

The fputwc() function writes a wide character into a stream, returning the character written, or WEOF in the case of an error.

NOTE
This function works only on systems, such as Windows NT, that support wide-character filenames.

Header File

```
#include <stdio.h>
```

Declaration

```
wint_t fputwc(wint_t c, FILE* stream);
```

- *c* — The wide character to write to the stream.
- *stream* — A pointer to the stream to which to write a character.

Example

The following program demonstrates how to use the fputwc() function. When run, the program attempts to open a file for writing and then writes 25 Xs to the file, displaying the characters as it goes. The program's output looks like this:

```
Data written to file:
XXXXXXXXXXXXXXXXXXXXXXXXX

Press any key to continue
```

Here is the program source code that produced the output:

```
#include "stdafx.h"
#include <stdio.h>
#include <iostream>

using namespace std;

int main(int argc, char* argv[])
{
```

```
FILE *file;

file = _wfopen(L"test.dat", L"w");
if (file == NULL)
    cout << "File open error" << endl;
else
{
    cout << "Data written to file:" << endl;
    for (int x=0; x<25; ++x)
    {
        wint_t result = fputwc('X', file);
        if (result == WEOF)
            cout << "fputwc() error" << endl;
        else
            wcout << (wchar_t)result;
    }

    cout << endl << endl;
    fclose(file);
}

return 0;
}
```

CROSS-REFERENCE

See also _close(), _creat(), _fcloseall(), _fdopen(), _fgetchar(), _fgetwchar(), _fileno(), _flushall(), _fputwchar(), _fsopen(), _getw(), _getws(), _lseeki64(), _open(), _putw(), _putws(), _read(), _rmtmp(), _tempnam(), _wcreat(), _wfdopen(), _wfopen(), _wfreopen(),_wfsopen(), _wopen(), _wtempnam(), _wtmpnam(), clearerr(), eof(), fclose(), feof(), ferror(), fflush(), fgetc(), fgetpos(), fgets(), fgetwc(), fgetws(), fopen(), fprintf(), fputc(), fputchar(), fputs(), fputws(), fread(), freopen(), fscanf(), fseek(), fsetpos(), ftell(), fwprintf(), fwrite(), fwscanf(), getc(), getchar(), gets(), getwc(), getwchar(), lseek(), putc(), putch(), putchar(), puts(), putwc(), putwchar(), rewind(), setbuf(), setvbuf(), tmpfile(), tmpnam(), ungetc(), ungetch(), ungetwc(), and write().

fputws()

Function

The fputws() function writes a wide-character string into a stream, returning a positive value if successful, or WEOF in the case of an error.

NOTE

This function works only on systems, such as Windows NT, that support wide-character filenames.

Header File

```
#include <stdio.h>
```

Declaration

```
int fputws(const wchar_t* string, FILE* stream);
```

- *stream* — A pointer to the stream to which to write the string.
- *string* — A pointer to the string to write to the stream.

Example

The following program demonstrates how to use the `fputws()` function. When run, the program attempts to open a file for writing and then writes ten strings to the file, displaying the strings as it goes. The program's output looks like this:

```
Data written to file:
String Output #0
String Output #1
String Output #2
String Output #3
String Output #4
String Output #5
String Output #6
String Output #7
String Output #8
String Output #9

Press any key to continue
```

Here is the program source code that produced the output:

```
#include "stdafx.h"
#include <stdio.h>
#include <iostream>

using namespace std;
```

```
int main(int argc, char* argv[])
{
    FILE *file;
    wchar_t str[81];

    file = _wfopen(L"test.dat", L"w");
    if (file == NULL)
        cout << "File open error" << endl;
    else
    {
        cout << "Data written to file:" << endl;
        for (int x=0; x<10; ++x)
        {
            swprintf(str, L"String Output #%d", x);
            int result = fputws(str, file);
            if (result == WEOF)
                cout << "fputws() error" << endl;
            else
                wcout << str << endl;
        }

        cout << endl << endl;
        fclose(file);
    }

    return 0;
}
```

CROSS-REFERENCE

See also _close(), _creat(), _fcloseall(), _fdopen(), _fgetchar(), _fgetwchar(), _fileno(), _flushall(), _fputwchar(), _fsopen(), _getw(), _getws(), _lseeki64(), _open(), _putw(), _putws(), _read(), _rmtmp(), _tempnam(), _wcreat(), _wfdopen(), _wfopen(), _wfreopen(),_wfsopen(), _wopen(), _wtempnam(), _wtmpnam(), clearerr(), eof(), fclose(), feof(), ferror(), fflush(), fgetc(), fgetpos(), fgets(), fgetwc(), fgetws(), fopen(), fprintf(), fputc(), fputchar(), fputs(), fputwc(), fread(), freopen(), fscanf(), fseek(), fsetpos(), ftell(), fwprintf(), fwrite(), fwscanf(), getc(), getchar(), gets(), getwc(), getwchar(), lseek(), putc(), putch(), putchar(), puts(), putwc(), putwchar(), rewind(), setbuf(), setvbuf(), tmpfile(), tmpnam(), ungetc(), ungetch(), ungetwc(), and write().

fread()

Function

The `fread()` function reads data from a stream, returning the number of data objects read.

Header File

```
#include <stdio.h>
```

Declaration

```
size_t fread(void *buffer, size_t size,
    size_t count, FILE *stream );
```

- *buffer* — A pointer to the buffer into which the data will be read.
- *count* — The maximum number of data objects to read.
- *size* — The size in bytes of the data object.
- *stream* — A pointer to the stream from which to read data.

Example

The following program demonstrates how to use the `fread()` function. When run, the program opens a file for reading and then reads and displays a 255-character string. The program's output looks like this:

```
Number of objects read: 1
Data read from file:
// fread.cpp : Defines the entry point for the console
application.
//

#include "stdafx.h"
#include <stdio.h>
#include <iostream>

using namespace std;

int main(int argc, char* argv[])
{
    FILE *file;
    char buf[256];
```

```
    file = fopen("fread.cpp",

Press any key to continue
```

Here is the program source code that produced the output:

```cpp
#include "stdafx.h"
#include <stdio.h>
#include <iostream>

using namespace std;

int main(int argc, char* argv[])
{
    FILE *file;
    char buf[256];

    file = fopen("fread.cpp", "r");
    if (file == NULL)
        cout << "File open error" << endl;
    else
    {
        int num = fread(buf, 255, 1, file);
        buf[255] = 0;
        cout << "Number of objects read: " << num << endl;
        cout << "Data read from file:" << endl;
        cout << "  " << buf << endl << endl;
        fclose(file);
    }

    return 0;
}
```

CROSS-REFERENCE

See also _close(), _creat(), _fcloseall(), _fdopen(), _fgetchar(), _fgetwchar(), _fileno(), _flushall(), _fputwchar(), _fsopen(), _getw(), _getws(), _lseeki64(), _open(), _putw(), _putws(), _read(), _rmtmp(), _tempnam(), _wcreat(), _wfdopen(), _wfopen(), _wfreopen(),_wfsopen(), _wopen(), _wtempnam(), _wtmpnam(), clearerr(), eof(), fclose(), feof(), ferror(), fflush(), fgetc(), fgetpos(), fgets(), fgetwc(), fgetws(), fopen(), fprintf(), fputc(), fputchar(), fputs(), fputwc(), fputws(), freopen(), fscanf(), fseek(), fsetpos(), ftell(), fwprintf(), fwrite(), fwscanf(), getc(), getchar(), gets(), getwc(), getwchar(), lseek(), putc(), putch(), putchar(), puts(), putwc(), putwchar(), rewind(), setbuf(), setvbuf(), tmpfile(), tmpnam(), ungetc(), ungetch(), ungetwc(), and write().

free()

Function

The free() function releases memory that was allocated by the calloc(), malloc(), and realloc() functions.

Header File

```
#include <stdlib.h>
```

Declaration

```
void free(void* memblock);
```

- *memblock* — The address of the memory block to free.

Example

The following program demonstrates how to use the free() function. When run, the program allocates enough memory to hold 256 integer values (1024 bytes), displaying a message that indicates whether the memory allocation was successful. After allocating the memory block, the program calls free() to release it. The program's output looks like this:

```
Memory allocated successfully
Freeing memory...
Memory freed
Press any key to continue
```

Here is the program source code that produced the output:

```
#include "stdafx.h"
#include <iostream>
#include <stdlib.h>

using namespace std;

int main(int argc, char* argv[])
{
    int* pMem = (int*)calloc(256, sizeof(int));

    if (pMem)
    {
        cout << "Memory allocated successfully" << endl;
```

```
            cout << "Freeing memory..." << endl;
            free(pMem);
            cout << "Memory freed" << endl;
        }
        else
            cout << "Memory allocation failed" << endl;

        return 0;
    }
```

CROSS-REFERENCE
See also calloc(), malloc(), and realloc().

freopen()

Function

The `freopen()` function creates a new file from an existing stream, returning a pointer to the new stream.

Header File

```
#include <stdio.h>
```

Declaration

```
FILE* freopen(const char *path,
    const char *mode, FILE *stream );
```

- *mode* — The file access mode, which can be one of the mode values from Table F-10. The extension mode values shown in Table F-11 can be combined with the mode.
- *path* — The name of the new file to create.
- *stream* — A pointer to the existing stream.

Table F-10 Mode Values for freopen()

Value	Description
"r"	Open for reading.
"w"	Open for writing, which erases the file if it already exists, or creates a new file if it doesn't exist.
"a"	Open for append, which writes to the end of an existing file, or creates the file if it doesn't already exist.
"r+"	Open for both reading and writing.
"w+"	Open for both reading and writing. If the file already exists, its contents are lost; if the file doesn't exist, it's created.
"a+"	Open for reading and appending. If the file doesn't exist, it's created.

Table F-11 Extension Mode Values for freopen()

Value	Description
t	Open for in text mode.
b	Open in binary mode.
c	Set the file's commit flag.
n	Turn off the file's commit flag.

Example

The following program demonstrates how to use the freopen() function. When run, the program attempts to open a file and reassign the stream to a new file, printing a status message as it goes. The program's output looks like this:

```
First file opened successfully.
Second file created successfully.
Press any key to continue
```

Here is the program source code that produced the output:

```cpp
#include "stdafx.h"
#include <stdio.h>
#include <iostream>

using namespace std;

int main(int argc, char* argv[])
{
    FILE* file = fopen("freopen.cpp", "r");
```

```
        if (file == NULL)
        {
            cout << "File open error." << endl;
            exit(1);
        }

        cout << "First file opened successfully." << endl;
        FILE* newFile = freopen("freopen.dup", "w", file);

        if (newFile == NULL)
        {
            cout << "File creation error." << endl;
            exit(1);
        }

        cout << "Second file created successfully." << endl;
        fcloseall();

        return 0;
    }
```

CROSS-REFERENCE

See also _close(), _creat(), _fcloseall(), _fdopen(), _fgetchar(), _fgetwchar(), _fileno(), _flushall(), _fputwchar(), _fsopen(), _getw(), _getws(), _lseeki64(), _open(), _putw(), _putws(), _read(), _rmtmp(), _tempnam(), _wcreat(), _wfdopen(), _wfopen(), _wfreopen(),_wfsopen(), _wopen(), _wtempnam(), _wtmpnam(), clearerr(), eof(), fclose(), feof(), ferror(), fflush(), fgetc(), fgetpos(), fgets(), fgetwc(), fgetws(), fopen(), fprintf(), fputc(), fputchar(), fputs(), fputwc(), fputws(), fread(), fscanf(), fseek(), fsetpos(), ftell(), fwprintf(), fwrite(), fwscanf(), getc(), getchar(), gets(), getwc(), getwchar(), lseek(), putc(), putch(), putchar(), puts(), putwc(), putwchar(), rewind(), setbuf(), setvbuf(), tmpfile(), tmpnam(), ungetc(), ungetch(), ungetwc(), and write().

frexp()

Function

The frexp() function gets the mantissa and exponent of a double floating-point value, returning the mantissa.

Header File

```
#include <math.h>
```

Declaration

```
double frexp(double x, int *expptr);
```

- *expptr* — A pointer to the storage area for the exponent.
- *x* — The value for which to get the mantissa and exponent.

Example

The following program demonstrates how to use the frexp() function. When run, the program calculates the mantissa and exponent of the value 15.65. The program's output looks like this:

```
The value = 15.65
The mantissa = 0.978125
The exponent = 4
Press any key to continue
```

Here is the program source code that produced the output:

```
#include "stdafx.h"
#include <math.h>
#include <iostream>

using namespace std;

int main(int argc, char* argv[])
{
    double var1 = 15.65;
    int exp;

    cout << "The value = " << var1 << endl;
    double man = frexp(var1, &exp);
    cout << "The mantissa = " << man << endl;
    cout << "The exponent = " << exp << endl;

    return 0;
}
```

CROSS-REFERENCE
See also _logb(), frexpf(), frexpl(), ldexp(), modf(), and pow().

frexpf()

Function

The `frexpf()` function gets the mantissa and exponent of a floating-point value, returning the mantissa.

 NOTE
Borland does not support this function.

Header File

```
#include <math.h>
```

Declaration

```
float frexpf(float x, int *expptr);
```

- *expptr* — A pointer to the storage area for the exponent.
- *x* — The value for which to get the mantissa and exponent.

Example

The following program demonstrates how to use the `frexpf()` function. When run, the program calculates the mantissa and exponent of the value 15.65. The program's output looks like this:

```
The value = 15.65
The mantissa = 0.978125
The exponent = 4
Press any key to continue
```

Here is the program source code that produced the output:

```
#include "stdafx.h"
#include <math.h>
#include <iostream>

using namespace std;
```

```
int main(int argc, char* argv[])
{
    float var1 = 15.65;
    int exp;

    cout << "The value = " << var1 << endl;
    float man = frexpf(var1, &exp);
    cout << "The mantissa = " << man << endl;
    cout << "The exponent = " << exp << endl;

    return 0;
}
```

CROSS-REFERENCE
See also frexp(), frexpl(), ldexp(), modf(), and pow().

frexpl()

Function

The frexpl() function gets the mantissa and exponent of a long double value, returning the mantissa.

Header File

```
#include <math.h>
```

Declaration

```
long double frexpl(long double x, int *expptr);
```

- *expptr*—A pointer to the storage area for the exponent.
- *x*—The value for which to get the mantissa and exponent.

Example

The following program demonstrates how to use the frexpl() function. When run, the program calculates the mantissa and exponent of the value 15.65. The program's output looks like this:

```
The value = 15.65
The mantissa = 0.978125
```

```
The exponent = 4
Press any key to continue
```

Here is the program source code that produced the output:

```cpp
#include "stdafx.h"
#include <math.h>
#include <iostream>

using namespace std;

int main(int argc, char* argv[])
{
    long double var1 = 15.65;
    int exp;

    cout << "The value = " << var1 << endl;
    long double man = frexpl(var1, &exp);
    cout << "The mantissa = " << man << endl;
    cout << "The exponent = " << exp << endl;

    return 0;
}
```

CROSS-REFERENCE
See also frexp(), frexpf(), ldexp(), modf(), and pow().

friend

Keyword

The `friend` keyword enables a program to define a friend function or class, which is a function or class that has access to another class's private and protected data members and member functions.

CROSS-REFERENCE
See also Friend Functions and Classes.

Friend Functions and Classes

Technique

The friend keyword enables a program to define a friend function or class, which is a function or class that has access to another class's private and protected data members and member functions. The following sections show how to create both friend functions and friend classes.

Creating Friend Functions

The following program defines two classes, named MyClass1 and MyClass2. MyClass1 declares that MyClass2's member function ShowClass1() is a friend function with access to MyClass1's private data member val1. When run, the program's output looks like this:

```
mc1.val1 = 25
Press any key to continue
```

Here is the program source code that produced the output:

```cpp
#include "stdafx.h"
#include <iostream>

using namespace std;

class MyClass1;

class MyClass2
{
public:
    MyClass2() {}
    ~MyClass2() {}
    void ShowClass1(MyClass1& mc1);
};

class MyClass1
{
private:
    int val1;
    friend void MyClass2::ShowClass1(MyClass1& mc1);

public:
    MyClass1(int v) { val1 = v; }
    ~MyClass1() {}
};
```

```
void MyClass2::ShowClass1(MyClass1& mc1)
{
    cout << "mc1.val1 = ";
    cout << mc1.val1 << endl;
}

int main(int argc, char* argv[])
{
    MyClass1 myClass1(25);
    MyClass2 myClass2;
    myClass2.ShowClass1(myClass1);

    return 0;
}
```

Creating a Friend Class

In the previous case, only the MyClass2 member function ShowClass1() can access MyClass1's private and protected members. Other member functions that might be added to MyClass2 cannot. However, if all of a class's member functions need access to another class's private and protected members, the entire class can be declared as a friend class. The following program demonstrates a friend class. The program's output looks like this:

```
mc1.val1 = 25
mc1.val1 = 25
Press any key to continue
```

Here is the program source code that produced the output:

```
#include "stdafx.h"
#include <iostream>

using namespace std;

class MyClass1;

class MyClass2
{
public:
    MyClass2() {}
    ~MyClass2() {}
    void ShowClass1(MyClass1& mc1);
    void ShowClass1Again(MyClass1& mc1);
};
```

```
class MyClass1
{
private:
    int val1;
    friend class MyClass2;

public:
    MyClass1(int v) { val1 = v; }
    ~MyClass1() {}
};

void MyClass2::ShowClass1(MyClass1& mc1)
{
    cout << "mc1.val1 = ";
    cout << mc1.val1 << endl;
}

void MyClass2::ShowClass1Again(MyClass1& mc1)
{
    cout << "mc1.val1 = ";
    cout << mc1.val1 << endl;
}

int main(int argc, char* argv[])
{
    MyClass1 myClass1(25);
    MyClass2 myClass2;
    myClass2.ShowClass1(myClass1);
    myClass2.ShowClass1Again(myClass1);

    return 0;
}
```

Global Friend Functions

Finally, a friend function doesn't have to be related to a class. Such a function can also be a typical global function, as demonstrated in the following program, whose output looks like this:

```
mc1.val1 = 25
Press any key to continue
```

Here is the program source code that produced the output:

```
#include "stdafx.h"
```

```
#include <iostream>

using namespace std;

class MyClass1
{
private:
    int val1;
    friend void ShowClass1(MyClass1& mc1);

public:
    MyClass1(int v) { val1 = v; }
    ~MyClass1() {}
};

void ShowClass1(MyClass1& mc1)
{
    cout << "mc1.val1 = ";
    cout << mc1.val1 << endl;
}

int main(int argc, char* argv[])
{
    MyClass1 myClass1(25);
    ShowClass1(myClass1);

    return 0;
}
```

CROSS-REFERENCE
See also class, Constructor, Creating a Class, and Destructor.

fscanf()

Function

The fscanf() reads a formatted string from a stream, returning the number of data objects received, or EOF in the case of an error.

Header File

```
#include <stdio.h>
```

Declaration

```
int fscanf(FILE *stream, const char *format
    [, argument ]...);
```

- *argument* — A list of data objects that match the format specifiers included in the format string *format*.
- *format* — The format string, which can include the format specifiers shown in Table F-12.
- *stream* — A pointer to the stream from which to read the string.

Table F-12 Format Specifiers for fscanf()

Specifier	Description
%c	Specifies a character.
%C	Specifies a wide character (printf()) or single-byte character (wprintf()).
%d	Specifies a signed decimal integer.
%e	Specifies a signed double-precision floating-point value using scientific notation with a lowercase e.
%E	Specifies a signed double-precision floating-point value using scientific notation with an uppercase E.
%f	Specifies a signed double-precision floating-point value.
%g	Specifies a signed double-precision floating-point value using either normal notation or scientific notation with a lowercase e.
%G	Specifies a signed double-precision floating-point value using either normal notation or scientific notation with an uppercase E.
%I	Specifies a signed decimal integer.
%n	Specifies an integer pointer.
%o	Specifies an unsigned octal integer.
%p	Specifies a void pointer.
%s	Specifies a string.
%S	Specifies a wide-character string (printf()) or single-byte-character string (wprintf()).
%u	Specifies an unsigned decimal integer.
%x	Specifies an unsigned hexadecimal integer with lowercase letters.
%X	Specifies an unsigned hexadecimal integer with uppercase letters.

Example

The following program demonstrates how to use the `fscanf()` function. When run, the program reads three data objects from the standard input stream. The program's output looks like this:

```
Enter two integers and a string:
25 69 test

You entered 3 data objects:
var1 = 25
var2 = 69
str = test

Press any key to continue
```

Here is the program source code that produced the output:

```cpp
#include "stdafx.h"
#include <stdio.h>
#include <iostream>

using namespace std;

int main(int argc, char* argv[])
{
    int var1;
    int var2;
    char str[81];

    cout << "Enter two integers and a string: " << endl;
    int num = fscanf(stdin, "%d %d %s",
        &var1, &var2, str);
    cout << endl;
    cout << "You entered " << num << " data objects:" << endl;
    cout << "var1 = " << var1 << endl;
cout << "var2 = " << var2 << endl;
    cout << "str = " << str << endl << endl;

    return 0;
}
```

CROSS-REFERENCE
See also _close(), _creat(), _fcloseall(), _fdopen(), _fgetchar(), _fgetwchar(), _fileno(), _flushall(), _fputwchar(), _fsopen(), _getw(), _getws(), _lseeki64(), _open(), _putw(), _putws(), _read(), _rmtmp(), _tempnam(), _wcreat(),

_wfdopen(), _wfopen(), _wfreopen(),_wfsopen(), _wopen(), _wtempnam(), _wtmpnam(), clearerr(), eof(), fclose(), feof(), ferror(), fflush(), fgetc(), fgetpos(), fgets(), fgetwc(), fgetws(), fopen(), fprintf(), fputc(), fputchar(), fputs(), fputwc(), fputws(), fread(), freopen(), fseek(), fsetpos(), ftell(), fwprintf(), fwrite(), fwscanf(), getc(), getchar(), gets(), getwc(), getwchar(), lseek(), putc(), putch(), putchar(), puts(), putwc(), putwchar(), rewind(), setbuf(), setvbuf(), tmpfile(), tmpnam(), ungetc(), ungetch(), ungetwc(), and write().

fseek()

Function

The fseek() function sets the position of the file pointer, returning 0 if successful, or a nonzero value if unsuccessful.

Header File

```
#include <stdio.h>
```

Declaration

```
int fseek(FILE *stream, long offset, int origin);
```

- *offset* — The number of bytes from *origin* to offset the file pointer.
- *origin* — The position from which the offset should be added.
- *stream* — A pointer to the stream for which to set the position of the file pointer.

Example

The following program demonstrates how to use the fseek() function. When run, the program opens a file, sets the file position of the file pointer to 50, and reads the next available line of text, displaying the file position as it goes. The program's output looks like this:

```
51 52 53 54 55 56 57 58 59 60 61 62 63 64 65 66 67
sole application.
Press any key to continue
```

Here is the program source code that produced the output:

```
#include "stdafx.h"
#include <stdio.h>
```

```cpp
#include <iostream>

using namespace std;

int main(int argc, char* argv[])
{
    char buf[81];
    FILE *file;
    fpos_t pos = 50;

    file = fopen("fseek.cpp", "r");
    if (file == NULL)
        cout << "File open error" << endl;
    else
    {
        fseek(file, pos, 0);
        int i = 0;
        int ch = fgetc(file);
        while (ch != '\n')
        {
            int result = fgetpos(file, &pos);
            if (result != 0)
                cout << "fgetpos() error" << endl;
            else
                cout << (int)pos << " ";

            buf[i] = (char)ch;
            ++i;
            ch = fgetc(file);
        }

        cout << endl;
        buf[i] = 0;
        cout << buf << endl;
        fclose(file);
    }

    return 0;
}
```

CROSS-REFERENCE
See also _close(), _creat(), _fcloseall(), _fdopen(), _fgetchar(), _fgetwchar(),
_fileno(), _flushall(), _fputwchar(), _fsopen(), _getw(), _getws(), _lseeki64(),
_open(), _putw(), _putws(), _read(), _rmtmp(), _tempnam(), _wcreat(),

_wfdopen(), _wfopen(), _wfreopen(),_wfsopen(), _wopen(), _wtempnam(), _wtmpnam(), clearerr(), eof(), fclose(), feof(), ferror(), fflush(), fgetc(), fgetpos(), fgets(), fgetwc(), fgetws(), fopen(), fprintf(), fputc(), fputchar(), fputs(), fputwc(), fputws(), fread(), freopen(), fscanf(), fsetpos(), ftell(), fwprintf(), fwrite(), fwscanf(), getc(), getchar(), gets(), getwc(), getwchar(), lseek(), putc(), putch(), putchar(), puts(), putwc(), putwchar(), rewind(), setbuf(), setvbuf(), tmpfile(), tmpnam(), ungetc(), ungetch(), ungetwc(), and write().

fsetpos()

Function

The fsetpos() function sets the position of the file pointer, returning 0 if successful, or a nonzero value if unsuccessful.

Header File

```
#include <stdio.h>
```

Declaration

```
int fsetpos(FILE* stream, fpos_t* pos);
```

- *pos* — A pointer to the variable that holds the new stream position.
- *stream* — A pointer to the stream for which to set the file position of the file pointer.

Example

The following program demonstrates how to use the fsetpos() function. When run, the program opens a file, sets the file position to 50, and reads the next available line of text, displaying the position of the file pointer as it goes. The program's output looks like this:

```
51 52 53 54 55 56 57 58 59 60 61 62 63 64 65 66 67 68 69
onsole application.
Press any key to continue
```

Here is the program source code that produced the output:

```
#include "stdafx.h"
#include <stdio.h>
#include <iostream>
```

```cpp
using namespace std;

int main(int argc, char* argv[])
{
    char buf[81];
    FILE *file;
    fpos_t pos = 50;

    file = fopen("fsetpos.cpp", "r");
    if (file == NULL)
        cout << "File open error" << endl;
    else
    {
        fsetpos(file, &pos);
        int i = 0;
        int ch = fgetc(file);
        while (ch != '\n')
        {
            int result = fgetpos(file, &pos);
            if (result != 0)
                cout << "fgetpos() error" << endl;
            else
                cout << (int)pos << " ";

            buf[i] = (char)ch;
            ++i;
            ch = fgetc(file);
        }

        cout << endl;
        buf[i] = 0;
        cout << buf << endl;
        fclose(file);
    }

    return 0;
}
```

CROSS-REFERENCE

See also _close(), _creat(), _fcloseall(), _fdopen(), _fgetchar(), _fgetwchar(), _fileno(), _flushall(), _fputwchar(), _fsopen(), _getw(), _getws(), _lseeki64(), _open(), _putw(), _putws(), _read(), _rmtmp(), _tempnam(), _wcreat(), _wfdopen(), _wfopen(), _wfreopen(),_wfsopen(), _wopen(), _wtempnam(), _wtmpnam(), clearerr(), eof(), fclose(), feof(), ferror(), fflush(), fgetc(), fgetpos(), fgets(), fgetwc(), fgetws(), fopen(), fprintf(), fputc(), fputchar(), fputs(), fputwc(), fputws(), fread(), freopen(), fscanf(), fseek(), ftell(), fwprintf(), fwrite(), fwscanf(), getc(), getchar(), gets(), getwc(), getwchar(), lseek(), putc(), putch(), putchar(), puts(), putwc(), putwchar(), rewind(), setbuf(), setvbuf(), tmpfile(), tmpnam(), ungetc(), ungetch(), ungetwc(), and write().

fstat()

Function

The `fstat()` retrieves status information about an open file, returning 0 if the information is obtained successfully, or –1 in the case of an error. The file information is returned into a `stat` structure, which is defined as follows:

```
struct stat
{
    _dev_t st_dev;    // Device handle or 0
    _ino_t st_ino;
    unsigned short st_mode; // File mode bit mask
    short st_nlink;   // Always 1 on non-NFTS
    short st_uid;
    short st_gid;
    _dev_t st_rdev;   // Device handle or 0
    _off_t st_size;   // File size
    time_t st_atime;  // Time of last access
    time_t st_mtime;  // Time of last modification
    time_t st_ctime;  // Creation time
};
```

NOTE

Borland users should refer to the `ftime()` function later in this chapter.

Header File

```
#include <sys/types.h>
#include <sys/stat.h>
```

Declaration

```
int fstat(int handle, struct _stat *buffer);
```

- *buffer*—A pointer to the _stat structure that will hold the returned status information.
- *handle*—The handle of the file for which to acquire status information.

Example

The following program demonstrates how to use the fstat() function. When run, the program acquires and displays size and time status information on a file. The program's output looks like this:

```
File Size: 772
Time: Wed Mar 10 00:00:00 1999
Press any key to continue
```

Here is the program source code that produced the output:

```
#pragma hdrstop
#include <condefs.h>
#include <fcntl.h>
#include <io.h>
#include <sys/types.h>
#include <sys/stat.h>
#include <time.h>
#include <iostream>


//—————————————————————————————————
#pragma argsused
int main(int argc, char **argv)
{
    struct stat statInfo;

    int fileHandle = open( "fstat.cpp", O_RDONLY);

    if(fileHandle ==  -1)
        cout << "File open error." << endl;
    else
    {
        int result = fstat(fileHandle, &statInfo);
        if(result == 0)
        {
            cout << "File Size: " << statInfo.st_size << endl;
            cout << "Time: " << ctime(&statInfo.st_atime);
        }
        else
```

```
                cout << "fstat() error" << endl;
        }
        close(fileHandle);

        cout << "Press Enter to continue" << endl;
        getchar();

        return 0;
    }
```

CROSS-REFERENCE
See also _stat(), _stati64(), _wstat(), _wstati64, and stat().

fstream

Class

The fstream class provides the functionality for file I/O using streams.

Class Declaration

```
class _CRTIMP fstream : public iostream {
public:
    fstream();
    fstream(const char *, int, int = filebuf::openprot);
    fstream(filedesc);
    fstream(filedesc, char *, int);
    ~fstream();

    streambuf * setbuf(char *, int);
    filebuf* rdbuf() const { return (filebuf*)
        ostream::rdbuf(); }

    void attach(filedesc);
    filedesc fd() const { return rdbuf()->fd(); }

    int is_open() const { return rdbuf()->is_open(); }
    void open(const char *, int, int = filebuf::openprot);
    void close();
    int setmode(int mode = filebuf::text)
        { return rdbuf()->setmode(mode); }
};
```

Class Members

Table F-13 lists and describes the members of fstream.

Table F-13 Members of fstream

Member	Description
attach( )	Associates the stream with a file.
close( )	Closes the file.
fd( )	Returns the stream's file descriptor.
is_open( )	Returns TRUE if the file associated with the stream is open.
open( )	Opens a file.
rdbuf( )	Returns a pointer to the stream's buffer object.
setbuf( )	Sets the filebuf object's buffer.
setmode( )	Sets the stream's mode.

CROSS-REFERENCE
See also ifstream, iostream, istream, ofstream, and ostream.

fstream

Standard C++ Library Header File

The fstream standard header file defines stream template functions and classes, including the template classes basic_ifstream, basic_ofstream, and basic_fstream.

ftell()

Function

The ftell() function gets the position of the file pointer, returning −1 if unsuccessful.

Header File

```
#include <stdio.h>
```

Declaration

```
long ftell(FILE* stream);
```

- *stream* — A pointer to the stream for which to get the file position.

Example

The following program demonstrates how to use the ftell() function. When run, the program opens a file and reads the first line of text, displaying the file position of the file pointer as it goes. The program's output looks like this:

```
1 2 3 4 5 6 7 8 9 10 11 12 13 14 15 16 17 18 19 20 21 22 23 24
25 26 27 28 29 30 31 32 33 34 35 36 37 38 39 40 41 42 43 44 45
46 47 48 49 50 51 52 53 54 55 56 57 58 59 60 61 62 63 64 65 66
67
// ftell.cpp : Defines the entry point for the console
application.
Press any key to continue
```

Here is the program source code that produced the output:

```cpp
#include "stdafx.h"
#include <stdio.h>
#include <iostream>

using namespace std;

int main(int argc, char* argv[])
{
    char buf[81];
    FILE *file;

    file = fopen("ftell.cpp", "r");
    if (file == NULL)
        cout << "File open error" << endl;
    else
    {
        int i = 0;
        int ch = fgetc(file);
        while (ch != '\n')
        {
            long pos = ftell(file);
            if (pos == -1)
                cout << "ftell() error" << endl;
            else
```

```
                cout << (int)pos << " ";

            buf[i] = (char)ch;
            ++i;
            ch = fgetc(file);
        }

        cout << endl;
        buf[i] = 0;
        cout << buf << endl;
        fclose(file);
    }

    return 0;
}
```

CROSS-REFERENCE

See also _close(), _creat(), _fcloseall(), _fdopen(), _fgetchar(), _fgetwchar(), _fileno(), _flushall(), _fputwchar(), _fsopen(), _getw(), _getws(), _lseeki64(), _open(), _putw(), _putws(), _read(), _rmtmp(), _tempnam(), _wcreat(), _wfdopen(), _wfopen(), _wfreopen(),_wfsopen(), _wopen(), _wtempnam(), _wtmpnam(), clearerr(), eof(), fclose(), feof(), ferror(), fflush(), fgetc(), fgetpos(), fgets(), fgetwc(), fgetws(), fopen(), fprintf(), fputc(), fputchar(), fputs(), fputwc(), fputws(), fread(), freopen(), fscanf(), fseek(), fsetpos(), fwprintf(), fwrite(), fwscanf(), getc(), getchar(), gets(), getwc(), getwchar(), lseek(), putc(), putch(), putchar(), puts(), putwc(), putwchar(), rewind(), setbuf(), setvbuf(), tmpfile(), tmpnam(), ungetc(), ungetch(), ungetwc(), and write().

ftime()

Function

The ftime() retrieves the current time. The function returns the time into a timeb structure, which is defined as follows:

```
struct timeb
{
    time_t time;     // Time in seconds since midnight 1/1/1970
    unsigned short millitm; // Milliseconds
    short timezone; // Difference from UTC in minutes
    short dstflag;  // Non-zero for DST
};
```

Header File

```
#include <sys/types.h>
#include <sys/timeb.h>
```

Declaration

```
void ftime(struct _timeb *timeptr);
```

- *timeptr*—A pointer to the timeb structure that will hold the returned time information.

Example

The following program demonstrates how to use the ftime() function. When run, the program acquires and displays time information. The program's output looks like this:

```
The current time is:
  Thu Mar 11 00:39:07 1999
```

```
Press any key to continue
```

Here is the program source code that produced the output:

```cpp
#include "stdafx.h"
#include <sys/types.h>
#include <sys/timeb.h>
#include <time.h>
#include <iostream>

using namespace std;

int main(int argc, char* argv[])
{
    struct timeb tb;

    cout << "The current time is:" << endl;
    ftime(&tb);
    char* str = ctime(&tb.time);
    cout << "  " << str << endl;

    return 0;
}
```

CROSS-REFERENCE
See also _ftime(), asctime(), ctime(), gmtime(), localtime(), and time().

fwprintf()

Function

The `fwprintf()` writes a formatted wide-character string to a stream, returning the number of bytes written, or a negative value in the case of an error.

Header File

```
#include <stdio.h>
```

Declaration

```
int fwprintf(FILE *stream, const wchar_t *format
    [, argument ]...);
```

- *argument*—A list of data items that match the format specifiers included in the format string *format*.
- *format*—The format string, which can include the format specifiers shown in Table F-14.
- *stream*—A pointer to the stream to which to write the string.

Table F-14 Format Specifiers for fwprintf()

Specifier	Description
%c	Specifies a character.
%C	Specifies a wide character (`printf()`) or single-byte character (`wprintf()`).
%d	Specifies a signed decimal integer.
%e	Specifies a signed double-precision floating-point value using scientific notation with a lowercase e.
%E	Specifies a signed double-precision floating-point value using scientific notation with an uppercase E.
%f	Specifies a signed double-precision floating-point value.
%g	Specifies a signed double-precision floating-point value using either normal notation or scientific notation with a lowercase e.

Continued

Table F-14 *Continued*

Specifier	Description
%G	Specifies a signed double-precision floating-point value using either normal notation or scientific notation with an uppercase E.
%I	Specifies a signed decimal integer.
%n	Specifies an integer pointer.
%o	Specifies an unsigned octal integer.
%p	Specifies a void pointer.
%s	Specifies a string.
%S	Specifies a wide-character string (printf()) or single-byte-character string (wprintf()).
%u	Specifies an unsigned decimal integer.
%x	Specifies an unsigned hexadecimal integer with lowercase letters.
%X	Specifies an unsigned hexadecimal integer with uppercase letters.

Example

The following program demonstrates how to use the fwprintf() function. When run, the program attempts to open a file for writing and then writes a formatted string to the file, displaying the string as it goes. The program's output looks like this:

```
Writing the following string:
var1 = 25 and var2 = 25.758
Press any key to continue
```

Here is the program source code that produced the output:

```
#include "stdafx.h"
#include <stdio.h>
#include <iostream>

using namespace std;

int main(int argc, char* argv[])
{
    FILE *file;
    int var1 = 25;
    double var2 = 25.758;

    file = fopen("test.txt", "w");
    if (file == NULL)
```

```
            cout << "File open error" << endl;
        else
        {
            cout << "Writing the following string:" << endl;
            cout << "var1 = " << var1;
            cout << " and var2 = " << var2 << endl;
            fwprintf(file, L"var1 = %d and var2 = %f\n",
                var1, var2);
            fclose(file);
        }

        return 0;
    }
```

CROSS-REFERENCE

See also _close(), _creat(), _fcloseall(), _fdopen(), _fgetchar(), _fgetwchar(), _fileno(), _flushall(), _fputwchar(), _fsopen(), _getw(), _getws(), _lseeki64(), _open(), _putw(), _putws(), _read(), _rmtmp(), _tempnam(), _wcreat(), _wfdopen(), _wfopen(), _wfreopen(),_wfsopen(), _wopen(), _wtempnam(), _wtmpnam(), clearerr(), eof(), fclose(), feof(), ferror(), fflush(), fgetc(), fgetpos(), fgets(), fgetwc(), fgetws(), fopen(), fprintf(), fputc(), fputchar(), fputs(), fputwc(), fputws(), fread(), freopen(), fscanf(), fseek(), fsetpos(), ftell(), fwrite(), fwscanf(), getc(), getchar(), gets(), getwc(), getwchar(), lseek(), putc(), putch(), putchar(), puts(), putwc(), putwchar(), rewind(), setbuf(), setvbuf(), tmpfile(), tmpnam(), ungetc(), ungetch(), ungetwc(), and write().

fwrite()

Function

The `fwrite()` function writes data to a stream, returning the number of data objects written.

Header File

```
#include <stdio.h>
```

Declaration

```
size_t fwrite(void *buffer, size_t size,
    size_t count, FILE *stream);
```

- *buffer*—A pointer to the buffer from which the data will be written.
- *count*—The maximum number of data objects to write.
- *size*—The size in bytes of the data object.
- *stream*—A pointer to the stream to which to write the string.

Example

The following program demonstrates how to use the `fwrite()` function. When run, the program opens a file for writing and then writes a string to the file. The program's output looks like this:

```
Number of objects written: 1
Data written to file:
  This is a test

Press any key to continue
```

Here is the program source code that produced the output:

```cpp
#include "stdafx.h"
#include <stdio.h>
#include <iostream>

using namespace std;

int main(int argc, char* argv[])
{
    FILE *file;
    char buf[] = "This is a test";

    file = fopen("test.txt", "w");
    if (file == NULL)
        cout << "File open error" << endl;
    else
    {
        int num = fwrite(buf, sizeof(buf), 1, file);
        cout << "Number of objects written: " << num << endl;
        cout << "Data written to file:" << endl;
        cout << "  " << buf << endl << endl;
        fclose(file);
    }

    return 0;
}
```

CROSS-REFERENCE
See also _close(), _creat(), _fcloseall(), _fdopen(), _fgetchar(), _fgetwchar(), _fileno(), _flushall(), _fputwchar(), _fsopen(), _getw(), _getws(), _lseeki64(), _open(), _putw(), _putws(), _read(), _rmtmp(), _tempnam(), _wcreat(), _wfdopen(), _wfopen(), _wfreopen(),_wfsopen(), _wopen(), _wtempnam(), _wtmpnam(), clearerr(), eof(), fclose(), feof(), ferror(), fflush(), fgetc(), fgetpos(), fgets(), fgetwc(), fgetws(), fopen(), fprintf(), fputc(), fputchar(), fputs(), fputwc(), fputws(), fread(), freopen(), fscanf(), fseek(), fsetpos(), ftell(), fwprintf(), fwscanf(), getc(), getchar(), gets(), getwc(), getwchar(), lseek(), putc(), putch(), putchar(), puts(), putwc(), putwchar(), rewind(), setbuf(), setvbuf(), tmpfile(), tmpnam(), ungetc(), ungetch(), ungetwc(), and write().

fwscanf()

Function

The `fwscanf()` reads a formatted wide-character string from a stream, returning the number of data objects received, or `WEOF` in the case of an error.

Header File

```
#include <stdio.h>
```

Declaration

```
int fwscanf(FILE *stream, const wchar_t *format
    [, argument ]...);
```

- *argument* — A list of data objects that match the format specifiers included in the format string *format*.
- *format* — The format string, which can include the format specifiers shown in Table F-15.
- *stream* — A pointer to the stream from which to read the wide-character string.

Table F-15 Format Specifiers for fwscanf()

Specifier	Description
%c	Specifies a character.
%C	Specifies a wide character (`printf()`) or single-byte character (`wprintf()`).

Continued

Table F-15 *Continued*

Specifier	Description
%d	Specifies a signed decimal integer.
%e	Specifies a signed double-precision floating-point value using scientific notation with a lowercase e.
%E	Specifies a signed double-precision floating-point value using scientific notation with an uppercase E.
%f	Specifies a signed double-precision floating-point value.
%g	Specifies a signed double-precision floating-point value using either normal notation or scientific notation with a lowercase e.
%G	Specifies a signed double-precision floating point-value using either normal notation or scientific notation with an uppercase E.
%I	Specifies a signed decimal integer.
%n	Specifies an integer pointer.
%o	Specifies an unsigned octal integer.
%p	Specifies a void pointer.
%s	Specifies a string.
%S	Specifies a wide-character string (`printf()`) or single-byte-character string (`wprintf()`).
%u	Specifies an unsigned decimal integer.
%x	Specifies an unsigned hexadecimal integer with lowercase letters.
%X	Specifies an unsigned hexadecimal integer with uppercase letters.

Example

The following program demonstrates how to use the `fwscanf()` function. When run, the program reads three data objects from the standard input stream. The program's output looks like this:

```
Enter two integers and a string:
25 69 test

You entered 3 data objects:
var1 = 25
var2 = 69
str = test

Press any key to continue
```

Here is the program source code that produced the output:

```
#include "stdafx.h"
```

```cpp
#include <stdio.h>
#include <iostream>

using namespace std;

int main(int argc, char* argv[])
{
    int var1;
    int var2;
    wchar_t str[81];

    cout << "Enter two integers and a string: " << endl;
    int num = fwscanf(stdin, L"%d %d %s",
        &var1, &var2, str);
    cout << endl;
    cout << "You entered " << num << " data objects:" << endl;
    cout << "var1 = " << var1 << endl;
cout << "var2 = " << var2 << endl;
    cout << "str = ";
    wcout << str << endl << endl;

    return 0;
}
```

CROSS-REFERENCE

See also _close(), _creat(), _fcloseall(), _fdopen(), _fgetchar(), _fgetwchar(), _fileno(), _flushall(), _fputwchar(), _fsopen(), _getw(), _getws(), _lseeki64(), _open(), _putw(), _putws(), _read(), _rmtmp(), _tempnam(), _wcreat(), _wfdopen(), _wfopen(), _wfreopen(),_wfsopen(), _wopen(), _wtempnam(), _wtmpnam(), clearerr(), eof(), fclose(), feof(), ferror(), fflush(), fgetc(), fgetpos(), fgets(), fgetwc(), fgetws(), fopen(), fprintf(), fputc(), fputchar(), fputs(), fputwc(), fputws(), fread(), freopen(), fscanf(), fseek(), fsetpos(), ftell(), fwprintf(), fwrite(), getc(), getchar(), gets(), getwc(), getwchar(), lseek(), putc(), putch(), putchar(), puts(), putwc(), putwchar(), rewind(), setbuf(), setvbuf(), tmpfile(), tmpnam(), ungetc(), ungetch(), ungetwc(), and write().

_gcvt()

Function

The _gcvt() function converts a floating-point value to a string of digits, including the decimal point and sign. The function returns a pointer to the buffer containing the converted digits.

Header File

```
#include <stdlib.h>
```

Declaration

```
char* _gcvt(double value, int count, char* buf);
```

- *buf* — A pointer to the buffer that will receive the converted digits.
- *count* — The number of digits to return.
- *value* — The value to convert.

Example

The following program demonstrates how to use the _gcvt() function. When run, the program converts a floating-point value to a string of digits, and then displays the converted value. The program's output looks like the following:

```
Buffer: 2435.8756
Press any key to continue
```

Here is the program source code that produced the output:

```
#include "stdafx.h"
#include <iostream>
#include <stdlib.h>

using namespace std;
```

```
int main(int argc, char* argv[])
{
    char buf[81];

    _gcvt(2435.87564, 8, buf);
    cout << "Buffer: " << buf << endl;

    return 0;
}
```

CROSS-REFERENCE
See also _ecvt(), _fcvt(), atof(), and gcvt().

_get_osfhandle()

Function

The _get_osfhandle() function returns the operating-system file handle for a file associated with a stream. A return value of –1 indicates an error.

Header File

```
#include <io.h>
```

Declaration

```
long _get_osfhandle(int fileHandle);
```

- *fileHandle* — The file's handle.

Example

The following program demonstrates how to call the _get_osfhandle() function. When run, the program opens a file and associates it with a stream. The program then retrieves and displays the operating system file handle. The program's output looks like the following:

```
Handle: 20
Press any key to continue
```

Here is the program source code that produced the output:

```
#include "stdafx.h"
#include <iostream>
#include <fcntl.h>
#include <io.h>

using namespace std;

int main(int argc, char* argv[])
{
    FILE *file;
    int  fileHandle;

    fileHandle = _open("get_osfhandle.cpp", O_RDONLY);
    if (fileHandle != -1)
    {
        file = _fdopen(fileHandle, "r");
        if (file != NULL )
        {
            long osfHandle = _get_osfhandle(fileHandle);
            cout << "Handle: " << osfHandle << endl;
        }
        fclose(file);
    }

    return 0;
}
```

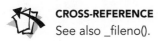

CROSS-REFERENCE
See also _fileno().

_getch()

Function

The _getch() function gets a character from the console without echoing the character on the console.

Header File

```
#include <conio.h>
```

Declaration

```
int _getch(void);
```

Example

The following program demonstrates how to use the _getch() function. When run, the program accepts a string from the console and then displays the results. The program's output looks something like the following:

```
Type a string and press Enter:
You typed:
   This is a test
Press any key to continue
```

Here is the program source code that produced the output:

```cpp
#include "stdafx.h"
#include <conio.h>
#include <iostream>

const CR = 13;

using namespace std;

int main(int argc, char* argv[])
{
    char buf[256];

    cout << "Type a string and press Enter:" << endl;
    int index = 0;
    int ch = _getch();
    while (ch != CR)
    {
        buf[index] = (char)ch;
        ++index;
        ch = _getch();
    }

    buf[index] = 0;
    cout << "You typed:" << endl;
    cout << "   " << buf << endl;

    return 0;
}
```

CROSS-REFERENCE
See also _getche(), _ungetch(), getc(), getch(), getchar(), getche(), getwc(), and getwchar().

_getche()

Function

The _getche() function gets a character from the console echoing the character on the console.

NOTE
Borland users should refer to the getche() function later in this chapter.

Header File

```
#include <conio.h>
```

Declaration

```
int _getche(void);
```

Example

The following program demonstrates how to use the _getche() function. When run, the program accepts a string from the console and then displays the results. The program's output looks something like the following:

```
Type a string and press Enter:
This is a test

You typed:
  This is a test

Press any key to continue
```

Here is the program source code that produced the output:

```
#include "stdafx.h"
#include <conio.h>
#include <iostream>

const CR = 13;
```

```
using namespace std;

int main(int argc, char* argv[])
{
    char buf[256];

    cout << "Type a string and press Enter:" << endl;
    int index = 0;
    int ch = _getche();
    while (ch != CR)
    {
        buf[index] = (char)ch;
        ++index;
        ch = _getche();
    }

    buf[index] = 0;
    cout << endl << endl << "You typed:" << endl;
    cout << "   " << buf << endl << endl;

    return 0;
}
```

CROSS-REFERENCE
See also _getch(),_ungetch(), getc(), getch(), getchar(), getche(), getwc(), and getwchar().

_getcwd()

Function

The _getcwd() function retrieves the default drive's current working directory, returning a pointer to the buffer containing the directory string. The function returns NULL in the case of an error.

NOTE
Borland users should refer to the getcwd() function later in this chapter.

Header File

```
#include <direct.h>
```

Declaration

```
char* _getcwd(char *buffer, int maxlen);
```

- *buffer* — A pointer to the buffer in which to store the directory string.
- *maxlen* — The maximum number of characters in the path.

Example

By retrieving and displaying the current working directory, the following program demonstrates how to use the _getcwd() function. The program's output looks something like the following:

```
Working directory: C:\Microsoft\G\_getcwd
Press any key to continue
```

Here is the program source code that produced the output:

```cpp
#include "stdafx.h"
#include <direct.h>
#include <iostream>

using namespace std;

int main(int argc, char* argv[])
{
    char buf[_MAX_PATH];

    char* path = _getcwd(buf, _MAX_PATH);
    if (path != NULL)
    {
        cout << "Working directory: ";
        cout << buf << endl;
    }
    else
        cout << "Error" << endl;

    return 0;
}
```

CROSS-REFERENCE

See also _chdrive(), _getdcwd(), _getdrive(), _mkdir(), _rmdir(), _searchenv(), _wchdir(), _wgetcwd(), _wgetdcwd(), _wmkdir(), _wrmdir(), _wsearchenv(), chdir(), and getcwd().

_getdcwd()

Function

The _getdcwd() function retrieves a disk drive's full current working directory path, returning a pointer to the buffer containing the directory string. The function returns NULL in the case of an error.

Header File

```
#include <direct.h>
```

Declaration

```
char* _getdcwd(int drive, char *buffer, int maxlen);
```

- *buffer* — A pointer to the buffer in which to store the directory string.
- *drive* — The drive for which to get the current working directory path, where 1 is A, 2 is B, 3 is C, and so forth.
- *maxlen* — The maximum number of characters in the path.

Example

By retrieving and displaying the current working directory for drive C, the following program demonstrates how to use the _getdcwd() function. The program's output looks something like the following:

```
Working directory: C:\Microsoft\G\_getdcwd
Press any key to continue
```

Here is the program source code that produced the output:

```
#include "stdafx.h"
#include <direct.h>
#include <iostream>

using namespace std;

int main(int argc, char* argv[])
{
    char buf[_MAX_PATH];

    char* path = _getdcwd(3, buf, _MAX_PATH);
```

```
    if (path != NULL)
    {
        cout << "Working directory: ";
        cout << buf << endl;
    }
    else
        cout << "Error" << endl;

    return 0;
}
```

CROSS-REFERENCE

See also _chdrive(), _getcwd(), _getdrive(), _mkdir(), _rmdir(), _searchenv(), _wchdir(), _wgetcwd(), _wgetdcwd(), _wmkdir(), _wrmdir(), _wsearchenv(), chdir(), and getcwd().

_getdrive()

Function

The _getdrive() function retrieves the current disk drive, where 1 is A, 2 is B, 3 is C, and so forth.

Header File

```
#include <direct.h>
```

NOTE

Borland users should include the dos.h header file.

Declaration

```
int _getdrive(void);
```

Example

By retrieving and displaying the current drive, the following program demonstrates how to use the _getdrive() function. The program's output looks something like the following:

```
Current Drive: 3
Press any key to continue
```

Here is the program source code that produced the output:

```
#include "stdafx.h"
#include <direct.h>
#include <iostream>

using namespace std;

int main(int argc, char* argv[])
{
    int drv = _getdrive();
    cout << "Current Drive: " << drv << endl;

    return 0;
}
```

CROSS-REFERENCE

See also _chdrive(), _getcwd(), _getdcwd(), _mkdir(), _rmdir(), _searchenv(), _wchdir(), _wgetcwd(), _wgetdcwd(), _wmkdir(), _wrmdir(), _wsearchenv(), chdir(), and getcwd().

_getpid()

Function

The _getpid() function retrieves the process ID.

NOTE

Borland users should refer to the getpid() function later in this chapter.

Header File

```
#include <process.h>
```

Declaration

```
int _getpid(void);
```

Example

By retrieving and displaying the process ID, the following program demonstrates how to use the _getpid() function. The program's output looks something like the following:

```
Process ID: -725041
Press any key to continue
```

Here is the program source code that produced the output:

```
#include "stdafx.h"
#include <process.h>
#include <iostream>

using namespace std;

int main(int argc, char* argv[])
{
    int pid = _getpid();
    cout << "Process ID: " << pid << endl;

    return 0;
}
```

CROSS-REFERENCE
See also getpid().

_getw()

Function

The _getw() function reads an integer from a stream.

Header File

```
#include <stdio.h>
```

Declaration

```
int _getw(FILE* stream);
```

- *stream* — A pointer to the stream from which to read an integer.

Example

The following program demonstrates how to use the _getw() function. When run, the program opens a file and reads and displays ten integers. The program's output looks something like the following:

```
Value #0: 1595944751
Value #1: 2004116839
Value #2: 1886413614
Value #3: 1142962720
Value #4: 1852401253
Value #5: 1948283749
Value #6: 1696621928
Value #7: 2037544046
Value #8: 1768910880
Value #9: 1713402990
Press any key to continue
```

Here is the program source code that produced the output:

```cpp
#include "stdafx.h"
#include <stdio.h>
#include <iostream>

using namespace std;

int main(int argc, char* argv[])
{
    FILE* file = fopen("_getw.cpp", "rb");

    if (file != NULL)
    {
        for (int x=0; x<10; ++x)
        {
            int val = _getw(file);
            int error = ferror(file);
            if (!error)
            {
                cout << "Value #" << x << ": ";
                cout << val << endl;
            }
            else
                cout << "Error reading file" << endl;
        }
        fclose(file);
    }
```

```
    else
        cout << "Error opening file" << endl;

    return 0;
}
```

CROSS-REFERENCE

See also _close(), _creat(), _fdopen(), _fgetchar(), _fgetwchar(), _fileno(), _flushall(), _fputwchar(), _fsopen(), _getw(), _getws(), _open(), _putch(), _putw(), _putws(), _read(), _rmtmp(), _tempnam(), _wcreat(), _wfdopen(), _wfopen(), _wfreopen(), _wfsopen(), _wopen(), _wtempnam(), _wtmpnam(), clearerr(), eof(), fclose(), feof(), ferror(), fflush(), fgetc(), fgetpos(), fgets(), fgetwc(), fgetws(), fopen(), fprintf(), fputc(), fputchar(), fputs(), fputwc(), fputws(), fread(), freopen(), fscanf(), fseek(), fsetpos(), ftell(), fwprintf(), fwrite(), fwscanf(), getc(), getchar(), gets(), getw(), getwc(), getwchar(), lseek(), lseeki64(), putc(), putch(), putchar(), puts(), putwc(), putwchar(), rewind(), setbuf(), setvbuf(), tmpfile(), tmpnam(), ungetc(), ungetch(), ungetwc(), and write().

_getws()

Function

The _getws() function reads a wide-character string from the stdin stream, returning a pointer to the string or returning NULL in the case of an error.

Header File

```
#include <stdio.h>
```

Declaration

```
wchar_t* _getws(wchar_t* buffer);
```

- *buffer*—A pointer to the buffer that will receive the string.

Example

The following program demonstrates how to use the _getws() function. When run, the program accepts a string from the console and displays the string. The program's output looks something like the following:

```
Enter a string below:
This is a test
```

```
You entered the following: This is a test
Press any key to continue
```

Here is the program source code that produced the output:

```
#include "stdafx.h"
#include <stdio.h>
#include <iostream>

using namespace std;

int main(int argc, char* argv[])
{
    wchar_t buf[81];

    cout << "Enter a string below: " << endl;
    _getws(buf);
    cout << "You entered the following: ";
    wcout << buf << endl;

    return 0;
}
```

CROSS-REFERENCE
See also _close(), _creat(), _fdopen(), _fgetchar(), _fgetwchar(), _fileno(), _flushall(), _fputwchar(), _fsopen(), _getw(), _open(), _putch(), _putw(), _putws(), _read(), _rmtmp(), _tempnam(), _wcreat(), _wfdopen(), _wfopen(), _wfreopen(), _wfsopen(), _wopen(), _wtempnam(), _wtmpnam(), clearerr(), eof(), fclose(), feof(), ferror(), fflush(), fgetc(), fgetpos(), fgets(), fgetwc(), fgetws(), fopen(), fprintf(), fputc(), fputchar(), fputs(), fputwc(), fputws(), fread(), freopen(), fscanf(), fseek(), fsetpos(), ftell(), fwprintf(), fwrite(), fwscanf(), getc(), getchar(), gets(), getw(), getwc(), getwchar(), lseek(), lseeki64(), putc(), putch(), putchar(), puts(), putwc(), putwchar(), rewind(), setbuf(), setvbuf(), tmpfile(), tmpnam(), ungetc(), ungetch(), ungetwc(), and write().

gcvt()

Function

The gcvt() function converts a floating-point value to a string of digits, including the decimal point and sign. The function returns a pointer to the buffer containing the converted digits.

Header File

```
#include <stdlib.h>
```

Declaration

```
char* gcvt(double value, int count, char* buf);
```

- *buf* — A pointer to the buffer that will receive the converted digits.
- *count* — The number of digits to return.
- *value* — The value to convert.

Example

The following program demonstrates how to use the gcvt() function. When run, the program converts a floating-point value to a string of digits, and then displays the converted value. The program's output looks like the following:

```
Buffer: 2435.8756
Press any key to continue
```

Here is the program source code that produced the output:

```
#include "stdafx.h"
#include <iostream>
#include <stdlib.h>

using namespace std;

int main(int argc, char* argv[])
{
    char buf[81];

    gcvt(2435.87564, 8, buf);
    cout << "Buffer: " << buf << endl;

    return 0;
}
```

CROSS-REFERENCE
See also _ecvt(), _fcvt(), _gcvt(), and atof().

getc()

Function

The getc() function reads a character from a stream, returning EOF in the event of an error or when at the end of the file.

Header File

```
#include <stdio.h>
```

Declaration

```
int getc(FILE* stream);
```

- *stream* — A pointer to the stream from which to read a character.

Example

The following program demonstrates how to use the getc() function. When run, the program opens a file and reads and displays ten characters. The program's output looks something like the following:

```
Character #0: /
Character #1: /
Character #2:
Character #3: g
Character #4: e
Character #5: t
Character #6: c
Character #7: .
Character #8: c
Character #9: p
Press any key to continue
```

Here is the program source code that produced the output:

```
#include "stdafx.h"
#include <stdio.h>
#include <iostream>

using namespace std;

int main(int argc, char* argv[])
{
```

```
FILE* file = fopen("getc.cpp", "rb");

if (file != NULL)
{
    for (int x=0; x<10; ++x)
    {
        int ch = getc(file);
        int error = ferror(file);
        if (!error)
        {
            cout << "Character #" << x << ": ";
            cout << (char)ch << endl;
        }
        else
            cout << "Error reading file" << endl;
    }
    fclose(file);
}
else
    cout << "Error opening file" << endl;

return 0;
}
```

CROSS-REFERENCE

See also _close(), _creat(), _fdopen(), _fgetchar(), _fgetwchar(), _fileno(), _flushall(), _fputwchar(), _fsopen(), _getw(), _getws(), _open(), _putch(), _putw(), _putws(), _read(), _rmtmp(), _tempnam(), _wcreat(), _wfdopen(), _wfopen(), _wfreopen(), _wfsopen(), _wopen(), _wtempnam(), _wtmpnam(), clearerr(), eof(), fclose(), feof(), ferror(), fflush(), fgetc(), fgetpos(), fgets(), fgetwc(), fgetws(), fopen(), fprintf(), fputc(), fputchar(), fputs(), fputwc(), fputws(), fread(), freopen(), fscanf(), fseek(), fsetpos(), ftell(), fwprintf(), fwrite(), fwscanf(), getchar(), gets(), getw(), getwc(), getwchar(), lseek(), lseeki64(), putc(), putch(), putchar(), puts(), putwc(), putwchar(), rewind(), setbuf(), setvbuf(), tmpfile(), tmpnam(), ungetc(), ungetch(), ungetwc(), and write().

getch()

Function

The getch() function gets a character from the console without echoing the character on the console.

Header File

```
#include <conio.h>
```

Declaration

```
int getch(void);
```

Example

The following program demonstrates how to use the getch() function. When run, the program accepts a string from the console and then displays the results. The program's output looks something like the following:

```
Type a string and press Enter:
You typed:
   This is a test
Press any key to continue
```

Here is the program source code that produced the output:

```
#include "stdafx.h"
#include <conio.h>
#include <iostream>

const CR = 13;

using namespace std;

int main(int argc,
char* argv[])
{
    char buf[256];

    cout << "Type a string and press Enter:" << endl;
    int index = 0;
    int ch = getch();
    while (ch != CR)
    {
        buf[index] = (char)ch;
        ++index;
        ch = getch();
    }

    buf[index] = 0;
```

```
        cout << "You typed:" << endl;
        cout << "   " << buf << endl;

        return 0;
    }
```

CROSS-REFERENCE

See also _getch(), _getche(), _ungetch(), getc(), getchar(), getwc(), and getwchar().

getchar()

Function

The getchar() function gets a character from the stdin stream.

Header File

```
#include <stdio.h>
```

Declaration

```
int getchar(void);
```

Example

The following program demonstrates how to use the getchar() function. When run, the program accepts a string from the console and then displays the results. The program's output looks something like the following:

```
Type a string and press Enter:
This is a test

You typed:
   This is a test

Press any key to continue
```

Here is the program source code that produced the output:

```
#include "stdafx.h"
#include <stdio.h>
```

```cpp
#include <iostream>

using namespace std;

int main(int argc,
char* argv[])
{
    char buf[256];

    cout << "Type a string and press Enter:" << endl;
    int index = 0;
    int ch = getchar();
    while (ch != '\n')
    {
        buf[index] = (char)ch;
        ++index;
        ch = getchar();
    }

    buf[index] = 0;
    cout << endl << "You typed:" << endl;
    cout << "   " << buf << endl << endl;

    return 0;
}
```

 CROSS-REFERENCE
See also _getch(), _getche(), _ungetch(), getc(), getch(), getwc(), and getwchar().

getche()

Function

The getche() function gets a character from the console echoing the character on the console.

Header File

```cpp
#include <conio.h>
```

Declaration

```
int getche(void);
```

Example

The following program demonstrates how to use the `getche()` function. When run, the program accepts a string from the console and then displays the results. The program's output looks something like the following:

```
Type a string and press Enter:
This is a test

You typed:
  This is a test

Press any key to continue
```

Here is the program source code that produced the output:

```cpp
#include "stdafx.h"
#include <conio.h>
#include <iostream>

const CR = 13;

using namespace std;

int main(int argc,
char* argv[])
{
    char buf[256];

    cout << "Type a string and press Enter:" << endl;
    int index = 0;
    int ch = getche();
    while (ch != CR)
    {
        buf[index] = (char)ch;
        ++index;
        ch = getche();
    }

    buf[index] = 0;
    cout << endl << endl << "You typed:" << endl;
```

f
g
h

```
cout << "   " << buf << endl << endl;

    return 0;
}
```

CROSS-REFERENCE

See also _getch(), _getche(), _ungetch(), getc(), getch(), getchar(), getwc(), and getwchar().

getcwd()

Function

The getcwd() function retrieves the default drive's current working directory, returning a pointer to the buffer containing the directory string. The function returns NULL in the case of an error.

Header File

```
#include <direct.h>
```

Declaration

```
char* getcwd(char *buffer, int maxlen);
```

- *buffer*—A pointer to the buffer in which to store the directory string.
- *maxlen*—The maximum number of characters in the path.

Example

By retrieving and displaying the current working directory, the following program demonstrates how to use the getcwd() function. The program's output looks something like the following:

```
Working directory: C:\Microsoft\G\getcwd
Press any key to continue
```

Here is the program source code that produced the output:

```
#include "stdafx.h"
#include <direct.h>
```

```
#include <iostream>

using namespace std;

int main(int argc, char* argv[])
{
    char buf[_MAX_PATH];

    char* path = getcwd(buf, _MAX_PATH);
    if (path != NULL)
    {
        cout << "Working directory: ";
        cout << buf << endl;
    }
    else
        cout << "Error" << endl;

    return 0;
}
```

CROSS-REFERENCE

See also _chdrive(), _getdcwd(), _getdrive(), _mkdir(), _rmdir(), _searchenv(),
_wchdir(), _wgetcwd(), _wgetdcwd(), _wmkdir(), _wrmdir(), _wsearchenv(), chdir(),
and getcwd().

getenv()

Function

The getenv() function retrieves the value of the specified environment variable, returning a pointer to the buffer containing the environment string. The
function returns NULL in the case of an error.

Header File

```
#include <stdlib.h>
```

Declaration

```
char* getenv(char *varname);
```

- *varname* — The name of the environment variable for which to get
the value.

Example

By retrieving and displaying the PATH variable's current setting, the following program demonstrates how to use the getenv() function. The program's output looks something like the following:

```
PATH: C:\WINDOWS;C:\WINDOWS\COMMAND
Press any key to continue
```

Here is the program source code that produced the output:

```cpp
#include "stdafx.h"
#include <stdlib.h>
#include <iostream>

using namespace std;

int main(int argc, char* argv[])
{
    char* value = getenv("PATH");
    if (value != NULL)
    {
        cout << "PATH: ";
        cout << value << endl;
    }
    else
        cout << "Error" << endl;

    return 0;
}
```

CROSS-REFERENCE
See also _wputenv(), putenv(), and wgetenv().

getpid()

Function

The getpid() function retrieves the process ID.

Header File

```cpp
#include <process.h>
```

Declaration

```
int getpid(void);
```

Example

By retrieving and displaying the process ID, the following program demonstrates how to use the getpid() function. The program's output looks something like the following:

```
Process ID: -725041
Press any key to continue
```

Here is the program source code that produced the output:

```
#include "stdafx.h"
#include <process.h>
#include <iostream>

using namespace std;

int main(int argc, char* argv[])
{
    int pid = getpid();
    cout << "Process ID: " << pid << endl;

    return 0;
}
```

CROSS-REFERENCE
See also _getpid().

getw()

Function

The getw() function reads an integer from a stream.

Header File

```
#include <stdio.h>
```

Declaration

```
int getw(FILE* stream);
```

- *stream* — A pointer to the stream from which to read an integer.

Example

The following program demonstrates how to use the getw() function. When run, the program opens a file and reads and displays ten integers. The program's output looks something like the following:

```
Value #0: 1595944751
Value #1: 2004116839
Value #2: 1886413614
Value #3: 1142962720
Value #4: 1852401253
Value #5: 1948283749
Value #6: 1696621928
Value #7: 2037544046
Value #8: 1768910880
Value #9: 1713402990
Press any key to continue
```

Here is the program source code that produced the output:

```cpp
#include "stdafx.h"
#include <stdio.h>
#include <iostream>

using namespace std;

int main(int argc, char* argv[])
{
    FILE* file = fopen("getw.cpp", "rb");

    if (file != NULL)
    {
        for (int x=0; x<10; ++x)
        {
            int val = getw(file);
            int error = ferror(file);
            if (!error)
            {
                cout << "Value #" << x << ": ";
```

```
                cout << val << endl;
            }
        else
            cout << "Error reading file" << endl;
        }
        fclose(file);
    }
    else
        cout << "Error opening file" << endl;

    return 0;
}
```

CROSS-REFERENCE

See also _close(), _creat(), _fdopen(), _fgetchar(), _fgetwchar(), _fileno(), _flushall(), _fputwchar(), _fsopen(), _getw(), _getws(), _open(), _putch(), _putw(), _putws(), _read(), _rmtmp(), _tempnam(), _wcreat(), _wfdopen(), _wfopen(), _wfreopen(), _wfsopen(), _wopen(), _wtempnam(), _wtmpnam(), clearerr(), eof(), fclose(), feof(), ferror(), fflush(), fgetc(), fgetpos(), fgets(), fgetwc(), fgetws(), fopen(), fprintf(), fputc(), fputchar(), fputs(), fputwc(), fputws(), fread(), freopen(), fscanf(), fseek(), fsetpos(), ftell(), fwprintf(), fwrite(), fwscanf(), getc(), getchar(), gets(), getwc(), getwchar(), lseek(), lseeki64(), putc(), putch(), putchar(), puts(), putwc(), putwchar(), rewind(), setbuf(), setvbuf(), tmpfile(), tmpnam(), ungetc(), ungetch(), ungetwc(), and write().

getwc()

Function

The `getwc()` function reads a wide character from a stream, returning `WEOF` in the event of an error or when at the end of the file.

Header File

```
#include <stdio.h>
```

Declaration

```
wint_t getwc(FILE* stream);
```

- *stream* — A pointer to the stream from which to read a character.

Example

The following program demonstrates how to use the getwc() function. When run, the program opens a file and reads and displays ten characters. The program's output looks something like the following:

```
Character #0: /
Character #1:
Character #2: e
Character #3: w
Character #4: .
Character #5: p
Character #6:
Character #7:
Character #8: e
Character #9: i
Press any key to continue
```

Note that only every other character in the file appears in the output because wide characters are twice as large as normal characters. Here is the program source code that produced the output:

```cpp
#include "stdafx.h"
#include <stdio.h>
#include <iostream>

using namespace std;

int main(int argc, char* argv[])
{
    FILE* file = fopen("getwc.cpp", "rb");

    if (file != NULL)
    {
        for (int x=0; x<10; ++x)
        {
            wint_t ch = getwc(file);
            int error = ferror(file);
            if (!error)
            {
                cout << "Character #" << x << ": ";
                cout << (char)ch << endl;
```

```
            }
        else
            cout << "Error reading file" << endl;
        }
        fclose(file);
    }
    else
        cout << "Error opening file" << endl;

    return 0;
}
```

CROSS-REFERENCE

See also _close(), _creat(), _fdopen(), _fgetchar(), _fgetwchar(), _fileno(), _flushall(), _fputwchar(), _fsopen(), _getw(), _getws(), _open(), _putch(), _putw(), _putws(), _read(), _rmtmp(), _tempnam(), _wcreat(), _wfdopen(), _wfopen(), _wfreopen(), _wfsopen(), _wopen(), _wtempnam(), _wtmpnam(), clearerr(), eof(), fclose(), feof(), ferror(), fflush(), fgetc(), fgetpos(), fgets(), fgetwc(), fgetws(), fopen(), fprintf(), fputc(), fputchar(), fputs(), fputwc(), fputws(), fread(), freopen(), fscanf(), fseek(), fsetpos(), ftell(), fwprintf(), fwrite(), fwscanf(), getc(), getchar(), gets(), getw(), getwchar(), lseek(), lseeki64(), putc(), putch(), putchar(), puts(), putwc(), putwchar(), rewind(), setbuf(), setvbuf(), tmpfile(), tmpnam(), ungetc(), ungetch(), ungetwc(), and write().

getwchar()

Function

The getwchar() function gets a wide character from the stdin stream.

Header File

```
#include <stdio.h>
```

Declaration

```
wint_t getwchar(void);
```

Example

The following program demonstrates how to use the getwchar() function. When run, the program accepts a string from the console and then displays the results. The program's output looks something like the following:

```
Type a string and press Enter:
This is a test

You typed:
  This is a test

Press any key to continue
```

Here is the program source code that produced the output:

```cpp
#include "stdafx.h"
#include <stdio.h>
#include <iostream>

using namespace std;

int main(int argc, char* argv[])
{
    char buf[256];

    cout << "Type a string and press Enter:" << endl;
    int index = 0;
    wint_t ch = getwchar();
    while (ch != '\n')
    {
        buf[index] = (char)ch;
        ++index;
        ch = getwchar();
    }

    buf[index] = 0;
    cout << endl << "You typed:" << endl;
    cout << "  " << buf << endl << endl;

    return 0;
}
```

CROSS-REFERENCE
See also _getch(), _getche(), _ungetch(), getc(), getch(), getchar(), and getwc().

gmtime()

Function

The gmtime() function creates a tm structure from a time value.

Header File

```
#include <time.h>
```

Declaration

```
struct tm* gmtime(const time_t* timer);
```

- *timer* — A pointer to the variable holding the time value.

Example

The following program demonstrates how to use the gmtime() function. When run, the program gets the system time, converts it to a structure, and displays the results. The program's output looks something like the following:

```
Time: 19:16:39

Press any key to continue
```

Here is the program source code that produced the output:

```
#include "stdafx.h"
#include <time.h>
#include <iostream>

using namespace std;

int main(int argc, char* argv[])
{
    time_t curTime;
    struct tm* timeStruct;

    curTime = time(&curTime);
    timeStruct = gmtime(&curTime);
    cout << "Time: ";
    cout << timeStruct->tm_hour << ":";
    cout << timeStruct->tm_min << ":";
```

```
        cout << timeStruct->tm_sec << endl << endl;

        return 0;
    }
```

 CROSS-REFERENCE
See also _ftime(), asctime(), ctime(), localtime(), mktime(), and time().

_heapchk()

Function

The _heapchk() function checks for errors in the heap and returns one of the values listed in Table H-1.

Table H-1 Return Values for _heapchk()

Value	Description
_HEAPBADBEGIN	Problems with the heap header.
_HEAPBADNODE	The heap has a bad node.
_HEAPBADPTR	The heap pointer is bad.
_HEAPEMPTY	The heap is empty.
_HEAPOK	The heap is OK.

Header File

```
#include <malloc.h>
```

Declaration

```
int _heapchk(void);
```

Example

The following program demonstrates how to call the _heapchk() function. When run, the program allocates a block of memory and then checks the consistency of the heap, displaying the results in a message. The program's output looks like this:

```
Heap is OK
Press any key to continue
```

497

Here is the program source code that produced the output:

```cpp
#include "stdafx.h"
#include <malloc.h>
#include <iostream>

using namespace std;

int main(int argc, char* argv[])
{
    char* buf = (char *) malloc(1024);
    if (buf != NULL)
    {
        int heapChk = _heapchk();
        switch( heapChk )
        {
            case _HEAPBADPTR:
                cout << "Heap pointer bad" << endl;
                break;
            case _HEAPBADBEGIN:
                cout << "Heap start bad" << endl;
                break;
            case _HEAPEMPTY:
                cout << "Heap is empty" << endl;
                break;
            case _HEAPBADNODE:
                cout << "Bad heap node" << endl;
                break;
            case _HEAPOK:
                cout << "Heap is OK" << endl;
                break;
        }
        free(buf);
    }

    return 0;
}
```

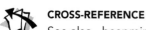

CROSS-REFERENCE
See also _heapmin(), _heapset(), and _heapwalk().

_heapmin()

Function

The _heapmin() function returns all unused memory to the operating system. This function returns an error value of –1 on every platform except Windows NT. A return value of 0 indicates that the function call was successful.

Header File

```
#include <malloc.h>
```

Declaration

```
int _heapmin(void);
```

Example

The following program demonstrates how to call the _heapmin() function. When run, the program allocates a block of memory and then returns all unused memory to the operating system. This program will return an error on all systems except Windows NT. The program's output looks like this on Windows 98:

```
_heapmin() not successful
Press any key to continue
```

Here is the program source code that produced the output:

```
#include "stdafx.h"
#include <malloc.h>
#include <iostream>

using namespace std;

int main(int argc, char* argv[])
{
    char* buf = (char *) malloc(1024);
    if (buf != NULL)
    {
        int result = _heapmin();
        if (result == 0)
```

```
                    cout << "_heapmin() successful" << endl;
            else
                    cout << "_heapmin() not successful" << endl;
            free(buf);
        }

        return 0;
    }
```

CROSS-REFERENCE
See also _heapchk(), _heapset(), _heapwalk(), free().

_heapset()

Function

The _heapset() function checks for heap errors and then initializes free memory to a specified value. With Visual C++, this function returns only _HEAPOK on every platform except Windows NT. If the function call is successful on Windows NT, it returns one of the values listed in Table H-2.

Table H-2 Return Values for _heapset()

Value	Description
_HEAPBADBEGIN	Problems with the heap header.
_HEAPBADNODE	The heap has a bad node.
_HEAPEMPTY	The heap is empty.
_HEAPOK	The heap is OK.

Header File

```
#include <malloc.h>
```

Declaration

```
int _heapset(unsigned int fill);
```

- *fill*—The value with which to initialize free memory

Example

The following program demonstrates how to call the _heapset() function. When run, the program allocates a block of memory and then calls _heapset(). The program's output looks like this:

```
Heap is OK
Press any key to continue
```

Here is the program source code that produced the output:

```cpp
#include "stdafx.h"
#include <malloc.h>
#include <iostream>

using namespace std;

int main(int argc, char* argv[])
{
    char* buf = (char *) malloc(1024);
    if (buf != NULL)
    {
        int result = _heapset(0);
        switch (result)
        {
            case _HEAPBADBEGIN:
                cout << "Heap start bad" << endl;
                break;
            case _HEAPEMPTY:
                cout << "Heap is empty" << endl;
                break;
            case _HEAPBADNODE:
                cout << "Bad heap node" << endl;
                break;
            case _HEAPOK:
                cout << "Heap is OK" << endl;
                break;
        }
        free(buf);
    }
    else
        cout << "Memory allocation failure" << endl;

    return 0;
}
```

CROSS-REFERENCE
See also _heapchk(), _heapmin(), _heapwalk(), and free().

_heapwalk()

Function

The _heapwalk() function examines each entry in the heap. With Visual C++, this function returns only _HEAPEND on every platform except Windows NT. If the function call is successful, it returns one of the values listed in Table H-3.

Table H-3 Return Values for the _heapwalk() Function

Value	Description
_HEAPBADBEGIN	Problems with the heap header.
_HEAPBADNODE	The heap has a bad node.
_HEAPBADPTR	There is no valid pointer in the _HEAPINFO structure.
_HEAPEMPTY	The heap is empty.
_HEAPEND	Reached the end of the heap.
_HEAPOK	The heap is OK.

Header File

```
#include <malloc.h>
```

Declaration

```
int _heapwalk(_HEAPINFO* heapInfo);
```

- *heapInfo* — A pointer to a _HEAPINFO structure

Example

The following program demonstrates how to call the _heapwalk() function. When run, the program allocates a block of memory and then calls _heapwalk() repeatedly until it reaches the end of the heap. The program's output looks like this:

```
Walking the heap...
Reached end of heap
```

```
Press any key to continue
```

Here is the program source code that produced the output:

```cpp
#include "stdafx.h"
#include <malloc.h>
#include <iostream>

using namespace std;

int main(int argc, char* argv[])
{
    int result;
    _HEAPINFO heapInfo;
    heapInfo._pentry = NULL;

    char* buf = (char *) malloc(1024);
    if (buf != NULL)
    {
        cout << "Walking the heap..." << endl;
        do
            result = _heapwalk(&heapInfo);
        while (result == _HEAPOK);

        switch (result)
        {
            case _HEAPBADBEGIN:
                cout << "Heap start bad" << endl;
                break;
            case _HEAPEMPTY:
                cout << "Heap is empty" << endl;
                break;
            case _HEAPBADNODE:
                cout << "Bad heap node" << endl;
                break;
            case _HEAPBADPTR:
                cout << "Bad heap pointer" << endl;
                break;
            case _HEAPEND:
                cout << "Reached end of heap" << endl;
                break;
        }
        free(buf);
    }
}
```

g
h
i

```
        else
            cout << "Memory allocation failure" << endl;

        return 0;
    }
```

CROSS-REFERENCE
See also _heapchk(), _heapmin(), _heapset(), and free().

_hypot()

Function

The _hypot() function calculates the hypotenuse of a triangle.

NOTE
Borland users should refer to the hypot() function later in this chapter.

Header File

```
#include <math.h>
```

Declaration

```
double _hypot(double x, double y);
```

- *x* — The size of the first side of the triangle.
- *y* — The size of the second side of the triangle.

Example

The following program demonstrates how to call the _hypot() function. When run, the program calculates the hypotenuse of a right triangle with sides of size 5 and 3. The program's output looks like this:

```
The hypotenuse is 5.83095
Press any key to continue
```

Here is the program source code that produced the output:

```
#include "stdafx.h"
#include <math.h>
```

```
#include <iostream>

using namespace std;

int main(int argc, char* argv[])
{
    double side1 = 5;
    double side2 = 3;

    double hypt = _hypot(side1, side2);
    cout << "The hypotenuse is " << hypt << endl;

    return 0;
}
```

CROSS-REFERENCE

See also acos(), asin(), atan(), atan2(), cos(), cosh(), hypot(), sin(), sinh(), tan(), and tanh().

Header Files

Concept

Header files are source-code files that contain information about classes, functions, constants, and other types of data that a program needs to compile successfully. For example, when a program uses the cout I/O object to display data on the screen, the program's source code must include the header file in which the cout object is defined, like this:

```
#include <iostream>
```

When defining classes, the usual practice is to declare the class in a header file and define the class in an implementation file. The header file usually has the .h filename extension, whereas the implementation file has the .cpp filename extension. The first listing below (stored as MyClass.h) declares a class in a header file, and the second listing (stored as MyClass.cpp) defines the class in an implementation file. The third listing (stored as header_files.cpp) is a program that uses the class and so must include the class's header file. The program's output looks like this:

```
Class value: 10
Press any key to continue
```

Here is the program source code that produced the output:

```cpp
// Class header file.
class MyClass
{
protected:
    int value;

public:
    MyClass(int val);
    ~MyClass();
    int GetValue();
};

// Class implementation file.
#include "stdafx.h"
#include "MyClass.h"

MyClass::MyClass(int val)
{
    value = val;
}

MyClass::~MyClass()
{
}

int MyClass::GetValue()
{
    return value;
}

// Program to test MyClass.
#include "stdafx.h"
#include <iostream>
#include "MyClass.h"

using namespace std;

int main(int argc, char* argv[])
{
    MyClass myClass(10);
    cout << "Class value: " << myClass.GetValue() << endl;
    return 0;
}
```

CROSS-REFERENCE
See also Implementation File.

hex

Manipulator

The hex manipulator causes numerical data to be output in hexadecimal form. For example, the following program displays the value 16 in hexadecimal form (10). The program's output looks like this:

```
10
Press any key to continue.
```

Here is the program source code that produced the output:

```
#include "stdafx.h"
#include <iostream>

using namespace std;

int main(int argc, char* argv[])
{
    cout << hex << 16 << endl;
    return 0;
}
```

CROSS-REFERENCE
See also binary, dec, and oct.

hypot()

Function

The hypot() function calculates the hypotenuse of a triangle.

Header File

```
#include <math.h>
```

Declaration

```
double hypot(double x, double y);
```

- ■ *x* — The size of the first side of a triangle.
- ■ *y* — The size of the second side of a triangle.

Example

The following program demonstrates how to call the hypot() function. When run, the program calculates the hypotenuse of a right triangle with sides of size 5 and 3. The program's output looks like this:

```
The hypotenuse is 5.83095
Press any key to continue
```

Here is the program source code that produced the output:

```cpp
#include "stdafx.h"
#include <math.h>
#include <iostream>

using namespace std;

int main(int argc, char* argv[])
{
    double side1 = 5;
    double side2 = 3;

    double hypt = hypot(side1, side2);
    cout << "The hypotenuse is " << hypt << endl;

    return 0;
}
```

CROSS-REFERENCE

See also _hypot(), acos(), asin(), atan(), atan2(), cos(), cosh(), sin(), sinh(), tan(), and tanh().

#if

Directive

The #if directive enables the compiler to manage conditional compilation, in which the program specifies different blocks of code to be compiled under given conditions. For example, the following example of the #if directive, along with the #else and #endif directives, prints a message depending on whether the symbol DEBUG has been defined. The program's output looks like the following:

```
Debugging is off.
Press any key to continue
```

Here is the program source code that produced the output:

```cpp
#include "stdafx.h"
#include <iostream>

#define DEBUG 0

using namespace std;

int main(int argc, char* argv[])
{
#if DEBUG
    cout << "Debugging is on." << endl;
#else
    cout << "Debugging is off." << endl;
#endif

    return 0;
}
```

CROSS-REFERENCE
See also #elif, #else, #endif, #ifdef, and #ifndef.

#ifdef

Directive

The #ifdef enables the compiler to manage conditional compilation, in which the program specifies different blocks of code to be compiled under given conditions. For example, the following example of the #ifdef directive, along with the #else and #endif directives, prints a message depending on whether the symbol VALUE has been defined. The program's output looks like the following:

```
VALUE is defined
Press any key to continue
```

Here is the program source code that produced the output:

```cpp
#include "stdafx.h"
#include <iostream>

#define VALUE

using namespace std;

int main(int argc, char* argv[])
{
#ifdef VALUE
    cout << "VALUE is defined" << endl;
#else
    cout << "VALUE is not defined" << endl;
#endif

    return 0;
}
```

 CROSS-REFERENCE
See also #elif, #else, #endif, #if, and #ifndef.

#ifndef

Directive

The #ifndef directive enables the compiler to manage conditional compilation, in which the program specifies different blocks of code to be compiled under given conditions. For example, the following example of the #ifndef directive, along with the #else and #endif directives, prints a message depending on whether the symbol VALUE has been defined. The program's output looks like the following:

```
VALUE is not defined
Press any key to continue
```

Here is the program source code that produced the output:

```
#include "stdafx.h"
#include <iostream>

//#define VALUE

using namespace std;

int main(int argc, char* argv[])
{
#ifndef VALUE
    cout << "VALUE is not defined" << endl;
#else
    cout << "VALUE is defined" << endl;
#endif

    return 0;
}
```

CROSS-REFERENCE
See also #elif, #else, #endif, #if, and #ifdef.

#include

Directive

The #include directive enables a program to include other source code files in its compilation. Usually, the #include directive is used to include, into a program, function definitions, objects, constants, and other symbols defined in a header file. For example, the following program includes the header file iostream into the program's code that gives the compiler the information it needs to compile the reference to the cout object. The program's output looks like the following:

```
A message from iostream!
Press any key to continue
```

Here is the program source code that produced the output:

```
#include "stdafx.h"
#include <iostream>

using namespace std;

int main(int argc, char* argv[])
{
    cout << "A message from iostream!" << endl;

    return 0;
}
```

__int16

keyword

The __int16 keyword specifies that the declared integer should be 16 bits in length. For example, the following line declares a 16-bit integer named var1:

```
__int16 var1;
```

 CROSS-REFERENCE
See also __int32, __int64, and __int8.

__int32

keyword

The __int32 keyword specifies that the declared integer should be 32 bits in length. For example, the following line declares a 32-bit integer named var1:

```
__int32 var1;
```

 CROSS-REFERENCE
See also __int16, __int64, and __int8.

__int64

keyword

The __int64 keyword specifies that the declared integer should be 64 bits in length. For example, the following line declares a 64-bit integer named var1:

```
__int64 var1;
```

 CROSS-REFERENCE
See also __int16, __int32, and __int8.

__int8

keyword

The __int8 keyword specifies that the declared integer should be 8 bits in length. For example, the following line declares a 8-bit integer named var1:

```
__int8 var1;
```

 CROSS-REFERENCE
See also __int16, __int32, and __int64.

__isascii()

Function

The __isascii() function returns true if the given value is an ASCII character. Otherwise, the function returns false.

 NOTE
Borland users should refer to the isascii() function later in this chapter.

Header File

```
#include <ctype.h>
```

Declaration

```
int __isascii(int c);
```

- *c* — The value to examine.

Example

The following program demonstrates how to use the __isascii() function. The program's output looks like the following:

```
val1 is ASCII.
Press any key to continue
```

Here is the program source code that produced the output:

```
#include "stdafx.h"
#include <iostream>

using namespace std;

int main(int argc, char* argv[])
{
    int val1 = 65;
    int result;

    result = __isascii(val1);
    if (result)
        cout << "val1 is ASCII." << endl;
    else
        cout << "val1 is not ASCII." << endl;

    return 0;
}
```

CROSS-REFERENCE

See also _ismbbalpha(), _ismbbgraph(), _ismbbkalnum(), _ismbbkana(), _ismbbkprint(), _ismbbkpunct(), _ismbblead(), _ismbbprint(), _ismbbpunct(), _ismbbtrail(), _ismbcalnum(), _ismbcalpha(), _ismbcdigit(), _ismbcgraph(), _ismbchira(), _ismbckata(), _ismbcl0(), _ismbcl1(), _ismbcl2(), _ismbclegal(), _ismbclower(), _ismbcprint(), _ismbcpunct(), _ismbcspace(), _ismbcsymbol(), _ismbcupper(), isalnum(), isalpha(), isascii(), isdigit(), isgraph(), isleadbyte(), islower(), isprint(), ispunct(), isspace(), isupper(), iswalnum(), iswalpha(), iswascii(), iswcntrl(), iswdigit(), iswgraph(), iswlower(), iswprint(), iswpunct(), iswspace(), iswupper(), iswxdigit(), and isxdigit().

__i64toa()

Function

The _i64toa() function converts a 64-bit integer to a string and returns a pointer to the resultant string.

Header File

```
#include <stdlib.h>
```

Declaration

```
char *_i64toa(__int64 value, char *string, int radix);
```

- *radix* — The number base to be used in the conversion. Must be a value from 2 to 36.
- *string* — A pointer to the buffer that will receive the string.
- *value* — The value to convert.

Example

The following program demonstrates how to use the _i64toa() function. When run, the program displays the value 23,543 in decimal, binary, and hexadecimal representations. The program's output looks like the following:

```
Decimal: 23543
Binary: 101101111110111
Hexadecimal: 5bf7
Press any key to continue
```

Here is the program source code that produced the output:

```
#include "stdafx.h"
#include <iostream>
#include <stdlib.h>

using namespace std;

int main(int argc, char* argv[])
{
    __int64 value = 23543;
    char buf[81];
```

```
_i64toa(value, buf, 10);
cout << "Decimal: " << buf << endl;
_i64toa(value, buf, 2);
cout << "Binary: " << buf << endl;
_i64toa(value, buf, 16);
cout << "Hexadecimal: " << buf << endl;

return 0;
}
```

CROSS-REFERENCE
See also _ecvt(), _fcvt(), _gcvt(), _i64tow(), _itoa(), _itow(), _ui64toa(), _ui64tow(), itoa(), ltoa(), and ultoa().

_i64tow()

Function

The _i64tow() function converts a 64-bit integer to a wide-character string and returns a pointer to the resultant string.

Header File

```
#include <stdlib.h>
```

Declaration

```
char *_i64tow(__int64 value, wchar_t *string, int radix);
```

- *radix* — The number base to be used in the conversion. Must be a value from 2 to 36.
- *string* — A pointer to the buffer that will receive the string.
- *value* — The value to convert.

Example

The following program demonstrates how to use the _i64tow() function. When run, the program displays the value 23,543 in decimal, binary, and hexadecimal representations. The program's output looks like the following:

```
Decimal: 23543
Binary: 101101111110111
Hexadecimal: 5bf7
Press any key to continue
```

Here is the program source code that produced the output:

```cpp
#include "stdafx.h"
#include <iostream>
#include <stdlib.h>

using namespace std;

int main(int argc, char* argv[])
{
    __int64 value = 23543;
    wchar_t buf[81];

    _i64tow(value, buf, 10);
    wprintf(L"Decimal: %s\n", buf);
    _i64tow(value, buf, 2);
    wprintf(L"Binary: %s\n", buf);
    _i64tow(value, buf, 16);
    wprintf(L"Hexadecimal: %s\n", buf);

    return 0;
}
```

CROSS-REFERENCE
See also _ecvt(), _fcvt(), _gcvt(), _i64toa(), _itoa(), _itow(), _ui64toa(), _ui64tow(), itoa(), ltoa(), and ultoa().

_isatty()

Function

The `_isatty()` function returns true if the given device handle is associated with a character device. Otherwise, the function returns false.

NOTE
Borland users should refer to the `isatty()` function later in this chapter.

Header File

```
#include <io.h>
```

Declaration

```
int _isatty(int handle);
```

- *handle* — The device handle.

Example

The following program demonstrates how to use the `_isatty()` function. When run, the program checks whether the `stdin` stream is currently associated with a character device. The program's output looks like the following:

```
This is a character device
Press any key to continue
```

Here is the program source code that produced the output:

```cpp
#include "stdafx.h"
#include <io.h>
#include <iostream>

using namespace std;

int main(int argc, char* argv[])
{
    int fileHandle = _fileno(stdin);
    int result = _isatty(fileHandle);
    if (result)
        cout << "This is a character device" << endl;
    else
        cout << "This is not a character device" << endl;

    return 0;
}
```

CROSS-REFERENCE

See also _access(), _chmod(), _chsize(), _filelength(), _fileno(), _fstat(), _fstati64(), _fullpath(), _get_osfhandle(), _locking(), _makepath(), _mktemp(), _open_osfhandle(), _splitpath(), _stat(), _stati64(), _umask(), _unlink(), _waccess(), _wchmod(), _wfullpath(), _wmakepath(), _wmktemp(), _wremove(), _wrename(), _wsplitpath(), _wstat(), _wstati64(), _wunlink(), isatty(), remove(), and rename().

_ismbbalnum()

Function

The _ismbbalnum() function returns true if the given value represents an alphanumeric character.

Header File

```
#include <mbctype.h>
```

Declaration

```
int _ismbbalnum(unsigned int ch);
```

- *ch* — The value to examine.

Example

The following program demonstrates how to use the _ismbbalnum() function. When run, the program checks whether a value represents an alphanumeric character and displays the result. The program's output looks like the following:

```
result = 1
Press any key to continue
#include "stdafx.h"
#include <iostream>
#include <mbctype.h>

using namespace std;

int main(int argc, char* argv[])
{
    int result = _ismbbalnum(65);
    cout << "result = " << result << endl;

    return 0;
}
```

CROSS-REFERENCE

See also __isascii(), _ismbbalpha(), _ismbbgraph(), _ismbbkalnum(), _ismbbkana(), _ismbbkprint(), _ismbbkpunct(), _ismbblead(), _ismbbprint(), _ismbbpunct(), _ismbbtrail(), _ismbcalnum(), _ismbcalpha(), _ismbcdigit(), _ismbcgraph(), _ismbchira(), _ismbckata(), _ismbcl0(), _ismbcl1(), _ismbcl2(), _ismbclegal(), _ismbclower(), _ismbcprint(), _ismbcpunct(), _ismbcspace(), _ismbcsymbol(), _ismbcupper(), isalnum(), isalpha(), isascii(), isdigit(), isgraph(), isleadbyte(), islower(), isprint(), ispunct(), isspace(), isupper(), iswalnum(), iswalpha(), iswascii(), iswcntrl(), iswdigit(), iswgraph(), iswlower(), iswprint(), iswpunct(), iswspace(), iswupper(), iswxdigit(), and isxdigit().

_ismbbalpha()

Function

The `_ismbbalpha()` function returns true if the given value represents an alphabetic character.

Header File

```
#include <mbctype.h>
```

Declaration

```
int _ismbbalpha(unsigned int ch);
```

- *ch* — The value to examine.

Example

The following program demonstrates how to use the `_ismbbalpha()` function. When run, the program checks whether a value represents an alphabetic character and displays the result. The program's output looks like the following:

```
result = 1
Press any key to continue
```

Here is the program source code that produced the output:

```
#include "stdafx.h"
#include <iostream>
#include <mbctype.h>

using namespace std;
```

```
int main(int argc, char* argv[])
{
    int result = _ismbbalpha(65);
    cout << "result = " << result << endl;

    return 0;
}
```

CROSS-REFERENCE

See also __isascii(), _ismbbalnum(), _ismbbgraph(), _ismbbkalnum(), _ismbbkana(), _ismbbkprint(), _ismbbkpunct(), _ismbblead(), _ismbbprint(), _ismbbpunct(), _ismbbtrail(), _ismbcalnum(), _ismbcalpha(), _ismbcdigit(), _ismbcgraph(), _ismbchira(), _ismbckata(), _ismbcl0(), _ismbcl1(), _ismbcl2(), _ismbclegal(), _ismbclower(), _ismbcprint(), _ismbcpunct(), _ismbcspace(), _ismbcsymbol(), _ismbcupper(), isalnum(), isalpha(), isascii(), isdigit(), isgraph(), isleadbyte(), islower(), isprint(), ispunct(), isspace(), isupper(), iswalnum(), iswalpha(), iswascii(), iswcntrl(), iswdigit(), iswgraph(), iswlower(), iswprint(), iswpunct(), iswspace(), iswupper(), iswxdigit(), and isxdigit().

_ismbbgraph()

Function

The `_ismbbgraph()` function returns true if the given value represents an ASCII or Katakana character other than a whitespace character.

Header File

```
#include <mbctype.h>
```

Declaration

```
int _ismbbgraph(unsigned int ch);
```

- *ch* — The value to examine.

Example

The following program demonstrates how to use the `_ismbbgraph()` function. When run, the program checks whether a value represents an ASCII or

Katakana character and displays the result. The program's output looks like the following:

```
result = 1
Press any key to continue
```

Here is the program source code that produced the output:

```cpp
#include "stdafx.h"
#include <iostream>
#include <mbctype.h>

using namespace std;

int main(int argc, char* argv[])
{
    int result = _ismbbgraph(50);
    cout << "result = " << result << endl;

    return 0;
}
```

CROSS-REFERENCE

See also _isascii(), _ismbbalnum(), _ismbbalpha(), _ismbbkalnum(), _ismbbkana(), _ismbbkprint(), _ismbbkpunct(), _ismbblead(), _ismbbprint(), _ismbbpunct(), _ismbbtrail(), _ismbcalnum(), _ismbcalpha(), _ismbcdigit(), _ismbcgraph(), _ismbchira(), _ismbckata(), _ismbcl0(), _ismbcl1(), _ismbcl2(), _ismbclegal(), _ismbclower(), _ismbcprint(), _ismbcpunct(), _ismbcspace(), _ismbcsymbol(), _ismbcupper(), isalnum(), isalpha(), isascii(), isdigit(), isgraph(), isleadbyte(), islower(), isprint(), ispunct(), isspace(), isupper(), iswalnum(), iswalpha(), iswascii(), iswcntrl(), iswdigit(), iswgraph(), iswlower(), iswprint(), iswpunct(), iswspace(), iswupper(), iswxdigit(), and isxdigit().

_ismbbkalnum()

Function

The _ismbbkalnum() function returns true if the given value represents a non-ASCII character, not including punctuation.

NOTE

Borland does not support this function.

Header File

```
#include <mbctype.h>
```

Declaration

```
int _ismbbkalnum(unsigned int ch);
```

- *ch* — The value to examine.

Example

The following program demonstrates how to use the `_ismbbkalnum()` function. When run, the program checks whether a value represents a non-ASCII character (not including punctuation) and displays the result. The program's output looks like the following:

```
result = 0
Press any key to continue
```

Here is the program source code that produced the output:

```cpp
#include "stdafx.h"
#include <iostream>
#include <mbctype.h>

using namespace std;

int main(int argc, char* argv[])
{
    int result = _ismbbkalnum(50);
    cout << "result = " << result << endl;

    return 0;
}
```

CROSS-REFERENCE

See also __isascii(), _ismbbalnum(), _ismbbalpha(), _ismbbgraph(), _ismbbkana(), _ismbbkprint(), _ismbbkpunct(), _ismbblead(), _ismbbprint(), _ismbbpunct(), _ismbbtrail(), _ismbcalnum(), _ismbcalpha(), _ismbcdigit(), _ismbcgraph(), _ismbchira(), _ismbckata(), _ismbcl0(), _ismbcl1(), _ismbcl2(), _ismbclegal(), _ismbclower(), _ismbcprint(), _ismbcpunct(), _ismbcspace(), _ismbcsymbol(), _ismbcupper(), isalnum(), isalpha(), isascii(), isdigit(), isgraph(), isleadbyte(), islower(), isprint(), ispunct(), isspace(), isupper(), iswalnum(), iswalpha(), iswascii(), iswcntrl(), iswdigit(), iswgraph(), iswlower(), iswprint(), iswpunct(), iswspace(), iswupper(), iswxdigit(), and isxdigit().

_ismbbkana()

Function

The _ismbbkana() function returns true if the given value represents a Katakana character.

Header File

```
#include <mbctype.h>
```

Declaration

```
int _ismbbkana(unsigned int ch);
```

- *ch* — The value to examine.

Example

The following program demonstrates how to use the _ismbbkana() function. When run, the program checks whether a value represents a Katakana character and displays the result. The program's output looks like the following:

```
result = 0
Press any key to continue
```

Here is the program source code that produced the output:

```
#include "stdafx.h"
#include <iostream>
#include <mbctype.h>

using namespace std;

int main(int argc, char* argv[])
{
    int result = _ismbbkana(50);
    cout << "result = " << result << endl;

    return 0;
}
```

CROSS-REFERENCE

See also __isascii(), _ismbbalnum(), _ismbbalpha(), _ismbbgraph(), _ismbbkalnum(), _ismbbkprint(), _ismbbkpunct(), _ismbblead(), _ismbbprint(), _ismbbpunct(), _ismbbtrail(), _ismbcalnum(), _ismbcalpha(), _ismbcdigit(), _ismbcgraph(), _ismbchira(), _ismbckata(), _ismbcl0(), _ismbcl1(), _ismbcl2(), _ismbclegal(), _ismbclower(), _ismbcprint(), _ismbcpunct(), _ismbcspace(), _ismbcsymbol(), _ismbcupper(), isalnum(), isalpha(), isascii(), isdigit(), isgraph(), isleadbyte(), islower(), isprint(), ispunct(), isspace(), isupper(), iswalnum(), iswalpha(), iswascii(), iswcntrl(), iswdigit(), iswgraph(), iswlower(), iswprint(), iswpunct(), iswspace(), iswupper(), iswxdigit(), and isxdigit.

_ismbbkprint()

Function

The _ismbbkprint() function returns true if the given value represents a non-ASCII text character, including punctuation.

NOTE
Borland does not support this function.

Header File

```
#include <mbctype.h>
```

Declaration

```
int _ismbbkprint(unsigned int ch);
```

- *ch* — The value to examine.

Example

The following program demonstrates how to use the _ismbbkprint() function. When run, the program checks whether a value represents a non-ASCII text character (including punctuation) and displays the result. The program's output looks like the following:

```
result = 0
Press any key to continue
```

Here is the program source code that produced the output:

```
#include "stdafx.h"
#include <iostream>
#include <mbctype.h>

using namespace std;

int main(int argc, char* argv[])
{
    int result = _ismbbkprint(1287);
    cout << "result = " << result << endl;

    return 0;
}
```

CROSS-REFERENCE

See also __isascii(), _ismbbalnum(), _ismbbalpha(), _ismbbgraph(), _ismbbkalnum(), _ismbbkana(), _ismbbkpunct(), _ismbblead(), _ismbbprint(), _ismbbpunct(), _ismbbtrail(), _ismbcalnum(), _ismbcalpha(), _ismbcdigit(), _ismbcgraph(), _ismbchira(), _ismbckata(), _ismbcl0(), _ismbcl1(), _ismbcl2(), _ismbclegal(), _ismbclower(), _ismbcprint(), _ismbcpunct(), _ismbcspace(), _ismbcsymbol(), _ismbcupper(), isalnum(), isalpha(), isascii(), isdigit(), isgraph(), isleadbyte(), islower(), isprint(), ispunct(), isspace(), isupper(), iswalnum(), iswalpha(), iswascii(), iswcntrl(), iswdigit(), iswgraph(), iswlower(), iswprint(), iswpunct(), iswspace(), iswupper(), iswxdigit(), and isxdigit().

_ismbbkpunct()

Function

The _ismbbkpunct() function returns true if the given value represents a non-ASCII punctuation character.

Header File

```
#include <mbctype.h>
```

Declaration

```
int _ismbbkpunct(unsigned int ch);
```

- *ch* — The value to examine.

Example

The following program demonstrates how to use the _ismbbkpunct() function. When run, the program checks whether a value represents a non-ASCII punctuation character and displays the result. The program's output looks like the following:

```
result = 0
Press any key to continue
```

Here is the program source code that produced the output:

```cpp
#include "stdafx.h"
#include <iostream>
#include <mbctype.h>

using namespace std;

int main(int argc, char* argv[])
{
    int result = _ismbbkpunct(1287);
    cout << "result = " << result << endl;

    return 0;
}
```

CROSS-REFERENCE

See also __isascii(), _ismbbalnum(), _ismbbalpha(), _ismbbgraph(), _ismbbkalnum(), _ismbbkana(), _ismbbkprint(), _ismbblead(), _ismbbprint(), _ismbbpunct(), _ismbbtrail(), _ismbcalnum(), _ismbcalpha(), _ismbcdigit(), _ismbcgraph(), _ismbchira(), _ismbckata(), _ismbcl0(), _ismbcl1(), _ismbcl2(), _ismbclegal(), _ismbclower(), _ismbcprint(), _ismbcpunct(), _ismbcspace(), _ismbcsymbol(), _ismbcupper(), isalnum(), isalpha(), isascii(), isdigit(), isgraph(), isleadbyte(), islower(), isprint(), ispunct(), isspace(), isupper(), iswalnum(), iswalpha(), iswascii(), iswcntrl(), iswdigit(), iswgraph(), iswlower(), iswprint(), iswpunct(), iswspace(), iswupper(), iswxdigit(), and isxdigit().

_ismbblead()

Function

The _ismbblead() function returns true if the given value represents the leading (first) byte of a multibyte character.

Header File

```
#include <mbctype.h>
```

Declaration

```
int _ismbblead(unsigned int ch);
```

- *ch* — The value to examine.

Example

The following program demonstrates how to use the _ismbblead() function. When run, the program checks whether a value represents the first byte of a multibyte character and displays the result. The program's output looks like the following:

```
result = 0
Press any key to continue
```

Here is the program source code that produced the output:

```
#include "stdafx.h"
#include <iostream>
#include <mbctype.h>

using namespace std;

int main(int argc, char* argv[])
{
    int result = _ismbblead(65);
    cout << result << endl;

    return 0;
}
```

CROSS-REFERENCE

See also __isascii(), _ismbbalnum(), _ismbbalpha(), _ismbbgraph(), _ismbbkalnum(), _ismbbkana(), _ismbbkprint(), _ismbbkpunct(), _ismbbprint(), _ismbbpunct(), _ismbbtrail(), _ismbcalnum(), _ismbcalpha(), _ismbcdigit(), _ismbcgraph(), _ismbchira(), _ismbckata(), _ismbcl0(), _ismbcl1(), _ismbcl2(), _ismbclegal(), _ismbclower(), _ismbcprint(), _ismbcpunct(), _ismbcspace(), _ismbcsymbol(), _ismbcupper(), isalnum(), isalpha(), isascii(), isdigit(), isgraph(), isleadbyte(), islower(), isprint(), ispunct(), isspace(), isupper(), iswalnum(), iswalpha(), iswascii(), iswcntrl(), iswdigit(), iswgraph(), iswlower(), iswprint(), iswpunct(), iswspace(), iswupper(), iswxdigit(), and isxdigit().

_ismbbprint()

Function

The _ismbbprint() function returns true if the given value represents an ASCII or Katakana printable character. Also includes whitespace characters.

Header File

```
#include <mbctype.h>
```

Declaration

```
int _ismbbprint(unsigned int ch);
```

- *ch* — The value to examine.

Example

The following program demonstrates how to use the _ismbbprint() function. When run, the program checks whether a value represents a printable ASCII or Katakana character and displays the result. The program's output looks like the following:

```
result = 1
Press any key to continue
```

Here is the program source code that produced the output:

```
#include "stdafx.h""
#include <iostream>
#include <mbctype.h>

using namespace std;

int main(int argc, char* argv[])
{
    int result = _ismbbprint(65);
    cout << result << endl;

    return 0;
}
```

CROSS-REFERENCE
See also __isascii(), _ismbbalnum(), _ismbbalpha(), _ismbbgraph(), _ismbbkalnum(), _ismbbkana(), _ismbbkprint(), _ismbbkpunct(), _ismbblead(), _ismbbpunct(), _ismbbtrail(), _ismbcalnum(), _ismbcalpha(), _ismbcdigit(), _ismbcgraph(), _ismbchira(), _ismbckata(), _ismbcl0(), _ismbcl1(), _ismbcl2(), _ismbclegal(), _ismbclower(), _ismbcprint(), _ismbcpunct(), _ismbcspace(), _ismbcsymbol(), _ismbcupper(), isalnum(), isalpha(), isascii(), isdigit(), isgraph(), isleadbyte(), islower(), isprint(), ispunct(), isspace(), isupper(), iswalnum(), iswalpha(), iswascii(), iswcntrl(), iswdigit(), iswgraph(), iswlower(), iswprint(), iswpunct(), iswspace(), iswupper(), iswxdigit(), and isxdigit().

_ismbbpunct()

Function

The _ismbbpunct() function returns true if the given value represents an ASCII or Katakana punctuation character.

Header File

```
#include <mbctype.h>
```

Declaration

```
int _ismbbpunct(unsigned int ch);
```

- *ch* — The value to examine.

Example

The following program demonstrates how to use the _ismbbpunct() function. When run, the program checks whether a value represents an ASCII or Katakana punctuation character and displays the result. The program's output looks like the following:

```
result = 1
Press any key to continue
```

Here is the program source code that produced the output:

```
#include "stdafx.h"
#include <iostream>
#include <mbctype.h>
```

```
using namespace std;

int main(int argc, char* argv[])
{
    int result = _ismbbpunct(33);
    cout << "result = " << result << endl;

    return 0;
}
```

CROSS-REFERENCE

See also __isascii(), _ismbbalnum(), _ismbbalpha(), _ismbbgraph(), _ismbbkalnum(), _ismbbkana(), _ismbbkprint(), _ismbbkpunct(), _ismbblead(), _ismbbprint(), _ismbbtrail(), _ismbcalnum(), _ismbcalpha(), _ismbcdigit(), _ismbcgraph(), _ismbchira(), _ismbckata(), _ismbcl0(), _ismbcl1(), _ismbcl2(), _ismbclegal(), _ismbclower(), _ismbcprint(), _ismbcpunct(), _ismbcspace(), _ismbcsymbol(), _ismbcupper(), isalnum(), isalpha(), isascii(), isdigit(), isgraph(), isleadbyte(), islower(), isprint(), ispunct(), isspace(), isupper(), iswalnum(), iswalpha(), iswascii(), iswcntrl(), iswdigit(), iswgraph(), iswlower(), iswprint(), iswpunct(), iswspace(), iswupper(), iswxdigit(), and isxdigit().

_ismbbtrail()

Function

The _ismbbtrail() function returns true if the given value represents the trailing (second) byte of a multibyte character.

Header File

```
#include <mbctype.h>
```

Declaration

```
int _ismbbtrail(unsigned int ch);
```

- *ch* — The value to examine.

Example

The following program demonstrates how to use the _ismbbtrail() function. When run, the program checks whether a value represents the second byte of a multibyte character and displays the result. The program's output looks like the following:

```
result = 0
Press any key to continue
```

Here is the program source code that produced the output:

```
#include "stdafx.h"
#include <iostream>
#include <mbctype.h>

using namespace std;

int main(int argc, char* argv[])
{
    int result = _ismbbtrail(65);
    cout << "result = " << result << endl;

    return 0;
}
```

CROSS-REFERENCE
See also __isascii(), _ismbbalnum(), _ismbbalpha(), _ismbbgraph(), _ismbbkalnum(), _ismbbkana(), _ismbbkprint(), _ismbbkpunct(), _ismbblead(), _ismbbprint(), _ismbbpunct(), _ismbcalnum(), _ismbcalpha(), _ismbcdigit(), _ismbcgraph(), _ismbchira(), _ismbckata(), _ismbcl0(), _ismbcl1(), _ismbcl2(), _ismbclegal(), _ismbclower(), _ismbcprint(), _ismbcpunct(), _ismbcspace(), _ismbcsymbol(), _ismbcupper(), isalnum(), isalpha(), isascii(), isdigit(), isgraph(), isleadbyte(), islower(), isprint(), ispunct(), isspace(), isupper(), iswalnum(), iswalpha(), iswascii(), iswcntrl(), iswdigit(), iswgraph(), iswlower(), iswprint(), iswpunct(), iswspace(), iswupper(), iswxdigit(), and isxdigit().

_ismbcalnum()

Function

The _ismbcalnum() function returns true if the given value represents a single-byte ASCII character.

Header File

```
#include <mbstring.h>
```

Declaration

```
int _ismbcalnum(unsigned int ch);
```

- *ch* — The value to examine.

Example

The following program demonstrates how to use the _ismbcalnum() function. When run, the program checks whether a value represents an alphanumeric character and displays the result. The program's output looks like the following:

```
result = 1
Press any key to continue
```

Here is the program source code that produced the output:

```cpp
#include "stdafx.h"
#include <iostream>
#include <mbstring.h>

using namespace std;

int main(int argc, char* argv[])
{
    int result = _ismbcalnum(65);
    cout << "result = " << result << endl;

    return 0;
}
```

CROSS-REFERENCE

See also __isascii(), _ismbbalnum(), _ismbbalpha(), _ismbbgraph(), _ismbbkalnum(), _ismbbkana(), _ismbbkprint(), _ismbbkpunct(), _ismbblead(), _ismbbprint(), _ismbbpunct(), _ismbbtrail(), _ismbcalpha(), _ismbcdigit(), _ismbcgraph(), _ismbchira(), _ismbckata(), _ismbcl0(), _ismbcl1(), _ismbcl2(), _ismbclegal(), _ismbclower(), _ismbcprint(), _ismbcpunct(), _ismbcspace(), _ismbcsymbol(), _ismbcupper(), isalnum(), isalpha(), isascii(), isdigit(), isgraph(), isleadbyte(), islower(), isprint(), ispunct(), isspace(), isupper(), iswalnum(), iswalpha(), iswascii(), iswcntrl(), iswdigit(), iswgraph(), iswlower(), iswprint(), iswpunct(), iswspace(), iswupper(), iswxdigit(), and isxdigit().

_ismbcalpha()

Function

The _ismbcalpha() function returns true if the given value represents a single-byte alphabetic character.

Header File

```
#include <mbstring.h>
```

Declaration

```
int _ismbcalpha(unsigned int ch);
```

- *ch* — The value to examine.

Example

The following program demonstrates how to use the _ismbcalpha() function. When run, the program checks whether a value represents an alphabetic character and displays the result. The program's output looks like the following:

```
result = 1
Press any key to continue
```

Here is the program source code that produced the output:

```
#include "stdafx.h"
#include <iostream>
#include <mbstring.h>

using namespace std;

int main(int argc, char* argv[])
{
    int result = _ismbcalpha(65);
    cout << "result = " << result << endl;

    return 0;
}
```

CROSS-REFERENCE
See also __isascii(), _ismbbalnum(), _ismbbalpha(), _ismbbgraph(), _ismbbkalnum(), _ismbbkana(), _ismbbkprint(), _ismbbkpunct(), _ismbblead(), _ismbbprint(), _ismbbpunct(), _ismbbtrail(), _ismbcalnum(), _ismbcdigit(), _ismbcgraph(), _ismbchira(), _ismbckata(), _ismbcl0(), _ismbcl1(), _ismbcl2(), _ismbclegal(), _ismbclower(), _ismbcprint(), _ismbcpunct(), _ismbcspace(), _ismbcsymbol(), _ismbcupper(), isalnum(), isalpha(), isascii(), isdigit(), isgraph(), isleadbyte(), islower(), isprint(), ispunct(), isspace(), isupper(), iswalnum(), iswalpha(), iswascii(), iswcntrl(), iswdigit(), iswgraph(), iswlower(), iswprint(), iswpunct(), iswspace(), iswupper(), iswxdigit(), and isxdigit().

_ismbcdigit()

Function

The `_ismbcdigit()` function returns true if the given value represents a digit character.

Header File

```
#include <mbstring.h>
```

Declaration

```
int _ismbcdigit(unsigned int ch);
```

- *ch* — The value to examine.

Example

The following program demonstrates how to use the `_ismbcdigit()` function. When run, the program checks whether a value represents a digit character and displays the result. The program's output looks like the following:

```
result = 4
Press any key to continue
```

Here is the program source code that produced the output:

```
#include "stdafx.h"
#include <iostream>
#include <mbstring.h>

using namespace std;
```

```
int main(int argc, char* argv[])
{
    int result = _ismbcdigit(50);
    cout << "result = " << result << endl;

    return 0;
}
```

CROSS-REFERENCE

See also __isascii(), _ismbbalnum(), _ismbbalpha(), _ismbbgraph(), _ismbbkalnum(), _ismbbkana(), _ismbbkprint(), _ismbbkpunct(), _ismbblead(), _ismbbprint(), _ismbbpunct(), _ismbbtrail(), _ismbcalnum(), _ismbcalpha(), _ismbcgraph(), _ismbchira(), _ismbckata(), _ismbcl0(), _ismbcl1(), _ismbcl2(), _ismbclegal(), _ismbclower(), _ismbcprint(), _ismbcpunct(), _ismbcspace(), _ismbcsymbol(), _ismbcupper(), isalnum(), isalpha(), isascii(), isdigit(), isgraph(), isleadbyte(), islower(), isprint(), ispunct(), isspace(), isupper(), iswalnum(), iswalpha(), iswascii(), iswcntrl(), iswdigit(), iswgraph(), iswlower(), iswprint(), iswpunct(), iswspace(), iswupper(), iswxdigit(), and isxdigit().

_ismbcgraph()

Function

The _ismbcgraph() function returns true if the given value represents a single-byte ASCII or Katakana character other than a whitespace character.

Header File

```
#include <mbstring.h>
```

Declaration

```
int _ismbcgraph(unsigned int ch);
```

- *ch* — The value to examine.

Example

The following program demonstrates how to use the _ismbcgraph() function. When run, the program checks whether a value represents an ASCII or

Katakana character and displays the result. The program's output looks like the following:

```
result = 1
Press any key to continue
```

Here is the program source code that produced the output:

```
#include "stdafx.h"
#include <iostream>
#include <mbstring.h>

using namespace std;

int main(int argc, char* argv[])
{
    int result = _ismbcgraph(50);
    cout << "result = " << result << endl;

    return 0;
}
```

CROSS-REFERENCE

See also __isascii(), _ismbbalnum(), _ismbbalpha(), _ismbbgraph(), _ismbbkalnum(), _ismbbkana(), _ismbbkprint(), _ismbbkpunct(), _ismbblead(), _ismbbprint(), _ismbbpunct(), _ismbbtrail(), _ismbcalnum(), _ismbcalpha(), _ismbcdigit(), _ismbchira(), _ismbckata(), _ismbcl0(), _ismbcl1(), _ismbcl2(), _ismbclegal(), _ismbclower(), _ismbcprint(), _ismbcpunct(), _ismbcspace(), _ismbcsymbol(), _ismbcupper(), isalnum(), isalpha(), isascii(), isdigit(), isgraph(), isleadbyte(), islower(), isprint(), ispunct(), isspace(), isupper(), iswalnum(), iswalpha(), iswascii(), iswcntrl(), iswdigit(), iswgraph(), iswlower(), iswprint(), iswpunct(), iswspace(), iswupper(), iswxdigit(), and isxdigit().

_ismbchira()

Function

The _ismbchira() function returns true if the given value represents a double-byte Hiragana character.

Header File

```
#include <mbstring.h>
```

Declaration

```
int _ismbchira(unsigned int ch);
```

- *ch* — The value to examine.

Example

The following program demonstrates how to use the _ismbchira() function. When run, the program checks whether a value represents a single-byte ASCII or Katakana character and displays the result. The program's output looks like the following:

```
result = 0
Press any key to continue
```

Here is the program source code that produced the output:

```
#include "stdafx.h"
#include <iostream>
#include <mbstring.h>

using namespace std;

int main(int argc, char* argv[])
{
    int result = _ismbchira(50);
    cout << "result = " << result << endl;

    return 0;
}
```

CROSS-REFERENCE

See also __isascii(), _ismbbalnum(), _ismbbalpha(), _ismbbgraph(), _ismbbkalnum(), _ismbbkana(), _ismbbkprint(), _ismbbkpunct(), _ismbblead(), _ismbbprint(), _ismbbpunct(), _ismbbtrail(), _ismbcalnum(), _ismbcalpha(), _ismbcdigit(), _ismbcgraph(), _ismbckata(), _ismbcl0(), _ismbcl1(), _ismbcl2(), _ismbclegal(), _ismbclower(), _ismbcprint(), _ismbcpunct(), _ismbcspace(), _ismbcsymbol(), _ismbcupper(), isalnum(), isalpha(), isascii(), isdigit(), isgraph(), isleadbyte(), islower(), isprint(), ispunct(), isspace(), isupper(), iswalnum(), iswalpha(), iswascii(), iswcntrl(), iswdigit(), iswgraph(), iswlower(), iswprint(), iswpunct(), iswspace(), iswupper(), iswxdigit(), and isxdigit().

_ismbckata()

Function

The _ismbckata() function returns true if the given value represents a double-byte Katakana character.

Header File

```
#include <mbstring.h>
```

Declaration

```
int _ismbckata(unsigned int ch);
```

- *ch* — The value to examine.

Example

The following program demonstrates how to use the _ismbckata() function. When run, the program checks whether a value represents a double-byte Katakana character and displays the result. The program's output looks like the following:

```
result = 0
Press any key to continue
```

Here is the program source code that produced the output:

```
#include "stdafx.h"
#include <iostream>
#include <mbstring.h>

using namespace std;

int main(int argc, char* argv[])
{
    int result = _ismbckata(50);
    cout << "result = " << result << endl;

    return 0;
}
```

CROSS-REFERENCE
See also __isascii(), _ismbbalnum(), _ismbbalpha(), _ismbbgraph(), _ismbbkalnum(),
_ismbbkana(), _ismbbkprint(), _ismbbkpunct(), _ismbblead(), _ismbbprint(),
_ismbbpunct(), _ismbbtrail(), _ismbcalnum(), _ismbcalpha(), _ismbcdigit(),
_ismbcgraph(), _ismbchira(), _ismbcl0(), _ismbcl1(), _ismbcl2(), _ismbclegal(),
_ismbclower(), _ismbcprint(), _ismbcpunct(), _ismbcspace(), _ismbcsymbol(),
_ismbcupper(), isalnum(), isalpha(), isascii(), isdigit(), isgraph(), isleadbyte(),
islower(), isprint(), ispunct(), isspace(), isupper(), iswalnum(), iswalpha(),
iswascii(), iswcntrl(), iswdigit(), iswgraph(), iswlower(), iswprint(), iswpunct(),
iswspace(), iswupper(), iswxdigit(), and isxdigit().

_ismbcl0()

Function

The _ismbcl0() function returns true if the given value represents a JIS non-Kanji character.

Header File

```
#include <mbstring.h>
```

Declaration

```
int _ismbcl0(unsigned int ch);
```

- *ch* — The value to examine.

Example

The following program demonstrates how to use the _ismbcl0() function. When run, the program checks whether a value represents a JIS non-Kanji character and displays the result. The program's output looks like the following:

```
result = 0
Press any key to continue
```

Here is the program source code that produced the output:

```
#include "stdafx.h"
#include <iostream>
#include <mbstring.h>
```

```
using namespace std;

int main(int argc, char* argv[])
{
    int result = _ismbcl0(0x7042);
    cout << "result = " << result << endl;

    return 0;
}
```

CROSS-REFERENCE

See also __isascii(), _ismbbalnum(), _ismbbalpha(), _ismbbgraph(), _ismbbkalnum(), _ismbbkana(), _ismbbkprint(), _ismbbkpunct(), _ismbblead(), _ismbbprint(), _ismbbpunct(), _ismbbtrail(), _ismbcalnum(), _ismbcalpha(), _ismbcdigit(), _ismbcgraph(), _ismbchira(), _ismbckata(), _ismbcl1(), _ismbcl2(), _ismbclegal(), _ismbclower(), _ismbcprint(), _ismbcpunct(), _ismbcspace(), _ismbcsymbol(), _ismbcupper(), isalnum(), isalpha(), isascii(), isdigit(), isgraph(), isleadbyte(), islower(), isprint(), ispunct(), isspace(), isupper(), iswalnum(), iswalpha(), iswascii(), iswcntrl(), iswdigit(), iswgraph(), iswlower(), iswprint(), iswpunct(), iswspace(), iswupper(), iswxdigit(), and isxdigit().

_ismbcl1()

Function

The _ismbcl1() function returns true if the given value represents a JIS level-1 character.

Header File

```
#include <mbstring.h>
```

Declaration

```
int _ismbcl1(unsigned int ch);
```

- *ch*—The value to examine.

Example

The following program demonstrates how to use the _ismbcl1() function. When run, the program checks whether a value represents a JIS level-1 character and displays the result. The program's output looks like the following:

```
result = 0
Press any key to continue
```

Here is the program source code that produced the output:

```cpp
#include "stdafx.h"
#include <iostream>
#include <mbstring.h>

using namespace std;

int main(int argc, char* argv[])
{
    int result = _ismbcl1(0x8142);
    cout << "result = " << result << endl;

    return 0;
}
```

CROSS-REFERENCE

See also __isascii(), _ismbbalnum(), _ismbbalpha(), _ismbbgraph(), _ismbbkalnum(), _ismbbkana(), _ismbbkprint(), _ismbbkpunct(), _ismbblead(), _ismbbprint(), _ismbbpunct(), _ismbbtrail(), _ismbcalnum(), _ismbcalpha(), _ismbcdigit(), _ismbcgraph(), _ismbchira(), _ismbckata(), _ismbcl0(), _ismbcl2(), _ismbclegal(), _ismbclower(), _ismbcprint(), _ismbcpunct(), _ismbcspace(), _ismbcsymbol(), _ismbcupper(), isalnum(), isalpha(), isascii(), isdigit(), isgraph(), isleadbyte(), islower(), isprint(), ispunct(), isspace(), isupper(), iswalnum(), iswalpha(), iswascii(), iswcntrl(), iswdigit(), iswgraph(), iswlower(), iswprint(), iswpunct(), iswspace(), iswupper(), iswxdigit(), and isxdigit().

_ismbcl2()

Function

The _ismbcl2() function returns true if the given value represents a JIS level-2 character.

Header File

```
#include <mbstring.h>
```

Declaration

```
int _ismbcl2(unsigned int ch);
```

- *ch* — The value to examine.

Example

The following program demonstrates how to use the _ismbcl2() function. When run, the program checks whether a value represents a JIS level-2 character and displays the result. The program's output looks like the following:

```
result = 0
Press any key to continue
```

Here is the program source code that produced the output:

```
#include "stdafx.h"
#include <iostream>
#include <mbstring.h>

using namespace std;

int main(int argc, char* argv[])
{
    int result = _ismbcl2(0x8142);
    cout << "result = " << result << endl;

    return 0;
}
```

CROSS-REFERENCE

See also __isascii(), _ismbbalnum(), _ismbbalpha(), _ismbbgraph(), _ismbbkalnum(), _ismbbkana(), _ismbbkprint(), _ismbbkpunct(), _ismbblead(), _ismbbprint(), _ismbbpunct(), _ismbbtrail(), _ismbcalnum(), _ismbcalpha(), _ismbcdigit(), _ismbcgraph(), _ismbchira(), _ismbckata(), _ismbcl0(), _ismbcl1(), _ismbclegal(), _ismbclower(), _ismbcprint(), _ismbcpunct(), _ismbcspace(), _ismbcsymbol(), _ismbcupper(), isalnum(), isalpha(), isascii(), isdigit(), isgraph(), isleadbyte(), islower(), isprint(), ispunct(), isspace(), isupper(), iswalnum(), iswalpha(), iswascii(), iswcntrl(), iswdigit(), iswgraph(), iswlower(), iswprint(), iswpunct(), iswspace(), iswupper(), iswxdigit(), and isxdigit().

_ismbclegal()

Function

The _ismbclegal() function returns true if the given value represents a legal multibyte symbol character.

Header File

```
#include <mbstring.h>
```

Declaration

```
int _ismbclegal(unsigned int ch);
```

- *ch* — The value to examine.

Example

The following program demonstrates how to use the _ismbclegal() function. When run, the program checks whether a value represents a multibyte symbol character and displays the result. The program's output looks like the following:

```
result = 0
Press any key to continue
```

Here is the program source code that produced the output:

```cpp
#include "stdafx.h"
#include <iostream>
#include <mbstring.h>

using namespace std;

int main(int argc, char* argv[])
{
    int result = _ismbclegal(0x7043);
    cout << "result = " << result << endl;

    return 0;
}
```

CROSS-REFERENCE
See also __isascii(), _ismbbalnum(), _ismbbalpha(), _ismbbgraph(), _ismbbkalnum(), _ismbbkana(), _ismbbkprint(), _ismbbkpunct(), _ismbblead(), _ismbbprint(), _ismbbpunct(), _ismbbtrail(), _ismbcalnum(), _ismbcalpha(), _ismbcdigit(), _ismbcgraph(), _ismbchira(), _ismbckata(), _ismbcl0(), _ismbcl1(), _ismbcl2(), _ismbclower(), _ismbcprint(), _ismbcpunct(), _ismbcspace(), _ismbcsymbol(), _ismbcupper(), isalnum(), isalpha(), isascii(), isdigit(), isgraph(), isleadbyte(), islower(), isprint(), ispunct(), isspace(), isupper(), iswalnum(), iswalpha(), iswascii(), iswcntrl(), iswdigit(), iswgraph(), iswlower(), iswprint(), iswpunct(), iswspace(), iswupper(), iswxdigit(), and isxdigit().

_ismbclower()

Function

The `_ismbclower()` function returns true if the given value represents a single-byte, lowercase letter.

Header File

```
#include <mbstring.h>
```

Declaration

```
int _ismbclower(unsigned int ch);
```

- *ch* — The value to examine.

Example

The following program demonstrates how to use the `_ismbclower()` function. When run, the program checks whether two values represent lowercase, single-byte characters and displays the result. The program's output looks like the following:

```
result = 1
result = 0
Press any key to continue
```

Here is the program source code that produced the output:

```
#include "stdafx.h"
#include <iostream>
#include <mbstring.h>
```

```
using namespace std;

int main(int argc, char* argv[])
{
    int result = _ismbclower(100);
    cout << "result = " << result << endl;
    result = _ismbclower(64);
    cout << "result = " << result << endl;

    return 0;
}
```

CROSS-REFERENCE

See also __isascii(), _ismbbalnum(), _ismbbalpha(), _ismbbgraph(), _ismbbkalnum(), _ismbbkana(), _ismbbkprint(), _ismbbkpunct(), _ismbblead(), _ismbbprint(), _ismbbpunct(), _ismbbtrail(), _ismbcalnum(), _ismbcalpha(), _ismbcdigit(), _ismbcgraph(), _ismbchira(), _ismbckata(), _ismbcl0(), _ismbcl1(), _ismbcl2(), _ismbclegal(), _ismbcprint(), _ismbcpunct(), _ismbcspace(), _ismbcsymbol(), _ismbcupper(), isalnum(), isalpha(), isascii(), isdigit(), isgraph(), isleadbyte(), islower(), isprint(), ispunct(), isspace(), isupper(), iswalnum(), iswalpha(), iswascii(), iswcntrl(), iswdigit(), iswgraph(), iswlower(), iswprint(), iswpunct(), iswspace(), iswupper(), iswxdigit(), and isxdigit().

_ismbcprint()

Function

The _ismbcprint() function returns true if the given value represents a single-byte ASCII or Katakana printable character. Also includes whitespace characters.

Header File

```
#include <mbstring.h>
```

Declaration

```
int _ismbcprint(unsigned int ch);
```

- *ch* — The value to examine.

Example

The following program demonstrates how to use the _ismbcprint() function. When run, the program checks whether a value represents a printable ASCII or Katakana character and displays the result. The program's output looks like the following:

```
result = 1
Press any key to continue
```

Here is the program source code that produced the output:

```cpp
#include "stdafx.h"
#include <iostream>
#include <mbstring.h>

using namespace std;

int main(int argc, char* argv[])
{
    int result = _ismbcprint(65);
    cout << "result = " << result << endl;

    return 0;
}
```

CROSS-REFERENCE

See also __isascii(), _ismbbalnum(), _ismbbalpha(), _ismbbgraph(), _ismbbkalnum(), _ismbbkana(), _ismbbkprint(), _ismbbkpunct(), _ismbblead(), _ismbbprint(), _ismbbpunct(), _ismbbtrail(), _ismbcalnum(), _ismbcalpha(), _ismbcdigit(), _ismbcgraph(), _ismbchira(), _ismbckata(), _ismbcl0(), _ismbcl1(), _ismbcl2(), _ismbclegal(), _ismbclower(), _ismbcpunct(), _ismbcspace(), _ismbcsymbol(), _ismbcupper(), isalnum(), isalpha(), isascii(), isdigit(), isgraph(), isleadbyte(), islower(), isprint(), ispunct(), isspace(), isupper(), iswalnum(), iswalpha(), iswascii(), iswcntrl(), iswdigit(), iswgraph(), iswlower(), iswprint(), iswpunct(), iswspace(), iswupper(), iswxdigit(), and isxdigit().

_ismbcpunct()

Function

The _ismbcpunct() function returns true if the given value represents a single-byte ASCII or Katakana punctuation character.

Header File

```
#include <mbstring.h>
```

Declaration

```
int _ismbcpunct(unsigned int ch);
```

- *ch* — The value to examine.

Example

The following program demonstrates how to use the _ismbcpunct() function. When run, the program checks whether a value represents a single-byte ASCII or Katakana punctuation character and displays the result. The program's output looks like the following:

```
result = 1
Press any key to continue
```

Here is the program source code that produced the output:

```
#include "stdafx.h"
#include <iostream>
#include <mbstring.h>

using namespace std;

int main(int argc, char* argv[])
{
    int result = _ismbcpunct(33);
    cout << "result = " << result << endl;

    return 0;
}
```

CROSS-REFERENCE

See also __isascii(), _ismbbalnum(), _ismbbalpha(), _ismbbgraph(), _ismbbkalnum(), _ismbbkana(), _ismbbkprint(), _ismbbkpunct(), _ismbblead(), _ismbbprint(), _ismbbpunct(), _ismbbtrail(), _ismbcalnum(), _ismbcalpha(), _ismbcdigit(), _ismbcgraph(), _ismbchira(), _ismbckata(), _ismbcl0(), _ismbcl1(), _ismbcl2(), _ismbclegal(), _ismbclower(), _ismbcprint(), _ismbcspace(), _ismbcsymbol(), _ismbcupper(), isalnum(), isalpha(), isascii(), isdigit(), isgraph(), isleadbyte(), islower(), isprint(), ispunct(), isspace(), isupper(), iswalnum(), iswalpha(), iswascii(), iswcntrl(), iswdigit(), iswgraph(), iswlower(), iswprint(), iswpunct(), iswspace(), iswupper(), iswxdigit(), and isxdigit().

_ismbcspace()

Function

The _ismbcspace() function returns true if the given value represents a whitespace character, such as a space or a tab.

Header File

```
#include <mbstring.h>
```

Declaration

```
int _ismbcspace(unsigned int ch);
```

- *ch* — The value to examine.

Example

The following program demonstrates how to use the _ismbcspace() function. When run, the program checks whether two values represent whitespace characters and displays the result. The program's output looks like the following:

```
result = 8
result = 0
Press any key to continue
```

Here is the program source code that produced the output:

```cpp
#include "stdafx.h"
#include <iostream>
#include <mbstring.h>

using namespace std;

int main(int argc, char* argv[])
{
    int result = _ismbcspace(32);
    cout << "result = " << result << endl;
    result = _ismbcspace(65);
    cout << "result = " << result << endl;

    return 0;
}
```

CROSS-REFERENCE
See also __isascii(), _ismbbalnum(), _ismbbalpha(), _ismbbgraph(), _ismbbkalnum(), _ismbbkana(), _ismbbkprint(), _ismbbkpunct(), _ismbblead(), _ismbbprint(), _ismbbpunct(), _ismbbtrail(), _ismbcalnum(), _ismbcalpha(), _ismbcdigit(), _ismbcgraph(), _ismbchira(), _ismbckata(), _ismbcl0(), _ismbcl1(), _ismbcl2(), _ismbclegal(), _ismbclower(), _ismbcprint(), _ismbcpunct(), _ismbcsymbol(), _ismbcupper(), isalnum(), isalpha(), isascii(), isdigit(), isgraph(), isleadbyte(), islower(), isprint(), ispunct(), isspace(), isupper(), iswalnum(), iswalpha(), iswascii(), iswcntrl(), iswdigit(), iswgraph(), iswlower(), iswprint(), iswpunct(), iswspace(), iswupper(), iswxdigit(), and isxdigit().

_ismbcsymbol()

Function

The _ismbcsymbol() function returns true if the given value represents a multibyte symbol character in the range of 0x8141 to 0x81AC.

Header File

```
#include <mbstring.h>
```

Declaration

```
int _ismbcsymbol(unsigned int ch);
```

- *ch* — The value to examine.

Example

The following program demonstrates how to use the _ismbcsymbol() function. When run, the program checks whether a value represents a multibyte symbol character in the required range and displays the result. The program's output looks like the following:

```
result = 0
Press any key to continue
```

Here is the program source code that produced the output:

```
#include "stdafx.h"
#include <iostream>
#include <mbstring.h>
```

```
using namespace std;

int main(int argc, char* argv[])
{
    int result = _ismbcsymbol(0x8110);
    cout << "result = " << result << endl;

    return 0;
}
```

CROSS-REFERENCE

See also __isascii(), _ismbbalnum(), _ismbbalpha(), _ismbbgraph(), _ismbbkalnum(), _ismbbkana(), _ismbbkprint(), _ismbbkpunct(), _ismbblead(), _ismbbprint(), _ismbbpunct(), _ismbbtrail(), _ismbcalnum(), _ismbcalpha(), _ismbcdigit(), _ismbcgraph(), _ismbchira(), _ismbckata(), _ismbcl0(), _ismbcl1(), _ismbcl2(), _ismbclegal(), _ismbclower(), _ismbcprint(), _ismbcpunct(), _ismbcspace(), _ismbcupper(), isalnum(), isalpha(), isascii(), isdigit(), isgraph(), isleadbyte(), islower(), isprint(), ispunct(), isspace(), isupper(), iswalnum(), iswalpha(), iswascii(), iswcntrl(), iswdigit(), iswgraph(), iswlower(), iswprint(), iswpunct(), iswspace(), iswupper(), iswxdigit(), isxdigit().

_ismbcupper()

Function

The _ismbcupper() function returns true if the given value represents a single-byte, uppercase letter.

Header File

```
#include <mbstring.h>
```

Declaration

```
int _ismbcupper(unsigned int ch);
```

- *ch* — The value to examine.

Example

The following program demonstrates how to use the _ismbcupper() function. When run, the program checks whether two values represent uppercase, single-byte characters and displays the result. The program's output looks like the following:

```
result = 0
result = 1
Press any key to continue
```

Here is the program source code that produced the output:

```
#include "stdafx.h"
#include <iostream>
#include <mbstring.h>

using namespace std;

int main(int argc, char* argv[])
{
    int result = _ismbcupper(100);
    cout << "result = " << result << endl;
    result = _ismbcupper(65);
    cout << "result = " << result << endl;

    return 0;
}
```

CROSS-REFERENCE

See also __isascii(), _ismbbalnum(), _ismbbalpha(), _ismbbgraph(), _ismbbkalnum(), _ismbbkana(), _ismbbkprint(), _ismbbkpunct(), _ismbblead(), _ismbbprint(), _ismbbpunct(), _ismbbtrail(), _ismbcalnum(), _ismbcalpha(), _ismbcdigit(), _ismbcgraph(), _ismbchira(), _ismbckata(), _ismbcl0(), _ismbcl1(), _ismbcl2(), _ismbclegal(), _ismbclower(), _ismbcprint(), _ismbcpunct(), _ismbcspace(), _ismbcsymbol(), isalnum(), isalpha(), isascii(), isdigit(), isgraph(), isleadbyte(), islower(), isprint(), ispunct(), isspace(), isupper(), iswalnum(), iswalpha(), iswascii(), iswcntrl(), iswdigit(), iswgraph(), iswlower(), iswprint(), iswpunct(), iswspace(), iswupper(), iswxdigit(), and isxdigit().

_isnan()

Function

The _isnan() function returns true if the given double value cannot be represented in IEEE format.

Header File

```
#include <float.h>
```

Declaration

```
int _isnan(double value);
```

- *value* — The value to test.

Example

The following program demonstrates how to use the _isnan() function. When run, the program checks whether a value is NaN (not a number) and displays the result. The program's output looks like the following:

```
Result = 0
Press any key to continue
```

Here is the program source code that produced the output:

```
#include "stdafx.h"
#include <iostream>
#include <float.h>

using namespace std;

int main(int argc, char* argv[])
{
    double value = 25469.574830089;

    int result = _isnan(value);
    cout << "Result = " << result << endl;

    return 0;
}
```

CROSS-REFERENCE
See also _finite() and _fpclass().

_itoa()

Function

The _itoa() function converts an integer value to a string.

NOTE
Borland users should refer to the itoa() function later in this chapter.

Header File

```
#include <stdlib.h>
```

Declaration

```
char* _itoa(int value, char* string, int radix);
```

- *radix* — The value number base (typically 10).
- *string* — A pointer to the buffer in which to store the string.
- *value* — The integer value to convert.

Example

The following program demonstrates how to use the _itoa() function. When run, the program converts a value into several number-base formats and displays the results. The program's output looks like the following:

```
This is 19,564 in base 10: 19564
This is 19,564 in base 16: 4c6c
This is 19,564 in base 2: 100110001101100
This is 19,564 in base 8: 46154

Press any key to continue
```

Here is the program source code that produced the output:

```
#include "stdafx.h"
#include <iostream>
#include <stdlib.h>

using namespace std;

int main(int argc, char* argv[])
{
```

```
char str[81];

char* result = _itoa(19564, str, 10);
cout << "This is 19,564 in base 10: ";
cout << result << endl;

result = _itoa(19564, str, 16);
cout << "This is 19,564 in base 16: ";
cout << result << endl;

result = _itoa(19564, str, 2);
cout << "This is 19,564 in base 2: ";
cout << result << endl;

result = itoa(19564, str, 8);
cout << "This is 19,564 in base 8: ";
cout << result << endl;
cout << endl;

return 0;
}
```

CROSS-REFERENCE

See also _ecvt(), _fcvt(), _gcvt(), _i64toa(), _i64tow(), _itow(), _ui64toa(), _ui64tow(), itoa(), ltoa(), and ultoa().

_itow()

Function

The _itow() function converts an integer to a wide-character string and returns a pointer to the resultant string.

Header File

```
#include <stdlib.h>
```

Declaration

```
wchar_t* _itow(int value, wchar_t *string, int radix);
```

- *radix*—The number base to be used in the conversion. Must be a value from 2 to 36.
- *string*—A pointer to the buffer that will receive the string.
- *value*—The value to convert.

Example

The following program demonstrates how to use the _itow() function. When run, the program displays the value 23,543 in decimal, binary, and hexadecimal representations. The program's output looks like the following:

```
Decimal: 23543
Binary: 101101111110111
Hexadecimal: 5bf7
Press any key to continue
```

Here is the program source code that produced the output:

```
#include "stdafx.h"
#include <iostream>
#include <stdlib.h>
using namespace std;

int main(int argc, char* argv[])
{
    int value = 23543;
    wchar_t buf[81];

    _itow(value, buf, 10);
    wprintf(L"Decimal: %s\n", buf);
    _itow(value, buf, 2);
    wprintf(L"Binary: %s\n", buf);
    _itow(value, buf, 16);
    wprintf(L"Hexadecimal: %s\n", buf);

    return 0;
}
```

CROSS-REFERENCE

See also _ecvt(), _fcvt(), _gcvt(), _i64toa(), _i64tow(), _itoa(), _ui64toa(), _ui64tow(), itoa(), ltoa(), and ultoa().

if

Keyword

The if keyword is part of the if statement, which enables a program to control the path of execution based on the result of an expression. If the given expression evaluates to true, the body of the if statement executes; otherwise, the body of the if statement is ignored.

CROSS-REFERENCE
If Statements.

If Statements

Technique

The if keyword is part of the if statement, which enables a program to control the path of execution based on the result of an expression. If the given expression evaluates to true, the body of the if statement executes; otherwise, the body of the if statement is ignored. For example, the following program requests the user to enter the value 1 or 2. The program uses if statements to tell the user which value she chose. The program's output looks like the following:

```
Enter the value 1 or 2:
2
You entered 2.

Press any key to continue
```

Here is the program source code that produced the output:

```
#include "stdafx.h"
#include <iostream>

using namespace std;

int main(int argc, char* argv[])
{
    int val;

    cout << "Enter the value 1 or 2:" << endl;
    cin > val;
```

```
    if (val == 1)
        cout << "You entered 1." << endl << endl;

    if (val == 2)
        cout << "You entered 2." << endl << endl;

    return 0;
}
```

If the user enters a value other than 1 or 2, the body of neither if statement executes. The program's output looks like the following:

```
Enter the value 1 or 2:
5

Press any key to continue
```

Multiple If Statements

Multiple if statements can be streamlined using the else and else if clauses. For example, a better version of the previous program follows:

```
#include "stdafx.h"
#include <iostream>

using namespace std;

int main(int argc, char* argv[])
{
    int val;

    cout << "Enter the value 1 or 2:" << endl;
    cin > val;

    if (val == 1)
        cout << "You entered 1." << endl << endl;
    else if (val == 2)
        cout << "You entered 2." << endl << endl;
    else
        cout << "Invalid entry." << endl;

    return 0;
}
```

In this version of the program, if val equals 1, program execution skips over the else clauses, making this program more efficient than the first version. The final `else` clause executes if the user enters any value other than 1 or 2. This program's output is identical to the first, except in the case when the user enters a value other than 1 or 2. In this case, the program's output looks like the following:

```
Enter the value 1 or 2:
5
Invalid entry.

Press any key to continue
```

Multiple Statements in a Clause

Finally, the body of an `if` statement can include multiple statements when the statements are enclosed by braces, as shown in the following program:

```cpp
#include "stdafx.h"
#include <iostream>

using namespace std;

int main(int argc, char* argv[])
{
    int val;
    int val2 = 0;

    cout << "Enter the value 1 or 2:" << endl;
    cin > val;

    if (val == 1)
    {
        val2 = val;
        cout << "You entered 1." << endl << endl;
    }
    else if (val == 2)
    {
        val2 = val;
        cout << "You entered 2." << endl << endl;
    }
    else
        cout << "Invalid entry." << endl;

    return 0;
}
```

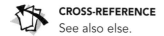

CROSS-REFERENCE
See also else.

ifstream

Class

The ifstream class provides the functionality for file input streams.

Class Declaration

```
class _CRTIMP ifstream : public istream {
public:
    ifstream();
    ifstream(const char *, int =ios::in,
        int = filebuf::openprot);
    ifstream(filedesc);
    ifstream(filedesc, char *, int);
    ~ifstream();

    streambuf * setbuf(char *, int);
    filebuf* rdbuf() const { return (filebuf*) ios::rdbuf(); }

    void attach(filedesc);
    filedesc fd() const { return rdbuf()->fd(); }

    int is_open() const { return rdbuf()->is_open(); }
    void open(const char *, int =ios::in,
        int = filebuf::openprot);
    void close();
    int setmode(int mode = filebuf::text)
        { return rdbuf()->setmode(mode); }
};
```

Class Members

Table I-1 lists and describes the members of the ifstream class.

Table I-1 Members of the ifstream Class

Member	Description
Attach()	Associates the stream with a file.
Close()	Closes the file.
fd()	Returns the stream's file descriptor.
is_open()	Returns TRUE if the file associated with the stream is open.
Open()	Opens a file.
Rdbuf()	Returns a pointer to the stream's buffer object.
Setbuf()	Sets the filebuf object's buffer.
Setmode()	Sets the stream's mode.

CROSS-REFERENCE

See also fstream, iostream, istream, ofstream, and ostream.

Implementation File

Concept

Implementation files are source-code files that contain definitions of classes, functions, and other data that a program needs in order to create its object files and link successfully. For example, when defining classes, the usual practice is to declare the class in a header file and define the class in an implementation file. The header file usually has the .h file-name extension, whereas the implementation file has the .cpp file-name extension. The first listing below (stored as MyClass.h) declares a class in a header file, and the second listing (stored as MyClass.cpp) defines the class in an implementation file. The third listing (stored as header_files.cpp) is a program that uses the class and therefore must include the class header file. The program's output looks like the following:

```
Class value: 10
Press any key to continue
```

Here is the program source code that produced the output:

```
// Class header file.
class MyClass
{
protected:
    int value;
```

```
public:
    MyClass(int val);
    ~MyClass();
    int GetValue();
};


//S Class implementation file.
#include "stdafx.h"
#include "MyClass.h"

MyClass::MyClass(int val)
{
    value = val;
}

MyClass::~MyClass()
{
}

int MyClass::GetValue()
{
    return value;
}


// Program to test MyClass.
#include "stdafx.h"
#include <iostream>
#include "MyClass.h"

using namespace std;

int main(int argc, char* argv[])
{
    MyClass myClass(10);
    cout << "Class value: " << myClass.GetValue() << endl;
    return 0;
}
```

CROSS-REFERENCE
See also Header Files.

Inheritance

Technique

Inheritance, along with *encapsulation* and *polymorphism*, is one of the most important features of object-oriented programming. Using inheritance, you can create a new custom class from an existing class, with the new class inheriting all the features of the original class (called the *base class*). In the following sections, you'll learn to use inheritance.

Creating the Base Class

Consider the following program, which defines a class named MyClass and tests the class in the main() function. The MyClass class will be the base class from which other classes can be created. The program's output looks like the following:

```
Class value: 10
Setting class value...
Class value: 25
Press any key to continue
```

Here is the program source code that produced the output:

```cpp
#include "stdafx.h"
#include <iostream>

using namespace std;

////////////////////////////////////////////
// MyClass
////////////////////////////////////////////
class MyClass
{
protected:
    int value;

public:
    MyClass(int val);
    ~MyClass();
    void SetValue(int val);
    int GetValue();
};

MyClass::MyClass(int val)
{
```

```
        value = val;
    }

    MyClass::~MyClass()
    {
    }

    void MyClass::SetValue(int val)
    {
        value = val;
    }

    int MyClass::GetValue()
    {
        return value;
    }


    /////////////////////////////////////////////
    // Main program
    /////////////////////////////////////////////
    int main(int argc, char* argv[])
    {
        MyClass myClass(10);
        int val = myClass.GetValue();
        cout << "Class value: " << val << endl;
        cout << "Setting class value..." << endl;
        myClass.SetValue(25);
        val = myClass.GetValue();
        cout << "Class value: " << val << endl;

        return 0;
    }
```

Inheriting from the Base Class

Now, suppose that you want to create a new class named MyCustomClass that is similar to MyClass, but has an additional data member named value2 along with the member functions required to set and get the value of value2. You can derive MyCustomClass directly from MyClass. When you do, MyCustomClass automatically inherits the value, SetValue(), and GetValue() members. All you have to do is add the additional members you need in the new MyCustomClass class. For example, the following program shows how to derive the MyCustomClass class from the MyClass class. The program's output looks like the following:

```
Class value: 10
Setting class value...
Class value: 25

Custom class value: 10
Custom class value2: 20
Setting custom class values...
Custom class value: 25
Custom class value2: 35

Press any key to continue
```

Here is the program source code that produced the output:

```cpp
#include "stdafx.h"
#include <iostream>

using namespace std;

//////////////////////////////////////////////
// MyClass
//////////////////////////////////////////////
class MyClass
{
protected:
    int value;

public:
    MyClass(int val);
    ~MyClass();
    void SetValue(int val);
    int GetValue();
};

MyClass::MyClass(int val)
{
    value = val;
}

MyClass::~MyClass()
{
}

void MyClass::SetValue(int val)
{
```

```
        value = val;
    }

    int MyClass::GetValue()
    {
        return value;
    }

    //////////////////////////////////////////////
    // MyCustomClass
    //////////////////////////////////////////////
    class MyCustomClass : public MyClass
    {
    protected:
        int value2;

    public:
        MyCustomClass(int val1, int val2);
        ~MyCustomClass();
        void SetValue2(int val);
        int GetValue2();
    };

    MyCustomClass::MyCustomClass(int val1, int val2) :
        MyClass(val1)
    {
        value2 = val2;
    }

    MyCustomClass::~MyCustomClass()
    {
    }

    void MyCustomClass::SetValue2(int val)
    {
        value2 = val;
    }

    int MyCustomClass::GetValue2()
    {
        return value2;
    }

    //////////////////////////////////////////////
```

```
// Main program
///////////////////////////////////////////////
int main(int argc, char* argv[])
{
    MyClass myClass(10);
    int val = myClass.GetValue();
    cout << "Class value: " << val << endl;
    cout << "Setting class value..." << endl;
    myClass.SetValue(25);
    val = myClass.GetValue();
    cout << "Class value: " << val << endl << endl;

    MyCustomClass myCustomClass(10, 20);
    val = myCustomClass.GetValue();
    cout << "Custom class value: " << val << endl;
    val = myCustomClass.GetValue2();
    cout << "Custom class value2: " << val << endl;
    cout << "Setting custom class values..." << endl;
    myCustomClass.SetValue(25);
    myCustomClass.SetValue2(35);
    val = myCustomClass.GetValue();
    cout << "Custom class value: " << val << endl;
    val = myCustomClass.GetValue2();
    cout << "Custom class value2: " << val << endl << endl;

    return 0;
}
```

CROSS-REFERENCE

See also Class Hierarchies and Creating a Class.

inline

Keyword

The `inline` keyword specifies that a function's complete implementation be placed into the object code wherever the function is called. This technique eliminates the need for the program to make inefficient function calls. However, when a function is declared as inline, the compiler doesn't necessarily comply, depending on whether the compiler determines that the inlined function will be more efficient than a normal function call. The following function is declared as inline:

```
inline int MyFunc(int val)
{
    return val * 2;
}
```

 CROSS-REFERENCE
See also Inline Functions.

Inline Functions

Technique

The `inline` keyword specifies that a function's complete implementation be placed into the object code wherever the function is called. This technique eliminates the need for the program to make inefficient function calls. However, when a function is declared as inline, the compiler doesn't necessarily comply, depending on whether the compiler determines that the inlined function will be more efficient than a normal function call. The following sections describe both inline functions and inline member functions.

Create an Inline Function

The following program demonstrates how to use the `inline` keyword. The program's output looks like the following:

```
result = 10
result = 20
result = 40
Press any key to continue
```

Here is the program source code that produced the output:

```
#include "stdafx.h"
#include <iostream>

using namespace std;

inline int MyFunc(int val)
{
    return val * 2;
}
```

```
int main(int argc, char* argv[])
{
    int result = MyFunc(5);
    cout << "result = " << result << endl;
    result = MyFunc(10);
    cout << "result = " << result << endl;
    result = MyFunc(20);
    cout << "result = " << result << endl;

    return 0;
}
```

When compiling this program, the compiler will (if it determines that there will be an efficiency gain) place the complete code of the MyFunc() function in place of the three calls to MyFunc() in main(). However, this substitution means that there will be three complete copies of the function in the object code, making the final executable file larger.

Inline Member Functions

A class's member functions can also be inline. However, you don't need to use the inline keyword to specify an inline function. Instead, define the complete function in the class declaration, rather than outside of the declaration. For example, the following program demonstrates how a class's member functions can be inline:

```
#include "stdafx.h"
#include <iostream>

using namespace std;

///////////////////////////////////////////////
// MyClass
///////////////////////////////////////////////
class MyClass
{
protected:
    int value;

public:
    MyClass(int val) { value = val; }
    ~MyClass() {}
    void SetValue(int val) { value = val; }
    int GetValue() { return value; }
```

```
};

/////////////////////////////////////////////
// Main program
/////////////////////////////////////////////
int main(int argc, char* argv[])
{
    MyClass myClass(10);
    int val = myClass.GetValue();
    cout << "Class value: " << val << endl;
    cout << "Setting class value..." << endl;
    myClass.SetValue(25);
    val = myClass.GetValue();
    cout << "Class value: " << val << endl << endl;

    return 0;
}
```

The program's output looks like the following:

```
Class value: 10
Setting class value...
Class value: 25


Press any key to continue
```

The same program written without inline member functions in the MyClass class looks like the following:

```
#include "stdafx.h"
#include <iostream>

using namespace std;

/////////////////////////////////////////////
// MyClass
/////////////////////////////////////////////
class MyClass
{
protected:
    int value;

public:
    MyClass(int val);
    ~MyClass();
    void SetValue(int val);
```

```
    int GetValue();
};

MyClass::MyClass(int val)
{
    value = val;
}

MyClass::~MyClass()
{
}

void MyClass::SetValue(int val)
{
    value = val;
}

int MyClass::GetValue()
{
    return value;
}

/////////////////////////////////////////////
// Main program
/////////////////////////////////////////////
int main(int argc, char* argv[])
{
    MyClass myClass(10);
    int val = myClass.GetValue();
    cout << "Class value: " << val << endl;
    cout << "Setting class value..." << endl;
    myClass.SetValue(25);
    val = myClass.GetValue();
    cout << "Class value: " << val << endl << endl;

    return 0;
}
```

int

Keyword

The int keyword enables a program to declare integer values, which are positive or negative whole numbers. The actual range of values for an integer depends upon the system on which the program is being run. The following line declares and defines an integer variable named val:

```
int val = 10;
```

 CROSS-REFERENCE
See also char, double, float, long, short, signed, unsigned.

ios

Class

The ios class is the base class for all the other stream classes, including istream and ostream, which are the basic input and output stream classes, respectively.

Class Declaration

```
class _CRTIMP ios {

public:
    enum io_state {  goodbit = 0x00,
                     eofbit  = 0x01,
                     failbit = 0x02,
                     badbit  = 0x04 };

    enum open_mode { in        = 0x01,
                     out       = 0x02,
                     ate       = 0x04,
                     app       = 0x08,
                     trunc     = 0x10,
                     nocreate  = 0x20,
                     noreplace = 0x40,
                     binary    = 0x80 };

    enum seek_dir { beg=0, cur=1, end=2 };
```

```
enum {  skipws      = 0x0001,
        left        = 0x0002,
        right       = 0x0004,
        internal    = 0x0008,
        dec         = 0x0010,
        oct         = 0x0020,
        hex         = 0x0040,
        showbase    = 0x0080,
        showpoint   = 0x0100,
        uppercase   = 0x0200,
        showpos     = 0x0400,
        scientific  = 0x0800,
        fixed       = 0x1000,
        unitbuf     = 0x2000,
        stdio       = 0x4000
                                    };

static const long basefield;
static const long adjustfield;
static const long floatfield;
ios(streambuf*);
virtual ~ios();

inline long flags() const;
inline long flags(long _l);

inline long setf(long _f,long _m);
inline long setf(long _l);
inline long unsetf(long _l);

inline int width() const;
inline int width(int _i);

inline ostream* tie(ostream* _os);
inline ostream* tie() const;

inline char fill() const;
inline char fill(char _c);

inline int precision(int _i);
inline int precision() const;

inline int rdstate() const;
inline void clear(int _i = 0);
```

```
//   inline operator void*() const;
     operator void *() const { if(state&(badbit|failbit) )
         return 0; return (void *)this; }
     inline int operator!() const;

     inline int  good() const;
     inline int  eof() const;
     inline int  fail() const;
     inline int  bad() const;

     inline streambuf* rdbuf() const;

     inline long & iword(int) const;
     inline void * & pword(int) const;

     static long bitalloc();
     static int xalloc();
     static void sync_with_stdio();

#ifdef  _MT
     inline void __cdecl setlock();
     inline void __cdecl clrlock();
     void __cdecl lock()
         { if (LockFlg<0) _mtlock(lockptr()); };
     void __cdecl unlock()
         { if (LockFlg<0) _mtunlock(lockptr()); }
     inline void __cdecl lockbuf();
     inline void __cdecl unlockbuf();
#else
     void __cdecl lock() { }
     void __cdecl unlock() { }
     void __cdecl lockbuf() { }
     void __cdecl unlockbuf() { }
#endif

protected:
     ios();
     ios(const ios&);
     ios& operator=(const ios&);
     void init(streambuf*);

     enum { skipping, tied };
     streambuf*  bp;
```

```
    int     state;
    int     ispecial;
    int     ospecial;
    int     isfx_special;
    int     osfx_special;
    int     x_delbuf;

    ostream* x_tie;
    long    x_flags;
    int     x_precision;
    char    x_fill;
    int     x_width;

    static void (*stdioflush)();

#ifdef _MT
    static void lockc() { _mtlock(& x_lockc); }
    static void unlockc() { _mtunlock( & x_lockc); }
    _PCRT_CRITICAL_SECTION lockptr() { return & x_lock; }
#else
    static void lockc() { }
    static void unlockc() { }
#endif

public:
    int delbuf() const { return x_delbuf; }
    void    delbuf(int _i) { x_delbuf = _i; }

private:
    static long x_maxbit;
    static int x_curindex;
    static int sunk_with_stdio;
#ifdef _MT
#define MAXINDEX 7
    static long x_statebuf[MAXINDEX+1];
    static int fLockcInit;
    static _CRT_CRITICAL_SECTION x_lockc;
    int LockFlg;
    _CRT_CRITICAL_SECTION x_lock;
#else
    static long * x_statebuf;
#endif
};
```

Class Members

Table I-2 lists and describes the members of the ios class.

Table I-2 Members of the ios Class

Member	Description
adjustfield	Mask used when getting the left, right, and internal field padding flags.
bad()	Returns a nonzero value if the stream's status is bad.
basefield	Mask used when getting the dec, oct, and hex conversion base flags.
binary	A manipulator that formats data in binary format.
bitalloc()	Gets a mask for unused bits in the stream flags.
clear()	Toggles the error flags for the stream.
dec	A manipulator that formats data in decimal format.
delbuf()	Determines whether the stream buffer is deleted upon stream destruction.
eof()	Returns a nonzero value if the stream is at the end of the file.
fail()	Returns a nonzero value in the event of an error.
fill()	Sets or gets the fill character for the stream.
flags()	Mask used when getting the scientific or fixed numeric formats.
floatfield	Mask used when getting the scientific or fixed numeric formats.
good()	Returns a nonzero value if the stream's status is good.
hex	A manipulator that formats data in hexadecimal format.
iword()	Generates a reference from the index value returned by xalloc().
oct	A manipulator that formats data in octal format.
precision()	Sets or gets the precision for the stream's floating-point format.
pword()	Generates a pointer from the index value returned by xalloc().
rdbuf()	Gets a pointer to the stream buffer object.
rdstate()	Gets the error flags for the stream.
resetiosflags	A manipulator that resets the stream's format flags.
setf()	Sets the stream format flags.
setfill	A manipulator that sets the fill character for the stream.
setiosflags	A manipulator that sets the stream's format flags.
setprecision	A manipulator that sets the floating-point precision for the stream.
setw	A manipulator that sets the field width for the stream.
sync_with_stdio()	Synchronizes the cin, cout, cerr, and clog stream objects with the standard I/O system.
text	A manipulator that formats data in text format.
tie()	Associates an ostream object with the stream.

Member	Description
unsetf()	Unsets the stream format flags.
width()	Sets or gets the output field width for the stream.
xalloc()	Gets an index to an unused word in the special-purpose stream state variables.

CROSS-REFERENCE
See also ifstream, iostream, istream, istrstream, ofstream, ostream, ostrstream, stdiostream, and streambuf.

iostream

Class

The iostream class defines the functionality required to manipulate stream input and output.

Class Declaration

```
class _CRTIMP iostream : public istream, public ostream {
public:
    iostream(streambuf*);
    virtual ~iostream();
protected:
    iostream();
    iostream(const iostream&);
inline iostream& operator=(streambuf*);
inline iostream& operator=(iostream&);
private:
    iostream(ios&);
    iostream(istream&);
    iostream(ostream&);
};
```

Class Members

The iostream class defines no class members of its own (outside of the constructor and destructor), inheriting all members from its istream and ostream base classes.

CROSS-REFERENCE
See also ifstream, ios, istream, istrstream, ofstream, ostream, ostrstream, stdiostream, and streambuf.

isalnum()

Function

The isalnum() function returns true if the given value represents an alphanumeric character.

Header File

```
#include <ctype.h>
```

Declaration

```
int isalnum(int ch);
```

- *ch* — The value to examine.

Example

The following program demonstrates how to use the isalnum() function. When run, the program checks whether a value represents an alphanumeric character and displays the result. The program's output looks like the following:

```
result = 1
Press any key to continue
```

Here is the program source code that produced the output:

```
#include "stdafx.h"
#include <iostream>
#include <ctype.h>

using namespace std;

int main(int argc, char* argv[])
{
    int result = isalnum(65);
    cout << "result = " << result << endl;
```

```
        return 0;
    }
```

CROSS-REFERENCE

See also __isascii(), _ismbbalnum(), _ismbbalpha(), _ismbbgraph(), _ismbbkalnum(), _ismbbkana(), _ismbbkprint(), _ismbbkpunct(), _ismbblead(), _ismbbprint(), _ismbbpunct(), _ismbbtrail(), _ismbcalnum(), _ismbcalpha(), _ismbcdigit(), _ismbcgraph(), _ismbchira(), _ismbckata(), _ismbcl0(), _ismbcl1(), _ismbcl2(), _ismbclegal(), _ismbclower(), _ismbcprint(), _ismbcpunct(), _ismbcspace(), _ismbcsymbol(), _ismbcupper(), isalpha(), isascii(), isdigit(), isgraph(), isleadbyte(), islower(), isprint(), ispunct(), isspace(), isupper(), iswalnum(), iswalpha(), iswascii(), iswcntrl(), iswctype(), iswdigit(), iswgraph(), iswlower(), iswprint(), iswpunct(), iswspace(), iswupper(), iswxdigit(), and isxdigit().

isalpha()

Function

The isalpha() function returns true if the given value represents an alphabetic character.

Header File

```
#include <ctype.h>
```

Declaration

```
int isalpha(int ch);
```

- *ch* — The value to examine.

Example

The following program demonstrates how to use the isalpha() function. When run, the program checks whether a value represents an alphabetic character and displays the result. The program's output looks like the following:

```
result = 1
Press any key to continue
```

Here is the program source code that produced the output:

```
#include "stdafx.h
```

```
#include <iostream>
#include <ctype.h>

using namespace std;

int main(int argc, char* argv[])
{
    int result = isalpha(65);
    cout << "result = " << result << endl;

    return 0;
}
```

CROSS-REFERENCE

See also __isascii(), _ismbbalnum(), _ismbbalpha(), _ismbbgraph(), _ismbbkalnum(), _ismbbkana(), _ismbbkprint(), _ismbbkpunct(), _ismbblead(), _ismbbprint(), _ismbbpunct(), _ismbbtrail(), _ismbcalnum(), _ismbcalpha(), _ismbcdigit(), _ismbcgraph(), _ismbchira(), _ismbckata(), _ismbcl0(), _ismbcl1(), _ismbcl2(), _ismbclegal(), _ismbclower(), _ismbcprint(), _ismbcpunct(), _ismbcspace(), _ismbcsymbol(), _ismbcupper(), isalnum(), isascii(), isdigit(), isgraph(), isleadbyte(), islower(), isprint(), ispunct(), isspace(), isupper(), iswalnum(), iswalpha(), iswascii(), iswcntrl(), iswdigit(), iswgraph(), iswlower(), iswprint(), iswpunct(), iswspace(), iswupper(), iswxdigit(), and isxdigit().

isascii()

Function

The isascii() function returns true if the given value is an ASCII character. Otherwise, the function returns false.

Header File

```
#include <ctype.h>
```

Declaration

```
int isascii(int c);
```

- *c*—The value to examine.

Example

The following program demonstrates how to use the `isascii()` function. The program's output looks like the following:

```
val1 is ASCII.
Press any key to continue
```

Here is the program source code that produced the output:

```cpp
#include "stdafx.h"
#include <iostream>

using namespace std;

int main(int argc, char* argv[])
{
    int val1 = 64;
    int result;

    result = isascii(val1);
    if (result)
        cout << "val1 is ASCII." << endl;
    else
        cout << "val1 is not ASCII." << endl;

    return 0;
}
```

CROSS-REFERENCE

See also __isascii(), _ismbbalnum(), _ismbbalpha(), _ismbbgraph(), _ismbbkalnum(), _ismbbkana(), _ismbbkprint(), _ismbbkpunct(), _ismbblead(), _ismbbprint(), _ismbbpunct(), _ismbbtrail(), _ismbcalnum(), _ismbcalpha(), _ismbcdigit(), _ismbcgraph(), _ismbchira(), _ismbckata(), _ismbcl0(), _ismbcl1(), _ismbcl2(), _ismbclegal(), _ismbclower(), _ismbcprint(), _ismbcpunct(), _ismbcspace(), _ismbcsymbol(), _ismbcupper(), isalnum(), isalpha(), isdigit(), isgraph(), isleadbyte(), islower(), isprint(), ispunct(), isspace(), isupper(), iswalnum(), iswalpha(), iswascii(), iswcntrl(), iswdigit(), iswgraph(), iswlower(), iswprint(), iswpunct(), iswspace(), iswupper(), iswxdigit(), and isxdigit().

isatty()

Function

The isatty() function returns true if the given device handle is associated with a character device. Otherwise, the function returns false.

Header File

```
#include <io.h>
```

Declaration

```
int isatty(int handle);
```

- *handle* — The device handle.

Example

The following program demonstrates how to use the isatty() function. When run, the program checks whether the stdin stream is currently associated with a character device. The program's output looks like the following:

```
This is a character device
Press any key to continue
```

Here is the program source code that produced the output:

```cpp
#include "stdafx.h"
#include <io.h>
#include <iostream>

using namespace std;

int main(int argc, char* argv[])
{
    int fileHandle = _fileno(stdin);
    int result = isatty(fileHandle);
    if (result)
        cout << "This is a character device" << endl;
    else
        cout << "This is not a character device" << endl;

    return 0;
}
```

CROSS-REFERENCE
See also _access(), _chmod(), _chsize(), _filelength(), _fileno(), _fstat(), _fstati64(), _fullpath(), _get_osfhandle(), _isatty(), _locking(), _makepath(), _mktemp(), _open_osfhandle(), _splitpath(), _stat(), _stati64(), _umask(), _unlink(), _waccess(), _wchmod(), _wfullpath(), _wmakepath(), _wmktemp(), _wremove(), _wrename(), _wsplitpath(), _wstat(), _wstati64(), _wunlink(), remove(), and rename().

iscntrl()

Function

The iscntrl() function returns true if the given value represents a control character.

Header File

```
#include <ctype.h>
```

Declaration

```
int iscntrl(int ch);
```

- *ch* — The value to examine.

Example

The following program demonstrates how to use the iscntrl() function. When run, the program checks whether a value represents a control character and displays the result. The program's output looks like the following:

```
result = 32
Press any key to continue
```

Here is the program source code that produced the output:

```
#include "stdafx.h"
#include <iostream>
#include <ctype.h>

using namespace std;

int main(int argc, char* argv[])
{
    int result = iscntrl(13);
```

```
        cout << "result = " << result << endl;

        return 0;
    }
```

CROSS-REFERENCE

See also __isascii(), _ismbbalnum(), _ismbbalpha(), _ismbbgraph(), _ismbbkalnum(), _ismbbkana(), _ismbbkprint(), _ismbbkpunct(), _ismbblead(), _ismbbprint(), _ismbbpunct(), _ismbbtrail(), _ismbcalnum(), _ismbcalpha(), _ismbcdigit(), _ismbcgraph(), _ismbchira(), _ismbckata(), _ismbcl0(), _ismbcl1(), _ismbcl2(), _ismbclegal(), _ismbclower(), _ismbcprint(), _ismbcpunct(), _ismbcspace(), _ismbcsymbol(), _ismbcupper(), isalnum(), isalpha(), isascii(), isdigit(), isgraph(), isleadbyte(), islower(), isprint(), ispunct(), isspace(), isupper(), iswalnum(), iswalpha(), iswascii(), iswcntrl(), iswdigit(), iswgraph(), iswlower(), iswprint(), iswpunct(), iswspace(), iswupper(), iswxdigit(), and isxdigit().

isdigit()

Function

The isdigit() function returns true if the given value represents a digit.

Header File

```
#include <ctype.h>
```

Declaration

```
int isdigit(int ch);
```

- *ch* — The value to examine.

Example

The following program demonstrates how to use the isdigit() function. When run, the program checks whether a value represents a digit and displays the result. The program's output looks like the following:

```
result = 4
Press any key to continue
```

Here is the program source code that produced the output:

```
#include "stdafx.h"
#include <iostream>
#include <ctype.h>

using namespace std;

int main(int argc, char* argv[])
{
    int result = isdigit(55);
    cout << "result = " << result << endl;

    return 0;
}
```

CROSS-REFERENCE

See also __isascii(), _ismbbalnum(), _ismbbalpha(), _ismbbgraph(), _ismbbkalnum(), _ismbbkana(), _ismbbkprint(), _ismbbkpunct(), _ismbblead(), _ismbbprint(), _ismbbpunct(), _ismbbtrail(), _ismbcalnum(), _ismbcalpha(), _ismbcdigit(), _ismbcgraph(), _ismbchira(), _ismbckata(), _ismbcl0(), _ismbcl1(), _ismbcl2(), _ismbclegal(), _ismbclower(), _ismbcprint(), _ismbcpunct(), _ismbcspace(), _ismbcsymbol(), _ismbcupper(), isalnum(), isalpha(), isascii(), isgraph(), isleadbyte(), islower(), isprint(), ispunct(), isspace(), isupper(), iswalnum(), iswalpha(), iswascii(), iswcntrl(), iswdigit(), iswgraph(), iswlower(), iswprint(), iswpunct(), iswspace(), iswupper(), iswxdigit(), and isxdigit().

isgraph()

Function

The isgraph() function returns true if the given value represents any printable character except a space.

Header File

```
#include <ctype.h>
```

Declaration

```
int isgraph(int ch);
```

- *ch* — The value to examine.

Example

The following program demonstrates how to use the `isgraph()` function. When run, the program checks whether a value represents a digit and displays the result. The program's output looks like the following:

```
result = 0
Press any key to continue
```

Here is the program source code that produced the output:

```cpp
#include "stdafx.h"
#include <iostream>
#include <ctype.h>

using namespace std;

int main(int argc, char* argv[])
{
    int result = isgraph(32);
    cout << "result = " << result << endl;

    return 0;
}
```

CROSS-REFERENCE

See also __isascii(), _ismbbalnum(), _ismbbalpha(), _ismbbgraph(), _ismbbkalnum(), _ismbbkana(), _ismbbkprint(), _ismbbkpunct(), _ismbblead(), _ismbbprint(), _ismbbpunct(), _ismbbtrail(), _ismbcalnum(), _ismbcalpha(), _ismbcdigit(), _ismbcgraph(), _ismbchira(), _ismbckata(), _ismbcl0(), _ismbcl1(), _ismbcl2(), _ismbclegal(), _ismbclower(), _ismbcprint(), _ismbcpunct(), _ismbcspace(), _ismbcsymbol(), _ismbcupper(), isalnum(), isalpha(), isascii(), iscntrl(), isdigit(), isleadbyte(), islower(), isprint(), ispunct(), isspace(), isupper(), iswalnum(), iswalpha(), iswascii(), iswcntrl(), iswdigit(), iswgraph(), iswlower(), iswprint(), iswpunct(), iswspace(), iswupper(), iswxdigit(), and isxdigit().

isleadbyte()

Function

The `isleadbyte()` function returns true if the given value represents the first (or lead) byte of a multibyte character.

NOTE

Borland does not support this function.

Header File

```
#include <ctype.h>
```

Declaration

```
int isleadbyte(int ch);
```

- *ch* — The value to examine.

Example

The following program demonstrates how to use the `isleadbyte()` function. When run, the program checks whether a value represents a lead byte and displays the result. The program's output looks like the following:

```
result = 0
Press any key to continue
```

Here is the program source code that produced the output:

```cpp
#include "stdafx.h"
#include <iostream>
#include <ctype.h>

using namespace std;

int main(int argc, char* argv[])
{
    int result = isleadbyte(25);
    cout << "result = " << result << endl;

    return 0;
}
```

CROSS-REFERENCE
See also __isascii(), _ismbbalnum(), _ismbbalpha(), _ismbbgraph(), _ismbbkalnum(), _ismbbkana(), _ismbbkprint(), _ismbbkpunct(), _ismbblead(), _ismbbprint(), _ismbbpunct(), _ismbbtrail(), _ismbcalnum(), _ismbcalpha(), _ismbcdigit(), _ismbcgraph(), _ismbchira(), _ismbckata(), _ismbcl0(), _ismbcl1(), _ismbcl2(), _ismbclegal(), _ismbclower(), _ismbcprint(), _ismbcpunct(), _ismbcspace(), _ismbcsymbol(), _ismbcupper(), isalnum(), isalpha(), isascii(), iscntrl(), isdigit(), isgraph(), islower(), isprint(), ispunct(), isspace(), isupper(), iswalnum(), iswalpha(), iswascii(), iswcntrl(), iswdigit(), iswgraph(), iswlower(), iswprint(), iswpunct(), iswspace(), iswupper(), iswxdigit(), and isxdigit().

islower()

Function

The islower() function returns true if the given value represents a lowercase character.

Header File

```
#include <ctype.h>
```

Declaration

```
int islower(int ch);
```

- *ch* — The value to examine.

Example

The following program demonstrates how to use the islower() function. When run, the program checks whether a value represents a lowercase character and displays the result. The program's output looks like the following:

```
result = 2
Press any key to continue
```

Here is the program source code that produced the output:

```
#include "stdafx.h"
#include <iostream>
#include <ctype.h>

using namespace std;

int main(int argc, char* argv[])
{
    int result = islower(97);
    cout << "result = " << result << endl;

    return 0;
}
```

CROSS-REFERENCE

See also __isascii(), _ismbbalnum(), _ismbbalpha(), _ismbbgraph(), _ismbbkalnum(), _ismbbkana(), _ismbbkprint(), _ismbbkpunct(), _ismbblead(), _ismbbprint(), _ismbbpunct(), _ismbbtrail(), _ismbcalnum(), _ismbcalpha(), _ismbcdigit(), _ismbcgraph(), _ismbchira(), _ismbckata(), _ismbcl0(), _ismbcl1(), _ismbcl2(), _ismbclegal(), _ismbclower(), _ismbcprint(), _ismbcpunct(), _ismbcspace(), _ismbcsymbol(), _ismbcupper(), isalnum(), isalpha(), isascii(), iscntrl(), isdigit(), isgraph(), isleadbyte(), isprint(), ispunct(), isspace(), isupper(), iswalnum(), iswalpha(), iswascii(), iswcntrl(), iswdigit(), iswgraph(), iswlower(), iswprint(), iswpunct(), iswspace(), iswupper(), iswxdigit(), and isxdigit().

isprint()

Function

The isprint() function returns true if the given value represents a printable character, including the space character.

Header File

```
#include <ctype.h>
```

Declaration

```
int isprint(int ch);
```

- *ch* — The value to examine.

Example

The following program demonstrates how to use the isprint() function. When run, the program checks whether a value represents a printable character and displays the result. The program's output looks like the following:

```
result = 64
Press any key to continue
```

Here is the program source code that produced the output:

```
#include "stdafx.h"
#include <iostream>
#include <ctype.h>

using namespace std;
```

```
int main(int argc, char* argv[])
{
    int result = isprint(32);
    cout << "result = " << result << endl;

    return 0;
}
```

 CROSS-REFERENCE
See also __isascii(), _ismbbalnum(), _ismbbalpha(), _ismbbgraph(), _ismbbkalnum(),
_ismbbkana(), _ismbbkprint(), _ismbbkpunct(), _ismbblead(), _ismbbprint(),
_ismbbpunct(), _ismbbtrail(), _ismbcalnum(), _ismbcalpha(), _ismbcdigit(),
_ismbcgraph(), _ismbchira(), _ismbckata(), _ismbcl0(), _ismbcl1(), _ismbcl2(),
_ismbclegal(), _ismbclower(), _ismbcprint(), _ismbcpunct(), _ismbcspace(),
_ismbcsymbol(), _ismbcupper(), isalnum(), isalpha(), isascii(), iscntrl(), isdigit(),
isgraph(), isleadbyte(), islower(), ispunct(), isspace(), isupper(), iswalnum(),
iswalpha(), iswascii(), iswcntrl(), iswdigit(), iswgraph(), iswlower(), iswprint(),
iswpunct(), iswspace(), iswupper(), iswxdigit(), and isxdigit().

ispunct()

Function

The ispunct() function returns true if the given value represents a punctuation character.

Header File

```
#include <ctype.h>
```

Declaration

```
int ispunct(int ch);
```

- *ch* — The value to examine.

Example

The following program demonstrates how to use the ispunct() function. When run, the program checks whether a value represents a punctuation character and displays the result. The program's output looks like the following:

```
result = 16
Press any key to continue
```

Here is the program source code that produced the output:

```cpp
#include "stdafx.h"
#include <iostream>
#include <ctype.h>

using namespace std;

int main(int argc, char* argv[])
{
    int result = ispunct(63);
    cout << "result = " << result << endl;

    return 0;
}
```

CROSS-REFERENCE

See also __isascii(), _ismbbalnum(), _ismbbalpha(), _ismbbgraph(), _ismbbkalnum(), _ismbbkana(), _ismbbkprint(), _ismbbkpunct(), _ismbblead(), _ismbbprint(), _ismbbpunct(), _ismbbtrail(), _ismbcalnum(), _ismbcalpha(), _ismbcdigit(), _ismbcgraph(), _ismbchira(), _ismbckata(), _ismbcl0(), _ismbcl1(), _ismbcl2(), _ismbclegal(), _ismbclower(), _ismbcprint(), _ismbcpunct(), _ismbcspace(), _ismbcsymbol(), _ismbcupper(), isalnum(), isalpha(), isascii(), iscntrl(), isdigit(), isgraph(), isleadbyte(), islower(), isprint(), isspace(), isupper(), iswalnum(), iswalpha(), iswascii(), iswcntrl(), iswdigit(), iswgraph(), iswlower(), iswprint(), iswpunct(), iswspace(), iswupper(), iswxdigit(), and isxdigit().

isspace()

Function

The isspace() function returns true if the given value represents a white-space character.

Header File

```cpp
#include <ctype.h>
```

Declaration

```
int isspace(int ch);
```

- *ch* — The value to examine.

Example

The following program demonstrates how to use the isspace() function. When run, the program checks whether a value represents a whitespace character and displays the result. The program's output looks like the following:

```
result = 8
Press any key to continue
```

Here is the program source code that produced the output:

```cpp
#include "stdafx.h"
#include <iostream>
#include <ctype.h>

using namespace std;

int main(int argc, char* argv[])
{
    int result = isspace(32);
    cout << "result = " << result << endl;

    return 0;
}
```

CROSS-REFERENCE

See also __isascii(), _ismbbalnum(), _ismbbalpha(), _ismbbgraph(), _ismbbkalnum(), _ismbbkana(), _ismbbkprint(), _ismbbkpunct(), _ismbblead(), _ismbbprint(), _ismbbpunct(), _ismbbtrail(), _ismbcalnum(), _ismbcalpha(), _ismbcdigit(), _ismbcgraph(), _ismbchira(), _ismbckata(), _ismbcl0(), _ismbcl1(), _ismbcl2(), _ismbclegal(), _ismbclower(), _ismbcprint(), _ismbcpunct(), _ismbcspace(), _ismbcsymbol(), _ismbcupper(), isalnum(), isalpha(), isascii(), iscntrl(), isdigit(), isgraph(), isleadbyte(), islower(), isprint(), ispunct(), isupper(), iswalnum(), iswalpha(), iswascii(), iswcntrl(), iswdigit(), iswgraph(), iswlower(), iswprint(), iswpunct(), iswspace(), iswupper(), iswxdigit(), and isxdigit().

istream

Class

The `istream` class defines the functionality required to manipulate stream input.

Class Declaration

```
class _CRTIMP istream : virtual public ios {
public:
    istream(streambuf*);
    virtual ~istream();

    int  ipfx(int =0);
    void isfx() { unlockbuf(); unlock(); }

    inline istream& operator>(istream&
        (__cdecl * _f)(istream&));
    inline istream& operator>(ios& (__cdecl * _f)(ios&));
    istream& operator>(char *);
    inline istream& operator>(unsigned char *);
    inline istream& operator>(signed char *);
    istream& operator>(char &);
    inline istream& operator>(unsigned char &);
    inline istream& operator>(signed char &);
    istream& operator>(short &);
    istream& operator>(unsigned short &);
    istream& operator>(int &);
    istream& operator>(unsigned int &);
    istream& operator>(long &);
    istream& operator>(unsigned long &);
    istream& operator>(float &);
    istream& operator>(double &);
    istream& operator>(long double &);
    istream& operator>(streambuf*);

    int get();

    inline istream& get(char *,int,char ='\n');
    inline istream& get(unsigned char *,int,char ='\n');
    inline istream& get(signed char *,int,char ='\n');

    istream& get(char &);
```

```
        inline istream& get(unsigned char &);
        inline istream& get(signed char &);

        istream& get(streambuf&,char ='\n');
        inline istream& getline(char *,int,char ='\n');
        inline istream& getline(unsigned char *,int,char ='\n');
        inline istream& getline(signed char *,int,char ='\n');

        inline istream& ignore(int =1,int =EOF);
        istream& read(char *,int);
        inline istream& read(unsigned char *,int);
        inline istream& read(signed char *,int);

        int gcount() const { return x_gcount; }
        int peek();
        istream& putback(char);
        int sync();

        istream& seekg(streampos);
        istream& seekg(streamoff,ios::seek_dir);
        streampos tellg();

        void eatwhite();

protected:
        istream();
        istream(const istream&);
        istream& operator=(streambuf* _isb);
        istream& operator=(const istream& _is)
            { return operator=(_is.rdbuf()); }
        istream& get(char *, int, int);
         int do_ipfx(int);

private:
        istream(ios&);
        int getint(char *);
        int getdouble(char *, int);
        int _fGline;
        int x_gcount;
};
```

Class Members

Tabe I-3 lists and describes the members of the istream class.

Table I-3 Members of the istream Class

Member	Description
eatwhite()	Removes leading whitespace characters in the stream.
gcount()	Returns the extraction count.
get()	Retrieves data from the stream.
getline()	Retrieves a line of data from the stream.
ignore()	Retrieves and ignores data from the stream.
ipfx()	Prepares the stream for input.
isfx()	Performs cleanup after data transfer.
peek()	Retrieves the next data element from the stream buffer.
putback()	Places a data element back in the stream.
read()	Reads a given number of data elements from the stream.
readsome()	Reads a given number of data elements from the stream.
seekg()	Changes the position in the stream, returning a pointer to the stream.
sync()	Synchronizes the stream with any external streams, returning 0 if successful or –1 if unsuccessful.
tellg()	Changes the position in the stream, returning the new position.
ws	Manipulator that removes leading whitespace characters.

CROSS-REFERENCE
See also ifstream, ios, iostream, istrstream, ofstream, ostream, ostrstream, and stdiostream.

istrstream

Class

The istrstream class defines the functionality required to manipulate stream input for string data.

Class Declaration

```
class _CRTIMP istrstream : public istream {
public:
    istrstream(char *);
    istrstream(char *, int);
    ~istrstream();
```

```
inline  strstreambuf* rdbuf() const
    { return (strstreambuf*) ios::rdbuf(); }
inline  char * str() { return rdbuf()->str(); }
};
```

Class Members

Table I-4 lists and describes the members of the istrstream class.

Table I-4 Members of the istrstream Class

Member	Description
rdbuf()	Gets a pointer to the stream's buffer object.
str()	Gets a pointer to the character data.

CROSS-REFERENCE
See also ifstream, ios, iostream, istream, ofstream, ostream, ostrstream, and stdiostream.

isupper()

Function

The isupper() function returns true if the given value represents an uppercase character.

Header File

```
#include <ctype.h>
```

Declaration

```
int isupper(int ch);
```

- *ch* — The value to examine.

Example

The following program demonstrates how to use the isupper() function. When run, the program checks whether a value represents an uppercase character and displays the result. The program's output looks like the following:

```
result = 1
Press any key to continue
```

Here is the program source code that produced the output:

```
#include "stdafx.h"
#include <iostream>
#include <ctype.h>

using namespace std;

int main(int argc, char* argv[])
{
    int result = isupper(65);
    cout << "result = " << result << endl;

    return 0;
}
```

CROSS-REFERENCE

See also __isascii(), _ismbbalnum(), _ismbbalpha(), _ismbbgraph(), _ismbbkalnum(), _ismbbkana(), _ismbbkprint(), _ismbbkpunct(), _ismbblead(), _ismbbprint(), _ismbbpunct(), _ismbbtrail(), _ismbcalnum(), _ismbcalpha(), _ismbcdigit(), _ismbcgraph(), _ismbchira(), _ismbckata(), _ismbcl0(), _ismbcl1(), _ismbcl2(), _ismbclegal(), _ismbclower(), _ismbcprint(), _ismbcpunct(), _ismbcspace(), _ismbcsymbol(), _ismbcupper(), isalnum(), isalpha(), isascii(), iscntrl(), isdigit(), isgraph(), isleadbyte(), islower(), isprint(), ispunct(), isspace(), iswalnum(), iswalpha(), iswascii(), iswcntrl(), iswdigit(), iswgraph(), iswlower(), iswprint(), iswpunct(), iswspace(), iswupper(), iswxdigit(), and isxdigit().

iswalnum()

Function

The iswalnum() function returns true if the given value represents an alphanumeric wide character.

Header File

```
#include <ctype.h>
```

Declaration

```
int iswalnum(wint_t ch);
```

- *ch*—The value to examine.

Example

The following program demonstrates how to use the `iswalnum()` function. When run, the program checks whether a value represents an alphanumeric wide character and displays the result. The program's output looks like the following:

```
result = 1
Press any key to continue
```

Here is the program source code that produced the output:

```
#include "stdafx.h"
#include <iostream>
#include <ctype.h>

using namespace std;

int main(int argc, char* argv[])
{
    int result = iswalnum(65);
    cout << "result = " << result << endl;

    return 0;
}
```

CROSS-REFERENCE

See also __isascii(), _ismbbalnum(), _ismbbalpha(), _ismbbgraph(), _ismbbkalnum(), _ismbbkana(), _ismbbkprint(), _ismbbkpunct(), _ismbblead(), _ismbbprint(), _ismbbpunct(), _ismbbtrail(), _ismbcalnum(), _ismbcalpha(), _ismbcdigit(), _ismbcgraph(), _ismbchira(), _ismbckata(), _ismbcl0(), _ismbcl1(), _ismbcl2(), _ismbclegal(), _ismbclower(), _ismbcprint(), _ismbcpunct(), _ismbcspace(), _ismbcsymbol(), _ismbcupper(), isalnum(), isalpha(), isascii(), iscntrl(), isdigit(), isgraph(), isleadbyte(), islower(), isprint(), ispunct(), isspace(), isupper(), iswalpha(), iswascii(), iswcntrl(), iswdigit(), iswgraph(), iswlower(), iswprint(), iswpunct(), iswspace(), iswupper(), iswxdigit(), and isxdigit().

iswalpha()

Function

The `iswalpha()` function returns true if the given value represents an alphabetic wide character.

Header File

```
#include <ctype.h>
```

Declaration

```
int iswalpha(wint_t ch);
```

- *ch* — The value to examine.

Example

The following program demonstrates how to use the `iswalpha()` function. When run, the program checks whether a value represents an alphabetic wide character and displays the result. The program's output looks like the following:

```
result = 1
Press any key to continue
```

Here is the program source code that produced the output:

```cpp
#include "stdafx.h"
#include <iostream>
#include <ctype.h>

using namespace std;

int main(int argc, char* argv[])
{
    int result = iswalpha(65);
    cout << "result = " << result << endl;

    return 0;
}
```

CROSS-REFERENCE

See also __isascii(), _ismbbalnum(), _ismbbalpha(), _ismbbgraph(), _ismbbkalnum(), _ismbbkana(), _ismbbkprint(), _ismbbkpunct(), _ismbblead(), _ismbbprint(), _ismbbpunct(), _ismbbtrail(), _ismbcalnum(), _ismbcalpha(), _ismbcdigit(), _ismbcgraph(), _ismbchira(), _ismbckata(), _ismbcl0(), _ismbcl1(), _ismbcl2(), _ismbclegal(), _ismbclower(), _ismbcprint(), _ismbcpunct(), _ismbcspace(), _ismbcsymbol(), _ismbcupper(), isalnum(), isalpha(), isascii(), iscntrl(), isdigit(), isgraph(), isleadbyte(), islower(), isprint(), ispunct(), isspace(), isupper(), iswalnum(), iswascii(), iswcntrl(), iswdigit(), iswgraph(), iswlower(), iswprint(), iswpunct(), iswspace(), iswupper(), iswxdigit(), and isxdigit().

iswascii()

Function

The iswascii() function returns true if the given value is an ASCII wide character.

Header File

```
#include <ctype.h>
```

Declaration

```
int iswascii(wint_t c);
```

- *c* — The value to examine.

Example

The following program demonstrates how to use the iswascii() function and displays the result. The program's output looks like the following:

```
val1 is ASCII.
Press any key to continue
```

Here is the program source code that produced the output:

```
#include "stdafx.h"
#include <ctype.h>
#include <iostream>

using namespace std;
```

```
int main(int argc, char* argv[])
{
   int val1 = 65;

    int result = iswascii(val1);
   if (result)
      cout << "val1 is ASCII." << endl;
   else
      cout << "val1 is not ASCII." << endl;

   return 0;
}
```

CROSS-REFERENCE

See also __isascii(), _ismbbalnum(), _ismbbalpha(), _ismbbgraph(), _ismbbkalnum(),
_ismbbkana(), _ismbbkprint(), _ismbbkpunct(), _ismbblead(), _ismbbprint(),
_ismbbpunct(), _ismbbtrail(), _ismbcalnum(), _ismbcalpha(), _ismbcdigit(),
_ismbcgraph(), _ismbchira(), _ismbckata(), _ismbcl0(), _ismbcl1(), _ismbcl2(),
_ismbclegal(), _ismbclower(), _ismbcprint(), _ismbcpunct(), _ismbcspace(),
_ismbcsymbol(), _ismbcupper(), isalnum(), isalpha(), isascii(), iscntrl(), isdigit(),
isgraph(), isleadbyte(), islower(), isprint(), ispunct(), isspace(), isupper(), iswalnum(),
iswalpha(), iswcntrl(), iswdigit(), iswgraph(), iswlower(), iswprint(), iswpunct(),
iswspace(), iswupper(), iswxdigit(), and isxdigit().

iswcntrl()

Function

The iswcntrl() function returns true if the given value represents a wide-character control character.

Header File

```
#include <ctype.h>
```

Declaration

```
int iswcntrl(wint_t ch);
```

- *ch* — The value to examine.

Example

The following program demonstrates how to use the iswcntrl() function. When run, the program checks whether a value represents a wide-character control character and displays the result. The program's output looks like the following:

```
result = 32
Press any key to continue
```

Here is the program source code that produced the output:

```cpp
#include "stdafx.h"
#include <iostream>
#include <ctype.h>

using namespace std;

int main(int argc, char* argv[])
{
    int result = iswcntrl(13);
    cout << "result = " << result << endl;

    return 0;
}
```

CROSS-REFERENCE

See also __isascii(), _ismbbalnum(), _ismbbalpha(), _ismbbgraph(), _ismbbkalnum(), _ismbbkana(), _ismbbkprint(), _ismbbkpunct(), _ismbblead(), _ismbbprint(), _ismbbpunct(), _ismbbtrail(), _ismbcalnum(), _ismbcalpha(), _ismbcdigit(), _ismbcgraph(), _ismbchira(), _ismbckata(), _ismbcl0(), _ismbcl1(), _ismbcl2(), _ismbclegal(), _ismbclower(), _ismbcprint(), _ismbcpunct(), _ismbcspace(), _ismbcsymbol(), _ismbcupper(), isalnum(), isalpha(), isascii(), iscntrl(), isdigit(), isgraph(), isleadbyte(), islower(), isprint(), ispunct(), isspace(), isupper(), iswalnum(), iswalpha(), iswascii(), iswdigit(), iswgraph(), iswlower(), iswprint(), iswpunct(), iswspace(), iswupper(), iswxdigit(), and isxdigit().

iswdigit()

Function

The iswdigit() function returns true if the given value represents a wide-character digit.

Header File

```
#include <ctype.h>
```

Declaration

```
int iswdigit(wint_t ch);
```

- *ch* — The value to examine.

Example

The following program demonstrates how to use the `iswdigit()` function. When run, the program checks whether a value represents a wide-character digit and displays the result. The program's output looks like the following:

```
result = 4
Press any key to continue
```

Here is the program source code that produced the output:

```
#include "stdafx.h"
#include <iostream>
#include <ctype.h>

using namespace std;

int main(int argc, char* argv[])
{
    int result = iswdigit(55);
    cout << "result = " << result << endl;

    return 0;
}
```

CROSS-REFERENCE

See also __isascii(), _ismbbalnum(), _ismbbalpha(), _ismbbgraph(), _ismbbkalnum(), _ismbbkana(), _ismbbkprint(), _ismbbkpunct(), _ismbblead(), _ismbbprint(), _ismbbpunct(), _ismbbtrail(), _ismbcalnum(), _ismbcalpha(), _ismbcdigit(), _ismbcgraph(), _ismbchira(), _ismbckata(), _ismbcl0(), _ismbcl1(), _ismbcl2(), _ismbclegal(), _ismbclower(), _ismbcprint(), _ismbcpunct(), _ismbcspace(), _ismbcsymbol(), _ismbcupper(), isalnum(), isalpha(), isascii(), iscntrl(), isdigit(), isgraph(), isleadbyte(), islower(), isprint(), ispunct(), isspace(), isupper(), iswalnum(), iswalpha(), iswascii(), iswcntrl(), iswgraph(), iswlower(), iswprint(), iswpunct(), iswspace(), iswupper(), iswxdigit(), and isxdigit().

iswgraph()

Function

The iswgraph() function returns true if the given value represents any printable wide character except a space.

Header File

```
#include <ctype.h>
```

Declaration

```
int iswgraph(wint_t ch);
```

- *ch* — The value to examine.

Example

The following program demonstrates how to use the iswgraph() function. When run, the program checks whether a value represents a wide-character digit and displays the result. The program's output looks like the following:

```
result = 0
Press any key to continue
```

Here is the program source code that produced the output:

```
#include "stdafx.h"
#include <iostream>
#include <ctype.h>

using namespace std;

int main(int argc, char* argv[])
{
    int result = iswgraph(32);
    cout << "result = " << result << endl;

    return 0;
}
```

CROSS-REFERENCE

See also __isascii(), _ismbbalnum(), _ismbbalpha(), _ismbbgraph(), _ismbbkalnum(), _ismbbkana(), _ismbbkprint(), _ismbbkpunct(), _ismbblead(), _ismbbprint(), _ismbbpunct(), _ismbbtrail(), _ismbcalnum(), _ismbcalpha(), _ismbcdigit(), _ismbcgraph(), _ismbchira(), _ismbckata(), _ismbcl0(), _ismbcl1(), _ismbcl2(), _ismbclegal(), _ismbclower(), _ismbcprint(), _ismbcpunct(), _ismbcspace(), _ismbcsymbol(), _ismbcupper(), isalnum(), isalpha(), isascii(), iscntrl(), isdigit(), isgraph(), isleadbyte(), islower(), isprint(), ispunct(), isspace(), isupper(), iswalnum(), iswalpha(), iswascii(), iswcntrl(), iswdigit(), iswlower(), iswprint(), iswpunct(), iswspace(), iswupper(), iswxdigit(), and isxdigit().

iswlower()

Function

The iswlower() function returns true if the given value represents a lowercase wide character.

Header File

```
#include <ctype.h>
```

Declaration

```
int iswlower(wint_t ch);
```

- *ch* — The value to examine.

Example

The following program demonstrates how to use the iswlower() function. When run, the program checks whether a value represents a lowercase wide character and displays the result. The program's output looks like the following:

```
result = 2
Press any key to continue
```

Here is the program source code that produced the output:

```
#include "stdafx.h"
#include <iostream>
#include <ctype.h>
```

```
using namespace std;

int main(int argc, char* argv[])
{
    int result = iswlower(97);
    cout << "result = " << result << endl;

    return 0;
}
```

CROSS-REFERENCE
See also __isascii(), _ismbbalnum(), _ismbbalpha(), _ismbbgraph(), _ismbbkalnum(), _ismbbkana(), _ismbbkprint(), _ismbbkpunct(), _ismbblead(), _ismbbprint(), _ismbbpunct(), _ismbbtrail(), _ismbcalnum(), _ismbcalpha(), _ismbcdigit(), _ismbcgraph(), _ismbchira(), _ismbckata(), _ismbcl0(), _ismbcl1(), _ismbcl2(), _ismbclegal(), _ismbclower(), _ismbcprint(), _ismbcpunct(), _ismbcspace(), _ismbcsymbol(), _ismbcupper(), isalnum(), isalpha(), isascii(), iscntrl(), isdigit(), isgraph(), isleadbyte(), islower(), isprint(), ispunct(), isspace(), isupper(), iswalnum(), iswalpha(), iswascii(), iswcntrl(), iswdigit(), iswgraph(), iswprint(), iswpunct(), iswspace(), iswupper(), iswxdigit(), and isxdigit().

iswprint()

Function

The iswprint() function returns true if the given value represents a printable wide character, including the space character.

Header File

```
#include <ctype.h>
```

Declaration

```
int iswprint(wint_t ch);
```

- *ch* — The value to examine.

Example

The following program demonstrates how to use the iswprint() function. When run, the program checks whether a value represents a printable wide character and displays the result. The program's output looks like the following:

```
result = 64
Press any key to continue
```

Here is the program source code that produced the output:

```
#include "stdafx.h"
#include <iostream>
#include <ctype.h>

using namespace std;

int main(int argc, char* argv[])
{
    int result = iswprint(32);
    cout << "result = " << result << endl;

    return 0;
}
```

CROSS-REFERENCE

See also __isascii(), _ismbbalnum(), _ismbbalpha(), _ismbbgraph(), _ismbbkalnum(), _ismbbkana(), _ismbbkprint(), _ismbbkpunct(), _ismbblead(), _ismbbprint(), _ismbbpunct(), _ismbbtrail(), _ismbcalnum(), _ismbcalpha(), _ismbcdigit(), _ismbcgraph(), _ismbchira(), _ismbckata(), _ismbcl0(), _ismbcl1(), _ismbcl2(), _ismbclegal(), _ismbclower(), _ismbcprint(), _ismbcpunct(), _ismbcspace(), _ismbcsymbol(), _ismbcupper(), isalnum(), isalpha(), isascii(), iscntrl(), isdigit(), isgraph(), isleadbyte(), islower(), isprint(), ispunct(), isspace(), isupper(), iswalnum(), iswalpha(), iswascii(), iswcntrl(), iswdigit(), iswgraph(), iswlower(), iswpunct(), iswspace(), iswupper(), iswxdigit(), and isxdigit().

iswpunct()

Function

The iswpunct() function returns true if the given value represents a punctuation wide character.

Header File

```
#include <ctype.h>
```

Declaration

```
int iswpunct(wint_t ch);
```

- *ch* — The value to examine.

Example

The following program demonstrates how to use the iswpunct() function. When run, the program checks whether a value represents a punctuation wide character and displays the result. The program's output looks like the following:

```
result = 16
Press any key to continue
```

Here is the program source code that produced the output:

```
#include "stdafx.h"
#include <iostream>
#include <ctype.h>

using namespace std;

int main(int argc, char* argv[])
{
    int result = iswpunct(63);
    cout << "result = " << result << endl;

    return 0;
}
```

CROSS-REFERENCE

See also __isascii(), _ismbbalnum(), _ismbbalpha(), _ismbbgraph(), _ismbbkalnum(), _ismbbkana(), _ismbbkprint(), _ismbbkpunct(), _ismbblead(), _ismbbprint(), _ismbbpunct(), _ismbbtrail(), _ismbcalnum(), _ismbcalpha(), _ismbcdigit(), _ismbcgraph(), _ismbchira(), _ismbckata(), _ismbcl0(), _ismbcl1(), _ismbcl2(), _ismbclegal(), _ismbclower(), _ismbcprint(), _ismbcpunct(), _ismbcspace(), _ismbcsymbol(), _ismbcupper(), isalnum(), isalpha(), isascii(), iscntrl(), isdigit(), isgraph(), isleadbyte(), islower(), isprint(), ispunct(), isspace(), isupper(), iswalnum(), iswalpha(), iswascii(), iswcntrl(), iswdigit(), iswgraph(), iswlower(), iswprint(), iswspace(), iswupper(), iswxdigit(), and isxdigit().

iswspace()

Function

The iswspace() function returns true if the given value represents a wide whitespace character.

Header File

```
#include <ctype.h>
```

Declaration

```
int iswspace(wint_t ch);
```

- *ch* — The value to examine.

Example

The following program demonstrates how to use the iswspace() function. When run, the program checks whether a value represents a wide white-space character and displays the result. The program's output looks like the following:

```
result = 8
Press any key to continue
```

Here is the program source code that produced the output:

```
#include "stdafx.h"
#include <iostream>
#include <ctype.h>

using namespace std;

int main(int argc, char* argv[])
{
    int result = iswspace(32);
    cout << "result = " << result << endl;

    return 0;
}
```

CROSS-REFERENCE

See also __isascii(), _ismbbalnum(), _ismbbalpha(), _ismbbgraph(), _ismbbkalnum(), _ismbbkana(), _ismbbkprint(), _ismbbkpunct(), _ismbblead(), _ismbbprint(), _ismbbpunct(), _ismbbtrail(), _ismbcalnum(), _ismbcalpha(), _ismbcdigit(), _ismbcgraph(), _ismbchira(), _ismbckata(), _ismbcl0(), _ismbcl1(), _ismbcl2(), _ismbclegal(), _ismbclower(), _ismbcprint(), _ismbcpunct(), _ismbcspace(), _ismbcsymbol(), _ismbcupper(), isalnum(), isalpha(), isascii(), iscntrl(), isdigit(), isgraph(), isleadbyte(), islower(), isprint(), ispunct(), isspace(), isupper(), iswalnum(), iswalpha(), iswascii(), iswcntrl(), iswdigit(), iswgraph(), iswlower(), iswprint(), iswpunct(), iswupper(), iswxdigit(), and isxdigit().

iswupper()

Function

The `iswupper()` function returns true if the given value represents an upper-case wide character.

Header File

```
#include <ctype.h>
```

Declaration

```
int iswupper(wint_t ch);
```

- *ch* — The value to examine.

Example

The following program demonstrates how to use the `iswupper()` function. When run, the program checks whether a value represents an uppercase wide character and displays the result. The program's output looks like the following:

```
result = 1
Press any key to continue
```

Here is the program source code that produced the output:

```
#include "stdafx.h"
#include <iostream>
#include <ctype.h>
```

```
using namespace std;

int main(int argc, char* argv[])
{
    int result = iswupper(65);
    cout << "result = " << result << endl;

    return 0;
}
```

CROSS-REFERENCE
See also __isascii(), _ismbbalnum(), _ismbbalpha(), _ismbbgraph(), _ismbbkalnum(), _ismbbkana(), _ismbbkprint(), _ismbbkpunct(), _ismbblead(), _ismbbprint(), _ismbbpunct(), _ismbbtrail(), _ismbcalnum(), _ismbcalpha(), _ismbcdigit(), _ismbcgraph(), _ismbchira(), _ismbckata(), _ismbcl0(), _ismbcl1(), _ismbcl2(), _ismbclegal(), _ismbclower(), _ismbcprint(), _ismbcpunct(), _ismbcspace(), _ismbcsymbol(), _ismbcupper(), isalnum(), isalpha(), isascii(), iscntrl(), isdigit(), isgraph(), isleadbyte(), islower(), isprint(), ispunct(), isspace(), isupper(), iswalnum(), iswalpha(), iswascii(), iswcntrl(), iswdigit(), iswgraph(), iswlower(), iswprint(), iswpunct(), iswspace(), iswxdigit(), and isxdigit().

iswxdigit()

Function

The iswxdigit() function returns true if the given value represents a wide-character hexadecimal digit.

Header File

```
#include <ctype.h>
```

Declaration

```
int iswxdigit(wint_t ch);
```

- *ch* — The value to examine.

Example

The following program demonstrates how to use the iswxdigit() function. When run, the program checks whether a value represents a wide-character hexadecimal digit and displays the result. The program's output looks like the following:

```
result = 128
Press any key to continue
```

Here is the program source code that produced the output:

```
#include "stdafx.h"
#include <iostream>
#include <ctype.h>

using namespace std;

int main(int argc, char* argv[])
{
    int result = iswxdigit(65);
    cout << "result = " << result << endl;

    return 0;
}
```

CROSS-REFERENCE

See also __isascii(), _ismbbalnum(), _ismbbalpha(), _ismbbgraph(), _ismbbkalnum(), _ismbbkana(), _ismbbkprint(), _ismbbkpunct(), _ismbblead(), _ismbbprint(), _ismbbpunct(), _ismbbtrail(), _ismbcalnum(), _ismbcalpha(), _ismbcdigit(), _ismbcgraph(), _ismbchira(), _ismbckata(), _ismbcl0(), _ismbcl1(), _ismbcl2(), _ismbclegal(), _ismbclower(), _ismbcprint(), _ismbcpunct(), _ismbcspace(), _ismbcsymbol(), _ismbcupper(),isalnum(), isalpha(), isascii(), iscntrl(), isdigit(), isgraph(), isleadbyte(), islower(), isprint(), ispunct(), isspace(), isupper(), iswalnum(), iswalpha(), iswascii(), iswcntrl(), iswdigit(), iswgraph(), iswlower(), iswprint(), iswpunct(), iswspace(), iswupper(), and isxdigit().

isxdigit()

Function

The isxdigit() function returns true if the given value represents a hexadecimal digit.

Header File

```
#include <ctype.h>
```

Declaration

```
int isxdigit(int ch);
```

- *ch*—The value to examine.

Example

The following program demonstrates how to use the `isxdigit()` function. When run, the program checks whether a value represents a hexadecimal digit and displays the result. The program's output looks like the following:

```
result = 128
Press any key to continue
```

Here is the program source code that produced the output:

```
#include "stdafx.h"
#include <iostream>
#include <ctype.h>

using namespace std;

int main(int argc, char* argv[])
{
    int result = isxdigit(65);
    cout << "result = " << result << endl;

    return 0;
}
```

CROSS-REFERENCE

See also __isascii(), _ismbbalnum(), _ismbbalpha(), _ismbbgraph(), _ismbbkalnum(), _ismbbkana(), _ismbbkprint(), _ismbbkpunct(), _ismbblead(), _ismbbprint(), _ismbbpunct(), _ismbbtrail(), _ismbcalnum(), _ismbcalpha(), _ismbcdigit(), _ismbcgraph(), _ismbchira(), _ismbckata(), _ismbcl0(), _ismbcl1(), _ismbcl2(), _ismbclegal(), _ismbclower(), _ismbcprint(), _ismbcpunct(), _ismbcspace(), _ismbcsymbol(), _ismbcupper(), isalnum(), isalpha(), isascii(), iscntrl(), isdigit(), isgraph(), isleadbyte(), islower(), isprint(), ispunct(), isspace(), isupper(), iswalnum(), iswalpha(), iswascii(), iswcntrl(), iswdigit(), iswgraph(), iswlower(), iswprint(), iswpunct(), iswspace(), iswupper(), and iswxdigit().

itoa()

Function

The itoa() function converts an integer value to a string.

Header File

```
#include <stdlib.h>
```

Declaration

```
char* itoa(int value, char* string, int radix);
```

- *radix* — The value number base (typically 10).
- *string* — A pointer to the buffer in which to store the string.
- *value* — The value to convert.

Example

The following program demonstrates how to use the itoa() function. When run, the program converts a value into several number-base formats and displays the results. The program's output looks like the following:

```
This is 19,564 in base 10: 19564
This is 19,564 in base 16: 4c6c
This is 19,564 in base 2: 100110001101100
This is 19,564 in base 8: 46154

Press any key to continue
```

Here is the program source code that produced the output:

```
#include "stdafx.h"
#include <iostream>
#include <stdlib.h>

using namespace std;

int main(int argc, char* argv[])
{
    char str[81];

    char* result = itoa(19564, str, 10);
```

```
        cout << "This is 19,564 in base 10: ";
        cout << result << endl;

        result = itoa(19564, str, 16);
        cout << "This is 19,564 in base 16: ";
        cout << result << endl;

        result = itoa(19564, str, 2);
        cout << "This is 19,564 in base 2: ";
        cout << result << endl;

        result = itoa(19564, str, 8);
        cout << "This is 19,564 in base 8: ";
        cout << result << endl;
        cout << endl;

        return 0;
    }
```

CROSS-REFERENCE

See also _ecvt(), _fcvt(), _gcvt(), _i64toa(), _i64tow(), _itoa(), _itow(), _ui64toa(), _ui64tow(), ltoa(), and ultoa().

_kbhit()

Function

The _kbhit() function returns a non-zero if a character is available at the console. Otherwise, the function returns 0.

NOTE

Borland users should refer to the kbhit() function later in this chapter.

Header File

```
#include <conio.h>
```

Declaration

```
int _kbhit(void);
```

Example

The following program demonstrates how to use the _kbhit() function. When run, the program loops until a character is available at the console, at which time the program displays the character. The program's output looks something like the following:

```
17331833193320332133223323332433253326332733283329333033313332
33333334333533363337333833393334033413342334333443345334633473
4833493350335133523353335435533563357335833593360336133623363
33643365336633673368336933703371337233733374337533763377337833
79338033813382338333843385338633873388338933903391339233933393
39533963397339833993400340134023403340434053406340734083409341
03411341234133414341534163417341834193420342134223423342434253
42634273428342934303431343234333434343534363437343834393440344
13442344334443445344634473448344934503451345234533454345534564
57345834593460346134623463346434653466346734683469347034713472
```

```
347334743475347634773478347934803481348234833484348534863487348734
883489349034913492349334943495349634973498349935003501350235033503
35043505350635073508350935103511351235133514351535163517
```

You typed: k

Press any key to continue

Here is the program source code that produced the output:

```cpp
#include "stdafx.h"
#include <iostream>
#include <conio.h>

using namespace std;

int main(int argc, char* argv[])
{
    int x = 0;

    cout << "Press a key" << endl;
    while (!_kbhit())
    {
        cout << x;
        ++x;
    }

    char ch = (char)_getch();

    cout << endl << endl;
    cout << "You typed: " << ch << endl << endl;

    return 0;
}
```

CROSS-REFERENCE

See also _cgets(), _cprintf(), _cputs(), _cscanf(), _getch(), _getche(), _ungetch(), _putch(), kbhit(), and putch().

kbhit()

Function

The kbhit() function returns a non-zero if a character is available at the console. Otherwise, the function returns 0.

Header File

```
#include <conio.h>
```

Declaration

```
int kbhit(void);
```

Example

The following program demonstrates how to use the kbhit() function. When run, the program loops until a character is available at the console, at which time the program displays the character. The program's output looks something like the following:

```
17331833193320332133223323332433253326332733283329333033313332
33333334333533363337333833393334033413342334333443345334633473
33834933503351335233533335343355335633573358335933603361336233363
33643365336633673368336933703371337233733374337533763377337833
79338033813382338333843385338633873388338933903391339233933393
395339633973398339934003401340234033404340534063407340834093341
034113412341334143415341634173418341934203421342234233342434253
42634273428342934303431343234333434343534363437343834393440344
134423443344434453446344734483449345034513452345334543455345564
57345834593460346134623463346434653466346734683469347034713472
34733474347534763477347834793480348134823483348434853486348734
88348934903491349234933349434953496349734983499350035013502350335
35043505350635073508350935103511351235133514351535163
```

```
You typed: k
```

```
Press any key to continue
```

Here is the program source code that produced the output:

```cpp
#include "stdafx.h"
#include <iostream>
#include <conio.h>

using namespace std;

int main(int argc, char* argv[])
{
    int x = 0;

    cout << "Press a key" << endl;
    while (!kbhit())
    {
        cout << x;
        ++x;
    }

    char ch = (char)_getch();

    cout << endl << endl;
    cout << "You typed: " << ch << endl << endl;

    return 0;
}
```

CROSS-REFERENCE

See also _cgets(), _cprintf(), _cputs(), _cscanf(), _getch(), _getche(), _kbhit(), _putch(), and _ungetch().

#line

Directive

The #line directive enables a program to change the current line number and file name used internally by the compiler. For example, the following program displays the currently stored line number and file name (using the __LINE__ and __FILE__ macros), changes the line number and file name, and then displays the new values. The program's output looks like the following:

```
Line: 11
File: C:\all code\Microsoft\L\#line\line.cpp
Line: 1
File: stdafx
Press any key to continue
```

Here is the program source code that produced the output:

```cpp
#include "stdafx.h"
#include <iostream>

using namespace std;

int main(int argc, char* argv[])
{
    cout << "Line: " << __LINE__ << endl;
    cout << "File: " << __FILE__ << endl;

#line 0 "stdafx"

    cout << "Line: " << __LINE__ << endl;
    cout << "File: " << __FILE__ << endl;

    return 0;
}
```

_lfind()

Function

The _lfind() function searches a list of values for a given key, returning a pointer to the key in the list, if found, or returning NULL if not found.

NOTE

Borland users should refer to the lfind() function later in this chapter.

Header File

```
#include <search.h>
```

Declaration

```
void* _lfind(const void *key, const void *base,
    unsigned int *num, unsigned int width,
    int (__cdecl *compare)(const void *elem1,
        const void *elem2));
```

- *base* — A pointer to the data in which to search for *key*.
- *compare* — A pointer to the function that will compare values. This function must return 0 if two elements match or return a nonzero value if two elements do not match.
- *elem1* — A pointer to a variable containing the key for which to search.
- *elem2* — A pointer to the element in *base* with which to compare *key*.
- *key* — A pointer to the value for which to search.
- *num* — A pointer to a variable containing the number of elements in *base*.
- *width* — The size of each element in *base*.

Example

The following program demonstrates how to use the _lfind() function. When run, the program displays the values in a list of integers and then requests the user to enter a value. The program then tells the user whether the value she entered matches a value in the list. The program's output looks something like the following:

```
Values in list:
  1 45 65 28 124 58 4 10

Enter a number: 58
58 is in the list.

Press any key to continue
```

Here is the program source code that produced the output:

```cpp
#include "stdafx.h"
#include <iostream>
#include <search.h>

using namespace std;

int compare(const void *num1, const void *num2)
{
    int val1 = *(int*)num1;
    int val2 = *(int*)num2;

    if (val1 == val2)
        return 0;
    else
        return 1;
}

int main(int argc, char* argv[])
{
    int list[] = {1, 45, 65, 28, 124, 58, 4, 10};
    int num;
    unsigned int count = 8;

    cout << "Values in list: " << endl;
    cout << "  ";
    for (int x=0; x<count; ++x)
        cout << list[x] << " ";

    cout << endl << endl << "Enter a number: ";
    scanf("%d", &num);

    void* result = _lfind(&num, list, &count,
        sizeof(int), compare);

    if (result)
```

```
        {
            cout << *(int*)result << " is in the list.";
            cout << endl << endl;
        }
        else
            cout << num << " not in list." << endl << endl;

        return 0;
    }
```

CROSS-REFERENCE
See also _lsearch(), bsearch(), lfind(), and qsort().

_locking()

Function

The _locking() function locks the requested number of bytes in a file, making those bytes inaccessible to other processes and returning 0 if successful or returning –1 if an error occurs. The current position of the file pointer indicates the first byte to be locked.

NOTE
Borland users should refer to the locking() function later in this chapter.

Header Files

```
#include <io.h>
#include <sys/locking.h>
```

Declaration

```
int _locking(int handle, int mode, long nbytes);
```

- *handle* — The file handle of the file to lock.
- *mode* — The locking mode, which can be one of the values from Table L-1.
- *nbytes* — The number of bytes to lock in the file.

Table L-1 Locking Modes for _locking()

Mode	Description
_LK_LOCK	Locks the given number of bytes, and, if the lock fails, retries ten times, after which the function returns an error.
_LK_NBLCK	Locks the given number of bytes, and, if the lock fails, returns an error.
_LK_NBRLCK	Performs the same function as _LK_NBLCK.
_LK_RLCK	Performs the same function as _LK_LOCK.
_LK_UNLCK	Unlocks the given number of locked bytes.

Example

The following program demonstrates how to use the _locking() function. When run, the program opens a file, locks 128 bytes in the file, and then unlocks the bytes, displaying messages as it goes. The program's output looks something like the following:

```
Opening the _locking.cpp file...
File opened successfully.
Now locking 128 bytes in file...
128 bytes locked successfully.
Now unlocking bytes...
Bytes now unlocked.

Press any key to continue
```

Here is the program source code that produced the output:

```
#include "stdafx.h"
#include <iostream>
#include <io.h>
#include <sys/stat.h>
#include <sys/locking.h>
#include <share.h>
#include <fcntl.h>

using namespace std;

int main(int argc, char* argv[])
{
    cout << "Opening the _locking.cpp file..." << endl;
    int fileHandle = _sopen("_locking.cpp",
```

```
                        _O_RDWR, _SH_DENYNO, _S_IREAD | _S_IWRITE);

            if (fileHandle != -1 )
            {
                cout << "File opened successfully." << endl;
                cout << "Now locking 128 bytes in file..." << endl;
                int result = _locking(fileHandle, _LK_NBLCK, 128L);
                if(result != -1 )
                {
                    cout << "128 bytes locked successfully." << endl;
                    cout << "Now unlocking bytes..." << endl;
                    _locking(fileHandle, _LK_UNLCK, 128L);
                    cout << "Bytes now unlocked." << endl;
                }
                else
                    cout << "Could not lock bytes." << endl;
            }
            else
                cout << "Could not open file." << endl;

            cout << endl;

            _close(fileHandle);

            return 0;
        }
```

CROSS-REFERENCE

See also _access(), _chmod(), _chsize(), _filelength(), _fstat(), _fstati64(), _fullpath(), _get_osfhandle(), _isatty(), _makepath(), _mktemp(), _open_osfhandle(), _setmode(), _splitpath(), _stat(), _stati64(), _umask(), _unlink(), _waccess(), _wchmod(), _wfullpath(), _wmakepath(), _wmktemp(), _wremove(), _wrename(), _wsplitpath(), _wstat(), _wstati64(), _wunlink(), locking(), remove(), and rename().

_lrotl()

Function

The _lrotl() function left rotates the bits of a long value, returning the resultant value.

Header Files

```
#include <stdlib.h>
```

Declaration

```
unsigned long _lrotl(unsigned long value, int shift);
```

- *shift* — The number of bits the given value should be left rotated.
- *value* — The value to be left rotated.

Example

The following program demonstrates how to use the _lrotl() function. When run, the program left rotates the value 1 from 0 to 16 bits, displaying the results as it goes. The program's output looks something like the following:

```
Rotated 0 bits: 1
Rotated 1 bits: 2
Rotated 2 bits: 4
Rotated 3 bits: 8
Rotated 4 bits: 16
Rotated 5 bits: 32
Rotated 6 bits: 64
Rotated 7 bits: 128
Rotated 8 bits: 256
Rotated 9 bits: 512
Rotated 10 bits: 1024
Rotated 11 bits: 2048
Rotated 12 bits: 4096
Rotated 13 bits: 8192
Rotated 14 bits: 16384
Rotated 15 bits: 32768
Rotated 16 bits: 65536
Press any key to continue
```

Here is the program source code that produced the output:

```
#include "stdafx.h"
#include <iostream>
#include <stdlib.h>

using namespace std;

int main(int argc, char* argv[])
```

```
{
    int x;
    unsigned long result;
    unsigned long value = 1;

    for (x=0; x<17; ++x)
    {
        result = _lrotl(value, x);
        cout << "Rotated " << x << " bits: ";
        cout << result << endl;
    }

    return 0;
}
```

CROSS-REFERENCE

See also _lrotr(), _rotl(), and _rotr().

_lrotr()

Function

The _lrotr() function right rotates the bits of a long value, returning the resultant value.

Header Files

```
#include <stdlib.h>
```

Declaration

```
unsigned long _lrotr(unsigned long value, int shift);
```

- *shift*—The number of bits the given value should be right rotated.
- *value*—The value to be right rotated.

Example

The following program demonstrates how to use the _lrotr() function. When run, the program right rotates the value 65,536 from 0 to 16 bits, displaying the results as it goes. The program's output looks something like the following:

```
Rotated 0 bits: 65536
Rotated 1 bits: 32768
Rotated 2 bits: 16384
Rotated 3 bits: 8192
Rotated 4 bits: 4096
Rotated 5 bits: 2048
Rotated 6 bits: 1024
Rotated 7 bits: 512
Rotated 8 bits: 256
Rotated 9 bits: 128
Rotated 10 bits: 64
Rotated 11 bits: 32
Rotated 12 bits: 16
Rotated 13 bits: 8
Rotated 14 bits: 4
Rotated 15 bits: 2
Rotated 16 bits: 1
Press any key to continue
```

Here is the program source code that produced the output:

```cpp
#include "stdafx.h"
#include <iostream>
#include <stdlib.h>

using namespace std;

int main(int argc, char* argv[])
{
    int x;
    unsigned long result;
    unsigned long value = 65536;

    for (x=0; x<17; ++x)
    {
        result = _lrotr(value, x);
        cout << "Rotated " << x << " bits: ";
        cout << result << endl;
    }

    return 0;
}
```

CROSS-REFERENCE

See also _lrotl(), _rotl(), and _rotr().

_lsearch()

Function

The _lsearch() function searches a list of values for a given key, returning a pointer to the matching value in the list. If the key is not found, _lsearch() adds the key to the end of the list and returns a pointer to the new list entry, and increments the element count found in the *num* argument.

 NOTE
Borland users should refer to the lsearch() function later in this chapter.

Header File

```
#include <search.h>
```

Declaration

```
void* _lsearch(const void *key, void *base,
    unsigned int *num, unsigned int width,
    int (__cdecl *compare)(const void *elem1,
        const void *elem2));
```

- *base* — A pointer to the data in which to search for *key*.
- *compare* — A pointer to the function that will compare values. This function must return 0 if two elements match or return a nonzero value if two elements do not match.
- *elem1* — A pointer to a variable containing the key for which to search.
- *elem2* — A pointer to the element in *base* with which to compare *key*.
- *key* — A pointer to the value for which to search.
- *num* — A pointer to a variable containing the number of elements in *base*.
- *width* — The size of each element in *base*.

Example

The following program demonstrates how to use the _lsearch() function. When run, the program displays the values in a list of integers and then requests the user to enter a value. The program then tells the user whether the

value she entered matches a value in the list, or else adds the value to the list.
The program's output looks something like the following:

```
Values in list:
  1 45 65 28 124 58 4 10

Enter a number: 99
99 added to list.

Values in list:
  1 45 65 28 124 58 4 10 99


Press any key to continue
```

Here is the program source code that produced the output:

```cpp
#include "stdafx.h"
#include <iostream>
#include <search.h>

using namespace std;

int compare(const void *num1, const void *num2)
{
    int val1 = *(int*)num1;
    int val2 = *(int*)num2;

    if (val1 == val2)
        return 0;
    else
        return 1;
}

void displayValues(int* list, int count)
{
    cout << "Values in list: " << endl;
    cout << "  ";
    for (int x=0; x<count; ++x)
        cout << list[x] << " ";
    cout << endl;
}

int main(int argc, char* argv[])
{
```

```
int list[20] = {1, 45, 65, 28, 124, 58, 4, 10};
int num;
unsigned int count = 8;

displayValues(list, count);

cout << endl << "Enter a number: ";
scanf("%d", &num);

void* result = _lsearch(&num, list, &count,
    sizeof(int), compare);

if (count == 8)
{
    cout << *(int*)result << " is in the list.";
    cout << endl << endl;
}
else
{
    cout << *(int*)result << " added to list.";
    cout << endl << endl;
    displayValues(list, count);
    cout << endl;
}

return 0;
}
```

CROSS-REFERENCE
See also _lfind() , bsearch(), lsearch(), and qsort().

_lseek()

Function

The _lseek() function sets the position of the file pointer, returning the new offset if successful or returning –1 if unsuccessful.

Header File

```
#include <io.h>
```

Declaration

```
long _lseek(int handle, long offset, int origin);
```

- *handle* — The handle of an open file.
- *offset* — The number of bytes from *origin* to offset the file pointer.
- *origin* — The position from which the offset should be added. This can be one of the values from Table L-2.

Table L-2 Origin Values for _lseek()

Value	Description
SEEK_CUR	Seek from the current position.
SEEK_END	Seek from the end of the file.
SEEK_SET	Seek from the beginning of the file.

Example

The following program demonstrates how to use the `_lseek()` function. When run, the program opens a file and sets the file position to 50, displaying messages as it goes. The program's output looks something like the following:

```
Opening the file...
File opened successfully.
Seeking to new position...
Seek was successful.
Press any key to continue
```

Here is the program source code that produced the output:

```cpp
#include "stdafx.h"
#include <stdio.h>
#include <fcntl.h>
#include <io.h>
#include <iostream>

using namespace std;

int main(int argc, char* argv[])
{
    fpos_t pos = 50;

    cout << "Opening the file..." << endl;
```

```
int fileHandle = open("_lseek.cpp", _O_RDONLY);

if (fileHandle == -1)
    cout << "File open error" << endl;
else
{
    cout << "File opened successfully." << endl;
    cout << "Seeking to new position..." << endl;
    long result = _lseek(fileHandle, pos, SEEK_SET);

    if (result != -1)
        cout << "Seek was successful." << endl;
    else
        cout << "Seek was unsuccessful." << endl;

    close(fileHandle);
}

return 0;
}
```

 CROSS-REFERENCE
See also _close(), _creat(), _fcloseall(), _fdopen(), _fgetchar(), _fgetwchar(), _fileno(), _flushall(), _fputwchar(), _fsopen(), _getw(), _getws(), _lseeki64(), _open(), _putw(), _putws(), _read(), _rmtmp(), _tempnam(), _wcreat(), _wfdopen(), _wfopen(), _wfreopen(), _wfsopen(), _wopen(), _wtempnam(), _wtmpnam(), clearerr(), eof(), fclose(), feof(), ferror(), fflush(), fgetc(), fgetpos(), fgets(), fgetwc(), fgetws(), fopen(), fprintf(), fputc(), fputchar(), fputs(), fputwc(), fputws(), fread(), freopen(), fscanf(), fsetpos(), ftell(), fwprintf(), fwrite(), fwscanf(), getc(), getchar(), gets(), getwc(), getwchar(), lseek(), putc(), putch(), putchar(), puts(), putwc(), putwchar(), rewind(), setbuf(), setvbuf(), tmpfile(), tmpnam(), ungetc(), ungetch(), ungetwc(), and write().

_lseeki64()

Function

The _lseeki64() function sets the position of the file pointer, returning (as a 64-bit integer) the new offset if successful or returning –1 if unsuccessful.

 NOTE
Borland does not support this function.

Header File

```
#include <io.h>
```

Declaration

```
__int64 _lseeki64(int handle, __int64 offset, int origin);
```

- *handle* — The handle of a open file.
- *offset* — The number of bytes from *origin* to offset the file pointer.
- *origin* — The position from which the offset should be added. This can be one of the values from Table L-3.

Table L-3 Origin Values for _lseeki64()

Value	Description
SEEK_CUR	Seek from the current position.
SEEK_END	Seek from the end of the file.
SEEK_SET	Seek from the beginning of the file.

Example

The following program demonstrates how to use the _lseeki64() function. When run, the program opens a file and sets the file position to 50, displaying messages as it goes. The program's output looks something like the following:

```
Opening the file...
File opened successfully.
Seeking to new position...
Seek was successful.
Press any key to continue
```

Here is the program source code that produced the output:

```
#include "stdafx.h"
#include <stdio.h>
#include <fcntl.h>
#include <io.h>
#include <iostream>

using namespace std;

int main(int argc, char* argv[])
```

```
{
    __int64 pos = 50;

    cout << "Opening the file..." << endl;
    int fileHandle = open("_lseeki64.cpp", _O_RDONLY);

    if (fileHandle == -1)
        cout << "File open error" << endl;
    else
    {
        cout << "File opened successfully." << endl;
        cout << "Seeking to new position..." << endl;
        __int64 result = _lseeki64(fileHandle, pos, SEEK_SET);

        if (result != -1)
            cout << "Seek was successful." << endl;
        else
            cout << "Seek was unsuccessful." << endl;

        close(fileHandle);
    }

    return 0;
}
```

CROSS-REFERENCE

See also _close(), _creat(), _fcloseall(), _fdopen(), _fgetchar(), _fgetwchar(), _fileno(), _flushall(), _fputwchar(), _fsopen(), _getw(), _getws(), _lseek(), _open(), _putw(), _putws(), _read(), _rmtmp(), _tempnam(), _wcreat(), _wfdopen(), _wfopen(), _wfreopen(), _wfsopen(), _wopen(), _wtempnam(), _wtmpnam(), clearerr(), eof(), fclose(), feof(), ferror(), fflush(), fgetc(), fgetpos(), fgets(), fgetwc(), fgetws(), fopen(), fprintf(), fputc(), fputchar(), fputs(), fputwc(), fputws(), fread(), freopen(), fscanf(), fsetpos(), ftell(), fwprintf(), fwrite(), fwscanf(), getc(), getchar(), gets(), getwc(), getwchar(), lseek(), putc(), putch(), putchar(), puts(), putwc(), putwchar(), rewind(), setbuf(), setvbuf(), tmpfile(), tmpnam(), ungetc(), ungetch(), ungetwc(), and write().

_ltoa()

Function

The _ltoa() function converts a long integer value to a string.

Header File

```
#include <stdlib.h>
```

Declaration

```
char* _ltoa(long value, char* string, int radix);
```

- *radix* — The value number base (typically 10).
- *string* — A pointer to the buffer in which to store the string.
- *value* — The value to convert.

Example

The following program demonstrates how to use the _ltoa() function. When run, the program converts a long-integer value into several number-base formats and displays the results. The program's output looks like the following:

```
This is 19,564 in base 10: 19564
This is 19,564 in base 16: 4c6c
This is 19,564 in base 2: 100110001101100
This is 19,564 in base 8: 46154

Press any key to continue
```

Here is the program source code that produced the output:

```cpp
#include "stdafx.h"
#include <iostream>
#include <stdlib.h>

using namespace std;

int main(int argc, char* argv[])
{
    char str[81];
    long value = 19564;

    char* result = _ltoa(value, str, 10);
    cout << "This is 19,564 in base 10: ";
    cout << result << endl;

    result = _ltoa(value, str, 16);
    cout << "This is 19,564 in base 16: ";
    cout << result << endl;
```

```
    result = _ltoa(value, str, 2);
    cout << "This is 19,564 in base 2: ";
    cout << result << endl;

    result = _ltoa(value, str, 8);
    cout << "This is 19,564 in base 8: ";
    cout << result << endl;
    cout << endl;

    return 0;
}
```

CROSS-REFERENCE

See also _ecvt(), _fcvt(), _gcvt(), _i64toa(), _i64tow(), _itow(), _ltow(), _ui64toa(), _ui64tow(), itoa(), ltoa(), and ultoa().

_ltow()

Function

The _ltow() function converts a long integer value to a wide-character string.

Header File

```
#include <stdlib.h>
```

Declaration

```
wchar_t* _ltow(long value, wchar_t* string, int radix);
```

- *radix* — The value number base (typically 10).
- *string* — A pointer to the buffer in which to store the string.
- *value* — The value to convert.

Example

The following program demonstrates how to use the _ltow() function. When run, the program converts a long-integer value into several wide-character number-base formats and displays the results. The program's output looks like the following:

```
This is 19,564 in base 10: 19564
This is 19,564 in base 16: 4c6c
This is 19,564 in base 2: 100110001101100
This is 19,564 in base 8: 46154

Press any key to continue
```

Here is the program source code that produced the output:

```
#include "stdafx.h"
#include <iostream>
#include <stdlib.h>

using namespace std;

int main(int argc, char* argv[])
{
    wchar_t str[81];
    long value = 19564;

    wchar_t* result = _ltow(value, str, 10);
    cout << "This is 19,564 in base 10: ";
    wcout << result << endl;

    result = _ltow(value, str, 16);
    cout << "This is 19,564 in base 16: ";
    wcout << result << endl;

    result = _ltow(value, str, 2);
    cout << "This is 19,564 in base 2: ";
    wcout << result << endl;

    result = _ltow(value, str, 8);
    cout << "This is 19,564 in base 8: ";
    wcout << result << endl;
    cout << endl;

    return 0;
}
```

CROSS-REFERENCE

See also _ecvt(), _fcvt(), _gcvt(), _i64toa(), _i64tow(), _itoa(), _ltoa(), _ui64toa(),
_ui64tow(), itoa(), ltoa(), and ultoa().

labs()

Function

The labs() function returns the absolute value of its long integer argument.

Header File

```
#include <stdlib.h>
```

Declaration

```
long labs(long num)
```

- *num* — The number for which to return the absolute value.

Example

The following program demonstrates how to use the labs() function. The program's output looks like the following:

```
The absolute value of -25 is 25
Press any key to continue
```

Here is the program source code that produced the output:

```
#include "stdafx.h"
#include <stdlib.h>
#include <iostream>

using namespace std;

int main(int argc, char* argv[])
{
    long var1 = -25;
    long result = labs(var1);
    cout << "The absolute value of " << var1;
    cout << " is " << result << endl;

    return 0;
}
```

CROSS-REFERENCE
See also _cabs(), abs(), fabs(), and fabsl().

ldexp()

Function

The ldexp() function returns the result of a number times 2 raised to the given power (x * 2^exp).

Header File

```
#include <math.h>
```

Declaration

```
double ldexp(double x, int exp)
```

- *exp* — The exponent by which 2 should be raised.
- *x* — The value that should be multiplied times 2 to the power of *exp*.

Example

The following program demonstrates how to use the ldexp() function. The program's output looks like the following:

```
Enter the value for x:
5
Enter the value for the exponent:
2
Result = 20

Press any key to continue
```

Here is the program source code that produced the output:

```
#include "stdafx.h"
#include <math.h>
#include <iostream>

using namespace std;

int main(int argc, char* argv[])
{
    float x;
    int exp;

    cout << "Enter the value for x: " << endl;
```

```
scanf("%f", &x);
cout << "Enter the value for the exponent: " << endl;
scanf("%d", &exp);
double result = ldexp(x, exp);
cout << "Result = " << result << endl << endl;

return 0;
}
```

CROSS-REFERENCE
See also _cabs(), _cabsl(), _hypot(), abs(), acos(), asin(), atan(), atan2(), ceil(), cos(), cosh(), div(), exp(), fabs(), fabsf(), fabsl(), floor(), fmod(), frexp(), labs(), ldexpl(), ldiv(), log(), log10(), pow(), sin(), sinh(), sqrt(), tan(), and tanh().

ldexpf()

Function

The ldexpf() function returns, as a float value, the result of a number times 2 raised to the given power ($x * 2^{exp}$).

NOTE
Borland does not support this function.

Header File

```
#include <math.h>
```

Declaration

```
float ldexpf(float x, int exp)
```

- *exp*—The exponent by which 2 should be raised.
- *x*—The value that should be multiplied times 2 to the power of *exp*.

Example

The following program demonstrates how to use the ldexpf() function. The program's output looks like the following:

```
Result = 8
```

```
Press any key to continue
```

Here is the program source code that produced the output:

```
#include "stdafx.h"
#include <math.h>
#include <iostream>

using namespace std;

int main(int argc, char* argv[])
{
    float x = 2;
    int exp = 2;

    float result = ldexpf(x, exp);
    cout << "Result = " << result << endl << endl;

    return 0;
}
```

CROSS-REFERENCE

See also _cabs(), _cabsl(), _hypot(), abs(), acos(), asin(), atan(), atan2(), ceil(), cos(), cosh(), div(), exp(), fabs(), fabsf(), fabsl(), floor(), fmod(), frexp(), labs(), ldexp(), ldiv(), log(), log10(), pow(), sin(), sinh(), sqrt(), tan(), and tanh().

ldexpl()

Function

The ldexpl() function returns, as a long double, the result of a number times 2 raised to the given power (x * 2^{exp}).

Header File

```
#include <math.h>
```

Declaration

```
long double ldexpl(long double x, int exp)
```

- *exp* — The exponent by which 2 should be raised.
- *x* — The value that should be multiplied times 2 to the power of *exp*.

Example

The following program demonstrates how to use the `ldexpl()` function. The program's output looks like the following:

```
Result = 8

Press any key to continue
```

Here is the program source code that produced the output:

```cpp
#include "stdafx.h"
#include <math.h>
#include <iostream>

using namespace std;

int main(int argc, char* argv[])
{
    long double x = 2;
    int exp = 2;

    long double result = ldexpl(x, exp);
    cout << "Result = " << result << endl << endl;

    return 0;
}
```

CROSS-REFERENCE
See also _cabs(), _cabsl(), _hypot(), abs(), acos(), asin(), atan(), atan2(), ceil(), cos(), cosh(), div(), exp(), fabs(), fabsf(), fabsl(), floor(), fmod(), frexp(), labs(), ldexp(), ldiv(), log(), log10(), pow(), sin(), sinh(), sqrt(), tan(), and tanh().

ldiv()

Function

The ldiv() performs a division and returns the quotient and remainder in an ldiv_t structure.

Header File

```
#include <stdlib.h>
```

Declaration

```
ldiv_t ldiv(long int numer, long int denom);
```

- *denom* — The value by which numer should be divided.
- *numer* — The value to be divided by denom.

Example

The following program demonstrates how to use the ldiv() function. When run, the program calls the ldiv() function to perform a division and displays the results. The program's output looks like the following:

```
Quotient: 4
Remainder: 1
Press any key to continue
```

Here is the program source code that produced the output:

```
#include "stdafx.h"
#include <iostream>
#include <stdlib.h>

using namespace std;

int main(int argc, char* argv[])
{
    long int val1 = 21;
    long int val2 = 5;

    ldiv_t result = ldiv(val1, val2);
```

```
        cout << "Quotient: " << result.quot << endl;
        cout << "Remainder: " << result.rem << endl;

        return 0;
}
```

CROSS-REFERENCE
See also _cabs(), _cabsl(), _hypot(), abs(), acos(), asin(), atan(), atan2(), ceil(), cos(), cosh(), div(), exp(), fabs(), fabsf(), fabsl(), floor(), fmod(), frexp(), labs(), ldexp(), ldexpl(), log(), log10(), pow(), sin(), sinh(), sqrt(), tan(), and tanh().

lfind()

Function

The lfind() function searches a list of values for a given key, returning a pointer to the key in the list, if found, or returning NULL if not found.

Header File

```
#include <search.h>
```

Declaration

```
void* lfind(const void *key, const void *base,
    unsigned int *num, unsigned int width,
    int (__cdecl *compare)(const void *elem1,
        const void *elem2));
```

- *base* — A pointer to the data in which to search for *key*.
- *compare* — A pointer to the function that will compare values. This function must return 0 if two elements match or return a nonzero value if two elements do not match.
- *elem1* — A pointer to a variable containing the key for which to search.
- *elem2* — A pointer to the element in *base* with which to compare *key*.
- *key* — A pointer to the value for which to search.
- *num* — A pointer to a variable containing the number of elements in *base*.
- *width* — The size of each element in *base*.

Example

The following program demonstrates how to use the `lfind()` function. When run, the program displays the values in a list of integers and then requests the user to enter a value. The program then tells the user whether the value she entered matches a value in the list. The program's output looks something like the following:

```
Values in list:
  1 45 65 28 124 58 4 10

Enter a number: 58
58 is in the list.

Press any key to continue
```

Here is the program source code that produced the output:

```cpp
#include "stdafx.h"
#include <iostream>
#include <search.h>

using namespace std;

int compare(const void *num1, const void *num2)
{
    int val1 = *(int*)num1;
    int val2 = *(int*)num2;

    if (val1 == val2)
        return 0;
    else
        return 1;
}

int main(int argc, char* argv[])
{
    int list[] = {1, 45, 65, 28, 124, 58, 4, 10};
    int num;
    unsigned int count = 8;

    cout << "Values in list: " << endl;
    cout << "  ";
    for (int x=0; x<count; ++x)
        cout << list[x] << " ";

    cout << endl << endl << "Enter a number: ";
```

```
    scanf("%d", &num);

    void* result = lfind(&num, list, &count,
      sizeof(int), compare);

    if (result)
    {
        cout << *(int*)result << " is in the list.";
        cout << endl << endl;
    }
    else
        cout << num << " not in list." << endl << endl;

    return 0;
}
```

CROSS-REFERENCE
See also _lfind(), _lsearch(), bsearch(), and qsort().

limits.h

Standard C Library Header File

The limits.h header file defines a set of constants that define implementation-dependent numerical limits.

Defined Constants

_I128_MAX	ARG_MAX
_I128_MIN	CHAR_BIT
_I16_MAX	CHAR_MAX
_I16_MIN	CHAR_MIN
_I32_MAX	INT_MAX
_I32_MIN	INT_MIN
_I64_MAX	LINK_MAX
_I64_MIN	LONG_MAX
_I8_MAX	LONG_MIN
_I8_MIN	MAX_CANON
_POSIX_ARG_MAX	MAX_INPUT

_POSIX_CHILD_MAX	MB_LEN_MAX
_POSIX_LINK_MAX	NAME_MAX
_POSIX_MAX_CANON	NGROUPS_MAX
_POSIX_MAX_INPUT	OPEN_MAX
_POSIX_NAME_MAX	PATH_MAX
_POSIX_NGROUPS_MAX	PIPE_BUF
_POSIX_OPEN_MAX	SCHAR_MAX
_POSIX_PATH_MAX	SCHAR_MIN
_POSIX_PIPE_BUF	SHRT_MAX
_POSIX_SSIZE_MAX	SHRT_MIN
_POSIX_STREAM_MAX	SSIZE_MAX
_POSIX_TZNAME_MAX	STREAM_MAX
_UI128_MAX	TZNAME_MAX
_UI16_MAX	UCHAR_MAX
_UI32_MAX	UINT_MAX
_UI64_MAX	ULONG_MAX
_UI8_MAX	USHRT_MAX

list

Template Class

The list template class represents a bi-directional linked list. The list of elments is of varying length.

Class Declaration

```
template<class T, class A = allocator<T> >
    class list {
public:
    typedef A allocator_type;
    typedef A::size_type size_type;
    typedef A::difference_type difference_type;
    typedef A::reference reference;
    typedef A::const_reference const_reference;
    typedef A::value_type value_type;
    typedef T0 iterator;
    typedef T1 const_iterator;
    typedef reverse_bidirectional_iterator<iterator,
```

```
            value_type, reference, A::pointer,
                difference_type> reverse_iterator;
    typedef reverse_bidirectional_iterator<const_iterator,
            value_type, const_reference, A::const_pointer,
                difference_type> const_reverse_iterator;
    explicit list(const A& al = A());
    explicit list(size_type n, const T& v = T(),
        const A& al = A());
    list(const list& x);
    list(const_iterator first, const_iterator last,
        const A& al = A());
    iterator begin();
    const_iterator begin() const;
    iterator end();
    iterator end() const;
    reverse_iterator rbegin();
    const_reverse_iterator rbegin() const;
    reverse_iterator rend();
    const_reverse_iterator rend() const;
    void resize(size_type n, T x = T());
    size_type size() const;
    size_type max_size() const;
    bool empty() const;
    A get_allocator() const;
    reference front();
    const_reference front() const;
    reference back();
    const_reference back() const;
    void push_front(const T& x);
    void pop_front();
    void push_back(const T& x);
    void pop_back();
    void assign(const_iterator first, const_iterator last);
    void assign(size_type n, const T& x = T());
    iterator insert(iterator it, const T& x = T());
    void insert(iterator it, size_type n, const T& x);
    void insert(iterator it,
        const_iterator first, const_iterator last);
    void insert(iterator it,
        const T *first, const T *last);
    iterator erase(iterator it);
    iterator erase(iterator first, iterator last);
    void clear();
    void swap(list x);
```

```
        void splice(iterator it, list& x);
        void splice(iterator it, list& x, iterator first);
        void splice(iterator it, list& x,
            iterator first, iterator last);
        void remove(const T& x);
        void remove_if(binder2nd<not_equal_to<T> > pr);
        void unique();
        void unique(not_equal_to<T> pr);
        void merge(list& x);
        void merge(list& x, greater<T> pr);
        void sort();
        template<class Pred>
            void sort(greater<T> pr);
        void reverse();
    protected:
        A allocator;
        };
```

Class Members

Table L-4 lists and describes the members of the list template class.

Table L-4 Members of the list Template Class

Member	Description
allocator_type	A synonym for the template's A parameter.
assign()	Assigns values to the elements of the list.
back()	Gets a reference to the last element in the list.
begin()	Returns a bi-directional iterator that points to the list's first elment.
clear()	Removes all elements from the list.
const_iterator	Object type for a constant bi-directional iterator.
const_reference	Refers to an element reference.
const_reverse_iterator	Object type for a constant reverse iterator.
difference_type	Represents the difference between two element addresses.
empty()	Returns true if the list is empty.
end()	Returns a bi-directional iterator that points to the next element beyond the end of the sequence.
erase()	Erases an element.
front()	Gets a reference to the first element in the list.
get_allocator()	Returns the allocator.

Continued

Table L-4 *Continued*

Member	Description
insert()	Inserts an element into the list.
iterator	Object type for a bi-directional iterator.
max_size()	Returns the maximum possible size of a list.
merge()	Merges one list into another.
pop_back()	Removes the last element in the list.
pop_front()	Removes the first element in the list.
push_back()	Adds an element to the end of the list.
push_front()	Adds an element to the front of the list.
rbegin()	Returns a reverse bi-directional iterator that points to the next element beyond the end of the sequence.
reference	A synonym for A as an element reference.
remove()	Removes specified elements from the list.
rend()	Returns a reverse bi-directional iterator that points to the sequence's first element.
resize()	Sets the size of the list to a given value.
reverse()	Reverses the order of the elements that comprise the list.
reverse_iterator	Object type for a reverse bi-directional iterator.
size()	Returns the length of the list.
size_type	Represents an unsigned integer used to represent the size of the list.
sort()	Sorts the elements of the list.
splice	Moves specified elements of a list to another list.
swap()	Swaps one list with another.
unique()	Removes non-unique elements from the list.
value_type	Represents a data type for an element in the set.

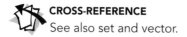

CROSS-REFERENCE
See also set and vector.

locale

Standard C++ Library Header File

The locale C++ header file defines a set of template classes and template functions for managing locale information.

Defined Template Classes

codecvt	money_get
codecvt_base	money_put
codecvt_byname	moneypunct
collate	moneypunct_byname
collate_byname	num_get
ctype	num_put
ctype_base	numpunct
ctype_byname	numpunct_byname
has_facet	time_base
locale	time_get
messages	time_get_byname
messages_base	time_put
messages_byname	time_put_byname
money_base	use_facet

Defined Template Functions

isalnum()	ispunct()
isalpha()	isspace()
iscntrl()	isupper()
isdigit()	isxdigit()
isgraph()	tolower()
islower()	toupper()
isprint()	

locale.h

Standard C Library Header File

The locale.h header file defines constants, functions, type definitions, and structures used to manage locale information.

Defined Constants

_CRTAPI1	LC_MIN
LC_ALL	LC_MONETARY
LC_COLLATE	LC_NUMERIC
LC_CTYPE	LC_TIME
LC_MAX	NULL

Defined Functions

```
_wsetlocale()
localeconv()
setlocale()
```

Defined Type Definitions

```
wchar_t
```

Defined Structures

```
struct lconv {
    char *decimal_point;
    char *thousands_sep;
    char *grouping;
    char *int_curr_symbol;
    char *currency_symbol;
    char *mon_decimal_point;
    char *mon_thousands_sep;
    char *mon_grouping;
    char *positive_sign;
    char *negative_sign;
    char int_frac_digits;
    char frac_digits;
    char p_cs_precedes;
    char p_sep_by_space;
    char n_cs_precedes;
    char n_sep_by_space;
    char p_sign_posn;
    char n_sign_posn;
};
```

Defined Macros

```
_CRTIMP
```

localtime()

Function

The `localtime()` function converts a time value to a `tm` structure, correcting for local time. The function returns a pointer to the `tm` structure containing the result or returns `NULL` if the given date precedes 1/1/1970. The `tm` structure is defined as follows:

```
struct tm {
    int tm_sec;     /* Seconds after the minute   */
    int tm_min;     /* Minutes after the hour     */
    int tm_hour;    /* Hours since midnight        */
    int tm_mday;    /* Day of the month           */
    int tm_mon;     /* Months since January       */
    int tm_year;    /* Years since 1900           */
    int tm_wday;    /* Days since Sunday          */
    int tm_yday;    /* Days since January 1       */
    int tm_isdst;   /* Daylight savings time flag */
};
```

Header Files

```
#include <time.h>
```

Declaration

```
struct tm* localtime(const time_t *timer);
```

- *timer* — A pointer to the time value to convert.

Example

The following program demonstrates how to use the `localtime()` function. When run, the program gets a time value from the system, converts it to a `tm` structure, and displays the results. The program's output looks something like the following:

```
Getting time value...
Converting time value...
```

```
Time: 12:35
Press any key to continue
```

Here is the program source code that produced the output:

```
#include "stdafx.h"
#include <iostream>
#include <time.h>

using namespace std;

int main(int argc, char* argv[])
{
    time_t timeVal;

    cout << "Getting time value..." << endl;
    time(&timeVal);
    cout << "Converting time value..." << endl;
    struct tm* locTime = localtime(&timeVal);
    if (locTime)
    {
        cout << "Time: " << locTime->tm_hour;
        cout << ":" << locTime->tm_min << endl;
    }
    else
        cout << "Could not convert time value." << endl;

    return 0;
}
```

CROSS-REFERENCE
See also _ftime(), _futime(), _strdate(), _strtime(), _utime(), _wasctime(), _wctime(), _wstrdate(), _wstrtime(), _wutime(), asctime(), clock(), ctime(), difftime(), gmtime(), mktime(), strftime(), time(), and wcsftime().

locking()

Function

The locking() function locks the requested number of bytes in a file, making those bytes inaccessible to other processes and returning 0 if successful or −1 if an error occurs. The current position of the file pointer indicates the first byte to be locked.

Header Files

```
#include <io.h>
#include <sys/locking.h>
```

Declaration

```
int locking(int handle, int mode, long nbytes);
```

- *handle* — The file handle of the file to lock.
- *mode* — The locking mode, which can be one of the values from Table L-5.
- *nbytes* — The number of bytes to lock in the file.

Table L-5 Locking Modes for locking()

Mode	Description
LK_LOCK	Locks the given number of bytes, and, if the lock fails, retries ten times, after which the function returns an error.
LK_NBLCK	Locks the given number of bytes, and, if the lock fails, returns an error.
LK_NBRLCK	Performs the same function as LK_NBLCK.
LK_RLCK	Performs the same function as LK_LOCK.
LK_UNLCK	Unlocks the given number of locked bytes.

Example

The following program demonstrates how to use the locking() function. When run, the program opens a file, locks 128 bytes in the file, and then unlocks the bytes, displaying messages as it goes. The program's output looks something like the following:

```
Opening the locking.cpp file...
File opened successfully.
Now locking 128 bytes in file...
128 bytes locked successfully.
Now unlocking bytes...
Bytes now unlocked.

Press any key to continue
```

Here is the program source code that produced the output:

```cpp
#include "stdafx.h"
#include <iostream>
#include <io.h>
#include <sys/stat.h>
#include <sys/locking.h>
#include <share.h>
#include <fcntl.h>

using namespace std;

int main(int argc, char* argv[])
{
    cout << "Opening the locking.cpp file..." << endl;
    int fileHandle = _sopen("locking.cpp",
        O_RDWR, SH_DENYNO, S_IREAD | S_IWRITE);

    if (fileHandle != -1 )
    {
        cout << "File opened successfully." << endl;
        cout << "Now locking 128 bytes in file..." << endl;
        int result = locking(fileHandle, LK_NBLCK, 128L);
        if(result != -1 )
        {
            cout << "128 bytes locked successfully." << endl;
            cout << "Now unlocking bytes..." << endl;
            locking(fileHandle, LK_UNLCK, 128L);
            cout << "Bytes now unlocked." << endl;
        }
        else
            cout << "Could not lock bytes." << endl;
    }
    else
        cout << "Could not open file." << endl;

    cout << endl;

    _close(fileHandle);

    return 0;
}
```

CROSS-REFERENCE
See also _access(), _chmod(), _chsize(), _filelength(), _fstat(), _fstati64(), _fullpath(), _get_osfhandle(), _isatty(), _locking(), _makepath(), _mktemp(), _open_osfhandle(), _setmode(), _splitpath(), _stat(), _stati64(), _umask(), _unlink(), _waccess(), _wchmod(), _wfullpath(), _wmakepath(), _wmktemp(), _wremove(), _wrename(), _wsplitpath(), _wstat(), _wstati64(), _wunlink(), remove(), and rename().

log()

Function

The log() function calculates the natural logarithm of a specified value.

Header Files

```
#include <math.h>
```

Declaration

```
double log(double x);
```

- x — The value for which to calculate the logarithm.

Example

The following program demonstrates how to use the log() function. When run, the program requests a value and then displays the logarithm of the value. The program's output looks something like the following:

```
Enter a value:
10
Result = 2.30259

Press any key to continue
```

Here is the program source code that produced the output:

```
#include "stdafx.h"
#include <math.h>
#include <iostream>

using namespace std;
```

```
int main(int argc, char* argv[])
{
    float x;

    cout << "Enter a value: " << endl;
    scanf("%f", &x);
    double result = log(x);
    cout << "Result = " << result << endl << endl;

    return 0;
}
```

CROSS-REFERENCE

See also _cabs(), _cabsl(), _hypot(), abs(), acos(), asin(), atan(), atan2(), ceil(), cos(), cosh(), div(), exp(), fabs(), fabsf(), fabsl(), floor(), fmod(), frexp(), labs(), ldexp(), ldexpl(), ldiv(), log10(), log10f(), log10l(), logf(), logl(), pow(), sin(), sinh(), sqrt(), tan(), and tanh().

log10()

Function

The log10() function calculates the base-10 logarithm of a specified value.

Header Files

```
#include <math.h>
```

Declaration

```
double log10(double x);
```

- *x* — The value for which to calculate the logarithm.

Example

The following program demonstrates how to use the log10() function. When run, the program requests a value and then displays the logarithm of the value. The program's output looks something like the following:

```
Enter a value:
10
```

```
Result = 1

Press any key to continue
```

Here is the program source code that produced the output:

```cpp
#include "stdafx.h"
#include <math.h>
#include <iostream>

using namespace std;

int main(int argc, char* argv[])
{
    float x;

    cout << "Enter a value: " << endl;
    scanf("%f", &x);
    double result = log10(x);
    cout << "Result = " << result << endl << endl;

    return 0;
}
```

CROSS-REFERENCE
See also _cabs(), _cabsl(), _hypot(), abs(), acos(), asin(), atan(), atan2(), ceil(), cos(), cosh(), div(), exp(), fabs(), fabsf(), fabsl(), floor(), fmod(), frexp(), labs(), ldexp(), ldexpl(), ldiv(), log(), pow(), sin(), sinh(), sqrt(), tan(), and tanh().

log10f()

Function

The `log10f()` function calculates the base-10 logarithm of a specified value, returning the result as a `float`.

NOTE
Borland does not support this function.

Header Files

```cpp
#include <math.h>
```

Declaration

```
float log10f(float x);
```

- x—The value for which to calculate the logarithm.

Example

The following program demonstrates how to use the `log10f()` function. When run, the program requests a value and then displays the logarithm of the value. The program's output looks something like the following:

```
Enter a value:
10
Result = 1

Press any key to continue
```

Here is the program source code that produced the output:

```cpp
#include "stdafx.h"
#include <math.h>
#include <iostream>

using namespace std;

int main(int argc, char* argv[])
{
    float x;

    cout << "Enter a value: " << endl;
    scanf("%f", &x);
    float result = log10f(x);
    cout << "Result = " << result << endl << endl;

    return 0;
}
```

CROSS-REFERENCE

See also _cabs(), _cabsl(), _hypot(), abs(), acos(), asin(), atan(), atan2(), ceil(), cos(), cosh(), div(), exp(), fabs(), fabsf(), fabsl(), floor(), fmod(), frexp(), labs(), ldexp(), ldexpl(), ldiv(), log(), log10(), log10l(), pow(), sin(), sinh(), sqrt(), tan(), and tanh().

log10l()

Function

The log10l() function calculates the base-10 logarithm of a specified value, returning the result as a long double.

Header Files

```
#include <math.h>
```

Declaration

```
long double log10l(long double x);
```

- *x* — The value for which to calculate the logarithm.

Example

The following program demonstrates how to use the log10l() function. When run, the program requests a value and then displays the logarithm of the value. The program's output looks something like the following:

```
Enter a value:
10
Result = 1

Press any key to continue
```

Here is the program source code that produced the output:

```
#include "stdafx.h"
#include <math.h>
#include <iostream>

using namespace std;

int main(int argc, char* argv[])
{
    float x;

    cout << "Enter a value: " << endl;
    scanf("%f", &x);
    long double result = log10l(x);
```

```
        cout << "Result = " << result << endl << endl;

        return 0;
}
```

CROSS-REFERENCE
See also _cabs(), _cabsl(), _hypot(), abs(), acos(), asin(), atan(), atan2(), ceil(), cos(),
cosh(), div(), exp(), fabs(), fabsf(), fabsl(), floor(), fmod(), frexp(), labs(), ldexp(),
ldexpl(), ldiv(), log(), log10(), log10f(), pow(), sin(), sinh(), sqrt(), tan(), and tanh().

logf()

Function

The logf() function calculates the natural logarithm of a specified value,
returning the result as a float.

NOTE
Borland does not support this function.

Header Files

```
#include <math.h>
```

Declaration

```
float logf(float x);
```

- *x* — The value for which to calculate the logarithm.

Example

The following program demonstrates how to use the logf() function. When
run, the program requests a value and then displays the logarithm of the value.
The program's output looks something like the following:

```
Enter a value:
10
Result = 2.30259

Press any key to continue
```

Here is the program source code that produced the output:

```
#include "stdafx.h"
#include <math.h>
#include <iostream>

using namespace std;

int main(int argc, char* argv[])
{
    float x;

    cout << "Enter a value: " << endl;
    scanf("%f", &x);
    float result = logf(x);
    cout << "Result = " << result << endl << endl;

    return 0;
}
```

CROSS-REFERENCE
See also _cabs(), _cabsl(), _hypot(), abs(), acos(), asin(), atan(), atan2(), ceil(), cos(), cosh(), div(), exp(), fabs(), fabsf(), fabsl(), floor(), fmod(), frexp(), labs(), ldexp(), ldexpl(), ldiv(), log(), log10(), log10f(), log10l(), logl(), pow(), sin(), sinh(), sqrt(), tan(), and tanh().

logl()

Function

The `logl()` function calculates the natural logarithm of a specified value, returning the result as a `long double`.

Header Files

```
#include <math.h>
```

Declaration

```
long double logl(long double x);
```

- *x* — The value for which to calculate the logarithm.

Example

The following program demonstrates how to use the `logl()` function. When run, the program requests a value and then displays the logarithm of the value. The program's output looks something like the following:

```
Enter a value:
10
Result = 2.30259

Press any key to continue
```

Here is the program source code that produced the output:

```
#include "stdafx.h"
#include <math.h>
#include <iostream>

using namespace std;

int main(int argc, char* argv[])
{
    float x;

    cout << "Enter a value: " << endl;
    scanf("%f", &x);
    long double result = logl(x);
    cout << "Result = " << result << endl << endl;

    return 0;
}
```

CROSS-REFERENCE
See also _cabs(), _cabsl(), _hypot(), abs(), acos(), asin(), atan(), atan2(), ceil(), cos(), cosh(), div(), exp(), fabs(), fabsf(), fabsl(), floor(), fmod(), frexp(), labs(), ldexp(), ldexpl(), ldiv(), log(), log10(), log10f(), log10l(), logf(), pow(), sin(), sinh(), sqrt(), tan(), and tanh().

long

Keyword

The `long` keyword enables a program to define large or more precise values. For example, the following line declares a variable named `longValue` as a long integer, which can hold values from –2,147,483,648 to 2,147,483,647:

```
long longValue;
```

On the other hand, an unsigned long integer, which the following line declares, can hold values from 0 to 4,294,967,295:

```
unsigned long longValue;
```

CROSS-REFERENCE
See also __int16, __int32, __int64, __int8, char, double, float, int, short, and unsigned.

longjmp()

Function

The longjmp() function restores the current stack environment (and thus a program's status) saved by the setjmp() function.

Header File

```
#include <setjmp.h>
```

Declaration

```
void longjmp(jmp_buf env, int value);
```

- *env* — The area in which the stack environment is saved.
- *value* — The value that should be returned to setjmp().

Example

The following program demonstrates how to use the longjmp() function. When run, the program saves the stack environment and then calls a function that restores the stack environment. Restoring the stack environment causes program execution to jump back to the setjmp() call, which now returns the value specified in the call to longjmp(). The program's output looks like the following:

```
Saving stack environment...
Calling MyFunc()...
Press a key to restore stack environment...
setjmp() returned 1
Press any key to continue
```

Here is the program source code that produced the output:

```cpp
#include "stdafx.h"
#include <conio.h>
#include <setjmp.h>
#include <iostream>

using namespace std;

void MyFunc(jmp_buf jmpbuf)
{
    cout << "Press a key to restore ";
    cout << "stack environment..." << endl;
    getch();
    longjmp(jmpbuf, 1);
}

int main(int argc, char* argv[])
{
    jmp_buf jmpbuf;

    cout << "Saving stack environment..." << endl;
    int result = setjmp(jmpbuf);
    if (result != 0)
    {
        cout << "setjmp() returned " << result << endl;
        exit(0);
    }

    cout << "Calling MyFunc()..." << endl;
    MyFunc(jmpbuf);

    return 0;

    return 0;
}
```

CROSS-REFERENCE
See also setjmp().

lsearch()

Function

The lsearch() function searches a list of values for a given key, returning a pointer to the matching value in the list. If the key is not found, lsearch() adds the key to the end of the list and returns a pointer to the new list entry, and increments the element count found in the *num* argument.

Header File

```
#include <search.h>
```

Declaration

```
void* lsearch(const void *key, void *base,
    unsigned int *num, unsigned int width,
    int (__cdecl *compare)(const void *elem1,
        const void *elem2));
```

- *base* — A pointer to the data in which to search for *key*.
- *compare* — A pointer to the function that will compare values. This function must return 0 if two elements match or return a nonzero value if two elements do not match.
- *elem1* — A pointer to a variable containing the key for which to search.
- *elem2* — A pointer to the element in *base* with which to compare *key*.
- *key* — A pointer to the value for which to search.
- *num* — A pointer to a variable containing the number of elements in *base*.
- *width* — The size of each element in *base*.

Example

The following program demonstrates how to use the lsearch() function. When run, the program displays the values in a list of integers and then requests the user to enter a value. The program then tells the user whether the value she entered matches a value in the list, or else adds the value to the list. The program's output looks something like the following:

```
Values in list:
 1 45 65 28 124 58 4 10
```

```
Enter a number: 99
99 added to list.

Values in list:
  1 45 65 28 124 58 4 10 99

Press any key to continue
```

Here is the program source code that produced the output:

```cpp
#include "stdafx.h"
#include <iostream>
#include <search.h>

using namespace std;

int compare(const void *num1, const void *num2)
{
    int val1 = *(int*)num1;
    int val2 = *(int*)num2;

    if (val1 == val2)
        return 0;
    else
        return 1;
}

void displayValues(int* list, int count)
{
    cout << "Values in list: " << endl;
    cout << "  ";
    for (int x=0; x<count; ++x)
        cout << list[x] << " ";
    cout << endl;
}

int main(int argc, char* argv[])
{
    int list[20] = {1, 45, 65, 28, 124, 58, 4, 10};
    int num;
    unsigned int count = 8;

    displayValues(list, count);
```

```
        cout << endl << "Enter a number: ";
        scanf("%d", &num);

        void* result = lsearch(&num, list, &count,
            sizeof(int), compare);

        if (count == 8)
        {
            cout << *(int*)result << " is in the list.";
            cout << endl << endl;
        }
        else
        {
            cout << *(int*)result << " added to list.";
            cout << endl << endl;
            displayValues(list, count);
            cout << endl;
        }

        return 0;
}
```

CROSS-REFERENCE
See also _lfind(), _lsearch(), bsearch(), and qsort().

lseek()

Function

The lseek() function sets the position of the file pointer, returning the new offset if successful or returning –1 if unsuccessful.

Header File

```
#include <io.h>
```

Declaration

```
long lseek(int handle, long offset, int origin);
```

- *handle*—The handle of an open file.

- *offset* — The number of bytes from *origin* to offset the file pointer.
- *origin* — The position from which the offset should be added. This can be one of the values from Table L-6.

Table L-6 Origin Values for the lseek() Function

Value	Description
SEEK_CUR	Seek from the current position.
SEEK_END	Seek from the end of the file.
SEEK_SET	Seek from the beginning of the file.

Example

The following program demonstrates how to use the lseek() function. When run, the program opens a file and sets the file position to 50, displaying messages as it goes. The program's output looks something like the following:

```
Opening the file...
File opened successfully.
Seeking to new position...
Seek was successful.
Press any key to continue
```

Here is the program source code that produced the output:

```cpp
#include "stdafx.h"
#include <stdio.h>
#include <fcntl.h>
#include <io.h>
#include <iostream>

using namespace std;

int main(int argc, char* argv[])
{
    fpos_t pos = 50;

    cout << "Opening the file..." << endl;
    int fileHandle = open("lseek.cpp", _O_RDONLY);

    if (fileHandle == -1)
```

```
            cout << "File open error" << endl;
        else
        {
            cout << "File opened successfully." << endl;
            cout << "Seeking to new position..." << endl;
            long result = lseek(fileHandle, pos, SEEK_SET);

            if (result != -1)
                cout << "Seek was successful." << endl;
            else
                cout << "Seek was unsuccessful." << endl;

            close(fileHandle);
        }

        return 0;
    }
```

CROSS-REFERENCE

See also _close(), _creat(), _fcloseall(), _fdopen(), _fgetchar(), _fgetwchar(), _fileno(), _flushall(), _fputwchar(), _fsopen(), _getw(), _getws(), _lseek(), _lseeki64(), _open(), _putw(), _putws(), _read(), _rmtmp(), _tempnam(), _wcreat(), _wfdopen(), _wfopen(), _wfreopen(), _wfsopen(), _wopen(), _wtempnam(), _wtmpnam(), clearerr(), eof(), fclose(), feof(), ferror(), fflush(), fgetc(), fgetpos(), fgets(), fgetwc(), fgetws(), fopen(), fprintf(), fputc(), fputchar(), fputs(), fputwc(), fputws(), fread(), freopen(), fscanf(), fsetpos(), ftell(), fwprintf(), fwrite(), fwscanf(), getc(), getchar(), gets(), getwc(), getwchar(), lseek(), putc(), putch(), putchar(), puts(), putwc(), putwchar(), rewind(), setbuf(), setvbuf(), tmpfile(), tmpnam(), ungetc(), ungetch(), ungetwc(), and write().

ltoa()

Function

The ltoa() function converts a long integer value to a string.

Header File

```
#include <stdlib.h>
```

Declaration

```
char* ltoa(long value, char* string, int radix);
```

- *radix* — The value number base (typically 10).
- *string* — A pointer to the buffer in which to store the string.
- *value* — The value to convert.

Example

The following program demonstrates how to use the `ltoa()` function. When run, the program converts a long-integer value into several number-base formats and displays the results. The program's output looks like the following:

```
This is 19,564 in base 10: 19564
This is 19,564 in base 16: 4c6c
This is 19,564 in base 2: 100110001101100
This is 19,564 in base 8: 46154

Press any key to continue
```

Here is the program source code that produced the output:

```
#include "stdafx.h"
#include <iostream>
#include <stdlib.h>

using namespace std;

int main(int argc, char* argv[])
{
    char str[81];
    long value = 19564;

    char* result = ltoa(value, str, 10);
    cout << "This is 19,564 in base 10: ";
    cout << result << endl;

    result = ltoa(value, str, 16);
    cout << "This is 19,564 in base 16: ";
    cout << result << endl;

    result = ltoa(value, str, 2);
    cout << "This is 19,564 in base 2: ";
    cout << result << endl;
```

```
        result = ltoa(value, str, 8);
        cout << "This is 19,564 in base 8: ";
        cout << result << endl;
        cout << endl;

        return 0;
    }
```

CROSS-REFERENCE

See also _ecvt(), _fcvt(), _gcvt(), _i64toa(), _i64tow(), _itow(), _ltoa(), _ltow(), _ui64toa(), _ui64tow(), itoa(), and ultoa().

_makepath()

Function

The _makepath() function assembles a full path from various path elements.

Header File

```
#include <stdlib.h>
```

Declaration

```
void _makepath(char *path, const char *drive,
    const char *dir, const char *fname,
    const char *ext);
```

- *dir* — The final path's directory element.
- *drive* — The final path's drive letter.
- *ext* — The final path's file name extension element.
- *fname* — The final path's file name element.
- *path* — A pointer to the character array that will hold the final path.

Example

The following program demonstrates how to use the _makepath() function. When run, the program creates and displays the full path for the various given elements. The program's output looks like this:

```
Full Path:
c:\Windows\System\sysedit.exe
Press any key to continue
```

Here is the program source code that produced the output:

```cpp
#include "stdafx.h"
#include <stdlib.h>
#include <iostream>

using namespace std;

int main(int argc, char* argv[])
{
    char fullPath[_MAX_PATH];
    char drive[] = "c";
    char dir[] = "\\Windows\\System";
    char fileName[] = "sysedit";
    char ext[] = "exe";

    _makepath(fullPath, drive, dir, fileName, ext);
    if (fullPath == NULL)
        cout << "Error in path" << endl;
    else
    {
        cout << "Full Path: " << endl;
        cout << fullPath << endl;
    }

    return 0;
}
```

CROSS-REFERENCE

See also _fullpath(), _getcwd(), _getdcwd(), _splitpath(), _wfullpath(), _wgetcwd(), _wgetdcwd(), _wmakepath(), and _wsplitpath().

_matherr()

function

The _matherr() function enables a program to respond to mathematical run-time errors.

Header File

```cpp
#include <math.h>
```

Declaration

```
int _matherr(struct _exception *except);
```

- *except* — A pointer to the _exception structure that holds information about the error.

Example

The following program demonstrates how to use the _matherr() function. When run, the program passes an illegal value to the sqrt() function, which causes a mathematical error. This error causes the _matherr() function to be called, where the error is handled, correcting the illegal value. Notice how setting the _exception object's retval member determines the corrected result of the original call to the sqrt() function in main(). The program's output looks like this:

```
Argument domain type error
Can't get the square root of a negative number.
Changing arg1 to positive.
Result = 5
Press any key to continue
```

Here is the program source code that produced the output:

```
#include "stdafx.h"
#include <math.h>
#include <iostream>

using namespace std;

int _matherr( struct _exception *except )
{
    double newValue;
    int result;

    switch (except->type)
    {
    case DOMAIN:
        cout << "Argument domain type error" << endl;
        result = strcmp("sqrt", except->name);
        if (!result)
        {
            if (except->arg1 < 0)
            {
                cout << "Can't get the square root ";
                cout << "of a negative number." << endl;
```

```
                          cout << "Changing arg1 to positive." << endl;
                          newValue = -(except->arg1);
                      }
                  else
                      newValue = except->arg1;
                  except->retval = sqrt(newValue);
              }
          return 1;
      case SING:
          cout << "Argument singularity type error" << endl;
          // Handle the error here.
          return 1;
      case OVERFLOW:
          cout << "Overflow range type error" << endl;
          // Handle the error here.
          return 1;
      case PLOSS:
          cout << "Partial significance type error" << endl;
          // Handle the error here.
          return 1;
      case TLOSS:
          cout << "Total significance type error " << endl;
          // Handle the error here.
          return 1;
      case UNDERFLOW:
          cout << "Underflow type error" << endl;
          // Handle the error here.
          return 1;
      }

      return 0;
}

int main(int argc, char* argv[])
{
    double val = -25.0;
    double result = sqrt(val);
    cout << "Result = " << result << endl;

    return 0;
}
```

CROSS-REFERENCE
See also _cabs(), _cabsl(), _hypot(), abs(), acos(), asin(), atan(), atan2, ceil(), cos(),
cosh(), div(), exp(), fabs(), fabsf(), fabsl(), floor(), fmod(), frexp(), labs(), ldexpl(),
ldiv(), log(), log10(), pow(), sin(), sinh(), sqrt(), tan(), and tanh().

_matherrl()

function

The _matherrl() function is the long-double version of the _matherr() function, which enables a program to respond to mathematical run-time errors.

Header File

```
#include <math.h>
```

Declaration

```
int _matherrl(struct _exceptionl *except);
```

- *except*—A pointer to the _exceptionl structure that holds
  information about the error.

Example

The following example demonstrates how to write the _matherrl() function.

```
int _matherrl(struct _exceptionl *except)
{
    switch (except->type)
    {
    case DOMAIN:
        cout << "Domain type error" << endl;
        // Handle the error here.
        return 1;
    case SING:
        cout << "Argument singularity type error" << endl;
        // Handle the error here.
        return 1;
    case OVERFLOW:
        cout << "Overflow range type error" << endl;
        // Handle the error here.
        return 1;
```

```
case PLOSS:
    cout << "Partial significance type error" << endl;
    // Handle the error here.
    return 1;
case TLOSS:
    cout << "Total significance type error " << endl;
    // Handle the error here.
    return 1;
case UNDERFLOW:
    cout << "Underflow type error" << endl;
    // Handle the error here.
    return 1;
}

return 0;
}
```

CROSS-REFERENCE
See also _cabs(), _cabsl(), _hypot(), _matherr(), abs(), acos(), asin(), atan(), atan2(), ceil(), cos(), cosh(), div(), exp(), fabs(), fabsf(), fabsl(), floor(), fmod(), frexp(), labs(), ldexpl(), ldiv(), log(), log10(), pow(), sin(), sinh(), sqrt(), tan(), and tanh().

_mbbtombc()

Function

The _mbbtombc() function converts a single-byte multibyte character to a multibyte character, returning the converted character, or, if unable to perform the conversion, returning the original character.

Header Files

```
#include <mbstring.h>
```

Declaration

```
unsigned short _mbbtombc(unsigned short c);
```

- c — The character value to convert.

Example

The following program demonstrates how to use the _mbbtombc() function. When run, the program converts the values of an array and displays the results. The program's output looks like this:

```
Converting values...
Conversion on value 1 not performed.
Conversion on value 2 not performed.
Conversion on value 3 not performed.
Conversion on value 4 not performed.
Conversion on value 5 not performed.
Conversion on value 53428 performed.
    Converted to 65460.
Conversion on value 52429 performed.
    Converted to 65485.
Conversion on value 52410 performed.
    Converted to 65466.
Conversion on value 52411 performed.
    Converted to 65467.
Conversion on value 52412 performed.
    Converted to 65468.
Press any key to continue
```

Here is the program source code that produced the output:

```cpp
#include "stdafx.h"
#include <mbstring.h>
#include <mbctype.h>
#include <iostream>

using namespace std;

int main(int argc, char* argv[])
{
    int x;
    unsigned short dat[] =
    {
        1, 2, 3, 4, 5,
        53428, 52429, 52410, 52411, 52412
    };

    cout << "Converting values..." << endl;

    for (x=0; x<10; ++x)
    {
```

```
            char result = _mbbtombc(dat[x]);
            if (result == dat[x])
            {
                cout << "Conversion on value ";
                cout << dat[x] << " not performed." << endl;
            }
            else
            {
                cout << "Conversion on value ";
                cout << dat[x] << " performed." << endl;
                cout << "    Converted to ";
                cout << (unsigned short)result << "." << endl;
            }
        }

        return 0;
    }
```

CROSS-REFERENCE

See also _ismbbalnum(), _ismbbalpha(), _ismbbgraph(), _ismbbkalnum(), _ismbbkana(), _ismbbkprint(), _ismbbkpunct(), _ismbblead(), _ismbbprint(), _ismbbpunct(), _ismbbtrail(), _mbbtype(), _mbccpy(), _mbcjistojms(), _mbcjmstojis(), _mbclen(), _mbctohira(), _mbctokata(), _mbctolower(), _mbctombb(), _mbctoupper(), _mbsbtype, _mbscat(), _mbschr(), _mbscmp(), _mbscoll(), _mbscpy(), _mbscspn(), _mbsdec(), _mbsdup(), _mbsicmp(), _mbsicoll(), _mbsinc(), _mbslen(), _mbslwr(), _mbsnbcat(), _mbsnbcmp(), _mbsnbcnt(), _mbsnbcoll(), _mbsnbcpy(), _mbsnbicmp(), _mbsnbicoll(), _mbsnbset(), _mbsncat(), _mbsnccnt(), _mbsncmp(), _mbsncoll(), _mbsncpy(), _mbsnextc(), _mbsnicmp(), _mbsnicoll(), _mbsninc(), _mbsnset(), _mbspbrk(), _mbsrchr(), _mbsrev(), _mbsset(), _mbsspn(), _mbsspnp(), _mbsstr(), _mbstok(), _mbstrlen(), _mbsupr(), isleadbyte(), mblen(), mbstowcs(), and mbtowc().

_mbbtype()

Function

The _mbbtype() function tests a character value to determine whether it is a valid single-byte character, valid multibyte-character lead byte, or valid multibyte-character trailing byte. The function returns the _MBC_SINGLE, _MBC_LEAD, _MBC_TRAIL, or _MBC_ILLEGAL values.

Header Files

```
#include <mbstring.h>
#include <mbctype.h>
```

Declaration

```
int _mbbtype(unsigned char c, int type);
```

- *c* — The character value to test.
- *type* — The type of value for which to test, where 1 tests for a trailing byte and any other value tests for a single or lead byte.

Example

The following program demonstrates how to use the _mbbtype() function. When run, the program tests the bytes of a string (including the null at the end of the string) and displays the results. The program's output looks like this:

```
Testing characters in the string...
Valid single byte: 84
Valid single byte: 104
Valid single byte: 105
Valid single byte: 115
Valid single byte: 32
Valid single byte: 105
Valid single byte: 115
Valid single byte: 32
Valid single byte: 97
Valid single byte: 32
Valid single byte: 116
Valid single byte: 101
Valid single byte: 115
Valid single byte: 116
Invalid byte: 0
Press any key to continue
```

Here is the program source code that produced the output:

```
#include "stdafx.h"
#include <mbstring.h>
#include <mbctype.h>
#include <iostream>

using namespace std;
```

```
int main(int argc, char* argv[])
{
    int x;
    char str[] = "This is a test";

    cout << "Testing characters in the string..." << endl;

    for (x=0; x<sizeof(str); ++x)
    {
        int result = _mbbtype(str[x], 0);
        if (result == _MBC_SINGLE)
        {
            cout << "Valid single byte: ";
            cout << (int)str[x] << endl;
        }
        else if (result == _MBC_LEAD)
        {
            cout << "Valid lead byte: ";
            cout << (int)str[x] << endl;
        }
        else
        {
            cout << "Invalid byte: ";
            cout << (int)str[x] << endl;
        }
    }

    return 0;
}
```

CROSS-REFERENCE

See also _ismbbalnum(), _ismbbalpha(), _ismbbgraph(), _ismbbkalnum(), _ismbbkana(), _ismbbkprint(), _ismbbkpunct(), _ismbblead(), _ismbbprint(), _ismbbpunct(), _ismbbtrail(), _mbbtombc(), _mbccpy(), _mbcjistojms(), _mbcjmstojis(), _mbclen(), _mbctohira(), _mbctokata(), _mbctolower(), _mbctombb(), _mbctoupper(), _mbsbtype, _mbscat(), _mbschr(), _mbscmp(), _mbscoll(), _mbscpy(), _mbscspn(), _mbsdec(), _mbsdup(), _mbsicmp(), _mbsicoll(), _mbsinc(), _mbslen(), _mbslwr(), _mbsnbcat(), _mbsnbcmp(), _mbsnbcnt(), _mbsnbcoll(), _mbsnbcpy(), _mbsnbicmp(), _mbsnbicoll(), _mbsnbset(), _mbsncat(), _mbsnccnt(), _mbsncmp(), _mbsncoll(), _mbsncpy(), _mbsnextc(), _mbsnicmp(), _mbsnicoll(), _mbsninc(), _mbsnset(), _mbspbrk(), _mbsrchr(), _mbsrev(), _mbsset(), _mbsspn(), _mbsspnp(), _mbsstr(), _mbstok(), _mbstrlen(), _mbsupr(), isleadbyte(), mblen(), mbstowcs(), and mbtowc().

_mbccpy()

Function

The _mbccpy() function copies one multibyte character to another. If the source character is invalid (that is, the source character is not the lead byte of a multibyte character), the function does not perform the copy.

Header Files

```
#include <mbctype.h>
```

Declaration

```
void _mbccpy(unsigned char *dest, const unsigned char *src);
```

- *dest* — A pointer to the destination character.
- *src* — A pointer to the source character.

Example

The following program demonstrates how to use the _mbccpy() function. When run, the program copies the character values from one array to another. The program's output looks like this:

```
Copying values...
Copied value A
Copied value B
Copied value C
Copied value D
Copied value E
Copied value F
Copied value G
Copied value H
Copied value I
Copied value J
New data: ABCDEFGHIJ
Press any key to continue
```

Here is the program source code that produced the output:

```
#include "stdafx.h"
#include <mbstring.h>
#include <mbctype.h>
#include <iostream>
```

```cpp
using namespace std;

int main(int argc, char* argv[])
{
    int x;
    unsigned char dat[] =
    {
        65, 66, 67, 68, 69,
        70, 71, 72, 73, 74
    };

    unsigned char newDat[128];
    memset(newDat, 0, sizeof(newDat));

    cout << "Copying values..." << endl;

    for (x=0; x<10; ++x)
    {
        _mbccpy(&newDat[x], &dat[x]);
        if (newDat[x] == 0)
        {
            cout << "Copying of value ";
            cout << dat[x] << " not performed." << endl;
        }
        else
        {
            cout << "Copied value ";
            cout << dat[x] << endl;
        }
    }

    cout << "New data: " << newDat << endl;

    return 0;
}
```

CROSS-REFERENCE

See also _ismbbalnum(), _ismbbalpha(), _ismbbgraph(), _ismbbkalnum(), _ismbbkana(), _ismbbkprint(), _ismbbkpunct(), _ismbblead(), _ismbbprint(), _ismbbpunct(), _ismbbtrail(), _mbbtombc(), _mbbtype(), _mbcjistojms(), _mbcjmstojis(), _mbclen(), _mbctohira(), _mbctokata(), _mbctolower(), _mbctombb(), _mbctoupper(), _mbsbtype, _mbscat(), _mbschr(), _mbscmp(), _mbscoll(), _mbscpy(), _mbscspn(), _mbsdec(), _mbsdup(), _mbsicmp(), _mbsicoll(), _mbsinc(), _mbslen(), _mbslwr(), _mbsnbcat(), _mbsnbcmp(), _mbsnbcnt(), _mbsnbcoll(), _mbsnbcpy(), _mbsnbicmp(), _mbsnbicoll(), _mbsnbset(), _mbsncat(), _mbsnccnt(), _mbsncmp(), _mbsncoll(), _mbsncpy(), _mbsnextc(), _mbsnicmp(), _mbsnicoll(), _mbsninc(), _mbsnset(), _mbspbrk(), _mbsrchr(), _mbsrev(), _mbsset(), _mbsspn(), _mbsspnp(), _mbsstr(), _mbstok(), _mbstrlen(), _mbsupr(), isleadbyte(), mblen(), mbstowcs(), and mbtowc().

_mbcjistojms()

Function

The _mbcjistojms() function converts a JIS (Japan Industry Standard) character to a Shift JIS (Kanji) character, returning the converted character, or returning 0 in the case of an error.

Header Files

```
#include <mbstring.h>
```

Declaration

```
unsigned int _mbcjistojms(unsigned int c);
```

- *c* — The character to convert.

Example

The following program demonstrates how to call the _mbcjistojms() function. When run, the program converts the character values in an array, displaying the results as it goes. The program's output looks like this:

```
Converting values...
Conversion on value 8529 performed.
Conversion on value 8530 performed.
Conversion on value 8531 performed.
Conversion on value 8532 performed.
Conversion on value 8533 performed.
Conversion on value 8534 performed.
Conversion on value 8535 performed.
Conversion on value 8536 performed.
Conversion on value 8537 performed.
Conversion on value 8538 performed.
Press any key to continue
```

Here is the program source code that produced the output:

```
#include "stdafx.h"
#include <mbstring.h>
#include <mbctype.h>
#include <iostream>

using namespace std;

int main(int argc, char* argv[])
{
    int x;
    unsigned int dat[] =
    {
        0x2151, 0x2152, 0x2153, 0x2154, 0x2155,
        0x2156, 0x2157, 0x2158, 0x2159, 0x215a,
    };

    cout << "Converting values..." << endl;

    for (x=0; x<10; ++x)
    {
        unsigned int result = _mbcjistojms(dat[x]);
        if (result == 0)
        {
            cout << "Conversion on value ";
            cout << dat[x] << " not performed." << endl;
        }
        else
        {
            cout << "Conversion on value ";
            cout << dat[x] << " performed." << endl;
        }
    }

    return 0;
}
```

CROSS-REFERENCE

See also _ismbbalnum(), _ismbbalpha(), _ismbbgraph(), _ismbbkalnum(), _ismbbkana(), _ismbbkprint(), _ismbbkpunct(), _ismbblead(), _ismbbprint(), _ismbbpunct(), _ismbbtrail(), _mbbtombc(), _mbbtype(), _mbccpy(), _mbcjmstojis(), _mbclen(), _mbctohira(), _mbctokata(), _mbctolower(), _mbctombb(), _mbctoupper(), _mbsbtype, _mbscat(), _mbschr(), _mbscmp(), _mbscoll(), _mbscpy(), _mbscspn(), _mbsdec(), _mbsdup(), _mbsicmp(), _mbsicoll(), _mbsinc(), _mbslen(), _mbslwr(), _mbsnbcat(), _mbsnbcmp(), _mbsnbcnt(), _mbsnbcoll(), _mbsnbcpy(), _mbsnbicmp(), _mbsnbicoll(), _mbsnbset(), _mbsncat(), _mbsnccnt(), _mbsncmp(), _mbsncoll(), _mbsncpy(), _mbsnextc(), _mbsnicmp(), _mbsnicoll(), _mbsninc(), _mbsnset(), _mbspbrk(), _mbsrchr(), _mbsrev(), _mbsset(), _mbsspn(), _mbsspnp(), _mbsstr(), _mbstok(), _mbstrlen(), _mbsupr(), isleadbyte(), mblen(), mbstowcs(), and mbtowc().

_mbcjmstojis()

Function

The `_mbcjmstojis()` function converts a Shift JIS (Kanji) character to a JIS (Japan Industry Standard) character, returning the converted character, or returning 0 in the case of an error.

Header Files

```
#include <mbstring.h>
```

Declaration

```
unsigned int _mbcjmstojis(unsigned int c);
```

- *c* — The character to convert.

Example

The following program demonstrates how to call the `_mbcjmstojis()` function. When run, the program converts the character values in an array, displaying the results as it goes. The program's output looks like this:

```
Converting values...
Conversion on value 33248 performed.
Conversion on value 33249 performed.
Conversion on value 33250 performed.
Conversion on value 33251 performed.
Conversion on value 33252 performed.
Conversion on value 33253 performed.
Conversion on value 33254 performed.
Conversion on value 33255 performed.
Conversion on value 33256 performed.
Conversion on value 33257 performed.
```

```
Press any key to continue
```

Here is the program source code that produced the output:

```cpp
#include "stdafx.h"
#include <mbstring.h>
#include <mbctype.h>
#include <iostream>

using namespace std;

int main(int argc, char* argv[])
{
    int x;
    unsigned int dat[] =
    {
        0x81e0, 0x81e1, 0x81e2, 0x81e3, 0x81e4,
        0x81e5, 0x81e6, 0x81e7, 0x81e8, 0x81e9
    };

    cout << "Converting values..." << endl;

    for (x=0; x<10; ++x)
    {
        unsigned int result = _mbcjmstojis(dat[x]);
        if (result == 0)
        {
            cout << "Conversion on value ";
            cout << dat[x] << " not performed." << endl;
        }
        else
        {
            cout << "Conversion on value ";
            cout << dat[x] << " performed." << endl;
        }
    }

    return 0;
}
```

CROSS-REFERENCE

See also _ismbbalnum(), _ismbbalpha(), _ismbbgraph(), _ismbbkalnum(), _ismbbkana(), _ismbbkprint(), _ismbbkpunct(), _ismbblead(), _ismbbprint(), _ismbbpunct(), _ismbbtrail(), _mbbtombc(), _mbbtype(), _mbccpy(), _mbcjistojms(), _mbclen(), _mbctohira(), _mbctokata(), _mbctolower(), _mbctombb(), _mbctoupper(), _mbsbtype, _mbscat(), _mbschr(), _mbscmp(), _mbscoll(), _mbscpy(), _mbscspn(), _mbsdec(), _mbsdup(), _mbsicmp(), _mbsicoll(), _mbsinc(), _mbslen(), _mbslwr(), _mbsnbcat(), _mbsnbcmp(), _mbsnbcnt(), _mbsnbcoll(), _mbsnbcpy(), _mbsnbicmp(), _mbsnbicoll(), _mbsnbset(), _mbsncat(), _mbsnccnt(), _mbsncmp(), _mbsncoll(), _mbsncpy(), _mbsnextc(), _mbsnicmp(), _mbsnicoll(), _mbsninc(), _mbsnset(), _mbspbrk(), _mbsrchr(), _mbsrev(), _mbsset(), _mbsspn(), _mbsspnp(), _mbsstr(), _mbstok(), _mbstrlen(), _mbsupr(), isleadbyte(), mblen(), mbstowcs(), and mbtowc().

_mbclen()

Function

The _mbclen() function returns the length of a multibyte character.

Header Files

```
#include <mbstring.h>
```

Declaration

```
size_t _mbclen(const unsigned char *c);
```

- *c*—A pointer to the source character.

Example

The following program demonstrates how to use the _mbclen() function. When run, the program displays the length in bytes of the character values in an array. The program's output looks like this:

```
Testing values...
Length of character A is 1.
Length of character B is 1.
Length of character C is 1.
Length of character D is 1.
Length of character E is 1.
Length of character F is 1.
Length of character G is 1.
Length of character H is 1.
Length of character I is 1.
Length of character J is 1.
Press any key to continue
```

Here is the program source code that produced the output:

```
#include "stdafx.h"
#include <mbstring.h>
#include <mbctype.h>
#include <iostream>

using namespace std;

int main(int argc, char* argv[])
{
    int x;
    unsigned char dat[] =
    {
        65, 66, 67, 68, 69,
        70, 71, 72, 73, 74
    };

    cout << "Testing values..." << endl;

    for (x=0; x<10; ++x)
    {
        size_t result = _mbclen(&dat[x]);
        cout << "Length of character " << dat[x];
        cout << " is " << result << "." << endl;
    }

    return 0;
}
```

CROSS-REFERENCE

See also _ismbbalnum(), _ismbbalpha(), _ismbbgraph(), _ismbbkalnum(), _ismbbkana(), _ismbbkprint(), _ismbbkpunct(), _ismbblead(), _ismbbprint(), _ismbbpunct(), _ismbbtrail(), _mbbtombc(), _mbbtype(), _mbccpy(), _mbcjistojms(), _mbcjmstojis(), _mbctohira(), _mbctokata(), _mbctolower(), _mbctombb(), _mbctoupper(), _mbsbtype, _mbscat(), _mbschr(), _mbscmp(), _mbscoll(), _mbscpy(), _mbscspn(), _mbsdec(), _mbsdup(), _mbsicmp(), _mbsicoll(), _mbsinc(), _mbslen(), _mbslwr(), _mbsnbcat(), _mbsnbcmp(), _mbsnbcnt(), _mbsnbcoll(), _mbsnbcpy(), _mbsnbicmp(), _mbsnbicoll(), _mbsnbset(), _mbsncat(), _mbsnccnt(), _mbsncmp(), _mbsncoll(), _mbsncpy(), _mbsnextc(), _mbsnicmp(), _mbsnicoll(), _mbsninc(), _mbsnset(), _mbspbrk(), _mbsrchr(), _mbsrev(), _mbsset(), _mbsspn(), _mbsspnp(), _mbsstr(), _mbstok(), _mbstrlen(), _mbsupr(), isleadbyte(), mblen(), mbstowcs(), and mbtowc().

_mbctohira()

Function

The _mbctohira() function converts a multibyte katakana character to a multibyte hiragana character, returning the converted character, or returning the original character if the conversion could not be performed.

Header Files

```
#include <mbstring.h>
```

Declaration

```
unsigned int _mbctohira(unsigned int c);
```

- *c*— The character to convert.

Example

The following program demonstrates how to call the _mbctohira() function. When run, the program converts the character values in an array, displaying the results as it goes. The program's output looks like this:

```
Converting values...
result = 33248
result = 33249
result = 33250
result = 33251
result = 33252
result = 33253
result = 33254
result = 33255
result = 33256
result = 33257
Press any key to continue
```

Here is the program source code that produced the output:

```
#include "stdafx.h"
#include <mbstring.h>
#include <iostream>

using namespace std;
```

```
int main(int argc, char* argv[])
{
    unsigned int x;
    unsigned int dat[] =
    {
        0x81e0, 0x81e1, 0x81e2, 0x81e3, 0x81e4,
        0x81e5, 0x81e6, 0x81e7, 0x81e8, 0x81e9
    };

    cout << "Converting values..." << endl;

    for (x=0; x<10; ++x)
    {
        unsigned int result = _mbctohira(dat[x]);
        cout << "result = " << result << endl;
    }

    return 0;
}
```

CROSS-REFERENCE

See also _ismbbalnum(), _ismbbalpha(), _ismbbgraph(), _ismbbkalnum(), _ismbbkana(), _ismbbkprint(), _ismbbkpunct(), _ismbblead(), _ismbbprint(), _ismbbpunct(), _ismbbtrail(), _mbbtombc(), _mbbtype(), _mbccpy(), _mbcjistojms(), _mbcjmstojis(), _mbclen(), _mbctokata(), _mbctolower(), _mbctombb(), _mbctoupper(), _mbsbtype, _mbscat(), _mbschr(), _mbscmp(), _mbscoll(), _mbscpy(), _mbscspn(), _mbsdec(), _mbsdup(), _mbsicmp(), _mbsicoll(), _mbsinc(), _mbslen(), _mbslwr(), _mbsnbcat(), _mbsnbcmp(), _mbsnbcnt(), _mbsnbcoll(), _mbsnbcpy(), _mbsnbicmp(), _mbsnbicoll(), _mbsnbset(), _mbsncat(), _mbsnccnt(), _mbsncmp(), _mbsncoll(), _mbsncpy(), _mbsnextc(), _mbsnicmp(), _mbsnicoll(), _mbsninc(), _mbsnset(), _mbspbrk(), _mbsrchr(), _mbsrev(), _mbsset(), _mbsspn(), _mbsspnp(), _mbsstr(), _mbstok(), _mbstrlen(), _mbsupr(), isleadbyte(), mblen(), mbstowcs(), and mbtowc().

_mbctokata()

Function

The _mbctokata() function converts a multibyte hiragana character to a multibyte katakana character, returning the converted character, or returning the original character if the conversion could not be performed.

Header Files

```
#include <mbstring.h>
```

Declaration

```
unsigned int _mbctokata(unsigned int c);
```

- *c* — The character to convert.

Example

The following program demonstrates how to call the `_mbctokata()` function. When run, the program converts the character values in an array, displaying the results as it goes. The program's output looks like this:

```
Converting values...
result = 33248
result = 33249
result = 33250
result = 33251
result = 33252
result = 33253
result = 33254
result = 33255
result = 33256
result = 33257
Press any key to continue
```

Here is the program source code that produced the output:

```
#include "stdafx.h"
#include <mbstring.h>
#include <iostream>

using namespace std;

int main(int argc, char* argv[])
{
    unsigned int x;
    unsigned int dat[] =
    {
        0x81e0, 0x81e1, 0x81e2, 0x81e3, 0x81e4,
        0x81e5, 0x81e6, 0x81e7, 0x81e8, 0x81e9
    };
```

```
cout << "Converting values..." << endl;

for (x=0; x<10; ++x)
{
    unsigned int result = _mbctokata(dat[x]);
    cout << "result = " << result << endl;
}

return 0;
}
```

CROSS-REFERENCE
See also _ismbbalnum(), _ismbbalpha(), _ismbbgraph(), _ismbbkalnum(),
_ismbbkana(), _ismbbkprint(), _ismbbkpunct(), _ismbblead(), _ismbbprint(),
_ismbbpunct(), _ismbbtrail(), _mbbtombc(), _mbbtype(), _mbccpy(), _mbcjistojms(),
_mbcjmstojis(), _mbclen(), _mbctohira(), _mbctolower(), _mbctombb(),
_mbctoupper(), _mbsbtype, _mbscat(), _mbschr(), _mbscmp(), _mbscoll(),
_mbscpy(), _mbscspn(), _mbsdec(), _mbsdup(), _mbsicmp(), _mbsicoll(), _mbsinc(),
_mbslen(), _mbslwr(), _mbsnbcat(), _mbsnbcmp(), _mbsnbcnt(), _mbsnbcoll(),
_mbsnbcpy(), _mbsnbicmp(), _mbsnbicoll(), _mbsnbset(), _mbsncat(), _mbsnccnt(),
_mbsncmp(), _mbsncoll(), _mbsncpy(), _mbsnextc(), _mbsnicmp(), _mbsnicoll(),
_mbsninc(), _mbsnset(), _mbspbrk(), _mbsrchr(), _mbsrev(), _mbsset(), _mbsspn(),
_mbsspnp(), _mbsstr(), _mbstok(), _mbstrlen(), _mbsupr(), isleadbyte(), mblen(),
mbstowcs(), and mbtowc().

_mbctolower()

Function

The _mbctolower() function converts a multibyte character to lowercase,
returning the converted character, or returning the original character if the
conversion could not be performed.

Header Files

```
#include <mbstring.h>
```

Declaration

```
unsigned int _mbctolower(unsigned int c);
```

- *c* — The character to convert.

Example

The following program demonstrates how to call the _mbctolower() function. When run, the program converts the character values in an array to lowercase, displaying the results as it goes. The program's output looks like this:

```
Converting values...
Original value: 65    A
Converted value: 97    a
Original value: 66    B
Converted value: 98    b
Original value: 67    C
Converted value: 99    c
Original value: 68    D
Converted value: 100    d
Original value: 69    E
Converted value: 101    e
Original value: 70    F
Converted value: 102    f
Original value: 71    G
Converted value: 103    g
Original value: 72    H
Converted value: 104    h
Original value: 73    I
Converted value: 105    i
Original value: 74    J
Converted value: 106    j
Press any key to continue
```

Here is the program source code that produced the output:

```
#include "stdafx.h"
#include <mbstring.h>
#include <iostream>

using namespace std;

int main(int argc, char* argv[])
{
    unsigned int x;
    unsigned int dat[] =
    {
        65, 66, 67, 68, 69,
        70, 71, 72, 73, 74
    };
```

```
            cout << "Converting values..." << endl;

            for (x=0; x<10; ++x)
            {
                cout << "Original value: " << dat[x];
                cout << "    " << (char)dat[x] << endl;
                unsigned int result = _mbctolower(dat[x]);
                cout << "Converted value: " << result;
                cout << "    " << (char)result << endl;
            }

            return 0;
        }
```

CROSS-REFERENCE

See also _ismbbalnum(), _ismbbalpha(), _ismbbgraph(), _ismbbkalnum(), _ismbbkana(), _ismbbkprint(), _ismbbkpunct(), _ismbblead(), _ismbbprint(), _ismbbpunct(), _ismbbtrail(), _mbbtombc(), _mbbtype(), _mbccpy(), _mbcjistojms(), _mbcjmstojis(), _mbclen(), _mbctohira(), _mbctokata(), _mbctombb(), _mbctoupper(), _mbsbtype, _mbscat(), _mbschr(), _mbscmp(), _mbscoll(), _mbscpy(), _mbscspn(), _mbsdec(), _mbsdup(), _mbsicmp(), _mbsicoll(), _mbsinc(), _mbslen(), _mbslwr(), _mbsnbcat(), _mbsnbcmp(), _mbsnbcnt(), _mbsnbcoll(), _mbsnbcpy(), _mbsnbicmp(), _mbsnbicoll(), _mbsnbset(), _mbsncat(), _mbsnccnt(), _mbsncmp(), _mbsncoll(), _mbsncpy(), _mbsnextc(), _mbsnicmp(), _mbsnicoll(), _mbsninc(), _mbsnset(), _mbspbrk(), _mbsrchr(), _mbsrev(), _mbsset(), _mbsspn(), _mbsspnp(), _mbsstr(), _mbstok(), _mbstrlen(), _mbsupr(), isleadbyte(), mblen(), mbstowcs(), and mbtowc().

_mbctombb()

Function

The _mbctombb() function converts a multibyte character to a single-byte multibyte character, returning the converted character, or, if unable to perform the conversion, returning the original character.

Header Files

```
#include <mbstring.h>
```

Declaration

```
unsigned int _mbctombb(unsigned int c);
```

- *c*—The character value to convert.

Example

The following program demonstrates how to use the `_mbctombb()` function. When run, the program converts the values of an array first from wide-character data to multibyte character data, and then to single-byte multibyte data, displaying the results as it goes. The program's output looks like this:

```
Converting values...
Converted value: 65    A
Converted value: 66    B
Converted value: 67    C
Converted value: 68    D
Converted value: 69    E
Converted value: 70    F
Converted value: 71    G
Converted value: 72    H
Converted value: 73    I
Converted value: 74    J
Press any key to continue
```

Here is the program source code that produced the output:

```
#include "stdafx.h"
#include <mbstring.h>
#include <iostream>

using namespace std;

int main(int argc, char* argv[])
{
    unsigned int x;
    wchar_t wstr[] = L"ABCDEFGHIJ";
    char mbc;

    cout << "Converting values..." << endl;

    for (x=0; x<10; ++x)
    {
        wctomb(&mbc, wstr[x]);
        unsigned int result = _mbctombb(mbc);
```

```
            cout << "Converted value: " << result;
            cout << "    " << (char)result << endl;
        }

        return 0;
    }
```

CROSS-REFERENCE
See also _ismbbalnum(), _ismbbalpha(), _ismbbgraph(), _ismbbkalnum(), _ismbbkana(), _ismbbkprint(), _ismbbkpunct(), _ismbblead(), _ismbbprint(), _ismbbpunct(), _ismbbtrail(), _mbbtombc(), _mbbtype(), _mbccpy(), _mbcjistojms(), _mbcjmstojis(), _mbclen(), _mbctohira(), _mbctokata(), _mbctolower(), _mbctoupper(), _mbsbtype, _mbscat(), _mbschr(), _mbscmp(), _mbscoll(), _mbscpy(), _mbscspn(), _mbsdec(), _mbsdup(), _mbsicmp(), _mbsicoll(), _mbsinc(), _mbslen(), _mbslwr(), _mbsnbcat(), _mbsnbcmp(), _mbsnbcnt(), _mbsnbcoll(), _mbsnbcpy(), _mbsnbicmp(), _mbsnbicoll(), _mbsnbset(), _mbsncat(), _mbsnccnt(), _mbsncmp(), _mbsncoll(), _mbsncpy(), _mbsnextc(), _mbsnicmp(), _mbsnicoll(), _mbsninc(), _mbsnset(), _mbspbrk(), _mbsrchr(), _mbsrev(), _mbsset(), _mbsspn(), _mbsspnp(), _mbsstr(), _mbstok(), _mbstrlen(), _mbsupr(), isleadbyte(), mblen(), mbstowcs(), and mbtowc().

_mbctoupper()

Function

The _mbctoupper() function converts a multibyte character to uppercase, returning the converted character, or returning the original character if the conversion could not be performed.

Header Files

```
#include <mbstring.h>
```

Declaration

```
unsigned int _mbctoupper(unsigned int c);
```

- *c*—The character to convert.

Example

The following program demonstrates how to call the _mbctoupper() function. When run, the program converts the character values in an array, displaying the results as it goes. The program's output looks like this:

```
Converting values...
Original value: 97    a
Converted value: 65    A
Original value: 98    b
Converted value: 66    B
Original value: 99    c
Converted value: 67    C
Original value: 100    d
Converted value: 68    D
Original value: 101    e
Converted value: 69    E
Original value: 102    f
Converted value: 70    F
Original value: 103    g
Converted value: 71    G
Original value: 104    h
Converted value: 72    H
Original value: 105    i
Converted value: 73    I
Original value: 106    j
Converted value: 74    J
Press any key to continue
```

Here is the program source code that produced the output:

```cpp
#include "stdafx.h"
#include <mbstring.h>
#include <iostream>

using namespace std;

int main(int argc, char* argv[])
{
    unsigned int x;
    unsigned int dat[] =
    {
        97, 98, 99, 100, 101,
        102, 103, 104, 105, 106
    };
```

```
        cout << "Converting values..." << endl;

        for (x=0; x<10; ++x)
        {
            cout << "Original value: " << dat[x];
            cout << "      " << (char)dat[x] << endl;
            unsigned int result = _mbctoupper(dat[x]);
            cout << "Converted value: " << result;
            cout << "     " << (char)result << endl;
        }

        return 0;
    }
```

CROSS-REFERENCE

See also _ismbbalnum(), _ismbbalpha(), _ismbbgraph(), _ismbbkalnum(), _ismbbkana(), _ismbbkprint(), _ismbbkpunct(), _ismbblead(), _ismbbprint(), _ismbbpunct(), _ismbbtrail(), _mbbtombc(), _mbbtype(), _mbccpy(), _mbcjistojms(), _mbcjmstojis(), _mbclen(), _mbctohira(), _mbctokata(), _mbctolower(), _mbctombb(), _mbsbtype, _mbscat(), _mbschr(), _mbscmp(), _mbscoll(), _mbscpy(), _mbscspn(), _mbsdec(), _mbsdup(), _mbsicmp(), _mbsicoll(), _mbsinc(), _mbslen(), _mbslwr(), _mbsnbcat(), _mbsnbcmp(), _mbsnbcnt(), _mbsnbcoll(), _mbsnbcpy(), _mbsnbicmp(), _mbsnbicoll(), _mbsnbset(), _mbsncat(), _mbsnccnt(), _mbsncmp(), _mbsncoll(), _mbsncpy(), _mbsnextc(), _mbsnicmp(), _mbsnicoll(), _mbsninc(), _mbsnset(), _mbspbrk(), _mbsrchr(), _mbsrev(), _mbsset(), _mbsspn(), _mbsspnp(), _mbsstr(), _mbstok(), _mbstrlen(), _mbsupr(), isleadbyte(), mblen(), mbstowcs(), and mbtowc().

_mbsbtype()

Function

The _mbsbtype() function tests a character value to determine whether it is a valid single-byte character, valid multibyte-character lead byte, or valid multibyte-character trailing byte. The function returns the _MBC_SINGLE, _MBC_LEAD, _MBC_TRAIL, or _MBC_ILLEGAL values.

Header Files

```
#include <mbstring.h>
#include <mbctype.h>
```

Declaration

```
int _mbsbtype(const unsigned char* mbstr, size_t count);
```

- *count* — The offset from the start of the string at which to test a character.
- *mbstr* — The address of a multibyte-character string.

Example

The following program demonstrates how to use the _mbsbtype() function. When run, the program tests the bytes of a string (including the null at the end of the string) and displays the results. The program's output looks like this:

```
Testing characters in the string...
Valid single byte: 84
Valid single byte: 104
Valid single byte: 105
Valid single byte: 115
Valid single byte: 32
Valid single byte: 105
Valid single byte: 115
Valid single byte: 32
Valid single byte: 97
Valid single byte: 32
Valid single byte: 116
Valid single byte: 101
Valid single byte: 115
Valid single byte: 116
Valid single byte: 0
Press any key to continue
```

Here is the program source code that produced the output:

```
#include "stdafx.h"
#include <mbstring.h>
#include <mbctype.h>
#include <iostream>

using namespace std;

int main(int argc, char* argv[])
{
    int x;
    unsigned char str[] = "This is a test";
```

```
cout << "Testing characters in the string..." << endl;

for (x=0; x<sizeof(str); ++x)
{
    int result = _mbsbtype(str, x);
    if (result == _MBC_SINGLE)
    {
        cout << "Valid single byte: ";
        cout << (int)str[x] << endl;
    }
    else if (result == _MBC_LEAD)
    {
        cout << "Valid lead byte: ";
        cout << (int)str[x] << endl;
    }
    else
    {
        cout << "Invalid byte: ";
        cout << (int)str[x] << endl;
    }
}

return 0;
}
```

CROSS-REFERENCE

See also _ismbbalnum(), _ismbbalpha(), _ismbbgraph(), _ismbbkalnum(), _ismbbkana(), _ismbbkprint(), _ismbbkpunct(), _ismbblead(), _ismbbprint(), _ismbbpunct(), _ismbbtrail(), _mbbtombc(), _mbbtype(), _mbccpy(), _mbcjistojms(), _mbcjmstojis(), _mbclen(), _mbctohira(), _mbctokata(), _mbctolower(), _mbctombb(), _mbctoupper(), _mbscat(), _mbschr(), _mbscmp(), _mbscoll(), _mbscpy(), _mbscspn(), _mbsdec(), _mbsdup(), _mbsicmp(), _mbsicoll(), _mbsinc(), _mbslen(), _mbslwr(), _mbsnbcat(), _mbsnbcmp(), _mbsnbcnt(), _mbsnbcoll(), _mbsnbcpy(), _mbsnbicmp(), _mbsnbicoll(), _mbsnbset(), _mbsncat(), _mbsnccnt(), _mbsncmp(), _mbsncoll(), _mbsncpy(), _mbsnextc(), _mbsnicmp(), _mbsnicoll(), _mbsninc(), _mbsnset(), _mbspbrk(), _mbsrchr(), _mbsrev(), _mbsset(), _mbsspn(), _mbsspnp(), _mbsstr(), _mbstok(), _mbstrlen(), _mbsupr(), isleadbyte(), mblen(), mbstowcs(), and mbtowc().

_mbscat()

Function

The _mbscat() function concatenates (joins together) multibyte-character strings, returning a pointer to the destination string.

Header File

```
#include <mbstring.h>
```

Declaration

```
unsigned char* _mbscat(unsigned char *strDestination,
    const unsigned char *strSource);
```

- *strDestination* — The string to which to concatenate *strSource*.
- *strSource* — The string to concatenate to *strDestination*.

Example

The following program demonstrates how to use the _mbscat() function. When run, the program concatenates the string "ABC" to the string "DEF". The output looks like this:

```
str1 = ABC
str2 = DEF
Result: ABCDEF
Press any key to continue
```

Here is the program source code that produced the output:

```
#include "stdafx.h"
#include <iostream>
#include <mbstring.h>

using namespace std;

int main(int argc, char* argv[])
{
    unsigned char str1[81] = {65, 66, 67, 0};
    unsigned char str2[81] = {68, 69, 70, 0};

    cout << "str1 = " << str1 << endl;
    cout << "str2 = " << str2 << endl;
    _mbscat(str1, str2);
```

```
        cout << "Result: " << str1 << endl;

        return 0;
    }
```

CROSS-REFERENCE

See also _ismbbalnum(), _ismbbalpha(), _ismbbgraph(), _ismbbkalnum(), _ismbbkana(), _ismbbkprint(), _ismbbkpunct(), _ismbblead(), _ismbbprint(), _ismbbpunct(), _ismbbtrail(), _mbbtombc(), _mbbtype(), _mbccpy(), _mbcjistojms(), _mbcjmstojis(), _mbclen(), _mbctohira(), _mbctokata(), _mbctolower(), _mbctombb(), _mbctoupper(), _mbsbtype, _mbschr(), _mbscmp(), _mbscoll(), _mbscpy(), _mbscspn(), _mbsdec(), _mbsdup(), _mbsicmp(), _mbsicoll(), _mbsinc(), _mbslen(), _mbslwr(), _mbsnbcat(), _mbsnbcmp(), _mbsnbcnt(), _mbsnbcoll(), _mbsnbcpy(), _mbsnbicmp(), _mbsnbicoll(), _mbsnbset(), _mbsncat(), _mbsnccnt(), _mbsncmp(), _mbsncoll(), _mbsncpy(), _mbsnextc(), _mbsnicmp(), _mbsnicoll(), _mbsninc(), _mbsnset(), _mbspbrk(), _mbsrchr(), _mbsrev(), _mbsset(), _mbsspn(), _mbsspnp(), _mbsstr(), _mbstok(), _mbstrlen(), _mbsupr(), isleadbyte(), mblen(), mbstowcs(), and mbtowc().

_mbschr()

Function

The _mbschr() function locates a character in a multibyte string, returning a pointer to the character.

Header File

```
#include <mbstring.h>
```

Declaration

```
unsigned char* _mbschr(const unsigned char *string,
    unsigned int c);
```

- *c* — The character for which to search.
- *string* — A pointer to the string in which to search for *c*.

Example

The following program demonstrates how to use the _mbschr() function. When run, the program locates the first occurrence of the letter E in the string

"ABCDEFGHIJ" and displays the string starting with the located letter. The program's output looks like this:

```
Original string = ABCDEFGHIJ
Searching for E...
Result: EFGHIJ
Press any key to continue
```

Here is the program source code that produced the output:

```cpp
#include "stdafx.h"
#include <iostream>
#include <mbstring.h>

using namespace std;

int main(int argc, char* argv[])
{
    unsigned char str1[81]
        = {65, 66, 67, 68, 69,
           70, 71, 72, 73, 74, 0};

    unsigned char ch = 69;
    cout << "Original string = " << str1 << endl;
    cout << "Searching for E..." << endl;
    unsigned char* pChr = _mbschr(str1, ch);
    cout << "Result: " << pChr << endl;

    return 0;
}
```

CROSS-REFERENCE

See also _ismbbalnum(), _ismbbalpha(), _ismbbgraph(), _ismbbkalnum(), _ismbbkana(), _ismbbkprint(), _ismbbkpunct(), _ismbblead(), _ismbbprint(), _ismbbpunct(), _ismbbtrail(), _mbbtombc(), _mbbtype(), _mbccpy(), _mbcjistojms(), _mbcjmstojis(), _mbclen(), _mbctohira(), _mbctokata(), _mbctolower(), _mbctombb(), _mbctoupper(), _mbsbtype, _mbscat(), _mbscmp(), _mbscoll(), _mbscpy(), _mbscspn(), _mbsdec(), _mbsdup(), _mbsicmp(), _mbsicoll(), _mbsinc(), _mbslen(), _mbslwr(), _mbsnbcat(), _mbsnbcmp(), _mbsnbcnt(), _mbsnbcoll(), _mbsnbcpy(), _mbsnbicmp(), _mbsnbicoll(), _mbsnbset(), _mbsncat(), _mbsnccnt(), _mbsncmp(), _mbsncoll(), _mbsncpy(), _mbsnextc(), _mbsnicmp(), _mbsnicoll(), _mbsninc(), _mbsnset(), _mbspbrk(), _mbsrchr(), _mbsrev(), _mbsset(), _mbsspn(), _mbsspnp(), _mbsstr(), _mbstok(), _mbstrlen(), _mbsupr(), isleadbyte(), mblen(), mbstowcs(), and mbtowc().

_mbscmp()

Function

The _mbscmp() function compares two multibyte-character strings, returning a value from Table M-1.

Table M-1 Return Values for _mbscmp()

Value	Description
Less than 0	string1 is alphabetically less than string2.
0	The two strings are equal.
Greater than 0	string1 is alphabetically greater than string2.
_NLSCMPERROR	Error.

Header File

```
#include <mbstring.h>
```

Declaration

```
int _mbscmp(const unsigned char *string1,
    const unsigned char *string2);
```

- *string1* — The first string to compare.
- *string2* — The second string to compare.

Example

The following program demonstrates how to use the _mbscmp() function. When run, the program compares several strings and displays the result of the comparisons. The output looks like this:

```
ABC equals ABC
ABC is less than abc
abc is greater than AbC
Press any key to continue
```

Here is the program source code that produced the output:

```cpp
#include "stdafx.h"
#include <iostream>
#include <mbstring.h>

using namespace std;

void cmp(unsigned char* s1, unsigned char* s2)
{
    int result = _mbscmp(s1, s2);
    if (result < 0 )
    {
        cout << s1 << " is less than ";
        cout << s2 << endl;
    }
    else if (result > 0)
    {
        cout << s1 << " is greater than ";
        cout << s2 << endl;
    }
    else
    {
        cout << s1 << " equals ";
        cout << s2 << endl;
    }
}

int main(int argc, char* argv[])
{
    unsigned char str1[] = {65, 66, 67, 0};
    unsigned char str2[] = {65, 66, 67, 0};
    unsigned char str3[] = {97, 98, 99, 0};
    unsigned char str4[] = {65, 98, 67, 0};

    cmp(str1, str2);
    cmp(str2, str3);
    cmp(str3, str4);

    return 0;
}
```

CROSS-REFERENCE
See also _ismbbalnum(), _ismbbalpha(), _ismbbgraph(), _ismbbkalnum(), _ismbbkana(), _ismbbkprint(), _ismbbkpunct(), _ismbblead(), _ismbbprint(), _ismbbpunct(), _ismbbtrail(), _mbbtombc(), _mbbtype(), _mbccpy(), _mbcjistojms(), _mbcjmstojis(), _mbclen(), _mbctohira(), _mbctokata(), _mbctolower(), _mbctombb(), _mbctoupper(), _mbsbtype, _mbscat(), _mbschr(), _mbscoll(), _mbscpy(), _mbscspn(), _mbsdec(), _mbsdup(), _mbsicmp(), _mbsicoll(), _mbsinc(), _mbslen(), _mbslwr(), _mbsnbcat(), _mbsnbcmp(), _mbsnbcnt(), _mbsnbcoll(), _mbsnbcpy(), _mbsnbicmp(), _mbsnbicoll(), _mbsnbset(), _mbsncat(), _mbsnccnt(), _mbsncmp(), _mbsncoll(), _mbsncpy(), _mbsnextc(), _mbsnicmp(), _mbsnicoll(), _mbsninc(), _mbsnset(), _mbspbrk(), _mbsrchr(), _mbsrev(), _mbsset(), _mbsspn(), _mbsspnp(), _mbsstr(), _mbstok(), _mbstrlen(), _mbsupr(), isleadbyte(), mblen(), mbstowcs(), and mbtowc().

_mbscoll()

Function

The _mbscoll() function compares two multibyte-character strings for the current locale, returning a value from Table M-2.

Table M-2 Return Values for _mbscoll()

Value	Description
Less than 0	string1 is alphabetically less than string2.
0	The two strings are equal.
Greater than 0	string1 is alphabetically greater than string2.
_NLSCMPERROR	Error.

Header File

```
#include <mbstring.h>
```

Declaration

```
int _mbscoll(const unsigned char *string1,
    const unsigned char *string2);
```

- *string1* — The first string to compare.
- *string2* — The second string to compare.

Example

The following program demonstrates how to use the _mbscoll() function. When run, the program compares several pairs of strings and displays the result of the comparisons. The program's output looks like this:

```
ABC equals ABC
ABC is greater than abc
abc is less than AbC
Press any key to continue
```

Here is the program source code that produced the output:

```cpp
#include "stdafx.h"
#include <iostream>
#include <mbstring.h>

using namespace std;

void cmp(unsigned char* s1, unsigned char* s2)
{
    int result = _mbscoll(s1, s2);
    if (result < 0 )
    {
        cout << s1 << " is less than ";
        cout << s2 << endl;
    }
    else if (result > 0)
    {
        cout << s1 << " is greater than ";
        cout << s2 << endl;
    }
    else
    {
        cout << s1 << " equals ";
        cout << s2 << endl;
    }
}

int main(int argc, char* argv[])
{
    unsigned char str1[] = {65, 66, 67, 0};
    unsigned char str2[] = {65, 66, 67, 0};
    unsigned char str3[] = {97, 98, 99, 0};
    unsigned char str4[] = {65, 98, 67, 0};
```

```
        cmp(str1, str2);
        cmp(str2, str3);
        cmp(str3, str4);

        return 0;
    }
```

CROSS-REFERENCE

See also _ismbbalnum(), _ismbbalpha(), _ismbbgraph(), _ismbbkalnum(), _ismbbkana(), _ismbbkprint(), _ismbbkpunct(), _ismbblead(), _ismbbprint(), _ismbbpunct(), _ismbbtrail(), _mbbtombc(), _mbbtype(), _mbccpy(), _mbcjistojms(), _mbcjmstojis(), _mbclen(), _mbctohira(), _mbctokata(), _mbctolower(), _mbctombb(), _mbctoupper(), _mbsbtype, _mbscat(), _mbschr(), _mbscmp(), _mbscpy(), _mbscspn(), _mbsdec(), _mbsdup(), _mbsicmp(), _mbsicoll(), _mbsinc(), _mbslen(), _mbslwr(), _mbsnbcat(), _mbsnbcmp(), _mbsnbcnt(), _mbsnbcoll(), _mbsnbcpy(), _mbsnbicmp(), _mbsnbicoll(), _mbsnbset(), _mbsncat(), _mbsnccnt(), _mbsncmp(), _mbsncoll(), _mbsncpy(), _mbsnextc(), _mbsnicmp(), _mbsnicoll(), _mbsninc(), _mbsnset(), _mbspbrk(), _mbsrchr(), _mbsrev(), _mbsset(), _mbsspn(), _mbsspnp(), _mbsstr(), _mbstok(), _mbstrlen(), _mbsupr(), isleadbyte(), mblen(), mbstowcs(), and mbtowc().

_mbscpy()

Function

The _mbscpy() function copies one multibyte-character string to another, returning a pointer to the destination string. The source and destination strings cannot overlap.

Header File

```
#include <mbstring.h>
```

Declaration

```
unsigned char* _mbscpy(unsigned char *strDestination,
    const unsigned char *strSource);
```

- *strDestination*—A pointer to the destination string.
- *strSource*—A pointer to the source string.

Example

The following program demonstrates how to use the _mbscpy() function. When run, the program copies one string to another and displays the result. The program's output looks like this:

```
Source string = ABCDE
Destination string = ABCDE
Press any key to continue
```

Here is the program source code that produced the output:

```cpp
#include "stdafx.h"
#include <iostream>
#include <mbstring.h>

using namespace std;

int main(int argc, char* argv[])
{
    unsigned char destStr[81];
    unsigned char srcStr[] = {65, 66, 67, 68, 69, 0};

    unsigned char* pResult = _mbscpy(destStr, srcStr);
    cout << "Source string = " << srcStr << endl;
    cout << "Destination string = " << pResult << endl;

    return 0;
}
```

CROSS-REFERENCE

See also _ismbbalnum(), _ismbbalpha(), _ismbbgraph(), _ismbbkalnum(), _ismbbkana(), _ismbbkprint(), _ismbbkpunct(), _ismbblead(), _ismbbprint(), _ismbbpunct(), _ismbbtrail(), _mbbtombc(), _mbbtype(), _mbccpy(), _mbcjistojms(), _mbcjmstojis(), _mbclen(), _mbctohira(), _mbctokata(), _mbctolower(), _mbctombb(), _mbctoupper(), _mbsbtype, _mbscat(), _mbschr(), _mbscmp(), _mbscoll(), _mbscspn(), _mbsdec(), _mbsdup(), _mbsicmp(), _mbsicoll(), _mbsinc(), _mbslen(), _mbslwr(), _mbsnbcat(), _mbsnbcmp(), _mbsnbcnt(), _mbsnbcoll(), _mbsnbcpy(), _mbsnbicmp(), _mbsnbicoll(), _mbsnbset(), _mbsncat(), _mbsnccnt(), _mbsncmp(), _mbsncoll(), _mbsncpy(), _mbsnextc(), _mbsnicmp(), _mbsnicoll(), _mbsninc(), _mbsnset(), _mbspbrk(), _mbsrchr(), _mbsrev(), _mbsset(), _mbsspn(), _mbsspnp(), _mbsstr(), _mbstok(), _mbstrlen(), _mbsupr(), isleadbyte(), mblen(), mbstowcs(), and mbtowc().

_mbscspn()

Function

The _mbscspn() function locates the first occurrence of a character in a multi-byte-character string, returning the length of the substring preceding the matching character.

Header File

```
#include <mbstring.h>
```

Declaration

```
size_t _mbscspn(const unsigned char *string,
    const unsigned char *strCharSet);
```

- *strCharSet*—A pointer to the set of characters for which to search.
- *string*—A pointer to the string to search.

Example

The following program demonstrates how to use the _mbscspn() function. When run, the program locates, in a string, the first character in a set and displays the result, indicating the located character with a caret (^). The program's output looks like this:

```
Source String: This is a test
Search characters: ast
Searching...

Result:
This is a test
   ^
Press any key to continue
```

Here is the program source code that produced the output:

```
#include "stdafx.h"
#include <iostream>
#include <mbstring.h>

using namespace std;
```

```
int main(int argc, char* argv[])
{
    unsigned char srcStr[] = "This is a test";
    unsigned char chrSet[] = "ast";

    cout << "Source String: " << srcStr << endl;
    cout << "Search characters: " << chrSet << endl;
    cout << "Searching..." << endl << endl;
    size_t len = _mbscspn(srcStr, chrSet);
    cout << "Result:" << endl;
    cout << srcStr << endl;
    for (unsigned x=0; x<len; ++x)
        cout << " ";
    cout << "^" << endl;

    return 0;
}
```

CROSS-REFERENCE

See also _ismbbalnum(), _ismbbalpha(), _ismbbgraph(), _ismbbkalnum(), _ismbbkana(), _ismbbkprint(), _ismbbkpunct(), _ismbblead(), _ismbbprint(), _ismbbpunct(), _ismbbtrail(), _mbbtombc(), _mbbtype(), _mbccpy(), _mbcjistojms(), _mbcjmstojis(), _mbclen(), _mbctohira(), _mbctokata(), _mbctolower(), _mbctombb(), _mbctoupper(), _mbsbtype, _mbscat(), _mbschr(), _mbscmp(), _mbscoll(), _mbscpy(), _mbsdec(), _mbsdup(), _mbsicmp(), _mbsicoll(), _mbsinc(), _mbslen(), _mbslwr(), _mbsnbcat(), _mbsnbcmp(), _mbsnbcnt(), _mbsnbcoll(), _mbsnbcpy(), _mbsnbicmp(), _mbsnbicoll(), _mbsnbset(), _mbsncat(), _mbsnccnt(), _mbsncmp(), _mbsncoll(), _mbsncpy(), _mbsnextc(), _mbsnicmp(), _mbsnicoll(), _mbsninc(), _mbsnset(), _mbspbrk(), _mbsrchr(), _mbsrev(), _mbsset(), _mbsspn(), _mbsspnp(), _mbsstr(), _mbstok(), _mbstrlen(), _mbsupr(), isleadbyte(), mblen(), mbstowcs(), and mbtowc().

_mbsdec()

Function

The _mbsdec() function returns a pointer to the previous character in a multi-byte-character string or NULL if the previous character cannot be determined.

Header File

```
#include <mbstring.h>
```

Declaration

```
unsigned char* _mbsdec(const unsigned char *start,
    const unsigned char *current);
```

- *current* — A pointer to the character for which to return the previous character.
- *start* — A pointer to the start of the string.

Example

The following program demonstrates how to use the _mbsdec() function. When run, the program locates the character that precedes the fifth character in a string and displays the result. The program's output looks like this:

```
Source String = This is a test
Result = s is a test
Press any key to continue
```

Here is the program source code that produced the output:

```
#include "stdafx.h"
#include <iostream>
#include <mbstring.h>

using namespace std;

int main(int argc, char* argv[])
{
    unsigned char srcStr[] = "This is a test";

    unsigned char* result = _mbsdec(srcStr, &srcStr[4]);
    cout << "Source String = " << srcStr << endl;
    cout << "Result = " << result << endl;

    return 0;
}
```

CROSS-REFERENCE
See also _ismbbalnum(), _ismbbalpha(), _ismbbgraph(), _ismbbkalnum(), _ismbbkana(), _ismbbkprint(), _ismbbkpunct(), _ismbblead(), _ismbbprint(), _ismbbpunct(), _ismbbtrail(), _mbbtombc(), _mbbtype(), _mbccpy(), _mbcjistojms(), _mbcjmstojis(), _mbclen(), _mbctohira(), _mbctokata(), _mbctolower(), _mbctombb(), _mbctoupper(), _mbsbtype, _mbscat(), _mbschr(), _mbscmp(), _mbscoll(), _mbscpy(), _mbscspn(), _mbsdup(), _mbsicmp(), _mbsicoll(), _mbsinc(), _mbslen(), _mbslwr(), _mbsnbcat(), _mbsnbcmp(), _mbsnbcnt(), _mbsnbcoll(), _mbsnbcpy(), _mbsnbicmp(), _mbsnbicoll(), _mbsnbset(), _mbsncat(), _mbsnccnt(), _mbsncmp(), _mbsncoll(), _mbsncpy(), _mbsnextc(), _mbsnicmp(), _mbsnicoll(), _mbsninc(), _mbsnset(), _mbspbrk(), _mbsrchr(), _mbsrev(), _mbsset(), _mbsspn(), _mbsspnp(), _mbsstr(), _mbstok(), _mbstrlen(), _mbsupr(), isleadbyte(), mblen(), mbstowcs(), and mbtowc().

_mbsdup()

Function

The _mbsdup() function duplicates a multibyte-character string, returning a pointer to the new string.

Header File

```
#include <mbstring.h>
```

Declaration

```
unsigned char* _mbsdup(const unsigned char *strSource);
```

- *strSource* — A pointer to the source string.

Example

The following program demonstrates how to use the _mbsdup() function. When run, the program duplicates the given string and displays the result. The program's output looks like this:

```
Source string = This is a test
New string = This is a test
Press any key to continue
```

Here is the program source code that produced the output:

```
#include "stdafx.h"
#include <iostream>
#include <mbstring.h>

using namespace std;

int main(int argc, char* argv[])
{
    unsigned char srcStr[] = "This is a test";

    unsigned char* destStr = _mbsdup(srcStr);
    cout << "Source string = " << srcStr << endl;
    cout << "New string = " << destStr << endl;

    return 0;
}
```

CROSS-REFERENCE
See also _ismbbalnum(), _ismbbalpha(), _ismbbgraph(), _ismbbkalnum(), _ismbbkana(), _ismbbkprint(), _ismbbkpunct(), _ismbblead(), _ismbbprint(), _ismbbpunct(), _ismbbtrail(), _mbbtombc(), _mbbtype(), _mbccpy(), _mbcjistojms(), _mbcjmstojis(), _mbclen(), _mbctohira(), _mbctokata(), _mbctolower(), _mbctombb(), _mbctoupper(), _mbsbtype, _mbscat(), _mbschr(), _mbscmp(), _mbscoll(), _mbscpy(), _mbscspn(), _mbsdec(), _mbsicmp(), _mbsicoll(), _mbsinc(), _mbslen(), _mbslwr(), _mbsnbcat(), _mbsnbcmp(), _mbsnbcnt(), _mbsnbcoll(), _mbsnbcpy(), _mbsnbicmp(), _mbsnbicoll(), _mbsnbset(), _mbsncat(), _mbsnccnt(), _mbsncmp(), _mbsncoll(), _mbsncpy(), _mbsnextc(), _mbsnicmp(), _mbsnicoll(), _mbsninc(), _mbsnset(), _mbspbrk(), _mbsrchr(), _mbsrev(), _mbsset(), _mbsspn(), _mbsspnp(), _mbsstr(), _mbstok(), _mbstrlen(), _mbsupr(), isleadbyte(), mblen(), mbstowcs(), and mbtowc().

_mbsicmp()

Function

The _mbsicmp() function compares two multibyte-character strings without regard for case (case-insensitive compare), returning a value from Table M-3.

Header File

```
#include <mbstring.h>
```

Table M-3 Return Values for _mbsicmp()

Value	Description
Less than 0	string1 is alphabetically less than string2.
0	The two strings are equal.
Greater than 0	string1 is alphabetically greater than string2.
_NLSCMPERROR	Error.

Declaration

```
int _mbsicmp(const unsigned char *string1,
    const char_t *string2);
```

- *string1* — The first string to compare.
- *string2* — The second string to compare.

Example

The following program demonstrates how to use the _mbsicmp() function. When run, the program compares several pairs of strings and displays the result of the comparisons. The output looks like this:

```
One Two Three equals one two three
one two three is greater than Four Five Six
Four Five Six is less than seven eight nine
Press any key to continue
```

Here is the program source code that produced the output:

```
#include "stdafx.h"
#include <iostream>
#include <mbstring.h>

using namespace std;

void cmp(unsigned char* s1, unsigned char* s2)
{
    int result = _mbsicmp(s1, s2);
    if (result < 0 )
    {
        cout << s1;
        cout << " is less than ";
        cout << s2 << endl;
    }
```

```
            else if (result > 0)
            {
                cout << s1;
                cout << " is greater than ";
                cout << s2 << endl;
            }
            else
            {
                cout << s1;
                cout << " equals ";
                cout << s2 << endl;
            }
        }

    int main(int argc, char* argv[])
    {
        unsigned char str1[] = "One Two Three";
        unsigned char str2[] = "one two three";
        unsigned char str3[] = "Four Five Six";
        unsigned char str4[] = "seven eight nine";

        cmp(str1, str2);
        cmp(str2, str3);
        cmp(str3, str4);

        return 0;
    }
```

CROSS-REFERENCE

See also _ismbbalnum(), _ismbbalpha(), _ismbbgraph(), _ismbbkalnum(), _ismbbkana(), _ismbbkprint(), _ismbbkpunct(), _ismbblead(), _ismbbprint(), _ismbbpunct(), _ismbbtrail(), _mbbtombc(), _mbbtype(), _mbccpy(), _mbcjistojms(), _mbcjmstojis(), _mbclen(), _mbctohira(), _mbctokata(), _mbctolower(), _mbctombb(), _mbctoupper(), _mbsbtype, _mbscat(), _mbschr(), _mbscmp(), _mbscoll(), _mbscpy(), _mbscspn(), _mbsdec(), _mbsdup(), _mbsicoll(), _mbsinc(), _mbslen(), _mbslwr(), _mbsnbcat(), _mbsnbcmp(), _mbsnbcnt(), _mbsnbcoll(), _mbsnbcpy(), _mbsnbicmp(), _mbsnbicoll(), _mbsnbset(), _mbsncat(), _mbsnccnt(), _mbsncmp(), _mbsncoll(), _mbsncpy(), _mbsnextc(), _mbsnicmp(), _mbsnicoll(), _mbsninc(), _mbsnset(), _mbspbrk(), _mbsrchr(), _mbsrev(), _mbsset(), _mbsspn(), _mbsspnp(), _mbsstr(), _mbstok(), _mbstrlen(), _mbsupr(), isleadbyte(), mblen(), mbstowcs(), and mbtowc().

_mbsicoll()

Function

The _mbsicoll() function compares two strings for the current locale without regard for case (case–insensitive compare), returning a value from Table M-4.

Table M-4 Return Values for _mbsicoll()

Value	Description
Less than 0	string1 is alphabetically less than string2.
0	The two strings are equal.
Greater than 0	string1 is alphabetically greater than string2.
_NLSCMPERROR	Error.

Header File

```
#include <mbstring.h>
```

Declaration

```
int _mbsicoll(const unsigned char *string1,
    const unsigned char *string2);
```

- *string1* — The first string to compare.
- *string2* — The second string to compare.

Example

The following program demonstrates how to use the _mbsicoll() function. When run, the program compares several pairs of strings and displays the result of the comparisons. The program's output looks like this:

```
One Two Three equals one two three
one two three is greater than Four Five Six
Four Five Six is less than seven eight nine
Press any key to continue
```

Here is the program source code that produced the output:

```
#include "stdafx.h"
#include <iostream>
#include <mbstring.h>
```

```
using namespace std;

void cmp(unsigned char* s1, unsigned char* s2)
{
    int result = _mbsicoll(s1, s2);
    if (result < 0 )
    {
        cout << s1;
        cout << " is less than ";
        cout << s2 << endl;
    }
    else if (result > 0)
    {
        cout << s1;
        cout << " is greater than ";
        cout << s2 << endl;
    }
    else
    {
        cout << s1;
        cout << " equals ";
        cout << s2 << endl;
    }
}

int main(int argc, char* argv[])
{
    unsigned char str1[] = "One Two Three";
    unsigned char str2[] = "one two three";
    unsigned char str3[] = "Four Five Six";
    unsigned char str4[] = "seven eight nine";

    cmp(str1, str2);
    cmp(str2, str3);
    cmp(str3, str4);

    return 0;
}
```

CROSS-REFERENCE

See also _ismbbalnum(), _ismbbalpha(), _ismbbgraph(), _ismbbkalnum(), _ismbbkana(), _ismbbkprint(), _ismbbkpunct(), _ismbblead(), _ismbbprint(), _ismbbpunct(), _ismbbtrail(), _mbbtombc(), _mbbtype(), _mbccpy(), _mbcjistojms(), _mbcjmstojis(), _mbclen(), _mbctohira(), _mbctokata(), _mbctolower(), _mbctombb(), _mbctoupper(), _mbsbtype, _mbscat(), _mbschr(), _mbscmp(), _mbscoll(), _mbscpy(), _mbscspn(), _mbsdec(), _mbsdup(), _mbsicmp(), _mbsinc(), _mbslen(), _mbslwr(), _mbsnbcat(), _mbsnbcmp(), _mbsnbcnt(), _mbsnbcoll(), _mbsnbcpy(), _mbsnbicmp(), _mbsnbicoll(), _mbsnbset(), _mbsncat(), _mbsnccnt(), _mbsncmp(), _mbsncoll(), _mbsncpy(), _mbsnextc(), _mbsnicmp(), _mbsnicoll(), _mbsninc(), _mbsnset(), _mbspbrk(), _mbsrchr(), _mbsrev(), _mbsset(), _mbsspn(), _mbsspnp(), _mbsstr(), _mbstok(), _mbstrlen(), _mbsupr(), isleadbyte(), mblen(), mbstowcs(), and mbtowc().

_mbsinc()

Function

The _mbsinc() function returns a pointer to the next character in a multibyte-character string, or NULL if the next character cannot be determined.

Header File

```
#include <mbstring.h>
```

Declaration

```
unsigned char* _mbsinc(const unsigned char *current);
```

- *current*—A pointer to the character for which to return the next character.

Example

The following program demonstrates how to use the _mbsinc() function. When run, the program locates the character that follows the fifth character in a string and displays the result. The program's output looks like this:

```
Source String = This is a test
Result = is a test
Press any key to continue
```

Here is the program source code that produced the output:

```
#include "stdafx.h"
#include <iostream>
#include <mbstring.h>

using namespace std;
```

```
int main(int argc, char* argv[])
{
    unsigned char srcStr[] = "This is a test";

    unsigned char* result = _mbsinc(&srcStr[4]);
    cout << "Source String = " << srcStr << endl;
    cout << "Result = " << result << endl;

    return 0;
}
```

CROSS-REFERENCE

See also _ismbbalnum(), _ismbbalpha(), _ismbbgraph(), _ismbbkalnum(), _ismbbkana(), _ismbbkprint(), _ismbbkpunct(), _ismbblead(), _ismbbprint(), _ismbbpunct(), _ismbbtrail(), _mbbtombc(), _mbbtype(), _mbccpy(), _mbcjistojms(), _mbcjmstojis(), _mbclen(), _mbctohira(), _mbctokata(), _mbctolower(), _mbctombb(), _mbctoupper(), _mbsbtype, _mbscat(), _mbschr(), _mbscmp(), _mbscoll(), _mbscpy(), _mbscspn(), _mbsdec(), _mbsdup(), _mbsicmp(), _mbsicoll(), _mbslen(), _mbslwr(), _mbsnbcat(), _mbsnbcmp(), _mbsnbcnt(), _mbsnbcoll(), _mbsnbcpy(), _mbsnbicmp(), _mbsnbicoll(), _mbsnbset(), _mbsncat(), _mbsnccnt(), _mbsncmp(), _mbsncoll(), _mbsncpy(), _mbsnextc(), _mbsnicmp(), _mbsnicoll(), _mbsninc(), _mbsnset(), _mbspbrk(), _mbsrchr(), _mbsrev(), _mbsset(), _mbsspn(), _mbsspnp(), _mbsstr(), _mbstok(), _mbstrlen(), _mbsupr(), isleadbyte(), mblen(), mbstowcs(), and mbtowc().

_mbslen()

Function

The _mbslen() function returns the length (the number of characters) of a multibyte-character string.

Header File

```
#include <mbstring.h>
```

Declaration

```
size_t _mbslen(const unsigned char *string);
```

- *string*—A pointer to the string for which to return the length.

Example

The following program demonstrates how to use the `_mbslen()` function. When run, the program calculates the length of a string and then uses the length to underline the source string. The program's output looks like this:

```
Source String:

This is a test
_____


Press any key to continue
```

Here is the program source code that produced the output:

```cpp
#include "stdafx.h"
#include <iostream>
#include <mbstring.h>

using namespace std;

int main(int argc, char* argv[])
{
    unsigned char srcStr[] = "This is a test";

    size_t len = _mbslen(srcStr);
    cout << "Source String:" << endl << endl;
    cout << srcStr << endl;
    for (unsigned x=0; x<len; ++x)
        cout << "-";
    cout << endl << endl;

    return 0;
}
```

CROSS-REFERENCE

See also _ismbbalnum(), _ismbbalpha(), _ismbbgraph(), _ismbbkalnum(), _ismbbkana(), _ismbbkprint(), _ismbbkpunct(), _ismbblead(), _ismbbprint(), _ismbbpunct(), _ismbbtrail(), _mbbtombc(), _mbbtype(), _mbccpy(), _mbcjistojms(), _mbcjmstojis(), _mbclen(), _mbctohira(), _mbctokata(), _mbctolower(), _mbctombb(), _mbctoupper(), _mbsbtype, _mbscat(), _mbschr(), _mbscmp(), _mbscoll(), _mbscpy(), _mbscspn(), _mbsdec(), _mbsdup(), _mbsicmp(), _mbsicoll(), _mbsinc(), _mbslwr(), _mbsnbcat(), _mbsnbcmp(), _mbsnbcnt(), _mbsnbcoll(), _mbsnbcpy(), _mbsnbicmp(), _mbsnbicoll(), _mbsnbset(), _mbsncat(), _mbsnccnt(), _mbsncmp(), _mbsncoll(), _mbsncpy(), _mbsnextc(), _mbsnicmp(), _mbsnicoll(), _mbsninc(), _mbsnset(), _mbspbrk(), _mbsrchr(), _mbsrev(), _mbsset(), _mbsspn(), _mbsspnp(), _mbsstr(), _mbstok(), _mbstrlen(), _mbsupr(), isleadbyte(), mblen(), mbstowcs(), and mbtowc().

_mbslwr()

Function

The _mbslwr() function converts a multibyte-character string to lowercase, returning a pointer to the new string.

Header File

```
#include <mbstring.h>
```

Declaration

```
unsigned char* _mbslwr(unsigned char *string);
```

■ *string* — The string to convert.

Example

The following program demonstrates how to use the _mbslwr() function. When run, the program converts several strings to lowercase and displays the results. The program's output looks like this:

```
Original String: One Two Three
Converted String: one two three

Original String: FOUR FIVE SIX
Converted String: four five six

Original String: seven eight nine
Converted String: seven eight nine

Press any key to continue
```

Here is the program source code that produced the output:

```
#include "stdafx.h"
#include <iostream>
#include <mbstring.h>

using namespace std;
```

```
void convert(unsigned char* s)
{
    cout << "Original String: " << s << endl;
    unsigned char* result = _mbslwr(s);
    cout << "Converted String: ";
    cout << result << endl << endl;
}

int main(int argc, char* argv[])
{
    unsigned char str1[] = "One Two Three";
    unsigned char str2[] = "FOUR FIVE SIX";
    unsigned char str3[] = "seven eight nine";

    convert(str1);
    convert(str2);
    convert(str3);

    return 0;
}
```

 CROSS-REFERENCE
See also _ismbbalnum(), _ismbbalpha(), _ismbbgraph(), _ismbbkalnum(), _ismbbkana(), _ismbbkprint(), _ismbbkpunct(), _ismbblead(), _ismbbprint(), _ismbbpunct(), _ismbbtrail(), _mbbtombc(), _mbbtype(), _mbccpy(), _mbcjistojms(), _mbcjmstojis(), _mbclen(), _mbctohira(), _mbctokata(), _mbctolower(), _mbctombb(), _mbctoupper(), _mbsbtype, _mbscat(), _mbschr(), _mbscmp(), _mbscoll(), _mbscpy(), _mbscspn(), _mbsdec(), _mbsdup(), _mbsicmp(), _mbsicoll(), _mbsinc(), _mbslen(), _mbsnbcat(), _mbsnbcmp(), _mbsnbcnt(), _mbsnbcoll(), _mbsnbcpy(), _mbsnbicmp(), _mbsnbicoll(), _mbsnbset(), _mbsncat(), _mbsnccnt(), _mbsncmp(), _mbsncoll(), _mbsncpy(), _mbsnextc(), _mbsnicmp(), _mbsnicoll(), _mbsninc(), _mbsnset(), _mbspbrk(), _mbsrchr(), _mbsrev(), _mbsset(), _mbsspn(), _mbsspnp(), _mbsstr(), _mbstok(), _mbstrlen(), _mbsupr(), isleadbyte(), mblen(), mbstowcs(), and mbtowc().

_mbsnbcat()

Function

The _mbsnbcat() function concatenates (joins together) multibyte-character strings, returning a pointer to the destination string.

Header File

```
#include <mbstring.h>
```

Declaration

```
unsigned char* _mbsnbcat(unsigned char *strDest,
    const unsigned char *strSource, size_t count);
```

- *count* — The number of bytes to concatenate.
- *strDest* — The string to which to concatenate *strSource*.
- *strSource* — The string to concatenate to *strDest*.

Example

The following program demonstrates how to use the _mbsnbcat() function. When run, the program concatenates the first six characters of the string "Four Five Six" to the string "One Two Three ". The program's output looks like this:

```
str1 = One Two Three
str2 = Four Five Six

Copying bytes from str1 to str2...

result = One Two Three Four F
str1 = One Two Three Four F

Press any key to continue
```

Here is the program source code that produced the output:

```
#include "stdafx.h"
#include <iostream>
#include <mbstring.h>

using namespace std;

int main(int argc, char* argv[])
{
    unsigned char str1[81] = "One Two Three ";
    unsigned char str2[] = "Four Five Six";
```

```
cout << "str1 = " << str1 << endl;
cout << "str2 = " << str2 << endl << endl;
cout << "Copying bytes from str1 to str2...";
cout << endl << endl;
unsigned char* result = _mbsnbcat(str1, str2, 6);
cout << "result = " << result << endl;
cout << "str1 = " << str1 << endl << endl;

return 0;
}
```

CROSS-REFERENCE

See also _ismbbalnum(), _ismbbalpha(), _ismbbgraph(), _ismbbkalnum(), _ismbbkana(), _ismbbkprint(), _ismbbkpunct(), _ismbblead(), _ismbbprint(), _ismbbpunct(), _ismbbtrail(), _mbbtombc(), _mbbtype(), _mbccpy(), _mbcjistojms(), _mbcjmstojis(), _mbclen(), _mbctohira(), _mbctokata(), _mbctolower(), _mbctombb(), _mbctoupper(), _mbsbtype, _mbscat(), _mbschr(), _mbscmp(), _mbscoll(), _mbscpy(), _mbscspn(), _mbsdec(), _mbsdup(), _mbsicmp(), _mbsicoll(), _mbsinc(), _mbslen(), _mbslwr(), _mbsnbcmp(), _mbsnbcnt(), _mbsnbcoll(), _mbsnbcpy(), _mbsnbicmp(), _mbsnbicoll(), _mbsnbset(), _mbsncat(), _mbsnccnt(), _mbsncmp(), _mbsncoll(), _mbsncpy(), _mbsnextc(), _mbsnicmp(), _mbsnicoll(), _mbsninc(), _mbsnset(), _mbspbrk(), _mbsrchr(), _mbsrev(), _mbsset(), _mbsspn(), _mbsspnp(), _mbsstr(), _mbstok(), _mbstrlen(), _mbsupr(), isleadbyte(), mblen(), mbstowcs(), and mbtowc().

_mbsnbcmp()

Function

The _mbsnbcmp() function compares a set of bytes in two multibyte-character strings, returning a value from Table M-5.

Table M-5 Return Values of _mbsnbcmp()

Value	Description
Less than 0	string1 is alphabetically less than string2.
0	The two strings are equal.
Greater than 0	string1 is alphabetically greater than string2.
_NLSCMPERROR	Error.

Header File

```
#include <mbstring.h>
```

Declaration

```
int _mbsnbcmp(const unsigned char *string1,
    const unsigned char *string2, size_t count);
```

- *count* — The number of characters to compare.
- *string1* — The first string to compare.
- *string2* — The second string to compare.

Example

The following program demonstrates how to use the _mbsnbcmp() function. When run, the program compares several pairs of strings and displays the result of the comparisons. The program's output looks like this:

```
For a length of 7 characters

One Two Three equals One Two Ten
One Two Ten is greater than Four Five Six
Four Five Six is greater than Four Eight Nine

Press any key to continue
```

Here is the program source code that produced the output:

```
#include "stdafx.h"
#include <iostream>
#include <mbstring.h>

using namespace std;

void cmp(unsigned char* s1,
        unsigned char* s2, size_t num)
{
    int result = _mbsnbcmp(s1, s2, num);

    if (result == _NLSCMPERROR)
        cout << "String compare error." << endl;
    else if (result < 0 )
    {
        cout << s1 << " is less than ";
```

```
            cout << s2 << endl;
        }
        else if (result > 0)
        {
            cout << s1 << " is greater than ";
            cout << s2 << endl;
        }
        else
        {
            cout << s1 << " equals ";
            cout << s2 << endl;
        }
    }

    int main(int argc, char* argv[])
    {
        unsigned char str1[] = "One Two Three";
        unsigned char str2[] = "One Two Ten";
        unsigned char str3[] = "Four Five Six";
        unsigned char str4[] = "Four Eight Nine";

        cout << "For a length of 7 characters" << endl << endl;
        cmp(str1, str2, 7);
        cmp(str2, str3, 7);
        cmp(str3, str4, 7);
        cout << endl;

        return 0;
    }
```

CROSS-REFERENCE

See also _ismbbalnum(), _ismbbalpha(), _ismbbgraph(), _ismbbkalnum(), _ismbbkana(), _ismbbkprint(), _ismbbkpunct(), _ismbblead(), _ismbbprint(), _ismbbpunct(), _ismbbtrail(), _mbbtombc(), _mbbtype(), _mbccpy(), _mbcjistojms(), _mbcjmstojis(), _mbclen(), _mbctohira(), _mbctokata(), _mbctolower(), _mbctombb(), _mbctoupper(), _mbsbtype, _mbscat(), _mbschr(), _mbscmp(), _mbscoll(), _mbscpy(), _mbscspn(), _mbsdec(), _mbsdup(), _mbsicmp(), _mbsicoll(), _mbsinc(), _mbslen(), _mbslwr(), _mbsnbcat(), _mbsnbcnt(), _mbsnbcoll(), _mbsnbcpy(), _mbsnbicmp(), _mbsnbicoll(), _mbsnbset(), _mbsncat(), _mbsnccnt(), _mbsncmp(), _mbsncoll(), _mbsncpy(), _mbsnextc(), _mbsnicmp(), _mbsnicoll(), _mbsninc(), _mbsnset(), _mbspbrk(), _mbsrchr(), _mbsrev(), _mbsset(), _mbsspn(), _mbsspnp(), _mbsstr(), _mbstok(), _mbstrlen(), _mbsupr(), isleadbyte(), mblen(), mbstowcs(), and mbtowc().

_mbsnbcnt()

Function

The _mbsnbcnt() function returns the number of bytes in a portion of a multibyte-character string.

Header File

```
#include <mbstring.h>
```

Declaration

```
size_t _mbsnbcnt(const unsigned char *string, size_t number);
```

- *number*—The number of characters to examine.
- *string*—A pointer to the character string to examine.

Example

The following program demonstrates how to use the _mbsnbcnt() function. When run, the program determines the number of bytes in the first four characters of a string and displays the result. The program's output looks like this:

```
Source String = This is a test
Result = 4
Press any key to continue
```

Here is the program source code that produced the output:

```
#include "stdafx.h"
#include <iostream>
#include <mbstring.h>

using namespace std;

int main(int argc, char* argv[])
{
    unsigned char srcStr[] = "This is a test";

    size_t result = _mbsnbcnt(srcStr, 4);
    cout << "Source String = " << srcStr << endl;
    cout << "Result = " << result << endl;

    return 0;
}
```

CROSS-REFERENCE
See also _ismbbalnum(), _ismbbalpha(), _ismbbgraph(), _ismbbkalnum(), _ismbbkana(), _ismbbkprint(), _ismbbkpunct(), _ismbblead(), _ismbbprint(), _ismbbpunct(), _ismbbtrail(), _mbbtombc(), _mbbtype(), _mbccpy(), _mbcjistojms(), _mbcjmstojis(), _mbclen(), _mbctohira(), _mbctokata(), _mbctolower(), _mbctombb(), _mbctoupper(), _mbsbtype, _mbscat(), _mbschr(), _mbscmp(), _mbscoll(), _mbscpy(), _mbscspn(), _mbsdec(), _mbsdup(), _mbsicmp(), _mbsicoll(), _mbsinc(), _mbslen(), _mbslwr(), _mbsnbcat(), _mbsnbcmp(), _mbsnbcoll(), _mbsnbcpy(), _mbsnbicmp(), _mbsnbicoll(), _mbsnbset(), _mbsncat(), _mbsnccnt(), _mbsncmp(), _mbsncoll(), _mbsncpy(), _mbsnextc(), _mbsnicmp(), _mbsnicoll(), _mbsninc(), _mbsnset(), _mbspbrk(), _mbsrchr(), _mbsrev(), _mbsset(), _mbsspn(), _mbsspnp(), _mbsstr(), _mbstok(), _mbstrlen(), _mbsupr(), isleadbyte(), mblen(), mbstowcs(), and mbtowc().

_mbsnbcoll()

Function

The _mbsnbcoll() function compares two multibyte-character strings for the current locale, returning a value from the Table M-6.

Table M-6 Return Values for _mbsnbcoll()

Value	Description
Less than 0	string1 is alphabetically less than string2.
0	The two strings are equal.
Greater than 0	string1 is alphabetically greater than string2.
_NLSCMPERROR	Error.

Header File

```
#include <mbstring.h>
```

Declaration

```
int _mbsnbcoll(const unsigned char *string1,
    const unsigned char *string2);
```

- *string1* — The first string to compare.
- *string2* — The second string to compare.

Example

The following program demonstrates how to use the _mbsnbcoll() function. When run, the program compares several pairs of strings and displays the result of the comparisons. The program's output looks like this:

```
One Two Three is greater than one two three
one two three is greater than Four Five Six
Four Five Six is less than seven eight nine
Press any key to continue
```

Here is the program source code that produced the output:

```cpp
#include "stdafx.h"
#include <iostream>
#include <mbstring.h>

using namespace std;

void cmp(unsigned char* s1,
         unsigned char* s2, size_t num)
{
    int result = _mbsnbcoll(s1, s2, num);
    if (result < 0 )
    {
        cout << s1;
        cout << " is less than ";
        cout << s2 << endl;
    }
    else if (result > 0)
    {
        cout << s1;
        cout << " is greater than ";
        cout << s2 << endl;
    }
    else
    {
        cout << s1;
        cout << " equals ";
        cout << s2 << endl;
    }
}

int main(int argc, char* argv[])
{
    unsigned char str1[] = "One Two Three";
```

```
unsigned char str2[] = "one two three";
unsigned char str3[] = "Four Five Six";
unsigned char str4[] = "seven eight nine";

cmp(str1, str2, 7);
cmp(str2, str3, 7);
cmp(str3, str4, 7);

return 0;
}
```

CROSS-REFERENCE

See also _ismbbalnum(), _ismbbalpha(), _ismbbgraph(), _ismbbkalnum(), _ismbbkana(), _ismbbkprint(), _ismbbkpunct(), _ismbblead(), _ismbbprint(), _ismbbpunct(), _ismbbtrail(), _mbbtombc(), _mbbtype(), _mbccpy(), _mbcjistojms(), _mbcjmstojis(), _mbclen(), _mbctohira(), _mbctokata(), _mbctolower(), _mbctombb(), _mbctoupper(), _mbsbtype, _mbscat(), _mbschr(), _mbscmp(), _mbscoll(), _mbscpy(), _mbscspn(), _mbsdec(), _mbsdup(), _mbsicmp(), _mbsicoll(), _mbsinc(), _mbslen(), _mbslwr(), _mbsnbcat(), _mbsnbcmp(), _mbsnbcnt(), _mbsnbcpy(), _mbsnbicmp(), _mbsnbicoll(), _mbsnbset(), _mbsncat(), _mbsnccnt(), _mbsncmp(), _mbsncoll(), _mbsncpy(), _mbsnextc(), _mbsnicmp(), _mbsnicoll(), _mbsninc(), _mbsnset(), _mbspbrk(), _mbsrchr(), _mbsrev(), _mbsset(), _mbsspn(), _mbsspnp(), _mbsstr(), _mbstok(), _mbstrlen(), _mbsupr(), isleadbyte(), mblen(), mbstowcs(), and mbtowc().

_mbsnbcpy()

Function

The _mbsnbcpy() function copies a specified number of bytes from one multi-byte-character string to another, returning a pointer to the destination string. The source and destination strings cannot overlap.

Header File

```
#include <mbstring.h>
```

Declaration

```
unsigned char* _mbsnbcpy(unsigned char *strDest,
    const unsigned char *strSource, size_t count);
```

- *count* — The number of bytes to copy.
- *strDest* — A pointer to the destination string.
- *strSource* — A pointer to the source string.

Example

The following program demonstrates how to use the _mbsnbcpy() function. When run, the program copies 11 bytes from one string to another and displays the result. The program's output looks like this:

```
Source string = This is a test
Destination string = This is a t
Press any key to continue
```

Here is the program source code that produced the output:

```cpp
#include "stdafx.h"
#include <iostream>
#include <mbstring.h>

using namespace std;

int main(int argc, char* argv[])
{
    unsigned char destStr[81];
    unsigned char srcStr[] = "This is a test";

    unsigned char* pResult = _mbsnbcpy(destStr, srcStr, 11);
    pResult[11] = 0;
    cout << "Source string = " << srcStr << endl;
    cout << "Destination string = " << pResult << endl;

    return 0;
}
```

CROSS-REFERENCE

See also _ismbbalnum(), _ismbbalpha(), _ismbbgraph(), _ismbbkalnum(), _ismbbkana(), _ismbbkprint(), _ismbbkpunct(), _ismbblead(), _ismbbprint(), _ismbbpunct(), _ismbbtrail(), _mbbtombc(), _mbbtype(), _mbccpy(), _mbcjistojms(), _mbcjmstojis(), _mbclen(), _mbctohira(), _mbctokata(), _mbctolower(), _mbctombb(), _mbctoupper(), _mbsbtype, _mbscat(), _mbschr(), _mbscmp(), _mbscoll(), _mbscpy(), _mbscspn(), _mbsdec(), _mbsdup(), _mbsicmp(), _mbsicoll(), _mbsinc(), _mbslen(), _mbslwr(), _mbsnbcat(), _mbsnbcmp(), _mbsnbcnt(), _mbsnbcoll(), _mbsnbicmp(), _mbsnbicoll(), _mbsnbset(), _mbsncat(), _mbsnccnt(), _mbsncmp(), _mbsncoll(), _mbsncpy(), _mbsnextc(), _mbsnicmp(), _mbsnicoll(), _mbsninc(), _mbsnset(), _mbspbrk(), _mbsrchr(), _mbsrev(), _mbsset(), _mbsspn(), _mbsspnp(), _mbsstr(), _mbstok(), _mbstrlen(), _mbsupr(), isleadbyte(), mblen(), mbstowcs(), and mbtowc().

_mbsnbicmp()

Function

The _mbsnbicmp() function compares a set of bytes in two multibyte-character strings without regard to character case (case–insensitive compare), returning a value from Table M-7.

Table M-7 Return Values for _mbsnbicmp()

Value	Description
Less than 0	string1 is alphabetically less than string2.
0	The two strings are equal.
Greater than 0	string1 is alphabetically greater than string2.
_NLSCMPERROR	Error.

Header File

```
#include <mbstring.h>
```

Declaration

```
int _mbsnbicmp(const unsigned char *string1,
    const unsigned char *string2, size_t count);
```

- *count* — The number of characters to compare.
- *string1* — The first string to compare.
- *string2* — The second string to compare.

Example

The following program demonstrates how to use the _mbsnbicmp() function. When run, the program compares several pairs of strings and displays the result of the comparisons. The program's output looks like this:

```
For a length of 7 characters
```

```
One Two Three equals One Two Ten
One Two Ten is greater than Four Five Six
Four Five Six is greater than Four Eight Nine
Four Eight Nine equals FOUR EIGHT NINE

Press any key to continue
```

Here is the program source code that produced the output:

```
#include "stdafx.h"
#include <iostream>
#include <mbstring.h>

using namespace std;

void cmp(unsigned char* s1,
         unsigned char* s2, size_t num)
{
    int result = _mbsnbicmp(s1, s2, num);

    if (result == _NLSCMPERROR)
        cout << "String compare error." << endl;
    else if (result < 0 )
    {
        cout << s1 << " is less than ";
        cout << s2 << endl;
    }
    else if (result > 0)
    {
        cout << s1 << " is greater than ";
        cout << s2 << endl;
    }
    else
    {
        cout << s1 << " equals ";
        cout << s2 << endl;
    }
}

int main(int argc, char* argv[])
{
    unsigned char str1[] = "One Two Three";
    unsigned char str2[] = "One Two Ten";
    unsigned char str3[] = "Four Five Six";
    unsigned char str4[] = "Four Eight Nine";
```

```
unsigned char str5[] = "FOUR EIGHT NINE";

cout << "For a length of 7 characters" << endl << endl;
cmp(str1, str2, 7);
cmp(str2, str3, 7);
cmp(str3, str4, 7);
cmp(str4, str5, 7);
cout << endl;

return 0;
}
```

CROSS-REFERENCE

See also _ismbbalnum(), _ismbbalpha(), _ismbbgraph(), _ismbbkalnum(),
_ismbbkana(), _ismbbkprint(), _ismbbkpunct(), _ismbblead(), _ismbbprint(),
_ismbbpunct(), _ismbbtrail(), _mbbtombc(), _mbbtype(), _mbccpy(), _mbcjistojms(),
_mbcjmstojis(), _mbclen(), _mbctohira(), _mbctokata(), _mbctolower(),
_mbctombc(), _mbctoupper(), _mbsbtype, _mbscat(), _mbschr(), _mbscmp(),
_mbscoll(), _mbscpy(), _mbscspn(), _mbsdec(), _mbsdup(), _mbsicmp(), _mbsicoll(),
_mbsinc(), _mbslen(), _mbslwr(), _mbsnbcat(), _mbsnbcmp(), _mbsnbcnt(),
_mbsnbcoll(), _mbsnbcpy(), _mbsnbicoll(), _mbsnbset(), _mbsncat(), _mbsnccnt(),
_mbsncmp(), _mbsncoll(), _mbsncpy(), _mbsnextc(), _mbsnicmp(), _mbsnicoll(),
_mbsninc(), _mbsnset(), _mbspbrk(), _mbsrchr(), _mbsrev(), _mbsset(), _mbsspn(),
_mbsspnp(), _mbsstr(), _mbstok(), _mbstrlen(), _mbsupr(), isleadbyte(), mblen(),
mbstowcs(), and mbtowc().

_mbsnbicoll()

Function

The _mbsnbicoll() function compares two multibyte-character strings for
the current locale without regard for case (case-insensitive compare), returning a value from Table M-8.

Table M-8 Return Values for _mbsnbicoll()

Value	Description
Less than 0	string1 is alphabetically less than string2.
0	The two strings are equal.
Greater than 0	string1 is alphabetically greater than string2.
_NLSCMPERROR	Error.

Header File

```
#include <mbstring.h>
```

Declaration

```
int _mbsnbicoll(const unsigned char *string1,
    const unsigned char *string2);
```

- *string1* — The first string to compare.
- *string2* — The second string to compare.

Example

The following program demonstrates how to use the _mbsnbicoll() function. When run, the program compares several pairs of strings and displays the result of the comparisons. The program's output looks like this:

```
One Two Three equals one two three
one two three is greater than Four Five Six
Four Five Six is less than seven eight nine
Press any key to continue
```

Here is the program source code that produced the output:

```
#include "stdafx.h"
#include <iostream>
#include <mbstring.h>

using namespace std;

void cmp(unsigned char* s1,
        unsigned char* s2, size_t num)
{
    int result = _mbsnbicoll(s1, s2, num);
    if (result < 0 )
    {
        cout << s1;
        cout << " is less than ";
        cout << s2 << endl;
    }
    else if (result > 0)
```

```
    {
        cout << s1;
        cout << " is greater than ";
        cout << s2 << endl;
    }
    else
    {
        cout << s1;
        cout << " equals ";
        cout << s2 << endl;
    }
}

int main(int argc, char* argv[])
{
    unsigned char str1[] = "One Two Three";
    unsigned char str2[] = "one two three";
    unsigned char str3[] = "Four Five Six";
    unsigned char str4[] = "seven eight nine";

    cmp(str1, str2, 7);
    cmp(str2, str3, 7);
    cmp(str3, str4, 7);

    return 0;
}
```

CROSS-REFERENCE

See also _ismbbalnum(), _ismbbalpha(), _ismbbgraph(), _ismbbkalnum(), _ismbbkana(), _ismbbkprint(), _ismbbkpunct(), _ismbblead(), _ismbbprint(), _ismbbpunct(), _ismbbtrail(), _mbbtombc(), _mbbtype(), _mbccpy(), _mbcjistojms(), _mbcjmstojis(), _mbclen(), _mbctohira(), _mbctokata(), _mbctolower(), _mbctombb(), _mbctoupper(), _mbsbtype, _mbscat(), _mbschr(), _mbscmp(), _mbscoll(), _mbscpy(), _mbscspn(), _mbsdec(), _mbsdup(), _mbsicmp(), _mbsicoll(), _mbsinc(), _mbslen(), _mbslwr(), _mbsnbcat(), _mbsnbcmp(), _mbsnbcnt(), _mbsnbcoll(), _mbsnbcpy(), _mbsnbicmp(), _mbsnbset(), _mbsncat(), _mbsnccnt(), _mbsncmp(), _mbsncoll(), _mbsncpy(), _mbsnextc(), _mbsnicmp(), _mbsnicoll(), _mbsninc(), _mbsnset(), _mbspbrk(), _mbsrchr(), _mbsrev(), _mbsset(), _mbsspn(), _mbsspnp(), _mbsstr(), _mbstok(), _mbstrlen(), _mbsupr(), isleadbyte(), mblen(), mbstowcs(), and mbtowc().

_mbsnbset()

Function

The _mbsnbset() function sets a portion of the contents of a multibyte-character string to a given character, returning a pointer to the new string.

Header File

```
#include <mbstring.h>
```

Declaration

```
unsigned char* _mbsnbset(const unsigned char *string,
    unsigned int c, size_t count);
```

- *c* — The character with which to fill the string.
- *count* — The number of characters to set.
- *string* — The string to convert.

Example

The following program demonstrates how to use the _mbsnbset() function. When run, the program sets several strings to various symbols and displays the results. The program's output looks like this:

```
Original String: One Two Three
Converted String: ??? Two Three

Original String: FOUR FIVE SIX
Converted String: *******VE SIX

Original String: seven eight nine
Converted String: #################

Press any key to continue
```

Here is the program source code that produced the output:

```
#include "stdafx.h"
#include <iostream>
```

```cpp
#include <mbstring.h>

using namespace std;

void convert(unsigned char* s,
            unsigned int c, size_t num)
{
    cout << "Original String: ";
    cout << s << endl;
    unsigned char* result = _mbsnbset(s, c, num);
    cout << "Converted String: ";
    cout << result << endl << endl;
}

int main(int argc, char* argv[])
{
    unsigned char str1[] = "One Two Three";
    unsigned char str2[] = "FOUR FIVE SIX";
    unsigned char str3[] = "seven eight nine";

    convert(str1, '?', 3);
    convert(str2, '*', 7);
    convert(str3, '#', 16);

    return 0;
}
```

CROSS-REFERENCE

See also _ismbbalnum(), _ismbbalpha(), _ismbbgraph(), _ismbbkalnum(), _ismbbkana(), _ismbbkprint(), _ismbbkpunct(), _ismbblead(), _ismbbprint(), _ismbbpunct(), _ismbbtrail(), _mbbtombc(), _mbbtype(), _mbccpy(), _mbcjistojms(), _mbcjmstojis(), _mbclen(), _mbctohira(), _mbctokata(), _mbctolower(), _mbctombb(), _mbctoupper(), _mbsbtype, _mbscat(), _mbschr(), _mbscmp(), _mbscoll(), _mbscpy(), _mbscspn(), _mbsdec(), _mbsdup(), _mbsicmp(), _mbsicoll(), _mbsinc(), _mbslen(), _mbslwr(), _mbsnbcat(), _mbsnbcmp(), _mbsnbcnt(), _mbsnbcoll(), _mbsnbcpy(), _mbsnbicmp(), _mbsnbicoll(), _mbsncat(), _mbsnccnt(), _mbsncmp(), _mbsncoll(), _mbsncpy(), _mbsnextc(), _mbsnicmp(), _mbsnicoll(), _mbsninc(), _mbsnset(), _mbspbrk(), _mbsrchr(), _mbsrev(), _mbsset(), _mbsspn(), _mbsspnp(), _mbsstr(), _mbstok(), _mbstrlen(), _mbsupr(), isleadbyte(), mblen(), mbstowcs(), and mbtowc().

_mbsncat()

Function

The _mbsncat() function concatenates (joins together) multibyte-character strings, returning a pointer to the destination string.

Header File

```
#include <mbstring.h>
```

Declaration

```
unsigned char* _mbsncat(unsigned char *strDest,
    const unsigned char *strSource, size_t count);
```

- *count* — The number of characters to concatenate.
- *strDest* — The string to which to concatenate *strSource*.
- *strSource* — The string to concatenate to *strDest*.

Example

The following program demonstrates how to use the _mbsncat() function. When run, the program concatenates the first six characters of the string "Four Five Six" to the string "One Two Three". The program's output looks like this:

```
str1 = One Two Three
str2 = Four Five Six

Performing concatenation...

result = One Two Three Four F
str1 = One Two Three Four F

Press any key to continue
```

Here is the program source code that produced the output:

```
#include "stdafx.h"
#include <iostream>
#include <mbstring.h>
```

```
using namespace std;

int main(int argc, char* argv[])
{
    unsigned char str1[81] = "One Two Three ";
    unsigned char str2[] = "Four Five Six";

    cout << "str1 = " << str1 << endl;
    cout << "str2 = " << str2 << endl << endl;
    cout << "Performing concatenation..." << endl << endl;
    unsigned char* result = _mbsncat(str1, str2, 6);
    cout << "result = " << result << endl;
    cout << "str1 = " << str1 << endl << endl;

    return 0;
}
```

CROSS-REFERENCE

See also _ismbbalnum(), _ismbbalpha(), _ismbbgraph(), _ismbbkalnum(), _ismbbkana(), _ismbbkprint(), _ismbbkpunct(), _ismbblead(), _ismbbprint(), _ismbbpunct(), _ismbbtrail(), _mbbtombc(), _mbbtype(), _mbccpy(), _mbcjistojms(), _mbcjmstojis(), _mbclen(), _mbctohira(), _mbctokata(), _mbctolower(), _mbctombb(), _mbctoupper(), _mbsbtype, _mbscat(), _mbschr(), _mbscmp(), _mbscoll(), _mbscpy(), _mbscspn(), _mbsdec(), _mbsdup(), _mbsicmp(), _mbsicoll(), _mbsinc(), _mbslen(), _mbslwr(), _mbsnbcat(), _mbsnbcmp(), _mbsnbcnt(), _mbsnbcoll(), _mbsnbcpy(), _mbsnbicmp(), _mbsnbicoll(), _mbsnbset(), _mbsnccnt(), _mbsncmp(), _mbsncoll(), _mbsncpy(), _mbsnextc(), _mbsnicmp(), _mbsnicoll(), _mbsninc(), _mbsnset(), _mbspbrk(), _mbsrchr(), _mbsrev(), _mbsset(), _mbsspn(), _mbsspnp(), _mbsstr(), _mbstok(), _mbstrlen(), _mbsupr(), isleadbyte(), mblen(), mbstowcs(), and mbtowc().

_mbsnccnt()

Function

The _mbsnccnt() function returns the number of characters in a portion of a multibyte-character string.

Header File

```
#include <mbstring.h>
```

Declaration

```
size_t _mbsnccnt(const unsigned char *string, size_t number);
```

- *number*—The number of bytes to examine.
- *string*—A pointer to the string to examine.

Example

The following program demonstrates how to use the _mbsnccnt() function. When run, the program determines the number of characters in the first four bytes of a string and displays the result. The program's output looks like this:

```
Source String = This is a test
Result = 4
Press any key to continue
```

Here is the program source code that produced the output:

```cpp
#include "stdafx.h"
#include <iostream>
#include <mbstring.h>

using namespace std;

int main(int argc, char* argv[])
{
    unsigned char srcStr[] = "This is a test";

    size_t result = _mbsnccnt(srcStr, 4);
    cout << "Source String = " << srcStr << endl;
    cout << "Result = " << result << endl;

    return 0;
}
```

CROSS-REFERENCE

See also _ismbbalnum(), _ismbbalpha(), _ismbbgraph(), _ismbbkalnum(), _ismbbkana(), _ismbbkprint(), _ismbbkpunct(), _ismbblead(), _ismbbprint(), _ismbbpunct(), _ismbbtrail(), _mbbtombc(), _mbbtype(), _mbccpy(), _mbcjistojms(), _mbcjmstojis(), _mbclen(), _mbctohira(), _mbctokata(), _mbctolower(), _mbctombb(), _mbctoupper(), _mbsbtype, _mbscat(), _mbschr(), _mbscmp(), _mbscoll(), _mbscpy(), _mbscspn(), _mbsdec(), _mbsdup(), _mbsicmp(), _mbsicoll(), _mbsinc(), _mbslen(), _mbslwr(), _mbsnbcat(), _mbsnbcmp(), _mbsnbcnt(), _mbsnbcoll(), _mbsnbcpy(), _mbsnbicmp(), _mbsnbicoll(), _mbsnbset(), _mbsncat(), _mbsncmp(), _mbsncoll(), _mbsncpy(), _mbsnextc(), _mbsnicmp(), _mbsnicoll(), _mbsninc(), _mbsnset(), _mbspbrk(), _mbsrchr(), _mbsrev(), _mbsset(), _mbsspn(), _mbsspnp(), _mbsstr(), _mbstok(), _mbstrlen(), _mbsupr(), isleadbyte(), mblen(), mbstowcs(), and mbtowc().

_mbsncmp()

Function

The _mbsncmp() function compares characters in two multibyte-character strings, returning a value from Table M-9.

Table M-9 Return Values for _mbsncmp()

Value	Description
Less than 0	string1 is alphabetically less than string2.
0	The two strings are equal.
Greater than 0	string1 is alphabetically greater than string2.
_NLSCMPERROR	Error.

Header File

```
#include <mbstring.h>
```

Declaration

```
int _mbsncmp(const unsigned char *string1,
    const unsigned char *string2, size_t count);
```

- *count* — The number of characters to compare.
- *string1* — The first string to compare.
- *string2* — The second string to compare.

Example

The following program demonstrates how to use the _mbsncmp() function. When run, the program compares several pairs of strings and displays the result of the comparisons. The program's output looks like this:

```
For a length of 7 characters
```

```
One Two Three equals One Two Ten
One Two Ten is greater than Four Five Six
Four Five Six is greater than Four Eight Nine
Four Eight Nine is greater than FOUR EIGHT NINE

Press any key to continue
```

Here is the program source code that produced the output:

```
#include "stdafx.h"
#include <iostream>
#include <mbstring.h>

using namespace std;

void cmp(unsigned char* s1,
         unsigned char* s2, size_t num)
{
    int result = _mbsncmp(s1, s2, num);

    if (result == _NLSCMPERROR)
        cout << "String compare error." << endl;
    else if (result < 0 )
    {
        cout << s1 << " is less than ";
        cout << s2 << endl;
    }
    else if (result > 0)
    {
        cout << s1 << " is greater than ";
        cout << s2 << endl;
    }
    else
    {
        cout << s1 << " equals ";
        cout << s2 << endl;
    }
}

int main(int argc, char* argv[])
{
    unsigned char str1[] = "One Two Three";
    unsigned char str2[] = "One Two Ten";
    unsigned char str3[] = "Four Five Six";
    unsigned char str4[] = "Four Eight Nine";
```

```
unsigned char str5[] = "FOUR EIGHT NINE";

cout << "For a length of 7 characters" << endl << endl;
cmp(str1, str2, 7);
cmp(str2, str3, 7);
cmp(str3, str4, 7);
cmp(str4, str5, 7);
cout << endl;

return 0;
}
```

CROSS-REFERENCE
See also _ismbbalnum(), _ismbbalpha(), _ismbbgraph(), _ismbbkalnum(), _ismbbkana(), _ismbbkprint(), _ismbbkpunct(), _ismbblead(), _ismbbprint(), _ismbbpunct(), _ismbbtrail(), _mbbtombc(), _mbbtype(), _mbccpy(), _mbcjistojms(), _mbcjmstojis(), _mbclen(), _mbctohira(), _mbctokata(), _mbctolower(), _mbctombb(), _mbctoupper(), _mbsbtype, _mbscat(), _mbschr(), _mbscmp(), _mbscoll(), _mbscpy(), _mbscspn(), _mbsdec(), _mbsdup(), _mbsicmp(), _mbsicoll(), _mbsinc(), _mbslen(), _mbslwr(), _mbsnbcat(), _mbsnbcmp(), _mbsnbcnt(), _mbsnbcoll(), _mbsnbcpy(), _mbsnbicmp(), _mbsnbicoll(), _mbsnbset(), _mbsncat(), _mbsnccnt(), _mbsncoll(), _mbsncpy(), _mbsnextc(), _mbsnicmp(), _mbsnicoll(), _mbsninc(), _mbsnset(), _mbspbrk(), _mbsrchr(), _mbsrev(), _mbsset(), _mbsspn(), _mbsspnp(), _mbsstr(), _mbstok(), _mbstrlen(), _mbsupr(), isleadbyte(), mblen(), mbstowcs(), and mbtowc().

_mbsncoll()

Function

The _mbsncoll() function compares two multibyte-character strings for the current locale, returning a value from Table M-10.

Table M-10 _mbsncoll() Return Values

Value	Description
Less than 0	string1 is alphabetically less than string2.
0	The two strings are equal.
Greater than 0	string1 is alphabetically greater than string2.
_NLSCMPERROR	Error.

Header File

```
#include <mbstring.h>
```

Declaration

```
int _mbsncoll(const unsigned char *string1,
    const unsigned char *string2, size_t count);
```

- *count* — The number of characters to compare.
- *string1* — The first string to compare.
- *string2* — The second string to compare.

Example

The following program demonstrates how to use the _mbsncoll() function. When run, the program compares several pairs of strings and displays the result of the comparisons. The program's output looks like this:

```
One Two Three equals One Two three
One Two three is greater than one Two Three
one Two Three is less than SEVEN EIGHT nine
SEVEN EIGHT nine is greater than seven eight nine
Press any key to continue
```

Here is the program source code that produced the output:

```cpp
#include "stdafx.h"
#include <iostream>
#include <mbstring.h>

using namespace std;

void cmp(unsigned char* s1,
         unsigned char* s2, size_t num)
{
    int result = _mbsncoll(s1, s2, num);
    if (result < 0 )
    {
        cout << s1;
        cout << " is less than ";
        cout << s2 << endl;
    }
```

```
        else if (result > 0)
        {
            cout << s1;
            cout << " is greater than ";
            cout << s2 << endl;
        }
        else
        {
            cout << s1;
            cout << " equals ";
            cout << s2 << endl;
        }
    }

    int main(int argc, char* argv[])
    {
        unsigned char str1[] = "One Two Three";
        unsigned char str2[] = "One Two three";
        unsigned char str3[] = "one Two Three";
        unsigned char str4[] = "SEVEN EIGHT nine";
        unsigned char str5[] = "seven eight nine";

        cmp(str1, str2, 7);
        cmp(str2, str3, 7);
        cmp(str3, str4, 7);
        cmp(str4, str5, 7);

        return 0;
    }
```

CROSS-REFERENCE

See also _ismbbalnum(), _ismbbalpha(), _ismbbgraph(), _ismbbkalnum(), _ismbbkana(), _ismbbkprint(), _ismbbkpunct(), _ismbblead(), _ismbbprint(), _ismbbpunct(), _ismbbtrail(), _mbbtombc(), _mbbtype(), _mbccpy(), _mbcjistojms(), _mbcjmstojis(), _mbclen(), _mbctohira(), _mbctokata(), _mbctolower(), _mbctombb(), _mbctoupper(), _mbsbtype, _mbscat(), _mbschr(), _mbscmp(), _mbscoll(), _mbscpy(), _mbscspn(), _mbsdec(), _mbsdup(), _mbsicmp(), _mbsicoll(), _mbsinc(), _mbslen(), _mbslwr(), _mbsnbcat(), _mbsnbcmp(), _mbsnbcnt(), _mbsnbcoll(), _mbsnbcpy(), _mbsnbicmp(), _mbsnbicoll(), _mbsnbset(), _mbsncat(), _mbsnccnt(), _mbsncmp(), _mbsncpy(), _mbsnextc(), _mbsnicmp(), _mbsnicoll(), _mbsninc(), _mbsnset(), _mbspbrk(), _mbsrchr(), _mbsrev(), _mbsset(), _mbsspn(), _mbsspnp(), _mbsstr(), _mbstok(), _mbstrlen(), _mbsupr(), isleadbyte(), mblen(), mbstowcs(), and mbtowc().

_mbsncpy()

Function

The _mbsncpy() function copies a specified number of multibyte characters from one string to another, returning a pointer to the destination string. The source and destination strings cannot overlap.

Header File

```
#include <mbstring.h>
```

Declaration

```
unsigned char* _mbsncpy(unsigned char *strDest,
    const unsigned char *strSource, size_t count);
```

- *count*—The number of characters to copy.
- *strDest*—A pointer to the destination string.
- *strSource*—A pointer to the source string.

Example

The following program demonstrates how to use the _mbsncpy() function. When run, the program copies 11 characters from one string to another and displays the result. The program's output looks like this:

```
Source string = This is a test
Destination string = This is a t
Press any key to continue
```

Here is the program source code that produced the output:

```
#include "stdafx.h"
#include <iostream>
#include <mbstring.h>

using namespace std;

int main(int argc, char* argv[])
{
    unsigned char destStr[81];
    unsigned char srcStr[] = "This is a test";
```

```
unsigned char* pResult = _mbsncpy(destStr, srcStr, 11);
pResult[11] = 0;
cout << "Source string = " << srcStr << endl;
cout << "Destination string = " << pResult << endl;

return 0;
}
```

CROSS-REFERENCE

See also _ismbbalnum(), _ismbbalpha(), _ismbbgraph(), _ismbbkalnum(), _ismbbkana(), _ismbbkprint(), _ismbbkpunct(), _ismbblead(), _ismbbprint(), _ismbbpunct(), _ismbbtrail(), _mbbtombc(), _mbbtype(), _mbccpy(), _mbcjistojms(), _mbcjmstojis(), _mbclen(), _mbctohira(), _mbctokata(), _mbctolower(), _mbctombb(), _mbctoupper(), _mbsbtype, _mbscat(), _mbschr(), _mbscmp(), _mbscoll(), _mbscpy(), _mbscspn(), _mbsdec(), _mbsdup(), _mbsicmp(), _mbsicoll(), _mbsinc(), _mbslen(), _mbslwr(), _mbsnbcat(), _mbsnbcmp(), _mbsnbcnt(), _mbsnbcoll(), _mbsnbcpy(), _mbsnbicmp(), _mbsnbicoll(), _mbsnbset(), _mbsncat(), _mbsnccnt(), _mbsncmp(), _mbsncoll(), _mbsnextc(), _mbsnicmp(), _mbsnicoll(), _mbsninc(), _mbsnset(), _mbspbrk(), _mbsrchr(), _mbsrev(), _mbsset(), _mbsspn(), _mbsspnp(), _mbsstr(), _mbstok(), _mbstrlen(), _mbsupr(), isleadbyte(), mblen(), mbstowcs(), and mbtowc().

_mbsnextc()

Function

The _mbsnextc() function returns, as an integer, the value of the next character in a multibyte-character string.

Header File

```
#include <mbstring.h>
```

Declaration

```
unsigned int _mbsnextc(const unsigned char *string);
```

- *string* — A pointer to the source string.

Example

The following program demonstrates how to use the `_mbsnextc()` function. When run, the program determines the integer value of the fifth character in a string and displays the result. The program's output looks like this:

```
Source String = This is a test
Result = 32
Press any key to continue
```

Here is the program source code that produced the output:

```cpp
#include "stdafx.h"
#include <iostream>
#include <mbstring.h>

using namespace std;

int main(int argc, char* argv[])
{
    unsigned char srcStr[] = "This is a test";

    unsigned int result = _mbsnextc(&srcStr[4]);
    cout << "Source String = ";
    cout << srcStr << endl;
    cout << "Result = " << result << endl;

    return 0;
}
```

CROSS-REFERENCE

See also _ismbbalnum(), _ismbbalpha(), _ismbbgraph(), _ismbbkalnum(), _ismbbkana(), _ismbbkprint(), _ismbbkpunct(), _ismbblead(), _ismbbprint(), _ismbbpunct(), _ismbbtrail(), _mbbtombc(), _mbbtype(), _mbccpy(), _mbcjistojms(), _mbcjmstojis(), _mbclen(), _mbctohira(), _mbctokata(), _mbctolower(), _mbctombb(), _mbctoupper(), _mbsbtype, _mbscat(), _mbschr(), _mbscmp(), _mbscoll(), _mbscpy(), _mbscspn(), _mbsdec(), _mbsdup(), _mbsicmp(), _mbsicoll(), _mbsinc(), _mbslen(), _mbslwr(), _mbsnbcat(), _mbsnbcmp(), _mbsnbcnt(), _mbsnbcoll(), _mbsnbcpy(), _mbsnbicmp(), _mbsnbicoll(), _mbsnbset(), _mbsncat(), _mbsnccnt(), _mbsncmp(), _mbsncoll(), _mbsncpy(), _mbsnicmp(), _mbsnicoll(), _mbsninc(), _mbsnset(), _mbspbrk(), _mbsrchr(), _mbsrev(), _mbsset(), _mbsspn(), _mbsspnp(), _mbsstr(), _mbstok(), _mbstrlen(), _mbsupr(), isleadbyte(), mblen(), mbstowcs(), and mbtowc().

_mbsnicmp()

Function

The _mbsnicmp() function compares characters in two multibyte-character strings without regard to character case (case–insensitive compare), returning a value from Table M-11.

Table M-11 Return Values for _mbsnicmp()

Value	Description
Less than 0	string1 is alphabetically less than string2.
0	The two strings are equal.
Greater than 0	string1 is alphabetically greater than string2.
_NLSCMPERROR	Error.

Header File

```
#include <mbstring.h>
```

Declaration

```
int _mbsnicmp(const unsigned char *string1,
    const unsigned char *string2, size_t count);
```

- *count* — The number of characters to compare.
- *string1* — The first string to compare.
- *string2* — The second string to compare.

Example

The following program demonstrates how to use the _mbsnicmp() function. When run, the program compares several pairs of strings and displays the result of the comparisons. The program's output looks like this:

```
For a length of 7 characters

One Two Three equals One Two Ten
One Two Ten is greater than Four Five Six
Four Five Six is greater than Four Eight Nine
Four Eight Nine equals FOUR EIGHT NINE

Press any key to continue
```

Here is the program source code that produced the output:

```cpp
#include "stdafx.h"
#include <iostream>
#include <mbstring.h>

using namespace std;

void cmp(unsigned char* s1,
         unsigned char* s2, size_t num)
{
    int result = _mbsnicmp(s1, s2, num);

    if (result == _NLSCMPERROR)
        cout << "String compare error." << endl;
    else if (result < 0 )
    {
        cout << s1 << " is less than ";
        cout << s2 << endl;
    }
    else if (result > 0)
    {
        cout << s1 << " is greater than ";
        cout << s2 << endl;
    }
    else
    {
        cout << s1 << " equals ";
        cout << s2 << endl;
    }
}

int main(int argc, char* argv[])
{
    unsigned char str1[] = "One Two Three";
    unsigned char str2[] = "One Two Ten";
    unsigned char str3[] = "Four Five Six";
    unsigned char str4[] = "Four Eight Nine";
    unsigned char str5[] = "FOUR EIGHT NINE";

    cout << "For a length of 7 characters" << endl << endl;
    cmp(str1, str2, 7);
    cmp(str2, str3, 7);
    cmp(str3, str4, 7);
    cmp(str4, str5, 7);
```

```
        cout << endl;

        return 0;
    }
```

CROSS-REFERENCE

See also _ismbbalnum(), _ismbbalpha(), _ismbbgraph(), _ismbbkalnum(), _ismbbkana(), _ismbbkprint(), _ismbbkpunct(), _ismbblead(), _ismbbprint(), _ismbbpunct(), _ismbbtrail(), _mbbtombc(), _mbbtype(), _mbccpy(), _mbcjistojms(), _mbcjmstojis(), _mbclen(), _mbctohira(), _mbctokata(), _mbctolower(), _mbctombb(), _mbctoupper(), _mbsbtype, _mbscat(), _mbschr(), _mbscmp(), _mbscoll(), _mbscpy(), _mbscspn(), _mbsdec(), _mbsdup(), _mbsicmp(), _mbsicoll(), _mbsinc(), _mbslen(), _mbslwr(), _mbsnbcat(), _mbsnbcmp(), _mbsnbcnt(), _mbsnbcoll(), _mbsnbcpy(), _mbsnbicmp(), _mbsnbicoll(), _mbsnbset(), _mbsncat(), _mbsnccnt(), _mbsncmp(), _mbsncoll(), _mbsncpy(), _mbsnextc(), _mbsnicoll(), _mbsninc(), _mbsnset(), _mbspbrk(), _mbsrchr(), _mbsrev(), _mbsset(), _mbsspn(), _mbsspnp(), _mbsstr(), _mbstok(), _mbstrlen(), _mbsupr(), isleadbyte(), mblen(), mbstowcs(), and mbtowc().

_mbsnicoll()

Function

The _mbsnicoll() function compares two multibyte-character strings for the current locale without regard to character case (case–insensitive compare), returning a value from Table M-12.

Table M-12 Return Values for _mbsnicoll()

Value	Description
Less than 0	string1 is alphabetically less than string2.
0	The two strings are equal.
Greater than 0	string1 is alphabetically greater than string2.
_NLSCMPERROR	Error.

Header File

```
#include <mbstring.h>
```

Declaration

```
int _mbsnicoll(const unsigned char *string1,
    const unsigned char *string2, size_t count);
```

- *count* — The number of characters to compare.
- *string1* — The first string to compare.
- *string2* — The second string to compare.

Example

The following program demonstrates how to use the _mbsnicoll() function. When run, the program compares several pairs of strings and displays the result of the comparisons. The program's output looks like this:

```
One Two Three equals One Two three
One Two three equals one Two Three
one Two Three is less than SEVEN EIGHT nine
SEVEN EIGHT nine equals seven eight nine
Press any key to continue
```

Here is the program source code that produced the output:

```
#include "stdafx.h"
#include <iostream>
#include <mbstring.h>

using namespace std;

void cmp(unsigned char* s1,
        unsigned char* s2, size_t num)
{
    int result = _mbsnicoll(s1, s2, num);
    if (result < 0 )
    {
        cout << s1;
        cout << " is less than ";
        cout << s2 << endl;
    }
    else if (result > 0)
    {
        cout << s1;
```

```
        cout << " is greater than ";
        cout << s2 << endl;
    }
    else
    {
        cout << s1;
        cout << " equals ";
        cout << s2 << endl;
    }
}

int main(int argc, char* argv[])
{
    unsigned char str1[] = "One Two Three";
    unsigned char str2[] = "One Two three";
    unsigned char str3[] = "one Two Three";
    unsigned char str4[] = "SEVEN EIGHT nine";
    unsigned char str5[] = "seven eight nine";

    cmp(str1, str2, 7);
    cmp(str2, str3, 7);
    cmp(str3, str4, 7);
    cmp(str4, str5, 7);

    return 0;
}
```

CROSS-REFERENCE

See also _ismbbalnum(), _ismbbalpha(), _ismbbgraph(), _ismbbkalnum(), _ismbbkana(), _ismbbkprint(), _ismbbkpunct(), _ismbblead(), _ismbbprint(), _ismbbpunct(), _ismbbtrail(), _mbbtombc(), _mbbtype(), _mbccpy(), _mbcjistojms(), _mbcjmstojis(), _mbclen(), _mbctohira(), _mbctokata(), _mbctolower(), _mbctombb(), _mbctoupper(), _mbsbtype, _mbscat(), _mbschr(), _mbscmp(), _mbscoll(), _mbscpy(), _mbscspn(), _mbsdec(), _mbsdup(), _mbsicmp(), _mbsicoll(), _mbsinc(), _mbslen(), _mbslwr(), _mbsnbcat(), _mbsnbcmp(), _mbsnbcnt(), _mbsnbcoll(), _mbsnbcpy(), _mbsnbicmp(), _mbsnbicoll(), _mbsnbset(), _mbsncat(), _mbsnccnt(), _mbsncmp(), _mbsncoll(), _mbsncpy(), _mbsnextc(), _mbsnicmp(), _mbsninc(), _mbsnset(), _mbspbrk(), _mbsrchr(), _mbsrev(), _mbsset(), _mbsspn(), _mbsspnp(), _mbsstr(), _mbstok(), _mbstrlen(), _mbsupr(), isleadbyte(), mblen(), mbstowcs(), and mbtowc().

_mbsninc()

Function

The _mbsninc() function returns a pointer to the string that results from advancing the specified number of multibyte characters in the source string.

Header File

```
#include <mbstring.h>
```

Declaration

```
unsigned char* _mbsninc(const unsigned char *string,
    size_t count);
```

- *count* — The number of multibyte characters to advance in the source string.
- *string* — A pointer to the source string.

Example

The following program demonstrates how to use the _mbsninc() function. When run, the program locates the fifth character in a string and displays the result. The program's output looks like this:

```
Source String = This is a test
Result = is a test
Press any key to continue
```

Here is the program source code that produced the output:

```
#include "stdafx.h"
#include <iostream>
#include <mbstring.h>

using namespace std;

int main(int argc, char* argv[])
{
    unsigned char srcStr[] = "This is a test";

    unsigned char* result = _mbsninc(srcStr, 5);
```

```
        cout << "Source String = " << srcStr << endl;
        cout << "Result = " << result << endl;

        return 0;
    }
```

CROSS-REFERENCE

See also _ismbbalnum(), _ismbbalpha(), _ismbbgraph(), _ismbbkalnum(), _ismbbkana(), _ismbbkprint(), _ismbbkpunct(), _ismbblead(), _ismbbprint(), _ismbbpunct(), _ismbbtrail(), _mbbtombc(), _mbbtype(), _mbccpy(), _mbcjistojms(), _mbcjmstojis(), _mbclen(), _mbctohira(), _mbctokata(), _mbctolower(), _mbctombb(), _mbctoupper(), _mbsbtype, _mbscat(), _mbschr(), _mbscmp(), _mbscoll(), _mbscpy(), _mbscspn(), _mbsdec(), _mbsdup(), _mbsicmp(), _mbsicoll(), _mbsinc(), _mbslen(), _mbslwr(), _mbsnbcat(), _mbsnbcmp(), _mbsnbcnt(), _mbsnbcoll(), _mbsnbcpy(), _mbsnbicmp(), _mbsnbicoll(), _mbsnbset(), _mbsncat(), _mbsnccnt(), _mbsncmp(), _mbsncoll(), _mbsncpy(), _mbsnextc(), _mbsnicmp(), _mbsnicoll(), _mbsnset(), _mbspbrk(), _mbsrchr(), _mbsrev(), _mbsset(), _mbsspn(), _mbsspnp(), _mbsstr(), _mbstok(), _mbstrlen(), _mbsupr(), isleadbyte(), mblen(), mbstowcs(), and mbtowc().

_mbsnset()

Function

The _mbsnset() function sets a portion of the contents of a multibyte-character string to a given character, returning a pointer to the new string.

Header File

```
#include <mbstring.h>
```

Declaration

```
unsigned char* _mbsnset(const unsigned char *string,
    unsigned int c, size_t count);
```

- *c*—The character with which to fill the string.
- *count*—The number of characters to set.
- *string*—The string to convert.

Example

The following program demonstrates how to use the _mbsnset() function. When run, the program sets several strings to various symbols and displays the results. The program's output looks like this:

```
Original String: One Two Three
Converted String: ??? Two Three

Original String: FOUR FIVE SIX
Converted String: *******VE SIX

Original String: seven eight nine
Converted String: ################

Press any key to continue
```

Here is the program source code that produced the output:

```cpp
#include "stdafx.h"
#include <iostream>
#include <mbstring.h>

using namespace std;

void convert(unsigned char* s,
             unsigned int c, size_t num)
{
    cout << "Original String: " << s << endl;
    unsigned char* result = _mbsnset(s, c, num);
    cout << "Converted String: " << result;
    cout << endl << endl;
}

int main(int argc, char* argv[])
{
    unsigned char str1[81] = "One Two Three";
    unsigned char str2[81] = "FOUR FIVE SIX";
    unsigned char str3[81] = "seven eight nine";

    convert(str1, '?', 3);
    convert(str2, '*', 7);
    convert(str3, '#', 16);

    return 0;
}
```

CROSS-REFERENCE
See also _ismbbalnum(), _ismbbalpha(), _ismbbgraph(), _ismbbkalnum(), _ismbbkana(), _ismbbkprint(), _ismbbkpunct(), _ismbblead(), _ismbbprint(), _ismbbpunct(), _ismbbtrail(), _mbbtombc(), _mbbtype(), _mbccpy(), _mbcjistojms(), _mbcjmstojis(), _mbclen(), _mbctohira(), _mbctokata(), _mbctolower(), _mbctombb(), _mbctoupper(), _mbsbtype, _mbscat(), _mbschr(), _mbscmp(), _mbscoll(), _mbscpy(), _mbscspn(), _mbsdec(), _mbsdup(), _mbsicmp(), _mbsicoll(), _mbsinc(), _mbslen(), _mbslwr(), _mbsnbcat(), _mbsnbcmp(), _mbsnbcnt(), _mbsnbcoll(), _mbsnbcpy(), _mbsnbicmp(), _mbsnbicoll(), _mbsnbset(), _mbsncat(), _mbsnccnt(), _mbsncmp(), _mbsncoll(), _mbsncpy(), _mbsnextc(), _mbsnicmp(), _mbsnicoll(), _mbsninc(), _mbspbrk(), _mbsrchr(), _mbsrev(), _mbsset(), _mbsspn(), _mbsspnp(), _mbsstr(), _mbstok(), _mbstrlen(), _mbsupr(), isleadbyte(), mblen(), mbstowcs(), and mbtowc().

_mbspbrk()

Function

The _mbspbrk() function locates the first occurrence of a multibyte character in a string, returning a pointer to the substring starting with the matching character.

Header File

```
#include <mbstring.h>
```

Declaration

```
unsigned char* _mbspbrk(const unsigned char *string,
    const unsigned char *strCharSet);
```

- *strCharSet* — A pointer to the set of characters for which to search.
- *string* — A pointer to the string to search.

Example

The following program demonstrates how to use the _mbspbrk() function. When run, the program locates, in a string, the first character in a set and displays the result. The program's output looks like this:

```
Source String:
This is a test
```

```
Substring:
s is a test

Press any key to continue
```

Here is the program source code that produced the output:

```
#include "stdafx.h"
#include <iostream>
#include <mbstring.h>

using namespace std;

int main(int argc, char* argv[])
{
    unsigned char srcStr[] = "This is a test";
    unsigned char chrSet[] = "ast";

    unsigned char* pSubStr = _mbspbrk(srcStr, chrSet);
    cout << "Source String:" << endl;
    cout << srcStr << endl;
    cout << "Substring:" << endl;
    cout << pSubStr << endl << endl;

    return 0;
}
```

CROSS-REFERENCE

See also _ismbbalnum(), _ismbbalpha(), _ismbbgraph(), _ismbbkalnum(), _ismbbkana(), _ismbbkprint(), _ismbbkpunct(), _ismbblead(), _ismbbprint(), _ismbbpunct(), _ismbbtrail(), _mbbtombc(), _mbbtype(), _mbccpy(), _mbcjistojms(), _mbcjmstojis(), _mbclen(), _mbctohira(), _mbctokata(), _mbctolower(), _mbctombb(), _mbctoupper(), _mbsbtype, _mbscat(), _mbschr(), _mbscmp(), _mbscoll(), _mbscpy(), _mbscspn(), _mbsdec(), _mbsdup(), _mbsicmp(), _mbsicoll(), _mbsinc(), _mbslen(), _mbslwr(), _mbsnbcat(), _mbsnbcmp(), _mbsnbcnt(), _mbsnbcoll(), _mbsnbcpy(), _mbsnbicmp(), _mbsnbicoll(), _mbsnbset(), _mbsncat(), _mbsnccnt(), _mbsncmp(), _mbsncoll(), _mbsncpy(), _mbsnextc(), _mbsnicmp(), _mbsnicoll(), _mbsninc(), _mbsnset(), _mbsrchr(), _mbsrev(), _mbsset(), _mbsspn(), _mbsspnp(), _mbsstr(), _mbstok(), _mbstrlen(), _mbsupr(), isleadbyte(), mblen(), mbstowcs(), and mbtowc().

_mbsrchr()

Function

The _mbsrchr() function locates the last occurrence of a multibyte character in a string, returning a pointer to the substring starting with the matching character.

Header File

```
#include <mbstring.h>
```

Declaration

```
unsigned char* _mbsrchr(const unsigned char *string,
    unsigned int c);
```

- *c* — The character for which to search.
- *string* — A pointer to the string to search.

Example

The following program demonstrates how to use the _mbsrchr() function. When run, the program locates the last occurrence of the character "i" in a string and displays the result. The program's output looks like this:

```
Source String:
This is a test
Substring:
is a test

Press any key to continue
```

Here is the program source code that produced the output:

```
#include "stdafx.h"
#include <iostream>
#include <mbstring.h>

using namespace std;

int main(int argc, char* argv[])
{
    unsigned char srcStr[] = "This is a test";
```

```
unsigned char* pSubStr = _mbsrchr(srcStr, 'i');
cout << "Source String:" << endl;
cout << srcStr << endl;
cout << "Substring:" << endl;
cout << pSubStr << endl << endl;

return 0;
}
```

CROSS-REFERENCE

See also _ismbbalnum(), _ismbbalpha(), _ismbbgraph(), _ismbbkalnum(), _ismbbkana(), _ismbbkprint(), _ismbbkpunct(), _ismbblead(), _ismbbprint(), _ismbbpunct(), _ismbbtrail(), _mbbtombc(), _mbbtype(), _mbccpy(), _mbcjistojms(), _mbcjmstojis(), _mbclen(), _mbctohira(), _mbctokata(), _mbctolower(), _mbctombb(), _mbctoupper(), _mbsbtype, _mbscat(), _mbschr(), _mbscmp(), _mbscoll(), _mbscpy(), _mbscspn(), _mbsdec(), _mbsdup(), _mbsicmp(), _mbsicoll(), _mbsinc(), _mbslen(), _mbslwr(), _mbsnbcat(), _mbsnbcmp(), _mbsnbcnt(), _mbsnbcoll(), _mbsnbcpy(), _mbsnbicmp(), _mbsnbicoll(), _mbsnbset(), _mbsncat(), _mbsnccnt(), _mbsncmp(), _mbsncoll(), _mbsncpy(), _mbsnextc(), _mbsnicmp(), _mbsnicoll(), _mbsninc(), _mbsnset(), _mbspbrk(), _mbsrev(), _mbsset(), _mbsspn(), _mbsspnp(), _mbsstr(), _mbstok(), _mbstrlen(), _mbsupr(), isleadbyte(), mblen(), mbstowcs(), and mbtowc().

_mbsrev()

Function

The _mbsrev() function reverses the order of characters in a multibyte-character string, returning a pointer to the new string.

Header File

```
#include <mbstring.h>
```

Declaration

```
unsigned char* _mbsrev(const unsigned char *string);
```

- *string*—The string in which to reverse the order of characters.

Example

The following program demonstrates how to use the _mbsrev() function.
When run, the program reverses the order of characters in several strings and
displays the results. The program's output looks like this:

```
Original String: One Two Three
Converted String: eerhT owT enO

Original String: FOUR FIVE SIX
Converted String: XIS EVIF RUOF

Original String: seven eight nine
Converted String: enin thgie neves

Press any key to continue
```

Here is the program source code that produced the output:

```cpp
#include "stdafx.h"
#include <iostream>
#include <mbstring.h>

using namespace std;

void convert(unsigned char* s)
{
    cout << "Original String: ";
    cout << s << endl;
    unsigned char* result = _mbsrev(s);
    cout << "Converted String: ";
    cout << result << endl << endl;
}

int main(int argc, char* argv[])
{
    unsigned char str1[] = "One Two Three";
    unsigned char str2[] = "FOUR FIVE SIX";
    unsigned char str3[] = "seven eight nine";

    convert(str1);
    convert(str2);
    convert(str3);

    return 0;
}
```

CROSS-REFERENCE
See also _ismbbalnum(), _ismbbalpha(), _ismbbgraph(), _ismbbkalnum(), _ismbbkana(), _ismbbkprint(), _ismbbkpunct(), _ismbblead(), _ismbbprint(), _ismbbpunct(), _ismbbtrail(), _mbbtombc(), _mbbtype(), _mbccpy(), _mbcjistojms(), _mbcjmstojis(), _mbclen(), _mbctohira(), _mbctokata(), _mbctolower(), _mbctombb(), _mbctoupper(), _mbsbtype, _mbscat(), _mbschr(), _mbscmp(), _mbscoll(), _mbscpy(), _mbscspn(), _mbsdec(), _mbsdup(), _mbsicmp(), _mbsicoll(), _mbsinc(), _mbslen(), _mbslwr(), _mbsnbcat(), _mbsnbcmp(), _mbsnbcnt(), _mbsnbcoll(), _mbsnbcpy(), _mbsnbicmp(), _mbsnbicoll(), _mbsnbset(), _mbsncat(), _mbsnccnt(), _mbsncmp(), _mbsncoll(), _mbsncpy(), _mbsnextc(), _mbsnicmp(), _mbsnicoll(), _mbsninc(), _mbsnset(), _mbspbrk(), _mbsrchr(), _mbsset(), _mbsspn(), _mbsspnp(), _mbsstr(), _mbstok(), _mbstrlen(), _mbsupr(), isleadbyte(), mblen(), mbstowcs(), and mbtowc().

_mbsset()

Function

The _mbsset() function sets the contents of a multibyte-character string to a specified character, returning a pointer to the new string.

Header File

```
#include <mbstring.h>
```

Declaration

```
unsigned char* _mbsset(const unsigned char *string,
    unsigned int c);
```

- *c* — The character with which to fill the string.
- *string* — The string to convert.

Example

The following program demonstrates how to use the _mbsset() function. When run, the program sets several strings to question marks and displays the results. The program's output looks like this:

```
Original String: One Two Three
Converted String: ????????????
```

```
Original String: FOUR FIVE SIX
Converted String: ?????????????

Original String: seven eight nine
Converted String: ??????????????

Press any key to continue
```

Here is the program source code that produced the output:

```cpp
#include "stdafx.h"
#include <iostream>
#include <mbstring.h>

using namespace std;

void convert(unsigned char* s, unsigned int c)
{
    cout << "Original String: ";
    cout << s << endl;
    unsigned char* result = _mbsset(s, c);
    cout << "Converted String: ";
    cout << result << endl << endl;
}

int main(int argc, char* argv[])
{
    unsigned char str1[] = "One Two Three";
    unsigned char str2[] = "FOUR FIVE SIX";
    unsigned char str3[] = "seven eight nine";

    convert(str1, '?');
    convert(str2, '?');
    convert(str3, '?');

    return 0;
}
```

CROSS-REFERENCE

See also _ismbbalnum(), _ismbbalpha(), _ismbbgraph(), _ismbbkalnum(), _ismbbkana(), _ismbbkprint(), _ismbbkpunct(), _ismbblead(), _ismbbprint(), _ismbbpunct(), _ismbbtrail(), _mbbtombc(), _mbbtype(), _mbccpy(), _mbcjistojms(), _mbcjmstojis(), _mbclen(), _mbctohira(), _mbctokata(), _mbctolower(), _mbctombb(), _mbctoupper(), _mbsbtype, _mbscat(), _mbschr(), _mbscmp(), _mbscoll(), _mbscpy(), _mbscspn(), _mbsdec(), _mbsdup(), _mbsicmp(), _mbsicoll(), _mbsinc(), _mbslen(), _mbslwr(), _mbsnbcat(), _mbsnbcmp(), _mbsnbcnt(), _mbsnbcoll(), _mbsnbcpy(), _mbsnbicmp(), _mbsnbicoll(), _mbsnbset(), _mbsncat(), _mbsnccnt(), _mbsncmp(), _mbsncoll(), _mbsncpy(), _mbsnextc(), _mbsnicmp(), _mbsnicoll(), _mbsninc(), _mbsnset(), _mbspbrk(), _mbsrchr(), _mbsrev(), _mbsspn(), _mbsspnp(), _mbsstr(), _mbstok(), _mbstrlen(), _mbsupr(), isleadbyte(), mblen(), mbstowcs(), and mbtowc().

_mbsspn()

Function

The _mbsspn() function locates the first occurrence of a multibyte-character substring that starts with a character that is not included in the specified set. The function returns the index of the first nonmatching character.

Header File

```
#include <mbstring.h>
```

Declaration

```
size_t _mbsspn(const unsigned char *string,
    const unsigned char *strCharSet);
```

- *strCharSet* — A pointer to the set of characters for which to search.
- *string* — A pointer to the string to search.

Example

The following program demonstrates how to use the _mbsspn() function. When run, the program locates, in a string, the first character that is not in the specified set and displays the result, indicating the located character with a caret (^). The program's output looks like this:

```
Source string = This is a test
Character set = ahisT

Searching...

Results:
This is a test
    ^
```

Press any key to continue

Here is the program source code that produced the output:

```
#include "stdafx.h"
#include <iostream>
#include <mbstring.h>

using namespace std;

int main(int argc, char* argv[])
{
    unsigned char srcStr[] = "This is a test";
    unsigned char chrSet[] = "ahisT ";

    cout << "Source string = " << srcStr << endl;
    cout << "Character set = " << chrSet << endl;
    cout << endl;
    cout << "Searching..." << endl << endl;
    size_t len = _mbsspn(srcStr, chrSet);
    cout << "Results:" << endl;
    cout << srcStr << endl;
    for (unsigned x=0; x<len; ++x)
        cout << " ";
    cout << "^" << endl << endl;

    return 0;
}
```

CROSS-REFERENCE

See also _ismbbalnum(), _ismbbalpha(), _ismbbgraph(), _ismbbkalnum(), _ismbbkana(), _ismbbkprint(), _ismbbkpunct(), _ismbblead(), _ismbbprint(), _ismbbpunct(), _ismbbtrail(), _mbbtombc(), _mbbtype(), _mbccpy(), _mbcjistojms(), _mbcjmstojis(), _mbclen(), _mbctohira(), _mbctokata(), _mbctolower(), _mbctombb(), _mbctoupper(), _mbsbtype, _mbscat(), _mbschr(), _mbscmp(), _mbscoll(), _mbscpy(), _mbscspn(), _mbsdec(), _mbsdup(), _mbsicmp(), _mbsicoll(), _mbsinc(), _mbslen(), _mbslwr(), _mbsnbcat(), _mbsnbcmp(), _mbsnbcnt(), _mbsnbcoll(), _mbsnbcpy(), _mbsnbicmp(), _mbsnbicoll(), _mbsnbset(), _mbsncat(), _mbsnccnt(), _mbsncmp(), _mbsncoll(), _mbsncpy(), _mbsnextc(), _mbsnicmp(), _mbsnicoll(), _mbsninc(), _mbsnset(), _mbspbrk(), _mbsrchr(), _mbsrev(), _mbsset(), _mbsspnp(), _mbsstr(), _mbstok(), _mbstrlen(), _mbsupr(), isleadbyte(), mblen(), mbstowcs(), and mbtowc().

_mbsspnp()

Function

The _mbsspnp() function locates the first occurrence of a multibyte-character substring that starts with a character that is not included in the specified set. The function returns a pointer to the first nonmatching character.

Header File

```
#include <mbstring.h>
```

Declaration

```
unsigned char* _mbsspnp(const unsigned char *string,
    const unsigned char *strCharSet);
```

- *strCharSet* — A pointer to the set of characters for which to search.
- *string* — A pointer to the string to search.

Example

The following program demonstrates how to use the _mbsspnp() function. When run, the program locates, in a string, the first character that is not in the specified set and displays the results. The program's output looks like this:

```
Source String:
This is a test

Remaining String:
test

Press any key to continue
```

Here is the program source code that produced the output:

```
#include "stdafx.h"
#include <iostream>
#include <mbstring.h>

using namespace std;

int main(int argc, char* argv[])
{
```

```
unsigned char srcStr[] = "This is a test";
unsigned char chrSet[] = "ahisT ";

unsigned char* result = _mbsspnp(srcStr, chrSet);
cout << "Source String:" << endl;
cout << srcStr << endl << endl;
cout << "Remaining String:" << endl;
cout << result << endl << endl;

return 0;
}
```

CROSS-REFERENCE

See also _ismbbalnum(), _ismbbalpha(), _ismbbgraph(), _ismbbkalnum(), _ismbbkana(), _ismbbkprint(), _ismbbkpunct(), _ismbblead(), _ismbbprint(), _ismbbpunct(), _ismbbtrail(), _mbbtombc(), _mbbtype(), _mbccpy(), _mbcjistojms(), _mbcjmstojis(), _mbclen(), _mbctohira(), _mbctokata(), _mbctolower(), _mbctombb(), _mbctoupper(), _mbsbtype, _mbscat(), _mbschr(), _mbscmp(), _mbscoll(), _mbscpy(), _mbscspn(), _mbsdec(), _mbsdup(), _mbsicmp(), _mbsicoll(), _mbsinc(), _mbslen(), _mbslwr(), _mbsnbcat(), _mbsnbcmp(), _mbsnbcnt(), _mbsnbcoll(), _mbsnbcpy(), _mbsnbicmp(), _mbsnbicoll(), _mbsnbset(), _mbsncat(), _mbsnccnt(), _mbsncmp(), _mbsncoll(), _mbsncpy(), _mbsnextc(), _mbsnicmp(), _mbsnicoll(), _mbsninc(), _mbsnset(), _mbspbrk(), _mbsrchr(), _mbsrev(), _mbsset(), _mbsspn(), _mbsstr(), _mbstok(), _mbstrlen(), _mbsupr(), isleadbyte(), mblen(), mbstowcs(), and mbtowc().

_mbsstr()

Function

The _mbsstr() function returns a pointer to a specified substring within a multibyte-character string.

Header File

```
#include <mbstring.h>
```

Declaration

```
unsigned char* _mbsstr(const unsigned char *string,
    const unsigned char *strCharSet);
```

- *strCharSet*—A pointer to the substring for which to search.
- *string*—A pointer to the string to search.

Example

The following program demonstrates how to use the _mbsstr() function. When run, the program locates a specified substring and then displays the portion of the original string that begins with the substring. The program's output looks like this:

```
Source String:
This is a test

Substring:
is a test

Press any key to continue
```

Here is the program source code that produced the output:

```
#include "stdafx.h"
#include <iostream>
#include <mbstring.h>

using namespace std;

int main(int argc, char* argv[])
{
    unsigned char srcStr[] = "This is a test";
    unsigned char chrSet[] = "is a";

    unsigned char* pSubStr = _mbsstr(srcStr, chrSet);
    cout << "Source String:" << endl;
    cout << srcStr << endl << endl;
    cout << "Substring:" << endl;
    cout << pSubStr << endl << endl;

    return 0;
}
```

CROSS-REFERENCE
See also _ismbbalnum(), _ismbbalpha(), _ismbbgraph(), _ismbbkalnum(), _ismbbkana(), _ismbbkprint(), _ismbbkpunct(), _ismbblead(), _ismbbprint(), _ismbbpunct(), _ismbbtrail(), _mbbtombc(), _mbbtype(), _mbccpy(), _mbcjistojms(), _mbcjmstojis(), _mbclen(), _mbctohira(), _mbctokata(), _mbctolower(),

_mbctombb(), _mbctoupper(), _mbsbtype, _mbscat(), _mbschr(), _mbscmp(), _mbscoll(), _mbscpy(), _mbscspn(), _mbsdec(), _mbsdup(), _mbsicmp(), _mbsicoll(), _mbsinc(), _mbslen(), _mbslwr(), _mbsnbcat(), _mbsnbcmp(), _mbsnbcnt(), _mbsnbcoll(), _mbsnbcpy(), _mbsnbicmp(), _mbsnbicoll(), _mbsnbset(), _mbsncat(), _mbsnccnt(), _mbsncmp(), _mbsncoll(), _mbsncpy(), _mbsnextc(), _mbsnicmp(), _mbsnicoll(), _mbsninc(), _mbsnset(), _mbspbrk(), _mbsrchr(), _mbsrev(), _mbsset(), _mbsspn(), _mbsspnp(), _mbstok(), _mbstrlen(), _mbsupr(), isleadbyte(), mblen(), mbstowcs(), and mbtowc().

_mbstok()

Function

The _mbstok() function extracts tokens from a multibyte character string.

Header File

```
#include <mbstring.h>
```

Declaration

```
unsigned char* _mbstok(unsigned char *strToken,
    const unsigned char *strDelimit);
```

- *strDelimit* — A pointer to the string containing the characters (delimiters) that separate one token from another.
- *strToken* — A pointer to the string containing the tokens to extract.

Example

The following program demonstrates how to use the _mbstok() function. When run, the program extracts tokens from a string, displaying the results as it goes. The program's output looks like this:

```
Token Source String:
One,Two Three,Four*Five

Token Delimiter String:
, *

Tokens Found:
One
Two
```

```
        Three
        Four
        Five

        Press any key to continue
```

Here is the program source code that produced the output:

```cpp
#include "stdafx.h"
#include <iostream>
#include <mbstring.h>

using namespace std;

int main(int argc, char* argv[])
{
    unsigned char str[] = "One,Two Three,Four*Five";
    unsigned char delimit[] = ", *";
    unsigned char *tok;

    cout << "Token Source String:" << endl;
    cout << str << endl << endl;
    cout << "Token Delimiter String:" << endl;
    cout << delimit << endl << endl;
    cout << "Tokens Found:" << endl;

    tok = _mbstok(str, delimit);
    while(tok != NULL )
    {
        cout << tok << endl;
        tok = _mbstok(NULL, delimit);
    }

    cout << endl;

    return 0;
}
```

CROSS-REFERENCE

See also _ismbbalnum(), _ismbbalpha(), _ismbbgraph(), _ismbbkalnum(), _ismbbkana(), _ismbbkprint(), _ismbbkpunct(), _ismbblead(), _ismbbprint(), _ismbbpunct(), _ismbbtrail(), _mbbtombc(), _mbbtype(), _mbccpy(), _mbcjistojms(), _mbcjmstojis(), _mbclen(), _mbctohira(), _mbctokata(), _mbctolower(), _mbctombb(), _mbctoupper(), _mbsbtype, _mbscat(), _mbschr(), _mbscmp(), _mbscoll(), _mbscpy(), _mbscspn(), _mbsdec(), _mbsdup(), _mbsicmp(), _mbsicoll(), _mbsinc(), _mbslen(), _mbslwr(), _mbsnbcat(), _mbsnbcmp(), _mbsnbcnt(), _mbsnbcoll(), _mbsnbcpy(), _mbsnbicmp(), _mbsnbicoll(), _mbsnbset(), _mbsncat(), _mbsnccnt(), _mbsncmp(), _mbsncoll(), _mbsncpy(), _mbsnextc(), _mbsnicmp(), _mbsnicoll(), _mbsninc(), _mbsnset(), _mbspbrk(), _mbsrchr(), _mbsrev(), _mbsset(), _mbsspn(), _mbsspnp(), _mbsstr(), _mbstrlen(), _mbsupr(), isleadbyte(), mblen(), mbstowcs(), and mbtowc().

_mbstrlen()

Function

The _mbstrlen() function returns the length (the number of characters) of a multibyte-character string.

 NOTE
Borland does not support this function.

Header File

```
#include <mbstring.h>
```

Declaration

```
size_t _mbstrlen(const char *string);
```

- *string* — A pointer to the string for which to return the length.

Example

The following program demonstrates how to use the _mbstrlen() function. When run, the program calculates the length of a string and then uses the length to underline the source string. The program's output looks like this:

```
Source String:

This is a test
───────
```

```
Press any key to continue
```

Here is the program source code that produced the output:

```
#include "stdafx.h"
```

```
#include <iostream>
#include <mbstring.h>

using namespace std;

int main(int argc, char* argv[])
{
    char srcStr[] = "This is a test";

    size_t len = _mbstrlen(srcStr);
    cout << "Source String:" << endl << endl;
    cout << srcStr << endl;
    for (unsigned x=0; x<len; ++x)
        cout << "-";
    cout << endl << endl;

    return 0;
}
```

CROSS-REFERENCE

See also _ismbbalnum(), _ismbbalpha(), _ismbbgraph(), _ismbbkalnum(), _ismbbkana(), _ismbbkprint(), _ismbbkpunct(), _ismbblead(), _ismbbprint(), _ismbbpunct(), _ismbbtrail(), _mbbtombc(), _mbbtype(), _mbccpy(), _mbcjistojms(), _mbcjmstojis(), _mbclen(), _mbctohira(), _mbctokata(), _mbctolower(), _mbctombb(), _mbctoupper(), _mbsbtype, _mbscat(), _mbschr(), _mbscmp(), _mbscoll(), _mbscpy(), _mbscspn(), _mbsdec(), _mbsdup(), _mbsicmp(), _mbsicoll(), _mbsinc(), _mbslen(), _mbslwr(), _mbsnbcat(), _mbsnbcmp(), _mbsnbcnt(), _mbsnbcoll(), _mbsnbcpy(), _mbsnbicmp(), _mbsnbicoll(), _mbsnbset(), _mbsncat(), _mbsnccnt(), _mbsncmp(), _mbsncoll(), _mbsncpy(), _mbsnextc(), _mbsnicmp(), _mbsnicoll(), _mbsninc(), _mbsnset(), _mbspbrk(), _mbsrchr(), _mbsrev(), _mbsset(), _mbsspn(), _mbsspnp(), _mbsstr(), _mbstok(), _mbsupr(), isleadbyte(), mblen(), mbstowcs(), and mbtowc().

_mbsupr()

Function

The _mbsupr() function converts a multibyte-character string to uppercase, returning a pointer to the new string.

Header File

```
#include <mbstring.h>
```

Declaration

```
unsigned char* _mbsupr(unsigned char *string);
```

■ *string* — The string to convert.

Example

The following program demonstrates how to use the _mbsupr() function. When run, the program converts several strings to uppercase and displays the results. The program's output looks like this:

```
Original String: One Two Three
Converted String: ONE TWO THREE

Original String: FOUR FIVE SIX
Converted String: FOUR FIVE SIX

Original String: seven eight nine
Converted String: SEVEN EIGHT NINE

Press any key to continue
```

Here is the program source code that produced the output:

```
#include "stdafx.h"
#include <iostream>
#include <mbstring.h>

using namespace std;

void convert(unsigned char* s)
{
    cout << "Original String: ";
    cout << s << endl;
    unsigned char* result = _mbsupr(s);
    cout << "Converted String: ";
    cout << result << endl << endl;
}

int main(int argc, char* argv[])
{
    unsigned char str1[] = "One Two Three";
    unsigned char str2[] = "FOUR FIVE SIX";
    unsigned char str3[] = "seven eight nine";
```

```
convert(str1);
convert(str2);
convert(str3);

return 0;
}
```

CROSS-REFERENCE
See also _ismbbalnum(), _ismbbalpha(), _ismbbgraph(), _ismbbkalnum(), _ismbbkana(), _ismbbkprint(), _ismbbkpunct(), _ismbblead(), _ismbbprint(), _ismbbpunct(), _ismbbtrail(), _mbbtombc(), _mbbtype(), _mbccpy(), _mbcjistojms(), _mbcjmstojis(), _mbclen(), _mbctohira(), _mbctokata(), _mbctolower(), _mbctombb(), _mbctoupper(), _mbsbtype, _mbscat(), _mbschr(), _mbscmp(), _mbscoll(), _mbscpy(), _mbscspn(), _mbsdec(), _mbsdup(), _mbsicmp(), _mbsicoll(), _mbsinc(), _mbslen(), _mbslwr(), _mbsnbcat(), _mbsnbcmp(), _mbsnbcnt(), _mbsnbcoll(), _mbsnbcpy(), _mbsnbicmp(), _mbsnbicoll(), _mbsnbset(), _mbsncat(), _mbsnccnt(), _mbsncmp(), _mbsncoll(), _mbsncpy(), _mbsnextc(), _mbsnicmp(), _mbsnicoll(), _mbsninc(), _mbsnset(), _mbspbrk(), _mbsrchr(), _mbsrev(), _mbsset(), _mbsspn(), _mbsspnp(), _mbsstr(), _mbstok(), _mbstrlen(), isleadbyte(), mblen(), mbstowcs(), and mbtowc().

_memccpy()

Function

The `_memccpy()` function copies characters from one buffer to another, returning a pointer to the character following the last character copied.

NOTE
Borland users should refer to the `memccpy()` function later in this chapter.

Header Files

```
#include <memory.h>
```

Declaration

```
void* _memccpy(void *dest, const void *src,
    int c, size_t count);
```

- *c* — The last character to copy from *src* to *dest*.
- *count* — The maximum number of characters to copy.

- *dest* — A pointer to the destination buffer.
- *src* — A pointer to the source buffer.

Example

The following program demonstrates how to use the _memccpy() function. When run, the program copies a portion of one string to another string (stopping at the letter h) and displays the results. The program's output looks like this:

```
Source string:
   One Two Three
Destination string:
   One Two Th
Press any key to continue
```

Here is the program source code that produced the output:

```
#include "stdafx.h"
#include <iostream>
#include <memory.h>

using namespace std;

int main(int argc, char* argv[])
{
    char str1[] = "One Two Three";
    char str2[81];

    char* pResult = (char*)_memccpy(str2, str1, 'h', 13);
    pResult[0] = 0;
    cout << "Source string: " << endl;
    cout << "   " << str1 << endl;
    cout << "Destination string: " << endl;
    cout << "   " << str2 << endl;

    return 0;
}
```

CROSS-REFERENCE

See also _memicmp(), memccpy(), memchr(), memcmp(), memcpy(), memicmp(), memmove(), and memset().

_memicmp()

Function

The _memicmp() function compares the values in two buffers without regard for character case (case–insensitive compare), returning a value from Table M-13.

NOTE

Borland users should refer to the memicmp() function later in this chapter.

Table M-13 Return Values for _memicmp()

Value	Description
Less than 0	string1 is alphabetically less than string2.
0	The two strings are equal.
Greater than 0	string1 is alphabetically greater than string2.

Header Files

```
#include <memory.h>
```

Declaration

```
int _memicmp(const void *buf1,
    const void *buf2, size_t count);
```

- *buf1* — A pointer to the buffer to compare to *buf2*.
- *buf2* — A pointer to the buffer to compare to *buf1*.
- *count* — The number of buffer elements to compare.

Example

The following program demonstrates how to use the _memicmp() function. When run, the program compares two buffers and displays the results. The program's output looks like this:

```
The buffers are equal.
Press any key to continue
```

Here is the program source code that produced the output:

```
#include "stdafx.h"
#include <iostream>
```

```
#include <memory.h>

using namespace std;

int main(int argc, char* argv[])
{
    char str1[] = "One Two Three";
    char str2[] = "ONE TWO THREE";

    int result = _memicmp(str1, str2, sizeof(str1));
    if (result == 0)
        cout << "The buffers are equal." << endl;
    else if (result < 0)
        cout << "str1 is less than str2." << endl;
    else
        cout << "str1 is greater than str2." << endl;

    return 0;
}
```

CROSS-REFERENCE
See also _memccpy(), memccpy(), memchr(), memcmp(), memcpy(), memicmp(), memmove(), and memset().

_mkdir()

Function

The _mkdir() function creates a new disk directory. If the function is successful, it returns 0. Otherwise, it returns –1.

Header File

```
#include <direct.h>
```

Declaration

```
int _mkdir(const char* dirname)
```

- *dirname*— The path and name of the new directory.

Example

The following program demonstrates how to use the _mkdir() function by creating a new directory in drive C's root directory and then deleting the new directory. The program's output looks like this:

```
New directory created
Press any key to continue
```

Here is the program source code that produced the output:

```cpp
#include "stdafx.h"
#include <direct.h>
#include <iostream>

using namespace std;

int main(int argc, char* argv[])
{
    int result = _mkdir("c:\\TestDir");
    if (result != -1)
    {
        cout << "New directory created" << endl;
        _rmdir("c:\\TestDir");
    }
    else
        cout << "Directory create error" << endl;

    return 0;
}
```

CROSS-REFERENCE

See also _chdrive(), _getdcwd(), _getdrive(), _searchenv(), _wchdir(), _wgetcwd(), _wgetdcwd(), _wmkdir(), _wrmdir(), _wsearchenv(), chdir(), getcwd(), and rmdir().

_mktemp()

Function

The _mktemp() function generates a unique filename that can be used to create temporary files. If the function is successful, it returns a pointer to the filename. Otherwise, it returns NULL.

Header File

```
#include <io.h>
```

Declaration

```
char* _mktemp(char *template);
```

- *template* — A pointer to the template to be used to create the filename. This template must be in the form *base*XXXXXX, where *base* is the user-supplied characters for the filename and the Xs are placeholders for the characters that the _mktemp() function will supply.

Example

The following program demonstrates how to use the _mktemp() function by creating and displaying a unique temporary filename. The program's output looks like this:

```
Temp file name: tempa25913
Press any key to continue
```

Here is the program source code that produced the output:

```cpp
#include "stdafx.h"
#include <io.h>
#include <iostream>

using namespace std;

int main(int argc, char* argv[])
{
    char fileName[] = "tempXXXXXX";

    char* result = _mktemp(fileName);
    if (result == NULL)
        cout << "Error forming temp File name" << endl;
    else
    {
        cout << "Temp file name: ";
        cout << fileName << endl;
    }

    return 0;
}
```

CROSS-REFERENCE
See also _tempnam(), _wmktemp, _wtempnam(), _wtmpnam(), tmpfile(), and tmpnam().

_msize()

Function

The _msize() function returns the size of an allocated memory block.

Header File

```
#include <malloc.h>
```

Declaration

```
size_t _msize(void *memBlock);
```

- *memBlock* — A pointer to the memory block whose size should be returned.

Example

The following program demonstrates how to use the _msize() function. When run, the program allocates a block of memory and then calls the _msize() function to get the size of the allocated block, displaying the size in a message. The program's output looks like this:

```
Bytes allocated: 1024
Press any key to continue
```

Here is the program source code that produced the output:

```
#include "stdafx.h"
#include <iostream>
#include <malloc.h>

using namespace std;

int main(int argc, char* argv[])
{
    char* buf = (char *)calloc(1024, sizeof(char));

    if (buf != NULL )
```

```
    {
        size_t bufSize = _msize(buf);
        cout << "Bytes allocated: " << bufSize << endl;
        free(buf);
    }
    else
        cout << "Allocation error." << endl;

    return 0;
}
```

CROSS-REFERENCE
See also _expand(), _heapadd(), _heapchk(), _heapmin(), _heapset(), _heapwalk(), alloca(), calloc(), free(), malloc(), and realloc().

malloc()

Function

The `malloc()` function allocates a block of memory, returning a pointer to the memory if successful, or `NULL` if unsuccessful.

Header File

```
#include <malloc.h>
```

Declaration

```
void* malloc(size_t size);
```

- *size* — The number of bytes of memory to allocate.

Example

The following program demonstrates how to use the `malloc()` function. When run, the program allocates a block of memory and then calls the `_msize()` function to get the size of the allocated block, displaying the size in a message. The program's output looks like this:

```
Allocating 1024 bytes of memory...
Bytes allocated: 1024
Freeing allocated memory...
Press any key to continue
```

Here is the program source code that produced the output:

```
#include "stdafx.h"
#include <iostream>
#include <malloc.h>

#include "stdafx.h"
#include <iostream>
#include <malloc.h>

using namespace std;

int main(int argc, char* argv[])
{
    cout << "Allocating 1024 bytes of memory..." << endl;
    char* buf = (char *)malloc(1024);

    if (buf != NULL )
    {
        size_t bufSize = _msize(buf);
        cout << "Bytes allocated: " << bufSize << endl;
        cout << "Freeing allocated memory..." << endl;
        free(buf);
    }
    else
        cout << "Allocation error." << endl;

    return 0;
}
```

CROSS-REFERENCE
See also _expand(), _heapadd(), _heapchk(), _heapmin(), _heapset(), _heapwalk(), _msize(), alloca(), calloc(), free(), and realloc().

map

Template Class

The map template class, which is defined in the map Standard C++ header file, defines an object for organizing data pairs comprising a key and a data item associated with the key.

map • 791

Class Declaration

```
template<class Key, class T, class Pred = less<Key>,
    class A = allocator<T> >
    class map {
public:
    typedef Key key_type;
    typedef T referent_type;
    typedef Pred key_compare;
    typedef A allocator_type;
    typedef pair<const Key, T> value_type;
    class value_compare;
    typedef A::size_type size_type;
    typedef A::difference_type difference_type;
    typedef A::rebind<value_type>::other::reference reference;
    typedef A::rebind<value_type>::other::const_reference
        const_reference;
    typedef T0 iterator;
    typedef T1 const_iterator;
    typedef reverse_bidirectional_iterator<iterator,
        value_type, reference, A::pointer,
            difference_type> reverse_iterator;
    typedef reverse_bidirectional_iterator<const_iterator,
        value_type, const_reference, A::const_pointer,
            difference_type> const_reverse_iterator;
    explicit map(const Pred& comp = Pred(),
        const A& al = A());
    map(const map& x);
    map(const value_type *first, const value_type *last,
        const Pred& comp = Pred(),
            const A& al = A());
    iterator begin();
    const_iterator begin() const;
    iterator end();
    iterator end() const;
    reverse_iterator rbegin();
    const_reverse_iterator rbegin() const;
    reverse_iterator rend();
    const_reverse_iterator rend() const;
    size_type size() const;
    size_type max_size() const;
    bool empty() const;
    A get_allocator() const;
    A::reference operator[](const Key& key);
    pair<iterator, bool> insert(const value_type& x);
```

```
        iterator insert(iterator it, const value_type& x);
        void insert(const value_type *first,
            const value_type *last);
        iterator erase(iterator it);
        iterator erase(iterator first, iterator last);
        size_type erase(const Key& key);
        void clear();
        void swap(map x);
        key_compare key_comp() const;
        value_compare value_comp() const;
        iterator find(const Key& key);
        const_iterator find(const Key& key) const;
        size_type count(const Key& key) const;
        iterator lower_bound(const Key& key);
        const_iterator lower_bound(const Key& key) const;
        iterator upper_bound(const Key& key);
        const_iterator upper_bound(const Key& key) const;
        pair<iterator, iterator> equal_range(const Key& key);
        pair<const_iterator, const_iterator>
            equal_range(const Key& key) const;
    protected:
        A allocator;
        };
```

Class Members

Table M-14 lists and describes the members of the map templateclass.

Table M-14 Members of the map Template Class

Member	Description
allocator_type	A synonym for the template's A parameter.
begin()	Returns a bidirectional iterator that points to the sequence's first element.
clear()	Removes all elements from the map.
const_iterator	Object type for a constant bidirectional iterator.
const_reference	Refers to an element reference.
const_reverse_iterator	Object type for a constant reverse iterator.
count()	Returns the number of elements for a given key.
difference_type	Represents the difference between two element addresses.
empty()	Returns true if the sequence is empty.

Member	Description
end()	Returns a bidirectional iterator that points to the next element beyond the end of the sequence.
equal_range()	Returns a pair of iterators for lower_bound() and upper_bound().
erase()	Erases an element.
find()	Finds an element in the map.
get_allocator()	Returns the allocator.
insert()	Inserts an element into the set.
iterator	Object type for a bi-directional iterator.
key_comp	Represents a function for comparing keys.
key_compare()	Compares keys in the set.
key_type	Represents a data type for a sort key.
lower_bound()	Returns an iterator for the first element that doesn't match the given key.
max_size()	Returns the maximum possible size of a sequence.
rbegin()	Returns a reverse bidirectional iterator that points to the next element beyond the end of the sequence.
reference	A synonym for A as an element reference.
rend()	Returns a reverse bidirectional iterator that points to the sequence's first element.
reverse_iterator	Object type for a reverse iterator.
size()	Returns the length of the sequence.
size_type	Represents an unsigned integer used to represent the size of the map.
swap()	Swaps one sequence with another.
upper_bound()	Returns an iterator for the first element that matches the given key.
value_comp	Represents a function for comparing values.
value_compare()	Compares values in the set.
value_type	Represents a data type for an element in the set.

CROSS-REFERENCE
See also list, set, and vector.

math.h

Standard C Library Header File

The math.h header files defines the constants, functions, and structures required for performing mathematical calculations.

Defined Constants

_DOMAIN	EDOM
_OVERFLOW	ERANGE
_PLOSS	OVERFLOW
_SING	PLOSS
_TLOSS	SING
_UNDERFLOW	TLOSS
DOMAIN	UNDERFLOW

Defined Functions

_atold()	atan()
_cabs()	atan2()
_cabsl()	atan2f()
_hypot()	atan2l()
_hypotl()	atanf()
_j0()	atanl()
_j0l()	atof()
_j1()	cabs()
_j1l()	ceil()
_jn()	ceilf()
_jnl()	ceill()
_matherr()	cos()
_matherrl()	cosf()
_y0()	cosh()
_y0l()	coshf()
_y1()	coshl()
_y1l()	cosl()
_yn()	exp()
_ynl()	expf()
abs()	expl()
acosf()	fabs()
acosl()	fabsf()
asin()	fabsl()
asinf()	floor()
asinl()	floorf()

floorl()   modff()

fmod()   modfl()

fmodf()   pow()

fmodl()   powf()

frexp()   powl()

frexpf()   sin()

frexpl()   sinf()

hypot()   sinh()

hypotf()   sinhf()

j0()   sinhl()

j1()   sinl()

jn()   sqrt()

labs()   sqrtf()

ldexp()   sqrtl()

ldexpf()   tan()

ldexpl()   tanf()

log()   tanh()

log10()   tanhf()

log10f()   tanhl()

log10l()   tanl()

logf()   y0()

logl()   y1()

matherr()   yn()

modf()

Defined Structures

```
struct _complex {
        double x,y;
        } ;
#define complex _complex

struct _complexl {
        long double x,y;
} ;

struct _exception {
        int type;
        char *name;
```

```
                        double arg1;
                        double arg2;
                        double retval;
                        } ;

            struct _exception1 {
                        int type;
                        char *name;
                        long double arg1;
                        long double arg2;
                        long double retval;
            } ;
```

matherr()

function

The `matherr()` function enables a program to respond to mathematical run-time errors.

Header File

```
#include <math.h>
```

Declaration

```
int matherr(struct _exception *except);
```

- *except* — A pointer to the `_exception` structure that holds information about the error.

Example

The following program demonstrates how to use the `matherr()` function. When run, the program passes an illegal value to the `sqrt()` function, which causes a mathematical error. This error causes the `matherr()` function to be called, where the error is handled, correcting the illegal value. Notice how setting the `_exception` object's `retval` member determines the corrected result of the original call to the `sqrt()` function in `main()`. The program's output looks like this:

```
Argument domain type error
Can't get the square root of a negative number.
```

```
Changing arg1 to positive.
Result = 5
Press any key to continue
```

Here is the program source code that produced the output:

```cpp
#include "stdafx.h"
#include <math.h>
#include <iostream>

using namespace std;

int matherr( struct _exception *except )
{
    double newValue;
    int result;

    switch (except->type)
    {
    case DOMAIN:
        cout << "Argument domain type error" << endl;
        result = strcmp("sqrt", except->name);
        if (!result)
        {
            if (except->arg1 < 0)
            {
                cout << "Can't get the square root ";
                cout << "of a negative number." << endl;
                cout << "Changing arg1 to positive." << endl;
                newValue = -(except->arg1);
            }
            else
                newValue = except->arg1;
            except->retval = sqrt(newValue);
        }
        return 1;
    case SING:
        cout << "Argument singularity type error" << endl;
        // Handle the error here.
        return 1;
    case OVERFLOW:
        cout << "Overflow range type error" << endl;
        // Handle the error here.
        return 1;
    case PLOSS:
```

```
                    cout << "Partial significance type error" << endl;
                    // Handle the error here.
                    return 1;
                case TLOSS:
                    cout << "Total significance type error " << endl;
                    // Handle the error here.
                    return 1;
                case UNDERFLOW:
                    cout << "Underflow type error" << endl;
                    // Handle the error here.
                    return 1;
            }

            return 0;
        }

        int main(int argc, char* argv[])
        {
            double val = -25.0;
            double result = sqrt(val);
            cout << "Result = " << result << endl;

            return 0;
        }
```

CROSS-REFERENCE
See also _cabs(), _cabsl(), _hypot(), abs(), acos(), asin(), atan(), atan2, ceil(), cos(), cosh(), div(), exp(), fabs(), fabsf(), fabsl(), floor(), fmod(), frexp(), labs(), ldexpl(), ldiv(), log(), log10(), pow(), sin(), sinh(), sqrt(), tan(), and tanh().

mblen()

Function

The mblen() function returns the length of a multibyte character.

Header Files

```
#include <stdlib.h>
```

Declaration

```
int mblen(const unsigned char *c, size_t count);
```

- *c* — A pointer to the source character.
- *count* — The number of bytes to examine.

Example

The following program demonstrates how to use the `mblen()` function. When run, the program displays the length in bytes of the character values in an array. The program's output looks like this:

```
Testing values...
Length of character A is 1.
Length of character B is 1.
Length of character C is 1.
Length of character D is 1.
Length of character E is 1.
Length of character F is 1.
Length of character G is 1.
Length of character H is 1.
Length of character I is 1.
Length of character J is 1.
Press any key to continue
```

Here is the program source code that produced the output:

```cpp
#include "stdafx.h"
#include <stdlib.h>
#include <iostream>

using namespace std;

int main(int argc, char* argv[])
{
    int x;
    char dat[] =
    {
        65, 66, 67, 68, 69,
        70, 71, 72, 73, 74
    };
```

```
        cout << "Testing values..." << endl;

        for (x=0; x<10; ++x)
        {
            int result = mblen(&dat[x], 1);
            if (result == -1)
                cout << "Not a multibyte character." << endl;
            else
            {
                cout << "Length of character " << dat[x];
                cout << " is " << result << "." << endl;
            }
        }

        return 0;
    }
```

CROSS-REFERENCE

See also _ismbbalnum(), _ismbbalpha(), _ismbbgraph(), _ismbbkalnum(), _ismbbkana(), _ismbbkprint(), _ismbbkpunct(), _ismbblead(), _ismbbprint(), _ismbbpunct(), _ismbbtrail(), _mbbtombc(), _mbbtype(), _mbccpy(), _mbcjistojms(), _mbcjmstojis(), _mbclen(), _mbctohira(), _mbctokata(), _mbctolower(), _mbctombb(), _mbctoupper(), _mbsbtype, _mbscat(), _mbschr(), _mbscmp(), _mbscoll(), _mbscpy(), _mbscspn(), _mbsdec(), _mbsdup(), _mbsicmp(), _mbsicoll(), _mbsinc(), _mbslen(), _mbslwr(), _mbsnbcat(), _mbsnbcmp(), _mbsnbcnt(), _mbsnbcoll(), _mbsnbcpy(), _mbsnbicmp(), _mbsnbicoll(), _mbsnbset(), _mbsncat(), _mbsnccnt(), _mbsncmp(), _mbsncoll(), _mbsncpy(), _mbsnextc(), _mbsnicmp(), _mbsnicoll(), _mbsninc(), _mbsnset(), _mbspbrk(), _mbsrchr(), _mbsrev(), _mbsset(), _mbsspn(), _mbsspnp(), _mbsstr(), _mbstok(), _mbstrlen(), _mbsupr(), isleadbyte(), mbstowcs(), and mbtowc().

mbstowcs()

Function

The mbstowcs() function converts a multibyte-character string to a wide-character string, returning the number of characters converted, or returning −1 in the case of an error.

Header Files

```
#include <stdlib.h>
```

Declaration

```
size_t mbstowcs(wchar_t *wcstr,
    const char *mbstr, size_t count);
```

- *count* — The number of bytes to convert.
- *mbstr* — A pointer to the multibyte-character string.
- *wcstr* — A pointer to the wide-character string buffer.

Example

The following program demonstrates how to use the mbstowcs() function. When run, the program converts a string to a wide-character string, displaying the results as it goes. The program's output looks like this:

```
Transforming string...
Original string = This is a test
Wide-character string = This is a test
# of chars converted = 14
Press any key to continue
```

Here is the program source code that produced the output:

```cpp
#include "stdafx.h"
#include <stdlib.h>
#include <iostream>

using namespace std;

int main(int argc, char* argv[])
{
    const char mbstr[] = "This is a test";
    wchar_t wcstr[81];

    cout << "Transforming string..." << endl;
    size_t result = mbstowcs(wcstr, mbstr, 14);
    wcstr[14] = 0;
    cout << "Original string = " << mbstr << endl;
    cout << "Wide-character string = ";
    wcout << wcstr;
    cout << endl;
    cout << "# of chars converted = " << result << endl;

    return 0;
}
```

CROSS-REFERENCE

See also _ismbbalnum(), _ismbbalpha(), _ismbbgraph(), _ismbbkalnum(), _ismbbkana(), _ismbbkprint(), _ismbbkpunct(), _ismbblead(), _ismbbprint(), _ismbbpunct(), _ismbbtrail(), _mbbtombc(), _mbbtype(), _mbccpy(), _mbcjistojms(), _mbcjmstojis(), _mbclen(), _mbctohira(), _mbctokata(), _mbctolower(), _mbctombb(), _mbctoupper(), _mbsbtype, _mbscat(), _mbschr(), _mbscmp(), _mbscoll(), _mbscpy(), _mbscspn(), _mbsdec(), _mbsdup(), _mbsicmp(), _mbsicoll(), _mbsinc(), _mbslen(), _mbslwr(), _mbsnbcat(), _mbsnbcmp(), _mbsnbcnt(), _mbsnbcoll(), _mbsnbcpy(), _mbsnbicmp(), _mbsnbicoll(), _mbsnbset(), _mbsncat(), _mbsnccnt(), _mbsncmp(), _mbsncoll(), _mbsncpy(), _mbsnextc(), _mbsnicmp(), _mbsnicoll(), _mbsninc(), _mbsnset(), _mbspbrk(), _mbsrchr(), _mbsrev(), _mbsset(), _mbsspn(), _mbsspnp(), _mbsstr(), _mbstok(), _mbstrlen(), _mbsupr(), isleadbyte(), mblen(), and mbtowc().

mbtowc()

Function

The mbtowc() function converts a multibyte-character to a wide-character, returning the number of characters converted, or returning –1 in the case of an error.

Header Files

```
#include <stdlib.h>
```

Declaration

```
size_t mbtowc(wchar_t *wcstr,
    const char *mbstr, size_t count);
```

- *count* — The number of bytes to scan.
- *mbstr* — A pointer to the multibyte-character.
- *wcstr* — A pointer to the wide-character.

Example

The following program demonstrates how to use the mbtowc() function. When run, the program converts a string to a wide-character string, displaying the results as it goes. The program's output looks like this:

```
Transforming string...
Converting character #0
```

```
Converting character #1
Converting character #2
Converting character #3
Converting character #4
Converting character #5
Converting character #6
Converting character #7
Converting character #8
Converting character #9
Converting character #10
Converting character #11
Converting character #12
Converting character #13
Original string = This is a test
Wide-character string = This is a test
Press any key to continue
```

Here is the program source code that produced the output:

```cpp
#include "stdafx.h"
#include <stdlib.h>
#include <iostream>

using namespace std;

int main(int argc, char* argv[])
{
    int x;
    const char mbstr[] = "This is a test";
    wchar_t wcstr[81];

    cout << "Transforming string..." << endl;

    for (x=0; x<14; ++x)
    {
        cout << "Converting character #" << x << endl;
        int result = mbtowc(&wcstr[x], &mbstr[x], 1);
        if (result == -1)
        {
            cout << "Cannot convert string." << endl;
            break;
        }
    }
    wcstr[14] = 0;
    cout << "Original string = " << mbstr << endl;
```

```
        cout << "Wide-character string = ";
        wcout << wcstr;
        cout << endl;

        return 0;
    }
```

CROSS-REFERENCE

See also _ismbbalnum(), _ismbbalpha(), _ismbbgraph(), _ismbbkalnum(), _ismbbkana(), _ismbbkprint(), _ismbbkpunct(), _ismbblead(), _ismbbprint(), _ismbbpunct(), _ismbbtrail(), _mbbtombc(), _mbbtype(), _mbccpy(), _mbcjistojms(), _mbcjmstojis(), _mbclen(), _mbctohira(), _mbctokata(), _mbctolower(), _mbctombb(), _mbctoupper(), _mbsbtype, _mbscat(), _mbschr(), _mbscmp(), _mbscoll(), _mbscpy(), _mbscspn(), _mbsdec(), _mbsdup(), _mbsicmp(), _mbsicoll(), _mbsinc(), _mbslen(), _mbslwr(), _mbsnbcat(), _mbsnbcmp(), _mbsnbcnt(), _mbsnbcoll(), _mbsnbcpy(), _mbsnbicmp(), _mbsnbicoll(), _mbsnbset(), _mbsncat(), _mbsnccnt(), _mbsncmp(), _mbsncoll(), _mbsncpy(), _mbsnextc(), _mbsnicmp(), _mbsnicoll(), _mbsninc(), _mbsnset(), _mbspbrk(), _mbsrchr(), _mbsrev(), _mbsset(), _mbsspn(), _mbsspnp(), _mbsstr(), _mbstok(), _mbstrlen(), _mbsupr(), isleadbyte(), mblen(), and mbstowcs().

memccpy()

Function

The memccpy() function copies characters from one buffer to another, returning a pointer to the character following the last character copied.

Header Files

```
#include <memory.h>
```

Declaration

```
void* memccpy(void *dest, const void *src,
    int c, size_t count);
```

- *c* — The last character to copy from *src* to *dest*.
- *count* — The maximum number of characters to copy.

- *dest*—A pointer to the destination buffer.
- *src*—A pointer to the source buffer.

Example

The following program demonstrates how to use the memccpy() function. When run, the program copies a portion of one string to another string (stopping at the letter h) and displays the results. The program's output looks like this:

```
Source string:
   One Two Three
Destination string:
   One Two Th
Press any key to continue
```

Here is the program source code that produced the output:

```
#include "stdafx.h"
#include <iostream>
#include <memory.h>

using namespace std;

int main(int argc, char* argv[])
{
    char str1[] = "One Two Three";
    char str2[81];

    char* pResult = (char*)memccpy(str2, str1, 'h', 13);
    pResult[0] = 0;
    cout << "Source string: " << endl;
    cout << "    " << str1 << endl;
    cout << "Destination string: " << endl;
    cout << "    " << str2 << endl;

    return 0;
}
```

CROSS-REFERENCE

See also _memccpy(), _memicmp(), memchr(), memcmp(), memcpy(), memicmp(), memmove(), and memset().

memchr()

Function

The memchr() function searches for the first occurrence of a character in a buffer, returning a pointer to the character, or returning NULL if the character isn't found.

Header Files

```
#include <memory.h>
```

Declaration

```
void* memchr(const void *buf, int c, size_t count);
```

- *buf*—A pointer to the buffer to search.
- *c*—The value for which to search.
- *count*—The number of buffer elements to search.

Example

The following program demonstrates how to use the memchr() function. When run, the program searches for the first occurrence of the letter T and displays the results. The program's output looks like this:

```
Source string:
    One Two Three
Result:
    Two Three
Press any key to continue
```

Here is the program source code that produced the output:

```
#include "stdafx.h"
#include <iostream>
#include <memory.h>

using namespace std;

int main(int argc, char* argv[])
{
    char str1[] = "One Two Three";

    char* result = (char*)memchr(str1, 'T', 9);
    if (result == NULL)
        cout << "Character not found." << endl;
```

```
        else
        {
            cout << "Source string: " << endl;
            cout << "    " << str1 << endl;
            cout << "Result: " << endl;
            cout << "    " << result << endl;
        }


        return 0;
    }
```

CROSS-REFERENCE

See also _memccpy(), _memicmp(), memccpy(), memcmp(), memcpy(), memicmp(), memmove(), and memset().

memcmp()

Function

The memcmp() function compares the values in two buffers, returning a value from Table M-15.

Table M-15 Return Values for memcmp()

Value	Description
Less than 0	string1 is alphabetically less than string2.
0	The two strings are equal.
Greater than 0	string1 is alphabetically greater than string2.

Header Files

```
#include <memory.h>
```

Declaration

```
int memcmp(const void *buf1, const void *buf2, size_t count);
```

- *buf1* — A pointer to the buffer to compare to *buf2*.
- *buf2* — A pointer to the buffer to compare to *buf1*.
- *count* — The number of buffer elements to compare.

Example

The following program demonstrates how to use the `memcmp()` function. When run, the program compares two buffers and displays the results. The program's output looks like this:

```
The buffers are equal.
Press any key to continue
```

Here is the program source code that produced the output:

```cpp
#include "stdafx.h"
#include <iostream>
#include <memory.h>

using namespace std;

int main(int argc, char* argv[])
{
    char str1[] = "One Two Three";
    char str2[] = "One Two Three";

    int result = memcmp(str1, str2, sizeof(str1));
    if (result == 0)
        cout << "The buffers are equal." << endl;
    else if (result < 0)
        cout << "str1 is less than str2." << endl;
    else
        cout << "str1 is greater than str2." << endl;

    return 0;
}
```

CROSS-REFERENCE

See also _memccpy(), _memicmp(), memccpy(), memchr(), memcpy(), memicmp(), memmove(), and memset().

memcpy()

Function

The `memcpy()` function copies characters from one buffer to another, returning a pointer to the destination buffer. The source and destination buffers should not overlap.

Header Files

```
#include <memory.h>
```

Declaration

```
void* memcpy(void *dest, const void *src, size_t count);
```

- *count* — The number of characters to copy.
- *dest* — A pointer to the destination buffer.
- *src* — A pointer to the source buffer.

Example

The following program demonstrates how to use the memcpy() function. When run, the program copies a portion of one string to another string and displays the results. The program's output looks like this:

```
Source string:
    One Two Three
Destination string:
    One Two T
Press any key to continue
```

Here is the program source code that produced the output:

```
#include "stdafx.h"
#include <iostream>
#include <memory.h>

using namespace std;

int main(int argc, char* argv[])
{
    char str1[] = "One Two Three";
    char str2[81];

    memcpy(str2, str1, 9);
    str2[9] = 0;
    cout << "Source string: " << endl;
    cout << "    " << str1 << endl;
    cout << "Destination string: " << endl;
    cout << "    " << str2 << endl;

    return 0;
}
```

CROSS-REFERENCE

See also _memccpy(), _memicmp(), memccpy(), memchr(), memcmp(), memicmp(), memmove(), and memset().

memicmp()

Function

The memicmp() function compares the values in two buffers without regard for character case (case–insensitive compare), returning a value from Table M-16.

Table M-16 Return Values for memicmp()

Value	Description
Less than 0	string1 is alphabetically less than string2.
0	The two strings are equal.
Greater than 0	string1 is alphabetically greater than string2.

Header Files

```
#include <memory.h>
```

Declaration

```
int memicmp(const void *buf1,
    const void *buf2, size_t count);
```

- *buf1* — A pointer to the buffer to compare to *buf2*.
- *buf2* — A pointer to the buffer to compare to *buf1*.
- *count* — The number of buffer elements to compare.

Example

The following program demonstrates how to use the memicmp() function. When run, the program compares two buffers and displays the results. The program's output looks like this:

```
The buffers are equal.
Press any key to continue
```

Here is the program source code that produced the output:

```
#include "stdafx.h"
#include <iostream>
#include <memory.h>

using namespace std;

int main(int argc, char* argv[])
{
    char str1[] = "One Two Three";
    char str2[] = "ONE TWO THREE";

    int result = memicmp(str1, str2, sizeof(str1));
    if (result == 0)
        cout << "The buffers are equal." << endl;
    else if (result < 0)
        cout << "str1 is less than str2." << endl;
    else
        cout << "str1 is greater than str2." << endl;

    return 0;
}
```

CROSS-REFERENCE

See also _memccpy(), _memicmp(), memccpy(), memchr(), memcmp(), memcpy(), memmove(), and memset().

memmove()

Function

The memmove() function moves the contents of one buffer to another, returning a pointer to the destination buffer. The source and destination buffers can overlap.

Header Files

```
#include <memory.h>
```

Declaration

```
void* memmove(void *dest, const void *src, size_t count);
```

- *count* — The number of characters to copy.
- *dest* — A pointer to the destination buffer.
- *src* — A pointer to the source buffer.

Example

The following program demonstrates how to use the `memmove()` function. When run, the program copies a portion of one string to another string and displays the results. The program's output looks like this:

```
Source string:
    One Two Three
Destination string:
    One Two T
Press any key to continue
```

Here is the program source code that produced the output:

```cpp
#include "stdafx.h"
#include <iostream>
#include <memory.h>

using namespace std;

int main(int argc, char* argv[])
{
    char str1[] = "One Two Three";
    char str2[81];

    char* result = (char*)memmove(str2, str1, 9);
    str2[9] = 0;
    cout << "Source string: " << endl;
    cout << "    " << str1 << endl;
    cout << "Destination string: " << endl;
    cout << "    " << result << endl;

    return 0;
}
```

CROSS-REFERENCE

See also _memccpy(), _memicmp(), memccpy(), memchr(), memcmp(), memcpy(), memicmp(), and memset().

memset()

Function

The memset() function fills a buffer with a specified value, returning a pointer to the buffer. The source and destination buffers can overlap.

Header Files

```
#include <memory.h>
```

Declaration

```
void* memset(void *dest, int c, size_t count);
```

- *c* — The value with which to fill the buffer.
- *count* — The number of buffer elements to fill.
- *dest* — A pointer to the destination buffer.

Example

The following program demonstrates how to use the memset() function. When run, the program fills a portion of a string with asterisks. The program's output looks like this:

```
Source string:
    One Two Three
Result:
    *********hree
Press any key to continue
```

Here is the program source code that produced the output:

```
#include "stdafx.h"
#include <iostream>
#include <memory.h>

using namespace std;

int main(int argc, char* argv[])
{
    char str1[] = "One Two Three";

    cout << "Source string: " << endl;
```

```
cout << "    " << str1 << endl;
char* result = (char*)memset(str1, '*', 9);
cout << "Result: " << endl;
cout << "    " << result << endl;

return 0;
}
```

CROSS-REFERENCE

See also _memccpy(), _memicmp(), memccpy(), memchr(), memcmp(), memcpy(), memicmp(), and memmove().

mkdir()

Function

The mkdir() function creates a new disk directory. If the function is successful, it returns 0; otherwise, it returns –1.

Header File

```
#include <direct.h>
```

Declaration

```
int mkdir(const char* dirname)
```

■ *dirname* — The path and name of the new directory.

Example

The following program demonstrates how to use the mkdir() function by creating a new directory in drive C's root directory and then deleting the new directory. The program's output looks like this:

```
New directory created
Press any key to continue
```

Here is the program source code that produced the output:

```
#include "stdafx.h"
#include <direct.h>
#include <iostream>
```

```
using namespace std;

int main(int argc, char* argv[])
{
    int result = mkdir("c:\\TestDir");
    if (result != -1)
    {
        cout << "New directory created" << endl;
        _rmdir("c:\\TestDir");
    }
    else
        cout << "Directory create error" << endl;

    return 0;
}
```

CROSS-REFERENCE
See also _chdrive(), _getdcwd(), _getdrive(), _mkdir(), _searchenv(), _wchdir(), _wgetcwd(), _wgetdcwd(), _wmkdir(), _wrmdir(), _wsearchenv(), chdir(), getcwd(), and rmdir().

mktemp()

Function

The mktemp() function generates a unique filename that can be used to create temporary files. If the function is successful, it returns a pointer to the file name; otherwise, it returns NULL.

Header File

```
#include <io.h>
```

Declaration

```
char* mktemp(char *template);
```

- *template*—A pointer to the template to be used to create the filename. This template must be in the form *base*XXXXXX, where *base* is the user-supplied characters for the filename and the Xs are placeholders for the characters that the mktemp() function will supply.

Example

The following program demonstrates how to use the `mktemp()` function by creating and displaying a unique temporary filename. The program's output looks like this:

```
Temp file name: tempa25913
Press any key to continue
```

Here is the program source code that produced the output:

```cpp
#include "stdafx.h"
#include <io.h>
#include <iostream>

using namespace std;

int main(int argc, char* argv[])
{
    char fileName[] = "tempXXXXXX";

    char* result = mktemp(fileName);
    if (result == NULL)
        cout << "Error forming temp File name" << endl;
    else
    {
        cout << "Temp file name: ";
        cout << fileName << endl;
    }

    return 0;
}
```

CROSS-REFERENCE
See also _mktemp(), _tempnam(), _wmktemp _wtempnam(), _wtmpnam(), tmpfile(), and tmpnam().

mktime()

Function

The `mktime()` function converts a `tm` structure to a `time_t` value containing the calendar time. If the function fails, it returns `(time_t)-1` (−1 cast to the type `time_t`).

Header File

```
#include <time.h>
```

Declaration

```
time_t mktime(struct tm *timeptr);
```

- *timeptr* — A pointer to the `tm` structure that should be converted to a `time_t` value.

Example

The following program demonstrates how to use the `mktime()` function by manipulating the current time and displaying the results. The program's output looks like this:

```
Getting the current time...
Converting to a tm structure...
Converting back to a time_t value...
The time is Fri Apr 02 09:24:50 1999

Press any key to continue
```

Here is the program source code that produced the output:

```
#include "stdafx.h"
#include <time.h>
#include <iostream>

using namespace std;

int main(int argc, char* argv[])
{

    struct tm* tmStruct;
    time_t curTime;
    time_t result;

    cout << "Getting the current time..." << endl;
    time(&curTime);
    cout << "Converting to a tm structure..." << endl;
    tmStruct = localtime(&curTime);
    cout << "Converting back to a time_t value..." << endl;
    result = mktime(tmStruct);
    if( result == (time_t)-1 )
```

```
            cout << "mktime() error." << endl;
        else
            cout << "The time is " << asctime(tmStruct) << endl;

        return 0;
}
```

CROSS-REFERENCE
See also _ftime(), _futime(), _strdate(), _strtime(), _wasctime(), _wctime(), _wstrdate(), _wstrtime(), asctime(), ctime(), difftime(), gmtime(), localtime(), time(), and wcsftime().

modf()

Function

The modf() function extracts the integer and decimal portions of a double value, returning the decimal portion.

Header File

```
#include <math.h>
```

Declaration

```
double modf(double x, double *intptr);
```

- *intptr*—A pointer to the variable that will receive the decimal portion of *x*.
- *x*—The double value from which to extract the integer and decimal portions.

Example

The following program demonstrates how to use the modf() function, extracting and displaying the integer and decimal portions of the number 53.985. The program's output looks like this:

```
Original value = 53.985
Integer part = 53
Fractional part = 0.985
Press any key to continue
```

Here is the program source code that produced the output:

```
#include "stdafx.h"
#include <math.h>
#include <iostream>

using namespace std;

int main(int argc, char* argv[])
{
    double val1 = 53.985;
    double intPart;

    double frac = modf(val1, &intPart);
    cout << "Original value = " << val1 << endl;
    cout << "Integer part = " << intPart << endl;
    cout << "Fractional part = " << frac << endl;

    return 0;
}
```

CROSS-REFERENCE
See also _cabs(), _cabsl(), _hypot(), abs(), acos(), asin(), atan(), atan2, ceil(), cos(), cosh(), div(), exp(), fabs(), fabsf(), fabsl(), floor(), fmod(), frexp(), labs(), ldexpl(), ldiv(), log(), log10(), modff(), modfl(), pow(), sin(), sinh(), sqrt(), tan(), and tanh().

modff()

Function

The modff() function extracts the integer and decimal portions of a float value, returning the decimal portion.

NOTE
Borland does not support this function.

Header File

```
#include <math.h>
```

Declaration

```
float modff(float x, float *intptr);
```

- *intptr*—A pointer to the variable that will receive the decimal portion of *x*.
- *x*—The float value from which to extract the integer and decimal portions.

Example

The following program demonstrates how to use the `modff()` function, extracting and displaying the integer and decimal portions of the number 53.985. The program's output looks like this:

```
Original value = 53.985
Integer part = 53
Fractional part = 0.985001
Press any key to continue
```

Here is the program source code that produced the output:

```cpp
#include "stdafx.h"
#include <math.h>
#include <iostream>

using namespace std;

int main(int argc, char* argv[])
{
    float val1 = (float)53.985;
    float intPart;

    float frac = modff(val1, &intPart);
    cout << "Original value = " << val1 << endl;
    cout << "Integer part = " << intPart << endl;
    cout << "Fractional part = " << frac << endl;

    return 0;
}
```

CROSS-REFERENCE

See also _cabs(), _cabsl(), _hypot(), abs(), acos(), asin(), atan(), atan2(), ceil(), cos(), cosh(), div(), exp(), fabs(), fabsf(), fabsl(), floor(), fmod(), frexp(), labs(), ldexpl(), ldiv(), log(), log10(), modf(), modfl(), pow(), sin(), sinh(), sqrt(), tan(), and tanh().

modfl()

Function

The modfl() function extracts the integer and decimal portions of a long double value, returning the decimal portion.

 NOTE
Borland does not support this function.

Header File

```
#include <math.h>
```

Declaration

```
long double modfl(long double x, long double *intptr);
```

- *intptr*—A pointer to the variable that will receive the decimal portion of *x*.
- *x*—The long double value from which to extract the integer and decimal portions.

Example

The following program demonstrates how to use the modfl() function, extracting and displaying the integer and decimal portions of the number 53.985. The program's output looks like this:

```
Original value = 53.985
Integer part = 53
Fractional part = 0.985
Press any key to continue
```

Here is the program source code that produced the output:

```
#include "stdafx.h"
#include <math.h>
#include <iostream>

using namespace std;

int main(int argc, char* argv[])
{
```

```
    long double val1 = 53.985;
    long double intPart;

    long double frac = modfl(val1, &intPart);
    cout << "Original value = " << val1 << endl;
    cout << "Integer part = " << intPart << endl;
    cout << "Fractional part = " << frac << endl;

    return 0;
}
```

CROSS-REFERENCE

See also _cabs(), _cabsl(), _hypot(), abs(), acos(), asin(), atan(), atan2, ceil(), cos(), cosh(), div(), exp(), fabs(), fabsf(), fabsl(), floor(), fmod(), frexp(), labs(), ldexpl(), ldiv(), log(), log10(), modf(), modff(), pow(), sin(), sinh(), sqrt(), tan(), and tanh().

multiset

Template Class

The multiset template class, which is defined in the multiset Standard C++ header file, defines an object for organizing data, where each data item represents both a value and a key.

Class Declaration

```
template<class Key, class Pred = less<Key>,
    class A = allocator<Key> >
    class multiset {
public:
    typedef Key key_type;
    typedef Pred key_compare;
    typedef Key value_type;
    typedef Pred value_compare;
    typedef A allocator_type;
    typedef A::size_type size_type;
    typedef A::difference_type difference_type;
    typedef A::rebind<value_type>::other::const_reference
        reference;
    typedef A::rebind<value_type>::other::const_reference
```

```
        const_reference;
    typedef T0 iterator;
    typedef T1 const_iterator;
    typedef reverse_bidirectional_iterator<iterator,
        value_type, reference, A::const_pointer,
            difference_type> reverse_iterator;
    typedef reverse_bidirectional_iterator<const_iterator,
        value_type, const_reference, A::pointer,
            difference_type> const_reverse_iterator;
    explicit multiset(const Pred& comp = Pred(),
        const A& al = A());
    multiset(const multiset& x);
    multiset(const value_type *first, const value_type *last,
        const Pred& comp = Pred(), const A& al = A());
    const_iterator begin() const;
    iterator end() const;
    const_reverse_iterator rbegin() const;
    const_reverse_iterator rend() const;
    size_type size() const;
    size_type max_size() const;
    bool empty() const;
    A get_allocator() const;
    iterator insert(const value_type& x);
    iterator insert(iterator it, const value_type& x);
    void insert(const value_type *first,
        const value_type *last);
    iterator erase(iterator it);
    iterator erase(iterator first, iterator last);
    size_type erase(const Key& key);
    void clear();
    void swap(multiset x);
    key_compare key_comp() const;
    value_compare value_comp() const;
    const_iterator find(const Key& key) const;
    size_type count(const Key& key) const;
    const_iterator lower_bound(const Key& key) const;
    const_iterator upper_bound(const Key& key) const;
    pair<const_iterator, const_iterator>
        equal_range(const Key& key) const;
protected:
    A allocator;
    };
```

Class Members

Table M-17 lists and describes the members of the `multiset` template class.

Table M-17 Members of the Multiset Template Class

Member	Description
allocator_type	A synonym for the template's A parameter.
begin()	Returns a bidirectional iterator that points to the sequence's first element.
clear()	Removes all elements from the set.
const_iterator	Object type for a constant bidirectional iterator.
const_reference	Refers to an element reference.
const_reverse_iterator	Object type for a constant reverse iterator.
count()	Returns the number of elements for a given key.
difference_type	Represents the difference between two element addresses.
empty()	Returns true if the sequence is empty.
end()	Returns a bidirectional iterator that points to the next element beyond the end of the sequence.
equal_range()	Returns a pair of iterators for `lower_bound()` and `upper_bound()`.
erase()	Erases an element.
find()	Finds an element in the set.
get_allocator()	Returns the allocator.
insert()	Inserts an element into the set.
iterator	Object type for a bidirectional iterator.
key_comp	Represents a function for comparing keys.
key_compare()	Compares keys in the set.
key_type	Represents a data type for a sort key.
lower_bound()	Returns an iterator for the first element that doesn't match the given key.
max_size()	Returns the maximum possible size of a sequence.
rbegin()	Returns a reverse bidirectional iterator that points to the next element beyond the end of the sequence.
reference	A synonym for A as an element `reference`.
rend()	Returns a reverse bidirectional iterator that points to the sequence's first element.
reverse_iterator	Object type for a reverse iterator.
size()	Returns the length of the sequence.
size_type	Represents an unsigned integer used to represent the size of the set.
swap()	Swaps one sequence with another.

Member	Description
upper_bound()	Returns an iterator for the first element that matches the given key.
value_comp	Represents a function for comparing values.
value_compare()	Compares values in the set.
value_type	Represents a data type for an element in the set.

CROSS-REFERENCE
See also list, set, and vector.

mutable

Keyword

Normally, class member functions that have been declared as const cannot modify class data members. To enable such a function to modify a class member, the member must be declared as mutable. The following program demonstrates how this is done. The program defines a class with two integer data members, one of which (member1) is also declared as mutable. The const member function MyFunc() can modify the value of member1, but cannot modify the value of member2. If the line member2 = num + 1 in MyFunc() were not commented out, the program would not compile. The program's output looks like this:

```
member1 = 25
Press any key to continue
```

Here is the program source code that produced the output:

```
#include "stdafx.h"
#include <iostream>

using namespace std;

class MyClass
{
protected:
    mutable int member1;
    int member2;

public:
    MyClass(){}
```

```
        ~MyClass(){}

        void MyFunc(int num) const
        {
            member1 = num;
            //member2 = num + 1; // Error!
        }

        int GetMember1()
        {
            return member1;
        }
    };

    int main(int argc, char* argv[])
    {
        MyClass myClass;
        myClass.MyFunc(25);
        cout << "member1 = " << myClass.GetMember1();
        cout << endl;

        return 0;
    }
```

 CROSS-REFERENCE
See also Creating a Class.

namespace

Keyword

The `namespace` keyword enables a program to define a namespace, which is another layer of scope within a program. For example, these lines define a namespace called `mynamespace`:

```
namespace mynamespace
{
    int var1;
    int MyFunc(int num)
    {
        return num * 3;
    }
}
```

CROSS-REFERENCE
See also Namespaces

Namespaces

Technique

The `namespace` keyword enables a program to define a namespace, which is another layer of scope within a program. Namespaces prevent identical symbol names from colliding within the same program, providing a way for programmers to ensure that their symbols are unique. In the following sections, you see how to create namespaces.

Defining a Namespace

Defining a namespace is similar to defining a class, as shown here:

```
namespace test1
{
```

```
int var1;
int MyFunc(int num)
{
    return num * 3;
}
}
```

The `namespace` keyword is followed by the name of the namespace. The symbols to be defined are placed within the curly brackets that delineate the body of the namespace definition. In the previous example, a variable named `var1` and a function named `MyFunc()` are defined within the namespace `test1`. Note that a namespace must be defined either at file scope (global to the file) or within another namespace (nested).

Referencing Namespace Symbols

To reference symbols that have been defined in a namespace, preface the symbol name with the namespace name followed by the scope-resolution operator. For example, to assign a value to `var1` in the namespace `test1`, write:

```
test1::var1 = 2
```

Demonstrating Namespaces

The following program demonstrates namespaces by defining three `var1` and `MyFunc()` symbols all within the same program. The program defines the first set of symbols in a namespace named `test1`, defines the second set within a namespace named `test2`, and defines the third set as they might normally be defined in a program's main namespace. The main program shows how to access the various versions of the symbols. The program's output looks like this:

```
      var1 = 1
test1::var1 = 2
test2::var1 = 3

      MyFunc(2) = 4
test1::MyFunc(2) = 6
test2::MyFunc(2) = 8

Press any key to continue
```

Here is the program source code that produced the output:

```
#include "stdafx.h"
#include <iostream>
```

```
using namespace std;

namespace test1
{
    int var1;
    int MyFunc(int num)
    {
        return num * 3;
    }
}

namespace test2
{
    int var1;
    int MyFunc(int num)
    {
        return num * 4;
    }
}

int MyFunc(int num)
{
    return num * 2;
}

int main(int argc, char* argv[])
{
    int var1;
    int result;

    var1 = 1;
    test1::var1 = 2;
    test2::var1 = 3;
    cout << "        var1 = " << var1 << endl;
    cout << "test1::var1 = " << test1::var1 << endl;
    cout << "test2::var1 = " << test2::var1 << endl;
    cout << endl;

    result = MyFunc(2);
    cout << "        MyFunc(2) = " << result << endl;
    result = test1::MyFunc(2);
    cout << "test1::MyFunc(2) = " << result << endl;
    result = test2::MyFunc(2);
    cout << "test2::MyFunc(2) = " << result << endl;
```

```
        cout << endl;

        return 0;
    }
```

A namespace must be defined in the file scope or within another namespace. The previous program example illustrates namespaces defined at file scope. Now, here are the test1 and test2 namespaces rewritten with test2 nested within test1:

```
namespace test1
{
    int var1;
    int MyFunc(int num)
    {
        return num * 3;
    }

    namespace test2
    {
        int var1;
        int MyFunc(int num)
        {
            return num * 4;
        }
    }
}
```

To reference a symbol defined in test2, the program now must resolve the reference with both the test1 and test2 names like this:

```
test1::test2::var1 = 3;
```

The following program demonstrates how the nested namespaces work. The program's output looks like this:

```
                var1 = 1
        test1::var1 = 2
test1::test2::var1 = 3

            MyFunc(2) = 4
        test1::MyFunc(2) = 6
test1::test2::MyFunc(2) = 8

Press any key to continue
```

Here is the program source code that produced the output:

```cpp
#include "stdafx.h"
#include <iostream>

using namespace std;

namespace test1
{
    int var1;
    int MyFunc(int num)
    {
        return num * 3;
    }

    namespace test2
    {
        int var1;
        int MyFunc(int num)
        {
            return num * 4;
        }
    }
}

int MyFunc(int num)
{
    return num * 2;
}

int main(int argc, char* argv[])
{
    int var1;
    int result;

    var1 = 1;
    test1::var1 = 2;
    test1::test2::var1 = 3;
    cout << "                var1 = ";
    cout << var1 << endl;
    cout << "         test1::var1 = ";
    cout << test1::var1 << endl;
    cout << "test1::test2::var1 = ";
    cout << test1::test2::var1 << endl;
    cout << endl;
```

m

n

o

```
        result = MyFunc(2);
        cout << "                MyFunc(2) = ";
        cout << result << endl;
        result = test1::MyFunc(2);
        cout << "          test1::MyFunc(2) = ";
        cout << result << endl;
        result = test1::test2::MyFunc(2);
        cout << "test1::test2::MyFunc(2) = ";
        cout << result << endl;
        cout << endl;

        return 0;
}
```

new

Keyword

The new keyword enables a program to create a data object on the heap. For example, the following program defines a class named MyClass, allocates an object of the class on the heap, calls the class's single member function GetVar1(), and then uses the delete operator to release the object from memory. The program's output looks like this:

```
Creating an object on the heap...
Getting value of myClass::var1...
myClass::var1 = 25
Deleting the myClass object...
Press any key to continue
```

Here is the program source code that produced the output:

```
#include "stdafx.h"
#include <iostream>

using namespace std;

class MyClass
{
protected:
    int var1;

public:
```

```
    MyClass(int num){ var1 = num; }
    ~MyClass(){}
    int GetVar1() { return var1; }
};

int main(int argc, char* argv[])
{
    cout << "Creating an object on the heap..." << endl;
    MyClass* myClass = new MyClass(25);
    cout << "Getting value of myClass::var1..." << endl;
    int result = myClass->GetVar1();
    cout << "myClass::var1 = " << result << endl;
    cout << "Deleting the myClass object..." << endl;
    delete myClass;

    return 0;
}
```

CROSS-REFERENCE
See also delete.

m

n

o

_onexit()

function

The _onexit() function registers one or more functions that should run when the program exits normally. The function returns a pointer to the function if successful, or NULL if unsuccessful.

NOTE
Borland users should refer to the atexit() function.

Header File

```
#include <stdlib.h>
```

Declaration

```
_onexit_t _onexit(_onexit_t func);
```

- *func* — A pointer to the function that should execute.

Example

The following program demonstrates how to use the _onexit() function. The program displays the following output:

```
Registering exit functions...
Press Enter to exit main()

Hello from MyExitFunc2.
Press Enter to continue

Hello from MyExitFunc1.
Press Enter to continue
Press any key to continue
```

Here is the program source code that produced the output:

```cpp
#include "stdafx.h"
#include <stdlib.h>
#include <iostream>

using namespace std;

int MyExitFunc1()
{
    cout << endl << "Hello from MyExitFunc1.";
    cout << endl << "Press Enter to continue";
    getchar();
    return 0;
}

int MyExitFunc2()
{
    cout << endl << "Hello from MyExitFunc2.";
    cout << endl << "Press Enter to continue";
    getchar();
    return 0;
}

int main(int argc, char* argv[])
{
    cout << "Registering exit functions..." << endl;
    _onexit(MyExitFunc1);
    _onexit(MyExitFunc2);
    cout << "Press Enter to exit main()" << endl;
    getchar();

    return 0;
}
```

CROSS-REFERENCE
See also atexit().

_open()

Function

The _open() function opens a file, returning the file's handle if successful, or −1 if unsuccessful.

Header File

```
#include <io.h>
```

Declaration

```
int _open(const char* fileName, int flag);
```

- *fileName* — The name of the file to open.
- *flag* — A value (from Table O-1) that indicates whether the file is being opened for reading and/or writing.

Table O-1 File flags for _open()

Value	Description
O_APPEND	Positions the file pointer at the end of the file.
O_BINARY	Opens the file in binary mode.
O_CREAT	Creates and then opens a file.
O_CREAT | O_SHORT_LIVED	Creates a temporary file that is not flushed to disk.
O_CREAT | O_TEMPORARY	Creates a temporary file that is deleted when the last file is closed.
O_CREAT | O_EXCL	Creates a file, returning an error if the file already exists.
O_RANDOM	Enables random access.
O_RDONLY	Opens a file in read-only mode.
O_RDWR	Opens a file for both reading and writing.
O_SEQUENTIAL	Enables sequential file access.
O_TEXT	Opens a text file.
O_TRUNC	Opens a file and truncates the file length to 0.
O_WRONLY	Opens a file in write-only mode.

n
o
p

Example

The following program demonstrates how to use the _open() function. When run, the program opens a file in read-only mode and then closes a file, displaying appropriate messages as it goes. The program's output looks like this:

```
File opened successfully.
File closed successfully.
Press any key to continue
```

Here is the program source code that produced the output:

```cpp
#include "stdafx.h"
#include <fcntl.h>
#include <io.h>
#include <iostream>

using namespace std;

int main(int argc, char* argv[])
{
    int fileHandle = _open("open.cpp", O_RDONLY);

    if (fileHandle != -1)
    {
        cout << "File opened successfully." << endl;
        int result = _close(fileHandle);
        if (result == 0)
            cout << "File closed successfully." << endl;
        else
            cout << "File close error." << endl;
    }
    else
        cout << "File open error." << endl;

    return 0;
}
```

CROSS-REFERENCE
See also _close(), _creat(), _unlink(), and open().

_open_osfhandle()

Function

The _open_osfhandle() function creates a C run-time file handle from a given operating system file handle. The function returns the handle if successful or returns −1 if unsuccessful.

Header File

```
#include <io.h>
```

Declaration

```
int _open_osfhandle(long osfhandle, int flags);
```

- *flags* — The file mode for which to open the file. This can be a combination of O_APPEND, O_RDONLY, or O_TEXT.
- *osfhandle* — The operating-system file handle.

Example

The following program demonstrates how to call the _open_osfhandle() function. When run, the program opens a file and associates it with a stream. The program then retrieves and displays the operating system file handle. The program's output looks like this:

```
OS file handle = 20
C runtime file handle = 4
Press any key to continue
```

Here is the program source code that produced the output:

```
#include "stdafx.h"
#include <iostream>
#include <fcntl.h>
#include <io.h>

using namespace std;

int main(int argc, char* argv[])
{
    FILE *file;
    int  fileHandle;
```

```
fileHandle = _open("_open_osfhandle.cpp", O_RDONLY);
if (fileHandle != -1)
{
    file = _fdopen(fileHandle, "r");
    if (file != NULL )
    {
        long osfHandle = _get_osfhandle(fileHandle);
        cout << "OS file handle = " << osfHandle << endl;
        int handle = _open_osfhandle(osfHandle,
            O_RDONLY | O_TEXT);
        if (handle == -1)
            cout << "Failed" << endl;
        else
        {
            cout << "C runtime file handle = ";
            cout  << handle << endl;
        }
        fclose(file);
    }
    else
        cout << "Couldn't open stream." << endl;
}
else
    cout << "Could not open the file." << endl;

return 0;
}
```

CROSS-REFERENCE
See also _fileno() and _get_osfhandle().

oct

Manipulator

The oct manipulator causes numerical data to be output in octal (base 8) form. For example, the following program displays several numbers in octal form. The program's output looks like this:

```
8 in octal = 10
16 in octal = 20
256 in octal = 400
```

```
14356 in octal = 34024
Press any key to continue
```

Here is the program source code that produced the output:

```
#include "stdafx.h"
#include <iostream>

using namespace std;

int main(int argc, char* argv[])
{
    cout << "8 in octal = "<< oct << 8 << endl;
    cout << "16 in octal = "<< oct << 16 << endl;
    cout << "256 in octal = "<< oct << 256 << endl;
    cout << "14356 in octal = "<< oct << 14356 << endl;

    return 0;
}
```

CROSS-REFERENCE
See also binary, dec, and hex.

ofstream

Class

The ofstream class, which derives from the ostream class, represents a stream for disk output.

Class Declaration

```
class _CRTIMP ofstream : public ostream {
public:
        ofstream();
        ofstream(const char *, int =ios::out,
            int = filebuf::openprot);
        ofstream(filedesc);
        ofstream(filedesc, char *, int);
        ~ofstream();
```

```
streambuf * setbuf(char *, int);
filebuf* rdbuf() const
    { return (filebuf*) ios::rdbuf(); }

void attach(filedesc);
filedesc fd() const { return rdbuf()->fd(); }

int is_open() const { return rdbuf()->is_open(); }
void open(const char *, int =ios::out,
    int = filebuf::openprot);
void close();
int setmode(int mode = filebuf::text)
    { return rdbuf()->setmode(mode); }
};
```

Class Members

Table O-2 lists the members of the ofstream class.

Table O-2 Members of the ofstream Class

Member	Description
attach()	Associates the stream to a file.
close()	Closes the file after flushing output.
fd()	Gets the stream's file descriptor.
isopen()	Returns TRUE if the file is open.
open()	Opens the file.
rdbuf()	Gets a pointer to the buffer object.
setbuf()	Sets the stream's output buffer.
setmode()	Toggles the file mode between binary and text.

CROSS-REFERENCE

See also ifstream, ios, iostream, istream, istrstream, ostream, ostrstream, stdiostream, and streambuf.

onexit()

function

The onexit() function registers one or more functions that should run when the program exits normally. The function returns a pointer to the function if successful or returns NULL if unsuccessful.

 NOTE
Borland users should refer to the atexit() function.

Header File

```
#include <stdlib.h>
```

Declaration

```
onexit_t onexit(_onexit_t func);
```

- *func* — A pointer to the function that should execute.

Example

The following program demonstrates how to use the onexit() function. The program displays the following output:

```
Registering exit functions...
Press Enter to exit main()

Hello from MyExitFunc2.
Press Enter to continue

Hello from MyExitFunc1.
Press Enter to continue
Press any key to continue
```

Here is the program source code that produced the output:

```
#include "stdafx.h"
#include <stdlib.h>
#include <iostream>

using namespace std;

int MyExitFunc1()
```

```
    {
        cout << endl << "Hello from MyExitFunc1.";
        cout << endl << "Press Enter to continue";
        getchar();
        return 0;
    }

    int MyExitFunc2()
    {
        cout << endl << "Hello from MyExitFunc2.";
        cout << endl << "Press Enter to continue";
        getchar();
        return 0;
    }

    int main(int argc, char* argv[])
    {
        cout << "Registering exit functions..." << endl;
        onexit(MyExitFunc1);
        onexit(MyExitFunc2);
        cout << "Press Enter to exit main()" << endl;
        getchar();

        return 0;
    }
```

CROSS-REFERENCE
See also atexit().

open()

Function

The open() function opens a file, returning the file's handle if successful, or −1 if unsuccessful.

Header File

```
#include <io.h>
```

Declaration

```
int open(const char* fileName, int flag);
```

- *fileName* — The name of the file to open.
- *flag* — A value (from Table O-3) that indicates whether the file is being opened for reading and/or writing.

Table O-3 File Flags for open()

Value	Description
O_APPEND	Positions the file pointer at the end of the file.
O_BINARY	Opens the file in binary mode.
O_CREAT	Creates and then opens a file.
O_CREAT | O_SHORT_LIVED	Creates a temporary file that is not flushed to disk.
O_CREAT | O_TEMPORARY	Creates a temporary file that is deleted when the last file is closed.
O_CREAT | O_EXCL	Creates a file, returning an error if the file already exists.
O_RANDOM	Enables random access.
O_RDONLY	Opens a file in read-only mode.
O_RDWR	Opens a file for both reading and writing.
O_SEQUENTIAL	Enables sequential file access.
O_TEXT	Opens a text file.
O_TRUNC	Opens a file and truncates the file length to 0.
O_WRONLY	Opens a file in write-only mode.

Example

The following program demonstrates how to use the open() function. When run, the program opens a file in read-only mode and then closes a file, displaying appropriate messages as it goes. The program's output looks like this:

```
File opened successfully.
File closed successfully.
Press any key to continue
```

Here is the program source code that produced the output:

```
#include "stdafx.h"
#include <fcntl.h>
#include <io.h>
#include <iostream>
```

```
using namespace std;

int main(int argc, char* argv[])
{
    int fileHandle = open("open.cpp", O_RDONLY);

    if (fileHandle != -1)
    {
        cout << "File opened successfully." << endl;
        int result = close(fileHandle);
        if (result == 0)
            cout << "File closed successfully." << endl;
        else
            cout << "File close error." << endl;
    }
    else
        cout << "File open error." << endl;

    return 0;
}
```

CROSS-REFERENCE
See also _close(), _creat(), _open(), and _unlink().

operator

Keyword

The operator keyword enables a class to overload (redefine) operators and so creates operators that work a special way for the class. For example, the following program defines a class named MyClass that defines a + operator. The + operator enables a program to add values to an object of the class. In this case, the operator returns the sum of the class's value member and the given value. The program's output looks like this:

```
val = 10
val = 25
Press any key to continue
```

Here is the program source code that produced the output:

```
#include "stdafx.h"
#include <iostream>
```

```
using namespace std;

class MyClass
{
protected:
    int value;

public:
    MyClass(int num){ value = num;}
    ~MyClass(){}
    int SetValue() { return value; }
    int GetValue() { return value; }
    int operator+(int num) { return value + num; }
};

int main(int argc, char* argv[])
{
    MyClass myClass(10);
    int val = myClass.GetValue();
    cout << "val = " << val << endl;
    val = myClass + 15;
    cout << "val = " << val << endl;

    return 0;
}
```

CROSS-REFERENCE
See also Creating a Class.

ostream

Class

The ostream class, which derives from the ios class, represents a general output stream.

Class Declaration

```
class _CRTIMP ostream : virtual public ios {
public:
        ostream(streambuf*);
```

```
        virtual ~ostream();

        ostream& flush();
        int  opfx();
        void osfx();

inline  ostream& operator<<(ostream&
    (__cdecl * _f)(ostream&));
inline  ostream& operator<<(ios& (__cdecl * _f)(ios&));
        ostream& operator<<(const char *);
inline  ostream& operator<<(const unsigned char *);
inline  ostream& operator<<(const signed char *);
inline  ostream& operator<<(char);
        ostream& operator<<(unsigned char);
inline  ostream& operator<<(signed char);
        ostream& operator<<(short);
        ostream& operator<<(unsigned short);
        ostream& operator<<(int);
        ostream& operator<<(unsigned int);
        ostream& operator<<(long);
        ostream& operator<<(unsigned long);
inline  ostream& operator<<(float);
        ostream& operator<<(double);
        ostream& operator<<(long double);
        ostream& operator<<(const void *);
        ostream& operator<<(streambuf*);
inline  ostream& put(char);
        ostream& put(unsigned char);
inline  ostream& put(signed char);
        ostream& write(const char *,int);
inline  ostream& write(const unsigned char *,int);
inline  ostream& write(const signed char *,int);
        ostream& seekp(streampos);
        ostream& seekp(streamoff,ios::seek_dir);
        streampos tellp();

protected:
        ostream();
        ostream(const ostream&);        // treat as private
        ostream& operator=(streambuf*); // treat as private
        ostream& operator=(const ostream& _os)
            {return operator=(_os.rdbuf()); }
        int do_opfx(int);               // not used
        void do_osfx();                 // not used
```

```
    private:
            ostream(ios&);
            ostream& writepad(const char *, const char *);
            int x_floatused;
    };
```

Class Members

Table O-4 lists the members of the ostream class.

Table O-4 Members of the ostream Class

Member	Description
endl	Ends a line and flushes the buffer.
ends	Terminates a string with a NULL character.
flush()	Flushes the stream's buffer.
opfx()	Checks the stream for errors before output operations.
osfx()	Checks the stream after output operations.
put()	Places a single byte into the output stream.
seekp()	Sets the file pointer for the stream.
tellp()	Returns the value of the stream's file pointer.
write()	Places multiple bytes into the output stream.

CROSS-REFERENCE
See also ifstream, ios, iostream, istream, istrstream, ofstream, ostrstream, stdiostream, and streambuf.

ostrstream

Class

The ostrstream class, which derives from the iostream class, represents an output stream for string data.

Class Declaration

```
class _CRTIMP strstream : public iostream {
```

```
public:
    strstream();
    strstream(char *, int, int);
    ~strstream();

    inline int pcount() const
        { return rdbuf()->out_waiting(); }
    inline  strstreambuf* rdbuf() const
        { return (strstreambuf*) ostream::rdbuf(); }
    inline  char * str()
        { return rdbuf()->str(); }
};
```

Class Members

Table O-5 lists the members of the ostrstream class.

Table O-5 Members of the ostrstream Class

Member	Description
pcount()	Returns the number of bytes currently in the stream's buffer.
rdbuf()	Gets a pointer to the stream's buffer object.
str()	Gets a pointer to the character array that represents the string.

CROSS-REFERENCE

See also ifstream, ios, iostream, istream, istrstream, ofstream, ostream, stdiostream, and strstream.

_pclose()

Function

The _pclose() function closes a pipe associated with the command processor, also closing the associated stream. The function returns the command processor's exit status, or −1 in the case of an error.

Header File

```
#include <stdio.h>
```

Declaration

```
int _pclose(FILE* stream);
```

- *stream* — The FILE pointer returned by _popen().

Example

The following program demonstrates how to use the _pclose() function. The program first opens a pipe for the DIR command, and then reads all output from the pipe and closes the pipe, displaying messages as it goes. The program's output looks similar to this:

```
Opening pipe for dir command...
Pipe opened successfully.
Reading from the pipe...

 Volume in drive C has no label
 Volume Serial Number is 2F1D-1EED
 Directory of C:\all code\Microsoft\P\_pclose

.              <DIR>         04-07-99 12:58a .
..             <DIR>         04-07-99 12:58a ..
STDAFX   H            667    04-07-99 12:58a StdAfx.h
```

```
STDAFX    CPP              294   04-07-99  12:58a  StdAfx.cpp
_PCLOSE   DSW              539   04-07-99  12:58a  _pclose.dsw
_PCLOSE   CPP              988   04-07-99  12:59a  _pclose.cpp
README    TXT            1,214   04-07-99  12:58a  ReadMe.txt
_PCLOSE   NCB                0   04-07-99  12:58a  _pclose.ncb
_PCLOSE   DSP            4,548   04-07-99  12:58a  _pclose.dsp
DEBUG           <DIR>          04-07-99  12:58a  Debug
_PCLOSE   PLG            1,613   04-07-99  12:59a  _pclose.plg
            8 file(s)          9,863 bytes
            3 dir(s)       9,113.95 MB free

Closing pipe...
Pipe closed successfully.
Press any key to continue
```

Here is the program source code that produced the output:

```cpp
#include "stdafx.h"
#include <iostream>
#include <stdio.h>

using namespace std;

int main(int argc, char* argv[])
{
    char str[256];

    cout << "Opening pipe for dir command..." << endl;
    FILE* pipeHandle = _popen("DIR", "rt");
    if (pipeHandle != NULL)
    {
        cout << "Pipe opened successfully." << endl;
        cout << "Reading from the pipe..." << endl;
        char* pStr = fgets(str, sizeof(str), pipeHandle);
        while (pStr)
        {
            cout << pStr;
            pStr = fgets(str, sizeof(str), pipeHandle);
        }

        cout << endl << "Closing pipe..." << endl;
        int result = _pclose(pipeHandle);
        if (result != -1)
            cout << "Pipe closed successfully." << endl;
```

```
        else
            cout << "Error closing pipe." << endl;
    }
    else
        cout << "Couldn't open pipe." << endl;

    return 0;
}
```

 CROSS-REFERENCE
See also _popen() and _wpopen().

_popen()

Function

The _popen() function opens a pipe associated with the command processor, returning a pointer to the associated stream, or NULL in the case of an error.

Header File

```
#include <stdio.h>
```

Declaration

```
FILE* _popen(const char *command, const char *mode);
```

- *command*—A pointer to the command that should be executed.
- *stream*—The stream's mode, which can be a combination of r for read mode, w for write mode, t for test mode, and b for binary mode.

Example

The following program demonstrates how to use the _popen() function. The program first opens a pipe for the DIR command, and then reads all output from the pipe and closes the pipe, displaying messages as it goes. The program's output looks similar to this:

```
Opening pipe for dir command...
Pipe opened successfully.
```

```
Reading from the pipe...

 Volume in drive C has no label
 Volume Serial Number is 2F1D-1EED
 Directory of C:\Microsoft\0\_popen

 .              <DIR>        04-07-99 12:18a .
 ..             <DIR>        04-07-99 12:18a ..
 STDAFX   H              667 04-07-99 12:18a StdAfx.h
 STDAFX   CPP            293 04-07-99 12:18a StdAfx.cpp
 _POPEN   DSW            537 04-07-99 12:18a _popen.dsw
 _POPEN   CPP            967 04-07-99 12:30a _popen.cpp
 README   TXT          1,208 04-07-99 12:18a ReadMe.txt
 _POPEN   NCB              0 04-07-99 12:18a _popen.ncb
 _POPEN   DSP          4,536 04-07-99 12:18a _popen.dsp
 DEBUG            <DIR>        04-07-99 12:18a Debug
 _POPEN   PLG          1,239 04-07-99 12:30a _popen.plg
          8 file(s)         9,447 bytes
          3 dir(s)      9,337.27 MB free

Closing pipe...
Pipe closed successfully.
Press any key to continue
```

Here is the program source code that produced the output:

```cpp
#include "stdafx.h"
#include <iostream>
#include <stdio.h>

using namespace std;

int main(int argc, char* argv[])
{
    char str[256];

    cout << "Opening pipe for dir command..." << endl;
    FILE* pipeHandle = _popen("DIR", "rt");
    if (pipeHandle != NULL)
    {
        cout << "Pipe opened successfully." << endl;
        cout << "Reading from the pipe..." << endl;
        char* pStr = fgets(str, sizeof(str), pipeHandle);
        while (pStr)
```

```
        {
            cout << pStr;
            pStr = fgets(str, sizeof(str), pipeHandle);
        }

        cout << endl << "Closing pipe..." << endl;
        int result = _pclose(pipeHandle);
        if (result != -1)
            cout << "Pipe closed successfully." << endl;
        else
            cout << "Error closing pipe." << endl;
    }
    else
        cout << "Couldn't open pipe." << endl;

    return 0;
}
```

CROSS-REFERENCE
See also _pclose() and _wpopen().

_putch()

Function

The _putch() function writes a single character to the stdout stream, returning the character written if successful or returning EOF if unsuccessful.

NOTE
Borland users should refer to the putch() function later in this chapter.

Header File

```
#include <conio.h>
```

Declaration

```
int _putch(int c);
```

- *c*— The character to write.

Example

The following program demonstrates how to use the _putch() function. When run, the program uses _putch() to write four characters to the stdout stream. The program's output looks like this:

```
Writing to the console:
TEST
Press any key to continue
```

Here is the program source code that produced the output:

```cpp
#include "stdafx.h"
#include <conio.h>
#include <iostream>

using namespace std;

int main(int argc, char* argv[])
{
    cout << "Writing to the console: " << endl;
    _putch('T');
    _putch('E');
    _putch('S');
    _putch('T');
    cout << endl;

    return 0;
}
```

CROSS-REFERENCE

See also _close(), _creat(), _fdopen(), _fgetchar(), _fgetwchar(), _fileno(), _flushall(), _fputwchar(), _fsopen(), _getw(), _getws(), _open(), _putw(), _putws(), _read(), _rmtmp(), _tempnam(), _wcreat(), _wfdopen(), _wfopen(), _wfreopen(), _wfsopen(), _wopen(), _wtempnam(), _wtmpnam(), clearerr(), eof(), fclose(), feof(), ferror(), fflush(), fgetc(), fgetpos(), fgets(), fgetwc(), fgetws(), fopen(), fprintf(), fputc(), fputchar(), fputs(), fputwc(), fputws(), fread(), freopen(), fscanf(), fseek(), fsetpos(), ftell(), fwprintf(), fwrite(), fwscanf(), getc(), getchar(), gets(), getw(), getwc(), getwchar(), lseek(), putc(), putch(), putchar(), putw(), putwc(), putwchar(), rewind(), setbuf(), setvbuf(), tmpfile(), tmpnam(), ungetc(), ungetch(), ungetwc(), and write().

_putenv()

Function

The _putenv() function sets the value of an environment variable, returning a 0 if successful, or –1 if unsuccessful.

 NOTE
Borland users should refer to the putenv() function later in this chapter.

Header File

```
#include <stdlib.h>
```

Declaration

```
int _putenv(char *envstring);
```

- *envstring*—The string holding the environment variable's setting.

Example

The following program demonstrates how to use the _putenv() function by setting the PATH variable. The program's output looks similar to this:

```
Current PATH: C:\WINDOWS;C:\WINDOWS;C:\WINDOWS\COMMAND

New PATH: C:\

Restored PATH: C:\WINDOWS;C:\WINDOWS;C:\WINDOWS\COMMAND

Press any key to continue
```

Here is the program source code that produced the output:

```
#include "stdafx.h"
#include <stdlib.h>
#include <iostream>

using namespace std;

int main(int argc, char* argv[])
```

```
{
    char* oldValue = getenv("PATH");
    if (oldValue == NULL)
    {
        cout << "Error getting variable" << endl;
        exit(1);
    }

    cout << "Current PATH: ";
    cout << oldValue << endl << endl;

    int result = _putenv("PATH=C:\\");
    if (result == -1)
    {
        cout << "Error setting variable" << endl;
        exit(1);
    }

    char* value = getenv("PATH");
    cout << "New PATH: ";
    cout << value << endl << endl;
    char s[_MAX_PATH] = "PATH=";
    strcpy(&s[5], oldValue);
    _putenv(s);
    value = getenv("PATH");
    cout << "Restored PATH: ";
    cout << value << endl << endl;

    return 0;
}
```

CROSS-REFERENCE
See also _wgetenv(), _wputenv(), getenv(), and putenv().

_putw()

Function

The _putw() function writes an integer to a stream, returning the value written.

Header File

```
#include <stdio.h>
```

Declaration

```
int _putw(int binint, FILE* stream);
```

- *binint* — The integer to write to the stream.
- *stream* — A pointer to the stream to which to write the integer.

Example

The following program demonstrates how to use the _putw() function. When run, the program creates a file and writes and displays ten integers. The program's output looks like this:

```
Value 0 written.
Value 1 written.
Value 2 written.
Value 3 written.
Value 4 written.
Value 5 written.
Value 6 written.
Value 7 written.
Value 8 written.
Value 9 written.
Press any key to continue
```

Here is the program source code that produced the output:

```
#include "stdafx.h"
#include <stdio.h>
#include <iostream>

using namespace std;

int main(int argc, char* argv[])
{
    FILE* file = fopen("test.dat", "wb");

    if (file != NULL)
    {
```

```
                    for (int x=0; x<10; ++x)
                    {
                        _putw(x, file);
                        int error = ferror(file);
                        if (!error)
                        {
                            cout << "Value " << x << " written.";
                            cout << endl;
                        }
                        else
                            cout << "Write error." << endl;
                    }
                    fclose(file);
                }
                else
                    cout << "Error creating file" << endl;

                return 0;
            }
```

CROSS-REFERENCE

See also _close(), _creat(), _fdopen(), _fgetchar(), _fgetwchar(), _fileno(), _flushall(), _fputwchar(), _fsopen(), _getw(), _getws(), _open(), _putch(), _putws(), _read(), _rmtmp(), _tempnam(), _wcreat(), _wfdopen(), _wfopen(), _wfreopen(), _wfsopen(), _wopen(), _wtempnam(), _wtmpnam(), clearerr(), eof(), fclose(), feof(), ferror(), fflush(), fgetc(), fgetpos(), fgets(), fgetwc(), fgetws(), fopen(), fprintf(), fputc(), fputchar(), fputs(), fputwc(), fputws(), fread(), freopen(), fscanf(), fseek(), fsetpos(), ftell(), fwprintf(), fwrite(), fwscanf(), getc(), getchar(), gets(), getw(), getwc(), getwchar(), lseek(), putc(), putch(), putchar(), puts(), putw(), putwc(), putwchar(), rewind(), setbuf(), setvbuf(), tmpfile(), tmpnam(), ungetc(), ungetch(), ungetwc(), and write().

_putws()

Function

The _putws() function writes a wide-character string to the stdout stream, returning a negative value if successful, or WEOF if unsuccessful.

Header File

```
#include <stdio.h>
```

Declaration

```
int _putws(const wchar_t* string);
```

- *string* — A pointer to the string to write.

Example

The following program demonstrates how to use the `_putws()` function. When run, the program writes ten wide-character strings to the `stdout` stream. The program's output looks like this:

```
This is line #0.
This is line #1.
This is line #2.
This is line #3.
This is line #4.
This is line #5.
This is line #6.
This is line #7.
This is line #8.
This is line #9.
Press any key to continue
```

Here is the program source code that produced the output:

```
#include "stdafx.h"
#include <stdio.h>
#include <iostream>

using namespace std;

int main(int argc, char* argv[])
{
    wchar_t str[81];

    for (int x=0; x<10; ++x)
    {
        swprintf(str, L"This is line #%d.", x);
        int result = _putws(str);
        if (result == WEOF)
            cout << "Write error." << endl;
    }

    return 0;
}
```

o

p

q

CROSS-REFERENCE

See also _close(), _creat(), _fdopen(), _fgetchar(), _fgetwchar(), _fileno(), _flushall(), _fputwchar(), _fsopen(), _getw(), _getws(), _open(), _putch(), _putw(), _read(), _rmtmp(), _tempnam(), _wcreat(), _wfdopen(), _wfopen(), _wfreopen(), _wfsopen(), _wopen(), _wtempnam(), _wtmpnam(), clearerr(), eof(), fclose(), feof(), ferror(), fflush(), fgetc(), fgetpos(), fgets(), fgetwc(), fgetws(), fopen(), fprintf(), fputc(), fputchar(), fputs(), fputwc(), fputws(), fread(), freopen(), fscanf(), fseek(), fsetpos(), ftell(), fwprintf(), fwrite(), fwscanf(), getc(), getchar(), gets(), getw(), getwc(), getwchar(), lseek(), putc(), putch(), putchar(), putw(), putwc(), putwchar(), rewind(), setbuf(), setvbuf(), tmpfile(), tmpnam(), ungetc(), ungetch(), ungetwc(), and write().

perror()

Function

The perror() function prints an error message to the stderr stream, including both a user-supplied message and the associated system error message.

Header File

```
#include <stdio.h>
```

Declaration

```
void perror(const char *string);
```

- *string* — The error message to display.

Example

The following program demonstrates how to use the perror() function. When run, the program attempts to open a file, and if the file fails to open, displays an error message. The program's output looks like this:

```
File open error: No such file or directory
Press any key to continue
```

Here is the program source code that produced the output:

```
#include "stdafx.h"
#include <fcntl.h>
#include <io.h>
#include <stdio.h>
```

```
#include <iostream>

using namespace std;

int main(int argc, char* argv[])
{
    int fileHandle = open("nosuchfile.dat", O_RDONLY);

    if (fileHandle != -1)
    {
        cout << "File opened successfully." << endl;
        close(fileHandle);
    }
    else
        perror("File open error");


    return 0;
}
```

CROSS-REFERENCE
See also _wperror(), clearerr(), ferror(), and strerror().

Polymorphism

Technique

Polymorphism is an object-oriented programming (OOP) technique that enables a base class and a derived class to implement the same member function in different ways, even when calling that member function through a pointer to the base class. The following sections explain how polymorphism works.

The Base Class

Suppose you have a class that displays a string. The following program demonstrates such a class. The program's output looks like this:

```
This is a test
Press any key to continue
```

Here is the program source code that produced the output:

```
#include "stdafx.h"
#include <iostream>
```

```cpp
using namespace std;

/////////////////////////////
// Base class declaration.
/////////////////////////////
class MyClass
{
protected:
    char str[256];

public:
    MyClass(char* s);
    ~MyClass();
    virtual void ShowString();
};

/////////////////////////////
// Base class definition.
/////////////////////////////
MyClass::MyClass(char* s)
{
    strcpy(str, s);
}

MyClass::~MyClass()
{
}

void MyClass::ShowString()
{
    cout << str << endl;
}

/////////////////////////////
// Main program.
/////////////////////////////
int main(int argc, char* argv[])
{
    MyClass myClass("This is a test");
    myClass.ShowString();

    return 0;
}
```

Virtual Functions

If you look closely at the MyClass class, you see a function named ShowString() that's declared as virtual. A virtual function can be implemented in different ways in derived classes, and it is the virtual function that puts polymorphism to work. In the MyClass class, the ShowString() member function does nothing more than display the string. However, suppose you want to derive a new class from MyClass, one that displays its string inside a box. You might write the new version of the program that follows. The program's output looks like this:

```
This is a test

***********************
* This is also a test *
***********************

Press any key to continue
```

Here is the program source code that produced the output:

```cpp
#include "stdafx.h"
#include <iostream>

using namespace std;

/////////////////////////////
// Base class declaration.
/////////////////////////////
class MyClass
{
protected:
    char str[256];

public:
    MyClass(char* s);
    ~MyClass();
    virtual void ShowString();
};

/////////////////////////////
// Base class definition.
/////////////////////////////
MyClass::MyClass(char* s)
{
    strcpy(str, s);
```

```
    }

    MyClass::~MyClass()
    {
    }

    void MyClass::ShowString()
    {
        cout << str << endl;
    }

    ////////////////////////////
    // Derived class declaration.
    ////////////////////////////
    class MyDerivedClass : public MyClass
    {
    public:
        MyDerivedClass(char* s);
        ~MyDerivedClass();
        virtual void ShowString();
    };

    ////////////////////////////
    // Derived class definition.
    ////////////////////////////
    MyDerivedClass::MyDerivedClass(char* s) : MyClass(s)
    {
    }

    MyDerivedClass::~MyDerivedClass()
    {
    }

    void MyDerivedClass::ShowString()
    {
        int x;

        int len = strlen(str);
        for (x=0; x<len+4; ++x)
            cout << "*";
        cout << endl;
        cout << "* " << str << " *" << endl;
        for (x=0; x<len+4; ++x)
            cout << "*";
```

```
        cout << endl << endl;
    }


    /////////////////////////////
    // Main program.
    /////////////////////////////
    int main(int argc, char* argv[])
    {
        MyClass myClass("This is a test");
        myClass.ShowString();
        cout << endl;
        MyDerivedClass myDerivedClass("This is also a test");
        myDerivedClass.ShowString();

        return 0;
    }
```

Now you also have a class named MyDerivedClass, which is derived from
the base class MyClass. The MyDerivedClass class has its own version of the
virtual ShowString() function. This version displays its string within a box of
asterisks. If you look at the main() function, you can see that the program
should have no difficulty figuring out which version of ShowString() to call.
After all, the MyClass and MyDerivedClass classes each have their own object,
named myClass and myDerivedClass. This isn't really polymorphism at work;
this version of the program would work just fine if the virtual keywords were
removed from the two classes.

Polymorphism in Action

Consider the following version of main(), in which both class objects are represented by pointers to the base class MyClass:

```
    int main(int argc, char* argv[])
    {
        MyClass* myClass = new MyClass("This is a test");
        myClass->ShowString();
        cout << endl;
        MyClass* myDerivedClass =
            new MyDerivedClass("This is also a test");
        myDerivedClass->ShowString();

        return 0;
    }
```

This program's output is exactly the same as the previous versions. One of
the useful things about derived classes is that you can use a pointer to the base

class to represent an object of a derived class. In this new version of `main()`, both `myClass` and `myDerivedClass` are pointers to an object of the `MyClass` class, even though one pointer represents a `MyClass` object and the other represents a `MyDerivedClass` object. Thanks to the virtual function `ShowString()`, however, calls to the `ShowString()` function through either pointer work just fine. This is polymorphism in action.

To see the difference between regular member functions and virtual member functions, just remove the `virtual` keyword from the `MyClass` and `MyDerivedClass` classes, and then recompile and run the program. Without virtual functions, both calls through the object pointers resolve to the `ShowString()` function in `MyClass`, yielding the following output:

```
This is a test

This is also a test
Press any key to continue
```

CROSS-REFERENCE
See also Creating a Class, Deriving a Class, and Pure Virtual Function.

pow()

Function

The `pow()` function returns the result of a value raised to a power.

Header File

```
#include <math.h>
```

Declaration

```
double pow(double base, double exp);
```

- *base* — The base number.
- *exp* — The exponent.

Example

The following program demonstrates how to use the `pow()` function. When run, the program calculates the result of 5 to the power of 3. The program's output looks like this:

```
5 to the power of 3 = 125
Press any key to continue
```

Here is the program source code that produced the output:

```cpp
#include "stdafx.h"
#include <math.h>
#include <iostream>

using namespace std;

int main(int argc, char* argv[])
{
    double base = 5.0;
    double exp = 3.0;

    double result = pow(base, exp);
    cout << base << " to the power of ";
    cout << exp << " = " << result << endl;

    return 0;
}
```

CROSS-REFERENCE

See also _cabs(), _cabsl(), _finite(), _hypot(), _logb(), _scalb(), abs(), acos(), asin(), atan(), atan2(), atof(), cabs(), ceil(), cos(), cosh(), exp(), fabs(), floor(), fmod(), frexp(), labs(), ldexp(), log(), log10(), modf(), powf(), powl(), sin(), sinh(), sqrt(), tan(), and tanh().

powf()

Function

The powf() function returns, as a float value, the result of a value raised to a power.

NOTE

Borland does not support this function.

Header File

```cpp
#include <math.h>
```

Declaration

```
float powf(float base, float exp);
```

- *base* — The base number.
- *exp* — The exponent.

Example

The following program demonstrates how to use the powf() function. When run, the program calculates the result of 5 to the power of 3. The program's output looks like this:

```
5 to the power of 3 = 125
Press any key to continue
```

Here is the program source code that produced the output:

```
#include "stdafx.h"
#include <math.h>
#include <iostream>

using namespace std;

int main(int argc, char* argv[])
{
    float base = (float)5.0;
    float exp = (float)3.0;

    float result = powf(base, exp);
    cout << base << " to the power of ";
    cout << exp << " = " << result << endl;

    return 0;
}
```

CROSS-REFERENCE

See also _cabs(), _cabsl(), _finite(), _hypot(), _logb(), _scalb(), abs(), acos(), asin(), atan(), atan2(), atof(), cabs(), ceil(), cos(), cosh(), exp(), fabs(), floor(), fmod(), frexp(), labs(), ldexp(), log(), log10(), modf(), pow(), powl(), sin(), sinh(), sqrt(), tan(), and tanh().

powl()

Function

The powl() function returns, as a `long double` value, the result of a value raised to a power.

 NOTE
Borland does not support this function.

Header File

```
#include <math.h>
```

Declaration

```
long double powl(long double base, long double exp);
```

- *base* — The base number.
- *exp* — The exponent.

Example

The following program demonstrates how to use the powl() function. When run, the program calculates the result of 5 to the power of 3. The program's output looks like this:

```
5 to the power of 3 = 125
Press any key to continue
```

Here is the program source code that produced the output:

```
#include "stdafx.h"
#include <math.h>
#include <iostream>

using namespace std;

int main(int argc, char* argv[])
{
    long double base = 5.0;
    long double exp = 3.0;

    long double result = powl(base, exp);
```

o
p
q

```
        cout << base << " to the power of ";
        cout << exp << " = " << result << endl;

        return 0;
    }
```

CROSS-REFERENCE

See also _cabs(), _cabsl(), _finite(), _hypot(), _logb(), _scalb(), abs(), acos(), asin(), atan(), atan2(), atof(), cabs(), ceil(), cos(), cosh(), exp(), fabs(), floor(), fmod(), frexp(), labs(), ldexp(), log(), log10(), modf(), pow(), powf(), sin(), sinh(), sqrt(), tan(), and tanh().

printf()

Function

The printf() function prints a formatted string to the standard output stream. The function returns the number of characters displayed, or returns −1 in the case of an error.

Header File

```
#include <stdio.h>
```

Declaration

```
int printf(const char *format [, argument]...);
```

- *argument* — A list of data items that match the control codes included in the format string, *format*.
- *format* — The format string, which can include text, as well as the control codes shown in Table P-1.

Table P-1 Format Specifiers for printf()

Specifier	Description
%c	Specifies a character.
%C	Specifies a wide-character (printf()) or single-byte character (wprintf()).
%d	Specifies a signed decimal integer.

Specifier	Description
%e	Specifies a signed double-precision floating-point value using scientific notation with a lowercase e.
%E	Specifies a signed double-precision floating-point value using scientific notation with an uppercase E.
%f	Specifies a signed double-precision floating-point value.
%g	Specifies a signed double-precision floating-point value using either normal notation or scientific notation with a lowercase e.
%G	Specifies a signed double-precision floating-point value using either normal notation or scientific notation with an uppercase E.
%i	Specifies a signed decimal integer.
%n	Specifies an integer pointer.
%o	Specifies an unsigned octal integer.
%p	Specifies a void pointer.
%s	Specifies a string.
%S	Specifies a wide-character string (printf()) or single-byte-character string (wprintf()).
%u	Specifies an unsigned decimal integer.
%x	Specifies an unsigned hexadecimal integer with lowercase letters.
%X	Specifies an unsigned hexadecimal integer with uppercase letters.

Example

The following program demonstrates how to use the printf() function. When run, the program calls printf() to display a formatted string. The program's output looks like this:

```
var1 = 50    str1 = This is a test.
Number of characters displayed: 35
Press any key to continue
```

Here is the program source code that produced the output:

```
#include "stdafx.h"
#include <stdio.h>
#include <iostream>

using namespace std;

int main(int argc, char* argv[])
{
    int var1 = 50;
    char str1[] = "This is a test.";

    int numChars = printf("var1 = %i    str1 = %s\n",
```

```
        var1, str1);
    printf("Number of characters displayed: %i\n",
        numChars);

    return 0;
}
```

CROSS-REFERENCE
See also cprintf(), cscanf(), fprintf(), fscanf(), fwprintf(), scanf(), sscanf(), swprintf(), swscanf(), vfprintf(), vfwprintf(), vprintf(), vsprintf(), vswprintf(), vwprintf(), and wscanf().

priority_queue

Template Class

The priority_queue template class defines an object for organizing a set of data such that the largest data element is always immediately available.

Class Declaration

```
template<class T,
    class Cont = vector<T>,
    class Pred = less<Cont::value_type> >
    class priority_queue {
public:
    typedef Cont::allocator_type allocator_type;
    typedef Cont::value_type value_type;
    typedef Cont::size_type size_type;
    explicit priority_queue(const Pred& pr = Pred(),
        const allocator_type& al = allocator_type());
    priority_queue(const value_type *first,
        const value_type *last,
        const Pred& pr = Pred(),
        const allocator_type& al = allocator_type());
    bool empty() const;
    size_type size() const;
    allocator_type get_allocator() const;
    value_type& top();
    const value_type& top() const;
    void push(const value_type& x);
    void pop();
```

```
protected:
    Cont c;
    Pred comp;
    };
```

Class Members

Table P-2 lists and describes the members of the `priority_queue` template class.

Table P-2 Members of the priority_queue Template Class

Member	Description
allocator_type	A synonym for the template's allocator type.
empty()	Returns true if the sequence is empty.
get_allocator()	Returns the allocator.
pop()	Removes the first data element.
push()	Places an element into the queue.
size()	Returns the length of the sequence.
size_type	Represents a type used to represent the size of the set.
top()	Returns a reference to the largest element, which is always sorted to the top of the queue.
value_type	Represents a data type for an element in the set.

CROSS-REFERENCE
See also list, queue, set, stack, and vector.

private

Keyword

The `private` keyword is used to declare a private member in a class. A private member cannot be accessed from outside of the class, nor can a derived class inherit it. For example, the following program defines two classes, `MyClass` and `MyDerivedClass`. The program derives `MyDerivedClass` from `MyClass`. However, because `MyClass`'s `Count()` member function is declared as private, the `MyDerivedClass` class does not inherit `Count()` and cannot call it, as you can see in `MyDerivedClass`'s version of `ShowString()`. If you uncomment the call to `Count()` there, the compiler will generate an error. The program's output looks like this:

```
This is a test
Length = 14
Another test
Press any key to continue
```

Here is the program source code that produced the output:

```
#include "stdafx.h"
#include <iostream>

using namespace std;

/////////////////////////////
// Base class declaration.
/////////////////////////////
class MyClass
{
protected:
    char str[256];

public:
    MyClass(char* s);
    ~MyClass();
    void ShowString();

private:
    int Count();
};

/////////////////////////////
// Base class definition.
/////////////////////////////
MyClass::MyClass(char* s)
{
    strcpy(str, s);
}

MyClass::~MyClass()
{
}

void MyClass::ShowString()
{
    cout << str << endl;
    cout << "Length = " << Count() << endl;
```

```
}

int MyClass::Count()
{
    return strlen(str);
}

//////////////////////////////
// Derived class declaration.
//////////////////////////////
class MyDerivedClass : public MyClass
{
public:
    MyDerivedClass(char* s);
    ~MyDerivedClass();
    void ShowString();
};

//////////////////////////////
// Derived class definition.
//////////////////////////////
MyDerivedClass::MyDerivedClass(char* s) : MyClass(s)
{
}

MyDerivedClass::~MyDerivedClass()
{
}

void MyDerivedClass::ShowString()
{
    cout << str << endl;

    // This line will cause an error.
    //cout << "Length = " << Count() << endl;
}

//////////////////////////////
// Main program.
//////////////////////////////
int main(int argc, char* argv[])
{
    MyClass myClass("This is a test");
```

```
    myClass.ShowString();

    MyDerivedClass myDerivedClass("Another test");
    myDerivedClass.ShowString();

    return 0;
}
```

The private keyword can also be used to specify how members are inherited by a derived class. For example, the following class declaration specifies private when inheriting members from its base class, which means that all inherited public and protected members of the base class become private members of the derived class:

```
class MyDerivedClass : private MyClass
{
public:
    MyDerivedClass(char* s);
    ~MyDerivedClass();
    void ShowString();
};
```

CROSS-REFERENCE
See also protected and public.

protected

Keyword

The protected keyword is used to declare a protected member in a class. A protected member cannot be accessed from outside of the class, but a derived class can inherit it. For example, the following program defines two classes, MyClass and MyDerivedClass. The program derives MyDerivedClass from MyClass. However, because MyClass's Count() member function is declared as private, the MyDerivedClass class does not inherit Count() and cannot call it, as you can see in MyDerivedClass's version of ShowString(). Still, MyDerivedClass does inherit the protected data member str, as you can also see in that class's version of ShowString(). The program's output looks like this:

```
This is a test
Length = 14
Another test
Press any key to continue
```

Here is the program source code that produced the output:

```
#include "stdafx.h"
#include <iostream>

using namespace std;

/////////////////////////////
// Base class declaration.
/////////////////////////////
class MyClass
{
protected:
    char str[256];

public:
    MyClass(char* s);
    ~MyClass();
    void ShowString();

private:
    int Count();
};

/////////////////////////////
// Base class definition.
/////////////////////////////
MyClass::MyClass(char* s)
{
    strcpy(str, s);
}

MyClass::~MyClass()
{
}

void MyClass::ShowString()
{
    cout << str << endl;
    cout << "Length = " << Count() << endl;
}

int MyClass::Count()
{
    return strlen(str);
```

```
    }

    /////////////////////////////
    // Derived class declaration.
    /////////////////////////////
    class MyDerivedClass : public MyClass
    {
    public:
        MyDerivedClass(char* s);
        ~MyDerivedClass();
        void ShowString();
    };

    /////////////////////////////
    // Derived class definition.
    /////////////////////////////
    MyDerivedClass::MyDerivedClass(char* s) : MyClass(s)
    {
    }

    MyDerivedClass::~MyDerivedClass()
    {
    }

    void MyDerivedClass::ShowString()
    {
        cout << str << endl;

        // This line will cause an error.
        //cout << "Length = " << Count() << endl;
    }

    /////////////////////////////
    // Main program.
    /////////////////////////////
    int main(int argc, char* argv[])
    {
        MyClass myClass("This is a test");
        myClass.ShowString();

        MyDerivedClass myDerivedClass("Another test");
        myDerivedClass.ShowString();

        return 0;
    }
```

The `protected` keyword can also be used to specify how a derived class inherits members. For example, the following class declaration specifies `protected` when inheriting members from its base class, which means that all inherited public and protected members of the base class become protected members of the derived class:

```
class MyDerivedClass : protected MyClass
{
public:
    MyDerivedClass(char* s);
    ~MyDerivedClass();
    void ShowString();
};
```

CROSS-REFERENCE
See also private and public.

public

Keyword

The `public` keyword is used to declare a public member in a class. A public member can be accessed from outside of the class, and a derived class can inherit it. For example, the following program defines two classes, `MyClass` and `MyDerivedClass`. The program derives `MyDerivedClass` from `MyClass`. However, because `MyClass`'s `Count()` member function is declared as private, the `MyDerivedClass` class does not inherit `Count()` and cannot call it, as you can see in `MyDerivedClass`'s version of `ShowString()`. Neither can the main program call `Count()`. Still, `MyDerivedClass` does inherit the protected data member `str`, as you can also see in that class's version of `ShowString()`. However, any attempt to access `str` in the `main()` function will cause a compiler error. The class's `ShowString()` function is declared as public, so the program can call the function from outside of the class as seen in the `main()` function. The program's output looks like this:

```
This is a test
Length = 14
Another test
Press any key to continue
```

Here is the program source code that produced the output:

```
#include "stdafx.h"
#include <iostream>
```

```cpp
using namespace std;

////////////////////////////////
// Base class declaration.
////////////////////////////////
class MyClass
{
protected:
    char str[256];

public:
    MyClass(char* s);
    ~MyClass();
    void ShowString();

private:
    int Count();
};

////////////////////////////////
// Base class definition.
////////////////////////////////
MyClass::MyClass(char* s)
{
    strcpy(str, s);
}

MyClass::~MyClass()
{
}

void MyClass::ShowString()
{
    cout << str << endl;
    cout << "Length = " << Count() << endl;
}

int MyClass::Count()
{
    return strlen(str);
```

```
}

/////////////////////////////
// Derived class declaration.
/////////////////////////////
class MyDerivedClass : public MyClass
{
public:
    MyDerivedClass(char* s);
    ~MyDerivedClass();
    void ShowString();
};

/////////////////////////////
// Derived class definition.
/////////////////////////////
MyDerivedClass::MyDerivedClass(char* s) : MyClass(s)
{
}

MyDerivedClass::~MyDerivedClass()
{
}

void MyDerivedClass::ShowString()
{
    cout << str << endl;

    // This line will cause an error.
    //cout << "Length = " << Count() << endl;
}

/////////////////////////////
// Main program.
/////////////////////////////
int main(int argc, char* argv[])
{
    MyClass myClass("This is a test");
    myClass.ShowString();

    MyDerivedClass myDerivedClass("Another test");
```

```
    myDerivedClass.ShowString();

    return 0;
}
```

The `public` keyword can also be used to specify how a derived class inherits members. For example, the following class declaration specifies `public` when inheriting members from its base class, which means that all inherited public and protected members of the base class become public and protected members of the derived class:

```
class MyDerivedClass : protected MyClass
{
public:
    MyDerivedClass(char* s);
    ~MyDerivedClass();
    void ShowString();
};
```

 CROSS-REFERENCE
See also private and protected.

Pure Virtual Function

Concept

A *pure virtual function* is a virtual member function that has not been defined in the base class. Because the function has not yet been defined, the base class cannot be instantiated and any classes derived from the base class must define the pure virtual function. A base class that contains a pure virtual function is called an *abstract class*.

An example of a pure virtual function declaration follows:

```
virtual void ShowString() = 0;
```

Notice the equal sign and the zero that are appended to the function's name.

The following program defines an abstract class named `MyClass`, which contains the pure virtual function, `ShowString()`. The program also defines a derived class named `MyDerivedClass` that defines the `ShowString()` function and so can be instantiated in the main program. The program's output looks like this:

```
A classy message.
Press any key to continue
```

Here is the program source code that produced the output:

```cpp
#include "stdafx.h"
#include <iostream>

using namespace std;

/////////////////////////////
// Base class declaration.
/////////////////////////////
class MyClass
{
protected:
    char str[256];

public:
    MyClass(char* s);
    ~MyClass();

    // This is a pure virtual function.
    virtual void ShowString() = 0;

private:
    int Count();
};

/////////////////////////////
// Base class definition.
/////////////////////////////
MyClass::MyClass(char* s)
{
    strcpy(str, s);
}

MyClass::~MyClass()
{
}

void MyClass::ShowString()
{
    cout << str << endl;
    cout << "Length = " << Count() << endl;
}

int MyClass::Count()
```

```
{
    return strlen(str);
}

/////////////////////////////
// Derived class declaration.
/////////////////////////////
class MyDerivedClass : public MyClass
{
public:
    MyDerivedClass(char* s);
    ~MyDerivedClass();
    void ShowString();
};

/////////////////////////////
// Derived class definition.
/////////////////////////////
MyDerivedClass::MyDerivedClass(char* s) : MyClass(s)
{
}

MyDerivedClass::~MyDerivedClass()
{
}

void MyDerivedClass::ShowString()
{
    cout << str << endl;
}

/////////////////////////////
// Main program.
/////////////////////////////
int main(int argc, char* argv[])
{
    // Cannot instantiate MyClass, because
    // it's an abstract class.
    //MyClass myClass("This is a test");
    //myClass.ShowString();

    MyDerivedClass myDerivedClass("A classy message.");
```

```
        myDerivedClass.ShowString();

        return 0;
    }
```

 CROSS-REFERENCE
See also Creating a Class, Deriving a Class, and Polymorphism.

putc()

Function

The putc() function writes a character to a stream, returning the character written.

Header File

```
#include <stdio.h>
```

Declaration

```
int putc(int c, FILE* stream);
```

- *c* — The character to write to the stream.
- *stream* — A pointer to the stream to which to write a character.

Example

The following program demonstrates how to use the putc() function. When run, the program opens a file and writes and displays a string, one character at a time. The program's output looks like this:

```
Character #0: T
Character #1: h
Character #2: i
Character #3: s
Character #4:
Character #5: i
Character #6: s
Character #7:
```

```
Character #8: a
Character #9:
Character #10: t
Character #11: e
Character #12: s
Character #13: t
Character #14: .
Press any key to continue
```

Here is the program source code that produced the output:

```cpp
#include "stdafx.h"
#include <stdio.h>
#include <iostream>

using namespace std;

int main(int argc, char* argv[])
{
    char str[] = "This is a test.";

    FILE* file = fopen("test.txt", "wt");

    if (file != NULL)
    {
        int len = strlen(str);
        for (int x=0; x<len; ++x)
        {
            int ch = putc(str[x], file);
            int error = ferror(file);
            if (!error)
            {
                cout << "Character #" << x << ": ";
                cout << (char)ch << endl;
            }
            else
                cout << "Error writing file" << endl;
        }
        fclose(file);
    }
    else
        cout << "Error opening file" << endl;

    return 0;
}
```

CROSS-REFERENCE
See also _close(), _creat(), _fdopen(), _fgetchar(), _fgetwchar(), _fileno(), _flushall(), _fputwchar(), _fsopen(), _getw(), _getws(), _open(), _putch(), _putw(), _putws(), _read(), _rmtmp(), _tempnam(), _wcreat(), _wfdopen(), _wfopen(), _wfreopen(), _wfsopen(), _wopen(), _wtempnam(), _wtmpnam(), clearerr(), eof(), fclose(), feof(), ferror(), fflush(), fgetc(), fgetpos(), fgets(), fgetwc(), fgetws(), fopen(), fprintf(), fputc(), fputchar(), fputs(), fputwc(), fputws(), fread(), freopen(), fscanf(), fseek(), fsetpos(), ftell(), fwprintf(), fwrite(), fwscanf(), getchar(), gets(), getw(), getwc(), getwchar(), lseek(), putch(), putchar(), puts(), putw(), putwc(), putwchar(), rewind(), setbuf(), setvbuf(), tmpfile(), tmpnam(), ungetc(), ungetch(), ungetwc(), and write().

putch()

Function

The putch() function writes a single character to the stdout stream, returning the character written if successful, or EOF if unsuccessful.

Header File

```
#include <conio.h>
```

Declaration

```
int putch(int c);
```

- *c* — The character to write.

Example

The following program demonstrates how to use the putch() function. When run, the program uses putch() to write four characters to the stdout stream. The program's output looks like this:

```
Writing to the console:
TEST
Press any key to continue
```

Here is the program source code that produced the output:

```
#include "stdafx.h"
#include <conio.h>
```

```
#include <iostream>

using namespace std;

int main(int argc, char* argv[])
{
    cout << "Writing to the console: " << endl;
    putch('T');
    putch('E');
    putch('S');
    putch('T');
    cout << endl;

    return 0;
}
```

CROSS-REFERENCE

See also _close(), _creat(), _fdopen(), _fgetchar(), _fgetwchar(), _fileno(), _flushall(), _fputwchar(), _fsopen(), _getw(), _getws(), _open(), _putch(), _putw(), _putws(), _read(), _rmtmp(), _tempnam(), _wcreat(), _wfdopen(), _wfopen(), _wfreopen(), _wfsopen(), _wopen(), _wtempnam(), _wtmpnam(), clearerr(), eof(), fclose(), feof(), ferror(), fflush(), fgetc(), fgetpos(), fgets(), fgetwc(), fgetws(), fopen(), fprintf(), fputc(), fputchar(), fputs(), fputwc(), fputws(), fread(), freopen(), fscanf(), fseek(), fsetpos(), ftell(), fwprintf(), fwrite(), fwscanf(), getc(), getchar(), gets(), getw(), getwc(), getwchar(), lseek(), putc(), putch(), putchar(), putw(), putwc(), putwchar(), rewind(), setbuf(), setvbuf(), tmpfile(), tmpnam(), ungetc(), ungetch(), ungetwc(), and write().

putchar()

Function

The putchar() function writes a character to the stdout stream, returning the character written.

Header File

```
#include <stdio.h>
```

Declaration

```
int putchar(int c);
```

- *c* — The character to write to the stream.

Example

The following program demonstrates how to use the `putchar()` function. When run, the program writes and displays a string, one character at a time. The program's output looks like this:

```
TCharacter #0: T
hCharacter #1: h
iCharacter #2: i
sCharacter #3: s
 Character #4:
iCharacter #5: i
sCharacter #6: s
 Character #7:
aCharacter #8: a
 Character #9:
tCharacter #10: t
eCharacter #11: e
sCharacter #12: s
tCharacter #13: t
.Character #14: .
Press any key to continue
```

Here is the program source code that produced the output:

```
#include "stdafx.h"
#include <stdio.h>
#include <iostream>

using namespace std;

int main(int argc, char* argv[])
{
    char str[] = "This is a test.";

    int len = strlen(str);
    for (int x=0; x<len; ++x)
```

o
p
q

```
{
    int ch = putchar(str[x]);
    int error = ferror(stdout);
    if (!error)
    {
        cout << "Character #" << x << ": ";
        cout << (char)ch << endl;
    }
    else
        cout << "Error writing character" << endl;
}

return 0;
}
```

CROSS-REFERENCE

See also _close(), _creat(), _fdopen(), _fgetchar(), _fgetwchar(), _fileno(), _flushall(), _fputwchar(), _fsopen(), _getw(), _getws(), _open(), _putch(), _putw(), _putws(), _read(), _rmtmp(), _tempnam(), _wcreat(), _wfdopen(), _wfopen(), _wfreopen(), _wfsopen(), _wopen(), _wtempnam(), _wtmpnam(), clearerr(), eof(), fclose(), feof(), ferror(), fflush(), fgetc(), fgetpos(), fgets(), fgetwc(), fgetws(), fopen(), fprintf(), fputc(), fputchar(), fputs(), fputwc(), fputws(), fread(), freopen(), fscanf(), fseek(), fsetpos(), ftell(), fwprintf(), fwrite(), fwscanf(), getchar(), gets(), getw(), getwc(), getwchar(), lseek(), putc(), putch(), puts(), putw(), putwc(), putwchar(), rewind(), setbuf(), setvbuf(), tmpfile(), tmpnam(), ungetc(), ungetch(), ungetwc(), and write().

putenv()

Function

The putenv() function sets the value of an environment variable, returning a 0 if successful, or −1 if unsuccessful.

Header File

```
#include <stdlib.h>
```

Declaration

```
int putenv(char *envstring);
```

- *envstring* — The string holding the environment variable's setting.

Example

The following program demonstrates how to use the `putenv()` function by setting the PATH variable. The program's output looks similar to this:

```
Current PATH: C:\WINDOWS;C:\WINDOWS;C:\WINDOWS\COMMAND

New PATH: C:\

Restored PATH: C:\WINDOWS;C:\WINDOWS;C:\WINDOWS\COMMAND

Press any key to continue
```

Here is the program source code that produced the output:

```
#include "stdafx.h"
#include <stdlib.h>
#include <iostream>

using namespace std;

int main(int argc, char* argv[])
{
    char* oldValue = getenv("PATH");
    if (oldValue == NULL)
    {
        cout << "Error getting variable" << endl;
        exit(1);
    }

    cout << "Current PATH: ";
    cout << oldValue << endl << endl;

    int result = putenv("PATH=C:\\");
    if (result == -1)
    {
        cout << "Error setting variable" << endl;
        exit(1);
    }

    char* value = getenv("PATH");
    cout << "New PATH: ";
    cout << value << endl << endl;
    char s[_MAX_PATH] = "PATH=";
    strcpy(&s[5], oldValue);
    putenv(s);
    value = getenv("PATH");
```

```
        cout << "Restored PATH: ";
        cout << value << endl << endl;

        return 0;
}
```

CROSS-REFERENCE
See also _putenv(), _wgetenv(), _wputenv(), and getenv().

puts()

Function

The puts() function writes a string to the stdout stream, returning a negative value if successful, or EOF if unsuccessful.

Header File

```
#include <stdio.h>
```

Declaration

```
int puts(const char* string);
```

- *string* — A pointer to the string to write.

Example

The following program demonstrates how to use the puts() function. When run, the program writes ten strings to the stdout stream. The program's output looks like this:

```
This is line #0.
This is line #1.
This is line #2.
This is line #3.
This is line #4.
This is line #5.
This is line #6.
This is line #7.
This is line #8.
This is line #9.
Press any key to continue
```

Here is the program source code that produced the output:

```
#include "stdafx.h"
#include <stdio.h>
#include <iostream>

using namespace std;

int main(int argc, char* argv[])
{
    char str[81];

    for (int x=0; x<10; ++x)
    {
        sprintf(str, "This is line #%d.", x);
        int result = puts(str);
        if (result == EOF)
            cout << "Write error." << endl;
    }

    return 0;
}
```

CROSS-REFERENCE
See also _close(), _creat(), _fdopen(), _fgetchar(), _fgetwchar(), _fileno(), _flushall(), _fputwchar(), _fsopen(), _getw(), _getws(), _open(), _putch(), _putw(), _putws(), _read(), _rmtmp(), _tempnam(), _wcreat(), _wfdopen(), _wfopen(), _wfreopen(), _wfsopen(), _wopen(), _wtempnam(), _wtmpnam(), clearerr(), eof(), fclose(), feof(), ferror(), fflush(), fgetc(), fgetpos(), fgets(), fgetwc(), fgetws(), fopen(), fprintf(), fputc(), fputchar(), fputs(), fputwc(), fputws(), fread(), freopen(), fscanf(), fseek(), fsetpos(), ftell(), fwprintf(), fwrite(), fwscanf(), getc(), getchar(), gets(), getw(), getwc(), getwchar(), lseek(), putc(), putch(), putchar(), putw(), putwc(), putwchar(), rewind(), setbuf(), setvbuf(), tmpfile(), tmpnam(), ungetc(), ungetch(), ungetwc(), and write().

putw()

Function

The putw() function writes an integer to a stream, returning the value written.

Header File

```
#include <stdio.h>
```

Declaration

```
int putw(int binint, FILE* stream);
```

- *binint* — The integer to write to the stream.
- *stream* — A pointer to the stream to which to write the integer.

Example

The following program demonstrates how to use the putw() function. When run, the program creates a file and writes and displays ten integers. The program's output looks like this:

```
Value 0 written.
Value 1 written.
Value 2 written.
Value 3 written.
Value 4 written.
Value 5 written.
Value 6 written.
Value 7 written.
Value 8 written.
Value 9 written.
Press any key to continue
```

Here is the program source code that produced the output:

```
#include "stdafx.h"
#include <stdio.h>
#include <iostream>

using namespace std;

int main(int argc, char* argv[])
{
    FILE* file = fopen("test.dat", "wb");

    if (file != NULL)
    {
        for (int x=0; x<10; ++x)
        {
```

```
        putw(x, file);
        int error = ferror(file);
        if (!error)
        {
            cout << "Value " << x << " written.";
            cout << endl;
        }
        else
            cout << "Write error." << endl;
    }
    fclose(file);
}
else
    cout << "Error creating file" << endl;

return 0;
}
```

CROSS-REFERENCE

See also _close(), _creat(), _fdopen(), _fgetchar(), _fgetwchar(), _fileno(), _flushall(), _fputwchar(), _fsopen(), _getw(), _getws(), _open(), _putch(), _putw(), _putws(), _read(), _rmtmp(), _tempnam(), _wcreat(), _wfdopen(), _wfopen(), _wfreopen(), _wfsopen(), _wopen(), _wtempnam(), _wtmpnam(), clearerr(), eof(), fclose(), feof(), ferror(), fflush(), fgetc(), fgetpos(), fgets(), fgetwc(), fgetws(), fopen(), fprintf(), fputc(), fputchar(), fputs(), fputwc(), fputws(), fread(), freopen(), fscanf(), fseek(), fsetpos(), ftell(), fwprintf(), fwrite(), fwscanf(), getc(), getchar(), gets(), getw(), getwc(), getwchar(), lseek(), putc(), putch(), putchar(), puts(), putwc(), putwchar(), rewind(), setbuf(), setvbuf(), tmpfile(), tmpnam(), ungetc(), ungetch(), ungetwc(), and write().

putwc()

Function

The putwc() function writes a wide-character to a stream, returning the character written.

Header File

```
#include <stdio.h>
```

Declaration

```
wint_t putwc(wint_t c, FILE* stream);
```

- *c* — The character to write to the stream.
- *stream* — A pointer to the stream to which to write a character.

Example

The following program demonstrates how to use the `putwc()` function. When run, the program opens a file and writes and displays a string, one character at a time. The program's output looks something like this:

```
Character #0: T
Character #1: h
Character #2: i
Character #3: s
Character #4:
Character #5: i
Character #6: s
Character #7:
Character #8: a
Character #9:
Character #10: t
Character #11: e
Character #12: s
Character #13: t
Character #14: .
Press any key to continue
```

Here is the program source code that produced the output:

```cpp
#include "stdafx.h"
#include <stdio.h>
#include <iostream>

using namespace std;

int main(int argc, char* argv[])
{
    wchar_t str[] = L"This is a test.";

    FILE* file = fopen("test.txt", "wt");

    if (file != NULL)
    {
```

```
for (int x=0; x<15; ++x)
{
    wint_t ch = putwc(str[x], file);
    int error = ferror(file);
    if (!error)
    {
        cout << "Character #" << x << ": ";
        cout << (char)ch << endl;
    }
    else
        cout << "Error writing file" << endl;
}
    fclose(file);
}
else
    cout << "Error opening file" << endl;

return 0;
}
```

CROSS-REFERENCE

See also _close(), _creat(), _fdopen(), _fgetchar(), _fgetwchar(), _fileno(), _flushall(), _fputwchar(), _fsopen(), _getw(), _getws(), _open(), _putch(), _putw(), _putws(), _read(), _rmtmp(), _tempnam(), _wcreat(), _wfdopen(), _wfopen(), _wfreopen(), _wfsopen(), _wopen(), _wtempnam(), _wtmpnam(), clearerr(), eof(), fclose(), feof(), ferror(), fflush(), fgetc(), fgetpos(), fgets(), fgetwc(), fgetws(), fopen(), fprintf(), fputc(), fputchar(), fputs(), fputwc(), fputws(), fread(), freopen(), fscanf(), fseek(), fsetpos(), ftell(), fwprintf(), fwrite(), fwscanf(), getchar(), gets(), getw(), getwc(), getwchar(), lseek(), putch(), putchar(), puts(), putc(), putw(), putwchar(), rewind(), setbuf(), setvbuf(), tmpfile(), tmpnam(), ungetc(), ungetch(), ungetwc(), and write().

o

p

q

putwchar()

Function

The putwchar() function writes a wide-character to the stdout stream, returning the character written.

Header File

```
#include <stdio.h>
```

Declaration

```
wint_t putwchar(wint_t c);
```

- *c* — The character to write to the stream.

Example

The following program demonstrates how to use the `putwchar()` function. When run, the program writes and displays a string, one character at a time. The program's output looks like this:

```
TCharacter #0: T
hCharacter #1: h
iCharacter #2: i
sCharacter #3: s
 Character #4:
iCharacter #5: i
sCharacter #6: s
 Character #7:
aCharacter #8: a
 Character #9:
tCharacter #10: t
eCharacter #11: e
sCharacter #12: s
tCharacter #13: t
.Character #14: .
Press any key to continue
```

Here is the program source code that produced the output:

```cpp
#include "stdafx.h"
#include <stdio.h>
#include <iostream>

using namespace std;

int main(int argc, char* argv[])
{
    wchar_t str[] = L"This is a test.";

    for (int x=0; x<15; ++x)
    {
        wint_t ch = putwchar(str[x]);
        int error = ferror(stdout);
        if (!error)
```

```
        {
            cout << "Character #" << x << ": ";
            cout << (char)ch << endl;
        }
        else
            cout << "Error writing character" << endl;
    }

    return 0;
}
```

CROSS-REFERENCE

See also _close(), _creat(), _fdopen(), _fgetchar(), _fgetwchar(), _fileno(), _flushall(), _fputwchar(), _fsopen(), _getw(), _getws(), _open(), _putch(), _putw(), _putws(), _read(), _rmtmp(), _tempnam(), _wcreat(), _wfdopen(), _wfopen(), _wfreopen(), _wfsopen(), _wopen(), _wtempnam(), _wtmpnam(), clearerr(), eof(), fclose(), feof(), ferror(), fflush(), fgetc(), fgetpos(), fgets(), fgetwc(), fgetws(), fopen(), fprintf(), fputc(), fputchar(), fputs(), fputwc(), fputws(), fread(), freopen(), fscanf(), fseek(), fsetpos(), ftell(), fwprintf(), fwrite(), fwscanf(), getchar(), gets(), getw(), getwc(), getwchar(), lseek(), putc(), putch(), putchar(), puts(), putw(), putwc(), rewind(), setbuf(), setvbuf(), tmpfile(), tmpnam(), ungetc(), ungetch(), ungetwc(), and write().

o

p

q

qsort

Function

The qsort() function performs a quick sort on an array of values.

Header File

```
#include <stdlib.h>
```

Declaration

```
void qsort(void *base, size_t num, size_t width,
    int (__cdecl *compare)(const void *elem1,
    const void *elem2));
```

- *base*— The address of the data to sort.
- *compare*— The function that compares two elements.
- *elem1*— The address of the first element to compare.
- *elem2*— The address of the second element to compare.
- *num*— The number of elements in the data.
- *width*— The width of an element.

Example

The following program demonstrates how to use the qsort() function, sorting a string array and displaying messages as it goes. The program's output looks like this:

```
SORTING ITEMS...

SORTING COMPLETE:

apple
```

```
boat
cattle
diamond
eggs
flag
goat
hat
insect
junk
lamp

Press any key to continue
```

Here is the program source code that produced the output:

```cpp
#include "stdafx.h"
#include <iostream>
#include <stdlib.h>

using namespace std;

int compare(const void *arg1, const void *arg2)
{
    char* str1 = *(char**)arg1;
    char* str2 = *(char**)arg2;
    int result = strcmp(str1, str2);

    return result;
}

int main(int argc, char* argv[])
{
    int x;

    char* data[] = {
        "cattle", "apple", "diamond",
        "insect", "hat", "flag", "goat",
        "eggs", "boat", "junk", "lamp"
    };

    cout << "SORTING ITEMS..." << endl << endl;
    qsort((void *)data, 11, sizeof(char *), compare);

    cout << "SORTING COMPLETE:" << endl << endl;
    for (x=0; x<11; ++x)
```

```
            cout << data[x] << endl;
        cout << endl;

        return 0;
    }
```

CROSS-REFERENCE
See also _lfind(), _lsearch(), and bsearch().

queue

Template Class

The queue template class defines an object for organizing a set of data into a queue.

Class Declaration

```
template<class T,
    class Cont = deque<T> >
    class queue {
public:
    typedef Cont::allocator_type allocator_type;
    typedef Cont::value_type value_type;
    typedef Cont::size_type size_type;
    explicit queue(const allocator_type& al =
allocator_type()) const;
    bool empty() const;
    size_type size() const;
    allocator_type get_allocator() const;
    value_type& top();
    const value_type& top() const;
    void push(const value_type& x);
    void pop();
protected:
    Cont c;
    };
```

Class Members

Table Q-1 lists and describes the members of the queue template class.

Table Q-1 Members of the queue Template Class

Member	Description
Allocator_type	A synonym for the template's allocator type.
empty()	Returns true if the sequence is empty.
get_allocator()	Returns the allocator.
pop()	Removes the first data element.
push()	Places an element into the queue.
size()	Returns the length of the sequence.
size_type	Represents a type used to represent the size of the set.
top()	Returns a reference to the largest element, which is always sorted to the top of the queue.
value_type	Represents a data type for an element in the set.

CROSS-REFERENCE

See also list, priority_queue, set, stack, and vector.

_read()

Function

The _read() function reads data from an open file, returning the number of bytes actually read, or −1 if an error occurs. The function returns 0 if it attempts to read beyond the end of the file.

Header File

```
#include <io.h>
```

Declaration

```
int _read(int handle, void *buffer, unsigned int count);
```

- *buffer*—A pointer to the buffer that will receive the read data.
- *count*—The number of bytes to read.
- *handle*—The file handle returned by the function that opened the file.

Example

The following program demonstrates how to use the _read() function. When run, the program opens a file and reads 50 bytes from the file, displaying status messages as it goes. The program's output looks like this:

```
Opening the file...
File opened successfully.
Reading the file...
CHARACTERS READ:
// _read.cpp : Defines the entry point for the con

Press any key to continue
```

Here is the program source code that produced the output:

```cpp
// _read.cpp : Defines the entry point for the console
application.
//
#include "stdafx.h"
#include <stdlib.h>
#include <io.h>
#include <fcntl.h>
#include <sys/stat.h>
#include <iostream>

using namespace std;

int main(int argc, char* argv[])
{
    char str[81];

    cout << "Opening the file..." << endl;
    int fileHandle = _open("_read.cpp",
        O_RDONLY, S_IREAD);

    if (fileHandle != -1 )
    {
        cout << "File opened successfully." << endl;
        cout << "Reading the file..." << endl;
        int numBytes =
            _read(fileHandle, str, 50);

        if (numBytes != -1 )
        {
            str[numBytes] = 0;
            cout << "CHARACTERS READ:" << endl;
            cout << str << endl << endl;
        }
         else
             cout << "File read error." << endl;

        _close( fileHandle );
    }
    else
        cout << "File open error." << endl;

    return 0;
}
```

CROSS-REFERENCE

See also _close(), _creat(), _fcloseall(), _fdopen(), _fgetchar(), _fgetwchar(), _fileno(), _flushall(), _fputwchar(), _fsopen(), _getw(), _getws(), _lseeki64(), _open(), _putw(), _putws(), _rmtmp(), _tempnam(), _wcreat(), _wfdopen(), _wfopen(), _wfreopen(), _wfsopen(), _wopen(), _write(), _wtempnam(), _wtmpnam(), clearerr(), eof(), fclose(), feof(), ferror(), fflush(), fgetc(), fgetpos(), fgets(), fgetwc(), fgetws(), fopen(), fprintf(), fputc(), fputchar(), fputs(), fputwc(), fputws(), fread(), freopen(), fscanf(), fseek(), fsetpos(), ftell(), fwprintf(), fwrite(), fwscanf(), getc(), getchar(), gets(), getwc(), getwchar(), lseek(), putc(), putch(), putchar(), puts(), putwc(), putwchar(), rewind(), setbuf(), setvbuf(), tmpfile(), tmpnam(), ungetc(), ungetch(), ungetwc(), and write().

_rmdir()

Function

The _rmdir() function deletes a directory. If the function is successful, it returns 0; otherwise, it returns –1.

Header File

```
#include <direct.h>
```

Declaration

```
int _rmdir(const char* dirname);
```

- *dirname* — The path and name of the directory to remove.

Example

The following program demonstrates how to use the _rmdir() function by creating a new directory in drive C's root directory and then deleting the new directory. The program's output looks like this:

```
Making new directory...
New directory created.
Removing directory...
Directory removed.
Press any key to continue
```

Here is the program source code that produced the output:

```
#include "stdafx.h"
#include <direct.h>
```

```
#include <iostream>

using namespace std;

int main(int argc, char* argv[])
{
    cout << "Making new directory..." << endl;
    int result = _mkdir("c:\\TestDir");
    if (result != -1)
    {
        cout << "New directory created." << endl;
        cout << "Removing directory..." << endl;
        result = _rmdir("c:\\TestDir");
        if (result == 0)
            cout << "Directory removed." << endl;
        else
            cout << "Error removing directory." << endl;
    }
    else
        cout << "Directory create error" << endl;

    return 0;
}
```

CROSS-REFERENCE

See also _chdrive(), _getdcwd(), _getdrive(), _rmtmp(), _searchenv(), _wchdir(), _wgetcwd(), _wgetdcwd(), _wmkdir(), _wrmdir(), _wsearchenv(), chdir(), getcwd(), mkdir(), rmdir(), and tmpfile().

_rmtmp()

Function

The _rmtmp() function removes temporary files that were created with tmpfile(), returning the number of files removed.

Header File

```
#include <stdio.h>
```

Declaration

```
int _rmtmp(void);
```

Example

The following program demonstrates how to use the _rmtmp() function, by creating a temporary file and deleting it, displaying messages as it goes. The program's output looks like this:

```
Creating temp file...
Temp file created.
Deleting temp file...
1 file removed.
Press any key to continue
```

Here is the program source code that produced the output:

```cpp
#include "stdafx.h"
#include <iostream>
#include <stdio.h>

using namespace std;

int main(int argc, char* argv[])
{
    cout << "Creating temp file..." << endl;
    FILE* file = tmpfile();
    if (file != NULL)
    {
        cout << "Temp file created." << endl;
        cout << "Deleting temp file..." << endl;
        int result = _rmtmp();
        cout << result << " file removed." << endl;
    }
    else
        cout << "File create error." << endl;

    return 0;
}
```

CROSS-REFERENCE

See also _chdrive(), _getdcwd(), _getdrive(), _rmdir(), _searchenv(), _wchdir(), _wgetcwd(), _wgetdcwd(), _wmkdir(), _wrmdir(), _wsearchenv(), chdir(), getcwd(), mkdir(), rmdir(), rmtmp(), and tmpfile().

_rotl()

Function

The _rotl() function left rotates the bits of a value, returning the rotate value.

Header File

```
#include <stdlib.h>
```

Declaration

```
unsigned int _rotl(unsigned int value, int shift);
```

- *value* — The value to be rotated.
- *shift* — The number of bits to rotate *value*.

Example

The following program demonstrates how to use the _rotl() function by left rotating a value and displaying the result. The program's output looks like this:

```
val1 = 256
result = 2048
Press any key to continue
```

Here is the program source code that produced the output:

```
#include "stdafx.h"
#include <iostream>
#include <stdlib.h>

using namespace std;

int main(int argc, char* argv[])
{
    unsigned int val1 = 256;
    unsigned int result;

    cout << "val1 = " << val1 << endl;
    result = _rotl(val1, 3);
    cout << "result = " << result << endl;

    return 0;
}
```

CROSS-REFERENCE

See also _cabs(), _cabsl(), _finite(), _hypot(), _logb(), _rotr(), _scalb(), abs(), acos(), asin(), atan(), atan2(), atof(), cabs(), ceil(), cos(), cosh(), exp(), fabs(), floor(), fmod(), frexp(), labs(), ldexp(), log(), log10(), modf(), powf(), powl(), sin(), sinh(), sqrt(), tan(), and tanh().

_rotr()

Function

The _rotr() function right rotates the bits of a value, returning the rotated value.

Header File

```
#include <stdlib.h>
```

Declaration

```
unsigned int _rotr(unsigned int value, int shift);
```

- *value* — The value to be rotated.
- *shift* — The number of bits to rotate *value*.

Example

The following program demonstrates how to use the _rotr() function by right rotating a value and displaying the result. The program's output looks like this:

```
val1 = 256
result = 32
Press any key to continue
```

Here is the program source code that produced the output:

```
#include "stdafx.h"
#include <iostream>
#include <stdlib.h>

using namespace std;

int main(int argc, char* argv[])
```

```
{
    unsigned int val1 = 256;
    unsigned int result;

    cout << "val1 = " << val1 << endl;
    result = _rotr(val1, 3);
    cout << "result = " << result << endl;

    return 0;
}
```

CROSS-REFERENCE

See also _cabs(), _cabsl(), _finite(), _hypot(), _logb(), _rotl(), _scalb(), abs(), acos(), asin(), atan(), atan2(), atof(), cabs(), ceil(), cos(), cosh(), exp(), fabs(), floor(), fmod(), frexp(), labs(), ldexp(), log(), log10(), modf(), powf(), powl(), sin(), sinh(), sqrt(), tan(), and tanh().

rand()

Function

The rand() function returns a random number from 0 to RAND_MAX.

Header File

```
#include <stdlib.h>
```

Declaration

```
int rand(void);
```

Example

The following program demonstrates how to use the rand() function, by generating ten random numbers. The program's output looks like this:

```
Random range: 0 to 32767
Seeding random number generator...
Generating random numbers...
Random #0: 1340
Random #1: 20825
Random #2: 28273
```

```
Random #3: 25225
Random #4: 29972
Random #5: 15919
Random #6: 14620
Random #7: 31817
Random #8: 13007
Random #9: 31558
Press any key to continue
```

Here is the program source code that produced the output:

```cpp
#include "stdafx.h"
#include <iostream>
#include <stdlib.h>
#include <time.h>

using namespace std;

int main(int argc, char* argv[])
{
    int x;

    cout << "Random range: 0 to " << RAND_MAX << endl;
    cout << "Seeding random number generator..." << endl;
    time_t seed = time(NULL);
    srand((unsigned)seed);

    cout << "Generating random numbers..." << endl;
    for (x=0; x<10; ++x)
    {
        int randNum = rand();
        cout << "Random #" << x;
        cout << ": " << randNum << endl;
    }

    return 0;
}
```

CROSS-REFERENCE

See also srand().

read()

Function

The read() function reads data from an open file, returning the number of bytes actually read, or −1 if an error occurs. The function returns 0 if it attempts to read beyond the end of the file.

Header File

```
#include <io.h>
```

Declaration

```
int read(int handle, void *buffer, unsigned int count);
```

- *buffer*—A pointer to the buffer that will receive the read data.
- *count*—The number of bytes to read.
- *handle*—The file handle returned by the function that opened the file.

Example

The following program demonstrates how to use the read() function. When run, the program opens a file and reads 50 bytes from the file, displaying status messages as it goes. The program's output looks like this:

```
Opening the file...
File opened successfully.
Reading the file...
CHARACTERS READ:
// read.cpp : Defines the entry point for the cons

Press any key to continue
```

Here is the program source code that produced the output:

```
// read.cpp : Defines the entry point for the console
application.
//
#include "stdafx.h"
#include <stdlib.h>
#include <io.h>
#include <fcntl.h>
#include <sys/stat.h>
#include <iostream>
```

```
using namespace std;

int main(int argc, char* argv[])
{
    char str[81];

    cout << "Opening the file..." << endl;
    int fileHandle = open("read.cpp",
        O_RDONLY, S_IREAD);

    if (fileHandle != -1 )
    {
        cout << "File opened successfully." << endl;
        cout << "Reading the file..." << endl;
        int numBytes =
            read(fileHandle, str, 50);

        if (numBytes != -1 )
        {
            str[numBytes] = 0;
            cout << "CHARACTERS READ:" << endl;
            cout << str << endl << endl;
        }
         else
            cout << "File read error." << endl;

        close( fileHandle );
    }
    else
        cout << "File open error." << endl;

    return 0;
}
```

CROSS-REFERENCE
See also _close(), _creat(), _fcloseall(), _fdopen(), _fgetchar(), _fgetwchar(),
_fileno(), _flushall(), _fputwchar(), _fsopen(), _getw(), _getws(), _lseeki64(),
_open(), _putw(), _putws(), _read(), _rmtmp(), _tempnam(), _wcreat(), _wfdopen(),
_wfopen(),_wfreopen(), _wfsopen(), _wopen(), _write(), _wtempnam(), _wtmp-
nam(), clearerr(), eof(), fclose(), feof(), ferror(), fflush(), fgetc(), fgetpos(), fgets(),
fgetwc(), fgetws(), fopen(), fprintf(), fputc(), fputchar(), fputs(), fputwc(), fputws(),
fread(), freopen(), fscanf(), fseek(), fsetpos(), ftell(), fwprintf(), fwrite(), fwscanf(),
getc(), getchar(), gets(), getwc(), getwchar(), lseek(), putc(), putch(), putchar(),
puts(), putwc(), putwchar(), rewind(), setbuf(), setvbuf(), tmpfile(), tmpnam(),
ungetc(), ungetch(), ungetwc(), and write().

realloc()

Function

The `realloc()` function reallocates and resizes memory blocks, returning a `void` pointer to the memory block, or `NULL` if an error occurs.

Header File

```
#include <malloc.h>
```

Declaration

```
void* realloc(void *memblock, size_t size);
```

- *memblock* — A pointer to the memory block to reallocate.
- *size* — The number of bytes to allocate.

Example

The following program demonstrates how to use the `realloc()` function. The program allocates a block of memory, displays the address of the allocated memory, reallocates the memory, and redisplays the address. (The reallocation process may or may not move a block of memory.) The program's output looks something like this:

```
Allocating memory...
Block size: 1024
Block address: 007C09A4

Reallocating memory...
Block size: 4096
Block address: 006C4260

Press any key to continue
```

Here is the program source code that produced the output:

```
#include "stdafx.h"
#include <malloc.h>
#include <iostream>

using namespace std;
```

```cpp
int main(int argc, char* argv[])
{
    cout << "Allocating memory..." << endl;
    int* buf = (int*)malloc(256*sizeof(int));

    if (buf == NULL)
    {
        cout << "Allocation failure." << endl;
        exit(1);
    }

    size_t size = _msize(buf);
    cout << "Block size: " << size << "   " << endl;
    cout << "Block address: " << buf << endl << endl;;

    cout << "Reallocating memory..." << endl;
    buf = (int*)realloc(buf, 1024*sizeof(int));

    if(buf ==  NULL)
    {
        cout << "Reallocation failure." << endl;
        exit(1);
    }

    size = _msize(buf);
    cout << "Block size: " << size << "   " << endl;
    cout << "Block address: " << buf << endl << endl;;

    free(buf);

    return 0;
}
```

CROSS-REFERENCE

See also alloca(), calloc(), and malloc().

register

Keyword

The `register` keyword requests that a variable be located in a hardware register, rather than in memory. For example, the following line requests that the variable `value` be stored in a register:

```
register int value;
```

 CROSS-REFERENCE
See also auto, extern, and static.

remove()

Function

The `remove()` function deletes a file, returning 0 if successful, or −1 if unsuccessful.

Header File

```
#include <stdio.h>
```

Declaration

```
int remove(const char* path);
```

- *path* — The path and name of the file to delete.

Example

The following program demonstrates how to use the `remove()` function, by creating a new file in drive C's root directory and then deleting the new file. The program's output looks like this:

```
Creating a new file...
New file created.
Renaming new file...
File renamed successfully.
Deleting new file...
New file deleted.
Press any key to continue
```

Here is the program source code that produced the output:

```
#include "stdafx.h"
#include <stdio.h>
#include <io.h>
#include <fcntl.h>
#include <iostream>
#include <sys\stat.h>

using namespace std;

int main(int argc, char* argv[])
{
    cout << "Creating a new file..." << endl;
    int fileHandle = open("c:\\TestFile",
        O_CREAT, S_IREAD | S_IWRITE);

    if (fileHandle != -1)
    {
        cout << "New file created." << endl;
        close(fileHandle);

        cout << "Renaming new file..." << endl;
        int result = rename("c:\\TestFile", "c:\\MyFile");
        if (result != 0)
            cout << "File rename error." << endl;
        else
            cout << "File renamed successfully." << endl;

        cout << "Deleting new file..." << endl;
        result = remove("c:\\MyFile");
        if (result == -1)
            cout << "Remove file error." << endl;
        else
            cout << "New file deleted." << endl;
    }
    else
        cout << "File create error" << endl;

    return 0;
}
```

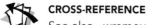

CROSS-REFERENCE
See also _wremove(), _wrename(), and rename().

rename()

Function

The rename() function renames a file, returning 0 if successful, or a nonzero value if unsuccessful.

Header File

```
#include <stdio.h>
```

Declaration

```
int rename(const char* oldname, const char* newname);
```

- *newname* — The new file name.
- *oldname* — The path and old file name.

Example

The following program demonstrates how to use the rename() function, by creating a new file in drive C's root directory, renaming the file, and then deleting the new file. The program's output looks like this:

```
New file created.
File renamed successfully.
New file deleted.
Press any key to continue
```

Here is the program source code that produced the output:

```
#include "stdafx.h"
#include <stdio.h>
#include <io.h>
#include <fcntl.h>
#include <iostream>
#include <sys\stat.h>

using namespace std;
```

```
int main(int argc, char* argv[])
{
    cout << "Creating a new file..." << endl;
    int fileHandle = open("c:\\TestFile",
        O_CREAT, S_IREAD | S_IWRITE);

    if (fileHandle != -1)
    {
        cout << "New file created." << endl;
        close(fileHandle);

        cout << "Renaming new file..." << endl;
        int result = rename("c:\\TestFile", "c:\\MyFile");
        if (result != 0)
            cout << "File rename error." << endl;
        else
            cout << "File renamed successfully." << endl;

        cout << "Deleting new file..." << endl;
        result = remove("c:\\MyFile");
        if (result == -1)
            cout << "Remove file error." << endl;
        else
            cout << "New file deleted." << endl;
    }
    else
        cout << "File create error" << endl;

    return 0;
}
```

CROSS-REFERENCE
See also _wremove() and remove().

return

Keyword

The return keyword exits a function, returning program execution to the calling function. If the returning function specifies a return data type, the value to be returned must be included in the return statement's parentheses. For example, the following function returns one of several integers:

```
int MyFunc(int num)
{
    if (num == 1)
        return(3);
    else if (num == 2)
        return(4);
    else
        return(5);
}
```

A function is not required to return a value. Such a function is declared as void and might look something like the following:

```
void MyFunc(int num)
{
    if (num == 1)
        return;

    // Do something here.
}
```

rewind()

Function

The rewind() function sets a file's pointer back to the beginning of the file.

Header File

```
#include <stdio.h>
```

Declaration

```
void rewind(FILE *stream);
```

- *stream* — A pointer to the stream that's associated with the file to rewind.

Example

The following program demonstrates how to use the rewind() function by reading from a file, rewinding the file, and reading the same data from the file a second time. The program's output looks like this:

```
Opening the file...
Reading from the file...
File input: //
Rewinding the file...
Reading from the file...
File input: //
Press any key to continue
```

Here is the program source code that produced the output:

```cpp
// rewind.cpp : Entry point for the console application.
//

#include "stdafx.h"
#include <stdio.h>
#include <iostream>

using namespace std;

int main(int argc, char* argv[])
{
    char str[256];

    cout << "Opening the file..." << endl;
    FILE* file = fopen("rewind.cpp","r");
    cout << "Reading from the file..." << endl;
    fscanf(file,"%s",str);
    cout << "File input: " << str << endl;
    cout << "Rewinding the file..." << endl;
    rewind(file);
    cout << "Reading from the file..." << endl;
    fscanf(file,"%s",str);
    cout << "File input: " << str << endl;
    fclose(file);

    return 0;
}
```

CROSS-REFERENCE

See also _close(), _creat(), _fcloseall(), _fdopen(), _fgetchar(), _fgetwchar(), _fileno(), _flushall(), _fputwchar(), _fsopen(), _getw(), _getws(), _lseeki64(), _open(), _putw(), _putws(), _read(), _rmtmp(), _tempnam(), _wcreat(), _wfdopen(), _wfopen(), _wfreopen(), _wfsopen(), _wopen(), _wtempnam(), _wtmpnam(), clearerr(), eof(), fclose(), feof(), ferror(), fflush(), fgetc(), fgetpos(), fgets(), fgetwc(), fgetws(), fprintf(), fputc(), fputchar(), fputs(), fputwc(), fputws(), fread(), freopen(), fscanf(), fseek(), fsetpos(), ftell(), fwprintf(), fwrite(), fwscanf(), getc(), getchar(), gets(), getwc(), getwchar(), lseek(), putc(), putch(), putchar(), puts(), putwc(), putwchar(), setbuf(), setvbuf(), tmpfile(), tmpnam(), ungetc(), ungetch(), ungetwc(), and write().

rmdir()

Function

The rmdir() function deletes a directory. If the function is successful, it returns 0; otherwise, it returns –1.

Header File

```
#include <direct.h>
```

Declaration

```
int rmdir(const char* dirname);
```

- *dirname* — The path and name of the directory to remove.

Example

The following program demonstrates how to use the rmdir() function by creating a new directory in drive C's root directory and then deleting the new directory. The program's output looks like this:

```
Making new directory...
New directory created.
Removing directory...
Directory removed.
Press any key to continue
```

Here is the program source code that produced the output:

```
#include "stdafx.h"
#include <direct.h>
#include <iostream>

using namespace std;

int main(int argc, char* argv[])
{
```

```
        cout << "Making new directory..." << endl;
        int result = mkdir("c:\\TestDir");
        if (result != -1)
        {
            cout << "New directory created." << endl;
            cout << "Removing directory..." << endl;
            result = rmdir("c:\\TestDir");
            if (result == 0)
                cout << "Directory removed." << endl;
            else
                cout << "Error removing directory." << endl;
        }
        else
            cout << "Directory create error" << endl;

        return 0;
    }
```

CROSS-REFERENCE
See also _chdrive(), _getdcwd(), _getdrive(), _rmdir(), _searchenv(), _wchdir(), _wgetcwd(), _wgetdcwd(), _wmkdir(), _wrmdir(), _wsearchenv(), chdir(), getcwd(), mkdir(), rmtmp(), and tmpfile().

rmtmp()

Function

The rmtmp() function removes temporary files that were created with tmpfile(), returning the number of files removed.

Header File

```
#include <stdio.h>
```

Declaration

```
int rmtmp(void);
```

Example

The following program demonstrates how to use the rmtmp() function by creating a temporary file and deleting it, displaying messages as it goes. The program's output looks like this:

```
Creating temp file...
Temp file created.
Deleting temp file...
1 file removed.
Press any key to continue
```

Here is the program source code that produced the output:

```cpp
#include "stdafx.h"
#include <iostream>
#include <stdio.h>

using namespace std;

int main(int argc, char* argv[])
{
    cout << "Creating temp file..." << endl;
    FILE* file = tmpfile();
    if (file != NULL)
    {
        cout << "Temp file created." << endl;
        cout << "Deleting temp file..." << endl;
        int result = rmtmp();
        cout << result << " file removed." << endl;
    }
    else
        cout << "File create error." << endl;

    return 0;
}
```

CROSS-REFERENCE

See also _chdrive(), _getdcwd(), _getdrive(), _rmdir(), _rmtmp, _searchenv(), _wchdir(), _wgetcwd(), _wgetdcwd(), _wmkdir(), _wrmdir(), _wsearchenv(), chdir(), getcwd(), mkdir(), rmdir(), and tmpfile().

_searchenv()

Function

The _searchenv() function locates a file using the paths specified in a environment variable.

Header File

```
#include <stdlib.h>
```

Declaration

```
void _searchenv(const char *filename,
    const char *varname, char *pathname);
```

- *filename* — A pointer to the file name for which to search.
- *pathname* — A pointer to the buffer in which to store the resultant path.
- *varname* — A pointer to the environment variable to use in the search.

Example

The following program demonstrates how to use the _searchenv() function, by locating a file using the PATH environment variable. The program's output looks like this:

```
Current PATH: C:\WINDOWS;C:\WINDOWS;C:\WINDOWS\COMMAND

New PATH: C:\Windows\System\

Located path: C:\Windows\System\sysedit.exe

Restored PATH: C:\WINDOWS;C:\WINDOWS;C:\WINDOWS\COMMAND
```

```
Press any key to continue
```

Here is the program source code that produced the output:

```cpp
#include "stdafx.h"
#include <stdlib.h>
#include <iostream>

using namespace std;

int main(int argc, char* argv[])
{
    char buf[_MAX_PATH];

    char* oldValue = getenv("PATH");
    if (oldValue == NULL)
    {
        cout << "Error getting variable" << endl;
        exit(1);
    }

    cout << "Current PATH: ";
    cout << oldValue << endl << endl;

    int result = putenv("PATH=C:\\Windows\\System\\");
    if (result == -1)
    {
        cout << "Error setting variable" << endl;
        exit(1);
    }

    char* value = getenv("PATH");
    cout << "New PATH: ";
    cout << value << endl << endl;

    _searchenv("sysedit.exe", "PATH", buf);
    cout << "Located path: ";
    cout << buf << endl << endl;

    char s[_MAX_PATH] = "PATH=";
    strcpy(&s[5], oldValue);
    putenv(s);
    value = getenv("PATH");
```

```
        cout << "Restored PATH: ";
        cout << value << endl << endl;

        return 0;
    }
```

CROSS-REFERENCE
See also _wsearchenv(), getenv(), and putenv().

_setjmp()

Function

The _setjmp() function saves the current stack environment (and thus a program's status).

NOTE
Borland users should refer to the setjmp() function later in this chapter.

Header File

```
#include <setjmp.h>
```

Declaration

```
int _setjmp(jmp_buf env);
```

- *env* — The area in which the stack environment is saved.

Example

The following program demonstrates how to use the _setjmp() function. The program's output looks like this:

```
Saving stack environment
Press any key to continue
```

Here is the program source code that produced the output:

```
#include "stdafx.h"
#include <setjmp.h>
```

```
#include <iostream>

using namespace std;

int main(int argc, char* argv[])
{
    jmp_buf stackEnv;

    cout << "Saving stack environment" << endl;
    int result = _setjmp(stackEnv);

    return 0;
}
```

CROSS-REFERENCE
See also longjmp() and setjmp().

_setmode()

Function

The _setmode() function sets the translation mode for a file, returning the previous mode if successful, or –1 if unsuccessful.

NOTE
Borland users should refer to the setmode() function later in this chapter.

Header File
```
#include <io.h>
```

Declaration
```
int _setmode(int handle, int mode);
```

- *handle* — The handle of the file whose mode will be reset.
- *mode* — The new translation mode, which must be _O_BINARY or _O_TEXT.

Example

The following program demonstrates how to use the _setmode() function, by setting the stdin stream's translation mode to binary. The program's output looks like this:

```
Getting handle for stdin...
Setting stdin stream to binary mode...
Mode successfully set.
Press any key to continue
```

Here is the program source code that produced the output:

```cpp
#include "stdafx.h"
#include <io.h>
#include <fcntl.h>
#include <iostream>

using namespace std;

int main(int argc, char* argv[])
{
    cout << "Getting handle for stdin..." << endl;
    int handle = _fileno(stdin);
    cout << "Setting stdin stream to binary mode..." << endl;
    int result = _setmode(handle, _O_BINARY);
    if (result != -1 )
        cout << "Mode successfully set." << endl;
    else
        cout << "Mode set error." << endl;

    return 0;
}
```

CROSS-REFERENCE
See also setmode().

_snprintf()

Function

The _snprintf() function creates a formatted string.

NOTE
Borland does not support this function.

Header File

```
#include <stdio.h>
```

Declaration

```
int _snprintf(char *buffer, size_t count,
    const char *format [, argument] ... );
```

- *argument*—A list of arguments that match the format specifiers in the format string.
- *buffer*—A pointer to the buffer that will receive the formatted string.
- *count*—The number of characters to write to the string.
- *format*—The format string, which can use the format specifiers shown in Table S-1.

Table S-1 Format Specifiers for _snprintf()

Specifier	Description
%c	Specifies a character.
%C	Specifies a wide character (printf()) or single-byte character (wprintf()).
%d	Specifies a signed decimal integer.
%e	Specifies a signed double-precision floating-point value using scientific notation with a lowercase e.
%E	Specifies a signed double-precision floating-point value using scientific notation with an uppercase E.
%f	Specifies a signed double-precision floating-point value.
%g	Specifies a signed double-precision floating-point value using either normal notation or scientific notation with a lowercase e.
%G	Specifies a signed double-precision floating-point value using either normal notation or scientific notation with an uppercase E.
%I	Specifies a signed decimal integer.
%n	Specifies an integer pointer.
%o	Specifies an unsigned octal integer.
%p	Specifies a void pointer.
%s	Specifies a string.

Specifier	Description
%S	Specifies a wide-character string (printf()) or single-byte-character string (wprintf()).
%u	Specifies an unsigned decimal integer.
%x	Specifies an unsigned hexadecimal integer with lowercase letters.
%X	Specifies an unsigned hexadecimal integer with uppercase letters.

Example

The following program demonstrates how to use the _snprintf() function, by comparing _snprintf()'s output to that of sprintf(). The program's output looks like this:

```
sprintf() results:
  This is a test: 256


_snprintf() results:
  This


Press any key to continue
```

Here is the program source code that produced the output:

```
#include "stdafx.h"
#include <stdio.h>
#include <iostream>

using namespace std;

int main(int argc, char* argv[])
{
    char dstStr[81];

    memset(dstStr, 0, sizeof(dstStr));
    sprintf(dstStr, "This is a test: %i\n", 256);
    cout << "sprintf() results: " << endl;
    cout << "   " << dstStr << endl;

    memset(dstStr, 0, sizeof(dstStr));
    _snprintf(dstStr, 4, "This is a test: %i\n", 256);
    cout << "_snprintf() results: " << endl;
    cout << "   " << dstStr << endl << endl;

    return 0;
}
```

r
s
t

CROSS-REFERENCE

See also _fputchar(), _fputwchar(), _snwprintf(), _vsnprintf(), _vsnwprintf(), fprintf(), fputc(), fputs(), fputwc(), fputws(), fwprintf(), printf(), vfprintf(), vfwprintf(), vprintf(), vsprintf(), vswprintf(), vwprintf(), and wprintf().

_snwprintf()

Function

The _snwprintf() function is the wide-character version of _snprintf(), which creates a formatted string.

NOTE

Borland does not support this function.

Header File

```
#include <stdio.h>
```

Declaration

```
int _snwprintf(wchar_t *buffer, size_t count,
    const wchar_t *format [, argument] ... );
```

- *argument* — A list of arguments that match the format specifiers in the format string.
- *buffer* — A pointer to the buffer that will receive the formatted string.
- *count* — The number of characters to write to the string.
- *format* — The format string, which can use the format specifiers shown in Table S-2.

Table S-2 Format Specifiers for _snwprintf()

Specifier	Description
%c	Specifies a character.
%C	Specifies a wide character (printf()) or single-byte character (wprintf()).
%d	Specifies a signed decimal integer.
%e	Specifies a signed double-precision floating-point value using scientific notation with a lowercase e.

Specifier	Description
%E	Specifies a signed double-precision floating-point value using scientific notation with an uppercase E.
%f	Specifies a signed double-precision floating-point value.
%g	Specifies a signed double-precision floating-point value using either normal notation or scientific notation with a lowercase e.
%G	Specifies a signed double-precision floating-point value using either normal notation or scientific notation with an uppercase E.
%i	Specifies a signed decimal integer.
%n	Specifies an integer pointer.
%o	Specifies an unsigned octal integer.
%p	Specifies a void pointer.
%s	Specifies a string.
%S	Specifies a wide-character string (printf()) or single-byte-character string (wprintf()).
%u	Specifies an unsigned decimal integer.
%x	Specifies an unsigned hexadecimal integer with lowercase letters.
%X	Specifies an unsigned hexadecimal integer with uppercase letters.

Example

The following program demonstrates how to use the _snwprintf() function, by comparing _snwprintf()'s output to that of swprintf(). The program's output looks like this:

```
swprintf() results:
  This is a test: 256


_snwprintf() results:
  This


Press any key to continue
```

Here is the program source code that produced the output:

```
#include "stdafx.h"
#include <stdio.h>
#include <iostream>

using namespace std;

int main(int argc, char* argv[])
{
```

```
        wchar_t dstStr[81];

        memset(dstStr, 0, sizeof(dstStr));
        swprintf(dstStr, L"This is a test: %i\n", 256);
        cout << "swprintf() results: " << endl << "  ";
        wcout << dstStr << endl;

        memset(dstStr, 0, sizeof(dstStr));
        _snwprintf(dstStr, 4, L"This is a test: %i\n", 256);
        cout << "_snwprintf() results: " << endl << "  ";
        wcout << dstStr << endl << endl;

        return 0;
    }
```

CROSS-REFERENCE

see also _fputchar(), _fputwchar(), _vsnprintf(), _vsnwprintf(), fprintf(), fputc(), fputs(), fputwc(), fputws(), fwprintf(), printf(), vfprintf(), vfwprintf(), vprintf(), vsprintf(), vswprintf(), vwprintf(), and wprintf().

_sopen()

Function

The _sopen() function opens a file with file sharing, returning the file's handle if successful, or –1 if unsuccessful.

Header File

```
#include <io.h>
```

Declaration

```
int _sopen(const char *filename, int oflag,
    int shflag [, int pmode ]);
```

- *filename* — The name of the file to open.
- *pmode* — The value S_IWRITE, S_IREAD, or S_IREAD | S_IWRITE. Needed only when using the O_CREAT file flag.
- *oflag* — A value (from Table S-3) that indicates how the file is to be opened.
- *shflag* — A value (from Table S-4) that indicates the file's share flag.

Table S-3 File Flag Values for _sopen()

Value	Description
O_APPEND	Positions the file pointer at the end of the file.
O_BINARY	Opens the file in binary mode.
O_CREAT	Creates and then opens a file.
O_CREAT | O_SHORT_LIVED	Creates a temporary file that is not flushed to disk.
O_CREAT | O_TEMPORARY	Creates a temporary file that is deleted when the last file is closed.
O_CREAT | O_EXCL	Creates a file, returning an error if the file already exists.
O_RANDOM	Enables random access.
O_RDONLY	Opens a file in read-only mode.
O_RDWR	Opens a file for both reading and writing.
O_SEQUENTIAL	Enables sequential file access.
O_TEXT	Opens a text file.
O_TRUNC	Opens a file and truncates the file length to 0.
O_WRONLY	Opens a file in write-only mode.

Table S-4 File Sharing Flag Values for _sopen()

Value	Description
SH_COMPAT	Compatibility mode setting for 16-bit applications.
SH_DENYNO	Read and write access.
SH_DENYRD	No read access.
SH_DENYRW	No read or write access.
SH_DENYWR	No write access.

Example

The following program demonstrates how to use the _sopen() function. When run, the program opens a file in read-only mode and then closes the file, displaying appropriate messages as it goes. The program's output looks like this:

```
File opened successfully.
Press any key to continue
```

Here is the program source code that produced the output:

```
#include "stdafx.h"
#include <fcntl.h>
```

```
#include <io.h>
#include <share.h>
#include <iostream>

using namespace std;

int main(int argc, char* argv[])
{
    int fileHandle = _sopen("_sopen.cpp",
        O_RDONLY, SH_DENYWR);

    if (fileHandle != -1)
    {
        cout << "File opened successfully." << endl;
        _close(fileHandle);
    }
    else
        cout << "File open error." << endl;

    return 0;
}
```

CROSS-REFERENCE

See also _close(), _creat(), _fcloseall(), _fdopen(), _fgetchar(), _fgetwchar(), _fileno(), _flushall(), _fputwchar(), _fsopen(), _getw(), _getws(), _lseeki64(),_open(), _putw(), _putws(), _read(), _rmtmp(), _sopen(), _tempnam(), _wcreat(), _wfdopen(), _wfopen(), _wfreopen(), _wopen(), _wsopen(), _wtempnam(), _wtmpnam(), clearerr(), eof(), fclose(), feof(), ferror(), fflush(), fgetc(), fgetpos(), fgets(), fgetwc(), fgetws(), fopen(), fprintf(), fputc(), fputchar(), fputs(), fputwc(), fputws(), fread(), freopen(), fscanf(), fseek(), fsetpos(), ftell(), fwprintf(), fwrite(), fwscanf(), getc(), getchar(), gets(), getwc(), getwchar(), lseek(), putc(), putch(), putchar(), puts(), putwc(), putwchar(), rewind(), setbuf(), setvbuf(), tmpfile(), tmpnam(), ungetc(), ungetch(), ungetwc(), and write().

_splitpath()

Function

The _splitpath() function divides a full path into its various path elements.

Header File

```
#include <stdlib.h>
```

Declaration

```
void _splitpath(const char *path, char *drive,
    char *dir, char *fname, char *ext);
```

- *dir* — A pointer to the character array that will contain the directory path element.
- *drive* — A pointer to the character array that will contain the drive letter path element.
- *ext* — A pointer to the character array that will contain the file name extension path element.
- *fname* — A pointer to the character array that will contain the file name path element.
- *path* — A pointer to the character array that contains the full path.

Example

The following program demonstrates how to use the _splitpath() function. When run, the program extracts and displays the elements of the supplied full path. The program's output looks like this:

```
Full Path: c:\Windows\System\sysedit.exe
Drive: c:
Directory: \Windows\System\
File name: sysedit
Extension: .exe
Press any key to continue
```

Here is the program source code that produced the output:

```
#include "stdafx.h"
#include <stdlib.h>
#include <iostream>

using namespace std;

int main(int argc, char* argv[])
{
    char fullPath[_MAX_PATH] =
        "c:\\Windows\\System\\sysedit.exe";
    char drive[_MAX_DRIVE];
    char dir[_MAX_DIR];
    char fileName[_MAX_FNAME];
```

```
        char ext[_MAX_EXT];

        _splitpath(fullPath, drive, dir, fileName, ext);
        cout << "Full Path: " << fullPath << endl;
        cout << "Drive: " << drive << endl;
        cout << "Directory: " << dir << endl;
        cout << "File name: " << fileName << endl;
        cout << "Extension: " << ext << endl;

        return 0;
    }
```

 CROSS-REFERENCE
See also _fullpath(), _getcwd(), _getdcwd(), _makepath(), _wfullpath(), _wgetcwd(), _wgetdcwd(), _wmakepath(), and _wsplitpath().

_stat()

Function

The _stat() function acquires status information about a file. The function returns 0 if successful, or –1 if unsuccessful.

Header File

```
#include <sys\systypes.h>
#include <sys\stat.h>
```

Declaration

```
int _stat(const char *path, struct _stat *buffer);
```

- *buffer* — A pointer to the _stat structure that will hold the returned status information.
- *path* — The path to the file for which to acquire status information.

Example

The following program demonstrates how to use the _stat() function. When run, the program acquires and displays size and time status information on a file. The program's output looks like this:

```
File Size: 550
Time: Wed Feb 24 00:00:00 1999
Press any key to continue
```

Here is the program source code that produced the output:

```cpp
#include "stdafx.h"
#include <sys\types.h>
#include <sys\stat.h>
#include <time.h>
#include <iostream>

using namespace std;

int main(int argc, char* argv[])
{
    struct _stat statInfo;

    int result = _stat( "_stat.cpp", &statInfo );
    if(result == 0)
    {
        cout << "File Size: " << statInfo.st_size << endl;
        cout << "Time: " << ctime(&statInfo.st_atime);
    }
    else
        cout << " _stat() error" << endl;

    return 0;
}
```

CROSS-REFERENCE
See also _stati64(), _wstat(), and _wstati64.

_stati64()

Function

The _stati64() function acquires status information about a file. The function returns a 64-bit integer of 0 if successful, or –1 if unsuccessful.

Header File

```
#include <sys\systypes.h>
#include <sys\stat.h>
```

Declaration

```
__int64 _stati64(const char *path, struct _stat *buffer);
```

- *buffer*—A pointer to the _stat structure that will hold the returned status information.
- *path*—The path to the file for which to acquire status information.

Example

The following program demonstrates how to use the _stati64() function. When run, the program acquires and displays size and time status information on a file. The program's output looks like this:

```
File Size: 571
Time: Wed Feb 24 00:00:00 1999
Press any key to continue
```

Here is the program source code that produced the output:

```cpp
#include "stdafx.h"
#include <sys\types.h>
#include <sys\stat.h>
#include <time.h>
#include <iostream>

using namespace std;

int main(int argc, char* argv[])
{
    struct _stati64 statInfo;

    __int64 result = _stati64( "_stati64.cpp", &statInfo );
    if(result == 0)
    {
        cout << "File Size: ";
        cout << (int)statInfo.st_size << endl;
        cout << "Time: " << ctime(&statInfo.st_atime);
    }
    else
        cout << " _stat() error" << endl;

    return 0;
}
```

CROSS-REFERENCE
See also _stat(), _wstat(), and _wstati64.

_status87()

Function

The _status87() function retrieves the value of the floating-point status word.

Header File

```
#include <float.h>
```

Declaration

```
unsigned int _status87(void);
```

Example

The following program demonstrates how to use the _status87() function. When run, the program causes a floating-point error (underflow) and displays the results of a call to _status87() after the error. The program's output looks like this:

```
Status = 3
Press any key to continue
```

Here is the program source code that produced the output:

```
#include "stdafx.h"
#include <iostream>
#include <float.h>

using namespace std;

int main(int argc, char* argv[])
{
    double var1 = 1e-60;
    float var2 = var1;

    unsigned int result = _status87();
```

```
            cout << "Status = " << result << endl;

            _clear87();

            return 0;
        }
```

CROSS-REFERENCE
See also _clear87(), _control87(), _fpclass(), _fpreset(), and _statusfp().

_statusfp()

Function

The _statusfp() function is a platform-independent version of _status87(), which retrieves the value of the floating-point status word.

NOTE
Borland does not support this function.

Header File

```
#include <float.h>
```

Declaration

```
unsigned int _statusfp(void);
```

Example

The following program demonstrates how to use the _statusfp() function. When run, the program causes a floating-point error (underflow) and displays the results of a call to _statusfp() after the error. The program's output looks like this:

```
Status = 3
Press any key to continue
```

Here is the program source code that produced the output:

```
#include "stdafx.h"
#include <iostream>
```

```
#include <float.h>

using namespace std;

int main(int argc, char* argv[])
{
    double var1 = 1e-60;
    float var2 = var1;

    unsigned int result = _statusfp();
    cout << "Status = " << result << endl;

    _clearfp();

    return 0;
}
```

CROSS-REFERENCE
See also _clear87(), _control87(), _fpclass(), _fpreset(), and _status87().

_strdate()

Function

The _strdate() function copies the date to a supplied buffer, returning a pointer to the buffer.

Header File

```
#include <time.h>
```

Declaration

```
char* _strdate(char *datestr);
```

- *datestr* — A pointer to the buffer that will receive the date string.

Example

The following program demonstrates how to use the _strdate() function. When run, the program copies the current date into a buffer named buf and then displays the result. The program's output looks like this:

```
Current Date: 02/16/99
Press any key to continue
```

Here is the program source code that produced the output:

```
#include "stdafx.h"
#include <time.h>
#include <iostream>

using namespace std;

int main(int argc, char* argv[])
{
    char buf[256];

    char* result = _strdate(buf);
    cout << "Current Date: " << result << endl;

    return 0;
}
```

CROSS-REFERENCE
See also _ftime(), _futime(), _strtime(), _utime(), _wasctime(), _wctime(), _wstrdate(), _wstrtime(), _wutime(), asctime(), ctime(), difftime(), gmtime(), localtime(), mktime(), strftime(), time(), and wcsftime().

_strdec()

Function

The _strdec() function returns a pointer to the previous character in a string, or NULL if the previous character cannot be determined.

NOTE
You cannot call _strdec() directly in your programs. The _tcsdec() function, which is used in the example program below, maps to the _strdec() function, unless the _UNICODE or _MBCS symbol is defined. This mapping occurs in the tchar.h header file.

Header File

```
#include <tchar.h>
```

Declaration

```
char* _strdec(const char *start, const char *current);
```

- *current* — A pointer to the character for which to return the previous character.
- *start* — A pointer to the start of the string.

Example

The following program demonstrates how to use the _strdec() function. When run, the program locates the character that precedes the fifth character in a string and displays the result. The program's output looks like this:

```
Source String = This is a test
Result = s is a test
Press any key to continue
```

Here is the program source code that produced the output:

```
#include "stdafx.h"
#include <iostream>
#include <tchar.h>

using namespace std;

int main(int argc, char* argv[])
{
    char* srcStr = "This is a test";

    char* result = _tcsdec(srcStr, &srcStr[4]);
    cout << "Source String = " << srcStr << endl;
    cout << "Result = " << result << endl;

    return 0;
}
```

CROSS-REFERENCE

See also _mbscat(), _mbschr(), _mbscmp(), _mbscoll(), _mbscpy(), _mbscspn(), _mbsdec(), _mbsdup(), _mbsicmp(), _mbsicoll(), _mbsinc(), _mbslen(), _mbslwr(), _mbsnbcat(), _mbsnbcmp(), _mbsnbcnt(), _mbsnbcoll(), _mbsnbcpy(), _mbsnbicmp(), _mbsnbicoll(), _mbsnbset(), _mbsnccnt(), _mbsncmp(), _mbsncoll(), _mbsncpy(), _mbsnextc(), _mbsnicmp(), _mbsnicoll(), _mbsninc(), _mbsnset(), _mbspbrk(), _mbsrchr(), _mbsrev(), _mbsset(), _mbsspn(), _mbsspnp(), _mbsstr(), _mbstok(), _mbstrlen(), _mbsupr(), _stricoll(), _strinc(), _strlwr(), _strncnt(), _strncoll(), _strnextc(), _strnicmp(), _strnicoll(), _strninc(), _strnset(), _strset(), _strspnp(), _strupr(), _tcsdec(), _tcsinc(), _tcsnccnt(), _tcsninc(), _tcsspnp(), _wcsdec(), _wcsicmp(), _wcsicoll(), _wcslwr(), _wcsncnt(), _wcsncoll(), _wcsnicmp(), _wcsnicoll(), _wcsninc(), _wcsnset(), _wcsrev(), _wcsset(), _wcsspnp(), _wcsupr(), strcat(), strchr(), strcmp(), strcoll(), strcpy(), strcspn(), strdup(), stricmp(), strlen(), strlwr(), strncat(), strncmp(), strncpy(), strnicmp(), strnset(), strpbrk(), strrchr(), strrev(), strset(), strspn(), strstr(), strtod(), strtok(), strtol(), strtoul(), strupr(), wcscat(), wcschr(), wcscmp(), wcscoll(), wcscpy(), wcscspn(), wcslen(), wcsncat(), wcsncmp(), wcsncpy(), wcspbrk(), wcsrchr(), wcsspn(), wcsstr(), wcstod(), wcstok(), wcstol(), and wcstoul().

_strerror()

Function

The _strerror() function returns a pointer to an error-message string.

Header File

```
#include <string.h>
```

Declaration

```
char* _strerror(const char *strErrMsg);
```

- *strErrMsg*—A pointer to the error message to display.

Example

The following program demonstrates how to use the _strerror() function. When run, the program generates an error by attempting to run a nonexistent program and displays the error's results. The program's output looks like this:

```
Running TestProg.exe

File not found
Current Error Msg:
    ERROR: No such file or directory

Press any key to continue
```

Here is the program source code that produced the output:

```
#include "stdafx.h"
```

```cpp
#include <iostream>
#include <process.h>
#include <errno.h>
#include <string.h>

using namespace std;

int main(int argc, char* argv[])
{
    cout << "Running TestProg.exe" << endl << endl;

    int result = spawnl(P_WAIT, "TestProg.exe",
        "TestProg.exe", "arg2", "arg3", NULL);
    if (result == -1)
    {
        switch(errno)
        {
        case ENOEXEC:
            cout << "Not an executable file" << endl;
            break;
        case E2BIG:
            cout << "Space required exceeds 32K" << endl;
            break;
        case ENOMEM:
            cout << "Not enough memory" << endl;
            break;
        case EINVAL:
            cout << "Bad execution mode" << endl;
            break;
        case ENOENT:
            cout << "File not found" << endl;
        }
    }

    cout << "Current Error Msg: " << endl;
    cout << "       " << _strerror("ERROR") << endl << endl;

    return 0;
}
```

CROSS-REFERENCE

See also clearerr(), ferror(), perror(), and strerror().

_stricoll()

Function

The _stricoll() function compares two strings for the current locale without regard for case (case–insensitive compare), returning a value from Table S-5:

Table S-5 Return Values for _stricoll()

Value	Description
Less than 0	string1 is alphabetically less than string2.
0	The two strings are equal.
Greater than 0	string1 is alphabetically greater than string2.

Header File

```
#include <string.h>
```

Declaration

```
int _stricoll(const char *string1, const char *string2);
```

- *string1* — The first string to compare.
- *string2* — The second string to compare.

Example

The following program demonstrates how to use the _stricoll() function. When run, the program compares several pairs of strings and displays the result of the comparisons. The program's output looks like this:

```
One Two Three equals one two three
one two three is greater than Four Five Six
Four Five Six is less than seven eight nine
Press any key to continue
```

Here is the program source code that produced the output:

```
#include "stdafx.h"
#include <iostream>
#include <string.h>

using namespace std;
```

```cpp
void cmp(char* s1, char* s2)
{
    int result = _stricoll(s1, s2);
    if (result < 0 )
    {
        cout << s1;
        cout << " is less than ";
        cout << s2 << endl;
    }
    else if (result > 0)
    {
        cout << s1;
        cout << " is greater than ";
        cout << s2 << endl;
    }
    else
    {
        cout << s1;
        cout << " equals ";
        cout << s2 << endl;
    }
}

int main(int argc, char* argv[])
{
    char* str1 = "One Two Three";
    char* str2 = "one two three";
    char* str3 = "Four Five Six";
    char* str4 = "seven eight nine";

    cmp(str1, str2);
    cmp(str2, str3);
    cmp(str3, str4);

    return 0;
}
```

 CROSS-REFERENCE

See also _mbscat(), _mbschr(), _mbscmp(), _mbscoll(), _mbscpy(), _mbscspn(), _mbsdec(), _mbsdup(), _mbsicmp(), _mbsicoll(), _mbsinc(), _mbslen(), _mbslwr(), _mbsnbcat(), _mbsnbcmp(), _mbsnbcnt(), _mbsnbcoll(), _mbsnbcpy(), _mbsnbicmp(), _mbsnbicoll(), _mbsnbset(), _mbsnccnt(), _mbsncmp(), _mbsncoll(), _mbsncpy(), _mbsnextc(), _mbsnicmp(), _mbsnicoll(), _mbsninc(),

_mbsnset(), _mbspbrk(), _mbsrchr(), _mbsrev(), _mbsset(), _mbsspn(), _mbsspnp(), _mbsstr(), _mbstok(), _mbstrlen(), _mbsupr(), _strdec(), _strinc(), _strlwr(), _strncnt(), _strncoll(), _strnextc(), _strnicmp(), _strnicoll(), _strninc(), _strnset(), _strset(), _strspnp(), _strupr(), _tcsdec(), _tcsinc(), _tcsnccnt(), _tcsninc(), _tcsspnp(), _wcsdec(), _wcsicmp(), _wcsicoll(), _wcslwr(), _wcsncnt(), _wcsncoll(), _wcsnicmp(), _wcsnicoll(), _wcsninc(), _wcsnset(), _wcsrev(), _wcsset(), _wcsspnp(), _wcsupr(), strcat(), strchr(), strcmp(), strcoll(), strcpy(), strcspn(), strdup(), stricmp(), strlen(), strlwr(), strncat(), strncmp(), strncpy(), strnicmp(), strnset(), strpbrk(), strrchr(), strrev(), strset(), strspn(), strstr(), strtod(), strtok(), strtol(), strtoul(), strupr(), wcscat(), wcschr(), wcscmp(), wcscoll(), wcscpy(), wcscspn(), wcslen(), wcsncat(), wcsncmp(), wcsncpy(), wcspbrk(), wcsrchr(), wcsspn(), wcsstr(), wcstod(), wcstok(), wcstol(), and wcstoul().

_strinc()

Function

The _strinc() function returns a pointer to the next character in a wide-character string, or NULL if the next character cannot be determined.

NOTE

You cannot call _strinc() directly in your programs. The _tcsinc() function, which is used in the example program below, maps to the _strinc() function, unless either the _UNICODE or _MBCS symbols are defined. This mapping occurs in the tchar.h header file.

Header File

```
#include <tchar.h>
```

Declaration

```
char* _strinc(const char *current);
```

- *current* — A pointer to the character for which to return the next character.

Example

The following program demonstrates how to use the _strinc() function. When run, the program locates the character that follows the fifth character in a string and displays the result. The program's output looks like this:

```
Source String = This is a test
Result = is a test
Press any key to continue
```

Here is the program source code that produced the output:

```
#include "stdafx.h"
#include <iostream>
#include <tchar.h>

using namespace std;

int main(int argc, char* argv[])
{
    char* srcStr = "This is a test";

char* result = _tcsinc(&srcStr[4]);
    cout << "Source String = " << srcStr << endl;
    cout << "Result = " << result << endl;

    return 0;
}
```

CROSS-REFERENCE

See also _mbscat(), _mbschr(), _mbscmp(), _mbscoll(), _mbscpy(), _mbscspn(), _mbsdec(), _mbsdup(), _mbsicmp(), _mbsicoll(), _mbsinc(), _mbslen(), _mbslwr(), _mbsnbcat(), _mbsnbcmp(), _mbsnbcnt(), _mbsnbcoll(), _mbsnbcpy(), _mbsnbicmp(), _mbsnbicoll(), _mbsnbset(), _mbsnccnt(), _mbsncmp(), _mbsncoll(), _mbsncpy(), _mbsnextc(), _mbsnicmp(), _mbsnicoll(), _mbsninc(), _mbsnset(), _mbspbrk(), _mbsrchr(), _mbsrev(), _mbsset(), _mbsspn(), _mbsspnp(), _mbsstr(), _mbstok(), _mbstrlen(), _mbsupr(), _strdec(), _stricoll(), _strlwr(), _strncnt(), _strncoll(), _strnextc(), _strnicmp(), _strnicoll(), _strninc(), _strnset(), _strset(), _strspnp(), _strupr(), _tcsdec(), _tcsinc(), _tcsnccnt(), _tcsninc(), _tcsspnp(), _wcsdec(), _wcsicmp(), _wcsicoll(), _wcslwr(), _wcsncnt(), _wcsncoll(), _wcsnicmp(), _wcsnicoll(), _wcsninc(), _wcsnset(), _wcsrev(), _wcsset(), _wcsspnp(), _wcsupr(), strcat(), strchr(), strcmp(), strcoll(), strcpy(), strcspn(), strdup(), stricmp(), strlen(), strlwr(), strncat(), strncmp(), strncpy(), strnicmp(), strnset(), strpbrk(), strrchr(), strrev(), strset(), strspn(), strstr(), strtod(), strtok(), strtol(), strtoul(), strupr(), wcscat(), wcschr(), wcscmp(), wcscoll(), wcscpy(), wcscspn(), wcslen(), wcsncat(), wcsncmp(), wcsncpy(), wcspbrk(), wcsrchr(), wcsspn(), wcsstr(), wcstod(), wcstok(), wcstol(), and wcstoul().

_strlwr()

Function

The _strlwr() function converts a string to lowercase, returning a pointer to the new string.

 NOTE
Borland users should refer to the strlwr() function later in this chapter.

Header File

```
#include <string.h>
```

Declaration

```
char* _strlwr(const char *string);
```

- *string* — The string to convert.

Example

The following program demonstrates how to use the _strlwr() function. When run, the program converts several strings to lowercase and displays the results. The program's output looks like this:

```
Original String: One Two Three
Converted String: one two three

Original String: FOUR FIVE SIX
Converted String: four five six

Original String: seven eight nine
Converted String: seven eight nine

Press any key to continue
```

Here is the program source code that produced the output:

```
#include "stdafx.h"
#include <iostream>
#include <string.h>

using namespace std;
```

```
void convert(char* s)
{
    cout << "Original String: " << s << endl;
    char* result = _strlwr(s);
    cout << "Converted String: ";
    cout << result << endl << endl;
}

int main(int argc, char* argv[])
{
    char str1[81];
    strcpy(str1, "One Two Three");
    char str2[81];
    strcpy(str2, "FOUR FIVE SIX");
    char str3[81];
    strcpy(str3, "seven eight nine");

    convert(str1);
    convert(str2);
    convert(str3);

    return 0;
}
```

CROSS-REFERENCE

See also _mbscat(), _mbschr(), _mbscmp(), _mbscoll(), _mbscpy(), _mbscspn(), _mbsdec(), _mbsdup(), _mbsicmp(), _mbsicoll(), _mbsinc(), _mbslen(), _mbslwr(), _mbsnbcat(), _mbsnbcmp(), _mbsnbcnt(), _mbsnbcoll(), _mbsnbcpy(), _mbsnbicmp(), _mbsnbicoll(), _mbsnbset(), _mbsnccnt(), _mbsncmp(), _mbsncoll(), _mbsncpy(), _mbsnextc(), _mbsnicmp(), _mbsnicoll(), _mbsninc(), _mbsnset(), _mbspbrk(), _mbsrchr(), _mbsrev(), _mbsset(), _mbsspn(), _mbsspnp(), _mbsstr(), _mbstok(), _mbstrlen(), _mbsupr(), _strdec(), _stricoll(), _strinc(), _strncnt(), _strncoll(), _strnextc(), _strnicmp(), _strnicoll(), _strninc(), _strnset(), _strset(), _strspnp(), _strupr(), _tcsdec(), _tcsinc(), _tcsnccnt(), _tcsninc(), _tcsspnp(), _wcsdec(), _wcsicmp(), _wcsicoll(), _wcslwr(), _wcsncnt(), _wcsncoll(), _wcsnicmp(), _wcsnicoll(), _wcsninc(), _wcsnset(), _wcsrev(), _wcsset(), _wcsspnp(), _wcsupr(), strcat(), strchr(), strcmp(), strcoll(), strcpy(), strcspn(), strdup(), stricmp(), strlen(), strlwr(), strncat(), strncmp(), strncpy(), strnicmp(), strnset(), strpbrk(), strrchr(), strrev(), strset(), strspn(), strstr(), strtod(), strtok(), strtol(), strtoul(), strupr(), wcscat(), wcschr(), wcscmp(), wcscoll(), wcscpy(), wcscspn(), wcslen(), wcsncat(), wcsncmp(), wcsncpy(), wcspbrk(), wcsrchr(), wcsspn(), wcsstr(), wcstod(), wcstok(), wcstol(), and wcstoul().

_strncnt()

Function

The _strncnt() function returns the number of characters in a portion of a string.

NOTE

You cannot call _strncnt() directly in your programs. The _tcsnccnt() function, which is used in the example program below, maps to the _strncnt() function, unless either the _UNICODE or _MBCS symbols are defined. This mapping occurs in the tchar.h header file.

Header File

```
#include <tchar.h>
```

Declaration

```
size_t _strncnt(const char *string, size_t number);
```

- *number* — The number of characters to examine.
- *string* — A pointer to the string to examine.

Example

The following program demonstrates how to use the _strncnt() function. When run, the program determines the number of characters in the first four bytes of a string and displays the result. The program's output looks like this:

```
Source String = This is a test
Result = 4
Press any key to continue
```

Here is the program source code that produced the output:

```
#include "stdafx.h"
#include <iostream>
#include <tchar.h>

using namespace std;

int main(int argc, char* argv[])
{
```

```
char* srcStr = "This is a test";

size_t result = _tcsnccnt(srcStr, 4);
cout << "Source String = " << srcStr << endl;
cout << "Result = " << result << endl;

return 0;
}
```

CROSS-REFERENCE

See also _mbscat(), _mbschr(), _mbscmp(), _mbscoll(), _mbscpy(), _mbscspn(), _mbsdec(), _mbsdup(), _mbsicmp(), _mbsicoll(), _mbsinc(), _mbslen(), _mbslwr(), _mbsnbcat(), _mbsnbcmp(), _mbsnbcnt(), _mbsnbcoll(), _mbsnbcpy(), _mbsnbicmp(), _mbsnbicoll(), _mbsnbset(), _mbsnccnt(), _mbsncmp(), _mbsncoll(), _mbsncpy(), _mbsnextc(), _mbsnicmp(), _mbsnicoll(), _mbsninc(), _mbsnset(), _mbspbrk(), _mbsrchr(), _mbsrev(), _mbsset(), _mbsspn(), _mbsspnp(), _mbsstr(), _mbstok(), _mbstrlen(), _mbsupr(), _strdec(), _stricoll(), _strinc(), _strlwr(), _strncoll(), _strnextc(), _strnicmp(), _strnicoll(), _strninc(), _strnset(), _strset(), _strspnp(), _strupr(), _tcsdec(), _tcsinc(), _tcsnccnt(), _tcsninc(), _tcsspnp(), _wcsdec(), _wcsicmp(), _wcsicoll(), _wcslwr(), _wcsncnt(), _wcsncoll(), _wcsnicmp(), _wcsnicoll(), _wcsninc(), _wcsnset(), _wcsrev(), _wcsset(), _wcsspnp(), _wcsupr(), strcat(), strchr(), strcmp(), strcoll(), strcpy(), strcspn(), strdup(), stricmp(), strlen(), strlwr(), strncat(), strncmp(), strncpy(), strnicmp(), strnset(), strpbrk(), strrchr(), strrev(), strset(), strspn(), strstr(), strtod(), strtok(), strtol(), strtoul(), strupr(), wcscat(), wcschr(), wcscmp(), wcscoll(), wcscpy(), wcscspn(), wcslen(), wcsncat(), wcsncmp(), wcsncpy(), wcspbrk(), wcsrchr(), wcsspn(), wcsstr(), wcstod(), wcstok(), wcstol(), and wcstoul().

_strncoll()

Function

The _strncoll() function compares two strings for the current locale, returning a value from Table S-6:

Table S-6 Return Values for _strncoll()

Value	Description
Less than 0	string1 is alphabetically less than string2.
0	The two strings are equal.
Greater than 0	string1 is alphabetically greater than string2.

Header File

```
#include <string.h>
```

Declaration

```
int _strncoll(const char *string1,
    const char *string2, size_t count);
```

- *count* — The number of characters to compare.
- *string1* — The first string to compare.
- *string2* — The second string to compare.

Example

The following program demonstrates how to use the _strncoll() function. When run, the program compares several pairs of strings and displays the result of the comparisons. The program's output looks like this:

```
One Two Three equals One Two three
One Two three is less than one Two Three
one Two Three is greater than SEVEN EIGHT nine
SEVEN EIGHT nine is less than seven eight nine
Press any key to continue
```

Here is the program source code that produced the output:

```
#include "stdafx.h"
#include <iostream>
#include <string.h>

using namespace std;

void cmp(char* s1, char* s2, size_t num)
{
    int result = _strncoll(s1, s2, num);
    if (result < 0 )
    {
        cout << s1;
        cout << " is less than ";
        cout << s2 << endl;
    }
    else if (result > 0)
    {
        cout << s1;
```

```
            cout << " is greater than ";
            cout << s2 << endl;
        }
        else
        {
            cout << s1;
            cout << " equals ";
            cout << s2 << endl;
        }
    }

    int main(int argc, char* argv[])
    {
        char* str1 = "One Two Three";
        char* str2 = "One Two three";
        char* str3 = "one Two Three";
        char* str4 = "SEVEN EIGHT nine";
        char* str5 = "seven eight nine";

        cmp(str1, str2, 7);
        cmp(str2, str3, 7);
        cmp(str3, str4, 7);
        cmp(str4, str5, 7);

        return 0;
    }
```

CROSS-REFERENCE

See also _mbscat(), _mbschr(), _mbscmp(), _mbscoll(), _mbscpy(), _mbscspn(), _mbsdec(), _mbsdup(), _mbsicmp(), _mbsicoll(), _mbsinc(), _mbslen(), _mbslwr(), _mbsnbcat(), _mbsnbcmp(), _mbsnbcnt(), _mbsnbcoll(), _mbsnbcpy(), _mbsnbicmp(), _mbsnbicoll(), _mbsnbset(), _mbsnccnt(), _mbsncmp(), _mbsncoll(), _mbsncpy(), _mbsnextc(), _mbsnicmp(), _mbsnicoll(), _mbsninc(), _mbsnset(), _mbspbrk(), _mbsrchr(), _mbsrev(), _mbsset(), _mbsspn(), _mbsspnp(), _mbsstr(), _mbstok(), _mbstrlen(), _mbsupr(), _strdec(), _stricoll(), _strinc(), _strlwr(), _strncnt(), _strnextc(), _strnicmp(), _strnicoll(), _strninc(), _strnset(), _strset(), _strspnp(), _strupr(), _tcsdec(), _tcsinc(), _tcsnccnt(), _tcsninc(), _tcsspnp(), _wcsdec(), _wcsicmp(), _wcsicoll(), _wcslwr(), _wcsncnt(), _wcsncoll(), _wcsnicmp(), _wcsnicoll(), _wcsninc(), _wcsnset(), _wcsrev(), _wcsset(), _wcsspnp(), _wcsupr(), strcat(), strchr(), strcmp(), strcoll(), strcpy(), strcspn(), strdup(), stricmp(), strlen(), strlwr(), strncat(), strncmp(), strncpy(), strnicmp(), strnset(), strpbrk(), strrchr(), strrev(), strset(), strspn(), strstr(), strtod(), strtok(), strtol(), strtoul(), strupr(), wcscat(), wcschr(), wcscmp(), wcscoll(), wcscpy(), wcscspn(), wcslen(), wcsncat(), wcsncmp(), wcsncpy(), wcspbrk(), wcsrchr(), wcsspn(), wcsstr(), wcstod(), wcstok(), wcstol(), and wcstoul().

_strnextc()

Function

The _strnextc() function returns, as an integer, the value of the next character in a wide-character string.

NOTE

You cannot call _strnextc() directly in your programs. The _tcsnextc() function, which is used in the example program below, maps to the _strnextc() function, unless either the _UNICODE or _MBCS symbols are defined. This mapping occurs in the tchar.h header file.

Header File

```
#include <tchar.h>
```

Declaration

```
unsigned int _strnextc(const char *string);
```

- *string* — A pointer to the source string.

Example

The following program demonstrates how to use the _strnextc() function. When run, the program determines the integer value of the fifth character in a wide-character string and displays the result. The program's output looks like this:

```
Source String = This is a test
Result = 32
Press any key to continue
```

Here is the program source code that produced the output:

```
#include "stdafx.h"
#include <iostream>
#include <tchar.h>
```

```
using namespace std;

int main(int argc, char* argv[])
{
    char* srcStr = "This is a test";

    unsigned int result = _tcsnextc(&srcStr[4]);
    cout << "Source String = ";
    cout << srcStr << endl;
    cout << "Result = " << result << endl;

    return 0;
}
```

CROSS-REFERENCE
See also _mbscat(), _mbschr(), _mbscmp(), _mbscoll(), _mbscpy(), _mbscspn(), _mbsdec(), _mbsdup(), _mbsicmp(), _mbsicoll(), _mbsinc(), _mbslen(), _mbslwr(), _mbsnbcat(), _mbsnbcmp(), _mbsnbcnt(), _mbsnbcoll(), _mbsnbcpy(), _mbsnbicmp(), _mbsnbicoll(), _mbsnbset(), _mbsnccnt(), _mbsncmp(), _mbsncoll(), _mbsncpy(), _mbsnextc(), _mbsnicmp(), _mbsnicoll(), _mbsninc(), _mbsnset(), _mbspbrk(), _mbsrchr(), _mbsrev(), _mbsset(), _mbsspn(), _mbsspnp(), _mbsstr(), _mbstok(), _mbstrlen(), _mbsupr(), _strdec(), _stricoll(), _strinc(), _strlwr(), _strncnt(), _strncoll(), _strnicmp(), _strnicoll(), _strninc(), _strnset(), _strset(), _strspnp(), _strupr(), _tcsdec(), _tcsinc(), _tcsnccnt(), _tcsninc(), _tcsspnp(), _wcsdec(), _wcsicmp(), _wcsicoll(), _wcslwr(), _wcsncnt(), _wcsncoll(), _wcsnicmp(), _wcsnicoll(), _wcsninc(), _wcsnset(), _wcsrev(), _wcsset(), _wcsspnp(), _wcsupr(), strcat(), strchr(), strcmp(), strcoll(), strcpy(), strcspn(), strdup(), stricmp(), strlen(), strlwr(), strncat(), strncmp(), strncpy(), strnicmp(), strnset(), strpbrk(), strrchr(), strrev(), strset(), strspn(), strstr(), strtod(), strtok(), strtol(), strtoul(), strupr(), wcscat(), wcschr(), wcscmp(), wcscoll(), wcscpy(), wcscspn(), wcslen(), wcsncat(), wcsncmp(), wcsncpy(), wcspbrk(), wcsrchr(), wcsspn(), wcsstr(), wcstod(), wcstok(), wcstol(), and wcstoul().

_strnicmp()

Function

The _strnicmp() function compares two strings without regard for case (case–insensitive compare), returning a value from Table S-7.

NOTE
Borland users should refer to the strnicmp() function later in this chapter.

Table S-7 Return Values for _strnicmp()

Value	Description
Less than 0	string1 is alphabetically less than string2.
0	The two strings are equal.
Greater than 0	string1 is alphabetically greater than string2.

Header File

```
#include <string.h>
```

Declaration

```
int _strnicmp(const char *string1,
    const char *string2, size_t count);
```

- *count* — The number of characters to compare.
- *string1* — The first string to compare.
- *string2* — The second string to compare.

Example

The following program demonstrates how to use the _strnicmp() function. When run, the program compares several pairs of strings and displays the result of the comparisons. The program's output looks like this:

```
One Two Three equals One Two three
One Two three equals one Two Three
one Two Three is less than SEVEN EIGHT nine
SEVEN EIGHT nine equals seven eight nine
Press any key to continue
```

Here is the program source code that produced the output:

```
#include "stdafx.h"
#include <iostream>
#include <string.h>

using namespace std;
```

```
void cmp(char* s1, char* s2, size_t num)
{
    int result = _strnicmp(s1, s2, num);
    if (result < 0 )
    {
        cout << s1;
        cout << " is less than ";
        cout << s2 << endl;
    }
    else if (result > 0)
    {
        cout << s1;
        cout << " is greater than ";
        cout << s2 << endl;
    }
    else
    {
        cout << s1;
        cout << " equals ";
        cout << s2 << endl;
    }
}

int main(int argc, char* argv[])
{
    char* str1 = "One Two Three";
    char* str2 = "One Two three";
    char* str3 = "one Two Three";
    char* str4 = "SEVEN EIGHT nine";
    char* str5 = "seven eight nine";

    cmp(str1, str2, 7);
    cmp(str2, str3, 7);
    cmp(str3, str4, 7);
    cmp(str4, str5, 7);

    return 0;
}
```

CROSS-REFERENCE
See also _mbscat(), _mbschr(), _mbscmp(), _mbscoll(), _mbscpy(), _mbscspn(), _mbsdec(), _mbsdup(), _mbsicmp(), _mbsicoll(), _mbsinc(), _mbslen(), _mbslwr(), _mbsnbcat(), _mbsnbcmp(), _mbsnbcnt(), _mbsnbcoll(), _mbsnbcpy(),

_mbsnbicmp(), _mbsnbicoll(), _mbsnbset(), _mbsnccnt(), _mbsncmp(), _mbsncoll(), _mbsncpy(), _mbsnextc(), _mbsnicmp(), _mbsnicoll(), _mbsninc(), _mbsnset(), _mbspbrk(), _mbsrchr(), _mbsrev(), _mbsset(), _mbsspn(), _mbsspnp(), _mbsstr(), _mbstok(), _mbstrlen(), _mbsupr(), _strdec(), _stricoll(), _strinc(), _strlwr(), _strncnt(), _strncoll(), _strnextc(), _strnicoll(), _strninc(), _strnset(), _strset(), _strspnp(), _strupr(), _tcsdec(), _tcsinc(), _tcsnccnt(), _tcsninc(), _tcsspnp(), _wcsdec(), _wcsicmp(), _wcsicoll(), _wcslwr(), _wcsncnt(), _wcsncoll(), _wcsnicmp(), _wcsnicoll(), _wcsninc(), _wcsnset(), _wcsrev(), _wcsset(), _wcsspnp(), _wcsupr(), strcat(), strchr(), strcmp(), strcoll(), strcpy(), strcspn(), strdup(), stricmp(), strlen(), strlwr(), strncat(), strncmp(), strncpy(), strnicmp(), strnset(), strpbrk(), strrchr(), strrev(), strset(), strspn(), strstr(), strtod(), strtok(), strtol(), strtoul(), strupr(), wcscat(), wcschr(), wcscmp(), wcscoll(), wcscpy(), wcscspn(), wcslen(), wcsncat(), wcsncmp(), wcsncpy(), wcspbrk(), wcsrchr(), wcsspn(), wcsstr(), wcstod(), wcstok(), wcstol(), and wcstoul().

_strnicoll()

Function

The _strnicoll() function compares two strings for the current locale without regard to case (case–insensitive compare), returning a value from Table S-8:

Table S-8 Return Values for _strnicoll()

Value	Description
Less than 0	string1 is alphabetically less than string2.
0	The two strings are equal.
Greater than 0	string1 is alphabetically greater than string2.

Header File

```
#include <string.h>
```

Declaration

```
int _strnicoll(const char *string1,
    const char *string2, size_t count);
```

- *count* — The number of characters to compare.
- *string1* — The first string to compare.
- *string2* — The second string to compare.

Example

The following program demonstrates how to use the _strnicoll() function. When run, the program compares several pairs of strings and displays the result of the comparisons. The program's output looks like this:

```
One Two Three equals One Two three
One Two three equals one Two Three
one Two Three is less than SEVEN EIGHT nine
SEVEN EIGHT nine equals seven eight nine
Press any key to continue
```

Here is the program source code that produced the output:

```cpp
#include "stdafx.h"
#include <iostream>
#include <string.h>

using namespace std;

void cmp(char* s1, char* s2, size_t num)
{
    int result = _strnicoll(s1, s2, num);
    if (result < 0 )
    {
        cout << s1;
        cout << " is less than ";
        cout << s2 << endl;
    }
    else if (result > 0)
    {
        cout << s1;
        cout << " is greater than ";
        cout << s2 << endl;
    }
    else
    {
        cout << s1;
        cout << " equals ";
        cout << s2 << endl;
    }
}

int main(int argc, char* argv[])
{
    char* str1 = "One Two Three";
    char* str2 = "One Two three";
```

```
char* str3 = "one Two Three";
char* str4 = "SEVEN EIGHT nine";
char* str5 = "seven eight nine";

cmp(str1, str2, 7);
cmp(str2, str3, 7);
cmp(str3, str4, 7);
cmp(str4, str5, 7);

return 0;
}
```

CROSS-REFERENCE

See also _mbscat(), _mbschr(), _mbscmp(), _mbscoll(), _mbscpy(), _mbscspn(), _mbsdec(), _mbsdup(), _mbsicmp(), _mbsicoll(), _mbsinc(), _mbslen(), _mbslwr(), _mbsnbcat(), _mbsnbcmp(), _mbsnbcnt(), _mbsnbcoll(), _mbsnbcpy(), _mbsnbicmp(), _mbsnbicoll(), _mbsnbset(), _mbsnccnt(), _mbsncmp(), _mbsncoll(), _mbsncpy(), _mbsnextc(), _mbsnicmp(), _mbsnicoll(), _mbsninc(), _mbsnset(), _mbspbrk(), _mbsrchr(), _mbsrev(), _mbsset(), _mbsspn(), _mbsspnp(), _mbsstr(), _mbstok(), _mbstrlen(), _mbsupr(), _strdec(), _stricoll(), _strinc(), _strlwr(), _strncnt(), _strncoll(), _strnextc(), _strnicmp(), _strninc(), _strnset(), _strset(), _strspnp(), _strupr(), _tcsdec(), _tcsinc(), _tcsnccnt(), _tcsninc(), _tcsspnp(), _wcsdec(), _wcsicmp(), _wcsicoll(), _wcslwr(), _wcsncnt(), _wcsncoll(), _wcsnicmp(), _wcsnicoll(), _wcsninc(), _wcsnset(), _wcsrev(), _wcsset(), _wcsspnp(), _wcsupr(), strcat(), strchr(), strcmp(), strcoll(), strcpy(), strcspn(), strdup(), stricmp(), strlen(), strlwr(), strncat(), strncmp(), strncpy(), strnicmp(), strnset(), strpbrk(), strrchr(), strrev(), strset(), strspn(), strstr(), strtod(), strtok(), strtol(), strtoul(), strupr(), wcscat(), wcschr(), wcscmp(), wcscoll(), wcscpy(), wcscspn(), wcslen(), wcsncat(), wcsncmp(), wcsncpy(), wcspbrk(), wcsrchr(), wcsspn(), wcsstr(), wcstod(), wcstok(), wcstol(), and wcstoul().

_strninc()

Function

The _strninc() function returns a pointer to the string that results from advancing the specified number of characters in the source string.

NOTE

You cannot call _strninc() directly in your programs. The _tcsninc() function, which is used in the example program below, maps to the _strninc() function, unless either the _UNICODE or _MBCS symbols are defined. This mapping occurs in the tchar.h header file.

Header File

```
#include <tchar.h>
```

Declaration

```
char* _strninc(const char *string, size_t count);
```

- *count* — The number of characters to advance in the source string.
- *string* — A pointer to the source string.

Example

The following program demonstrates how to use the _strninc() function. When run, the program locates the fifth character in a string and displays the result. The program's output looks like this:

```
Source String = This is a test
Result = is a test
Press any key to continue
```

Here is the program source code that produced the output:

```
#include "stdafx.h"
#include <iostream>
#include <tchar.h>

using namespace std;

int main(int argc, char* argv[])
{
    char* srcStr = "This is a test";

char* result = _tcsninc(srcStr, 5);
    cout << "Source String = " << srcStr << endl;
    cout << "Result = " << result << endl;

    return 0;
}
```

CROSS-REFERENCE
See also _mbscat(), _mbschr(), _mbscmp(), _mbscoll(), _mbscpy(), _mbscspn(), _mbsdec(), _mbsdup(), _mbsicmp(), _mbsicoll(), _mbsinc(), _mbslen(), _mbslwr(), _mbsnbcat(), _mbsnbcmp(), _mbsnbcnt(), _mbsnbcoll(), _mbsnbcpy(), _mbsnbicmp(), _mbsnbicoll(), _mbsnbset(), _mbsnccnt(), _mbsncmp(),

_mbsncoll(), _mbsncpy(), _mbsnextc(), _mbsnicmp(), _mbsnicoll(), _mbsninc(), _mbsnset(), _mbspbrk(), _mbsrchr(), _mbsrev(), _mbsset(), _mbsspn(), _mbsspnp(), _mbsstr(), _mbstok(), _mbstrlen(), _mbsupr(), _strdec(), _stricoll(), _strinc(), _strlwr(), _strncnt(), _strncoll(), _strnextc(), _strnicmp(), _strnicoll(), _strnset(), _strset(), _strspnp(), _strupr(), _tcsdec(), _tcsinc(), _tcsnccnt(), _tcsninc(), _tcsspnp(), _wcsdec(), _wcsicmp(), _wcsicoll(), _wcslwr(), _wcsncnt(), _wcsncoll(), _wcsnicmp(), _wcsnicoll(), _wcsninc(), _wcsnset(), _wcsrev(), _wcsset(), _wcsspnp(), _wcsupr(), strcat(), strchr(), strcmp(), strcoll(), strcpy(), strcspn(), strdup(), stricmp(), strlen(), strlwr(), strncat(), strncmp(), strncpy(), strnicmp(), strnset(), strpbrk(), strrchr(), strrev(), strset(), strspn(), strstr(), strtod(), strtok(), strtol(), strtoul(), strupr(), wcscat(), wcschr(), wcscmp(), wcscoll(), wcscpy(), wcscspn(), wcslen(), wcsncat(), wcsncmp(), wcsncpy(), wcspbrk(), wcsrchr(), wcsspn(), wcsstr(), wcstod(), wcstok(), wcstol(), and wcstoul().

_strnset()

Function

The _strnset() function sets a portion of the contents of a string to a given character, returning a pointer to the new string.

NOTE
Borland users should refer to the strnset() function later in this chapter.

Header File

```
#include <string.h>
```

Declaration

```
char* _strnset(const char *string, char c, size_t count);
```

- *c* — The character with which to fill the string.
- *count* — The number of characters to set.
- *string* — The string to set.

Example

The following program demonstrates how to use the _strnset() function. When run, the program sets several strings to various symbols and displays the results. The program's output looks like this:

```
Original String: One Two Three
Converted String: ??? Two Three

Original String: FOUR FIVE SIX
Converted String: *******VE SIX

Original String: seven eight nine
Converted String: ################

Press any key to continue
```

Here is the program source code that produced the output:

```cpp
#include "stdafx.h"
#include <iostream>
#include <string.h>

using namespace std;

void convert(char* s, char c, size_t num)
{
    cout << "Original String: ";
    cout << s << endl;
    char* result = _strnset(s, c, num);
    cout << "Converted String: ";
    cout << result << endl << endl;
}

int main(int argc, char* argv[])
{
    char str1[81];
    strcpy(str1, "One Two Three");
    char str2[81];
    strcpy(str2, "FOUR FIVE SIX");
    char str3[81];
    strcpy(str3, "seven eight nine");

    convert(str1, '?', 3);
    convert(str2, '*', 7);
    convert(str3, '#', 16);

    return 0;
}
```

CROSS-REFERENCE

See also _mbscat(), _mbschr(), _mbscmp(), _mbscoll(), _mbscpy(), _mbscspn(), _mbsdec(), _mbsdup(), _mbsicmp(), _mbsicoll(), _mbsinc(), _mbslen(), _mbslwr(), _mbsnbcat(), _mbsnbcmp(), _mbsnbcnt(), _mbsnbcoll(), _mbsnbcpy(), _mbsnbicmp(), _mbsnbicoll(), _mbsnbset(), _mbsnccnt(), _mbsncmp(), _mbsncoll(), _mbsncpy(), _mbsnextc(), _mbsnicmp(), _mbsnicoll(), _mbsninc(), _mbsnset(), _mbspbrk(), _mbsrchr(), _mbsrev(), _mbsset(), _mbsspn(), _mbsspnp(), _mbsstr(), _mbstok(), _mbstrlen(), _mbsupr(), _strdec(), _stricoll(), _strinc(), _strlwr(), _strncnt(), _strncoll(), _strnextc(), _strnicmp(), _strnicoll(), _strninc(), _strset(), _strspnp(), _strupr(), _tcsdec(), _tcsinc(), _tcsnccnt(), _tcsninc(), _tcsspnp(), _wcsdec(), _wcsicmp(), _wcsicoll(), _wcslwr(), _wcsncnt(), _wcsncoll(), _wcsnicmp(), _wcsnicoll(), _wcsninc(), _wcsnset(), _wcsrev(), _wcsset(), _wcsspnp(), _wcsupr(), strcat(), strchr(), strcmp(), strcoll(), strcpy(), strcspn(), strdup(), stricmp(), strlen(), strlwr(), strncat(), strncmp(), strncpy(), strnicmp(), strnset(), strpbrk(), strrchr(), strrev(), strset(), strspn(), strstr(), strtod(), strtok(), strtol(), strtoul(), strupr(), wcscat(), wcschr(), wcscmp(), wcscoll(), wcscpy(), wcscspn(), wcslen(), wcsncat(), wcsncmp(), wcsncpy(), wcspbrk(), wcsrchr(), wcsspn(), wcsstr(), wcstod(), wcstok(), wcstol(), and wcstoul().

_strset()

Function

The _strset() function sets the contents of a string to a specified character, returning a pointer to the new string.

NOTE

Borland users should refer to the strset() function later in this chapter.

Header File

```
#include <string.h>
```

Declaration

```
char* _strset(const char *string, char c);
```

- *c* — The character with which to fill the string.
- *string* — The string to set.

Example

The following program demonstrates how to use the _strset() function. When run, the program sets several strings to question marks and displays the results. The program's output looks like this:

```
Original String: One Two Three
Converted String: ?????????????

Original String: FOUR FIVE SIX
Converted String: ?????????????

Original String: seven eight nine
Converted String: ???????????????

Press any key to continue
```

Here is the program source code that produced the output:

```cpp
#include "stdafx.h"
#include <iostream>
#include <string.h>

using namespace std;

void convert(char* s, char c)
{
    cout << "Original String: ";
    cout << s << endl;
    char* result = _strset(s, c);
    cout << "Converted String: ";
    cout << result << endl << endl;
}

int main(int argc, char* argv[])
{
    char str1[81];
    strcpy(str1, "One Two Three");
    char str2[81];
    strcpy(str2, "FOUR FIVE SIX");
    char str3[81];
    strcpy(str3, "seven eight nine");

    convert(str1, '?');
    convert(str2, '?');
```

```
        convert(str3, '?');

        return 0;
    }
```

CROSS-REFERENCE

See also _mbscat(), _mbschr(), _mbscmp(), _mbscoll(), _mbscpy(), _mbscspn(), _mbsdec(), _mbsdup(), _mbsicmp(), _mbsicoll(), _mbsinc(), _mbslen(), _mbslwr(), _mbsnbcat(), _mbsnbcmp(), _mbsnbcnt(), _mbsnbcoll(), _mbsnbcpy(), _mbsnbicmp(), _mbsnbicoll(), _mbsnbset(), _mbsnccnt(), _mbsncmp(), _mbsncoll(), _mbsncpy(), _mbsnextc(), _mbsnicmp(), _mbsnicoll(), _mbsninc(), _mbsnset(), _mbspbrk(), _mbsrchr(), _mbsrev(), _mbsset(), _mbsspn(), _mbsspnp(), _mbsstr(), _mbstok(), _mbstrlen(), _mbsupr(), _strdec(), _stricoll(), _strinc(), _strlwr(), _strncnt(), _strncoll(), _strnextc(), _strnicmp(), _strnicoll(), _strninc(), _strnset(), _strspnp(), _strupr(), _tcsdec(), _tcsinc(), _tcsnccnt(), _tcsninc(), _tcsspnp(), _wcsdec(), _wcsicmp(), _wcsicoll(), _wcslwr(), _wcsncnt(), _wcsncoll(), _wcsnicmp(), _wcsnicoll(), _wcsninc(), _wcsnset(), _wcsrev(), _wcsset(), _wcsspnp(), _wcsupr(), strcat(), strchr(), strcmp(), strcoll(), strcpy(), strcspn(), strdup(), stricmp(), strlen(), strlwr(), strncat(), strncmp(), strncpy(), strnicmp(), strnset(), strpbrk(), strrchr(), strrev(), strset(), strspn(), strstr(), strtod(), strtok(), strtol(), strtoul(), strupr(), wcscat(), wcschr(), wcscmp(), wcscoll(), wcscpy(), wcscspn(), wcslen(), wcsncat(), wcsncmp(), wcsncpy(), wcspbrk(), wcsrchr(), wcsspn(), wcsstr(), wcstod(), wcstok(), wcstol(), and wcstoul().

_strspnp()

Function

The _strspnp() function locates the first occurrence of a substring that starts with a character not included in the specified set. The function returns a pointer to the first nonmatching character.

NOTE

You cannot call _strspnp() directly in your programs. The _tcsspnp() function, which is used in the example program below, maps to the _strspnp() function, unless either the _UNICODE or _MBCS symbols are defined. This mapping occurs in the tchar.h header file.

Header File

```
#include <tchar.h>
```

Declaration

```
char* _strspnp(const char *string, const char *strCharSet);
```

- *strCharSet*—A pointer to the set of characters for which to search.
- *string*—A pointer to the string to search.

Example

The following program demonstrates how to use the _strspnp() function. When run, the program locates, in a string, the first character not in the specified set and displays the results. The program's output looks like this:

```
Source String:
This is a test

Remaining String:
test

Press any key to continue
```

Here is the program source code that produced the output:

```
#include "stdafx.h"
#include <iostream>
#include <tchar.h>

using namespace std;

int main(int argc, char* argv[])
{
    char* srcStr = "This is a test";
    char* chrSet = "ahisT ";

char* result = _tcsspnp(srcStr, chrSet);
    cout << "Source String:" << endl;
    cout << srcStr << endl << endl;
    cout << "Remaining String:" << endl;
    cout << result << endl << endl;

    return 0;
}
```

CROSS-REFERENCE

See also _mbscat(), _mbschr(), _mbscmp(), _mbscoll(), _mbscpy(), _mbscspn(), _mbsdec(), _mbsdup(), _mbsicmp(), _mbsicoll(), _mbsinc(), _mbslen(), _mbslwr(), _mbsnbcat(), _mbsnbcmp(), _mbsnbcnt(), _mbsnbcoll(), _mbsnbcpy(), _mbsnbicmp(), _mbsnbicoll(), _mbsnbset(), _mbsnccnt(), _mbsncmp(), _mbsncoll(), _mbsncpy(), _mbsnextc(), _mbsnicmp(), _mbsnicoll(), _mbsninc(), _mbsnset(), _mbspbrk(), _mbsrchr(), _mbsrev(), _mbsset(), _mbsspn(), _mbsspnp(), _mbsstr(), _mbstok(), _mbstrlen(), _mbsupr(), _strdec(), _stricoll(), _strinc(), _strlwr(), _strncnt(), _strncoll(), _strnextc(), _strnicmp(), _strnicoll(), _strninc(), _strnset(), _strset(), _strupr(), _tcsdec(), _tcsinc(), _tcsnccnt(), _tcsninc(), _tcsspnp(), _wcsdec(), _wcsicmp(), _wcsicoll(), _wcslwr(), _wcsncnt(), _wcsncoll(), _wcsnicmp(), _wcsnicoll(), _wcsninc(), _wcsnset(), _wcsrev(), _wcsset(), _wcsspnp(), _wcsupr(), strcat(), strchr(), strcmp(), strcoll(), strcpy(), strcspn(), strdup(), stricmp(), strlen(), strlwr(), strncat(), strncmp(), strncpy(), strnicmp(), strnset(), strpbrk(), strrchr(), strrev(), strset(), strspn(), strstr(), strtod(), strtok(), strtol(), strtoul(), strupr(), wcscat(), wcschr(), wcscmp(), wcscoll(), wcscpy(), wcscspn(), wcslen(), wcsncat(), wcsncmp(), wcsncpy(), wcspbrk(), wcsrchr(), wcsspn(), wcsstr(), wcstod(), wcstok(), wcstol(), and wcstoul().

_strtime()

Function

The _strtime() function copies the time to a supplied buffer, returning a pointer to the buffer.

Header File

```
#include <time.h>
```

Declaration

```
char* _strtime(char *timestr);
```

- *timestr*—A pointer to the buffer that will receive the time string.

Example

The following program demonstrates how to use the _strtime() function. When run, the program copies the current time into a buffer named buf and then displays the result. The program's output looks something like this:

```
Current Time: 14:56:42
Press any key to continue
```

Here is the program source code that produced the output:

```
#include "stdafx.h"
#include <time.h>
#include <iostream>

using namespace std;

int main(int argc, char* argv[])
{
    char buf[256];

    char* result = _strtime(buf);
    cout << "Current Time: " << result << endl;

    return 0;
}
```

CROSS-REFERENCE
See also _ftime(), _futime(), _strdate(), _tzset(), _utime(), _wasctime(), _wctime(), _wstrdate(), _wstrtime(), _wutime(), asctime(), ctime(), difftime(), gmtime(), localtime(), mktime(), strftime(), time(), and wcsftime().

_strupr()

Function

The _strupr() function converts a string to uppercase, returning a pointer to the new string.

NOTE
Borland users should refer to the strupr() function later in this chapter.

Header File

```
#include <string.h>
```

Declaration

```
char* _strupr(const char *string);
```

- *string*—The string to convert.

Example

The following program demonstrates how to use the _strupr() function. When run, the program converts several strings to uppercase and displays the results. The program's output looks like this:

```
Original String: One Two Three
Converted String: ONE TWO THREE

Original String: FOUR FIVE SIX
Converted String: FOUR FIVE SIX

Original String: seven eight nine
Converted String: SEVEN EIGHT NINE

Press any key to continue
```

Here is the program source code that produced the output:

```
#include "stdafx.h"
#include <iostream>
#include <string.h>

using namespace std;

void convert(char* s)
{
    cout << "Original String: ";
    cout << s << endl;
    char* result = _strupr(s);
    cout << "Converted String: ";
    cout << result << endl << endl;
}

int main(int argc, char* argv[])
{
    char str1[81];
    strcpy(str1, "One Two Three");
    char str2[81];
    strcpy(str2, "FOUR FIVE SIX");
    char str3[81];
    strcpy(str3, "seven eight nine");

    convert(str1);
    convert(str2);
```

```
    convert(str3);

    return 0;
}
```

CROSS-REFERENCE

See also _mbscat(), _mbschr(), _mbscmp(), _mbscoll(), _mbscpy(), _mbscspn(), _mbsdec(), _mbsdup(), _mbsicmp(), _mbsicoll(), _mbsinc(), _mbslen(), _mbslwr(), _mbsnbcat(), _mbsnbcmp(), _mbsnbcnt(), _mbsnbcoll(), _mbsnbcpy(), _mbsnbicmp(), _mbsnbicoll(), _mbsnbset(), _mbsnccnt(), _mbsncmp(), _mbsncoll(), _mbsncpy(), _mbsnextc(), _mbsnicmp(), _mbsnicoll(), _mbsninc(), _mbsnset(), _mbspbrk(), _mbsrchr(), _mbsrev(), _mbsset(), _mbsspn(), _mbsspnp(), _mbsstr(), _mbstok(), _mbstrlen(), _mbsupr(), _strdec(), _stricoll(), _strinc(), _strlwr(), _strncnt(), _strncoll(), _strnextc(), _strnicmp(), _strnicoll(), _strninc(), _strnset(), _strset(), _strspnp(), _tcsdec(), _tcsinc(), _tcsnccnt(), _tcsninc(), _tcsspnp(), _wcsdec(), _wcsicmp(), _wcsicoll(), _wcslwr(), _wcsncnt(), _wcsncoll(), _wcsnicmp(), _wcsnicoll(), _wcsninc(), _wcsnset(), _wcsrev(), _wcsset(), _wcsspnp(), _wcsupr(), strcat(), strchr(), strcmp(), strcoll(), strcpy(), strcspn(), strdup(), stricmp(), strlen(), strlwr(), strncat(), strncmp(), strncpy(), strnicmp(), strnset(), strpbrk(), strrchr(), strrev(), strset(), strspn(), strstr(), strtod(), strtok(), strtol(), strtoul(), strupr(), wcscat(), wcschr(), wcscmp(), wcscoll(), wcscpy(), wcscspn(), wcslen(), wcsncat(), wcsncmp(), wcsncpy(), wcspbrk(), wcsrchr(), wcsspn(), wcsstr(), wcstod(), wcstok(), wcstol(), and wcstoul().

_swab()

Function

The _swab() function swaps pairs of bytes in a string. The function returns no value.

NOTE
Borland users should refer to the swab() function later in this chapter.

Header File

```
#include <stdlib.h>
```

Declaration

```
void _swab(char *src, char *dest, int n);
```

- *dest* — A pointer to the destination string.
- *n* — The number of bytes to swap.
- *src* — A pointer to the source string.

Example

The following program demonstrates how to use the _swab() function. When run, the program swaps bytes in a string and displays the results. The program's output looks like this:

```
Source string: 1234567890
Destination string:

Source string: 1234567890
Destination string: 2143658709

Press any key to continue
```

Here is the program source code that produced the output:

```
#include "stdafx.h"
#include <stdlib.h>
#include <iostream>

using namespace std;

int main(int argc, char* argv[])
{
    char srcStr[] = "1234567890";
    char dstStr[14] = "";

    cout << "Source string: " << srcStr << endl;
    cout << "Destination string: " << dstStr << endl;
    cout << endl;

    swab(srcStr, dstStr, 10);

    cout << "Source string: " << srcStr << endl;
    cout << "Destination string: " << dstStr << endl;
    cout << endl;

    return 0;
}
```

CROSS-REFERENCE
See also _mbsdup(), _mbsicmp(), _mbsicoll(), _mbsinc(), _memccpy(), _memicmp(), memchr(), memcmp(), memcpy(), memmove(), memset(), and swab().

scanf()

Function

The scanf() function accepts formatted data from the standard input stream. The function returns the number of data items successfully received.

Header File

```
#include <stdio.h>
```

Declaration

```
int scanf(const char *format [, argument]...);
```

- *argument* — A list of data items that match the control codes included in the format string *format*.
- *format* — The format string, which can include the format specifiers shown in Table S-9.

Table S-9 Format Specifiers for scanf()

Specifier	Description
%c	Specifies a character.
%C	Specifies a wide character (printf()) or single-byte character (wprintf()).
%d	Specifies a signed decimal integer.
%e	Specifies a signed double-precision floating-point value using scientific notation with a lowercase e.
%E	Specifies a signed double-precision floating-point value using scientific notation with an uppercase E
%f	Specifies a signed double-precision floating-point value.
%g	Specifies a signed double-precision floating-point value using either normal notation or scientific notation with a lowercase e.

Continued

Table S-9 *Continued*

Specifier	Description
%G	Specifies a signed double-precision floating-point value using either normal notation or scientific notation with an uppercase E.
%I	Specifies a signed decimal integer.
%n	Specifies an integer pointer.
%o	Specifies an unsigned octal integer.
%p	Specifies a void pointer.
%s	Specifies a string.
%S	Specifies a wide-character string (printf()) or single-byte-character string (wprintf()).
%u	Specifies an unsigned decimal integer.
%x	Specifies an unsigned hexadecimal integer with lowercase letters.
%X	Specifies an unsigned hexadecimal integer with uppercase letters.

Example

The following program demonstrates how to use the scanf() function. When run, the program calls scanf() to input two data items: an integer and a string. The program's output looks something like this:

```
Enter an integer and a string:
234 test

You entered:
234 test
Number of items: 2

Press any key to continue
```

Here is the program source code that produced the output:

```
#include "stdafx.h"
#include <stdio.h>
#include <iostream>

using namespace std;

int main(int argc, char* argv[])
{
    int var1;
    char str1[81];

    printf("Enter an integer and a string:\n");
```

```
int numItems = scanf("%i %s", &var1, str1);
printf("\nYou entered:\n");
printf("%i %s\n", var1, str1);
printf("Number of items: %i\n\n", numItems);

return 0;
}
```

CROSS-REFERENCE

See also cprintf(), cscanf(), fprintf(), fscanf(), fwprintf(), printf(), sscanf(), vfprintf(), vfwprintf(), vprintf(), vsprintf(), vswprintf(), vwprintf(), wprintf(), and wscanf().

Scope

Technique

Scope determines the parts of a program in which data objects are visible. C++ supports file (or global), function, block, and prototype scope. The following sections describe the various types of scope.

File Scope

An identifier has file scope when the identifier is declared outside of all other functions, blocks, or parameter lists that are defined in the file. This type of identifier can be accessed from anywhere within the file. For example, the following program declares a variable named `fileVar`, which has file scope. In the program, both the `main()` and `func1()` functions can manipulate the value of the variable. The program's output looks like this:

```
fileVar in main() = 10
fileVar in func1() = 20
Press any key to continue
```

Here is the program source code that produced the output:

```
#include "stdafx.h"
#include <iostream>

using namespace std;

// This variable has file scope.
int fileVar;

void func1()
```

```
    {
        fileVar += 10;
        cout << "fileVar in func1() = " << fileVar;
        cout << endl;
    }

    int main(int argc, char* argv[])
    {
        fileVar = 10;
        cout << "fileVar in main() = " << fileVar;
         cout << endl;
        func1();

        return 0;
    }
```

Function Scope

An identifier that's declared inside a function but outside of any program blocks in the function is said to have function scope. Such an identifier can be accessed from anywhere in the function in which it's declared, but nowhere else in the program. The following program demonstrates function scope. The program's output looks like this:

```
fileVar in func1() = 10
Press any key to continue
```

Here is the program source code that produced the output:

```
#include "stdafx.h"
#include <iostream>

using namespace std;

// This variable has file scope.
void func1()
{
    // This variable has function scope.
    int fileVar = 0;

    fileVar += 10;
    cout << "fileVar in func1() = " << fileVar;
    cout << endl;
}

int main(int argc, char* argv[])
```

```
{
    // The following line would cause a compiler
    // error if it weren't commented out.
    //fileVar = 10;

    func1();

    return 0;
}
```

Block Scope

An identifier that's declared inside a program block is said to have block scope and is visible only within that program block. That is, the identifier cannot be referenced anywhere else in the program, including in the function that defined the program block (except within the block itself). The following program demonstrates block scope. The program's output looks like this:

```
x = 0
x = 1
x = 2
x = 3
x = 4
Press any key to continue
```

Here is the program source code that produced the output:

```
#include "stdafx.h"
#include <iostream>

using namespace std;

int main(int argc, char* argv[])
{
    // x has block scope.
    for (int x=0; x<5; ++x)
        cout << "x = " << x << endl;

    // The following line would cause a compiler
    // error if it weren't commented out.
    //x = 10;

    return 0;
}
```

Prototype Scope

Finally, an identifier that's declared inside a function prototype has prototype scope and is visible only within that prototype. The following program demonstrates prototype scope. The program's output looks like this:

```
var1 = 10
result = 20
Press any key to continue
```

Here is the program source code that produced the output:

```
#include "stdafx.h"
#include <iostream>

using namespace std;

// This is a function prototype. The num symbol
// has prototype scope.
int func1(int num);

int main(int argc, char* argv[])
{
    int var1 = 10;
    cout << "var1 = " << var1 << endl;
    int result = func1(var1);
    cout << "result = " << result << endl;

    return 0;
}

// This is the definition of the prototyped
// function. It doesn't even reference the
// original num identifier, using n instead.
int func1(int n)
{
    n *= 2;
    return n;
}
```

 CROSS-REFERENCE
See also auto, extern, register, and static.

set

Template Class

The set template class represents a group of elements that can be both a value and a sorting key. The set of elements is of varying length.

Class Declaration

```
template<class Key, class Pred = less<Key>,
    class A = allocator<Key> >
class set
{
public:
    typedef Key key_type;
    typedef Pred key_compare;
    typedef Key value_type;
    typedef Pred value_compare;
    typedef A allocator_type;
    typedef A::size_type size_type;
    typedef A::difference_type difference_type;
    typedef A::rebind<value_type>::
        other::const_reference reference;
    typedef A::rebind<value_type>::
        other::const_reference const_reference;
    typedef T0 iterator;
    typedef T1 const_iterator;
    typedef reverse_bidirectional_iterator<iterator,
        value_type, reference, A::pointer,
            difference_type> reverse_iterator;
    typedef reverse_bidirectional_iterator<const_iterator,
        value_type, const_reference, A::const_pointer,
            difference_type> const_reverse_iterator;
    explicit set(const Pred& comp = Pred(),
        const A& al = A());
    set(const set& x);
    set(const value_type *first, const value_type *last,
        const Pred& comp = Pred(), const A& al = A());
    const_iterator begin() const;
    iterator end() const;
    const_reverse_iterator rbegin() const;
    const_reverse_iterator rend() const;
```

```
        size_type size() const;
        size_type max_size() const;
        bool empty() const;
        A get_allocator() const;
        pair<iterator, bool> insert(const value_type& x);
        iterator insert(iterator it, const value_type& x);
        void insert(InIt first, InIt last);
        iterator erase(iterator it);
        iterator erase(iterator first, iterator last);
        size_type erase(const Key& key);
        void clear();
        void swap(set x);
        key_compare key_comp() const;
        value_compare value_comp() const;
        const_iterator find(const Key& key) const;
        size_type count(const Key& key) const;
        const_iterator lower_bound(const Key& key) const;
        const_iterator upper_bound(const Key& key) const;
        pair<const_iterator, const_iterator>
            equal_range(const Key& key) const;
    protected:
        A allocator;
    };
```

Class Members

Table S-10 lists and describes the members of the set template class.

Table S-10 Members of the set Template Class

Member	Description
allocator_type	A synonym for the template's A parameter.
begin()	Returns a random-access iterator that points to the sequence's first element.
clear()	Removes all elements from the list.
const_iterator	Object type for a constant random-access iterator.
const_reference	Refers to an element reference.
const_reverse_ iterator	Object type for a constant reverse iterator.
count()	Returns the number of elements for a given key.
difference_type	Represents the difference between two element addresses.
empty()	Returns true if the sequence is empty.
end()	Returns a random-access iterator that points to the next element beyond the end of the sequence.

Member	Description
equal_range()	Returns a pair of iterators for lower_bound() and upper_bound().
erase()	Erases an element.
find()	Finds an element in the set.
get_allocator()	Returns the allocator.
insert()	Inserts an element into the set.
iterator	Object type for a random-access iterator.
key_compare	Represents a function for comparing keys.
key_compare()	Compares keys in the set.
key_type	Represents a data type for a sort key.
lower_bound()	Returns an iterator for the first element that doesn't match the given key.
max_size()	Returns the maximum possible size of a sequence.
rbegin()	Returns a reverse iterator that points to the next element beyond the end of the sequence.
reference	A synonym for A as an element reference.
rend()	Returns a reverse iterator that points to the sequence's first element.
reverse_iterator	Object type for a reverse iterator.
size()	Returns the length of the sequence.
size_type	Represents an unsigned integer used to represent the size of the set.
swap()	Swaps one sequence with another.
upper_bound()	Returns an iterator for the first element that matches the given key.
value_compare	Represents a function for comparing values.
value_compare()	Compares values in the set.
value_type	Represents a data type for an element in the set.

CROSS-REFERENCE
See also list and vector.

set_terminate()

Function

The set_terminate() function sets the function called at program termination, returning a pointer to the last function that was registered by set_terminate().

Header File

```
#include <eh.h>
```

Declaration

```
terminate_function set_terminate
    (terminate_function term_func);
```

- *term_func* — The function to call upon program termination.

Example

The following program demonstrates how to use the set_terminate() function. The program's output looks something like this:

```
Inside MyTerm()
Press any key to continue
```

Here is the program source code that produced the output:

```
#include "stdafx.h"
#include <eh.h>
#include <iostream>

using namespace std;

void MyTerm()
{
    cout << "Inside MyTerm()" << endl;
    exit(0);
}

int main(int argc, char* argv[])
{
    terminate_function old = set_terminate(MyTerm);
    throw "Fake Exception";

    return 0;
}
```

CROSS-REFERENCE
See also abort() and set_unexpected().

set_unexpected()

Function

The set_unexpected() function sets the function called by unexpected(), returning a pointer to the last function that was registered by set_unexpected().

Header File

```
#include <eh.h>
```

Declaration

```
unexpected_function set_unexpected
    (unexpected_function unexp_func );
```

- *unexp_func* — The function to call on program termination.

Example

The following program demonstrates how to use the set_unexpected() function. The program's output looks like this:

```
Setting to the MyTerm() function...
Press any key to continue
```

Here is the program source code that produced the output:

```
#include "stdafx.h"
#include <eh.h>
#include <iostream>

using namespace std;

void MyTerm()
{
    cout << "Inside MyTerm()" << endl;
    exit(0);
}

int main(int argc, char* argv[])
{
    cout << "Setting to the MyTerm() function..." << endl;
```

r
s
t

```
        unexpected_function old = set_unexpected(MyTerm);

        return 0;
    }
```

CROSS-REFERENCE
See also abort() and set_terminate().

setbuf()

Function

The setbuf() function sets a stream to buffered or unbuffered.

Header File

```
#include <stdio.h>
```

Declaration

```
void setbuf(FILE *stream, char *buffer);
```

- *buffer* — A pointer to the memory to use for buffering data.
- *stream* — A pointer to the stream for which to set buffering.

Example

The following program demonstrates how to use the setbuf() function, by opening two streams and setting them to unbuffered and buffered, respectively. The program's output looks something like this:

```
Setting strm1 to unbuffered
Setting strm2 to buffered
Now closing files
Press any key to continue
```

Here is the program source code that produced the output:

```
#include "stdafx.h"
#include <stdio.h>
#include <iostream>

using namespace std;
```

```
int main(int argc, char* argv[])
{
    char buf[BUFSIZ];

    FILE* strm1 = fopen("file1", "w");
    FILE* strm2 = fopen("file2", "w" );
    if ((strm1 == NULL) || (strm2 == NULL))
        cout << "File error" << endl;
    else
    {
        cout << "Setting strm1 to unbuffered" << endl;
        setbuf(strm1, NULL);
        cout << "Setting strm2 to buffered" << endl;
        setbuf( strm2, buf);
        cout << "Now closing files" << endl;
        fclose(strm1);
        fclose(strm2);
    }

    return 0;
}
```

CROSS-REFERENCE
See also setvbuf().

setjmp()

Function

The setjmp() function saves the current stack environment (and thus a program's status).

Header File

```
#include <setjmp.h>
```

Declaration

```
int setjmp(jmp_buf env);
```

- *env* — The area in which the stack environment is saved.

Example

The following program demonstrates how to use the setjmp() function. The program's output looks like this:

```
Saving stack environment
Press any key to continue
```

Here is the program source code that produced the output:

```
#include "stdafx.h"
#include <setjmp.h>
#include <iostream>

using namespace std;

int main(int argc, char* argv[])
{
    jmp_buf stackEnv;

    cout << "Saving stack environment" << endl;
    int result = setjmp(stackEnv);

    return 0;
}
```

CROSS-REFERENCE
See also _setjmp() and longjmp().

setlocale()

Function

The setlocale() function sets various elements of the current locale, returning a pointer to a locale string, or NULL if the call is unsuccessful.

Header File

```
#include <locale.h>
```

Declaration

```
char* setlocale(int category, const char *locale);
```

- *category*— The element of the locale that should be changed, which can be a value from Table S-11.

- *locale*— A pointer to the name of the locale from the list in Table S-12. This can also be "C", which selects the default values for the system.

Table S-11 Locale Category Values for setlocale()

Value	Description
LC_ALL	Set all categories.
LC_COLLATE	Set the locale category associated with the strcoll( ), _stricoll( ), wcscoll( ), _wcsicoll( ), wcsxfrm( ), and strxfrm( ) functions.
LC_CTYPE	Set the locale category associated with character functions.
LC_MONETARY	Set the locale category that affects monetary formatting.
LC_NUMERIC	Set the locale category that affects decimal points.
LC_TIME	Set the locale category that affects time functions.

Table S-12 Locale Names for setlocale()

Language	Name
Chinese	"chinese"
Chinese (simplified)	"chinese-simplified" or "chs"
Chinese (traditional)	"chinese-traditional" or "cht"
Czech	"czech" or "csy"
Danish	"danish" or "dan"
Dutch	"dutch" or "nld"
Dutch (Belgian)	"belgian", "dutch-belgian", or "nlb"
English (default)	"english"
English (Australian)	"australian", "ena", or "english-aus"
English (Canadian)	"canadian", "enc", or "english-can"
English (New Zealand)	"english-nz" or "enz"
English (UK)	"english-uk", "eng", or "uk"
English (USA)	"american", "american english", "american-english", "english-american", "english-us", "english-usa", "enu", "us", or "usa"
Finnish	"finnish" or "fin"
French (default)	"french" or "fra"
French (Belgian)	"french-belgian" or "frb"

Continued

Table S-12 *Continued*

Language	Name
French (Canadian)	"french-canadian" or "frc"
French (Swiss)	"french-swiss" or "frs"
German (default)	"german" or "deu"
German (Austrian)	"german-austrian" or "dea"
German (Swiss)	"german-swiss", "des", or "swiss"
Greek	"greek" or "ell"
Hungarian	"hungarian" or "hun"
Icelandic	"icelandic" or "isl"
Italian (default)	"italian" or "ita"
Italian (Swiss)	"italian-swiss" or "its"
Japanese	"japanese" or "jpn"
Korean	"kor" or "korean"
Norwegian (default)	"norwegian"
Norwegian (Bokmal)	"norwegian-bokmal" or "nor"
Norwegian (Nynorsk)	"norwegian-nynorsk" or "non"
Polish	"polish" or "plk"
Portuguese (default)	"portuguese" or "ptg"
Portuguese (Brazilian)	"portuguese-brazilian" or "ptb"
Russian (default)	"russian" or "rus"
Slovak	"slovak" or "sky"
Spanish (default)	"spanish" or "esp"
Spanish (Mexican)	"spanish-mexican" or "esm"
Spanish (Modern)	"spanish-modern" or "esn"
Swedish	"swedish" or "sve"
Turkish	"turkish" or "trk"

Example

The following program demonstrates how to use the `setlocale()` function, by setting the locale for several languages and displaying date strings in the selected languages. The program's output looks like this:

```
Result: English_United States.1252
English Date: Tuesday, February 16, 1999

Result: Spanish - Traditional Sort_Spain.1252
Spanish Date: martes, 16 de febrero de 1999

Result: German_Germany.1252
```

German Date: Dienstag, 16. Februar 1999

Result: Dutch_Netherlands.1252
Dutch Date: dinsdag 16 februari 1999

Press any key to continue

Here is the program source code that produced the output:

```
#include "stdafx.h"
#include <locale.h>
#include <time.h>
#include <iostream>

using namespace std;

int main(int argc, char* argv[])
{
    char dateStr[81];
    time_t curTime;
    struct tm* tmTime;

    time (&curTime);
    tmTime = gmtime(&curTime);

    char* result = setlocale(LC_ALL, "English");
    if (result == NULL)
        cout << "Error setting locale" << endl;
    else
    {
        cout << "Result: ";
        cout << result << endl;
        strftime(dateStr, 80, "%#x", tmTime);
        cout << "English Date: ";
        cout << dateStr << endl << endl;
    }

    result = setlocale(LC_ALL, "Spanish");
    if (result == NULL)
        cout << "Error setting locale" << endl;
    else
    {
        cout << "Result: ";
        cout << result << endl;
        strftime(dateStr, 80, "%#x", tmTime);
```

```
                    cout << "Spanish Date: ";
                    cout << dateStr << endl << endl;
                }

                result = setlocale(LC_ALL, "German");
                if (result == NULL)
                    cout << "Error setting locale" << endl;
                else
                {
                    cout << "Result: ";
                    cout << result << endl;
                    strftime(dateStr, 80, "%#x", tmTime);
                    cout << "German Date: ";
                    cout << dateStr << endl << endl;
                }

                result = setlocale(LC_ALL, "Dutch");
                if (result == NULL)
                    cout << "Error setting locale" << endl;
                else
                {
                    cout << "Result: ";
                    cout << result << endl;
                    strftime(dateStr, 80, "%#x", tmTime);
                    cout << "Dutch Date: ";
                    cout << dateStr << endl << endl;
                }

                setlocale(LC_ALL, "C");

                return 0;
            }
```

 **CROSS-REFERENCE**
See also _wsetlocale().

setmode()

Function

The setmode() function sets the translation mode for a file, returning the previous mode if successful, or −1 if unsuccessful.

Header File

```
#include <io.h>
```

Declaration

```
int setmode(int handle, int mode);
```

- *handle* — The handle of the file whose mode will be reset.
- *mode* — The new translation mode, which must be O_BINARY or O_TEXT.

Example

The following program demonstrates how to use the setmode() function, by setting the stdin stream's translation mode to binary. The program's output looks like this:

```
Getting handle for stdin...
Setting stdin stream to binary mode...
Mode successfully set.
Press any key to continue
```

Here is the program source code that produced the output:

```
#include "stdafx.h"
#include <io.h>
#include <fcntl.h>
#include <iostream>

using namespace std;

int main(int argc, char* argv[])
{
    cout << "Getting handle for stdin..." << endl;
    int handle = _fileno(stdin);
    cout << "Setting stdin stream to binary mode..." << endl;
    int result = setmode(handle, O_BINARY);
    if (result != -1 )
        cout << "Mode successfully set." << endl;
    else
        cout << "Mode set error." << endl;

    return 0;
}
```

r
s
t

CROSS-REFERENCE
See also _setmode().

setvbuf()

Function

The setvbuf() function sets a stream to buffered or unbuffered, returning 0 if successful, or a nonzero value if unsuccessful.

Header File

```
#include <stdio.h>
```

Declaration

```
int setvbuf(FILE *stream, char *buffer,
    int mode, size_t size);
```

- *buffer* — A pointer to the memory to use for buffering data.
- *mode* — The buffering mode, which can be _IOFBF (full buffering), _IOLBF (MS-DOS full buffering), or _IONBF (no buffering).
- *size* — The size of the buffer in bytes.
- *stream* — A pointer to the stream for which to set buffering.

Example

The following program demonstrates how to use the setvbuf() function, by opening two streams and setting them to unbuffered and buffered, respectively. The program's output looks like this:

```
Setting strm1 to unbuffered
Setting strm2 to buffered
Now closing files
Press any key to continue
```

Here is the program source code that produced the output:

```
#include "stdafx.h"
#include <stdio.h>
#include <iostream>

using namespace std;
```

```
int main(int argc, char* argv[])
{
    char buf[BUFSIZ];

    FILE* strm1 = fopen("file1", "w");
    FILE* strm2 = fopen("file2", "w" );
    if ((strm1 == NULL) || (strm2 == NULL))
        cout << "File error" << endl;
    else
    {
        cout << "Setting strm1 to unbuffered" << endl;
        int result = setvbuf(strm1, NULL, _IONBF, 0);
        if (result != 0)
            cout << "setvbuf() error" << endl;
        cout << "Setting strm2 to buffered" << endl;
        result = setvbuf( strm2, buf, _IOFBF, sizeof(buf));
        if (result != 0)
            cout << "setvbuf() error" << endl;
        cout << "Now closing files" << endl;
        fclose(strm1);
        fclose(strm2);
    }

    return 0;
}
```

 CROSS-REFERENCE
See also setbuf().

short

Keyword

The short keyword is used to declare 2-byte integer values that can hold values in the range –32,768 to 32,767. For example, the following declares a variable named var1 as a short integer:

```
short var1;
```

 CROSS-REFERENCE
See also char, int, long, signed, and unsigned.

signal.h

Standard C Library Header File

The signal.h header file defines signal constants and signal functions.

Defined Constants

SIG_ACK	SIGBREAK
SIG_DFL	SIGFPE
SIG_ERR	SIGILL
SIG_IGN	SIGINT
SIG_SGE	SIGSEGV
SIGABRT	SIGTERM

Defined Functions

```
raise()
signal()
```

signed

Keyword

The signed keyword is used to declare integer values that can hold positive and negative values. For example, the following declares a variable named var1 as a signed short integer:

```
signed short int var1;
```

Unless specifically declared as unsigned, all integer values are by default signed, which makes it unnecessary to use the signed keyword.

CROSS-REFERENCE

See also char, int, long, short, and unsigned.

sin()

Function

The sin() function returns the sine of its argument.

Header File

```
#include <math.h>
```

Declaration

```
double sin(double num)
```

- *num* — The value for which to return the sine.

Example

The following program demonstrates how to use the sin() function. The program's output looks like this:

```
The sine of 1.387 is 0.983157
Press any key to continue
```

Here is the program source code that produced the output:

```
#include "stdafx.h"
#include <math.h>
#include <iostream>

using namespace std;

int main(int argc, char* argv[])
{
    double var1 = 1.387;
    double result = sin(var1);
    cout << "The sine of " << var1;
    cout << " is " << result << endl;

    return 0;
}
```

CROSS-REFERENCE
See also acos(), asin(), atan2(), cos(), cosh(), sinf(), sinh(), sinhf(), sinhl(), sinl(), tan(), and tanh().

sinf()

Function

The sinf() function returns, as a float value, the sine of its argument.

 NOTE
Borland does not support this function.

Header File

```
#include <math.h>
```

Declaration

```
float sinf(float num)
```

- *num* — The value for which to return the sine.

Example

The following program demonstrates how to use the sinf() function. The program's output looks like this:

```
The sine of 1.387 is 0.983157
Press any key to continue
```

Here is the program source code that produced the output:

```
#include "stdafx.h"
#include <math.h>
#include <iostream>

using namespace std;

int main(int argc, char* argv[])
{
    float var1 = (float)1.387;
    float result = sinf(var1);
    cout << "The sine of " << var1;
    cout << " is " << result << endl;

    return 0;
}
```

CROSS-REFERENCE

See also acos(), asin(), atan2(), cos(), cosh(), sin(), sinh(), sinhf(), sinhl(), sinl(), tan(), and tanh().

sinh()

Function

The `sinh()` function returns the hyperbolic sine of its argument.

Header File

```
#include <math.h>
```

Declaration

```
double sinh(double num)
```

- *num* — The value for which to return the hyperbolic sine.

Example

The following program demonstrates how to use the `sinh()` function. The program's output looks like this:

```
The hyperbolic sine of 1.387 is 1.8765
Press any key to continue
```

Here is the program source code that produced the output:

```
#include "stdafx.h"
#include <math.h>
#include <iostream>

using namespace std;

int main(int argc, char* argv[])
{
    double var1 = 1.387;
    double result = sinh(var1);
    cout << "The hyperbolic sine of " << var1;
    cout << " is " << result << endl;

    return 0;
}
```

CROSS-REFERENCE

See also acos(), asin(), atan2(), cos(), cosh(), sin(), sinf(), sinhf(), sinhl(), sinl(), tan(), and tanh().

sinhf()

Function

The sinhf() function returns, as a float value, the hyperbolic sine of its argument.

NOTE

Borland does not support this function.

Header File

```
#include <math.h>
```

Declaration

```
float sinhf(float num)
```

- *num* — The value for which to return the hyperbolic sine.

Example

The following program demonstrates how to use the sinhf() function. The program's output looks like this:

```
The hyperbolic sine of 1.387 is 1.8765
Press any key to continue
```

Here is the program source code that produced the output:

```
#include "stdafx.h"
#include <math.h>
#include <iostream>

using namespace std;

int main(int argc, char* argv[])
{
    float var1 = (float)1.387;
    float result = sinhf(var1);
```

```
cout << "The hyperbolic sine of " << var1;
cout << " is " << result << endl;

return 0;
}
```

CROSS-REFERENCE
See also acos(), asin(), atan2(), cos(), cosh(), sin(), sinf(), sinh(), sinhl(), sinl(), tan(), and tanh().

sinhl()

Function

The `sinhl()` function returns, as a `long double` value, the hyperbolic sine of its argument.

Header File

```
#include <math.h>
```

Declaration

```
long double sinhl(long double num)
```

- *num* — The value for which to return the hyperbolic sine.

Example

The following program demonstrates how to use the `sinhl()` function. The program's output looks like this:

```
The hyperbolic sine of 1.387 is 1.8765
Press any key to continue
```

Here is the program source code that produced the output:

```
#include "stdafx.h"
#include <math.h>
#include <iostream>

using namespace std;

int main(int argc, char* argv[])
```

```
    {
        long double var1 = 1.387;
        long double result = sinhl(var1);
        cout << "The hyperbolic sine of " << var1;
        cout << " is " << result << endl;

        return 0;
    }
```

CROSS-REFERENCE

See also acos(), asin(), atan2(), cos(), cosh(), sin(), sinf(), sinh(), sinhf(), sinl(), tan(), and tanh().

sinl()

Function

The sinf() function returns, as a long double value, the sine of its argument.

Header File

```
#include <math.h>
```

Declaration

```
long double sinl(long double num)
```

- *num* — The value for which to return the sine.

Example

The following program demonstrates how to use the sinl() function. The program's output looks like this:

```
The sine of 1.387 is 0.983157
Press any key to continue
```

Here is the program source code that produced the output:

```
#include "stdafx.h"
#include <math.h>
#include <iostream>

using namespace std;
```

```
int main(int argc, char* argv[])
{
    long double var1 = 1.387;
    long double result = sinl(var1);
    cout << "The sine of " << var1;
    cout << " is " << result << endl;

    return 0;
}
```

CROSS-REFERENCE
See also acos(), asin(), atan2(), cos(), cosh(), sin(), sinf(), sinh(), sinhf(), sinhl(), tan(), and tanh().

sizeof

Operator

The `sizeof` operator returns the size in bytes of a specified data object.

Syntax

```
sizeof(data)
```

- *data* — The data object for which to obtain the size.

Example

The following program displays the size of char, short int, int, and float values, as well as the size of the user-defined structure MyStruct. The program's output looks like this:

```
A char value is 1 byte
A short value is 2 bytes
An int value is 4 bytes
A float value is 4 bytes
MyStruct is 24 bytes
Press any key to continue
```

Here is the program source code that produced the output:

```
#include "stdafx.h"
```

```
#include <iostream>

using namespace std;

int main(int argc, char* argv[])
{
    struct MyStruct
    {
        int var1;
        int var2;
        int var3;
        double var4;
    } myStruct;

    size_t size = sizeof(char);
    cout << "A char value is " << size << " byte" << endl;
    size = sizeof(short);
    cout << "A short value is " << size << " bytes" << endl;
    size = sizeof(int);
    cout << "An int value is " << size << " bytes" << endl;
    size = sizeof(float);
    cout << "A float value is " << size << " bytes" << endl;
    size = sizeof(myStruct);
    cout << "MyStruct is " << size << " bytes" << endl;

    return 0;
}
```

spawnl()

Function

The spawnl() function runs a child process given the process's path and name and additional arguments. This function returns to the process that called it. If the process is called with the P_WAIT mode, the function returns the process's exit status. If the process is run with the P_NOWAIT or P_NOWAITO mode, the function returns the process handle. If the called process does not run successfully, the function returns –1. In this case, the errno global variable is set to one of the error values in Table S-13.

Table S-13 Error Values for spawnl()

Value	Description
E2BIG	The arguments and environment require more than 32K of space.
EINVAL	Bad execution mode.
ENOENT	The specified file cannot be found.
ENOEXEC	The specified file is not executable.
ENOMEM	Not enough memory to run the process.

Header File

```
#include <process.h>
```

Declaration

```
int spawnl(int mode, const char *cmdname, const char *arg0,
    const char *arg1, ... const char *argn, NULL);
```

- *arg0* — A pointer to the first argument.
- *arg1* — A pointer to the second argument.
- *argn* — A pointer to the last argument.
- *cmdname* — The path and file name of the process to run.
- *mode* — The process's execution mode, which can be P_WAIT, P_NOWAIT, or P_NOWAITO.

Example

The following program demonstrates how to use the spawnl() function. When run, the program runs a child process called TestProg.exe, displaying a message if an error occurs. The program's output looks like this:

```
Running TestProg.exe

Child process running.
Press any key to continue
```

Here is the program source code that produced the output:

```
#include "stdafx.h"
#include <iostream>
```

```cpp
#include <process.h>
#include <errno.h>

using namespace std;

int main(int argc, char* argv[])
{
    cout << "Running TestProg.exe" << endl;

    int result = spawnl(P_WAIT, "TestProg.exe",
        "TestProg.exe", "arg2", "arg3", NULL);
    if (result == -1)
    {
        switch(errno)
        {
        case ENOEXEC:
            cout << "Not an executable file" << endl;
            break;
        case E2BIG:
            cout << "Space required exceeds 32K" << endl;
            break;
        case ENOMEM:
            cout << "Not enough memory" << endl;
            break;
        case EINVAL:
            cout << "Bad execution mode" << endl;
            break;
        case ENOENT:
            cout << "File not found" << endl;
        }
    }

    return 0;
}
```

CROSS-REFERENCE

See also _wexecl(), _wexecle(), _wexeclp(), _wexeclpe(), _wexecv(), _wexecve(), _wexecvp(), _wexecvpe(), _wspawnl(), _wspawnle(), _wspawnlp(), _wspawnlpe(), _wspawnv(), _wspawnve(), _wspawnvp(),_wspawnvpe(), execl(), execle(), execlp(), execlpe(), execv(), execve(), execvp(), execvpe(), spawnle(), spawnlp(), spawnlpe(), spawnv(), spawnve(), spawnvp(), and spawnvpe().

spawnle()

Function

The `spawnle()` function runs a child process given the process's path and name, additional arguments, and environment settings. This function returns to the process that called it. If the process is called with the `P_WAIT` mode, the function returns the process's exit status. If the process is run with the `P_NOWAIT` or `P_NOWAITO` mode, the function returns the process handle. If the called process does not run successfully, the function returns –1. In this case, the `errno` global variable is set to one of the error values in Table S-14.

Table S-14 Error Values for spawnle()

value	Description
E2BIG	The arguments and environment require more than 32K of space.
EINVAL	Bad execution mode.
ENOENT	The specified file cannot be found.
ENOEXEC	The specified file is not executable.
ENOMEM	Not enough memory to run the process.

Header File

```
#include <process.h>
```

Declaration

```
int spawnle(int mode, const char *cmdname, const char *arg0,
    const char *arg1, ... const char *argn,
    NULL, const char *const *envp);
```

- *arg0* — A pointer to the first argument.
- *arg1* — A pointer to the second argument.
- *argn* — A pointer to the last argument.
- *cmdname* — The path and file name of the process to run.
- *envp* — A pointer to the environment settings.
- *mode* — The process's execution mode, which can be `P_WAIT`, `P_NOWAIT`, or `P_NOWAITO`.

r

s

t

Example

The following program demonstrates how to use the spawnle() function. When run, the program runs a child process called TestProg.exe, displaying a message if an error occurs. The program's output looks like this:

```
Running TestProg.exe

Child process running.
Press any key to continue
```

Here is the program source code that produced the output:

```cpp
#include "stdafx.h"
#include <iostream>
#include <process.h>
#include <errno.h>

using namespace std;

char *envir[] =
{
    "ENVIR1=environment setting 1",
    "ENVIR2=environment setting 2",
    "ENVIR3=environment setting 3",
     NULL
};

int main(int argc, char* argv[])
{
    cout << "Running TestProg.exe" << endl;

    int result = spawnle(P_WAIT, "TestProg.exe",
        "TestProg.exe", "arg2", "arg3", NULL, envir);
    if (result == -1)
    {
        switch(errno)
        {
        case ENOEXEC:
            cout << "Not an executable file" << endl;
            break;
        case E2BIG:
            cout << "Space required exceeds 32K" << endl;
            break;
        case ENOMEM:
            cout << "Not enough memory" << endl;
```

```
                break;
            case EINVAL:
                cout << "Bad execution mode" << endl;
                break;
            case ENOENT:
                cout << "File not found" << endl;
            }
        }

        return 0;
    }
```

CROSS-REFERENCE
See also _wexecl(), _wexecle(), _wexeclp(), _wexeclpe(), _wexecv(), _wexecve(), _wexecvp(), _wexecvpe(), _wspawnl(), _wspawnle(), _wspawnlp(), _wspawnlpe(), _wspawnv(), _wspawnve(), _wspawnvp(),_wspawnvpe(), execl(), execle(), execlp(), execlpe(), execv(), execve(), execvp(), execvpe(), spawnl(), spawnlp(), spawnlpe(), spawnv(), spawnve(), spawnvp(), and spawnvpe().

spawnlp()

Function

The spawnlp() function runs a child process given the process's path and name and additional arguments. This function returns to the process that called it. If the process is called with the P_WAIT mode, the function returns the process's exit status. If the process is run with the P_NOWAIT or P_NOWAITO mode, the function returns the process handle. If the called process does not run successfully, the function returns −1. In this case, the errno global variable is set to one of the error values in Table S-15.

Table S-15 Error Values forspawnlp()

Error	Description
E2BIG	The arguments and environment require more than 32K of space.
EINVAL	Bad execution mode.
ENOENT	The specified file cannot be found.
ENOEXEC	The specified file is not executable.
ENOMEM	Not enough memory to run the process.

r
s
t

Header File

```
#include <process.h>
```

Declaration

```
int spawnlp(int mode, const char *cmdname, const char *arg0,
    const char *arg1, ... const char *argn, NULL );
```

- *arg0* — A pointer to the first argument.
- *arg1* — A pointer to the second argument.
- *argn* — A pointer to the last argument.
- *cmdname* — The path and file name of the process to run.
- *mode* — The process's execution mode, which can be P_WAIT, P_NOWAIT, or P_NOWAITO.

Example

The following program demonstrates how to use the spawnlp() function. When run, the program runs a child process called TestProg.exe, displaying a message if an error occurs.

```
Running TestProg.exe

Child process running.
Press any key to continue
```

Here is the program source code that produced the output:

```
#include "stdafx.h"
#include <iostream>
#include <process.h>
#include <errno.h>

using namespace std;

int main(int argc, char* argv[])
{
    cout << "Running TestProg.exe" << endl;

    int result = spawnlp(P_WAIT, "TestProg.exe",
        "TestProg.exe", "arg2", "arg3", NULL);
    if (result == -1)
    {
```

```
        switch(errno)
        {
        case ENOEXEC:
            cout << "Not an executable file" << endl;
            break;
        case E2BIG:
            cout << "Space required exceeds 32K" << endl;
            break;
        case ENOMEM:
            cout << "Not enough memory" << endl;
            break;
        case EINVAL:
            cout << "Bad execution mode" << endl;
            break;
        case ENOENT:
            cout << "File not found" << endl;
        }
    }

    return 0;
}
```

CROSS-REFERENCE
See also _wexecl(), _wexecle(), _wexeclp(), _wexeclpe(), _wexecv(), _wexecve(), _wexecvp(), _wexecvpe(), _wspawnl(), _wspawnle(), _wspawnlp(), _wspawnlpe(), _wspawnv(), _wspawnve(), _wspawnvp(),_wspawnvpe(), execl(), execle(), execlp(), execlpe(), execv(), execve(), execvp(), execvpe(), spawnl(), spawnle(), spawnlpe(), spawnv(), spawnve(), spawnvp(), and spawnvpe().

spawnlpe()

Function

The spawnlpe() function runs a child process given the process's path and name, additional arguments, and environment settings. This function returns to the process that called it. If the process is called with the P_WAIT mode, the function returns the process's exit status. If the process is run with the P_NOWAIT or P_NOWAITO mode, the function returns the process handle. If the called process does not run successfully, the function returns –1. In this case, the errno global variable is set to one of the error values in Table S-16.

Table S-16 Error Values for spawnlpe()

Value	Description
E2BIG	The arguments and environment require more than 32K of space.
EINVAL	Bad execution mode.
ENOENT	The specified file cannot be found.
ENOEXEC	The specified file is not executable.
ENOMEM	Not enough memory to run the process.

Header File

```
#include <process.h>
```

Declaration

```
int spawnlpe(int mode, const char *cmdname, const char *arg0,
    const char *arg1, ... const char *argn,
    NULL, const char *const *envp);
```

- *arg0* — A pointer to the first argument.
- *arg1* — A pointer to the second argument.
- *argn* — A pointer to the last argument.
- *cmdname* — The path and file name of the process to run.
- *envp* — A pointer to the environment settings.
- *mode* — The process's execution mode, which can be P_WAIT, P_NOWAIT, or P_NOWAITO.

Example

The following program demonstrates how to use the spawnlpe() function. When run, the program runs a child process called TestProg.exe, displaying a message if an error occurs. The program's output looks like this:

```
Running TestProg.exe

Child process running.
Press any key to continue
```

Here is the program source code that produced the output:

```
#include "stdafx.h"
#include <iostream>
```

```cpp
#include <process.h>
#include <errno.h>

using namespace std;

char *envir[] =
{
   "ENVIR1=environment setting 1",
   "ENVIR2=environment setting 2",
   "ENVIR3=environment setting 3",
    NULL
};

int main(int argc, char* argv[])
{
    cout << "Running TestProg.exe" << endl;

    int result = spawnlpe(P_WAIT, "TestProg.exe",
        "TestProg.exe", "arg2", "arg3", NULL, envir);
    if (result == -1)
    {
        switch(errno)
        {
        case ENOEXEC:
            cout << "Not an executable file" << endl;
            break;
        case E2BIG:
            cout << "Space required exceeds 32K" << endl;
            break;
        case ENOMEM:
            cout << "Not enough memory" << endl;
            break;
        case EINVAL:
            cout << "Bad execution mode" << endl;
            break;
        case ENOENT:
            cout << "File not found" << endl;
        }
    }

    return 0;
}
```

CROSS-REFERENCE

See also _wexecl(), _wexecle(), _wexeclp(), _wexeclpe(), _wexecv(), _wexecve(), _wexecvp(), _wexecvpe(), _wspawnl(), _wspawnle(), _wspawnlp(), _wspawnlpe(), _wspawnv(), _wspawnve(), _wspawnvp(),_wspawnvpe(), execl(), execle(), execlp(), execlpe(), execv(), execve(), execvp(), execvpe(), spawnl(), spawnle(), spawnlp(), spawnv(), spawnve(), spawnvp(), and spawnvpe().

spawnv()

Function

The spawnv() function runs a child process given the process's path and name and additional arguments supplied as an array of char pointers. This function returns to the process that called it. If the process is called with the P_WAIT mode, the function returns the process's exit status. If the process is run with the P_NOWAIT or P_NOWAITO mode, the function returns the process handle. If the called process does not run successfully, the function returns –1. In this case, the errno global variable is set to one of the error values in Table S-17.

Table S-17 Error Values for spawnv()

Error	Description
E2BIG	The arguments and environment require more than 32K of space.
EINVAL	Bad execution mode.
ENOENT	The specified file cannot be found.
ENOEXEC	The specified file is not executable.
ENOMEM	Not enough memory to run the process.

Header File

```
#include <process.h>
```

Declaration

```
int spawnv(int mode, const char *cmdname,
    const char *const *argv);
```

- *argv* — A pointer to an array of char pointers that point to the arguments.
- *cmdname* — The path and file name of the process to run.

- *mode* — The process's execution mode, which can be P_WAIT, P_NOWAIT, or P_NOWAITO.

Example

The following program demonstrates how to use the spawnv() function. When run, the program runs a child process called TestProg.exe, displaying a message if an error occurs.

```
Running TestProg.exe

Child process running.
Press any key to continue
```

Here is the program source code that produced the output:

```cpp
#include "stdafx.h"
#include <iostream>
#include <process.h>
#include <errno.h>

using namespace std;

int main(int argc, char* argv[])
{
    char* args[] =
    {
        "TestProg.exe",
        "argument #1",
        "argument #2",
         NULL
    };

    cout << "Running TestProg.exe" << endl;

    int result = spawnv(P_WAIT, "TestProg.exe", args);
    if (result == -1)
    {
        switch(errno)
        {
        case ENOEXEC:
            cout << "Not an executable file" << endl;
            break;
        case E2BIG:
            cout << "Space required exceeds 32K" << endl;
            break;
```

```
                                case ENOMEM:
                                    cout << "Not enough memory" << endl;
                                    break;
                                case EINVAL:
                                    cout << "Bad execution mode" << endl;
                                    break;
                                case ENOENT:
                                    cout << "File not found" << endl;
                                }
                        }

                        return 0;
                }
```

CROSS-REFERENCE

See also _wexecl(), _wexecle(), _wexeclp(), _wexeclpe(), _wexecv(), _wexecve(), _wexecvp(), _wexecvpe(), _wspawnl(), _wspawnle(), _wspawnlp(), _wspawnlpe(), _wspawnv(), _wspawnve(), _wspawnvp(),_wspawnvpe(), execl(), execle(), execlp(), execlpe(), execv(), execve(), execvp(), execvpe(), spawnl(), spawnle(), spawnlp(), spawnlpe(), spawnve(), spawnvp(), and spawnvpe().

spawnve()

Function

The spawnve() function runs a child process given the process's path and name, and additional arguments and environment settings supplied as an array of char pointers. This function returns to the process that called it. If the process is called with the P_WAIT mode, the function returns the process's exit status. If the process is run with the P_NOWAIT or P_NOWAITO mode, the function returns the process handle. If the called process does not run successfully, the function returns –1. In this case, the errno global variable is set to one of the error values in Table S-18.

Table S-18 Error Values for spawnve()

Value	Description
E2BIG	The arguments and environment require more than 32K of space.
EINVAL	Bad execution mode.
ENOENT	The specified file cannot be found.
ENOEXEC	The specified file is not executable.
ENOMEM	Not enough memory to run the process.

Header File

```
#include <process.h>
```

Declaration

```
int spawnve(int mode, const char *cmdname,
    const char *const *argv, const char *const *envp);
```

- *argv* — A pointer to an array of `char` pointers that point to the arguments.
- *cmdname* — The path and file name of the process to run.
- *envp* — A pointer to an array of `char` pointers that point to the environment settings.
- *mode* — The process's execution mode, which can be `P_WAIT`, `P_NOWAIT`, or `P_NOWAITO`.

Example

The following program demonstrates how to use the `spawnve()` function. When run, the program runs a child process called TestProg.exe, displaying a message if an error occurs. The program's output looks like this:

```
Running TestProg.exe

Child process running.
Press any key to continue
```

Here is the program source code that produced the output:

```
#include "stdafx.h"
#include <iostream>
#include <process.h>
#include <errno.h>

using namespace std;

char* envir[] =
{
    "ENVIR1=environment setting 1",
    "ENVIR2=environment setting 2",
    "ENVIR3=environment setting 3",
    NULL
};
```

```
            char* args[] =
            {
                "TestProg.exe",
                "argument #1",
                "argument #2",
                 NULL
            };

            int main(int argc, char* argv[])
            {
                cout << "Running TestProg.exe" << endl;

                int result = spawnve(P_WAIT, "TestProg.exe",
                    args, envir);
                if (result == -1)
                {
                    switch(errno)
                    {
                    case ENOEXEC:
                        cout << "Not an executable file" << endl;
                        break;
                    case E2BIG:
                        cout << "Space required exceeds 32K" << endl;
                        break;
                    case ENOMEM:
                        cout << "Not enough memory" << endl;
                        break;
                    case EINVAL:
                        cout << "Bad execution mode" << endl;
                        break;
                    case ENOENT:
                        cout << "File not found" << endl;
                    }
                }

                return 0;
            }
```

CROSS-REFERENCE

See also _wexecl(), _wexecle(), _wexeclp(), _wexeclpe(), _wexecv(), _wexecve(), _wexecvp(), _wexecvpe(), _wspawnl(), _wspawnle(), _wspawnlp(), _wspawnlpe(), _wspawnv(), _wspawnve(), _wspawnvp(),_wspawnvpe(), execl(), execle(), execlp(), execlpe(), execv(), execve(), execvp(), execvpe(), spawnl(), spawnle(), spawnlp(), spawnlpe(), spawnv(), spawnvp(), and spawnvpe().

spawnvp()

Function

The `spawnvp()` function runs a child process given the process's path and name and additional arguments supplied as an array of `char` pointers. This function returns to the process that called it. If the process is called with the `P_WAIT` mode, the function returns the process's exit status. If the process is run with the `P_NOWAIT` or `P_NOWAITO` mode, the function returns the process handle. If the called process does not run successfully, the function returns −1. In this case, the `errno` global variable is set to one of the error values in Table S-19.

Table S-19 Error Values for spawnvp()

Value	Description
E2BIG	The arguments and environment require more than 32K of space.
EINVAL	Bad execution mode.
ENOENT	The specified file cannot be found.
ENOEXEC	The specified file is not executable.
ENOMEM	Not enough memory to run the process.

Header File

```
#include <process.h>
```

Declaration

```
int spawnvp(int mode, const char *cmdname,
    const char *const *argv);
```

- *argv* — A pointer to an array of `char` pointers that point to the arguments.
- *cmdname* — The path and file name of the process to run.
- *mode* — The process's execution mode, which can be `P_WAIT`, `P_NOWAIT`, or `P_NOWAITO`.

Example

The following program demonstrates how to use the `spawnvp()` function. When run, the program runs a child process called TestProg.exe, displaying a message if an error occurs. The program's output looks like this:

```
Running TestProg.exe

Child process running.
Press any key to continue
```

Here is the program source code that produced the output:

```cpp
#include "stdafx.h"
#include <iostream>
#include <process.h>
#include <errno.h>

using namespace std;

int main(int argc, char* argv[])
{
    char* args[] =
    {
        "TestProg.exe",
        "argument #1",
        "argument #2",
         NULL
    };

    cout << "Running TestProg.exe" << endl;

    int result = spawnvp(P_WAIT, "TestProg.exe", args);
    if (result == -1)
    {
        switch(errno)
        {
        case ENOEXEC:
            cout << "Not an executable file" << endl;
            break;
        case E2BIG:
            cout << "Space required exceeds 32K" << endl;
            break;
        case ENOMEM:
            cout << "Not enough memory" << endl;
            break;
        case EINVAL:
            cout << "Bad execution mode" << endl;
            break;
        case ENOENT:
```

```
                    cout << "File not found" << endl;
                }
            }

        return 0;
    }
```

CROSS-REFERENCE
See also _wexecl(), _wexecle(), _wexeclp(), _wexeclpe(), _wexecv(), _wexecve(),
_wexecvp(), _wexecvpe(), _wspawnl(), _wspawnle(), _wspawnlp(), _wspawnlpe(),
_wspawnv(), _wspawnve(), _wspawnvp(),_wspawnvpe(), execl(), execle(), execlp(),
execlpe(), execv(), execve(), execvp(), execvpe(), spawnl(), spawnle(), spawnlp(),
spawnlpe(), spawnv(), spawnve(), and spawnvpe().

spawnvpe()

Function

The spawnvpe() function runs a child process given the process's path and
name, and additional arguments and environment settings supplied as an
array of char pointers. This function returns to the process that called it. If the
process is called with the _P_WAIT mode, the function returns the process's
exit status. If the process is run with the _P_NOWAIT or _P_NOWAITO mode, the
function returns the process handle. If the called process does not run successfully, the function returns –1. In this case, the errno global variable is set
to one of the error values in Table S-20.

Table S-20 Error Values for spawnvpe()

Value	Description
E2BIG	The arguments and environment require more than 32K of space.
EINVAL	Bad execution mode.
ENOENT	The specified file cannot be found.
ENOEXEC	The specified file is not executable.
ENOMEM	Not enough memory to run the process.

Header File

```
#include <process.h>
```

Declaration

```
int spawnvpe(int mode, const char *cmdname,
    const char *const *argv, const char *const *envp);
```

- *argv* — A pointer to an array of `char` pointers that point to the arguments.
- *cmdname* — The path and file name of the process to run.
- *envp* — A pointer to an array of `char` pointers that point to the environment settings.
- *mode* — The process's execution mode, which can be `P_WAIT`, `P_NOWAIT`, or `P_NOWAITO`.

Example

The following program demonstrates how to use the `spawnvpe()` function. When run, the program runs a child process called TestProg.exe, displaying a message if an error occurs. The program's output looks like this:

```
Running TestProg.exe

Child process running.
Press any key to continue
```

Here is the program source code that produced the output:

```
#include "stdafx.h"
#include <iostream>
#include <process.h>
#include <errno.h>

using namespace std;

char* envir[] =
{
    "ENVIR1=environment setting 1",
    "ENVIR2=environment setting 2",
    "ENVIR3=environment setting 3",
     NULL
};

char* args[] =
{
    "TestProg.exe",
    "argument #1",
```

```cpp
        "argument #2",
        NULL
};

int main(int argc, char* argv[])
{
    cout << "Running TestProg.exe" << endl;

    int result = spawnvpe("TestProg.exe", args, envir);
    if (result == -1)
    {
        switch(errno)
        {
        case ENOEXEC:
            cout << "Not an executable file" << endl;
            break;
        case E2BIG:
            cout << "Space required exceeds 32K" << endl;
            break;
        case ENOMEM:
            cout << "Not enough memory" << endl;
            break;
        case EMFILE:
            cout << "Too many files open" << endl;
            break;
        case EACCES:
            cout << "Locking or sharing violation" << endl;
            break;
        case ENOENT:
            cout << "File not found" << endl;
        }
    }

    return 0;
}
```

CROSS-REFERENCE

See also _wexecl(), _wexecle(), _wexeclp(), _wexeclpe(), _wexecv(), _wexecve(),
_wexecvp(), _wexecvpe(), _wspawnl(), _wspawnle(), _wspawnlp(), _wspawnlpe(),
_wspawnv(), _wspawnve(), _wspawnvp(),_wspawnvpe(), execl(), execle(), execlp(),
execlpe(), execv(), execve(), execvp(), execvpe(), spawnl(), spawnle(), spawnlp(),
spawnlpe(), spawnv(), spawnve(), and spawnvp().

sprintf()

Function

The sprintf() function creates a formatted string, returning the number of bytes written to the string.

Header File

```
#include <stdio.h>
```

Declaration

```
int sprintf(char *buffer,
    const char *format [, argument] ...);
```

- *argument* — A list of arguments that match the format specifiers in the format string.
- *buffer* — A pointer to the buffer that will receive the formatted string.
- *format* — The format string, which can use the format specifiers shown in Table S-21.

Table S-21 Format Specifiers for sprintf()

Specifier	Description
%c	Specifies a character.
%C	Specifies a wide character (printf()) or single-byte character (wprintf()).
%d	Specifies a signed decimal integer.
%e	Specifies a signed double-precision floating-point value using scientific notation with a lowercase e.
%E	Specifies a signed double-precision floating-point value using scientific notation with an uppercase E.
%f	Specifies a signed double-precision floating-point value.
%g	Specifies a signed double-precision floating-point value using either normal notation or scientific notation with a lowercase e.
%G	Specifies a signed double-precision floating-point value using either normal notation or scientific notation with an uppercase E.
%I	Specifies a signed decimal integer.
%n	Specifies an integer pointer.
%o	Specifies an unsigned octal integer.
%p	Specifies a void pointer.

Specifier	Description
%s	Specifies a string.
%S	Specifies a wide-character string (printf( )) or single-byte-character string (wprintf( )).
%u	Specifies an unsigned decimal integer.
%x	Specifies an unsigned hexadecimal integer with lowercase letters.
%X	Specifies an unsigned hexadecimal integer with uppercase letters.

Example

The following program demonstrates how to use the sprintf() function. The program's output looks like this:

```
sprintf() results:
  This is a test: 256


Press any key to continue
```

Here is the program source code that produced the output:

```
#include "stdafx.h"
#include <stdio.h>
#include <iostream>

using namespace std;

int main(int argc, char* argv[])
{
    char dstStr[81];

    memset(dstStr, 0, sizeof(dstStr));
    sprintf(dstStr, "This is a test: %i\n", 256);
    cout << "sprintf() results: " << endl << "  ";
    cout << dstStr << endl;

    return 0;
}
```

CROSS-REFERENCE

See also _fputchar(), _fputwchar(), _vsnprintf(), _vsnwprintf(), fprintf(), fputc(), fputs(), fputwc(), fputws(), fwprintf(), printf(), swprintf(), vfprintf(), vfwprintf(), vprintf(), vsprintf(), vswprintf(), vwprintf(), and wprintf().

sqrt()

Function

The sqrt() function returns the square root of a given value.

Header File

```
#include <math.h>
```

Declaration

```
double sqrt(double x);
```

- x — The value for which to find the square root.

Example

The following program demonstrates how to use the sqrt() function. The program's output looks like this:

```
The square root of 25 is 5
The square root of 37.98 is 6.16279
Press any key to continue
```

Here is the program source code that produced the output:

```cpp
#include "stdafx.h"
#include <math.h>
#include <iostream>

using namespace std;

int main(int argc, char* argv[])
{
    int var1 = 25;
    double var2 = 37.98;
    double result = sqrt(var1);
    cout << "The square root of " << var1;
    cout << " is " << result << endl;
    result = sqrt(var2);
    cout << "The square root of " << var2;
    cout << " is " << result << endl;

    return 0;
}
```

CROSS-REFERENCE
See also exp(), log(), and pow().

srand()

Function

The srand() function seeds the random-number generator with the value at which random numbers should begin to be generated.

Header File

```
#include <stdlib.h>
```

Declaration

```
void srand(unsigned int seed);
```

- *seed*— The seed value for the random-number generator.

Example

The following program demonstrates how to use the srand() function, by seeding the random-number generator with the current time and then generating and displaying a few random numbers. The program's output looks like this:

```
Random number 0 is 21356
Random number 1 is 22846
Random number 2 is 11639
Random number 3 is 22319
Random number 4 is 8336
Press any key to continue
```

Here is the program source code that produced the output:

```
#include "stdafx.h"
#include <stdlib.h>
#include<time.h>
#include <iostream>

using namespace std;

int main(int argc, char* argv[])
```

```
{
    time_t curTime;

    time(&curTime);
    srand(curTime);

    for (int x=0; x<5; ++x)
    {
        int val = rand();
        cout << "Random number " << x;
        cout << " is " << val << endl;
    }

    return 0;
}
```

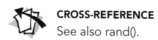

CROSS-REFERENCE
See also rand().

sscanf()

Function

The sscanf() function accepts formatted data from a string, transferring the data to variables based on the supplied format specifiers. The function returns the number of data items successfully received.

Header File

```
#include <stdio.h>
```

Declaration

```
int sscanf(const char *buffer,
    const char *format [, argument ] ...);
```

- *argument*—A list of data items that match the format specifiers included in the format string, *format*.
- *buffer*—The address of the buffer that contains the string to read.
- *format*—The format string, which can include the format specifiers shown in Table S-22.

Table S-22 Format Specifiers for sscanf()

Specifier	Description
%c	Specifies a character.
%C	Specifies a wide character (`printf()`) or single-byte character (`wprintf()`).
%d	Specifies a signed decimal integer.
%e	Specifies a signed double-precision floating-point value using scientific notation with a lowercase e.
%E	Specifies a signed double-precision floating-point value using scientific notation with an uppercase E.
%f	Specifies a signed double-precision floating-point value.
%g	Specifies a signed double-precision floating-point value using either normal notation or scientific notation with a lowercase e.
%G	Specifies a signed double-precision floating-point value using either normal notation or scientific notation with an uppercase E.
%I	Specifies a signed decimal integer.
%n	Specifies an integer pointer.
%o	Specifies an unsigned octal integer.
%p	Specifies a void pointer.
%s	Specifies a string.
%S	Specifies a wide-character string (`printf()`) or single-byte-character string (`wprintf()`).
%u	Specifies an unsigned decimal integer.
%x	Specifies an unsigned hexadecimal integer with lowercase letters.
%X	Specifies an unsigned hexadecimal integer with uppercase letters.

Example

The following program demonstrates how to use the `sscanf()` function. When run, the program calls `sscanf()` to input two data items: an integer and a string. The program's output looks like this:

```
str = Test
var1 = 25
Items received: 2

Press any key to continue
```

Here is the program source code that produced the output:

```
#include "stdafx.h"
#include <stdio.h>
```

```
#include <iostream>

using namespace std;

int main(int argc, char* argv[])
{
    char buf[] = "Test 25";
    char str[10];
    int var1;

    int num = sscanf(buf, "%s %d", str, &var1);
    cout << "str = " << str << endl;
    cout << "var1 = " << var1 << endl;
    cout << "Items received: " << num << endl << endl;

    return 0;
}
```

CROSS-REFERENCE
See also cprintf(), cscanf(), fprintf(), fscanf(), fwprintf(), printf(), scanf(), swprintf(), swscanf(), vfprintf(), vfwprintf(), vprintf(), vsprintf(), vswprintf(), vwprintf(), wprintf(), and wscanf().

sstream

Standard C++ Library Header File

The sstream library header file defines the `basic_stringbuf`, `basic_istringstream`, `basic_ostringstream`, and `basic_stringstream` template classes, which implement various iostream operations.

CROSS-REFERENCE
See also basic_istringstream, basic_ostringstream, basic_stringbuf, and basic_stringstream.

stack

Template class

The stack template class represents an object for manipulating data in a stack.

Class Declaration

```
template<class T,
    class Cont = deque<T> >
class stack
{
public:
    typedef Cont::allocator_type allocator_type;
    typedef Cont::value_type value_type;
    typedef Cont::size_type size_type;
    explicit stack(const allocator_type&
        al = allocator_type()) const;
    bool empty() const;
    size_type size() const;
    allocator_type get_allocator() const;
    value_type& top();
    const value_type& top() const;
    void push(const value_type& x);
    void pop();
protected:
    Cont c;
};
```

Class Members

Table S-23 lists and describes the members of the stack template class.

Table S-23 Members of the stack Template Class

Member	Description
allocator_type	Represents the allocator's data type.
empty()	Returns true if the stack is empty.
get_allocator()	Returns the allocator.
pop()	Removes an element from the stack.
push()	Places an element onto the stack.
size()	Returns the length of the sequence.
size_type	Represents an unsigned integer used to represent the size of the stack.
top()	Returns the value on the top of the stack.
value_type	Represents a data type for an element in the stack.

r
s
t

CROSS-REFERENCE
See also deque, list, and vector.

static

Keyword

The static keyword enables a program to declare that a variable should remain in memory from the moment the program starts to the moment it's terminated. This is called *static duration*. A static variable obeys the rules of scope, but its value is not lost when the variable goes out of scope because the variable is not deleted from memory. The following program shows how a static variable retains its value even when going out of scope. The program's output looks like this:

```
var1 = 1
var1 = 2
var1 = 3
var1 = 4
var1 = 5
Press any key to continue
```

Here is the program source code that produced the output:

```cpp
#include "stdafx.h"
#include <iostream>

using namespace std;

void MyFunc()
{
    static int var1 = 0;

    ++var1;
    cout << "var1 = " << var1 << endl;
}

int main(int argc, char* argv[])
{
    for (int x=0; x<5; ++x)
        MyFunc();

    return 0;
}
```

The `static` keyword can also be used with functions and class members. In the case of a function, the `static` keyword makes the function invisible from outside of the file in which it's defined. When a class data member is declared as `static`, only one copy of the member is shared between all objects instantiated from the class. Static member functions, on the other hand, can be called without instantiating an object of the class. However, such functions can call only other static member functions and access only static data members. This is because an instance of the class has not yet been created, which means that nonstatic members do not yet exist. The following program demonstrates a static member function in a class named `MyClass`. The program's output looks like this:

```
In MemFunc()
Press any key to continue
```

Here is the program source code that produced the output:

```cpp
#include "stdafx.h"
#include <iostream>

using namespace std;

class MyClass
{
public:
    MyClass(){};
    ~MyClass(){};

    static void MemFunc()
    {
        cout << "In MemFunc()" << endl;
    };
};

int main(int argc, char* argv[])
{
    MyClass::MemFunc();

    return 0;
}
```

Note the syntax used in `main()` to call the static member function `MemFunc()`. The function call starts with the name of the class and is followed by a double colon (`::`) and the name of the function. Note also that the program creates no instance of the `MyClass` class, but can still call the static member function.

CROSS-REFERENCE
See also auto, extern, register, and Scope.

static_cast

Operator

The `static_cast` operator enables a program to cast one type to another without regard to whether the conversion is safe.

Syntax

```
static_cast<typeid>(expression)
```

- *expression* — The data object to cast.
- *typeid* — The type to which to cast *expression*.

Example

The following program creates an instance of the `MyClass` class and then uses the `static_cast` operator to cast the `MyClass` pointer to a `MyDerivedClass` pointer. The program's output looks like this:

```
Performing cast...
Press any key to continue
```

Here is the program source code that produced the output:

```
#include "stdafx.h"
#include <iostream>

using namespace std;

class MyClass
{
public:
    MyClass(){};
    ~MyClass(){};
};

class MyDerivedClass: public MyClass
{
public:
```

```
        MyDerivedClass(){};
        ~MyDerivedClass(){};
    };

    int main(int argc, char* argv[])
    {
        MyClass* myClass = new MyClass;
        cout << "Performing cast..." << endl;
        MyDerivedClass* myDerivedClass =
            static_cast<MyDerivedClass*>(myClass);
        delete myClass;

        return 0;
    }
```

Note the syntax for the static_cast operator. The static_cast keyword is followed by angle brackets within which is specified the resultant type of the cast. That is followed by the source expression enclosed in parentheses. For example, in the sample program, the pointer myClass is being cast as a pointer to MyDerivedClass (which, by the way, is not a safe cast).

 CROSS-REFERENCE
See also dynamic_cast.

stdarg.h

Standard C Library Header File

The stdarg.h library header file defines the va_arg(), va_end(), and va_start() macros for implementing variable-length argument lists.

 CROSS-REFERENCE
See also va_arg(), va_end(), and va_start().

stddef.h

Standard C Library Header File

The stddef.h library header file defines frequently used constants, functions, and data types.

Defined Constants

```
NULL
```

Defined Functions

```
__threadid()
__threadhandle()
```

Defined Data Types

```
ptrdiff_t
size_t
wchar_t
```

stderr

Stream

The stderr stream is the standard error output stream, which, by default, displays its output on the screen. The following program, for example, displays the string "This is a test" on the screen. The program's output looks like this:

```
This is a test
Press any key to continue
```

Here is the program source code that produced the output:

```
#include "stdafx.h"
#include <iostream>

using namespace std;

int main(int argc, char* argv[])
{
    fputs("This is a test\n", stderr);

    return 0;
}
```

CROSS-REFERENCE
See also stdin and stdout.

stdexcept

Standard C++ Library Header File

The stdexcept library header file defines classes used for exception management. The classes defined are logic_error, domain_error, invalid_argument, length_error, out_of_range, runtime_error, range_error, overflow_error, and underflow_error.

CROSS-REFERENCE
See also exception.

stdin

Stream

The stdin stream is the standard input stream, which, by default, gets its input from the keyboard. The following program, for example, retrieves and displays a string from the keyboard. The program's output looks something like this:

```
Enter a string: This is a test
This is a test

Press any key to continue
```

Here is the program source code that produced the output:

```cpp
#include "stdafx.h"
#include <iostream>

using namespace std;

int main(int argc, char* argv[])
{
    char buf[81];

    cout << "Enter a string: ";
    fgets(buf, sizeof(buf), stdin);
    cout << buf << endl;

    return 0;
}
```

CROSS-REFERENCE
See also stderr and stdout.

stdio.h

Standard C Library Header File

The stdio.h library header file defines the common constants, functions, data types, structures, and macros needed for file I/O.

Defined Constants

_IOAPPEND	_SYS_OPEN
_IOB_ENTRIES	_SYS_OPEN
_IOEOF	_wP_tmpdir
_IOERR	BUFSIZ
_IOFBF	EOF
_IOLBF	FILENAME_MAX
_IOMYBUF	FOPEN_MAX
_IONBF	L_ctermid
_IOREAD	L_cuserid
_IORW	L_tmpnam
_IOSTRG	NULL
_IOWRT	SEEK_CUR
NSTREAM	SEEK_END
NSTREAM	SEEK_SET
_P_tmpdir	TMP_MAX
_P_tmpdir	WEOF

Defined Functions

_fcloseall()	fputchar()
_fdopen()	fputs()
_fgetchar()	fputwc()
_fgetwchar()	fputws()

`_filbuf()`	`fread()`
`_fileno()`	`freopen()`
`_flsbuf()`	`fscanf()`
`_flushall()`	`fseek()`
`_fputchar()`	`fsetpos()`
`_fputwchar()`	`ftell()`
`_fsopen()`	`fwprintf()`
`_getmaxstdio()`	`fwrite()`
`_getw()`	`fwscanf()`
`_getws()`	`getc()`
`_pclose()`	`getchar()`
`_popen()`	`gets()`
`_putw()`	`getw()`
`_putws()`	`getwc()`
`_rmtmp()`	`getwchar()`
`_setmaxstdio()`	`perror()`
`_snprintf()`	`printf()`
`_snwprintf()`	`putc()`
`_tempnam()`	`putchar()`
`_unlink()`	`puts()`
`_vsnprintf()`	`putw()`
`_vsnwprintf()`	`putwc()`
`_wfdopen()`	`putwchar()`
`_wfopen()`	`remove()`
`_wfreopen()`	`rename()`
`_wfsopen()`	`rewind()`
`_wperror()`	`rmtmp()`
`_wpopen()`	`scanf()`
`_wremove()`	`setbuf()`
`_wtempnam()`	`setvbuf()`
`_wtmpnam()`	`sprintf()`
`clearerr()`	`sscanf()`
`fclose()`	`swprintf()`
`fcloseall()`	`swscanf()`

r
s
t

```
fdopen()              tempnam()
feof()                tmpfile()
ferror()              tmpnam()
fflush()              ungetc()
fgetc()               ungetwc()
fgetchar()            unlink()
fgetpos()             vfprintf()
fgets()               vfwprintf()
fgetwc()              vprintf()
fgetws()              vsprintf()
fileno()              vswprintf()
flushall()            vwprintf()
fopen()               wprintf()
fprintf()             wscanf()
fputc()
```

Defined Data Types

```
size_t      va_list
wchar_t     FILE
wint_t      fpos_t
wctype_t
```

Defined Structures

```
struct _iobuf
{
    char *_ptr;
    int   _cnt;
    char *_base;
    int   _flag;
    int   _file;
    int   _charbuf;
    int   _bufsiz;
    char *_tmpfname;
};
```

Defined Macros

_fileno()	putc()
feof()	putchar()
ferror()	putwc()
getc()	putwchar()
getchar()	stderr
getwc()	stdin
getwchar()	stdout

stdiobuf

Class

The stdiobuf class implements buffering for the standard I/O streams.

Class Declaration

```
class _CRTIMP stdiobuf : public streambuf
{
public:
    stdiobuf(FILE* f);
    FILE* stdiofile() { return _str; }

    virtual int pbackfail(int c);
    virtual int overflow(int c = EOF);
    virtual int underflow();
    virtual streampos seekoff( streamoff,
        ios::seek_dir, int =ios::in|ios::out);
    virtual int sync();
    ~stdiobuf();
    int setrwbuf(int _rsize, int _wsize);

private:
        FILE * _str;
};
```

Class Members

Table S-24 lists and describes the members of the stdiobuf class.

Table S-24 Members of the stdiobuf Class

Member	Description
stdiofile()	Returns a pointer to the file associated with the object.
overflow()	Removes all elements from the output buffer.
pbackfail()	Places an element back into the input buffer, returning the element if successful or returning EOF if unsuccessful.
seekoff()	Repositions the next-element pointer for a buffer.
sync()	Removes all elements from the input and output buffers.
underflow()	Fills the input buffer.

CROSS-REFERENCE
See also stdiostream.

stdiostream

Class

The stdiostream class manages standard I/O streams through its associated stdiobuf object.

Class Declaration

```
class _CRTIMP stdiostream : public iostream
{
public:
    stdiostream(FILE *);
    ~stdiostream();
    stdiobuf* rdbuf() const
        { return (stdiobuf*) ostream::rdbuf(); }

private:
};
```

Class Members

The stdiostream class features a single member function, rdbuf(), which returns a pointer to the object's stdiobuf object.

CROSS-REFERENCE
See also stdiobuf.

stdlib.h

Standard C Library Header File

The stdlib.h library header file defines miscellaneous frequently used constants, functions, data types, structures, macros, and global variables.

Defined Constants

_MAX_DIR	_OUT_TO_STDERR
_MAX_DRIVE	_REPORT_ERRMODE
_MAX_EXT	EXIT_FAILURE
_MAX_FNAME	EXIT_SUCCESS
_MAX_PATH	MB_CUR_MAX
_OUT_TO_DEFAULT	NULL
_OUT_TO_MSGBOX	RAND_MAX

Defined Functions

_atoi64()	_wtol()
_atold()	abort()
_beep()	abs()
_ecvt()	atexit()
_exit()	atof()
_fcvt()	atoi()
_fullpath()	atol()
_gcvt()	bsearch()
_i64toa()	calloc()
_i64tow()	div()
_itoa()	ecvt()
_itow ()	exit()
_lrotl()	fcvt()
_lrotr()	free()
_ltoa()	gcvt()
_ltow ()	getenv()
_makepath()	itoa()
_mbstrlen()	labs()

_onexit()	ldiv()
_putenv()	ltoa()
_rotl()	malloc()
_rotr()	mblen()
_searchenv()	mbstowcs()
_set_error_mode()	mbtowc()
_seterrormode()	onexit()
_sleep()	perror()
_splitpath()	putenv()
_strtold()	qsort()
_swab()	rand()
_ui64toa()	realloc()
_ui64tow()	srand()
_ultoa()	strtod()
_ultow ()	strtol()
_wfullpath()	strtoul()
_wgetenv()	swab()
_wmakepath()	system()
_wperror()	ultoa()
_wputenv()	wcstod()
_wsearchenv()	wcstol()
_wsplitpath()	wcstombs()
_wsystem()	wcstoul()
_wtoi()	wctomb()
_wtoi64()	

Defined Data Types

```
size_t;
wchar_t;
```

Defined Structures

```
typedef struct _div_t {
        int quot;
        int rem;
```

```
      } div_t;

typedef struct _ldiv_t {
        long quot;
        long rem;
} ldiv_t;
```

Defined Macros

__max()	max()
__min()	min()

Defined Global Variables

__argc	_sys_errlist[]
__argv	_sys_nerr
__wargv	_winmajor
_doserrno	_winminor
_environ	_winver
_fileinfo	environ
_fmode	errno
_osver	sys_errlist
_pgmptr	sys_nerr

stdout

Stream

The stdout stream is the standard output stream, which, by default, displays its output on the screen. The following program, for example, displays the string "This is a test" on the screen. The program's output looks like this:

```
This is a test
Press any key to continue
```

Here is the program source code that produced the output:

```
#include "stdafx.h"
#include <iostream>
```

```
using namespace std;

int main(int argc, char* argv[])
{
    fputs("This is a test\n", stdout);

    return 0;
}
```

CROSS-REFERENCE
See also stderr and stdin.

strcat()

Function

The strcat() function concatenates (joins together) strings, returning a pointer to the destination string.

Header File

```
#include <string.h>
```

Declaration

```
char* strcat(char *strDestination, const char *strSource);
```

- *strDestination* — The string to which to concatenate *strSource*.
- *strSource* — The string to concatenate to *strDestination*.

Example

The following program demonstrates how to use the strcat() function. When run, the program concatenates the string "Four Five Six" to the string "One Two Three ". The program's output looks like this:

```
Result: One Two Three Four Five Six
Press any key to continue
```

Here is the program source code that produced the output:

```
#include "stdafx.h"
#include <iostream>
```

```
#include <string.h>

using namespace std;

int main(int argc, char* argv[])
{
    char str1[81];

    char* str2 = {"Four Five Six"};
    strcpy(str1, "One Two Three ");
    strcat(str1, str2);
    cout << "Result: " << str1 << endl;

    return 0;
}
```

CROSS-REFERENCE
See also _mbscat(), _mbschr(), _mbscmp(), _mbscoll(), _mbscpy(), _mbscspn(),
_mbsdec(), _mbsdup(), _mbsicmp(), _mbsicoll(), _mbsinc(), _mbslen(), _mbslwr(),
_mbsnbcat(), _mbsnbcmp(), _mbsnbcnt(), _mbsnbcoll(), _mbsnbcpy(),
_mbsnbicmp(), _mbsnbicoll(), _mbsnbset(), _mbsnccnt(), _mbsncmp(),
_mbsncoll(), _mbsncpy(), _mbsnextc(), _mbsnicmp(), _mbsnicoll(), _mbsninc(),
_mbsnset(), _mbspbrk(), _mbsrchr(), _mbsrev(), _mbsset(), _mbsspn(),
_mbsspnp(), _mbsstr(), _mbstok(), _mbstrlen(), _mbsupr(), _strdec(), _stricoll(),
_strinc(), _strlwr(), _strncnt(), _strncoll(), _strnextc(), _strnicmp(), _strnicoll(),
_strninc(), _strnset(), _strset(), _strspnp(), _strupr(), _tcsdec(), _tcsinc(), _tcsnccnt(),
_tcsninc(), _tcsspnp(), _wcsdec(), _wcsicmp(), _wcsicoll(), _wcslwr(), _wcsncnt(),
_wcsncoll(), _wcsnicmp(), _wcsnicoll(), _wcsninc(), _wcsnset(), _wcsrev(),
_wcsset(), _wcsspnp(), _wcsupr(), strchr(), strcmp(), strcoll(), strcpy(), strcspn(),
strdup(), stricmp(), strlen(), strlwr(), strncat(), strncmp(), strncpy(), strnicmp(),
strnset(), strpbrk(), strrchr(), strrev(), strset(), strspn(), strstr(), strtod(), strtok(),
strtol(), strtoul(), strupr(), wcscat(), wcschr(), wcscmp(), wcscoll(), wcscpy(),
wcscspn(), wcslen(), wcsncat(), wcsncmp(), wcsncpy(), wcspbrk(), wcsrchr(),
wcsspn(), wcsstr(), wcstod(), wcstok(), wcstol(), and wcstoul().

strchr()

Function

The strchr() function locates a character in a string, returning a pointer to
the character.

Header File

```
#include <string.h>
```

Declaration

```
char* strchr(const char *string, wint_t c);
```

- *c* — The character for which to search.
- *string* — A pointer to the string to search for *c*.

Example

The following program demonstrates how to use the strchr() function. When run, the program locates the first occurrence of the letter e in the string "One Two Three" and displays the string starting with the located letter. The program's output looks like this:

```
Result: e Two Three
Press any key to continue
```

Here is the program source code that produced the output:

```
#include "stdafx.h"
#include <iostream>
#include <string.h>

using namespace std;

int main(int argc, char* argv[])
{
    char ch = 'e';
    char* str1 = "One Two Three";
    char* pChr = strchr(str1, ch);
    cout << "Result: " << pChr << endl;

    return 0;
}
```

CROSS-REFERENCE

See also _mbscat(), _mbschr(), _mbscmp(), _mbscoll(), _mbscpy(), _mbscspn(), _mbsdec(), _mbsdup(), _mbsicmp(), _mbsicoll(), _mbsinc(), _mbslen(), _mbslwr(), _mbsnbcat(), _mbsnbcmp(), _mbsnbcnt(), _mbsnbcoll(), _mbsnbcpy(), _mbsnbicmp(), _mbsnbicoll(), _mbsnbset(), _mbsnccnt(), _mbsncmp(),

_mbsncoll(), _mbsncpy(), _mbsnextc(), _mbsnicmp(), _mbsnicoll(), _mbsninc(), _mbsnset(), _mbspbrk(), _mbsrchr(), _mbsrev(), _mbsset(), _mbsspn(), · _mbsspnp(), _mbsstr(), _mbstok(), _mbstrlen(), _mbsupr(), _strdec(), _stricoll(), _strinc(), _strlwr(), _strncnt(), _strncoll(), _strnextc(), _strnicmp(), _strnicoll(), _strninc(), _strnset(), _strset(), _strspnp(), _strupr(), _tcsdec(), _tcsinc(), _tcsnccnt(), _tcsninc(), _tcsspnp(), _wcsdec(), _wcsicmp(), _wcsicoll(), _wcslwr(), _wcsncnt(), _wcsncoll(), _wcsnicmp(), _wcsnicoll(), _wcsninc(), _wcsnset(), _wcsrev(), _wcsset(), _wcsspnp(), _wcsupr(), strcat(), strcmp(), strcoll(), strcpy(), strcspn(), strdup(), stricmp(), strlen(), strlwr(), strncat(), strncmp(), strncpy(), strnicmp(), strnset(), strpbrk(), strrchr(), strrev(), strset(), strspn(), strstr(), strtod(), strtok(), strtol(), strtoul(), strupr(), wcscat(), wcschr(), wcscmp(), wcscoll(), wcscpy(), wcscspn(), wcslen(), wcsncat(), wcsncmp(), wcsncpy(), wcspbrk(), wcsrchr(), wcsspn(), wcsstr(), wcstod(), wcstok(), wcstol(), and wcstoul().

strcmp()

Function

The strcmp() function compares two wide-character strings, returning a value from Table S-25.

Table S-25 Return Values for strcmp()

Value	Description
Less than 0	string1 is alphabetically less than string2.
0	The two strings are equal.
Greater than 0	string1 is alphabetically greater than string2.

Header File

```
#include <string.h>
```

Declaration

```
int strcmp(const char *string1, const char *string2);
```

- *string1* — The first string to compare.
- *string2* — The second string to compare.

Example

The following program demonstrates how to use the `strcmp()` function. When run, the program compares several pairs of strings and displays the result of the comparisons. The program's output looks like this:

```
One Two Three equals One Two Three
One Two Three is greater than Four Five Six
Four Five Six is less than Seven Eight Nine
Press any key to continue
```

Here is the program source code that produced the output:

```cpp
#include "stdafx.h"
#include <iostream>
#include <string.h>

using namespace std;

void cmp(char* s1, char* s2)
{
    int result = strcmp(s1, s2);
    if (result < 0 )
    {
        cout << s1 << " is less than ";
        cout << s2 << endl;
    }
    else if (result > 0)
    {
        cout << s1 << " is greater than ";
        cout << s2 << endl;
    }
    else
    {
        cout << s1 << " equals ";
        cout << s2 << endl;
    }
}

int main(int argc, char* argv[])
{
    char* str1 = "One Two Three";
    char* str2 = "One Two Three";
    char* str3 = "Four Five Six";
    char* str4 = "Seven Eight Nine";
```

```
    cmp(str1, str2);
    cmp(str2, str3);
    cmp(str3, str4);

    return 0;
}
```

CROSS-REFERENCE

See also _mbscat(), _mbschr(), _mbscmp(), _mbscoll(), _mbscpy(), _mbscspn(), _mbsdec(), _mbsdup(), _mbsicmp(), _mbsicoll(), _mbsinc(), _mbslen(), _mbslwr(), _mbsnbcat(), _mbsnbcmp(), _mbsnbcnt(), _mbsnbcoll(), _mbsnbcpy(), _mbsnbicmp(), _mbsnbicoll(), _mbsnbset(), _mbsnccnt(), _mbsncmp(), _mbsncoll(), _mbsncpy(), _mbsnextc(), _mbsnicmp(), _mbsnicoll(), _mbsninc(), _mbsnset(), _mbspbrk(), _mbsrchr(), _mbsrev(), _mbsset(), _mbsspn(), _mbsspnp(), _mbsstr(), _mbstok(), _mbstrlen(), _mbsupr(), _strdec(), _stricoll(), _strinc(), _strlwr(), _strncnt(), _strncoll(), _strnextc(), _strnicmp(), _strnicoll(), _strninc(), _strnset(), _strset(), _strspnp(), _strupr(), _tcsdec(), _tcsinc(), _tcsnccnt(), _tcsninc(), _tcsspnp(), _wcsdec(), _wcsicmp(), _wcsicoll(), _wcslwr(), _wcsncnt(), _wcsncoll(), _wcsnicmp(), _wcsnicoll(), _wcsninc(), _wcsnset(), _wcsrev(), _wcsset(), _wcsspnp(), _wcsupr(), strcat(), strchr(), strcoll(), strcpy(), strcspn(), strdup(), stricmp(), strlen(), strlwr(), strncat(), strncmp(), strncpy(), strnicmp(), strnset(), strpbrk(), strrchr(), strrev(), strset(), strspn(), strstr(), strtod(), strtok(), strtol(), strtoul(), strupr(), wcscat(), wcschr(), wcscmp(), wcscoll(), wcscpy(), wcscspn(), wcslen(), wcsncat(), wcsncmp(), wcsncpy(), wcspbrk(), wcsrchr(), wcsspn(), wcsstr(), wcstod(), wcstok(), wcstol(), and wcstoul().

strcoll()

Function

The `strcoll()` function compares two strings for the current locale, returning a value from Table S-26.

Table S-26 Return Values for strcoll()

Value	Description
Less than 0	`string1` is alphabetically less than `string2`.
0	The two strings are equal.
Greater than 0	`string1` is alphabetically greater than `string2`.

Header File

```
#include <string.h>
```

Declaration

```
int strcoll(const char *string1, const char *string2);
```

- *string1* — The first string to compare.
- *string2* — The second string to compare.

Example

The following program demonstrates how to use the strcoll() function. When run, the program compares several pairs of strings and displays the result of the comparisons. The program's output looks like this:

```
One Two Three equals One Two Three
One Two Three is greater than Four Five Six
Four Five Six is less than Seven Eight Nine
Press any key to continue
```

Here is the program source code that produced the output:

```
#include "stdafx.h"
#include <iostream>
#include <string.h>

using namespace std;

void cmp(char* s1, char* s2)
{
    int result = strcoll(s1, s2);
    if (result < 0 )
    {
        cout << s1 << " is less than ";
        cout << s2 << endl;
    }
    else if (result > 0)
    {
        cout << s1 << " is greater than ";
        cout << s2 << endl;
```

```
        }
    else
    {
        cout << s1 << " equals ";
        cout << s2 << endl;
    }
}

int main(int argc, char* argv[])
{
    char* str1 = "One Two Three";
    char* str2 = "One Two Three";
    char* str3 = "Four Five Six";
    char* str4 = "Seven Eight Nine";

    cmp(str1, str2);
    cmp(str2, str3);
    cmp(str3, str4);

    return 0;
}
```

CROSS-REFERENCE
See also _mbscat(), _mbschr(), _mbscmp(), _mbscoll(), _mbscpy(), _mbscspn(), _mbsdec(), _mbsdup(), _mbsicmp(), _mbsicoll(), _mbsinc(), _mbslen(), _mbslwr(), _mbsnbcat(), _mbsnbcmp(), _mbsnbcnt(), _mbsnbcoll(), _mbsnbcpy(), _mbsnbicmp(), _mbsnbicoll(), _mbsnbset(), _mbsnccnt(), _mbsncmp(), _mbsncoll(), _mbsncpy(), _mbsnextc(), _mbsnicmp(), _mbsnicoll(), _mbsninc(), _mbsnset(), _mbspbrk(), _mbsrchr(), _mbsrev(), _mbsset(), _mbsspn(), _mbsspnp(), _mbsstr(), _mbstok(), _mbstrlen(), _mbsupr(), _strdec(), _stricoll(), _strinc(), _strlwr(), _strncnt(), _strncoll(), _strnextc(), _strnicmp(), _strnicoll(), _strninc(), _strnset(), _strset(), _strspnp(), _strupr(), _tcsdec(), _tcsinc(), _tcsnccnt(), _tcsninc(), _tcsspnp(), _wcsdec(), _wcsicmp(), _wcsicoll(), _wcslwr(), _wcsncnt(), _wcsncoll(), _wcsnicmp(), _wcsnicoll(), _wcsninc(), _wcsnset(), _wcsrev(), _wcsset(), _wcsspnp(), _wcsupr(), strcat(), strchr(), strcmp(), strcpy(), strcspn(), strdup(), stricmp(), strlen(), strlwr(), strncat(), strncmp(), strncpy(), strnicmp(), strnset(), strpbrk(), strrchr(), strrev(), strset(), strspn(), strstr(), strtod(), strtok(), strtol(), strtoul(), strupr(), wcscat(), wcschr(), wcscmp(), wcscoll(), wcscpy(), wcscspn(), wcslen(), wcsncat(), wcsncmp(), wcsncpy(), wcspbrk(), wcsrchr(), wcsspn(), wcsstr(), wcstod(), wcstok(), wcstol(), and wcstoul().

strcpy()

Function

The strcpy() function copies one string to another, returning a pointer to the destination string. The source and destination strings cannot overlap.

Header File

```
#include <string.h>
```

Declaration

```
char* strcpy(char *strDestination, const char *strSource);
```

- *strDestination* — A pointer to the destination string.
- *strSource* — A pointer to the source string.

Example

The following program demonstrates how to use the strcpy() function. When run, the program copies one string to another and displays the result. The program's output looks like this:

```
Source string = This is a test
Destination string = This is a test
Press any key to continue
```

Here is the program source code that produced the output:

```
#include "stdafx.h"
#include <iostream>
#include <string.h>

using namespace std;

int main(int argc, char* argv[])
{
    char destStr[81];
    char* srcStr = "This is a test";

    char* pResult = strcpy(destStr, srcStr);
    cout << "Source string = " << srcStr << endl;
```

```
        cout << "Destination string = " << pResult << endl;

        return 0;
    }
```

CROSS-REFERENCE
See also _mbscat(), _mbschr(), _mbscmp(), _mbscoll(), _mbscpy(), _mbscspn(), _mbsdec(), _mbsdup(), _mbsicmp(), _mbsicoll(), _mbsinc(), _mbslen(), _mbslwr(), _mbsnbcat(), _mbsnbcmp(), _mbsnbcnt(), _mbsnbcoll(), _mbsnbcpy(), _mbsnbicmp(), _mbsnbicoll(), _mbsnbset(), _mbsnccnt(), _mbsncmp(), _mbsncoll(), _mbsncpy(), _mbsnextc(), _mbsnicmp(), _mbsnicoll(), _mbsninc(), _mbsnset(), _mbspbrk(), _mbsrchr(), _mbsrev(), _mbsset(), _mbsspn(), _mbsspnp(), _mbsstr(), _mbstok(), _mbstrlen(), _mbsupr(), _strdec(), _stricoll(), _strinc(), _strlwr(), _strncnt(), _strncoll(), _strnextc(), _strnicmp(), _strnicoll(), _strninc(), _strnset(), _strset(), _strspnp(), _strupr(), _tcsdec(), _tcsinc(), _tcsnccnt(), _tcsninc(), _tcsspnp(), _wcsdec(), _wcsicmp(), _wcsicoll(), _wcslwr(), _wcsncnt(), _wcsncoll(), _wcsnicmp(), _wcsnicoll(), _wcsninc(), _wcsnset(), _wcsrev(), _wcsset(), _wcsspnp(), _wcsupr(), strcat(), strchr(), strcmp(), strcoll(), strcspn(), strdup(), stricmp(), strlen(), strlwr(), strncat(), strncmp(), strncpy(), strnicmp(), strnset(), strpbrk(), strrchr(), strrev(), strset(), strspn(), strstr(), strtod(), strtok(), strtol(), strtoul(), strupr(), wcscat(), wcschr(), wcscmp(), wcscoll(), wcscpy(), wcscspn(), wcslen(), wcsncat(), wcsncmp(), wcsncpy(), wcspbrk(), wcsrchr(), wcsspn(), wcsstr(), wcstod(), wcstok(), wcstol(), and wcstoul().

strcspn()

Function

The strcspn() function locates the first occurrence of a character in a string, returning the length of the substring preceding a matching character.

Header File

```
#include <string.h>
```

Declaration

```
size_t strcspn(const char *string, const char *strCharSet);
```

- *strCharSet*—A pointer to the set of characters for which to search.
- *string*—A pointer to the string to search.

Example

The following program demonstrates how to use the `strcspn()` function. When run, the program locates, in a string, the first character in a set and displays the result, indicating the located character with a caret (^). The program's output looks like this:

```
Source String:
This is a test
    ^

Press any key to continue
```

Here is the program source code that produced the output:

```cpp
#include "stdafx.h"
#include <iostream>
#include <string.h>

using namespace std;

int main(int argc, char* argv[])
{
    char* srcStr = "This is a test";
    char* chrSet = "ast";

    size_t len = strcspn(srcStr, chrSet);
    cout << "Source String:" << endl;
    cout << srcStr << endl;
    for (unsigned x=0; x<len; ++x)
        cout << " ";
    cout << "^" << endl;

    return 0;
}
```

CROSS-REFERENCE

See also _mbscat(), _mbschr(), _mbscmp(), _mbscoll(), _mbscpy(), _mbscspn(), _mbsdec(), _mbsdup(), _mbsicmp(), _mbsicoll(), _mbsinc(), _mbslen(), _mbslwr(), _mbsnbcat(), _mbsnbcmp(), _mbsnbcnt(), _mbsnbcoll(), _mbsnbcpy(), _mbsnbicmp(), _mbsnbicoll(), _mbsnbset(), _mbsnccnt(), _mbsncmp(), _mbsncoll(), _mbsncpy(), _mbsnextc(), _mbsnicmp(), _mbsnicoll(), _mbsninc(), _mbsnset(), _mbspbrk(), _mbsrchr(), _mbsrev(), _mbsset(), _mbsspn(), _mbsspnp(), _mbsstr(), _mbstok(), _mbstrlen(), _mbsupr(), _strdec(), _stricoll(), _strinc(), _strlwr(), _strncnt(), _strncoll(), _strnextc(), _strnicmp(), _strnicoll(), _strninc(), _strnset(), _strset(), _strspnp(), _strupr(), _tcsdec(), _tcsinc(), _tcsnccnt(), _tcsninc(), _tcsspnp(), _wcsdec(), _wcsicmp(), _wcsicoll(), _wcslwr(), _wcsncnt(), _wcsncoll(), _wcsnicmp(), _wcsnicoll(), _wcsninc(), _wcsnset(), _wcsrev(), _wcsset(), _wcsspnp(), _wcsupr(), strcat(), strchr(), strcmp(), strcoll(), strcpy(), strdup(), stricmp(), strlen(), strlwr(), strncat(), strncmp(), strncpy(), strnicmp(), strnset(), strpbrk(), strrchr(), strrev(), strset(), strspn(), strstr(), strtod(), strtok(), strtol(), strtoul(), strupr(), wcscat(), wcschr(), wcscmp(), wcscoll(), wcscpy(), wcscspn(), wcslen(), wcsncat(), wcsncmp(), wcsncpy(), wcspbrk(), wcsrchr(), wcsspn(), wcsstr(), wcstod(), wcstok(), wcstol(), and wcstoul().

strdup()

Function

The `strdup()` function duplicates a string, returning a pointer to the new string.

Header File

```
#include <string.h>
```

Declaration

```
char* strdup(const char *strSource);
```

- *strSource* — A pointer to the source string.

Example

The following program demonstrates how to use the `strdup()` function. When run, the program duplicates the given string and displays the result. The program's output looks like this:

```
Source string = This is a test
New string = This is a test
Press any key to continue
```

Here is the program source code that produced the output:

```
#include "stdafx.h"
#include <iostream>
#include <string.h>

using namespace std;

int main(int argc, char* argv[])
```

```
{
    char* srcStr = "This is a test";

    char* destStr = strdup(srcStr);
    cout << "Source string = " << srcStr << endl;
    cout << "New string = " << destStr << endl;

    return 0;
}
```

CROSS-REFERENCE

See also _mbscat(), _mbschr(), _mbscmp(), _mbscoll(), _mbscpy(), _mbscspn(), _mbsdec(), _mbsdup(), _mbsicmp(), _mbsicoll(), _mbsinc(), _mbslen(), _mbslwr(), _mbsnbcat(), _mbsnbcmp(), _mbsnbcnt(), _mbsnbcoll(), _mbsnbcpy(), _mbsnbicmp(), _mbsnbicoll(), _mbsnbset(), _mbsnccnt(), _mbsncmp(), _mbsncoll(), _mbsncpy(), _mbsnextc(), _mbsnicmp(), _mbsnicoll(), _mbsninc(), _mbsnset(), _mbspbrk(), _mbsrchr(), _mbsrev(), _mbsset(), _mbsspn(), _mbsspnp(), _mbsstr(), _mbstok(), _mbstrlen(), _mbsupr(), _strdec(), _stricoll(), _strinc(), _strlwr(), _strncnt(), _strncoll(), _strnextc(), _strnicmp(), _strnicoll(), _strninc(), _strnset(), _strset(), _strspnp(), _strupr(), _tcsdec(), _tcsinc(), _tcsnccnt(), _tcsninc(), _tcsspnp(), _wcsdec(), _wcsicmp(), _wcsicoll(), _wcslwr(), _wcsncnt(), _wcsncoll(), _wcsnicmp(), _wcsnicoll(), _wcsninc(), _wcsnset(), _wcsrev(), _wcsset(), _wcsspnp(), _wcsupr(), strcat(), strchr(), strcmp(), strcoll(), strcpy(), strcspn(), stricmp(), strlen(), strlwr(), strncat(), strncmp(), strncpy(), strnicmp(), strnset(), strpbrk(), strrchr(), strrev(), strset(), strspn(), strstr(), strtod(), strtok(), strtol(), strtoul(), strupr(), wcscat(), wcschr(), wcscmp(), wcscoll(), wcscpy(), wcscspn(), wcslen(), wcsncat(), wcsncmp(), wcsncpy(), wcspbrk(), wcsrchr(), wcsspn(), wcsstr(), wcstod(), wcstok(), wcstol(), and wcstoul().

streambuf

Class

The streambuf abstract class represents the buffers—and the operations needed to manipulate those buffers—for data processed by stream classes.

Class Declaration

```
class _CRTIMP streambuf
{
public:

    virtual ~streambuf();
```

```
    inline int in_avail() const;
    inline int out_waiting() const;
    int sgetc();
    int snextc();
    int sbumpc();
    void stossc();

    inline int sputbackc(char);

    inline int sputc(int);
    inline int sputn(const char *,int);
    inline int sgetn(char *,int);

    virtual int sync();

    virtual streambuf* setbuf(char *, int);
    virtual streampos seekoff(streamoff,ios::seek_dir,
        int =ios::in|ios::out);
    virtual streampos seekpos(streampos,
        int =ios::in|ios::out);

    virtual int xsputn(const char *,int);
    virtual int xsgetn(char *,int);

    virtual int overflow(int =EOF) = 0;
    virtual int underflow() = 0;

    virtual int pbackfail(int);

    void dbp();

#ifdef  _MT
    void setlock() { LockFlg-; }
    void clrlock() { if (LockFlg <= 0) LockFlg++; }
    void lock() { if (LockFlg<0) _mtlock(lockptr()); };
    void unlock() { if (LockFlg<0) _mtunlock(lockptr()); }
#else
    void lock() { }
    void unlock() { }
#endif

protected:
    streambuf();
```

```
        streambuf(char *,int);

        inline char * base() const;
        inline char * ebuf() const;
        inline char * pbase() const;
        inline char * pptr() const;
        inline char * epptr() const;
        inline char * eback() const;
        inline char * gptr() const;
        inline char * egptr() const;
        inline int blen() const;
        inline void setp(char *,char *);
        inline void setg(char *,char *,char *);
        inline void pbump(int);
        inline void gbump(int);

        void setb(char *,char *,int =0);
        inline int unbuffered() const;
        inline void unbuffered(int);
        int allocate();
        virtual int doallocate();
#ifdef _MT
        _PCRT_CRITICAL_SECTION lockptr() { return & x_lock; }
#endif

private:
        int _fAlloc;
        int _fUnbuf;
        int x_lastc;
        char * _base;
        char * _ebuf;
        char * _pbase;
        char * _pptr;
        char * _epptr;
        char * _eback;
        char * _gptr;
        char * _egptr;
#ifdef _MT
        int LockFlg;                    // <0 indicates locking
required
        _CRT_CRITICAL_SECTION x_lock;        // lock needed only
for multi-thread operation
#endif
};
```

Class Members

Table S-27 lists and describes the members of the `streambuf` class.

Table S-27 Members of the streambuf Class

Member	Description
allocate()	Allocates a buffer.
base()	Gets a pointer to the reserve area's start.
blen()	Gets the reserve area's size.
dbp()	Displays debugging information for the class.
doallocate()	Allocates the reserve area.
eback()	Gets the input buffer's lower bound.
ebuf	Gets a pointer to the reserve area's end.
egptr()	Holds a pointer to the input buffer's end.
epptr()	Gets a pointer to the output buffer's end.
gbump	Increments the input buffer's next-element pointer.
gptr()	Holds a pointer to the input buffer.
in_avail()	Returns the number of available characters.
out_waiting()	Returns the number of characters waiting for output.
overflow()	Removes all elements from the output buffer.
pbackfail()	Places an element back into the input buffer, returning the element if successful, or EOF if unsuccessful.
pbase()	Gets a pointer to the output buffer's start.
pbump()	Increments the output buffer's next-element pointer.
pptr()	Gets the put pointer.
sbumpc()	Returns the current character before incrementing the buffer's next-element pointer.
seekoff()	Repositions the next-element pointer for a buffer.
seekpos()	Repositions the next-element pointer for a buffer.
setb()	Initializes the object's reserve area.
setbuf()	Attaches a reserve area to the object.
setg()	Sets all the input buffer pointers.
setp()	Sets all the output buffer pointers.
sgetc()	Returns the next character without repositioning the buffer's next-element pointer.
sgetn()	Retrieves a series of characters from the buffer.
snextc()	Returns the next character after incrementing the buffer's next-element pointer.
sputbackc()	Decrements the buffer's next-element pointer.
sputc()	Places a character in the output buffer.

Continued

r
s
t

Table S-27 *Continued*

Member	Description
sputn()	Places a series of characters in the output buffer.
stossc()	Increments the buffer's next-element pointer without returning a value.
sync()	Removes all elements from the input and output buffers.
unbuffered()	Manipulates the object's buffer-state variable.
underflow()	Fills the input buffer.

CROSS-REFERENCE
See also istrstream, ostrstream, strstream (class), and strstream (Standard C++ Library Header file).

streambuf

Standard C++ Library Header File

The streambuf header file defines the basic_streambuf template class, which supplies data type definitions and functions used by various other stream classes.

CROSS-REFERENCE
See also basic_streambuf, istream, ostream, and streambuf (class).

strerror()

Function

The strerror() function returns a pointer to an error-message string.

Header File

```
#include <string.h>
```

Declaration

```
char* strerror(int errnum);
```

- *errnum* — The error number for which to get an error message.

Example

The following program demonstrates how to use the strerror() function. When run, the program generates an error by attempting to run a nonexistent program and displays the error's results. The program's output looks like this:

```
Running TestProg.exe

File not found
Current Error Msg:
    No such file or directory

Press any key to continue
```

Here is the program source code that produced the output:

```cpp
#include "stdafx.h"
#include <iostream>
#include <process.h>
#include <errno.h>
#include <string.h>

using namespace std;

int main(int argc, char* argv[])
{
    cout << "Running TestProg.exe" << endl << endl;

    int result = spawnl(P_WAIT, "TestProg.exe",
        "TestProg.exe", "arg2", "arg3", NULL);
    if (result == -1)
    {
        switch(errno)
        {
        case ENOEXEC:
            cout << "Not an executable file" << endl;
            break;
        case E2BIG:
            cout << "Space required exceeds 32K" << endl;
            break;
        case ENOMEM:
            cout << "Not enough memory" << endl;
            break;
        case EINVAL:
            cout << "Bad execution mode" << endl;
```

```
            break;
        case ENOENT:
            cout << "File not found" << endl;
        }
    }

    cout << "Current Error Msg: " << endl;
    cout << "        " << strerror(errno) << endl << endl;

    return 0;
}
```

CROSS-REFERENCE
See also _strerror(), clearerr(), ferror(), and perror().

strftime()

Function

The strftime() function generates a formatted time string, returning the
number of characters in the string or returning 0 in the case of an error.

Header File

```
#include <time.h>
```

Declaration

```
size_t strftime(char *strDest, size_t maxsize,
    const char *format, const struct tm *timeptr);
```

- *format*—A pointer to the format string. Table S-28 shows the
  available format codes.
- *maxsize*—The maximum allowable length of the formatted string.
- *strDest*—A pointer to the buffer that will receive the formatted
  string.
- *timeptr*—A pointer to the tm structure that contains the time to
  format.

Table S-28 Format Codes for strftime()

Code	Description
%#%	Ignore the # flag.
%#a	Ignore the # flag.
%#A	Ignore the # flag.
%#b	Ignore the # flag.
%#B	Ignore the # flag.
%#c	Format as the current locale's long date and time.
%#d	Delete leading zeroes.
%#H	Delete leading zeroes.
%#I	Delete leading zeroes.
%#j	Delete leading zeroes.
%#m	Delete leading zeroes.
%#M	Delete leading zeroes.
%#p	Ignore the # flag.
%#S	Delete leading zeroes.
%#U	Delete leading zeroes.
%#w	Delete leading zeroes.
%#W	Delete leading zeroes.
%#X	Ignore the # flag.
%#x	Format as the current locale's long date.
%#y	Delete leading zeroes.
%#Y	Delete leading zeroes.
%#z	Ignore the # flag.
%#Z	Ignore the # flag.
%%	Display a percent sign.
%a	Format as an abbreviated weekday name.
%A	Format as a full weekday name.
%b	Format as an abbreviated month name.
%B	Format as a full month name.
%c	Format the date and time for the current locale.
%d	Format the day of the month as a number from 01 to 31.
%H	Format the hour in 24-hour style.
%I	Format the hour in the 12-hour style.
%j	Format the day of the year as a number from 001 to 366.
%m	Format the month as a number from 01 to 12.
%M	Format the minute as a number from 00 to 59.
%p	Use the AM/PM indicator for the current locale.
%S	Format the second as a number from 00 to 59.

Continued

Table S-28 *Continued*

Code	Description
%U	Format the week of the year as a number from 00 to 53, using Sunday as the first day of the week.
%w	Format the weekday as a number from 0 to 6, where 0 represents Sunday.
%W	Week of the year as a number from 00 to 53.
%x	Format the date for the current locale.
%X	Format the time for the current locale.
%y	Format the year as a two-digit number from 00 to 99.
%Y	Format the year as a four-digit number, for example 1999.
%z	Format the time zone name as an abbreviation.
%Z	Format the time zone name as a full name.

Example

The following program demonstrates how to use the `strftime()` function. The program initializes a `tm` structure, converts the structure to a string, and displays the result. The program's output looks like this:

```
Thu, January 21, 1999.

Press any key to continue
```

Here is the program source code that produced the output:

```
#include "stdafx.h"
#include <iostream>
#include <time.h>

using namespace std;

int main(int argc, char* argv[])
{
    char buf[256];
    struct tm tmTime;

    tmTime.tm_mday   = 21;
    tmTime.tm_mon    = 0;
    tmTime.tm_year   = 99;
    tmTime.tm_wday   = 4;
    tmTime.tm_yday   = 0;
    tmTime.tm_isdst  = 0;
    tmTime.tm_sec    = 0;
```

```
        tmTime.tm_min    = 17;
        tmTime.tm_hour   = 5;

        strftime(buf, 256, "%a, %B %d, %Y.\n", &tmTime);
        cout << buf << endl;

        return 0;
    }
```

CROSS-REFERENCE
See also asctime(), ctime(), difftime(), _ftime(), _futime(), gmtime(), localtime(), mktime(), _strdate(), _strtime(), time(), _utime(), _wasctime(), wcsftime(), _wctime(), _wstrtime(), and _wutime().

stricmp()

Function

The `stricmp()` function compares two strings without regard for case (case–insensitive compare), returning a value from Table S-29.

Table S-29 Return Values for stricmp()

Value	Description
Less than 0	`string1` is alphabetically less than `string2`.
0	The two strings are equal.
Greater than 0	`string1` is alphabetically greater than `string2`.

Header File

```
        #include <string.h>
```

Declaration

```
        int stricmp(const char *string1, const char *string2);
```

- *string1* — The first string to compare.
- *string2* — The second string to compare.

Example

The following program demonstrates how to use the `stricmp()` function. When run, the program compares several pairs of strings and displays the result of the comparisons. The program's output looks like this:

```
One Two Three equals one two three
one two three is greater than Four Five Six
Four Five Six is less than seven eight nine
Press any key to continue
```

Here is the program source code that produced the output:

```cpp
#include "stdafx.h"
#include <iostream>
#include <string.h>

using namespace std;

void cmp(char* s1, char* s2)
{
    int result = stricmp(s1, s2);
    if (result < 0 )
    {
        cout << s1;
        cout << " is less than ";
        cout << s2 << endl;
    }
    else if (result > 0)
    {
        cout << s1;
        cout << " is greater than ";
        cout << s2 << endl;
    }
    else
    {
        cout << s1;
        cout << " equals ";
        cout << s2 << endl;
    }
}

int main(int argc, char* argv[])
{
    char* str1 = "One Two Three";
    char* str2 = "one two three";
```

```
    char* str3 = "Four Five Six";
    char* str4 = "seven eight nine";

    cmp(str1, str2);
    cmp(str2, str3);
    cmp(str3, str4);

    return 0;
}
```

CROSS-REFERENCE

See also _mbscat(), _mbschr(), _mbscmp(), _mbscoll(), _mbscpy(), _mbscspn(), _mbsdec(), _mbsdup(), _mbsicmp(), _mbsicoll(), _mbsinc(), _mbslen(), _mbslwr(), _mbsnbcat(), _mbsnbcmp(), _mbsnbcnt(), _mbsnbcoll(), _mbsnbcpy(), _mbsnbicmp(), _mbsnbicoll(), _mbsnbset(), _mbsnccnt(), _mbsncmp(), _mbsncoll(), _mbsncpy(), _mbsnextc(), _mbsnicmp(), _mbsnicoll(), _mbsninc(), _mbsnset(), _mbspbrk(), _mbsrchr(), _mbsrev(), _mbsset(), _mbsspn(), _mbsspnp(), _mbsstr(), _mbstok(), _mbstrlen(), _mbsupr(), _strdec(), _stricoll(), _strinc(), _strlwr(), _strncnt(), _strncoll(), _strnextc(), _strnicmp(), _strnicoll(), _strninc(), _strnset(), _strset(), _strspnp(), _strupr(), _tcsdec(), _tcsinc(), _tcsnccnt(), _tcsninc(), _tcsspnp(), _wcsdec(), _wcsicmp(), _wcsicoll(), _wcslwr(), _wcsncnt(), _wcsncoll(), _wcsnicmp(), _wcsnicoll(), _wcsninc(), _wcsnset(), _wcsrev(), _wcsset(), _wcsspnp(), _wcsupr(), strcat(), strchr(), strcmp(), strcoll(), strcpy(), strcspn(), strdup(), strlen(), strlwr(), strncat(), strncmp(), strncpy(), strnicmp(), strnset(), strpbrk(), strrchr(), strrev(), strset(), strspn(), strstr(), strtod(), strtok(), strtol(), strtoul(), strupr(), wcscat(), wcschr(), wcscmp(), wcscoll(), wcscpy(), wcscspn(), wcslen(), wcsncat(), wcsncmp(), wcsncpy(), wcspbrk(), wcsrchr(), wcsspn(), wcsstr(), wcstod(), wcstok(), wcstol(), and wcstoul().

string.h

Standard C Library Header File

The string.h library header file defines the constants, functions, and data types needed to manipulate various types of character data.

Defined Constants

```
_NLSCMPERROR
NULL
```

Defined Functions

_c2pstr()	strerror()
_memccpy()	stricmp()
_memicmp()	strlen()
_p2cstr()	strlwr()
_strcmpi()	strncat()
_strdup()	strncmp()
_strerror()	strncpy()
_stricmp()	strnicmp()
_stricoll()	strnset()
_strlwr()	strpbrk()
_strncoll()	strrchr()
_strnicmp()	strrev()
_strnicoll()	strset()
_strnset()	strspn()
_strrev()	strstr()
_strset()	strtok()
_strupr()	strupr()
_wcsdup()	strxfrm()
_wcsicmp()	wcscat()
_wcsicoll()	wcschr()
_wcslwr()	wcscmp()
_wcsncoll()	wcscoll()
_wcsnicmp()	wcscpy()
_wcsnicoll()	wcscspn()
_wcsnset()	wcsdup()
_wcsrev()	wcsicmp()
_wcsset()	wcsicoll()
_wcsupr()	wcslen()
memccpy()	wcslwr()
memchr()	wcsncat()
memcmp()	wcsncmp()
memcpy()	wcsncpy()
memicmp()	wcsnicmp()
memmove()	wcsnset()
memset()	wcspbrk()

```
strcat()        wcsrchr()
strchr()        wcsrev()
strcmp()        wcsset()
strcmpi()       wcsspn()
strcoll()       wcsstr()
strcpy()        wcstok()
strcspn()       wcsupr()
strdup()        wcsxfrm()
```

Defined Data Types

```
size_t
wchar_t
```

strlen()

Function

The `strlen()` function returns the length (the number of characters) of a string.

Header File

```
#include <string.h>
```

Declaration

```
size_t strlen(const char *string);
```

- *string* — A pointer to the string for which to return the length.

Example

The following program demonstrates how to use the `strlen()` function. When run, the program calculates the length of a string and then uses the length to underline the source string. The program's output looks like this:

```
Source String:

This is a test
```

Press any key to continue

Here is the program source code that produced the output:

```cpp
#include "stdafx.h"
#include <iostream>
#include <string.h>

using namespace std;

int main(int argc, char* argv[])
{
    char* srcStr = "This is a test";

    size_t len = strlen(srcStr);
    cout << "Source String:" << endl << endl;
    cout << srcStr << endl;
    for (unsigned x=0; x<len; ++x)
        cout << "-";
    cout << endl << endl;

    return 0;
}
```

CROSS-REFERENCE

See also _mbscat(), _mbschr(), _mbscmp(), _mbscoll(), _mbscpy(), _mbscspn(), _mbsdec(), _mbsdup(), _mbsicmp(), _mbsicoll(), _mbsinc(), _mbslen(), _mbslwr(), _mbsnbcat(), _mbsnbcmp(), _mbsnbcnt(), _mbsnbcoll(), _mbsnbcpy(), _mbsnbicmp(), _mbsnbicoll(), _mbsnbset(), _mbsnccnt(), _mbsncmp(), _mbsncoll(), _mbsncpy(), _mbsnextc(), _mbsnicmp(), _mbsnicoll(), _mbsninc(), _mbsnset(), _mbspbrk(), _mbsrchr(), _mbsrev(), _mbsset(), _mbsspn(), _mbsspnp(), _mbsstr(), _mbstok(), _mbstrlen(), _mbsupr(), _strdec(), _stricoll(), _strinc(), _strlwr(), _strncnt(), _strncoll(), _strnextc(), _strnicmp(), _strnicoll(), _strninc(), _strnset(), _strset(), _strspnp(), _strupr(), _tcsdec(), _tcsinc(), _tcsnccnt(), _tcsninc(), _tcsspnp(), _wcsdec(), _wcsicmp(), _wcsicoll(), _wcslwr(), _wcsncnt(), _wcsncoll(), _wcsnicmp(), _wcsnicoll(), _wcsninc(), _wcsnset(), _wcsrev(), _wcsset(), _wcsspnp(), _wcsupr(), strcat(), strchr(), strcmp(), strcoll(), strcpy(), strcspn(), strdup(), stricmp(), strlwr(), strncat(), strncmp(), strncpy(), strnicmp(), strnset(), strpbrk(), strrchr(), strrev(), strset(), strspn(), strstr(), strtod(), strtok(), strtol(), strtoul(), strupr(), wcscat(), wcschr(), wcscmp(), wcscoll(), wcscpy(), wcscspn(), wcslen(), wcsncat(), wcsncmp(), wcsncpy(), wcspbrk(), wcsrchr(), wcsspn(), wcsstr(), wcstod(), wcstok(), wcstol(), and wcstoul().

strlwr()

Function

The strlwr() function converts a string to lowercase, returning a pointer to the new string.

Header File

```
#include <string.h>
```

Declaration

```
char* strlwr(const char *string);
```

- *string* — The string to convert.

Example

The following program demonstrates how to use the strlwr() function. When run, the program converts several strings to lowercase and displays the results. The program's output looks like this:

```
Original String: One Two Three
Converted String: one two three

Original String: FOUR FIVE SIX
Converted String: four five six

Original String: seven eight nine
Converted String: seven eight nine

Press any key to continue
```

Here is the program source code that produced the output:

```
#include "stdafx.h"
#include <iostream>
#include <string.h>

using namespace std;

void convert(char* s)
```

```
    {
        cout << "Original String: " << s << endl;
        char* result = strlwr(s);
        cout << "Converted String: ";
        cout << result << endl << endl;
    }

    int main(int argc, char* argv[])
    {
        char str1[81];
        strcpy(str1, "One Two Three");
        char str2[81];
        strcpy(str2, "FOUR FIVE SIX");
        char str3[81];
        strcpy(str3, "seven eight nine");

        convert(str1);
        convert(str2);
        convert(str3);

        return 0;
    }
```

CROSS-REFERENCE

See also _mbscat(), _mbschr(), _mbscmp(), _mbscoll(), _mbscpy(), _mbscspn(), _mbsdec(), _mbsdup(), _mbsicmp(), _mbsicoll(), _mbsinc(), _mbslen(), _mbslwr(), _mbsnbcat(), _mbsnbcmp(), _mbsnbcnt(), _mbsnbcoll(), _mbsnbcpy(), _mbsnbicmp(), _mbsnbicoll(), _mbsnbset(), _mbsnccnt(), _mbsncmp(), _mbsncoll(), _mbsncpy(), _mbsnextc(), _mbsnicmp(), _mbsnicoll(), _mbsninc(), _mbsnset(), _mbspbrk(), _mbsrchr(), _mbsrev(), _mbsset(), _mbsspn(), _mbsspnp(), _mbsstr(), _mbstok(), _mbstrlen(), _mbsupr(), _strdec(), _stricoll(), _strinc(), _strlwr(), _strncnt(), _strncoll(), _strnextc(), _strnicmp(), _strnicoll(), _strninc(), _strnset(), _strset(), _strspnp(), _strupr(), _tcsdec(), _tcsinc(), _tcsnccnt(), _tcsninc(), _tcsspnp(), _wcsdec(), _wcsicmp(), _wcsicoll(), _wcslwr(), _wcsncnt(), _wcsncoll(), _wcsnicmp(), _wcsnicoll(), _wcsninc(), _wcsnset(), _wcsrev(), _wcsset(), _wcsspnp(), _wcsupr(), strcat(), strchr(), strcmp(), strcoll(), strcpy(), strcspn(), strdup(), stricmp(), strlen(), strncat(), strncmp(), strncpy(), strnicmp(), strnset(), strpbrk(), strrchr(), strrev(), strset(), strspn(), strstr(), strtod(), strtok(), strtol(), strtoul(), strupr(), wcscat(), wcschr(), wcscmp(), wcscoll(), wcscpy(), wcscspn(), wcslen(), wcsncat(), wcsncmp(), wcsncpy(), wcspbrk(), wcsrchr(), wcsspn(), wcsstr(), wcstod(), wcstok(), wcstol(), and wcstoul().

strncat()

Function

The strncat() function concatenates strings, returning a pointer to the destination string.

Header File

```
#include <string.h>
```

Declaration

```
char* strncat(char *strDest,
    const char *strSource, size_t count);
```

- *count* — The number of characters to concatenate.
- *strDest* — The string to which to concatenate *strSource*.
- *strSource* — The string to concatenate to *strDest*.

Example

The following program demonstrates how to use the strncat() function. When run, the program concatenates the first six characters of the string "Four Five Six" to the string "One Two Three". The program's output looks like this:

```
Result: One Two Three Four F
Press any key to continue
```

Here is the program source code that produced the output:

```
#include "stdafx.h"
#include <iostream>
#include <string.h>

using namespace std;

int main(int argc, char* argv[])
{
    char str1[81];
```

```
        char* str2 = "Four Five Six";

        strcpy(str1, "One Two Three ");
        strncat(str1, str2, 6);
        cout << "Result: " << str1 << endl;

        return 0;
    }
```

CROSS-REFERENCE

See also _mbscat(), _mbschr(), _mbscmp(), _mbscoll(), _mbscpy(), _mbscspn(), _mbsdec(), _mbsdup(), _mbsicmp(), _mbsicoll(), _mbsinc(), _mbslen(), _mbslwr(), _mbsnbcat(), _mbsnbcmp(), _mbsnbcnt(), _mbsnbcoll(), _mbsnbcpy(), _mbsnbicmp(), _mbsnbicoll(), _mbsnbset(), _mbsnccnt(), _mbsncmp(), _mbsncoll(), _mbsncpy(), _mbsnextc(), _mbsnicmp(), _mbsnicoll(), _mbsninc(), _mbsnset(), _mbspbrk(), _mbsrchr(), _mbsrev(), _mbsset(), _mbsspn(), _mbsspnp(), _mbsstr(), _mbstok(), _mbstrlen(), _mbsupr(), _strdec(), _stricoll(), _strinc(), _strlwr(), _strncnt(), _strncoll(), _strnextc(), _strnicmp(), _strnicoll(), _strninc(), _strnset(), _strset(), _strspnp(), _strupr(), _tcsdec(), _tcsinc(), _tcsnccnt(), _tcsninc(), _tcsspnp(), _wcsdec(), _wcsicmp(), _wcsicoll(), _wcslwr(), _wcsncnt(), _wcsncoll(), _wcsnicmp(), _wcsnicoll(), _wcsninc(), _wcsnset(), _wcsrev(), _wcsset(), _wcsspnp(), _wcsupr(), strcat(), strchr(), strcmp(), strcoll(), strcpy(), strcspn(), strdup(), stricmp(), strlen(), strlwr(), strncmp(), strncpy(), strnicmp(), strnset(), strpbrk(), strrchr(), strrev(), strset(), strspn(), strstr(), strtod(), strtok(), strtol(), strtoul(), strupr(), wcscat(), wcschr(), wcscmp(), wcscoll(), wcscpy(), wcscspn(), wcslen(), wcsncat(), wcsncmp(), wcsncpy(), wcspbrk(), wcsrchr(), wcsspn(), wcsstr(), wcstod(), wcstok(), wcstol(), and wcstoul().

strncmp()

Function

The strncmp() function compares a set of characters in two strings, returning a value from Table S-30.

Table S-30 Return Values for strncmp()

Value	Description
Less than 0	string1 is alphabetically less than string2.
0	The two strings are equal.
Greater than 0	string1 is alphabetically greater than string2.

Header File

```
#include <string.h>
```

Declaration

```
int strncmp(const char *string1,
    const char *string2, size_t count);
```

- *count* — The number of characters to compare.
- *string1* — The first string to compare.
- *string2* — The second string to compare.

Example

The following program demonstrates how to use the strncmp() function. When run, the program compares several pairs of strings and displays the result of the comparisons. The program's output looks like this:

```
For a length of 7 characters

One Two Three equals One Two Ten
One Two Ten is greater than Four Five Six
Four Five Six is greater than Four Eight Nine

Press any key to continue
```

Here is the program source code that produced the output:

```
#include "stdafx.h"
#include <iostream>
#include <string.h>

using namespace std;

void cmp(char* s1, char* s2, size_t num)
{
    int result = strncmp(s1, s2, num);
    if (result < 0 )
    {
        cout << s1 << " is less than ";
        cout << s2 << endl;
    }
    else if (result > 0)
    {
```

```
            cout << s1 << " is greater than ";
            cout << s2 << endl;
        }
        else
        {
            cout << s1 << " equals ";
            cout << s2 << endl;
        }
    }

    int main(int argc, char* argv[])
    {
        char* str1 = "One Two Three";
        char* str2 = "One Two Ten";
        char* str3 = "Four Five Six";
        char* str4 = "Four Eight Nine";

        cout << "For a length of 7 characters" << endl << endl;
        cmp(str1, str2, 7);
        cmp(str2, str3, 7);
        cmp(str3, str4, 7);
        cout << endl;

        return 0;
    }
```

CROSS-REFERENCE

See also _mbscat(), _mbschr(), _mbscmp(), _mbscoll(), _mbscpy(), _mbscspn(), _mbsdec(), _mbsdup(), _mbsicmp(), _mbsicoll(), _mbsinc(), _mbslen(), _mbslwr(), _mbsnbcat(), _mbsnbcmp(), _mbsnbcnt(), _mbsnbcoll(), _mbsnbcpy(), _mbsnbicmp(), _mbsnbicoll(), _mbsnbset(), _mbsnccnt(), _mbsncmp(), _mbsncoll(), _mbsncpy(), _mbsnextc(), _mbsnicmp(), _mbsnicoll(), _mbsninc(), _mbsnset(), _mbspbrk(), _mbsrchr(), _mbsrev(), _mbsset(), _mbsspn(), _mbsspnp(), _mbsstr(), _mbstok(), _mbstrlen(), _mbsupr(), _strdec(), _stricoll(), _strinc(), _strlwr(), _strncnt(), _strncoll(), _strnextc(), _strnicmp(), _strnicoll(), _strninc(), _strnset(), _strset(), _strspnp(), _strupr(), _tcsdec(), _tcsinc(), _tcsnccnt(), _tcsninc(), _tcsspnp(), _wcsdec(), _wcsicmp(), _wcsicoll(), _wcslwr(), _wcsncnt(), _wcsncoll(), _wcsnicmp(), _wcsnicoll(), _wcsninc(), _wcsnset(), _wcsrev(), _wcsset(), _wcsspnp(), _wcsupr(), strcat(), strchr(), strcmp(), strcoll(), strcpy(), strcspn(), strdup(), stricmp(), strlen(), strlwr(), strncat(), strncpy(), strnicmp(), strnset(), strpbrk(), strrchr(), strrev(), strset(), strspn(), strstr(), strtod(), strtok(), strtol(), strtoul(), strupr(), wcscat(), wcschr(), wcscmp(), wcscoll(), wcscpy(), wcscspn(), wcslen(), wcsncat(), wcsncmp(), wcsncpy(), wcspbrk(), wcsrchr(), wcsspn(), wcsstr(), wcstod(), wcstok(), wcstol(), and wcstoul().

strncpy()

Function

The strncpy() function copies a specified number of characters from one string to another, returning a pointer to the destination string. The source and destination strings cannot overlap.

Header File

```
#include <string.h>
```

Declaration

```
char* strncpy(char *strDest,
    const char *strSource, size_t count);
```

- *count* — The number of characters to copy.
- *strDest* — A pointer to the destination string.
- *strSource* — A pointer to the source string.

Example

The following program demonstrates how to use the strncpy() function. When run, the program copies 11 characters from one string to another and displays the result. The program's output looks like this:

```
Source string = This is a test
Destination string = This is a t
Press any key to continue
```

Here is the program source code that produced the output:

```
#include "stdafx.h"
#include <iostream>
#include <string.h>

using namespace std;

int main(int argc, char* argv[])
{
    char destStr[81];
    char* srcStr = "This is a test";

    char* pResult = strncpy(destStr, srcStr, 11);
```

```
        pResult[11] = 0;
        cout << "Source string = " << srcStr << endl;
        cout << "Destination string = " << pResult << endl;

        return 0;
    }
```

CROSS-REFERENCE

See also _mbscat(), _mbschr(), _mbscmp(), _mbscoll(), _mbscpy(), _mbscspn(), _mbsdec(), _mbsdup(), _mbsicmp(), _mbsicoll(), _mbsinc(), _mbslen(), _mbslwr(), _mbsnbcat(), _mbsnbcmp(), _mbsnbcnt(), _mbsnbcoll(), _mbsnbcpy(), _mbsnbicmp(), _mbsnbicoll(), _mbsnbset(), _mbsnccnt(), _mbsncmp(), _mbsncoll(), _mbsncpy(), _mbsnextc(), _mbsnicmp(), _mbsnicoll(), _mbsninc(), _mbsnset(), _mbspbrk(), _mbsrchr(), _mbsrev(), _mbsset(), _mbsspn(), _mbsspnp(), _mbsstr(), _mbstok(), _mbstrlen(), _mbsupr(), _strdec(), _stricoll(), _strinc(), _strlwr(), _strncnt(), _strncoll(), _strnextc(), _strnicmp(), _strnicoll(), _strninc(), _strnset(), _strset(), _strspnp(), _strupr(), _tcsdec(), _tcsinc(), _tcsnccnt(), _tcsninc(), _tcsspnp(), _wcsdec(), _wcsicmp(), _wcsicoll(), _wcslwr(), _wcsncnt(), _wcsncoll(), _wcsnicmp(), _wcsnicoll(), _wcsninc(), _wcsnset(), _wcsrev(), _wcsset(), _wcsspnp(), _wcsupr(), strcat(), strchr(), strcmp(), strcoll(), strcpy(), strcspn(), strdup(), stricmp(), strlen(), strlwr(), strncat(), strncmp(), strnicmp(), strnset(), strpbrk(), strrchr(), strrev(), strset(), strspn(), strstr(), strtod(), strtok(), strtol(), strtoul(), strupr(), wcscat(), wcschr(), wcscmp(), wcscoll(), wcscpy(), wcscspn(), wcslen(), wcsncat(), wcsncmp(), wcsncpy(), wcspbrk(), wcsrchr(), wcsspn(), wcsstr(), wcstod(), wcstok(), wcstol(), and wcstoul().

strnicmp()

Function

The strnicmp() function compares two strings without regard for case (case–insensitive compare), returning a value from Table S-31.

Table S-31 Return Values for strnicmp()

Value	Description
Less than 0	string1 is alphabetically less than string2.
0	The two strings are equal.
Greater than 0	string1 is alphabetically greater than string2.

Header File

```
#include <string.h>
```

Declaration

```
int strnicmp(const char *string1,
    const char *string2, size_t count);
```

- *count* — The number of characters to compare.
- *string1* — The first string to compare.
- *string2* — The second string to compare.

Example

The following program demonstrates how to use the `strnicmp()` function. When run, the program compares several pairs of strings and displays the result of the comparisons. The program's output looks like this:

```
One Two Three equals One Two three
One Two three equals one Two Three
one Two Three is less than SEVEN EIGHT nine
SEVEN EIGHT nine equals seven eight nine
Press any key to continue
```

Here is the program source code that produced the output:

```
#include "stdafx.h"
#include <iostream>
#include <string.h>

using namespace std;

void cmp(char* s1, char* s2, size_t num)
{
    int result = _strnicmp(s1, s2, num);
    if (result < 0 )
    {
        cout << s1;
        cout << " is less than ";
        cout << s2 << endl;
    }
    else if (result > 0)
```

```
        {
            cout << s1;
            cout << " is greater than ";
            cout << s2 << endl;
        }
        else
        {
            cout << s1;
            cout << " equals ";
            cout << s2 << endl;
        }
    }

    int main(int argc, char* argv[])
    {
        char* str1 = "One Two Three";
        char* str2 = "One Two three";
        char* str3 = "one Two Three";
        char* str4 = "SEVEN EIGHT nine";
        char* str5 = "seven eight nine";

        cmp(str1, str2, 7);
        cmp(str2, str3, 7);
        cmp(str3, str4, 7);
        cmp(str4, str5, 7);

        return 0;
    }
```

 CROSS-REFERENCE

See also _mbscat(), _mbschr(), _mbscmp(), _mbscoll(), _mbscpy(), _mbscspn(), _mbsdec(), _mbsdup(), _mbsicmp(), _mbsicoll(), _mbsinc(), _mbslen(), _mbslwr(), _mbsnbcat(), _mbsnbcmp(), _mbsnbcnt(), _mbsnbcoll(), _mbsnbcpy(), _mbsnbicmp(), _mbsnbicoll(), _mbsnbset(), _mbsnccnt(), _mbsncmp(), _mbsncoll(), _mbsncpy(), _mbsnextc(), _mbsnicmp(), _mbsnicoll(), _mbsninc(), _mbsnset(), _mbspbrk(), _mbsrchr(), _mbsrev(), _mbsset(), _mbsspn(), _mbsspnp(), _mbsstr(), _mbstok(), _mbstrlen(), _mbsupr(), _strdec(), _stricoll(), _strinc(), _strlwr(), _strncnt(), _strncoll(), _strnextc(), _strnicmp(), _strnicoll(), _strninc(), _strnset(), _strset(), _strspnp(), _strupr(), _tcsdec(), _tcsinc(), _tcsnccnt(), _tcsninc(), _tcsspnp(), _wcsdec(), _wcsicmp(), _wcsicoll(), _wcslwr(), _wcsncnt(), _wcsncoll(), _wcsnicmp(), _wcsnicoll(), _wcsninc(), _wcsnset(), _wcsrev(), _wcsset(), _wcsspnp(), _wcsupr(), strcat(), strchr(), strcmp(), strcoll(), strcpy(), strcspn(), strdup(), stricmp(), strlen(), strlwr(), strncat(), strncmp(), strncpy(), strnset(), strpbrk(), strrchr(), strrev(), strset(), strspn(), strstr(), strtod(), strtok(), strtol(), strtoul(), strupr(), wcscat(), wcschr(), wcscmp(), wcscoll(), wcscpy(), wcscspn(), wcslen(), wcsncat(), wcsncmp(), wcsncpy(), wcspbrk(), wcsrchr(), wcsspn(), wcsstr(), wcstod(), wcstok(), wcstol(), and wcstoul().

strnset()

Function

The `strnset()` function sets a portion of the contents of a string to a given character, returning a pointer to the new string.

Header File

```
#include <string.h>
```

Declaration

```
char* strnset(const char *string, char c, size_t count);
```

- *c* — The character with which to fill the string.
- *count* — The number of characters to set.
- *string* — The string to set.

Example

The following program demonstrates how to use the `strnset()` function. When run, the program sets several strings to various symbols and displays the results. The program's output looks like this:

```
Original String: One Two Three
Converted String: ??? Two Three

Original String: FOUR FIVE SIX
Converted String: ******VE SIX

Original String: seven eight nine
Converted String: ################

Press any key to continue
```

Here is the program source code that produced the output:

```
#include "stdafx.h"
```

```
#include <iostream>
#include <string.h>

using namespace std;

void convert(char* s, char c, size_t num)
{
    cout << "Original String: ";
    cout << s << endl;
    char* result = strnset(s, c, num);
    cout << "Converted String: ";
    cout << result << endl << endl;
}

int main(int argc, char* argv[])
{
    char str1[81];
    strcpy(str1, "One Two Three");
    char str2[81];
    strcpy(str2, "FOUR FIVE SIX");
    char str3[81];
    strcpy(str3, "seven eight nine");

    convert(str1, '?', 3);
    convert(str2, '*', 7);
    convert(str3, '#', 16);

    return 0;
}
```

CROSS-REFERENCE

See also _mbscat(), _mbschr(), _mbscmp(), _mbscoll(), _mbscpy(), _mbscspn(), _mbsdec(), _mbsdup(), _mbsicmp(), _mbsicoll(), _mbsinc(), _mbslen(), _mbslwr(), _mbsnbcat(), _mbsnbcmp(), _mbsnbcnt(), _mbsnbcoll(), _mbsnbcpy(), _mbsnbicmp(), _mbsnbicoll(), _mbsnbset(), _mbsnccnt(), _mbsncmp(), _mbsncoll(), _mbsncpy(), _mbsnextc(), _mbsnicmp(), _mbsnicoll(), _mbsninc(), _mbsnset(), _mbspbrk(), _mbsrchr(), _mbsrev(), _mbsset(), _mbsspn(), _mbsspnp(), _mbsstr(), _mbstok(), _mbstrlen(), _mbsupr(), _strdec(), _stricoll(), _strinc(), _strlwr(), _strncnt(), _strncoll(), _strnextc(), _strnicmp(), _strnicoll(), _strninc(), _strnset(), _strset(), _strspnp(), _strupr(), _tcsdec(), _tcsinc(), _tcsnccnt(), _tcsninc(), _tcsspnp(), _wcsdec(), _wcsicmp(), _wcsicoll(), _wcslwr(), _wcsncnt(), _wcsncoll(), _wcsnicmp(), _wcsnicoll(), _wcsninc(), _wcsnset(), _wcsrev(), _wcsset(), _wcsspnp(), _wcsupr(), strcat(), strchr(), strcmp(), strcoll(), strcpy(), strcspn(), strdup(), stricmp(), strlen(), strlwr(), strncat(), strncmp(), strncpy(), strnicmp(), strpbrk(), strrchr(), strrev(), strset(), strspn(), strstr(), strtod(), strtok(), strtol(), strtoul(), strupr(), wcscat(), wcschr(), wcscmp(), wcscoll(), wcscpy(), wcscspn(), wcslen(), wcsncat(), wcsncmp(), wcsncpy(), wcspbrk(), wcsrchr(), wcsspn(), wcsstr(), wcstod(), wcstok(), wcstol(), and wcstoul().

strpbrk()

Function

The strpbrk() function locates the first occurrence of a character in a string, returning a pointer to the substring starting with the matching character.

Header File

```
#include <string.h>
```

Declaration

```
char* strpbrk(const char *string,
    const char *strCharSet);
```

- *strCharSet* — A pointer to the set of characters for which to search.
- *string* — A pointer to the string to search.

Example

The following program demonstrates how to use the strpbrk() function. When run, the program locates, in a string, the first character in a set and displays the result. The program's output looks like this:

```
Source String:
This is a test
Substring:
s is a test

Press any key to continue
```

Here is the program source code that produced the output:

```
#include "stdafx.h"
#include <iostream>
```

```
#include <string.h>

using namespace std;

int main(int argc, char* argv[])
{
    char* srcStr = "This is a test";
    char* chrSet = "ast";

    char* pSubStr = strpbrk(srcStr, chrSet);
    cout << "Source String:" << endl;
    cout << srcStr << endl;
    cout << "Substring:" << endl;
    cout << pSubStr << endl << endl;

    return 0;
}
```

CROSS-REFERENCE

See also _mbscat(), _mbschr(), _mbscmp(), _mbscoll(), _mbscpy(), _mbscspn(), _mbsdec(), _mbsdup(), _mbsicmp(), _mbsicoll(), _mbsinc(), _mbslen(), _mbslwr(), _mbsnbcat(), _mbsnbcmp(), _mbsnbcnt(), _mbsnbcoll(), _mbsnbcpy(), _mbsnbicmp(), _mbsnbicoll(), _mbsnbset(), _mbsnccnt(), _mbsncmp(), _mbsncoll(), _mbsncpy(), _mbsnextc(), _mbsnicmp(), _mbsnicoll(), _mbsninc(), _mbsnset(), _mbspbrk(), _mbsrchr(), _mbsrev(), _mbsset(), _mbsspn(), _mbsspnp(), _mbsstr(), _mbstok(), _mbstrlen(), _mbsupr(), _strdec(), _stricoll(), _strinc(), _strlwr(), _strncnt(), _strncoll(), _strnextc(), _strnicmp(), _strnicoll(), _strninc(), _strnset(), _strset(), _strspnp(), _strupr(), _tcsdec(), _tcsinc(), _tcsnccnt(), _tcsninc(), _tcsspnp(), _wcsdec(), _wcsicmp(), _wcsicoll(), _wcslwr(), _wcsncnt(), _wcsncoll(), _wcsnicmp(), _wcsnicoll(), _wcsninc(), _wcsnset(), _wcsrev(), _wcsset(), _wcsspnp(), _wcsupr(), strcat(), strchr(), strcmp(), strcoll(), strcpy(), strcspn(), strdup(), stricmp(), strlen(), strlwr(), strncat(), strncmp(), strncpy(), strnicmp(), strnset(), strrchr(), strrev(), strset(), strspn(), strstr(), strtod(), strtok(), strtol(), strtoul(), strupr(), wcscat(), wcschr(), wcscmp(), wcscoll(), wcscpy(), wcscspn(), wcslen(), wcsncat(), wcsncmp(), wcsncpy(), wcspbrk(), wcsrchr(), wcsspn(), wcsstr(), wcstod(), wcstok(), wcstol(), and wcstoul().

strrchr()

Function

The strrchr() function locates the last occurrence of a character in a string, returning a pointer to the substring starting with the matching character.

Header File

```
#include <string.h>
```

Declaration

```
char* strrchr(const char *string, int c);
```

- *c*—The character for which to search.
- *string*—A pointer to the string to search.

Example

The following program demonstrates how to use the strrchr() function. When run, the program locates the last occurrence of the character "i" in a string and displays the result. The program's output looks like this:

```
Source String:
This is a test
Substring:
is a test


Press any key to continue
```

Here is the program source code that produced the output:

```cpp
#include "stdafx.h"
#include <iostream>
#include <string.h>

using namespace std;

int main(int argc, char* argv[])
{
    char* srcStr = "This is a test";

    char* pSubStr = strrchr(srcStr, 'i');
    cout << "Source String:" << endl;
    cout << srcStr << endl;
    cout << "Substring:" << endl;
    cout << pSubStr << endl << endl;

    return 0;
}
```

r
s
t

CROSS-REFERENCE

See also _mbscat(), _mbschr(), _mbscmp(), _mbscoll(), _mbscpy(), _mbscspn(), _mbsdec(), _mbsdup(), _mbsicmp(), _mbsicoll(), _mbsinc(), _mbslen(), _mbslwr(), _mbsnbcat(), _mbsnbcmp(), _mbsnbcnt(), _mbsnbcoll(), _mbsnbcpy(), _mbsnbicmp(), _mbsnbicoll(), _mbsnbset(), _mbsnccnt(), _mbsncmp(), _mbsncoll(), _mbsncpy(), _mbsnextc(), _mbsnicmp(), _mbsnicoll(), _mbsninc(), _mbsnset(), _mbspbrk(), _mbsrchr(), _mbsrev(), _mbsset(), _mbsspn(), _mbsspnp(), _mbsstr(), _mbstok(), _mbstrlen(), _mbsupr(), _strdec(), _stricoll(), _strinc(), _strlwr(), _strncnt(), _strncoll(), _strnextc(), _strnicmp(), _strnicoll(), _strninc(), _strnset(), _strset(), _strspnp(), _strupr(), _tcsdec(), _tcsinc(), _tcsnccnt(), _tcsninc(), _tcsspnp(), _wcsdec(), _wcsicmp(), _wcsicoll(), _wcslwr(), _wcsncnt(), _wcsncoll(), _wcsnicmp(), _wcsnicoll(), _wcsninc(), _wcsnset(), _wcsrev(), _wcsset(), _wcsspnp(), _wcsupr(), strcat(), strchr(), strcmp(), strcoll(), strcpy(), strcspn(), strdup(), stricmp(), strlen(), strlwr(), strncat(), strncmp(), strncpy(), strnicmp(), strnset(), strpbrk(), strrev(), strset(), strspn(), strstr(), strtod(), strtok(), strtol(), strtoul(), strupr(), wcscat(), wcschr(), wcscmp(), wcscoll(), wcscpy(), wcscspn(), wcslen(), wcsncat(), wcsncmp(), wcsncpy(), wcspbrk(), wcsrchr(), wcsspn(), wcsstr(), wcstod(), wcstok(), wcstol(), and wcstoul().

strrev()

Function

The strrev() function reverses the order of characters in a string to upper-case, returning a pointer to the new string.

Header File

```
#include <string.h>
```

Declaration

```
char* strrev(const char *string);
```

- *string* — The string to reverse.

Example

The following program demonstrates how to use the strrev() function. When run, the program reverses several strings and displays the results. The program's output looks like this:

```
Original String: One Two Three
Converted String: eerhT owT enO

Original String: FOUR FIVE SIX
Converted String: XIS EVIF RUOF

Original String: seven eight nine
Converted String: enin thgie neves

Press any key to continue
```

Here is the program source code that produced the output:

```cpp
#include "stdafx.h"
#include <iostream>
#include <string.h>

using namespace std;

void convert(char* s)
{
    cout << "Original String: ";
    cout << s << endl;
    char* result = strrev(s);
    cout << "Converted String: ";
    cout << result << endl << endl;
}

int main(int argc, char* argv[])
{
    char str1[81];
    strcpy(str1, "One Two Three");
    char str2[81];
    strcpy(str2, "FOUR FIVE SIX");
    char str3[81];
    strcpy(str3, "seven eight nine");

    convert(str1);
    convert(str2);
    convert(str3);

    return 0;
}
```

CROSS-REFERENCE

See also _mbscat(), _mbschr(), _mbscmp(), _mbscoll(), _mbscpy(), _mbscspn(), _mbsdec(), _mbsdup(), _mbsicmp(), _mbsicoll(), _mbsinc(), _mbslen(), _mbslwr(), _mbsnbcat(), _mbsnbcmp(), _mbsnbcnt(), _mbsnbcoll(), _mbsnbcpy(), _mbsnbicmp(), _mbsnbicoll(), _mbsnbset(), _mbsnccnt(), _mbsncmp(), _mbsncoll(), _mbsncpy(), _mbsnextc(), _mbsnicmp(), _mbsnicoll(), _mbsninc(), _mbsnset(), _mbspbrk(), _mbsrchr(), _mbsrev(), _mbsset(), _mbsspn(), _mbsspnp(), _mbsstr(), _mbstok(), _mbstrlen(), _mbsupr(), _strdec(), _stricoll(), _strinc(), _strlwr(), _strncnt(), _strncoll(), _strnextc(), _strnicmp(), _strnicoll(), _strninc(), _strnset(), _strset(), _strspnp(), _strupr(), _tcsdec(), _tcsinc(), _tcsnccnt(), _tcsninc(), _tcsspnp(), _wcsdec(), _wcsicmp(), _wcsicoll(), _wcslwr(), _wcsncnt(), _wcsncoll(), _wcsnicmp(), _wcsnicoll(), _wcsninc(), _wcsnset(), _wcsrev(), _wcsset(), _wcsspnp(), _wcsupr(), strcat(), strchr(), strcmp(), strcoll(), strcpy(), strcspn(), strdup(), stricmp(), strlen(), strlwr(), strncat(), strncmp(), strncpy(), strnicmp(), strnset(), strpbrk(), strrchr(), strset(), strspn(), strstr(), strtod(), strtok(), strtol(), strtoul(), strupr(), wcscat(), wcschr(), wcscmp(), wcscoll(), wcscpy(), wcscspn(), wcslen(), wcsncat(), wcsncmp(), wcsncpy(), wcspbrk(), wcsrchr(), wcsspn(), wcsstr(), wcstod(), wcstok(), wcstol(), and wcstoul().

strset()

Function

The strset() function sets the contents of a string to a specified character, returning a pointer to the new string.

Header File

```
#include <string.h>
```

Declaration

```
char* strset(const char *string, char c);
```

- *c* — The character with which to fill the string.
- *string* — The string to set.

Example

The following program demonstrates how to use the strset() function. When run, the program sets several strings to question marks and displays the results. The program's output looks like this:

```
Original String: One Two Three
Converted String: ???????????????

Original String: FOUR FIVE SIX
Converted String: ????????????

Original String: seven eight nine
Converted String: ???????????????????

Press any key to continue
```

Here is the program source code that produced the output:

```cpp
#include "stdafx.h"
#include <iostream>
#include <string.h>

using namespace std;

void convert(char* s, char c)
{
    cout << "Original String: ";
    cout << s << endl;
    char* result = strset(s, c);
    cout << "Converted String: ";
    cout << result << endl << endl;
}

int main(int argc, char* argv[])
{
    char str1[81];
    strcpy(str1, "One Two Three");
    char str2[81];
    strcpy(str2, "FOUR FIVE SIX");
    char str3[81];
    strcpy(str3, "seven eight nine");

    convert(str1, '?');
    convert(str2, '?');
    convert(str3, '?');

    return 0;
}
```

CROSS-REFERENCE

See also _mbscat(), _mbschr(), _mbscmp(), _mbscoll(), _mbscpy(), _mbscspn(), _mbsdec(), _mbsdup(), _mbsicmp(), _mbsicoll(), _mbsinc(), _mbslen(), _mbslwr(), _mbsnbcat(), _mbsnbcmp(), _mbsnbcnt(), _mbsnbcoll(), _mbsnbcpy(), _mbsnbicmp(), _mbsnbicoll(), _mbsnbset(), _mbsnccnt(), _mbsncmp(), _mbsncoll(), _mbsncpy(), _mbsnextc(), _mbsnicmp(), _mbsnicoll(), _mbsninc(), _mbsnset(), _mbspbrk(), _mbsrchr(), _mbsrev(), _mbsset(), _mbsspn(), _mbsspnp(), _mbsstr(), _mbstok(), _mbstrlen(), _mbsupr(), _strdec(), _stricoll(), _strinc(), _strlwr(), _strncnt(), _strncoll(), _strnextc(), _strnicmp(), _strnicoll(), _strninc(), _strnset(), _strset(), _strspnp(), _strupr(), _tcsdec(), _tcsinc(), _tcsnccnt(), _tcsninc(), _tcsspnp(), _wcsdec(), _wcsicmp(), _wcsicoll(), _wcslwr(), _wcsncnt(), _wcsncoll(), _wcsnicmp(), _wcsnicoll(), _wcsninc(), _wcsnset(), _wcsrev(), _wcsset(), _wcsspnp(), _wcsupr(), strcat(), strchr(), strcmp(), strcoll(), strcpy(), strcspn(), strdup(), stricmp(), strlen(), strlwr(), strncat(), strncmp(), strncpy(), strnicmp(), strnset(), strpbrk(), strrchr(), strrev(), strspn(), strstr(), strtod(), strtok(), strtol(), strtoul(), strupr(), wcscat(),wcschr(), wcscmp(), wcscoll(), wcscpy(), wcscspn(), wcslen(), wcsncat(), wcsncmp(), wcsncpy(), wcspbrk(), wcsrchr(), wcsspn(), wcsstr(), wcstod(), wcstok(), wcstol(), and wcstoul().

strspn()

Function

The `strspn()` function locates the first occurrence of a substring that starts with a character not included in the specified set. The function returns the index of the first nonmatching character.

Header File

```
#include <string.h>
```

Declaration

```
size_t strspn(const char *string, const char *strCharSet);
```

- *strCharSet*—A pointer to the set of characters for which to search.
- *string*—A pointer to the string to search.

Example

The following program demonstrates how to use the strspn() function.
When run, the program locates, in a string, the first character not in the spec-
ified set and displays the result, indicating the located character with a caret
(^). The program's output looks like this:

```
Source String:
This is a test
           ^

Press any key to continue
```

Here is the program source code that produced the output:

```
#include "stdafx.h"
#include <iostream>
#include <string.h>

using namespace std;

int main(int argc, char* argv[])
{
    char* srcStr = "This is a test";
    char* chrSet = "ahisT ";

    size_t len = strspn(srcStr, chrSet);
    cout << "Source String:" << endl;
    cout << srcStr << endl;
    for (unsigned x=0; x<len; ++x)
        cout << " ";
    cout << "^" << endl;

    return 0;
}
```

CROSS-REFERENCE

See also _mbscat(), _mbschr(), _mbscmp(), _mbscoll(), _mbscpy(), _mbscspn(),
_mbsdec(), _mbsdup(), _mbsicmp(), _mbsicoll(), _mbsinc(), _mbslen(), _mbslwr(),
_mbsnbcat(), _mbsnbcmp(), _mbsnbcnt(), _mbsnbcoll(), _mbsnbcpy(),
_mbsnbicmp(), _mbsnbicoll(), _mbsnbset(), _mbsnccnt(), _mbsncmp(),
_mbsncoll(), _mbsncpy(), _mbsnextc(), _mbsnicmp(), _mbsnicoll(), _mbsninc(),
_mbsnset(), _mbspbrk(), _mbsrchr(), _mbsrev(), _mbsset(), _mbsspn(),
_mbsspnp(), _mbsstr(), _mbstok(), _mbstrlen(), _mbsupr(), _strdec(), _stricoll(),
_strinc(), _strlwr(), _strncnt(), _strncoll(), _strnextc(), _strnicmp(), _strnicoll(),
_strninc(), _strnset(), _strset(), _strspnp(), _strupr(), _tcsdec(), _tcsinc(), _tcsnccnt(),

_tcsninc(), _tcsspnp(), _wcsdec(), _wcsicmp(), _wcsicoll(), _wcslwr(), _wcsncnt(), _wcsncoll(), _wcsnicmp(), _wcsnicoll(), _wcsninc(), _wcsnset(), _wcsrev(), _wcsset(), _wcsspnp(), _wcsupr(), strcat(), strchr(), strcmp(), strcoll(), strcpy(), strcspn(), strdup(), stricmp(), strlen(), strlwr(), strncat(), strncmp(), strncpy(), strnicmp(), strnset(), strpbrk(), strrchr(), strrev(), strset(), strstr(), strtod(), strtok(), strtol(), strtoul(), strupr(), wcscat(), wcschr(), wcscmp(), wcscoll(), wcscpy(), wcscspn(), wcslen(), wcsncat(), wcsncmp(), wcsncpy(), wcspbrk(), wcsrchr(), wcsspn(), wcsstr(), wcstod(), wcstok(), wcstol(), and wcstoul().

strstr()

Function

The strstr() function returns a pointer to a specified substring within a string.

Header File

```
#include <string.h>
```

Declaration

```
char* strstr(const char *string, const char *strCharSet);
```

- *strCharSet* — A pointer to the substring for which to search.
- *string* — A pointer to the string to search.

Example

The following program demonstrates how to use the strstr() function. When run, the program locates a specified substring and displays the portion of the original string that begins with the substring. The program's output looks like this:

```
Source String:
This is a test

Substring:
is a test

Press any key to continue
```

Here is the program source code that produced the output:

```
#include "stdafx.h"
#include <iostream>
#include <string.h>

using namespace std;

int main(int argc, char* argv[])
{
    char* srcStr = "This is a test";
    char* chrSet = "is a";

    char* pSubStr = strstr(srcStr, chrSet);
    cout << "Source String:" << endl;
    cout << srcStr << endl << endl;
    cout << "Substring:" << endl;
    cout << pSubStr << endl << endl;

    return 0;
}
```

CROSS-REFERENCE

See also _mbscat(), _mbschr(), _mbscmp(), _mbscoll(), _mbscpy(), _mbscspn(), _mbsdec(), _mbsdup(), _mbsicmp(), _mbsicoll(), _mbsinc(), _mbslen(), _mbslwr(), _mbsnbcat(), _mbsnbcmp(), _mbsnbcnt(), _mbsnbcoll(), _mbsnbcpy(), _mbsnbicmp(), _mbsnbicoll(), _mbsnbset(), _mbsnccnt(), _mbsncmp(), _mbsncoll(), _mbsncpy(), _mbsnextc(), _mbsnicmp(), _mbsnicoll(), _mbsninc(), _mbsnset(), _mbspbrk(), _mbsrchr(), _mbsrev(), _mbsset(), _mbsspn(), _mbsspnp(), _mbsstr(), _mbstok(), _mbstrlen(), _mbsupr(), _strdec(), _stricoll(), _strinc(), _strlwr(), _strncnt(), _strncoll(), _strnextc(), _strnicmp(), _strnicoll(), _strninc(), _strnset(), _strset(), _strspnp(), _strupr(), _tcsdec(), _tcsinc(), _tcsnccnt(), _tcsninc(), _tcsspnp(), _wcsdec(), _wcsicmp(), _wcsicoll(), _wcslwr(), _wcsncnt(), _wcsncoll(), _wcsnicmp(), _wcsnicoll(), _wcsninc(), _wcsnset(), _wcsrev(), _wcsset(), _wcsspnp(), _wcsupr(), strcat(), strchr(), strcmp(), strcoll(), strcpy(), strcspn(), strdup(), stricmp(), strlen(), strlwr(), strncat(), strncmp(), strncpy(), strnicmp(), strnset(), strpbrk(), strrchr(), strrev(), strset(), strspn(), strtod(), strtok(), strtol(), strtoul(), strupr(), wcscat(), wcschr(), wcscmp(), wcscoll(), wcscpy(), wcscspn(), wcslen(), wcsncat(), wcsncmp(), wcsncpy(), wcspbrk(), wcsrchr(), wcsspn(), wcsstr(), wcstod(), wcstok(), wcstol(), and wcstoul().

strstream

Class

The `strstream` class represents a stream for string-type data.

Class Declaration

```
class strstream : public iostream
{
public:
    strstream();
    strstream(char *s, streamsize n,
        ios_base::openmode mode = ios_base::in |
        ios_base::out);
    strstreambuf *rdbuf() const;
    void freeze(bool frz = true);
    char *str();
    streamsize pcount() const;
};
```

Class Members

Table S-32 lists and describes the members of `strstream`.

Table S-32 Members of strstream

Member	Description
freeze()	Freezes the string's contents.
pcount()	Returns the number of elements written to the string.
rdbuf()	Returns the address of the string's buffer.
str()	Returns a pointer to the first element of the string's sequence.

CROSS-REFERENCE

See also istrstream, ostrstream, strstream (Standard C++ Library Header File), and strstreambuf.

strstream

Standard C++ Library Header File

The strstream library header file defines the classes used with string streams, including the istrstream, ostrstream, strstream, and strstreambuf classes.

CROSS-REFERENCE
See also istrstream, ostrstream, strstream (class), and strstreambuf.

strstreambuf

Class

The strstreambuf class represents a buffer for data manipulated with the string stream classes.

Class Declaration

```
class strstreambuf : public streambuf
{
public:
    explicit strstreambuf(streamsize n = 0);
    strstreambuf(void (*palloc)(size_t),
        void (*pfree)(void *));
    strstreambuf(char *gp, streamsize n,
        char *pp = 0);
    strstreambuf(signed char *gp, streamsize n,
        signed char *pp = 0);
    strstreambuf(unsigned char *gp, streamsize n,
        unsigned char *pp = 0);
    strstreambuf(const char *gp, streamsize n);
    strstreambuf(const signed char *gp, streamsize n);
    strstreambuf(const unsigned char *gp, streamsize n);
    void freeze(bool frz = true) const;
    char *str();
    streamsize pcount();
protected:
    virtual streampos seekoff(streamoff off,
        ios_base::seekdir way,
```

```
        ios_base::openmode which = ios_base::in |
        ios_base::out);
    virtual streampos seekpos(streampos sp,
        ios_base::openmode which = ios_base::in |
        ios_base::out);
    virtual int underflow();
    virtual int pbackfail(int c = EOF);
    virtual int overflow(int c = EOF);
};
```

Class Members

Table S-33 lists and describes the members of the `strstreambuf` class.

Table S-33 Members of the strstreambuf Class

Member	Description
freeze()	Freezes the string's contents.
overflow()	Inserts an element into the string buffer, returning c if successful, or EOF if not successful.
pbackfail()	Places an element back into the input buffer, returning c if successful, or EOF if unsuccessful.
pcount()	Returns the number of elements written to the string.
seekoff()	Sets a position in the stream.
seekpos()	Sets a position in the stream.
str()	Returns a pointer to the first element of the string's sequence.
underflow()	Removes an elements from the string buffer, returning the element if successful, or EOF if unsuccessful.

CROSS-REFERENCE

See also istrstream, ostrstream, strstream (class), and strstream (Standard C++ Library Header File).

strtod()

Function

The `strtod()` function converts a string to a double-precision floating-point value.

Header File

```
#include <string.h>
```

Declaration

```
double strtod(const char *nptr, char **endptr);
```

- *endptr* — The pointer that will hold the address of the portion of the string that cannot be converted.
- *nptr* — A pointer to the string to convert.

Example

The following program demonstrates how to use the `strtod()` function. When run, the program converts a portion of a string to a `double` value and displays the remainder of the string (the portion that could not be converted). The program's output looks like this:

```
Source String:
12345.5643This is a test

Result = 12345.6

Remaining string:
This is a test

Press any key to continue
```

Here is the program source code that produced the output:

```cpp
#include "stdafx.h"
#include <iostream>
#include <string.h>

using namespace std;

int main(int argc, char* argv[])
{
    char* srcStr = "12345.5643This is a test";
    char* str;

    double result = strtod(srcStr, &str);
    cout << "Source String:" << endl;
    cout << srcStr << endl << endl;
    cout << "Result = " << result << endl << endl;
```

```
        cout << "Remaining string:" << endl;
        cout << str << endl << endl;

        return 0;
    }
```

CROSS-REFERENCE

See also _mbscat(), _mbschr(), _mbscmp(), _mbscoll(), _mbscpy(), _mbscspn(), _mbsdec(), _mbsdup(), _mbsicmp(), _mbsicoll(), _mbsinc(), _mbslen(), _mbslwr(), _mbsnbcat(), _mbsnbcmp(), _mbsnbcnt(), _mbsnbcoll(), _mbsnbcpy(), _mbsnbicmp(), _mbsnbicoll(), _mbsnbset(), _mbsnccnt(), _mbsncmp(), _mbsncoll(), _mbsncpy(), _mbsnextc(), _mbsnicmp(), _mbsnicoll(), _mbsninc(), _mbsnset(), _mbspbrk(), _mbsrchr(), _mbsrev(), _mbsset(), _mbsspn(), _mbsspnp(), _mbsstr(), _mbstok(), _mbstrlen(), _mbsupr(), _strdec(), _stricoll(), _strinc(), _strlwr(), _strncnt(), _strncoll(), _strnextc(), _strnicmp(), _strnicoll(), _strninc(), _strnset(), _strset(), _strspnp(), _strupr(), _tcsdec(), _tcsinc(), _tcsnccnt(), _tcsninc(), _tcsspnp(), _wcsdec(), _wcsicmp(), _wcsicoll(), _wcslwr(), _wcsncnt(), _wcsncoll(), _wcsnicmp(), _wcsnicoll(), _wcsninc(), _wcsnset(), _wcsrev(), _wcsset(), _wcsspnp(), _wcsupr(), strcat(), strchr(), strcmp(), strcoll(), strcpy(), strcspn(), strdup(), stricmp(), strlen(), strlwr(), strncat(), strncmp(), strncpy(), strnicmp(), strnset(), strpbrk(), strrchr(), strrev(), strset(), strspn(), strstr(), strtok(), strtol(), strtoul(), strupr(), wcscat(), wcschr(), wcscmp(), wcscoll(), wcscpy(), wcscspn(), wcslen(), wcsncat(), wcsncmp(), wcsncpy(), wcspbrk(), wcsrchr(), wcsspn(), wcsstr(), wcstod(), wcstok(), wcstol(), and wcstoul().

strtok()

Function

The strtok() function extracts tokens from a string.

Header File

```
#include <string.h>
```

Declaration

```
char* strtok(char *strToken, const char *strDelimit);
```

- *strDelimit* — A pointer to the string containing the characters (delimiters) that separate one token from another.
- *strToken* — A pointer to the string containing the tokens to extract.

Example

The following program demonstrates how to use the strtok() function. When run, the program extracts tokens from a string, displaying the results as it goes. The program's output looks like this:

```
Token Source String:
One,Two Three,Four*Five

Token Delimiter String:
, *

Tokens Found:
One
Two
Three
Four
Five

Press any key to continue
```

Here is the program source code that produced the output:

```cpp
#include "stdafx.h"
#include <iostream>
#include <string.h>

using namespace std;

#include <stdio.h>

int main(int argc, char* argv[])
{
    char str[81];
    char delimit[10];
    char *tok;

    strcpy(str, "One,Two Three,Four*Five");
    strcpy(delimit, ", *");
    cout << "Token Source String:" << endl;
    cout << str << endl << endl;
    cout << "Token Delimiter String:" << endl;
    cout << delimit << endl << endl;
    cout << "Tokens Found:" << endl;

    tok = strtok(str, delimit);
```

```
while(tok != NULL )
{
    cout << tok << endl;
    tok = strtok(NULL, delimit);
}

cout << endl;

return 0;
}
```

CROSS-REFERENCE

See also _mbscat(), _mbschr(), _mbscmp(), _mbscoll(), _mbscpy(), _mbscspn(), _mbsdec(), _mbsdup(), _mbsicmp(), _mbsicoll(), _mbsinc(), _mbslen(), _mbslwr(), _mbsnbcat(), _mbsnbcmp(), _mbsnbcnt(), _mbsnbcoll(), _mbsnbcpy(), _mbsnbicmp(), _mbsnbicoll(), _mbsnbset(), _mbsnccnt(), _mbsncmp(), _mbsncoll(), _mbsncpy(), _mbsnextc(), _mbsnicmp(), _mbsnicoll(), _mbsninc(), _mbsnset(), _mbspbrk(), _mbsrchr(), _mbsrev(), _mbsset(), _mbsspn(), _mbsspnp(), _mbsstr(), _mbstok(), _mbstrlen(), _mbsupr(), _strdec(), _stricoll(), _strinc(), _strlwr(), _strncnt(), _strncoll(), _strnextc(), _strnicmp(), _strnicoll(), _strninc(), _strnset(), _strset(), _strspnp(), _strupr(), _tcsdec(), _tcsinc(), _tcsnccnt(), _tcsninc(), _tcsspnp(), _wcsdec(), _wcsicmp(), _wcsicoll(), _wcslwr(), _wcsncnt(), _wcsncoll(), _wcsnicmp(), _wcsnicoll(), _wcsninc(), _wcsnset(), _wcsrev(), _wcsset(), _wcsspnp(), _wcsupr(), strcat(), strchr(), strcmp(), strcoll(), strcpy(), strcspn(), strdup(), stricmp(), strlen(), strlwr(), strncat(), strncmp(), strncpy(), strnicmp(), strnset(), strpbrk(), strrchr(), strrev(), strset(), strspn(), strstr(), strtod(), strtol(), strtoul(), strupr(), wcscat(), wcschr(), wcscmp(), wcscoll(), wcscpy(), wcscspn(), wcslen(), wcsncat(), wcsncmp(), wcsncpy(), wcspbrk(), wcsrchr(), wcsspn(), wcsstr(), wcstod(), wcstok(), wcstol(), and wcstoul().

strtol()

Function

The strtol() function converts a string to a long integer value.

Header File

```
#include <string.h>
```

Declaration

```
long strtol(const char *nptr, char **endptr, int base);
```

- *base* — The number base to use in the conversion.
- *endptr* — The pointer that will hold the address of the portion of the string that cannot be converted.
- *nptr* — A pointer to the string to convert.

Example

The following program demonstrates how to use the strtol() function. When run, the program converts a portion of a string to a long integer value and displays the remainder of the string (the portion that could not be converted). The program's output looks like this:

```
Source String:
1234556This is a test

Result = 1234556

Remaining string:
This is a test

Press any key to continue
```

Here is the program source code that produced the output:

```cpp
#include "stdafx.h"
#include <iostream>
#include <string.h>

using namespace std;

int main(int argc, char* argv[])
{
    char* srcStr = "1234556This is a test";
    char* str;

    long result = strtol(srcStr, &str, 10);
    cout << "Source String:" << endl;
    cout << srcStr << endl << endl;
    cout << "Result = " << result << endl << endl;
```

```
cout << "Remaining string:" << endl;
cout << str << endl << endl;

return 0;
}
```

CROSS-REFERENCE

See also _mbscat(), _mbschr(), _mbscmp(), _mbscoll(), _mbscpy(), _mbscspn(), _mbsdec(), _mbsdup(), _mbsicmp(), _mbsicoll(), _mbsinc(), _mbslen(), _mbslwr(), _mbsnbcat(), _mbsnbcmp(), _mbsnbcnt(), _mbsnbcoll(), _mbsnbcpy(), _mbsnbicmp(), _mbsnbicoll(), _mbsnbset(), _mbsnccnt(), _mbsncmp(), _mbsncoll(), _mbsncpy(), _mbsnextc(), _mbsnicmp(), _mbsnicoll(), _mbsninc(), _mbsnset(), _mbspbrk(), _mbsrchr(), _mbsrev(), _mbsset(), _mbsspn(), _mbsspnp(), _mbsstr(), _mbstok(), _mbstrlen(), _mbsupr(), _strdec(), _stricoll(), _strinc(), _strlwr(), _strncnt(), _strncoll(), _strnextc(), _strnicmp(), _strnicoll(), _strninc(), _strnset(), _strset(), _strspnp(), _strupr(), _tcsdec(), _tcsinc(), _tcsnccnt(), _tcsninc(), _tcsspnp(), _wcsdec(), _wcsicmp(), _wcsicoll(), _wcslwr(), _wcsncnt(), _wcsncoll(), _wcsnicmp(), _wcsnicoll(), _wcsninc(), _wcsnset(), _wcsrev(), _wcsset(), _wcsspnp(), _wcsupr(), strcat(), strchr(), strcmp(), strcoll(), strcpy(), strcspn(), strdup(), stricmp(), strlen(), strlwr(), strncat(), strncmp(), strncpy(), strnicmp(), strnset(), strpbrk(), strrchr(), strrev(), strset(), strspn(), strstr(), strtod(), strtok(), strtoul(), strupr(), wcscat(), wcschr(), wcscmp(), wcscoll(), wcscpy(), wcscspn(), wcslen(), wcsncat(), wcsncmp(), wcsncpy(), wcspbrk(), wcsrchr(), wcsspn(), wcsstr(), wcstod(), wcstok(), wcstol(), and wcstoul().

strtoul()

Function

The strtoul() function converts a string to an unsigned long integer value.

Header File

```
#include <string.h>
```

Declaration

```
unsigned long strtoul(const char *nptr,
    char **endptr, int base);
```

■ *base*—The number base to use in the conversion.

- *endptr*—The pointer that will hold the address of the portion of the string that cannot be converted.
- *nptr*—A pointer to the string to convert.

Example

The following program demonstrates how to use the strtoul() function. When run, the program converts a portion of a string to an unsigned long integer value and displays the remainder of the string (the portion that could not be converted). The program's output looks like this:

```
Source String:
1234556This is a test

Result = 1234556

Remaining string:
This is a test

Press any key to continue
```

Here is the program source code that produced the output:

```cpp
#include "stdafx.h"
#include <iostream>
#include <string.h>

using namespace std;

int main(int argc, char* argv[])
{
    char* srcStr = "1234556This is a test";
    char* str;

    unsigned long result = strtoul(srcStr, &str, 10);
    cout << "Source String:" << endl;
    cout << srcStr << endl << endl;
    cout << "Result = " << result << endl << endl;
    cout << "Remaining string:" << endl;
    cout << str << endl << endl;

    return 0;
}
```

CROSS-REFERENCE

See also _mbscat(), _mbschr(), _mbscmp(), _mbscoll(), _mbscpy(), _mbscspn(), _mbsdec(), _mbsdup(), _mbsicmp(), _mbsicoll(), _mbsinc(), _mbslen(), _mbslwr(), _mbsnbcat(), _mbsnbcmp(), _mbsnbcnt(), _mbsnbcoll(), _mbsnbcpy(), _mbsnbicmp(), _mbsnbicoll(), _mbsnbset(), _mbsnccnt(), _mbsncmp(), _mbsncoll(), _mbsncpy(), _mbsnextc(), _mbsnicmp(), _mbsnicoll(), _mbsninc(), _mbsnset(), _mbspbrk(), _mbsrchr(), _mbsrev(), _mbsset(), _mbsspn(), _mbsspnp(), _mbsstr(), _mbstok(), _mbstrlen(), _mbsupr(), _strdec(), _stricoll(), _strinc(), _strlwr(), _strncnt(), _strncoll(), _strnextc(), _strnicmp(), _strnicoll(), _strninc(), _strnset(), _strset(), _strspnp(), _strupr(), _tcsdec(), _tcsinc(), _tcsnccnt(), _tcsninc(), _tcsspnp(), _wcsdec(), _wcsicmp(), _wcsicoll(), _wcslwr(), _wcsncnt(), _wcsncoll(), _wcsnicmp(), _wcsnicoll(), _wcsninc(), _wcsnset(), _wcsrev(), _wcsset(), _wcsspnp(), _wcsupr(), strcat(), strchr(), strcmp(), strcoll(), strcpy(), strcspn(), strdup(), stricmp(), strlen(), strlwr(), strncat(), strncmp(), strncpy(), strnicmp(), strnset(), strpbrk(), strrchr(), strrev(), strset(), strspn(), strstr(), strtod(), strtok(), strtol(), strupr(), wcscat(), wcschr(), wcscmp(), wcscoll(), wcscpy(), wcscspn(), wcslen(), wcsncat(), wcsncmp(), wcsncpy(), wcspbrk(), wcsrchr(), wcsspn(), wcsstr(), wcstod(), wcstok(), wcstol(), and wcstoul().

struct

Keyword

The `struct` keyword is used to define a structure, a data object that can hold fields (called members) of various data types. For example, the following shows how to declare a data structure named `MyStruct` that can store two integers, a double, and a string:

```
struct MyStruct
{
    int member1;
    int member2;
    double member3;
    char member4[81];
};
```

CROSS-REFERENCE

See also structures.

structures

Technique

The `struct` keyword is used to define a structure, a data object that can hold fields (called members) of various data types. For example, the following shows how to declare a data structure named `MyStruct` that can store two integers, a double, and a string:

```
struct MyStruct
{
    int member1;
    int member2;
    double member3;
    char member4[81];
};
```

Creating a Structure Instance

To use the structure, a program must first declare an instance of the structure. The following program demonstrates how to create an instance of a structure and how to manipulate the members of the structure. The program's output looks like this:

```
member1 = 10
member2 = 20
member3 = 36.23
member4 = This is a test

Press any key to continue
```

Here is the program source code that produced the output:

```
#include "stdafx.h"
#include <iostream>

using namespace std;

struct MyStruct
{
    int member1;
    int member2;
    double member3;
```

```
        char member4[81];
};

int main(int argc, char* argv[])
{
    MyStruct myStruct;

    myStruct.member1 = 10;
    myStruct.member2 = 20;
    myStruct.member3 = 36.23;
    strcpy(myStruct.member4, "This is a test");

    cout << "member1 = " << myStruct.member1 << endl;
    cout << "member2 = " << myStruct.member2 << endl;
    cout << "member3 = " << myStruct.member3 << endl;
    cout << "member4 = " << myStruct.member4 << endl;
    cout << endl;

    return 0;
}
```

Creating Single-Instance Structures

If you need only a single instance of the structure, you can define both the structure and the instance simultaneously by adding a tag to the structure definition. The following program demonstrates how this technique works. The program's output is identical to the output from the previous example.

```
#include "stdafx.h"
#include <iostream>

using namespace std;

int main(int argc, char* argv[])
{
    struct MyStruct
    {
        int member1;
        int member2;
        double member3;
        char member4[81];
    } myStruct;

    myStruct.member1 = 10;
```

```
        myStruct.member2 = 20;
        myStruct.member3 = 36.23;
        strcpy(myStruct.member4, "This is a test");

        cout << "member1 = " << myStruct.member1 << endl;
        cout << "member2 = " << myStruct.member2 << endl;
        cout << "member3 = " << myStruct.member3 << endl;
        cout << "member4 = " << myStruct.member4 << endl;
        cout << endl;

        return 0;
    }
```

CROSS-REFERENCE
See also class.

strupr()

Function

The `strupr()` function converts a string to uppercase, returning a pointer to the new string.

Header File

```
#include <string.h>
```

Declaration

```
char* strupr(const char *string);
```

- *string* — The string to convert.

Example

The following program demonstrates how to use the `strupr()` function. When run, the program converts several strings to uppercase and displays the results. The program's output looks like this:

```
Original String: One Two Three
Converted String: ONE TWO THREE
```

```
Original String: FOUR FIVE SIX
Converted String: FOUR FIVE SIX

Original String: seven eight nine
Converted String: SEVEN EIGHT NINE

Press any key to continue
```

Here is the program source code that produced the output:

```
#include "stdafx.h"
#include <iostream>
#include <string.h>

using namespace std;

void convert(char* s)
{
    cout << "Original String: ";
    cout << s << endl;
    char* result = strupr(s);
    cout << "Converted String: ";
    cout << result << endl << endl;
}

int main(int argc, char* argv[])
{
    char str1[81];
    strcpy(str1, "One Two Three");
    char str2[81];
    strcpy(str2, "FOUR FIVE SIX");
    char str3[81];
    strcpy(str3, "seven eight nine");

    convert(str1);
    convert(str2);
    convert(str3);

    return 0;
}
```

CROSS-REFERENCE

See also _mbscat(), _mbschr(), _mbscmp(), _mbscoll(), _mbscpy(), _mbscspn(), _mbsdec(), _mbsdup(), _mbsicmp(), _mbsicoll(), _mbsinc(), _mbslen(), _mbslwr(), _mbsnbcat(), _mbsnbcmp(), _mbsnbcnt(), _mbsnbcoll(), _mbsnbcpy(), _mbsnbicmp(), _mbsnbicoll(), _mbsnbset(), _mbsnccnt(), _mbsncmp(),

_mbsncoll(), _mbsncpy(), _mbsnextc(), _mbsnicmp(), _mbsnicoll(), _mbsninc(), _mbsnset(), _mbspbrk(), _mbsrchr(), _mbsrev(), _mbsset(), _mbsspn(), _mbsspnp(), _mbsstr(), _mbstok(), _mbstrlen(), _mbsupr(), _strdec(), _stricoll(), _strinc(), _strlwr(), _strncnt(), _strncoll(), _strnextc(), _strnicmp(), _strnicoll(), _strninc(), _strnset(), _strset(), _strspnp(), _strupr(), _tcsdec(), _tcsinc(), _tcsnccnt(), _tcsninc(), _tcsspnp(), _wcsdec(), _wcsicmp(), _wcsicoll(), _wcslwr(), _wcsncnt(), _wcsncoll(), _wcsnicmp(), _wcsnicoll(), _wcsninc(), _wcsnset(), _wcsrev(), _wcsset(), _wcsspnp(), _wcsupr(), strcat(), strchr(), strcmp(), strcoll(), strcpy(), strcspn(), strdup(), stricmp(), strlen(), strlwr(), strncat(), strncmp(), strncpy(), strnicmp(), strnset(), strpbrk(), strrchr(), strrev(), strset(), strspn(), strstr(), strtod(), strtok(), strtol(), strtoul(), wcscat(),wcschr(), wcscmp(), wcscoll(), wcscpy(), wcscspn(), wcslen(), wcsncat(), wcsncmp(), wcsncpy(), wcspbrk(), wcsrchr(), wcsspn(), wcsstr(), wcstod(), wcstok(), wcstol(), and wcstoul().

swab()

Function

The swab() function swaps pairs of bytes in a string. The function returns no value.

Header File

```
#include <stdlib.h>
```

Declaration

```
void swab(char *src, char *dest, int n);
```

- *dest* — A pointer to the destination string.
- *n* — The number of bytes to swap.
- *src* — A pointer to the source string.

Example

The following program demonstrates how to use the swab() function. When run, the program swaps bytes in a string and displays the results. The program's output looks like this:

```
Source string: 1234567890
Destination string:

Source string: 1234567890
```

```
Destination string: 2143658709

Press any key to continue
```

Here is the program source code that produced the output:

```cpp
#include "stdafx.h"
#include <stdlib.h>
#include <iostream>

using namespace std;

int main(int argc, char* argv[])
{
    char srcStr[] = "1234567890";
    char dstStr[14] = "";

    cout << "Source string: " << srcStr << endl;
    cout << "Destination string: " << dstStr << endl;
    cout << endl;

    swab(srcStr, dstStr, 10);

    cout << "Source string: " << srcStr << endl;
    cout << "Destination string: " << dstStr << endl;
    cout << endl;

    return 0;
}
```

CROSS-REFERENCE

See also _mbsdup(), _mbsicmp(), _mbsicoll(), _mbsinc(), _memccpy(), _memicmp(), _swab(), memchr(), memcmp(), memcpy(), memmove(), and memset().

switch

Keyword

The switch keyword begins the switch statement, which enables program branching based on the value of an expression. For example, the following switch statement displays a message based on the value of the variable var1. In this case, the case 3 portion of the statement executes, displaying the message "Three".

```
int var1 = 3;

switch (var1)
{
    case 1:
        cout << "One" << endl;
        break;
    case 2:
        cout << "Two" << endl;
        break;
    case 3:
        cout << "Three" << endl;
        break;
    case 4:
        cout << "Four" << endl;
        break;
    case 5:
        cout << "Five" << endl;
}
```

CROSS-REFERENCE
See also break, case, and for.

swprintf()

Function

The swprintf() function is the wide-character version of the sprintf() function, which creates a formatted string, returning the number of bytes written to the string.

Header File

```
#include <stdio.h>
```

Declaration

```
int swprintf(wchar_t *buffer,
    const wchar_t *format [, argument] ...);
```

- *argument* — A list of arguments that match the format specifiers in the format string.

- *buffer* — A pointer to the buffer that will receive the formatted string.
- *format* — The format string, which can use the format specifiers shown in Table S-34.

Table S-34 Format Specifiers for swprintf()

Specifier	Description
%c	Specifies a character.
%C	Specifies a wide character (printf()) or single-byte character (wprintf()).
%d	Specifies a signed decimal integer.
%e	Specifies a signed double-precision floating-point value using scientific notation with a lowercase e.
%E	Specifies a signed double-precision floating-point value using scientific notation with an uppercase E.
%f	Specifies a signed double-precision floating-point value.
%g	Specifies a signed double-precision floating-point value using either normal notation or scientific notation with a lowercase e.
%G	Specifies a signed double-precision floating-point value using either normal notation or scientific notation with an uppercase E.
%I	Specifies a signed decimal integer.
%n	Specifies an integer pointer.
%o	Specifies an unsigned octal integer.
%p	Specifies a void pointer.
%s	Specifies a string.
%S	Specifies a wide-character string (printf()) or single-byte-character string (wprintf()).
%u	Specifies an unsigned decimal integer.
%x	Specifies an unsigned hexadecimal integer with lowercase letters.
%X	Specifies an unsigned hexadecimal integer with uppercase letters.

Example

The following program demonstrates how to use the swprintf() function. The program's output looks something like this:

```
swprintf() results:
  This is a test: 256

Press any key to continue
```

Here is the program source code that produced the output:

```
#include "stdafx.h"
#include <stdio.h>
#include <iostream>

using namespace std;

int main(int argc, char* argv[])
{
    wchar_t dstStr[81];

    memset(dstStr, 0, sizeof(dstStr));
    swprintf(dstStr, L"This is a test: %i\n", 256);
    cout << "swprintf() results: " << endl << "   ";
    wcout << dstStr << endl;

    return 0;
}
```

CROSS-REFERENCE
See also _fputchar(), _fputwchar(), _vsnprintf(), _vsnwprintf(), fprintf(), fputc(), fputs(), fputwc(), fputws(), fwprintf(), printf(), sprintf(), swprintf(), vfprintf(), vfwprintf(), vprintf(), vsprintf(), vswprintf(), vwprintf(), and wprintf().

swscanf()

Function

The swscanf() function is the wide-character version of the sscanf() function, which accepts formatted data from a string, transferring the data to variables based on the supplied format specifiers. The function returns the number of data items successfully received.

Header File

```
#include <stdio.h>
```

Declaration

```
int swscanf(const wchar_t *buffer,
    const wchar_t *format [, argument ] ...);
```

- *argument*—A list of data items that match the format specifiers included in the format string *format*.
- *buffer*—The address of the buffer that contains the string to read.
- *format*—The format string, which can include the format specifiers shown in Table S-35.

Table S-35 Format Specifiers for swscanf()

Specifier	Description
%c	Specifies a character.
%C	Specifies a wide character (printf()) or single-byte character (wprintf()).
%d	Specifies a signed decimal integer.
%e	Specifies a signed double-precision floating-point value using scientific notation with a lowercase e.
%E	Specifies a signed double-precision floating-point value using scientific notation with an uppercase E.
%f	Specifies a signed double-precision floating-point value.
%g	Specifies a signed double-precision floating-point value using either normal notation or scientific notation with a lowercase e.
%G	Specifies a signed double-precision floating-point value using either normal notation or scientific notation with an uppercase E.
%I	Specifies a signed decimal integer.
%n	Specifies an integer pointer.
%o	Specifies an unsigned octal integer.
%p	Specifies a void pointer.
%s	Specifies a string.
%S	Specifies a wide-character string (printf()) or single-byte-character string (wprintf()).
%u	Specifies an unsigned decimal integer.
%x	Specifies an unsigned hexadecimal integer with lowercase letters.
%X	Specifies an unsigned hexadecimal integer with uppercase letters.

Example

The following program demonstrates how to use the swscanf() function. When run, the program calls swscanf() to input two data items: a string and an integer. The program's output looks like this:

```
str = Test
var1 = 25
```

```
Items received: 2

Press any key to continue
```

Here is the program source code that produced the output:

```cpp
#include "stdafx.h"
#include <stdio.h>
#include <iostream>

using namespace std;

int main(int argc, char* argv[])
{
    wchar_t buf[] = L"Test 25";
    wchar_t str[10];
    int var1;

    int num = swscanf(buf, L"%s %d", str, &var1);
    cout << "str = ";
    wcout << str << endl;
    cout << "var1 = " << var1 << endl;
    cout << "Items received: " << num << endl << endl;

    return 0;
}
```

CROSS-REFERENCE
See also cprintf(), cscanf(), fprintf(), fscanf(), fwprintf(), printf(), scanf(), sprintf(), sscanf(), swprintf(), vfprintf(), vfwprintf(), vprintf(), vsprintf(), vswprintf(), vwprintf(), wprintf(), and wscanf().

system()

Function

The system() function executes a given command, returning the value returned by the command interpreter or returning –1 in the case of an error. The function returns 0 and sets the errno global variable to ENOENT if the command interpreter cannot be found.

Header File

```cpp
#include <process.h>
```

Declaration

```
int system(const char *command);
```

- *command*—A pointer to the command to execute.

Example

The following program demonstrates how to use the system() function. When run, the program executes the DIR command and displays the results. The program's output looks like this:

```
Volume in drive C has no label
Volume Serial Number is 2F1D-1EED
Directory of C:\all code\Microsoft\S\system

.                    <DIR>         03-04-99  3:24a .
..                   <DIR>         03-04-99  3:24a ..
STDAFX    H              667       03-04-99  3:24a StdAfx.h
STDAFX    CPP            293       03-04-99  3:24a StdAfx.cpp
SYSTEM    DSW            537       03-04-99  3:24a system.dsw
SYSTEM    CPP            256       03-04-99  3:24a system.cpp
README    TXT          1,208       03-04-99  3:24a ReadMe.txt
SYSTEM    NCB              0       03-04-99  3:24a system.ncb
SYSTEM    DSP          4,536       03-04-99  3:24a system.dsp
DEBUG              <DIR>           03-04-99  3:24a Debug
SYSTEM    PLG          1,602       03-04-99  3:24a system.plg
          8 file(s)              9,099 bytes
          3 dir(s)          10,507.48 MB free
Press any key to continue
```

Here is the program source code that produced the output:

```cpp
#include "stdafx.h"
#include <process.h>
#include <iostream>

using namespace std;

int main(int argc, char* argv[])
{
    int result = system("dir");

    return 0;
}
```

CROSS-REFERENCE

See also _wexecl(), _wexecle(), _wexeclp(), _wexeclpe(), _wexecv(), _wexecve(), _wexecvp(), _wexecvpe(), _wspawnl(), _wspawnle(), _wspawnlp(), _wspawnlpe(), _wspawnv(), _wspawnve(), _wspawnvp(), _wsystem(), execl(), execle(), execlp(), execlpe(), execv(), execve(), execvp(), execvpe(), spawnl(), spawnle(), spawnlp(), spawnlpe(), spawnv(), spawnve(), spawnvp(), and spawnvpe().

r
s
t

__toascii()

Function

The __toascii() function converts an integer value to an ASCII character, returning an integer whose upper bits have been cleared to yield a value between 0 and 127.

NOTE
Borland users should refer to the toascii() function later in this chapter.

Header File

```
#include <ctype.h>
```

Declaration

```
int __toascii(int c);
```

- *c* — The value to convert to ASCII.

Example

The following program demonstrates how to use the __toascii() function. The program's output looks like the following:

```
Starting int value = 41281
Converting to ASCII...
New int value = 65
Character = A
Press any key to continue
```

Here's the program source code that created the output:

```
#include "stdafx.h"
#include <ctype.h>
#include <iostream>
```

```
using namespace std;

int main(int argc, char* argv[])
{
    int ch = 0xA141;
    cout << "Starting int value = " << ch << endl;
    cout << "Converting to ASCII..." << endl;
    int result = __toascii(ch);
    cout << "New int value = " << result << endl;
    cout << "Character = " << (char)result << endl;

    return 0;
}
```

CROSS-REFERENCE

See also _mbctolower(), _mbctoupper(), _tolower(), _toupper(), toascii(), toupper(), and towlower().

_tasctime()

Function

The _tasctime() function is the TCHAR version of the asctime() function, which converts the contents of a tm structure (which holds time and date information) to a string, returning a pointer to the string.

Header File

```
#include <time.h>
```

Declaration

```
TCHAR* _tasctime(const strict tm* pTm);
```

- *pTm*—A pointer to the tm structure that contains the time and date data to be converted to a string.

Example

The following program demonstrates how to use the `_tasctime()` function. The program initializes a `tm` structure, converts the structure to a string, and then displays the result. The program's output looks like the following:

```
Thu Jan 21 05:17:00 1999

Press any key to continue
```

Here is the program source code that produced the output:

```cpp
#include "stdafx.h"
#include <iostream>
#include <time.h>
#include <tchar.h>

using namespace std;

int main(int argc, char* argv[])
{
    struct tm tmTime;

    tmTime.tm_mday   = 21;
    tmTime.tm_mon    = 0;
    tmTime.tm_year   = 99;
    tmTime.tm_wday   = 4;
    tmTime.tm_yday   = 0;
    tmTime.tm_isdst  = 0;
    tmTime.tm_sec    = 0;
    tmTime.tm_min    = 17;
    tmTime.tm_hour   = 5;

    TCHAR* str = _tasctime(&tmTime);
    cout << str << endl;

    return 0;
}
```

CROSS-REFERENCE

See also _wasctime() and asctime().

_tcscat()

Function

The _tcscat() function is the TCHAR version of the strcat() function, which concatenates (joins together) strings, returning a pointer to the destination string. The behavior of this function depends on the definition of the _UNICODE and _MBCS symbols. If neither symbol is defined, the function compiles for ANSI (single-byte characters); if _UNICODE is defined, the function compiles for UNICODE (wide characters); and if _MBCS is defined, the function compiles for MBCS (multibyte characters).

Header File

```
#include <tchar.h>
```

Declaration

```
TCHAR* _tcscat(TCHAR *strDestination, const TCHAR *strSource);
```

- *strDestination* — The string to which to concatenate *strSource*.
- *strSource* — The string to concatenate to *strDestination*.

Example

The following program demonstrates how to use the _tcscat() function. When run, the program concatenates the string "Four Five Six" to the string "One Two Three ". The program's output looks like the following:

```
Result: One Two Three Four Five Six
Press any key to continue
```

Here is the program source code that produced the output:

```
#include "stdafx.h"
#include <iostream>
#include <tchar.h>

using namespace std;

int main(int argc, char* argv[])
{
    TCHAR str1[81];
```

```
TCHAR* str2 = {"Four Five Six"};
_tcscpy(str1, "One Two Three ");
_tcscat(str1, str2);
cout << "Result: " << str1 << endl;

return 0;
}
```

CROSS-REFERENCE

See also _mbscat(), _tasctime(), _tcschr(), _tcscmp(), _tcscoll(), _tcscpy(), _tcscspn(),
_tcsdec(), _tcsdup(), _tcsftime(), _tcsicmp(), _tcsicoll(), _tcsinc(), _tcslen(), _tcslwr(),
_tcsnbcnt(), _tcsncat(), _tcsnccmp(), _tcsnccnt(), _tcsnccoll(), _tcsnicmp(),
_tcsncmp(), _tcsncoll(), _tcsncpy(), _tcsnextc(), _tcsnicmp(), _tcsnicoll(), _tcsninc(),
_tcsnset(), _tcspbrk(), _tcsrchr(), _tcsrev(), _tcsset(), _tcsspn(), _tcsspnp(), _tcsstr(),
_tcstod(), _tcstok(), _tcstol(), _tcstoul(), _tcsupr(), _tcsxfrm(), _tctime(), _tell(),
_telli64(), _tempnam(), _tolower(), _toupper(), strcat(), and wcscat().

_tcschr()

Function

The _tcschr() function is the TCHAR version of the strchr() function, which
locates a character in a string, returning a pointer to the character. The behavior of this function depends on the definition of the _UNICODE and _MBCS symbols. If neither symbol is defined, the function compiles for ANSI (single-byte
characters); if _UNICODE is defined, the function compiles for UNICODE
(wide characters); and if _MBCS is defined, the function compiles for MBCS
(multibyte characters).

Header File

```
#include <tchar.h>
```

Declaration

```
TCHAR* _tcschr(const TCHAR *string, TCHAR c);
```

- *c*— The character for which to search.
- *string*— A pointer to the string to search for *c*.

Example

The following program demonstrates how to use the _tcschr() function. When run, the program locates the first occurrence of the letter "e" in the string "One Two Three" and displays the string starting with the located letter. The program's output looks like the following:

```
Result: e Two Three
Press any key to continue
```

Here is the program source code that produced the output:

```
#include "stdafx.h"
#include <iostream>
#include <tchar.h>

using namespace std;

int main(int argc, char* argv[])
{
    TCHAR ch = 'e';
    TCHAR* str1 = "One Two Three";
    TCHAR* pChr = _tcschr(str1, ch);
    cout << "Result: " << pChr << endl;

    return 0;
}
```

CROSS-REFERENCE

See also _mbschr(), _tasctime(), _tcscat(), _tcscmp(), _tcscoll(), _tcscpy(), _tcscspn(), _tcsdec(), _tcsdup(), _tcsftime(), _tcsicmp(), _tcsicoll(), _tcsinc(), _tcslen(), _tcslwr(), _tcsnbcnt(), _tcsncat(), _tcsnccmp(), _tcsnccnt(), _tcsnccoll(), _tcsnicmp(), _tcsncmp(), _tcsncoll(), _tcsncpy(), _tcsnextc(), _tcsnicmp(), _tcsnicoll(), _tcsninc(), _tcsnset(), _tcspbrk(), _tcsrchr(), _tcsrev(), _tcsset(), _tcsspn(), _tcsspnp(), _tcsstr(), _tcstod(), _tcstok(), _tcstol(), _tcstoul(), _tcsupr(), _tcsxfrm(), _tctime(), _tell(), _telli64(), _tempnam(), _tolower(), _toupper(), strchr(), and wcschr().

_tcscmp()

Function

The _tcscmp() function is the TCHAR version of the strcmp() function, which compares two strings, returning a value from Table T-1. The behavior of this function depends on the definition of the _UNICODE and _MBCS symbols. If neither symbol is defined, the function compiles for ANSI (single-byte characters); if _UNICODE is defined, the function compiles for UNICODE (wide characters); and if _MBCS is defined, the function compiles for MBCS (multibyte characters).

Table T-1 Return Values for _tcscmp()

Value	Description
Less than 0	string1 is alphabetically less than string2.
0	The two strings are equal.
Greater than 0	string1 is alphabetically greater than string2.

Header File

```
#include <tchar.h>
```

Declaration

```
int _tcscmp(const TCHAR *string1, const TCHAR *string2);
```

- *string1* — The first string to compare.
- *string2* — The second string to compare.

Example

The following program demonstrates how to use the _tcscmp() function. When run, the program compares several pairs of strings and displays the result of the comparisons. The program's output looks like the following:

```
One Two Three equals One Two Three
One Two Three is greater than Four Five Six
Four Five Six is less than Seven Eight Nine
Press any key to continue
```

Here is the program source code that produced the output:

```
#include "stdafx.h"
#include <iostream>
#include <tchar.h>

using namespace std;

void cmp(TCHAR* s1, TCHAR* s2)
```

```
        {
            int result = _tcscmp(s1, s2);
            if (result < 0 )
            {
                cout << s1 << " is less than ";
                cout << s2 << endl;
            }
            else if (result > 0)
            {
                cout << s1 << " is greater than ";
                cout << s2 << endl;
            }
            else
            {
                cout << s1 << " equals ";
                cout << s2 << endl;
            }
        }

        int main(int argc, TCHAR* argv[])
        {
            TCHAR* str1 = "One Two Three";
            TCHAR* str2 = "One Two Three";
            TCHAR* str3 = "Four Five Six";
            TCHAR* str4 = "Seven Eight Nine";

            cmp(str1, str2);
            cmp(str2, str3);
            cmp(str3, str4);

            return 0;
        }
```

CROSS-REFERENCE

See also _mbscmp(), _tasctime(), _tcscat(), _tcschr(), _tcscoll(), _tcscpy(), _tcscspn(), _tcsdec(), _tcsdup(), _tcsftime(), _tcsicmp(), _tcsicoll(), _tcsinc(), _tcslen(), _tcslwr(), _tcsnbcnt(), _tcsncat(), _tcsnccmp(), _tcsnccnt(), _tcsnccoll(), _tcsnicmp(), _tcsncmp(), _tcsncoll(), _tcsncpy(), _tcsnextc(), _tcsnicmp(), _tcsnicoll(), _tcsninc(), _tcsnset(), _tcspbrk(), _tcsrchr(), _tcsrev(), _tcsset(), _tcsspn(), _tcsspnp(), _tcsstr(), _tcstod(), _tcstok(), _tcstol(), _tcstoul(), _tcsupr(), _tcsxfrm(), _tctime(), _tell(), _telli64(), _tempnam(), _tolower(), _toupper(), strcmp(), and wcscmp().

_tcscoll()

Function

The _tcscoll() function is the TCHAR version of the strcoll() function, which compares two strings for the current locale, returning a value from Table T-2. The behavior of this function depends on the definition of the _UNICODE and _MBCS symbols. If neither symbol is defined, the function compiles for ANSI (single-byte characters); if _UNICODE is defined, the function compiles for UNICODE (wide characters); and if _MBCS is defined, the function compiles for MBCS (multibyte characters).

Table T-2 Return Values for _tcscoll()

Value	Description
Less than 0	string1 is alphabetically less than string2.
0	The two strings are equal.
Greater than 0	string1 is alphabetically greater than string2.

Header File

```
#include <tchar.h>
```

Declaration

```
int _tcscoll(const TCHAR *string1, const TCHAR *string2);
```

- *string1* — The first string to compare.
- *string2* — The second string to compare.

Example

The following program demonstrates how to use the _tcscoll() function. When run, the program compares several pairs of strings and displays the result of the comparisons. The program's output looks like the following:

```
One Two Three equals One Two Three
One Two Three is greater than Four Five Six
Four Five Six is less than Seven Eight Nine
Press any key to continue
```

Here is the program source code that produced the output:

```cpp
#include "stdafx.h"
#include <iostream>
#include <tchar.h>

using namespace std;

void cmp(TCHAR* s1, TCHAR* s2)
{
    int result = _tcscoll(s1, s2);
    if (result < 0 )
    {
        cout << s1 << " is less than ";
        cout << s2 << endl;
    }
    else if (result > 0)
    {
        cout << s1 << " is greater than ";
        cout << s2 << endl;
    }
    else
    {
        cout << s1 << " equals ";
        cout << s2 << endl;
    }
}

int main(int argc, TCHAR* argv[])
{
    TCHAR* str1 = "One Two Three";
    TCHAR* str2 = "One Two Three";
    TCHAR* str3 = "Four Five Six";
    TCHAR* str4 = "Seven Eight Nine";

    cmp(str1, str2);
    cmp(str2, str3);
    cmp(str3, str4);

    return 0;
}
```

CROSS-REFERENCE

See also _mbscoll(), _tasctime(), _tcscat(), _tcschr(), _tcscmp(), _tcscpy(), _tcscspn(),
_tcsdec(), _tcsdup(), _tcsftime(), _tcsicmp(), _tcsicoll(), _tcsinc(), _tcslen(), _tcslwr(),
_tcsnbcnt(), _tcsncat(), _tcsnccmp(), _tcsnccnt(), _tcsnccoll(), _tcsnicmp(),
_tcsncmp(), _tcsncoll(), _tcsncpy(), _tcsnextc(), _tcsnicmp(), _tcsnicoll(), _tcsninc(),
_tcsnset(), _tcspbrk(), _tcsrchr(), _tcsrev(), _tcsset(), _tcsspn(), _tcsspnp(), _tcsstr(),
_tcstod(), _tcstok(), _tcstol(), _tcstoul(), _tcsupr(), _tcsxfrm(), _tctime(), _tell(),
_telli64(), _tempnam(), _tolower(), _toupper(), strcoll(), and wcscoll().

_tcscpy()

Function

The _tcscpy() function is the TCHAR version of the strcpy() function, which
copies one string to another, returning a pointer to the destination string. The
source and destination strings cannot overlap. The behavior of this function
depends on the definition of the _UNICODE and _MBCS symbols. If neither
symbol is defined, the function compiles for ANSI (single-byte characters);
if _UNICODE is defined, the function compiles for UNICODE (wide characters); and if _MBCS is defined, the function compiles for MBCS (multibyte
characters).

Header File

```
#include <tchar.h>
```

Declaration

```
TCHAR* _tcscpy(TCHAR *strDestination, const TCHAR *strSource);
```

- *strDestination* — A pointer to the destination string.
- *strSource* — A pointer to the source string.

Example

The following program demonstrates how to use the _tcscpy() function.
When run, the program copies one string to another and displays the result.
The program's output looks like the following:

```
Source string = This is a test
Destination string = This is a test
Press any key to continue
```

Here is the program source code that produced the output:

```
#include "stdafx.h"
#include <iostream>
#include <tchar.h>

using namespace std;

int main(int argc, TCHAR* argv[])
{
    TCHAR destStr[81];
    TCHAR* srcStr = "This is a test";

    TCHAR* pResult = _tcscpy(destStr, srcStr);
    cout << "Source string = " << srcStr << endl;
    cout << "Destination string = " << pResult << endl;

    return 0;
}
```

CROSS-REFERENCE

See also _mbscpy(), _tasctime(), _tcscat(), _tcschr(), _tcscmp(), _tcscoll(), _tcscspn(), _tcsdec(), _tcsdup(), _tcsftime(), _tcsicmp(), _tcsicoll(), _tcsinc(), _tcslen(), _tcslwr(), _tcsnbcnt(), _tcsncat(), _tcsnccmp(), _tcsnccnt(), _tcsnccoll(), _tcsncicmp(), _tcsncmp(), _tcsncoll(), _tcsncpy(), _tcsnextc(), _tcsnicmp(), _tcsnicoll(), _tcsninc(), _tcsnset(), _tcspbrk(), _tcsrchr(), _tcsrev(), _tcsset(), _tcsspn(), _tcsspnp(), _tcsstr(), _tcstod(), _tcstok(), _tcstol(), _tcstoul(), _tcsupr(), _tcsxfrm(), _tctime(), _tell(), _telli64(), _tempnam(), _tolower(), _toupper(), strcpy(), and wcscpy().

_tcscspn()

Function

The _tcscspn() function is the TCHAR version of the strcspn() function, which locates the first occurrence of a character in a string, returning the length of the substring preceding a matching character. The behavior of this function depends on the definition of the _UNICODE and _MBCS symbols. If neither symbol is defined, the function compiles for ANSI (single-byte characters); if _UNICODE is defined, the function compiles for UNICODE (wide characters); and if _MBCS is defined, the function compiles for MBCS (multibyte characters).

Header File

```
#include <tchar.h>
```

Declaration

```
size_t _tcscspn(const TCHAR *string, const TCHAR *strCharSet);
```

- *strCharSet* — A pointer to the set of characters for which to search.
- *string* — A pointer to the string to search.

Example

The following program demonstrates how to use the _tcscspn() function. When run, the program locates, in a string, the first character in a set and displays the result, indicating the located character with a caret (^). The program's output looks like the following:

```
Source String:
This is a test
  ^
Press any key to continue
```

Here is the program source code that produced the output:

```
#include "stdafx.h"
#include <iostream>
#include <tchar.h>

using namespace std;

int main(int argc, char* argv[])
{
    TCHAR* srcStr = "This is a test";
    TCHAR* chrSet = "ast";

    size_t len = _tcscspn(srcStr, chrSet);
    cout << "Source String:" << endl;
    cout << srcStr << endl;
    for (unsigned x=0; x<len; ++x)
        cout << " ";
    cout << "^" << endl;

    return 0;
}
```

CROSS-REFERENCE

See also _mbscspn(), _tasctime(), _tcscat(), _tcschr(), _tcscmp(), _tcscoll(), _tcscpy(), _tcsdec(), _tcsdup(), _tcsftime(), _tcsicmp(), _tcsicoll(), _tcsinc(), _tcslen(), _tcslwr(), _tcsnbcnt(), _tcsncat(), _tcsnccmp(), _tcsnccnt(), _tcsnccoll(), _tcsnicmp(), _tcsncmp(), _tcsncoll(), _tcsncpy(), _tcsnextc(), _tcsnicmp(), _tcsnicoll(), _tcsninc(), _tcsnset(), _tcspbrk(), _tcsrchr(), _tcsrev(), _tcsset(), _tcsspn(), _tcsspnp(), _tcsstr(), _tcstod(), _tcstok(), _tcstol(), _tcstoul(), _tcsupr(), _tcsxfrm(), _tctime(), _tell(), _telli64(), _tempnam(), _tolower(), _toupper(), strcspn(), and wcscspn().

_tcsdec()

Function

The _tcsdec() function is the TCHAR version of the _strdec() function, which returns a pointer to the previous character in a string or NULL if the previous character cannot be determined. The behavior of this function depends on the definition of the _UNICODE and _MBCS symbols. If neither symbol is defined, the function compiles for ANSI (single-byte characters); if _UNICODE is defined, the function compiles for UNICODE (wide characters); and if _MBCS is defined, the function compiles for MBCS (multibyte characters).

Header File

```
#include <tchar.h>
```

Declaration

```
TCHAR* _tcsdec(const TCHAR *start, const TCHAR *current);
```

- *current* — A pointer to the character for which to return the previous character.
- *start* — A pointer to the start of the string.

Example

The following program demonstrates how to use the _tcsdec() function. When run, the program locates the character that precedes the fifth character in a string and displays the result. The program's output looks like the following:

```
Source String = This is a test
Result = s is a test
Press any key to continue
```

Here is the program source code that produced the output:

```
#include "stdafx.h"
#include <iostream>
#include <tchar.h>

using namespace std;

int main(int argc, char* argv[])
{
    char* srcStr = "This is a test";

    char* result = _tcsdec(srcStr, &srcStr[4]);
    cout << "Source String = " << srcStr << endl;
    cout << "Result = " << result << endl;

    return 0;
}
```

CROSS-REFERENCE

See also _mbsdec(), _strdec(), _tasctime(), _tcscat(), _tcschr(), _tcscmp(), _tcscoll(), _tcscpy(), _tcscspn(), _tcsdup(), _tcsftime(), _tcsicmp(), _tcsicoll(), _tcsinc(), _tcslen(), _tcslwr(), _tcsnbcnt(), _tcsncat(), _tcsnccmp(), _tcsnccnt(), _tcsnccoll(), _tcsnicmp(), _tcsncmp(), _tcsncoll(), _tcsncpy(), _tcsnextc(), _tcsnicmp(), _tcsnicoll(), _tcsninc(), _tcsnset(), _tcspbrk(), _tcsrchr(), _tcsrev(), _tcsset(), _tcsspn(), _tcsspnp(), _tcsstr(), _tcstod(), _tcstok(), _tcstol(), _tcstoul(), _tcsupr(), _tcsxfrm(), _tctime(), _tell(), _telli64(), _tempnam(), _tolower(), _toupper(), and _wcsdec().

_tcsdup()

The _tcsdup() function is the TCHAR version of the strdup() function, which duplicates a string, returning a pointer to the new string. The behavior of this function depends on the definition of the _UNICODE and _MBCS symbols. If neither symbol is defined, the function compiles for ANSI (single-byte characters); if _UNICODE is defined, the function compiles for UNICODE (wide characters); and if _MBCS is defined, the function compiles for MBCS (multibyte characters).

Header File

```
#include <tchar.h>
```

Declaration

```
TCHAR* _tcsdup(const TCHAR *strSource);
```

- *strSource* — A pointer to the source string.

Example

The following program demonstrates how to use the `_tcsdup()` function. When run, the program duplicates the given string and displays the result. The program's output looks like the following:

```
Source string = This is a test
New string = This is a test
Press any key to continue
```

Here is the program source code that produced the output:

```cpp
#include "stdafx.h"
#include <iostream>
#include <tchar.h>

using namespace std;

int main(int argc, TCHAR* argv[])
{
    TCHAR* srcStr = "This is a test";

    TCHAR* destStr = _tcsdup(srcStr);
    cout << "Source string = " << srcStr << endl;
    cout << "New string = " << destStr << endl;

    return 0;
}
```

CROSS-REFERENCE

See also _mbsdup(), _tasctime(), _tcscat(), _tcschr(), _tcscmp(), _tcscoll(), _tcscpy(), _tcscspn(), _tcsdec(), _tcsftime(), _tcsicmp(), _tcsicoll(), _tcsinc(), _tcslen(), _tcslwr(), _tcsnbcnt(), _tcsncat(), _tcsnccmp(), _tcsnccnt(), _tcsnccoll(), _tcsnicimp(), _tcsncmp(), _tcsncoll(), _tcsncpy(), _tcsnextc(), _tcsnicmp(), _tcsnicoll(), _tcsninc(), _tcsnset(), _tcspbrk(), _tcsrchr(), _tcsrev(), _tcsset(), _tcsspn(), _tcsspnp(), _tcsstr(), _tcstod(), _tcstok(), _tcstol(), _tcstoul(), _tcsupr(), _tcsxfrm(), _tctime(), _tell(), _telli64(), _tempnam(), _tolower(), _toupper(), _wcsdup(), and strdup().

_tcsftime()

Function

The _tcsftime() function is the TCHAR version of the strftime() function, which generates a formatted time string, returning the number of characters in the string or returning 0 in the case of an error. The behavior of this function depends on the definition of the _UNICODE and _MBCS symbols. If neither symbol is defined, the function compiles for ANSI (single-byte characters); if _UNICODE is defined, the function compiles for UNICODE (wide characters); and if _MBCS is defined, the function compiles for MBCS (multibyte characters).

Header File

```
#include <time.h>
```

Declaration

```
size_t _tcsftime(TCHAR *strDest, size_t maxsize,
    const TCHAR *format, const struct tm *timeptr);
```

- *format*—A pointer to the format string. Table T-3 shows the available format codes.
- *maxsize*—The maximum allowable length of the formatted string.
- *strDest*—A pointer to the buffer that will receive the formatted string.
- *timeptr*—A pointer to the tm structure that contains the time to format.

Table T-3 Format Codes for _tcsftime()

Code	Description
%#%	Ignore the # flag.
%#a	Ignore the # flag.
%#A	Ignore the # flag.
%#b	Ignore the # flag.
%#B	Ignore the # flag.
%#c	Format as the current locale's long date and time.
%#d	Delete leading zeroes.
%#H	Delete leading zeroes.

Continued

Table T-3 *Continued*

Code	Description
%#I	Delete leading zeroes.
%#j	Delete leading zeroes.
%#m	Delete leading zeroes.
%#M	Delete leading zeroes.
%#p	Ignore the # flag.
%#S	Delete leading zeroes.
%#U	Delete leading zeroes.
%#w	Delete leading zeroes.
%#W	Delete leading zeroes.
%#X	Ignore the # flag.
%#x	Format as the current locale's long date.
%#y	Delete leading zeroes.
%#Y	Delete leading zeroes.
%#z	Ignore the # flag.
%#Z	Ignore the # flag.
%%	Display a percent sign.
%a	Format as an abbreviated weekday name.
%A	Format as a full weekday name.
%b	Format as an abbreviated month name.
%B	Format as a full month name.
%c	Format the date and time for the current locale.
%d	Format the day of the month as a number from 01 to 31.
%H	Format the hour in 24-hour style.
%I	Format the hour in the 12-hour style.
%j	Format the day of the year as a number from 001 to 366.
%m	Format the month as a number from 01 to 12.
%M	Format the minute as a number from 00 to 59.
%p	Use the AM/PM indicator for the current locale.
%S	Format the second as a number from 00 to 59.
%U	Format the week of the year as a number from 00 to 53, using Sunday as the first day of the week.
%w	Format the weekday as a number from 0 to 6, where 0 represents Sunday.
%W	Week of the year as a number from 00 to 53.
%x	Format the date for the current locale.
%X	Format the time for the current locale.
%y	Format the year as a two-digit number from 00 to 99.
%Y	Format the year as a four-digit number (1999).
%z	Format the time zone name as an abbreviation.
%Z	Format the time zone name as a full name.

Example

The following program demonstrates how to use the `_tcsftime()` function. The program initializes a `tm` structure, converts the structure to a string, and then displays the result. The program's output looks like the following:

```
Thu, January 21, 1999.

Press any key to continue
```

Here is the program source code that produced the output:

```
#include "stdafx.h"
#include <iostream>
#include <time.h>
#include <tchar.h>

using namespace std;

int main(int argc, char* argv[])
{
    TCHAR buf[256];
    struct tm tmTime;

    tmTime.tm_mday  = 21;
    tmTime.tm_mon   = 0;
    tmTime.tm_year  = 99;
    tmTime.tm_wday  = 4;
    tmTime.tm_yday  = 0;
    tmTime.tm_isdst = 0;
    tmTime.tm_sec   = 0;
    tmTime.tm_min   = 17;
    tmTime.tm_hour  = 5;

    _tcsftime(buf, 256, "%a, %B %d, %Y.\n", &tmTime);
    cout << buf << endl;

    return 0;
}
```

CROSS-REFERENCE
See also _tasctime(), _tcscat(), _tcschr(), _tcscmp(), _tcscoll(), _tcscpy(), _tcscspn(), _tcsdec(), _tcsdup(), _tcsicmp(), _tcsicoll(), _tcsinc(), _tcslen(), _tcslwr(), _tcsnbcnt(), _tcsncat(), _tcsnccmp(), _tcsnccnt(), _tcsnccoll(), _tcsncicmp(), _tcsncmp(), _tcsncoll(), _tcsncpy(), _tcsnextc(), _tcsnicmp(), _tcsnicoll(), _tcsninc(), _tcsnset(), _tcspbrk(), _tcsrchr(), _tcsrev(), _tcsset(), _tcsspn(), _tcsspnp(), _tcsstr(), _tcstod(), _tcstok(), _tcstol(), _tcstoul(), _tcsupr(), _tcsxfrm(), _tctime(), _tell(), _telli64(), _tempnam(), _tolower(), _toupper(), strftime(), and wcsftime().

_tcsicmp()

Function

The _tcsicmp() function is the TCHAR version of the stricmp() function, which compares two strings without regard for case (case-insensitive), returning a value from Table T-4. The behavior of this function depends on the definition of the _UNICODE and _MBCS symbols. If neither symbol is defined, the function compiles for ANSI (single-byte characters); if _UNICODE is defined, the function compiles for UNICODE (wide characters); and if _MBCS is defined, the function compiles for MBCS (multibyte characters).

Table T-4 Return Values for _tcsicmp()

Value	Description
Less than 0	string1 is alphabetically less than string2.
0	The two strings are equal.
Greater than 0	string1 is alphabetically greater than string2.

Header File

```
#include <tchar.h>
```

Declaration

```
int _tcsicmp(const TCHAR *string1, const TCHAR *string2);
```

- *string1* — The first string to compare.
- *string2* — The second string to compare.

Example

The following program demonstrates how to use the _tcsicmp() function. When run, the program compares several pairs of strings and displays the result of the comparisons. The program's output looks like the following:

```
One Two Three equals one two three
One Two Three equals one two three
one two three is greater than Four Five Six
Four Five Six is less than seven eight nine
Press any key to continue
```

Here is the program source code that produced the output:

```cpp
#include "stdafx.h"
#include <iostream>
#include <tchar.h>

using namespace std;

void cmp(TCHAR* s1, TCHAR* s2)
{
    int result = _tcsicmp(s1, s2);
    if (result < 0 )
    {
        cout << s1;
        cout << " is less than ";
        cout << s2 << endl;
    }
    else if (result > 0)
    {
        cout << s1;
        cout << " is greater than ";
        cout << s2 << endl;
    }
    else
    {
        cout << s1;
        cout << " equals ";
        cout << s2 << endl;
    }
}

int main(int argc, TCHAR* argv[])
{
    TCHAR* str1 = "One Two Three";
    TCHAR* str2 = "one two three";
    TCHAR* str3 = "Four Five Six";
    TCHAR* str4 = "seven eight nine";

    cmp(str1, str2);
    cmp(str2, str3);
    cmp(str3, str4);

    return 0;
}
```

CROSS-REFERENCE

See also _mbsicmp(), _tasctime(), _tcscat(), _tcschr(), _tcscmp(), _tcscoll(), _tcscpy(), _tcscspn(), _tcsdec(), _tcsdup(), _tcsftime(), _tcsicoll(), _tcsinc(), _tcslen(), _tcslwr(), _tcsnbcnt(), _tcsncat(), _tcsnccmp(), _tcsnccnt(), _tcsnccoll(), _tcsncicmp(), _tcsncmp(), _tcsncoll(), _tcsncpy(), _tcsnextc(), _tcsnicmp(), _tcsnicoll(), _tcsninc(), _tcsnset(), _tcspbrk(), _tcsrchr(), _tcsrev(), _tcsset(), _tcsspn(), _tcsspnp(), _tcsstr(), _tcstod(), _tcstok(), _tcstol(), _tcstoul(), _tcsupr(), _tcsxfrm(), _tctime(), _tell(), _telli64(), _tempnam(), _tolower(), _toupper(), _wcsicmp(), and stricmp().

_tcsicoll()

Function

The _tcsicoll() function is the TCHAR version of the _stricoll() function, which compares two strings for the current locale without regard for case (case-insensitive), returning a value from Table T-5. The behavior of this function depends on the definition of the _UNICODE and _MBCS symbols. If neither symbol is defined, the function compiles for ANSI (single-byte characters); if _UNICODE is defined, the function compiles for UNICODE (wide characters); and if _MBCS is defined, the function compiles for MBCS (multibyte characters).

Table T-5 Return Values for _tcsicoll()

Value	Description
Less than 0	string1 is alphabetically less than string2.
0	The two strings are equal.
Greater than 0	string1 is alphabetically greater than string2.

Header File

```
#include <tchar.h>
```

Declaration

```
int _tcsicoll(const TCHAR *string1, const TCHAR *string2);
```

- *string1* — The first string to compare.
- *string2* — The second string to compare.

Example

The following program demonstrates how to use the _tcsicoll() function. When run, the program compares several pairs of strings and displays the result of the comparisons. The program's output looks like the following:

```
One Two Three equals one two three
One Two Three equals one two three
one two three is greater than Four Five Six
Four Five Six is less than seven eight nine
Press any key to continue
```

Here is the program source code that produced the output:

```cpp
#include "stdafx.h"
#include <iostream>
#include <tchar.h>

using namespace std;

void cmp(TCHAR* s1, TCHAR* s2)
{
    int result = _tcsicoll(s1, s2);
    if (result < 0 )
    {
        cout << s1;
        cout << " is less than ";
        cout << s2 << endl;
    }
    else if (result > 0)
    {
        cout << s1;
        cout << " is greater than ";
        cout << s2 << endl;
    }
    else
    {
        cout << s1;
        cout << " equals ";
        cout << s2 << endl;
    }
}

int main(int argc, TCHAR* argv[])
{
    TCHAR* str1 = "One Two Three";
```

```
        TCHAR* str2 = "one two three";
        TCHAR* str3 = "Four Five Six";
        TCHAR* str4 = "seven eight nine";

        cmp(str1, str2);
        cmp(str2, str3);
        cmp(str3, str4);

        return 0;
    }
```

 CROSS-REFERENCE
See also _mbsicoll(), _stricoll(), _tasctime(), _tcscat(), _tcschr(), _tcscmp(), _tcscoll(), _tcscpy(), _tcscspn(), _tcsdec(), _tcsdup(), _tcsftime(), _tcsicmp(), _tcsinc(), _tcslen(), _tcslwr(), _tcsnbcnt(), _tcsncat(), _tcsnccmp(), _tcsnccnt(), _tcsnccoll(), _tcsncicmp(), _tcsncmp(), _tcsncoll(), _tcsncpy(), _tcsnextc(), _tcsnicmp(), _tcsnicoll(), _tcsninc(), _tcsnset(), _tcspbrk(), _tcsrchr(), _tcsrev(), _tcsset(), _tcsspn(), _tcsspnp(), _tcsstr(), _tcstod(), _tcstok(), _tcstol(), _tcstoul(), _tcsupr(), _tcsxfrm(), _tctime(), _tell(), _telli64(), _tempnam(), _tolower(), _toupper(), and _wcsicoll().

_tcsinc()

Function

The _tcsinc() function is the TCHAR version of the _strinc() function, which returns a pointer to the next character in a string, or NULL if the next character cannot be determined. The behavior of this function depends on the definition of the _UNICODE and _MBCS symbols. If neither symbol is defined, the function compiles for ANSI (single-byte characters); if _UNICODE is defined, the function compiles for UNICODE (wide characters); and if _MBCS is defined, the function compiles for MBCS (multibyte characters).

Header File

```
#include <tchar.h>
```

Declaration

```
TCHAR* _tcsinc(const TCHAR *current);
```

- *current* — A pointer to the character for which to return the next character.

Example

The following program demonstrates how to use the _tcsinc() function. When run, the program locates the character that follows the fifth character in a string and displays the result. The program's output looks like the following:

```
Source String = This is a test
Result = is a test
Press any key to continue
```

Here is the program source code that produced the output:

```
#include "stdafx.h"
#include <iostream>
#include <tchar.h>

using namespace std;

int main(int argc, char* argv[])
{
    TCHAR* srcStr = "This is a test";

    TCHAR* result = _tcsinc(&srcStr[4]);
    cout << "Source String = " << srcStr << endl;
    cout << "Result = " << result << endl;

    return 0;
}
```

CROSS-REFERENCE
See also _mbsinc(), _strinc(), _tasctime(), _tcscat(), _tcschr(), _tcscmp(), _tcscoll(), _tcscpy(), _tcscspn(), _tcsdec(), _tcsdup(), _tcsftime(), _tcsicmp(), _tcsicoll(), _tcslen(), _tcslwr(), _tcsnbcnt(), _tcsncat(), _tcsnccmp(), _tcsnccnt(), _tcsnccoll(), _tcsncicmp(), _tcsncmp(), _tcsncoll(), _tcsncpy(), _tcsnextc(), _tcsnicmp(), _tcsnicoll(), _tcsninc(), _tcsnset(), _tcspbrk(), _tcsrchr(), _tcsrev(), _tcsset(), _tcsspn(), _tcsspnp(), _tcsstr(), _tcstod(), _tcstok(), _tcstol(), _tcstoul(), _tcsupr(), _tcsxfrm(), _tctime(), _tell(), _telli64(), _tempnam(), _tolower(), _toupper(), and _wcsinc().

_tcslen()

Function

The _tcslen() function is the TCHAR version of the strlen() function, which returns the length (the number of characters) of a string. The behavior of this function depends on the definition of the _UNICODE and _MBCS symbols. If neither symbol is defined, the function compiles for ANSI (single-byte characters); if _UNICODE is defined, the function compiles for UNICODE (wide characters); and if _MBCS is defined, the function compiles for MBCS (multibyte characters).

Header File

```
#include <tchar.h>
```

Declaration

```
size_t _tcslen(const TCHAR *string);
```

- *string* — A pointer to the string for which to return the length.

Example

The following program demonstrates how to use the _tcslen() function. When run, the program calculates the length of a string and then uses the length to underline the source string. The program's output looks like the following:

```
Source String:

This is a test
_____

Press any key to continue
```

Here is the program source code that produced the output:

```
#include "stdafx.h"
#include <iostream>
#include <tchar.h>

using namespace std;

int main(int argc, char* argv[])
{
```

```
TCHAR* srcStr = "This is a test";

size_t len = _tcslen(srcStr);
cout << "Source String:" << endl << endl;
cout << srcStr << endl;
for (unsigned x=0; x<len; ++x)
    cout << "-";
cout << endl << endl;

return 0;
}
```

CROSS-REFERENCE

See also _mbslen(), _tasctime(), _tcscat(), _tcschr(), _tcscmp(), _tcscoll(), _tcscpy(), _tcscspn(), _tcsdec(), _tcsdup(), _tcsftime(), _tcsicmp(), _tcsicoll(), _tcsinc(), _tcslwr(), _tcsnbcnt(), _tcsncat(), _tcsnccmp(), _tcsnccnt(), _tcsnccoll(), _tcsnicmp(), _tcsncmp(), _tcsncoll(), _tcsncpy(), _tcsnextc(), _tcsnicmp(), _tcsnicoll(), _tcsninc(), _tcsnset(), _tcspbrk(), _tcsrchr(), _tcsrev(), _tcsset(), _tcsspn(), _tcsspnp(), _tcsstr(), _tcstod(), _tcstok(), _tcstol(), _tcstoul(), _tcsupr(), _tcsxfrm(), _tctime(), _tell(), _telli64(), _tempnam(), _tolower(), _toupper(), strlen(), and wcslen().

_tcslwr()

Function

The _tcslwr() function is the TCHAR version of the strlwr() function, which converts a string to lowercase, returning a pointer to the new string. The behavior of this function depends on the definition of the _UNICODE and _MBCS symbols. If neither symbol is defined, the function compiles for ANSI (single-byte characters); if _UNICODE is defined, the function compiles for UNICODE (wide characters); and if _MBCS is defined, the function compiles for MBCS (multibyte characters).

Header File

```
#include <tchar.h>
```

Declaration

```
TCHAR* _tcslwr(const TCHAR *string);
```

- *string* — The string to convert.

Example

The following program demonstrates how to use the _tcslwr() function. When run, the program converts several strings to lowercase and displays the results. The program's output looks like the following:

```
Original String: One Two Three
Converted String: one two three

Original String: FOUR FIVE SIX
Converted String: four five six

Original String: seven eight nine
Converted String: seven eight nine

Press any key to continue
```

Here is the program source code that produced the output:

```cpp
#include "stdafx.h"
#include <iostream>
#include <tchar.h>

using namespace std;

void convert(TCHAR* s)
{
    cout << "Original String: " << s << endl;
    TCHAR* result = _tcslwr(s);
    cout << "Converted String: ";
    cout << result << endl << endl;
}

int main(int argc, TCHAR* argv[])
{
    TCHAR str1[81];
    _tcscpy(str1, "One Two Three");
    TCHAR str2[81];
    _tcscpy(str2, "FOUR FIVE SIX");
    TCHAR str3[81];
    _tcscpy(str3, "seven eight nine");

    convert(str1);
    convert(str2);
    convert(str3);
```

```
    return 0;
}
```

CROSS-REFERENCE
See also _mbslwr(), _tasctime(), _tcscat(), _tcschr(), _tcscmp(), _tcscoll(), _tcscpy(),
_tcscspn(), _tcsdec(), _tcsdup(), _tcsftime(), _tcsicmp(), _tcsicoll(), _tcsinc(),
_tcslen(), _tcsnbcnt(), _tcsncat(), _tcsnccmp(), _tcsnccnt(), _tcsnccoll(), _tcsncicmp(),
_tcsncmp(), _tcsncoll(), _tcsncpy(), _tcsnextc(), _tcsnicmp(), _tcsnicoll(), _tcsninc(),
_tcsnset(), _tcspbrk(), _tcsrchr(), _tcsrev(), _tcsset(), _tcsspn(), _tcsspnp(), _tcsstr(),
_tcstod(), _tcstok(), _tcstol(), _tcstoul(), _tcsupr(), _tcsxfrm(), _tctime(), _tell(),
_telli64(), _tempnam(), _tolower(), _toupper(),_wcslwr(), and strlwr().

_tcsnbcnt()

Function

The _tcsnbcnt() function is the TCHAR version of the _mbsnbcnt() function,
which returns the number of bytes in a portion of a multibyte-character string.
The behavior of this function depends on the definition of the _UNICODE and
_MBCS symbols. If neither symbol is defined, the function compiles for ANSI
(single-byte characters); if _UNICODE is defined, the function compiles for
UNICODE (wide characters); and if _MBCS is defined, the function compiles
for MBCS (multibyte characters).

Header File

```
#include <tchar.h>
```

Declaration

```
size_t _tcsnbcnt(const unsigned TCHAR *string, size_t number);
```

- *number*—The number of characters to examine.
- *string*—A pointer to the string to examine.

Example

The following program demonstrates how to use the _tcsnbcnt() function.
When run, the program determines the number of bytes in the first four char-

acters of a string and displays the result. The program's output looks like the following:

```
Source String = This is a test
Result = 4
Press any key to continue
```

Here is the program source code that produced the output:

```
#include "stdafx.h"
#include <iostream>
#include <tchar.h>

using namespace std;

int main(int argc, char* argv[])
{
    TCHAR srcStr[] = "This is a test";

    size_t result = _tcsnbcnt(srcStr, 4);
    cout << "Source String = " << srcStr << endl;
    cout << "Result = " << result << endl;

    return 0;
}
```

CROSS-REFERENCE

See also _mbsnbcnt(), _tasctime(), _tcscat(), _tcschr(), _tcscmp(), _tcscoll(), _tcscpy(), _tcscspn(), _tcsdec(), _tcsdup(), _tcsftime(), _tcsicmp(), _tcsicoll(), _tcsinc(), _tcslen(), _tcslwr(), _tcsncat(), _tcsnccmp(), _tcsnccnt(), _tcsnccoll(), _tcsnicmp(), _tcsncmp(), _tcsncoll(), _tcsncpy(), _tcsnextc(), _tcsnicmp(), _tcsnicoll(), _tcsninc(), _tcsnset(), _tcspbrk(), _tcsrchr(), _tcsrev(), _tcsset(), _tcsspn(), _tcsspnp(), _tcsstr(), _tcstod(), _tcstok(), _tcstol(), _tcstoul(), _tcsupr(), _tcsxfrm(), _tctime(), _tell(), _telli64(), _tempnam(), _tolower(), _toupper(), and _tscncicoll().

_tcsncat()

Function

The _tcsncat() function is the TCHAR version of the strncat() function, which concatenates (joins together) strings, returning a pointer to the destination string. The behavior of this function depends on the definition of the _UNICODE and _MBCS symbols. If neither symbol is defined, the function compiles for ANSI (single-byte characters); if _UNICODE is defined, the function compiles for UNICODE (wide characters); and if _MBCS is defined, the function compiles for MBCS (multibyte characters).

Header File

```
#include <tchar.h>
```

Declaration

```
TCHAR* _tcsncat(TCHAR *strDest,
    const TCHAR *strSource, size_t count);
```

- *count* — The number of characters to concatenate.
- *strDest* — The string to which to concatenate *strSource*.
- *strSource* — The string to concatenate to *strDest*.

Example

The following program demonstrates how to use the _tcsncat() function. When run, the program concatenates the first six characters of the string "Four Five Six" to the string "One Two Three ". The program's output looks like the following:

```
Result: One Two Three Four F
Press any key to continue
```

Here is the program source code that produced the output:

```
#include "stdafx.h"
#include <iostream>
#include <tchar.h>

using namespace std;

int main(int argc, char* argv[])
{
    TCHAR str1[81];
    TCHAR* str2 = "Four Five Six";

    _tcscpy(str1, "One Two Three ");
    _tcsncat(str1, str2, 6);
    cout << "Result: " << str1 << endl;

    return 0;
}
```

s
t
u

CROSS-REFERENCE

See also _mbsncat(), _tasctime(), _tcscat(), _tcschr(), _tcscmp(), _tcscoll(), _tcscpy(), _tcscspn(), _tcsdec(), _tcsdup(), _tcsftime(), _tcsicmp(), _tcsicoll(), _tcsinc(), _tcslen(), _tcslwr(), _tcsnbcnt(), _tcsnccmp(), _tcsnccnt(), _tcsnccoll(), _tcsncicmp(), _tcsncmp(), _tcsncoll(), _tcsncpy(), _tcsnextc(), _tcsnicmp(), _tcsnicoll(), _tcsninc(), _tcsnset(), _tcspbrk(), _tcsrchr(), _tcsrev(), _tcsset(), _tcsspn(), _tcsspnp(), _tcsstr(), _tcstod(), _tcstok(), _tcstol(), _tcstoul(), _tcsupr(), _tcsxfrm(), _tctime(), _tell(), _telli64(), _tempnam(), _tolower(), _toupper(), strncat(), and wcsncat().

_tcsnccmp()

Function

The _tcsncmmp() function compares a set of characters in two strings, returning a value from the following Table T-6. The behavior of this function depends on the definition of the _UNICODE and _MBCS symbols. If neither symbol is defined, the function compiles for ANSI (single-byte characters); if _UNICODE is defined, the function compiles for UNICODE (wide characters); and if _MBCS is defined, the function compiles for MBCS (multibyte characters).

Table T-6 Return Values for _tcsnccmp()

Value	Description
Less than 0	string1 is alphabetically less than string2.
0	The two strings are equal.
Greater than 0	string1 is alphabetically greater than string2.

Header File

```
#include <tchar.h>
```

Declaration

```
int _tcsnccmp(const TCHAR *string1,
    const TCHAR *string2, size_t count);
```

- *count* — The number of characters to compare.
- *string1* — The first string to compare.
- *string2* — The second string to compare.

Example

The following program demonstrates how to use the _tcsncmp() function. When run, the program compares several pairs of strings and displays the result of the comparisons. The output looks like the following:

```
For a length of 7 characters

One Two Three equals One Two Ten
One Two Ten is greater than Four Five Six
Four Five Six is greater than Four Eight Nine
Press any key to continue
```

Here is the program source code that produced the output:

```cpp
#include "stdafx.h"
#include <iostream>
#include <tchar.h>

using namespace std;

void cmp(TCHAR* s1, TCHAR* s2, size_t num)
{
    int result = _tcsnccmp(s1, s2, num);
    if (result < 0 )
    {
        cout << s1 << " is less than ";
        cout << s2 << endl;
    }
    else if (result > 0)
    {
        cout << s1 << " is greater than ";
        cout << s2 << endl;
    }
    else
    {
        cout << s1 << " equals ";
        cout << s2 << endl;
    }
}

int main(int argc, char* argv[])
{
    TCHAR* str1 = "One Two Three";
    TCHAR* str2 = "One Two Ten";
    TCHAR* str3 = "Four Five Six";
```

```
      TCHAR* str4 = "Four Eight Nine";

      cout << "For a length of 7 characters" << endl << endl;
      cmp(str1, str2, 7);
      cmp(str2, str3, 7);
      cmp(str3, str4, 7);
      cout << endl;

      return 0;
   }
```

CROSS-REFERENCE

See also _mbscat(), _mbsncmp(), _tasctime(), _tcscat(), _tcschr(), _tcscmp(), _tcscoll(), _tcscpy(), _tcscspn(), _tcsdec(), _tcsdup(), _tcsftime(), _tcsicmp(), _tcsicoll(), _tcsinc(), _tcslen(), _tcslwr(), _tcsnbcnt(), _tcsncat(), _tcsnccnt(), _tcsnccoll(), _tcsnicmp(), _tcsncmp(), _tcsncoll(), _tcsncpy(), _tcsnextc(), _tcsnicmp(), _tcsnicoll(), _tcsninc(), _tcsnset(), _tcspbrk(), _tcsrchr(), _tcsrev(), _tcsset(), _tcsspn(), _tcsspnp(), _tcsstr(), _tcstod(), _tcstok(), _tcstol(), _tcstoul(), _tcsupr(), _tcsxfrm(), _tctime(), _tell(), _telli64(), _tempnam(), _tolower(), _toupper(), strncmp(), and wcsncmp().

_tcsnccnt()

Function

The _tcsnccnt() function returns the number of characters in a portion of a character string.

Header File

```
#include <tchar.h>
```

Declaration

```
size_t _tcsnccnt(const TCHAR *string, size_t number);
```

- *number* — The number of bytes to examine.
- *string* — A pointer to the string to examine.

Example

The following program demonstrates how to use the _tcsnccnt() function. When run, the program determines the number of characters in the first four bytes of a string and displays the result. The program's output looks like the following:

```
Source String = This is a test
Result = 4
Press any key to continue
```

Here is the program source code that produced the output:

```cpp
#include "stdafx.h"
#include <iostream>
#include <tchar.h>

using namespace std;

int main(int argc, char* argv[])
{
    TCHAR srcStr[] = "This is a test";

    size_t result = _tcsnccnt(srcStr, 4);
    cout << "Source String = " << srcStr << endl;
    cout << "Result = " << result << endl;

    return 0;
}
```

CROSS-REFERENCE

See also _mbsncmp(), _tasctime(), _tcscat(), _tcschr(), _tcscmp(), _tcscoll(), _tcscpy(), _tcscspn(), _tcsdec(), _tcsdup(), _tcsftime(), _tcsicmp(), _tcsicoll(), _tcsinc(), _tcslen(), _tcslwr(), _tcsnbcnt(), _tcsncat(), _tcsnccoll(), _tcsncicmp(), _tcsncmp(), _tcsncoll(), _tcsncpy(), _tcsnextc(), _tcsnicmp(), _tcsnicoll(), _tcsninc(), _tcsnset(), _tcspbrk(), _tcsrchr(), _tcsrev(), _tcsset(), _tcsspn(), _tcsspnp(), _tcsstr(), _tcstod(), _tcstok(), _tcstol(), _tcstoul(), _tcsupr(), _tcsxfrm(), _tctime(), _tell(), _telli64(), _tempnam(), _tolower(), _toupper(), strncmp(), and wcsncmp().

_tcsnccoll()

Function

The _tcsnccoll() function compares two strings for the current locale, returning a value from Table T-7. The behavior of this function depends on the definition of the _UNICODE and _MBCS symbols. If neither symbol is defined, the function compiles for ANSI (single-byte characters); if _UNICODE is defined, the function compiles for UNICODE (wide characters); and if _MBCS is defined, the function compiles for MBCS (multibyte characters).

Table T-7 Return Values for _tcsnccoll()

Value	Description
Less than 0	string1 is alphabetically less than string2.
0	The two strings are equal.
Greater than 0	string1 is alphabetically greater than string2.

Header File

```
#include <tchar.h>
```

Declaration

```
int _tcsnccoll(const TCHAR *string1,
    const TCHAR *string2, size_t count);
```

- *count* — The number of characters to compare.
- *string1* — The first string to compare.
- *string2* — The second string to compare.

Example

The following program demonstrates how to use the _tcsnccoll() function. When run, the program compares several pairs of strings and displays the result of the comparisons. The program's output looks like the following:

```
One Two Three equals One Two three
One Two three is less than one Two Three
one Two Three is greater than SEVEN EIGHT nine
SEVEN EIGHT nine is less than seven eight nine
Press any key to continue
```

Here is the program source code that produced the output:

```
#include "stdafx.h"
#include <iostream>
#include <tchar.h>

using namespace std;

void cmp(TCHAR* s1, TCHAR* s2, size_t num)
{
    int result = _tcsnccoll(s1, s2, num);
    if (result < 0 )
    {
        cout << s1;
        cout << " is less than ";
        cout << s2 << endl;
    }
    else if (result > 0)
    {
        cout << s1;
        cout << " is greater than ";
        cout << s2 << endl;
    }
    else
    {
        cout << s1;
        cout << " equals ";
        cout << s2 << endl;
    }
}

int main(int argc, TCHAR* argv[])
{
    TCHAR* str1 = "One Two Three";
    TCHAR* str2 = "One Two three";
    TCHAR* str3 = "one Two Three";
    TCHAR* str4 = "SEVEN EIGHT nine";
    TCHAR* str5 = "seven eight nine";

    cmp(str1, str2, 7);
    cmp(str2, str3, 7);
    cmp(str3, str4, 7);
    cmp(str4, str5, 7);

    return 0;
}
```

CROSS-REFERENCE

See also _mbsncoll(), _strncoll(), _tasctime(), _tcscat(), _tcschr(), _tcscmp(), _tcscoll(), _tcscpy(), _tcscspn(), _tcsdec(), _tcsdup(), _tcsftime(), _tcsicmp(), _tcsicoll(), _tcsinc(), _tcslen(), _tcslwr(), _tcsnbcnt(), _tcsncat(), _tcsnccmp(), _tcsnccnt(), _tcsncicmp(), _tcsncmp(), _tcsncoll(), _tcsncpy(), _tcsnextc(), _tcsnicmp(), _tcsnicoll(), _tcsninc(), _tcsnset(), _tcspbrk(), _tcsrchr(), _tcsrev(), _tcsset(), _tcsspn(), _tcsspnp(), _tcsstr(), _tcstod(), _tcstok(), _tcstol(), _tcstoul(), _tcsupr(), _tcsxfrm(), _tctime(), _tell(), _telli64(), _tempnam(), _tolower(), _toupper(), and _wcsncoll().

_tcsncicmp()

Function

The _tcsncicmp() function compares two strings without regard for case (case-insensitive), returning a value from Table T-8. The behavior of this function depends on the definition of the _UNICODE and _MBCS symbols. If neither symbol is defined, the function compiles for ANSI (single-byte characters); if _UNICODE is defined, the function compiles for UNICODE (wide characters); and if _MBCS is defined, the function compiles for MBCS (multibyte characters).

Table T-8 Return Values for _tcsncicmp()

Value	Description
Less than 0	string1 is alphabetically less than string2.
0	The two strings are equal.
Greater than 0	string1 is alphabetically greater than string2.

Header File

```
#include <tchar.h>
```

Declaration

```
int _tcsncicmp(const TCHAR *string1,
    const TCHAR *string2, size_t count);
```

- *count* — The number of characters to compare.
- *string1* — The first string to compare.
- *string2* — The second string to compare.

Example

The following program demonstrates how to use the _tcsncicmp() function. When run, the program compares several pairs of strings and displays the result of the comparisons. The program's output looks like the following:

```
One Two Three equals One Two three
One Two three equals one Two Three
one Two Three is less than SEVEN EIGHT nine
SEVEN EIGHT nine equals seven eight nine
Press any key to continue
```

Here is the program source code that produced the output:

```cpp
#include "stdafx.h"
#include <iostream>
#include <tchar.h>

using namespace std;

void cmp(TCHAR* s1, TCHAR* s2, size_t num)
{
    int result = _tcsncicmp(s1, s2, num);
    if (result < 0 )
    {
        cout << s1;
        cout << " is less than ";
        cout << s2 << endl;
    }
    else if (result > 0)
    {
        cout << s1;
        cout << " is greater than ";
        cout << s2 << endl;
    }
    else
    {
        cout << s1;
        cout << " equals ";
        cout << s2 << endl;
    }
}

int main(int argc, TCHAR* argv[])
{
    TCHAR* str1 = "One Two Three";
```

```
TCHAR* str2 = "One Two three";
TCHAR* str3 = "one Two Three";
TCHAR* str4 = "SEVEN EIGHT nine";
TCHAR* str5 = "seven eight nine";

cmp(str1, str2, 7);
cmp(str2, str3, 7);
cmp(str3, str4, 7);
cmp(str4, str5, 7);

return 0;
}
```

CROSS-REFERENCE

See also _mbsnicmp(), _strnicmp(), _tasctime(), _tcscat(), _tcschr(), _tcscmp(), _tcscoll(), _tcscpy(), _tcscspn(), _tcsdec(), _tcsdup(), _tcsftime(), _tcsicmp(), _tcsicoll(), _tcsinc(), _tcslen(), _tcslwr(), _tcsnbcnt(), _tcsncat(), _tcsnccmp(), _tcsnccnt(), _tcsnccoll(), _tcsncmp(), _tcsncoll(), _tcsncpy(), _tcsnextc(), _tcsnicmp(), _tcsnicoll(), _tcsninc(), _tcsnset(), _tcspbrk(), _tcsrchr(), _tcsrev(), _tcsset(), _tcsspn(), _tcsspnp(), _tcsstr(), _tcstod(), _tcstok(), _tcstol(), _tcstoul(), _tcsupr(), _tcsxfrm(), _tctime(), _tell(), _telli64(), _tempnam(), _tolower(), _toupper(), and _wcsnicmp().

_tcsncmp()

Function

The _tcsncmp() function is the TCHAR version of the strncmp() function, which compares a set of characters in two strings, returning a value from Table T-9. The behavior of this function depends on the definition of the _UNICODE and _MBCS symbols. If neither symbol is defined, the function compiles for ANSI (single-byte characters); if _UNICODE is defined, the function compiles for UNICODE (wide characters); and if _MBCS is defined, the function compiles for MBCS (multibyte characters).

Table T-9 Return Values for _tcsncmp()

Value	Description
Less than 0	string1 is alphabetically less than string2.
0	The two strings are equal.
Greater than 0	string1 is alphabetically greater than string2.

Header File

```
#include <tchar.h>
```

Declaration

```
int _tcsncmp(const TCHAR *string1,
    const TCHAR *string2, size_t count);
```

- *count* — The number of characters to compare.
- *string1* — The first string to compare.
- *string2* — The second string to compare.

Example

The following program demonstrates how to use the _tcsncmp() function. When run, the program compares several pairs of strings and displays the result of the comparisons. The program's output looks like the following:

```
For a length of 7 characters

One Two Three equals One Two Ten
One Two Ten is greater than Four Five Six
Four Five Six is greater than Four Eight Nine

Press any key to continue
```

Here is the program source code that produced the output:

```
#include "stdafx.h"
#include <iostream>
#include <tchar.h>

using namespace std;

void cmp(TCHAR* s1, TCHAR* s2, size_t num)
{
    int result = _tcsncmp(s1, s2, num);
    if (result < 0 )
    {
        cout << s1 << " is less than ";
        cout << s2 << endl;
    }
    else if (result > 0)
    {
```

```
                    cout << s1 << " is greater than ";
                    cout << s2 << endl;
            }
            else
            {
                    cout << s1 << " equals ";
                    cout << s2 << endl;
            }
    }

    int main(int argc, TCHAR* argv[])
    {
        TCHAR* str1 = "One Two Three";
        TCHAR* str2 = "One Two Ten";
        TCHAR* str3 = "Four Five Six";
        TCHAR* str4 = "Four Eight Nine";

        cout << "For a length of 7 characters" << endl << endl;
        cmp(str1, str2, 7);
        cmp(str2, str3, 7);
        cmp(str3, str4, 7);
        cout << endl;

        return 0;
    }
```

 CROSS-REFERENCE

See also _mbsncmp(), _tasctime(), _tcscat(), _tcschr(), _tcscmp(), _tcscoll(), _tcscpy(), _tcscspn(), _tcsdec(), _tcsdup(), _tcsftime(), _tcsicmp(), _tcsicoll(), _tcsinc(), _tcslen(), _tcslwr(), _tcsnbcnt(), _tcsncat(), _tcsnccmp(), _tcsnccnt(), _tcsnccoll(), _tcsnicmp(), _tcsncoll(), _tcsncpy(), _tcsnextc(), _tcsnicmp(), _tcsnicoll(), _tcsninc(), _tcsnset(), _tcspbrk(), _tcsrchr(), _tcsrev(), _tcsset(), _tcsspn(), _tcsspnp(), _tcsstr(), _tcstod(), _tcstok(), _tcstol(), _tcstoul(), _tcsupr(), _tcsxfrm(), _tctime(), _tell(), _telli64(), _tempnam(), _tolower(), _toupper(), strncmp(), and wcsncmp().

_tcsncoll()

Function

The _tcsncoll() function is the TCHAR version of the _strncoll() function, which compares two strings for the current locale, returning a value from Table T-10. The behavior of this function depends on the definition of the

_UNICODE and _MBCS symbols. If neither symbol is defined, the function compiles for ANSI (single-byte characters); if _UNICODE is defined, the function compiles for UNICODE (wide characters); and if _MBCS is defined, the function compiles for MBCS (multibyte characters).

Table T-10 Return Values for _tcsncoll()

Value	Description
Less than 0	string1 is alphabetically less than string2.
0	The two strings are equal.
Greater than 0	string1 is alphabetically greater than string2.

Header File

```
#include <tchar.h>
```

Declaration

```
int _tcsncoll(const TCHAR *string1,
    const TCHAR *string2, size_t count);
```

- *count* — The number of characters to compare.
- *string1* — The first string to compare.
- *string2* — The second string to compare.

Example

The following program demonstrates how to use the _tcsncoll() function. When run, the program compares several pairs of strings and displays the result of the comparisons. The program's output looks like the following:

```
One Two Three equals One Two three
One Two three is less than one Two Three
one Two Three is greater than SEVEN EIGHT nine
SEVEN EIGHT nine is less than seven eight nine
Press any key to continue
```

Here is the program source code that produced the output:

```
#include "stdafx.h"
#include <iostream>
#include <tchar.h>
```

```
using namespace std;

void cmp(TCHAR* s1, TCHAR* s2, size_t num)
{
    int result = _tcsncoll(s1, s2, num);
    if (result < 0 )
    {
        cout << s1;
        cout << " is less than ";
        cout << s2 << endl;
    }
    else if (result > 0)
    {
        cout << s1;
        cout << " is greater than ";
        cout << s2 << endl;
    }
    else
    {
        cout << s1;
        cout << " equals ";
        cout << s2 << endl;
    }
}

int main(int argc, TCHAR* argv[])
{
    TCHAR* str1 = "One Two Three";
    TCHAR* str2 = "One Two three";
    TCHAR* str3 = "one Two Three";
    TCHAR* str4 = "SEVEN EIGHT nine";
    TCHAR* str5 = "seven eight nine";

    cmp(str1, str2, 7);
    cmp(str2, str3, 7);
    cmp(str3, str4, 7);
    cmp(str4, str5, 7);

    return 0;
}
```

CROSS-REFERENCE
See also _mbsncoll(), _strncoll(), _tasctime(), _tcscat(), _tcschr(), _tcscmp(), _tcscoll(),
_tcscpy(), _tcscspn(), _tcsdec(), _tcsdup(), _tcsftime(), _tcsicmp(), _tcsicoll(), _tcsinc(),
_tcslen(), _tcslwr(), _tcsnbcnt(), _tcsncat(), _tcsnccmp(), _tcsnccnt(), _tcsnccoll(),
_tcsnicmp(), _tcsncmp(), _tcsncpy(), _tcsnextc(), _tcsnicmp(), _tcsnicoll(), _tcsninc(),
_tcsnset(), _tcspbrk(), _tcsrchr(), _tcsrev(), _tcsset(), _tcsspn(), _tcsspnp(), _tcsstr(),
_tcstod(), _tcstok(), _tcstol(), _tcstoul(), _tcsupr(), _tcsxfrm(), _tctime(), _tell(),
_telli64(), _tempnam(), _tolower(), _toupper(), and _wcsncoll().

_tcsncpy()

Function

The _tcsncpy() function is the TCHAR version of the strncpy() function,
which copies a specified number of characters from one string to another,
returning a pointer to the destination string. The source and destination
strings cannot overlap. The behavior of this function depends on the definition
of the _UNICODE and _MBCS symbols. If neither symbol is defined, the function
compiles for ANSI (single-byte characters); if _UNICODE is defined, the function compiles for UNICODE (wide characters); and if _MBCS is defined, the
function compiles for MBCS (multibyte characters).

Header File

```
#include <tchar.h>
```

Declaration

```
TCHAR* _tcsncpy(TCHAR *strDest,
    const TCHAR *strSource, size_t count);
```

- *count*—The number of characters to copy.
- *strDest*—A pointer to the destination string.
- *strSource*—A pointer to the source string.

Example

The following program demonstrates how to use the _tcsncpy() function.
When run, the program copies 11 characters from one string to another and
displays the result. The program's output looks like the following:

```
Source string = This is a test
```

```
Destination string = This is a t
Press any key to continue
```

Here is the program source code that produced the output:

```
#include "stdafx.h"
#include <iostream>
#include <tchar.h>

using namespace std;

int main(int argc, char* argv[])
{
    TCHAR destStr[81];
    TCHAR* srcStr = "This is a test";

    TCHAR* pResult = _tcsncpy(destStr, srcStr, 11);
    pResult[11] = 0;
    cout << "Source string = " << srcStr << endl;
    cout << "Destination string = " << pResult << endl;

    return 0;
}
```

CROSS-REFERENCE

See also _mbsncpy(), _tasctime(), _tcscat(), _tcschr(), _tcscmp(), _tcscoll(), _tcscpy(), _tcscspn(), _tcsdec(), _tcsdup(), _tcsftime(), _tcsicmp(), _tcsicoll(), _tcsinc(), _tcslen(), _tcslwr(), _tcsnbcnt(), _tcsncat(), _tcsnccmp(), _tcsnccnt(), _tcsnccoll(), _tcsncicmp(), _tcsncmp(), _tcsncoll(), _tcsnextc(), _tcsnicmp(), _tcsnicoll(), _tcsninc(), _tcsnset(), _tcspbrk(), _tcsrchr(), _tcsrev(), _tcsset(), _tcsspn(), _tcsspnp(), _tcsstr(), _tcstod(), _tcstok(), _tcstol(), _tcstoul(), _tcsupr(), _tcsxfrm(), _tctime(), _tell(), _telli64(), _tempnam(), _tolower(), _toupper(), strncpy(), and wcsncpy().

_tcsnextc()

Function

The _tcsnextc() function is the TCHAR version of the _strnextc() function, which returns the value of the next character in a string. The behavior of this function depends on the definition of the _UNICODE and _MBCS symbols. If neither symbol is defined, the function compiles for ANSI (single-byte characters); if _UNICODE is defined, the function compiles for

UNICODE (wide characters); and if _MBCS is defined, the function compiles for MBCS (multibyte characters).

Header File

```
#include <tchar.h>
```

Declaration

```
unsigned int _tcsnextc(const TCHAR *string);
```

- *string* — A pointer to the source string.

Example

The following program demonstrates how to use the _tcsnextc() function. When run, the program determines the integer value of the fifth character in a string and displays the result. The program's output looks like the following:

```
Source String = This is a test
Result = 32
Press any key to continue
```

Here is the program source code that produced the output:

```
#include "stdafx.h"
#include <iostream>
#include <tchar.h>

using namespace std;

int main(int argc, char* argv[])
{
    TCHAR* srcStr = "This is a test";

    unsigned int result = _tcsnextc(&srcStr[4]);
    cout << "Source String = ";
    cout << srcStr << endl;
    cout << "Result = " << result << endl;

    return 0;
}
```

CROSS-REFERENCE

See also _mbsnextc(), _strnextc(), _tasctime(), _tcscat(), _tcschr(), _tcscmp(), _tcscoll(), _tcscpy(), _tcscspn(), _tcsdec(), _tcsdup(), _tcsftime(), _tcsicmp(), _tcsicoll(), _tcsinc(), _tcslen(), _tcslwr(), _tcsnbcnt(), _tcsncat(), _tcsnccmp(), _tcsnccnt(), _tcsnccoll(), _tcsnicmp(), _tcsncmp(), _tcsncoll(), _tcsncpy(), _tcsnicmp(), _tcsnicoll(), _tcsninc(), _tcsnset(), _tcspbrk(), _tcsrchr(), _tcsrev(), _tcsset(), _tcsspn(), _tcsspnp(), _tcsstr(), _tcstod(), _tcstok(), _tcstol(), _tcstoul(), _tcsupr(), _tcsxfrm(), _tctime(), _tell(), _telli64(), _tempnam(), _tolower(), _toupper(), and _wcsnextc().

_tcsnicmp()

Function

The _tcsnicmp() function is the TCHAR version of the _strnicmp() function, which compares two strings without regard for case (case-insensitive), returning a value from Table T-11. The behavior of this function depends on the definition of the _UNICODE and _MBCS symbols. If neither symbol is defined, the function compiles for ANSI (single-byte characters); if _UNICODE is defined, the function compiles for UNICODE (wide characters); and if _MBCS is defined, the function compiles for MBCS (multibyte characters).

Table T-11 Return Values for _tcsnicmp()

Value	Description
Less than 0	string1 is alphabetically less than string2.
0	The two strings are equal.
Greater than 0	string1 is alphabetically greater than string2.

Header File

```
#include <tchar.h>
```

Declaration

```
int _tcsnicmp(const TCHAR *string1,
    const TCHAR *string2, size_t count);
```

- *count* — The number of characters to compare.
- *string1* — The first string to compare.
- *string2* — The second string to compare.

Example

The following program demonstrates how to use the _tcsnicmp() function. When run, the program compares several pairs of strings and displays the result of the comparisons. The program's output looks like the following:

```
One Two Three equals One Two three
One Two three equals one Two Three
one Two Three is less than SEVEN EIGHT nine
SEVEN EIGHT nine equals seven eight nine
Press any key to continue
```

Here is the program source code that produced the output:

```cpp
#include "stdafx.h"
#include <iostream>
#include <tchar.h>

using namespace std;

void cmp(TCHAR* s1, TCHAR* s2, size_t num)
{
    int result = _tcsnicmp(s1, s2, num);
    if (result < 0 )
    {
        cout << s1;
        cout << " is less than ";
        cout << s2 << endl;
    }
    else if (result > 0)
    {
        cout << s1;
        cout << " is greater than ";
        cout << s2 << endl;
    }
    else
    {
        cout << s1;
        cout << " equals ";
        cout << s2 << endl;
    }
}

int main(int argc, TCHAR* argv[])
{
    TCHAR* str1 = "One Two Three";
```

```
TCHAR* str2 = "One Two three";
TCHAR* str3 = "one Two Three";
TCHAR* str4 = "SEVEN EIGHT nine";
TCHAR* str5 = "seven eight nine";

cmp(str1, str2, 7);
cmp(str2, str3, 7);
cmp(str3, str4, 7);
cmp(str4, str5, 7);

return 0;
}
```

CROSS-REFERENCE

See also _mbsnicmp(), _strnicmp(), _tasctime(), _tcscat(), _tcschr(), _tcscmp(), _tcscoll(), _tcscpy(), _tcscspn(), _tcsdec(), _tcsdup(), _tcsftime(), _tcsicmp(), _tcsicoll(), _tcsinc(), _tcslen(), _tcslwr(), _tcsnbcnt(), _tcsncat(), _tcsnccmp(), _tcsnccnt(), _tcsnccoll(), _tcsnicmp(), _tcsncmp(), _tcsncoll(), _tcsncpy(), _tcsnextc(), _tcsnicoll(), _tcsninc(), _tcsnset(), _tcspbrk(), _tcsrchr(), _tcsrev(), _tcsset(), _tcsspn(), _tcsspnp(), _tcsstr(), _tcstod(), _tcstok(), _tcstol(), _tcstoul(), _tcsupr(), _tcsxfrm(), _tctime(), _tell(), _telli64(), _tempnam(), _tolower(), _toupper(), and _wcsnicmp().

_tcsnicoll()

Function

The _tcsnicoll() function is the TCHAR version of the _strnicoll() function, which compares two strings for the current locale without regard to case (case-insensitive), returning a value from Table T-12. The behavior of this function depends on the definition of the _UNICODE and _MBCS symbols. If neither symbol is defined, the function compiles for ANSI (single-byte characters); if _UNICODE is defined, the function compiles for UNICODE (wide characters); and if _MBCS is defined, the function compiles for MBCS (multibyte characters).

Table T-12 Return Values for _tcsnicoll()

Value	Description
Less than 0	string1 is alphabetically less than string2.
0	The two strings are equal.
Greater than 0	string1 is alphabetically greater than string2.

Header File

```
#include <tchar.h>
```

Declaration

```
int _tcsnicoll(const TCHAR *string1,
    const TCHAR *string2, size_t count);
```

- *count* — The number of characters to compare.
- *string1* — The first string to compare.
- *string2* — The second string to compare.

Example

The following program demonstrates how to use the `_tcsnicoll()` function. When run, the program compares several pairs of strings and displays the result of the comparisons. The program's output looks like the following:

```
One Two Three equals One Two three
One Two three equals one Two Three
one Two Three is less than SEVEN EIGHT nine
SEVEN EIGHT nine equals seven eight nine
Press any key to continue
```

Here is the program source code that produced the output:

```
#include "stdafx.h"
#include <iostream>
#include <tchar.h>

using namespace std;

void cmp(TCHAR* s1, TCHAR* s2, size_t num)
{
    int result = _tcsnicoll(s1, s2, num);
    if (result < 0 )
    {
        cout << s1;
        cout << " is less than ";
        cout << s2 << endl;
    }
    else if (result > 0)
    {
        cout << s1;
        cout << " is greater than ";
```

```
                    cout << s2 << endl;
            }
            else
            {
                    cout << s1;
                    cout << " equals ";
                    cout << s2 << endl;
            }
    }

    int main(int argc, TCHAR* argv[])
    {
            TCHAR* str1 = "One Two Three";
            TCHAR* str2 = "One Two three";
            TCHAR* str3 = "one Two Three";
            TCHAR* str4 = "SEVEN EIGHT nine";
            TCHAR* str5 = "seven eight nine";

            cmp(str1, str2, 7);
            cmp(str2, str3, 7);
            cmp(str3, str4, 7);
            cmp(str4, str5, 7);

            return 0;
    }
```

CROSS-REFERENCE
See also _mbsnicoll(), _strnicoll(), _tasctime(), _tcscat(), _tcschr(), _tcscmp(),
_tcscoll(), _tcscpy(), _tcscspn(), _tcsdec(), _tcsdup(), _tcsftime(), _tcsicmp(),
_tcsicoll(), _tcsinc(), _tcslen(), _tcslwr(), _tcsnbcnt(), _tcsncat(), _tcsnccmp(),
_tcsnccnt(), _tcsnccoll(), _tcsnicmp(), _tcsncmp(), _tcsncoll(), _tcsncpy(),
_tcsnextc(), _tcsnicmp(), _tcsninc(), _tcsnset(), _tcspbrk(), _tcsrchr(), _tcsrev(),
_tcsset(), _tcsspn(), _tcsspnp(), _tcsstr(), _tcstod(), _tcstok(), _tcstol(), _tcstoul(),
_tcsupr(), _tcsxfrm(), _tctime(), _tell(), _telli64(), _tempnam(), _tolower(),
_toupper(), and _wcsnicoll().

_tcsninc()

Function

The _tcsninc() function is the TCHAR version of the _strninc() function,
which returns a pointer to the string that results from advancing the specified
number of characters in the source string. The behavior of this function

depends on the definition of the _UNICODE and _MBCS symbols. If neither symbol is defined, the function compiles for ANSI (single-byte characters); if _UNICODE is defined, the function compiles for UNICODE (wide characters); and if _MBCS is defined, the function compiles for MBCS (multibyte characters).

Header File

```
#include <tchar.h>
```

Declaration

```
TCHAR* _tcsninc(const TCHAR *string, size_t count);
```

- *count* — The number of characters to advance in the source string.
- *string* — A pointer to the source string.

Example

The following program demonstrates how to use the _tcsninc() function. When run, the program locates the fifth character in a string and displays the result. The program's output looks like the following:

```
Source String = This is a test
Result = is a test
Press any key to continue
```

Here is the program source code that produced the output:

```
#include "stdafx.h"
#include <iostream>
#include <tchar.h>

using namespace std;

int main(int argc, char* argv[])
{
    TCHAR* srcStr = "This is a test";

    TCHAR* result = _tcsninc(srcStr, 5);
    cout << "Source String = " << srcStr << endl;
    cout << "Result = " << result << endl;

    return 0;
}
```

CROSS-REFERENCE

See also _mbsninc(), _strninc(), _tasctime(), _tcscat(), _tcschr(), _tcscmp(), _tcscoll(), _tcscpy(), _tcscspn(), _tcsdec(), _tcsdup(), _tcsftime(), _tcsicmp(), _tcsicoll(), _tcsinc(), _tcslen(), _tcslwr(), _tcsnbcnt(), _tcsncat(), _tcsnccmp(), _tcsnccnt(), _tcsnccoll(), _tcsncicmp(), _tcsncmp(), _tcsncoll(), _tcsncpy(), _tcsnextc(), _tcsnicmp(), _tcsnicoll(), _tcsnset(), _tcspbrk(), _tcsrchr(), _tcsrev(), _tcsset(), _tcsspn(), _tcsspnp(), _tcsstr(), _tcstod(), _tcstok(), _tcstol(), _tcstoul(), _tcsupr(), _tcsxfrm(), _tctime(), _tell(), _telli64(), _tempnam(), _tolower(), _toupper(), and _wcsninc().

_tcsnset()

Function

The _tcsnset() function is the TCHAR version of _strnset(), which sets a portion of a string to a given character, returning a pointer to the new string. The behavior of this function depends on the definition of the _UNICODE and _MBCS symbols. If neither symbol is defined, the function compiles for ANSI (single-byte characters); if _UNICODE is defined, the function compiles for UNICODE (wide characters); and if _MBCS is defined, the function compiles for MBCS (multibyte characters).

Header File

```
#include <tchar.h>
```

Declaration

```
TCHAR* _tcsnset(const TCHAR *string,
    unsigned int c, size_t count);
```

- *c* — The character with which to fill the string.
- *count* — The number of characters to set.
- *string* — The string to set.

Example

The following program demonstrates how to use the _tcsnset() function. When run, the program sets several strings to various symbols and displays the results. The program's output looks like the following:

```
Original String: One Two Three
Converted String: ??? Two Three

Original String: FOUR FIVE SIX
Converted String: *******VE SIX

Original String: seven eight nine
Converted String: ################
```

Press any key to continue

Here is the program source code that produced the output:

```cpp
#include "stdafx.h"
#include <iostream>
#include <tchar.h>

using namespace std;

void convert(TCHAR* s, int c, size_t num)
{
    cout << "Original String: " << s << endl;
    TCHAR* result = _tcsnset(s, c, num);
    cout << "Converted String: " << result;
    cout << endl << endl;
}

int main(int argc, char* argv[])
{
    TCHAR str1[81] = "One Two Three";
    TCHAR str2[81] = "FOUR FIVE SIX";
    TCHAR str3[81] = "seven eight nine";

    convert(str1, '?', 3);
    convert(str2, '*', 7);
    convert(str3, '#', 16);

    return 0;
}
```

s
t
u

CROSS-REFERENCE

See also _mbsnset(), _strnset(), _tasctime(), _tcscat(), _tcschr(), _tcscmp(), _tcscoll(), _tcscpy(), _tcscspn(), _tcsdec(), _tcsdup(), _tcsftime(), _tcsicmp(), _tcsicoll(), _tcsinc(), _tcslen(), _tcslwr(), _tcsnbcnt(), _tcsncat(), _tcsnccmp(), _tcsnccnt(), _tcsnccoll(), _tcsncicmp(), _tcsncmp(), _tcsncoll(), _tcsncpy(), _tcsnextc(), _tcsnicmp(), _tcsnicoll(), _tcsninc(), _tcspbrk(), _tcsrchr(), _tcsrev(), _tcsset(), _tcsspn(), _tcsspnp(), _tcsstr(), _tcstod(), _tcstok(), _tcstol(), _tcstoul(), _tcsupr(), _tcsxfrm(), _tctime(), _tell(), _telli64(), _tempnam(), _tolower(), _toupper(), and _wcsnset().

_tcspbrk()

Function

The _tcspbrk() function is the TCHAR version of the strpbrk() function, which locates the first occurrence of a character in a string, returning a pointer to the substring starting with the matching character. The behavior of this function depends on the definition of the _UNICODE and _MBCS symbols. If neither symbol is defined, the function compiles for ANSI (single-byte characters); if _UNICODE is defined, the function compiles for UNICODE (wide characters); and if _MBCS is defined, the function compiles for MBCS (multibyte characters).

Header File

```
#include <tchar.h>
```

Declaration

```
TCHAR* _tcspbrk(const TCHAR *string,
    const TCHAR *strCharSet);
```

- *strCharSet* — A pointer to the set of characters for which to search.
- *string* — A pointer to the string to search.

Example

The following program demonstrates how to use the _tcspbrk() function. When run, the program locates, in a string, the first character in a set of characters and displays the result. The program's output looks like the following:

```
Source String:
This is a test
Substring:
s is a test
```

Press any key to continue

Here is the program source code that produced the output:

```cpp
#include "stdafx.h"
#include <iostream>
#include <tchar.h>

using namespace std;

int main(int argc, char* argv[])
{
    TCHAR* srcStr = "This is a test";
    TCHAR* chrSet = "ast";

    TCHAR* pSubStr = _tcspbrk(srcStr, chrSet);
    cout << "Source String:" << endl;
    cout << srcStr << endl;
    cout << "Substring:" << endl;
    cout << pSubStr << endl << endl;

    return 0;
}
```

CROSS-REFERENCE
See also _mbspbrk(), _tasctime(), _tcscat(), _tcschr(), _tcscmp(), _tcscoll(), _tcscpy(), _tcscspn(), _tcsdec(), _tcsdup(), _tcsftime(), _tcsicmp(), _tcsicoll(), _tcsinc(), _tcslen(), _tcslwr(), _tcsnbcnt(), _tcsncat(), _tcsnccmp(), _tcsnccnt(), _tcsnccoll(), _tcsncicmp(), _tcsncmp(), _tcsncoll(), _tcsncpy(), _tcsnextc(), _tcsnicmp(), _tcsnicoll(), _tcsninc(), _tcsnset(), _tcsrchr(), _tcsrev(), _tcsset(), _tcsspn(), _tcsspnp(), _tcsstr(), _tcstod(), _tcstok(), _tcstol(), _tcstoul(), _tcsupr(), _tcsxfrm(), _tctime(), _tell(), _telli64(), _tempnam(), _tolower(), _toupper(), strpbrk(), and wcspbrk().

_tcsrchr()

Function

The _tcsrchr() function is the TCHAR version of the strrchr() function, which locates the last occurrence of a character in a string, returning a pointer to the substring starting with the matching character. The behavior of this function depends on the definition of the _UNICODE and _MBCS symbols. If neither symbol is defined, the function compiles for ANSI (single-byte characters); if _UNICODE is defined, the function compiles for UNICODE (wide characters); and if _MBCS is defined, the function compiles for MBCS (multibyte characters).

Header File

```
#include <tchar.h>
```

Declaration

```
TCHAR* _tcsrchr(const TCHAR *string, int c);
```

- *c* — The character for which to search.
- *string* — A pointer to the string to search.

Example

The following program demonstrates how to use the _tcsrchr() function. When run, the program locates the last occurrence of the character *i* in a string and displays the result. The program's output looks like the following:

```
Source String:
This is a test
Substring:
is a test


Press any key to continue
```

Here is the program source code that produced the output:

```
#include "stdafx.h"
#include <iostream>
#include <tchar.h>

using namespace std;
```

```
int main(int argc, char* argv[])
{
    TCHAR* srcStr = "This is a test";

    TCHAR* pSubStr = _tcsrchr(srcStr, 'i');
    cout << "Source String:" << endl;
    cout << srcStr << endl;
    cout << "Substring:" << endl;
    cout << pSubStr << endl << endl;

    return 0;
}
```

CROSS-REFERENCE

See also _mbsrchr(), _tasctime(), _tcscat(), _tcschr(), _tcscmp(), _tcscoll(), _tcscpy(), _tcscspn(), _tcsdec(), _tcsdup(), _tcsftime(), _tcsicmp(), _tcsicoll(), _tcsinc(), _tcslen(), _tcslwr(), _tcsnbcnt(), _tcsncat(), _tcsnccmp(), _tcsnccnt(), _tcsnccoll(), _tcsncicmp(), _tcsncmp(), _tcsncoll(), _tcsncpy(), _tcsnextc(), _tcsnicmp(), _tcsnicoll(), _tcsninc(), _tcsnset(), _tcspbrk(), _tcsrev(), _tcsset(), _tcsspn(), _tcsspnp(), _tcsstr(), _tcstod(), _tcstok(), _tcstol(), _tcstoul(), _tcsupr(), _tcsxfrm(), _tctime(), _tell(), _telli64(), _tempnam(), _tolower(), _toupper(), strrchr(), and wcsrchr().

_tcsrev()

Function

The _tcsrev() function is the TCHAR version of the _strrev() function, which reverses the order of characters in a string, returning a pointer to the new string. The behavior of this function depends on the definition of the _UNICODE and _MBCS symbols. If neither symbol is defined, the function compiles for ANSI (single-byte characters); if _UNICODE is defined, the function compiles for UNICODE (wide characters); and if _MBCS is defined, the function compiles for MBCS (multibyte characters).

Header File

```
#include <tchar.h>
```

Declaration

```
TCHAR* _tcsrev(const TCHAR *string);
```

- *string* — The string to reverse.

Example

The following program demonstrates how to use the _tcsrev() function. When run, the program reverses the order of the characters in several strings and displays the results. The program's output looks like the following:

```
Original String: One Two Three
Converted String: eerhT owT enO

Original String: FOUR FIVE SIX
Converted String: XIS EVIF RUOF

Original String: seven eight nine
Converted String: enin thgie neve

Press any key to continue
```

Here is the program source code that produced the output:

```
#include "stdafx.h"
#include <iostream>
#include <tchar.h>

using namespace std;

void convert(TCHAR* s)
{
    cout << "Original String: ";
    cout << s << endl;
    TCHAR* result = _tcsrev(s);
    cout << "Converted String: ";
    cout << result << endl << endl;
}

int main(int argc, TCHAR* argv[])
{
    TCHAR str1[81] = "One Two Three";
    TCHAR str2[81] = "FOUR FIVE SIX";
    TCHAR str3[81]= "seven eight nine";
```

```
    convert(str1);
    convert(str2);
    convert(str3);

    return 0;
}
```

CROSS-REFERENCE

See also _mbsrev(), _strrev(), _tasctime(), _tcscat(), _tcschr(), _tcscmp(), _tcscoll(), _tcscpy(), _tcscspn(), _tcsdec(), _tcsdup(), _tcsftime(), _tcsicmp(), _tcsicoll(), _tcsinc(), _tcslen(), _tcslwr(), _tcsnbcnt(), _tcsncat(), _tcsnccmp(), _tcsnccnt(), _tcsnccoll(), _tcsncicmp(), _tcsncmp(), _tcsncoll(), _tcsncpy(), _tcsnextc(), _tcsnicmp(), _tcsnicoll(), _tcsninc(), _tcsnset(), _tcspbrk(), _tcsrchr(), _tcsset(), _tcsspn(), _tcsspnp(), _tcsstr(), _tcstod(), _tcstok(), _tcstol(), _tcstoul(), _tcsupr(), _tcsxfrm(), _tctime(), _tell(), _telli64(), _tempnam(), _tolower(), _toupper(), and _wcsrev().

_tcsset()

Function

The _tcsset() function is the TCHAR version of strset(), which sets the contents of a string to a specified character, returning a pointer to the new string. The behavior of this function depends on the definition of the _UNICODE and _MBCS symbols. If neither symbol is defined, the function compiles for ANSI (single-byte characters); if _UNICODE is defined, the function compiles for UNICODE (wide characters); and if _MBCS is defined, the function compiles for MBCS (multibyte characters).

Header File

```
#include <tchar.h>
```

Declaration

```
TCHAR* _tcsset(const TCHAR *string, char c);
```

- *c* — The character with which to fill the string.
- *string* — The string to set.

Example

The following program demonstrates how to use the _tcsset() function. When run, the program sets several strings to question marks and displays the results. The program's output looks like the following:

```
Original String: One Two Three
Converted String: ?????????????

Original String: FOUR FIVE SIX
Converted String: ?????????????

Original String: seven eight nine
Converted String: ???????????????

Press any key to continue
```

Here is the program source code that produced the output:

```cpp
#include "stdafx.h"
#include <iostream>
#include <tchar.h>

using namespace std;

void convert(TCHAR* s, TCHAR c)
{
    cout << "Original String: ";
    cout << s << endl;
    TCHAR* result = _tcsset(s, c);
    cout << "Converted String: ";
    cout << result << endl << endl;
}

int main(int argc, TCHAR* argv[])
{
    TCHAR str1[81] = "One Two Three";
    TCHAR str2[81] = "FOUR FIVE SIX";
    TCHAR str3[81] = "seven eight nine";

    convert(str1, '?');
    convert(str2, '?');
    convert(str3, '?');

    return 0;
}
```

CROSS-REFERENCE

See also _mbsset(), _strset(), _tasctime(), _tcscat(), _tcschr(), _tcscmp(), _tcscoll(), _tcscpy(), _tcscspn(), _tcsdec(), _tcsdup(), _tcsftime(), _tcsicmp(), _tcsicoll(), _tcsinc(), _tcslen(), _tcslwr(), _tcsnbcnt(), _tcsncat(), _tcsnccmp(), _tcsnccnt(), _tcsnccoll(), _tcsncicmp(), _tcsncmp(), _tcsncoll(), _tcsncpy(), _tcsnextc(), _tcsnicmp(), _tcsnicoll(), _tcsninc(), _tcsnset(), _tcspbrk(), _tcsrchr(), _tcsrev(), _tcsspn(), _tcsspnp(), _tcsstr(), _tcstod(), _tcstok(), _tcstol(), _tcstoul(), _tcsupr(), _tcsxfrm(), _tctime(), _tell(), _telli64(), _tempnam(), _tolower(), _toupper(), and _wcsset().

_tcsspn()

Function

The _tcsspn() function is the TCHAR version of the strspn() function, which locates the first occurrence of a substring that starts with a character not included in the specified set. The function returns the index of the first non-matching character. The behavior of this function depends on the definition of the _UNICODE and _MBCS symbols. If neither symbol is defined, the function compiles for ANSI (single-byte characters); if _UNICODE is defined, the function compiles for UNICODE (wide characters); and if _MBCS is defined, the function compiles for MBCS (multibyte characters).

Header File

```
#include <tchar.h>
```

Declaration

```
size_t _tcsspn(const TCHAR *string, const TCHAR *strCharSet);
```

- *strCharSet* — A pointer to the set of characters for which to search.
- *string* — A pointer to the string to search.

Example

The following program demonstrates how to use the _tcsspn() function. When run, the program locates, in a string, the first character not in the specified set and displays the result, indicating the located character with a caret (^). The program's output looks like the following:

```
Source String:
This is a test
```

```
                                  ^
      Press any key to continue
```

Here is the program source code that produced the output:

```
#include "stdafx.h"
#include <iostream>
#include <tchar.h>

using namespace std;

int main(int argc, char* argv[])
{
    TCHAR* srcStr = "This is a test";
    TCHAR* chrSet = "ahisT ";

    size_t len = _tcsspn(srcStr, chrSet);
    cout << "Source String:" << endl;
    cout << srcStr << endl;
    for (unsigned x=0; x<len; ++x)
        cout << " ";
    cout << "^" << endl;

    return 0;
}
```

CROSS-REFERENCE
See also _mbsspn(), _tasctime(), _tcscat(), _tcschr(), _tcscmp(), _tcscoll(), _tcscpy(), _tcscspn(), _tcsdec(), _tcsdup(), _tcsftime(), _tcsicmp(), _tcsicoll(), _tcsinc(), _tcslen(), _tcslwr(), _tcsnbcnt(), _tcsncat(), _tcsnccmp(), _tcsnccnt(), _tcsnccoll(), _tcsnicicmp(), _tcsncmp(), _tcsncoll(), _tcsncpy(), _tcsnextc(), _tcsnicmp(), _tcsnicoll(), _tcsninc(), _tcsnset(), _tcspbrk(), _tcsrchr(), _tcsrev(), _tcsset(), _tcsspnp(), _tcsstr(), _tcstod(), _tcstok(), _tcstol(), _tcstoul(), _tcsupr(), _tcsxfrm(), _tctime(), _tell(), _telli64(), _tempnam(), _tolower(), _toupper(), strspn(), and wcsspn().

_tcsspnp()

Function

The _tcsspnp() function is the TCHAR version of the _strspnp() function, which locates the first occurrence of a substring that starts with a character not included in the specified set. The function returns a pointer to the first non-matching character. The behavior of this function depends on the definition of the _UNICODE and _MBCS symbols. If neither symbol is defined, the function compiles for ANSI (single-byte characters); if _UNICODE is defined, the function compiles for UNICODE (wide characters); and if _MBCS is defined, the function compiles for MBCS (multibyte characters).

Header File

```
#include <tchar.h>
```

Declaration

```
TCHAR* _tcsspnp(const TCHAR *string, const TCHAR *strCharSet);
```

- *strCharSet*—A pointer to the set of characters for which to search.
- *string*—A pointer to the string to search.

Example

The following program demonstrates how to use the _tcsspnp() function. When run, the program locates, in a string, the first character not in the specified set and displays the substring that begins with the located character. The program's output looks like the following:

```
Source String:
This is a test

Remaining String:
test

Press any key to continue
```

Here is the program source code that produced the output:

```
#include "stdafx.h"
#include <iostream>
#include <tchar.h>

using namespace std;

int main(int argc, char* argv[])
{
    TCHAR* srcStr = "This is a test";
    TCHAR* chrSet = "ahisT ";
```

```
                    TCHAR* result = _tcsspnp(srcStr, chrSet);
                    cout << "Source String:" << endl;
                    cout << srcStr << endl << endl;
                    cout << "Remaining String:" << endl;
                    cout << result << endl << endl;

                    return 0;
                }
```

CROSS-REFERENCE

See also _mbsspnp(), _strspnp(), _tasctime(), _tcscat(), _tcschr(), _tcscmp(), _tcscoll(), _tcscpy(), _tcscspn(), _tcsdec(), _tcsdup(), _tcsftime(), _tcsicmp(), _tcsicoll(), _tcsinc(), _tcslen(), _tcslwr(), _tcsnbcnt(), _tcsncat(), _tcsnccmp(), _tcsnccnt(), _tcsnccoll(), _tcsnicmp(), _tcsncmp(), _tcsncoll(), _tcsncpy(), _tcsnextc(), _tcsnicmp(), _tcsnicoll(), _tcsninc(), _tcsnset(), _tcspbrk(), _tcsrchr(), _tcsrev(), _tcsset(), _tcsspn(), _tcsstr(), _tcstod(), _tcstok(), _tcstol(), _tcstoul(), _tcsupr(), _tcsxfrm(), _tctime(), _tell(), _telli64(), _tempnam(), _tolower(), _toupper(), and _wcsspnp().

_tcsstr()

Function

The _tcsstr() function is the TCHAR version of the strstr() function, which returns a pointer to a specified substring within a string. The behavior of this function depends on the definition of the _UNICODE and _MBCS symbols. If neither symbol is defined, the function compiles for ANSI (single-byte characters); if _UNICODE is defined, the function compiles for UNICODE (wide characters); and if _MBCS is defined, the function compiles for MBCS (multibyte characters).

Header File

```
#include <tchar.h>
```

Declaration

```
TCHAR* _tcsstr(const TCHAR *string, const TCHAR *strCharSet);
```

- *strCharSet*—A pointer to the substring for which to search.
- *string*—A pointer to the string to search.

Example

The following program demonstrates how to use the _tcsstr() function. When run, the program locates a specified substring, and then displays the portion of the original string that begins with the substring. The program's output looks like the following:

```
Source String:
This is a test

Substring:
is a test

Press any key to continue
```

Here is the program source code that produced the output:

```cpp
#include "stdafx.h"
#include <iostream>
#include <tchar.h>

using namespace std;

int main(int argc, char* argv[])
{
    TCHAR* srcStr = "This is a test";
    TCHAR* chrSet = "is a";

    TCHAR* pSubStr = _tcsstr(srcStr, chrSet);
    cout << "Source String:" << endl;
    cout << srcStr << endl << endl;
    cout << "Substring:" << endl;
    cout << pSubStr << endl << endl;

    return 0;
}
```

CROSS-REFERENCE
See also _mbsstr(), _tasctime(), _tcscat(), _tcschr(), _tcscmp(), _tcscoll(), _tcscpy(), _tcscspn(), _tcsdec(), _tcsdup(), _tcsftime(), _tcsicmp(), _tcsicoll(), _tcsinc(), _tcslen(), _tcslwr(), _tcsnbcnt(), _tcsncat(), _tcsnccmp(), _tcsnccnt(), _tcsnccoll(), _tcsnicmp(), _tcsncmp(), _tcsncoll(), _tcsncpy(), _tcsnextc(), _tcsnicmp(), _tcsnicoll(), _tcsninc(), _tcsnset(), _tcspbrk(), _tcsrchr(), _tcsrev(), _tcsset(), _tcsspn(), _tcsspnp(), _tcstod(), _tcstok(), _tcstol(), _tcstoul(), _tcsupr(), _tcsxfrm(), _tctime(), _tell(), _telli64(), _tempnam(), _tolower(), _toupper(), strstr(), and wcsstr().

_tcstod()

Function

The _tcstod() function is the TCHAR version of the strtod() function, which converts a string to a double-precision floating-point value. The behavior of this function depends on the definition of the _UNICODE and _MBCS symbols. If neither symbol is defined, the function compiles for ANSI (single-byte characters); if _UNICODE is defined, the function compiles for UNICODE (wide characters); and if _MBCS is defined, the function compiles for MBCS (multibyte characters).

Header File

```
#include <tchar.h>
```

Declaration

```
double _tcstod(const TCHAR *nptr, TCHAR **endptr);
```

- *endptr* — The pointer that will hold the address of the portion of the string that cannot be converted.
- *nptr* — A pointer to the string to convert.

Example

The following program demonstrates how to use the _tcstod() function. When run, the program converts a portion of a string to a double value, and then displays the remainder of the string (the portion that could not be converted). The program's output looks like the following:

```
Source String:
12345.5643This is a test

Result = 12345.6

Remaining string:
This is a test

Press any key to continue
```

Here is the program source code that produced the output:

```
#include "stdafx.h"
```

```
#include <iostream>
#include <tchar.h>

using namespace std;

int main(int argc, char* argv[])
{
    TCHAR* srcStr = "12345.5643This is a test";
    TCHAR* str;

    double result = _tcstod(srcStr, &str);
    cout << "Source String:" << endl;
    cout << srcStr << endl << endl;
    cout << "Result = " << result << endl << endl;
    cout << "Remaining string:" << endl;
    cout << str << endl << endl;

    return 0;
}
```

CROSS-REFERENCE

See also _tasctime(), _tcscat(), _tcschr(), _tcscmp(), _tcscoll(), _tcscpy(), _tcscspn(), _tcsdec(), _tcsdup(), _tcsftime(), _tcsicmp(), _tcsicoll(), _tcsinc(), _tcslen(), _tcslwr(), _tcsnbcnt(), _tcsncat(), _tcsnccmp(), _tcsnccnt(), _tcsnccoll(), _tcsnicmp(), _tcsncmp(), _tcsncoll(), _tcsncpy(), _tcsnextc(), _tcsnicmp(), _tcsnicoll(), _tcsninc(), _tcsnset(), _tcspbrk(), _tcsrchr(), _tcsrev(), _tcsset(), _tcsspn(), _tcsspnp(), _tcsstr(), _tcstok(), _tcstol(), _tcstoul(), _tcsupr(), _tcsxfrm(), _tctime(), _tell(), _telli64(), _tempnam(), _tolower(), _toupper(), strtod(), and wcstod().

_tcstok()

Function

The _tcstok() function is the TCHAR version of the strtok() function, which extracts tokens from a string. The behavior of this function depends on the definition of the _UNICODE and _MBCS symbols. If neither symbol is defined, the function compiles for ANSI (single-byte characters); if _UNICODE is defined, the function compiles for UNICODE (wide characters); and if _MBCS is defined, the function compiles for MBCS (multibyte characters).

Header File

```
#include <tchar.h>
```

Declaration

```
TCHAR* _tcstok(TCHAR *strToken, const TCHAR *strDelimit);
```

- *strDelimit* — A pointer to the string containing the characters (delimiters) that separate one token from another.
- *strToken* — A pointer to the string containing the tokens to extract.

Example

The following program demonstrates how to use the _tcstok() function. When run, the program extracts tokens from a string, displaying the results as it goes. The program's output looks like the following:

```
Token Source String:
One,Two Three,Four*Five

Token Delimiter String:
, *

Tokens Found:
One
Two
Three
Four
Five

Press any key to continue
```

Here is the program source code that produced the output:

```
#include "stdafx.h"
#include <iostream>
#include <tchar.h>

using namespace std;

int main(int argc, char* argv[])
{
    TCHAR str[] = "One,Two Three,Four*Five";
    TCHAR delimit[] = ", *";
```

```
        TCHAR *tok;

        cout << "Token Source String:" << endl;
        cout << str << endl << endl;
        cout << "Token Delimiter String:" << endl;
        cout << delimit << endl << endl;
        cout << "Tokens Found:" << endl;

        tok = _tcstok(str, delimit);
        while(tok != NULL )
        {
            cout << tok << endl;
            tok = _tcstok(NULL, delimit);
        }

        cout << endl;

        return 0;
    }
```

CROSS-REFERENCE

See also _mbstok(), _tasctime(), _tcscat(), _tcschr(), _tcscmp(), _tcscoll(), _tcscpy(), _tcscspn(), _tcsdec(), _tcsdup(), _tcsftime(), _tcsicmp(), _tcsicoll(), _tcsinc(), _tcslen(), _tcslwr(), _tcsnbcnt(), _tcsncat(), _tcsnccmp(), _tcsnccnt(), _tcsnccoll(), _tcsncicmp(), _tcsncmp(), _tcsncoll(), _tcsncpy(), _tcsnextc(), _tcsnicmp(), _tcsnicoll(), _tcsninc(), _tcsnset(), _tcspbrk(), _tcsrchr(), _tcsrev(), _tcsset(), _tcsspn(), _tcsspnp(), _tcsstr(), _tcstod(), _tcstol(), _tcstoul(), _tcsupr(), _tcsxfrm(), _tctime(), _tell(), _telli64(), _tempnam(), _tolower(), _toupper(), strtok(), and wcstok().

_tcstol()

Function

The _tcstol() function is the TCHAR version of the strtol() function, which converts a string to a long integer. The behavior of this function depends on the definition of the _UNICODE and _MBCS symbols. If neither symbol is defined, the function compiles for ANSI (single-byte characters); if _UNICODE is defined, the function compiles for UNICODE (wide characters); and if _MBCS is defined, the function compiles for MBCS (multibyte characters).

Header File

```
#include <tchar.h>
```

Declaration

```
long _tcstol(const TCHAR *nptr, TCHAR **endptr, int base);
```

- *base* — The number base to use in the conversion.
- *endptr* — The pointer that will hold the address of the portion of the string that cannot be converted.
- *nptr* — A pointer to the string to convert.

Example

The following program demonstrates how to use the _tcstol() function. When run, the program converts a portion of a string to a long value, and then displays the remainder of the string (the portion that could not be converted). The program's output looks like the following:

```
Source String:
1234556This is a test

Result = 1234556

Remaining string:
This is a test

Press any key to continue
```

Here is the program source code that produced the output:

```
#include "stdafx.h"
#include <iostream>
#include <tchar.h>

using namespace std;

int main(int argc, char* argv[])
{
    TCHAR* srcStr = "1234556This is a test";
    TCHAR* str;

    long result = _tcstol(srcStr, &str, 10);
    cout << "Source String:" << endl;
```

```
        cout << srcStr << endl << endl;
        cout << "Result = " << result << endl << endl;
        cout << "Remaining string:" << endl;
        cout << str << endl << endl;

        return 0;
    }
```

CROSS-REFERENCE

See also _tasctime(), _tcscat(), _tcschr(), _tcscmp(), _tcscoll(), _tcscpy(), _tcscspn(), _tcsdec(), _tcsdup(), _tcsftime(), _tcsicmp(), _tcsicoll(), _tcsinc(), _tcslen(), _tcslwr(), _tcsnbcnt(), _tcsncat(), _tcsnccmp(), _tcsnccnt(), _tcsnccoll(), _tcsncicmp(), _tcsncmp(), _tcsncoll(), _tcsncpy(), _tcsnextc(), _tcsnicmp(), _tcsnicoll(), _tcsninc(), _tcsnset(), _tcspbrk(), _tcsrchr(), _tcsrev(), _tcsset(), _tcsspn(), _tcsspnp(), _tcsstr(), _tcstod(), _tcstok(), _tcstoul(), _tcsupr(), _tcsxfrm(), _tctime(), _tell(), _telli64(), _tempnam(), _tolower(), _toupper(), strtol(), and wcstol().

_tcstoul()

Function

The _tcstoul() function is the TCHAR version of the strtoul() function, which converts a string to an unsigned long integer. The behavior of this function depends on the definition of the _UNICODE and _MBCS symbols. If neither symbol is defined, the function compiles for ANSI (single-byte characters); if _UNICODE is defined, the function compiles for UNICODE (wide characters); and if _MBCS is defined, the function compiles for MBCS (multibyte characters).

Header File

```
#include <tchar.h>
```

Declaration

```
unsigned long _tcstoul(const TCHAR *nptr,
    TCHAR **endptr, int base);
```

- *base* — The number base to use in the conversion.
- *endptr* — The pointer that will hold the address of the portion of the string that cannot be converted.
- *nptr* — A pointer to the string to convert.

Example

The following program demonstrates how to use the `_tcstoul()` function. When run, the program converts a portion of a string to a `long` value, and then displays the remainder of the string (the portion that could not be converted). The program's output looks like the following:

```
Source String:
1234556This is a test

Result = 1234556

Remaining string:
This is a test

Press any key to continue
```

Here is the program source code that produced the output:

```cpp
#include "stdafx.h"
#include <iostream>
#include <tchar.h>

using namespace std;

int main(int argc, char* argv[])
{
    TCHAR* srcStr = "1234556This is a test";
    TCHAR* str;

    unsigned long result = _tcstoul(srcStr, &str, 10);
    cout << "Source String:" << endl;
    cout << srcStr << endl << endl;
    cout << "Result = " << result << endl << endl;
    cout << "Remaining string:" << endl;
    cout << str << endl << endl;

    return 0;
}
```

CROSS-REFERENCE

See also _tasctime(), _tcscat(), _tcschr(), _tcscmp(), _tcscoll(), _tcscpy(), _tcscspn(), _tcsdec(), _tcsdup(), _tcsftime(), _tcsicmp(), _tcsicoll(), _tcsinc(), _tcslen(), _tcslwr(), _tcsnbcnt(), _tcsncat(), _tcsnccmp(), _tcsnccnt(), _tcsnccoll(), _tcsnicmp(), _tcsncmp(), _tcsncoll(), _tcsncpy(), _tcsnextc(), _tcsnicmp(), _tcsnicoll(), _tcsninc(), _tcsnset(), _tcspbrk(), _tcsrchr(), _tcsrev(), _tcsset(), _tcsspn(), _tcsspnp(), _tcsstr(), _tcstod(), _tcstok(), _tcstol(), _tcsupr(), _tcsxfrm(), _tctime(), _tell(), _telli64(), _tempnam(), _tolower(), _toupper(), strtoul(), and wcstoul().

_tcsupr()

Function

The _tcsupr() function is the TCHAR version of the strupr() function, which converts a string to uppercase, returning a pointer to the new string. The behavior of this function depends on the definition of the _UNICODE and _MBCS symbols. If neither symbol is defined, the function compiles for ANSI (single-byte characters); if _UNICODE is defined, the function compiles for UNICODE (wide characters); and if _MBCS is defined, the function compiles for MBCS (multibyte characters).

Header File

```
#include <tchar.h>
```

Declaration

```
TCHAR* _tcsupr(const TCHAR *string);
```

- *string* — The string to convert.

Example

The following program demonstrates how to use the _tcsupr() function. When run, the program converts several strings to uppercase and displays the results. The program's output looks like the following:

```
Original String: One Two Three
Converted String: ONE TWO THREE

Original String: FOUR FIVE SIX
Converted String: FOUR FIVE SIX

Original String: seven eight nine
Converted String: SEVEN EIGHT NINE

Press any key to continue
```

Here is the program source code that produced the output:

```
#include "stdafx.h"
#include <iostream>
#include <tchar.h>
```

```
using namespace std;

void convert(TCHAR* s)
{
    cout << "Original String: ";
    cout << s << endl;
    TCHAR* result = _tcsupr(s);
    cout << "Converted String: ";
    cout << result << endl << endl;
}

int main(int argc, char* argv[])
{
    TCHAR str1[] = "One Two Three";
    TCHAR str2[] = "FOUR FIVE SIX";
    TCHAR str3[] = "seven eight nine";

    convert(str1);
    convert(str2);
    convert(str3);

    return 0;
}
```

CROSS-REFERENCE

See also _mbsupr(), _tasctime(), _tcscat(), _tcschr(), _tcscmp(), _tcscoll(), _tcscpy(), _tcscspn(), _tcsdec(), _tcsdup(), _tcsftime(), _tcsicmp(), _tcsicoll(), _tcsinc(), _tcslen(), _tcslwr(), _tcsnbcnt(), _tcsncat(), _tcsnccmp(), _tcsnccnt(), _tcsnccoll(), _tcsncicmp(), _tcsncmp(), _tcsncoll(), _tcsncpy(), _tcsnextc(), _tcsnicmp(), _tcsnicoll(), _tcsninc(), _tcsnset(), _tcspbrk(), _tcsrchr(), _tcsrev(), _tcsset(), _tcsspn(), _tcsspnp(), _tcsstr(), _tcstod(), _tcstok(), _tcstol(), _tcsxfrm(), _tctime(), _tell(), _telli64(), _tempnam(), _tolower(), _toupper(), _wcsupr(), and strupr().

_tcsxfrm()

Function

The _tcsxfrm() function is the TCHAR version of the strxfrm() function, which transforms a string using locale information. The function returns the length of the string if successful or returns –1 if unsuccessful. The behavior of this function depends on the definition of the _UNICODE and _MBCS symbols. If neither symbol is defined, the function compiles for ANSI (single-byte characters); if _UNICODE is defined, the function compiles for UNICODE (wide characters); and if _MBCS is defined, the function compiles for MBCS (multibyte characters).

Header File

```
#include <tchar.h>
```

Declaration

```
size_t _tcsxfrm(TCHAR *strDest,
    const TCHAR *strSource, size_t count);
```

- *count* — The maximum number of characters in *strDest*.
- *strDest* — A pointer to the buffer that will receive the string.
- *strSource* — A pointer to the source string.

Example

The following program demonstrates how to use the _tcsxfrm() function. When run, the program sets a locale and converts a string. The program's output looks like the following:

```
Press any key to continue
```

Here is the program source code that produced the output:

```
#include "stdafx.h"
#include <locale.h>
#include <tchar.h>
#include <iostream>

using namespace std;

int main(int argc, char* argv[])
{
    TCHAR str[81];

    TCHAR* result = setlocale(LC_COLLATE, "Spanish");
    if (result == NULL)
        cout << "Error setting locale" << endl;
    else
        _tcsxfrm(str, "This is a test", 81);
```

```
        setlocale(LC_ALL, "C");

        return 0;
    }
```

CROSS-REFERENCE

See also _tasctime(), _tcscat(), _tcschr(), _tcscmp(), _tcscoll(), _tcscpy(), _tcscspn(), _tcsdec(), _tcsdup(), _tcsftime(), _tcsicmp(), _tcsicoll(), _tcsinc(), _tcslen(), _tcslwr(), _tcsnbcnt(), _tcsncat(), _tcsnccmp(), _tcsnccnt(), _tcsnccoll(), _tcsnicmp(), _tcsncmp(), _tcsncoll(), _tcsncpy(), _tcsnextc(), _tcsnicmp(), _tcsnicoll(), _tcsninc(), _tcsnset(), _tcspbrk(), _tcsrchr(), _tcsrev(), _tcsset(), _tcsspn(), _tcsspnp(), _tcsstr(), _tcstod(), _tcstok(), _tcstol(), _tctime(), _tell(), _telli64(), _tempnam(), _tolower(), _toupper(), strxfrm(), and wcsxfrm().

_tctime()

Function

The _tctime() function is the TCHAR version of the ctime() function, which converts the contents of a time_t structure to a string.

Header Files

```
#include <tchar.h>
#include <time.h>
```

Declaration

```
TCHAR* _tctime(const time_t* time);
```

- *time* — The address of the time_t structure that should be converted to a string.

Example

The following program demonstrates how to use the _tctime() function. When run, the program calls the time() function to get the current time in a time_t structure, and then converts the structure to a string for display. The program's output looks something like the following:

```
Mon Jan 11 15:29:21 1999

Press any key to continue
```

Here is the program source code that produced the output:

```cpp
#include "stdafx.h"
#include <iostream>
#include <time.h>
#include <tchar.h>

using namespace std;

int main(int argc, char* argv[])
{
    time_t curTime;
    time(&curTime);
    TCHAR* timeStr = _tctime(&curTime);
    cout << timeStr << endl;

    return 0;
}
```

CROSS-REFERENCE
See also _ftime(), _futime(), _strdate(), _strtime(), _utime(), _wasctime(), _wctime(), _wstrtime(), _wutime(), asctime(), ctime(), difftime(), gmtime(), localtime(), mktime(), strftime(), time(), and wcsftime().

_tell()

Function

The _tell() function returns the position of the file pointer or returns –1L in the case of an error.

NOTE
Borland users should refer to the tell() function later in this chapter.

Header Files

```cpp
#include <io.h>
```

Declaration

```
long _tell(int handle);
```

- *handle* — The file handle.

Example

The following program demonstrates how to use the _tell() function. When run, the program opens and reads from a file, and gets the position of the file pointer, displaying messages as it goes. The program's output looks something like the following:

```
Opening the file...
File opened successfully.
Getting file pointer...
File pointer = 0
Reading 64 bytes from the file...
Buffer = // _tell.cpp : Defines the entry
File pointer = 32
File closed successfully.
Press any key to continue
```

Here is the program source code that produced the output:

```cpp
#include "stdafx.h"
#include <fcntl.h>
#include <io.h>
#include <iostream>

using namespace std;

int main(int argc, char* argv[])
{
    char buf[64];

    cout << "Opening the file..." << endl;
    int fileHandle = _open("_tell.cpp", O_RDONLY);

    if (fileHandle != -1)
    {
        cout << "File opened successfully." << endl;
        cout << "Getting file pointer..." << endl;
        long pos = _tell(fileHandle);
        cout << "File pointer = " << pos << endl;
        cout << "Reading 64 bytes from the file..." << endl;
```

```
        int bytes = _read(fileHandle, buf, 32);
        buf[bytes] = 0;
        cout << "Buffer = " << buf << endl;
        pos = _tell(fileHandle);
        cout << "File pointer = " << pos << endl;
        int result = _close(fileHandle);
        if (result == 0)
            cout << "File closed successfully." << endl;
        else
            cout << "File close error." << endl;
    }
    else
        cout << "File open error." << endl;

    return 0;
}
```

CROSS-REFERENCE

See also _close(), _creat(), _dup(), _dup2(), _eof(), _lseek(), _lseeki64(), _open(), _read(), _sopen(), _telli64(), _umask(), _wcreat(), _wopen(), _write(), _wsopen(), and tell().

_telli64()

Function

The `_telli64()` function returns the position of the file pointer (as a 64-bit integer) or returns –1L in the case of an error.

NOTE

Borland does not support this function.

Header Files

```
#include <io.h>
```

Declaration

```
__int64 _telli64(int handle);
```

■ *handle* — The file handle.

Example

The following program demonstrates how to use the _telli64() function. When run, the program opens and reads from a file, and gets the position of the file pointer, displaying messages as it goes. The program's output looks like the following:

```
Opening the file...
File opened successfully.
Getting file pointer...
File pointer = 0
Reading 64 bytes from the file...
Buffer = // _telli64.cpp : Defines the en
File pointer = 32
File closed successfully.
Press any key to continue
```

Here is the program source code that produced the output:

```cpp
#include "stdafx.h"
#include <fcntl.h>
#include <io.h>
#include <iostream>

using namespace std;

int main(int argc, char* argv[])
{
    char buf[64];

    cout << "Opening the file..." << endl;
    int fileHandle = _open("_telli64.cpp", O_RDONLY);

    if (fileHandle != -1)
    {
        cout << "File opened successfully." << endl;
        cout << "Getting file pointer..." << endl;
        __int64 pos = _telli64(fileHandle);
        cout << "File pointer = " << (int)pos << endl;
        cout << "Reading 64 bytes from the file..." << endl;
        int bytes = _read(fileHandle, buf, 32);
        buf[bytes] = 0;
        cout << "Buffer = " << buf << endl;
        pos = _telli64(fileHandle);
        cout << "File pointer = " << (int)pos << endl;
        int result = _close(fileHandle);
```

```
        if (result == 0)
            cout << "File closed successfully." << endl;
        else
            cout << "File close error." << endl;
    }
    else
        cout << "File open error." << endl;

    return 0;
}
```

CROSS-REFERENCE
See also _close(), _commit(), _creat(), _dup(), _dup2(), _eof(), _lseek(), _lseeki64(), _open(), _read(), _sopen(), _tell(), _umask(), _wcreat(), _wopen(), _write(), and _wsopen().

_tempnam()

Function

The _tempnam() function generates a unique file name that can be used to create a temporary file. If the function is successful, it returns a pointer to the file name. Otherwise, it returns NULL.

Header File

```
#include <stdio.h>
```

Declaration

```
char* _tempnam(char *dir, char *prefix);
```

- *dir*—A pointer to a string containing the directory to use if the variable TMP is undefined.
- *prefix*—The characters supplied by the user to be used in the file name.

Example

By creating and displaying a unique temporary file name, the following program demonstrates how to use the _tempnam() function. The program's output looks something like the following:

```
Temp file name: C:\WINDOWS\TEMP\temp2
Press any key to continue
```

Here is the program source code that produced the output:

```
#include "stdafx.h"
#include <stdio.h>
#include <iostream>

using namespace std;

int main(int argc, char* argv[])
{
    char dir[] = "c:\\Windows";
    char prefix[] = "temp";

    char* result = _tempnam(dir, prefix);
    if (result == NULL)
        cout << "Error forming temp File name" << endl;
    else
        cout << "Temp file name: " << result << endl;

    return 0;
}
```

CROSS-REFERENCE
See also _mktemp(), _wmktemp(), _wtempnam(), _wtmpnam(), tempnam(), tmpfile(), and tmpnam().

_tolower()

Function

The _tolower() function converts a character to lowercase, returning the converted character.

Header File

```
#include <ctype.h>
```

Declaration

```
int _tolower(int c);
```

- *c*—The character to convert.

Example

The following program demonstrates how to use the `_tolower()` function. The program's output looks like the following:

```
Original character = A
Converted character = a
Press any key to continue
```

Here is the program source code that produced the output:

```
#include "stdafx.h"
#include <ctype.h>
#include <iostream>

using namespace std;

int main(int argc, char* argv[])
{
    char ch = 'A';

    cout << "Original character = " << ch << endl;
    char result = (char)_tolower(ch);
    cout << "Converted character = " << result << endl;

    return 0;
}
```

CROSS-REFERENCE

See also _mbctolower(), _mbctoupper(), _toupper(), tolower(), toupper(), and towlower().

_toupper()

Function

The _toupper() function converts a character to uppercase, returning the converted character.

Header File

```
#include <ctype.h>
```

Declaration

```
int _toupper(int c);
```

- *c* — The character to convert.

Example

The following program demonstrates how to use the _toupper() function. The program's output looks like the following:

```
Original character = a
Converted character = A
Press any key to continue
```

Here is the program source code that produced the output:

```
#include "stdafx.h"
#include <ctype.h>
#include <iostream>

using namespace std;

int main(int argc, char* argv[])
{
    char ch = 'a';

    cout << "Original character = " << ch << endl;
    char result = (char)_toupper(ch);
    cout << "Converted character = " << result << endl;

    return 0;
}
```

CROSS-REFERENCE
See also _mbctolower(), _mbctoupper(), _tolower(), tolower(), toupper(), and towlower().

tan()

Function

The tan() function returns the tangent of its argument.

Header File

```
#include <math.h>
```

Declaration

```
double tan(double num);
```

- *num* — The number for which to return the tangent.

Example

The following program demonstrates how to use the tan() function. The program's output looks like the following:

```
The tangent of 98.5 is 2.01752
Press any key to continue
```

Here is the program source code that produced the output:

```
#include "stdafx.h"
#include <math.h>
#include <iostream>

using namespace std;

int main(int argc, char* argv[])
{
    double var1 = 98.5;
    double result = tan(var1);
    cout << "The tangent of " << var1;
    cout << " is " << result << endl;

    return 0;
}
```

s
t
u

CROSS-REFERENCE
See also acos(), asin(), atan(), atan2(), cos(), cosh(), sin(), sinh(), tanf(), tanh(), tanhf(), tanhl(), and tanl().

tanf()

Function

The tanf() function returns as a float the tangent of its argument.

NOTE
Borland does not support this function.

Header File

```
#include <math.h>
```

Declaration

```
float tanf(float num);
```

- *num* — The number for which to return the tangent.

Example

The following program demonstrates how to use the tanf() function. The program's output looks like the following:

```
The tangent of 98.5 is 2.01752
Press any key to continue
```

Here is the program source code that produced the output:

```
#include "stdafx.h"
#include <math.h>
#include <iostream>

using namespace std;

int main(int argc, char* argv[])
{
    float var1 = (float)98.5;
    float result = tanf(var1);
```

```
        cout << "The tangent of " << var1;
        cout << " is " << result << endl;

        return 0;
    }
```

CROSS-REFERENCE
See also acos(), asin(), atan(), atan2(), cos(), cosh(), sin(), sinh(), tan(), tanh(), tanhf(), tanhl(), and tanl().

tanh()

Function

The `tanh()` function returns the hyperbolic tangent of its argument.

Header File

```
#include <math.h>
```

Declaration

```
double tanh(double num);
```

- *num* — The number for which to return the hyperbolic tangent.

Example

The following program demonstrates how to use the `tanh()` function. The program's output looks like the following:

```
The hyperbolic tangent of 98.5 is 1
Press any key to continue
```

Here is the program source code that produced the output:

```
#include "stdafx.h"
#include <math.h>
#include <iostream>

using namespace std;

int main(int argc, char* argv[])
```

s
t
u

```
{
    double var1 = 98.5;
    double result = tanh(var1);
    cout << "The hyperbolic tangent of " << var1;
    cout << " is " << result << endl;

    return 0;
}
```

CROSS-REFERENCE
See also acos(), asin(), atan(), atan2(), cos(), cosh(), sin(), sinh(), tan(), tanf(), tanhf(), tanhl(), and tanl().

tanhf()

Function

The tanhf() function returns as a float the hyperbolic tangent of its argument.

NOTE
Borland does not support this function.

Header File

```
#include <math.h>
```

Declaration

```
float tanhf(float num);
```

- *num* — The number for which to return the hyperbolic tangent.

Example

The following program demonstrates how to use the tanhf() function. The program's output looks like the following:

```
The hyperbolic tangent of 98.5 is 1
Press any key to continue
```

Here is the program source code that produced the output:

```
#include "stdafx.h"
```

```
#include <math.h>
#include <iostream>

using namespace std;

int main(int argc, char* argv[])
{
    float var1 = (float)98.5;
    float result = tanhf(var1);
    cout << "The hyperbolic tangent of " << var1;
    cout << " is " << result << endl;

    return 0;
}
```

CROSS-REFERENCE
See also acos(), asin(), atan(), atan2(), cos(), cosh(), sin(), sinh(), tan(), tanf(), tanh(),
tanhl(), and tanl().

tanhl()

Function

The tanhl() function returns as a long double the hyperbolic tangent of
its argument.

Header File

```
#include <math.h>
```

Declaration

```
long double tanhl(long double num);
```

- *num* — The number for which to return the hyperbolic tangent.

Example

The following program demonstrates how to use the tanhl() function. The
program's output looks like the following:

```
The hyperbolic tangent of 98.5 is 1
Press any key to continue
```

Here is the program source code that produced the output:

```
#include "stdafx.h"
#include <math.h>
#include <iostream>

using namespace std;

int main(int argc, char* argv[])
{
    long double var1 = 98.5;
    long double result = tanhl(var1);
    cout << "The hyperbolic tangent of " << var1;
    cout << " is " << result << endl;

    return 0;
}
```

CROSS-REFERENCE
See also acos(), asin(), atan(), atan2(), cos(), cosh(), sin(), sinh(), tan(), tanf(), tanh(), tanhf(), and tanl().

tanl()

Function

The tanl() function returns as a long double the tangent of its argument.

Header File

```
#include <math.h>
```

Declaration

```
long double tanl(long double num);
```

- *num* — The number for which to return the tangent.

Example

The following program demonstrates how to use the tanl() function. The program's output looks like the following:

```
The tangent of 98.5 is 2.01752
Press any key to continue
```

Here is the program source code that produced the output:

```
#include "stdafx.h"
#include <math.h>
#include <iostream>

using namespace std;

int main(int argc, char* argv[])
{
    long double var1 = 98.5;
    long double result = tanl(var1);
    cout << "The tangent of " << var1;
    cout << " is " << result << endl;

    return 0;
}
```

CROSS-REFERENCE

See also acos(), asin(), atan(), atan2(), cos(), cosh(), sin(), sinh(), tan(), tanf(), tanh(), tanhf(), and tanhl().

tell()

Function

The tell() function returns the position of the file pointer or returns –1L in the case of an error.

Header File

```
#include <io.h>
```

Declaration

```
long tell(int handle);
```

- *handle* — The file handle.

Example

The following program demonstrates how to use the `tell()` function. When run, the program opens and reads from a file, and gets the position of the file pointer, displaying messages as it goes. The program's output looks something like the following:

```
Opening the file...
File opened successfully.
Getting file pointer...
File pointer = 0
Reading 64 bytes from the file...
Buffer = // _tell.cpp : Defines the entry
File pointer = 32
File closed successfully.
Press any key to continue
```

Here is the program source code that produced the output:

```cpp
#include "stdafx.h"
#include <fcntl.h>
#include <io.h>
#include <iostream>

using namespace std;

int main(int argc, char* argv[])
{
    char buf[64];

    cout << "Opening the file..." << endl;
    int fileHandle = open("tell.cpp", O_RDONLY);

    if (fileHandle != -1)
    {
        cout << "File opened successfully." << endl;
        cout << "Getting file pointer..." << endl;
        long pos = tell(fileHandle);
        cout << "File pointer = " << pos << endl;
        cout << "Reading 64 bytes from the file..." << endl;
        int bytes = read(fileHandle, buf, 32);
        buf[bytes] = 0;
        cout << "Buffer = " << buf << endl;
        pos = tell(fileHandle);
        cout << "File pointer = " << pos << endl;
        int result = close(fileHandle);
```

```
        if (result == 0)
            cout << "File closed successfully." << endl;
        else
            cout << "File close error." << endl;
    }
    else
        cout << "File open error." << endl;

    return 0;
}
```

CROSS-REFERENCE

See also _close(), _commit(), _creat(), _dup(), _dup2(), _eof(), _lseek(), _lseeki64(), _open(), _read(), _sopen(), _tell(), _telli64(), _umask(), _wcreat(), _wopen(), _write(), and _wsopen().

template

Keyword

The `template` keyword is used to define template functions and classes. A *template function* enables a program to call the same function with different types of arguments. The compiler determines which types are being used and generates the appropriate code from the template. For example, the following lines define a template function:

```
template<class T>
T MyFunc(T num)
{
    return num*2;
}
```

CROSS-REFERENCE

See also Templates.

Templates

Technique

The `template` keyword is used to define template functions and classes. A *template function* enables a program to call the same function with different types of arguments. The compiler determines which types are being used and generates the appropriate code from the template. In the following sections, you see how to create template functions and classes.

Creating Template Functions

For example, the following program defines a template function named MyFunc(). The program's output looks like the following:

```
val1 = 20
val2 = 50
Press any key to continue
```

Here is the program source code that produced the output:

```
#include "stdafx.h"
#include <iostream>

using namespace std;

template<class T>
T MyFunc(T num)
{
    return num*2;
}

int main(int argc, char* argv[])
{
    int val1 = MyFunc(10);
    double val2 = MyFunc(25);
    cout << "val1 = " << val1 << endl;
    cout << "val2 = " << val2 << endl;

    return 0;
}
```

Note how the template function is written, which the T representing whatever data type needs to be substituted by the compiler. In main(), the program calls MyFunc() twice, once with an int argument and once with a double argument.

Creating Template Classes

A *template class* enables a program to create objects from the same class with different types of arguments. The compiler determines which types are being used and generates the appropriate code from the template. For example, the following program defines a template class named `MyClass()`. The program's output looks like the following:

```
myClass1.num = 10
myClass2.num = 3463.05
Press any key to continue
```

Here is the program source code that produced the output:

```cpp
#include "stdafx.h"
#include <iostream>

using namespace std;

template<class T>
class MyClass
{
protected:
    T num;

public:
    MyClass(T n) {num = n;}
    ~MyClass(){}

    T GetNum() { return num; }
};

int main(int argc, char* argv[])
{
    int val1 = 10;
    double val2 = 3463.0475;

    MyClass<int> myClass1(val1);
    int n1 = myClass1.GetNum();
    cout << "myClass1.num = " << n1 << endl;

    MyClass<double> myClass2(val2);
    double n2 = myClass2.GetNum();
    cout << "myClass2.num = " << n2 << endl;

    return 0;
}
```

Notice how the template class is defined similarly to a template function, with the T representing the data type to be substituted by the compiler. As you can see in `main()`, you must also supply the data type when instantiating an object of the class.

tempnam()

Function

The `tempnam()` function generates a unique file name that can be used to create a temporary file. If the function is successful, it returns a pointer to the file name. Otherwise, it returns `NULL`.

Header File

```
#include <stdio.h>
```

Declaration

```
char* tempnam(char *dir, char *prefix);
```

- *dir* — A pointer to a string containing the directory to use if the variable TMP is undefined.
- *prefix* — The characters supplied by the user to be used in the file name.

Example

By creating and displaying a unique temporary file name, the following program demonstrates how to use the `tempnam()` function. The program's output looks something like the following:

```
Temp file name: C:\WINDOWS\TEMP\temp2
Press any key to continue
```

Here is the program source code that produced the output:

```
#include "stdafx.h"
#include <stdio.h>
#include <iostream>

using namespace std;

int main(int argc, char* argv[])
{
    char dir[] = "c:\\Windows";
    char prefix[] = "temp";

    char* result = tempnam(dir, prefix);
```

```
    if (result == NULL)
        cout << "Error forming temp File name" << endl;
    else
        cout << "Temp file name: " << result << endl;

    return 0;
}
```

CROSS-REFERENCE

See also _mktemp(), _tempnam(), _wmktemp(), _wtempnam(), _wtmpnam(), tmpfile(), and tmpnam().

this

Keyword

The `this` keyword represents an object pointer available only within the object itself. Even though it doesn't appear in the parameter list, the `this` pointer is passed to an object's member functions automatically as an invisible argument. For example, the following member function of the `MyClass` class sets the `value` member to an integer passed to the function:

```
void MyClass::setNum(int num)
{
    value = num;
}
```

This function could also be written using the `this` pointer, as shown in the following:

```
void MyClass::setNum(int num)
{
    this->value = num;
}
```

throw

Keyword

The `throw` keyword enables a program to pass exception objects when runtime errors occur. For example, the following `try` program block throws an exception if the `calloc()` function fails to allocate the requested block of memory:

```
try
{
    buf = (char*)calloc(256, sizeof(char));
    if (buf == NULL)
        throw *errorMsg;
    else
        free(buf);
}
catch (char* exception)
{
    cout << exception << endl;
}
```

CROSS-REFERENCE
See also Exception Handling.

time()

Function

The time() function gets the system time as a time_t value. This value represents the number of seconds since January 1, 1970.

Header File

```
#include <time.h>
```

Declaration

```
time_t time(time_t *timer);
```

- *timer*—A pointer to the storage location for the time value.

Example

By retrieving and displaying the time value, the following program demonstrates how to use the time() function. The program's output looks something like the following:

```
Seconds = 925240568
Press any key to continue
```

Here is the program source code that produced the output:

```cpp
#include "stdafx.h"
#include <time.h>
#include <iostream>

using namespace std;

int main(int argc, char* argv[])
{
    time_t curTime;

    time(&curTime);
    cout << "Seconds = " << curTime << endl;

    return 0;
}
```

CROSS-REFERENCE

See also _ftime(), _futime(), _strdate(), _strtime(), _utime(), _wasctime(), _wctime(), _wstrdate(), _wstrtime(), _wutime(), asctime(), clock(), ctime(), difftime(), gmtime(), localtime(), mktime(), strftime(), and wcsftime().

tmpfile()

Function

The `tmpfile()` function creates a temporary file in binary read-and-write mode, returning a pointer to the stream associated with the file or returning `NULL` in the case of an error. The file created by `tmpfile()` is deleted automatically when the file is closed.

Header File

```cpp
#include <stdio.h>
```

Declaration

```cpp
FILE* tmpfile(void);
```

Example

By creating and removing a temporary file, the following program demon-strates how to use the `tmpfile()` function. The program's output looks like the following:

```
Creating a temp file...
File created successfully.
Closing and deleting the file...
Press any key to continue
```

Here is the program source code that produced the output:

```cpp
#include "stdafx.h"
#include <stdio.h>
#include <iostream>

using namespace std;

int main(int argc, char* argv[])
{
    cout << "Creating a temp file..." << endl;
    FILE* file = tmpfile();
    if (file)
    {
        cout << "File created successfully." << endl;
        cout << "Closing and deleting the file..." << endl;
        fclose(file);
    }
    else
        cout << "Cannot create the file." << endl;

    return 0;
}
```

CROSS-REFERENCE

See also _mktemp(), _tempnam(), _wmktemp(), _wtempnam(), _wtmpnam(), tempnam(), and tmpnam().

tmpnam()

Function

The `tmpnam()` function generates a unique file name that can be used to create a temporary file. If the function is successful, it returns a pointer to the file name. Otherwise, it returns `NULL`.

Header File

```
#include <stdio.h>
```

Declaration

```
char* tmpnam(char *string);
```

- *string* — A pointer to the temporary name or `NULL` if the program supplies no buffer.

Example

By creating and displaying a unique temporary file name, the following program demonstrates how to use the `tmpnam()` function. The program's output looks something like the following:

```
Temp file name: \s3vv8omt.
Press any key to continue
```

Here is the program source code that produced the output:

```
#include "stdafx.h"
#include <stdio.h>
#include <iostream>

using namespace std;

int main(int argc, char* argv[])
{
    char buf[256];

    char* result = tmpnam(buf);
    if (result == NULL)
        cout << "Error creating temp File name" << endl;
    else
        cout << "Temp file name: " << result << endl;
```

```
            return 0;
     }
```

CROSS-REFERENCE

See also _mktemp(), _tempnam(), _wmktemp(), _wtempnam(), _wtmpnam(), tempnam(), tmpfile().

toascii()

Function

The `toascii()` function converts an integer value to an ASCII character, returning an integer whose upper bits have been cleared to yield a value between 0 and 127.

Header File

```
#include <ctype.h>
```

Declaration

```
int toascii(int c);
```

- *c*—The value to convert to ASCII.

Example

The following program demonstrates how to use the `toascii()` function. The program's output looks like the following:

```
Starting int value = 41281
Converting to ASCII...
New int value = 65
Character = A
Press any key to continue
```

Here is the program source code that produced the output:

```
#include "stdafx.h"
#include <ctype.h>
#include <iostream>

using namespace std;
```

```
int main(int argc, char* argv[])
{
    int ch = 0xA141;
    cout << "Starting int value = " << ch << endl;
    cout << "Converting to ASCII..." << endl;
    int result = toascii(ch);
    cout << "New int value = " << result << endl;
    cout << "Character = " << (char)result << endl;

    return 0;
}
```

CROSS-REFERENCE

See also __toascii(), _mbctolower(), _mbctoupper(), _tolower(), _toupper(), toupper(), and towlower().

tolower()

Function

The tolower() function converts a character to lowercase only if the character needs conversion, returning the converted character.

Header File

```
#include <ctype.h>
```

Declaration

```
int tolower(int c);
```

- *c* — The character to convert.

Example

The following program demonstrates how to use the tolower() function. The program's output looks like the following:

```
Original character = A
Converted character = a
Press any key to continue
```

Here is the program source code that produced the output:

```
#include "stdafx.h"
#include <ctype.h>
#include <iostream>

using namespace std;

int main(int argc, char* argv[])
{
    char ch = 'A';

    cout << "Original character = " << ch << endl;
    char result = (char)tolower(ch);
    cout << "Converted character = " << result << endl;

    return 0;
}
```

CROSS-REFERENCE

See also _mbctolower(), _mbctoupper(), _tolower(), _toupper(), toupper(), and towlower().

toupper()

Function

The toupper() function converts a character to uppercase only if the character needs converting, returning the converted character.

Header File

```
#include <ctype.h>
```

Declaration

```
int toupper(int c);
```

- *c* — The character to convert.

Example

The following program demonstrates how to use the `toupper()` function. The program's output looks like the following:

```
Original character = a
Converted character = A
Press any key to continue
```

Here is the program source code that produced the output:

```cpp
#include "stdafx.h"
#include <ctype.h>
#include <iostream>

using namespace std;

int main(int argc, char* argv[])
{
    char ch = 'a';

    cout << "Original character = " << ch << endl;
    char result = (char)toupper(ch);
    cout << "Converted character = " << result << endl;

    return 0;
}
```

CROSS-REFERENCE
See also _mbctolower(), _mbctoupper(), _tolower(), _toupper(), tolower(), and towlower().

towlower()

Function

The `towlower()` function converts a wide character to lowercase only if the character needs conversion, returning the converted character.

Header File

```cpp
#include <ctype.h>
```

Declaration

```
int towlower(wint_t c);
```

- *c*—The character to convert.

Example

The following program demonstrates how to use the `towlower()` function. The program's output looks like the following:

```
Original character = A
Converted character = a
Press any key to continue
```

Here is the program source code that produced the output:

```cpp
#include "stdafx.h"
#include <ctype.h>
#include <iostream>

using namespace std;

int main(int argc, char* argv[])
{
    wint_t ch = 'A';

    cout << "Original character = " << (char)ch << endl;
    char result = (char)towlower(ch);
    cout << "Converted character = " << result << endl;

    return 0;
}
```

 CROSS-REFERENCE

See also _mbctolower(), _mbctoupper(), _tolower(), _toupper(), tolower(), toupper(), and towupper().

towupper()

Function

The `towupper()` function converts a wide character to uppercase only if the character needs conversion, returning the converted character.

Header File

```
#include <ctype.h>
```

Declaration

```
int towupper(wint_t c);
```

- *c*—The character to convert.

Example

The following program demonstrates how to use the `towupper()` function. The program's output looks like the following:

```
Original character = a
Converted character = A
Press any key to continue
```

Here is the program source code that produced the output:

```
#include "stdafx.h"
#include <ctype.h>
#include <iostream>

using namespace std;

int main(int argc, char* argv[])
{
    wint_t ch = 'a';

    cout << "Original character = " << (char)ch << endl;
    char result = (char)towupper(ch);
    cout << "Converted character = " << result << endl;

    return 0;
}
```

CROSS-REFERENCE

See also _mbctolower(), _mbctoupper(), _tolower(), _toupper(), tolower(), toupper(), and towlower().

s
t
u

true

Keyword

The `true` keyword represents the true value of a Boolean data object. For example, the following program sets a Boolean variable to false and another Boolean variable to true. The program then displays the variables' values on the screen. The output looks like the following:

```
var1 = 0
var2 = 1
Press any key to continue
```

The program source code that produced the output follows:

```
#include "stdafx.h"
#include <iostream>

using namespace std;

int main(int argc, char* argv[])
{
    bool var1 = false;
    bool var2 = true;

    cout << "var1 = " << var1 << endl;
    cout << "var2 = " << var2 << endl;

    return 0;
}
```

 CROSS-REFERENCE
See also bool and false.

try

Keyword

The `try` keyword is used as part of a `try` statement, which enables a program to respond to exceptions that may be generated by the code in a `try` program block. The general syntax for a `try` statement follows:

```
try
{
    // Code that may cause an exception
```

```
    // goes here.
}
catch( ... )
{
    // Code that responds to the exception
    // goes here.
}
```

 CROSS-REFERENCE
See also Exception Handling.

typedef

Keyword

The typedef keyword associates a symbol with an existing data type. This name can be used as an alias for the declared type. For example, the following structure uses the typedef keyword to assign the name test to a structure:

```
typedef struct teststruct
{
    int x;
    int y;
} test;
```

An instance of the data type can then be defined as follows:

```
test myTest;
myTest.x = 10;
myTest.y = 20;
```

s
t
u

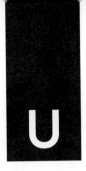

#undef

Directive

The #undef directive undefines a previously defined symbol. For example, the following program defines a symbol named TEST_SYMBOL. Because TEST_SYMBOL is defined at the time the compiler reaches the first #ifdef TEST_SYM-BOL directive, the compiler compiles the line cout << "TEST_SYMBOL defined." << endl. However, the program then undefines TEST_SYMBOL, so that when the compiler reaches the second #ifdef directive, TEST_SYMBOL is no longer defined and the compiler ignores the cout << "TEST_SYMBOL not defined." << endl line. The program's output looks like this:

```
TEST_SYMBOL defined.
Press any key to continue
```

Here is the program source code that produced the output:

```
#include "stdafx.h"
#include <iostream>

using namespace std;

int main(int argc, char* argv[])
{
#define TEST_SYMBOL
#ifdef TEST_SYMBOL
    cout << "TEST_SYMBOL defined." << endl;
#endif

#undef TEST_SYMBOL
#ifdef TEST_SYMBOL
    cout << "TEST_SYMBOL not defined." << endl;
#endif

    return 0;
}
```

CROSS-REFERENCE
See also #define, #endif, #ifdef, and #ifndef.

_ui64toa()

Function

The _ui64toa() function converts an unsigned 64-bit integer to a string and returns a pointer to the resultant string.

Header File

```
#include <stdlib.h>
```

Declaration

```
char *_ui64toa(unsigned __int64 value,
    char *string, int radix);
```

- *radix* — The number base to be used in the conversion. Must be a value from 2 to 36.
- *string* — A pointer to the buffer that will receive the string.
- *value* — The value to convert.

Example

The following program demonstrates how to use the _ui64toa() function. When run, the program displays the value 23,543 in decimal, binary, and hexadecimal representations. The program's output looks like this:

```
Decimal: 23543
Binary: 101101111110111
Hexadecimal: 5bf7
Press any key to continue
```

Here is the program source code that produced the output:

```
#include "stdafx.h"
#include <iostream>
#include <stdlib>

using namespace std;
```

```
int main(int argc, char* argv[])
{
    unsigned __int64 value = 23543;
    char buf[81];

    _ui64toa(value, buf, 10);
    cout << "Decimal: " << buf << endl;
    _ui64toa(value, buf, 2);
    cout << "Binary: " << buf << endl;
    _ui64toa(value, buf, 16);
    cout << "Hexadecimal: " << buf << endl;

    return 0;
}
```

CROSS-REFERENCE

See also _ecvt(), _fcvt(), _gcvt(), _i64toa(), _i64tow(), _itow(), _ui64tow(), _ultow(), itoa(), and ultoa().

_ui64tow()

Function

The _ui64tow() function converts an unsigned 64-bit integer to a wide-character string and returns a pointer to the resultant string.

Header File

```
#include <stdlib.h>
```

Declaration

```
char *_ui64tow(unsigned __int64 value,
    wchar_t *string, int radix);
```

- *radix* — The number base to be used in the conversion. Must be a value from 2 to 36.
- *string* — A pointer to the buffer that will receive the string.
- *value* — The value to convert.

Example

The following program demonstrates how to use the `_ui64tow()` function. When run, the program displays the value 23,543 in decimal, binary, and hexadecimal representations. The program's output looks like this:

```
Decimal: 23543
Binary: 101101111110111
Hexadecimal: 5bf7
Press any key to continue
```

Here is the program source code that produced the output:

```
#include "stdafx.h"
#include <iostream>
#include <stdlib.h>

using namespace std;

int main(int argc, char* argv[])
{
    unsigned __int64 value = 23543;
    wchar_t buf[81];

    _ui64tow(value, buf, 10);
    wprintf(L"Decimal: %s\n", buf);
    _ui64tow(value, buf, 2);
    wprintf(L"Binary: %s\n", buf);
    _ui64tow(value, buf, 16);
    wprintf(L"Hexadecimal: %s\n", buf);

    return 0;
}
```

CROSS-REFERENCE
See also _ecvt(), _fcvt(), _gcvt(), _i64toa(), _itow(), _ui64toa(), _ultow(), itoa(), and ultoa().

_ultoa()

Function

The `_ultoa()` function converts an unsigned long integer value to a string, returning a pointer to the resultant string.

NOTE
Borland users should refer to the ultoa() function later in this chapter.

Header File

```
#include <stdlib.h>
```

Declaration

```
char* _ultoa(unsigned long value, char* string, int radix);
```

- *radix* — The value number base (typically 10).
- *string* — A pointer to the buffer in which to store the string.
- *value* — The value to convert.

Example

The following program demonstrates how to use the _ultoa() function. When run, the program converts an unsigned long-integer value into several number-base formats and displays the results. The program's output looks like this:

```
This is 19,564 in base 10: 19564
This is 19,564 in base 16: 4c6c
This is 19,564 in base 2: 100110001101100
This is 19,564 in base 8: 46154

Press any key to continue
```

Here is the program source code that produced the output:

```cpp
#include "stdafx.h"
#include <iostream>
#include <stdlib.h>

using namespace std;

int main(int argc, char* argv[])
{
    char str[81];
    unsigned long value = 19564;

    char* result = _ultoa(value, str, 10);
    cout << "This is 19,564 in base 10: ";
```

```
        cout << result << endl;

        result = _ultoa(value, str, 16);
        cout << "This is 19,564 in base 16: ";
        cout << result << endl;

        result = _ultoa(value, str, 2);
        cout << "This is 19,564 in base 2: ";
        cout << result << endl;

        result = _ultoa(value, str, 8);
        cout << "This is 19,564 in base 8: ";
        cout << result << endl;
        cout << endl;

        return 0;
    }
```

CROSS-REFERENCE

See also _ecvt(), _fcvt(), _gcvt(), _i64toa(), _i64tow(), _itow(), _ui64toa(), _ui64tow(), itoa(), ltoa(), and ultoa().

_ultow()

Function

The _ultow() function converts an unsigned long integer to a wide-character string and returns a pointer to the resultant string.

Header File

```
#include <stdlib.h>
```

Declaration

```
char *_ultow(unsigned long value,
    wchar_t *string, int radix);
```

- *radix* — The number base to be used in the conversion. Must be a value from 2 to 36.
- *string* — A pointer to the buffer that will receive the string.

■ *value* — The value to convert.

Example

The following program demonstrates how to use the _ultow() function. When run, the program displays the value 23,543 in decimal, binary, and hexadecimal representations. The program's output looks like this:

```
Decimal: 23543
Binary: 101101111110111
Hexadecimal: 5bf7
Press any key to continue
```

Here is the program source code that produced the output:

```
#include "stdafx.h"
#include <iostream>
#include <stdlib.h>

using namespace std;

int main(int argc, char* argv[])
{
    unsigned long value = 23543;
    wchar_t buf[81];

    _ultow(value, buf, 10);
    wprintf(L"Decimal: %s\n", buf);
    _ultow(value, buf, 2);
    wprintf(L"Binary: %s\n", buf);
    _ultow(value, buf, 16);
    wprintf(L"Hexadecimal: %s\n", buf);

    return 0;
}
```

CROSS-REFERENCE

See also _ecvt(), _fcvt(), _gcvt(), _i64toa(), _i64tow(), _itow(), _ui64toa(), _ui64tow(), itoa(), itow(), and ultoa().

_umask()

Function

The _umask() function sets the default file-access mode, which determines the read and write access of newly created files. The function returns the previous default file mode.

 NOTE
Borland users should refer to the umask() function later in this chapter.

Header File

```
#include <io.h>
#include <sys\stat.h>
```

Declaration

```
int _umask(int mode);
```

- *mode* — The new default mode which can be one or both of _S_IREAD (which disallows reading from the file) or _S_IWRITE (which disallows writing to the file).

Example

The following program demonstrates how to use the _umask() function. When run, the program sets the default mode to _S_WRITE, which disallows writing to a new file. The program then creates a new file, specifying both read and write access. However, because the default access has been set to disallow writes, the created file is read-only. (Before running the program, be sure that the file test.txt doesn't already exist in the program's directory.) The program's output looks like this:

```
Making read-only the default mode...
Opening the file for writing...
Closing file...
Checking file mode...
File is read-only.
Press any key to continue
```

Here is the program source code that produced the output:

```
#include "stdafx.h"
#include <io.h>
```

```
#include <stdio.h>
#include <sys\stat.h>
#include <iostream>

using namespace std;

int main(int argc, char* argv[])
{
    struct _stat statStruct;

    cout << "Making read-only the default mode...";
    cout << endl;
    unsigned oldMask = _umask(_S_IWRITE);

    cout << "Opening the file for writing..." << endl;
    FILE* file = fopen("test.txt","w+");

    if (file == NULL)
        cout << "File open error." << endl;
    else
    {
        cout << "Closing file..." << endl;
        fclose(file);
        cout << "Checking file mode..." << endl;
        _stat("test.txt",&statStruct);

        if (statStruct.st_mode & _S_IWRITE)
            cout << "File is still writable." << endl;
        else
            cout << "File is read-only." << endl;
    }

    return 0;
}
```

CROSS-REFERENCE
See also _stat() and umask().

_ungetch()

Function

The _ungetch() function gives a character back to the console, returning the character, or EOF in the case of an error.

 NOTE
Borland users should refer to the ungetch() function later in this chapter.

Header File

```
#include <conio.h>
```

Declaration

```
int _ungetch();
```

Example

The following program demonstrates how to use the _ungetch() function. When run, the program accepts a character from the console, reads the character, gives the character back to the console, and reads it a second time. The program's output looks like this:

```
Type a character:
A
Your character: A
Putting character back...
Getting the character...
Your character: A
Press any key to continue
```

Here is the program source code that produced the output:

```
#include "stdafx.h"
#include <conio.h>
#include <iostream>

using namespace std;

int main(int argc, char* argv[])
{
    cout << "Type a character:" << endl;
```

```
    int ch = _getche();
    cout << endl << "Your character: ";
    cout << (char)ch << endl;

    cout << "Putting character back..." << endl;
    _ungetch(ch);

    cout << "Getting the character..." << endl;
    ch = _getche();
    cout << "Your character: ";
    cout << (char)ch << endl;

    return 0;
}
```

CROSS-REFERENCE

See also _getche(), getc(), getch(), getchar(), getche(), getwc(), getwchar(), and ungetch().

_unlink()

Function

The _unlink() function deletes a file, returning 0 if successful, or –1 if an error occurs.

Header File

```
#include <io.h>
```

Declaration

```
int _unlink(const char *filename);
```

- *filename* — The file to delete.

Example

The following program demonstrates how to use the _unlink() function. When run, the program attempts to create and delete a file, displaying messages as it goes. The program's output looks like this:

```
Creating a file...
File created successfully.
Closing the new file...
Deleting the new file...
File deleted successfully.
Press any key to continue
```

Here is the program source code that produced the output:

```cpp
#include "stdafx.h"
#include <io.h>
#include <sys\stat.h>
#include <iostream>

using namespace std;

int main(int argc, char* argv[])
{
    cout << "Creating a file..." << endl;
    int fileHandle = _creat("test.dat", S_IREAD | S_IWRITE);

    if (fileHandle != -1)
    {
        cout << "File created successfully." << endl;
        cout << "Closing the new file..." << endl;
        _close(fileHandle);

        cout << "Deleting the new file..." << endl;
        int result = _unlink("test.dat");
        if (result == 0)
            cout << "File deleted successfully." << endl;
        else
        {
            cout << "File delete error: ";
            if (errno == EACCES)
                cout << "Read-only file" << endl;
            else if (errno == ENOENT)
                cout << "File not found" << endl;
            else
                cout << "Unknown error" << endl;
        }
    }
    else
```

```
        cout << "File create error." << endl;

    return 0;
}
```

CROSS-REFERENCE
See also _access(), _chmod(), _fullpath(), _get_osfhandle(), _makepath(), _mktemp(), _open_osfhandle(), _splitpath(), _stat(), _stati64(), _umask(), _waccess(), _wchmod(), _wfullpath(), _wmakepath(), _wmktemp(), _wremove(), _wrename(), _wsplitpath(), _wstat(), _wstati64(), _wunlink(), remove(), rename(), and unlink().

_utime()

Function

The _utime() function sets the time when a file was last modified. The function returns 0 if successful, or −1 if an error occurs.

Header File

```
#include <sys\utime.h>
```

Declaration

```
int _utime(char *filename, struct _utimbuf *times);
```

- *filename* — The file for which to change the modification time.
- *times* — A pointer to an initialized _utimebuf structure containing the new modification time or NULL to change the modification time to the current time.

Example

The following program demonstrates how to use the _utime() function. When run, the program attempts to change a file's modification time and displays the results. The program's output looks like this:

```
Modification time successfully changed
Press any key to continue
```

Here is the program source code that produced the output:

```cpp
#include "stdafx.h"
#include <sys\utime.h>
#include <iostream>

using namespace std;

int main(int argc, char* argv[])
{
    int result = _utime("_utime.cpp", NULL);
    if (result == 0)
        cout << "Modification time successfully changed" <<
endl;
    else
    {
        cout << "Modification time change error: ";
        switch (errno)
        {
        case EACCES:
            cout << "Read-only file" << endl;
            break;
        case EINVAL:
            cout << "Invalid time" << endl;
            break;
        case EMFILE:
            cout << "Too many open files" << endl;
            break;
        case ENOENT:
            cout << "File not found" << endl;
            break;
        default:
            cout << "Unknown error" << endl;
        }
    }

    return 0;
}
```

CROSS-REFERENCE
See also _ftime(), _futime(), _strdate(), _strtime(), _wasctime(), _wctime(), _wstrtime(), _wutime(), asctime(), ctime(), difftime(), gmtime(), localtime(), mktime(), strftime(), time(), utime(), and wcsftime().

ultoa()

Function

The `ultoa()` function converts an unsigned long integer value to a string, returning a pointer to the resultant string.

Header File

```
#include <stdlib.h>
```

Declaration

```
char* ultoa(unsigned long value, char* string, int radix);
```

- *radix* — The value number base (typically 10).
- *string* — A pointer to the buffer in which to store the string.
- *value* — The value to convert.

Example

The following program demonstrates how to use the `ultoa()` function. When run, the program converts an unsigned long-integer value into several number-base formats and displays the results. The program's output looks like this:

```
This is 19,564 in base 10: 19564
This is 19,564 in base 16: 4c6c
This is 19,564 in base 2: 100110001101100
This is 19,564 in base 8: 46154

Press any key to continue
```

Here is the program source code that produced the output:

```
#include "stdafx.h"
#include <iostream>
#include <stdlib.h>

using namespace std;

int main(int argc, char* argv[])
{
    char str[81];
```

```
unsigned long value = 19564;

char* result = ultoa(value, str, 10);
cout << "This is 19,564 in base 10: ";
cout << result << endl;

result = ultoa(value, str, 16);
cout << "This is 19,564 in base 16: ";
cout << result << endl;

result = ultoa(value, str, 2);
cout << "This is 19,564 in base 2: ";
cout << result << endl;

result = ultoa(value, str, 8);
cout << "This is 19,564 in base 8: ";
cout << result << endl;
cout << endl;

return 0;
}
```

CROSS-REFERENCE

See also _ecvt(), _fcvt(), _gcvt(), _i64toa(), _i64tow(), _itow(), _ui64toa(), _ui64tow(), _ultoa(), itoa(), and ltoa().

umask()

Function

The umask() function sets the default file-access mode, which determines the read and write access of newly created files. The function returns the previous default file mode.

Header File

```
#include <io.h>
#include <sys\stat.h>
```

Declaration

```
int umask(int mode);
```

- *mode* — The new default mode, which can be one or both of S_IREAD (which disallows reading from the file) or S_IWRITE (which disallows writing to the file).

Example

The following program demonstrates how to use the umask() function. When run, the program sets the default mode to S_WRITE, which disallows writing to a new file. The program then creates a new file, specifying both read and write access. However, because the default access has been set to disallow writes, the created file is read-only. (Before running the program, be sure that the file test.txt doesn't already exist in the program's directory.) The program's output looks like this:

```
Making read-only the default mode...
Opening the file for writing...
Closing file...
Checking file mode...
File is read-only.
Press any key to continue
```

Here is the program source code that produced the output:

```
#include "stdafx.h"
#include <io.h>
#include <stdio.h>
#include <sys\stat.h>
#include <iostream>

using namespace std;

int main(int argc, char* argv[])
{
    struct stat statStruct;

    cout << "Making read-only the default mode...";
    cout << endl;
    unsigned oldMask = umask(S_IWRITE);

    cout << "Opening the file for writing..." << endl;
    FILE* file = fopen("test.txt","w+");

    if (file == NULL)
        cout << "File open error." << endl;
    else
```

t
> u
v

```
        {
            cout << "Closing file..." << endl;
            fclose(file);
            cout << "Checking file mode..." << endl;
            stat("test.txt",&statStruct);

            if (statStruct.st_mode & S_IWRITE)
                cout << "File is still writable." << endl;
            else
                cout << "File is read-only." << endl;
        }

        return 0;
    }
```

CROSS-REFERENCE
See also _stat() and _umask().

ungetc()

Function

The ungetc() function places a character back into a stream, returning the character, or EOF in the event of an error.

Header File

```
#include <stdio.h>
```

Declaration

```
int ungetc(int c, FILE* stream);
```

- *c* — The character to place back into the stream.
- *stream* — A pointer to the stream.

Example

The following program demonstrates how to use the ungetc() function. When run, the program opens a file, reads a character, returns the character to the stream, and then rereads the character. The program's output looks similar to this:

```
Opening the file...
Getting a character...
Character: /
Returning the character...
Getting the character again...
Character: /
Press any key to continue
```

Here is the program source code that produced the output:

```cpp
#include "stdafx.h"
#include <stdio.h>
#include <iostream>

using namespace std;

int main(int argc, char* argv[])
{
    cout << "Opening the file..." << endl;
    FILE* file = fopen("ungetc.cpp", "rb");

    if (file != NULL)
    {
        cout << "Getting a character..." << endl;
        int ch = getc(file);
        int error = ferror(file);
        if (!error)
        {
            cout << "Character: ";
            cout << (char)ch << endl;
            cout << "Returning the character..." << endl;
            ungetc(ch, file);
            cout << "Getting the character again..." << endl;
            ch = getc(file);
            cout << "Character: ";
            cout << (char)ch << endl;
        }
        else
            cout << "Error reading file" << endl;

        fclose(file);
    }
    else
```

```
                    cout << "Error opening file" << endl;

            return 0;
        }
```

CROSS-REFERENCE
See also _close(), _creat(), _fdopen(), _fgetchar(), _fgetwchar(), _fileno(), _flushall(), _fputwchar(), _fsopen(), _getw(), _getws(), _open(), _putw(), _putws(), _read(), _rmtmp(), _tempnam(), _wcreat(), _wfdopen(), _wfopen(), _wfreopen(), _wfsopen(), _wopen(), _wtempnam(), _wtmpnam(), clearerr(), eof(), fclose(), feof(), ferror(), fflush(), fgetc(), fgetpos(), fgets(), fgetwc(), fgetws(), fopen(), fprintf(), fputc(), fputchar(), fputs(), fputwc(), fputws(), fread(), freopen(), fscanf(), fseek(), fsetpos(), ftell(), fwprintf(), fwrite(), fwscanf(), getc(), getchar(), gets(), getw(), getwc(), getwchar(), lseek(), putc(), putch(), putchar(), puts(), putwc(), putwchar(), rewind(), setbuf(), setvbuf(), tmpfile(), tmpnam(), ungetch(), ungetwc(), and write().

ungetch()

Function

The ungetch() function gives a character back to the console, returning the character, or EOF in the case of an error.

Header File

```
#include <conio.h>
```

Declaration

```
int ungetch();
```

Example

The following program demonstrates how to use the ungetch() function. When run, the program accepts a character from the console, reads the character, gives the character back to the console, and reads it a second time. The program's output looks like this:

```
Type a character:
A
Your character: A
```

```
Putting character back...
Getting the character...
Your character: A
Press any key to continue
```

Here is the program source code that produced the output:

```cpp
#include "stdafx.h"
#include <conio.h>
#include <iostream>

using namespace std;

int main(int argc, char* argv[])
{
    cout << "Type a character:" << endl;
    int ch = getche();
    cout << endl << "Your character: ";
    cout << (char)ch << endl;

    cout << "Putting character back..." << endl;
    ungetch(ch);

    cout << "Getting the character..." << endl;
    ch = getche();
    cout << "Your character: ";
    cout << (char)ch << endl;

    return 0;
}
```

CROSS-REFERENCE

See also _getche(), _ungetch(), getc(), getch(), getchar(), getche(), getwc(), and getwchar().

ungetwc()

Function

The ungetwc() function places a wide-character back into a stream, returning the character, or WEOF in the event of an error.

Header File

```
#include <stdio.h>
```

Declaration

```
wint_t ungetwc(wint_t c, FILE* stream);
```

- *c* — The character to place back into the stream.
- *stream* — A pointer to the stream.

Example

The following program demonstrates how to use the ungetwc() function. When run, the program opens a file, reads a character, returns the character to the stream, and then rereads the character. The program's output looks similar to this:

```
Opening the file...
Getting a character...
Character: 12079
Returning the character...
Getting the character again...
Character: 12079
Press any key to continue
```

Here is the program source code that produced the output:

```
#include "stdafx.h"
#include <stdio.h>
#include <iostream>

using namespace std;

int main(int argc, char* argv[])
{
    cout << "Opening the file..." << endl;
FILE* file = fopen("ungetwc.cpp", "rb");

    if (file != NULL)
    {
        cout << "Getting a character..." << endl;
        wint_t ch = getwc(file);
        int error = ferror(file);
        if (!error)
```

```
        {
            cout << "Character: ";
            wcout << (wchar_t)ch << endl;
            cout << "Returning the character..." << endl;
            ungetwc(ch, file);
            cout << "Getting the character again..." << endl;
            ch = getwc(file);
            cout << "Character: ";
            wcout << (wchar_t)ch << endl;
        }
        else
            cout << "Error reading file" << endl;

        fclose(file);
    }
    else
        cout << "Error opening file" << endl;

    return 0;
}
```

CROSS-REFERENCE

See also _close(), _creat(), _fdopen(), _fgetchar(), _fgetwchar(), _fileno(), _flushall(), _fputwchar(), _fsopen(), _getw(), _getws(), _open(), _putw(), _putws(), _read(), _rmtmp(), _tempnam(), _wcreat(), _wfdopen(), _wfopen(), _wfreopen(), _wfsopen(), _wopen(), _wtempnam(), _wtmpnam(), clearerr(), eof(), fclose(), feof(), ferror(), fflush(), fgetc(), fgetpos(), fgets(), fgetwc(), fgetws(), fopen(), fprintf(), fputc(), fputchar(), fputs(), fputwc(), fputws(), fread(), freopen(), fscanf(), fseek(), fsetpos(), ftell(), fwprintf(), fwrite(), fwscanf(), getc(), getchar(), gets(), getw(), getwc(), getwchar(), lseek(), putc(), putch(), putchar(), puts(), putwc(), putwchar(), rewind(), setbuf(), setvbuf(), tmpfile(), tmpnam(), ungetc(), ungetch(), and write().

union

Keyword

The union keyword enables a program to define a special type of structure named a union. A *union* specifies two or more data types as members. However, because all members of a union share the same memory, only a single member at a time can hold a valid value. For example, the following program defines a union named test_union, which declares an integer and a character as members. The program first sets the integer member, and then displays the integer's value and address. The program then sets the character member's value, and displays both the integer and character members. The integer value of 65 shows that setting the character to A also changed the value of the integer, because both members are located at the same address. The program also displays the character member's address, proving that it's the same as the integer member's. The program's output looks like this:

```
union1.x = 12
Address of x = 006AFDF4
union1.x = 65
union1.c = A
Address of c = 006AFDF4
Press any key to continue
```

Here is the program source code that produced the output:

```cpp
#include "stdafx.h"
#include <iostream>

using namespace std;

int main(int argc, char* argv[])
{
    union test_union
    {
        int x;
        char c;
    } union1;

    union1.x = 12;
    cout << "union1.x = " << union1.x << endl;
    int* pInt = &union1.x;
    cout << "Address of x = " << pInt << endl;
    union1.c = 'A';
    cout << "union1.x = " << union1.x << endl;
    cout << "union1.c = " << union1.c << endl;
    char* pChar = &union1.c;
    cout << "Address of c = " << (int*)pChar << endl;

    return 0;
}
```

 **CROSS-REFERENCE**
See also struct.

unlink()

Function

The `unlink()` function deletes a file, returning 0 if successful, or –1 if an error occurs.

Header File

```
#include <io.h>
```

Declaration

```
int unlink(const char *filename);
```

- *filename* — The file to delete.

Example

The following program demonstrates how to use the `unlink()` function. When run, the program attempts to create and delete a file, displaying messages as it goes. The program's output looks like this:

```
Creating a file...
File created successfully.
Closing the new file...
Deleting the new file...
File deleted successfully.
Press any key to continue
```

Here is the program source code that produced the output:

```
#include "stdafx.h"
#include <io.h>
#include <sys\stat.h>
#include <iostream>

using namespace std;

int main(int argc, char* argv[])
{
```

```
cout << "Creating a file..." << endl;
int fileHandle = creat("test.dat", S_IREAD | S_IWRITE);

if (fileHandle != -1)
{
    cout << "File created successfully." << endl;
    cout << "Closing the new file..." << endl;
    close(fileHandle);

    cout << "Deleting the new file..." << endl;
    int result = unlink("test.dat");
    if (result == 0)
        cout << "File deleted successfully." << endl;
    else
    {
        cout << "File delete error: ";
        if (errno == EACCES)
            cout << "Read-only file" << endl;
        else if (errno == ENOENT)
            cout << "File not found" << endl;
        else
            cout << "Unknown error" << endl;
    }
}
else
    cout << "File create error." << endl;

return 0;
}
```

CROSS-REFERENCE

See also _access(), _chmod(), _fullpath(), _get_osfhandle(), _makepath(), _mktemp(), _wmktemp(), _open_osfhandle(), _splitpath(), _stat(), _stati64(), _umask(), _unlink(), _waccess(), _wchmod(), _wfullpath(), _wmakepath(), _wsplitpath(), _wremove(), _wrename(), _wstat(), _wstati64(), _wunlink(), remove(), and rename().

unsigned

Keyword

The unsigned keyword enables a program to declare values that are unsigned. Unsigned values cannot be negative and therefore can hold larger positive values than their signed counterparts. This is because the bit that is normally used to indicate the value's sign can be used instead as another data bit. The following line shows how to define an unsigned integer:

```
unsigned int value = 1245;
```

 CROSS-REFERENCE
See also char, double, float, int, long, short, and signed.

utime()

Function

The utime() function sets the time when a file was last modified. The function returns 0 if successful, or −1 if an error occurs.

Header File

```
#include <sys\utime.h>
```

Declaration

```
int utime(char *filename, struct _utimbuf *times);
```

- *filename* — The file for which to change the modification time.
- *times* — A pointer to an initialized _utimbuf structure containing the new modification time or NULL to change the modification time to the current time.

Example

The following program demonstrates how to use the utime() function. When run, the program attempts to change a file's modification time and displays the results. The program's output looks like this:

```
Modification time successfully changed
```

```
Press any key to continue
```

Here is the program source code that produced the output:

```cpp
#include "stdafx.h"
#include <sys\utime.h>
#include <iostream>

using namespace std;

int main(int argc, char* argv[])
{
    int result = utime("utime.cpp", NULL);
    if (result == 0)
        cout << "Modification time successfully changed" <<
endl;
    else
    {
        cout << "Modification time change error: ";
        switch (errno)
        {
        case EACCES:
            cout << "Read-only file" << endl;
            break;
        case EINVAL:
            cout << "Invalid time" << endl;
            break;
        case EMFILE:
            cout << "Too many open files" << endl;
            break;
        case ENOENT:
            cout << "File not found" << endl;
            break;
        default:
            cout << "Unknown error" << endl;
        }
    }

    return 0;
}
```

CROSS-REFERENCE

See also _ftime(), _futime(), gmtime(), localtime(), mktime(), _strdate(), strftime(), _strtime(), time(), _tzset(), _utime(), _wasctime(), _wctime(), wcsftime(), _wstrtime(), _wutime(), asctime(), ctime(), and difftime().

_vsnprintf()

Function

The `_vsnprintf()` function writes formatted data to a buffer from a variable argument list, returning the number of bytes written, or a negative number in the case of an error.

NOTE
Borland does not support this function.

Header File

```
#include <stdio.h>
```

Declaration

```
int _vsnprintf(char *buffer, size_t count,
    const char *format, va_list argptr);
```

- *argptr* — The argument list.
- *buffer* — A pointer to the buffer that will receive the formatted data.
- *count* — The maximum number of characters to write to the buffer.
- n format — A pointer to the format string, which can contain format specifiers from Table V-1.

Table V-1 Format Specifiers for _vsnprintf()

Specifier	Description
%c	Specifies a character.
%C	Specifies a single-byte character or wide character.
%d	Specifies a signed decimal integer.

Continued

Table V-1 *Continued*

Specifier	Description
%e	Specifies a signed double-precision floating-point value using scientific notation with a lowercase e.
%E	Specifies a signed double-precision floating-point value using scientific notation with an uppercase E.
%f	Specifies a signed double-precision floating-point value.
%g	Specifies a signed double-precision floating-point value using either normal notation or scientific notation with a lowercase e.
%G	Specifies a signed double-precision floating-point value using either normal notation or scientific notation with an uppercase E.
%i	Specifies a signed decimal integer.
%n	Specifies an integer pointer.
%o	Specifies an unsigned octal integer.
%p	Specifies a void pointer.
%s	Specifies a string.
%S	Specifies a single-byte-character string or wide-character string.
%u	Specifies an unsigned decimal integer.
%x	Specifies an unsigned hexadecimal integer with lowercase letters.
%X	Specifies an unsigned hexadecimal integer with uppercase letters.

Example

The following program demonstrates how to use the _vsnprintf() function. When run, the program writes a variable argument list containing four values to a buffer, displaying messages as it goes. The program's output looks like this:

```
Writing values to buffer...
Number of characters written: 39
Contents of the buffer:
    199.990000 — 99 — A — This is a test
Press any key to continue
```

Here is the program source code that produced the output:

```
#include "stdafx.h"
#include <stdio.h>
#include <stdarg.h>
#include <iostream>

using namespace std;
```

```cpp
int write_args(char* buf, char* fmtStr, ...)
{
    va_list args;

    va_start(args, fmtStr);
    int result = _vsnprintf(buf, 81,
        fmtStr, args);
    va_end(args);

    return(result);
}

int main(int argc, char* argv[])
{
    char buf[81];

    cout << "Writing values to buffer..." << endl;
    int result = write_args(buf, "%f - %d - %c - %s",
        199.99, 99, 'A', "This is a test");
    if (result > 0)
    {
        cout << "Number of characters written: ";
        cout << result << endl;
        cout << "Contents of the buffer: " << endl;
        cout << "    " << buf << endl;
    }
    else
        cout << "Write error." << endl;

    return 0;
}
```

 CROSS-REFERENCE
See also _vsnwprintf(), _vsprintf(), cprintf(), cscanf(), fprintf(), fscanf(), fwprintf(), printf(), scanf(), sscanf(), swprintf(), swscanf(), va_arg(), va_end(), va_list(), va_start(), vfprintf(), vfwprintf(), vprintf(), vsprintf(), vswprintf(), vwprintf(), wprintf(), and wscanf().

u
v
w

_vsnwprintf()

Function

The _vsnwprintf() function writes formatted wide-character data to a buffer from a variable argument list, returning the number of bytes written, or a negative number in the case of an error.

 NOTE
Borland does not support this function.

Header File

```
#include <stdio.h>
```

Declaration

```
int _vsnwprintf(wchar_t *buffer, size_t count,
    const wchar_t *format, va_list argptr);
```

- *argptr* — The argument list.
- *buffer* — A pointer to the buffer that will receive the formatted data.
- *count* — The maximum number of characters to write to the buffer.
- *format* — A pointer to the format string, which can contain format specifiers from Table V-2.

Table V-2 Format Specifiers for _vsnwprintf()

Specifier	Description
%c	Specifies a character.
%C	Specifies a single-byte character or wide character.
%d	Specifies a signed decimal integer.
%e	Specifies a signed double-precision floating-point value using scientific notation with a lowercase e.
%E	Specifies a signed double-precision floating-point value using scientific notation with an uppercase E.
%f	Specifies a signed double-precision floating-point value.
%g	Specifies a signed double-precision floating-point value using either normal notation or scientific notation with a lowercase e.
%G	Specifies a signed double-precision floating-point value using either normal notation or scientific notation with an uppercase E.

Specifier	Description
%i	Specifies a signed decimal integer.
%n	Specifies an integer pointer.
%o	Specifies an unsigned octal integer.
%p	Specifies a void pointer.
%s	Specifies a string.
%S	Specifies a single-byte-character string or wide-character string.
%u	Specifies an unsigned decimal integer.
%x	Specifies an unsigned hexadecimal integer with lowercase letters.
%X	Specifies an unsigned hexadecimal integer with uppercase letters.

Example

The following program demonstrates how to use the _vsnwprintf() function. When run, the program writes a variable argument list containing four values to a buffer, displaying messages as it goes. The program's output looks like this:

```
Writing values to buffer...
Number of characters written: 39
Contents of the buffer:
   199.990000 — 99 — A — This is a test
Press any key to continue
```

Here is the program source code that produced the output:

```
#include "stdafx.h"
#include <stdio.h>
#include <stdarg.h>
#include <iostream>

using namespace std;

int write_args(wchar_t* buf, wchar_t* fmtStr, ...)
{
    va_list args;

    va_start(args, fmtStr);
    int result = _vsnwprintf(buf, 81,
        fmtStr, args);
    va_end(args);

    return(result);
}
```

```
int main(int argc, char* argv[])
{
    wchar_t buf[81];

    cout << "Writing values to buffer..." << endl;
    int result = write_args(buf, L"%f - %d - %c - %s",
        199.99, 99, 'A', L"This is a test");
    if (result > 0)
    {
        cout << "Number of characters written: ";
        cout << result << endl;
        cout << "Contents of the buffer: " << endl;
        cout << "    ";
        wcout << buf << endl;
    }
    else
        cout << "Write error." << endl;

    return 0;
}
```

CROSS-REFERENCE

See also _vsnprintf(), _vsprintf(), cprintf(), cscanf(), fprintf(), fscanf(), fwprintf(), printf(), scanf(), sscanf(), swprintf(), swscanf(), va_arg(), va_end(), va_list, va_start(), vfprintf(), vfwprintf(), vprintf(), vsprintf(), vswprintf(), vwprintf(), wprintf(), and wscanf().

va_arg()

Macro

The va_arg() macro returns the current argument in an argument list, updating the argument pointer to the next argument after returning the current one. For example, the following code example calls va_arg() within a for loop, extracting and displaying the arguments in the argument list:

```
va_start(args, count);
for (x=0; x<count; ++x)
{
    char* arg = va_arg(args, char*);
    cout << arg << endl;
}
va_end(args);
```

The `va_arg()` macro's two arguments are the argument list and the type of the argument to retrieve.

CROSS-REFERENCE

See also va_end(), va_list, va_start(), and Variable Argument Lists.

va_end()

Macro

The `va_end()` macro, which should be called after completing the extraction of arguments with the `va_arg()` macro, closes and resets an argument list. For example, the following code example calls `va_end()` after extracting and displaying all the arguments in an argument list:

```
va_start(args, count);
for (x=0; x<count; ++x)
{
    char* arg = va_arg(args, char*);
    cout << arg << endl;
}
va_end(args);
```

The `va_end()` macro's single argument is the argument list.

CROSS-REFERENCE

See also va_arg(), va_list, va_start(), and Variable Argument Lists.

va_list

Structure

The `va_list` structure holds the information needed by the `va_start()`, `va_arg()`, and `va_end()` macros to extract arguments from an argument list. For example, the following function has, as its second parameter, an argument list, which is represented by an ellipsis. The arguments are available in the function's `va_list` variable. For example, the following function implements an argument list:

```
void write_args(int count, ...)
{
    va_list args;
```

u
v
w

```
    int x;

    va_start(args, count);
    for (x=0; x<count; ++x)
    {
        char* arg = va_arg(args, char*);
        cout << arg << endl;
    }
    va_end(args);
}
```

CROSS-REFERENCE

See also va_arg(), va_end(), va_start(), and Variable Argument Lists.

va_start()

Macro

The va_start() macro, which should be called before extracting arguments with the va_arg() macro, initializes the argument list, making the first argument in the list current. For example, the following code example calls va_start() before extracting and displaying all the arguments in an argument list named args:

```
void write_args(int count, ...)
{
    va_list args;
    int x;

    va_start(args, count);
    for (x=0; x<count; ++x)
    {
        char* arg = va_arg(args, char*);
        cout << arg << endl;
    }
    va_end(args);
}
```

The va_start() macro's two arguments are the argument list and the name of the last fixed parameter that was passed to the function that received the variable argument list.

CROSS-REFERENCE
See also va_arg(), va_end(), va_list, and Variable Argument Lists.

valarray

Template class

The `valarray` template class defines an object for organizing a set in an array-like structure that supports various types of arithmetic operations between stored elements.

Class Declaration

```
template<class T>
    class valarray {
public:
    typedef T value_type;
    valarray();
    explicit valarray(size_t n);
    valarray(const T& val, size_t n));
    valarray(const T *p, size_t n);
    valarray(const slice_array<T>& sa);
    valarray(const gslice_array<T>& ga);
    valarray(const mask_array<T>& ma);
    valarray(const indirect_array<T>& ia);
    valarray<T>& operator=(const valarray<T>& va);
    valarray<T>& operator=(const T& x);
    valarray<T>& operator=(const slice_array<T>& sa);
    valarray<T>& operator=(const gslice_array<T>& ga);
    valarray<T>& operator=(const mask_array<T>& ma);
    valarray<T>& operator=(const indirect_array<T>& ia);
    T operator[](size_t n) const;
    T& operator[](size_t n);
    valarray<T> operator[](slice sa) const;
    slice_array<T> operator[](slice sa);
    valarray<T> operator[](const gslice& ga) const;
    gslice_array<T> operator[](const gslice& ga);
    valarray<T> operator[](const valarray<bool>& ba) const;
    mask_array<T> operator[](const valarray<bool>& ba);
    valarray<T> operator[](const valarray<size_t>& xa) const;
    indirect_array<T> operator[](const valarray<size_t>& xa);
    valarray<T> operator+();
```

u

▶ v

w

```
            valarray<T> operator-();
            valarray<T> operator~();
            valarray<bool> operator!();
            valarray<T>& operator*=(const valarray<T>& x);
            valarray<T>& operator*=(const T& x);
            valarray<T>& operator/=(const valarray<T>& x);
            valarray<T>& operator/=(const T& x);
            valarray<T>& operator%=(const valarray<T>& x);
            valarray<T>& operator%=(const T& x);
            valarray<T>& operator+=(const valarray<T>& x);
            valarray<T>& operator+=(const T& x);
            valarray<T>& operator-=(const valarray<T>& x);
            valarray<T>& operator-=(const T& x);
            valarray<T>& operator^=(const valarray<T>& x);
            valarray<T>& operator^=(const T& x);
            valarray<T>& operator&=(const valarray<T>& x);
            valarray<T>& operator&=(const T& x);
            valarray<T>& operator|=(const valarray<T>& x);
            valarray<T>& operator|=(const T& x);
            valarray<T>& operator<<=(const valarray<T>& x);
            valarray<T>& operator<<=(const T& x);
            valarray<T>& operator>=(const valarray<T>& x);
            valarray<T>& operator>=(const T& x);
            size_t size() const;
            T sum() const;
            T max() const;
            T min() const;
            valarray<T> shift(int n) const;
            valarray<T> cshift(int n) const;
            valarray<T> apply(T fn(T)) const;
            valarray<T> apply(T fn(const T&)) const;
            void fill(const T& val);
            void free();
            void resize(size_t n, const T& c = T());
            };
```

Class Members

Table V-3 lists and describes the members of the `valarray` template class.

Table V-3 Members of the valarray Template Class

Member	Description
apply()	Applies a function to the elements in the array.
cshift()	Performs a circular shift on the elements of the array.
fill()	Fills the array with a specified value.
free()	Removes all elements from the array.
max()	Returns the largest element in the array.
min()	Returns the smallest element in the array.
resize()	Changes the size of the array.
shift()	Shifts the elements of the array.
size()	Returns the size (the number of elements) of the array.
sum()	Returns the sum of all elements in the array.
value_type	Represents a data type for an element in the set.

CROSS-REFERENCE
See also list, queue, set, stack, and vector.

Variable Argument Lists

Technique

Variable argument lists enable a function to receive a variable number of arguments. To implement a variable argument list, you must be familiar with the va_list structure and with the va_start(), va_arg(), and va_end() macros. The following sections show how to implement variable argument lists.

The va_list Structure

The va_list structure holds the argument list that's received by a function. Suppose you need a function that can print a list of strings, but the number of strings received by the function will vary from one call to another. For example, two calls to the function might look like this:

```
write_strs(5, "One", "Two", "Three", "Four", "Five");
write_strs(3, "Robin", "Alice", "Greta");
```

The first argument in both functions is the number of strings being passed as arguments. The first function call passes five string arguments, whereas the second function call passes only three string arguments. To write a function that can receive this variable number of arguments, you might start like this:

```
void write_strs(int count, ...)
{
    va_list args;


}
```

The `write_strs()` function's first parameter is the argument count that's passed to the function by the function call's first argument. The second parameter — the ellipsis — represents the argument list, which contains all other arguments passed to the function. This argument list is accessible through the function's `args` variable, which is defined as type `va_list`.

The va_start Macro

To access the argument list, you must first initialize the list by calling the `va_start()` macro with the name of the list and the name of the last fixed parameter received by the function, like this:

```
va_start(args, count);
```

The va_arg Macro

At this point, your program can start processing the argument list by calling the `va_arg()` macro:

```
char* arg = va_arg(args, char*);
```

This macro returns the current argument and then advances the argument pointer to the next argument. Therefore, each time you call `va_arg()` you get the next argument in the list. The macro's two arguments are the name of the argument list and the data type to return.

The va_end Macro

After retrieving the arguments in the argument list, the list is closed by calling the `va_end()` macro, which sets the list pointer to `NULL`:

```
va_end(args);
```

This macro's single argument is the name of the argument list.

A Variable Argument List in Action

The following program puts variable argument lists to the test. The program's `write_strs()` function can display any number of strings passed as a variable argument list, as is proven by the three calls to write_strs() in main(). The program's output looks like this:

```
Sending argument list...
One
Two
Three
Four
Five
Six
Seven
Eight
Nine
Ten
Sending argument list...
Robin
Alice
Greta
Sending argument list...
Cow
Horse
Cat
Dog
Bird
Press any key to continue
```

Here is the program source code that produced the output:

```
#include "stdafx.h"
#include <stdlib.h>
#include <stdarg.h>
#include <iostream>

using namespace std;

void write_strs(int count, ...)
{
    va_list args;
    int x;

    va_start(args, count);
    for (x=0; x<count; ++x)
    {
        char* arg = va_arg(args, char*);
        cout << arg << endl;
    }
}
```

```
        va_end(args);
    }

    int main(int argc, char* argv[])
    {
        cout << "Sending argument list..." << endl;
        write_strs(10, "One", "Two", "Three", "Four", "Five",
            "Six", "Seven", "Eight", "Nine", "Ten");
        cout << "Sending argument list..." << endl;
        write_strs(3, "Robin", "Alice", "Greta");
        cout << "Sending argument list..." << endl;
        write_strs(5, "Cow", "Horse", "Cat", "Dog", "Bird");

        return 0;
    }
```

CROSS-REFERENCE
See also va_arg(), va_end(), va_list, and va_start().

vector

Template class

The vector template class defines an object that implements a variable-size array.

Class Declaration

```
    template<class T, class A = allocator<T> >
        class vector {
    public:
        typedef A allocator_type;
        typedef A::size_type size_type;
        typedef A::difference_type difference_type;
        typedef A::reference reference;
        typedef A::const_reference const_reference;
        typedef A::value_type value_type;
        typedef T0 iterator;
        typedef T1 const_iterator;
        typedef reverse_iterator<iterator, value_type,
            reference, A::pointer, difference_type>
                reverse_iterator;
        typedef reverse_iterator<const_iterator, value_type,
```

```
        const_reference, A::const_pointer, difference_type>
            const_reverse_iterator;
    explicit vector(const A& al = A());
    explicit vector(size_type n, const T& v = T(),
        const A& al = A());
    vector(const vector& x);
    vector(const_iterator first, const_iterator last,
        const A& al = A());
    void reserve(size_type n);
    size_type capacity() const;
    iterator begin();
    const_iterator begin() const;
    iterator end();
    iterator end() const;
    reverse_iterator rbegin();
    const_reverse_iterator rbegin() const;
    reverse_iterator rend();
    const_reverse_iterator rend() const;
    void resize(size_type n, T x = T());
    size_type size() const;
    size_type max_size() const;
    bool empty() const;
    A get_allocator() const;
    reference at(size_type pos);
    const_reference at(size_type pos) const;
    reference operator[](size_type pos);
    const_reference operator[](size_type pos);
    reference front();
    const_reference front() const;
    reference back();
    const_reference back() const;
    void push_back(const T& x);
    void pop_back();
    void assign(const_iterator first, const_iterator last);
    void assign(size_type n, const T& x = T());
    iterator insert(iterator it, const T& x = T());
    void insert(iterator it, size_type n, const T& x);
    void insert(iterator it,
        const_iterator first, const_iterator last);
    iterator erase(iterator it);
    iterator erase(iterator first, iterator last);
    void clear();
    void swap(vector x);
protected:
```

```
    A allocator;
    };
```

Class Members

Table V-4 lists and describes the members of the vector template class.

Table V-4 Members of the vector Template Class

Member	Description
allocator_type	A synonym for the template's A parameter.
assign()	Replaces the current sequence with the given sequence.
at()	Returns a reference to the specified element.
back()	Returns a reference to the last element in the array.
begin()	Returns a random-access iterator that points to the sequence's first element.
capacity()	Returns the amount of allocated storage for a sequence.
clear()	Erases all elements from the array.
const_iterator	Object type for a constant random-access iterator.
const_reference	A synonym for A converted to const_reference.
const_reverse_ iterator	Object type for a constant reverse iterator.
difference_type	A synonym for A converted to difference_type.
empty()	Returns true if the sequence is empty.
end()	Returns a random-access iterator that points to the next element beyond the end of the sequence.
erase()	Erases a portion of the sequence.
front()	Returns a reference to the first element in the array.
get_allocator()	Returns the allocator.
insert()	Inserts a given sequence into the current sequence.
iterator	Object type for a random-access iterator.
max_size()	Returns the maximum possible size of a sequence.
pop_back()	Removes the last element from the array.
push_back()	Places an element at the end of the array.
rbegin()	Returns a reverse iterator that points to the next element beyond the end of the sequence.
reference	A synonym for A converted to reference.
rend()	Returns a reverse iterator that points to the sequence's first element.
reserve()	Sets the amount of allocated storage for a sequence.
resize()	Resizes the sequence.
reverse_iterator	Object type for a reverse iterator.
size()	Returns the length of the sequence.

Member	Description
size_type	A synonym for A converted to size_type
swap()	Swaps one sequence with another.
value_type	A synonym for the template's E parameter.

CROSS-REFERENCE
See also list, queue, set, stack, and valarray.

vfprintf()

Function

The vfprintf() function writes formatted data to a stream from a variable argument list, returning the number of bytes written or returning a negative number in the case of an error.

Header File

```
#include <stdio.h>
```

Declaration

```
int vfprintf(FILE *stream,
    const char *format, va_list argptr);
```

- *argptr*—The argument list.
- *format*—A pointer to the format string, which can contain format specifiers from Table V-5.
- *stream*—A pointer to the stream to which to write the data.

Table V-5 Format Specifiers for vfprintf()

Specifier	Description
%c	Specifies a character.
%C	Specifies a single-byte character or wide-character.
%d	Specifies a signed decimal integer.

Continued

u
v
w

Table V-5 *Continued*

Specifier	Description
%e	Specifies a signed double-precision floating-point value using scientific notation with a lowercase e.
%E	Specifies a signed double-precision floating-point value using scientific notation with an uppercase E.
%f	Specifies a signed double-precision floating-point value.
%g	Specifies a signed double-precision floating-point value using either normal notation or scientific notation with a lowercase e.
%G	Specifies a signed double-precision floating-point value using either normal notation or scientific notation with an uppercase E.
%i	Specifies a signed decimal integer.
%n	Specifies an integer pointer.
%o	Specifies an unsigned octal integer.
%p	Specifies a void pointer.
%s	Specifies a string.
%S	Specifies a single-byte-character string or wide-character string.
%u	Specifies an unsigned decimal integer.
%x	Specifies an unsigned hexadecimal integer with lowercase letters.
%X	Specifies an unsigned hexadecimal integer with uppercase letters.

Example

The following program demonstrates how to use the `vfprintf()` function. When run, the program opens a temporary file, writes a variable argument list containing four values to the file, and then closes the file, displaying messages as it goes. The program's output looks like this:

```
Creating a temp file...
File created successfully.
Writing values to file...
Number of characters written: 31
File closed.
Press any key to continue
```

Here is the program source code that produced the output:

```
#include "stdafx.h"
#include <stdio.h>
#include <stdarg.h>
#include <iostream>

using namespace std;
```

```cpp
int write_args(FILE* file, char *fmtStr, ...)
{
   va_list args;

   va_start(args, fmtStr);
   int result = vfprintf(file, fmtStr, args);
   va_end(args);

   return(result);
}

int main(int argc, char* argv[])
{
    cout << "Creating a temp file..." << endl;
    FILE* file = tmpfile();
    if (file != NULL)
    {
        cout << "File created successfully." << endl;
        cout << "Writing values to file..." << endl;
        int result = write_args(file,
            " %f %d %c %s", 199.99, 99,
            'A', "This is a test");
        if (result > 0)
        {
            cout << "Number of characters written: ";
            cout << result << endl;
            fclose(file);
            cout << "File closed." << endl;
        }
        else
            cout << "Write error." << endl;
    }
    else
        cout << "Error creating file." << endl;

    return 0;
}
```

u
v
w

CROSS-REFERENCE
See also _vsnprintf(), _vsnwprintf(), _vsprintf(), cprintf(), cscanf(), fprintf(), fscanf(), fwprintf(), printf(), scanf(), sscanf(), swprintf(), swscanf(), va_arg(), va_end(), va_list, va_start(), vfwprintf(), vprintf(), vsprintf(), vswprintf(), vwprintf(), wprintf(), and wscanf().

vfwprintf()

Function

The `vfwprintf()` function writes formatted wide-character data to a stream from a variable argument list, returning the number of bytes written or returning a negative number in the case an error.

Header File

```
#include <stdio.h>
```

Declaration

```
int vfwprintf(FILE *stream,
    const wchar_t *format, va_list argptr);
```

- *argptr* — The argument list.
- *format* — A pointer to the format string, which can contain format specifiers from Table V-6.
- *stream* — A pointer to the stream to which to write the data.

Table V-6 Format Specifiers for vfwprintf()

Specifier	Description
%c	Specifies a character.
%C	Specifies a single-byte character or wide-character.
%d	Specifies a signed decimal integer.
%e	Specifies a signed double-precision floating-point value using scientific notation with a lowercase e.
%E	Specifies a signed double-precision floating-point value using scientific notation with an uppercase E.
%f	Specifies a signed double-precision floating-point value.
%g	Specifies a signed double-precision floating-point value using either normal notation or scientific notation with a lowercase e.
%G	Specifies a signed double-precision floating-point value using either normal notation or scientific notation with an uppercase E.
%I	Specifies a signed decimal integer.
%n	Specifies an integer pointer.
%o	Specifies an unsigned octal integer.
%p	Specifies a void pointer.
%s	Specifies a string.

Specifier	Description
%S	Specifies a single-byte-character string or wide-character string.
%u	Specifies an unsigned decimal integer.
%x	Specifies an unsigned hexadecimal integer with lowercase letters.
%X	Specifies an unsigned hexadecimal integer with uppercase letters.

Example

The following program demonstrates how to use the vfwprintf() function. When run, the program opens a temporary file, writes a variable argument list containing four values to the file, and then closes the file, displaying messages as it goes. The program's output looks like this:

```
Creating a temp file...
File created successfully.
Writing values to file...
Number of characters written: 23
File closed.
Press any key to continue
```

Here is the program source code that produced the output:

```cpp
#include "stdafx.h"
#include <stdio.h>
#include <stdarg.h>
#include <iostream>

using namespace std;

int write_args(FILE* file, wchar_t *fmtStr, ...)
{
    va_list args;

    va_start(args, fmtStr);
    int result = vfwprintf(file, fmtStr, args);
    va_end(args);

    return(result);
}

int main(int argc, char* argv[])
{
    cout << "Creating a temp file..." << endl;
    FILE* file = tmpfile();
```

```
if (file != NULL)
{
    cout << "File created successfully." << endl;
    cout << "Writing values to file..." << endl;
    int result = write_args(file,
        L"%f %d %c %s", 199.99, 99,
        (wchar_t)'A', "This is a test");
    if (result > 0)
    {
        cout << "Number of characters written: ";
        cout << result << endl;
        fclose(file);
        cout << "File closed." << endl;
    }
    else
        cout << "Write error." << endl;
}
else
    cout << "Error creating file." << endl;

return 0;
}
```

CROSS-REFERENCE

See also _vsnprintf(), _vsnwprintf(), _vsprintf(), cprintf(), cscanf(), fprintf(), fscanf(), fwprintf(), printf(), scanf(), sscanf(), swprintf(), swscanf(), va_arg(), va_end(), va_list(), va_start(), vfprintf(), vprintf(), vsprintf(), vswprintf(), vwprintf(), wprintf(), and wscanf().

virtual

Keyword

The virtual keyword enables a program to declare virtual functions, which are important to the implementation of polymorphism in object-oriented programming (OOP). For example, the following class declares one of its functions as virtual:

```
class MyClass
{
protected:
    char str[256];
```

```
public:
    MyClass(char* s);
    ~MyClass();
    virtual void ShowString();
};
```

CROSS-REFERENCE
See also Polymorphism and Virtual Functions.

Virtual Functions

Concept

Virtual functions are the main tool used to implement polymorphism with classes. Polymorphism is an object-oriented programming (OOP) technique that enables a base class and a derived class to implement the same member function in different ways, even when calling that member function through a pointer to the base class. The following program demonstrates virtual functions and polymorphism. The program's output looks like this:

```
This is a test

***********************
* This is also a test *
***********************

Press any key to continue
```

Here is the program source code that produced the output:

```
#include "stdafx.h"
#include <iostream>

using namespace std;

////////////////////////////
// Base class declaration.
////////////////////////////
class MyClass
{
protected:
    char str[256];

public:
```

u
v
w

```
    MyClass(char* s);
    ~MyClass();
    virtual void ShowString();
};

/////////////////////////////
// Base class definition.
/////////////////////////////
MyClass::MyClass(char* s)
{
    strcpy(str, s);
}

MyClass::~MyClass()
{
}

void MyClass::ShowString()
{
    cout << str << endl;
}

/////////////////////////////
// Derived class declaration.
/////////////////////////////
class MyDerivedClass : public MyClass
{
public:
    MyDerivedClass(char* s);
    ~MyDerivedClass();
    virtual void ShowString();
};

/////////////////////////////
// Derived class definition.
/////////////////////////////
MyDerivedClass::MyDerivedClass(char* s) : MyClass(s)
{
}

MyDerivedClass::~MyDerivedClass()
{
}
```

```
void MyDerivedClass::ShowString()
{
    int x;

    int len = strlen(str);
    for (x=0; x<len+4; ++x)
        cout << "*";
    cout << endl;
    cout << "* " << str << " *" << endl;
    for (x=0; x<len+4; ++x)
        cout << "*";
    cout << endl << endl;
}

/////////////////////////////
// Main program.
/////////////////////////////
int main(int argc, char* argv[])
{
    MyClass* myClass = new MyClass("This is a test");
    myClass->ShowString();
    cout << endl;
    MyClass* myDerivedClass =
        new MyDerivedClass("This is also a test");
    myDerivedClass->ShowString();

    return 0;
}
```

In this program, the class MyDerivedClass is derived from the base class MyClass. MyClass uses its ShowString() member function to display a single line of text. The MyDerivedClass class has its own version of the virtual ShowString() function. This version displays its string within a box of asterisks. One useful thing about derived classes is that you can use a pointer to the base class to represent an object of a derived class. In main(), both myClass and myDerivedClass are pointers to an object of the MyClass class, even though one pointer represents a MyClass object and the other represents a MyDerivedClass object. Thanks to the virtual function ShowString(), however, calls to the ShowString() function through either pointer work just fine.

CROSS-REFERENCE

See also Creating a Class, Deriving a Class, and Polymorphism.

void

Keyword

There are three ways to use the void keyword. The first is to declare that a function returns no value, as shown in the following example:

```
void MyFunc(int num)
{
    // Do something here.
}
```

The second way that the void keyword can be used is to declare a function as receiving no parameters, as shown in this example:

```
int MyFunc(void)
{
    // Do something here.

    return result;
}
```

Finally, the void keyword can be used to declare a pointer that can point to any type of data. For example, the following line calls the calloc() function to allocate a block of memory. The calloc() function returns a pointer to void:

```
void* buf = calloc(1024, sizeof(char));
```

Before a void pointer can be used to access data, the pointer must be cast to a data type. For example, if you wanted to allocate a block of memory to hold a string, you might do this:

```
char* buf = (char*)calloc(1024, sizeof(char));
```

volatile

Keyword

The volatile keyword specifies to the compiler that a data object can be modified by processes external to the running program. Such an external process might be another thread, an interrupt, or the hardware. The following line declares an integer variable as volatile:

```
volatile int value;
```

vprintf()

Function

The `vprintf()` function writes formatted data to the `stdout` stream from a variable argument list, returning the number of bytes written, or a negative number in the case of an error.

Header File

```
#include <stdio.h>
```

Declaration

```
int vprintf(const char *format, va_list argptr);
```

- *argptr* — The argument list.
- *format* — A pointer to the format string, which can contain format specifiers from Table V-7.

Table V-7 Format Specifiers for vprintf()

Specifier	Description
%c	Specifies a character.
%C	Specifies a single-byte character or wide character.
%d	Specifies a signed decimal integer.
%e	Specifies a signed double-precision floating-point value using scientific notation with a lowercase e.
%E	Specifies a signed double-precision floating-point value using scientific notation with an uppercase E.
%f	Specifies a signed double-precision floating-point value.
%g	Specifies a signed double-precision floating-point value using either normal notation or scientific notation with a lowercase e.
%G	Specifies a signed double-precision floating-point value using either normal notation or scientific notation with an uppercase E.
%I	Specifies a signed decimal integer.
%n	Specifies an integer pointer.
%o	Specifies an unsigned octal integer.
%p	Specifies a void pointer.
%s	Specifies a string.
%S	Specifies a single-byte-character string or wide-character string.

Continued

Table V-7 *Continued*

%u	Specifies an unsigned decimal integer.
%x	Specifies an unsigned hexadecimal integer with lowercase letters.
%X	Specifies an unsigned hexadecimal integer with uppercase letters.

Example

The following program demonstrates how to use the vprintf() function. When run, the program writes a variable argument list that contains four values to stdout, displaying messages as it goes. The program's output looks like this:

```
Writing values to stream...
199.990000 — 99 — A — This is a test
Number of characters written: 39
Press any key to continue
```

Here is the program source code that produced the output:

```cpp
#include "stdafx.h"
#include <stdio.h>
#include <stdarg.h>
#include <iostream>

using namespace std;

int write_args(char *fmtStr, ...)
{
    va_list args;

    va_start(args, fmtStr);
    int result = vprintf(fmtStr, args);
    va_end(args);

    return(result);
}

int main(int argc, char* argv[])
{
    cout << "Writing values to stream..." << endl;
    int result = write_args("%f — %d — %c — %s",
        199.99, 99, 'A', "This is a test");
    if (result > 0)
    {
```

```
            cout << endl;
            cout << "Number of characters written: ";
            cout << result << endl;
        }
        else
            cout << "Write error." << endl;

        return 0;
    }
```

CROSS-REFERENCE
See also _vsnprintf(), _vsnwprintf(), _vsprintf(), cprintf(), cscanf(), fprintf(), fscanf(), fwprintf(), printf(), scanf(), sscanf(), swprintf(), swscanf(), va_arg(), va_end(), va_list, va_start(), vfprintf(), vfwprintf(), vsprintf(), vswprintf(), vwprintf(), wprintf(), and wscanf().

vsprintf()

Function

The vsprintf() function writes formatted data to a buffer from a variable argument list, returning the number of bytes written, or a negative number in the case of an error.

Header File

```
#include <stdio.h>
```

Declaration

```
int vsprintf(char *buffer,
    const char *format, va_list argptr);
```

- *argptr*—The argument list.
- *buffer*—A pointer to the buffer that will receive the formatted data.
- *format*—A pointer to the format string, which can contain format specifiers from Table V-8.

u
v
w

Table V-8 Format Specifiers for vsprintf()

Specifier	Description
%c	Specifies a character.
%C	Specifies a single-byte character or wide character.
%d	Specifies a signed decimal integer.
%e	Specifies a signed double-precision floating-point value using scientific notation with a lowercase e.
%E	Specifies a signed double-precision floating-point value using scientific notation with an uppercase E.
%f	Specifies a signed double-precision floating-point value.
%g	Specifies a signed double-precision floating-point value using either normal notation or scientific notation with a lowercase e.
%G	Specifies a signed double-precision floating-point value using either normal notation or scientific notation with an uppercase E.
%I	Specifies a signed decimal integer.
%n	Specifies an integer pointer.
%o	Specifies an unsigned octal integer.
%p	Specifies a void pointer.
%s	Specifies a string.
%S	Specifies a single-byte-character string or wide-character string.
%u	Specifies an unsigned decimal integer.
%x	Specifies an unsigned hexadecimal integer with lowercase letters.
%X	Specifies an unsigned hexadecimal integer with uppercase letters.

Example

The following program demonstrates how to use the vsprintf() function. When run, the program writes a variable argument list containing four values to a buffer, displaying messages as it goes. The program's output looks like this:

```
Writing values to buffer...
Number of characters written: 39
Contents of the buffer:
   199.990000 — 99 — A — This is a test
Press any key to continue
```

Here is the program source code that produced the output:

```
#include "stdafx.h"
#include <stdio.h>
#include <stdarg.h>
#include <iostream>
```

```
using namespace std;

int write_args(char* buf, char* fmtStr, ...)
{
    va_list args;

    va_start(args, fmtStr);
    int result = vsprintf(buf, fmtStr, args);
    va_end(args);

    return(result);
}

int main(int argc, char* argv[])
{
    char buf[81];

    cout << "Writing values to buffer..." << endl;
    int result = write_args(buf, "%f - %d - %c - %s",
        199.99, 99, 'A', "This is a test");
    if (result > 0)
    {
        cout << "Number of characters written: ";
        cout << result << endl;
        cout << "Contents of the buffer: " << endl;
        cout << "    " << buf << endl;
    }
    else
        cout << "Write error." << endl;

    return 0;
}
```

CROSS-REFERENCE

See also _vsnprintf(), _vsnwprintf(), _vsprintf(), cprintf(), cscanf(), fprintf(), fscanf(), fwprintf(), printf(), scanf(), sscanf(), swprintf(), swscanf(), va_arg(), va_end(), va_list, va_start(), vfprintf(), vfwprintf(), vprintf(), vswprintf(), vwprintf(), wprintf(), and wscanf().

u
v
w

vswprintf()

Function

The vswprintf() function writes formatted wide-character data to a buffer from a variable argument list, returning the number of bytes written, or a negative number in the case of an error.

Header File

```
#include <stdio.h>
```

Declaration

```
int vswprintf(wchar_t *buffer,
    const wchar_t *format, va_list argptr);
```

- *argptr*—The argument list.
- *buffer*—A pointer to the buffer that will receive the formatted data.
- *format*—A pointer to the format string, which can contain format specifiers from Table V-9.

Table V-9 Format Specifiers for vswprintf()

Specifier	Description
%c	Specifies a character.
%C	Specifies a single-byte character or wide character.
%d	Specifies a signed decimal integer.
%e	Specifies a signed double-precision floating-point value using scientific notation with a lowercase e.
%E	Specifies a signed double-precision floating-point value using scientific notation with an uppercase E.
%f	Specifies a signed double-precision floating-point value.
%g	Specifies a signed double-precision floating-point value using either normal notation or scientific notation with a lowercase e.
%G	Specifies a signed double-precision floating-point value using either normal notation or scientific notation with an uppercase e.
%I	Specifies a signed decimal integer.
%n	Specifies an integer pointer.
%o	Specifies an unsigned octal integer.
%p	Specifies a void pointer.
%s	Specifies a string.

Specifier	Description
%S	Specifies a single-byte-character string or wide-character string.
%u	Specifies an unsigned decimal integer.
%x	Specifies an unsigned hexadecimal integer with lowercase letters.
%X	Specifies an unsigned hexadecimal integer with uppercase letters.

Example

The following program demonstrates how to use the vswprintf() function. When run, the program writes a variable argument list containing four values to a buffer, displaying messages as it goes. The program's output looks like this:

```
Writing values to buffer...
Number of characters written: 39
Contents of the buffer:
   199.990000 - 99 - A - This is a test
Press any key to continue
```

Here is the program source code that produced the output:

```
#include "stdafx.h"
#include <stdio.h>
#include <stdarg.h>
#include <iostream>

using namespace std;

int write_args(wchar_t* buf, wchar_t* fmtStr, ...)
{
    va_list args;

    va_start(args, fmtStr);
    int result = vswprintf(buf, fmtStr, args);
    va_end(args);

    return(result);
}

int main(int argc, char* argv[])
{
    wchar_t buf[81];

    cout << "Writing values to buffer..." << endl;
```

```
int result = write_args(buf, L"%f — %d — %c — %s",
    199.99, 99, 'A', L"This is a test");
if (result > 0)
{
    cout << "Number of characters written: ";
    cout << result << endl;
    cout << "Contents of the buffer: " << endl;
    cout << "    ";
    wcout << buf << endl;
}
else
    cout << "Write error." << endl;

return 0;
}
```

CROSS-REFERENCE

See also _vsnprintf(), _vsnwprintf(), _vsprintf(), cprintf(), cscanf(), fprintf(), fscanf(), fwprintf(), printf(), scanf(), sscanf(), swprintf(), swscanf(), va_arg(), va_end(), va_list, va_start(), vfprintf(), vfwprintf(), vprintf(), vsprintf(), vwprintf(), wprintf(), and wscanf().

vwprintf()

Function

The vwprintf() function writes formatted wide-character data to the stdout stream from a variable argument list, returning the number of bytes written, or a negative number in the case of an error.

Header File

```
#include <stdio.h>
```

Declaration

```
int vwprintf(const wchar_t *format, va_list argptr);
```

- *argptr*—The argument list.
- *format*—A pointer to the format string, which can contain format specifiers from Table V-10.

Table V-10 Format Specifiers for vwprintf()

Specifier	Description
%c	Specifies a character.
%C	Specifies a single-byte character or wide character.
%d	Specifies a signed decimal integer.
%e	Specifies a signed double-precision floating-point value using scientific notation with a lowercase e.
%E	Specifies a signed double-precision floating-point value using scientific notation with an uppercase E.
%f	Specifies a signed double-precision floating-point value.
%g	Specifies a signed double-precision floating-point value using either normal notation or scientific notation with a lowercase e.
%G	Specifies a signed double-precision floating-point value using either normal notation or scientific notation with an uppercase E.
%i	Specifies a signed decimal integer.
%n	Specifies an integer pointer.
%o	Specifies an unsigned octal integer.
%p	Specifies a void pointer.
%s	Specifies a string.
%S	Specifies a single-byte-character string or wide-character string.
%u	Specifies an unsigned decimal integer.
%x	Specifies an unsigned hexadecimal integer with lowercase letters.
%X	Specifies an unsigned hexadecimal integer with uppercase letters.

Example

The following program demonstrates how to use the vwprintf() function. When run, the program writes a variable argument list containing four values to stdout, displaying messages as it goes. The program's output looks like this:

```
Writing values to stream...
199.990000 — 99 — A — This is a test
Number of characters written: 39
Press any key to continue
```

Here is the program source code that produced the output:

```
#include "stdafx.h"
#include <stdio.h>
#include <stdarg.h>
#include <iostream>

using namespace std;
```

```
int write_args(wchar_t *fmtStr, ...)
{
   va_list args;

   va_start(args, fmtStr);
   int result = vwprintf(fmtStr, args);
   va_end(args);

   return(result);
}

int main(int argc, char* argv[])
{
    cout << "Writing values to stream..." << endl;
    int result = write_args(L"%f - %d - %c - %s",
        199.99, 99, 'A', L"This is a test");
    if (result > 0)
    {
        cout << endl;
        cout << "Number of characters written: ";
        cout << result << endl;
    }
    else
        cout << "Write error." << endl;

    return 0;
}
```

CROSS-REFERENCE

See also _vsnprintf(), _vsnwprintf(), _vsprintf(), cprintf(), cscanf(), fprintf(), fscanf(), fwprintf(), printf(), scanf(), sscanf(), swprintf(), swscanf(), va_arg(), va_end(), va_list, va_start(), vfprintf(), vfwprintf(), vprintf(), vsprintf(), vswprintf(), wprintf(), and wscanf().

_waccess()

Function

The _waccess() function is the wide-character version of the access() function and returns information about the accessibility of a file. The function returns 0 if the access checked for is valid, or –1 if it is not.

NOTE
This function works only on systems, such as Windows NT, that support wide-character filenames.

Header File

```
#include <io.h>
```

Declaration

```
int _waccess(const wchar_t* fileName, int access)
```

- *access* — The type of access for which to check. Can be 0 (existence), 2 (write), 4 (read), 6 (read and write).
- *fileName* — The path to the file to check.

Example

The following program demonstrates how to use the _waccess() function. The program's output looks like this:

```
The file exists.
The file can be written to.
Press any key to continue
```

Here is the program source code that produced the output:

```
#include "stdafx.h"
```

```
#include <io.h>
#include <iostream>

using namespace std;

int main(int argc, char* argv[])
{
    int result = _waccess(L"access.cpp", 0);
    if (result != -1)
    {
        cout << "The file exists." << endl;
        result = access("access.cpp", 2);
        if (result != -1)
            cout << "The file can be written to." << endl;
        else
            cout << "The file cannot be written to." << endl;
    }
    else
        cout << "The file does not exist." << endl;

    return 0;
}
```

CROSS-REFERENCE
See also _chmod(), _wchmod(), and access().

_wasctime()

Function

The _wasctime() function is the wide-character version of the asctime() function and converts the contents of a tm structure (which holds time and date information) to a string, returning a pointer to the string.

Header File

```
#include <time.h>
```

Declaration

```
wchar_t* _wasctime(const strict tm* pTm)
```

- *pTm*—A pointer to the tm structure that contains the time and date data to be converted to a string.

Example

The following program demonstrates how to use the _wasctime() function. The program initializes a tm structure, converts the structure to a string, and then displays the result. The program's output looks like this:

```
Thu Jan 21 05:17:00 1999

Press any key to continue
```

Here is the program source code that produced the output:

```
#include "stdafx.h"
#include <iostream>
#include <time.h>

using namespace std;

int main(int argc, char* argv[])
{
    struct tm tmTime;

    tmTime.tm_mday   = 21;
    tmTime.tm_mon    = 0;
    tmTime.tm_year   = 99;
    tmTime.tm_wday   = 4;
    tmTime.tm_yday   = 0;
    tmTime.tm_isdst  = 0;
    tmTime.tm_sec    = 0;
    tmTime.tm_min    = 17;
    tmTime.tm_hour   = 5;

    wchar_t* str = _wasctime(&tmTime);
    wcout << str << endl;

    return 0;
}
```

CROSS-REFERENCE

See also _ftime(), _futime(), _strdate(), _strtime(), _utime(), _wctime(), _wstrtime(), _wutime(), asctime(), ctime(), difftime(), gmtime(), localtime(), mktime(), strftime(), time(), and wcsftime().

_wchdir()

Function

The _wchdir() function is the wide-character version of the chdir() function and changes the current directory. If the function is successful, it returns 0; otherwise, it returns –1.

 NOTE
This function works only on systems, such as Windows NT, that support wide-character filenames.

Header File

```
#include <direct.h>
```

Declaration

```
int _wchdir(const wchar_t* dir)
```

- *dir* — The path of the new current directory.

Example

The following program demonstrates how to use the _wchdir() function by changing the current directory to C:\Windows. The program's output looks like this:

```
Current directory is now c:\Windows
Press any key to continue
```

Here is the program source code that produced the output:

```
#include "stdafx.h"
#include <direct.h>
#include <iostream>

using namespace std;

int main(int argc, char* argv[])
{
    int result = _wchdir(L"c:\\Windows");
    if (result != -1)
    {
        cout << "Current directory is now c:\\Windows";
```

```
            cout << endl;
        }
        else
            cout << "Directory doesn't exist" << endl;

        return 0;
    }
```

CROSS-REFERENCE
See also _chdrive(), _getcwd(), _getdcwd(), _getdrive(), _mkdir(), _rmdir(), _searchenv(), _wgetcwd(), _wgetdcwd(), _wmkdir(), _wrmdir(), and _wsearchenv().

_wchmod()

Function

The _wchmod() function changes the access permission of a specified file, whose name must be specified as a wide-character string. The function returns 0 if the function call is successful, or −1 if unsuccessful.

NOTE
This function works only on systems, such as Windows NT, that support wide-character filenames.

Header File

```
#include <io.h>
#include <sys\stat.h>
```

Declaration

```
int _wchmod(const wchar_t* fileName, int pMode);
```

- *fileName*— The name of the file whose access permission is to be changed.
- *pMode*— The access to which to set the file. Can be S_IREAD and/or S_IWRITE, both of which are defined in the stat.h header.

V
W
X

Example

The following program demonstrates how to use the _wchmod() function. When run, the program changes the access permission on the wchmod.cpp file to allow both reading and writing. The program's output looks like this:

```
File permission changed.
Press any key to continue
```

Here is the program source code that produced the output:

```cpp
#include "stdafx.h"
#include <iostream>
#include <io.h>
#include <sys\stat.h>

using namespace std;

int main(int argc, char* argv[])
{
    wchar_t* fileName = {L"wchmod.cpp"};

    int result = _wchmod(fileName, S_IWRITE);
    if (result == 0)
        cout << "File permission changed." << endl;
    else
        cout << "File not found." << endl;

    return 0;
}
```

CROSS-REFERENCE
See also _chmod().

_wcreat()

Function

The _wcreat() function creates a file, returning the file's handle if successful, or –1 if unsuccessful. Unlike the _creat() function, _wcreat() requires a wide-character format filename.

NOTE

This function works only on systems, such as Windows NT, that support wide-character filenames.

Header File

```
#include <io.h>
#include <sys\stat.h>
```

Declaration

```
int _wcreat(const wchar_t* fileName, int mode);
```

- *fileName* — The name of the file to create.
- *mode* — A value that specifies the file-creation mode. This can be one or both of S_IREAD and S_IWRITE, which are defined in the stat.h header file.

Example

The following program demonstrates how to use the _wcreat() function. When run, the program creates a file in read-and-write mode and then closes a file, displaying appropriate messages as it goes. The program's output looks like this:

```
File permission changed.
Press any key to continue
```

Here is the program source code that produced the output:

```
#include "stdafx.h"
#include <fcntl.h>
#include <sys\stat.h>
#include <io.h>
#include <iostream>

using namespace std;

int main(int argc, char* argv[])
{
    int fileHandle = _wcreat(L"test.dat", S_IREAD | S_IWRITE);

    if (fileHandle != -1)
    {
```

V

W

X

```
                cout << "File created successfully." << endl;
                _close(fileHandle);
            }
            else
                cout << "File create error." << endl;

            return 0;
        }
```

CROSS-REFERENCE

See also _close(), _creat(), _fcloseall(), _fdopen(), _fgetchar(), _fgetwchar(), _fileno(), _flushall(), _fputwchar(), _fsopen(), _getw(), _getws(), _lseeki64(), _open(), _putw(), _putws(), _read(), _rmtmp(), _tempnam(), _wfdopen(), _wfopen(), _wfreopen(), _wfsopen(), _wopen(), _wtempnam(), _wtmpnam(), clearerr(), eof(), fclose(), feof(), ferror(), fflush(), fgetc(), fgetpos(), fgets(), fgetwc(), fgetws(), fopen(), fprintf(), fputc(), fputchar(), fputs(), fputwc(), fputws(), fread(), freopen(), fscanf(), fseek(), fsetpos(), ftell(), fwprintf(), fwrite(), fwscanf(), getc(), getchar(), gets(), getwc(), getwchar(), lseek(), putc(), putch(), putchar(), puts(), putwc(), putwchar(), rewind(), setbuf(), setvbuf(), tmpfile(), tmpnam(), ungetc(), ungetch(), ungetwc(), and write().

_wcsdec()

Function

The _wcsdec() function returns a pointer to the previous character in a wide-character string, or NULL if the previous character cannot be determined.

Header File

```
#include <tchar.h>
```

Declaration

```
wchar_t* _wcsdec(const wchar_t *start,
    const wchar_t *current);
```

- *current*—A pointer to the character for which to return the previous character.
- *start*—A pointer to the start of the string.

Example

The following program demonstrates how to use the _wcsdec() function. When run, the program locates the character that precedes the fifth character in a wide-character string and displays the result. The program's output looks like this:

```
Source String = This is a test
Result = s is a test
Press any key to continue
```

Here is the program source code that produced the output. (To access the _wcsdec() function, you must define the _UNICODE symbol.)

```
#include "stdafx.h"
#include <iostream>
#define _UNICODE
#include <tchar.h>

using namespace std;

int main(int argc, char* argv[])
{
    wchar_t* srcStr = {L"This is a test"};

    wchar_t* result = _wcsdec(srcStr, &srcStr[4]);
    cout << "Source String = ";
    wcout << srcStr << endl;
    cout << "Result = ";
    wcout << result << endl;

    return 0;
}
```

CROSS-REFERENCE

See also _mbscat(), _mbschr(), _mbscmp(), _mbscoll(), _mbscpy(), _mbscspn(), _mbsdec(), _mbsdup(), _mbsicmp(), _mbsicoll(), _mbsinc(), _mbslen(), _mbslwr(), _mbsnbcat(), _mbsnbcmp(), _mbsnbcnt(), _mbsnbcoll(), _mbsnbcpy(), _mbsnbicmp(), _mbsnbicoll(), _mbsnbset(), _mbsnccnt(), _mbsncmp(), _mbsncoll(), _mbsncpy(), _mbsnextc(), _mbsnicmp(), _mbsnicoll(), _mbsninc(), _mbsnset(), _mbspbrk(), _mbsrchr(), _mbsrev(), _mbsset(), _mbsspn(), _mbsspnp(), _mbsstr(), _mbstok(), _mbstrlen(), _mbsupr(), _wcsdup(), _wcsicmp(), _wcsicoll(), _wcsinc(), _wcslwr(), _wcsncnt(), _wcsncoll(), _wcsnextc(), _wcsnicmp(), _wcsnicoll(), _wcsninc(), _wcsnset(), _wcsrev(), _wcsset(), _wcsspnp(), _wcsupr(), strcat(), strchr(), strcmp(), strcoll(), strcpy(), strcspn(), strlen(), strncmp(), strncpy(), strpbrk(), strrchr(), strspn(), strstr(), strtod(), strtok(), strtol(), strtoul(), strxfrm(), wcscat(), wcschr(), wcscmp(), wcscoll(), wcscpy(), wcscspn(), wcslen(), wcsncmp(), wcsncpy(), wcspbrk(), wcsrchr(), wcsspn(), wcsstr(), wcstod(), wcstok(), wcstol(), wcstoul(), and wcsxfrm().

_wcsdup()

Function

The _wcsdup() function duplicates a wide-character string, returning a pointer to the new string.

Header File

```
#include <string.h>
```

Declaration

```
wchar_t* _wcsdup(const wchar_t *strSource);
```

- *strSource*—A pointer to the source string.

Example

The following program demonstrates how to use the _wcsdup() function. When run, the program duplicates the given string and displays the result. The program's output looks like this:

```
Source string = This is a test
New string = This is a test
Press any key to continue
```

Here is the program source code that produced the output:

```
#include "stdafx.h"
#include <iostream>
#include <string.h>

using namespace std;

int main(int argc, char* argv[])
{
    wchar_t* srcStr = {L"This is a test"};

    wchar_t* destStr = _wcsdup(srcStr);
```

```
        cout << "Source string = ";
        wcout << srcStr << endl;
        cout << "New string = ";
        wcout << destStr << endl;

        return 0;
    }
```

CROSS-REFERENCE

See also _mbscat(), _mbschr(), _mbscmp(), _mbscoll(), _mbscpy(), _mbscspn(), _mbsdec(), _mbsdup(), _mbsicmp(), _mbsicoll(), _mbsinc(), _mbslen(), _mbslwr(), _mbsnbcat(), _mbsnbcmp(), _mbsnbcnt(), _mbsnbcoll(), _mbsnbcpy(), _mbsnbicmp(), _mbsnbicoll(), _mbsnbset(), _mbsnccnt(), _mbsncmp(), _mbsncoll(), _mbsncpy(), _mbsnextc(), _mbsnicmp(), _mbsnicoll(), _mbsninc(), _mbsnset(), _mbspbrk(), _mbsrchr(), _mbsrev(), _mbsset(), _mbsspn(), _mbsspnp(), _mbsstr(), _mbstok(), _mbstrlen(), _mbsupr(), _wcsdec(), _wcsicmp(), _wcsicoll(), _wcsinc(), _wcslwr(), _wcsncnt(), _wcsncoll(), _wcsnextc(), _wcsnicmp(), _wcsnicoll(), _wcsninc(), _wcsnset(), _wcsrev(), _wcsset(), _wcsspnp(), _wcsupr(), strcat(), strchr(), strcmp(), strcoll(), strcpy(), strcspn(), strlen(), strncmp(), strncpy(), strpbrk(), strrchr(), strspn(), strstr(), strtod(), strtok(), strtol(), strtoul(), strxfrm(), wcscat(), wcschr(), wcscmp(), wcscoll(), wcscpy(), wcscspn(), wcslen(), wcsncmp(), wcsncpy(), wcspbrk(), wcsrchr(), wcsspn(), wcsstr(), wcstod(), wcstok(), wcstol(), wcstoul(), and wcsxfrm().

_wcsicmp()

Function

The _wcsicmp() function compares two wide-character strings without regard for case (case–insensitive compare), returning a value from Table W-1.

Table W-1 Return Values for _wcsicmp()

Value	Description
Less than 0	string1 is alphabetically less than string2.
0	The two strings are equal.
Greater than 0	string1 is alphabetically greater than string2.

Header File

```
#include <string.h>
```

Declaration

```
int _wcsicmp(const wchar_t *string1, const wchar_t *string2);
```

- *string1* — The first string to compare.
- *string2* — The second string to compare.

Example

The following program demonstrates how to use the _wcsicmp() function. When run, the program compares several pairs of strings and displays the result of the comparisons. The program's output looks like this:

```
One Two Three equals one two three
one two three is greater than Four Five Six
Four Five Six is less than seven eight nine
Press any key to continue
```

Here is the program source code that produced the output:

```
#include "stdafx.h"
#include <iostream>
#include <string.h>

using namespace std;

void cmp(wchar_t* s1, wchar_t* s2)
{
    int result = _wcsicmp(s1, s2);
    if (result < 0 )
    {
        wcout << s1;
        cout << " is less than ";
        wcout << s2 << endl;
    }
    else if (result > 0)
    {
        wcout << s1;
```

```
        cout << " is greater than ";
        wcout << s2 << endl;
    }
    else
    {
        wcout << s1;
        cout << " equals ";
        wcout << s2 << endl;
    }
}

int main(int argc, char* argv[])
{
    wchar_t* str1 = {L"One Two Three"};
    wchar_t* str2 = {L"one two three"};
    wchar_t* str3 = {L"Four Five Six"};
    wchar_t* str4 = {L"seven eight nine"};

    cmp(str1, str2);
    cmp(str2, str3);
    cmp(str3, str4);

    return 0;
}
```

CROSS-REFERENCE

See also _mbscat(), _mbschr(), _mbscmp(), _mbscoll(), _mbscpy(), _mbscspn(), _mbsdec(), _mbsdup(), _mbsicmp(), _mbsicoll(), _mbsinc(), _mbslen(), _mbslwr(), _mbsnbcat(), _mbsnbcmp(), _mbsnbcnt(), _mbsnbcoll(), _mbsnbcpy(), _mbsnbicmp(), _mbsnbicoll(), _mbsnbset(), _mbsnccnt(), _mbsncmp(), _mbsncoll(), _mbsncpy(), _mbsnextc(), _mbsnicmp(), _mbsnicoll(), _mbsninc(), _mbsnset(), _mbspbrk(), _mbsrchr(), _mbsrev(), _mbsset(), _mbsspn(), _mbsspnp(), _mbsstr(), _mbstok(), _mbstrlen(), _mbsupr(), _wcsdec(), _wcsdup(), _wcsicoll(), _wcsinc(), _wcslwr(), _wcsncnt(), _wcsncoll(), _wcsnextc(), _wcsnicmp(), _wcsnicoll(), _wcsninc(), _wcsnset(), _wcsrev(), _wcsset(), _wcsspnp(), _wcsupr(), strcat(), strchr(), strcmp(), strcoll(), strcpy(), strcspn(), strlen(), strncmp(), strncpy(), strpbrk(), strrchr(), strspn(), strstr(), strtod(), strtok(), strtol(), strtoul(), strxfrm(), wcscat(), wcschr(), wcscmp(), wcscoll(), wcscpy(), wcscspn(), wcslen(), wcsncmp(), wcsncpy(), wcspbrk(), wcsrchr(), wcsspn(), wcsstr(), wcstod(), wcstok(), wcstol(), wcstoul(), and wcsxfrm().

v
w
x

_wcsicoll()

Function

The _wcsicoll() function compares two wide-character strings for the current locale without regard for case (case–insensitive compare), returning a value from Table W-2.

Table W-2 Return Values for _wcsicoll()

Value	Description
Less than 0	string1 is alphabetically less than string2.
0	The two strings are equal.
Greater than 0	string1 is alphabetically greater than string2.

Header File

```
#include <string.h>
```

Declaration

```
int _wcsicoll(const wchar_t *string1, const wchar_t *string2);
```

- *string1* — The first string to compare.
- *string2* — The second string to compare.

Example

The following program demonstrates how to use the _wcsicoll() function. When run, the program compares several pairs of strings and displays the result of the comparisons. The program's output looks like this:

```
One Two Three equals one two three
One Two Three is greater than Four Five Six
Four Five Six is less than seven eight nine
Press any key to continue
```

Here is the program source code that produced the output:

```
#include "stdafx.h"
#include <iostream>
#include <string.h>
```

```cpp
using namespace std;

void cmp(wchar_t* s1, wchar_t* s2)
{
    int result = _wcsicoll(s1, s2);
    if (result < 0 )
    {
        wcout << s1;
        cout << " is less than ";
        wcout << s2 << endl;
    }
    else if (result > 0)
    {
        wcout << s1;
        cout << " is greater than ";
        wcout << s2 << endl;
    }
    else
    {
        wcout << s1;
        cout << " equals ";
        wcout << s2 << endl;
    }
}

int main(int argc, char* argv[])
{
    wchar_t* str1 = L"One Two Three";
    wchar_t* str2 = L"one two three";
    wchar_t* str3 = L"Four Five Six";
    wchar_t* str4 = L"seven eight nine";

    cmp(str1, str2);
    cmp(str2, str3);
    cmp(str3, str4);

    return 0;
}
```

CROSS-REFERENCE

See also _mbscat(), _mbschr(), _mbscmp(), _mbscoll(), _mbscpy(), _mbscspn(), _mbsdec(), _mbsdup(), _mbsicmp(), _mbsicoll(), _mbsinc(), _mbslen(), _mbslwr(), _mbsnbcat(), _mbsnbcmp(), _mbsnbcnt(), _mbsnbcoll(), _mbsnbcpy(), _mbsnbicmp(), _mbsnbicoll(), _mbsnbset(), _mbsnccnt(), _mbsncmp(), _mbsncoll(), _mbsncpy(), _mbsnextc(), _mbsnicmp(), _mbsnicoll(), _mbsninc(), _mbsnset(), _mbspbrk(), _mbsrchr(), _mbsrev(), _mbsset(), _mbsspn(), _mbsspnp(), _mbsstr(), _mbstok(), _mbstrlen(), _mbsupr(), _wcsdec(), _wcsdup(), _wcsicmp(), _wcsinc(), _wcslwr(), _wcsncnt(), _wcsncoll(), _wcsnextc(), _wcsnicmp(), _wcsnicoll(), _wcsninc(), _wcsnset(), _wcsrev(), _wcsset(), _wcsspnp(), _wcsupr(), strcat(), strchr(), strcmp(), strcoll(), strcpy(), strcspn(), strlen(), strncmp(), strncpy(), strpbrk(), strrchr(), strspn(), strstr(), strtod(), strtok(), strtol(), strtoul(), strxfrm(), wcscat(), wcschr(), wcscmp(), wcscoll(), wcscpy(), wcscspn(), wcslen(), wcsncmp(), wcsncpy(), wcspbrk(), wcsrchr(), wcsspn(), wcsstr(), wcstod(), wcstok(), wcstol(), wcstoul(), and wcsxfrm().

_wcsinc()

Function

The _wcsinc() function returns a pointer to the next character in a wide-character string, or NULL if the next character cannot be determined.

Header File

```
#include <tchar.h>
```

Declaration

```
wchar_t* _wcsinc(const wchar_t *current);
```

- *current*—A pointer to the character for which to return the next character.

Example

The following program demonstrates how to use the _wcsinc() function. When run, the program locates the character that follows the fifth character in a wide-character string and displays the result. The program's output looks like this:

```
Source String = This is a test
Result = is a test
Press any key to continue
```

Here is the program source code that produced the output. (To access the _wcsinc() function, you must define the _UNICODE symbol.)

```
#include "stdafx.h"
#include <iostream>
#define _UNICODE
#include <tchar.h>

using namespace std;

int main(int argc, char* argv[])
{
    wchar_t* srcStr = {L"This is a test"};

    wchar_t* result = _wcsinc(&srcStr[4]);
    cout << "Source String = ";
    wcout << srcStr << endl;
    cout << "Result = ";
    wcout << result << endl;

    return 0;
}
```

CROSS-REFERENCE
See also _mbscat(), _mbschr(), _mbscmp(), _mbscoll(), _mbscpy(), _mbscspn(), _mbsdec(), _mbsdup(), _mbsicmp(), _mbsicoll(), _mbsinc(), _mbslen(), _mbslwr(), _mbsnbcat(), _mbsnbcmp(), _mbsnbcnt(), _mbsnbcoll(), _mbsnbcpy(), _mbsnbicmp(), _mbsnbicoll(), _mbsnbset(), _mbsnccnt(), _mbsncmp(), _mbsncoll(), _mbsncpy(), _mbsnextc(), _mbsnicmp(), _mbsnicoll(), _mbsninc(), _mbsnset(), _mbspbrk(), _mbsrchr(), _mbsrev(), _mbsset(), _mbsspn(), _mbsspnp(), _mbsstr(), _mbstok(), _mbstrlen(), _mbsupr(), _wcsdec(), _wcsdup(), _wcsicmp(), _wcsicoll(), _wcslwr(), _wcsncnt(), _wcsncoll(), _wcsnextc(), _wcsnicmp(), _wcsnicoll(), _wcsninc(), _wcsnset(), _wcsrev(), _wcsset(), _wcsspnp(), _wcsupr(), strcat(), strchr(), strcmp(), strcoll(), strcpy(), strcspn(), strlen(), strncmp(), strncpy(), strpbrk(), strrchr(), strspn(), strstr(), strtod(), strtok(), strtol(), strtoul(), strxfrm(), wcscat(), wcschr(), wcscmp(), wcscoll(), wcscpy(), wcscspn(), wcslen(), wcsncmp(), wcsncpy(), wcspbrk(), wcsrchr(), wcsspn(), wcsstr(), wcstod(), wcstok(), wcstol(), wcstoul(), and wcsxfrm().

V
W
X

_wcslwr()

Function

The _wcslwr() function converts a wide-character string to lowercase, return-ing a pointer to the new string.

Header File

```
#include <string.h>
```

Declaration

```
wchar_t* _wcslwr(const wchar_t *string);
```

- *string* — The string to convert.

Example

The following program demonstrates how to use the _wcslwr() function. When run, the program converts several strings to lowercase and displays the results. The program's output looks like this:

```
Original String: One Two Three
Converted String: one two three

Original String: FOUR FIVE SIX
Converted String: four five six

Original String: seven eight nine
Converted String: seven eight nine

Press any key to continue
```

Here is the program source code that produced the output:

```
#include "stdafx.h"
#include <iostream>
#include <string.h>

using namespace std;
```

```
void convert(wchar_t* s)
{
    cout << "Original String: ";
    wcout << s << endl;
    wchar_t* result = _wcslwr(s);
    cout << "Converted String: ";
    wcout << result << endl << endl;
}

int main(int argc, char* argv[])
{
    wchar_t str1[81];
    wcscpy(str1, L"One Two Three");
    wchar_t str2[81];
    wcscpy(str2, L"FOUR FIVE SIX");
    wchar_t str3[81];
    wcscpy(str3, L"seven eight nine");

    convert(str1);
    convert(str2);
    convert(str3);

    return 0;
}
```

CROSS-REFERENCE

See also _mbscat(), _mbschr(), _mbscmp(), _mbscoll(), _mbscpy(), _mbscspn(), _mbsdec(), _mbsdup(), _mbsicmp(), _mbsicoll(), _mbsinc(), _mbslen(), _mbslwr(), _mbsnbcat(), _mbsnbcmp(), _mbsnbcnt(), _mbsnbcoll(), _mbsnbcpy(), _mbsnbicmp(), _mbsnbicoll(), _mbsnbset(), _mbsnccnt(), _mbsncmp(), _mbsncoll(), _mbsncpy(), _mbsnextc(), _mbsnicmp(), _mbsnicoll(), _mbsninc(), _mbsnset(), _mbspbrk(), _mbsrchr(), _mbsrev(), _mbsset(), _mbsspn(), _mbsspnp(), _mbsstr(), _mbstok(), _mbstrlen(), _mbsupr(), _wcsdec(), _wcsdup(), _wcsicmp(), _wcsicoll(), _wcsinc(), _wcsncnt(), _wcsncoll(), _wcsnextc(), _wcsnicmp(), _wcsnicoll(), _wcsninc(), _wcsnset(), _wcsrev(), _wcsset(), _wcsspnp(), _wcsupr(), strcat(), strchr(), strcmp(), strcoll(), strcpy(), strcspn(), strlen(), strncmp(), strncpy(), strpbrk(), strrchr(), strspn(), strstr(), strtod(), strtok(), strtol(), strtoul(), strxfrm(), wcscat(), wcschr(), wcscmp(), wcscoll(), wcscpy(), wcscspn(), wcslen(), wcsncmp(), wcsncpy(), wcspbrk(), wcsrchr(), wcsspn(), wcsstr(), wcstod(), wcstok(), wcstol(), wcstoul(), and wcsxfrm().

V
W
X

_wcsncnt()

Function

The _wcsncnt() function returns the number of characters in a portion of a wide-character string.

Header File

```
#include <tchar.h>
```

Declaration

```
size_t _wcsncnt(const wchar_t *string, size_t number);
```

- *number* — The number of characters to examine.
- *string* — A pointer to the string to examine.

Example

The following program demonstrates how to use the _wcsncnt() function. When run, the program determines the number of bytes in the first four characters of a wide-character string and displays the result. The program's output looks like this:

```
Source String = This is a test
Result = 4
Press any key to continue
```

Here is the program source code that produced the output. (To access the _wcsncnt() function, you must define the _UNICODE symbol.)

```
#include "stdafx.h"
#include <iostream>
#define _UNICODE
#include <tchar.h>

using namespace std;

int main(int argc, char* argv[])
{
    wchar_t* srcStr = {L"This is a test"};

    size_t result = _wcsncnt(srcStr, 4);
```

```
cout << "Source String = ";
wcout << srcStr << endl;
cout << "Result = " << result << endl;

return 0;
}
```

CROSS-REFERENCE

See also _mbscat(), _mbschr(), _mbscmp(), _mbscoll(), _mbscpy(), _mbscspn(), _mbsdec(), _mbsdup(), _mbsicmp(), _mbsicoll(), _mbsinc(), _mbslen(), _mbslwr(), _mbsnbcat(), _mbsnbcmp(), _mbsnbcnt(), _mbsnbcoll(), _mbsnbcpy(), _mbsnbicmp(), _mbsnbicoll(), _mbsnbset(), _mbsnccnt(), _mbsncmp(), _mbsncoll(), _mbsncpy(), _mbsnextc(), _mbsnicmp(), _mbsnicoll(), _mbsninc(), _mbsnset(), _mbspbrk(), _mbsrchr(), _mbsrev(), _mbsset(), _mbsspn(), _mbsspnp(), _mbsstr(), _mbstok(), _mbstrlen(), _mbsupr(), _wcsdec(), _wcsdup(), _wcsicmp(), _wcsicoll(), _wcsinc(), _wcslwr(), _wcsncoll(), _wcsnextc(), _wcsnicmp(), _wcsnicoll(), _wcsninc(), _wcsnset(), _wcsrev(), _wcsset(), _wcsspnp(), _wcsupr(), strcat(), strchr(), strcmp(), strcoll(), strcpy(), strcspn(), strlen(), strncmp(), strncpy(), strpbrk(), strrchr(), strspn(), strstr(), strtod(), strtok(), strtol(), strtoul(), strxfrm(), wcscat(), wcschr(), wcscmp(), wcscoll(), wcscpy(), wcscspn(), wcslen(), wcsncmp(), wcsncpy(), wcspbrk(), wcsrchr(), wcsspn(), wcsstr(), wcstod(), wcstok(), wcstol(), wcstoul(), and wcsxfrm().

_wcsncoll()

Function

The _wcsncoll() function compares two wide-character strings for the current locale, returning a value from Table W-3.

Table W-3 Return Values for _wcsncoll()

Value	Description
Less than 0	string1 is alphabetically less than string2.
0	The two strings are equal.
Greater than 0	string1 is alphabetically greater than string2.

Header File

```
#include <string.h>
```

Declaration

```
int _wcsncoll(const wchar_t *string1,
    const wchar_t *string2, size_t count);
```

- *count* — The number of characters to compare.
- *string1* — The first string to compare.
- *string2* — The second string to compare.

Example

The following program demonstrates how to use the _wcsncoll() function. When run, the program compares several pairs of strings and displays the result of the comparisons. The program's output looks like this:

```
One Two Three equals One Two three
One Two three is less than one Two Three
one Two Three is greater than SEVEN EIGHT nine
SEVEN EIGHT nine is less than seven eight nine
Press any key to continue
```

Here is the program source code that produced the output:

```
#include "stdafx.h"
#include <iostream>
#include <string.h>

using namespace std;

void cmp(wchar_t* s1, wchar_t* s2, size_t num)
{
    int result = _wcsncoll(s1, s2, num);
    if (result < 0 )
    {
        wcout << s1;
        cout << " is less than ";
        wcout << s2 << endl;
    }
    else if (result > 0)
    {
        wcout << s1;
```

```
            cout << " is greater than ";
            wcout << s2 << endl;
        }
        else
        {
            wcout << s1;
            cout << " equals ";
            wcout << s2 << endl;
        }
    }

    int main(int argc, char* argv[])
    {
        wchar_t* str1 = L"One Two Three";
        wchar_t* str2 = L"One Two three";
        wchar_t* str3 = L"one Two Three";
        wchar_t* str4 = L"SEVEN EIGHT nine";
        wchar_t* str5 = L"seven eight nine";

        cmp(str1, str2, 7);
        cmp(str2, str3, 7);
        cmp(str3, str4, 7);
        cmp(str4, str5, 7);

        return 0;
    }
```

CROSS-REFERENCE

See also _mbscat(), _mbschr(), _mbscmp(), _mbscoll(), _mbscpy(), _mbscspn(), _mbsdec(), _mbsdup(), _mbsicmp(), _mbsicoll(), _mbsinc(), _mbslen(), _mbslwr(), _mbsnbcat(), _mbsnbcmp(), _mbsnbcnt(), _mbsnbcoll(), _mbsnbcpy(), _mbsnbicmp(), _mbsnbicoll(), _mbsnbset(), _mbsnccnt(), _mbsncmp(), _mbsncoll(), _mbsncpy(), _mbsnextc(), _mbsnicmp(), _mbsnicoll(), _mbsninc(), _mbsnset(), _mbspbrk(), _mbsrchr(), _mbsrev(), _mbsset(), _mbsspn(), _mbsspnp(), _mbsstr(), _mbstok(), _mbstrlen(), _mbsupr(), _wcsdec(), _wcsdup(), _wcsicmp(), _wcsicoll(), _wcsinc(), _wcslwr(), _wcsncnt(), _wcsnextc(), _wcsnicmp(), _wcsnicoll(), _wcsninc(), _wcsnset(), _wcsrev(), _wcsset(), _wcsspnp(), _wcsupr(), strcat(), strchr(), strcmp(), strcoll(), strcpy(), strcspn(), strlen(), strncmp(), strncpy(), strpbrk(), strrchr(), strspn(), strstr(), strtod(), strtok(), strtol(), strtoul(), strxfrm(), wcscat(), wcschr(), wcscmp(), wcscoll(), wcscpy(), wcscspn(), wcslen(), wcsncmp(), wcsncpy(), wcspbrk(), wcsrchr(), wcsspn(), wcsstr(), wcstod(), wcstok(), wcstol(), wcstoul(), and wcsxfrm().

V
W
X

_wcsnextc()

Function

The _wcsnextc() function returns, as an integer, the value of the next character in a wide-character string.

Header File

```
#include <tchar.h>
```

Declaration

```
unsigned int _wcsnextc(const wchar_t *string);
```

- *string* — A pointer to the source string.

Example

The following program demonstrates how to use the _wcsnextc() function. When run, the program determines the integer value of the fifth character in a wide-character string and displays the result. The program's output looks like this:

```
Source String = This is a test
Result = 32
Press any key to continue
```

Here is the program source code that produced the output follows. (To access the _wcsinc() function, you must define the _UNICODE symbol.)

```
#include "stdafx.h"
#include <iostream>
#define _UNICODE
#include <tchar.h>

using namespace std;

int main(int argc, char* argv[])
{
    wchar_t* srcStr = {L"This is a test"};

    unsigned int result = _wcsnextc(&srcStr[4]);
    cout << "Source String = ";
    wcout << srcStr << endl;
```

```
        cout << "Result = " << result << endl;

        return 0;
}
```

CROSS-REFERENCE

See also _mbscat(), _mbschr(), _mbscmp(), _mbscoll(), _mbscpy(), _mbscspn(),
_mbsdec(), _mbsdup(), _mbsicmp(), _mbsicoll(), _mbsinc(), _mbslen(), _mbslwr(),
_mbsnbcat(),   _mbsnbcmp(),   _mbsnbcnt(),   _mbsnbcoll(),   _mbsnbcpy(),
_mbsnbicmp(),   _mbsnbicoll(),   _mbsnbset(),   _mbsnccnt(),   _mbsncmp(),
_mbsncoll(), _mbsncpy(), _mbsnextc(), _mbsnicmp(), _mbsnicoll(), _mbsninc(),
_mbsnset(),   _mbspbrk(),   _mbsrchr(),   _mbsrev(),   _mbsset(),   _mbsspn(),
_mbsspnp(), _mbsstr(), _mbstok(), _mbstrlen(), _mbsupr(), _wcsdec(), _wcsdup(),
_wcsicmp(), _wcsicoll(), _wcsinc(), _wcslwr(), _wcsncnt(), _wcsncoll(), _wcsnicmp(),
_wcsnicoll(), _wcsninc(), _wcsnset(), _wcsrev(), _wcsset(), _wcsspnp(), _wcsupr(),
strcat(), strchr(), strcmp(), strcoll(), strcpy(), strcspn(), strlen(), strncmp(), strncpy(),
strpbrk(), strrchr(), strspn(), strstr(), strtod(), strtok(), strtol(), strtoul(), strxfrm(),
wcscat(), wcschr(), wcscmp(), wcscoll(), wcscpy(), wcscspn(), wcslen(), wcsncmp(),
wcsncpy(), wcspbrk(), wcsrchr(), wcsspn(), wcsstr(), wcstod(), wcstok(), wcstol(),
wcstoul(), and wcsxfrm().

_wcsnicmp()

Function

The _wcsnicmp() function compares two wide-character strings without
regard for case (case–insensitive compare), returning a value from Table W-4.

Table W-4 Return Values for _wcsnicmp()

Value	Description
Less than 0	string1 is alphabetically less than string2.
0	The two strings are equal.
Greater than 0	string1 is alphabetically greater than string2.

Header File

```
#include <string.h>
```

Declaration

```
int _wcsnicmp(const wchar_t *string1,
    const wchar_t *string2, size_t count);
```

- *count* — The number of characters to compare.
- *string1* — The first string to compare.
- *string2* — The second string to compare.

Example

The following program demonstrates how to use the _wcsnicmp() function. When run, the program compares several pairs of strings and displays the result of the comparisons. The program's output looks like this:

```
One Two Three equals One Two three
One Two three equals one Two Three
one Two Three is less than SEVEN EIGHT nine
SEVEN EIGHT nine equals seven eight nine
Press any key to continue
```

Here is the program source code that produced the output:

```
#include "stdafx.h"
#include <iostream>
#include <string.h>

using namespace std;

void cmp(wchar_t* s1, wchar_t* s2, size_t num)
{
    int result = _wcsnicmp(s1, s2, num);
    if (result < 0 )
    {
        wcout << s1;
        cout << " is less than ";
        wcout << s2 << endl;
    }
    else if (result > 0)
    {
        wcout << s1;
        cout << " is greater than ";
```

```
            wcout << s2 << endl;
        }
        else
        {
            wcout << s1;
            cout << " equals ";
            wcout << s2 << endl;
        }
    }

    int main(int argc, char* argv[])
    {
        wchar_t* str1 = L"One Two Three";
        wchar_t* str2 = L"One Two three";
        wchar_t* str3 = L"one Two Three";
        wchar_t* str4 = L"SEVEN EIGHT nine";
        wchar_t* str5 = L"seven eight nine";

        cmp(str1, str2, 7);
        cmp(str2, str3, 7);
        cmp(str3, str4, 7);
        cmp(str4, str5, 7);

        return 0;
    }
```

CROSS-REFERENCE

See also _mbscat(), _mbschr(), _mbscmp(), _mbscoll(), _mbscpy(), _mbscspn(), _mbsdec(), _mbsdup(), _mbsicmp(), _mbsicoll(), _mbsinc(), _mbslen(), _mbslwr(), _mbsnbcat(), _mbsnbcmp(), _mbsnbcnt(), _mbsnbcoll(), _mbsnbcpy(), _mbsnbicmp(), _mbsnbicoll(), _mbsnbset(), _mbsnccnt(), _mbsncmp(), _mbsncoll(), _mbsncpy(), _mbsnextc(), _mbsnicmp(), _mbsnicoll(), _mbsninc(), _mbsnset(), _mbspbrk(), _mbsrchr(), _mbsrev(), _mbsset(), _mbsspn(), _mbsspnp(), _mbsstr(), _mbstok(), _mbstrlen(), _mbsupr(), _wcsdec(), _wcsdup(), _wcsicmp(), _wcsicoll(), _wcsinc(), _wcslwr(), _wcsncnt(), _wcsncoll(), _wcsnextc(), _wcsnicoll(), _wcsninc(), _wcsnset(), _wcsrev(), _wcsset(), _wcsspnp(), _wcsupr(), strcat(), strchr(), strcmp(), strcoll(), strcpy(), strcspn(), strlen(), strncmp(), strncpy(), strpbrk(), strrchr(), strspn(), strstr(), strtod(), strtok(), strtol(), strtoul(), strxfrm(), wcscat(), wcschr(), wcscmp(), wcscoll(), wcscpy(), wcscspn(), wcslen(), wcsncmp(), wcsncpy(), wcspbrk(), wcsrchr(), wcsspn(), wcsstr(), wcstod(), wcstok(), wcstol(), wcstoul(), and wcsxfrm().

V
W
X

_wcsnicoll()

Function

The _wcsnicoll() function compares two wide-character strings for the current locale without regard to case (case–insensitive compare), returning a value from Table W-5.

Table W-5 Return Values for _wcsnicoll()

Value	Description
Less than 0	string1 is alphabetically less than string2.
0	The two strings are equal.
Greater than 0	string1 is alphabetically greater than string2.

Header File

```
#include <string.h>
```

Declaration

```
int _wcsnicoll(const wchar_t *string1,
    const wchar_t *string2, size_t count);
```

- *count* — The number of characters to compare.
- *string1* — The first string to compare.
- *string2* — The second string to compare.

Example

The following program demonstrates how to use the _wcsnicoll() function. When run, the program compares several pairs of strings and displays the result of the comparisons. The program's output looks like this:

```
One Two Three equals One Two three
One Two three equals one Two Three
one Two Three is less than SEVEN EIGHT nine
SEVEN EIGHT nine equals seven eight nine
Press any key to continue
```

Here is the program source code that produced the output:

```
#include "stdafx.h"
#include <iostream>
#include <string.h>

using namespace std;

void cmp(wchar_t* s1, wchar_t* s2, size_t num)
{
    int result = _wcsnicoll(s1, s2, num);
    if (result < 0 )
    {
        wcout << s1;
        cout << " is less than ";
        wcout << s2 << endl;
    }
    else if (result > 0)
    {
        wcout << s1;
        cout << " is greater than ";
        wcout << s2 << endl;
    }
    else
    {
        wcout << s1;
        cout << " equals ";
        wcout << s2 << endl;
    }
}

int main(int argc, char* argv[])
{
    wchar_t* str1 = L"One Two Three";
    wchar_t* str2 = L"One Two three";
    wchar_t* str3 = L"one Two Three";
    wchar_t* str4 = L"SEVEN EIGHT nine";
    wchar_t* str5 = L"seven eight nine";

    cmp(str1, str2, 7);
    cmp(str2, str3, 7);
    cmp(str3, str4, 7);
    cmp(str4, str5, 7);

    return 0;
}
```

CROSS-REFERENCE

See also _mbscat(), _mbschr(), _mbscmp(), _mbscoll(), _mbscpy(), _mbscspn(), _mbsdec(), _mbsdup(), _mbsicmp(), _mbsicoll(), _mbsinc(), _mbslen(), _mbslwr(), _mbsnbcat(), _mbsnbcmp(), _mbsnbcnt(), _mbsnbcoll(), _mbsnbcpy(), _mbsnbicmp(), _mbsnbicoll(), _mbsnbset(), _mbsnccnt(), _mbsncmp(), _mbsncoll(), _mbsncpy(), _mbsnextc(), _mbsnicmp(), _mbsnicoll(), _mbsninc(), _mbsnset(), _mbspbrk(), _mbsrchr(), _mbsrev(), _mbsset(), _mbsspn(), _mbsspnp(), _mbsstr(), _mbstok(), _mbstrlen(), _mbsupr(), _wcsdec(), _wcsdup(), _wcsicmp(), _wcsicoll(), _wcsinc(), _wcslwr(), _wcsncnt(), _wcsncoll(), _wcsnextc(), _wcsnicmp(), _wcsninc(), _wcsnset(), _wcsrev(), _wcsset(), _wcsspnp(), _wcsupr(), strcat(), strchr(), strcmp(), strcoll(), strcpy(), strcspn(), strlen(), strncmp(), strncpy(), strpbrk(), strrchr(), strspn(), strstr(), strtod(), strtok(), strtol(), strtoul(), strxfrm(), wcscat(), wcschr(), wcscmp(), wcscoll(), wcscpy(), wcscspn(), wcslen(), wcsncmp(), wcsncpy(), wcspbrk(), wcsrchr(), wcsspn(), wcsstr(), wcstod(), wcstok(), wcstol(), wcstoul(), and wcsxfrm().

_wcsninc()

Function

The _wcsninc() function returns a pointer to the string that results from advancing the specified number of characters in the source string.

Header File

```
#include <tchar.h>
```

Declaration

```
wchar_t* _wcsninc(const wchar_t *string, size_t count);
```

- *count* — The number of characters to advance in the source string.
- *string* — A pointer to the source string.

Example

The following program demonstrates how to use the _wcsninc() function. When run, the program locates the fifth character in a wide-character string and displays the result. The program's output looks like this:

```
Source String = This is a test
Result = is a test
Press any key to continue
```

Here is the program source code that produced the output. (To access the _wcsninc() function, you must define the _UNICODE symbol.)

```
#include "stdafx.h"
#include <iostream>
#define _UNICODE
#include <tchar.h>

using namespace std;

int main(int argc, char* argv[])
{
    wchar_t* srcStr = {L"This is a test"};

    wchar_t* result = _wcsninc(srcStr, 5);
    cout << "Source String = ";
    wcout << srcStr << endl;
    cout << "Result = ";
    wcout << result << endl;

    return 0;
}
```

CROSS-REFERENCE

See also _mbscat(), _mbschr(), _mbscmp(), _mbscoll(), _mbscpy(), _mbscspn(), _mbsdec(), _mbsdup(), _mbsicmp(), _mbsicoll(), _mbsinc(), _mbslen(), _mbslwr(), _mbsnbcat(), _mbsnbcmp(), _mbsnbcnt(), _mbsnbcoll(), _mbsnbcpy(), _mbsnbicmp(), _mbsnbicoll(), _mbsnbset(), _mbsnccnt(), _mbsncmp(), _mbsncoll(), _mbsncpy(), _mbsnextc(), _mbsnicmp(), _mbsnicoll(), _mbsninc(), _mbsnset(), _mbspbrk(), _mbsrchr(), _mbsrev(), _mbsset(), _mbsspn(), _mbsspnp(), _mbsstr(), _mbstok(), _mbstrlen(), _mbsupr(), _wcsdec(), _wcsdup(), _wcsicmp(), _wcsicoll(), _wcsinc(), _wcslwr(), _wcsncnt(), _wcsncoll(), _wcsnextc(), _wcsnicmp(), _wcsnicoll(), _wcsnset(), _wcsrev(), _wcsset(), _wcsspnp(), _wcsupr(), strcat(), strchr(), strcmp(), strcoll(), strcpy(), strcspn(), strlen(), strncmp(), strncpy(), strpbrk(), strrchr(), strspn(), strstr(), strtod(), strtok(), strtol(), strtoul(), strxfrm(), wcscat(), wcschr(), wcscmp(), wcscoll(), wcscpy(), wcscspn(), wcslen(), wcsncmp(), wcsncpy(), wcspbrk(), wcsrchr(), wcsspn(), wcsstr(), wcstod(), wcstok(), wcstol(), wcstoul(), and wcsxfrm().

V

W

X

_wcsnset()

Function

The _wcsnset() function sets a portion of the contents of a wide-character string to a given character, returning a pointer to the new string.

Header File

```
#include <string.h>
```

Declaration

```
wchar_t* _wcsnset(const wchar_t *string,
    wchar_t c, size_t count);
```

- *c* — The character with which to fill the string.
- *count* — The number of characters to set.
- *string* — The string to set.

Example

The following program demonstrates how to use the _wcsnset() function. When run, the program sets several strings to question marks and displays the results. The program's output looks like this:

```
Original String: One Two Three
Converted String: ??? Two Three

Original String: FOUR FIVE SIX
Converted String: *******VE SIX

Original String: seven eight nine
Converted String: #################

Press any key to continue
```

Here is the program source code that produced the output:

```
#include "stdafx.h"
#include <iostream>xx
#include <string.h>

using namespace std;
```

```cpp
void convert(wchar_t* s, wchar_t c, size_t num)
{
    cout << "Original String: ";
    wcout << s << endl;
    wchar_t* result = _wcsnset(s, c, num);
    cout << "Converted String: ";
    wcout << result << endl << endl;
}

int main(int argc, char* argv[])
{
    wchar_t str1[81];
    wcscpy(str1, L"One Two Three");
    wchar_t str2[81];
    wcscpy(str2, L"FOUR FIVE SIX");
    wchar_t str3[81];
    wcscpy(str3, L"seven eight nine");

    convert(str1, '?', 3);
    convert(str2, '*', 7);
    convert(str3, '#', 16);

    return 0;
}
```

CROSS-REFERENCE

See also _mbscat(), _mbschr(), _mbscmp(), _mbscoll(), _mbscpy(), _mbscspn(), _mbsdec(), _mbsdup(), _mbsicmp(), _mbsicoll(), _mbsinc(), _mbslen(), _mbslwr(), _mbsnbcat(), _mbsnbcmp(), _mbsnbcnt(), _mbsnbcoll(), _mbsnbcpy(), _mbsnbicmp(), _mbsnbicoll(), _mbsnbset(), _mbsnccnt(), _mbsncmp(), _mbsncoll(), _mbsncpy(), _mbsnextc(), _mbsnicmp(), _mbsnicoll(), _mbsninc(), _mbsnset(), _mbspbrk(), _mbsrchr(), _mbsrev(), _mbsset(), _mbsspn(), _mbsspnp(), _mbsstr(), _mbstok(), _mbstrlen(), _mbsupr(), _wcsdec(), _wcsdup(), _wcsicmp(), _wcsicoll(), _wcsinc(), _wcslwr(), _wcsncnt(), _wcsncoll(), _wcsnextc(), _wcsnicmp(), _wcsnicoll(), _wcsninc(), _wcsrev(), _wcsset(), _wcsspnp(), _wcsupr(), strcat(), strchr(), strcmp(), strcoll(), strcpy(), strcspn(), strlen(), strncmp(), strncpy(), strpbrk(), strrchr(), strspn(), strstr(), strtod(), strtok(), strtol(), strtoul(), strxfrm(), wcscat(), wcschr(), wcscmp(), wcscoll(), wcscpy(), wcscspn(), wcslen(), wcsncmp(), wcsncpy(), wcspbrk(), wcsrchr(), wcsspn(), wcsstr(), wcstod(), wcstok(), wcstol(), wcstoul(), and wcsxfrm().

_wcsrev()

Function

The _wcsrev() function reverses the order of characters in a wide-character string, returning a pointer to the new string.

Header File

```
#include <string.h>
```

Declaration

```
wchar_t* _wcsrev(const wchar_t *string);
```

- *string* — The string to reverse.

Example

The following program demonstrates how to use the _wcsrev() function. When run, the program reverses several strings and displays the results. The program's output looks like this:

```
Original String: One Two Three
Converted String: eerhT owT enO

Original String: FOUR FIVE SIX
Converted String: XIS EVIF RUOF

Original String: seven eight nine
Converted String: enin thgie neves

Press any key to continue
```

Here is the program source code that produced the output:

```
#include "stdafx.h"
#include <iostream>
#include <string.h>

using namespace std;
```

```
void convert(wchar_t* s)
{
    cout << "Original String: ";
    wcout << s << endl;
    wchar_t* result = _wcsrev(s);
    cout << "Converted String: ";
    wcout << result << endl << endl;
}

int main(int argc, char* argv[])
{
    wchar_t str1[81];
    wcscpy(str1, L"One Two Three");
    wchar_t str2[81];
    wcscpy(str2, L"FOUR FIVE SIX");
    wchar_t str3[81];
    wcscpy(str3, L"seven eight nine");

    convert(str1);
    convert(str2);
    convert(str3);

    return 0;
}
```

CROSS-REFERENCE
See also _mbscat(), _mbschr(), _mbscmp(), _mbscoll(), _mbscpy(), _mbscspn(), _mbsdec(), _mbsdup(), _mbsicmp(), _mbsicoll(), _mbsinc(), _mbslen(), _mbslwr(), _mbsnbcat(), _mbsnbcmp(), _mbsnbcnt(), _mbsnbcoll(), _mbsnbcpy(), _mbsnbicmp(), _mbsnbicoll(), _mbsnbset(), _mbsnccnt(), _mbsncmp(), _mbsncoll(), _mbsncpy(), _mbsnextc(), _mbsnicmp(), _mbsnicoll(), _mbsninc(), _mbsnset(), _mbspbrk(), _mbsrchr(), _mbsrev(), _mbsset(), _mbsspn(), _mbsspnp(), _mbsstr(), _mbstok(), _mbstrlen(), _mbsupr(), _wcsdec(), _wcsdup(), _wcsicmp(), _wcsicoll(), _wcsinc(), _wcslwr(), _wcsncnt(), _wcsncoll(), _wcsnextc(), _wcsnicmp(), _wcsnicoll(), _wcsninc(), _wcsnset(), _wcsset(), _wcsspnp(), _wcsupr(), strcat(), strchr(), strcmp(), strcoll(), strcpy(), strcspn(), strlen(), strncmp(), strncpy(), strpbrk(), strrchr(), strspn(), strstr(), strtod(), strtok(), strtol(), strtoul(), strxfrm(), wcscat(), wcschr(), wcscmp(), wcscoll(), wcscpy(), wcscspn(), wcslen(), wcsncmp(), wcsncpy(), wcspbrk(), wcsrchr(), wcsspn(), wcsstr(), wcstod(), wcstok(), wcstol(), wcstoul(), and wcsxfrm().

V

W

X

_wcsset()

Function

The _wcsset() function sets the contents of a wide-character string to a specified character, returning a pointer to the new string.

Header File

```
#include <string.h>
```

Declaration

```
wchar_t* _wcsset(const wchar_t *string, wchar_t c);
```

- *c* — The character with which to fill the string.
- *string* — The string to set.

Example

The following program demonstrates how to use the _wcsset() function. When run, the program sets several strings to question marks and displays the results. The program's output looks like this:

```
Original String: One Two Three
Converted String: ????????????

Original String: FOUR FIVE SIX
Converted String: ?????????????

Original String: seven eight nine
Converted String: ??????????????????

Press any key to continue
```

Here is the program source code that produced the output:

```
#include "stdafx.h"
#include <iostream>
#include <string.h>

using namespace std;
```

```
void convert(wchar_t* s, wchar_t c)
{
    cout << "Original String: ";
    wcout << s << endl;
    wchar_t* result = _wcsset(s, c);
    cout << "Converted String: ";
    wcout << result << endl << endl;
}

int main(int argc, char* argv[])
{
    wchar_t str1[81];
    wcscpy(str1, L"One Two Three");
    wchar_t str2[81];
    wcscpy(str2, L"FOUR FIVE SIX");
    wchar_t str3[81];
    wcscpy(str3, L"seven eight nine");

    convert(str1, '?');
    convert(str2, '?');
    convert(str3, '?');

    return 0;
}
```

CROSS-REFERENCE

See also _mbscat(), _mbschr(), _mbscmp(), _mbscoll(), _mbscpy(), _mbscspn(), _mbsdec(), _mbsdup(), _mbsicmp(), _mbsicoll(), _mbsinc(), _mbslen(), _mbslwr(), _mbsnbcat(), _mbsnbcmp(), _mbsnbcnt(), _mbsnbcoll(), _mbsnbcpy(), _mbsnbicmp(), _mbsnbicoll(), _mbsnbset(), _mbsnccnt(), _mbsncmp(), _mbsncoll(), _mbsncpy(), _mbsnextc(), _mbsnicmp(), _mbsnicoll(), _mbsninc(), _mbsnset(), _mbspbrk(), _mbsrchr(), _mbsrev(), _mbsset(), _mbsspn(), _mbsspnp(), _mbsstr(), _mbstok(), _mbstrlen(), _mbsupr(), _wcsdec(), _wcsdup(), _wcsicmp(), _wcsicoll(), _wcsinc(), _wcslwr(), _wcsncnt(), _wcsncoll(), _wcsnextc(), _wcsnicmp(), _wcsnicoll(), _wcsninc(), _wcsnset(), _wcsrev(), _wcsspnp(), _wcsupr(), strcat(), strchr(), strcmp(), strcoll(), strcpy(), strcspn(), strlen(), strncmp(), strncpy(), strpbrk(), strrchr(), strspn(), strstr(), strtod(), strtok(), strtol(), strtoul(), strxfrm(), wcscat(), wcschr(), wcscmp(), wcscoll(), wcscpy(), wcscspn(), wcslen(), wcsncmp(), wcsncpy(), wcspbrk(), wcsrchr(), wcsspn(), wcsstr(), wcstod(), wcstok(), wcstol(), wcstoul(), and wcsxfrm().

V
W
X

_wcsspnp()

Function

The _wcsspnp() function locates the first occurrence, in a wide-character string, of a substring that starts with a character not included in the specified set. The function returns a pointer to the first nonmatching character.

Header File

```
#include <tchar.h>
```

Declaration

```
wchar_t* _wcsspnp(const wchar_t *string,
    const wchar_t *strCharSet);
```

- *strCharSet*—A pointer to the set of characters for which to search.
- *string*—A pointer to the string to search.

Example

The following program demonstrates how to use the _wcsspnp() function. When run, the program locates, in a string, the first character not in the specified set and displays the results. The program's output looks like this:

```
Source String:
This is a test

Remaining String:
test

Press any key to continue
```

Here is the program source code that produced the output. (To recognize the _wcsspnp() function, your program must define the _UNICODE symbol.)

```
#include "stdafx.h"
#include <iostream>
#define _UNICODE
#include <tchar.h>

using namespace std;
```

```
int main(int argc, char* argv[])
{
    wchar_t* srcStr = {L"This is a test"};
    wchar_t* chrSet = {L"ahisT "};

    wchar_t* result = _wcsspnp(srcStr, chrSet);
    cout << "Source String:" << endl;
    wcout << srcStr << endl << endl;
    cout << "Remaining String:" << endl;
    wcout << result << endl << endl;

    return 0;
}
```

CROSS-REFERENCE

See also _mbscat(), _mbschr(), _mbscmp(), _mbscoll(), _mbscpy(), _mbscspn(), _mbsdec(), _mbsdup(), _mbsicmp(), _mbsicoll(), _mbsinc(), _mbslen(), _mbslwr(), _mbsnbcat(), _mbsnbcmp(), _mbsnbcnt(), _mbsnbcoll(), _mbsnbcpy(), _mbsnbicmp(), _mbsnbicoll(), _mbsnbset(), _mbsnccnt(), _mbsncmp(), _mbsncoll(), _mbsncpy(), _mbsnextc(), _mbsnicmp(), _mbsnicoll(), _mbsninc(), _mbsnset(), _mbspbrk(), _mbsrchr(), _mbsrev(), _mbsset(), _mbsspn(), _mbsspnp(), _mbsstr(), _mbstok(), _mbstrlen(), _mbsupr(), _wcsdec(), _wcsdup(), _wcsicmp(), _wcsicoll(), _wcsinc(), _wcslwr(), _wcsncnt(), _wcsncoll(), _wcsnextc(), _wcsnicmp(), _wcsnicoll(), _wcsninc(), _wcsnset(), _wcsrev(), _wcsset(), _wcsupr(), strcat(), strchr(), strcmp(), strcoll(), strcpy(), strcspn(), strlen(), strncmp(), strncpy(), strpbrk(), strrchr(), strspn(), strstr(), strtod(), strtok(), strtol(), strtoul(), strxfrm(), wcscat(), wcschr(), wcscmp(), wcscoll(), wcscpy(), wcscspn(), wcslen(), wcsncmp(), wcsncpy(), wcspbrk(), wcsrchr(), wcsspn(), wcsstr(), wcstod(), wcstok(), wcstol(), wcstoul(), and wcsxfrm().

_wcsupr()

Function

The _wcsupr() function converts a wide-character string to uppercase, returning a pointer to the new string.

Header File

```
#include <string.h>
```

Declaration

```
wchar_t* _wcsupr(const wchar_t *string);
```

- *string* — The string to convert.

Example

The following program demonstrates how to use the _wcsupr() function. When run, the program converts several strings to uppercase and displays the results. The program's output looks like this:

```
Original String: One Two Three
Converted String: ONE TWO THREE

Original String: FOUR FIVE SIX
Converted String: FOUR FIVE SIX

Original String: seven eight nine
Converted String: SEVEN EIGHT NINE

Press any key to continue
```

Here is the program source code that produced the output:

```
#include "stdafx.h"
#include <iostream>
#include <string.h>

using namespace std;

void convert(wchar_t* s)
{
    cout << "Original String: ";
    wcout << s << endl;
    wchar_t* result = _wcsupr(s);
    cout << "Converted String: ";
    wcout << result << endl << endl;
}

int main(int argc, char* argv[])
{
    wchar_t str1[81];
    wcscpy(str1, L"One Two Three");
    wchar_t str2[81];
    wcscpy(str2, L"FOUR FIVE SIX");
```

```
        wchar_t str3[81];
        wcscpy(str3, L"seven eight nine");

        convert(str1);
        convert(str2);
        convert(str3);

        return 0;
    }
```

CROSS-REFERENCE

See also _mbscat(), _mbschr(), _mbscmp(), _mbscoll(), _mbscpy(), _mbscspn(), _mbsdec(), _mbsdup(), _mbsicmp(), _mbsicoll(), _mbsinc(), _mbslen(), _mbslwr(), _mbsnbcat(), _mbsnbcmp(), _mbsnbcnt(), _mbsnbcoll(), _mbsnbcpy(), _mbsnbicmp(), _mbsnbicoll(), _mbsnbset(), _mbsnccnt(), _mbsncmp(), _mbsncoll(), _mbsncpy(), _mbsnextc(), _mbsnicmp(), _mbsnicoll(), _mbsninc(), _mbsnset(), _mbspbrk(), _mbsrchr(), _mbsrev(), _mbsset(), _mbsspn(), _mbsspnp(), _mbsstr(), _mbstok(), _mbstrlen(), _mbsupr(), _wcsdec(), _wcsdup(), _wcsicmp(), _wcsicoll(), _wcsinc(), _wcslwr(), _wcsncnt(), _wcsncoll(), _wcsnextc(), _wcsnicmp(), _wcsnicoll(), _wcsninc(), _wcsnset(), _wcsrev(), _wcsset(), _wcsspnp(), strcat(), strchr(), strcmp(), strcoll(), strcpy(), strcspn(), strlen(), strncmp(), strncpy(), strpbrk(), strrchr(), strspn(), strstr(), strtod(), strtok(), strtol(), strtoul(), strxfrm(), wcscat(), wcschr(), wcscmp(), wcscoll(), wcscpy(), wcscspn(), wcslen(), wcsncmp(), wcsncpy(), wcspbrk(), wcsrchr(), wcsspn(), wcsstr(), wcstod(), wcstok(), wcstol(), wcstoul(), and wcsxfrm().

_wctime()

Function

The _wctime() function is a wide-character version of the ctime() function and converts the contents of a time_t structure to a string.

Header File

```
#include <time.h>
```

Declaration

```
wchar_t* _wctime(const time_t* time);
```

■ *time*—The address of the `time_t` structure that should be converted to a string.

Example

The following program demonstrates how to use the `_wctime()` function. When run, the program calls the `time()` function to get the current time in a `time_t` structure, and then converts the structure to a string for display. The program's output looks like this:

```
Mon Jan 11 15:29:21 1999

Press any key to continue
```

Here is the program source code that produced the output:

```
#include "stdafx.h"
#include <iostream>
#include <time.h>

using namespace std;

int main(int argc, char* argv[])
{
    time_t curTime;
    time(&curTime);
    wchar_t* timeStr = _wctime(&curTime);
    wcout << timeStr << endl;

    return 0;
}
```

CROSS-REFERENCE
See also _ftime(), _futime(), _strdate(), _strtime(), _utime(), _wasctime(), _wstrtime(), _wutime(), asctime(), ctime(), difftime(), gmtime(), localtime(), mktime(), strftime(), and time().

_wexecl()

Function

The `_wexecl()` function runs a child process given the process's path and name and additional arguments (all using wide-character arguments). This function does not return to the process that called it. If the called process does not run successfully, the function returns –1. In this case, the `errno` global variable is set to one of the error values in Table W-6.

NOTE
This function works only on systems, such as Windows NT, that support wide-character filenames.

Table W-6 Error Values for _wexecl()

Value	Description
E2BIG	The arguments and environment require more than 32K of space.
EACCES	There has been a sharing or locking violation.
EMFILE	Too many files are open.
ENOENT	The specified file cannot be found.
ENOEXEC	The specified file is not executable.
ENOMEM	Not enough memory to run the process.

Header File

```
#include <process.h>
```

Declaration

```
int _wexecl(const wchar_t *cmdname,
    const wchar_t *arg0, ... const wchar_t *argn, NULL);
```

- *arg0* — A pointer to the first argument.
- *argn* — A pointer to the last argument.
- *cmdname* — The path and filename of the process to run.

Example

The following program demonstrates how to use the _wexecl() function. When run, the program runs a child process called TestProg.exe, displaying messages as it goes. The program's output looks like this:

```
Running TestProg.exe
```

```
Child process running.
Press any key to continue
```

Here is the program source code that produced the output:

```cpp
#include "stdafx.h"
#include <iostream>
#include <process.h>
#include <errno.h>

using namespace std;

int main(int argc, char* argv[])
{
    cout << "Running TestProg.exe" << endl;

    int result = _wexecl(L"TestProg.exe", L"TestProg.exe",
        L"arg2", L"arg3", NULL);
    if (result == -1)
    {
        switch(errno)
        {
        case ENOEXEC:
            cout << "Not an executable file" << endl;
            break;
        case E2BIG:
            cout << "Space required exceeds 32K" << endl;
            break;
        case ENOMEM:
            cout << "Not enough memory" << endl;
            break;
        case EMFILE:
            cout << "Too many files open" << endl;
            break;
        case EACCES:
            cout << "Locking or sharing violation" << endl;
            break;
        case ENOENT:
            cout << "File not found" << endl;
        }
    }

    return 0;
}
```

CROSS-REFERENCE
See also _wexecle(), _wexeclp(), _wexeclpe(), _wexecv(), _wexecve(), _wexecvp(),
_wexecvpe(), _wspawnl(), _wspawnle(), _wspawnlp(), _wspawnlpe(), _wspawnv(),
_wspawnve(), _wspawnvp(), _wspawnvpe(), execl(), execle(), execlp(), execlpe(),
execv(), execve(), execvp(), execvpe(), spawnl(), spawnle(), spawnlp(), spawnlpe(),
spawnv(), spawnve(), spawnvp(), and spawnvpe().

_wexecle()

Function

The _wexecle() function runs a child process given the process's path and
name, additional arguments, and environment settings (using wide-character
arguments). This function does not return to the process that called it. If the
called process does not run successfully, the function returns –1. In this case,
the errno global variable will be set to one of the error values in Table W-7.

NOTE
This function works only on systems, such as Windows NT, that support wide-
character filenames.

Table W-7 Error Values for _wexecle()

Value	Description
E2BIG	The arguments and environment require more than 32K of space.
EACCES	There has been a sharing or locking violation.
EMFILE	Too many files are open.
ENOENT	The specified file cannot be found.
ENOEXEC	The specified file is not executable.
ENOMEM	Not enough memory to run the process.

Header File

```
#include <process.h>
```

Declaration

```
int _wexecle(const wchar_t *cmdname,
```

```
      const wchar_t *arg0, ... const wchar_t *argn,
      NULL, const wchar_t *const *envp)
```

- *arg0* — A pointer to the first argument.
- *argn* — A pointer to the last argument.
- *cmdname* — The path and filename of the process to run.
- *envp* — A pointer to the environment settings.

Example

The following program demonstrates how to use the _wexecle() function. When run, the program runs a child process called TestProg.exe, displaying messages as it goes. The program's output looks like this:

```
Running TestProg.exe
Press any key to continue
Child process running.
```

Here is the program source code that produced the output:

```
#include "stdafx.h"
#include <iostream>
#include <process.h>
#include <errno.h>

using namespace std;

char *envir[] =
{
   "ENVIR1=environment setting 1",
   "ENVIR2=environment setting 2",
   "ENVIR3=environment setting 3",
    NULL
};

int main(int argc, char* argv[])
{
    cout << "Running TestProg.exe" << endl;

    int result = _wexecle(L"TestProg.exe", L"TestProg.exe",
        L"arg2", L"arg3", NULL, envir);
    if (result == -1)
    {
        switch(errno)
```

```
        {
        case ENOEXEC:
            cout << "Not an executable file" << endl;
            break;
        case E2BIG:
            cout << "Space required exceeds 32K" << endl;
            break;
        case ENOMEM:
            cout << "Not enough memory" << endl;
            break;
        case EMFILE:
            cout << "Too many files open" << endl;
            break;
        case EACCES:
            cout << "Locking or sharing violation" << endl;
            break;
        case ENOENT:
            cout << "File not found" << endl;
        }
    }

    return 0;
}
```

CROSS-REFERENCE
See also _wexecl(), _wexeclp(), _wexeclpe(), _wexecv(), _wexecve(), _wexecvp(),
_wexecvpe(), _wspawnl(), _wspawnle(), _wspawnlp(), _wspawnlpe(), _wspawnv(),
_wspawnve(), _wspawnvp(), _wspawnvpe(), execl(), execle(), execlp(), execlpe(),
execv(), execve(), execvp(), execvpe(), spawnl(), spawnle(), spawnlp(), spawnlpe(),
spawnv(), spawnve(), spawnvp(), and spawnvpe().

_wexeclp()

Function

The _wexeclp() function runs a child process given the process's path and
name and additional arguments (using wide-character arguments). This function does not return to the process that called it. If the called process does not
run successfully, the function returns –1. In this case, the errno global variable
is set to one of the error values in Table W-8.

NOTE

This function works only on systems, such as Windows NT, that support wide-character filenames.

Table W-8 Error Values for _wexeclp()

Value	Description
E2BIG	The arguments and environment require more than 32K of space.
EACCES	There has been a sharing or locking violation.
EMFILE	Too many files are open.
ENOENT	The specified file cannot be found.
ENOEXEC	The specified file is not executable.
ENOMEM	Not enough memory to run the process.

Header File

```
#include <process.h>
```

Declaration

```
int _wexeclp(const wchar_t *cmdname,
    const wchar_t *arg0, ... const wchar_t *argn, NULL);
```

- *arg0* — A pointer to the first argument.
- *argn* — A pointer to the last argument.
- *cmdname* — The path and filename of the process to run.

Example

The following program demonstrates how to use the _wexeclp() function. When run, the program runs a child process called TestProg.exe, displaying messages as it goes. The program's output looks like this:

```
Running TestProg.exe

Child process running.
Press any key to continue
```

Here is the program source code that produced the output:

```cpp
#include "stdafx.h"
#include <iostream>
#include <process.h>
#include <errno.h>

using namespace std;

int main(int argc, char* argv[])
{
    cout << "Running TestProg.exe" << endl;

    int result = _wexeclp(L"TestProg.exe", L"TestProg.exe",
        L"arg2", L"arg3", NULL);
    if (result == -1)
    {
        switch(errno)
        {
        case ENOEXEC:
            cout << "Not an executable file" << endl;
            break;
        case E2BIG:
            cout << "Space required exceeds 32K" << endl;
            break;
        case ENOMEM:
            cout << "Not enough memory" << endl;
            break;
        case EMFILE:
            cout << "Too many files open" << endl;
            break;
        case EACCES:
            cout << "Locking or sharing violation" << endl;
            break;
        case ENOENT:
            cout << "File not found" << endl;
        }
    }

    return 0;
}
```

CROSS-REFERENCE

See also _wexecle(), _wexecle(), _wexeclpe(), _wexecv(), _wexecve(), _wexecvp(), _wexecvpe(), _wspawnl(), _wspawnle(), _wspawnlp(), _wspawnlpe(), _wspawnv(), _wspawnve(), _wspawnvp(), _wspawnvpe(), execl(), execle(), execlp(), execlpe(), execv(), execve(), execvp(), execvpe(), spawnl(), spawnle(), spawnlp(), spawnlpe(), spawnv(), spawnve(), spawnvp(), and spawnvpe().

_wexeclpe()

Function

The _wexeclpe() function runs a child process given the process's path and name, additional arguments, and environment settings (all using wide-character arguments). This function does not return to the process that called it. If the called process does not run successfully, the function returns −1. In this case, the errno global variable is set to one of the error values in Table W-9.

NOTE

This function works only on systems, such as Windows NT, that support wide-character filenames.

Table W-9 Error Values for _wexeclpe()

Value	Description
E2BIG	The arguments and environment require more than 32K of space.
EACCES	There has been a sharing or locking violation.
EMFILE	Too many files are open.
ENOENT	The specified file cannot be found.
ENOEXEC	The specified file is not executable.
ENOMEM	Not enough memory to run the process.

Header File

```
#include <process.h>
```

Declaration

```
int _wexeclpe(const wchar_t *cmdname,
    const wchar_t *arg0, ... const wchar_t *argn,
    NULL, const wchar_t *const *envp)
```

- *arg0* — A pointer to the first argument.
- *argn* — A pointer to the last argument.
- *cmdname* — The path and filename of the process to run.
- *envp* — A pointer to the environment settings.

Example

The following program demonstrates how to use the `_wexeclpe()` function. When run, the program runs a child process called TestProg.exe, displaying messages as it goes. The program's output looks like this:

```
Running TestProg.exe

Child process running.
Press any key to continue
```

Here is the program source code that produced the output:

```cpp
#include "stdafx.h"
#include <iostream>
#include <process.h>
#include <errno.h>

using namespace std;

char *envir[] =
{
    "ENVIR1=environment setting 1",
    "ENVIR2=environment setting 2",
    "ENVIR3=environment setting 3",
     NULL
};

int main(int argc, char* argv[])
{
    cout << "Running TestProg.exe" << endl;

    int result = _wexeclpe(L"TestProg.exe", L"TestProg.exe",
        L"arg2", L"arg3", NULL, envir);
    if (result == -1)
    {
        switch(errno)
        {
        case ENOEXEC:
```

```
                cout << "Not an executable file" << endl;
                break;
            case E2BIG:
                cout << "Space required exceeds 32K" << endl;
                break;
            case ENOMEM:
                cout << "Not enough memory" << endl;
                break;
            case EMFILE:
                cout << "Too many files open" << endl;
                break;
            case EACCES:
                cout << "Locking or sharing violation" << endl;
                break;
            case ENOENT:
                cout << "File not found" << endl;
        }
    }

    return 0;
}
```

CROSS-REFERENCE

See also _wexecl(), _wexecle(), _wexeclp(), _wexecv(), _wexecve(), _wexecvp(),
_wexecvpe(), _wspawnl(), _wspawnle(), _wspawnlp(), _wspawnlpe(), _wspawnv(),
_wspawnve(), _wspawnvp(), _wspawnvpe(), execl(), execle(), execlp(), execlpe(),
execv(), execve(), execvp(), execvpe(), spawnl(), spawnle(), spawnlp(), spawnlpe(),
spawnv(), spawnve(), spawnvp(), and spawnvpe().

_wexecv()

Function

The _wexecv() function runs a child process given the process's path and
name (using wide-character strings) and additional arguments supplied as an
array of wchar_t pointers. This function does not return to the process that
called it. If the called process does not run successfully, the function returns
−1. In this case, the errno global variable is set to one of the error values in
Table W-10.

NOTE
This function works only on systems, such as Windows NT, that support wide-character filenames.

Table W-10 Error Values for _wexecv()

Value	Description
E2BIG	The arguments and environment require more than 32K of space.
EACCES	There has been a sharing or locking violation.
EMFILE	Too many files are open.
ENOENT	The specified file cannot be found.
ENOEXEC	The specified file is not executable.
ENOMEM	Not enough memory to run the process.

Header File

```
#include <process.h>
```

Declaration

```
int _wexecv(const wchar_t *cmdname,
    const wchar_t *const *argv)
```

- *argv* — A pointer to an array of wchar_t pointers that point to the arguments.
- *cmdname* — The path and filename of the process to run.

Example

The following program demonstrates how to use the _wexecv() function. When run, the program runs a child process called TestProg.exe, displaying messages as it goes. The program's output looks like this:

```
Running TestProg.exe
Press any key to continue
Child process running.
```

Here is the program source code that produced the output:

```
#include "stdafx.h"
#include <iostream>
```

V
W
X

```cpp
#include <process.h>
#include <errno.h>

using namespace std;

int main(int argc, char* argv[])
{
    wchar_t* args[] =
    {
        L"TestProg.exe",
        L"argument #1",
        L"argument #2",
         NULL
    };

    cout << "Running TestProg.exe" << endl;

    int result = _wexecv(L"TestProg.exe", args);
    if (result == -1)
    {
        switch(errno)
        {
        case ENOEXEC:
            cout << "Not an executable file" << endl;
            break;
        case E2BIG:
            cout << "Space required exceeds 32K" << endl;
            break;
        case ENOMEM:
            cout << "Not enough memory" << endl;
            break;
        case EMFILE:
            cout << "Too many files open" << endl;
            break;
        case EACCES:
            cout << "Locking or sharing violation" << endl;
            break;
        case ENOENT:
            cout << "File not found" << endl;
        }
    }

    return 0;
}
```

CROSS-REFERENCE

See also _wexecl(), _wexecle(), _wexeclp(), _wexeclpe(), _wexecve(), _wexecvp(),
_wexecvpe(), _wspawnl(), _wspawnle(), _wspawnlp(), _wspawnlpe(), _wspawnv(),
_wspawnve(), _wspawnvp(), _wspawnvpe(), execl(), execle(), execlp(), execlpe(),
execv(), execve(), execvp(), execvpe(), spawnl(), spawnle(), spawnlp(), spawnlpe(),
spawnv(), spawnve(), spawnvp(), and spawnvpe().

_wexecve()

Function

The _wexecve() function runs a child process given the process's path and
name (as wide-character strings), and additional arguments and environment
settings supplied as an array of wchar_t pointers. This function does not
return to the process that called it. If the called process does not run successfully, the function returns –1. In this case, the errno global variable is set to
one of the error values in Table W-11.

NOTE

This function works only on systems, such as Windows NT, that support wide-
character filenames.

Table W-11 Error Values for _wexecve()

Error	Description
E2BIG	The arguments and environment require more than 32K of space.
EACCES	There has been a sharing or locking violation.
EMFILE	Too many files are open.
ENOENT	The specified file cannot be found.
ENOEXEC	The specified file is not executable.
ENOMEM	Not enough memory to run the process.

Header File

```
#include <process.h>
```

V
W
X

Declaration

```
int _wexecve(const wchar_t *cmdname,
    const wchar_t *const *argv,
    const wchar_t *const *envp);
```

- *argv* — A pointer to an array of wchar_t pointers that point to the arguments.
- *cmdname* — The path and filename of the process to run.
- *envp* — A pointer to an array of wchar_t pointers that point to the environment settings.

Example

The following program demonstrates how to use the _wexecve() function. When run, the program runs a child process called TestProg.exe, displaying messages as it goes. The program's output looks like this:

```
Running TestProg.exe

Child process running.
Press any key to continue
```

Here is the program source code that produced the output:

```
#include "stdafx.h"
#include <iostream>
#include <process.h>
#include <errno.h>

using namespace std;

wchar_t *envir[] =
{
    L"ENVIR1=environment setting 1",
    L"ENVIR2=environment setting 2",
    L"ENVIR3=environment setting 3",
     NULL
};

wchar_t* args[] =
{
    L"TestProg.exe",
    L"argument #1",
```

```
        L"argument #2",
         NULL
};

int main(int argc, char* argv[])
{
    cout << "Running TestProg.exe" << endl;

    int result = _wexecve(L"TestProg.exe", args, envir);
    if (result == -1)
    {
        switch(errno)
        {
        case ENOEXEC:
            cout << "Not an executable file" << endl;
            break;
        case E2BIG:
            cout << "Space required exceeds 32K" << endl;
            break;
        case ENOMEM:
            cout << "Not enough memory" << endl;
            break;
        case EMFILE:
            cout << "Too many files open" << endl;
            break;
        case EACCES:
            cout << "Locking or sharing violation" << endl;
            break;
        case ENOENT:
            cout << "File not found" << endl;
        }
    }

    return 0;
}
```

CROSS-REFERENCE

See also _wexecl(), _wexecle(), _wexeclp(), _wexeclpe(), _wexecv(), _wexecvp(), _wexecvpe(), _wspawnl(), _wspawnle(), _wspawnlp(), _wspawnlpe(), _wspawnv(), _wspawnve(), _wspawnvp(), _wspawnvpe(), execl(), execle(), execlp(), execlpe(), execv(), execve(), execvp(), execvpe(), spawnl(), spawnle(), spawnlp(), spawnlpe(), spawnv(), spawnve(), spawnvp(), and spawnvpe().

_wexecvp()

Function

The _wexecvp() function runs a child process given the process's path and name (as wide-character strings) and additional arguments supplied as an array of wchar_t pointers. This function does not return to the process that called it. If the called process does not run successfully, the function returns –1. In this case, the errno global variable is set to one of the error values in Table W-12.

NOTE

This function works only on systems, such as Windows NT, that support wide-character filenames.

Table W-12 Error Values for _wexecvp()

Value	Description
E2BIG	The arguments and environment require more than 32K of space.
EACCES	There has been a sharing or locking violation.
EMFILE	Too many files are open.
ENOENT	The specified file cannot be found.
ENOEXEC	The specified file is not executable.
ENOMEM	Not enough memory to run the process.

Header File

```
#include <process.h>
```

Declaration

```
int _wexecvp(const wchar_t *cmdname,
    const wchar_t *const *argv)
```

- *argv* — A pointer to an array of wchar_t pointers that point to the arguments.
- *cmdname* — The path and filename of the process to run.

Example

The following program demonstrates how to use the _wexecvp() function. When run, the program runs a child process called TestProg.exe, displaying messages as it goes. The program's output looks like this:

```
Running TestProg.exe
Press any key to continue
Child process running.
```

Here is the program source code that produced the output:

```cpp
#include "stdafx.h"
#include <iostream>
#include <process.h>
#include <errno.h>

using namespace std;

int main(int argc, char* argv[])
{
    wchar_t* args[] =
    {
        L"TestProg.exe",
        L"argument #1",
        L"argument #2",
         NULL
    };

    cout << "Running TestProg.exe" << endl;

    int result = _wexecvp(L"TestProg.exe", args);
    if (result == -1)
    {
        switch(errno)
        {
        case ENOEXEC:
            cout << "Not an executable file" << endl;
            break;
        case E2BIG:
            cout << "Space required exceeds 32K" << endl;
            break;
        case ENOMEM:
            cout << "Not enough memory" << endl;
            break;
        case EMFILE:
```

```
                            cout << "Too many files open" << endl;
                            break;
                      case EACCES:
                            cout << "Locking or sharing violation" << endl;
                            break;
                      case ENOENT:
                            cout << "File not found" << endl;
                      }
                }

                return 0;
          }
```

CROSS-REFERENCE

See also _wexecl(), _wexecle(), _wexeclp(), _wexeclpe(), _wexecv(), _wexecve(), _wexecvpe(), _wspawnl(), _wspawnle(), _wspawnlp(), _wspawnlpe(), _wspawnv(), _wspawnve(), _wspawnvp(), _wspawnvpe(), execl(), execle(), execlp(), execlpe(), execv(), execve(), execvp(), execvpe(), spawnl(), spawnle(), spawnlp(), spawnlpe(), spawnv(), spawnve(), spawnvp(), and spawnvpe().

_wexecvpe()

Function

The _wexecvpe() function runs a child process given the process's path and name (as wide-character strings), and additional arguments and environment settings supplied as an array of wchar_t pointers. This function does not return to the process that called it. If the called process does not run successfully, the function returns –1. In this case, the errno global variable is set to one of the error values in Table W-13.

NOTE

This function works only on systems, such as Windows NT, that support wide-character filenames.

Table W-13 Error Values for _wexecvpe()

Value	Description
E2BIG	The arguments and environment require more than 32K of space.
EACCES	There has been a sharing or locking violation.
EMFILE	Too many files are open.

Value	Description
ENOENT	The specified file cannot be found.
ENOEXEC	The specified file is not executable.
ENOMEM	Not enough memory to run the process.

Header File

```
#include <process.h>
```

Declaration

```
int _wexecvpe(const wchar_t *cmdname,
    const wchar_t *const *argv,
    const wchar_t *const *envp);
```

- *argv* — A pointer to an array of wchar_t pointers that point to the arguments.
- *cmdname* — The path and filename of the process to run.
- *envp* — A pointer to an array of wchar_t pointers that point to the environment settings.

Example

The following program demonstrates how to use the _wexecvpe() function. When run, the program runs a child process called TestProg.exe, displaying messages as it goes. The program's output looks like this:

```
Running TestProg.exe

Child process running.
Press any key to continue
```

Here is the program source code that produced the output:

```
#include "stdafx.h"
#include <iostream>
#include <process.h>
#include <errno.h>

using namespace std;

wchar_t *envir[] =
```

```
{
    L"ENVIR1=environment setting 1",
    L"ENVIR2=environment setting 2",
    L"ENVIR3=environment setting 3",
     NULL
};

wchar_t* args[] =
{
    L"TestProg.exe",
    L"argument #1",
    L"argument #2",
     NULL
};

int main(int argc, char* argv[])
{
    cout << "Running TestProg.exe" << endl;

    int result = _wexecvpe(L"TestProg.exe", args, envir);
    if (result == -1)
    {
        switch(errno)
        {
        case ENOEXEC:
            cout << "Not an executable file" << endl;
            break;
        case E2BIG:
            cout << "Space required exceeds 32K" << endl;
            break;
        case ENOMEM:
            cout << "Not enough memory" << endl;
            break;
        case EMFILE:
            cout << "Too many files open" << endl;
            break;
        case EACCES:
            cout << "Locking or sharing violation" << endl;
            break;
        case ENOENT:
            cout << "File not found" << endl;
        }
    }

    return 0;
```

```
    }
```

CROSS-REFERENCE

See also _wexecl(), _wexecle(), _wexeclp(), _wexeclpe(), _wexecv(), _wexecve(),
_wexecvp(), _wspawnl(), _wspawnle(), _wspawnlp(), _wspawnlpe(), _wspawnv(),
_wspawnve(), _wspawnvp(), _wspawnvpe(), execl(), execle(), execlp(), execlpe(),
execv(), execve(), execvp(), execvpe(), spawnl(), spawnle(), spawnlp(), spawnlpe(),
spawnv(), spawnve(), spawnvp(), and spawnvpe().

_wfdopen()

Function

The _wfdopen() function associates a stream with an open file, returning a
pointer to the stream.

Header File

```
#include <stdio.h>
```

Declaration

```
FILE* _wfdopen(int handle, const wchar_t *mode);
```

- *handle* — A handle to the open file.
- *mode* — The file access mode, which can be one of the mode values
  in Table W-14. The extension mode values shown in Table W-15 can
  be combined with the mode.

Table W.14 Mode Values for _wfdopen()

Value	Description
"r"	Open for reading.
"w"	Open for writing, which erases the file if it already exists or creates a new file if it doesn't exist.
"a"	Open for append, which writes to the end of an existing file or creates the file if it doesn't already exist.
"r+"	Open for both reading and writing.
"w+"	Open for both reading and writing. If the file already exists, its contents are lost; if the file doesn't exist, it's created.
"a+"	Open for reading and appending. If the file doesn't exist, it's created.

V
W
X

Table W-15 Extension Mode Values for _wfdopen()

Value	Description
T	Open for in text mode.
B	Open in binary mode.
C	Set the file's commit flag.
N	Turn off the file's commit flag.

Example

The following program demonstrates how to use the _wfdopen() function. When run, the program opens a file for reading and then associates a stream with the open file, printing status messages as it goes. The program's output looks like this:

```
Stream created successfully.
Press any key to continue
```

Here is the program source code that produced the output:

```cpp
#include "stdafx.h"
#include <fcntl.h>
#include <io.h>
#include <stdio.h>
#include <iostream>

using namespace std;

int main(int argc, char* argv[])
{
    int fileHandle = _open("_wfdopen.cpp", O_RDONLY);

    if (fileHandle == -1)
        cout << "File open error." << endl;
    else
    {
        FILE* file = _wfdopen(fileHandle, L"r");

        if(file == NULL )
            cout << "Stream creation error." << endl;
        else
        {
            cout << "Stream created successfully." << endl;
            fclose(file);
        }
    }
```

```
        }

        return 0;
    }
```

CROSS-REFERENCE

See also _close(), _creat(), _fcloseall(), _fdopen(), _fgetchar(), _fgetwchar(), _fileno(), _flushall(), _fputwchar(), _fsopen(), _getw(), _getws(), _lseeki64(), _open(), _putw(), _putws(), _read(), _rmtmp(), _tempnam(), _wcreat(), _wfopen(), _wfreopen(), _wfsopen(), _wopen(), _wtempnam(), _wtmpnam(), clearerr(), eof(), fclose(), feof(), ferror(), fflush(), fgetc(), fgetpos(), fgets(), fgetwc(), fgetws(), fopen(), fprintf(), fputc(), fputchar(), fputs(), fputwc(), fputws(), fread(), freopen(), fscanf(), fseek(), fsetpos(), ftell(), fwprintf(), fwrite(), fwscanf(), getc(), getchar(), gets(), getwc(), getwchar(), lseek(), putc(), putch(), putchar(), puts(), putwc(), putwchar(), rewind(), setbuf(), setvbuf(), tmpfile(), tmpnam(), ungetc(), ungetch(), ungetwc(), and write().

_wfindfirst()

Function

The _wfindfirst() function finds the first file that matches the given specification, returning a handle to the file. If the function fails, it returns –1, and the errno global variable is set to either ENOENT (no matching files) or EINVAL (invalid file specification).

NOTE

This function works only on systems, such as Windows NT, that support wide-character filenames.

Header File

```
#include <io.h>
```

Declaration

```
long _wfindfirst(wchar_t *filespec,
    struct _wfinddata_t *fileinfo);
```

- *fileinfo* — A pointer to a _wfinddata_t structure in which the function will store information about the requested file.
- *filespec* — The file specification.

Example

The following program demonstrates how to use the _wfindfirst() function. When run, the program looks for all files in the current directory, printing each file's name and size. The program's output looks like this:

```
FILE: . - 0 bytes
FILE: .. - 0 bytes
FILE: StdAfx.h - 667 bytes
FILE: StdAfx.cpp - 297 bytes
FILE: ReadMe.txt - 1232 bytes
FILE: _wfindfirst.dsw - 545 bytes
FILE: _wfindfirst.cpp - 828 bytes
FILE: Debug - 0 bytes
FILE: _wfindfirst.dsp - 4584 bytes
FILE: _wfindfirst.ncb - 0 bytes
FILE: _wfindfirst.plg - 1275 bytes
Press any key to continue
```

Here is the program source code that produced the output:

```cpp
#include "stdafx.h"
#include <io.h>
#include <iostream>

using namespace std;

int main(int argc, char* argv[])
{
    struct _wfinddata_t fileData;

    long fileHandle = _wfindfirst(L"*.*", &fileData);

    if(fileHandle == -1L)
        cout << "No files found." << endl;
    else
    {
        cout << "FILE: ";
        wcout << fileData.name;
        cout << " - ";
        wcout << fileData.size;
        cout << " bytes" << endl;

        int result = _wfindnext(fileHandle, &fileData);
        while(result == 0 )
        {
```

```
            cout << "FILE: ";
            wcout << fileData.name;
            cout << " - ";
            wcout << fileData.size;
            cout << " bytes";
            cout << endl;
            result = _wfindnext(fileHandle, &fileData);
        }

        _findclose(fileHandle);
    }

    return 0;
}
```

CROSS-REFERENCE

See also _findclose(), _findfirst(), _findfirsti64(), _findnext(), _wfindfirsti64(), _wfindnext(), _wfindnexti64, and findnexti64().

_wfindfirsti64()

Function

The _wfindfirsti64() function finds the first file that matches the given specification, returning a handle to the file. If the function fails, it returns −1, and the errno global variable is set to either ENOENT (no matching files) or EINVAL (invalid file specification).

NOTE

Borland does not support this function. Also, this function works only on systems, such as Windows NT, that support wide-character filenames.

Header File

```
#include <io.h>
```

Declaration

```
__int64 _wfindfirsti64(wchar_t *filespec,
    struct _wfinddatai64_t *fileinfo);
```

■ *fileinfo* — A pointer to a _wfinddatai64_t structure in which the function will store information about the requested file.

■ *filespec* — The file specification.

Example

The following program demonstrates how to use the _wfindfirsti64() function. When run, the program looks for all files in the current directory, printing each file's name and size. The program's output looks like this:

```
FILE: . — 0 bytes
FILE: .. — 0 bytes
FILE: StdAfx.h — 667 bytes
FILE: StdAfx.cpp — 300 bytes
FILE: ReadMe.txt — 1250 bytes
FILE: _wfindfirsti64.dsw — 551 bytes
FILE: _wfindfirsti64.cpp — 878 bytes
FILE: Debug — 0 bytes
FILE: _wfindfirsti64.dsp — 4620 bytes
FILE: _wfindfirsti64.ncb — 0 bytes
FILE: _wfindfirsti64.plg — 1302 bytes
Press any key to continue
```

Here is the program source code that produced the output:

```cpp
#include "stdafx.h"
#include <io.h>
#include <iostream>

using namespace std;

int main(int argc, char* argv[])
{
    struct _wfinddatai64_t fileData;

    __int64 fileHandle = _wfindfirsti64(L"*.*", &fileData);

    if(fileHandle == -1)
        cout << "No files found." << endl;
    else
    {
        cout << "FILE: ";
        wcout << fileData.name;
        cout << " — ";
        wcout << (int)fileData.size;
```

```
        cout << " bytes" << endl;

        __int64 result = _wfindnexti64(fileHandle, &fileData);
        while(result == 0 )
        {
            cout << "FILE: ";
            wcout << fileData.name;
            cout << " - ";
            wcout << (int)fileData.size << " bytes";
            cout << endl;
            result = _wfindnexti64(fileHandle, &fileData);
        }

        _findclose(fileHandle);
    }

    return 0;
}
```

CROSS-REFERENCE
See also _findclose(), _findfirst(), _findfirsti64(), _findnext(), _wfindfirst(), _wfindnext(), _wfindnexti64, and findnexti64().

_wfindnext()

Function

The _wfindnext() function finds the next file that matches the given specification, returning a handle to the file. If the function fails, it returns −1, and the errno global variable is set to ENOENT (no matching files).

NOTE
This function works only on systems, such as Windows NT, that support wide-character filenames.

Header File

```
#include <io.h>
```

V
W
X

Declaration

```
int _wfindnext(long handle, struct _wfinddata_t *fileinfo);
```

- *fileinfo* — A pointer to a _wfinddata_t structure in which the function will store information about the requested file.
- *handle* — The file handle returned by _findfirst().

Example

The following program demonstrates how to use the _wfindnext() function. When run, the program looks for all files in the current directory, printing each file's name and size. The program's output looks like this:

```
FILE: . — 0 bytes
FILE: .. — 0 bytes
FILE: StdAfx.h — 667 bytes
FILE: StdAfx.cpp — 296 bytes
FILE: _wfindnext.dsw — 543 bytes
FILE: _wfindnext.cpp — 844 bytes
FILE: ReadMe.txt — 1226 bytes
FILE: _wfindnext.ncb — 0 bytes
FILE: _wfindnext.dsp — 4572 bytes
FILE: Debug — 0 bytes
FILE: _wfindnext.plg — 1266 bytes
Press any key to continue
```

Here is the program source code that produced the output:

```cpp
#include "stdafx.h"
#include <io.h>
#include <iostream>

using namespace std;

int main(int argc, char* argv[])
{
    struct _wfinddata_t fileData;

    long fileHandle = _wfindfirst(L"*.*", &fileData);

    if(fileHandle == -1L)
        cout << "No files found." << endl;
    else
    {
        cout << "FILE: ";
```

```
        wcout << fileData.name;
        cout << " - ";
        wcout << fileData.size;
        cout << " bytes" << endl;

        int result = _wfindnext(fileHandle, &fileData);
        while(result == 0 )
        {
            cout << "FILE: ";
            wcout << fileData.name;
            cout << " - ";
            wcout << fileData.size;
            cout << " bytes";
            cout << endl;
            result = _wfindnext(fileHandle, &fileData);
        }

        _findclose(fileHandle);
    }

    return 0;
}
```

CROSS-REFERENCE
See also _findclose(), _findfirst(), _findfirsti64(), _findnext(), _wfindfirst(), _wfindfirsti64(), _wfindnexti64, and findnexti64().

_wfindnexti64()

Function

The _wfindnexti64() function finds the next file that matches the given spec-ification, returning a handle to the file. If the function fails, it returns –1, and the errno global variable is set to ENOENT (no matching files).

NOTE
Borland does not support this function. Also, this function works only on sys-tems, such as Windows NT, that support wide-character filenames.

Header File

```
#include <io.h>
```

Declaration

```
__int64 _wfindnexti64(long handle,
    struct _wfinddatai64_t *fileinfo);
```

- *fileinfo*—A pointer to a _wfinddatai64_t structure in which the function will store information about the requested file.
- *handle*—The file handle returned by _findfirsti64().

Example

The following program demonstrates how to use the _wfindnexti64() function. When run, the program looks for all files in the current directory, printing each file's name and size. The program's output looks like this:

```
FILE: . — 0 bytes
FILE: .. — 0 bytes
FILE: StdAfx.h — 667 bytes
FILE: StdAfx.cpp — 299 bytes
FILE: ReadMe.txt — 1244 bytes
FILE: _wfindnexti64.dsw — 549 bytes
FILE: _wfindnexti64.cpp — 892 bytes
FILE: Debug — 0 bytes
FILE: _wfindnexti64.dsp — 4608 bytes
FILE: _wfindnexti64.ncb — 0 bytes
FILE: _wfindnexti64.plg — 1668 bytes
Press any key to continue
```

Here is the program source code that produced the output:

```cpp
#include "stdafx.h"
#include <io.h>
#include <iostream>

using namespace std;

int main(int argc, char* argv[])
{
    struct _wfinddatai64_t fileData;

    __int64 fileHandle = _wfindfirsti64(L"*.*", &fileData);

    if(fileHandle == -1)
        cout << "No files found." << endl;
    else
    {
```

```
cout << "FILE: ";
wcout << fileData.name;
cout << " - ";
wcout << (int)fileData.size;
cout << " bytes" << endl;

__int64 result = _wfindnexti64(fileHandle, &fileData);
while(result == 0 )
{
    cout << "FILE: ";
    wcout << fileData.name;
    cout << " - ";
    wcout << (int)fileData.size;
    wcout << " bytes";
    cout << endl;
    result = _wfindnexti64(fileHandle, &fileData);
}

    _findclose(fileHandle);
}

    return 0;
}
```

CROSS-REFERENCE
See also _findclose(), _findfirst(), _findfirsti64(), _findnext(), _wfindfirst(), _wfindfirsti64(), _wfindnext(), and findnexti64().

_wfopen()

Function

The _wfopen() function opens a file as a stream, returning a pointer to the stream.

NOTE
This function works only on systems, such as Windows NT, that support wide-character filenames.

Header File

```
#include <stdio.h>
```

V

W

X

Declaration

```
FILE* _wfopen(const wchar_t *filename, const wchar_t *mode);
```

- *filename* — The name of the file to open.
- *mode* — The file access mode, which can be one of the mode values from Table W-16. The extension mode values shown in Table W-17 can be combined with the mode.

Table W-16 Mode Values for _wfopen()

Value	Description
"r"	Open for reading.
"w"	Open for writing, which erases the file if it already exists or creates a new file if it doesn't exist.
"a"	Open for append, which writes to the end of an existing file or creates the file if it doesn't already exist.
"r+"	Open for both reading and writing.
"w+"	Open for both reading and writing. If the file already exists, its contents are lost; if the file doesn't exist, it's created.
"a+"	Open for reading and appending. If the file doesn't exist, it's created.

Table W-17 Extension Mode Values for _wfopen()

Value	Description
T	Open for in text mode.
B	Open in binary mode.
C	Set the file's commit flag.
N	Turn off the file's commit flag.

Example

The following program demonstrates how to use the `_wfopen()` function. When run, the program attempts to open a file, prints a status message, and then closes the file if it opened successfully. The program's output looks like this:

```
File opened successfully.
Press any key to continue
```

Here is the program source code that produced the output:

```
#include "stdafx.h"
```

```
#include <stdio.h>
#include <iostream>

using namespace std;

int main(int argc, char* argv[])
{
    FILE* file = _wfopen(L"fopen.cpp", L"r");

    if (file != NULL)
    {
        cout << "File opened successfully." << endl;
        fclose(file);
    }
    else
        cout << "File failed to open." << endl;

    return 0;
}
```

CROSS-REFERENCE
See also _close(), _creat(), _fcloseall(), _fdopen(), _fgetchar(), _fgetwchar(), _fileno(), _flushall(), _fputwchar(), _fsopen(), _getw(), _getws(), _lseeki64(), _open(), _putw(), _putws(), _read(), _rmtmp(), _tempnam(), _wcreat(), _wfdopen(), _wfreopen(), _wfsopen(), _wopen(), _wtempnam(), _wtmpnam(), clearerr(), eof(), fclose(), feof(), ferror(), fflush(), fgetc(), fgetpos(), fgets(), fgetwc(), fgetws(), fopen(), fprintf(), fputc(), fputchar(), fputs(), fputwc(), fputws(), fread(), freopen(), fscanf(), fseek(), fsetpos(), ftell(), fwprintf(), fwrite(), fwscanf(), getc(), getchar(), gets(), getwc(), getwchar(), lseek(), putc(), putch(), putchar(), puts(), putwc(), putwchar(), rewind(), setbuf(), setvbuf(), tmpfile(), tmpnam(), ungetc(), ungetch(), ungetwc(), and write().

_wfreopen()

Function

The _wfreopen() function creates a new file from an existing stream, returning a pointer to the new stream.

NOTE
This function works only on systems, such as Windows NT, that support wide-character filenames.

Header File

```
#include <stdio.h>
```

Declaration

```
FILE* _wfreopen(const wchar_t *path,
    const wchar_t *mode, FILE *stream );
```

- *mode* — The file access mode, which can be one of the mode values from Table W-18. The extension mode values shown in Table W-19 can be combined with the mode.
- *path* — The name of the new file to create.
- *stream* — A pointer to the existing stream.

Table W-18 Mode Values for _wfreopen()

Value	Description
"r"	Open for reading.
"w"	Open for writing, which erases the file if it already exists or creates a new file if it doesn't exist.
"a"	Open for append, which writes to the end of an existing file or creates the file if it doesn't already exist.
"r+"	Open for both reading and writing.
"w+"	Open for both reading and writing. If the file already exists, its contents are lost; if the file doesn't exist, it's created.
"a+"	Open for reading and appending. If the file doesn't exist, it's created.

Table W-19 Extension Mode Values for _wfreopen()

Value	Description
t	Open for in text mode.
b	Open in binary mode.
c	Set the file's commit flag.
n	Turn off the file's commit flag.

Example

The following program demonstrates how to use the _wfreopen() function. When run, the program attempts to open a file and reassign the stream to a new file, printing status messages as it goes. The program's output looks like this:

```
First file opened successfully.
Second file created successfully.
Press any key to continue
```

Here is the program source code that produced the output:

```cpp
#include "stdafx.h"
#include <stdio.h>
#include <iostream>

using namespace std;

int main(int argc, char* argv[])
{
    FILE* file = _wfopen(L"_wfreopen.cpp", L"r");

    if (file == NULL)
    {
        cout << "File open error." << endl;
        exit(1);
    }

    cout << "First file opened successfully." << endl;
    FILE* newFile = _wfreopen(L"_wfreopen.dup", L"w", file);

    if (newFile == NULL)
    {
        cout << "File creation error." << endl;
        exit(1);
    }

    cout << "Second file created successfully." << endl;
    fcloseall();

    return 0;
}
```

CROSS-REFERENCE
See also _close(), _creat(), _fcloseall(), _fdopen(), _fgetchar(), _fgetwchar(), _fileno(), _flushall(), _fputwchar(), _fsopen(), _getw(), _getws(), _lseeki64(), _open(), _putw(), _putws(), _read(), _rmtmp(), _tempnam(), _wcreat(), _wfdopen(), _wfopen(), _wfsopen(), _wopen(), _wtempnam(), _wtmpnam(), clearerr(), eof(), fclose(), feof(), ferror(), fflush(), fgetc(), fgetpos(), fgets(), fgetwc(), fgetws(), fopen(), fprintf(), fputc(), fputchar(), fputs(), fputwc(), fputws(), fread(), freopen(), fscanf(), fseek(), fsetpos(), ftell(), fwprintf(), fwrite(), fwscanf(), getc(), getchar(), gets(), getwc(), getwchar(), lseek(), putc(), putch(), putchar(), puts(), putwc(), putwchar(), rewind(), setbuf(), setvbuf(), tmpfile(), tmpnam(), ungetc(), ungetch(), ungetwc(), and write().

_wfsopen()

Function

The _wfsopen() function opens a stream using file sharing.

NOTE
This function works only on systems, such as Windows NT, that support wide-character filenames.

Header File

```
#include <stdio.h>
```

Declaration

```
FILE* _wfsopen(const wchar_t *filename,
    const wchar_t *mode, int shflag);
```

- *filename* — The name of the file to open.
- *mode* — The file access mode, which can be one of the mode values from Table W-20. The values shown in Table W-21 can be combined with the mode.
- *shflag* — The sharing flag for the stream, which can be an extension mode value (defined in share.h) from Table W-22.

Table W-20 Mode Values for the _wfsopen() function

Value	Description
"r"	Open for reading.
"w"	Open for writing, which erases the file if it already exists or creates a new file if it doesn't exist.
"a"	Open for append, which writes to the end of an existing file or creates the file if it doesn't already exist.
"r+"	Open for both reading and writing.
"w+"	Open for both reading and writing. If the file already exists, its contents are lost; if the file doesn't exist, it's created.
"a+"	Open for reading and appending. If the file doesn't exist, it's created.

Table W-21 Extension Mode Values for _wfsopen()

Value	Description
T	Open for in text mode.
B	Open in binary mode.
C	Set the file's commit flag.
N	Turn off the file's commit flag.

Table W-22 File-Sharing Flag Values for _wfsopen()

Value	Description
SH_COMPAT	Compatibility mode setting for 16-bit applications.
SH_DENYO	Read and write access.
SH_DENYRD	No read access.
SH_DENYRW	No read or write access.
SH_DENYWR	No write access.

Example

The following program demonstrates how to use the _wfsopen() function. When run, the program attempts to open a file that denies write access, prints a status message, and then closes the file if it opened successfully. The program's output looks like this:

```
File opened successfully.
Press any key to continue
```

Here is the program source code that produced the output:

```
#include "stdafx.h"
#include <stdio.h>
#include <iostream>
#include <share.h>

using namespace std;

int main(int argc, char* argv[])
{
    FILE* file = _wfsopen(L"_fsopen.cpp", L"r", SH_DENYWR);

    if (file != NULL)
    {
        cout << "File opened successfully." << endl;

     fclose(file);
    }
    else
        cout << "File failed to open." << endl;

    return 0;
}
```

CROSS-REFERENCE
See also _close(), _creat(), _fcloseall(), _fdopen(), _fgetchar(), _fgetwchar(), _fileno(), _flushall(), _fputwchar(), _fsopen(), _getw(), _getws(), _lseeki64(), _open(), _putw(), _putws(), _read(), _rmtmp(), _tempnam(), _wcreat(), _wfdopen(), _wfopen(), _wfreopen(), _wopen(), _wtempnam(), _wtmpnam(), clearerr(), eof(), fclose(), feof(), ferror(), fflush(), fgetc(), fgetpos(), fgets(), fgetwc(), fgetws(), fopen(), fprintf(), fputc(), fputchar(), fputs(), fputwc(), fputws(), fread(), freopen(), fscanf(), fseek(), fsetpos(), ftell(), fwprintf(), fwrite(), fwscanf(), getc(), getchar(), gets(), getwc(), getwchar(), lseek(), putc(), putch(), putchar(), puts(), putwc(), putwchar(), rewind(), setbuf(), setvbuf(), tmpfile(), tmpnam(), ungetc(), ungetch(), ungetwc(), and write().

_wfullpath()

Function

The _wfullpath() function is the wide-character version of _fullpath(), which creates a full path from a relative path name.

NOTE
This function works only on systems, such as Windows NT, that support wide-character filenames.

Header File

```
#include <stdlib.h>
```

Declaration

```
wchar_t* _wfullpath(wchar_t *absPath,
    const wchar_t *relPath, size_t maxLength);
```

- *absPath* — A pointer to the character array that will hold the final path.
- *relPath* — The relative path for which the function should find the absolute path.
- *maxLength* — The maximum number of characters to return in the absolute path name.

Example

The following program demonstrates how to use the _wfullpath() function. When run, the program creates and displays the full path for the program's source code file. The program's output looks like this:

```
Full Path:
C:\Microsoft\W\_wfullpath\_wfullpath.cpp
Press any key to continue
```

Here is the program source code that produced the output:

```
#include "stdafx.h"
#include <stdio.h>
#include <iostream>

using namespace std;

int main(int argc, char* argv[])
{
    wchar_t fullPath[_MAX_PATH];

    _wfullpath(fullPath, L"_wfullpath.cpp", _MAX_PATH);
    if (fullPath == NULL)
```

V

W

X

```
            cout << "Error in path" << endl;
        else
        {
            cout << "Full Path: " << endl;
            wcout << fullPath << endl;
        }

        return 0;
    }
```

CROSS-REFERENCE

See also _fullpath(), _getcwd(), _getdcwd(), _makepath(), _splitpath(), _wgetcwd(), _wgetdcwd(), _wmakepath(), and _wsplitpath().

_wgetcwd()

Function

The _wgetcwd() function retrieves the default drive's current working directory, returning a pointer to the buffer containing the directory string. The function returns NULL in the case of an error.

NOTE

This function works only on systems, such as Windows NT, that support wide-character filenames.

Header File

```
#include <direct.h>
```

Declaration

```
wchar_t* _wgetcwd(wchar_t *buffer, int maxlen);
```

- *buffer* — A pointer to the buffer in which to store the directory string.
- *maxlen* — The maximum number of characters in the path.

Example

The following program demonstrates how to use the _wgetcwd() function by retrieving and displaying the current working directory. The program's output looks like this:

```
Working directory: C:\Microsoft\W\_wgetcwd
Press any key to continue
```

Here is the program source code that produced the output:

```cpp
#include "stdafx.h"
#include <direct.h>
#include <iostream>

using namespace std;

int main(int argc, char* argv[])
{
    wchar_t buf[_MAX_PATH];

    wchar_t* path = _wgetcwd(buf, _MAX_PATH);
    if (path != NULL)
    {
        cout << "Working directory: ";
        wcout << buf << endl;
    }
    else
        cout << "Error" << endl;

    return 0;
}
```

CROSS-REFERENCE
See also chdir(), chdrive(), getcwd(), getdcwd(), getdrive(), _mkdir(), _rmdir(), _searchenv(), _wchdir(), _wgetdcwd(), _wmkdir(), _wrmdir(), and _wsearchenv().

_wgetdcwd()

Function

The _wgetdcwd() function retrieves a disk drive's full, current, working-directory path, returning a pointer to the buffer containing the directory string. The function returns NULL in the case of an error.

NOTE
This function works only on systems, such as Windows NT, that support wide-character filenames.

Header File

```
#include <direct.h>
```

Declaration

```
wchar_t* _wgetdcwd(int drive, wchar_t *buffer, int maxlen);
```

- *buffer* — A pointer to the buffer in which to store the directory string.
- *drive* — The drive for which to get the current working-directory path, where 1 is A, 2 is B, 3 is C, and so on.
- *maxlen* — The maximum number of characters in the path.

Example

The following program demonstrates how to use the _wgetdcwd() function by retrieving and displaying the current working directory for drive C. The program's output looks like this:

```
Working directory: C:\Microsoft\W\_wgetdcwd
Press any key to continue
```

Here is the program source code that produced the output:

```
#include "stdafx.h"
#include <direct.h>
#include <iostream>

using namespace std;

int main(int argc, char* argv[])
{
    wchar_t buf[_MAX_PATH];

    wchar_t* path = _wgetdcwd(3, buf, _MAX_PATH);
    if (path != NULL)
    {
        cout << "Working directory: ";
        wcout << buf << endl;
```

```
    }
    else
        cout << "Error" << endl;

    return 0;
}
```

CROSS-REFERENCE

See also _chdir(), _chdrive(), getcwd(), _getdcwd(), getdrive(), _mkdir(), _rmdir(), _searchenv(), _wchdir(), _wgetcwd(), _wgetdcwd(), _wmkdir(), _wrmdir(), and _wsearchenv().

_wgetenv()

Function

The _wgetenv() function retrieves the value of the specified environment variable, returning a pointer to the buffer containing the environment string. The function returns NULL in the case of an error.

Header File

```
#include <stdlib.h>
```

Declaration

```
wchar_t* _wgetenv(wchar_t *varname);
```

- *varname* — The name of the environment variable for which to get the value.

Example

The following program demonstrates how to use the _wgetenv() function, by retrieving and displaying the PATH variable's current setting. The program's output looks something like this:

```
PATH: C:\WINDOWS;C:\WINDOWS\COMMAND
Press any key to continue
```

Here is the program source code that produced the output:

```
#include "stdafx.h"
#include <stdlib.h>
```

```
#include <iostream>

using namespace std;

int main(int argc, char* argv[])
{
    wchar_t* value = _wgetenv(L"PATH");
    if (value != NULL)
    {
        cout << "PATH: ";
        wcout << value << endl;
    }
    else
        cout << "Error" << endl;

    return 0;
}
```

CROSS-REFERENCE
See also _wputenv(), getenv(), and putenv().

_wmakepath()

Function

The _wmakepath() function is the wide-character version of _makepath(), which assembles a full path from various path elements.

Header File

```
#include <stdlib.h>
```

Declaration

```
void _wmakepath(wchar_t *path, const wchar_t *drive,
    const wchar_t *dir, const wchar_t *fname,
    const wchar_t *ext);
```

- *dir* — The final path's directory element.
- *drive* — The final path's drive letter.
- *ext* — The final path's filename extension element.

- *fname* — The final path's filename element.
- *path* — A pointer to the character array that will hold the final path.

Example

The following program demonstrates how to use the _wmakepath() function. When run, the program creates and displays the full path for the various given elements. The program's output looks like this:

```
Full Path:
c:Windows\System\sysedit.exe
Press any key to continue
```

Here is the program source code that produced the output:

```
#include "stdafx.h"
#include <stdio.h>
#include <iostream>

using namespace std;

int main(int argc, char* argv[])
{
    wchar_t fullPath[_MAX_PATH];
    wchar_t drive[] = L"c";
    wchar_t dir[] = L"Windows\\System";
    wchar_t fileName[] = L"sysedit";
    wchar_t ext[] = L"exe";

    _wmakepath(fullPath, drive, dir, fileName, ext);
    if (fullPath == NULL)
        cout << "Error in path" << endl;
    else
    {
        cout << "Full Path: " << endl;
        wcout << fullPath << endl;
    }

    return 0;
}
```

V
W
X

CROSS-REFERENCE

See lso _fullpath(), _getcwd(), _getdcwd(), _makepath(), _splitpath(), _wfullpath(), _wgetcwd(), _wgetdcwd(), and _wsplitpath().

_wmkdir()

Function

The _wmkdir() function is the wide-character version of mkdir(), which creates a new directory. If the function is successful, it returns 0; otherwise, it returns −1.

NOTE

This function works only on systems, such as Windows NT, that support wide-character filenames.

Header File

```
#include <direct.h>
```

Declaration

```
int _wmkdir(const wchar_t* dirname)
```

- *dirname* — The path and name of the new current directory.

Example

The following program demonstrates how to use the _wmkdir() function, by creating a new directory in drive C's root directory and then deleting the new directory. The program's output looks like this:

```
New directory created
Press any key to continue
```

Here is the program source code that produced the output:

```
#include "stdafx.h"
#include <direct.h>
#include <iostream>

using namespace std;
```

```
int main(int argc, char* argv[])
{
    int result = _wmkdir(L"c:\\TestDir");
    if (result != -1)
    {
        cout << "New directory created" << endl;
        _wrmdir(L"c:\\TestDir");
    }
    else
        cout << "Directory create error" << endl;

    return 0;
}
```

CROSS-REFERENCE

See also _searchenv(), _wchdir(), _wgetcwd(), _wgetdcwd(), _wrmdir(), _wsearchenv(), chdir(), chdrive(), getcwd(), _getdcwd(), getdrive(), mkdir(), and rmdir().

_wmktemp()

Function

The _wmktemp() function is the wide-character version of _mktemp(), which generates a unique filename that can be used to create temporary file. If the function is successful, it returns a pointer to the filename; otherwise, it returns NULL.

Header File

```
#include <io.h>
```

Declaration

```
wchar_t* _wmktemp(wchar_t *template);
```

- *template* — A pointer to the template to be used to create the filename. This template must be in the form *base*XXXXXX, where *base* is the user-supplied characters for the filename and the X's are placeholders for the characters that the _wmktemp() function will supply.

Example

The following program demonstrates how to use the _wmktemp() function, by creating and displaying a unique temporary filename. The program's output looks like this:

```
Temp file name: tempa46901
Press any key to continue
Here is the program source code that produced the output:
#include "stdafx.h"
#include <io.h>
#include <iostream>

using namespace std;

int main(int argc, char* argv[])
{
    wchar_t* result;
    wchar_t fileName[] = L"tempXXXXXX";

    result = _wmktemp(fileName);
    if (result == NULL)
        cout << "Error forming temp File name" << endl;
    else
    {
        cout << "Temp file name: ";
        wcout << fileName << endl;
    }

    return 0;
}
```

 CROSS-REFERENCE
See also _mktemp(), _tempnam(), _wtempnam(), _wtmpnam(), tmpfile(), and tmpnam().

_wopen()

Function

The _wopen() function opens a file, returning the file's handle if successful, or –1 if unsuccessful. Unlike the _open() function, _wopen() requires its filename argument to be in wide-character format.

NOTE
This function works only on systems, such as Windows NT, that support wide-character filenames.

Header File

```
#include <io.h>
```

Declaration

```
int _wopen(const wchar_t* fileName, int flag);
```

- *fileName* — The name of the file to open.
- *flag* — A flag value (from Table W-23) that indicates whether the file is being opened for reading and/or writing.

Table W-23 File Flag Values for _wopen()

Value	Description
O_APPEND	Positions the file pointer at the end of the file.
O_BINARY	Opens the file in binary mode.
O_CREAT	Creates and then opens a file.
O_CREAT | O_SHORT_LIVED	Creates a temporary file that is not flushed to disk.
O_CREAT | O_TEMPORARY	Creates a temporary file that is deleted when the last file is closed.
O_CREAT | O_EXCL	Creates a file, returning an error if the file already exists.
O_RANDOM	Enables random access.
O_RDONLY	Opens a file in read-only mode.
O_RDWR	Opens a file for both reading and writing.
O_SEQUENTIAL	Enables sequential file access.
O_TEXT	Opens a text file.
O_TRUNC	Opens a file and truncates the file length to 0.
O_WRONLY	Opens a file in write-only mode.

V
W
X

Example

The following program demonstrates how to use the _wopen() function. When run, the program opens a file in read-only mode and then closes the file, displaying appropriate messages as it goes. The program's output looks like this:

```
File opened successfully.
Press any key to continue
```

Here is the program source code that produced the output:

```cpp
#include "stdafx.h"
#include <fcntl.h>
#include <io.h>
#include <iostream>

using namespace std;

int main(int argc, char* argv[])
{
    int fileHandle = _wopen(L"open.cpp", O_RDONLY);

    if (fileHandle != -1)
    {
        cout << "File opened successfully." << endl;
        int result = _close(fileHandle);
    }
    else
        cout << "File open error." << endl;

    return 0;
}
```

CROSS-REFERENCE

See also _close(), _creat(), _fcloseall(), _fdopen(), _fgetchar(), _fgetwchar(), _fileno(), _flushall(), _fputwchar(), _fsopen(), _getw(), _getws(), _lseeki64(), _open(), _putw(), _putws(), _read(), _rmtmp(), _tempnam(), _wcreat(), _wfdopen(), _wfopen(), _wfreopen(), _wfsopen(), _wtempnam(), _wtmpnam(), clearerr(), eof(), fclose(), feof(), ferror(), fflush(), fgetc(), fgetpos(), fgets(), fgetwc(), fgetws(), fopen(), fprintf(), fputc(), fputchar(), fputs(), fputwc(), fputws(), fread(), freopen(), fscanf(), fseek(), fsetpos(), ftell(), fwprintf(), fwrite(), fwscanf(), getc(), getchar(), gets(), getwc(), getwchar(), lseek(), putc(), putch(), putchar(), puts(), putwc(), putwchar(), rewind(), setbuf(), setvbuf(), tmpfile(), tmpnam(), ungetc(), ungetch(), ungetwc(), and write().

_wperror()

Function

The _wperror() function is the wide-character version of the perror() function, which prints an error message to the stderr stream.

Header File

```
#include <stdio.h>
```

Declaration

```
void _wperror(const wchar_t *string);
```

- *string*—The error message to display.

Example

The following program demonstrates how to use the _wperror() function. When run, the program attempts to open a file, and if the file fails to open, displays an error message. The program's output looks like this:

```
File open error: Bad file descriptor
Press any key to continue
```

Here is the program source code that produced the output:

```
#include "stdafx.h"
#include <fcntl.h>
#include <io.h>
#include <stdio.h>
#include <iostream>

using namespace std;

int main(int argc, char* argv[])
{
    int fileHandle = _wopen(L"_wperror.cpp", O_RDONLY);

    if (fileHandle != -1)
    {
        cout << "File opened successfully." << endl;
        int result = _close(fileHandle);
    }
```

```
        else
            _wperror(L"File open error");


        return 0;
    }
```

CROSS-REFERENCE
See also clearerr(), ferror(), perror(), and strerror().

_wpopen()

Function

The _wpopen() function is the wide-character version of the _popen() function, which opens a pipe associated with a command's standard input or output, returning a stream if successful. or NULL if unsuccessful.

NOTE
This function works only on systems, such as Windows NT, that support wide-character filenames.

Header File

```
#include <stdio.h>
```

Declaration

```
FILE* _wpopen(const wchar_t *command, const wchar_t *mode);
```

- *command* — The command string to execute.
- *mode* — The requested mode for the stream, which can be a one or a combination of the following: "r", "w", "t", and "b". These modes stand for read, write, text, and binary, respectively.

Example

The following program demonstrates how to use the _wpopen() function. When run, the program calls, reads, and displays its own source code file, as shown below:

```
#include "stdafx.h"
#include <fcntl.h>
#include <io.h>
#include <stdio.h>
#include <iostream>

using namespace std;

int main(int argc, char* argv[])
{
    FILE    *file;
    char    buf[81];
    int result;

    file = _wpopen(L"type _wpopen.cpp", L"rt");

    if (file != NULL )
    {
        result = feof(file);

        while (!result)
        {
            char* str = fgets(buf, 80, file);
            if (str != NULL )
                cout << str;
            result = feof(file);
        }

        _pclose(file);
    }
    else
        cout << "Error opening pipe." << endl;

    return 0;
}
```

CROSS-REFERENCE
See also _pclose() and _popen().

V
W
X

_wputenv()

Function

The _wputenv() function sets the value of an environment variable, returning a 0 if successful, or –1 if not successful.

Header File

```
#include <stdlib.h>
```

Declaration

```
int _wputenv(wchar_t *envstring);
```

- *envstring* — The string holding the environment variable's setting.

Example

The following program demonstrates how to use the _wputenv() function by setting the PATH variable. The program's output looks like this:

```
Current PATH: C:\WINDOWS;C:\WINDOWS\COMMAND

New PATH: C:\

Restored PATH: C:\WINDOWS;C:\WINDOWS\COMMAND

Press any key to continue
```

Here is the program source code that produced the output:

```
#include "stdafx.h"
#include <stdlib.h>
#include <iostream>

using namespace std;

int main(int argc, char* argv[])
{
    wchar_t* oldValue = _wgetenv(L"PATH");
    if (oldValue == NULL)
    {
        cout << "Error getting variable" << endl;
        exit(1);
```

```
        }

        cout << "Current PATH: ";
        wcout << oldValue << endl << endl;

        int result = _wputenv(L"PATH=C:\\");
        if (result == -1)
        {
            cout << "Error setting variable" << endl;
            exit(1);
        }

        wchar_t* value = _wgetenv(L"PATH");
        cout << "New PATH: ";
        wcout << value << endl << endl;
        wchar_t s[_MAX_PATH] = L"PATH=";
        wcscpy(&s[5], oldValue);
        _wputenv(s);
        value = _wgetenv(L"PATH");
        cout << "Restored PATH: ";
        wcout << value << endl << endl;

        return 0;
    }
```

CROSS-REFERENCE
See also _wgetenv(), getenv(), and putenv().

_wremove()

Function

The _wremove() function is the wide-character version of the remove() function, which deletes a file. If the function is successful, it returns 0; otherwise, it returns −1.

NOTE
This function works only on systems, such as Windows NT, that support wide-character filenames.

Header File

```
#include <stdio.h>
```

Declaration

```
int _wremove(const wchar_t* path)
```

- *path* — The path and name of the file to delete.

Example

The following program demonstrates how to use the _wremove() function by creating a new file in drive C's root directory and then deleting the new file. The program's output looks like this:

```
New file created
New file deleted.
Press any key to continue
```

Here is the program source code that produced the output:

```
#include "stdafx.h"
#include <stdio.h>
#include <io.h>
#include <fcntl.h>
#include <iostream>
#include <sys\stat.h>

using namespace std;

int main(int argc, char* argv[])
{
    int fileHandle = _wopen(L"c:\\TestFile",
        O_CREAT, S_IREAD | S_IWRITE);
    if (fileHandle != -1)
    {
        cout << "New file created" << endl;
        close(fileHandle);
        int result = _wremove(L"c:\\TestFile");
        if (result == -1)
            cout << "Remove file error." << endl;
        else
            cout << "New file deleted." << endl;
    }
    else
```

```
            cout << "File create error" << endl;

        return 0;
    }
```

CROSS-REFERENCE
See also _wrename(), remove(), and rename().

_wrename()

Function

The _wrename() function is the wide-character version of the rename() function, which renames a file. If the function is successful, it returns 0; otherwise, it returns a nonzero value.

NOTE
This function works only on systems, such as Windows NT, that support wide-character filenames.

Header File

```
#include <stdio.h>
```

Declaration

```
int _wrename(const wchar_t* oldname, const wchar_t* newname)
```

- *newname* — The new filename.
- *oldname* — The path and old filename.

Example

The following program demonstrates how to use the _wrename() function by creating a new file in drive C's root directory, renaming the file, and then deleting the new file. The program's output looks like this:

```
New file created.
File renamed successfully.
Remove file error.
Press any key to continue
```

Here is the program source code that produced the output:

```cpp
#include "stdafx.h"
#include <stdio.h>
#include <io.h>
#include <fcntl.h>
#include <iostream>
#include <sys\stat.h>

using namespace std;

int main(int argc, char* argv[])
{
    int fileHandle = _wopen(L"c:\\TestFile",
        O_CREAT, S_IREAD | S_IWRITE);
    if (fileHandle != -1)
    {
        cout << "New file created." << endl;
        close(fileHandle);

        int result = _wrename(L"c:\\TestFile", L"MyFile");
        if (result != 0)
            cout << "File rename error." << endl;
        else
            cout << "File renamed successfully." << endl;

        result = _wremove(L"c:\\TestFile");
        if (result == -1)
            cout << "Remove file error." << endl;
        else
            cout << "New file deleted." << endl;
    }
    else
        cout << "File create error" << endl;

    return 0;
}
```

CROSS-REFERENCE

See also _wremove(), remove(), and rename().

_write()

Function

The _write() function writes data to an open file, returning the number of bytes written, or –1 if an error occurs.

Header File

```
#include <io.h>
```

Declaration

```
int _write(int handle, const void *buffer,
    unsigned int count);
```

- *buffer* — A pointer to the data to write.
- *count* — The number of bytes to write.
- *handle* — The file handle returned by the function that opened the file.

Example

The following program demonstrates how to use the _write() function. When run, the program creates a file and writes 14 bytes to the file, displaying status messages as it goes. The program's output looks like this:

```
File written successfully
Press any key to continue
```

Here is the program source code that produced the output:

```
#include "stdafx.h"
#include <stdlib.h>
#include <io.h>
#include <fcntl.h>
#include <sys/stat.h>
#include <iostream>

using namespace std;

int main(int argc, char* argv[])
{
    int numBytes;
```

```
int fileHandle;

fileHandle = _open("MyFile.dat",
    O_RDWR | O_CREAT, S_IREAD | S_IWRITE);

if (fileHandle != -1 )
{
    numBytes = _write(fileHandle, "This is a test", 14);

    if (numBytes != -1 )
        cout << "File written successfully" << endl;
    else
        cout << "File write error." << endl;

    _close( fileHandle );
}
else
    cout << "File open error." << endl;

return 0;
}
```

CROSS-REFERENCE
See also _close(), _creat(), _fcloseall(), _fdopen(), _fgetchar(), _fgetwchar(), _fileno(), _flushall(), _fputwchar(), _fsopen(), _getw(), _getws(), _lseeki64(), _open(), _putw(), _putws(), _read(), _rmtmp(), _tempnam(), _wcreat(), _wfdopen(), _wfopen(), _wfreopen(), _wfsopen(), _wopen(), _wtempnam(), _wtmpnam(), clearerr(), eof(), fclose(), feof(), ferror(), fflush(), fgetc(), fgetpos(), fgets(), fgetwc(), fgetws(), fopen(), fprintf(), fputc(), fputchar(), fputs(), fputwc(), fputws(), fread(), freopen(), fscanf(), fseek(), fsetpos(), ftell(), fwprintf(), fwrite(), fwscanf(), getc(), getchar(), gets(), getwc(), getwchar(), lseek(), putc(), putch(), putchar(), puts(), putwc(), putwchar(), rewind(), setbuf(), setvbuf(), tmpfile(), tmpnam(), ungetc(), ungetch(), ungetwc(), and write().

_wrmdir()

Function

The _wrmdir() function is the wide-character version of the rmdir() function, which deletes a directory. If the function is successful, it returns 0; otherwise it returns −1.

NOTE
This function works only on systems, such as Windows NT, that support wide-character filenames.

Header File

```
#include <direct.h>
```

Declaration

```
int _wrmdir(const wchar_t* dirname)
```

- *dirname* — The path and name of the directory to remove.

Example

The following program demonstrates how to use the _wrmdir() function by creating a new directory in drive C's root directory and then deleting the new directory. The program's output looks like this:

```
New directory created
Press any key to continue
#include "stdafx.h"
#include <direct.h>
#include <iostream>

using namespace std;

int main(int argc, char* argv[])
{
    int result = _wmkdir(L"c:\\TestDir");
    if (result != -1)
    {
        cout << "New directory created" << endl;
        _wrmdir(L"c:\\TestDir");
    }
    else
        cout << "Directory create error" << endl;

    return 0;
}
```

CROSS-REFERENCE
See also _chdir(), _chdrive(), _getcwd(), _getdcwd(), _getdrive(), _mkdir(), _rmdir(), _searchenv(), _wchdir(), _wgetcwd(), _wgetdcwd(), _wmkdir(), and _wsearchenv().

_wsearchenv()

Function

The _wsearchenv() function is the wide-character version of the _searchenv() function, which locates a file using the paths specified in a environment variable.

Header File

```
#include <stdlib.h>
```

Declaration

```
void _wsearchenv(const wchar_t *filename,
    const wchar_t *varname, wchar_t *pathname);
```

- *filename*—A pointer to the filename for which to search.
- *pathname*—A pointer to the buffer in which to store the resultant path.
- *varname*—A pointer to the environment variable to use in the search.

Example

The following program demonstrates how to use the _wsearchenv() function by locating a file using the PATH environment variable. The program's output looks like this:

```
Current PATH: C:\WINDOWS;C:\WINDOWS\COMMAND

New PATH: C:\Windows\System\

Located path: C:\Windows\System\sysedit.exe

Restored PATH: C:\WINDOWS;C:\WINDOWS\COMMAND

Press any key to continue
```

Here is the program source code that produced the output:

```cpp
#include "stdafx.h"
#include <stdlib.h>
#include <iostream>

using namespace std;

int main(int argc, char* argv[])
{
    wchar_t buf[_MAX_PATH];

    wchar_t* oldValue = _wgetenv(L"PATH");
    if (oldValue == NULL)
    {
        cout << "Error getting variable" << endl;
        exit(1);
    }

    cout << "Current PATH: ";
    wcout << oldValue << endl << endl;

    int result = _wputenv(L"PATH=C:\\Windows\\System\\");
    if (result == -1)
    {
        cout << "Error setting variable" << endl;
        exit(1);
    }

    wchar_t* value = _wgetenv(L"PATH");
    cout << "New PATH: ";
    wcout << value << endl << endl;

    _wsearchenv(L"sysedit.exe", L"PATH", buf);
    cout << "Located path: ";
    wcout << buf << endl << endl;

    wchar_t s[_MAX_PATH] = L"PATH=";
    wcscpy(&s[5], oldValue);
    _wputenv(s);
    value = _wgetenv(L"PATH");
    cout << "Restored PATH: ";
    wcout << value << endl << endl;

    return 0;
}
```

CROSS-REFERENCE

See also _chdir(), _chdrive(), _getcwd(), _getdcwd(), _getdrive(), _mkdir(), _rmdir(), _searchenv(), _wchdir(), _wgetcwd(), _wgetdcwd(), _wmkdir(), and _wrmdir().

_wsetlocale()

Function

The _wsetlocale() function is the wide-character version of the setlocale() function, which sets various elements of the current locale, returning a pointer to a locale string, or NULL if the call is unsuccessful.

Header File

```
#include <locale.h>
```

Declaration

```
wchar_t* _wsetlocale(int category, const wchar_t *locale);
```

- *category* — The element of the locale that should be changed, which can be a value from Table W-24.
- *locale* — A pointer to the name of the locale, values for which are listed in Table W-25. This can also be "C", which selects the default values for the system.

Table W-24 Locale Category Values for _wsetlocale()

Value	Description
LC_ALL	Set all categories.
LC_COLLATE	Set the locale category associated with the _stricoll(), _wcsicoll(), strcoll(), strxfrm(), wcscoll(), and wcsxfrm() functions.
LC_CTYPE	Set the locale category associated with character functions.
LC_MONETARY	Set the locale category that affects monetary formatting.
LC_NUMERIC	Set the locale category that affects decimal points.
LC_TIME	Set the locale category that affects time functions.

Table W-25 Locale Names for _wsetlocale()

Language	Name
Chinese	"chinese"
Chinese (simplified)	"chinese-simplified" or "chs"
Chinese (traditional)	"chinese-traditional" or "cht"
Czech	"czech" or "csy"
Danish	"danish" or "dan"
Dutch	"dutch" or "nld"
Dutch (Belgian)	"belgian", "dutch-belgian", or "nlb"
English (default)	"english"
English (Australian)	"australian", "ena", or "english-aus"
English (Canadian)	"canadian", "enc", or "english-can"
English (New Zealand)	"english-nz" or "enz"
English (UK)	"english-uk", "eng", or "uk"
English (USA)	"american", "american english", "american-english", "english-american", "english-us", "english-usa", "enu", "us", or "usa"
Finnish	"finnish" or "fin"
French (default)	"french" or "fra"
French (Belgian)	"french-belgian" or "frb"
French (Canadian)	"french-canadian" or "frc"
French (Swiss)	"french-swiss" or "frs"
German (default)	"german" or "deu"
German (Austrian)	"german-austrian" or "dea"
German (Swiss)	"german-swiss", "des", or "swiss"
Greek	"greek" or "ell"
Hungarian	"hungarian" or "hun"
Icelandic	"icelandic" or "isl"
Italian (default)	"italian" or "ita"
Italian (Swiss)	"italian-swiss" or "its"
Japanese	"japanese" or "jpn"
Korean	"kor" or "korean"
Norwegian (default)	"norwegian"
Norwegian Norwegian (Bokmal)	"norwegian-bokmal" or "nor"
Norwegian Norwegian (Nynorsk)	"norwegian-nynorsk" or "non"
Polish	"polish" or "plk"
Portuguese (default)	"portuguese" or "ptg"
Portuguese (Brazilian)	"portuguese-brazilian" or "ptb"
Russian (default)	"russian" or "rus"
Slovak	"slovak" or "sky"

Continued

Table W-25 *Continued*

Language	Name
Spanish (default)	"spanish" or "esp"
Spanish (Mexican)	"spanish-mexican" or "esm"
Spanish (Modern)	"spanish-modern" or "esn"
Swedish	"swedish" or "sve"
Turkish	"turkish" or "trk"

Example

The following program demonstrates how to use the `_wsetlocale()` function by setting the locale for several languages and displaying date strings in the selected languages. The program's output looks like this:

```
Result: English_United States.1252
English Date: Tuesday, February 16, 1999

Result: Spanish - Traditional Sort_Spain.1252
Spanish Date: martes, 16 de febrero de 1999

Result: German_Germany.1252
German Date: Dienstag, 16. Februar 1999

Result: Dutch_Netherlands.1252
Dutch Date: dinsdag 16 februari 1999


Press any key to continue
```

Here is the program source code that produced the output:

```
#include "stdafx.h"
#include <locale.h>
#include <time.h>
#include <iostream>

using namespace std;

int main(int argc, char* argv[])
{
    wchar_t dateStr[81];
    time_t curTime;
    struct tm* tmTime;
```

```cpp
time (&curTime);
tmTime = gmtime(&curTime);

wchar_t* result = _wsetlocale(LC_ALL, L"English");
if (result == NULL)
    cout << "Error setting locale" << endl;
else
{
    cout << "Result: ";
    wcout << result << endl;
    wcsftime(dateStr, 80, L"%#x", tmTime);
    cout << "English Date: ";
    wcout << dateStr << endl << endl;
}

result = _wsetlocale(LC_ALL, L"Spanish");
if (result == NULL)
    cout << "Error setting locale" << endl;
else
{
    cout << "Result: ";
    wcout << result << endl;
    wcsftime(dateStr, 80, L"%#x", tmTime);
    cout << "Spanish Date: ";
    wcout << dateStr << endl << endl;
}

result = _wsetlocale(LC_ALL, L"German");
if (result == NULL)
    cout << "Error setting locale" << endl;
else
{
    cout << "Result: ";
    wcout << result << endl;
    wcsftime(dateStr, 80, L"%#x", tmTime);
    cout << "German Date: ";
    wcout << dateStr << endl << endl;
}

result = _wsetlocale(LC_ALL, L"Dutch");
if (result == NULL)
    cout << "Error setting locale" << endl;
else
{
```

v
w
x

```
                          cout << "Result: ";
                          wcout << result << endl;
                          wcsftime(dateStr, 80, L"%#x", tmTime);
                          cout << "Dutch Date: ";
                          wcout << dateStr << endl << endl;
                  }

                  _wsetlocale(LC_ALL, L"C");

                  return 0;
          }
```

CROSS-REFERENCE
See also setlocale().

_wsopen()

Function

The _wsopen() function opens a file with file sharing, returning the file's handle if successful, or –1 if unsuccessful.

NOTE
This function works only on systems, such as Windows NT, that support wide-character filenames.

Header File

```
#include <io.h>
```

Declaration

```
int _wsopen(const wchar_t *filename, int oflag,
     int shflag [, int pmode ]);
```

- *filename* — The name of the file to open.
- *pmode* — The value S_IWRITE, S_IREAD, or S_IREAD | S_IWRITE. Needed only when using the O_CREAT file flag.
- *oflag* — A value (from Table W-26) that indicates whether the file is being opened for reading and/or writing.
- *shflag* — A value (from Table W-27) that indicates the file's share flag.

Table W-26 File Flag Values for _wsopen()

Value	Description
O_APPEND	Positions the file pointer at the end of the file.
O_BINARY	Opens the file in binary mode.
O_CREAT	Creates and then opens a file.
O_CREAT | O_SHORT_LIVED	Creates a temporary file that is not flushed to disk.
O_CREAT | O_TEMPORARY	Creates a temporary file that is deleted when the last file is closed.
O_CREAT | O_EXCL	Creates a file, returning an error if the file already exists.
O_RANDOM	Enables random access.
O_RDONLY	Opens a file in read-only mode.
O_RDWR	Opens a file for both reading and writing.
O_SEQUENTIAL	Enables sequential file access.
O_TEXT	Opens a text file.
O_TRUNC	Opens a file and truncates the file length to 0.
O_WRONLY	Opens a file in write-only mode.

Table W-27 File-Sharing Flag Values for _wsopen()

Value	Description
SH_COMPAT	Compatibility mode setting for 16-bit applications.
SH_DENYNO	Read and write access.
SH_DENYRD	No read access.
SH_DENYRW	No read or write access.
SH_DENYWR	No write access.

Example

The following program demonstrates how to use the _wsopen() function. When run, the program opens a file in read-only mode and then closes the file, displaying appropriate messages as it goes. The program's output looks like this:

```
File opened successfully.
Press any key to continue
```

Here is the program source code that produced the output:

```
#include "stdafx.h"
#include <fcntl.h>
#include <io.h>
```

```
#include <share.h>
#include <iostream>

using namespace std;

int main(int argc, char* argv[])
{
    int fileHandle = _wsopen(L"_wsopen.cpp",
        O_RDONLY, SH_DENYWR);

    if (fileHandle != -1)
    {
        cout << "File opened successfully." << endl;
        _close(fileHandle);
    }
    else
        cout << "File open error." << endl;

    return 0;
}
```

CROSS-REFERENCE

See also _close(), _creat(), _fcloseall(), _fdopen(), _fgetchar(), _fgetwchar(), _fileno(), _flushall(), _fputwchar(), _fsopen(), _getw(), _getws(), _lseeki64(), _open(), _putw(), _putws(), _read(), _rmtmp(), _tempnam(), _wcreat(), _wfdopen(), _wfopen(), _wfreopen(), _wfsopen(), _wopen(), _wtempnam(), _wtmpnam(), clearerr(), eof(), fclose(), feof(), ferror(), fflush(), fgetc(), fgetpos(), fgets(), fgetwc(), fgetws(), fopen(), fprintf(), fputc(), fputchar(), fputs(), fputwc(), fputws(), fread(), freopen(), fscanf(), fseek(), fsetpos(), ftell(), fwprintf(), fwrite(), fwscanf(), getc(), getchar(), gets(), getwc(), getwchar(), lseek(), putc(), putch(), putchar(), puts(), putwc(), putwchar(), rewind(), setbuf(), setvbuf(), tmpfile(), tmpnam(), ungetc(), ungetch(), ungetwc(), and write().

_wspawnl()

Function

The _wspawnl() function runs a child process given the process's path and name and additional arguments (all using wide-character arguments). This function returns to the process that called it. If the process is called with the P_WAIT mode, the function returns the process's exit status. If the process is run with either the P_NOWAIT or P_NOWAITO mode, the function returns the process handle. If the called process does not run successfully, the function returns –1. In this case, the errno global variable is set to one of the error values Table W-28.

NOTE

This function works only on systems, such as Windows NT, that support wide-character filenames.

Table W-28 Error Values for _wspawnl()

Value	Description
E2BIG	The arguments and environment require more than 32K of space.
EINVAL	Bad execution mode.
ENOENT	The specified file cannot be found.
ENOEXEC	The specified file is not executable.
ENOMEM	Not enough memory to run the process.

Header File

```
#include <process.h>
```

Declaration

```
int _wspawnl(int mode, const wchar_t *cmdname,
    const wchar_t *arg0, const wchar_t *arg1,
    ... const wchar_t *argn, NULL);
```

- *arg0* — A pointer to the first argument.
- *arg1* — A pointer to the second argument.
- *argn* — A pointer to the last argument.
- *cmdname* — The path and filename of the process to run.
- *mode* — The process's execution mode, which can be P_WAIT, P_NOWAIT, or P_NOWAITO.

Example

The following program demonstrates how to use the _wspawnl() function. When run, the program runs a child process called TestProg.exe, displaying a message if an error occurs. The program's output looks like this:

```
Running TestProg.exe

Child process running.
Press any key to continue
```

Here is the program source code that produced the output:

```
#include "stdafx.h"
#include <iostream>
#include <process.h>
#include <errno.h>

using namespace std;

int main(int argc, char* argv[])
{
    cout << "Running TestProg.exe" << endl;

    int result = _wspawnl(P_WAIT,
        L"TestProg.exe", L"TestProg.exe",
        L"arg2", L"arg3", NULL);
    if (result == -1)
    {
        switch(errno)
        {
        case ENOEXEC:
            cout << "Not an executable file" << endl;
            break;
        case E2BIG:
            cout << "Space required exceeds 32K" << endl;
            break;
        case ENOMEM:
            cout << "Not enough memory" << endl;
            break;
        case EINVAL:
            cout << "Bad execution mode" << endl;
            break;
        case ENOENT:
            cout << "File not found" << endl;
        }
    }

    return 0;
}
```

CROSS-REFERENCE
See also _wexcel(), _wexecle(), _wexeclp(), _wexeclpe(), _wexecv(), _wexecve(),
_wexecvp(), _wexecvpe(), _wspawnle(), _wspawnlp(), _wspawnlpe(), _wspawnv(),
_wspawnve(), _wspawnvp(), _wspawnvpe(), execl, execle(), execlp(), execlpe(),
execv(), execve(), execvp(), execvpe(), spawnl(), spawnle(), spawnlp(), spawnlpe(),
spawnv(), spawnve(), spawnvp(), and spawnvpe().

_wspawnle()

Function

The _wspawnle() function runs a child process given the process's path and
name, additional arguments, and environment settings (using wide-character
arguments). This function returns to the process that called it. If the process
is called with the P_WAIT mode, the function returns the process's exit status.
If the process is run with either the P_NOWAIT or P_NOWAITO mode, the function
returns the process handle. If the called process does not run successfully, the
function returns –1. In this case, the errno global variable is set to one of the
error values in Table W-29.

NOTE
This function works only on systems, such as Windows NT, that support wide-
character filenames.

Table W-29 Error Values for _wspawnle()

Value	Description
E2BIG	The arguments and environment require more than 32K of space.
EINVAL	Bad execution mode.
ENOENT	The specified file cannot be found.
ENOEXEC	The specified file is not executable.
ENOMEM	Not enough memory to run the process.

Header File

```
#include <process.h>
```

Declaration

```
int _wspawnle(int mode, const wchar_t *cmdname,
```

```
const wchar_t *arg0, const wchar_t *arg1,
... const wchar_t *argn, NULL,
const wchar_t *const *envp);
```

- *arg0* — A pointer to the first argument.
- *arg1* — A pointer to the second argument.
- *argn* — A pointer to the last argument.
- *cmdname* — The path and filename of the process to run.
- *envp* — A pointer to the environment settings.
- *mode* — The process's execution mode, which can be P_WAIT, P_NOWAIT, or P_NOWAITO.

Example

The following program demonstrates how to use the _wspawnle() function. When run, the program runs a child process called TestProg.exe, displaying a message if an error occurs. The program's output looks like this:

```
Running TestProg.exe

Child process running.
Press any key to continue
```

Here is the program source code that produced the output:

```
#include "stdafx.h"
#include <iostream>
#include <process.h>
#include <errno.h>

using namespace std;

wchar_t *envir[] =
{
   L"ENVIR1=environment setting 1",
   L"ENVIR2=environment setting 2",
   L"ENVIR3=environment setting 3",
    NULL
};

int main(int argc, char* argv[])
{
    cout << "Running TestProg.exe" << endl;
```

```
int result = _wspawnle(P_WAIT, L"TestProg.exe",
    L"TestProg.exe", L"arg2", L"arg3", NULL, envir);
if (result == -1)
{
    switch(errno)
    {
    case ENOEXEC:
        cout << "Not an executable file" << endl;
        break;
    case E2BIG:
        cout << "Space required exceeds 32K" << endl;
        break;
    case ENOMEM:
        cout << "Not enough memory" << endl;
        break;
    case EINVAL:
        cout << "Bad execution mode" << endl;
        break;
    case ENOENT:
        cout << "File not found" << endl;
    }
}

return 0;
}
```

CROSS-REFERENCE

See also _wexcel(), _wexecle(), _wexeclp(), _wexeclpe(), _wexecv(), _wexecve(), _wexecvp(), _wexecvpe(), _wspawnl(), wspawnlp(), _wspawnlpe(), _wspawnv(), _wspawnve(), _wspawnvp(), _wspawnvpe(), execl, execle(), execlp(), execlpe(), execv(), execve(), execvp(), execvpe(), spawnl(), spawnle(), spawnlp(), spawnlpe(), spawnv(), spawnve(), spawnvp(), and spawnvpe().

_wspawnlp()

Function

The _wspawnlp() function runs a child process given the process's path and name and additional arguments (using wide-character arguments). This function returns to the process that called it. If the process is called with the P_WAIT mode, the function returns the process's exit status. If the process is run with either the P_NOWAIT or P_NOWAITO mode, the function returns the process handle. If the called process does not run successfully, the function returns −1. In this case, the errno global variable is set to one of the error values in Table W-30.

 NOTE
This function works only on systems, such as Windows NT, that support wide-character filenames.

Table W-30 Error Values for _wspawnlp()

Value	Description
E2BIG	The arguments and environment require more than 32K of space.
EINVAL	Bad execution mode.
ENOENT	The specified file cannot be found.
ENOEXEC	The specified file is not executable.
ENOMEM	Not enough memory to run the process.

Header File

```
#include <process.h>
```

Declaration

```
int _wspawnlp(int mode, const wchar_t *cmdname,
    const wchar_t *arg0, const wchar_t *arg1,
    ... const wchar_t *argn, NULL);
```

- *arg0*—A pointer to the first argument.
- *arg1*—A pointer to the second argument.
- *argn*—A pointer to the last argument.
- *cmdname*—The path and filename of the process to run.
- *mode*—The process's execution mode, which can be P_WAIT, P_NOWAIT, or P_NOWAITO.

Example

The following program demonstrates how to use the _wspawnlp() function. When run, the program runs a child process called TestProg.exe, displaying a message if an error occurs. The program's output looks like this:

```
Running TestProg.exe
```

```
Child process running.
Press any key to continue
```

Here is the program source code that produced the output:

```cpp
#include "stdafx.h"
#include <iostream>
#include <process.h>
#include <errno.h>

using namespace std;

int main(int argc, char* argv[])
{
    cout << "Running TestProg.exe" << endl;

    int result = _wspawnlp(P_WAIT, L"TestProg.exe",
        L"TestProg.exe", L"arg2", L"arg3", NULL);
    if (result == -1)
    {
        switch(errno)
        {
        case ENOEXEC:
            cout << "Not an executable file" << endl;
            break;
        case E2BIG:
            cout << "Space required exceeds 32K" << endl;
            break;
        case ENOMEM:
            cout << "Not enough memory" << endl;
            break;
        case EINVAL:
            cout << "Bad execution mode" << endl;
            break;
        case ENOENT:
            cout << "File not found" << endl;
        }
    }

    return 0;
}
```

CROSS-REFERENCE
See also _wexcel(), _wexecle(), _wexeclp(), _wexeclpe(), _wexecv(), _wexecve(), _wexecvp(), _wexecvpe(), _wspawnl(), _wspawnle(), _wspawnlpe(), _wspawnv(), _wspawnve(), _wspawnvp(), _wspawnvpe(), execl, execle(), execlp(), execlpe(), execv(), execve(), execvp(), execvpe(), spawnl(), spawnle(), spawnlp(), spawnlpe(), spawnv(), spawnve(), spawnvp(), and spawnvpe().

_wspawnlpe()

Function

The _wspawnlpe() function runs a child process given the process's path and name, additional arguments, and environment settings (all using wide-character arguments). This function returns to the process that called it. If the process is called with the P_WAIT mode, the function returns the process's exit status. If the process is run with either the P_NOWAIT or P_NOWAITO mode, the function returns the process handle. If the called process does not run successfully, the function returns –1. In this case, the errno global variable is set to one of the error values in Table W-31.

NOTE
This function works only on systems, such as Windows NT, that support wide-character filenames.

Table W-31 Error Values for _wspawnlpe()

Value	Description
E2BIG	The arguments and environment require more than 32K of space.
EINVAL	Bad execution mode.
ENOENT	The specified file cannot be found.
ENOEXEC	The specified file is not executable.
ENOMEM	Not enough memory to run the process.

Header File

```
#include <process.h>
```

Declaration

```
int _wspawnlpe(int mode, const wchar_t *cmdname,
    const wchar_t *arg0, const wchar_t *arg1,
    ... const wchar_t *argn, NULL,
    const wchar_t *const *envp);
```

- *arg0* — A pointer to the first argument.
- *arg1* — A pointer to the second argument.
- *argn* — A pointer to the last argument.
- *cmdname* — The path and filename of the process to run.
- *envp* — A pointer to the environment settings.
- *mode* — The process's execution mode, which can be P_WAIT, P_NOWAIT, or P_NOWAITO.

Example

The following program demonstrates how to use the _wspawnlpe() function. When run, the program runs a child process called TestProg.exe, displaying a message if an error occurs. The program's output looks like this:

```
Running TestProg.exe

Child process running.
Press any key to continue
```

Here is the program source code that produced the output:

```
#include "stdafx.h"
#include <iostream>
#include <process.h>
#include <errno.h>

using namespace std;

char *envir[] =
{
    "ENVIR1=environment setting 1",
    "ENVIR2=environment setting 2",
    "ENVIR3=environment setting 3",
     NULL
};

int main(int argc, char* argv[])
{
```

```
cout << "Running TestProg.exe" << endl;

int result = _wspawnlpe(P_WAIT, L"TestProg.exe",
    L"TestProg.exe", L"arg2", L"arg3", NULL, envir);
if (result == -1)
{
    switch(errno)
    {
    case ENOEXEC:
        cout << "Not an executable file" << endl;
        break;
    case E2BIG:
        cout << "Space required exceeds 32K" << endl;
        break;
    case ENOMEM:
        cout << "Not enough memory" << endl;
        break;
    case EINVAL:
        cout << "Bad execution mode" << endl;
        break;
    case ENOENT:
        cout << "File not found" << endl;
    }
}

return 0;
}
```

 CROSS-REFERENCE
See also _wexcel(), _wexecle(), _wexeclp(), _wexeclpe(), _wexecv(), _wexecve(), _wexecvp(), _wexecvpe(), _wspawnl(), _wspawnle(), _wspawnlp(), _wspawnv(), _wspawnve(), _wspawnvp(), _wspawnvpe(), execl, execle(), execlp(), execlpe(), execv(), execve(), execvp(), execvpe(), spawnl(), spawnle(), spawnlp(), spawnlpe(), spawnv(), spawnve(), spawnvp(), and spawnvpe().

_wspawnv()

Function

The _wspawnv() function runs a child process given the process's path and name (using wide-character strings) and additional arguments supplied as an array of wchar_t pointers. This function returns to the process that called it. If the process is called with the P_WAIT mode, the function returns the process's exit status. If the process is run with either the P_NOWAIT or P_NOWAITO mode, the function returns the process handle. If the called process does not run successfully, the function returns -1. In this case, the errno global variable will be set to one of the error values in Table W-32.

 NOTE
This function works only on systems, such as Windows NT, that support wide-character filenames.

Table W-32 Error Values for _wspawnv()

Value	Description
E2BIG	The arguments and environment require more than 32K of space.
EINVAL	Bad execution mode.
ENOENT	The specified file cannot be found.
ENOEXEC	The specified file is not executable.
ENOMEM	Not enough memory to run the process.

Header File

```
#include <process.h>
```

Declaration

```
int _wspawnv(int mode, const wchar_t *cmdname,
    const wchar_t *const *argv);
```

- *argv* — A pointer to an array of wchar_t pointers that point to the arguments.
- *cmdname* — The path and filename of the process to run.
- *mode* — The process's execution mode, which can be P_WAIT, P_NOWAIT, or P_NOWAITO.

Example

The following program demonstrates how to use the _wspawnv() function. When run, the program runs a child process called TestProg.exe, displaying a message if an error occurs. The program's output looks like this:

```
Running TestProg.exe
```

```
Child process running.
Press any key to continue
```

Here is the program source code that produced the output:

```cpp
#include "stdafx.h"
#include <iostream>
#include <process.h>
#include <errno.h>

using namespace std;

int main(int argc, char* argv[])
{
    wchar_t* args[] =
    {
        L"TestProg.exe",
        L"argument #1",
        L"argument #2",
         NULL
    };

    cout << "Running TestProg.exe" << endl;

    int result = _wspawnv(P_WAIT, L"TestProg.exe", args);
    if (result == -1)
    {
        switch(errno)
        {
        case ENOEXEC:
            cout << "Not an executable file" << endl;
            break;
        case E2BIG:
            cout << "Space required exceeds 32K" << endl;
            break;
        case ENOMEM:
            cout << "Not enough memory" << endl;
            break;
        case EINVAL:
            cout << "Bad execution mode" << endl;
            break;
        case ENOENT:
            cout << "File not found" << endl;
```

```
            }
        }

        return 0;
    }
```

CROSS-REFERENCE
See also _wexecl(), _wexecle(), _wexeclp(), _wexeclpe(), _wexecv(), _wexecve(),
_wexecvp(), _wexecvpe(), _wspawnl(), _wspawnle(), _wspawnlp(), _wspawnlpe(),
_wspawnve(), _wspawnvp(), _wspawnvpe(), execl, execle(), execlp(), execlpe(),
execv(), execve(), execvp(), execvpe(), spawnl(), spawnle(), spawnlp(), spawnlpe(),
spawnv(), spawnve(), spawnvp(), and spawnvpe().

_wspawnve()

Function

The _wspawnve() function runs a child process given the process's path and
name (as wide-character strings), and additional arguments and environment
settings supplied as an array of wchar_t pointers. This function returns to the
process that called it. If the process is called with the P_WAIT mode, the function returns the process's exit status. If the process is run with either the
P_NOWAIT or P_NOWAITO mode, the function returns the process handle. If the
called process does not run successfully, the function returns –1. In this case,
the errno global variable is set to one of the error values in Table W-33.

NOTE
This function works only on systems, such as Windows NT, that support wide-
character filenames.

Table W-33 Error Values for _wspawnve()

Value	Description
E2BIG	The arguments and environment require more than 32K of space.
EINVAL	Bad execution mode.
ENOENT	The specified file cannot be found.
ENOEXEC	The specified file is not executable.
ENOMEM	Not enough memory to run the process.

V
W
X

Header File

```
#include <process.h>
```

Declaration

```
int _wspawnve(int mode, const wchar_t *cmdname,
    const wchar_t *const *argv, const wchar_t *const *envp);
```

- *argv* — A pointer to an array of wchar_t pointers that point to the arguments.
- *cmdname* — The path and filename of the process to run.
- *envp* — A pointer to an array of wchar_t pointers that point to the environment settings.
- *mode* — The process's execution mode, which can be P_WAIT, P_NOWAIT, or P_NOWAITO.

Example

The following program demonstrates how to use the _wspawnve() function. When run, the program runs a child process called TestProg.exe, displaying a message if an error occurs. The program's output looks like this:

```
Running TestProg.exe

Child process running.
Press any key to continue
```

Here is the program source code that produced the output:

```
#include "stdafx.h"
#include <iostream>
#include <process.h>
#include <errno.h>

using namespace std;

wchar_t *envir[] =
{
   L"ENVIR1=environment setting 1",
   L"ENVIR2=environment setting 2",
   L"ENVIR3=environment setting 3",
    NULL
};
```

```
wchar_t* args[] =
{
    L"TestProg.exe",
    L"argument #1",
    L"argument #2",
     NULL
};

int main(int argc, char* argv[])
{
    cout << "Running TestProg.exe" << endl;

    int result = _wspawnve(P_WAIT, L"TestProg.exe",
        args, envir);
    if (result == -1)
    {
        switch(errno)
        {
        case ENOEXEC:
            cout << "Not an executable file" << endl;
            break;
        case E2BIG:
            cout << "Space required exceeds 32K" << endl;
            break;
        case ENOMEM:
            cout << "Not enough memory" << endl;
            break;
        case EINVAL:
            cout << "Bad execution mode" << endl;
            break;
        case ENOENT:
            cout << "File not found" << endl;
        }
    }

    return 0;
}
```

CROSS-REFERENCE

See also _wexcel(), _wexecle(), _wexeclp(), _wexeclpe(), _wexecv(), _wexecve(),
_wexecvp(), _wexecvpe(), _wspawnl(), _wspawnle(), _wspawnlp(), _wspawnlpe(),
_wspawnv(), _wspawnvp(), _wspawnvpe(), execl, execle(), execlp(), execlpe(),
execv(), execve(), execvp(), execvpe(), spawnl(), spawnle(), spawnlp(), spawnlpe(),
spawnv(), spawnve(), spawnvp(), and spawnvpe().

_wspawnvp()

Function

The _wspawnvp() function runs a child process given the process's path and name (as wide-character strings) and additional arguments supplied as an array of wchar_t pointers. This function returns to the process that called it. If the process is called with the P_WAIT mode, the function returns the process's exit status. If the process is run with either the P_NOWAIT or P_NOWAITO mode, the function returns the process handle. If the called process does not run successfully, the function returns –1. In this case, the errno global variable is set to one of the error values in Table W-34.

 NOTE

This function works only on systems, such as Windows NT, that support wide-character filenames.

Table W-34 Error Values for _wspawnvp()

Value	Description
E2BIG	The arguments and environment require more than 32K of space.
EINVAL	Bad execution mode.
ENOENT	The specified file cannot be found.
ENOEXEC	The specified file is not executable.
ENOMEM	Not enough memory to run the process.

Header File

```
#include <process.h>
```

Declaration

```
int _wspawnvp(int mode, const wchar_t *cmdname,
    const wchar_t *const *argv );
```

- *argv* — A pointer to an array of wchar_t pointers that point to the arguments.
- *cmdname* — The path and filename of the process to run.
- *mode* — The process's execution mode, which can be P_WAIT, P_NOWAIT, or P_NOWAITO.

Example

The following program demonstrates how to use the _wspawnvp() function. When run, the program runs a child process called TestProg.exe, displaying a message if an error occurs. The program's output looks like this:

```
Running TestProg.exe

Child process running.
Press any key to continue
```

Here is the program source code that produced the output:

```cpp
#include "stdafx.h"
#include <iostream>
#include <process.h>
#include <errno.h>

using namespace std;

int main(int argc, char* argv[])
{
    wchar_t* args[] =
    {
        L"TestProg.exe",
        L"argument #1",
        L"argument #2",
         NULL
    };

    cout << "Running TestProg.exe" << endl;

    int result = _wspawnvp(P_WAIT, L"TestProg.exe", args);
    if (result == -1)
    {
        switch(errno)
        {
        case ENOEXEC:
            cout << "Not an executable file" << endl;
            break;
        case E2BIG:
            cout << "Space required exceeds 32K" << endl;
            break;
        case ENOMEM:
            cout << "Not enough memory" << endl;
            break;
```

```
                    case EINVAL:
                        cout << "Bad execution mode" << endl;
                        break;
                    case ENOENT:
                        cout << "File not found" << endl;
                    }
                }

            return 0;
        }
```

CROSS-REFERENCE

See also _wexcel(), _wexecle(), _wexeclp(), _wexeclpe(), _wexecv(), _wexecve(), _wexecvp(), _wexecvpe(), _wspawnl(), _wspawnle(), _wspawnlp(), _wspawnlpe(), _wspawnv(), _wspawnve(), _wspawnvpe(), execl, execle(), execlp(), execlpe(), execv(), execve(), execvp(), execvpe(), spawnl(), spawnle(), spawnlp(), spawnlpe(), spawnv(), spawnve(), spawnvp(), and spawnvpe().

_wspawnvpe()

Function

The _wspawnvpe() function runs a child process given the process's path and name (as wide-character strings), and additional arguments and environment settings supplied as an array of wchar_t pointers. This function returns to the process that called it. If the process is called with the _P_WAIT mode, the function returns the process's exit status. If the process is run with the _P_NOWAIT or _P_NOWAITO modes, the function returns the process handle. If the called process does not run successfully, the function returns −1. In this case, the errno global variable is set to one of the error values in Table W-35.

NOTE

This function works only on systems, such as Windows NT, that support wide-character filenames.

Table W-35 Error Values for _wspawnvpe()

Value	Description
E2BIG	The arguments and environment require more than 32K of space.
EINVAL	Bad execution mode.
ENOENT	The specified file cannot be found.

Value	Description
ENOEXEC	The specified file is not executable.
ENOMEM	Not enough memory to run the process.

Header File

```
#include <process.h>
```

Declaration

```
int _wspawnvpe(int mode, const wchar_t *cmdname,
    const wchar_t *const *argv, const wchar_t *const *envp);
```

- *argv* — A pointer to an array of wchar_t pointers that point to the arguments.
- *cmdname* — The path and filename of the process to run.
- *envp* — A pointer to an array of wchar_t pointers that point to the environment settings.
- *mode* — The process's execution mode, which can be P_WAIT, P_NOWAIT, or P_NOWAITO.

Example

The following program demonstrates how to use the _wspawnvpe() function. When run, the program runs a child process called TestProg.exe, displaying a message if an error occurs. The program's output looks like this:

```
Running TestProg.exe

Child process running.
Press any key to continue
```

Here is the program source code that produced the output:

```
#include "stdafx.h"
#include <iostream>
#include <process.h>
#include <errno.h>

using namespace std;

wchar_t *envir[] =
{
```

```
            L"ENVIR1=environment setting 1",
            L"ENVIR2=environment setting 2",
            L"ENVIR3=environment setting 3",
             NULL
        };

        wchar_t* args[] =
        {
            L"TestProg.exe",
            L"argument #1",
            L"argument #2",
             NULL
        };

        int main(int argc, char* argv[])
        {
            cout << "Running TestProg.exe" << endl;

            int result = _wspawnvpe(P_WAIT, L"TestProg.exe",
                args, envir);
            if (result == -1)
            {
                switch(errno)
                {
                case ENOEXEC:
                    cout << "Not an executable file" << endl;
                    break;
                case E2BIG:
                    cout << "Space required exceeds 32K" << endl;
                    break;
                case ENOMEM:
                    cout << "Not enough memory" << endl;
                    break;
                case EINVAL:
                    cout << "Bad process mode" << endl;
                    break;
                case ENOENT:
                    cout << "File not found" << endl;
                }
            }

            return 0;
        }
```

CROSS-REFERENCE
See also _wexcel(), _wexecle(), _wexeclp(), _wexeclpe(), _wexecv(), _wexecve(), _wexecvp(), _wexecvpe(), _wspawnl(), _wspawnle(), _wspawnlp(), _wspawnlpe(), _wspawnv(), _wspawnve(), _wspawnvp(), execl, execle(), execlp(), execlpe(), execv(), execve(), execvp(), execvpe(), spawnl(), spawnle(), spawnlp(), spawnlpe(), spawnv(), spawnve(), spawnvp(), and spawnvpe().

_wsplitpath()

Function

The _wsplitpath() function is the wide-character version of the _splitpath() function, which divides a full path into its various path elements.

Header File

```
#include <stdlib.h>
```

Declaration

```
void _wsplitpath(const wchar_t *path, wchar_t *drive,
    wchar_t *dir, wchar_t *fname, wchar_t *ext);
```

- *dir* — A pointer to the character array that will contain directory path element.
- *drive* — A pointer to the character array that will contain the drive letter path element.
- *ext* — A pointer to the character array that will contain the filename extension path element.
- *fname* — A pointer to the character array that will contain the filename path element.
- *path* — A pointer to the character array that contains the full path.

Example

The following program demonstrates how to use the _wsplitpath() function. When run, the program extracts and displays the elements of the supplied full path. The program's output looks like this:

```
Full Path: c:\Windows\System\sysedit.exe
Drive: c:
```

V
W
X

```
Directory: \Windows\System\
File name: sysedit
Extension: .exe
Press any key to continue
```

Here is the program source code that produced the output:

```cpp
#include "stdafx.h"
#include <stdlib.h>
#include <iostream>

using namespace std;

int main(int argc, char* argv[])
{
    wchar_t fullPath[_MAX_PATH] =
        L"c:\\Windows\\System\\sysedit.exe";
    wchar_t drive[_MAX_DRIVE];
    wchar_t dir[_MAX_DIR];
    wchar_t fileName[_MAX_FNAME];
    wchar_t ext[_MAX_EXT];

    _wsplitpath(fullPath, drive, dir, fileName, ext);
    cout << "Full Path: ";
    wcout << fullPath << endl;
    cout << "Drive: ";
    wcout << drive << endl;
    cout << "Directory: ";
    wcout << dir << endl;
    cout << "File name: ";
    wcout << fileName << endl;
    cout << "Extension: ";
    wcout << ext << endl;

    return 0;
}
```

CROSS-REFERENCE

See also _fullpath(), _getcwd(), _getdcwd(), _makepath(), _splitpath(), _wfullpath(), _wgetcwd(), _wgetdcwd(), and _wmakepath().

_wstat()

Function

The _wstat() function is the wide-character version of the _stat() function, which acquires status information about a file. The function returns 0 if successful or –1 if unsuccessful.

NOTE
This function works only on systems, such as Windows NT, that support wide-character filenames.

Header File

```
#include <sys\systypes.h>
#include <sys\stat.h>
```

Declaration

```
int _wstat(const wchar_t *path, struct _stat *buffer);
```

- *buffer*—A pointer to the _stat structure that will hold the returned status information.
- *path*—The path to the file for which to acquire status information.

Example

The following program demonstrates how to use the _wstat() function. When run, the program acquires and displays size and time status information on a file. The program's output looks something like this:

```
File Size: 599
Time: Mon May 03 00:00:00 1999
Press any key to continue
```

Here is the program source code that produced the output:

```
#include "stdafx.h"
#include <sys/types.h>
#include <sys/stat.h>
#include <time.h>
#include <iostream>

using namespace std;
```

```
int main(int argc, char* argv[])
{
    struct _stat statInfo;

    int result = _wstat( L"_wstat.cpp", &statInfo );
    if(result == 0)
    {
        cout << "File Size: " << statInfo.st_size << endl;
        cout << "Time: " << ctime(&statInfo.st_atime);
    }
    else
        cout << " _wstat() error" << endl;

    return 0;
}
```

CROSS-REFERENCE
See also _stat(), _stati64(), and _wstati64.

_wstati64()

Function

The _wstati64() function is the wide-character version of _stati64(), which acquires status information about a file. The function returns 0 if successful, or –1 if unsuccessful.

NOTE
This function works only on systems, such as Windows NT, that support wide-character filenames.

Header File

```
#include <sys\systypes.h>
#include <sys\stat.h>
```

Declaration

```
__int64 _wstati64(const wchar_t *path,
    struct _stati64 *buffer);
```

- *buffer* — A pointer to the _stati64 structure that will hold the returned status information.
- *path* — The path to the file for which to acquire status information.

Example

The following program demonstrates how to use the _wstati64() function. When run, the program acquires and displays size and time status information on a file. The program's output looks like this:

```
File Size: 599
Time: Mon May 03 00:00:00 1999
Press any key to continue
```

Here is the program source code that produced the output:

```cpp
#include "stdafx.h"
#include <sys/types.h>
#include <sys/stat.h>
#include <time.h>
#include <iostream>

using namespace std;

int main(int argc, char* argv[])
{
    struct _stati64 statInfo;

    __int64 result = _wstati64(L"_wstat.cpp", &statInfo);
    if(result == 0)
    {
        cout << "File Size: " << (int)statInfo.st_size << endl;
        cout << "Time: " << ctime(&statInfo.st_atime);
    }
    else
        cout << " _wstati64() error" << endl;

    return 0;
}
```

CROSS-REFERENCE

See also _stat(), _stati64(), and _wstat().

_wstrdate()

Function

The _wstrdate() function is the wide-character version of the _strdate() function, which copies the date to a supplied buffer, returning a pointer to the buffer.

Header File

```
#include <time.h>
```

Declaration

```
wchar_t* _wstrdate(wchar_t *datestr);
```

- *datestr* — A pointer to the buffer that will receive the date string.

Example

The following program demonstrates how to use the _wstrdate() function. When run, the program copies the current date into a buffer named buf and then displays the result. The program's output looks like this:

```
Current Date: 02/16/99
Press any key to continue
```

Here is the program source code that produced the output:

```
#include "stdafx.h"
#include <time.h>
#include <iostream>

using namespace std;

int main(int argc, char* argv[])
{
    wchar_t buf[256];

    wchar_t* result = _wstrdate(buf);
    cout << "Current Date: ";
    wcout << result << endl;

    return 0;
}
```

CROSS-REFERENCE
See also _ftime(), _futime(), _strtime(), _utime(), _wasctime, _wctime(), _wstrtime(), _wutime(), asctime(), ctime(), difftime(), gmtime(), localtime(), mktime(), strftime(), time(), and wcsftime().

_wstrtime()

Function

The _wstrtime() function is the wide-character version of the _strtime() function, which copies the time to a supplied buffer, returning a pointer to the buffer.

Header File

```
#include <time.h>
```

Declaration

```
wchar_t* _wstrtime(wchar_t *timestr);
```

- *timestr*—A pointer to the buffer that will receive the date string.

Example

The following program demonstrates how to use the _wstrtime() function. When run, the program copies the current time into a buffer named buf and then displays the result. The program's output looks like this:

```
Current Time: 14:56:42
Press any key to continue
```

Here is the program source code that produced the output:

```
#include "stdafx.h"
#include <time.h>
#include <iostream>

using namespace std;

int main(int argc, char* argv[])
{
    wchar_t buf[256];
```

```
        wchar_t* result = _wstrtime(buf);
        cout << "Current Date: ";
        wcout << result << endl;

        return 0;
}
```

CROSS-REFERENCE
See also _ftime(), _futime(), _strdate(), _strtime(), _utime(), _wasctime, _wctime(), _wstrdate(), _wutime(), asctime(), ctime(), difftime(), gmtime(), localtime(), mktime(), strftime(), time(), and wcsftime().

_wsystem()

Function

The _wsystem() function is the wide-character version of the _system() function, which executes a given command, returning the value returned by the command interpreter, or –1 in the case of an error. The function returns 0 and sets the errno global variable to ENOENT if the command interpreter cannot be found.

NOTE
This function works only on systems, such as Windows NT, that support wide-character filenames.

Header File

```
#include <process.h>
```

Declaration

```
int _wsystem(const wchar_t *command);
```

- *command*—A pointer to the command to execute.

Example

The following program demonstrates how to use the _wsystem() function. When run, the program executes the DIR command and displays the results. The program's output looks something like this:

```
Volume in drive C has no label
Volume Serial Number is 07CE-0C0B
Directory of C:\all code\Microsoft\W\_wsystem

.                <DIR>        02-16-99  3:07p .
..               <DIR>        02-16-99  3:07p ..
STDAFX    H            667  02-16-99  3:07p StdAfx.h
STDAFX    CPP          295  02-16-99  3:07p StdAfx.cpp
_WSYSTEM  DSW          541  02-16-99  3:07p _wsystem.dsw
_WSYSTEM  CPP          255  02-16-99  3:11p _wsystem.cpp
README    TXT        1,220  02-16-99  3:07p ReadMe.txt
_WSYSTEM  NCB            0  02-16-99  3:07p _wsystem.ncb
_WSYSTEM  DSP        4,560  02-16-99  3:07p _wsystem.dsp
DEBUG            <DIR>        02-16-99  3:07p Debug
_WSYSTEM  PLG        1,257  02-16-99  3:11p _wsystem.plg
         8 file(s)         8,795 bytes
         3 dir(s)     10,302.81 MB free
Press any key to continue
```

Here is the program source code that produced the output:

```cpp
#include "stdafx.h"
#include <process.h>
#include <iostream>

using namespace std;

int main(int argc, char* argv[])
{
    int result = _wsystem(L"dir");

    return 0;
}
```

CROSS-REFERENCE

See also _system(), _wexcel(), _wexecle(), _wexeclp(), _wexeclpe(), _wexecv(), _wexecve(), _wexecvp(), _wexecvpe(), _wspawnl(), _wspawnle(), _wspawnlp(), _wspawnlpe(), _wspawnv(), _wspawnve(), _wspawnvp(), _wspawnvpe(), execl, execle(), execlp(), execlpe(), execv(), execve(), execvp(), execvpe(), spawnl(), spawnle(), spawnlp(), spawnlpe(), spawnv(), spawnve(), spawnvp(), and spawnvpe().

_wtempnam()

Function

The _wtempnam() function is the wide-character version of the _tempnam() function, which generates a unique filename that can be used to create a temporary file. If the function is successful, it returns a pointer to the filename; otherwise, it returns NULL.

Header File

```
#include <stdio.h>
```

Declaration

```
wchar_t* _wtempnam(wchar_t *dir, wchar_t *prefix);
```

- *dir*—A pointer to a string containing the directory to use if the variable TMP is undefined.
- *prefix*—The characters supplied by the user to be used in the filename.

Example

The following program demonstrates how to use the _wtempnam() function by creating and displaying a unique temporary filename. The program's output looks like this:

```
Temp file name: C:\WINDOWS\TEMP\temp2
Press any key to continue
```

Here is the program source code that produced the output:

```
#include "stdafx.h"
#include <stdio.h>
#include <iostream>

using namespace std;

int main(int argc, char* argv[])
{
    wchar_t* result;
    wchar_t dir[] = L"c:\\Windows";
    wchar_t prefix[] = L"temp";
```

```
result = _wtempnam(dir, prefix);
if (result == NULL)
    cout << "Error forming temp File name" << endl;
else
{
    cout << "Temp file name: ";
    wcout << result << endl;
}

return 0;
}
```

CROSS-REFERENCE

See also _mktemp(), _tempnam(), _wmktemp(), _wtmpnam(), tmpfile(), and tmpnam().

_wtmpnam()

Function

The _wtmpnam() function is the wide-character version of the tmpnam() function, which generates a unique filename that can be used to create a temporary file. If the function is successful, it returns a pointer to the filename; otherwise, it returns NULL.

Header File

```
#include <stdio.h>
```

Declaration

```
wchar_t* _wtmpnam(wchar_t *string);
```

- *string*—A pointer to a string that will contain the generated temporary filename.

Example

The following program demonstrates how to use the _wtmpnam() function by creating and displaying a temporary filename. The program's output looks like this:

```
Temp file name: \s3vv75jr.
Press any key to continue
```

Here is the program source code that produced the output:

```
#include "stdafx.h"
#include <stdio.h>
#include <iostream>

using namespace std;

int main(int argc, char* argv[])
{
    wchar_t fileName[_MAX_FNAME];
    wchar_t* result;

    result = _wtmpnam(fileName);
    if (result == NULL)
        cout << "Error forming temp File name" << endl;
    else
    {
        cout << "Temp file name: ";
        wcout << result << endl;
    }

    return 0;
}
```

CROSS-REFERENCE
See also _mktemp(), _tempnam(), _wmktemp(), _wtempnam(), tmpfile(), and tmpnam().

_wtoi()

Function

The _wtoi() function converts a wide-character string to an integer, returning the resultant integer. If the string cannot be interpreted as an integer, _wtoi() returns 0.

Header File

```
#include <stdlib.h>
```

Declaration

```
int _wtoi(const wchar_t *string);
```

- *string* — The string to convert.

Example

The following program demonstrates how to use the _wtoi() function. When run, the program converts the string "5000" to an integer and displays the result. The program's output looks like this:

```
Result = 5000
Press any key to continue
```

Here is the program source code that produced the output:

```
#include "stdafx.h"
#include <iostream>
#include <stdlib.h>

using namespace std;

int main(int argc, char* argv[])
{
    int result = _wtoi(L"5000");
    cout << "Result = " << result << endl;

    return 0;
}
```

CROSS-REFERENCE
See also _wtoi64(), _wtol(), atof(), atoi(), and atol().

_wtoi64()

Function

The _wtoi64() function converts a wide-character string to a 64-bit integer, returning the resultant integer. If the string cannot be interpreted as an integer, _wtoi64() returns 0.

V

W

X

Header File

```
#include <stdlib.h>
```

Declaration

```
__int64 _wtoi64(const wchar_t *string);
```

- *string* — The string to convert.

Example

The following program demonstrates how to use the _wtoi64() function. When run, the program converts the string "5000" to a 64-bit integer and displays the result. The program's output looks like this:

```
Result = 5000
Press any key to continue
```

Here is the program source code that produced the output:

```cpp
#include "stdafx.h"
#include <iostream>
#include <stdlib.h>

using namespace std;

int main(int argc, char* argv[])
{
    __int64 result = _wtoi64(L"5000");
    cout << "Result = " << (int)result << endl;

    return 0;
}
```

CROSS-REFERENCE
See also _wtoi(), _wtol(), atof(), atoi(), and atol().

_wtol()

Function

The _wtol() function converts a wide-character string to a long integer, returning the resultant integer. If the string cannot be interpreted as an integer, _wtol() returns 0.

Header File

```
#include <stdlib.h>
```

Declaration

```
long _wtol(const wchar_t *string);
```

- *string* — The string to convert.

Example

The following program demonstrates how to use the _wtol() function. When run, the program converts the string "5000" to a long integer and displays the result. The program's output looks like this:

```
Result = 5000
Press any key to continue
```

Here is the program source code that produced the output:

```
#include "stdafx.h"
#include <iostream>
#include <stdlib.h>

using namespace std;

int main(int argc, char* argv[])
{
    long result = _wtol(L"5000");
    cout << "Result = " << result << endl;

    return 0;
}
```

V

W

X

CROSS-REFERENCE
See also _wtoi(), _wtoi64(), atof(), atoi(), and atol().

_wunlink()

Function

The _wunlink() function is the wide-character version of the _unlink() function, which deletes a file, returning 0 if successful or –1 if an error occurs.

NOTE
This function works only on systems, such as Windows NT, that support wide-character filenames.

Header File

```
#include <io.h>
```

Declaration

```
int _wunlink(const wchar_t *filename);
```

■ *filename* — The file to delete.

Example

The following program demonstrates how to use the _wunlink() function. When run, the program attempts to delete a file and displays the results. The program's output looks like this:

```
File deleted successfully
Press any key to continue
```

Here is the program source code that produced the output:

```
#include "stdafx.h"
#include <io.h>
#include <iostream>

using namespace std;

int main(int argc, char* argv[])
{
```

```
int result = _wunlink(L"c:\\MyFile.txt");
if (result == 0)
    cout << "File deleted successfully" << endl;
else
{
    cout << "File delete error: ";
    if (errno == EACCES)
        cout << "Read-only file" << endl;
    else if (errno == ENOENT)
        cout << "File not found" << endl;
    else
        cout << "Unknown error" << endl;
}

return 0;
}
```

CROSS-REFERENCE

See also _access(), _chmod(), _fullpath(), _get_osfhandle(), _makepath(), _mktemp(), _open_osfhandle(), _splitpath(), _stat(), _stati64(),_umask(), _unlink(), _waccess(), _wchmod(), _wfullpath(), _wmakepath(), _wmktemp(), _wremove(), _wrename(), _wsplitpath(), _wstat(), and _wstati64(), remove(), and rename().

_wutime()

Function

The _wutime() function is the wide-character version of the _utime() function, which sets the time when a file was last modified. The function returns 0 if successful, or –1 if an error occurs.

NOTE

This function works only on systems, such as Windows NT, that support wide-character filenames.

Header File

```
#include <sys\utime.h>
```

Declaration

```
int _wutime(wchar_t *filename, struct _utimbuf *times);
```

- *filename*—The file for which to change the modification time.
- *times*—A pointer to an initialized _utimebuf structure that contains the new modification time or NULL to change the modification time to the current time.

Example

The following program demonstrates how to use the _wutime() function. When run, the program attempts to change a file's modification time and displays the results. The program's output looks like this:

```
Modification time successfully changed
Press any key to continue
```

Here is the program source code that produced the output:

```cpp
#include "stdafx.h"
#include <sys\utime.h>
#include <iostream>

using namespace std;

int main(int argc, char* argv[])
{
    int result = _wutime(L"_wutime.cpp", NULL);
    if (result == 0)
        cout << "Modification time successfully changed" <<
endl;
    else
    {
        cout << "Modification time change error: ";
        switch (errno)
        {
        case EACCES:
            cout << "Read-only file" << endl;
            break;
        case EINVAL:
            cout << "Invalid time" << endl;
            break;
        case EMFILE:
            cout << "Too many open files" << endl;
            break;
```

```
                case ENOENT:
                    cout << "File not found" << endl;
                    break;
                default:
                    cout << "Unknown error" << endl;
                }
        }

        return 0;
}
```

CROSS-REFERENCE

See also _ftime(), _futime(), _strdate(), _strtime(), _tzset(), _utime(), _wasctime, _wctime(), _wstrdate(), _wstrtime(), asctime(), ctime(), difftime(), gmtime(), localtime(), mktime(), strftime(), time(), and wcsftime().

wcerr

Stream Object

The wcerr stream object is a wide-character version of the cerr stream object, which is a predefined object of the ostream class that places output into the standard error output stream.

Header File

```
#include <iostream.h>
```

Example

The following program demonstrates how to use the wcerr stream object by displaying an error message if a value doesn't fit a required range. The program's output looks like this:

```
Enter a value from 1 to 5:
7
ERROR: Value out of range!

Press any key to continue
```

Here is the program source code that produced the output. endl is a stream manipulator that places a carriage return and line feed onto the stream. Other manipulators include hex for obtaining hexadecimal output (cout << hex << 2000 << endl), oct for obtaining octal output (cout << oct << 2000 << endl), and dec for obtaining decimal output (cout << dec << 2000 << endl).

```
#include "stdafx.h"
#include <iostream>

using namespace std;

int main(int argc, char* argv[])
{
    char s[81];
    wchar_t msg[] = L"ERROR: Value out of range!";

    cout << "Enter a value from 1 to 5:" << endl;
    cin > s;
    int val = atoi(s);
    if ((val < 1) || (val > 5))
        wcerr << msg << endl << endl;
    else
        cout << "Value OK" << endl << endl;

    return 0;
}
```

CROSS-REFERENCE
See also cin, clog, cout, istream, ostream, wcin, and wcout.

wchar.h

Standard C library header file

The wchar.h header file defines the constants, functions, and data types needed to manipulate wide data.

Defined Constants

NULL	WCHAR_MAX
WCHAR_MIN	WEOF

Defined Functions

btowc()	wcscpy()
fgetwc()	wcscspn()
fgetws()	wcsftime()
fputwc()	wcslen()
fputws()	wcsncat()
fwide()	wcsncmp()
fwprintf()	wcsncpy()
fwscanf()	wcspbrk()
getwc()	wcsrchr()
getwchar()	wcsrtombs()
mbrlen()	wcsspn()
mbrtowc()	wcsstr()
mbsinit()	wcstod()
mbsrtowcs()	wcstok()
putwc()	wcstol()
putwchar()	wcstoul()
swprintf()	wcsxfrm()
swscanf()	wctob()
ungetwc()	wmemchr()
vfwprintf()	wmemchr()
vswprintf()	wmemchr()
vwprintf()	wmemcmp()
wcrtomb()	wmemcpy()
wcscat()	wmemmove()
wcschr()	wmemset()
wcscmp()	wprintf()
wcscoll()	wscanf()

Defined Data Types

mbstate_t	wchar_t
size_t	wint_t
tm	

wcin

Stream Object

The wcin stream object is a predefined object of the ostream class that can be used to retrieve wide-character data from the standard input stream.

Header File

```
#include <iostream.h>
```

Example

The following program demonstrates how to use the wcin stream object by retrieving a string from the user and redisplaying the acquired string on the screen. The program's output looks like this:

```
Enter a string below:
abcdefghijklmnopqrstuvwxyz

You typed the following:
abcdefghijklmnopqrstuvwxyz

Press any key to continue
```

Here is the program source code that produced the output. endl is a stream manipulator that places a carriage return and line feed onto the stream. Other manipulators include hex for obtaining hexadecimal output (wcout << hex << 2000 << endl), oct for obtaining octal output (wcout << oct << 2000 << endl), and dec for obtaining decimal output (wcout << dec << 2000 << endl).

```
#include "stdafx.h"
#include <iostream>

using namespace std;

int main(int argc, char* argv[])
{
    wchar_t str[81];

    cout << "Enter a string below:" << endl;
    wcin > str;
    cout << endl << "You typed the following:" << endl;
    wcout << str << endl << endl;
```

```
        return 0;
    }
```

CROSS-REFERENCE
See also cerr, cin, and wcerr.

wclog

Stream Object

The wclog stream object is a predefined object of the ostream class that places buffered wide-character output into the standard error output stream.

Header File

```
#include <iostream.h>
```

Example

The following program demonstrates how to use the wclog stream object by displaying an error message if a value doesn't fit a required range. The program's output looks something like this:

```
Enter a value from 1 to 5:
7
ERROR: Value out of range!

Press any key to continue
```

Here is the program source code that produced the output. endl is a stream manipulator that places a carriage return and line feed onto the stream. Other manipulators include hex for obtaining hexadecimal output (cout << hex << 2000 << endl), oct for obtaining octal output (cout << oct << 2000 << endl), and dec for obtaining decimal output (cout << dec << 2000 << endl).

```
#include "stdafx.h"
#include <iostream>

using namespace std;

int main(int argc, char* argv[])
```

```
    {
        wchar_t s[81];
        wchar_t* str;

        cout << "Enter a value from 1 to 5:" << endl;
        wcin > s;
        long val = wcstol(s, &str, 10);
        if ((val < 1) || (val > 5))
            wclog << L"ERROR: Value out of range!" << endl <<
endl;
        else
            cout << "Value OK" << endl << endl;

        return 0;
    }
```

CROSS-REFERENCE
See also cerr, cin, cout, istream, ostream, wcin, and wcout.

wcout

Stream Object

The wcout stream object is a predefined object of the ostream class that can be used to send wide-character output to the standard output stream.

Header File

```
#include <iostream.h>
```

Example

The following program demonstrates how to use the wcout stream object by retrieving a string from the user and redisplaying the acquired string on the screen using the wcout object. The program's output looks like this:

```
Enter a string below:
abcdefghijklmnopqrstuvwxyz

You typed the following:
abcdefghijklmnopqrstuvwxyz
```

```
Press any key to continue
```

Here is the program source code that produced the output. endl is a stream manipulator that places a carriage return and line feed onto the stream. Other manipulators include hex for obtaining hexadecimal output (wcout << hex << 2000 << endl), oct for obtaining octal output (wcout << oct << 2000 << endl), and dec for obtaining decimal output (wcout << dec << 2000 << endl).

```cpp
#include "stdafx.h"
#include <iostream>

using namespace std;

int main(int argc, char* argv[])
{
    wchar_t str[81];

    cout << "Enter a string below:" << endl;
    wcin > str;
    cout << endl << "You typed the following:" << endl;
    wcout << str << endl << endl;

    return 0;
}
```

CROSS-REFERENCE
See also cerr, cin, wcerr, and wcin.

wcscat()

Function

The wcscat() function concatenates wide-character strings, returning a pointer to the destination string.

Header File

```
#include <string.h>
```

Declaration

```
wchar_t *wcscat(wchar_t *strDestination,
```

```
        const wchar_t *strSource);
```

- *strDestination* — The string to which to concatenate *strSource*.
- *strSource* — The string to concatenate to *strDestination*.

Example

The following program demonstrates how to use the `wcscat()` function. When run, the program concatenates the wide-character string "Four Five Six" to the wide-character string "One Two Three ". The program's output looks like this:

```
Result: One Two Three Four Five Six
Press any key to continue
```

Here is the program source code that produced the output:

```cpp
#include "stdafx.h"
#include <iostream>
#include <string.h>

using namespace std;

int main(int argc, char* argv[])
{
    wchar_t str1[81];

    wchar_t* str2 = {L"Four Five Six"};
    wcscpy(str1, L"One Two Three ");
    wcscat(str1, str2);
    cout << "Result: ";
    wcout << str1 << endl;

    return 0;
}
```

CROSS-REFERENCE

See also _mbscat(), _mbschr(), _mbscmp(), _mbscoll(), _mbscpy(), _mbscspn(), _mbsdec(), _mbsdup(), _mbsicmp(), _mbsicoll(), _mbsinc(), _mbslen(), _mbslwr(), _mbsnbcat(), _mbsnbcmp(), _mbsnbcnt(), _mbsnbcoll(), _mbsnbcpy(), _mbsnbicmp(), _mbsnbicoll(), _mbsnbset(), _mbsnccnt(), _mbsncmp(), _mbsncoll(), _mbsncpy(), _mbsnextc(), _mbsnicmp(), _mbsnicoll(), _mbsninc(), _mbsnset(), _mbspbrk(), _mbsrchr(), _mbsrev(), _mbsset(), _mbsspn(), _mbsspnp(), _mbsstr(), _mbstok(), _mbstrlen(), _mbsupr(), _wcsdec(), _wcsdup(), _wcsicmp(), _wcsicoll(), _wcsinc(), _wcslwr(), _wcsncnt(), _wcsncoll(), _wcsnextc(), _wcsnicmp(), _wcsnicoll(), _wcsninc(), _wcsnset(), _wcsrev(), _wcsset(), _wcsspnp(), _wcsupr(), strcat(), strchr(), strcmp(), strcoll(), strcpy(), strcspn(), strlen(), strncmp(), strncpy(), strpbrk(), strrchr(), strspn(), strstr(), strtod(), strtok(), strtol(), strtoul(), strxfrm(), wcschr(), wcscmp(), wcscoll(), wcscpy(), wcscspn(), wcslen(), wcsncmp(), wcsncpy(), wcspbrk(), wcsrchr(), wcsspn(), wcsstr(), wcstod(), wcstok(), wcstol(), and wcstoul().

wcschr()

Function

The wcschr() function locates a character in a wide-character string, returning a pointer to the character.

Header File

```
#include <string.h>
```

Declaration

```
wchar_t* wcschr(const wchar_t *string, wint_t c);
```

- *c* — The character for which to search.
- *string* — A pointer to the string to search for *c*.

Example

The following program demonstrates how to use the wcschr() function. When run, the program locates the first occurrence of the letter e in the string "One Two Three" and displays the string starting with the located letter. The program's output looks like this:

```
Result: e Two Three
Press any key to continue
```

Here is the program source code that produced the output:

```
#include "stdafx.h"
#include <iostream>
#include <string.h>

using namespace std;
```

```
int main(int argc, char* argv[])
{
    wint_t ch = 'e';
    wchar_t* str1 = {L"One Two Three"};
    wchar_t* pChr = wcschr(str1, ch);
    cout << "Result: ";
    wcout << pChr << endl;

    return 0;
}
```

CROSS-REFERENCE

See also _mbscat(), _mbschr(), _mbscmp(), _mbscoll(), _mbscpy(), _mbscspn(), _mbsdec(), _mbsdup(), _mbsicmp(), _mbsicoll(), _mbsinc(), _mbslen(), _mbslwr(), _mbsnbcat(), _mbsnbcmp(), _mbsnbcnt(), _mbsnbcoll(), _mbsnbcpy(), _mbsnbicmp(), _mbsnbicoll(), _mbsnbset(), _mbsnccnt(), _mbsncmp(), _mbsncoll(), _mbsncpy(), _mbsnextc(), _mbsnicmp(), _mbsnicoll(), _mbsninc(), _mbsnset(), _mbspbrk(), _mbsrchr(), _mbsrev(), _mbsset(), _mbsspn(), _mbsspnp(), _mbsstr(), _mbstok(), _mbstrlen(), _mbsupr(), _wcsdec(), _wcsdup(), _wcsicmp(), _wcsicoll(), _wcsinc(), _wcslwr(), _wcsncnt(), _wcsncoll(), _wcsnextc(), _wcsnicmp(), _wcsnicoll(), _wcsninc(), _wcsnset(), _wcsrev(), _wcsset(), _wcsspnp(), _wcsupr(), strcat(), strchr(), strcmp(), strcoll(), strcpy(), strcspn(), strlen(), strncmp(), strncpy(), strpbrk(), strrchr(), strspn(), strstr(), strtod(), strtok(), strtol(), strtoul(), strxfrm(), wcscat(), wcscmp(), wcscoll(), wcscpy(), wcscspn(), wcslen(), wcsncmp(), wcsncpy(), wcspbrk(), wcsrchr(), wcsspn(), wcsstr(), wcstod(), wcstok(), wcstol(), and wcstoul().

wcscmp()

Function

The wcscmp() function compares two wide-character strings, returning a value from Table W-36.

Table W-36 Return Values for wcscmp()

Value	Description
Less than 0	string1 is alphabetically less than string2.
0	The two strings are equal.
Greater than 0	string1 is alphabetically greater than string2.

Header File

```
#include <string.h>
```

Declaration

```
int wcscmp(const wchar_t *string1, const wchar_t *string2);
```

- *string1* — The first string to compare.
- *string2* — The second string to compare.

Example

The following program demonstrates how to use the `wcscmp()` function. When run, the program compares several pairs of strings and displays the result of the comparisons. The program's output looks like this:

```
One Two Three equals One Two Three
One Two Three is greater than Four Five Six
Four Five Six is less than Seven Eight Nine
Press any key to continue
```

Here is the program source code that produced the output:

```
#include "stdafx.h"
#include <iostream>
#include <string.h>

using namespace std;

void cmp(wchar_t* s1, wchar_t* s2)
{
    int result = wcscmp(s1, s2);
    if (result < 0 )
    {
        wcout << s1;
        cout << " is less than ";
        wcout << s2 << endl;
    }
    else if (result > 0)
    {
        wcout << s1;
        cout << " is greater than ";
```

V

W

X

```
            wcout << s2 << endl;
        }
        else
        {
            wcout << s1;
            cout << " equals ";
            wcout << s2 << endl;
        }
    }

    int main(int argc, char* argv[])
    {
        wchar_t* str1 = {L"One Two Three"};
        wchar_t* str2 = {L"One Two Three"};
        wchar_t* str3 = {L"Four Five Six"};
        wchar_t* str4 = {L"Seven Eight Nine"};

        cmp(str1, str2);
        cmp(str2, str3);
        cmp(str3, str4);

        return 0;
    }
```

CROSS-REFERENCE

See also _mbscat(), _mbschr(), _mbscmp(), _mbscoll(), _mbscpy(), _mbscspn(), _mbsdec(), _mbsdup(), _mbsicmp(), _mbsicoll(), _mbsinc(), _mbslen(), _mbslwr(), _mbsnbcat(), _mbsnbcmp(), _mbsnbcnt(), _mbsnbcoll(), _mbsnbcpy(), _mbsnbicmp(), _mbsnbicoll(), _mbsnbset(), _mbsnccnt(), _mbsncmp(), _mbsncoll(), _mbsncpy(), _mbsnextc(), _mbsnicmp(), _mbsnicoll(), _mbsninc(), _mbsnset(), _mbspbrk(), _mbsrchr(), _mbsrev(), _mbsset(), _mbsspn(), _mbsspnp(), _mbsstr(), _mbstok(), _mbstrlen(), _mbsupr(), _wcsdec(), _wcsdup(), _wcsicmp(), _wcsicoll(), _wcsinc(), _wcslwr(), _wcsncnt(), _wcsncoll(), _wcsnextc(), _wcsnicmp(), _wcsnicoll(), _wcsninc(), _wcsnset(), _wcsrev(), _wcsset(), _wcsspnp(), _wcsupr(), strcat(), strchr(), strcmp(), strcoll(), strcpy(), strcspn(), strlen(), strncmp(), strncpy(), strpbrk(), strrchr(), strspn(), strstr(), strtod(), strtok(), strtol(), strtoul(), strxfrm(), wcscat(), wcschr(), wcscoll(), wcscpy(), wcscspn(), wcslen(), wcsncmp(), wcsncpy(), wcspbrk(), wcsrchr(), wcsspn(), wcsstr(), wcstod(), wcstok(), wcstol(), and wcstoul().

wcscoll()

Function

The `wcscoll()` function compares two wide-character strings for the current locale, returning a value from Table W-37.

Table W-37 Return Values for wcscoll()

Value	Description
Less than 0	`string1` is alphabetically less than `string2`.
0	The two strings are equal.
Greater than 0	`string1` is alphabetically greater than `string2`.

Header File

```
#include <string.h>
```

Declaration

```
int wcscoll(const wchar_t *string1, const wchar_t *string2);
```

- *string1* — The first string to compare.
- *string2* — The second string to compare.

Example

The following program demonstrates how to use the `wcscoll()` function. When run, the program compares several pairs of strings and displays the result of the comparisons. The program's output looks like this:

```
One Two Three equals One Two Three
One Two Three is greater than Four Five Six
Four Five Six is less than Seven Eight Nine
Press any key to continue
```

Here is the program source code that produced the output:

```
#include "stdafx.h"
#include <iostream>
#include <string.h>

using namespace std;
```

```
void cmp(wchar_t* s1, wchar_t* s2)
{
    int result = wcscoll(s1, s2);
    if (result < 0 )
    {
        wcout << s1;
        cout << " is less than ";
        wcout << s2 << endl;
    }
    else if (result > 0)
    {
        wcout << s1;
        cout << " is greater than ";
        wcout << s2 << endl;
    }
    else
    {
        wcout << s1;
        cout << " equals ";
        wcout << s2 << endl;
    }
}

int main(int argc, char* argv[])
{
    wchar_t* str1 = {L"One Two Three"};
    wchar_t* str2 = {L"One Two Three"};
    wchar_t* str3 = {L"Four Five Six"};
    wchar_t* str4 = {L"Seven Eight Nine"};

    cmp(str1, str2);
    cmp(str2, str3);
    cmp(str3, str4);

    return 0;
}
```

CROSS-REFERENCE

See also _mbscat(), _mbschr(), _mbscmp(), _mbscoll(), _mbscpy(), _mbscspn(), _mbsdec(), _mbsdup(), _mbsicmp(), _mbsicoll(), _mbsinc(), _mbslen(), _mbslwr(), _mbsnbcat(), _mbsnbcmp(), _mbsnbcnt(), _mbsnbcoll(), _mbsnbcpy(), _mbsnbicmp(), _mbsnbicoll(), _mbsnbset(), _mbsnccnt(), _mbsncmp(), _mbsncoll(), _mbsncpy(), _mbsnextc(), _mbsnicmp(), _mbsnicoll(), _mbsninc(),

_mbsnset(), _mbspbrk(), _mbsrchr(), _mbsrev(), _mbsset(), _mbsspn(), _mbsspnp(), _mbsstr(), _mbstok(), _mbstrlen(), _mbsupr(), _wcsdec(), _wcsdup(), _wcsicmp(), _wcsicoll(), _wcsinc(), _wcslwr(), _wcsncnt(), _wcsncoll(), _wcsnextc(), _wcsnicmp(), _wcsnicoll(), _wcsninc(), _wcsnset(), _wcsrev(), _wcsset(), _wcsspnp(), _wcsupr(), strcat(), strchr(), strcmp(), strcoll(), strcpy(), strcspn(), strlen(), strncmp(), strncpy(), strpbrk(), strrchr(), strspn(), strstr(), strtod(), strtok(), strtol(), strtoul(), strxfrm(), wcscat(), wcschr(), wcscmp(), wcscpy(), wcscspn(), wcslen(), wcsncmp(), wcsncpy(), wcspbrk(), wcsrchr(), wcsspn(), wcsstr(), wcstod(), wcstok(), wcstol(), and wcstoul().

wcscpy()

Function

The wcscpy() function copies one wide-character string to another, returning a pointer to the destination string. The source and destination strings cannot overlap.

Header File

```
#include <string.h>
```

Declaration

```
wchar_t* wcscpy(wchar_t *strDestination,
    const wchar_t *strSource );
```

- *strDestination* — A pointer to the destination string.
- *strSource* — A pointer to the source string.

Example

The following program demonstrates how to use the wcscpy() function. When run, the program copies one string to another and displays the result. The program's output looks like this:

```
Source string = This is a test
Destination string = This is a test
Press any key to continue
```

Here is the program source code that produced the output:

```
#include "stdafx.h"
```

```
#include <iostream>
#include <string.h>

using namespace std;

int main(int argc, char* argv[])
{
    wchar_t destStr[81];
    wchar_t* srcStr = {L"This is a test"};

    wchar_t* pResult = wcscpy(destStr, srcStr);
    cout << "Source string = ";
    wcout << srcStr << endl;
    cout << "Destination string = ";
    wcout << pResult << endl;

    return 0;
}
```

CROSS-REFERENCE

See also _mbscat(), _mbschr(), _mbscmp(), _mbscoll(), _mbscpy(), _mbscspn(), _mbsdec(), _mbsdup(), _mbsicmp(), _mbsicoll(), _mbsinc(), _mbslen(), _mbslwr(), _mbsnbcat(), _mbsnbcmp(), _mbsnbcnt(), _mbsnbcoll(), _mbsnbcpy(), _mbsnbicmp(), _mbsnbicoll(), _mbsnbset(), _mbsnccnt(), _mbsncmp(), _mbsncoll(), _mbsncpy(), _mbsnextc(), _mbsnicmp(), _mbsnicoll(), _mbsninc(), _mbsnset(), _mbspbrk(), _mbsrchr(), _mbsrev(), _mbsset(), _mbsspn(), _mbsspnp(), _mbsstr(), _mbstok(), _mbstrlen(), _mbsupr(), _wcsdec(), _wcsdup(), _wcsicmp(), _wcsicoll(), _wcsinc(), _wcslwr(), _wcsncnt(), _wcsncoll(), _wcsnextc(), _wcsnicmp(), _wcsnicoll(), _wcsninc(), _wcsnset(), _wcsrev(), _wcsset(), _wcsspnp(), _wcsupr(), strcat(), strchr(), strcmp(), strcoll(), strcpy(), strcspn(), strlen(), strncmp(), strncpy(), strpbrk(), strrchr(), strspn(), strstr(), strtod(), strtok(), strtol(), strtoul(), strxfrm(), wcscat(), wcschr(), wcscmp(), wcscoll(), wcscspn(), wcslen(), wcsncmp(), wcsncpy(), wcspbrk(), wcsrchr(), wcsspn(), wcsstr(), wcstod(), wcstok(), wcstol(), and wcstoul().

wcscspn()

Function

The wcscspn() function locates the first occurrence of a character in a wide-character string, returning the length of the substring preceding a matching character.

Header File

```
#include <string.h>
```

Declaration

```
size_t wcscspn(const wchar_t *string,
    const wchar_t *strCharSet);
```

- *strCharSet*—A pointer to the set of characters for which to search.
- *string*—A pointer to the string to search.

Example

The following program demonstrates how to use the wcscspn() function. When run, the program locates, in a string, the first character in a set and displays the result, indicating the located character with a caret (^). The program's output looks like this:

```
Source String:
This is a test
     ^
Press any key to continue
```

Here is the program source code that produced the output:

```
#include "stdafx.h"
#include <iostream>
#include <string.h>

using namespace std;

int main(int argc, char* argv[])
{
    wchar_t* srcStr = {L"This is a test"};
    wchar_t* chrSet = {L"ast"};

    size_t len = wcscspn(srcStr, chrSet);
    cout << "Source String:" << endl;
    wcout << srcStr << endl;
    for (unsigned x=0; x<len; ++x)
        cout << " ";
    cout << "^" << endl;

    return 0;
}
```

V

W

X

CROSS-REFERENCE
See also _mbscat(), _mbschr(), _mbscmp(), _mbscoll(), _mbscpy(), _mbscspn(), _mbsdec(), _mbsdup(), _mbsicmp(), _mbsicoll(), _mbsinc(), _mbslen(), _mbslwr(), _mbsnbcat(), _mbsnbcmp(), _mbsnbcnt(), _mbsnbcoll(), _mbsnbcpy(), _mbsnbicmp(), _mbsnbicoll(), _mbsnbset(), _mbsnccnt(), _mbsncmp(), _mbsncoll(), _mbsncpy(), _mbsnextc(), _mbsnicmp(), _mbsnicoll(), _mbsninc(), _mbsnset(), _mbspbrk(), _mbsrchr(), _mbsrev(), _mbsset(), _mbsspn(), _mbsspnp(), _mbsstr(), _mbstok(), _mbstrlen(), _mbsupr(), _wcsdec(), _wcsdup(), _wcsicmp(), _wcsicoll(), _wcsinc(), _wcslwr(), _wcsncnt(), _wcsncoll(), _wcsnextc(), _wcsnicmp(), _wcsnicoll(), _wcsninc(), _wcsnset(), _wcsrev(), _wcsset(), _wcsspnp(), _wcsupr(), strcat(), strchr(), strcmp(), strcoll(), strcpy(), strcspn(), strlen(), strncmp(), strncpy(), strpbrk(), strrchr(), strspn(), strstr(), strtod(), strtok(), strtol(), strtoul(), strxfrm(), wcscat(), wcschr(), wcscmp(), wcscoll(), wcscpy(), wcslen(), wcsncmp(), wcsncpy(), wcspbrk(), wcsrchr(), wcsspn(), wcsstr(), wcstod(), wcstok(), wcstol(), and wcstoul().

wcsftime()

Function

The `wcsftime()` function is the wide-character version of the `strftime()` function, which generates a formatted time string, returning the number of characters in the string, or 0 in the case of an error.

Header File

```
#include <time.h>
```

Declaration

```
size_t wcsftime(wchar_t *strDest, size_t maxsize,
    const wchar_t *format, const struct tm *timeptr);
```

- *format*—A pointer to the format string. Table W-38 shows the available format codes.
- *maxsize*—The maximum allowable length of the formatted string.
- *strDest*—A pointer to the buffer that will receive the formatted string.
- *timeptr*—A pointer to the `tm` structure that contains the time to format.

Table W-38 Format Codes for wcsftime()

Code	Description
%#%	Ignore the # flag.
%#a	Ignore the # flag.
%#A	Ignore the # flag.
%#b	Ignore the # flag.
%#B	Ignore the # flag.
%#c	Format as the current locale's long date and time.
%#d	Delete leading zeroes.
%#H	Delete leading zeroes.
%#I	Delete leading zeroes.
%#j	Delete leading zeroes.
%#m	Delete leading zeroes.
%#M	Delete leading zeroes.
%#p	Ignore the # flag.
%#S	Delete leading zeroes.
%#U	Delete leading zeroes.
%#w	Delete leading zeroes.
%#W	Delete leading zeroes.
%#X	Ignore the # flag.
%#x	Format as the current locale's long date.
%#y	Delete leading zeroes.
%#Y	Delete leading zeroes.
%#z	Ignore the # flag.
%#Z	Ignore the # flag.
%%	Display a percent sign.
%a	Format as an abbreviated weekday name.
%A	Format as a full weekday name.
%b	Format as an abbreviated month name.
%B	Format as a full month name.
%c	Format the date and time for the current locale.
%d	Format the day of the month as a number from 01 to 31.
%H	Format the hour in 24-hour style.
%I	Format the hour in the 12-hour style.
%j	Format the day of the year as a number from 001 to 366.
%m	Format the month as a number from 01 to 12.
%M	Format the minute as a number from 00 to 59.
%p	Use the AM/PM indicator for the current locale.
%S	Format the second as a number from 00 to 59.

Continued

Table W-38 *Continued*

Code	Description
%U	Format the week of the year as a number from 00 to 53, using Sunday as the first day of the week.
%w	Format the weekday as a number from 0 to 6, where 0 represents Sunday.
%W	Week of the year as a number from 00 to 53.
%x	Format the date for the current locale.
%X	Format the time for the current locale.
%y	Format the year as a two-digit number from 00 to 99.
%Y	Format the year as a four-digit number, for example 1999.
%z	Format the time zone name as an abbreviation.
%Z	Format the time zone name as a full name.

Example

The following program demonstrates how to use the `wcsftime()` function. The program initializes a `tm` structure, converts the structure to a string, and then displays the result. The program's output looks like this:

```
Thu, January 21, 1999.

Press any key to continue
```

Here is the program source code that produced the output:

```
#include "stdafx.h"
#include <iostream>
#include <time.h>

using namespace std;

int main(int argc, char* argv[])
{
    wchar_t buf[256];
    struct tm tmTime;

    tmTime.tm_mday   = 21;
    tmTime.tm_mon    = 0;
    tmTime.tm_year   = 99;
    tmTime.tm_wday   = 4;
    tmTime.tm_yday   = 0;
```

```
        tmTime.tm_isdst  = 0;
        tmTime.tm_sec    = 0;
        tmTime.tm_min    = 17;
        tmTime.tm_hour   = 5;

        wcsftime(buf, 256, L"%a, %B %d, %Y.\n", &tmTime);
        wcout << buf << endl;

        return 0;
    }
```

CROSS-REFERENCE

See also _ftime(), _futime(), _strdate(), _strtime(), _tzset(), _utime(), _wasctime, _wctime(), _wstrdate(), _wstrtime(), _wutime(), asctime(), ctime(), difftime(), gmtime(), localtime(), mktime(), strftime(), and time().

wcslen()

Function

The wcslen() function returns the length (the number of characters) of a wide-character string.

Header File

```
#include <string.h>
```

Declaration

```
size_t wcslen(const wchar_t *string);
```

- *string*—A pointer to the string for which to return the length.

Example

The following program demonstrates how to use the wcslen() function. When run, the program calculates the length of a string and then uses the length to underline the source string. The program's output looks like this:

```
Source String:

This is a test
```

V
W
X

Press any key to continue

Here is the program source code that produced the output:

```
#include "stdafx.h"
#include <iostream>
#include <string.h>

using namespace std;

int main(int argc, char* argv[])
{
    wchar_t* srcStr = {L"This is a test"};

    size_t len = wcslen(srcStr);
    cout << "Source String:" << endl << endl;
    wcout << srcStr << endl;
    for (unsigned x=0; x<len; ++x)
        cout << "-";
    cout << endl << endl;

    return 0;
}
```

CROSS-REFERENCE

See also _mbscat(), _mbschr(), _mbscmp(), _mbscoll(), _mbscpy(), _mbscspn(), _mbsdec(), _mbsdup(), _mbsicmp(), _mbsicoll(), _mbsinc(), _mbslen(), _mbslwr(), _mbsnbcat(), _mbsnbcmp(), _mbsnbcnt(), _mbsnbcoll(), _mbsnbcpy(), _mbsnbicmp(), _mbsnbicoll(), _mbsnbset(), _mbsnccnt(), _mbsncmp(), _mbsncoll(), _mbsncpy(), _mbsnextc(), _mbsnicmp(), _mbsnicoll(), _mbsninc(), _mbsnset(), _mbspbrk(), _mbsrchr(), _mbsrev(), _mbsset(), _mbsspn(), _mbsspnp(), _mbsstr(), _mbstok(), _mbstrlen(), _mbsupr(), _wcsdec(), _wcsdup(), _wcsicmp(), _wcsicoll(), _wcsinc(), _wcslwr(), _wcsncnt(), _wcsncoll(), _wcsnextc(), _wcsnicmp(), _wcsnicoll(), _wcsninc(), _wcsnset(), _wcsrev(), _wcsset(), _wcsspnp(), _wcsupr(), strcat(), strchr(), strcmp(), strcoll(), strcpy(), strcspn(), strlen(), strncmp(), strncpy(), strpbrk(), strrchr(), strspn(), strstr(), strtod(), strtok(), strtol(), strtoul(), strxfrm(), wcscat(), wcschr(), wcscmp(), wcscoll(), wcscpy(), wcscspn(), wcsncmp(), wcsncpy(), wcspbrk(), wcsrchr(), wcsspn(), wcsstr(), wcstod(), wcstok(), wcstol(), and wcstoul().

wcsncat()

Function

The wcsncat() function concatenates wide-character strings, returning a pointer to the destination string.

Header File

```
#include <string.h>
```

Declaration

```
wchar_t* wcsncat(wchar_t *strDest,
    const wchar_t *strSource, size_t count);
```

- *count* — The number of characters to concatenate.
- *strDest* — The string to which to concatenate *strSource*.
- *strSource* — The string to concatenate to *strDest*.

Example

The following program demonstrates how to use the wcsncat() function. When run, the program concatenates the first six characters of the wide-character string "Four Five Six" to the wide-character string "One Two Three ". The program's output looks like this:

```
Result: One Two Three Four F
Press any key to continue
```

Here is the program source code that produced the output:

```
#include "stdafx.h"
#include <iostream>
#include <string.h>

using namespace std;

int main(int argc, char* argv[])
{
    wchar_t str1[81];
```

```
wchar_t* str2 = {L"Four Five Six"};
wcscpy(str1, L"One Two Three ");
wcsncat(str1, str2, 6);
cout << "Result: ";
wcout << str1 << endl;

return 0;
}
```

CROSS-REFERENCE

See also _mbscat(), _mbschr(), _mbscmp(), _mbscoll(), _mbscpy(), _mbscspn(), _mbsdec(), _mbsdup(), _mbsicmp(), _mbsicoll(), _mbsinc(), _mbslen(), _mbslwr(), _mbsnbcat(), _mbsnbcmp(), _mbsnbcnt(), _mbsnbcoll(), _mbsnbcpy(), _mbsnbicmp(), _mbsnbicoll(), _mbsnbset(), _mbsnccnt(), _mbsncmp(), _mbsncoll(), _mbsncpy(), _mbsnextc(), _mbsnicmp(), _mbsnicoll(), _mbsninc(), _mbsnset(), _mbspbrk(), _mbsrchr(), _mbsrev(), _mbsset(), _mbsspn(), _mbsspnp(), _mbsstr(), _mbstok(), _mbstrlen(), _mbsupr(), _wcsdec(), _wcsdup(), _wcsicmp(), _wcsicoll(), _wcsinc(), _wcslwr(), _wcsncnt(), _wcsncoll(), _wcsnextc(), _wcsnicmp(), _wcsnicoll(), _wcsninc(), _wcsnset(), _wcsrev(), _wcsset(), _wcsspnp(), _wcsupr(), strcat(), strchr(), strcmp(), strcoll(), strcpy(), strcspn(), strlen(), strncmp(), strncpy(), strpbrk(), strrchr(), strspn(), strstr(), strtod(), strtok(), strtol(), strtoul(), strxfrm(), wcscat(), wcschr(), wcscmp(), wcscoll(), wcscpy(), wcscspn(), wcslen(), wcsncmp(), wcsncpy(), wcspbrk(), wcsrchr(), wcsspn(), wcsstr(), wcstod(), wcstok(), wcstol(), and wcstoul().

wcsncmp()

Function

The wcsncmp() function compares a set of characters in two wide-character strings, returning a value from Table W-39.

Table W-39 Return Values for wcsncmp()

Value	Description
Less than 0	string1 is alphabetically less than string2.
0	The two strings are equal.
Greater than 0	string1 is alphabetically greater than string2.

Header File

```
#include <string.h>
```

Declaration

```
int wcsncmp(const wchar_t *string1,
    const wchar_t *string2, size_t count);
```

- *count* — The number of characters to compare.
- *string1* — The first string to compare.
- *string2* — The second string to compare.

Example

The following program demonstrates how to use the `wcsncmp()` function. When run, the program compares several pairs of strings and displays the result of the comparisons. The program's output looks like this:

```
For a length of 7 characters

One Two Three equals One Two Ten
One Two Ten is greater than Four Five Six
Four Five Six is greater than Four Eight Nine

Press any key to continue
```

Here is the program source code that produced the output:

```
#include "stdafx.h"
#include <iostream>
#include <string.h>

using namespace std;

void cmp(wchar_t* s1, wchar_t* s2, size_t num)
{
    int result = wcsncmp(s1, s2, num);
    if (result < 0 )
    {
        wcout << s1;
        cout << " is less than ";
        wcout << s2 << endl;
    }
    else if (result > 0)
```

V
W
X

```
    {
        wcout << s1;
        cout << " is greater than ";
        wcout << s2 << endl;
    }
    else
    {
        wcout << s1;
        cout << " equals ";
        wcout << s2 << endl;
    }
}

int main(int argc, char* argv[])
{
    wchar_t* str1 = {L"One Two Three"};
    wchar_t* str2 = {L"One Two Ten"};
    wchar_t* str3 = {L"Four Five Six"};
    wchar_t* str4 = {L"Four Eight Nine"};

    cout << "For a length of 7 characters" << endl << endl;
    cmp(str1, str2, 7);
    cmp(str2, str3, 7);
    cmp(str3, str4, 7);
    cout << endl;

    return 0;
}
```

CROSS-REFERENCE

See also _mbscat(), _mbschr(), _mbscmp(), _mbscoll(), _mbscpy(), _mbscspn(), _mbsdec(), _mbsdup(), _mbsicmp(), _mbsicoll(), _mbsinc(), _mbslen(), _mbslwr(), _mbsnbcat(), _mbsnbcmp(), _mbsnbcnt(), _mbsnbcoll(), _mbsnbcpy(), _mbsnbicmp(), _mbsnbicoll(), _mbsnbset(), _mbsnccnt(), _mbsncmp(), _mbsncoll(), _mbsncpy(), _mbsnextc(), _mbsnicmp(), _mbsnicoll(), _mbsninc(), _mbsnset(), _mbspbrk(), _mbsrchr(), _mbsrev(), _mbsset(), _mbsspn(), _mbsspnp(), _mbsstr(), _mbstok(), _mbstrlen(), _mbsupr(), _wcsdec(), _wcsdup(), _wcsicmp(), _wcsicoll(), _wcsinc(), _wcslwr(), _wcsncnt(), _wcsncoll(), _wcsnextc(), _wcsnicmp(), _wcsnicoll(), _wcsninc(), _wcsnset(), _wcsrev(), _wcsset(), _wcsspnp(), _wcsupr(), strcat(), strchr(), strcmp(), strcoll(), strcpy(), strcspn(), strlen(), strncmp(), strncpy(), strpbrk(), strrchr(), strspn(), strstr(), strtod(), strtok(), strtol(), strtoul(), strxfrm(), wcscat(), wcschr(), wcscmp(), wcscoll(), wcscpy(), wcscspn(), wcslen(), wcsncpy(), wcspbrk(), wcsrchr(), wcsspn(), wcsstr(), wcstod(), wcstok(), wcstol(), and wcstoul().

wcsncpy()

Function

The `wcsncpy()` function copies a specified number of characters from one wide-character string to another, returning a pointer to the destination string. The source and destination strings cannot overlap.

Header File

```
#include <string.h>
```

Declaration

```
wchar_t* wcsncpy(wchar_t *strDest,
    const wchar_t *strSource, size_t count);
```

- *count* — The number of characters to copy.
- *strDest* — A pointer to the destination string.
- *strSource* — A pointer to the source string.

Example

The following program demonstrates how to use the `wcsncpy()` function. When run, the program copies 11 characters from one string to another and displays the result. The program's output looks like this:

```
Source string = This is a test
Destination string = This is a t
Press any key to continue
```

Here is the program source code that produced the output:

```
#include "stdafx.h"
#include <iostream>
#include <string.h>

using namespace std;

int main(int argc, char* argv[])
{
    wchar_t destStr[81];
    wchar_t* srcStr = {L"This is a test"};
```

```
wchar_t* pResult = wcsncpy(destStr, srcStr, 11);
pResult[11] = 0;
cout << "Source string = ";
wcout << srcStr << endl;
cout << "Destination string = ";
wcout << pResult << endl;

return 0;
}
```

CROSS-REFERENCE

See also _mbscat(), _mbschr(), _mbscmp(), _mbscoll(), _mbscpy(), _mbscspn(), _mbsdec(), _mbsdup(), _mbsicmp(), _mbsicoll(), _mbsinc(), _mbslen(), _mbslwr(), _mbsnbcat(), _mbsnbcmp(), _mbsnbcnt(), _mbsnbcoll(), _mbsnbcpy(), _mbsnbicmp(), _mbsnbicoll(), _mbsnbset(), _mbsnccnt(), _mbsncmp(), _mbsncoll(), _mbsncpy(), _mbsnextc(), _mbsnicmp(), _mbsnicoll(), _mbsninc(), _mbsnset(), _mbspbrk(), _mbsrchr(), _mbsrev(), _mbsset(), _mbsspn(), _mbsspnp(), _mbsstr(), _mbstok(), _mbstrlen(), _mbsupr(), _wcsdec(), _wcsdup(), _wcsicmp(), _wcsicoll(), _wcsinc(), _wcslwr(), _wcsncnt(), _wcsncoll(), _wcsnextc(), _wcsnicmp(), _wcsnicoll(), _wcsninc(), _wcsnset(), _wcsrev(), _wcsset(), _wcsspnp(), _wcsupr(), strcat(), strchr(), strcmp(), strcoll(), strcpy(), strcspn(), strlen(), strncmp(), strncpy(), strpbrk(), strrchr(), strspn(), strstr(), strtod(), strtok(), strtol(), strtoul(), strxfrm(), wcscat(), wcschr(), wcscmp(), wcscoll(), wcscpy(), wcscspn(), wcslen(), wcsncmp(), wcspbrk(), wcsrchr(), wcsspn(), wcsstr(), wcstod(), wcstok(), wcstol(), and wcstoul().

wcspbrk()

Function

The wcspbrk() function locates the first occurrence of a character in a wide-character string, returning a pointer to the substring starting with the matching character.

Header File

```
#include <string.h>
```

Declaration

```
wchar_t* wcspbrk(const wchar_t *string,
    const wchar_t *strCharSet);
```

- *strCharSet*—A pointer to the set of characters for which to search.
- *string*—A pointer to the string to search.

Example

The following program demonstrates how to use the `wcspbrk()` function. When run, the program locates, in a string, the first character in a set and displays the result. The program's output looks like this:

```
Source String:
This is a test
Substring:
s is a test


Press any key to continue
```

Here is the program source code that produced the output:

```
#include "stdafx.h"
#include <iostream>
#include <string.h>

using namespace std;

int main(int argc, char* argv[])
{
    wchar_t* srcStr = {L"This is a test"};
    wchar_t* chrSet = {L"ast"};

    wchar_t* pSubStr = wcspbrk(srcStr, chrSet);
    cout << "Source String:" << endl;
    wcout << srcStr << endl;
    cout << "Substring:" << endl;
    wcout << pSubStr << endl << endl;

    return 0;
}
```

CROSS-REFERENCE

See also _mbscat(), _mbschr(), _mbscmp(), _mbscoll(), _mbscpy(), _mbscspn(), _mbsdec(), _mbsdup(), _mbsicmp(), _mbsicoll(), _mbsinc(), _mbslen(), _mbslwr(), _mbsnbcat(), _mbsnbcmp(), _mbsnbcnt(), _mbsnbcoll(), _mbsnbcpy(), _mbsnbicmp(), _mbsnbicoll(), _mbsnbset(), _mbsnccnt(), _mbsncmp(), _mbsncoll(), _mbsncpy(), _mbsnextc(), _mbsnicmp(), _mbsnicoll(), _mbsninc(),

_mbsnset(), _mbspbrk(), _mbsrchr(), _mbsrev(), _mbsset(), _mbsspn(), _mbsspnp(), _mbsstr(), _mbstok(), _mbstrlen(), _mbsupr(), _wcsdec(), _wcsdup(), _wcsicmp(), _wcsicoll(), _wcsinc(), _wcslwr(), _wcsncnt(), _wcsncoll(), _wcsnextc(), _wcsnicmp(), _wcsnicoll(), _wcsninc(), _wcsnset(), _wcsrev(), _wcsset(), _wcsspnp(), _wcsupr(), strcat(), strchr(), strcmp(), strcoll(), strcpy(), strcspn(), strlen(), strncmp(), strncpy(), strpbrk(), strrchr(), strspn(), strstr(), strtod(), strtok(), strtol(), strtoul(), strxfrm(), wcscat(), wcschr(), wcscmp(), wcscoll(), wcscpy(), wcscspn(), wcslen(), wcsncmp(), wcspbrk(), wcsrchr(), wcsspn(), wcsstr(), wcstod(), wcstok(), wcstol(), and wcstoul().

wcsrchr()

Function

The wcsrchr() function locates the last occurrence of a character in a wide-character string, returning a pointer to the substring starting with the matching character.

Header File

```
#include <string.h>
```

Declaration

```
char* wcsrchr(const wchar_t *string, int c);
```

- *c* — The character for which to search.
- *string* — A pointer to the string to search.

Example

The following program demonstrates how to use the wcsrchr() function. When run, the program locates the last occurrence of the character i in a string and displays the result. The program's output looks like this:

```
Source String:
This is a test
Substring:
is a test

Press any key to continue
```

Here is the program source code that produced the output:

```
#include "stdafx.h"
#include <iostream>
#include <string.h>

using namespace std;

int main(int argc, char* argv[])
{
    wchar_t* srcStr = {L"This is a test"};

    wchar_t* pSubStr = wcsrchr(srcStr, 'i');
    cout << "Source String:" << endl;
    wcout << srcStr << endl;
    cout << "Substring:" << endl;
    wcout << pSubStr << endl << endl;

    return 0;
}
```

CROSS-REFERENCE

See also _mbscat(), _mbschr(), _mbscmp(), _mbscoll(), _mbscpy(), _mbscspn(), _mbsdec(), _mbsdup(), _mbsicmp(), _mbsicoll(), _mbsinc(), _mbslen(), _mbslwr(), _mbsnbcat(), _mbsnbcmp(), _mbsnbcnt(), _mbsnbcoll(), _mbsnbcpy(), _mbsnbicmp(), _mbsnbicoll(), _mbsnbset(), _mbsnccnt(), _mbsncmp(), _mbsncoll(), _mbsncpy(), _mbsnextc(), _mbsnicmp(), _mbsnicoll(), _mbsninc(), _mbsnset(), _mbspbrk(), _mbsrchr(), _mbsrev(), _mbsset(), _mbsspn(), _mbsspnp(), _mbsstr(), _mbstok(), _mbstrlen(), _mbsupr(), _wcsdec(), _wcsdup(), _wcsicmp(), _wcsicoll(), _wcsinc(), _wcslwr(), _wcsncnt(), _wcsncoll(), _wcsnextc(), _wcsnicmp(), _wcsnicoll(), _wcsninc(), _wcsnset(), _wcsrev(), _wcsset(), _wcsspnp(), _wcsupr(), strcat(), strchr(), strcmp(), strcoll(), strcpy(), strcspn(), strlen(), strncmp(), strncpy(), strpbrk(), strrchr(), strspn(), strstr(), strtod(), strtok(), strtol(), strtoul(), strxfrm(), wcscat(), wcschr(), wcscmp(), wcscoll(), wcscpy(), wcscspn(), wcslen(), wcsncmp(), wcsncpy(), wcspbrk(), wcsspn(), wcsstr(), wcstod(), wcstok(), wcstol(), and wcstoul().

wcsspn()

Function

The wcsspn() function locates the first occurrence, in a wide-character string, of a substring that starts with a character not included in the specified set. The function returns the index of the first nonmatching character.

Header File

```
#include <string.h>
```

Declaration

```
size_t wcsspn(const wchar_t *string,
    const wchar_t *strCharSet);
```

- *strCharSet* — A pointer to the set of characters for which to search.
- *string* — A pointer to the string to search.

Example

The following program demonstrates how to use the wcsspn() function. When run, the program locates, in a string, the first character not in the specified set and displays the result, indicating the located character with a caret (^). The program's output looks like this:

```
Source String:
This is a test
       ^

Press any key to continue
```

Here is the program source code that produced the output:

```
#include "stdafx.h"
#include <iostream>
#include <string.h>

using namespace std;

int main(int argc, char* argv[])
{
    wchar_t* srcStr = {L"This is a test"};
    wchar_t* chrSet = {L"ahisT "};

    size_t len = wcsspn(srcStr, chrSet);
    cout << "Source String:" << endl;
    wcout << srcStr << endl;
    for (unsigned x=0; x<len; ++x)
        cout << " ";
    cout << "^" << endl;

    return 0;
}
```

CROSS-REFERENCE

See also _mbscat(), _mbschr(), _mbscmp(), _mbscoll(), _mbscpy(), _mbscspn(), _mbsdec(), _mbsdup(), _mbsicmp(), _mbsicoll(), _mbsinc(), _mbslen(), _mbslwr(), _mbsnbcat(), _mbsnbcmp(), _mbsnbcnt(), _mbsnbcoll(), _mbsnbcpy(), _mbsnbicmp(), _mbsnbicoll(), _mbsnbset(), _mbsnccnt(), _mbsncmp(), _mbsncoll(), _mbsncpy(), _mbsnextc(), _mbsnicmp(), _mbsnicoll(), _mbsninc(), _mbsnset(), _mbspbrk(), _mbsrchr(), _mbsrev(), _mbsset(), _mbsspn(), _mbsspnp(), _mbsstr(), _mbstok(), _mbstrlen(), _mbsupr(), _wcsdec(), _wcsdup(), _wcsicmp(), _wcsicoll(), _wcsinc(), _wcslwr(), _wcsncnt(), _wcsncoll(), _wcsnextc(), _wcsnicmp(), _wcsnicoll(), _wcsninc(), _wcsnset(), _wcsrev(), _wcsset(), _wcsspnp(), _wcsupr(), strcat(), strchr(), strcmp(), strcoll(), strcpy(), strcspn(), strlen(), strncmp(), strncpy(), strpbrk(), strrchr(), strspn(), strstr(), strtod(), strtok(), strtol(), strtoul(), strxfrm(), wcscat(), wcschr(), wcscmp(), wcscoll(), wcscpy(), wcscspn(), wcslen(), wcsncmp(), wcsncpy(), wcspbrk(), wcsrchr(), wcsstr(), wcstod(), wcstok(), wcstol(), and wcstoul().

wcsstr()

Function

The wcsstr() function returns a pointer to a specified substring within a wide-character string.

Header File

```
#include <string.h>
```

Declaration

```
wchar_t* wcsstr(const wchar_t *string,
    const wchar_t *strCharSet );
```

- *strCharSet*—A pointer to the substring for which to search.
- *string*—A pointer to the string to search.

Example

The following program demonstrates how to use the wcsstr() function. When run, the program locates, in a wide-character string, the specified substring, and then displays the portion of the original string that begins with the substring. The program's output looks like this:

```
Source String:
This is a test

Substring:
is a test

Press any key to continue
```

Here is the program source code that produced the output:

```
***OK —Clay#include "stdafx.h"
#include <iostream>
#include <string.h>

using namespace std;

int main(int argc, char* argv[])
{
    wchar_t* srcStr = {L"This is a test"};
    wchar_t* chrSet = {L"is a"};

    wchar_t* pSubStr = wcsstr(srcStr, chrSet);
    cout << "Source String:" << endl;
    wcout << srcStr << endl << endl;
    cout << "Substring:" << endl;
    wcout << pSubStr << endl << endl;

    return 0;
}
```

CROSS-REFERENCE

See also _mbscat(), _mbschr(), _mbscmp(), _mbscoll(), _mbscpy(), _mbscspn(), _mbsdec(), _mbsdup(), _mbsicmp(), _mbsicoll(), _mbsinc(), _mbslen(), _mbslwr(), _mbsnbcat(), _mbsnbcmp(), _mbsnbcnt(), _mbsnbcoll(), _mbsnbcpy(), _mbsnbicmp(), _mbsnbicoll(), _mbsnbset(), _mbsnccnt(), _mbsncmp(), _mbsncoll(), _mbsncpy(), _mbsnextc(), _mbsnicmp(), _mbsnicoll(), _mbsninc(), _mbsnset(), _mbspbrk(), _mbsrchr(), _mbsrev(), _mbsset(), _mbsspn(), _mbsspnp(), _mbsstr(), _mbstok(), _mbstrlen(), _mbsupr(), _wcsdec(), _wcsdup(), _wcsicmp(), _wcsicoll(), _wcsinc(), _wcslwr(), _wcsncnt(), _wcsncoll(), _wcsnextc(), _wcsnicmp(), _wcsnicoll(), _wcsninc(), _wcsnset(), _wcsrev(), _wcsset(), _wcsspnp(), _wcsupr(), strcat(), strchr(), strcmp(), strcoll(), strcpy(), strcspn(), strlen(), strncmp(), strncpy(), strpbrk(), strrchr(), strspn(), strstr(), strtod(), strtok(), strtol(), strtoul(), strxfrm(), wcscat(), wcschr(), wcscmp(), wcscoll(), wcscpy(), wcscspn(), wcslen(), wcsncmp(), wcsncpy(), wcspbrk(), wcsrchr(), wcsspn(), wcstod(), wcstok(), wcstol(), and wcstoul().

wcstod()

Function

The wcstod() function converts a wide-character string to a double-precision floating-point value.

Header File

```
#include <string.h>
```

Declaration

```
double wcstod(const wchar_t *nptr, wchar_t **endptr);
```

- *endptr*—The pointer that will hold the address of the portion of the string that cannot be converted.
- *nptr*—A pointer to the string to convert.

Example

The following program demonstrates how to use the wcstod() function. When run, the program converts a portion of a wide-character string to a double value, and then displays the remainder of the string (the portion that could not be converted). The program's output looks like this:

```
Source String:
12345.5643This is a test

Result = 12345.6

Remaining string:
This is a test

Press any key to continue
```

Here is the program source code that produced the output:

```
#include "stdafx.h"
#include <iostream>
#include <string.h>
```

V
W
X

```
using namespace std;

int main(int argc, char* argv[])
{
    wchar_t* srcStr = {L"12345.5643This is a test"};
    wchar_t* str;

    double result = wcstod(srcStr, &str);
    cout << "Source String:" << endl;
    wcout << srcStr << endl << endl;
    cout << "Result = " << result << endl << endl;
    cout << "Remaining string:" << endl;
    wcout << str << endl << endl;

    return 0;
}
```

CROSS-REFERENCE
See also _wtoi64(), _wtol(), atof(), atoi(), and atol().

wcstok()

Function

The wcstok() function extracts tokens from a wide-character string.

Header File

```
#include <string.h>
```

Declaration

```
wchar_t* wcstok(wchar_t *strToken,
    const wchar_t *strDelimit);
```

- *strDelimit* — A pointer to the string containing the characters (delimiters) that separate one token from another.
- *strToken* — A pointer to the string containing the tokens to extract.

Example

The following program demonstrates how to use the wcstok() function. When run, the program extracts tokens from a string, displaying the results as it goes. The program's output looks like this:

```
Token Source String:
One,Two Three,Four*Five

Token Delimiter String:
, *

Tokens Found:
One
Two
Three
Four
Five

Press any key to continue
```

Here is the program source code that produced the output:

```cpp
#include "stdafx.h"
#include <iostream>
#include <string.h>

using namespace std;

#include <stdio.h>

int main(int argc, char* argv[])
{
    wchar_t str[81];
    wchar_t delimit[10];
    wchar_t *tok;

    wcscpy(str, L"One,Two Three,Four*Five");
    wcscpy(delimit, L", *");
    cout << "Token Source String:" << endl;
    wcout << str << endl << endl;
    cout << "Token Delimiter String:" << endl;
    wcout << delimit << endl << endl;
    cout << "Tokens Found:" << endl;

    tok = wcstok(str, delimit);
```

```
while(tok != NULL )
{
    wcout << tok << endl;
    tok = wcstok(NULL, delimit);
}

cout << endl;

return 0;
}
```

CROSS-REFERENCE

See also _mbscat(), _mbschr(), _mbscmp(), _mbscoll(), _mbscpy(), _mbscspn(), _mbsdec(), _mbsdup(), _mbsicmp(), _mbsicoll(), _mbsinc(), _mbslen(), _mbslwr(), _mbsnbcat(), _mbsnbcmp(), _mbsnbcnt(), _mbsnbcoll(), _mbsnbcpy(), _mbsnbicmp(), _mbsnbicoll(), _mbsnbset(), _mbsnccnt(), _mbsncmp(), _mbsncoll(), _mbsncpy(), _mbsnextc(), _mbsnicmp(), _mbsnicoll(), _mbsninc(), _mbsnset(), _mbspbrk(), _mbsrchr(), _mbsrev(), _mbsset(), _mbsspn(), _mbsspnp(), _mbsstr(), _mbstok(), _mbstrlen(), _mbsupr(), _wcsdec(), _wcsdup(), _wcsicmp(), _wcsicoll(), _wcsinc(), _wcslwr(), _wcsncnt(), _wcsncoll(), _wcsnextc(), _wcsnicmp(), _wcsnicoll(), _wcsninc(), _wcsnset(), _wcsrev(), _wcsset(), _wcsspnp(), _wcsupr(), strcat(), strchr(), strcmp(), strcoll(), strcpy(), strcspn(), strlen(), strncmp(), strncpy(), strpbrk(), strrchr(), strspn(), strstr(), strtod(), strtok(), strtol(), strtoul(), strxfrm(), wcscat(), wcschr(), wcscmp(), wcscoll(), wcscpy(), wcscspn(), wcslen(), wcsncmp(), wcsncpy(), wcspbrk(), wcsrchr(), wcsspn(), wcsstr(), wcstod(), wcstol(), and wcstoul().

wcstol()

Function

The wcstol() function converts a wide-character string to a long integer.

Header File

```
#include <string.h>
```

Declaration

```
long wcstol(const wchar_t *nptr, wchar_t **endptr, int base);
```

- *base* — The number base to use in the conversion.

- *endptr* — The pointer that will hold the address of the portion of the string that cannot be converted.
- *nptr* — A pointer to the string to convert.

Example

The following program demonstrates how to use the wcstol() function. When run, the program converts a portion of a wide-character string to a long value, and then displays the remainder of the string (the portion that could not be converted). The program's output looks like this:

```
Source String:
1234556This is a test

Result = 1234556

Remaining string:
This is a test

Press any key to continue
```

Here is the program source code that produced the output:

```
#include "stdafx.h"
#include <iostream>
#include <string.h>

using namespace std;

int main(int argc, char* argv[])
{
    wchar_t* srcStr = {L"1234556This is a test"};
    wchar_t* str;

    long result = wcstol(srcStr, &str, 10);
    cout << "Source String:" << endl;
    wcout << srcStr << endl << endl;
    cout << "Result = " << result << endl << endl;
    cout << "Remaining string:" << endl;
    wcout << str << endl << endl;

    return 0;
}
```

CROSS-REFERENCE
See also _wtoi64(), _wtol(), atof(), atoi(), and atol().

wcstombs()

Function

The wcstombs() function converts a wide-character string to a multibyte string, returning the number of bytes written to the destination string.

Header File

```
#include <string.h>
```

Declaration

```
size_t wcstombs(char *mbstr,
    const wchar_t *wcstr, size_t count);
```

- *count* — The maximum number of bytes to write to the destination string.
- *mbstr* — A pointer to the string that will hold the converted multibyte characters.
- *wcstr* — A pointer to the wide-character source string.

Example

The following program demonstrates how to use the wcstombs() function. When run, the program converts a wide-character string to a multibyte string and displays the result. The program's output looks like this:

```
Original String: This is a test

Multibyte String: This is a test

Press any key to continue
```

Here is the program source code that produced the output:

```
#include "stdafx.h"
#include <iostream>
#include <string.h>
```

```
using namespace std;

int main(int argc, char* argv[])
{
    char mbStr[81];
    wchar_t *srcStr = L"This is a test";

    cout << "Original String: ";
    wcout << srcStr << endl << endl;
    wcstombs(mbStr, srcStr, 80);
    cout << "Multibyte String: ";
    cout << mbStr << endl << endl;

    return 0;
}
```

CROSS-REFERENCE

See also _mbscat(), _mbschr(), _mbscmp(), _mbscoll(), _mbscpy(), _mbscspn(), _mbsdec(), _mbsdup(), _mbsicmp(), _mbsicoll(), _mbsinc(), _mbslen(), _mbslwr(), _mbsnbcat(), _mbsnbcmp(), _mbsnbcnt(), _mbsnbcoll(), _mbsnbcpy(), _mbsnbicmp(), _mbsnbicoll(), _mbsnbset(), _mbsnccnt(), _mbsncmp(), _mbsncoll(), _mbsncpy(), _mbsnextc(), _mbsnicmp(), _mbsnicoll(), _mbsninc(), _mbsnset(), _mbspbrk(), _mbsrchr(), _mbsrev(), _mbsset(), _mbsspn(), _mbsspnp(), _mbsstr(), _mbstok(), _mbstrlen(), _mbsupr(), _wcsdec(), _wcsdup(), _wcsicmp(), _wcsicoll(), _wcsinc(), _wcslwr(), _wcsncnt(), _wcsncoll(), _wcsnextc(), _wcsnicmp(), _wcsnicoll(), _wcsninc(), _wcsnset(), _wcsrev(), _wcsset(), _wcsspnp(), _wcsupr(), strcat(), strchr(), strcmp(), strcoll(), strcpy(), strcspn(), strlen(), strncmp(), strncpy(), strpbrk(), strrchr(), strspn(), strstr(), strtod(), strtok(), strtol(), strtoul(), strxfrm(), wcscat(), wcschr(), wcscmp(), wcscoll(), wcscpy(), wcscspn(), wcslen(), wcsncmp(), wcsncpy(), wcspbrk(), wcsrchr(), wcsspn(), wcsstr(), wcstod(), wcstok(), wcstol(), and wcstoul().

wcstoul()

Function

The wcstoul() function converts a wide-character string to an unsigned long integer.

Header File

```
#include <string.h>
```

Declaration

```
unsigned long wcstoul(const wchar_t *nptr,
    wchar_t **endptr, int base);
```

- *base*—The number base to use in the conversion.
- *endptr*—The pointer that will hold the address of the portion of the string that cannot be converted.
- *nptr*—A pointer to the string to convert.

Example

The following program demonstrates how to use the wcstoul() function. When run, the program converts a portion of a wide-character string to a long value and then displays the remainder of the string (the portion that could not be converted). The program's output looks like this:

```
Source String:
1234556This is a test

Result = 1234556

Remaining string:
This is a test

Press any key to continue
```

Here is the program source code that produced the output:

```cpp
#include "stdafx.h"
#include <iostream>
#include <string.h>

using namespace std;

int main(int argc, char* argv[])
{
    wchar_t* srcStr = {L"1234556This is a test"};
    wchar_t* str;

    long result = wcstoul(srcStr, &str, 10);
    cout << "Source String:" << endl;
    wcout << srcStr << endl << endl;
    cout << "Result = " << result << endl << endl;
    cout << "Remaining string:" << endl;
```

```
        wcout << str << endl << endl;

        return 0;
    }
```

CROSS-REFERENCE
See also _wtoi64(), _wtol(), atof(), atoi(), and atol().

wctob()

Function

The wctob() function returns the given character as a 1-byte multibyte character, or returns WEOF if the character cannot be converted.

Header File

```
#include <wchar.h>
```

Declaration

```
int wctob(wint_t c);
```

- *c* — The character to convert.

Example

The following program demonstrates how to use the wctob() function. When run, the program converts a character to a single-byte multibyte character. The program's output looks like this:

```
result = 65
Press any key to continue
```

Here is the program source code that produced the output:

```
#include "stdafx.h"
#include <wchar.h>
#include <iostream>

using namespace std;

int main(int argc, char* argv[])
```

```
{
    wint_t c = 65;

    int result = wctob(c);
    cout << "result = " << result << endl;

    return 0;
}
```

CROSS-REFERENCE

See also _mbscat(), _mbschr(), _mbscmp(), _mbscoll(), _mbscpy(), _mbscspn(), _mbsdec(), _mbsdup(), _mbsicmp(), _mbsicoll(), _mbsinc(), _mbslen(), _mbslwr(), _mbsnbcat(), _mbsnbcmp(), _mbsnbcnt(), _mbsnbcoll(), _mbsnbcpy(), _mbsnbicmp(), _mbsnbicoll(), _mbsnbset(), _mbsnccnt(), _mbsncmp(), _mbsncoll(), _mbsncpy(), _mbsnextc(), _mbsnicmp(), _mbsnicoll(), _mbsninc(), _mbsnset(), _mbspbrk(), _mbsrchr(), _mbsrev(), _mbsset(), _mbsspn(), _mbsspnp(), _mbsstr(), _mbstok(), _mbstrlen(), _mbsupr(), _wcsdec(), _wcsdup(), _wcsicmp(), _wcsicoll(), _wcsinc(), _wcslwr(), _wcsncnt(), _wcsncoll(), _wcsnextc(), _wcsnicmp(), _wcsnicoll(), _wcsninc(), _wcsnset(), _wcsrev(), _wcsset(), _wcsspnp(), _wcsupr(), strcat(), strchr(), strcmp(), strcoll(), strcpy(), strcspn(), strlen(), strncmp(), strncpy(), strpbrk(), strrchr(), strspn(), strstr(), strtod(), strtok(), strtol(), strtoul(), strxfrm(), wcscat(), wcschr(), wcscmp(), wcscoll(), wcscpy(), wcscspn(), wcslen(), wcsncmp(), wcsncpy(), wcspbrk(), wcsrchr(), wcsspn(), wcsstr(), wcstod(), wcstok(), wcstol(), and wcstoul().

wctomb()

Function

The wctomb() function converts a wide-character to a multibyte character, returning the number of characters converted. The function returns –1 if unsuccessful.

Header File

```
#include <stdlib.h>
```

Declaration

```
int wctomb(char *mbchar, wchar_t wchar);
```

- *mbchar* – A pointer to the buffer that will hold the multibyte character.
- *wchar* – The wide character to convert.

Example

The following program demonstrates how to use the `wctomb()` function. When run, the program converts a wide character to a multibyte character and displays the results returned from the function. The program's output looks like this:

```
result = 1
Press any key to continue
```

Here is the program source code that produced the output:

```cpp
#include "stdafx.h"
#include <stdlib.h>
#include <iostream>

using namespace std;

int main(int argc, char* argv[])
{
    wchar_t ch = L'C';
    char mb[10];

    int result = wctomb(mb, ch);
    cout << "result = " << result << endl;

    return 0;
}
```

CROSS-REFERENCE
See also _mbbtombc(), _mbcjistojms(), _mbcjmstojis(), _mbctohira(), _mbctokata(), _mbctombb(), mblen(), mbstowcs(), mbtowc(), wcstombs(), and wctrans().

V
W
X

wctype.h

Standard C Library Header File

The wctype.h header file defines the constants, functions, and data types needed to manipulate wide data.

Defined Constants

_UPPER	_BLANK
_LOWER	_HEX
_DIGIT	_LEADBYTE
_SPACE	_ALPHA
_PUNCT	WEOF
_CONTROL	

Defined Functions

iswalpha()	iswcntrl()
iswupper()	iswascii()
iswlower()	isleadbyte()
iswdigit()	towupper()
iswxdigit()	towlower()
iswspace()	iswctype()
iswpunct()	towctrans()
iswalnum()	wctrans()
iswprint()	wctype()
iswgraph()	

Defined Data Types

wchar_t	wctype_t
wctrans_t	wint_t

while

Keyword

The while keyword is part of a while loop statement, which enables a program to execute a block of code repeatedly until a given condition becomes false. For example, the following program uses a while loop to increment a variable named index from 0 to 9. The program's output looks like this:

```
index = 0
index = 1
index = 2
index = 3
index = 4
index = 5
index = 6
index = 7
index = 8
index = 9
Press any key to continue
```

Here is the program source code that produced the output:

```
#include "stdafx.h"
#include <iostream>

using namespace std;

int main(int argc, char* argv[])
{
    int index = 0;
    while (index < 10)
    {
        cout << "index = " << index << endl;
        ++index;
    }

    return 0;
}
```

A similar program could be written using a do-while loop, which evaluates the loop control expression at the end of the loop rather than at the beginning:

```
#include "stdafx.h"
#include <iostream>

using namespace std;
```

```
int main(int argc, char* argv[])
{
    int index = 0;
    do
    {
        cout << "index = " << index << endl;
        ++index;
    }
    while (index < 10);

    return 0;
}
```

CROSS-REFERENCE
See also do and for.

wmemchr()

Function

The wmemchr() function locates a matching character in an array, returning a pointer to the character if found, or NULL if not found.

Header File

```
#include <wchar.h>
```

Declaration

```
wchar_t *wmemchr(wchar_t *s, wchar_t c, size_t n);
```

- *c* — The character for which to search.
- *n* — The size of the array *s*.
- *s* — A pointer to the array to search.

Example

The following program demonstrates how to use the wmemchr() function. When run, the program searches an array for the character i and displays the results. The program's output looks like this:

```
is is a test
Press any key to continue
```

Here is the program source code that produced the output:

```
#include "stdafx.h"
#include <iostream>
#include <wchar.h>

using namespace std;

int main(int argc, char* argv[])
{
    wchar_t str[] = L"This is a test";

    wchar_t* chr = wmemchr(str, L'i', sizeof(str));
    wcout << chr << endl;

    return 0;
}
```

CROSS-REFERENCE
See also wmemcmp(), wmemcpy(), wmemmove(), and wmemset().

wmemcmp()

Function

The wmemcmp() function compares two arrays, returning an integer that indicates whether the arrays are equal (0), the first array is greater than the second (a positive number), or the first array is less than the second (a negative number).

NOTE
Borland does not support this function.

Header File

```
#include <wchar.h>
```

Declaration

```
int wmemcmp(const wchar_t *s1, const wchar_t *s2, size_t n);
```

- *n* — The size of the arrays *s1* and *s2*.
- *s1* — A pointer to the first array to compare.
- *s2* — A pointer to the second array to compare.

Example

The following program demonstrates how to use the wmemcmp() function. When run, the program compares two arrays and displays the results. The program's output looks like this:

```
The second array is greater
Press any key to continue
```

Here is the program source code that produced the output:

```cpp
#include "stdafx.h"
#include <wchar.h>
#include <iostream>

using namespace std;

int main(int argc, char* argv[])
{
    wchar_t str1[] = L"abcdefg";
    wchar_t str2[] = L"abcdefh";

    int result = wmemcmp(str1, str2, sizeof(str1));
    if (result == 0)
        cout << "The arrays are equal" << endl;
    else if (result > 0)
        cout << "The first array is greater" << endl;
    else if (result < 0)
        cout << "The second array is greater" << endl;

    return 0;
}
```

CROSS-REFERENCE
See also wmemchr(), wmemcpy(), wmemmove(), and wmemset().

wmemcpy()

Function

The wmemcpy() function copies one array to another, returning a pointer to the destination array.

Header File

```
#include <wchar.h>
```

Declaration

```
wchar_t *wmemcpy(wchar_t *s1, const wchar_t *s2, size_t n);
```

- *n* — The size of the arrays *s1* and *s2*.
- *s1* — A pointer to the destination array.
- *s2* — A pointer to the source array.

Example

The following program demonstrates how to use the wmemcpy() function. When run, the program copies one array to another and displays the results. The program's output looks like this:

```
abcdefg
Press any key to continue
```

Here is the program source code that produced the output:

```cpp
#include "stdafx.h"
#include <wchar.h>
#include <iostream>

using namespace std;

int main(int argc, char* argv[])
{
    wchar_t str2[] = L"abcdefg";
    wchar_t str1[sizeof(str2)];

    wchar_t* dest = wmemcpy(str1, str2, sizeof(str2));
    wcout << dest << endl;

    return 0;
}
```

V

W

X

CROSS-REFERENCE
See also wmemchr(), wmemcmp(), wmemmove(), and wmemset().

wmemmove()

Function

The wmemmove() function copies one array to another, returning a pointer to the destination array. Overlapping arrays are valid arguments to this function.

NOTE
Borland does not support this function.

Header File

```
#include <wchar.h>
```

Declaration

```
wchar_t* wmemmove(wchar_t *s1, const wchar_t *s2, size_t n);
```

- *n* — The size of the arrays *s1* and *s2*.
- *s1* — A pointer to the destination array.
- *s2* — A pointer to the source array.

Example

The following program demonstrates how to use the wmemmove() function. When run, the program copies one array to another and displays the results. The program's output looks like this:

```
abcdefg
Press any key to continue
```

Here is the program source code that produced the output:

```
#include "stdafx.h"
#include <wchar.h>
#include <iostream>

using namespace std;
```

```
int main(int argc, char* argv[])
{
    wchar_t str2[] = L"abcdefg";
    wchar_t str1[sizeof(str2)];

    wchar_t* dest = wmemmove(str1, str2, sizeof(str2));
    wcout << dest << endl;

    return 0;
}
```

CROSS-REFERENCE
See also wmemchr(), wmemcmp(), wmemcpy(), and wmemset().

wmemset()

Function

The wmemset() function fills an array with a given character, returning a pointer to the destination array.

Header File

```
#include <wchar.h>
```

Declaration

```
wchar_t* wmemset(wchar_t *s, wchar_t c, size_t n);
```

- *c* — The character with which to fill the array.
- *n* — The size of the arrays *s1* and *s2*.
- *s* — A pointer to the destination array.

Example

The following program demonstrates how to use the wmemset() function. When run, the program fills an array with the character "X" and displays the results. The program's output looks like this:

```
XXXXXXXXXXXXXXXXXXXXXXXXXXXXXXX
Press any key to continue
```

V
W
X

Here is the program source code that produced the output:

```
#include "stdafx.h"
#include <wchar.h>
#include <iostream>

using namespace std;

int main(int argc, char* argv[])
{
    wchar_t str1[64];

    wchar_t* dest = wmemset(str1, L'X', 30);
    dest[32] = 0;
    wcout << dest << endl;

    return 0;
}
```

CROSS-REFERENCE
See also wmemchr(), wmemcmp(), wmemcpy(), and wmemmove().

wprintf()

Function

The `wprintf()` function is the wide-character version of the `printf()` function, which prints a formatted string to the standard output stream. The function returns the number of characters displayed, or –1 in the case of an error.

Header File

```
#include <stdio.h>
```

Declaration

```
int wprintf(const wchar_t *format [, argument]...);
```

- *argument*—A list of data items that match the control codes included in the format string *format*.
- *format*—The format string, which can include text, as well as the format specifiers shown in Table W-40.

Table W-40 Format Specifiers for wprintf()

Specifier	Description
%c	Specifies a character.
%C	Specifies a wide character (`printf()`) or single-byte character (`wprintf()`).
%d	Specifies a signed decimal integer.
%e	Specifies a signed double-precision floating-point value using scientific notation with a lowercase e.
%E	Specifies a signed double-precision floating-point value using scientific notation with an uppercase E.
%f	Specifies a signed double-precision floating-point value.
%g	Specifies a signed double-precision floating-point value using either normal notation or scientific notation with a lowercase e.
%G	Specifies a signed double-precision floating-point value using either normal notation or scientific notation with an uppercase E.
%i	Specifies a signed decimal integer.
%n	Specifies an integer pointer.
%o	Specifies an unsigned octal integer.
%p	Specifies a void pointer.
%s	Specifies a string.
%S	Specifies a wide-character string (`printf()`) or single-byte-character string (`wprintf()`).
%u	Specifies an unsigned decimal integer.
%x	Specifies an unsigned hexadecimal integer with lowercase letters.
%X	Specifies an unsigned hexadecimal integer with uppercase letters.

Example

The following program demonstrates how to use the `wprintf()` function. When run, the program calls `wprintf()` to display a formatted string. The program's output looks like this:

```
var1 = 50    str1 = This is a test.
Number of characters displayed: 35
Press any key to continue
```

Here is the program source code that produced the output:

```
#include "stdafx.h"
#include <stdio.h>
#include <iostream>

using namespace std;
```

```
int main(int argc, char* argv[])
{
    int var1 = 50;
    wchar_t str1[] = L"This is a test.";

    int numChars = wprintf(L"var1 = %i    str1 = %s\n",
        var1, str1);
    wprintf(L"Number of characters displayed: %i\n",
        numChars);

    return 0;
}
```

CROSS-REFERENCE

See also cprintf(), cscanf(), fprintf(), fscanf(), fwprintf(), printf(), scanf(), sscanf(), swprintf(), swscanf(), vfprintf(), vfwprintf(), vprintf(), vsprintf(), vswprintf(), vwprintf(), and wscanf().

write()

Function

The write() function writes data to an open file, returning the number of bytes written, or –1 if an error occurs.

Header File

```
#include <io.h>
```

Declaration

```
int write(int handle, const void *buffer,
    unsigned int count);
```

- *buffer* — A pointer to the data to write.
- *count* — The number of bytes to write.
- *handle* — The file handle returned by the function that opened the file.

Example

The following program demonstrates how to use the `write()` function. When run, the program creates a file and writes 14 bytes to the file, displaying status messages as it goes. The program's output looks like this:

```
File written successfully
Press any key to continue
```

Here is the program source code that produced the output:

```cpp
#include "stdafx.h"
#include <stdlib.h>
#include <io.h>
#include <fcntl.h>
#include <sys/stat.h>
#include <iostream>

using namespace std;

int main(int argc, char* argv[])
{
    int numBytes;
    int fileHandle;

    fileHandle = open("MyFile.dat",
        O_RDWR | O_CREAT, S_IREAD | S_IWRITE);

    if (fileHandle != -1 )
    {
        numBytes = write(fileHandle, "This is a test", 14);

        if (numBytes != -1 )
            cout << "File written successfully" << endl;
        else
            cout << "File write error." << endl;

        close( fileHandle );
    }
    else
        cout << "File open error." << endl;

    return 0;
}
```

CROSS-REFERENCE

See also _close(), _creat(), _fcloseall(), _fdopen(), _fgetchar(), _fgetwchar(), _fileno(), _flushall(), _fputwchar(), _fsopen(), _getw(), _getws(), _lseeki64(), _open(), _putw(), _putws(), _read(), _rmtmp(), _tempnam(), _wcreat(), _wfdopen(), _wfopen(), _wfreopen(), _wfsopen(), _wopen(), _wtempnam(), _wtmpnam(), clearerr(), eof(), fclose(), feof(), ferror(), fflush(), fgetc(), fgetpos(), fgets(), fgetwc(), fgetws(), fopen(), fprintf(), fputc(), fputchar(), fputs(), fputwc(), fputws(), fread(), freopen(), fscanf(), fseek(), fsetpos(), ftell(), fwprintf(), fwrite(), fwscanf(), getc(), getchar(), gets(), getwc(), getwchar(), lseek(), putc(), putch(), putchar(), puts(), putwc(), putwchar(), rewind(), setbuf(), setvbuf(), tmpfile(), tmpnam(), ungetc(), ungetch(), and ungetwc().

wscanf()

Function

The wscanf() function is the wide-character version of the scanf() function, which accepts formatted data from the standard input stream. The function returns the number of data items successfully received.

Header File

```
#include <stdio.h>
```

Declaration

```
int wscanf(const wchar_t *format [, argument]...);
```

- *argument* — A list of data items that match the control codes included in the format string *format*.
- *format* — The format string, which can include the format specifiers shown in Table W-41.

Table W-41 Format Specifiers for wscanf()

Specifier	Description
%c	Specifies a character.
%C	Specifies a wide character (printf()) or single-byte character (wprintf()).
%d	Specifies a signed decimal integer.

Specifier	Description
%e	Specifies a signed double-precision floating-point value using scientific notation with a lowercase e.
%E	Specifies a signed double-precision floating-point value using scientific notation with an uppercase E.
%f	Specifies a signed double-precision floating-point value.
%g	Specifies a signed double-precision floating-point value using either normal notation or scientific notation with a lowercase e.
%G	Specifies a signed double-precision floating-point value using either normal notation or scientific notation with an uppercase E.
%I	Specifies a signed decimal integer.
%n	Specifies an integer pointer.
%o	Specifies an unsigned octal integer.
%p	Specifies a void pointer.
%s	Specifies a string.
%S	Specifies a wide-character string (printf()) or single-byte-character string (wprintf()).
%u	Specifies an unsigned decimal integer.
%x	Specifies an unsigned hexadecimal integer with lowercase letters.
%X	Specifies an unsigned hexadecimal integer with uppercase letters.

Example

The following program demonstrates how to use the wscanf() function. When run, the program calls wscanf() to input two data items, an integer and a string. The program's output looks something like this:

```
Enter an integer and a string:
234 test

You entered:
234 test
Number of items: 2

Press any key to continue
```

Here is the program source code that produced the output:

```
#include "stdafx.h"
#include <stdio.h>
#include <iostream>

using namespace std;
```

```
int main(int argc, char* argv[])
{
    int var1;
    wchar_t str1[81];

    wprintf(L"Enter an integer and a string:\n");
    int numItems = wscanf(L"%i %s", &var1, str1);
    wprintf(L"\nYou entered:\n");
    wprintf(L"%i %s\n", var1, str1);
    wprintf(L"Number of items: %i\n\n", numItems);

    return 0;
}
```

CROSS-REFERENCE

See also cprintf(), cscanf(), fprintf(), fscanf(), fwprintf(), printf(), scanf(), sscanf(), swprintf(), swscanf(), vfprintf(), vfwprintf(), vprintf(), vsprintf(), vswprintf(), vwprintf(), and wprintf().

What's on the CD-ROM?

The CD-ROM that accompanies this book contains all the sample programs described in each chapter. These programs are organized in directories that are named after the chapters. That is, you can find the programs for Chapter A in the A folder, the programs for Chapter B in the B folder, and so on. Each program is located in its own directory, named after the appropriate entry in the book. For example, you can find the program for the `printf()` function in the Microsoft/P/printf or Borland/P/printf directory, depending on which version of the source code you need.

Each program on the CD-ROM includes not only the source code, but also all the project files generated by Visual C++ or Borland C++ Builder. To experiment with any program, copy the appropriate program directory to your hard drive and then double-click the program's .dsw (for Microsoft Visual C++ 6.0) or .bpr (for Borland C++ Builder 3) file to load the project into the programming environment. You can then modify the source code, compile the program, or do whatever you like with the project.

Please note that after you copy files from the CD-ROM to your hard drive, you'll need to shut off the read-only attribute on any files you plan to modify. (You won't need to do this if you install the entire CD-ROM contents, as described in the CD-ROM Installation Instructions at the end of this book.) Your programming environment cannot save modified files until you do this. To turn off the read-only attribute on a set of files (after copying them to your hard drive), highlight the files in Windows Explorer and right-click the group. Then, select the Properties command from the context menu, and turn off the Read-Only checkbox in the property sheet that appears.

IDG Books Worldwide, Inc. End-User License Agreement

READ THIS. You should carefully read these terms and conditions before opening the software packet(s) included with this book ("Book"). This is a license agreement ("Agreement") between you and IDG Books Worldwide, Inc. ("IDGB"). By opening the accompanying software packet(s), you acknowledge that you have read and accept the following terms and conditions. If you do not agree and do not want to be bound by such terms and conditions, promptly return the Book and the unopened software packet(s) to the place you obtained them for a full refund.

1. **License Grant.** IDGB grants to you (either an individual or entity) a nonexclusive license to use one copy of the enclosed software program(s) (collectively, the "Software") solely for your own personal or business purposes on a single computer (whether a standard computer or a workstation component of a multiuser network). The Software is in use on a computer when it is loaded into temporary memory (RAM) or installed into permanent memory (hard disk, CD-ROM, or other storage device). IDGB reserves all rights not expressly granted herein.

2. **Ownership.** IDGB is the owner of all right, title, and interest, including copyright, in and to the compilation of the Software recorded on the disk(s) or CD-ROM ("Software Media"). Copyright to the individual programs recorded on the Software Media is owned by the author or other authorized copyright owner of each program. Ownership of the Software and all proprietary rights relating thereto remain with IDGB and its licensers.

3. **Restrictions on Use and Transfer.**

   (a) You may only (i) make one copy of the Software for backup or archival purposes, or (ii) transfer the Software to a single hard disk, provided that you keep the original for backup or archival purposes. You may not (i) rent or lease the Software, (ii) copy or reproduce the Software through a LAN or other network system or through any computer subscriber system or bulletin-board system, or (iii) modify, adapt, or create derivative works based on the Software.

(b) You may not reverse engineer, decompile, or disassemble the Software. You may transfer the Software and user documentation on a permanent basis, provided that the transferee agrees to accept the terms and conditions of this Agreement and you retain no copies. If the Software is an update or has been updated, any transfer must include the most recent update and all prior versions.

4. **Restrictions on Use of Individual Programs.** You must follow the individual requirements and restrictions detailed for each individual program in the Appendix in this Book. These limitations are also contained in the individual license agreements recorded on the Software Media. These limitations may include a requirement that after using the program for a specified period of time, the user must pay a registration fee or discontinue use. By opening the Software packet(s), you will be agreeing to abide by the licenses and restrictions for these individual programs that are detailed in the Appendix and on the Software Media. None of the material on this Software Media or listed in this Book may ever be redistributed, in original or modified form, for commercial purposes.

5. **Limited Warranty.**

(a) IDGB warrants that the Software and Software Media are free from defects in materials and workmanship under normal use for a period of sixty (60) days from the date of purchase of this Book. If IDGB receives notification within the warranty period of defects in materials or workmanship, IDGB will replace the defective Software Media.

(b) **IDGB AND THE AUTHOR OF THE BOOK DISCLAIM ALL OTHER WARRANTIES, EXPRESS OR IMPLIED, INCLUDING WITHOUT LIMITATION IMPLIED WARRANTIES OF MERCHANTABILITY AND FITNESS FOR A PARTICULAR PURPOSE, WITH RESPECT TO THE SOFTWARE, THE PROGRAMS, THE SOURCE CODE CONTAINED THEREIN, AND/OR THE TECHNIQUES DESCRIBED IN THIS BOOK. IDGB DOES NOT WARRANT THAT THE FUNCTIONS CONTAINED IN THE SOFTWARE WILL MEET YOUR REQUIREMENTS OR THAT THE OPERATION OF THE SOFTWARE WILL BE ERROR FREE.**

(c) This limited warranty gives you specific legal rights, and you may have other rights that vary from jurisdiction to jurisdiction.

6. Remedies.

(a) IDGB's entire liability and your exclusive remedy for defects in materials and workmanship shall be limited to replacement of the Software Media, which may be returned to IDGB with a copy of your receipt at the following address: Software Media Fulfillment Department, Attn.: C++ Master Reference, IDG Books Worldwide, Inc., 7260 Shadeland Station, Ste. 100, Indianapolis, IN 46256, or call 1-800-762-2974. Please allow three to four weeks for delivery. This Limited Warranty is void if failure of the Software Media has resulted from accident, abuse, or misapplication. Any replacement Software Media will be warranted for the remainder of the original warranty period or thirty (30) days, whichever is longer.

(b) In no event shall IDGB or the author be liable for any damages whatsoever (including without limitation damages for loss of business profits, business interruption, loss of business information, or any other pecuniary loss) arising from the use of or inability to use the Book or the Software, even if IDGB has been advised of the possibility of such damages.

(c) Because some jurisdictions do not allow the exclusion or limitation of liability for consequential or incidental damages, the above limitation or exclusion may not apply to you.

7. U.S. Government Restricted Rights.
Use, duplication, or disclosure of the Software by the U.S. Government is subject to restrictions stated in paragraph (c)(1)(ii) of the Rights in Technical Data and Computer Software clause of DFARS 252.227-7013, and in subparagraphs (a) through (d) of the Commercial Computer—Restricted Rights clause at FAR 52.227-19, and in similar clauses in the NASA FAR supplement, when applicable.

8. General.
This Agreement constitutes the entire understanding of the parties and revokes and supersedes all prior agreements, oral or written, between them and may not be modified or amended except in a writing signed by both parties hereto that specifically refers to this Agreement. This Agreement shall take precedence over any other documents that may be in conflict herewith. If any one or more provisions contained in this Agreement are held by any court or tribunal to be invalid, illegal, or otherwise unenforceable, each and every other provision shall remain in full force and effect.

my2cents.idgbooks.com

Register This Book — And Win!

Visit **http://my2cents.idgbooks.com** to register this book and we'll automatically enter you in our fantastic monthly prize giveaway. It's also your opportunity to give us feedback: let us know what you thought of this book and how you would like to see other topics covered.

Discover IDG Books Online!

The IDG Books Online Web site is your online resource for tackling technology — at home and at the office. Frequently updated, the IDG Books Online Web site features exclusive software, insider information, online books, and live events!

10 Productive & Career-Enhancing Things You Can Do at www.idgbooks.com

- Nab source code for your own programming projects.
- Download software.
- Read Web exclusives: special articles and book excerpts by IDG Books Worldwide authors.
- Take advantage of resources to help you advance your career as a Novell or Microsoft professional.
- Buy IDG Books Worldwide titles or find a convenient bookstore that carries them.
- Register your book and win a prize.
- Chat live online with authors.
- Sign up for regular e-mail updates about our latest books.
- Suggest a book you'd like to read or write.
- Give us your 2¢ about our books and about our Web site.

You say you're not on the Web yet? It's easy to get started with IDG Books' *Discover the Internet,* available at local retailers everywhere.

CD-ROM Installation Instructions

The CD-ROM that accompanies this book includes a batch file for transferring all of the files on the CD-ROM to your hard drive. To transfer the files, perform the following steps:

1. Place the CD-ROM in your CD-ROM drive.

2. On Windows' Start menu, select the Run command. The Run dialog box appears.

3. In the dialog's Open box, type **A:\install A B**, where **A** is the letter for your CD-ROM drive and **B** is the destination drive. (Don't add colons to the drive letters.) Example: If your CD-ROM drive is drive D, and you want to copy the book's files to drive C, you'd type **D:\install D C** into the Run dialog's Open box.

4. A DOS window appears in which you can watch the batch file copy the book's files to your destination drive.

After the file copying is complete, you can find the book's program files in the CPPRef directory on your destination drive.